PENGUIN BOOKS

THE LIFE OF GRAHAM GREENE: VOLUME III, 1955–1991

Norman Sherry is a fellow of the Royal Society of Literature and the Mitchell Distinguished Professor of Literature at Trinity University in San Antonio, Texas. In addition to the first two volumes of *The Life of Graham Greene*, he is the author of *Conrad's Eastern World*, *Conrad's Western World*, *Charlotte and Emily Brontë*, and *Jane Austen*.

Praise for
The Life of Graham Greene: Volume III, 1955–1991

A *New York Times* Notable Book

"Norman Sherry has completed his enormous task. This mighty work will be the quarry, forever, for all who seek Greene the man, Greene the writer, Greene as lover and antagonist, Greene sacred and profane. We hear Graham in speech and in writing, in letters of ecstasy and love, friendship and fury—hear his own words and the testimony of his contemporaries. We follow his lifelong commentary on the difficulty of private being, and on the tumult of his tragic century.

"In mastering the huge story and allowing Greene's complexities to have their unnerving say, Sherry illumines the personalities, many and mercurial, of this strange, prodigious, and deeply literary figure, who—to borrow words he himself used of another writer—'belonged to the heroic age of English fiction and outlived it.'"
—Shirley Hazzard, National Book Award winner and author of *The Great Fire*

"About this ambiguous, complex writer, Dr. Sherry writes with insight, erudition, and humane objectivity—capturing the conscience that made an indelible mark on modern literature." —*The Dallas Morning News*

"Marked by sorrow and disappointment, but plenty of fascinating adventures. An exemplary biography, of profound interest to admirers of Greene's work and to students of contemporary letters."
—*Kirkus Reviews* (starred review)

"Sherry came to know Greene quite well, and his firsthand impressions enhance this portrait. It becomes clear . . . that this project has been a labor of love. With the publication of the third and final volume, Sherry brings to a close his ambitious attempt to account for the many aspects of Greene's life and work." —*Los Angeles Times*

"For anyone interested in Greene's life and work, this three-volume biography is incomparable; as an intellectual and political history of the twentieth century it is invaluable; as a literary journey, as well as a journey across the world, it is masterly; as a source book and rogues' gallery it is fascinating." —Paul Theroux, *The New York Times Book Review*

"Captivating . . . The most endearing aspect of *The Life of Graham Greene* is the humility of Sherry's recognition that in an odd, *Citizen Kane* sort of way, Greene's motives often remain a mystery." —*The Washington Post*

"To be open to the subject's experience . . . requires biography on an extraordinary scale. Sherry has himself become a fabled figure because of his willingness to retrace Greene's voyages to the ends of the earth." —*The New York Sun*

"One of the most comprehensive literary biographies of our time. . . . Sherry's assessment of Greene's eccentric religious notions is . . . superb." —*New York Newsday*

"A sympathetic but forthright account of the life of one of the most complex, enigmatic and fascinating figures of the twentieth-century literary world. . . . Sherry has written the definitive biography of Graham Greene, an English author of international status." —*America*

THE LIFE OF
GRAHAM
GREENE

Volume Three: 1955–1991

Norman Sherry

PENGUIN BOOKS

PENGUIN BOOKS

Published by the Penguin Group

Penguin Group (USA) Inc., 375 Hudson Street, New York, New York 10014, U.S.A.

Penguin Group (Canada), 90 Eglinton Avenue East, Suite 700, Toronto,
Ontario, Canada M4P 2Y3 (a division of Pearson Penguin Canada Inc.)

Penguin Books Ltd, 80 Strand, London WC2R 0RL, England

Penguin Ireland, 25 St Stephen's Green, Dublin 2, Ireland
(a division of Penguin Books Ltd)

Penguin Group (Australia), 250 Camberwell Road, Camberwell,
Victoria 3124, Australia (a division of Pearson Australia Group Pty Ltd)

Penguin Books India Pvt Ltd, 11 Community Centre,
Panchsheel Park, New Delhi – 110 017, India

Penguin Group (NZ), cnr Airborne and Rosedale Roads, Albany,
Auckland 1310, New Zealand (a division of Pearson New Zealand Ltd)

Penguin Books (South Africa) (Pty) Ltd, 24 Sturdee Avenue,
Rosebank, Johannesburg 2196, South Africa

Penguin Books Ltd, Registered Offices:
80 Strand, London WC2R 0RL, England

First published in the United States of America by Viking Penguin,
a member of Penguin Group (USA) Inc. 2004
Published in Penguin Books 2005

1   3   5   7   9   10   8   6   4   2

Copyright © Norman Sherry, 2004
All rights reserved

ISBN 0 14 30.3613 0

Printed in the United States of America
Set in Bembo

In memory of
the remarkable Walter Adams,
& the unforgettable Michael Meyer

For dear friends:
Nicholas Scheetz,
Jacqueline Loomis Quillen,
Bernard Lifshutz,
Russell E. Newell,
& George & Nannette Herrick

And the jewels in my crown:
Ileana Taylor Sherry
& John Michael Graham Sherry

Contents

· Contents ·

Illustrations

Picture Credits

Every effort has been made to obtain the necessary permissions with reference to copyright material. The publishers apologise if inadvertently any sources remain unacknowledged.

1 Norman Sherry; 2 Courtesy of Elisabeth Dennys; 3 Snowdon; 4 Courtesy of Carol Lynley; 5 Slim Aarons, Getty Images; 6 Courtesy of Anita Björk; 7 Greene/Walston Collection, Georgetown University; 8 *Express* Newspapers; 9 Getty Images; 10 Getty Images; 11 Time Life Pictures/Getty Images; 12 Photograph by Peter Stackpole © Time Life Pictures/Getty Images; 13 and 14 Courtesy of Dr Michel Lechat; 15 Courtesy of WHO; 16 Courtesy of Henri Vanderslaghmolen; 17 Courtesy of Dr Michel Lechat; 18 Courtesy of Chris Lipscomb; 19 Time Life Pictures/Getty Images; 20 Roger Wood Studio; 21 Courtesy of M. T. Danielsson; 22 Courtesy of Michael Meyer; 23 Courtesy of the Evelyn Waugh estate; 24 Photograph by Bern Schwartz, courtesy of Michael Meyer; 25 Courtesy of Harry Gottlieb; 26 Illustration by Pille Négron, Courtesy of Aubelin Jolicoeur; 27 Getty Images; 28 Associated Press; 29 *Telegraph* magazine; 30 Courtesy of Aubelin Jolicoeur; 31 Courtesy of Aiden Nichols OP. Reproduced here from *Dominican Gallery* by Aiden Nichols OP, Gracewing Publishing, 1997 and used with permission; 32 Graham Greene Archives; 33 Photograph by Douglas Miller, Hulton Archive/Getty Images; 34 Graham Greene Archives; 35 Norman Sherry; 36 Graham Greene Archives; 37 Photograph by G. R. Shand-Taylor; 38 Nisar Sheraly; 39 Malcolm W. Browne/*New York Times*; 40 and 41 Photograph by Carlos Reyes-Manzo/© Andes Press Agency; 42 Greene/Walston Collection, Georgetown University; 43 Boston College; 44 Courtesy of Bryan Forbes; 45 Georgetown

Finding Greene

Attempt the end, and never stand to doubt;
Nothing's so hard but search will find it out.
       — ROBERT HERRICK

BECAUSE Graham Greene's wide-ranging activities spanned most of the twentieth century, I found I was writing not only his story, but our history as well. Greene's life touched, and his work transfixed, as an insect in amber, many major events of our time: the First World War; the General Strike; the Great Depression; the Second World War; bitter civil wars in Liberia, Mexico and Vietnam; Mau Mau atrocities in Kenya; the War of the Running Dogs in Malaya; Cold War espionage; McCarthyism of the 1950s; the political strongmen of the postwar era – François 'Papa Doc' Duvalier of Haiti; Cuba's Castro; the Sandinistas of Nicaragua; Panama's General Omar Torrijos; and the Milieu (the French mafia) in Marseilles.

Greene's travels to the world's trouble spots bespeak an adventurous soul, his constant explorative journeys a throwback to Livingstone and Stanley, Burton and Speke – a Victorian schoolboy's dream fulfilled. Yet Greene was motivated by the daring of despair; he sought daredevilish disaster in lost, forgotten places with the persistence of a determined suicide. If death had come, his diaries reveal, he would have welcomed it.

Greene was a novelist with a massive curiosity. His method was to observe his age, and as that age changed from decade to decade, he reflected the changes in successive novels. He marched with the times, and his manic-depressive nature forced him to seek stimulation and diversion through events reflecting the dangerous extremes of the day. His urge to fence with a violent death made him a vital centre from which our age can be seen. Though there are in any age many centres, a passage from George Eliot's *Middlemarch* fits:

Your pier-glass or extensive surface of polished steel made to be rubbed . . . will be minutely and multitudinously scratched in all directions; but place now against it a lighted candle as a centre of illumination and lo! the scratches will seem to arrange themselves in a fine series of concentric circles round that little sun . . . These things are a parable. The scratches are events, and the candle is the egoism of [a] person.

Seeing biography as history from the singular perspective of a novelist, the standard of a research scientist, seeking truth without deviation, is imperative. As in science, biography involves constant testing of theories about the subject by the measurement of what one knows; and what one knows, over the years, grows and grows like the fabled beanstalk.

It would have been easier to have had a specific point of view, to have looked at Greene through a template of excessive admiration or excessive hate (and indeed, one memorialist has done the former, one biographer the latter). Such a method dramatically reduces the scope of research that is ultimately undertaken, since conclusions have already been reached before the research begins. If one is ready-armed to see only what one wishes to see, truth is never served. Using such a method, one is not looking for the complicated man standing there, but only for the partial evidence which will either glorify or beggar the writer's view of the nature of the subject.

The Greene whom his friends recognise is not to be seen. Given the variety of Greene's nature, it is not difficult to see him as someone who might be consumed by hatred, calculating in his malice – but he was not. It is never that easy. To use George Eliot's parable: the scratches are world events and Greene's reportage of them, so his scratches are to be found on many parts of the globe, and whilst he carried his singular personality around with him, its very singularity lies in its immense diversity. The research demanded even simply to touch upon the truth of Greene is perpetually challenging.

★

For many of us, Graham Greene was the most distinguished author of his era. Whatever his faults – he could be petty, he could be juvenile – he was yet magnanimous (the good often kept secret; his myriad kindnesses, alas, only inadvertently unearthed). His trips to brothels, his visits to opium dens in Vietnam, his smoking dope in London (yes, he did inhale), in retrospect seem minor misdeeds. He was special, unquestionably so, but also inevitably human and he suffered for his terrible curiosity about the world.

Greene's life was hounded by two contending elements in his nature: the strong conflict between his manic and his depressive sides. There were many occasions when Greene had an exuberant vitality, when to breathe was to enjoy. At such times, he was great good company, leaping from topic to topic seemingly with abandon. But his depressions were severe, and if he sometimes hated the world, then he hated himself more. Life became a dark tide; he felt the weight of every possible sin as he sank into the depths. On such occasions, one noticed how wooden and desperate and full of self-blame he seemed. And Roman Catholic convert though he was, he then doubted there was a God in the universe.

During these moments the plague spot of depression fostered his formidable desire for self-destruction. Sometimes he set the date for his death, saving up sleeping pills because he wanted a termination point for his unhappiness. For a long time, Greene could visualise not heaven − only hell, with any sort of intimacy, and it was the hell of James Joyce that he envisioned: 'There by reason of the great number of the damned, the prisoners are heaped together in their awful prison . . . the damned . . . are not even able to remove from the eye a worm that gnaws it . . . All the filth of the world, all the offal and scum . . . shall run there as to a vast reeking sewer.'

Even though Greene became a Catholic while an undergraduate − to induce the young Catholic Vivien Dayrell-Browning to marry him − there came a time in his life, within three years of the marriage, when he needed his Catholic God with a vengeance as he concerned himself with the struggle in the human soul between good and evil. His absorption with this struggle is best put by Frederic Raphael, as recalled to me by my dear friend Barbara Wall: 'If God could count every hair on your head, Greene did not fail to draw attention to the dandruff.' Like his character Bendrix in *The End of the Affair*, God was hounding Greene and Greene wanted this to be so. Greene's emotional pain and exhilaration were high at such moments. He took the Catholic creed to heart: 'Goodness has only once found a perfect incarnation in a human body, and never will again.'

*

I have a further purpose in writing biography. As in my earlier work on Joseph Conrad, I've tried to search out sources of Greene's work, seeking the origins, techniques and models that stand behind his fictional characters and settings. In this way, the author's originality is more effectively revealed, the operation of the creative imagination sometimes delicately pinned down.

I began with a withering notion that no man travels through life without leaving tracks, that nothing comes from nothing. So I sought, in visiting Mexico forty years after Greene had been there, to follow in his tracks, trying to recreate (which is only marginally possible) the total experience in a particular area at a particular time: to see and feel what Greene saw and felt, trying to submerge and steep myself in his life. To the extent that this can be done, we are in a position to see what Greene saw and, more important, to have a sense of what he used and what he discarded in his work.

Once the original events have been brought back from the black hole of lost time, we can observe those changes which a creative mind necessarily makes. We look over the writer's shoulder, watching his immersion in personal experience, based on common talk, report and rumour. Greene was particularly adept at seeking the inner truth of his material, getting at another's corruption (and his own), fleshing out the features of the characters he met: his and their pleasures, deep distresses, their fantasies, common and uncommon from childhood to dying.

This way, genuine inroads into a writer's secrets can be made and we may hope to contemplate an author's original and changing intentions. It lets us appreciate his skill in bringing together material from many sources, and thus we learn something of the psychology of composition. And sometimes with unusual good fortune one can actually find the originals.

In 1978, returning from the rainforests of Tabasco and mountains of Chiapas in south-west Mexico, in a little white mountain church I found the model for Greene's famous Judas figure, he who prowls sinister in *The Power and the Glory*. In the courtyard I saw Mexican men, white shirt-tails hanging, heads bowed and great sombreros in their hands, behind them a crude sign asserting 'the pay for a Christian is poor, but the rewards endless'. Sitting alone was a dirty, small-boned figure, his face unlined though he was seventy-six. In recent years he had lived rough, sleeping in the streets, and never washed. Perhaps it was grime that protected his gnome-like face from natural human wrinkles?

His name was Don Pelito. He wore a long black coat stretching well below his knees. It had large patch pockets in which he carried all his earthly belongings. His trouser legs were rolled up. When I shook hands with him, something on his palm crackled. It was only afterwards as I was interviewing him that I realised his hand was caked with dried excrement. What would he have thought if he had known that Greene, meeting him once fifty years before while Don Pelito was a clerk-typist in the Presidencia, had seen him instinctively as the type who would betray the Christ-like figure, the whisky priest?

The mannerisms Greene noted, including the scratching under his armpit, were repeated in my company, but his way of life made this understandable. His mouth was toothless, the two fangs described by Greene gone, so that what Greene saw and felt, I did not: 'a clerk I grew to loathe, a mestizo with curly sideburns and two yellow fangs at either end of his mouth. He had an awful . . . neighing laugh which showed the empty gums.' The neighing laugh he still had, but I did not find it so unpleasant as to make him a Judas who betrays the priest for the small sum of seven hundred pesos.

Though Greene used some minor physical aspects of Don Pelito to create his character, it was the utterly extraordinary nature of any betrayer which clearly fascinated him. Thus he substantially added to the character of Don Pelito. What Greene did with one sighting of Don Pelito was to recognise the possibilities of developing a Judas, secretly setting him against his scapegoat hero, the whisky priest, to betray the one who had given him succour. Without this Judas figure, Greene could not have created his masterpiece.

★

Greene was most remarkable: he refused to be fenced in, becoming a kind of Wandering Jew, a gypsy scholar. He travelled more than a migratory bird, more than a hundred migratory birds. He was one of fate's fugitives, living more in the air than on land, unrelentingly journeying across, around, backward and forward to every part of the globe, known and unknown, a man with an unparalleled wanderlust.

All and each adds to our knowledge of this strange man, or stranger of a man. I call him 'stranger' after twenty-nine years of continuous reflection because at the end of the day when his tale has been told, he remains just that. Greene was a man not easily caught in the act of greatness, and I knew him better, much better it seems, than I know the lines on my face. I still think (and this carries its own sadness) that Greene is as Edward Sackville-West once stated, an electric hare whom the greyhound critics (and alas, greyhound biographers too) are not *meant* to catch.

I am not thinking of Greene's many ambiguities, the false and conflicting stories which he himself contributed to the constant battery of those who reported on him for over fifty years. Rather, I'm thinking that in spite of my having spent a quarter of a lifetime on this biography, time has been too short for one to entirely encompass and comprehend, to give total and full expression to Greene, for it is a work that can never be entirely finished; to complete such is God's domain.

N.S.
San Antonio, Texas
2003

The Way It Was:
1904–1955

The Way It Was

1904–1939

BORN in Berkhamsted on 2 October 1904, the fourth of six children, Henry Graham Greene entered the cloistered world of upper-middle-class Edwardian society. His father, Charles Greene, headmaster of Berkhamsted School, was a man of sharp intelligence and naïve innocence. His mother, Marion, though somewhat remote, offered her children security and confidence.

Greene was an odd child, given to nightmares and a strange imagination, painfully sensitive, and very shy. These qualities proved to be an affliction when he moved from his family's home at School House to become a boarder at Berkhamsted. His physical awkwardness prevented him from excelling at games, and the total absence of solitude made life beyond the green baize door, that separation between home and school, unbearable.

His subsequent breakdown was brought about by a boy only three months older – Lionel Carter, who looked inoffensive but recognised the conflict between Greene's need to be loyal to his father and Greene's desire to befriend the boys at school.

Greene was different from the pack. He had a funny voice, with a bit of a lisp – the headmaster's son who could be suspected of being a spy and driven out. Isolated, disliked, distrusted, and fearing humiliation, Greene saw death as a release – the only way of escape. First he tried to saw open his knee and when that failed he swallowed potions in order to poison himself, including hyposulphite, hay-fever drops, a whole tin of hair pomade – even a bottle of eye-drops. He picked and ate of the deadly-nightshade plant but survived. When nothing worked, he took fourteen aspirins and swam in the school pool – his legs feeling like lead – but he did not drown. He couldn't know then, but he'd found the theme for his greatest novels and stories: 'In the lost boyhood of Judas / Christ was betrayed.'

Charles Greene sent his disturbed son to a London psychoanalyst, Kenneth Richmond, and the six months Greene spent under Richmond had a profound effect. Richmond and his wife, Zoe, were Jungian psychologists, spiritualists, involved in the London literary community. They presented Greene with his first experience of a family environment where every issue was open for discussion. Under the Richmonds' influence he explored the darker side of human nature and acquired his first literary contacts.

On his return to Berkhamsted, Greene was more assured and became rigorously keen in his observations, a characteristic which helped distinguish him as a novelist. In 1922 he went up to Oxford, to Balliol College, where he revelled in the escape from middle-class conventionality, and indulged in escapades reflecting his obsession to flee the creeping boredom of everyday life.

Fascination with disguise and espionage led Greene in 1924 on the first of many adventures in the world's trouble spots. The Ruhr Republic lured him under the sponsorship of German Intelligence. Greene covered his travel expenses by promising articles based on the journeys. With youthful recklessness, he ventured almost without care into pockets of turmoil.

At university Greene flirted with death. He played Russian roulette six times in five months. Greene's attempt to blow his head off was a necessary test of himself – the uninspired weakling on the playing fields of Berkhamsted becomes the inspired adventurer off them, an example of his need to experience what he called 'life reinforced by the propinquity of death'.

During his last two terms at Oxford his first volume of verse, *Babbling April*, was published and he began his first novel, *Anthony Sant* (never published). In 1925 he fell in love with nineteen-year-old Vivien Dayrell-Browning, who was employed by his publisher, Basil Blackwell. Vivien was handsome, independent and a devout Catholic convert. Greene deluged her with almost 2,000 letters in thirty months. Initially she treated him with reserve, but not surprisingly, her feelings for him gradually warmed.

After graduation Greene was in need of work. Uncertain whether to choose a domestic or a foreign job, he sought employment with the British American Tobacco Company, hoping to leave for China, but the tedium of the work, the crassness of one particular co-worker, and his fear of losing Vivien made his resignation inevitable. He turned to journalism, but, lacking experience, was unable to land a job with any London daily. Instead he accepted a position as a trainee, sub-editing on the *Nottingham Journal* without salary.

Nottingham provided Greene with a reservoir of experience of working-class life from which he created memorable, mysterious and often seedy characters. He received instruction from Father Trollope in preparation for his conversion to the Catholic Church – his motivation chiefly his love for Vivien. The domestic atmosphere of the sub-editors' room at the *Journal* provided a peaceful interlude, but Greene soon began seeking work in London.

In March 1926, with less than five months' experience on the *Nottingham Journal*, Greene was offered a post as sub-editor with *The Times*. By supplementing his income with reviews, marriage was within reach. However, Vivien's commitment to him was still in question. To deal with Vivien's fear of sex, Greene, extraordinarily, offered a celibate marriage.

It was while Greene was a sub-editor at *The Times* that the country experienced the General Strike, and London ground to a halt. Young Greene was exhilarated by working as a packer, manual labourer and a member of the newspaper's 'shock troops' during those nine days. But the excitement ended and monotony loomed. The possibility of unending years of sub-editing at *The Times* gave impetus to his literary efforts. He finished his second novel, *The Episode*, but encountered repeated rejections and the novel remained unpublished. Having forsaken any hope of his first two novels being published, he started a third, *The Man Within*.

Greene and Vivien were married on 15 October 1927. They honeymooned in France and returned to live in London at a house affectionately known as 'the basket', a reflection of Vivien's passion for cats.

At the age of twenty-four, still at *The Times*, and only ten days after *The Man Within* was submitted, Greene was telephoned with the news that his novel had been accepted. It was an immediate success, with two reprints sold before publication. Within six months the novel went into six impressions and was translated into five languages. On publication day in June 1929 a literary star had been discovered.

Overconfident as a result of his early success, Greene persuaded his publisher, Heinemann, to take him on salary in order to write full-time. He resigned from *The Times*, but his next two novels, *The Name of Action* and *Rumour at Nightfall*, were failures. *The Name of Action* hardly sold 2,000 copies and *Rumour at Nightfall* barely 1,200. Financial pressures forced Greene and Vivien to move from London to a primitive cottage in Chipping Campden. Greene became depressed by the growing debt to his publisher. For Vivien, the time of isolation and struggle was idyllic.

The 1930s were difficult times, and the Greenes were not unaffected by the Depression. Although temporarily elated that his next novel, *Stamboul Train*, was selected as a Book Society choice, Greene was forced to share the expense of reprinting twenty pages of it under threat of a libel action from J. B. Priestley, who concluded that Greene's character Mr Savoy was based on him. In spite of all that, *Stamboul Train* was the Christmas rage and a breakthrough success. Excellent reviews poured in, and by late January sales had passed the 16,000 mark. Greene continued to review for the *Spectator*.

After moving from Chipping Campden to Oxford and finishing *It's a Battlefield* (its central metaphor was life as 'a battlefield in which individuals, ignorant of the extent of the whole war, fought their own separate battles') Greene spent three weeks in Sweden trying to concoct a biography of the Swedish match king, Ivar Kreuger, but instead began *England Made Me*, set in Sweden, which condemned the antiquated precepts of 'honour' so central to the public school system in which he had suffered.

Shortly after his first child, Lucy Caroline, was born in December 1933, Greene impulsively decided to explore Liberia. Over a glass of champagne at a wedding, his twenty-three-year-old cousin, Barbara Greene, agreed to accompany him. The attraction of such a trip for Greene was that the most reliable map available still showed large blank areas with only the word 'Cannibals' written across.

At Freetown, Sierra Leone, he found everything ugly and seedy to be European, and everything beautiful to be native. At the start of the journey Greene was a novice African traveller, but by the time he reached Monrovia he was seasoned, overcoming endless difficulties, leading his small expedition with vigilance, walking hour after hour through perilous terrain, sometimes getting lost. In spite of the heat, he dutifully recorded his observations.

Greene pushed himself to the limit, physically and mentally, nearly exceeding even *his* formidable determination. He contracted a strange disease with a fever from sheer exhaustion of travel – one night, Barbara was sure her cousin was going to die, but next morning his fever broke, and he had a renewed interest in life. They had weeks more of jungle before reaching Grand Bassa, and by April they were back home in England. Greene's resulting book, *Journey Without Maps* (1936), is probably one of the best travel books of our time.

Greene moved from Oxford to London where his son Francis was born on 13 September 1936. London was the hub of publishing, and Greene began a thriller, *Brighton Rock*, edited the short-lived *Night and Day* magazine, and reviewed films for the *Spectator*. It was a review of Shirley Temple's *Wee Willie Winkie* that hastened the downfall of *Night and Day*. In its libel action, Twentieth Century Fox's bizarre claim was that Greene 'had accused [it] of "procuring" Miss Temple "for immoral purposes"'.

With *Brighton Rock* published and the libel suit threatening, Greene departed for Mexico under the patronage of Longman's to write about religious persecution. Greene journeyed by mule from Salto to Palenque, recording his extreme suffering.

In Villahermosa, decrees had been passed insisting that priests should marry. God was denounced from the pulpit, people were forced to destroy altars, religious ornaments were smashed, even torn from the wearer's neck. Priests in Tabasco were hunted down and eventually shot, except for one who wandered for ten years under cover in the forest and swamps and became the itinerant 'whisky' priest. Greene knew that 'The greatest saints have been men with more than normal capacity for evil and the most vicious men have sometimes narrowly evaded sanctity.'

1939–1955

Suffering from dysentery, Greene left Mexico City in May 1938, returning to the Shirley Temple case and work on *Brighton Rock*. Reflecting on his Mexican experience, he asserted: 'I hate this country and this people' – an attitude reflected in *The Lawless Roads* and, to a lesser extent, in his great novel, *The Power and the Glory*. After arriving in England later that month, his disdain waned, as English Catholicism paled in comparison to the compelling physical devotion of the Mexican peons. London was a shock: 'How could a world like this end in anything but war?' And as London prepared for the coming conflict, so did Greene. Worried about supporting his family once the fighting began, he forced himself to take on writing assignments while perfecting *The Power and the Glory*. Work was impossible at home with interruptions from children and the telephone, so he took a studio in Mecklenburgh Square, where he completed *The Confidential Agent* (which, despite Greene's doubts, was taken on by Warner Brothers and made into a notable feature film starring the inimitable Charles Boyer). Greene rented his workroom from Dorothy Glover, with whom he later began an affair.

War was declared on 3 September 1939, and though Greene evacuated his wife and children to his mother's home in Crowborough, he awaited the raids at the family home in Clapham Common. In late 1939 he was summoned to meet the draft board, but managed to delay his call-up until June 1940 so that he could finish *The Power and the Glory*. However, two months previously, he had accepted a post looking after the authors' section of the Ministry of Information, whose work he came to view as 'not done for its usefulness but . . . simply as an occupation'. After eight months, his position was abolished, and he looked for ways to do his bit in the war.

On 4 March 1940 – in the midst of the fighting – *The Power and the Glory* was published. It was not immediately the overwhelming success it was deservedly to become. The British public were more concerned about the fall of France and the Low Countries. Soon after moving his family inland to Oxford, and to Vivien's delight, Greene was hired as literary editor of the *Spectator*.

The London Blitz began on 7 September 1940 and continued for seventy-six consecutive nights. Greene spent many of those nights as an air-raid warden, watching for fires breaking out after bombs fell, with Dorothy. Some of his experiences during the Blitz were transferred to Rowe in his novel *The Ministry of Fear*, perhaps his most brilliant thriller, though Greene called it an 'entertainment'. He also wrote of this in *Ways of Escape*, particularly about 16 April 1941, known as 'The Wednesday', when, in a single night, 2,000 London civilians died and 100,000 homes were destroyed. His home in Clapham, 14 North Side, that beautiful 'Mozart opera' house (as described by Lady Read), received a direct hit. Greene's family were in Oxford that night, and he, living with Dorothy, did not know of the destruction until the next day. Vivien said: 'His life was saved because of his infidelity' – and with the bombing went her dreams of a traditional home life, though she did not know the finality of it at this time.

In 1941, with his sister Elisabeth's help (she was already a member of the SIS – the Secret Intelligence Service), Greene was accepted into MI6 and sent to West Africa under cover of a position in the Colonial Service. Though concerned for both his family and Dorothy, the prospects of helping to prosecute the war and of having an interesting and well-paid job were irresistible.

Greene travelled to the Dark Continent on a cargo ship with eleven other passengers. Between submarine and machine-gun watches and the frequent parties, Greene worked aboard on *British Dramatists* and observed his shipmates, gathering characters and scenes for future works. On 3 January 1942, the ship entered the port of Freetown, capital of Sierra Leone, which Greene later termed 'the Soupsweet Land'. He was flown to Lagos to complete his SIS training. Back in Freetown, he found a 'dingy little Creole villa about two miles out of town' to serve as both home and SIS base. This house and his life in Sierra Leone are luminously described in *The Heart of the Matter*.

After several potential covers failed to materialise, Greene became 'a vague attachment to the police force', and spent his time coding and decoding telegrams and reports, despite his efforts to initiate other MI6 schemes. He did make periodic trips up-country to find and check on agents, trips which 'saved my sanity' and were reflected in *The Heart of the Matter*. During this period, Greene read, walked about

Freetown, visited at least one whorehouse (which appeared in the novel) and wrote. In August, in addition to his SIS activities, he began working on *The Ministry of Fear*, and in order to protect his typescript from loss in the post during the return sea journeys (German U-boats were very active among British convoys), he sent the typescript to his publisher in three parts. By December, actually *before* it was even published, the story was bought by Paramount Pictures. In June, Vivien cabled him that *The Power and the Glory* had won the Hawthornden Prize, and that Paramount was making a film of his book *A Gun for Sale*. Greene's reputation was growing even while the war was at its height.

On 7 November 1942, Greene's father, Charles, died from diabetes. Graham received the news in two telegrams delivered in reverse order: he learned first of his father's death, and then of his illness. Feeling 'misery and remorse' at taking a job abroad (he'd had little option) while his father was so sick, Greene had a mass said for Charles and began planning to come home. Early in 1943, his relationship with his superior having deteriorated, and feeling he had accomplished all he could in Africa, Greene returned to England.

Towards the end of 1942, Greene, still in Africa, corresponded with his agent about the dramatisation in London of *Brighton Rock*, which had been on option for two years. War-jaded audiences were embracing frivolous, light-hearted productions, but Greene's agent felt the mood was changing. Greene returned to Dorothy's house at 19 Gower Mews. Knowing about Greene's love affair, Vivien could not bring herself to send his mail to Dorothy's home, and forwarded all of it to his club, the Reform.

Greene worked long hours at SIS headquarters in St Albans under Kim Philby, who was even then (though of course no one in SIS knew this) a Soviet agent. The purpose of Section VI was to counter enemy intelligence, and Greene proceeded 'quietly, coolly and competently' among the other non-professional agents in a casual atmosphere of 'sweaters and grey flannel trousers'. His time at St Albans and later at Ryder Street in London provided material for his stunning entertainment to come, *Our Man in Havana*. Then, just prior to the Allied invasion of Europe on 6 June 1944, Greene resigned from MI6 and transferred to the Political Intelligence Department, which had promised to send him to France. He also by this move avoided a promotion offered him by Kim Philby.

Greene and Dorothy Glover were now living in an extremely dangerous – and therefore cheap – top-floor flat in Gordon Square, but Greene's main concern was for his family: he sent Laurence Pollinger some suggestions for publication of his work in the event of his death, a very real possibility given his continuing work as an air-raid warden. He returned to duty as an SIS player in London.

On 14 July 1944, the war nearing its end, Greene wrote to his mother that he would be 'starting on Monday as a publisher', joining Eyre & Spottiswoode. Greene proved himself by persuading François Mauriac and Ford Madox Ford to allow Eyre & Spottiswoode to publish them. But he was to last only four years. A conflict over Anthony Powell with his senior director, Douglas Jerrold, spurred his 1948 resignation.

On VE Day, 8 May 1945, after Germany's unconditional surrender, Greene and Dorothy observed the subdued celebrations, an experience he gave to Sarah and Henry Miles in *The End of the Affair*. To make it up to Vivien for not being with her at this time, he took her on holiday. Knowing that her marriage was on shaky ground, Vivien was looking forward rather desperately to setting up housekeeping as a family again, now that the war was over. This was not to be.

From June to October 1945, as a critic, Greene wrote 'Graham Greene on Books' for the *Evening Standard*, generally denigrating popular writers (though he steadfastly supported George Orwell's *Animal Farm*). He continued working on what would be a masterpiece, *The Heart of the Matter*, after bringing out *Nineteen Stories*, a volume of short stories. Such was the speed of Greene's growing reputation, that early in 1946 Heinemann decided to publish a number of his books in a uniform edition.

In 1946, Vivien wrote to her husband about a wealthy married lady who'd been so influenced by his books that she was converting to Catholicism. This woman asked that Greene be her godfather. Thinking it a bit of a lark, Greene, though unable to get away himself, suggested that Vivien represent him at the lady's christening. This was Vivien's first contact with the beautiful and compelling Catherine Walston, who would become Greene's lover for the next thirteen years and more – the greatest passion of his life.

Catherine and Greene began a hectic affair, beginning on a vacation on the remote island of Achill, off the coast of Ireland – even though he was still living with Dorothy. He knew that he was no longer in love with Dorothy or Vivien, but guilt bound him to both. The first part of *The Heart of the Matter* bears witness to Greene's marital troubles; the second to his disturbed relationship with Dorothy, subtly disguised here. By the time Catherine came onto the scene, he was as unhappy and as suicidal as his character Scobie. She became Greene's complex and beautiful love, which he best revealed in his next novel, *The End of the Affair*.

The year 1947 marked Greene's first collaboration with film mogul Alexander Korda and director Carol Reed. Together the three produced two of the greatest films of the immediate postwar era, *The Fallen Idol* and *The Third Man*. For the latter film, Greene travelled to the 'smashed dreary city of Vienna'. From Vienna he went to Prague in search of a revolution, and then on to Rome to meet Catherine. It was on this trip to Italy that he found Rosaio, a small villa in Anacapri where parts of most of his later books were written. On Anacapri Greene found also some lasting friends, including writer Norman Douglas, Michael Richey, Shirley Hazzard and her husband Francis Steegmuller, and Dottoressa Moor (whom he later immortalised in *Travels with My Aunt*). Always missing Catherine, Greene went with Carol Reed to America to work on *The Third Man*.

Greene's continuing cohabitation with Dorothy strained his budding relationship with Catherine. He had great difficulty separating from Dorothy Glover because of guilt – she was without any other to love and support her. Greene tried to place her in situations where she might meet someone else. Meanwhile Catherine continued to have other clandestine affairs, fuelling Greene's own insecurity.

Finally, in November 1947, the long-suffering Vivien opened an undelivered letter from Graham to Catherine which had been returned to her house. She found she could no longer overlook his adulteries, and Greene left Vivien's house – and Vivien. She was utterly shocked at his departure. She thought she'd never see him again. As she described it to me, she went to the window and watched him walk away, 'He looked back for a minute – didn't wave, but looked back.' Eight years later, in *The Quiet American*, Greene uses this indelible picture: 'a fox, seen by an enemy flare . . . the body of a bayoneted Malay . . . my wife's face at a window when I came home to say goodbye for the last time'.

He continued to correspond with her and see her and the children regularly. They struggled throughout 1948 over what form their separation should take, but they remained married until Greene's death in 1991. Then, during a trip to Marrakech, Dorothy revealed knowledge of his affair with Catherine. Greene at last broke with Dorothy, and with Catherine's help procured a flat next to her own in St James's Street, London. Now there was only Catherine.

The publication of *The Heart of the Matter* brought Greene great fame and great controversy, making him a media figure, a status with which he was never comfortable and from which he longed to escape. In 1949, Greene emerged as a playwright with the dramatisation of *The Heart of the Matter*, which was withdrawn after only one performance.

Increasingly Greene pressured Catherine to leave her husband and marry him. Her husband Harry, in turn, began to limit Catherine's meetings with Greene. The indulgent Harry had initially received

Greene warmly, but when Catherine told him she was leaving to marry Greene, Harry – that remarkably good man – was reduced to tears, and Catherine couldn't go through with it.

Late in 1950, Greene went to Malaya at the invitation of his brother Hugh, who was head of Emergency Information Services during the 'War of the Running Dogs'. In preparation for a *Life* magazine article, Greene stayed with a rubber planter under siege by communist guerrillas, spent time with a railway superintendent whose line had endured forty derailments in less than a year, and patrolled with the Gurkhas for three arduous days through interminable foothills and thick jungle. He was constantly retching, and almost broken by these journeys.

Greene travelled from Malaya to Saigon in January 1951, and entered a world of civil war – nightly bombings, anonymous grenade tossing and frequent assassinations – and tall, elegant girls in white silk trousers. His melancholia lifted. It was in Vietnam that Greene began using opium, a drug that dulled at least his physical ache for Catherine, but could not alleviate his troublesome dreams of her. There he gathered notes, experiences and characters for *The Quiet American*.

Greene loved his first visit to Indo-China and wanted to return to Vietnam. By now Harry Walston had forbidden Greene from visiting their home. One reason for this was the imminent publication of *The End of the Affair*, dedicated in England 'To C.' (and few would know who 'C.' was) but in the American edition 'To Catherine with love'. Catherine apparently at this point suggested a platonic 'intellectual companionship', something Greene did not feel capable of; fear of losing Catherine had even stopped the compulsive writer from producing his daily 500 words. Catherine decreed that they not see each other for seven months. Greene, miserable, cruised the Aegean Sea on Alexander Korda's yacht *Elsewhere*, then proceeded directly back to Saigon, where he felt 'happy and at home'.

The Far East had a disturbing effect on Greene, raising questions about 'all one's beliefs' and stirring his death wish. The French were still in charge in Vietnam, and General de Lattre, who had once greeted Greene enthusiastically, now suspected him of being a British spy. This was a real possibility, as Alexander Korda had approached Greene about working in Vietnam for the SIS. *The Quiet American* (published in England in late 1955, in the US early 1956), with its accusations of American-sponsored terrorism in Vietnam, brought Greene unjustifiably his reputation for anti-Americanism.

Greene left Saigon rather sadly on 9 February 1952. He'd been denied a visa to the US after deliberately publicising his six-week membership at the age of nineteen in the communist party. He was eventually granted a visa to go to Hollywood to see about the filming of *The End of the Affair*, and travelled from there to New York, where newspaper interviews bore headlines like the *Herald Tribune*'s 'Graham Greene says US Lives in Red Obsessed "State of Fear"'. When Greene next applied for a visa, he was offered one for a mere eight weeks, rather than the customary one year.

While in Vietnam, Greene began writing his first stage play not derived from one of his previous works, *The Living Room*, which was accepted for production when offered to director Peter Glenville. *The Living Room* premiered in Stockholm in 1952 to mixed reviews, though Greene was not liked (and for very special reasons) in Sweden. It was a splendid success in Great Britain, though some Catholics did not like it.

In 1953, Greene flew to Kenya to report on the Mau Mau rebellion for the *Sunday Times*. Nairobi, the town and the colonials, didn't appeal to him; he wanted to get into the field. Though initially sympathetic to the underdog Mau Mau, he found that the brutality and horror of their actions under 'General' Kimathi forced him to write sympathetically about the settlers.

Absolutely *not* a communist, Greene nonetheless remained true to Kim Philby even after he defected to the Soviet Union in January 1963. He wrote an introduction to Philby's memoirs, and stayed in contact with him until Philby's death, perhaps enduring public scorn not just for friendship's sake, but most likely for the sake of whatever information their exchange of letters and meetings in Moscow brought Greene for the SIS. After all, Greene continued working for the British Secret Intelligence Service, if only part-time.

The possibility of losing Catherine Walston continued to worry Greene, and as the 1950s progressed he saw less and less of her. When they did meet, it was often abroad. Over 'a long night & a long morning' in Rome, Catherine suggested their affair should end. Though he loved other women, Greene lived 'on a precipice' overlooking the barren wasteland of life without the beautiful Catherine.

PART I

Novelist as Playwright

I

1991: Our Man Dying

Whatever day or night I was born,
I was born too late.
Whatever day or night I die,
I die too early.

          — NORMAN SHERRY

A FRIEND of mine coming out of Leicester Square underground at four o'clock on 3 April 1991 was suddenly confronted by huge black letters on a newspaper billboard: 'GRAHAM GREENE DEAD'. Not since the loss in 1989 of Laurence Olivier, the century's greatest actor, or when in 1965 the mighty Churchill died, had readers the world over been so moved. To find another writer receiving such attention one would have to go back to the death of Charles Dickens in 1870.

I was at my home in San Antonio, Texas, when Graham died. Ian Mayes, the obituary editor of the *Guardian*, phoned me at 5.30 a.m. (a perfectly respectable time in an England six hours ahead) asking if I had heard. From that moment on, the phone rang every three minutes. Calls were coming in from many parts of the world: New Zealand, France, Russia, Australia, Spain, Italy, Sweden, Holland, Canada and America. No one from Africa called – not Liberia, the source of his greatest travel book, *Journey Without Maps*; nor the Congo, the setting for *A Burnt-Out Case*. There weren't any calls from his old political hunting grounds: Panama – Torrijos and Chuchu dead before him; Nicaragua, Cuba or El Salvador. Still, much of the world, it seemed, wished to know the last thoughts, the last words of Graham Greene. As the calls poured in, I was at the same time trying to deal with my own pain. I had known he was terminally ill, yet the immense loss I felt astonished me. Up to that time, I'd had a certain hesitancy – not about the writer, but about the man.

In the great lecture halls of America when asked whether I liked Greene, I was somewhat cagey. I cloaked my reply with remarks about Greene's elder brother Raymond, a leading medical practitioner and

3

mountaineer; about his younger brother Sir Hugh, one-time Director-General of the BBC; and how I loved his younger sister Elisabeth, perhaps covertly suggesting that I did not overly favour Graham. Yet, on hearing of his death, the shock left me with the deepest grief and genuine pain, and an almost insupportable sense of loss.

Graham Greene had been a presence with readers since 1925, publishing a first book of poetry at Oxford. He was a person groomed for the longest life: an aunt approached her hundredth year, so it seemed likely that if he didn't commit suicide (a real possibility in his youth and in the 1950s and 60s), he, who was eighty-six at death, might rightly have expected to live another ten years with mind alert, pen poised, determined, if it were only possible, to write an account of his own death as the new millennium dawned.

And yet, Greene did not feel a desire for old age. Once on a plane with Alan Pryce-Jones, he turned and said: 'The trouble about life is that it goes on far too long.' In a private poem to Catherine Walston, the wife of politician Harry, later Lord Walston and Greene's great love, he repeated this notion more dramatically, again revealing a lurking courtship with death: 'O You who gave Man too the blessing to die/ shorten the term of our breath.'

There were moments when one could glimpse Greene's profound emptiness, moments of extreme depression when he was truly Conrad's hollow man, when he didn't like life, didn't like people. Querry, the mentally 'burnt-out case' in the novel of the same name, reflects this: he is spiritually dead. Something of the distance he felt he'd fallen from humanity shows early in *A Burnt-Out Case*. Querry has travelled on and on until the boat's last stop: a leper colony. To Dr Colin, the leper doctor, Querry confesses his condition: 'Self-expression is a hard and selfish thing. It eats everything, even the self. At the end you find you haven't even got a self to express.'[1]

This statement by the fictional Querry is a reflection of Greene's condition on different occasions in his life. His absolute resolve to give his life totally to his work had many times left a void – he did become consumed, truly a 'burnt-out case'. Yet here surely is the heroic side of Greene. Whilst he might have emptied himself of feeling (and almost of life itself) as if being eaten alive or suffering from Lesch-Nyhan Syndrome,* his novels are fundamentally enhancing, making a difference to millions. (Not for nothing have his works been translated into dozens of languages.) There are numerous scenes in his major novels of great imaginative power which justify his dedication and his pain.

* A genetic disease which leads the sufferer to self-mutilation.

In *The Heart of the Matter*, the hero Scobie visits a makeshift hospital treating survivors from a ship sunk by a German submarine, who have endured forty days in an open boat. At a point when Scobie is watching over a dying child, his prayers take on a bargaining tone. Scobie listens to the child's heavy, uneven breathing. He longs to help, thinking such worry must be what parents go through, seeing 'their children dying slowly every hour they live', and he is shrinking here from just a few minutes of it. He prays for God to give her peace:

> The breathing broke, choked, began again with terrible effort. Looking between his fingers he could see the six-year-old face convulsed like a navvy's with labour. 'Father,' he prayed, 'give her peace. Take away my peace for ever, but give her peace.'[2]

He hears her 'small scraping voice' from the bed: 'Father.' He watches her 'blue and bloodshot eyes watching him'. He sees her breast struggling for breath to repeat the word. He comforts her with a handkerchief, folded in the shape of a bunny's head on the wall.

> 'There's your rabbit,' he said, 'to go to sleep with.' . . . sweat poured down his face and tasted in his mouth as salt as tears. 'Sleep.' He moved the rabbit's ears up and down. Then he heard Mrs Bowles's voice speaking low just behind him. 'Stop that,' she said harshly, 'the child's dead.'[3]

Similarly, in part two, chapter three, of *The Power and the Glory*, we find the whisky priest picked up and jailed, not because he was recognised as a priest and therefore subject to arrest and execution, but because he had a brandy bottle in his pocket in a town where liquor is banned. So he is in jail under a false name: 'This place was very like the world: overcrowded with lust and crime and unhappy love, it stank to heaven.'[4] The priest is moved by an enormous and irrational affection for the inhabitants. They stand or lie tight together, one stranger pressed against another: 'He was just one criminal among a herd of criminals . . . He had a sense of companionship which he had never experienced in the old days when pious people came kissing his black cotton glove.'[5] In the darkness, 'somewhere against the far wall pleasure began again; it was unmistakable: the movements, the breathlessness, and then the cry. The pious woman said aloud with fury, "Why won't they stop it? The brutes, the animals!"'[6] As the whisky priest's compassion grows, the pious woman's hate swells at the sound of their 'hooded and cramped pleasure'. She accuses the priest of sympathising with these animals, at one time calling him a martyr and then ending with the words, 'The sooner you are dead the better.'[7] And the priest had 'always been worried by the fate of pious women', for they fed on illusion. He was frightened for them: they came to death so often in a 'state of invincible complacency'.[8] (That is not how Greene came to his death.)

> He couldn't see her in the darkness, but there were plenty of faces he could remember . . . When you visualised a man or woman carefully, you could always begin to feel pity . . . When you saw the lines at the corners of the eyes, the shape of the mouth, how the hair grew, it was impossible to hate. Hate was just a failure of imagination.[9]

The next morning, his suit fouled by the cell floor, he is forced to empty the pails of excrement and clean up vomit – ugly, grotesque, but edifying, even as Scobie's death in *The Heart of the Matter*. This is true in spite of the criticism by Greene's friend, Evelyn Waugh, of Scobie's suicide (the unforgivable sin which no true Catholic could ever commit whether 'persecuted, tortured, imprisoned, loveless, maimed, bankrupt or ruined'[10]) that 'the idea of willing' one's 'own damnation for the love of God is either a very loose poetical expression or a mad blasphemy'.[11]

*

At Graham's death, I suddenly felt I'd lost a father, brother, son (for there is something filial about being a biographer – you are your subject's last disciple). I was, we all are, a close witness to death's perpetual annihilation of the womb-born. In his final year, death approaching, Greene's spiritual problems were still unsolved. He was a Catholic who couldn't live a pure Catholic life; his continued sinning deeply troubled his conscience. Yet he did not seem afraid. He was fearless but played out, his leukaemia would allow him only a few months to live. This was his last battle: the great traveller was becoming frail. Lord William Russell (1639–83) when close to death and winding up his watch said, 'I have done with time, now I am going to eternity.'[12] Greene's calmness in the face of death reminds us of that peer.

Greene was a strange and disturbing child and adolescent; he was a strange and disturbing adult. As he approached death, he did not feel, as most might, like a cornered rat.

Creatively, Greene's words caught the bite, the note and very trick of life. Though it was difficult being Greene, he was, all his life, not only 'Our Man', but his own.

2

His Noble Head of Hair
(The Delilah Twist)

Judge not the play
before the play be done.
— SIR JOHN DAVIES

FEW readers would disagree that Graham Greene's masterpiece is
The Power and the Glory. But the theatre version of *The Power and
the Glory* was not Greene's, though he refers to it as early as February
1952, in a letter to his Swedish publisher, Ragnar Svanstrom: 'I finished
a play [*The Living Room*] while I was abroad (in the Far East) and the
dramatisation of *The Power and the Glory* is well-advanced.'[1] The initial
stage adaptation of *The Power and the Glory* was done by Denis Cannan
and Pierre Bost, but did not have its debut in London until 5 April
1956. They'd finished the play in 1952. Yet, two years later, it still hadn't
found a home. Looking the script over, Greene felt he could improve
it, and on 22 October he wrote to Natasha Brook (wife of director
Peter Brook) asking her to 'tell Peter that I have finished revising *The
Power & The Glory* . . . and that I will let him have it in the course of
the next few weeks'.[2] Natasha read the play before her husband, and
wrote that the 'new P. & G. seems very very good, and as soon as Peter
has a chance to write to you about it I'm sure he will'.[3] Brook did:*

> In a moment of respite I read the 'Power & G' . . . I was *immensely*
> impressed. I do think you've made all the difference in the world
> — the first act is superb and there are now only very minor weak-
> nesses in the prison and cantina scenes. The last scene is excel-
> lent too. Congratulations and thank God you took it over.[4]

Brook ended with a comic postscript: 'We've just arranged to import
an enchanting Italian girl for you in February.' Greene was glad Brook

---

* This was undated, as were all of Brook's letters to Greene.

'like[d] my final version of *The Power and the Glory* and that you are still keen on doing it', but responded to their half-joking offer: 'You can leave out the enchanting Italian girl so long as you bring yourselves back in February.'[5] It was another full year before the play was put on in London.

The production and the music were both done by Brook, who also chose a very young unknown to play the Lieutenant of Police: Harry H. Corbett. But without the right whisky priest, little could be achieved. Greene and Brook both wanted Paul Scofield for the part. Only thirty-four years of age, Scofield already looked craggy, his rough, sculptured face, and an odd voice, strangely plaintive yet never whining.

It was the time of the Brook–Scofield season of 1956 – *Hamlet, The Power and the Glory* and *The Family Reunion* at the Phoenix Theatre in Charing Cross Road. Brook and Scofield admired each other's work, and in his recollections, *Threads of Time*, Brook describes his 'discovery' of Paul Scofield:

As we shook hands, I looked into a face that unaccountably in a young man was streaked and mottled like an old rock, and I was instantly aware that something very deep lay hidden behind this ageless appearance. Paul was courteous, distant, but as we began to work an instant understanding arose between us, needing very few words, and I realised that beneath the gentle modesty of his behaviour lay the absolute assurance of a born artist.[6]

I have quoted Brook's description of Scofield's character – his absolute assurance of being a born artist – because I have heard from several sources, in particular from Greene's sister, Elisabeth Dennys, that there was something twin-like in character and creativity between Greene and the actor. (She offered me some curious advice: 'If you want to understand Graham – understand the nature of Paul.') The partnership between Brook and Scofield went on for some years. On this occasion, Brook recalls Scofield's difficulties:

We were responsible together for a season of plays at the Phoenix Theatre, and Paul was playing *Hamlet* at night while we rehearsed ... *The Power and the Glory* during the day. The part of the humble Mexican whisky-sodden priest attracted him greatly, and although in his imagination he saw the character with absolute clarity, somehow this never descended into his body.[7]

'During the last performances of *Hamlet*, as we drew near to the end of rehearsals,' Brook wrote, 'the author was desperate, I was alarmed, even Paul was truly worried – the alchemy of his secret art was failing, and he could not even achieve a convincing external imitation of the part.' Brook was aware that Scofield was suffering a creative block, and they were all profoundly anxious: *Hamlet* was closing on a Saturday and they were opening with *The Power and the Glory* the following Monday. Brook then describes a miraculous change:

> I spent Sunday in the auditorium with the sets and the lights, preparing for the dress rehearsal, and Paul went straight to his dressing room where a barber had been called to cut off the splendid romantic head of hair he had cultivated to play the prince. When the run-through started, I was sitting with Graham Greene and Denis Cannan . . . in the stalls. The curtain rose . . . Through a window there was a glimpse of a rusty steamer, a stagnant river, a Mexican sky . . . The door at the back of the set opened, and a small man entered. He was wearing a black suit, steel-rimmed glasses, and holding a suitcase. For a moment we wondered who this stranger was and why he was wandering on to our stage. Then we realised that it was Paul, transformed. His tall body had shrunk; he had become insignificant. The new character now possessed him entirely. The obstacle had been his, or rather Hamlet's, noble head of hair.[8]

Thus, one haircut reaped the opposite effect of Samson's shorn locks: the transmogrification of Greene's novel into a play sent it on its way to success, and Greene was no longer desperate.

Scofield's acting in the role was, by all accounts, astonishing. Benedict Nightingale adds to Brook's description: Scofield 'turned the whisky priest . . . into a shrunken, wizened figure, with a shambling walk and a dry, dead voice'.[9] And T. C. Worsley reports his experience of Scofield's performance that first night:

> This is a most persuasive piece of acting, in which the accumulation of small details – the shuffle, the twitch, the whisky voice, the glints in the eye – combine to carry us into complete belief in a derelict human being who yet remains, though unemphatically, unself-consciously, a special, dedicated creature.[10]

Gene D. Phillips, sj, at the time he was writing *Graham Greene: The Films of His Fiction*, had a letter from Scofield about his playing the priest: 'My experience . . . was a very profound one – it changed my whole attitude to my work as an actor, making me feel . . . that there is or should be a spiritual element in the relationship between actor and audience, and that the actor can if he wishes, and is provided with the right material by his author, heighten and bring into focus an awareness of an existence larger than our own. For this I shall always be indebted to Graham.'[11]

Sir Laurence Olivier, who once played the part of the whisky priest himself, admitted, perhaps a bit reluctantly, that Scofield's broken-down priest 'was the best performance I can remember . . . I was floored.'[12] In later years, Greene recalled vividly to me the sight of another great: John Gielgud, moved by Scofield's performance, weeping in his seat.

3
Greene on Broadway

14 – with infinite sex appeal.
– GRAHAM GREENE

CATHERINE had not gone out of his life; there was a going away and a coming back. In December 1955, Graham Greene (fifty-one years) and Catherine Walston (thirty-nine years) celebrated the publication of *The Quiet American* by smoking opium in Greene's rooms, C6 in the famed Albany chambers in London – a far cry from the Vietnamese setting where they had hit the opium dens together. Greene was exultant. He still had his beloved, and he had written a new and disturbing play, *The Potting Shed*. This, in two years' time, would see his return to London's West End as a successful playwright. Life found him in love, working well, and enjoying some amusing distractions.[*]

Greene's novels (and in this case a play) often have their origins in earlier work, found sometimes in the margins of a book or on a postcard[†] or scrap of paper. In this case the notes were written before he began his career as a novelist.

Soon after Greene went down from Balliol and began as an apprentice on the *Nottingham Journal*, he sent a story to his then sweetheart,

---

[*] Two years earlier, through Churchill's friend Lord Bracken, Greene became a director of the Greene King brewery. Bracken wrote to Greene on 1 May 1953 admitting that piercing the mysteries of the brewery was not easy, but he had the task of devising a way for the most eminent of the Greenes to be restored to the business. He added that in desiring to become a brewer, Greene was following in the footsteps of Dr Johnson, trustee of the Thrale Brewery. Johnson said at the sale of the brewery: 'We are not here to sell a parcel of boilers and vats, but the potentiality of growing rich, beyond the dreams of avarice.' However nephew Graham Carleton Greene, a director of the brewery himself, does not think his uncle became a director.
[†] The first page of Greene's short story 'The Man Who Stole the Eiffel Tower' was written on a picture postcard of the Eiffel Tower. The story appeared in *Punch* on 19 September 1956.

Vivien. His juvenile style (he was callow for his age) was flamboyant and full of vague philosophising, speaking of 'heaven uprearing her head in a cloud of miraculous towers', of the 'lonely walker's tread, to cross the moat & dare the dangerous uttermost stair'.[1] The wonderfully taut, often wry Greeneian style, like chipped granite, had yet to be born. However, one day he would use a derivative of the title of this insignificant piece, for, oddly, he called this knightly romance *Night by the Potting Shed*.

The success of Greene's first play, *The Living Room* (1953), tweaked some journalists' envy. The *Daily Express* wrote that Greene 'writes about chill misery', but 'sells like hot cakes'.[2] Another said people were 'hypnotised by the name of Graham Greene' and described the play as 'an orgy of sin, suffering and tragedy in the true Graham Greene manner'.[3] When *The Living Room* opened at Wyndham's Theatre, the play and the acting brought forth an astonishing fourteen curtain calls. Greene wouldn't have been human if he hadn't begun to think of a second play and another success, especially as newspaper critics spoke of 'his unerring sense of theatre'.[4]

'Graham came June 12th [1953],' Evelyn Waugh states in his diary. 'He is full of theatrical projects, but, it seemed, in an unhappy state . . . He told me the plot of his new play is a priest who "sacrifices" his faith in order to restore a boy to life. But very sweet and modest. Always judging people by kindness.'[5]

So Greene had in mind the main features of his second play, *The Potting Shed*, but despite the tremendous success of *The Living Room*, he still was in an 'unhappy state'. Could such a frame of mind have been because Catherine Walston had again rejected him? And if so, it looks as if Greene's Catholicism, in large measure, depended on his love for her. Waugh records that Greene 'told the Italian ambassador, as excuse for not visiting conference at Florence, that he was "no longer a practising Catholic". He asked for a biscuit before Mass as though to provide (like his hero in *Heart of the Matter*) a reason for not taking communion, but went off to early train fasting on Monday.'[6]

In spite of having the basic notion of his next play, Greene did not begin writing immediately. There were many reasons for this. For one thing, he needed to think this play through carefully: two of the major characters – the boy and the priest – are each, in their very different ways, lost souls. We have another tormented character in the role of James Callifer's mother. And as in *The Living Room*, there are personal elements in *The Potting Shed*. I was unable to discover any model for the priest, Father William Callifer. But Mrs Callifer – the mother of James – and the dying atheist father, the brother, Miss Connolly (Father

Callifer's housekeeper), and even the lowly dog, all had origins in Graham's life. Such autobiographical material must have made him cautious as to how to proceed.

Other activities intervened to hold up his second play. In 1953 Greene travelled to Kenya to write about the Mau Mau for the *Sunday Times*. In 1954 he went to Indo-China again for the *Sunday Times*, also for *Le Figaro*. In the same year, he began visiting Cuba and Haiti, countries about which he would write important articles and, later, significant novels.

In 1955, he took time out to write a minor novel with the Hemingwayesque title *Loser Takes All*, which contains a sketch of his friend, film mogul Alexander Korda, under the name Dreuther. That same year *The Quiet American* appeared. Waugh, writing in his diary (almost under his breath), mentioned he had *The Quiet American* for review: 'a masterly but base work'.[7] A week later, Greene sent his friend a copy to which Waugh replied: 'I have already read it with deep admiration & wrote a review . . . I am afraid I let my dislike of Fowler run away with me. What a shit he is!'[8]

The Potting Shed lay fallow in Greene's mind, and with two novels out of the way, he returned to it. He'd begun writing it in Jamaica, during a holiday in 1954, with Catherine Walston. In February 1955 he was in Hong Kong on his way to Hanoi – his fourth and last visit to Vietnam. He was to interview Ho Chi Minh, though the contents of that interview were not revealed. I asked Greene to discuss it with me. He would not. While waiting in Saigon for permission to go to Hanoi, he went off to his local where he had nine pipes in an opium den, all alone. Missing Catherine, he was determined to smoke himself inert before going to sleep, eating only biscuits, and drinking only lemonade. He admits to 'working a bit rewriting *The Potting Shed*, especially the part I did in Jamaica'.[9] He turns candid: 'The play will never be producible, but it is good practise.'

The month that *The Quiet American* appeared in America (March 1956), he wrote to his friend, the indomitable navigator Michael Richey, that he was deeply immersed in writing the play. 'I am sorry I couldn't see more of you at Brighton the other day, but I am absolutely punch drunk with work . . . and not fit for human company.'[10]

★

The Potting Shed, Greene's most celebrated play, had its world premiere unexpectedly in America. Unexpectedly, because Greene had experienced difficulty in getting a visa. Even before the 1956 US publication of *The Quiet American*, a novel thought to be anti-American, Greene desired to have a go at the United States, playing David in battle against this latter-day Goliath. In 1954 he decided to test the infamous McCarran Act* on immigration. Travelling from Haiti, Greene landed at Puerto Rico and found himself being deported. He revelled in the deportation – not his first nor his last attempt to singe Uncle Sam's beard.

Tilting at American windmills caused him to be classified a prohibited immigrant to the United States, during the period of Senator Joseph McCarthy's grim campaign against 'communists' and 'subversives'.

Greene's trouble began in 1951, when an interview with him appeared in *Time* magazine (29 October). In his cover portrait Greene looks pensive, inward, shrewd. In the very power of his wet blue eyes there is a suggestion of mad determination. In the interview, Greene mentioned that when a student in Oxford, he had, as a prank, become a dues-paying member of the communist party for no more than six weeks. When he found that party membership would not get him a free trip to Moscow, he dropped out. Greene must have known this little tidbit would force the guardians of the McCarran Act to make him *persona non grata*. Except for a short time in 1957 for *The Potting Shed*, he remained so.

Greene had a particular purpose in releasing this information. He'd been told by an important official at the American embassy in Brussels that the State Department was anxious for cases which would expose the absurdity of the McCarran Act. He was already aware that philosopher Michael Polyanin, novelist Alberto Moravia and anti-communist novelist Arthur Koestler had all at different times been excluded from visiting America. Such men could look after themselves. Greene wished to place himself under the McCarran ban because many others were 'excluded by this Act and are unable in their anonymity and poverty to bring their case before the Attorney-General . . . I applied for a visa because I was in a position to secure a measure of publicity against McCarthy and McCarran.'[11]

He got more than he bargained for. Throughout the fifties he was blacklisted. This meant that whenever Greene wanted to visit the United States he had to get permission from the Attorney-General in Washington which usually took three weeks, and his stay was limited to one month. The State Department made things impossible: he had to let the authorities know on which plane he would arrive and leave, and his hard-won visa was stamped with 'mysterious letters and numbers' ensuring long delays at immigration.[12]

---

* The Internal Security Act of 1950, known popularly as the McCarran Act, required all communist, communist-dominated or communist-linked organisations to register with the federal government the names of all members and contributors, and allowed emergency detention of 'potentially dangerous' persons.

In *Ways of Escape*, Greene writes that he 'rather enjoyed the game'.[13] I doubt it. Jacques Barzun, provost and doyen of Columbia University deans, and a writer of brilliance, recalled an occasion when Greene was visiting his American publisher. Having been delayed by immigration officials, he arrived at the Viking party 'looking grim and not at all appreciative of the proffered hospitality'. The guests offered their 'commiseration and regret and assured Greene that the rest of his visit would be one continuous welcome: these promises fell on deaf ears. Mr Greene did not smile and manifestly did not believe: he had come to an unfriendly and bigoted Philistine country.'[14]

In the summer of 1956 (only a few months after the US publication of *The Quiet American*, then a *cause célèbre*) an alert New York director-producer heard that Greene was nearly finished writing a second play. It all began when Carmen Capalbo read in a gossip column a line from Ed Sullivan, stating that Greene was working on a play:

> I wanted to leave right away and try to see Greene, but I knew
> I needed an introduction. I . . . couldn't find anyone who knew
> him, but then one man said he . . . knew someone who did and
> he gave me the phone number of Mary Pritchett in Connecticut.[15]

Capalbo could not have had a better contact. Mary, once Greene's literary agent, was a terrific character; her sharp mind and reliable judgment earned Greene's trust. She wrote to him that she'd 'like to introduce two brilliant young men who wish to discuss a project with you'.[16]

Young Capalbo came with his partner, Stanley Chase, already a successful team. (Their *Threepenny Opera*, produced at the Theater de Lys in Manhattan, ran for seven years.) Armed with Mary Pritchett's introduction (without which they most assuredly would not have made it through the door), they took a plane to England the next day. They didn't contact Greene until they were in London, no doubt thinking he couldn't easily refuse to see two young men with a business proposition who'd paid their own way across the Atlantic. What a risk they took, since Greene was rarely out of a plane himself. They telephoned, and Greene told them to call the next day; thus they bore down on Greene's London residence. He greeted them affably, appearing tall, slim, with thin blond-grey hair, pink complexion and slightly bloodshot pale blue eyes, in 'a gray flannel double-breasted suit of excellent cut, a cream silk shirt with a plain green silk tie and good, English brown bluchers'.[17]

Capalbo recalled Greene's quirky, springy walk made him awkward like a 'gangly schoolboy'. They talked about anything and everything, but did not speak of why they had come, despite the advantage of having in hand their letter of introduction.

The morning over, the young Americans had yet to broach their subject – and Greene didn't ask them, though they did present him with the original cast album of *The Threepenny Opera*. Greene took them to lunch in Piccadilly and afterwards to a private strip-joint: 'We arrived at a squalid, curving little street off Piccadilly Circus. As we entered, Greene took out a card from his wallet and offered it to the doorman who recognised Greene and exclaimed, "Ah. Good afternoon, Mr Tench."'* It was pitch-black in the nightclub. At one end was a stripper, 'plump, not to say fat, and not unattractive. She started taking off her clothes, the spotlight upon her.' Capalbo recalled:

> In those days her nipples [and below] were covered . . . she went through her bumping and grinding . . . a squeaky three-piece band, off-key musicians, tired at that time in the afternoon, no doubt from having played half the night – and Greene was loving it.[18]

'Since then', as Capalbo wryly put it, 'we've all seen better strippers in high school productions of *Gypsy*.'[19]

After dinner at the Café Royal, they returned to c6 Albany for a nightcap. On Greene's walls Capalbo noticed paintings by Jack Yeats, Graham Sutherland and Ben Nicholson. Apart from these, the walls were lined with books. It was at this point, and only at this point, that Greene asked why they'd come. When they told him, he was surprised that they knew about the play. Admitting he had finished Greene added: '"I don't think much of it." He was so self-effacing. He blushed a little. He had a tendency to blush.'[20]

The young men took *The Potting Shed* back to their hotel and stayed up half the night reading. They knew at once they wanted to produce it (Capalbo to direct) and wanted, in fact, to persuade Greene to let them give the play its world premiere on Broadway rather than in London. There was much to do. They began by telephoning Greene the next morning. He was amazed that the two Americans liked it.

When Capalbo and Chase finally succeeded in getting Greene's second play on Broadway, everyone in the business was surprised. Capalbo remembered: 'These were exciting times. Having got Greene to agree, we were by no means finished. We worked very hard in

---

* Tench is the dentist in *The Power and the Glory* (1940). It was Greene's habit to carry a number of business cards with fictional names taken from lead characters in his novels. I saw one with Major Scobie, the suicidal hero of *The Heart of the Matter*, on it. There must have been others.

London during the next two days . . . It was essential to get the right person to play the extraordinary mother in this play.'[21]

Capalbo and Chase had bearded the literary lion in his den; now they approached the grande dame of the theatre, Dame Sybil Thorndike, then aged seventy-three, whose remarkable career had spanned fifty years. They expected to be turned away. Instead, Dame Sybil spoke of her admiration for Greene and said she'd love to be in his play. So great was her hope that the part would be suitable for her that she wanted to come to their hotel at once to read the manuscript, rather than expecting the young men to go to her. Dame Sybil read it, was delighted and willing to travel to America (which she'd last visited in 1938). Before she actually committed, she asked if they had a part for her husband Lewis Casson (a question often raised). They had.

Ultimately, they had to get in touch with Greene's British manager, Donald Albery, who had produced *The Living Room*, to gain his permission to take the play to New York. Albery was amazed that Greene was letting these young pups kidnap the play, but he was in favour of the project. He was further amazed that they'd already hauled aboard Dame Sybil. Within less than a week Capalbo and Chase had crossed most of the hurdles and persuaded Greene to allow the world premiere in New York, on the way to Broadway. But what on earth was Greene thinking? *The Potting Shed*, sombre, grim, brilliant, was not, absolutely not, a typical Broadway play.

In a short letter to his friend René Berval, Greene updated him: 'I am finishing off a film script of Shaw's *Saint Joan* for Otto Preminger, doing last revisions of a play which comes on in New York this winter called *The Potting Shed*.'[22]

Winter it was, since the play went into rehearsals in late December 1956, six months after Capalbo and Chase met Greene in London. The final cast: Dame Sybil Thorndike; her husband Sir Lewis Casson; Robert Flemyng as the troubled son; Leueen MacGrath as the son's ex-wife; and Frank Conroy, who unexpectedly ran away with the part of the priest. Capalbo had to seek Conroy out in a country hideaway. He'd found him profoundly depressed, virtually at the point of suicide, having lost confidence. Capalbo had a genius for knowing whom to cast and persuaded Conroy, much against his will, to play the broken-down priest. Later, the *New York Times* critic wrote of Conroy, 'He plays . . . with a warmth and humility that are overwhelming, and give *The Potting Shed* its finest moments on the stage.'[23] Conroy won a Tony for 'Best Featured Actor in a Play'.

The role of the forward, brilliantly alive child detective (another of Greene's mature children, who by their honesty, openness and pragmatism seem able to solve problems beyond their elders) went to the beautiful young Carol Lynley. On a poster for the play which Greene sent to Catherine Walston, he wrote beside the lissom figure of the tender-aged Miss Lynley: '14 – with infinite sex appeal'.

★

Capalbo and the actors felt that although the first two acts were splendid, the third needed attention. Uncharacteristically, Greene was willing to rewrite, but couldn't come to New York because of trouble with his visa. As an alternative, he flew to Montreal and presented himself daily at Capalbo's hotel. They went over the play line by line. Greene's revisions in blue ink (it was much later in life that he began using green) were in the 'tiniest hand[writing] I have ever seen', Capalbo said. At first Capalbo found Greene's reputation intimidating and it interfered with his own ability to advise as director, until Greene told him to forget he was a novelist and 'deal with me as you would any novice'. They had done much, but still 'hadn't licked the third act'.[24]

After two weeks of rehearsing the first two acts, Capalbo tackled the difficult third. The second act ends with a superb revelation scene; the third and final providing the intellectual resolution of the play. Yet it lacked bite. Capalbo felt that the problem was that the son was playing the final intimate scene to his mother, not to his estranged wife. American audiences would not readily relate to that. And his two leading ladies, Leueen MacGrath and Dame Sybil Thorndike, agreed with Capalbo, though it meant that Dame Sybil as the mother had a smaller part in the final act.

Capalbo somewhat anxiously phoned Greene and told him what they were trying to do and why. Greene shouted down the mouthpiece: 'Of course, why didn't we think of it before?'[25] Greene seemed, at least until *The Potting Shed*'s English premiere, wildly enthusiastic about the change.

★

Further rewriting made it necessary for Greene to visit New York. But how could he overcome his visa problems? Chase had the answer. He hired an extremely skilled and well-connected attorney in Washington who called Chase back *in one hour* to say it was all cleared up, the State Department agreeing that 'what had happened in the past happened in the past'.[26] These were the Eisenhower years and Joseph McCarthy, his cause lost, was in the process of being sent into the political wilderness.* Capalbo called Greene within hours to tell him jubilantly that

---

* McCarthy died soon afterwards on 2 May 1957, the year *The Potting Shed* opened on Broadway.

an entry visa had been granted. He left the next day for New York. At the Algonquin Hotel he rewrote the third act in three days.

Greene said he did not wish to stay for the opening night. Indeed he'd left town before the premiere and never received Terence Rattigan's* kind telegram at the Bijou Theatre: 'Very best wishes for a great success tonight.'[27] Capalbo and Chase threw a send-off party for the departing author. The next night, just before the penultimate preview, suddenly in front of the theatre a strange figure came upon them, coat over his head. It was Greene, who with childish glee shouted 'Boo!' From under the coat he laughed: 'I couldn't say goodbye to New York without another look at the play.'[28] His last-minute change of plans meant that Greene was able to witness the almost magical effect his play had on the Broadway audience.

---

* Terence Rattigan was one of England's most popular dramatists, whose later plays *The Winslow Boy* (1946), *The Browning Version* (1948) and *The Deep Blue Sea* (1952) show a deepening psychological insight. He was knighted in 1971.

4

Secrets of *The Potting Shed*

But the child's sob in the silence curses deeper
than the strong man in his wrath.
— ELIZABETH BARRETT BROWNING

F ROM the beginning, the play fascinated, and for twelve weeks the theatre was packed to the brim. The central enigma is the secret nature of the hero — a nature profoundly mysterious even to the hero himself. An intensifying suspense throughout the first two acts culminates in the second scene of the second act — surely one of the most memorable moments of a play in our time.

This comes about when James Callifer, the disturbed son of an authoritarian mother, seeks out his uncle, a priest whom he's not seen since childhood. James and his uncle both inhabit damaged souls: Father William Callifer had lost his faith many years earlier under extraordinary circumstances. Thus, there are two mysteries, one hinging upon, and determined by, the other. In both cases, the journey backtracks from *effect* to *cause*. Ingeniously, Greene leads us back through the labyrinth of suggestion to the source of his hero's perpetual torment.

James Callifer's bizarre tale baffles. Now middle-aged, he's never been able to love or give affection, even when married. He meets his former wife, Sara, again in his mother's home just before his father dies, and says with absolute honesty: 'I love nothing', to which she, like a stern bell striking the same clear note, agrees: 'You do indeed. In the night you'd wake loving Nothing. You went looking for Nothing everywhere. When you came in at night I could see you had been with Nothing all day. I was jealous of Nothing as though it was a woman; and now you sleep with Nothing every night.'[1]

James has felt a void since an unexplained illness as a boy of thirteen. Whatever happened, he remembers nothing. The play, right up to the end of the second act, creates almost a fever to know the source of the son's malady, for here must lie the origin of James's personal tragedy.

20

James Callifer's family in the play is irrevocably separated from him. He has worked on a provincial newspaper as sub-editor for five years. His father, a renowned atheist, friend of Bertrand Russell and H. G. Wells, according to James, 'killed [religious] superstition for his generation'. In James's young life, 'God was taboo.'[2]

And the situation? A mother who engineers the isolation of her youngest son. At the same time, James, living in the provinces, desperately tries to discover what happened to him as a child. His psychiatrist makes great efforts to take him back in time, seeking the event in his childhood by means of Methedrine. Yet the nature of his crisis seems beyond recall. He remembers nothing before the age of fourteen.

It is his father's approaching death that brings James home. It's not his mother's wish that he return. Whatever sin he committed as a teenager has not been forgiven. The telegram signalling his father's imminent death comes from his niece of thirteen, who wonders why word was sent to her father, her grandfather's friend Dr Baston, and to her Uncle James's ex-wife, but not to Uncle James. She asks Dr Baston: 'Is he a criminal? . . . Or wicked? . . . Or mad? . . . Is [he] a hunchback?'[3] Believing he cannot be any of these, she sends James a telegram.

What has James done to disgrace himself? Why does his mother refuse him contact with the rest of his family? He is the black sheep, the 'pariah among the Callifers'.

★

From his very first novel (*The Man Within*, in 1929) to his last (*The Captain and the Enemy*, in 1988), Greene felt compelled to create characters psychologically maimed, tenuous survivors in a hostile world, often flawed, as is James. They are ill at ease – strangers to themselves. Some live beyond the law. The character Father Callifer borrows from Shakespeare so aptly: 'They scoff at scars who never felt a wound.'[4]

Greene's feeling for victims was an obsession. He would not sacrifice a storyline just to make it seem more natural or moving to his audience. This was the reason Capalbo suggested changes – a wife/husband reunion instead of a final mother/son understanding. It was also a more satisfying ending for theatregoers who had been kept on the edges of their seats after supping on at least one horror.★

We have seen that Greene was willing to change his third act, transferring the dramatic conversation between James and his mother to

---

★ Capalbo told me in April 2002 that he felt the change would make a more 'convincing [finish] for an audience's acceptance of a grown man's attempts to prove his sanity by relating once more to his wife – a mature action – rather than to his mother. It was a resolution of the *play's* dilemma.'

James and his wife. But when the play was produced over a year later at the Globe in London, Greene changed back to the original version. He writes: 'For the English production we have reverted to the last Act as it was originally written and this is the only version authorised for Great Britain.'[5]*

Greene felt he had to do his best to reflect a genuine real-life conflict; it was a conflict comparable to one in his own family. Here lies true Greeneland: truth, however insalubrious, must be told. Greene's truth is in his fiction, and the autobiographical sources are there, if subtly disguised. Greene was aware that if fiction were concocted without a leavening of real experience, language would lose intensity and urgency. This is especially true in *The Potting Shed*.

*

Graham had two brilliant brothers: Raymond, a distinguished Harley Street specialist and mountaineer; and Hugh, the Director-General of the BBC. But there was another brother, Herbert, the black sheep of the family (see Volume One), who caused his family great heart-ache.

That stringent devotion to work coupled with a determination to be successful and independent, Graham's own creed, was absent in Herbert. He was always getting jobs abroad and then losing them; always speaking of *resigning* when he'd actually been *sacked*. He bore, as his brother described it, 'the knobs, excrescences, [and] fungi of a dozen careers'.[6] But Herbert's greatest weakness was that he drank to excess. Sir Cecil Parrott, Graham's contemporary at Berkhamsted School, recalled to me that Herbert 'had to be carried home every night and a coach was specially kept for him'.[7]

Herbert's first post was in Santos, Brazil, in his uncle's coffee firm. There, he got a girl pregnant. Greene describes his brother's lechery: 'His humorous friendly shifty eyes raked her like the headlamps of a second-hand car which had been painted and polished to deceive.'[8] Herbert signed chits around town to show he was a big man; his uncle had to foot the bill. He gambled and got everyone working for his uncle to gamble too, and when his uncle had to fire him he went to Argentina. After Argentina, money was found for Herbert to start a tobacco farm in Rhodesia. That venture collapsed. Herbert and his wife moved closer to the capital, Salisbury. Further financial help was

---

* Capalbo also stressed his belief that 'the reason Graham changed the third act revision for London is that he couldn't deal with James coming to terms with his wife, as Graham was unable to do the same thing in his own life with Vivien. That would have been hypocritical, and so resolving his differences with the mother was an easier way out.'

provided to start a chicken farm. The chickens died of tuberculosis! It was one damned thing after another.

Graham came almost to hate Herbert for his fecklessness. Sometimes Greene is venomous, calling him 'an utter bounder' who was practically living on his people for thirty years. Graham hoped something might happen to him in Argentina: 'I know it's . . . horrid . . . but if he'd had the self respect of a louse he'd have done himself in by this time.'[9]

Three weeks later, a further letter: 'My eldest brother's "broken out" again. His is a case where I can't help feeling that suicide far from being sinful would be meritorious.'[10] But Herbert had no leaning towards suicide. And his failures went on for years: 'More trouble about H. It's knocked my father up physically . . . I shouldn't be in the least surprised if that bounder literally killed him.'[11]

It is easy to understand Graham's family closing ranks against the eldest son. They all, especially his mother, whose love for her husband was paramount, made Herbert an outcast from the family, in order to protect his father. In *The Potting Shed*, James Callifer is similarly excluded by his mother, who controls the Callifer household. James feels his ostracism intensely and is often deeply depressed, his black moods leaving him suicidal. In the Greene household, there must have been many subterfuges employed to keep Herbert away. Felix Greene, Graham's cousin, told me that the Greenes, in setting Herbert up in Rhodesia, were actually shipping him out. 'He's a trouble, send him off.'[12] Yet in spite of Graham's being pleased that Herbert was out of the way, according to Graham Carleton Greene, Graham's nephew: 'Whoever was best off in the family used to help him fairly regularly.'

Why did Graham, himself guilty of alienating Herbert, now write with such sympathy about James and his troubling exile? When he began writing *The Potting Shed*, Herbert was ill with Parkinson's disease, which would eventually kill him. But was there another reason for the playwright's sympathy?

*

The niece's telegram announcing that his father is dying arrives while James Callifer is undergoing psychological treatment. In spite of Dr Kreuzer's efforts, James is no better.

Dr Kreuzer had a model in Graham's childhood therapist, Kenneth Richmond,* a natural psychologist, with an admirable record of helping

---

* Charles Greene sent Graham to Richmond for six months in 1921 on the recommendation of his son Raymond − then a medical student − when Graham's crisis became known to the family. (See Volume One.) Greene had tried to commit suicide on several occasions and then finally ran away from school.

disturbed schoolboys who responded to his Jungian method of a face-to-face interview between patient and therapist, sitting opposite each other, two human beings trying to solve a problem as friends. But Richmond had limited success with Greene, hence, Dr Kreuzer's admission of failure: 'For six months now I've been trying to find out, and you haven't given me a clue.'[13] James says to Kreuzer: 'I've talked myself dry. Six months of talking. It hasn't got us far.'[14]

Greene would not have actually said this to his therapist, but he carried this sentiment into adulthood. Richmond's impressive widow Zoe echoed her husband's appraisal: 'In Graham's case, he wanted to commit suicide in the end because he couldn't love himself or anybody else.'[15]

In the play, James Callifer strives to discover the source of his misery and, with the help of his niece, runs to earth the mystery which has torn his family apart. The secret lies in what happened in the potting shed, and at its centre, a miracle. He discovers within himself a strange fear: 'It was dark. I was carrying water for my dog. And I didn't have the courage even to come within sight of the door [of the family shed].'[16] 'What', he asks, 'could have happened that was so terrible it wiped out all memory? I was a boy, doctor. What a boy can do is very limited.'[17]

★

James's mother cruelly bars his entry to the dying father's bedroom; the old man dies without seeing his youngest son.

JAMES:	Can I go up?
MRS CALLIFER:	Please wait. The nurse has to let me know.
JAMES:	There's not much time, is there?
MRS CALLIFER:	He mustn't have a shock – now. [*Sara comes in with Anne.*] Go upstairs quickly, dear. Both of you. [*She steps aside for them and they go out.*]
JAMES:	I thought we had to wait for the nurse?
MRS CALLIFER:	[*Slowly, bracing herself for the plain truth.*] James, I don't want you to see him.
JAMES:	But why? I've come for that.
MRS CALLIFER:	I didn't send the telegram.
JAMES:	I know. I'm going to see him, though. [*He moves towards the open door, but Mrs Callifer shuts it and stands with her fingers on the handle.*]
MRS CALLIFER:	I don't want to be harsh. That's why I meant to let you know afterwards. But he's got to die in peace.
JAMES:	Why should I destroy his peace?
MRS CALLIFER:	[*pleadingly*] I love him, James. I want so much to

24

	see the last of him. Promise me you won't move from here.
JAMES:	No! [*He shakes his head.*]
MRS CALLIFER:	Then I stay. [*She leans wearily against the door.*]
JAMES:	Mother, if you love me –
MRS CALLIFER:	I love him more.
JAMES:	Give me one reason. [*She doesn't answer, but she is crying.*] All right. You've won, Mother. I promise not to come.[18]

★

There is another outcast in the play's atheist Callifer family: the dying father's brother. Long ago James's uncle, a Catholic priest, loved James almost as a son. But Father William Callifer might as well be an atheist himself, for he has completely lost his faith. He performs his priestly tasks by rote.

James tracks down Uncle William and, waiting in the hall, overhears the conversation between priest and housekeeper. Miss Connolly has known many priests and has 'learnt only too well to distinguish between the office and the man'.[19] At one point she chastises the good priest who is without faith: 'The people here have a right to a priest with the faith', to which the Father answers with a question: 'Do you think I want to get up every morning at six in time to make my meditation before Mass? Meditation on what? The reason why I'm going on with this slave-labour? They give prisoners useless tasks, don't they, digging pits and filling them up again. Like mine.'[20]

Prior to finding his uncle, James learns from Mrs Potter, the gardener's widow, the horrible hidden event from childhood: 'You were hanging there, sir. You'd used a cord from the play-room. [Mr Potter] cut you down . . . There wasn't any life in you, sir.' The gardener tried artificial respiration. 'It wasn't any use he said. Your heart was stopped.' James 'was beyond human aid, Potter said . . . Potter left the door open, and he looked up and saw your uncle was there. "Master James has killed himself," Potter said. You were stretched out there on the ground and you had no more breath, Potter said, than a dead fish.'[21]

But James was not dead, or, if dead, he revived. So the wonder of what happened in the potting shed cast shadows of doubt on the atheist's universe. James's mother was especially aware that if the story spread, a miracle in a famous atheist's backyard, what nonsense it would make of the life of a rationalist. Even more terrible, her atheist husband *believes* the miracle. She has seen it in his eyes. Thus James is banned from the house because he would be a permanent reminder to her husband of the uselessness of his life.

After hearing what happened to him, James seeks out his uncle, the priest, who speaks of his brother, James's father:

FR CALLIFER: He was a very clever man. Older and cleverer than I was. He took everything I told you and made fun of it. He made me a laughing stock before you. I had taught you about the Virgin birth and he cured you with physiology.

JAMES: Was that why I tried to kill myself?

FR CALLIFER: So you know about that, do you? He was a bit too rough. A child can't stand confusion.[22]

James presses further. It seems his uncle, the priest, did not feel it was a miracle: 'How could you have been dead? . . . It was a coma. Just a coma. The doctor said so.'[23] But the boy had recovered before the doctor arrived. When James asks if the gardener could possibly be right, his uncle asks how it could be – if you had been dead, and then were not, it would have been a miracle, and if it were a miracle, God would have to exist. 'That hideous [religious] picture there would have a meaning. But if God existed, why should He take away His faith from me?'[24] Then Father Callifer remembers the shed and his nephew lying there and Potter struggling to revive him:

I prayed. I was a model priest, you see, with all the beliefs and conventions. Besides, I loved you . . . I couldn't have a child and I suppose you took his place.

He had taken James on his knees and felt a terrible pain:

So terrible I don't think I could go through it again. It was just as though I was the one who was strangled – I could feel the cord round my neck. I couldn't breathe, I couldn't speak, I had to pray in my mind, and then your breath came back, and it was just as though I had died instead. So I went away to bury myself in rooms like this.[25]

And what did his uncle pray for? James needs to know. He and his uncle have suffered too many years of despair.

FR CALLIFER: I'd have given my life for you – but what could I do? I could only pray. I suppose I

offered something in return. Something I
valued – not spirits. I really thought I loved
God in those days. I said, 'Let him live, God. I
love him. Let him live. I will give you anything
if you will let him live.' But what had I got to
give Him? I was a poor man. I said, 'Take away
what I love most. Take – take –' [*He can't
remember.*]

JAMES: 'Take away my faith but let him live'?

FR CALLIFER: Did you hear me?

JAMES: Yes. You were speaking a long way off, and I
came towards you through a cave of darkness. I
didn't want to come. I struggled not to come.
But something pushed me to you.

FR CALLIFER: Something?

JAMES: Or somebody. [*Callifer begins to weep.*] Uncle, can
I help?

FR CALLIFER: I even forgot what I said to Him, until you
came. He answered my prayer, didn't He? He
took my offer.

JAMES: Do you really believe . . . ?

FR CALLIFER: . . . You must forgive me. I'm tired and a little
drunk. I haven't thought about that day for
thirty years. Will you see me to my room? It's
dark on the landing. [*He gets up, and then pauses
and looks up at the hideous picture.*] I thought I
had lost Him forever.[26]

★

Greene first tried suicide at the same age as James Callifer tried to
hang himself, but Greene's methods were more varied, and some a bit
less severe: sawing his knee open; swallowing different potions to poison
himself, including hyposulphite, hay-fever drops, a whole tin of hair
pomade, a bottle of eye drops. He survived the ingestion of a deadly-
nightshade plant, and he swallowed fourteen aspirin tablets before
swimming in the school pool, his legs like lead.

Graham as a child was acutely sensitive, and whether his resentment
was justified or not, he was troubled by his mother always putting his
father first. And while the young Graham *was* suicidal, he never
attempted to hang himself, although that is not to suggest that such
an attempt hadn't crossed his mind.

It is James's parents who have driven our hero to attempt to take
his life. We've seen that Mrs Callifer has a model in Greene's mother,

but there are also parallels between Mr Callifer and Greene's father, Charles Greene, headmaster of Berkhamsted School.

Now Graham Greene's father was absolutely not an atheist. In speeches to his school, he was given to high rhetoric, often with reference to Scripture. He was somewhat naïve, certainly unworldly, and protected by his motherly wife, but he was intelligent; he and his whole family were looked upon by Charles's younger brother Edward as the 'intellectual Greenes'. So the remark made by Father Callifer fits: 'He was a very clever man. Older and cleverer than I was. He took everything I told you and made fun of it. He made me a laughing stock before you.'[27] This is not Charles Greene, but the family of Charles's younger brother, Edward Greene, and Edward himself, who felt in awe of Charles *and* Marion Greene, and even their family.

Certainly Charles Greene was no ogre, nor was he unwilling to believe. He gave a sermon at the beginning of every term, very often on a theme of purity. An entry in the diary of James Wilson (a contemporary of Greene's at Berkhamsted) reads: 'Charles preached a very vehement sermon against filthiness.' His answer to the problems of young men was to 'follow the rules of the Church'.[28] Charles Greene, according to Graham's cousin Ben, was 'bewildered by sex'.[29] He, like many headmasters during the Victorian and Edwardian period right up to and beyond the First World War, feared not religion nor atheism, but homosexuality.

In the play, James Callifer's father has certain characteristics of Charles. During Charles Greene's retirement, his wife read to him daily, censoring material, including their son's novels, to spare him. The character of Mrs Callifer speaks about her husband in a way which, while sharp, probably reflects Marion Greene's notion of her role: 'For nearly fifty years I've looked after his laundry. I've seen to his household. I've paid attention to his – allergies. He wasn't a leader. I can see that now. He was someone I protected. And now I'm unemployed.'[30]

*

After its New York success, Greene set about having *The Potting Shed* performed in England. The first try: 'A record breaking week at Brighton', he wrote to his son Francis on 7 February, and added: '[a] reasonably good first night in London but the press, as I expect you've seen, has been a bit mixed, varying from the downright bad in the Beaverbrook and Rothermere crowd of reporters, to a rave notice on the Third Programme.'[31]

As we've seen, for the London stage, Greene returned the third act to its original form. But we learn more of his earlier mood by looking at a little-known interview that he gave in New York ten days before opening night on Broadway. Henry Hewes, who showed himself aware of Greene's unhappiness, thought the fifty-two-year-old writer 'spoke with the apprehensiveness of a man who has mastered one craft and thus recognizes how far he is from mastering another. "I'm not loosened up enough yet," he says, "And I don't take sufficient advantage of the director's technique."' Hewes then speaks of the major changes made in the third act. It 'originally lacked the reunion of James and his wife. The new, less pessimistic ending obviously pleases Mr Greene, who is quite proud of the fact that in France he is considered an optimist.'[32]

On 10 January, Evelyn Waugh invited Greene down to his home, Combe Florey: 'If for any reason you feel like coming here for a night or two before Feb 6th you would be welcomed with open arms & bottles,'[33] and three weeks later Waugh wrote how 'jolly decent' Greene was to include him 'among the host of your friends clamouring for admission last night'.

He tells Greene it was 'an enthralling evening' but complains mildly: 'I am not theologian enough to understand the theological basis', and suggests, in a clever dismissive line, that Greene should turn the play into a full-length novel, 'explaining more fully to simple people like me'.[34] To his wife, Laura, Waugh was disdainful: 'The play is great nonsense theologically & will puzzle people needlessly';[35] to Ann Fleming, he was more direct: 'The theme is great balls theologically', and adds that while the reviewers asserted '"only Roman Catholics will understand it[,]" [w]e are just the people who don't'.[36]*

In contrast, Edith Sitwell loved the play and stood her ground as a fierce convert. She had been profoundly moved: 'Such beauty and tenderness, journeying beyond despair! It is a great, compassionate yet terrifying play . . . I thank you for a great experience, which will always remain with me.'[37]

★

Greene had grave concerns about Father Callifer's making a contract with God: 'Take away what I love most. Take – Take –' Thirty years after the event James completes the priest's sentence: 'Take away my faith but let him live.'[38] This is Greene's supreme example of sacrificial love. And perhaps Greene himself thought his play's theme was 'great balls theologically', for at least in front of the American journalists,

---

*This was a concern which some of the play's production people wondered about. Carmen Capalbo said, in April 2002, that the audience members, a great many of them Jewish, sat 'quietly enthralled by the play at every performance – and many Jews were among [the play's] most fervent champions'. He goes on to say that they also invited Catholic clergy, and their response was 'overwhelmingly positive'.

Greene discussed the priest's curious bargain (though he'd used the same gambit in *The Power and the Glory*, in *The Heart of the Matter* and *The End of the Affair*); aware that he needed to make some sort of explanation of the offer to relinquish faith in return for a life, he called it 'a contract made in the dark'.

> When the boy lives, the priest only imagines that God has accepted his offer. But faith is 'a gift from God, not a merit, and therefore was not his to give away', as is proved when he recovers his faith.[39]

Yet God does not abandon the believer. The believer does the deserting. Father Callifer does not deliberately repudiate God. Surely Greene was not so naïve as to think he could cut a deal with the Almighty.

There is a more terrifying way to look at this bargain: since God doesn't ever take away faith from a believer, Father Callifer's loss of faith was his own choice, a device of his own making. God never entered into the transaction. Allowing a young man to return from the dead, and in the bargain taking away the priest's faith for thirty years is too coarse a trade for God to make. That is what we might think. But there is a dream of Greene's on the night of 2 October 1966, even more wrenching:

> Terribly distressed because a small child of three months already showed signs of [indecipherable]. Such children have died of that at six months. I beat my fists against the wall and prayed angrily that I should die instead.

It is easy to see here, as in the similar case in *The End of the Affair* and *The Heart of the Matter*, that this attempted bargaining with God was strong within him. Greene's sympathy was almost saintly; he was willing to offer not his faith, or as in the parallel case of a six-year-old dying child in *The Heart of the Matter*, his peace of mind, but his very life.

★

The play was applauded by many. Greene's American publishers, Viking, had the text of *The Potting Shed* out in the bookstores in the same month as the play was running. Richard Watts, Jr, of the *New York Post*, 10 February 1957, felt Greene's play was impressive as dramatic suspense, containing scenes 'not far from overwhelming', which were a combination of 'intellectual suspense, drama and scourging contemplation of inner spiritual conflict; it is at once enthralling, sensitive, disturbing, darkly beautiful and curiously moving'.[40] Indeed, *The Potting Shed* is a wonderful thriller – a search for a boy's lost nature, a trek backwards to discover why he has no feeling, no ability to love – the first of Greene's hollow men.

Greene deserved his fame as a novelist, but with *The Potting Shed* he became a dramatist of great promise. Who could have believed his power as a playwright would be so fleeting?

PART 2

Little Miss Lolita

5

Is It Pornography?

Till the devil whispered behind the leaves,
'It's pretty, but is it art?'
— RUDYARD KIPLING

I N the early 1950s there was in England a new drive against obscenity in literature. At first the prosecutions were against hole-in-the-corner publishers known to deal in pornography, but then the net spread wider and began to encompass more serious works. One study of prostitution provoked such a disturbance that frightened publishers started withdrawing books to avoid legal penalties. It was argued that in such a climate, Greene's own *The End of the Affair* could have been successfully prosecuted. In 1954, on 5 June, there appeared a letter from Greene in *The Times*:

> All this has happened before, about 10 years after a great war. Blake's drawings were impounded by police officers in a raid on a London art gallery (the fact that they had made a mistake did not make their action less absurd), copies of Joyce's *Ulysses* were seized by the Customs, the publishers of *The Well of Loneliness** were prosecuted and condemned. Must we have the whole nonsense over again? One is tempted to call it Manichaean nonsense, for it seems to condemn any description of man's sexual nature as though sex in itself were ugly. *Ulysses* is now openly published; *The Well of Loneliness* can be obtained in the uniform edition of Miss Radclyffe Hall's works. Is the whole dreary routine to be followed once more – books to be condemned and then resuscitated when a more reasonable official attitude prevails? . . .

* Radclyffe Hall's novel *The Well of Loneliness* is about the love of one woman for another. After its appearance in 1928, a London magistrate judged the book an 'obscene libel' and ordered copies to be destroyed. The British ban was eventually overturned on appeal after the author's death in 1943.

It is with a sincere desire that our magistrates and judges should take no rash risk that one writes this letter.[1]

According to Ronald Matthews, Greene was a bit tipsy when he wrote this in Monte Carlo, but I see no hint of that. On the contrary, his argument is crystal clear. But no one could have known, certainly not Greene, that this missive was, in a sense, the initial shot across the bows in the battle of censorship. And it was but a skirmish then, not to become a war for at least a year and a half. Greene's weapon was humour, in a cunning assault against what he saw as censorship of legitimate literature.

It began innocently enough: Greene had been asked by the *Sunday Times* to choose the three best books of 1955. He had done this for years, either for the *Sunday Times* or the *Observer*. On this occasion Greene chose *Boswell on the Grand Tour*, Herbert Luthy's *State of France* and Vladimir Nabokov's *Lolita*, the story of paedophile Humbert Humbert, a European intellectual who develops an obsessive love and lust for Lolita, a twelve-year-old nymphet. That love is consummated, Lolita being indeed his willing inamorata.

Up to this point, Nabokov had had very little success in persuading American publishers to accept *Lolita*. Edmund Wilson, the distinguished American critic, tried to place the novel with Farrar, Straus, but Roger Straus gave it a firm rejection because of the subject matter, advising Nabokov not to publish it even pseudonymously. Wilson (despite his initial dislike of the book, though it is true he'd only read half of it) next introduced his visiting friend Jason Epstein, an important Doubleday editor, to Nabokov's recent work with the words: 'Here's a manuscript by my friend . . . Nabokov. It's repulsive, but you should read it.'[2] Epstein was impressed and wanted to publish it, but the president of Doubleday wouldn't hear of it. By then Nabokov had been rejected by Viking, New Directions and Simon & Schuster.

Nabokov next sought a French publisher. After all, *Ulysses* was published in France long before either England or America allowed it. Nabokov sent *Lolita* to Doussia Ergaz, asking her to show it to Sylvia Beach, who'd brought out *Ulysses*, but Beach was too old to fight further literary battles. Ergaz then gave it to publisher Maurice Girodias's Olympia Press. (Nabokov did not know that Girodias dealt in borderline sleaze.) But Girodias did have in his list some worthy, and even great, writers: Beckett, Durrell, Henry Miller. As Nabokov's biographer Brian Boyd put it: 'Three-quarters of his list was pornographic trash, but he accepted the title of pornographer' – he is quoting Girodias himself – 'with joy and pride.'[3] Because Olympia was a lowly press and since Girodias didn't advertise, *Lolita* received no reviews.

Almost accidentally Nabokov learned that Graham Greene had picked *Lolita* as one of his books of the year. According to Andrew Field, Nabokov read by chance of Greene's choice in the *New York Times Book Review* in mid-January 1956. Nothing else was heard until 26 February 1956, when, again in the *New York Times*, Nabokov learned more from Harvey Breit's column, 'In and Out of Books':

> Looking at the English papers . . . we notice that Mr Graham Greene, fine novelist and hater of all things American except Texas, is riding again. In the *Sunday Express*, columnist John Gordon writes of his shock at reading a book, *Lolita*, a long French novel about nymphets, recommended by Mr Greene . . . 'Sheer unrestrained pornography,' wrote Mr Gordon and lectured Mr Greene severely.[4]

Breit missed out some powerful lines from the *Sunday Express* editor-in-chief John Gordon's sudden and unexpected attack on Greene and Nabokov: 'Without doubt it is the filthiest book I have ever read . . . the entire book is devoted to an exhaustive, uninhibited, and utterly disgusting description of his [Humbert's] pursuits and successes . . . Anyone who published it or sold it here would certainly go to prison.'[5] Evelyn Waugh, in a letter to Nancy Mitford on 11 January 1956, reported that 'Graham Greene recommended a pornographic book in the *Sunday Times*. I mean the sort of book you go to jug for.'[6]

Instead of responding to John Gordon in kind, Greene had the genius to reply tongue-in-cheek. Greene's friend John Sutro gives an account in the *Spectator* of how Greene decided to deal with Gordon: he would laugh him out of court. Greene decided to form a joke organisation, to play upon Gordon's inborn Scottish puritanism. Thus the John Gordon Society was born, its arrival announced in the *Spectator*:

> In recognition of the struggle he has maintained for so many years against the insidious menace of pornography, in defence of our hearths and homes and the purity of public life, the signatories propose to form the John Gordon Society if sufficient support is forthcoming. The main object of the Society will be to represent the ideals of Mr Gordon in active form, in the presentation of family films, the publication of family books, and in lectures which will fearlessly attack the social evils of our time, and to form a body of competent censors, unaffected by commercial considerations, to examine and if necessary to condemn all

offensive books, plays, films, strip cartoons, musical compositions, paintings, sculptures, and ceramics.

Yours faithfully,
Graham Greene, President
John Sutro, Vice-president[7]

This was followed by a note from the editor of the *Spectator* saying that he would 'gladly forward applications' for the new Society. Greene wrote another, mischievous letter to the *Spectator*, commenting on an admission which had appeared in Gordon's own column:

Since the publication of Mr John Gordon's confession that he has several times 'shamefacedly' smuggled pornographic books into this country in his suitcase, I have received several letters (including three from a doctor, a lawyer and a clergyman of the Church of England) protesting that our Society cannot under the circumstances continue with its present name. An alternative title suggested by one correspondent is the Joynson-Hicks Society to commemorate that great Home Secretary who purged our youthful shelves.

Personally (and I feel sure I speak for Mr Sutro too) I honour Mr Gordon all the more for his public confession, startling though it may have seemed to those who have for years admired his stand against the prevailing looseness of morals. It is so much easier to admit a spectacular and major sin than to plead guilty, as he has done, to a 'shamefaced' misdemeanour more common among schoolboys than men of maturer years. None the less certain members feel that the title of the Society will have to be subject to debate at the first General Meeting on March 6, and therefore we are unable to invite the attendance of Mr Gordon himself on that occasion. I have little doubt that the point at issue will be honourably settled ('he that is without sin among you cast the first stone'), and that members, already numbering half a century, will continue to pursue their great objectives under the proud and unstained title of the John Gordon Society.[8]

Greene asked Catherine Walston if she'd seen his letter: 'This is a reply to John Gordon's attack on me the other day for "recommending" pornography – i.e. *Lolita*.' And Greene added: 'I am getting tired of Beaverbrook's gutter boys & feel like hitting back.'[9]

John Sutro, in an article many years later, recalled that some people didn't like this teasing of Gordon. Sutro gives one example from B. A. Young of Fulham:

Before your clever readers bust themselves with laughing at Mr John Gordon, may I be allowed a humble and, I fear, old-fashioned word in his defence? In an age when books and newspapers are available not only to the adult population of all classes but also to kiddies, it is not a bad thing to have at least one responsible journalist on the side of decent thinking and moral living. Mr Greene and his sycophants may sneer as they will; but John Gordon's column in the Sunday Express is courageous, Christian, and almost always accurate. To make fun of it is the act of a snob and a cad.[10]

Sutro recalls they were 'deluged with correspondence, [and] cables to POGO LONDON and stamped addressed envelopes were strewn around like autumn leaves'.[11] Another letter addressed to the society's fictitious secretary asserts, 'I wish to enrol as a life member (and a life after death member if that is possible) of the John Gordon Society, and I wish you and Mr Gordon every success in your great crusade.'[12] Someone is pulling someone else's leg.

At the inaugural meeting, there were sixty first-comers. John Sutro mentions the leading members who arrived at Greene's flat: bookseller Helen Winick; Venetia Murray of the *Picture Post*; Christopher Chataway of Independent Television News; David Farrer of Secker & Warburg; Christopher Isherwood, Greene's cousin; director and friend Peter Brook; Ian Gilmour and his wife, owners of the *Spectator*; Alexander Frere, head of Heinemann and a favourite of Greene's; and Baroness Budberg, one-time lover of communist writer Maxim Gorky, H. G. Wells and the philosopher A. J. Ayer.

Greene wrote an account of that first meeting for the *Spectator*.

Mr Frere and other publishers present offered co-operation in submitting proofs of forthcoming books to the Society and agreed to indicate by means of a band the Society's disapproval if it proved impossible for them to withdraw the books after condemnation . . . Another member felt that the Society might well approach the manufacturers of the game 'Scrabble' and persuade them to include in each set a pledge to be signed by the purchaser that no words would be allowable other than those in the *Concise Oxford Dictionary*.* Yet another proposal was for a plaque to be placed by the Society on the wall of the house occupied by Mr Gordon's predecessor, the late James Douglas – famous for his statement worthy of an ancient Roman, 'I

---

* The Concise (9th edition) is no longer afraid of four-letter words, though it still feels the need to indicate that they are 'coarse slang'.

would rather give poison to my daughter than place in her hands a copy of *The Well of Loneliness*.'[13]

The Society invited John Gordon himself to the second meeting, asking him to deliver a lecture. With that, the hilarious initial meeting broke up. Clearly Greene won the first round. There are doubts that he won the second, for John Gordon was a bonnie fighter and absolutely no pushover.

The Society tried to persuade Gordon that his lecture should be on censorship. Gordon sidestepped that neatly in his letter of 5 May 1956. He wrote: 'I propose instead that we make the subject "Pornography" which was the original, and I presume still is, the main interest of your Society.' Then came the kicker: 'I suggest instead of a lecture that your distinguished President, Mr Graham Greene, undertakes to defend Pornography in books and newspapers while I oppose it . . . As the subject is of wide public interest and . . . of considerable importance to the community, I think attendance at the debate should not be restricted to members of the Society. I suggest that it should be open to all who wish to participate.'[14] We can see the direction of Gordon's thoughts: Greene had filled the first meeting with his acolytes; Gordon was determined to fill the second with his.

In reply to Gordon, 'Miss Thompson' stressed that Greene would not be willing 'to defend pornography, and the discussion would be more likely to proceed on the lines of what exactly pornography was, about which there is obviously some disagreement between you and the President'. But Gordon would not be led 'as a lamb to the slaughter'. After some manoeuvrings, the meeting was arranged for 25 July at the Horseshoe Inn in Tottenham Court Road. And, wrote Gordon, 'Of course invite the Press. The more publicity we get the better. After all isn't the real object publicity?' But then he came back to the need for a large audience:

> I undertake to give you the widest possible publicity before the meeting, and thus I hope 'drum up' a substantial audience eager to meet you all and to join in the fun. Even at the cost of becoming members. It is for that reason that I hope you may agree upon a room big enough to cope with a good attendance.

He got a last dig in: 'I don't think you need to have any worries about any possible difference of opinion between your President and myself regarding what pornography is. I am sure we both know exactly what it is.'[15]

Greene and Sutro were worried their prize goose wouldn't turn up. Sutro recalled that as they stood with their backs to the door, 'a tall figure slipped in. Everything about him was grey, hair, face and suit. "Am I in the right room for the John Gordon Society dinner?" he asked. "Yes," we said. "I am John Gordon." [16]

John Sutro recalled that dinner when I interviewed him and his wife Gillian in Monte Carlo on 10 May 1977:

> It was the funniest evening Gillian spent in her life. We were in a private room in the Horseshoe Inn and the dinner party consisted of Antonia Fraser and her husband, Graham Greene, John Gordon . . . He arrived first and then there was a party of about 11 people . . . an extraordinary dinner party with Gillian next to John Gordon, Graham and so on. Gillian charmed John Gordon and he told her he had a speech he was going to make about her husband but now he had met Gillian, he wouldn't make it. And kept his word . . .
>
> I was the Chairman – Randolph Churchill was there quite drunk. It was full of people who had all come in from the street because it was open to anyone, you see. It was packed with people. I was supposed to be the Chairman, Frere was there, who was attacked. It was a mad, mad evening. At the end of the evening, the manager of the place said to me that it was the most distinguished company he'd ever had inside his place. It was uproarious. John Gordon had the *Sunday Express* backing him. We had only the *Spectator* behind us and all because Graham had chosen *Lolita* as his book of the year.

Three and a half years after the event, Graham wrote to Leonard Russell, then Literary Editor of the *Sunday Times*, telling him: 'the final public meeting at the Horseshoe Tavern was a royal success and those on the platform, John Gordon, myself, Frere, and John Sutro, had to reach it by climbing up a fire escape.' [17]

William Barkeley gave an account the following day in the *Daily Express*:

> The John Gordon Society made a splendid start in the Horseshoe, Tottenham Court-road, last night – and probably a glorious finish . . .
>
> There [was John Gordon] . . . with Mr Graham Greene sitting at his right side. Said [Gordon]: 'It was a book so dirty it was printed in Paris. No publisher in this country is willing to print it. It is the story of a man who devoted his life to seducing young girls. Let me read you this description . . .'
>
> Loud cheers went up from the crowded audience as Mr Gordon read the passage in a solemn voice.

41

'More, more,' shouted the audience. 'Give us it at dictation speed.'

This did not embarrass John Gordon. He was not the chairman, but he took the chairman's gavel and banged for order.

Gordon next tried to catch Greene with a clever move, trying to probe into Greene's past when, eighteen years before, he'd reviewed a Shirley Temple film, referring to the nine-year-old's 'dubious coquetry',[18] for which he'd been sued and had lost.

If I were Mr Graham Greene, after that salutary experience I would not get myself mixed up with this sort of thing again.

Greene was about to reply when Winston Churchill's son entered the fray:

At this stage Mr Randolph Churchill, who had been interrupting a great deal at the back of the hall, moved forward. He went on interrupting – and being interrupted by members of the audience.

One voice shouted: 'Is he being paid for the number of inter-ruptions he makes?'

John Gordon wound up: 'I hope what I have said will give food for reflection to people who began this thing as a joke, and will bring some of them to the penitent's stool.'

. . . Randolph Churchill went on bouncing up.

John Gordon: 'I happen to be a shareholder [in the Beaverbrook press]' (loud shouts and laughter) 'whose money has to be spent on Randolph Churchill in very large sums over many years. A majority of us in the organisation would be glad to see the payments stopped.'

Loud was the laughter when Randolph Churchill shouted back: 'Sell your shares.'[19]

The evening wore on, but not without Randolph Churchill bringing the house down. He seemed more Gordon's opponent than Greene's – Barkeley again:

Amid uproar it became suddenly revealed that Randolph Churchill was not just a public visitor but a fully paid-up member of the John Gordon Society.

John Gordon was disgusted to hear this. He said, 'It is the first time anybody got any money out of him.'

Randolph Churchill then protested that the whole object of the society was being ruined because the saint around whom it had been built had said he wouldn't favour a censorship of books.

'This is heresy from the man whom we have all gathered to support. We should dissolve the society,' he proclaimed.

Amid loud laughter, the chairman, Mr John Sutro, announced that the committee would carefully consider the point raised by Randolph Churchill.[20]

On the following Sunday, 29 July 1956, Gordon admitted in the *Sunday Express*: '[my] greatest help through the hilarious evening was Mr Randolph Churchill, who presented himself to me as a stooge. I can never adequately express my thanks to him. He strode up and down the centre aisle of the packed hall, looking for all the world like a pompous ducal butler laying down the law to the peasants in "the local".'[21]

In a letter to Michael Richey on 3 August 1956, Greene described the Horseshoe as 'packed to overflowing with people standing all down the stairs and only about a quarter . . . were members of the Society . . . However John Gordon had miscalculated and found that his public were against him.' (This view is opposed to Barkeley's, but Barkeley had, I suppose, to pitch it in his boss's direction.) Greene adds: 'If it hadn't been for Randolph Churchill overdoing his attacks on Gordon all the sympathy would have been against Gordon. Anyway it was all great fun and didn't in fact reach the point of razor blades or fists.'

★

At the end of the year, Greene received a sad letter from Vladimir Nabokov:

From various friends I keep receiving heart-warming reports on your kindness to my books. This is New Year's Eve, and I feel I would like to talk to you.

My poor Lolita is having a rough time. The pity is that if I had made her a boy, or a cow, or a bicycle, Philistines might never have flinched. On the other hand, Olympia Press informs me that amateurs (amateurs!) are disappointed with the tame turn my story takes in the second volume, and do not buy it. I have been sent copies of the article, in which, about a year ago, a Mr Gordon with your witty assistance made such a fool of himself. It would seem, however, that a clean vulgar mind makes [Gordon's] wonderfully strong, for my French agent tells me that the book (the English original) is now banned by governmental decree in France . . .

This is an extraordinary situation. I could patter on like this till next year. Wishing you a very happy New one, I remain,

Yours very sincerely[22]

Greene wrote with some bitterness on the subject in the *Spectator*, whilst showing his desire to continue the charade of the John Gordon Society, his support paper-thin: 'Now Mr [Rab] Butler . . . has come to the support of Mr Gordon in his condemnation of *Lolita*, the distinguished novel by Professor Vladimir Nabokov of Cornell University. The Home Office seem to have brought pressure to bear on the French authorities and induced them to suppress the series in which *Lolita* happens to appear from publication in English in France.'[23]

Greene returns to the farce of being in favour of Gordon's puritanism, and proposes that Mr Butler be elected Honorary Vice-President. 'Whatever differences of opinion we may have about his action, we cannot but admire his temerity in extending the control exercised by his Ministry across the Channel.' He went on:

> In the days when Baudelaire's poems were condemned by a French court there was no British Home Secretary with the courage to work behind the scenes in defence of our tourists' morality. The Society looks forward to the day when the Minister of the Interior in Paris will reciprocate Mr Butler's activities and arrange the suppression in London of any French books liable to excite the passions of . . . Monsieur Jean Gordon on holiday.[24]

★

America's obscenity laws were then much fiercer than England's, yet *Lolita* was published first in America. How did this come about? At the second meeting of the John Gordon Society, Walter Minton, a representative of G. P. Putnam & Sons, happened to be in London and just for kicks turned up at the Horsehoe Inn. Immediately he recognised that he must take up the challenge and publish *Lolita*.

The novel appeared in America on 18 August 1958. Some critics were outraged, but others enormously impressed. Orville Prescott argued in the *New York Times* that the arrival of *Lolita* was bad news in the world of books ('The first [objection] is that it is dull, dull, dull in a pretentious, florid and archly fatuous fashion. The second is that it is repulsive . . . highbrow pornography'[25]), but nothing could stop the passion for *Lolita*, as Walter Minton's letter to Nabokov effectively proved: 'I telegraphed you this AM there were over 300 reorders on publication day. It is now 3:00 PM and there are over 1000!'[26] The '1000' was crossed out and '1400' written underneath.

★

The war as to who would publish in England heated up – it seemed an impossible task. A few years after Greene chose *Lolita* as one of his

1955 books of the year, The Bodley Head's Max Reinhardt wrote to Nabokov, at a time when to publish such a work could mean prosecution. Greene's secretary had written to Reinhardt, 'He [Greene] says that all that has transpired is that Putnam's are publishing it in the U.S. and there was some sort of proposal that Weidenfeld [& Nicolson] should publish it in England, but it was felt that Nabokov would prefer Mr Greene to have first refusal for The Bodley Head if he wished.'[27] Exactly two months later, on 3 November 1958, Max wrote to Greene about a letter he'd received from Walter Minton:

I cannot understand why the book MUST be published in collaboration with another publisher, but his letter has crossed mine when I said that we would only be interested if we did it on our own. Evidently it is a clash between the Olympia Press [in France] and Nabokov, and should there also be a clash between Minton and Nabokov then perhaps we will get the book after all, but doubtful.[28]

It was Greene's view that The Bodley Head would be able to publish *Lolita* or, as he put it, 'I wouldn't be surprised if we got LOLITA yet if we keep a firm stand against collaboration.'[29] But The Bodley Head did not get the book, as we can tell from Greene's inside knowledge: 'I have just heard news . . . that makes the way we were treated over *Lolita* more than ever unsatisfactory. Apparently Weidenfeld consulted counsel, John Forster, and as a result the book is appearing in a vulgarised version with several pages cut out. One doesn't know whether Nabokov realises this or has given his consent to it.'[30]

Reinhardt took a further two months to write to Nabokov (that fact alone is astonishing), but like every other publisher, Max could sense the danger from the scare word 'pornography':* 'Graham Greene told me today [he'd heard] LOLITA was going to be published with some severe cuts. As he is about to go abroad he asked me to . . . tell you that if this were so it would be a great shame and he thinks that it would detract from the quality of the book. I don't know what arrangements you and Mr Minton have finally made. So far as we are concerned we made what we thought was a substantial offer and agreed to publish the book as it is and without any cuts whatsoever. This offer still stands if you are at all interested.'[31] And then Reinhardt offered

* Graham's nephew, Graham Carleton Greene, joined Secker & Warburg in January 1958. He was asked to read *Lolita* and 'nearly lost my job over it', he told me. He said it was the funniest book he'd ever read, but made no suggestion there might be any legal difficulties. Fred Warburg thought Graham Carleton should have alerted them to the danger, but he said, 'at 21, what did I know about that sort of thing?'

what should have been, if contracts had not been already signed, a clincher, for it was another example of Greene's stunning courage and risk-taking:

> There is here a very real danger of prosecution when the book is published and so far our laws do not allow for the defence to bring in the literary merit of a book. On the other hand the person who is prosecuted in the publishing company publishing the book is one who actually signs the contract. If The Bodley Head published LOLITA it was the intention for Graham Greene to sign the contract on our behalf. Although one could not bring in a witness for the defence to prove the literary merit of the book he could use the arguments himself for his own defence. I seriously feel that if this were known the dangers of prosecution would be less.

In his reply, Nabokov stated categorically that *Lolita* wouldn't be cut, and though he'd have liked to be published by The Bodley Head, he was sorry but it was now too late. This was a colossal disappointment to Greene and Reinhardt, and Greene never quite forgave Nabokov, though in a recent letter to me, Reinhardt gave other reasons why it went to Weidenfeld:

> Graham was very keen that we should publish Nabokov's *Lolita* as he had written in praise of it . . . but there was some dissent on the Board at The Bodley Head and eventually Weidenfeld & Nicolson published it via the French publisher Maurice Girodias. George Weidenfeld offered to publish it jointly with The Bodley Head but I refused as I did not want to appear to need the support of another publisher.[32]

Perhaps a minor loss of face would have been financially worthwhile, since great profits were made in England in bringing out *Lolita*, but there was great danger as well. The Bodley Head should have joined forces with Weidenfeld & Nicolson.

The attacks on Greene did not stop. At the end of 1958, Robert Pitman used the *Sunday Express* book page to repeat more or less the charges against Greene which his editor, Gordon, had employed, but spiked them with a dash of yellow journalism:

> Two weeks ago on this page I mentioned that the British firm, Weidenfeld and Nicolson, were proposing to publish *Lolita*. I gave some indication of *Lolita*'s outline (to say that its 450 pages deal

in gloating detail with the debauching of little girls aged between nine and 12 . . .)[33]

Pitman then reports that he telephoned the publisher asking them to reconsider the decision to print. They angrily rejected him:

The *Lolita* brigade have been alarmed and angry. Who are they? Foremost there is Vladimir Nabokov's friend, Mr GRAHAM GREENE. Unlike many would-be-liberals, Mr Greene is a genuinely good humoured and tolerant man. And he is a genius in his own right.

For any one of his novels I would forgive him all his follies. Which of course is saying something.

Pitman repeated the Shirley Temple slur used during the debate at the Horseshoe Inn, and then took another tack:

Mr Greene saw nothing wrong in writing a long commendation of opium smoking. A daring undergraduate might have written it at 20. Mr Greene was nearer 50. (The first whiff of the drug, he enthused, was like '*the first sight of a beautiful woman with whom one realises a relationship is possible . . .*')

That presumably was why Mr Greene first commended *Lolita* three years ago when it was merely just another dirty book printed by a Paris publisher named Girodias.

Greene was only the first — the popular politician Lord Boothby had his wrist slapped. Then Pitman pitched into the publisher George Weidenfeld, and finally the Conservative member of Parliament for Bournemouth, Nigel Nicolson (son of Harold Nicolson and Vita Sackville-West), came in for a pummelling:

Mr Nicolson has explained in the House of Commons that he is publishing *Lolita* as a matter of conscience. The House in recent years has heard a lot about Mr Nicolson's conscience . . . Movingly he praised Nabokov to the assembled M.P.s . . . 'His books have been acclaimed by distinguished critics all over the world.'[34]

What had Nicolson, a good and honest man, actually said? Speaking in his Bournemouth constituency, he acknowledged that some were accusing him of publishing pornographic books. He responded to the *Sunday Express*'s calling *Lolita* obscene, asking what was meant by that term. The legal definition was 'a book which could' corrupt a reader.

Lolita could not possibly corrupt anybody. It is the very opposite of corrupting. It condemns what it describes, just as a murder story implicitly condemns murder. A book which describes a wicked man is not therefore itself wicked. It is usually the opposite. It holds him up as an example of what *not* to do, by describing the consequences of his wickedness. That is exactly what *Lolita* does.[35]

The *Express* kept pressing its opposition:

[*Lolita*] . . . was finally accepted by Weidenfeld & Nicolson. But W. & N. decided to hold up publication pending possible modification of British vague pornography law, which gives any constable the right to seize books or have booksellers prosecuted if in his own judgment a book is obscene.[36]

The Labour MP, Roy Jenkins – the late Lord Jenkins of Hillhead – introduced a bill to modify the law to allow prosecution 'only if a book as a whole, rather than in individual passages, is judged obscene, [which] would also allow the defence to summon expert witnesses on literary merit'. The *Express* went on to say that if the reform failed, 'the publishers risk prosecution should they bring out *Lolita*'. The *Express* also interviewed a 'local politico' living in Bournemouth, whose view was definite: 'A director of a firm intending to publish this vulgar novel is no fitting representative for good Bournemouth citizens.'[37] And indeed, Nicolson was not re-adopted as a candidate for the next election, for whatever reasons.

Lolita finally appeared in England in November 1959. Given Greene's 'discovery' of Nabokov and the ensuing controversy, it was natural for newspapers to appeal to him to review what fast became a bestseller in England, too. He steadfastly refused. Weidenfeld & Nicolson were able to take the risk of prosecution because by the autumn the new and more liberal Obscene Publications Act had taken effect. After that, *Lolita* was gathered into every library's bosom and Nabokov's fortune was made. Greene was left out in the cold.

PART 3

Affairs Won

6

Love's Blind Dance

Trip no further . . .
Journeys end in lovers meeting,
Every wise man's son doth know.
— SHAKESPEARE

AFTER having finished *The Potting Shed* in December 1955, Greene's world was again blossoming. But in early 1956, the wilting began.

He'd been 'grumpy over the telephone', which in a letter to Catherine he blamed on too much whisky with Dorothy Glover, Alexander Korda's death (23 January 1956), a press cutting and 'disappointment about the holiday [one of the first of many cancelled by Catherine], worry about the P & the G'* combined. Referring to the coming election in which Catherine's husband Harry Walston was a candidate, Greene understands her reason for staying by her husband's side: '& if there's anything specific I can do (which wouldn't cause scandal), do let me know. Good luck anyway to both of you.' Then, 'Why don't we take Noël Coward's house [in Jamaica] in April [1956]? I love you in spite of *my* (!) bad moods & bad behaviour.'[1]

In addition, Greene was worried about his health. Eric Strauss, his physician, assumed he had cancer. The day before, he'd had a blood test: 'I shall know the result on Thursday. If it's really bad (as Eric on the phone so cheerfully assumes) there would be only two alternatives — killing oneself or taking no action. The Church would prefer the second!'[2]

Dottoressa Moor, Greene's old friend in Capri, diagnosed several possibilities. Her therapies seemed worse than the disease: 'Life without drink or you would be real hell.' But then a sudden mood swing — he who was always the more ardent of the two, uncharacteristically wrote in dismissive manner:

---

* The play of *The Power and the Glory* — see Chapter 2.

We are still in touch because of a bargain I made in Rome. I see no possibility of carrying out my end before the winter – too much work at the moment to get anything started. If therefore you want to call off your side of the bargain & leave me, I can't blame you.

And then, 'About the 19th . . . you'll certainly have the curse. Not exactly a "party" date.'[3] Greene seemed inexplicably acquiescent to the chance of losing Catherine. This is worth noting. Of course, he is bitter that none of their arrangements ever came off. Then he suddenly offers another suggestion – a long holiday in Madrid in October. 'After all we lost more than a week & all the plans for Paris, Lisbon, Stockholm, & even London to make up have gone by the board.'[4] But why the atypical willingness to let Catherine leave him given his lovesick nature?

Greene turned to his physician brother, who ordered more blood tests; he awaited the results. When Catherine telephoned, she found him 'peevish & unreasonable . . . Raymond had promised to ring me at 12 & I hung on . . . with no result. Then came back feeling a bit cross with wine & waiting & got your call.'[5] Explanations, excuses and rationalisations, these were now constants. But Greene was given a reprieve: 'If there was anything wrong with my liver it's cured – so anyway I can drink again. But I had hoped for *some* physical explan-ation of my melancholia & general beastliness to you – & now it simply seems that I am beastly & that's that.' And then a sad comment, 'I love you dearly & *I hate myself so much* – & it's the second half that seems to cause the trouble . . . there's nothing in life one values like you – *not work or children or books.*'

His depression continued: 'Just after you'd rung up a parcel of . . . *The End of the Affair* turned up – *that book of ill omen.*' His postscript: 'I wish I could stop being a bastard.'[6] Greene's anguish over what he sees as Catherine's withdrawal must be one reason for his moods. 'You sometimes think I'm angry with you when I'm only sad & disap-pointed with fate.'[7] Another letter, dated simply 'Thursday', invites her to London: 'Let's go to a flicker & have supper at the Casanova – but mostly I want to lie beside you (& under you & over you) on this great barren bed.'[8]*

*

Greene's friend Edward Sackville-West was sure that the melancholy Greene would commit suicide. What kept him from such a deed? I

---

* This was their famous blue bed; their lovers' bed.

am sure it was *not* because he was suddenly intensely aware that time was slipping under his feet. He often wished to die.

I think it was the numerous physical and sensual adventures deliberately sought all over the globe, part of the struggle to allay misery. His debilitating spells were tied to him as inevitably as a tail to a dog. Greene's mood disorders are among the best examples in our time, as Byron's were in his, of manic episodes characterised by high energy levels, irritability, enthusiasm and increased productivity, followed by deep, black depressions, dark nights of the mind.

Graham's depression is described just prior to his final visit to Vietnam, early in 1955, in a letter to Catherine only days before his departure. Wanting to see her he admitted passing through a melancholic spell for days, thinking about his early love life, his marriage, reflections 'more distant than childhood. It even comes into my dreams . . . One looks back across a huge chasm . . . I wish I didn't have so much to be remorseful about.'

He is enduring awful weather in Brighton with no one to talk to and 'unloads' on her. He contemplates leaving England, and staying away so that 'the past is even smaller – right out of sight'. But he tells her he needs to write to someone, and she is the only person he comfortably shares his thoughts with. A few days after reaching Vietnam, he writes to her from the Hotel Majestic in Saigon: 'Nearly three weeks & one letter from you. It doesn't seem worth keeping up a one-sided conversation. But I'm feeling so depressed that I have to speak to someone.' This is a broken record, skipping maddeningly over the same line of song. How burdensome it must have been to Catherine. He tells her he's practically given up drink and complains that being sober makes him 'see too clearly too many things', and that he feels 'a sense of the other person's indifference'. But it doesn't stop the chorus being repeated over and over: 'Forgive a dreary letter, but one can't always hide one's thoughts.'[9] He was compelled to reach out to her no matter what.

His motto (strange for a writer) was 'Set a watch, O Lord, before my mouth and a door round about my lips', for Greene trusted few, despite his assertion that 'To go through life without trust is to be imprisoned in the worst cell of all, oneself'. He was often conscious of being so imprisoned.

One of the trusted few was his sister Elisabeth, who worked as his secretary in later years. But during his mid-fifties he revealed his darker side only to Catherine Walston, who, by her spirit, could single-handedly banish his indifference to life. He could become morose, then lively, then gentle, then most gentle, then extremely irritable. He was volatile and contradictory, anger following warm emotions, or, if he felt he had been unfair, deep compassion. His chivalrous willingness to apologise (deeply repenting his anger), and his morbid irascibility of temper, oscillated with the gentler side of his nature.

*

If Catherine and Greene's relationship was complex, the relationship between Graham and Harry Walston was bizarre. Sometimes the three of them came to town together. Catherine and Greene were not allowed to meet too often in London, and rarely (by this time) at the Walstons' country home, Newton Hall, near Cambridge. Harry had political aspirations – it was essential for them to be discreet. But Greene refers to an extraordinary meeting between himself and Harry: 'I had a very nice dinner with Harry & he seemed quite happy about your leaving on the 30th [to meet Greene]. He also thought there was a definite obligation.'[10] (Now there's a perfect English gentleman!)

Finally, a trip is worked out: they decide on the jaunt to Jamaica, to Noël Coward's home, but a letter dated 9 February 1956 is again lugubrious, and Greene apparently had not kept his spirits up: 'Sorry if I seemed too depressed & unhelpful over the telephone, & I always seem to forget the listening ears' (presumably Catherine's children). By now he'd had four X-rays: 'My fifth tomorrow. I shall be surprised from my general aches & pains if they don't find *something*.' He was wondering if his medical problems could be psychosomatic, a result of not seeing Catherine: '1955 was a poor year & 1956 hasn't begun well. I wish one day we could have again a peaceful uninterrupted uncurtailed holiday with both of us working at something.' Greene ends: 'God bless you, dear. I love you, you know.' According to a postscript, he seems to have made friends among the diplomatic corps: '"Nice" dinner at Swedish Embassy to look forward to on 15th [February].'[11]

No sooner had the wonderful holiday been set up than Catherine had further problems. There had been no holiday since 1954. He complained: 'Last year we saw less of each other than we'd ever done.'[12] Jamaica is off. Instead, Catherine suggests they rent a yacht, but Greene does not want the responsibility. Still, he does not turn it down definitely, though 'There's also with a yacht always the danger from Press gutter boys'.[13] He offers Switzerland as an alternative. It provided a better centre for the walks he hoped to take with his brother Hugh, on their 'old Burgundy trip'.* Greene is calculating her menstrual

---

* Graham and his brother Hugh had taken a trip to Burgundy in 1931 where, according to Hugh, 'We were in an old fashioned third class carriage with the partition between the carriages only going half way up, and as I remember it there was somebody with his elbow and his hand laid out on the partition fast asleep in the next carriage, and just before we got out at the station, Graham very quietly fitted a French-letter on one of his fingers.' (See Volume One, p. 487.)

cycle: 'but if it was possible the "calendar" indicates Thursday the 23rd as a more fun day. I always remind you of these things – not because I only want to see you when I can sleep with you, but because it's always so good doing both & waking in the night & finding you there.'[14]

★

Greene's medical woes persisted. On Monday he was scheduled for a barium enema, and on Tuesday his gall bladder had to be examined. 'Indications (touch wood) are so far against "organic" trouble, but I gather from the nurse [that Raymond is] "concerned" about the gall-bladder.' His longing comes out: 'If only I can fit any operation into our dead period & be well to walk & work & sleep with you in June.'[15] He next suggests they go to a friend's pub in Kent, the Rose and Crown Hotel in Brinchley. He did try to fill every moment, even going to a Danny Kaye movie with Dorothy Glover.* He tells Catherine he can't work with all the suspense about the X-rays, so he 'got through nearly all the books I'd put aside for Jamaica'.[16]

Just when he thinks he is not going to persuade Catherine to see him, she says yes to Paris: 'Telegram from Hotel de Paris – all well April 18–22.'[17] He is worried about his gall bladder and conscious of a two-day session of X-rays: 'I'll be glad of a holiday after all this if they don't have to cut me up instead.' But as usual Greene was working and writing, most probably on *Our Man in Havana*, which would take him two years to complete and publish. He called it a 'very funny plot which if it comes off will make a footnote to history like the Captain of Kopenick.† Will tell you one day, but we are being very security minded!'[18]

★

Suddenly their relationship seems to be in jeopardy, and Greene is not apologetic. He writes in anger and pain, suggesting again that he should leave England to live abroad. So disturbed is Greene that he seriously considers ending with Catherine. In a letter postmarked 7 March 1956, dated as 'In bed. Wed. 3 p.m.', Greene reveals the depths of his love, guilt, uncertainty and unhappiness and this crisis he fears 'may be more serious than Rome'.[19]

---

* Likely *The Court Jester*, 1956.
† A 1931 play by the German dramatist Carl Zuckmayer, also made into a film in 1956 – it is a satire on Prussian militarism. Political pressure forced Zuckmayer to emigrate to the US in 1939.

The Rome quarrel had been their nadir, and by it Greene measured all future disagreements.* But then comes a softening, asking forgiveness after aquavits and beer, offering some thinking points:

a) whether we want to simplify enough to separate – except as friends who meet occasionally and
b) whether it's possible to simplify & not lose each other, and
c) of course whether we want to stay together, because if we don't there's no point in worrying about a) & b).

And then something curious. Apparently, Greene had seen something he shouldn't have:

I do want you to feel that this letter has nothing – or only a remote connexion with – one's view through the window last night. It has far more connexion with Rome ... Call it a neurosis if you like, but I have the desire to be of use to someone ... I have felt of little use & possibly of real harm to you.

He told her she had no responsibility to him, nor he to her, but that their desire was probably to need and be needed. And he felt selfish: 'You might have been happier now if you'd had your wish in Rome.'[20] Greene harks back to their original relationship, before it turned into the typical life of the wealthy. He mourns their past uncomplicated love, initiated on the island of Achill, a barren bit of land, but to them idyllic. The bucolic life, where writing and love seemed immutable, was paradise. Yet, if bliss, it was bliss lived under a corrugated roof, with no running water, a cold tap outside.† He disdains their luxury hotel holidays: 'now [we] think in terms of Hong Kong or Tahiti. Soon we'll have to think in terms of a rocket to the moon. You are so right to go walking in Ireland or ... Switzerland. We ... want to simplify, but can we?'[21] And he begins to see love in terms of giving rather than taking. He tells Catherine she might think she's

---

* In Rome, Catherine elected to sleep in a separate bed, and even more devastating, she told Greene that in the unlikely event of both of their spouses dying, she would not marry him. Greene was profoundly upset by this and he refers to 'Rome' often in his letters, feeling guilty because at least twice he fought against finishing, even though he thought it might have been better for her. He saw the trouble as both wanting to 'simplify our lives (even your feeling for walking in Ireland or Switzerland may be part of it) & yet if you simplify you can only do it by excluding me (after all I'm a kind of barnacle on your boat) & if I should simplify it would be by excluding you (living abroad etc.)'.
† Vivien Greene, very much aware that the love her husband bore for Catherine began at Achill, imagined, given Catherine's wealth, that the cottage floor must have had 'the softest white lambskin rugs on it'. It did not.

of no use to him, but he feels certain he is no use to her. Greene wants them both to think it over: 'you in Ireland & me on the Continent & say nothing until we are both back. Then we can "try" to decide what to do.'[22]

We don't know how Catherine reacted, though that she did react is clear: 'Thank you so much for your long letters.'[23] Greene's own correspondence for some time well into 1956 is unusually brief. Catherine seems to be getting postcards instead of love letters.

★

In April 1956, Greene was in Canada when A. J. Liebling's attack on *The Quiet American* appeared in the *New Yorker*. Liebling masked his anger at Greene's portrayal of Vietnam under a contemptuous air. He denied that Greene's protagonist, the artless but loveable Alden Pyle, could be an American, asserting that he was, rather, 'a perfect specimen of a French author's idea of an Englishman': 'a naïve chap who speaks bad French, eats tasteless food and is only accidentally and episodically heterosexual', who is 'earnest, in an obtuse way, and physically brave, through a lack of imagination . . . Pyle's choice of idiom convinced me that he is a thinly disguised Englishman.'[24]

Saying that Liebling's article goes too far and that the critic and the magazine 'look rather silly', Greene is nevertheless troubled. In the process of buying his daughter, Lucy Caroline, a ranch in Canada, he needs as much money as possible, and he fears that 'the violence of the *New Yorker*' will 'frighten off the film people'.[25] Still he cannot avoid the usual complaint: 'But what a long time it is since we had a real long quiet holiday together. October 1954?'[26]

Casino cards for the two of them proved the trip was to Monte Carlo. They were gambling, but it was with their future.

★

Their holiday over, Greene was back in Europe on 11 May, in Paris in fact, his manic imagination holding sway: 'Crowds of police. I suppose Tito's on the way, & I've mislaid my bomb.' He then recalls a pretty girl at a cocktail party, who 'turned out to be the daughter of old Balliol friend, Robin Turton, Minister of Health. Next room also in hotel, not that that was any comfort!'[27] A month later on 19 June, he is travelling in Portugal: 'I like Portugal in a way better than Spain – it's cleaner, quieter, less dramatic, but the bull fights – I went to one – so feeble, no killing at all & no real risk.'[28]

Graham and Catherine planned to get back together for a longer period than the Monte Carlo jaunt, though nothing was fixed: 'About the holiday – I want a final talk with you. What about a Town Isle cottage & Haiti.' But incredibly, unless letters have gone astray, Greene seems to be writing only once a month. One's suspicion grows.

★

He tried to lure Catherine with interesting and engaging invitations, once dangling dinner with Anita Loos (famous author of *Gentlemen Prefer Blondes)*. These enticements failed.

Another month went by and, from the Royal Albion in Brighton, Greene wrote, 'Darling . . . Drank too much last night after finishing second version of script [*St Joan*] . . . Friday week to France for a few days . . . probably with art director.'[29] He was bogged down with work for Otto Preminger and wanted it over.

Greene took especial comfort in knowing his schedule in advance. He filled his life to the brim to avoid the dark melancholy which gripped him. We can watch his mind organising the rest of 1956 from the middle of August on, asking Catherine about the Far East for the autumn. And, 'if you can manage Paris for two or three nights next month, which?'[30]

His neurosis is at work. When there were no empty spaces on his calendar, he could temporarily cast out the devil of depression, and avoid the cave of darkness.

★

In 1949, Greene had attempted suicide over his failure to persuade Catherine to marry him. In spite of his offers of houses and boats, and in spite of her genuine love for Greene, she was not going to leave her children or her husband. She also recognised that life with Greene would be a spiky experience. She understood his troubled nature: 'Graham's misery is as real as an illness.'[31] 'He is very shy and cannot conceive of anyone wanting him. He is a strange tormented person. I love him very much and wish . . . he did not suffer so much with a very real melancholia.'[32]

Knowing he was never to be allowed Catherine in any permanent way – 'the depression comes down when I think of the years ahead, with scraps and bits of you, probably smaller scraps & bits'[33] – Greene dealt with it by adding two dozen aspirins to half a pint of whisky. He thought to bring an end to his pain. He later remembered his near-happiness as he stirred the few grains of aspirin left at the bottom of the glass until they had dissolved. He pictured death coming quickly, that his heart would stop suddenly as a clock, that he'd be swiftly struck down. Only deep sleep, not death, struck him down.

He attempted to subdue his neuroses: 'I need a flick of the whip to keep me going.' And Greene admitted that he tired of everything, even of the Russian roulette played as a young undergraduate at Oxford. 'The moment the finger depresses the trigger, the surge of adrenalin through the system has the effect of dissipating boredom', but 'I grew tired of Russian roulette as of everything else.'[34]

But he never seemed to tire of Catherine. Over the long affair, he would woo, promise, flatter, threaten, and even butt heads with her. Yet she could win him back so easily:

> From the depths of gin blues I was suddenly ready to kiss any beggar's sores from sheer happiness when your letter arrived.[35]

★

Trouble continued. An undated letter (probably 31 August 1956) begins with an apology, always a bad sign, blaming his feeling low on being up until 2 a.m. with Otto Preminger and a set designer. Greene was afraid that Harry wouldn't agree to their October/November plans, and he needed to decide if he could attend rehearsals of *The Potting Shed* in America. He notices her contradictions: 'You were not allowed to go to Paris . . . but apparently an island off Wales is less strenuous than lying in bed most of the day at the Ritz, & from your account of life at Newton it seems unlikely that our "wild" Parisian life would be more tiring. But let's leave that.'

Catherine had told him she would come for something 'important'. But he just wanted to be with her, that was the important thing for Graham – and surely for most lovers. Then two things she'd said during their lovemaking in Rome troubled him. Catherine wanted the affair to end and had remarked (as noted in the previous chapter):

> in the wildly unlikely hypothetical case that our respective part-ners died, you would not marry me. Now I've always felt that from the Catholic point of view there was an excuse for us, in that we would marry if we could. But if that's not the case, what is our affair – except nights on the tiles? and that's awfully un-important to believe against breaking the rules.

Greene confesses:

> My darling, I'd rather be 500 miles from you than 50 miles from you when I can't see you . . . I love you very very dearly. God bless you. G.[36]

Catherine made amends and they met, Greene writing on 6 September 1956: 'Darling, Thank you for a lovely sweet exciting happy evening.' And he was off to Portugal. From there he lists for Catherine the cast of *The Potting Shed* and bluntly asks: 'Do we or don't we get to first night?'[37] Catherine did not come, and Greene, having made a stubborn promise not to attend if she did not accompany him, missed the first night of his own play.

7

Actress in the Wings

Love comes in the window and goes out the door.
— ANCIENT PROVERB

LATE in 1956, Catherine Walston was suddenly overwhelmed. She, the recipient of some of the most passionate love letters in the language, heard from Greene that he, her lover of almost ten years, was deceiving her. It was no casual interlude, but a serious affair with the young, beautiful, elfin Swedish actress Anita Björk. Anita had lost her husband, one of Sweden's finest writers, Stig Dagerman, who'd committed suicide in December 1954. Greene wrote on 19 December 1955 to Father Caraman: 'Could you find time to include among your masses the name of a young Swede, Stig Dagerman? His wife is a friend of mine, & although not a Catholic, would like this to be done.'

Greene's long delay in telling Catherine was itself a further betrayal. She knew that he was making more frequent trips to Stockholm, but he had a publisher there. She never imagined his visits were to further trysts. But by December 1955, Greene had become the lover of Anita Björk; now, twelve months later (the letter undated), Greene let the cat out of the bag.

Dear dear Catherine,
I've just got your note about Jamaica – one of the dearest you've ever written to me, and now I've *got* to write to you. I've been postponing too long, hoping that things would somehow settle. I love you so much & no one has ever been or can ever be, what you've been to me. Nine years are more packed with memory than the rest of life.

At this point, Catherine, then forty-two, must have felt a sense of foreboding. Indeed, he confesses that the previous November he 'fell a little in love with a girl (of 33)'. He hadn't intended for it to happen, but she came to London and they slept together once. He agreed to see her after Christmas. Then he tells Catherine he went to Stockholm to 'work it out of my system', but the rumours began so they went to Portugal (this was while he was pleading with Catherine to go to the first night of *The Potting Shed* in New York). Then, the rational-ising begins: 'Ever since Rome & that awful long night I've been afraid of pressing you. It had nothing to do with this other business . . . I was hoping . . . to kill the other feeling.' He expounds his case:

> I love 'making love' with you more than I've ever done with anyone else, & yet I'm caught with this quieter love. She's like a child . . . & is, I suppose, lonely . . . I have no confidence in myself any more. I've kept this dark too long because I don't want to lose either of you. I think it would be worse to lose you (like losing a world), but I flinch too at losing her. I don't know what to do, darling. I hoped so much it would die out before you got to know, & that I'd tell it to you one day as something dead. Now perhaps you won't even give me the choice. I wouldn't blame you.
>
> I love you in my mind & my heart & my body, & yet I've gone & done this. I love her too & mucked her up. That's why the death-wish came back − I hadn't had it for years.
> Dear Catherine
>   G.
> If I fail you, I'll fail everybody.[1]

He showed some courage in finally being truthful, though there's a suggestion that the story had already broken, at least in Sweden. Vivien Greene told me that the newspapers got hold of the story that Graham Greene was going around with a young Swedish film star. So perhaps Greene had to forestall journalists, who, he must have felt, would have done irreparable damage.

Knowing about his affair with Anita, we can now look differently at the casually expressed postscript in the preceding chapter: '"Nice" dinner at Swedish Embassy to look forward to on 15th.'[2] One can assume that when Anita came to London over Christmas she intro-duced Greene to members of the Swedish embassy. Certainly it was at this moment in London that the affair between Anita and Greene bloomed. Michael Meyer introduced them. He stated later that their affair began at Christmas 1955, and 'was to last, with considerable inten-sity on both sides, for nearly four years'.[3]

Of course, it was splendid to have a new and charming mistress, a brilliant actress to boot. But a new love for Greene did not mean he wanted to give up Catherine. He struggled to tempt her to come to his play, to Macau or Hong Kong after his visit to China, or to a Malayan bungalow on an unspoiled beach, just a few of the arrows in his quiver to try to bring her back.

Greene finally persuaded Catherine to meet him in Paris, but not until after Easter. Still he carried on his campaign of letters hoping to bring her to the Far East, tempting her with promises of fun, sun and pipes of opium. It was to no avail. Catherine was not going to forgive easily. Perhaps she never really forgave him, even though she herself had casual affairs, at times at the highest point of their love.

Yet Greene needed Catherine to see him through his low points. He never wrote better than when they had working holidays, perfect writing holidays. She was his ideal: an exciting and graceful woman. If only she would come out to play whenever the famous author cast his net. But she had legitimate excuses for not going on holiday with him. Three separate times, her husband tried to win a seat in Parliament. As long as there was hope of Harry's success, she had to assist him. But her explanations helped to wear Greene down.

★

Catherine's initial (though not lasting) reaction to Greene's admission of guilt seems to have been mild. We can assume this from his response, admitting he was 'selfish, unintelligent and unimaginative', and felt he deserved to be left, and that he'd give up Anita for her. He told her how sweet and generous she'd been, and how:

> Nobody can mean as much to me as you in the head, the heart, the body – any way. I would have . . . sent a telegram to Stockholm only it's a first night there . . . I mustn't add to her nerves . . . But I'll try to clear everything up – if I haven't the courage on Sunday, then when I get to Canada . . . if I've ruined things tell me. I love you terribly.

Then he asks her to write, aching to make plans together. He is still owned by her – 'Your photograph is in my bedroom – please don't take away the ring.' He tells her: 'I wish to God we'd been able to marry. Nothing important would have gone wrong then.'[4] The letter is unsigned.

But two days later, after reaching Amsterdam at midnight, Greene finds two letters from Catherine. He is now made painfully aware that telling her of his affair was a mistake. His reply is carefully constructed as he strives to overcome Catherine's resistance, telling her they love each other, and asking if they could just ride it out. Again he remembers Rome, and states that that time was 'worse because you didn't love me, so none of my words seemed to carry any weight that night & morning'. He tries to be honest, but it doesn't make anything better: 'I *know* I love you more than this girl (hadn't we now better give a name to her, Anita Björk?) She's honest & sweet . . . but she's not *you*.' And he doesn't want to live in Sweden. He feels that he and Anita have nothing in common except loneliness. He muses: 'With loneliness gone where would we be? I love her, but I'm not so much *in* love with her even as I am with you.'

Five days later, in Montreal to meet Capalbo to work on the script of *The Potting Shed*, Greene tries to keep his foot in the door. He makes a curious distinction in what he will tell Catherine: 'I hesitate to write till I hear from you, but I'll only write news – it seems unnatural not to write to you.' He says his plane landed first in Ireland, but he didn't know anything about it because 'I slept like the drunken log I was'.[5] In Montreal, eight days before Christmas, he criticises the blatant merchandising: the 'Christmas horror . . . down the central aisle [of the main street] Christmas trees . . . & along the sides life sized choristers singing tinned carols, life sized camels, shepherds, magi'.[6]

Greene pleads with Catherine to meet him in New York or Paris. But there was no response. He writes a week later about his daughter's ranch, 'a lovely spot. Rolling ground & flat valley with a wonderful view of the Rockies', then comes back to memories of his love for Catherine: 'but these were the best years of my life – even the unhappy bits . . . Don't let's lose each other. Come to Paris.'[7]

His Christmas Day letter from Montreal begins sadly, for he has discovered that on the previous Saturday, Catherine had visited a Paris shop where he'd just been, and he mentions passing a restaurant which he's never noticed before but from which Catherine would sometimes write to him. He then continues making excuses for Anita:

I can never lose you – even if you should prefer to lose me. You make me happier than anyone has ever done, only I thought I was making you less & less happy, & I snatched at a substitute.

Dear heart, let me buy you your smalls until you as well as I are doddering with age. I never want to leave you – unless you want me to.[8]

Then there comes a chance to meet as promised, in Paris or Cuba: 'We'd go to Santiago which is on the sea & perhaps find a small place. I want to be with you.'[9]

Right at the end of the year, a sentimental Greene writes again:

Everything belongs to you – my brief case with ROF,* my pyjamas . . . even my shaving box, & all parts of the world except this seem to be yours . . . Stay with me. I am breaking up everything else. If only you would come to Paris . . . I could show you. Love of you is the only thing that lasts. All last night I dreamt of you. You were wearing the ring & I *felt* it on your finger. It's seldom one feels in a dream . . . Please come back to me. I've come back to you.

At 7.30 that night, he wrote again. He says he's never loved her more, and that she'd 'be very welcome on Tuesday night at the St J. & Albany if something detained you. I feel like somebody who's had a fever.'[10]

There was no reply.

*

By 9 January 1957, Greene was in New York, staying at the Algonquin. *The Potting Shed* was in rehearsal, and he watched *Around the World in Eighty Days* – the best film I've ever seen'[11] (which is saying something from this former film critic). But his first night in New York seemed 'almost like London' because he met British celebrities: 'Saw Ian Fleming there, just after running into Gracie [Fields] & Boris! Then at supper Margaret Leighton was at the next table!'[12]

On 11 January, he must have felt he'd opened a pathway to Catherine, for it appears there was a slight relenting. He finally received a 'very dear letter' from her, though it refused him his opening night. He thought she was wrong not come to New York, not 'for talk, just for fun'. He was disturbed. He wants her, but said he also wanted friendship, companionship, too, not just 'eight weeks a year of sex only'. He wants 'new memories, not just hanging on to the old ones'. It is all so sad: 'I'm not made to be a lover only.'[13] Greene ends his letter: 'I'm so weary & bored of New York.' But before posting it, he received a cable from Catherine, not full of good news:

1.15 a.m Jan 12
Just been woken by your cable, so ignore all the parts of this letter which deal with the first night. I'll celebrate it in London or Paris, & if I come back to London before you go, I'll be careful not to run in to you or phone you. When you want to see me,

---

* I suggested in Volume Two that this was one of their codes. I guessed it meant 'Right of Fuck'.

send me a line. I'll always want to see you. But I can't fight any more.

Poor dear, you learned over the Lowell episode* that the truth doesn't pay, & I've learned it over this . . . I suppose your decision too will go against Cuba, so perhaps I'll go there in February & March. A bit of opium & debauchery might be good for me![14]

★

But Greene kept on writing to Catherine out of a habit of ten years' standing. On 18 January 1957, longing to leave New York and knowing he'd arrive in Rome or Paris on 25 January and fly to London the next day, he wrote at full throttle, brimming over with love and longing. He asks her about meeting in Paris, 'Surely people shouldn't "divorce" for this – that morning in Tunbridge Wells is still to me the only real marriage I ever had.'[15] I've come across this reference often, alluding to a wedding ceremony. Greene continues: 'If there's no hope there's no hope, & one will go on somehow, but if you can give me hope, do give it.'

At one point in their correspondence, Catherine refers to Greene's deception about Anita. Greene responds:

> I always meant to tell you when it was over – & dear there were no elaborate schemes in Jamaica [though we know he took Anita to Noël Coward's old home in Jamaica, Catherine and Graham's previous hunting grounds] – one simply didn't write (except the postcards), that was all.[16]

No one can doubt that Catherine was the single most important person to his writing. What a harvest of work she oversaw:

> Dear love, believe this – that in all our trips this year I was happy being with you – I'm not happy away from you. You are the biggest thing in my life & remain so – even if you left me as I deserve. And what fruitful years they have been for work – 3 films, 2 plays, 2 novels. I am going ahead planning for Cuba this summer & the novelette to be written while you lie in bed. Unless you'd rather go to Capri.[17]

By now, another reason Catherine and Greene did not meet often was her husband Harry's concern about her excessive drinking when she

---

* This was a minor affair of Catherine's with Senator Lowell Weicker, then in the American armed forces in Europe, soon after the Second World War.

was with Greene. So Greene wrote, advising her to rest, get some sun, and get well. He feels no pity, just 'love & desire & regret at failing you & hope to be with you again. A character in my play says, "I don't pity you. I'm not that proud. One doesn't pity an equal."'

He was going to Stockholm, not on a 'happy leching expedition', but to disengage. He did feel some pity there, and wanted to detach gently, in order to stay friends. He describes it as 'more tenderness than sex', chalking it up to the father–daughter age difference, and admits that 'when someone loves you, it's always difficult not to respond, unless they are boring or repulsive.' He wishes Catherine happy birthday and asks her to 'come back to me, & when we meet, let it be for a matter of days – at the Ritz or here. Not just an evening or a drink. I love you.'[18]

★

All through 1957, Greene wrote to Catherine. In a letter of 15 February, he sent photos which reminded him of 'a very happy day . . . huge all-gin dry Martinis at lunch'.[19] He was in high spirits over the reviews of *The Potting Shed*, some of which he sent. In the *New York Times*, Sunday, 10 February 1957, an advertisement mustered parts of reviews from several papers into one enthusiastic paean:

> An absorbing and fascinating drama with original characters and provocative ideas, set down in brilliantly effective theatrical terms. It has bite . . . drive . . . wit, and above all, it has characters who are not the same old shapes filched out of the stencil pile. A detective story for grown ups, it has ingenious suspense, and, by the evening's end, the first-nighters were brought to the edges of their seats.

All the actors were praised, along with Capalbo and Chase, 'managers whose ambitions go beyond routine theatricality . . . [We] salute young producers of vision and courage. *The Potting Shed* is a distinguished event in our theatrical season.'[20] Greene sent Catherine the review from *Newsweek*, drew a line under one sentence, 'Two days before his *The Potting Shed* opened in New York last week, Graham Greene unexplainedly flew to Paris',[21] and wrote in the margin: 'I could have explained. I never want to go to a first night with anybody but you.'[22] And he did not.

After speaking about his 'worse stomach – bleeding all the time, but that seems over too. (I'll have a check up before China)'[23] – he asks Catherine if he could dedicate the first edition of *The Potting Shed* to her, and again realises what a help she has been: 'I've done so much

67

with you. The end of *The Heart of the Matter, The End of the Affair,** *The Quiet American, The Fallen Idol, The Third Man, Loser Takes All, The Living Room, The Potting Shed*. And now I want to do *A House of Reputation* with you too.'[24]

If in later years Greene revealed himself as a different (and by no means better) writer, it was because there was no longer a Catherine.

Then Greene makes another promise to Catherine about Anita Björk: 'Of course we must talk. Only I wish we could talk away from people, together, Paris, Brighton . . . I love you so dearly & what I want to explain to you is this: that *even if you won't come back to me, I'd break with Sweden*.'[25] From this moment on, he called Anita 'Sweden' to Catherine, and turned a bit cruel. He told Catherine he was bored with Anita, and assured her she'd never bored him, not once. 'I'm alive with you, but I'm pretending to be alive with Anita. So if I can't mend the damage I've done, I'll just have to go off by myself. Only let me try first.'[26]

In a private conversation Michael Meyer, who knew Anita for more than forty years, told me that the affair with Anita was more complicated, and Greene's term 'more tenderness than sex' was just blowing smoke:

> She has just about everything – [she is] beautiful, talented, highly intelligent, a linguist and very sweet natured – and very sexy, for I had a friend who had an affair with her and he said she was highly passionate in bed. I remember once when I picked Graham up at the airport as usual and drove him out to her house . . . they could hardly wait to get into bed, so much so that I, who was hoping for a drink or a cup of tea after my drive to the airport and then out to that suburb, was surprised to hear Anita say, with one of her most charming smiles, after about one and a half minutes: 'Please go.'

Since Catherine wouldn't see Greene, he makes a trip to Sweden, just before going off to China on 8 April, for a last visit with Anita. In Stockholm, perhaps in Anita's company, or when she's not far away, he writes to Catherine: 'I want you more than anyone & I was sad when not even a picture postcard came from Megève . . . I wish we could have met in Hong Kong & had a solid month together. We aren't allowing time for sores to heal. They can only heal together. I love you so much, dear Catherine, & I want *you* to be happy more

---

* Catherine's influence was paramount here, both in that the major female character, Sarah, is closely based on her, and also, incredibly, that Greene (so he hinted to me) used an extract from Catherine's own diary to describe the hero, Bendrix, who is basically Greene.

than anybody else . . . I have no companionship without you & life becomes desperately lonely . . . Come to Capri.'[27]

He is not entirely without companionship, for a postcard to Catherine dated 30 March 1957 shows the Royal Palace at Stockholm, a shot taken at night with the lights of the palace shining on the lake and his writing: 'The awful thing is that I've never been so happy here as I was with you.'[28]

Would he honour his 'Sweden' promise to Catherine? He was spared the opium and debauchery in Cuba he'd hinted at, but a new venture was upon him, to China. Yet, he still saw Catherine as his ultimate love and for him, the perfect carnal trinity: 'the only complete relation I've ever had – my head, my heart, my balls all working together'.[29]

PART 4

Spy Mission: More Clouseau than Bond

8

Cursing the Dragon

Shhhhh . . . There Could Be Spies Among Us!

He goes like one on a secret errand.
— WALTER PATER

JOURNEYS were Greene's means of controlling depression. He often came out of melancholy with a sudden eagerness for new ventures. When he spoke of ways of escape, Greene meant an escape from self – a self which felt there was nothing in life worth having, nothing worth doing, until he reached the point where the seeds of inspiration of what he had seen and heard, what he'd experienced, could be cultivated into the landscape of Greeneland.

But in the spring of 1957, Greene's new adventure was China. On 15 February he wrote to Catherine that 'Jack Huntingdon & I & Edith Sitwell (!) and a few others are invited to China in April'. Greene's interest would be measured by Catherine's reaction, 'But if it's going to give us pipes & fun & sun I'd do it. It would probably mean your being in the Far East from around May 15 to June 15 roughly. Please come.'[1]

With or without Catherine, Greene was intent on going. To his friend Prince Chula of Thailand, he wrote on 26 March 1957: 'the Earl and Countess [the writer Margaret Lane] of Huntingdon expect to arrive in Bangkok on May 25 & to stay for about one week, when they hope to go up to Angkor* . . . They will be staying at the Oriental hotel.'[2] It was through the Huntingdons that Greene first was asked to go, unaware of the turbulent time which lay ahead: the countess, a friend, telephoned to invite him, 'subject to the consent of the Chinese

---

* Site of several capitals of the Khmer empire which flourished in the latter part of the ninth century. Angkor Wat, surely one of the most imposing shrines in the world to the divinity of the monarch – such delicate sculptural ornamentation surrounds the centred object: the monarch's stone penis.

73

authorities, to join a little party including herself and her husband for a month's visit to China'.³ Greene left England for China on 8 April.

Almost thirty years after the event, on 27 May 1985, Greene published an article in *The Times* about his trip to China, entitled 'A Weed Among the Flowers', making the point that *he* was the weed 'during that deceptively hopeful season of the Hundred Flowers'.⁴ But there was something niggling just under the surface.

We get more of his feelings after his trip to China in a letter to the poet Edmund Blunden* on 16 May, shortly after returning. Blunden had sent Greene a programme of *Twelfth Night* with a poem in it. Greene wrote, praising Blunden for his ability, and letting him know he'd hoped to be in Hong Kong that spring, but got only as far as Peking. He much preferred the Chinese overseas to the Chinese in their own country, although they were 'very kind and hospitable. Pekin [*sic*] seemed to be so much less Eastern than Hong Kong, but all the same there were still some two-hundred-year-old restaurants where one could eat extremely well.'⁵ Did Greene simply not like the home-grown variety of Chinese, or was there something in China that disturbed him?

*

On 26 March, Jack Dribbon, secretary of the British-China Friendship Association, gave Greene an itinerary for travel via Amsterdam, Prague, Moscow and Irkutsk. Greene's delegation included Lord Chorley and Professor Joseph Lauwerys. Members of the Huntingdon group included the Scottish poet (and communist) Hugh MacDiarmid. The two delegations were to meet in China. Delegates were warned that though hotel services were efficient, 'this should not encourage . . . gratuities',⁶ which the new communist government frowned upon. Mrs Evelyn Brown, a colleague of Dribbon and member of the Association, was assigned to 'help', but probably was there to keep a sharp eye on the Greene–Chorley–Lauwerys group. One suspects that Mrs Brown was the Association's spy – each group of visitors had at least one. In 'A Weed Among the Flowers' Greene identifies Mrs Brown as 'Mrs Smith', a cautious change.

Dribbon wrote to the group suggesting they meet prior to departure, at a 'get-together' at Mrs Brown's flat where a representative of the office of the Chargé d' Affaires and others with a knowledge of

---

* Blunden (1896–1974), with whom Greene had many opium sessions, was then holder of the Chair of English at the University of Hong Kong. He had been a friend of Graham's brother Hugh when Hugh was an undergraduate and Blunden a Fellow at Merton College, Oxford. In December 1932, when Greene was still in his twenties, Blunden (and others) chose *Stamboul Train* as the Book Society's Book of the Month.

China would be present to answer any questions. 'A chat over a glass of sherry will make for a good beginning, to what, I am confident, will prove a most exciting experience.'[7]

★

At the time Dribbon was writing to Greene, Greene was writing to the Catholic authorities. Enter Father Timothy Connolly of the St Columban's foreign service, and Father McGrath of the Missionary Society in Ireland.

On 27 March, a letter from Connolly to McGrath about Greene was passed on to Greene by McGrath, a worthy but unwise action. 'I feel an obligation to send on to you the letter which I received from my Superior General and I sincerely hope that you will understand our position':

Dear Fr McGrath,

I am happy to hear that Mr Graham Greene is to go to China. He is a man of great moral and physical courage and will, I am sure, present independent views. It is thoughtful of him to seek assistance from Fr MacElroy and you. While, personally, I admire Mr Greene and appreciate the value of his published work, you will realise that, in the interest of our own work, I must advise certain precautions.

On at least two public occasions, Mr Greene seems to have misunderstood and consequently misinterpreted the views of missionary priests connected with us. I do not question at all the honesty of his own opinion nor his right to it, but I feel that in your contact with him the presence of a third party acceptable to both of you and capable of bearing witness, in case of necessity, to what transpires would be desirable. I wonder if Mr Woodruff would act in this capacity. We, at least, would be eminently satisfied in that case.[8]

On 5 April, three days before he left for China, Greene's arrow of contempt flew straight:

I suppose that Father Connolly — although he refers to 'at least two public occasions' — is referring to a single case of a priest whom I never met personally and whose work as a journalist, not as a priest, I considered was damaging to the Catholic community in Indo-China by its inaccuracy and bias.

He adds that he gave up six lines out of three articles to this unnamed man, as he did not wish to offend him. He concludes he had no intention of interviewing the priests.

*I wished only to receive advice on what embarrassing or useful questions
I might ask in China to serve the Catholic cause.* I should have
welcomed Mr Woodruff or Mr Derrick at our meeting as a friend
and guest, but certainly not in the capacity of a third person
guarding you against the dangers of what I might say. The tone
of Father Connolly's letter certainly leads me to suppose that I
should have gained nothing from our meeting. Perhaps in China
you have been used to the dangers of misinterpretation, but I
think that it is a mistake to take your lack of trust into the West
and I for one will not submit to it.[9]

Greene did not meet with either McGrath or the Superior General.

*

But Greene did seek advice on what to ask in China 'to serve the
Catholic cause'. China was a relentless enemy of Catholicism. In 1948
there had been 5,916 foreign missionaries there; at the time of Greene's
visit, twenty-five were left. Imprisoned in Shanghai were the Americans
Father Joseph McCormack (Maryknoll), Father John Houle (Jesuit),
Father Charles McCarthy (Jesuit) and Father Cyril Wagner (Franciscan);
in Harbin were the Koreans Rev Kim and Rev Yen.

In Greene's archives in his sister Elisabeth's home is a file entitled
'Various Points'. This material most certainly could not have been put
together by the Missionary Society. It's of an entirely different kidney,
suggesting that the questions and the details were derived from Britain's
Secret Intelligence Service. If this can be assumed, Greene went to
China with at least one specific purpose: to spy. He was ultimately
unsuccessful, despite his spy-tuned nature. He was outwitted by the
communists who'd been alerted to the dangers of having Greene in
their country.

I believe that what the SIS wanted could have been obtained, but
it entailed serious risks. Perhaps the SIS felt that since the famous
Greene had been given delegate status, the communist authorities would
not place him under arrest or put him in harm's way.

A reference in a letter to Catherine posted on 27 March suggests
that just before leaving, Greene met with a member of the intelligence
community, an old friend. 'Tomorrow a duty lunch (how I dread them)
with Eric [Greene's physician] & dinner F[oreign] O[ffice] people.'[10]
Greene would have offered his services to the SIS; he was not inclined
to love a communist country determined to destroy the Catholic
Church. In the notes from Greene's archives it is proposed that he
should approach the well-known correspondent of the British communist newspaper the *Daily Worker*, Alan Winnington, then in Peking,

claiming that 'they' have information that Winnington 'is rumoured to be having doubts', presumably about China's communism in particular or communism in general. They recommended that Greene should approach 'other foreign correspondents' as well, and asked him for 'Any comments obtainable from official or unofficial sources on RUSSIAN AID. Reports of considerable economic difficulties re raw materials etc. Since Russian assistance and planning is much advertised. How do they get round the fact that it is so unsuccessful?' More difficult tasks included trying to see political trials in the more remote districts, to find out whether a proper defence was allowed:

> Is it possible to get evidence from officials of any people who have successfully appealed, or defended themselves? If so how did they succeed? . . . Watch for signs of forced labour in the remoter districts. Groups of 20 or 30 may not always be accompanied by armed guards. They often have Chinese characters on their backs . . . If invited to visit Cooperative farms try to avoid usual ones, e.g. Kaokang, but seek further afield! Same with state-owned factories or workshops, avoid An-Shan which is the show place.[11]

★

The same religious persecution Greene dealt with in *The Power and the Glory* in Mexico in the 1930s was taking place in the fifties in China. Mexico had drawn Greene to its shores because it was a battlefield between paganism and Christianity, 'the fiercest . . . since the reign of [Queen] Elizabeth', he wrote in *The Lawless Roads*.[12] It involved the desecration and destruction of churches and cathedrals, the hunting down and killing of priests. Graves were plain earth mounds without crosses as markers, and with numbers, not names, over them. Thus, a systematic creation of a Godless country.

By going into atheist China, Greene felt he was being recalled to an earlier battlefield. As in Mexico, there would be many, priests included, who would save their skins and follow, or at least pretend to follow, the communist way, for in that direction alone lay physical safety. But Chinese Catholics found at least two willing martyrs. On Greene's preparation sheet, he listed (or had listed for him) two men who refused to capitulate: Father John Tung Tse-tse and Hu Feng. Greene writes: 'Fr. John Tung Tse-tse, last heard of in a prison for counter-revolutionaries just outside Chungking. Until Robert Ford brought us news last September nothing had been heard of him since his arrest in July 1951.'[13]

In the Greene archives, a pamphlet entitled *Religious Freedom in China* tells how Father John Tung Tse-tse stood up to be counted even when senior Catholic officials sank to their knees with a rattle or a thud in fear. Just one month after his reaffirmation of faith in the Catholic Church, Tung was arrested as he was preparing to say mass, bound hand and foot, and driven off in a lorry under armed escort. Information about Tung then filtered out of China. There were also well-documented files of Greene's about the other martyr, Hu Feng.

★

Greene left London on 8 April 1957 on the first leg of his journey and arrived in Peking on the 10th, the delegation having spent the night of the 9th at Irkutsk. It was a laconic first postcard Greene sent to Catherine: 'Shared a room with the Peer & the Professor. Only the former snored.'[14] Later he speaks of the journey: '26 hours late so far. Somewhere on the way to Ormsk. O, for C6 Albany & the Ritz Paris & you.'[15] They stopped one night in Moscow and then left at 1 a.m. to travel in slow two-engined planes across Russia. In Greene's plane were Mongols, Germans and a nice old Bulgarian professor:

> Breakfast at 6 a.m. & no more to eat until about midnight when our plane having petered out, we were transferred to another & got to Irkutsk . . . in Mongolia a great crowd . . . waiting for their relatives home from the great distant city – all kinds of costumes & colours. No village to be seen – only the new clean little airport & the brown distances. We were in a Chinese plane now & bumped over the Great Wall (a lovely view) into Pekin [*sic*] in the afternoon.[16]

His later article in *The Times* shows the nonsensical bravura of the communist air hostess: 'It was a very rough descent to Peking and I asked the air hostess why we didn't wear safety belts. "Oh," she said, "of course we had safety belts at first, but now our pilots are so reliable." '[17]

The delegation were kept so busy that it must have been impossible for Greene to do any business for the Foreign Office. He tells Catherine: 'I keep my clock at London time – it's 10.25 a.m. with me & 2.25 a.m. with you – almost yesterday. My companions have gone off to see the new Peking University, but I have struck. Yesterday we had a long day – the Temple of Heaven in the morning, the Forbidden City in the afternoon, the Peking Opera in the evening . . . after five days here we go to Sian, the old imperial city, then to Chungking & four nights on a boat down the Yang-tse gorges to Hankow.'

Greene was not enamoured of China or diverted by what they were seeing – delegations, after all, are really controlled tourists: 'When one sees so much,' he shrewdly records, 'one has nothing to write about.' He came to the conclusion that one loves a city only because of associations or because 'one is with someone one loves. I love you & long for Paris. Please let it happen – even if the film [*St Joan*] were postponed.'[18]

By 16 April 1957, his first week over, Greene is tired of the whole show. He had visited the 'Summer Palace [which] would have made a beautiful bird cage . . . seen the Forbidden City, the Temple of Heaven etc . . . I start back on the 4th [May], stay a few days in Moscow, & I'll be home on the 8th or the 9th.'[19]

All the time, his thoughts were of Catherine. He heads his letter to her 'Sian – somewhere in China. Holy Saturday', his nerves on edge as he speaks of servants cleaning up, 'O God, *five* boys are doing my room & bathroom while I write, naturally taking twice as long as one French maid . . . I think I'm too old for new places except for a very short spell. In fact after ten days I'm *bored* with no [urge] even to relieve boredom with fear.'[20] Neither is his boredom relieved by sightseeing.

'My companions have gone off to see factories, but I've refused. I've been spoilt for companions – I'm so used to being by myself or with you.'[21] In his article, he wrote of how in Sian his companions 'got involved with serious visits to factories and education establishments and scientific institutes',[22] but he was able to excuse himself, no doubt hoping to do a little spying on his own. 'I made friends with a gigantic tricycle driver who was ready to take me shopping in the back lanes of the old city. He was probably a police informer, but what did I care? I was innocent of any espionage intentions.'[23] In spite of his denials, the Chinese would have suspected Greene, and they would have been right. Greene was a famous Catholic in a country where Catholics were under severe attack. He was being watched.

The Chinese method was simple: keep the delegates on a tight schedule – the Forbidden City, the Great Wall, the Ming Tombs, the Chinese opera. (Surely they'd need to do little else to outwit possible candidates for espionage.) As for Greene, even the Catholics themselves didn't trust their celebrated convert. The Chinese had no difficulty turning the potential shark into a minnow.

While his fellow travellers were touring around, Greene tried to follow up some of the suggestions of the SIS. He failed. He discovered that the tricycle driver 'spoke a bit of English which made it even more probable that he was an informer'. 'Perhaps,' he writes, 'my desire to be alone justified a certain suspicion.'[24]

Felix Greene, Graham's cousin, told me in interview (Felix was a great lover of the Chinese people, and he didn't care for his famous relative) that he was particularly concerned with Graham's narrow scope of interests during this trip. According to Felix, Greene shocked the many Chinese officials he met. Graham's statement in every place he went was: 'There are two things I want, a pretty girl to sleep with, and to know where I can get some opium.'[25]

Greene, his sexual curiosity nagging at him, began questioning his male guide about contraception. Told it was encouraged and widely practised, Greene then asked the guide (was he an informer too?) to buy a condom for him. Chinese delicacy dictated the reply: 'That I cannot do. You see, I do not know your size.'[26]

*

The delegation began to gnaw on Graham's nerves. Professor Lauwerys pushed him almost to the breaking point. Greene was irritated by this man who thought he knew

> absolutely everything (he was in China before for 3 weeks ten years ago). He speaks in sentences, paragraphs, & conditional clauses, pronouncing his words as carefully & slowly as Gladstone chewed his food. We try never to ask even a simple question ('Do you like this pork?') because the answer will grow & grow, until it has included the Chinese theory of cooking, a meal he once had in Nanking, the constituents of sweet & sour sauce, & the nature of the meals he offers to privileged friends at his home . . . I find I tease him with less & less mercy & become intolerable myself. [Lord] Chorley is just a bore, amiable & quiet, & Mrs Brown, the stout Jewess, is rather [a] grande dame & sentimental about anything Chinese. But oh, oh, the professor.
>
> Tomorrow Chungking & then four days on the Yangtse which I would look forward to by myself, but with these three . . . Bring the Ritz & Paris soon, soon.

But at least he could tolerate the guides and interpreters: 'a young man with a missing front tooth & delicate, & a girl like a Pekinese are both sweet. I'd much rather be alone with them.'[27]

Nine days later, on 28 April 1957, Greene was preparing to leave for Moscow (then on to Paris and Catherine), but first he tried to go to mass in Peking. He recalled watching great crowds from his hotel window the night before after thirty hours in the train from Hankow. He had a lovely view of the rehearsal for the May Day parade – coloured searchlights, pale rose and white and slate blue, with fireworks and the throngs of people, 'like carpets of colour . . . moving along the great road by the Forbidden Palace. Off to Mass now.' And then he writes: 'Failed. Only man who knew the way my one-eyed trishaw man . . . & I can't find him.'[28]

So Greene had failed, at least in Peking, to discover how many attended mass. I do not doubt that his journeys with the other delegates provided some useful intelligence to the West, but the fact remains that Greene's espionage attempts in China fizzled.

I suspect also that his heart wasn't in it. He wanted to leave the delegation and go to Paris to attend the opening night of Shaw's *St Joan* (he'd written the screenplay), and perhaps see Catherine. Once he'd decided to cut short his trip and spend only twenty days in China, he knew he'd go home with duties unfulfilled. Incredibly, here was Greene going out with a whimper. Yet, suddenly the tables turned.

★

In his three weeks in China, Greene had been a frustrated spy. Normally courteous, he suddenly broke rank, and aggressively asked pointed questions about persecuted Catholics and the martyr Hu Feng. Greene entered the lists to do battle, only to discover that his own colleagues stood alongside the enemy.

We can get some notion of his troubles, and assuredly those of his tour mates, from a letter which his interpreter Tu Nan wrote to Greene on 27 June 1957: 'What a great pleasure it is for me to have . . . travelled three weeks with you. It is . . . always extremely interesting to hear . . . Englishmen talking, debating and quarrelling . . . an experience I . . . certainly will not forget. I hope you have enjoyed your visit to China in spite of the ignorance and inefficiency of your interpreters'[29] – this last phrase a nice example of stylised Chinese modesty.

If he made a secret report, Greene would never divulge it, so we cannot measure his success. However, the letter from Tu Nan makes it clear that Greene's group fought and we know more from a note to Catherine: 'Friction between the four fellow travellers increases, but the explosion at Chungking when I threatened to leave [the delegation] has not been repeated!'[30]

In an account in *The Times* written after his return, Greene tells us that he 'had been asked by London [SIS or Catholic authorities?] to inquire into the fate of an imprisoned writer . . . Hu Feng'.[31] Greene had gone to China well versed about the case, and must have been poised throughout his three weeks there to speak about Hu Feng in public at the appropriate time. He chose to make his attack in the city of Chungking. It was there that Hu Feng had lived and where he was first imprisoned without trial. We might never have known about what happened at Chungking at all, if Greene's venting spleen had not suddenly brought the case dramatically into prominence a month after the delegation's return to London.

He must still have been stinging from the turn of events in Chungking, and felt forced on principle to reveal the hitherto private conflict. The quarrel played itself out in the *Daily Telegraph*. Suddenly it became possible to speak out and catch his unexpected British adversary, Lord Chorley, on the hip. The correspondence between Greene and Chorley, and a letter from Professor Lauwerys, entered the public arena.

In the *Telegraph*, Greene supported the British Security Services (this in itself was somewhat curious), and attacked, not the 'impossible Professor', but rather Lord Chorley, 'a bore, amiable & quiet'. Greene made his comments in the newspaper on 4 June 1957. Thinking Chorley was inconsistent and illogical in his attack on the Security Services, he let off the first shot: 'I was, of course, sympathetic with his thesis, though . . . I could not help suspecting, in view of the three weeks I had recently spent in his company in China, that he had got his facts a little jumbled . . . Rather in the spirit of Lord Chorley's recent speech I had been cross examining our Chinese host on the imprisonment without trial of the Chinese author, Mr Hu Feng.'

Green quotes from the dinner party:

> Our host had been a personal friend of Mr Hu Feng, and so I suggested what a happy conclusion it would be if at his eventual trial Mr Hu Feng were proved to be innocent. That, our host said, was an impossibility: a man was not arrested unless he were known to be guilty.*
>
> At this point Lord Chorley came to the rescue of our host. In times of war or revolution, he declared, we all recognised that the rights of the individual must lapse before the needs of the State. China was 'overrun' (a delightful phrase) with agents of Formosa, and he expressed his sympathetic understanding with the Chinese security authorities in their treatment of Mr Hu Feng. In fact he had been studying the papers in the case 'for a year'.

Greene admits he overreacted. He'd spoken of the shame and disgust he felt listening to Lord Chorley, a distinguished British jurist, defending imprisonment without trial. And Greene satirically described Chorley as belonging 'with the great comic figures of fiction – Don Quixote perhaps with more than a touch of Mrs Malaprop'.[32]

In his later account Greene's recall of the incident is more effective

---

* This sounds like Kafka's short story, 'The Penal Colony'.

and he makes fun of Lord Chorley's comments at the dinner given by
the mayor of Chungking, when Chorley spoke up to ease the embarrassment, only making matters worse:

'All of us here . . . realise the special difficulties you suffer from
in the People's Republic, overrun as you are by spies from Taiwan.'
    The image of the *Times* map flashed before my eyes – the huge
white patch of China extending from Canton in the south to the
wastes of Sinkiang and in the far north to Mongolia and off-set,
like a little green ear drop, Taiwan. China 'overrun' by spies? Excited
as I was no doubt by the Mou-Tai [a very powerful local brew to
which Greene became attached] I too scrambled to my feet. I was
deeply shocked, I said, to hear an English lawyer speak in such
outrageous terms. Was a man considered in his eyes to be guilty
without being tried? In that case I must refuse to travel any further
in Lord Chorley's company. The dinner party broke up.[33]

Lord Chorley replied four days later to Greene's *Daily Telegraph*
letter: 'Mr Graham Greene's account of what happened at the dinner
party at Chungking is hardly recognisable. After all, he is one of our
leading writers of fiction.' Chorley is himself evasive: 'I do not want
to quarrel with [Greene]. The occasion was private, and I was under
the impression that we had shaken hands after our little difference of
opinion.' According to Chorley, his criticism of the Security Services
in his own country was expressed because they had employed 'university teachers . . . to spy on their colleagues in college, which was the
gravamen of my case in the university debate'. He went on to say
that 'there is very little similarity between the postponement of the
trial of Mr Hu Feng . . . and the employment of university teachers
as security agents'.[34]
    But Greene would not allow Lord Chorley an easy escape: 'Perhaps
a novelist is more trained in accuracy than a politician, and depends
more on a good memory. My account of Lord Chorley's defence of
Mr Hu Feng's imprisonment without trial was true in detail, and I
would not describe our passage of arms on such a subject as "a small
difference of opinion". Lord Chorley's concern for human rights varies
with the country he finds himself in.'[35]
    Greene took issue with Chorley's suggestion that Hu Feng's impris-
onment for over a year was merely a postponement of a trial, and
attacked Chorley's point that 'the case against Mr Hu Feng is well-
known; it has been made public'. Greene's riposte was: 'It certainly has.
Instead of a trial in open court the authorities have tried him on the
bookstalls: at least two works have been issued in Chinese giving the

case *against* Mr Hu Feng. Is this Lord Chorley's idea of justice? Does he believe that anyone could issue a book in China giving the case *for* Mr Hu Feng?' And then a low blow: 'Perhaps he does. For he seems prepared to swallow anything on a free holiday abroad.'[36]

Chorley responded on 20 June 1957, arguing that civil liberties depended on the conditions prevailing, and again seemed to support the communist cause:

> Most people would agree that the liberties we enjoy in this country in time of peace could hardly be expected to prevail in a country which has just been through a revolution, and which still has an active enemy, well armed and well trained ... strategically placed not many miles from its coastline – an enemy which can and does land its spies and saboteurs on that long coastline, and which is receiving constant support and aid from the strongest Power in the world.

Chorley speaks of Britain's wartime 'Regulation 18b', which 'suspended trials in cases coming under it. This was an argument which I put very forcibly to Mr Greene . . . but he had no use for 18b, which he condemned out of hand, as of course he had a perfect right to do, and indeed could hardly not do, as he described himself to our Chinese hosts as an "anarchist".'[37]

Drunk or not, Greene felt, as he did on countless occasions, the need to speak on behalf of the underdog, for voiceless victims. He took the risk of standing up against the known barbarities of the communists in China. Communist China has never taken much notice of the West, but by airing the case of Hu Feng, Greene's words might have strengthened those facing the humiliations and indignities of the tyrant's stroke.

The present Lord Chorley is the son of Greene's opponent. His comments in a letter to me provide an understandable, and British, point of view. He argues that the group had been invited by the PRC government and that 'Greene was I understand drunk a lot of the time. He was (I think) extremely rude about his hosts – publicly – at a formal dinner and my father put him down.'[38]

Greene and Chorley did make up while in China. On Easter Sunday, Greene attended mass in the Catholic cathedral in Chungking. He returned to his hotel and felt guilt, intensified when Lord Chorley met him and offered his hand, apologising. Greene acknowledges that: 'The apology of course should have been mine. However, we shook hands and forgave each other and next day found us quite amicably sharing a cabin on the boat to Hangkow.'[39]

On 24 June, the 'third man' of the party sent a dutiful letter to the *Daily Telegraph*. The loquacious Professor Lauwerys, poor fellow, supported everyone:

It was a cheerful and convivial affair which gave us all ample opportunity of testing with appreciation the remarkable technical progress which has been made in the distilleries of China. The discussion in consequence became somewhat animated, and at a certain stage it turned to the case of Mr Hu Feng.

Mr Graham Greene spoke with a passion and warmth which I admired. He defended the principles of Western democracy, the importance of civic rights and of personal freedom. This pleased me mightily and I was delighted to support him.

My own impression is that Lord Chorley had not been paying very much attention to this particular discussion, but it may well be that he thought the argument was becoming a little acrimonious and it was time to intervene. My memory is that he pointed out that always and everywhere civil liberties dwindled at times of civil strife. He gave instances from our own past history.

I am inclined to think that the heat of the debate may have led him into a position which he would not really wish to defend. Certainly, for my part, I did not take this very seriously.

Having travelled with Lord Chorley and Mr Graham Greene for four weeks, I am certain that both, in different ways, are admirable defenders of democratic freedoms. Nor are they sparing in their criticisms of other political systems . . . Nor are they more inconsistent than the rest of us.[40]

But after the events of that evening, Greene was still angry – perhaps drunkenly so, and mostly with the professor. Though written thirty years later, 'A Weed Among the Flowers' evokes his displeasure with the long-winded academic:

I could bear the Professor's paragraphs no longer. Our voices were raised. I forget what terms I used, they must have been severe, for the Professor threatened to throw me into the Yangtze-kiang . . .

In the middle of the night I was woken by extraordinary noises, as though somebody was being strangled. They seemed to come from next door and I thought at once of the dangerous Professor. He too had drunk a lot of Mou-Tai. Was he assaulting his cabin companion, our young and friendly guide? The choking sounds continued. I looked across the cabin at Lord Chorley. He was sleeping peacefully. Something had to be done. I got up and went into the corridor and banged furiously on the Professor's door. 'Stop that fucking noise, you bugger,' I shouted. There was silence and I went back to bed.

I fell asleep, but when I woke again it was to the same strangled cries . . . this time they seemed to come from the deck above. Had our guide escaped there and been pursued by the murderous Professor? Would he, as a substitute for me, be flung into the Yangtze-kiang?[41]

Greene checked on the peacefully slumbering professor, and then went sleuthing – he thought he might be preventing a murder. But it was wholly unnecessary; the violent, garbled sounds were coming from two cooks talking in the kitchen. It was simply the guttural nature of the Chinese language.

PART 5

Affairs Lost

9

I Only Have Eyes
for You . . . and You

Life lived at the level of the Adam's apple,
not the pants.
                              — GRAHAM GREENE

As we follow the struggles of Greene's heart, we are tracking events
using the only source available — Greene's private letters to
Catherine Walston — and thus we hear only one end of a conversation. Greene's letters to Anita Björk are not available, whilst Catherine's
to Greene — he told me — were destroyed.

We left Greene with a promise to Catherine to 'break with Sweden'.
He would retreat as promised, but he wished to relinquish her deli-
cately — standards of civilised behaviour would be retained and he and
Anita would remain friends.

However, in July, a most extraordinary thing: Greene has taken Anita
to Martinique for a holiday and while they are there, Catherine also
decides to visit the island. He writes to her, suggesting that she should
'drive by the coast road to St Pierre . . .'[1] Nothing indicates that Greene
and Catherine met secretly, and I suspect they did not. But it is bizarre
that Greene's beloved two should be on the same tropical island at the
same time. And there is absolutely no inkling that his affair with Anita
is waning.

When writing to Catherine just before her arrival, Greene expressed
reservations about Martinique: 'it's really hopeless trying to get away
from a hotel . . . We spent two nights at Madame's fishing cottage —
nice bathing, nice fishermen, but hot & mosquitoey & an awful starving
kitten that licked all the food & jumped about all the time grabbing
things.'[2]

Then Greene tells Catherine that he and Anita arranged to rent a
house for three weeks, but it was inhospitable and they 'packed up and
went back to the hotel'. The holiday was unlike Jamaica in every way
and he longed to be back with Catherine for 'our long mornings &

dry Martinis and walking' to lunch. And not just the holiday suffers in comparison with others he's had with Catherine, but sadly, so does Anita: 'I'm longing for this holiday to end. Ours always go like lightning, but this so drags.'[3]

On 18 July 1957 he reports that he 'heard & watched' Catherine's plane come in and that: 'I was quite quiet & happy, lovely water & I make a good rum punch now, but the nights very long – hot and sticky under mosquito nets with no douche to work off the . . . sand.' He is going to St Kitts to see his grand-uncle's grave before flying from Guadeloupe on the 30th. 'Present plans I return to London Aug 4, but yesterday A. got a cable wanting her to start a film on Aug 5, so we may return earlier.'[4] The difference between this letter and those sent shortly after he broke the news of his affair with Anita is astonishing. Has Catherine given Greene some kind of reprieve? Or did he simply let Catherine's anguish gradually dissolve until the transgression was, if not forgotten, forgiven?

Only a few weeks earlier Greene had been telling Catherine how he'd been able to write well and successfully because Catherine was to be with him. Now he refers to working well on *A House of Reputation* and *Our Man in Havana* while on holiday with Anita, feeling it's gone better over the previous week, looking towards finishing the second act of the play.

By the 27th, six days later, he'd had his fill of Martinique. He and Anita had driven around almost every spot on the island, but he tells Catherine: 'it would give me the creeps to live here. Poisonings far from rare. One white man was given a steak made from a putrefying baby dug up for the purpose [of poisoning him].' Then suddenly at the end of the letter he writes: 'No news . . . of the Russian visa.'[5]

★

On 17 August 1957, Greene wrote from Moscow. He'd taken his son, Francis, along with him for his twenty-first birthday. Greene describes their visit to Tolstoy's home at Yasnaya Polyana which, even before Tolstoy died in 1910 at the age of eighty-three, had become a place of pilgrimage – the rooms kept exactly as they were. In the garden the 'same flowerbeds with the same flowers as in Tolstoy's time . . . I was given a bouquet, but the roses have already died. It was strangely moving . . . Off to Leningrad tomorrow.'[6] Greene sent Catherine dried rose petals in the letter – the stains are still visible on the paper.

Visiting Leningrad, they went to art galleries as they had in Moscow. Greene sent Catherine a postcard showing a celebrated Delacroix. 'This is a lovely city & I miss you especially when Francis gets a bit on the nerves. Come to Vienna soon.'[7] Another card says: 'hope your boat is a success', and remarks on a fall that Catherine had suffered, hoping 'your poor ribs healed. Back on 26th. So much love.'[8] The postcard arrived in England the day of his return. From there he wrote Catherine about the strain Vivien was putting on him. This emotionally charged letter shows just how enormously upset he could get, in his own British way. It also emphasises his need for *peace* in which to write – the most important thing in his life. He complains that Vivien's been on the phone 'filling me with vague unease about Lucy – who "has reason to feel left out" – (my God, when she's been handed [a] 1000 acre ranch & her heart's desire). I think it's more likely Vivien than Lucy who's the trouble. Before that it was Francis who was "left out". O God. O Montreal, I must have diverted more than £20,000 towards them in the last three years in spite of taxation & only having writing to do it with.' He gets down to brass tacks:

> No, dear dear Catherine, I don't need or want emotional cock-tails. If it hadn't been for the peace I've had with you two months a year, I couldn't have worked enough to keep all this going.

He describes his need for calm:

> You – when we are together – give peace for work from worry, & so in a smaller way does Anita. Neither of you are emotional cocktails. Neither of you make demands.

And then, the confession:

> I meant to tell you today [at lunch] that I'm going for three nights to Stockholm on Sunday – I partly forgot because of talking of other things & partly was afraid. I love you more but I love her too, & it seemed so cold blooded going away for five weeks & then not seeing her at all for months & this is the last chance for a longish while. Now I hate myself for making excuses.[9]

This is a different Greene. He's on a treadmill, and must be, if only to keep his family financially. And the promise to leave 'Sweden' has still not been fulfilled.

On the other hand, Greene is pleased with his son, who came back alone from Russia under his own steam. Listen to a proud father: 'Francis turned up – having penetrated beyond the Caucasus, through Armenia, to the borders of Turkey! He could have got to Samarkand but hadn't time.'[10] Francis was enjoying his birthday, but was still at the stage when young men break out in pimples, as his father noted in Leningrad: 'I was very encouraged by Francis in general, & pleased to notice that girls were inclined to look twice at him in spite of spots!'[11]

Shortly after his return to London, Greene mentions a 'Drinking evening with FO man'.[12] The fact that he was seeing the Foreign Office probably means he was reporting on his journey to Moscow and Leningrad. But at this time he was planning a visit to Cuba, and would be reporting about that or being advised as to what they would like him to see. Clearly Cuba was on the cards for discussion, as a postcard to Catherine only a couple of days later suggests: 'Party went off well but oh what a price! Have heard nothing yet from Cuban Ambassador.'[13]

Greene feels better about Catherine than he has in a long time, thinking that for more than a year before the affair with Anita happened she'd 'stopped talking to me about things'. Now he feels they are closer than they have been since 1955, and adds: 'I see no reason why we shouldn't book hunt together & go to pubs together & talk about anything under the sun. It was in 1955 that I began to invent excuses to get you to London – films, first nights etc – because you seemed to have gone so far away – and that was before A. Now I *feel* you close again, even though you say you aren't!'[14]

But Greene's letter must have met with some thorny resistance, for his response to Catherine's next letter is quite firm and dismissive. He tells her he understands a great deal of what she says, and that he was just trying to play it her way. When that approach doesn't work, he suggests they be conventional and not see one another. He admits he's still in love with her, but that the meeting in Vienna, which he's had his tongue hanging out for, might be a mistake. Then a Catholic brush-off: 'God bless you. I do very much love you, but I'm no good to you any longer. G.'[15] A rejection by Graham as opposed to the usual rejection by Catherine – this is new. But he is soon playing the same old song: 'Still here, so I needn't have put things at their roughest . . . I *am* going [to Stockholm] tomorrow for the rest of the week – back Sunday. I hate hurting you, & I go on doing it.'[16]

Greene keeps in perpetual motion. 'Dinner with Michael Anderson [director of *Around the World in Eighty Days*] . . . With Hugh & Elaine Greene to the Metropole & nearly wept at the old [music hall] songs. Just a chance of selling film rights of *The Potting Shed* in USA in which case there'd be no hurry about Cuba & I could postpone in the hope of your consenting to come with me in the spring. On the 17th I'm going to have an eating–drinking night in Paris with Michael Meyer who's never been! 16th Vivien in London. I've asked Mrs Young to arrange a Kenneth–Islay*–you reunion, preferably dinner.'[17]

★

Upon returning to London from Stockholm Greene writes: 'Not knowing that you were about, I went & drank with the director at the Savile [Club] & now I've just returned from a solitary meal at the Café [Royal] . . . Down to Crowborough Saturday. *Now* I have Vivien next Wednesday evening instead. O God, O Montreal. I could have had lunch today with Katharine Hepburn – who asked for me – if I hadn't muddled Vivien.'[18]

Five days later, on 22 October 1957, he tells Catherine he's leaving for a while: 'This afternoon . . . I couldn't even remember my way between Piccadilly Circus & Charing Cross Road!' And he has a gripe: 'O God, Vivien tomorrow who wants me to go shopping with her!'[19]

In his next letter, we learn that Catherine has at last dumped him. He wishes she'd waited until he'd come home. She is jumping to conclusions and he is nervy, telling her: 'If there were tears in my eyes it was because I love you so much. I shall always love you, & the ten years *are the only part of my life I'd like to live again. You* are the last attachment – it's exaggeration to call [being with Anita] an attachment except technically – & it's already weakening.' He admits it's his own fault. He quotes Othello: 'Like the base Indian who flung a pearl away'.[20]

The same day he writes Catherine another letter: 'I'm sorry about everything. It's my fault & I had it coming . . .'[21] But two weeks later, he's banging on the same back door: 'Do you mind my writing? I've tried not to, but you are the only person to whom I can write . . .'[22]

He is going off to Havana, and is afraid. 'Two days ago in NY the story [*Our Man in Havana*] began to grow & I even thought it might grow into something good – funny & sad & exciting, but now the feeling has slipped away.'[23] He goes back to his obsessions: Catherine and Anita.

★

By 8 November, he is holidaying with Anita in Havana, once a very special place for Catherine. He criticises her reading choices, and her

---

* Author Kenneth McPherson and photographer Islay Lyons, friends of Greene and Catherine from Capri. McPherson edited Dottoressa Moor's memoirs until his death, when Greene took over – see Chapter 37.

'stupid questions & I get impatient & won't answer'. Then there was his pretending to be happy about a pregnancy slip-up, but 'secretly I made a promise that if there were no baby I would consider . . . going somewhere like Stonyhurst [a Catholic retreat] when the play was over for three weeks or three months. There wasn't a baby & now I don't see how it's to be done.'

He tells Catherine, 'You are the only real life there was: everything else was a drug to keep me going until you were with me . . . I've got 26 books with me, but again there's no You to say I like this or I don't like that, do read this, don't you think this metaphor's good.' He has regrets: 'I was so harsh on the phone . . . I don't see love in quite the same sense as you . . . If you don't want me to write, tell me.' And then a long postscript: 'Now I must get up & wander round & tomorrow I must try to begin "Our Man in Havana". It won't come as easily & happily as The Third Man. I have an awful fear that work won't work without you – what I did in Martinique was hopeless.'[24]

Usually, a writer writes at a desk. But look at Greene's constant careening around the world. How could he work under such conditions? The fact is he did. Greene made the world his workplace, any strange hotel his study, and as long as Catherine was with him he was centred, at peace, so he could write. In Catherine's company he could draw on the unknown measure of himself, find his own secret amplitude. She was his constant; she galvanised his genius. His obsession for her goes on and on.

If after ten years Greene did not need Catherine's body quite so much, he certainly needed her company and her mind's unrivalled exhilarations. Two days before Christmas, he begins another letter from his daughter's ranch: 'I loved your Christmas card, dear heart. I've dreamed twice of you & me making love. I never dream of anyone else. I can't believe we won't be together again. I've been such a hopeless fool & now I don't know how to manage.'[25] Greene refuses to accept the obvious: to have Catherine, he must give up Anita.

Greene sent a telegram to Newton Hall: 'HAPPY XMAS TO ALL / AND SO MUCH LOVE TO YOU = GRAHAM',[26] but he ended his 23 December letter with a financial plan, his mind always looking at the world and his place in it: 'I've got a scheme of selling all my north American rights . . . for 3,000 dollars a year until the age of 70. I think in the first years anyway they can make a good profit.'[27] Unless such a scheme had been index-related, this would have been financially disastrous.

★

The year 1958 dawned and still no break with Anita. His first letter to Catherine in the new year is on stationery from the Grand Hotel,

Stockholm. Greene didn't stay there, but ate his meals in the restaurant and used the hotel notepaper, an open advertisement that he was still with Anita. He asks Catherine to come to a movie in London, and gives her a choice of days. He offers to change a date with his Australian girlfriend, Jocelyn Rickards, and asks Catherine to think about coming to Brighton: 'it would be something to have one time together before you go away.'[28]

He tells Catherine that Vivien had come up from Oxford for an evening, then 'went off quite happily'. After seeing Vivien to the station Greene returned to Albany. He and Catherine had rooms there, so they were close to each other when both were in London. His letter continues: 'I longed to ring you as your light was *on*, but didn't.' Then a cryptic note: 'A. busy with film & play rehearsals. Trying to work.'[29]

Catherine must have written a letter of absolute rejection. He was brought down so low, and is at a loss how to respond. He simply asks her to phone, 'even if I do cry afterwards in the bath as I did yesterday'. Catherine probably told him she was going away for an extended period in order to bring this painful affair to a close. They agree to a final meeting before her departure, but Greene conjures up images of despair: 'I'll probably have to dash from the room & maybe we better not go to a public restaurant but have some food at home – I don't want to make a fool of myself in public.' He stresses for the umpteenth time that he still is thoroughly in love with Catherine, 'head, heart and body', and suggests for the second time that perhaps the only solution would be for him to clear out of England altogether 'where there is too much to remind me of you'. And he adds in undertone: 'I'm arranging for Svanstrom to buy Rosaio'[30] (his home in Anacapri, where he and Catherine shared some of their most compelling moments). Greene is stripping himself of every reminder of her, as every lost lover must . . . but this lover just can't hack it.

But Greene fails to see Catherine's difficulty, which is extraordinary. In *The End of the Affair*, had he not had Bendrix say to his lover, Sarah: 'I'd rather be dead or see you dead . . . than with another man. I'm not eccentric. That's ordinary human love . . . Anybody who loves is jealous'?[31] Greene seems to have forgotten his own injunction. He admits to a possible suicide plan, saying it was wildly silly, but now that she has gone away from him, he has put his feet 'in so deep that I can't see how I can ever get them out short of a proverbial plane crash'.[32] He had considered suicide during 1947, when he was juggling Catherine and Vivien; he told Vivien he'd stored away 'five hundred Nembutal tablets and I can solve the whole business with that'.[33]

He's as immovable over Anita as he had been over Catherine ten years earlier, and thus twists helplessly in the breeze: 'When people inquire after you I never know whether to tell them you've left me. The female vultures gather here at the scent of death – so I suppose Anita will be the next one I'll fail. The death wish is very strong.'[34] What he should do stares him in the face. He turns a blind eye to giving up Anita. Instead, he'd rather face death – suicide as his exit of choice?

★

In the middle of these arguments, Greene had a visit from Sir Oliver Crosthwaite-Eyre, a major shareholder of the publishing firm of Eyre & Spottiswoode. Sir Oliver had retired to South Africa but came to England specially to see Greene. On the night before the first night of *The Potting Shed* in Brighton, he and Greene engaged in an enormous binge. In the morning, he called on Greene: 'He wanted me to take over E. & S. in place of Douglas Jerrold – salary round £6000 I think! It was really an effort to say No, but I know I couldn't stand being bound to London & that yearly visit to New York.' Then Greene astonishes: 'All the same it would have been nice to be secure from the necessity of writing.' He describes their night together, drinking dry martinis – Graham's special concoction, and then they went pubbing with Oliver's chauffeur 'and had 3 pink gins each'. Then they went to the Lyric for a bottle and a half of wine. Incredibly, Graham admits: 'In spite of that I did 400 words in bed this morning.'[35]

While Greene was involved in London rehearsals for *The Potting Shed*, he was also getting up at 7.30 to work on *Our Man in Havana* and on a radio play about the former Master of Balliol College, Benjamin Jowett: 'Finished Jowett (which you wouldn't like).' He also went by himself to see a film about Picasso: 'one feels a slight distaste of an artist who is such a good actor.'[36]

He tells Catherine he's reading his friend Sir Harold Acton (though they were not close as undergraduates) as well as the former vice-chancellor of Oxford, Maurice Bowra: 'some Acton with interest (O for more of his kind) & Bowra dutifully & with boredom – he writes so badly.' And then the contents of his postbag: 'Letter from Peter Glenville, in California wanting me to do the script of a book about North Africa – I've said No but I'm reading the book. William Wyler has also turned up in trouble with *Ben Hur* & in company with a producer called superbly Mr Zimbalist – I'm lunching with them on Friday – I might help if there's a lot of money & if my name was kept out. On Saturday I visit Stockholm.'[37] Again, Anita. Why does he rub Catherine's nose in it?

Yet Catherine had gone with him to see the opening of his play in Brighton, so he had broken down her resistance, without giving up

Anita. He writes: 'Please can I see you soon when you get back? I've
felt close to you again since our two movies & Brighton.' He stays
busy, writing that 'Capalbo's . . . wife has turned up. [She had parted
from her husband.] I'm giving her lunch . . . Tonight I have . . . dress
rehearsal – apparently we broke the theatre record at Brighton.' And
a final cryptic note: 'I'll send you a quick line on the way to
Crowborough [where he was visiting his mother and Dorothy Glover]
about how things went.'[38]

It was Catherine's birthday on 12 February, and Greene was again
in Stockholm. Then on the 14th he sent an unexpected telegram to
Catherine at the Marquis Estate in St Lucia:

LAST NIGHT EVERYTHING FINISHED STOCKHOLM MUTUAL AGREE-
MENT WILL WRITE WHEN LESS EXHAUSTED HOW I WISH WE WERE
TOGETHER CAN WE HAVE FEW DAYS WHEN YOU RETURN MUCH
WANT ADVICE ALSO ABOUT OLIVERS OFFER LOVE[39]

Greene sent this telegram from London. It's as if he had come home
wounded from the war:

THANK YOU DEAR CABLE TOO TIRED TO WRITE YET BUT WILL SO
MUCH LOVE[40]

*

Almost two weeks after his first telegram Greene writes to Catherine
about the Anita breakup:

I caught an aeroplane back next morning & poor Anita went
off to a rehearsal looking 60 years old. No quarrel & the ten
days that followed were awful – not as awful as I felt with you:
two years is a lot less than ten & we had never been so close,
but the days were empty enough. Jocelyn, the Sutros & Jeanne
Stonor have all helped by going to cinemas & plays – & now
suddenly this morning I feel what the hell and have done 500
words.[41]

In London he fills every moment to help him recover from his loss,
taking his son to the ballet, where the curtain was 'delayed for half an
hour till Mike Todd & Elizabeth Taylor had taken their seats just in
front.* Then John [Sutro], Gillian & I had a box for Margot [Fonteyn]

---

* Taylor and Todd married in 1957; Todd died in a plane accident later in the year.

in *Sylvia* & drank hock in the intervals & ate delicious sandwiches. I'm going with Jocelyn tomorrow to the *Charley's Aunt* musical & next week with Jeanne to *The Iceman Cometh*.[42]

He is having trouble living without Anita, and he suffers. Graham again tells Catherine what Catherine would not wish to know:

> until this morning I've been filletted & lived on drink & sleeping pills. Anyway my weight's gone down 3 lbs. *I never knew I'd miss the girl so much* . . . The book [*Our Man in Havana*] has reached 41,000 words – 3000 below schedule (I was working well when the fuse blew).[43]

Greene tells Catherine that Mrs Young is booking them up for *The Potting Shed* in London, asks if they could have a few days after Easter: 'Paris & the Ritz & Maxim's?' Writing that he wished he hadn't lent out his Capri place to his Swedish publisher from May to July, he adds in a sort of *sotto voce*: 'I wish a lot of things hadn't happened or even begun', and continues: 'I've been a bloody fool.'[44]

And then a next-to-final comment in his postscript: 'I wish we were beside Coward's bathing pool drinking fresh lime (here it's snowing). Just ordered the final life of Byron (in three volumes & I shall love every volume).' Then something he has not done since his Vietnam days: he draws five signs of a kiss, so spread out that they indicate he is kissing her cheeks, two crosses, then another two further down indicating he is kissing her breasts; the final kiss – her pudendum.

He's trying to fill time with pain-dulling pursuits. 'So the first night's over,' he writes, and though the letter is undated it is presumably 5 or 6 February 1958, the London opening of *The Potting Shed*. He mentions that Evelyn Waugh attended, as did other friends: 'In the end I had quite a party drinking champagne & I missed you all the more: Evelyn (in a sombre rather death-wish mood on his way to Rhodesia over the life of Knox [Greene had no love for the Catholic theologian Ronald Knox; Waugh's life came out in 1959] – how I detest that man, leaving Evelyn all the work & not a penny of money)', then more about the play and those who attended: the Sutros, Pat and Frere, Eric Strauss, Jocelyn and Freddie [A. J. Ayer].

> The audience was very sticky, the performances A–, reception good. The notices have been mixed, the serious [is] reasonably good, & the little reporter chap's bad – but the 3rd programme [BBC] last night, a superb 'rave' notice comparing me to Montaigne![45]

98

He took John Hayward to see *The Potting Shed* and gave him supper afterwards: 'Oh, how glad I am to be finished with it all. I feel really tired & have had to give up working in bed for the last three days.'[46]

★

Oliver Crosthwaite-Eyre wrote to Greene on 4 March 1958, while *The Potting Shed* was still flying high. He had not forgotten Greene's brilliance as a publisher when working as a director under Douglas Jerrold at Eyre & Spottiswoode and had a strong determination to have Greene take over the firm. By 1958 Eyre & Spottiswoode had joined with Methuen and Associated British Publishers and had flourished. Crosthwaite-Eyre offered him the opportunity of a lifetime, running a real family business which would perhaps have allowed Greene's son Francis in due course to take over a distinguished publishing house. Arrangements would be made for Douglas to retire in the autumn, and '[you would] join us as Managing and Editorial Director of the Publishers . . . [and] also join the board of Associated British Publishers and that of Eyre & Spottiswoode Limited'.[47]

In earlier days Greene, in a conflict with Douglas Jerrold, had himself retired rather suddenly as a result of a disagreement over the novelist Anthony Powell.* Greene's relationship with Jerrold was uncertain and we sense something of the strain that Jerrold felt working with Greene simply from the title of an article Jerrold wrote for *Harper's* in August 1952: 'Graham Greene, Pleasure-Hater.'

My reading of the situation is that Jerrold forced Greene out of the firm in 1948 because of the trouble with Powell. This was of no economic consequence to Graham, because that year he had tremendous success with *The Heart of the Matter*. Still, it must have given Greene secret pleasure to receive such a letter, a decade later, from the former Chairman of the Board.

Sir Oliver brought to Greene's attention a young man he thought would make a good lieutenant, someone to 'run the show' when Greene was out of the country. No doubt Crosthwaite-Eyre gave much thought to his selection, hoping he'd chosen the right person to give Greene confidence. It did not work. Greene describes to Catherine the weekend at Crosthwaite-Eyre's place in the country:

It was a nice weekend – Eric & Thomas (whom I liked very much . . .) & a nice Austrian count, but a young married couple who were very intense & intellectual & tiresome (life lived at the level of the adam's apple, not the pants) – they were brought

* Though Greene in interview denied this was the prime cause; see Volume Two, pp. 200–3.

there for me to look at, because if I took the job (which Oliver is keeping open for me anyway till April) he could be my second-in-command. I don't know that I could stand it – it would be such a lonely job without someone to laugh & drink with.[48]

Greene is exhausted, feeling battered because Oliver drinks 'enormously all the time – our drinking nothing in comparison'.[49]

Catherine continued to write, so his pleading continued, wishing to 'forget the stupidities of the past two years', and he admits he feels old, and

> that it's all my fault doesn't help . . . Dear Catherine, come back soon. I feel like someone clinging by his nails to a window ledge waiting for a net to be spread below. The net is still such a long time away.[50]

On the back of the envelope, he adds: 'Depressed to find how bad the Havana story is turning out.' He was desperate to get back to Catherine – the only one he could love. But then the door slammed shut.

★

Having a scare after hearing that Catherine had been swept off the rocks at the Marquis Estate, he admits: 'I can't imagine how one could go on living without you being part of life.' He is terribly lonely and continues to accept every invitation. So far he'd 'been to five theatres & two ballets'.[51] Also, people he met in New York during production of *The Potting Shed* keep landing on his doorstep: 'Just before I went to Stockholm [he had written 'Paris' but then wrote above 'Stockholm'] Mrs Capalbo turned up & I gave her lunch as I told you & then soon after I returned Leueen [MacGrath] appeared . . . I went away . . . & when I came back she was under dope in a nursing home . . . What a lot of lame ducks we are (I don't mean you.)'

On Saturday he was 'disturbed' by

> a cable from Stockholm simply saying one word 'Anita'. A bit of whimsy, I thought, but I wished you were here, so that I wasn't tempted to do anything silly out of loneliness.[52]

He missed Catherine: 'It seems so much longer that you've been away . . . What a life you are leading. Dear Catherine, don't disappear into it.'[53] But a letter dated Tuesday, 25 March, 1.30 p.m., suggests that Catherine had at last returned, but Greene couldn't keep his date with her: 'Welcome home. I am stuck in Amsterdam by weather in London.' His loneliness had indeed made him do something silly:

> I'm sorry, dear dear Catherine, but things got complicated again on Saturday – a message from Anita – another week & I probably wouldn't have gone, but I cancelled the weekend engagements & went . . . Now things have gone back to what they were or more so. I feel hopelessly muddled. I missed [Anita] more than I thought I would, but now that's healed, it's you I miss. Am I crazy or do I just happen to love two women as I never have before?[54]

He is cornered, truth dripping slow.

10

Lovers Come Tumbling Down

So we must keep apart,
You there, I here,
With just the door ajar . . .
— EMILY DICKINSON

I N January 1958, as rehearsals began for the London production of *The Potting Shed*, Greene's relationship with Catherine Walston continued its downward spiral. Catherine is about to break off for good. Using the epistolary method, rich in the nectar of drama, we see the fluid nature of their affection – and anger – as Greene tries to hold on to two women. Unlike Catherine, Anita was no letter writer; she could be many things, but not his secret sharer in the written word.

The implication from Greene's letters to Catherine is that she felt Anita had grown too important, or perhaps she was fed up with Greene's two-, three- (and maybe more-) timing. Nonetheless, during all of 1958, their ten-year affair was off again/on again. There is quarrelling, making up, and quarrelling again. But it is not until the close of the year, when Anita finally decides to end the relationship, that Greene feels the deepest despair.

★

Greene began working on *Our Man in Havana* in October 1956.[1] On 2 January 1958 he wrote to his Swedish publisher Ragnar Svanstrom that he was writing a short novel – about 55,000 words. On 22 April 1958, having been asked to write an introduction for another writer's book he declined because he was 'very pressed for time as I have to finish a book by the end of May and I simply can't be distracted from it'. Greene added: 'Writing is always difficult for me and a preface like that would take up probably a week's time which I [can't afford].'[2]

On 4 June, Greene wrote to Catherine in a short note that he'd 'Finished revision on Monday for better for worse'.[3] *Our Man in Havana* was complete. He sent Catherine a copy of the typescript, asking her to tell him how she found it – for his part: 'I think it stinks.'[4] Despite his doubts, he delivered the novel on time.

By 14 July, he was 'working a bit on the dentist play' (*The Complaisant Lover*, produced by Sir John Gielgud at the Globe Theatre on 18 June 1959) and also writing *A House of Reputation*, a play not produced until September 2000 by the Graham Greene Birthplace Trust in Berkhamsted.*

Three months before *Our Man in Havana* appeared on the bookstalls telegrams from film companies started arriving. Greene wrote that his American agent, Monica McCall, wanted to sell it for $125,000, and that Cary Grant was reading it. Greene was edging towards working with his friend Carol Reed, as he had done so successfully on *The Fallen Idol* and *The Third Man*. Hopes were high that with Reed as director and Greene as scriptwriter, they could perform a hat-trick. Greene was giving up a lot of money to work with a friend, to write a funny, ingenious film script based on a funny, ingenious novel.

Alfred Hitchcock was at first interested in *Our Man in Havana*, and was willing to pay £25,000 for the rights, but when McCall wanted to double the asking price, he backed off. Greene didn't want Hitchcock. In his film reviews in the 1930s Greene could not hide his contempt for the renowned filmmaker: 'as a producer he had no sense of continuity and as a writer he had no sense of life.'[5]† So, the old firm of Graham Greene and Carol Reed were again riding high.

*

Our Man in Havana was published in England and America simultaneously in October 1958. It was appropriate that the novel became a film, because Greene's original idea, which he'd had in mind for years, was for it to be a movie script. Just after the Second World War, Greene's friend Alberto Cavalcanti asked for a screenplay. Greene thought immediately of a story just waiting to be written: the activities of spies working

---

* Writer/director Bryan Forbes also did a revival of *The Living Room* in October 1987 at the Royalty Theatre in Queensway. Bryan told me in a letter of 24 December 2001 that Graham brought Elisabeth to the performance, and pronounced it a 'wonderful production'. They ate dinner at Rules. Altogether an enjoyable evening in spite of, or perhaps because of, his last comment, 'We drank quite a bit, I remember.'

† He is even more critical in *Ways of Escape*, ignoring the director's popularity with audiences, and calling Hitchcock's 'inadequate sense of reality' irritating and pronouncing *The Thirty-Nine Steps* spoilt in his hands: 'His films consist of a series of small "amusing" melodramatic situations: the murderer's button dropped on the baccarat board; the strangled organist's hands prolonging the notes in the empty church . . . very perfunctorily he builds up to these tricky situations (paying no attention on the way to inconsistencies, loose ends, psychological absurdities) and then drops them: they mean nothing: they lead to nothing.' (*Ways of Escape*, Lester & Orpen Dennys, 1980, p. 85.)

for the German secret service, the Abwehr, in Portugal. In chapter 12 we see more of the extraordinary origins of this story.

The skeleton of the story Greene concocted and the page he offered to Cavalcanti were sent to the British censors. They turned it down on the grounds that no certificate could be issued which permitted making fun of the Secret Service. When Greene visited Havana, it suddenly struck him that in that city, 'where every vice was permissible and every trade possible, lay the true background for my comedy. I realised I had been planning the wrong situation . . . at the wrong period. The shadows in 1938 of the war to come had been too dark for comedy; the reader could feel no sympathy for [a spy] who was cheating his country in Hitler's day.'[6]

*

After the Amsterdam airport letter in which Greene admitted he was back again with Anita, a month went by before he wrote to Catherine again.[7] In that time, a deterioration had set in. He told Catherine not to meet him at Brighton. I assume a later meeting in Brussels was also scrapped. Greene suddenly felt himself to be in the driving seat, telling her not to confuse the issue and giving some indication of how difficult it was to be Graham Greene, and why he found relationships at this stage in life difficult. 'Part of my nerves is that I love & miss you . . . Dear Catherine please believe we won't always be out of step.'

Attached (perhaps by Catherine) to this letter is another from Marie Biche, Greene's French literary agent and friend. Marie is trying to patch things up between the two, reassuring Catherine that *she* is the most important person to Greene, that he wished Catherine had been in England when he broke up with Anita as he would not have started up again with her, but gone back to Catherine. Marie asked Greene if he could ever go back; his answer, she says, was given without a second's hesitation: '"One knows one could, like that, with Catherine."'[8]

Greene and Catherine do meet in London and have a wonderful evening, with Anita still very much in the ascendancy, even though Greene is at pains to deny it. After a particularly pleasant evening with Catherine, he ends his short letter telling her he'll be waiting when she returns from yet another trip to St Lucia, and adds: 'We are always – somehow – going to be together.'[9]

It is at this time, the summer of 1958, that he buys Anita a house in the Swedish archipelago. He has been too busy, helping Anita move, to write to Catherine. In another letter, sudden contempt: 'I'm beginning really to dislike Swedes – with the exception of Anita of course.'[10] He'd planned to escape for a few days to see the American theatre director Sam Wanamaker in Liverpool, but couldn't go because 'Anita wants to go to a small island in the archipelago for a week – a two-roomed cottage, the children sleeping in the kitchen'. The trouble was that it was in a defence area and Greene, a foreigner, had to seek special permission to visit.

Having made a commitment to Anita, Greene begins to have doubts: 'I don't know how this will work out . . . I can't really believe that life in a foreign country will be possible.' We know from this undated letter how far he had gone with Anita: 'I've landed myself with an obligation though to try – but nothing is as good as being *with* you. I don't say that it's not better than being without you.' He admits, for the first time, to himself regarding Anita: 'For once I don't think I'll have done harm – I've brought her out of the cave she was a bit living in after [her husband's] suicide.'[11]

Greene describes the holiday in the archipelago as a 'terribly chaste one', in a one-room hut with primitive facilities including a lavatory seat over a hole in the ground in the woods. While using it, 'the mosquitoes descend in clouds & eat one's bottom. One sleeps in a narrow little hard berth so high up that one nearly puts one's leg out jumping down . . . One washes in the sea.'[12]

Again come the comparisons with his and Catherine's wonderful first days, so often referred to. If we are tiring of Greene's ardent correspondence, think of the onslaught on Catherine. He writes of her in his diary. In 1958: it was 'all about you & the longing & pain & happiness . . . Dear Catherine, I am ruined for anyone else.'[13] Still on holiday in early July with Anita, Greene becomes restless: 'There's nothing to do – not even making love! & it's restful, but so boring, so boring.' He again promises to leave Anita: '*You* are the last attachment.'[14]

By 9 July, he and Anita have returned from the archipelago to Stockholm and Greene starts right in: 'We both agree it's not working . . . but there's no emotion . . . I'm sure the decision will stick.' He asks Catherine to meet him in Capri in October. He's staying in Stockholm as a 'family friend', he says, because if he left at once, Anita would immediately vacate the home he'd bought her. He is generous: 'I do want her to come out of this episode better than she went in . . . I've told V[ivien] the affair is in liquidation.'[15] But his letters continue to snipe at Anita. Required to be 'a kind of marmalade blonde for her next film', they colour her hair and she looks 'ten years older. It's awful that a little thing like that can add to one's indifference.'[16] And he can't easily suffer children: 'The small boy is away with his grandparents & the little girl is much less nuisance alone & in a house.'[17]

So the Anita affair is finally winding down. Halfway into July, he writes from Stockholm that he'll be back on 1 August, and he wants Catherine to 'think it over while I'm away'.[18]

What is Catherine to think over? Is she herself engaged in another affair? On 8 August she hears from him: 'What a lot of mystery! Surely this is not the right period for getting together . . . Wait until you . . . don't have to have secrets. After all I ruined things with my secrets.' And then he tells her: 'Now I pass the ball to you, & I'll leave it to you to choose the time – whether in a week, a month or a year.'[19] The mystery remains a mystery – for now.

*

Greene's entertainment, *Our Man in Havana*, was well reviewed, and in some cases, exultingly so. We have the author's usual disclaimer: 'In a fairy-story like this, set at some indeterminate date in the future, it seems unnecessary to disclaim any connexion between my characters and living people.' He asserts that 'there is no police officer like Captain Segura in Cuba today'.[20] But in *Ways of Escape*, Greene links Segura to Ventura, the head of Batista's secret police, adding that *Our Man in Havana* did him little good with the new rulers in Cuba, because by poking fun at the British Secret Service he'd minimised the terror of the dictator Batista. Greene did not want to blacken the background for his comedy, but, 'those who had suffered during the years of dictatorship could hardly be expected to appreciate that my real subject was the absurdity of the British agent and not the justice of a revolution, nor did my aesthetic reasons for changing a savage Captain Ventura into a cynical Captain Segura appeal to them.'[21]

Another former secret agent, the well-known Malcolm Muggeridge, praised Greene: 'He was tremendously good at dealing with agents and working out cover plans . . . and justifiably was very highly thought of.' And Muggeridge applauded *Our Man in Havana*: 'He understood what he was about as . . . *Our Man in Havana* shows. It's the most brilliant book on intelligence that's ever been written because it gets inside the whole fantasy . . . [the] feeling of it, the ludicrousness . . . the way people get caught up in it. You have to take it seriously and yet it's all based on a fantasy.'[22]

*

While *Our Man in Havana* is waxing, Anita is waning. Anita is busy working:

> Then we say goodbye for keeps . . . It's pouring with rain . . . All rather dreary. This is the way the world ends, not with a bang but a whimper. To add a final ironic touch she has the curse – an advantage also of course.[23]

It was in this mood that Greene decided he'd write the script for *Our Man in Havana* with Carol Reed as both producer and director. Reed had assembled an impressive cast: Alec Guinness as Wormold; Burl Ives as Dr Hasselbacher; Maureen O'Hara as Beatrice; Ernie Kovacs as Segura; Ralph Richardson as 'C', head of British Intelligence; and the inimitable Noël Coward taking the part of the English intelligence officer Hawthorne. Greene tries to link arms, heart and body to Catherine, and tells her he's off to Havana, tempting her with two or three weeks in Rome and Anacapri; he wants to check on his house there. He asks her to 'Leave a note behind for me in London & I'll start booking seats etc. I plan to finish the script by the end of the year & then perhaps I can finance Tahiti – or anywhere.'[24]

But when Michael Meyer returned from the Far East in the summer of 1958, Greene suggested *he* accompany him to Cuba, then still under Batista. Meyer met Greene in Stockholm at the end of August. Greene wrote into a copy of his play *The Potting Shed*: 'On what could be a sad occasion – the last *smorgasbord*.'[25] Things were going badly. After the long summer decline, thoughts of Anita seem finally to have receded. Greene writes to Catherine and shows what kind of Catholic he's been in the past: 'I must say I half begin to believe in the sacraments! Things on that line have been made so easy for me here.'[26] Again the immortal: 'I think it must be recognised that I married you one morning in Tunbridge Wells.'[27] Catherine still refused to go to Cuba.

The *Observer* asked him to report on Algeria* in September or October 1958, but the film *Our Man in Havana* loomed. In the days before he went to New York and then with Carol Reed to Havana for a first look at the terrain, he made a few jaunts. For a break he went to Paris and tried to get himself in better physical condition: 'Been missing lunch & walking everywhere.'[28] He looked up Vietnam friends, dined on a riverboat, and repeated his old Vietnam habit: 'I went & smoked four pipes of opium with old Indo-China hands.'[29]

He had time for a quick visit to Capri, this time with Catherine. She was finally aware of his genuine need of her now that he and Anita had parted. Upon their return, she sent a note which cheered him greatly. In a letter dated simply 'Wednesday' (though the envelope helps us out with the date), he wrote: 'I loved our time in Capri & was only sad that it was short . . . Let's try & see each other if only for five minutes on Thursday.'[30]

Greene then refers to the fact that Catherine is going away yet

---

* In May 1958, European colonists in Algeria ended the Fourth French Republic and returned General de Gaulle to power.

again. How could she expect to keep him? Anita was barely over, yet off Catherine was going to St Lucia and Rat Island. Greene tells her: 'I'll write again soon from Havana. Could we have one outing even if it was only one night at Brighton before you go away for such a long time?'[31]

Then at last Greene and Reed are in Havana, and in his first note he tells Catherine of his gambling at the Tropicana: 'Won 70 dollars here with one 25 cent piece in a machine. You've never seen such a jackpot!'[32] (In *Ways of Escape*, Greene writes of 'the fruit machines spilling out jackpots of silver dollars'.[33]) When he returns to England on 24 October, he and Carol Reed go to Brighton to work on the film script of *Our Man in Havana*. From there Greene sent Catherine a telegram: 'FAIR WINDS AND HAPPY LANDFALL LOVE GRAHAM'.[34] He tells Michael Meyer he's back, tired and depressed. He confesses: 'I find after all these weeks that I'm just as much in love with Anita as ever . . . I wish to God that she'd live half her time here [London] – then I could stand half in Sweden, but I'm afraid the affair's gone flat for her.'[35] On 15 November 1958 he writes again to Meyer. He'd sent Anita his latest play, *The Complaisant Lover*, but she hadn't acknowledged it. Greene feels he can't ring her in case a 'stranger is now installed'. He says: 'I can't *pester* the girl' and asks Meyer to tell her she's still 'in the bloodstream and I'm quite unable to look for a successor'. He ends his letter by admitting: 'Anyway she's one of the nicest people I've ever met, and my only regret is losing her.'[36] (Almost twenty years later, Meyer wrote to Anita Björk to arrange an interview with me. She felt it would be difficult to talk to a stranger about Greene. She told me: 'I loved that man but he was too "cynical" for me at that time. I was too childish.'[37])

Greene knows that Anita is irrecoverable. Meyer had prompted a final letter from Anita, admitting she was living with someone – presumably one of her 'lame ducks'.* He then goes on: 'An expensive affair it's been! I think your analysis was a good one. Ironically one neglected her a good deal because one had to earn money quickly for the house – having exhausted one's Swedish royalties by allowing her to use them without her knowing it through Ragnar. No more actresses and no more Swedes.'[38]

At this time, he was 'terribly anxious about Catherine . . . somewhere in the South Atlantic in a small sailing boat her husband bought between the Cararines & St Lucia where it was being taken by the

---

* Anita often seemed to gravitate to those who had great need of her, Stig Dagerman for one, and another man who also became her husband and who, like Dagerman, committed suicide.

crew. She's alone & wasn't at all well before she left. I'll be sick with anxiety if I don't get a cable by Monday . . . [Film] script finished today. I dread the finish as now there's nothing to do but brood. Why can't one fall out of love as easily as one falls into it?'[39] A month later, he sent Catherine a telegram at St Lucia:

JUST GOT WONDERFUL LETTER THANK GOD YOU ARE IN REACH AGAIN NO SUBSTITUTE AND LIFE HAS NOT CHANGED TO ME LETS MAKE PLANS LOVE[40]

PART 6

From London Books to Cuban Crooks

11

Publishing Redux

Publish and be damned!
— DUKE OF WELLINGTON

WHEN Max Reinhardt became Managing Director of The Bodley
Head publishers, he decided that his friendship with Graham
Greene should be paramount. The first evidence comes in an apologetic letter dated 5 June 1957, responding to Greene's dislike of a first
proof copy:

> The book was accepted by the previous management and as we
> took over the list . . . we just went ahead with . . . all the books
> . . . however, I am re-considering the whole matter and for the
> time being I am postponing publication.

This was in itself amazing on Reinhardt's part. I thought perhaps it
was one of those editions Greene periodically published for friends,
not a book meant to go on sale – that would have meant Greene had
dispensed with Heinemann as his publisher. But in a letter dated 30
September 1998, Reinhardt stressed: 'The letter dated 5 June 1957 to
Graham refers to a proof copy I had sent him of a Bodley Head book
by someone whose name I cannot remember which Graham had not
liked. It would not have been a book by Graham.'

Assuming Max's memory is sound here, what can be inferred is
that Greene was dissatisfied with the quality of the printing and
perhaps also the design. Nevertheless, Max's next letter to Greene on
7 June 1957 seems as sudden as it is astonishing, announcing that at
a special meeting of the board Greene had been elected a director:
'May I say, on behalf of all of us, how delighted we are to have you
on the Board, and how very much we look forward to your advice
on refashioning our list.' And Greene was to be allowed surprising

freedoms: 'I realise that you may be abroad a certain amount and therefore not always able to attend our Board Meetings, but we are very happy to have this arrangement as flexible as is convenient to you.'

Max informed Greene that board meetings were held on the last Tuesday of every month (to enable the accounts department to prepare the previous month's figures) and editorial meetings every Tuesday, and added that he'd be welcome at their weekly meetings, even though they weren't expecting him to turn up often. The meetings were of a more general, policy-making nature: 'You will be particularly welcome at these meetings, but I realise that you will be abroad [for] the first one.' Reinhardt asks Greene to lunch to show him their offices, but only 'if you can spare the time'.

Reinhardt must have felt he had good reason to give Greene special treatment. He told me that one of the motivations was that Greene had been 'an editor [and Director] at Eyre & Spottiswoode and I asked him to join us [at] The Bodley Head as I needed some literary weight . . . to counter-balance the bankers who were only interested in the financial aspects of the business'.[1] Greene did turn up for a tour of the offices.

The next day, just before leaving for Martinique, as usual working until the last minute, Greene sent Reinhardt random but well thought out suggestions as a result of glancing at the 'Complete Catalogue' of The Bodley Head:

1. What about combining Rex Warner's translations of Euripides of which you have published three into one volume at a reasonable price, the *Helen*, the *Hippolytus* and the *Medea*. An Omnibus volume of this kind would at any rate get noticed in the respectable press and might have a steady sale.

2. I have a strong feeling that the moment is ripe with all these books that are appearing on the Victorian wars for a life of Kinglake [1809–91; author of *Eothen*, a classic book of Eastern travel] who covers not only the Crimea and the Middle East of his time but also the early days in Algeria. I don't know why I'd suggest Beechcroft as somebody who might be interested as it's quite different from any of his short stories, on the other hand Beechcroft is under the surface a literary writer.

3. Query. I suppose we've lost André Maurois for good and all.

4. What is the position today of Kenneth Grahame who was an idol of one's childhood? Is he a regular seller at 6/- or is he due for a revival in say Penguins?

5. Barbara Comyns. She's a crazy but interesting novelist whom I started when I was at Eyre & Spottiswoode but whom [Douglas] Jerrold abandoned with all my other authors except Mauriac when I left. I haven't read the one listed in the general catalogue, but I think it's worth keeping an eye on her.

6. Georges Bernanos. *The Diary of a Country Priest*. Does this continue to have a good regular sale or ought it to be jerked up with a paperback – Penguin or Pan?

7. Marcel Aymé. If we still have rights in his books I do think some kind of concerted drive should be made to put him over to the English.[2]

Greene didn't expect a response from this 'passing list'. He wasn't in touch with The Bodley Head for three months, going first, as we've seen, to Martinique with Anita Björk, then on 30 July to St Kitts to see family graves. He was back in London on 4 August, awaiting his Russian visa. And by 17 August, he was in Moscow with his son Francis. He was finally back in London on 26 August and wrote to Max Reinhardt about taking up the author Nathanael West, who had died in a motor accident in 1940. Greene writes on 2 September, after checking his own library shelves: 'it was the Grey Walls Press which did *Miss Lonelyhearts* and *The Day of the Locust*. Presumably these are out of print now. The complete works with an introduction by Alan Ross are published in America by Farrar Straus and Cudahy. It includes besides the two books mentioned *The Dream Life of Balso Snell* and *A Cool Million*.'

★

And then, unexpectedly, a big fish swam close by. Greene (and at the same time Reinhardt) saw a notice in a newspaper about Charlie Chaplin's autobiography. Greene wrote first. The undated letter was sent to the Savoy Hotel, London, where Chaplin had been staying for a few days:

Am now connected with publishing house The Bodley Head and would be delighted if allowed [to] make competitive offer for your autobiography.

Affectionately Graham Greene.[3]

Greene received no reply. Reinhardt then sent a telegram to Chaplin. Still no reply. What neither man knew was that Chaplin never read letters with no return address.

By December 1957, during the time he was in Stockholm with Anita, Greene received a letter from Reinhardt telling him that the board had authorised an offer to Chaplin of up to '10,000 pounds advance for his autobiography'.[4] Reinhardt telegraphed Switzerland: again, no reply. He got in touch with Chaplin's manager, explaining they would like to see Chaplin. In March, Reinhardt asked Greene to go along; the dice wouldn't roll without him: '[if Chaplin] is at all prepared to talk would [you] care perhaps to fly over with me for a day or so'[5] to meet with him, the implication being that with Greene's help, the big fish might get snagged in The Bodley Head's net in Vevey.*

Greene's contact with Chaplin, as Reinhardt knew, began years earlier during a visit to Hollywood. Greene had come to Chaplin's aid when he was unceremoniously booted out of America. By the time that happened, Chaplin had lived in the United States for nearly forty years, but he was suspect: he'd addressed a crowd as 'Comrades', which to the paranoid witch-hunters of those dangerous times was tantamount to being a communist.

Chaplin had left the country on 15 September 1952 and was two days out on the *Queen Elizabeth* when he learned from a radio message that the US Attorney-General had ordered him detained by the Immigration and Naturalization Service upon his return to America. Greene took up the cudgels on Chaplin's behalf, writing an open letter which appeared in the *New Statesman and Nation* on 27 September 1952:

Your films have always been compassionate towards the weak and the underprivileged; they have always punctured the bully. To our pain and astonishment you paid the United States the highest compliment in your power by settling within her borders, and now we feel pain . . . at the response . . . from those authorities who seem to take their orders from such men as McCarthy.[6]

---

* It was a kind of 'Appointment in Samarra', for, years later, Chaplin was to die in Switzerland at Vevey (on Christmas Day 1977); still further on, Greene too met his death in Vevey, on 3 April 1991.

The letter spoke of the 'great pyramid of friendly letters that must be awaiting you in London' for he was England's favourite son.

Reinhardt knew how much Chaplin owed Greene. Now was the time to collect the debt. Of course, nothing of that would be mentioned. But it was essential for Greene to go with Reinhardt to Vevey in March 1958.

★

Chaplin's autobiography took a long time to get off the ground. In 1960, Chaplin told Ian Fleming that he'd finished 500 pages. Two years earlier, Leonard Russell of the *Sunday Times* – the newspaper that finally bought the serialisation of Chaplin's autobiography – asked if Chaplin was using a 'ghost'. Chaplin's latter-day biographer, David Robinson, quotes the following from the *Sunday Times*: 'Mr Reinhardt looked shocked, offended even. Surely we couldn't think that Chaplin, a man who wrote his own scripts, directed his own films, composed his own music, would seek outside help with his own memoirs.'[7]

And Reinhardt pulled off a tremendous coup: Chaplin was in his corral. Later he and Chaplin became close friends, but it was Greene who made it possible, through his dramatic and early support. And Reinhardt acknowledges Greene's importance in the negotiations in a letter: 'I understand that everybody is after him, naturally, and if he gave us the book it would not necessarily be only for the money *but for our association with you*.'[8] So Greene, Reinhardt, and Reinhardt's wife, Joan, met in Geneva on 16 March. Reinhardt told Greene: 'I have ordered a car to meet us at the airport at Geneva and I will then drive you and Joan to Vevey.'[9]

Max and Joan had been to a publishers' congress in Vienna, where Greene joined them. They travelled home by way of Switzerland. They saw both Charlie and his wife Oona. Late that evening when the women had gone to bed, Chaplin asked Graham and Max if they wanted to hear what he'd written of his autobiography. As Max remembers it, 'Tears came to his eyes as he read about his mother and his half-brother and the poverty-stricken life they had led',[10] for he was one of the people of the abyss, brought up in a workhouse and charity institutions, with an alcoholic father and a mentally disturbed mother.

Recalling that propitious meeting and the following morning, Max told me how he and Greene strolled around the grounds of the Chaplin estate. Greene said: 'I think it could be a wonderful book.' Later Greene, speaking from the heart, confronted Max in his strange, soft voice – a touch of the diffident scholar. His strained serious face revealed no falsity behind his words: 'Good writing is one of the few things he believed in [and think of the significance of that] and what Charlie had written so far was first-rate.'

★

Upon returning home, Greene wrote to his son about enjoying himself at Chaplin's home. He pronounced the autobiography 'really extraordinarily good' but added with his usual caution: 'what he has written so far'.[11]

And just as Greene had worked for very many years, out of genuine kindness, correcting the manuscripts of his friend, the Indian novelist R. K. Narayan, he was similarly willing to work on Chaplin's autobiography. The fact that Greene had been politically useful to Chaplin in the past, and was willing to work over Chaplin's manuscript in the present, clinched the day at Vevey, and made Chaplin determined that The Bodley Head should be his publisher.

The promised date of publication was 1962, but the memoirs took another two years to appear. Greene and Reinhardt stood midwives to the novice Chaplin. On stage and film, Chaplin gave spontaneous imitations, recitations, pantomimes with the ease of genius, but he was, nevertheless, self-taught. His struggle to rise from the depths was a mighty thing, but he sometimes felt that the British secretary he employed knew English better than he.

When it was known that Chaplin's book was going to The Bodley Head, offers came in. Simon & Schuster were willing to offer £10,000 for the American rights and the Scandinavian publishers, Norstedt, offered The Bodley Head £14,000. Reinhardt at once doubled his offer to Chaplin to an advance of £20,000. It was not unreasonable, for the secret was out and, as Chaplin's biographer Robinson puts it, 'frenzied and fantastic offers for the serial rights'[12] came from all over the world. In the meantime, Chaplin kept writing and rewriting.

★

Greene continued letters of revision of The Bodley Head catalogue, and his own passions had their play. He did turn up for some editorial meetings, and as in the past, had disagreements with J. B. Priestley, who was also on the Board of Directors: Greene was out to bring back into print a favourite of his, Ford Madox Ford, and he succeeded, despite Priestley's doubts. Reinhardt, in letting Greene have his head, pulled off yet another coup. He accepted the notion that the best of Ford should be brought out, but persuaded Greene to edit *The Bodley Head Ford Madox Ford*. Greene felt compelled to edit all the volumes and then wrote separate introductions to the first and third volumes. Two volumes appeared in 1962 and a further two in 1963.

Greene's adulation of Ford was intense. He admired Ford's attention to craft, but there was much else in Ford that attracted, in particular his sheer involvement in his themes. Of the novel he saw as Ford's masterpiece Greene wrote: 'A novelist is not a vegetable absorbing nourishment mechanically from soil and air: material is not easily or painlessly gained, and one cannot help wondering what agonies of frustration and error lay behind [*The Good Soldier*].'[13]

★

Ever a watchdog for the firm, Greene bombarded The Bodley Head with suggestions. In a letter of 17 October 1957 he wrote:

> In the November issue [of the *London Magazine*] there is a story which seems to me quite up to the Salinger level called 'The Dormouse Child' by A. E. Ellis. Apparently Ellis has never published anything before outside undergraduate magazines but he has completed a novel. Probably this novel has been taken but shouldn't we write and ask to see it?

He goes on to mention Siobhan Lynam, attached to the British embassy in Paris. Spot up-to-date, he tells The Bodley Head she's had a novel published in the States but not in Britain, and adds: 'One wonders whether it has been turned down by several publishers and whether it would not be worth writing to her.' Though Greene's publisher is Heinemann and he will publish forthcoming non-fiction and novels with them, we are beginning to see a lowering of loyalties, for in his letter to Reinhardt he adds: 'I imagine that Heinemann as they now are the distributors and owners of the *London Magazine* are watching it closely for new authors, but Heinemann may well slip up and I think we should keep a very careful eye on the magazine.'

As we saw earlier, this was the time that Greene went off to Havana with Anita Björk. Sometime while there, he suggested that Max should publish Stig Dagerman.* Dagerman, Anita's late husband, was an important Swedish writer, and the fact that Greene recommended his publication in English by a company on whose board he sat had nothing to do with Greene's relationship with his widow. Greene never indulged in nepotism, in the strictest or broadest sense of the term. He was at times a cruel critic and didn't praise friends' work just because they were friends. (There was an exception: Dorothy Glover's illustrations

---

* Dagerman published *The Serpent* in 1945 and *The Island of the Doomed* in the following year. These existential novels were concerned with terror and the need to face it directly. He had enjoyed a great success in 1948 with his play *The Condemned*.

for a children's book. But she was more than a friend, and he always felt he had helped ruin her life.)

In early December he went to Alberta to visit his daughter's ranch. On 18 December, Max wrote to Greene enclosing The Bodley Head list for the first six months of 1957, and mentioning that he had seen the Swedish publisher Ragnar Svanstrom who, like Max, was a member of the Savile Club in London. The two publishers had agreed to do a one-volume selection of Dagerman's work, the book to be partly subsidised by the Trustees of the Anglo-Swedish Literary Foundation, and arranged for Norstedt (Svanstrom's company) to buy from them some copies of the English edition. Max was excited: 'Here is a book with lots of prestige on which we really cannot go wrong. Thank you again for this idea.'

Greene (who never stopped writing, never stopped thinking, never stopped reading) helped build The Bodley Head. Early in January 1958, he came up with a new find:

1. Have you come across the fascinating Judge Dee mysteries written in English by a Dutchman called Robert van Gulik who is an authority on the Far East? They are . . . founded on old fourth century Chinese detective stories with illustrations by the author in the Ming manner. The first of these which I . . . encountered in Cuba is an actual classical Chinese story of Judge Dee but I can let you see the Chinese Maze Murders which are the first of the invented ones. I found this book enthralling. They are published curiously enough in English in Holland and Tokyo and I don't know whether anybody has obtained the English rights, but I think they would be . . . worth having . . . The Dutch publisher is W. Van Hoever Lt., The Hague.

He adds a caveat:

Incidentally Agatha Christie has done jacket blurb for the Chinese Maze Murders which may mean that the rights have gone.

2. Seeing a new Arsène Lupin film produced by the French, and a very good film too, it occurred to me that the time might have arrived for an Arsène Lupin omnibus if the rights can be picked up. Presumably the film will be shown soon in London. T. S. Eliot is a great admirer of Arsène Lupin and I wonder whether he could be induced to write a Preface. (It suddenly occurs to me that you may not be an Arsène Lupin fan and

may not realise that he is a famous gentleman burglar.) The five Lupin books which I possess are published by Hurst & Blackett, Eveleigh Nash, Cassell, and Mills & Boon. I don't know when Maurice Leblanc, the author, died,* and whether possibly the books are approaching limited copyright. The translations I possess range in date from 1909 to 1922.[14]

A final paragraph expresses his hope of attending the board meeting on 28 January, but adds: '[as] my play [*The Potting Shed*] opens at Brighton on the 27th it rather depends whether there are some last-minute changes to be made.'

*

Max was in his element to have brought such a dynamo into his firm. After all, Greene was not working for The Bodley Head full-time – his suggestions were made when he could afford to leave his novel writing. A copy of Greene's *The Lost Childhood*, a collection of essays first published in 1951, containing the autobiographical essay of the same name, persuaded Max that he must bring out a reissue of Greene's favourite childhood book, Marjorie Bowen's† *The Viper of Milan*, which Greene insisted determined him as a boy of four-teen to become a writer: 'I think it was Miss Bowen's apparent zest that made me want to write. One could not read her without believing that to write was to live and to enjoy, and before one had discovered one's mistake it was too late – the first book one does enjoy.'

But Marjorie Bowen's book had another purpose. It explained Greene's world: '[S]he had given me my pattern – religion might later explain it to me in other terms, but the pattern was already there – perfect evil walking the world where perfect good can never walk again, and only the pendulum ensures that after all in the end justice is done.' He realised that 'Goodness has only once found a perfect incarnation in a human body and never will again, but evil can always find a home there. Human nature is not black and white but black and grey. I read all that in *The Viper of Milan* and I looked round and I saw that it was so.'[15]

Max was as good as his word, though *The Viper of Milan* was not brought out until late in 1959. On 19 August of that year, Max wrote to Greene: 'Our Children's department has decided to publish *The Viper of Milan*.' Max, not missing a trick, asked to use Greene's account

---

* Leblanc died in Paris on 6 November 1941.
† A pseudonym of Gabrielle Campbell (1886–1952).

of Bowen in *The Lost Childhood* as an introduction to the book, and went on to suggest: 'we would be thrilled to take over your children's books or publish any that have been out of print, and I think you would find that we would sell them well.'

Greene responded a month later. His play *The Complaisant Lover* (first put on at the Globe on 18 June 1959) was a great success, and he had gone to Austria for a break. He was alone. He'd written to Catherine, tiring of seeing her so rarely: 'I want to have someone other than myself to look after – not with a cheque-book or at the end of a phone.'[16] On 17 August, he tells her he's off to Nice and staying close to a friend's home, but nothing more is said. Perhaps her suspicions should have been alerted.

On 22 September, he hears that his mother has died. Two days after, he informs Max that they can use *The Lost Childhood* without charge.

Greene then goes straight into a business discussion of his children's stories: 'The one most worth reprinting . . . as it contains the best illustrations, is *The Little Fire Engine*.' He addresses the question of colours in the illustrations, as the original's three colours would be too expensive for a reprint. Greene thought it might be useful to purchase the plates back from Jarrolds.

> *The Little Train*, which was the first and was originally published by Eyre & Spottiswoode, is also nicely illustrated, but Max Parrish has put out an inferior version in two colours and a different format and spoilt the market. The third was *The Little Horse Bus* but the artist was forced to use only two colours and I don't think the drawings are up to her proper form . . . The same applies to *The Little Steam-Roller* (and in this case the author was not up to his proper form either). I rather doubt whether you would get away with one of a series but if you remain interested, let's talk it over with a vodka on the rocks.[17]

Greene then sailed the Atlantic and arrived in New York followed by shoals of mail commiserating with him over the death of his mother. He was bored by the sheer number of letters he had to write. One feels that her loss exposed a cold spot in his heart. He responded to Max Reinhardt's letter of condolence in curious Greeneian terms: 'Thank you both for your note. I was very glad when it was all over – my mother was very tired & bored.'[18]

Max replied with a short note, innocuous and diplomatic as always:

Dear Graham,

We would very much like to publish *The Little Train* but would it be possible to do so with new illustrations? I hope so, and perhaps we can talk about it when we meet.[19]

Greene responded immediately:

Sorry it would be quite impossible to publish *The Little Train* with new illustrations. That would be an insult to an old friend who collaborated in the whole affair. Would you return my file copy sometime.[20]

So the deal fell through out of Greene's fierce loyalty. That 'old friend' was, of course, Dorothy Glover, well on her way to becoming an alcoholic. Greene was not going to harm his former lover by dropping her third-rate illustrations. Max's desire for new ones was understandable, but he could not know the depth of Greene's protectiveness for those he'd loved. After Dorothy died (in 1971), the way was open for Max to publish Greene's children's novels. In 1973 *The Little Train* appeared, the illustrations done brilliantly by Edward Ardizzone, who in the same year illustrated *The Little Fire Engine* and, in the following year, *The Little Horse Bus*.

*

On 15 November 1958, Max went off to Paris to meet with Marie Biche, Greene's French literary agent. Greene had involved Max in the translation of Charles du Bos's life of Benjamin Constant. Before leaving, Max tells Greene: 'If you happen to be there [Paris] it would be splendid, and if you would like us to make any bookings at the hotel, on the plane or for a play do let me know', offering a totally free holiday for Greene if he wished. It could not be. Greene was working on a film script of his novel *Our Man in Havana*. He had just returned from Cuba and was working with Carol Reed at the Hotel Metropole in Brighton. They had a suite with interconnecting doors plus a room with a secretary between them. The last sentence of Max's letter points to Greene's contribution to the firm: 'Our turnover for October will be about 35,000 pounds, so that I hope we shall be beating our target of 180,000 pounds a year.'[21]

Since Greene's suggestions often turned to gold, Max listened carefully to his acceptances and rejections:

1.   The novel by Hugh Sykes Davies. I am against publishing this. It seems to be a lifeless piece of work. Written in a style which

the author obviously considers cultivated. He has no power to write dialogue and the whole thing seems to me phoney.

2.   *Le Petit Ami.*＊ I should say the translation was all right, but I do think that our editorial man ought to go through it carefully making suggestions to the translator. There are examples of translator's English in it. I am not very happy at the idea of a book being called *Le Petit Ami* in English. What about *The Child of Montmartre*.[22]

On 23 January Greene writes asking Max to apologise to the board for his upcoming absence: 'Circumstances have arisen which make it desirable for me to leave earlier for the Belgian Congo and I shall not be able to come.'

Greene began his return from Africa, flying from Douala to meet Catherine Walston in Paris for three days. Then he went to London for rehearsals of *The Complaisant Lover*. During his absence, Max and his board agreed to the new title, *The Child of Montmartre*, and upon his return Max asked Greene for a quote, which he wrote on the day the request arrived. Despite suffering eye trouble he came up with:

> Léautaud was not among the giants of French literature, but he was a man who could have dined with the giants. He has taken for his own a particular area of human life and no one is his rival there. It was the same area that Toulouse-Lautrec painted: the bars and brothels of Montmartre, the ugly, the beautiful and ravaged faces of the aging coquettes. He 'judges not as a judge judges'; he only notices with the clear curious impartial eye of a child.[23]

Max also asked Greene to read Richard Wright's *Pagan Spain*, adding a warning about the attitude of his board to the book: 'As you know, opinions are very divided about it and feelings are strong.'[24] Greene replied three days later from his flat in Albany, his eye trouble resolving more quickly than his oculist had predicted – his judgment as straight as a die: 'Interesting, but rather slight', yet on the whole he advised publishing:

> If Pritchett would give it his imprimatur on the cover. I rather wish it had been called something like *Negro in Spain* as the

---

＊ Written by Paul Léautaud (1872–1956) in 1903.

interest in the book lies in the point of view. I was disappointed
to find nothing offensive in it to me as a Catholic![25]

On 11 August 1959 Greene again apologises for missing the meeting
of directors on the 13th: 'As I told you I am going to be in transit
from Paris that day.' Suddenly, Greene changes tack. He's found another
book: an autobiography of Gracie Fields, the tremendously popular
English entertainer who had given ten command performances, first
to King George VI and then to his daughter, Queen Elizabeth II before
retiring to Capri. Gracie Fields' autobiography had been written with
the help of a minor journalist and appeared in a women's magazine.
Catherine Walston read it there and Greene thought there was something worth pursuing. There was no English publisher in the picture
yet, so Greene suggested: 'If we acted quickly enough – and perhaps
we don't want to act at all – I am sure we could obtain the rights.
She is a modest creature and would have no objection, I am certain,
to having this put into better form. In fact she rather objected to what
they had done as so often they wrote something untrue which was
less interesting . . . than the truth. I imagine there might be a very
good provincial sale anyway for a book of this kind.'

Greene knew Gracie well and liked seeing her on Capri. Max sent
Greene a draft letter which Greene altered. This letter is dated 18
August 1959 and reveals that Catherine had torn out all the instal-
ments of the book. Greene had shown them to Max, who was keen
to publish. Greene told Gracie it would give him great pleasure to
look after her book. Then, the rub:

> There is one difficulty: we feel that the treatment of the story
> that appears in *Woman* would have to be changed fairly drasti-
> cally to make it suitable for publication as a book. Perhaps there
> was an original draft which *Woman* edited to fit their require-
> ments, but I seem to remember that you had some reason to
> complain . . . [about the] journalist . . . If there is an original
> draft we should . . . like to see it in the hope that it could be
> published more or less as it stands, but otherwise would you be
> willing to let us employ [an editor] . . . ? If you agree with all
> this we shall be glad to make you an offer for the volume rights.

Gracie Fields' memoirs, *Sing As We Go*, came out in 1960.

On 10 December Greene came up with two more possibilities. The
first was Horace Gregory's *The World of James Whistler*. 'Gregory is quite
a good minor poet as I expect you know in the States and the book
may be quite interesting here.' The second was the life of Dr Hubert

Eaton, the man who made the 'ghastly Forest Lawn Cemetery'* in California:

> *First Step Up Towards Heaven* published in the US by Prentice Hall
> . . . It seems to be full of unconscious humour as he has taken
> [himself] quite seriously and I wondered if we got the book
> whether we couldn't get Evelyn Waugh to do a preface or let us
> reprint his original essay in the *Tablet* on which *The Loved One*
> was founded.

Waugh's bitter fun about Forest Lawn Cemetery and its activities is worthy of Swift. He's mordantly satiric about the activities of the mortician, modelled on Dr Eaton. It was astonishing that Eaton did not sue, though he did write a modest letter: 'It is becoming more and more evident that people in the United States who have never visited Forest Lawn Cemetery [Waugh called it Whispering Glades] believe that Evelyn Waugh's book *The Loved One* is a true depiction of Forest Lawn Memorial Park.'[26] But it was. When Waugh's novel appeared, *Time* described Waugh as being 'caught between laughter and vomiting'.[27]

There were books Greene rejected. His one-time intelligence colleague during the war, Leslie Nicholson, sent a manuscript and asked for his advice, unaware that Greene was a publisher now. Greene speaks directly but not unkindly, saying there was a great deal in it which he liked very much, and many shared memories: 'Members of the old firm will appreciate its authenticity. I, too, as you probably know, suffered from the same paymaster!' Then he added that he felt that the 'narrative is not sufficiently compulsive for the ordinary reader. God knows one doesn't want to publish melodramatic spy stories, but there are pages and pages . . . which really are no more than travelogue . . . In my opinion they don't add up to a book at present. Anyway I may be completely wrong and let's talk about it when I come back from France.'[28]

Next, Chaplin is back in the news. Max sends Greene copies of letters

---

* More than '300 acres dotted with white sculptures and quaint English chapels . . . Forest Lawn attracts over a million visitors per year. Over 60,000 people have actually been *married* there . . . Where else can you see the final resting places of multiple movie stars, visit a replica of Rudyard Kipling's church, watch white swans glide across a lake, see a mosaic of "The Signing of the Declaration of Independence," view the world's largest religious painting in a state-of-the-art theater, and discover replicas of *all* of Michelangelo's major works in one place? . . . Eaton, a firm believer in a joyous life after death, became convinced that most current cemeteries were "unsightly, depressing stoneyards," and pledged to create one that . . . would be as unlike other cemeteries "as sunlight is unlike darkness, as eternal life is unlike death."' (www.seeing-stars.com)

he intends sending to Chaplin for approval, remarking that the typescript is at long last being copied (it will be another four years before the book appears) to be sent to Greene. Greene had at this time gone to Jamaica to stay at Ian Fleming's home, Goldeneye, on a working holiday with Catherine Walston, so the affair seems, at least briefly, to be on again.

At first he could not get on with the Chaplin script because, as he said in a postcard, he was busy revising Narayan's latest novel (probably *The Man-Eater of Malgudi*). Then, Greene, having begun work on the Chaplin script, sent Max an urgent telegram: 'PROFOUNDLY WORRIED ABOUT [the Chaplin] BOOK STOP SUGGEST HEDGING STOP GRAHAM STOP'. Max was not worried and sent Greene a return telegram: 'INCREASING FIRM OFFERS STILL POURING IN BUT NO COMMITMENTS YET MADE STOP IMPOSSIBLE FOR US TO LOSE FINANCIALLY STOP MAX'.

Back from Jamaica, Greene wrote to Max from his Albany flat on 5 December 1960 letting him know that he had to go unexpectedly to Paris and would miss the next meeting and suggesting they should meet on his return to talk about Chaplin. He tells Max it took two weeks to go through the Chaplin manuscript (and Greene always worked at incredible speed), but that he had made only rough corrections: 'I find I have shortened it by about 15,000 words.' This was a sacrifice of two valuable weeks to a writer who'd had terrible difficulty finishing *A Burnt-Out Case*. Max congratulated Greene on his editing job: 'I had not realised you had worked so much on the typescript and how very much you have improved it . . . I hope Chaplin will accept our recommendations.'[29]

After the book came out, the rumour went round the world that Greene had ghost-written it. That was untrue. Chaplin ignored Greene's suggestions for cutting down (and cutting out) irrelevancies. It was a case of one genius unable to listen to another.

★

Two final projects: the first relates to Stephen Crane; the second to Greene's cousin, Robert Louis Stevenson.

Crane's *The Red Badge of Courage* brought him immediate and deserved fame in 1895. His first novel, entitled *Maggie: A Girl of the Streets*, a study of a slum girl's descent into prostitution, had been published under a pseudonym two years earlier. Crane's fascination with prostitution ran parallel to his own life, for in the mid-1890s he set up house with Cora Taylor who ran a brothel in Florida. Crane had joined up with her on his way to report the war in Cuba. Taylor styled herself his (common-law) wife, and they lived briefly in Sussex at the end of the nineteenth century before Crane died of tuberculosis in 1900 at the age of twenty-eight. Now, sixty years afterwards,

Greene writes to Max about Lillian Gilkes's scholarly life of Cora Crane, issued by Indiana University Press. There were some amusing photographs, unpublished, of Henry James 'who was one of their visitors and friends, along with Wells, Conrad, Hueffer etc. *The Red Badge of Courage* with selected short stories has just been published in the World Classics and I think there is a continuing interest.' Greene notes that Crane's collected letters had been recently published and he felt that, from a prestige point of view, an offer to Indiana University Press should be made. Cora had gone 'back at the end of her life to managing a brothel in Louisiana. The book won't set the Thames on fire, but it should rate interesting reviews.'[30]

Max responded: 'I have checked up with the representative of Indiana University Press about Cora Crane . . . The book is on offer elsewhere . . . but if the present publisher turns it down it will be offered to us. Thanks for spotting it.'[31]

The key to Greene's shrewdness lay in his deep and subtle knowledge of the book world, not perhaps greatly superior to that of any thoughtful, active publisher – but he was a novelist, not a publisher. The final example of his knack for choosing well is evident in correspondence with Yale University Library. He wrote remembering his days at Eyre & Spottiswoode when, on a 1948 trip to New York, he met a man in Scribner's antique department. They held corrected proofs of Robert Louis Stevenson's *The Wrong Box*. Scribner's had been awaiting corrected proofs for months. Not having received any, they just went ahead and published. Only after printing did the proofs arrive from the South Seas:

> There are very heavy corrections – in fact towards the end I seem to remember one chapter is almost rewritten. Scribner's promised Stevenson to put this right in a future edition and never did so, so that all editions now in print of *The Wrong Box* do not represent the book as Stevenson wanted it.

Greene wrote to Eyre & Spottiswoode suggesting that Scribner should join in publishing the proper version. Scribner's could not be budged. They feared such action would reduce the value of the manuscript. Greene thought:

> They had no legal right to possess it. These proof sheets have now gone to Yale . . . when an American professor who is editing Stevenson's letters came to see me the other day he suggested I should write to them. This is the correspondence. The question of *The Amateur Emigrant* is . . . different. It would certainly be

interesting but it wouldn't have the same general appeal as the first real version of *The Wrong Box*. I do hope you'll agree with me that this is a project of commercial as well as prestige value.

The ever-vigilant Greene adds: 'The book of course is by now out of copyright.'

★

For ten years, until 1968, Greene remained an active director of The Bodley Head. If he'd taken over Eyre & Spottiswoode, as Sir Oliver Crosthwaite-Eyre devoutly wished, Greene could have been a sterling publisher, literature a mighty loser.

12

Heroes and Heroines

Revolutions are not made with rose-water.
— BULWER LYTTON

O UR *Man in Havana* starts out with what must have seemed a highly improbable situation. Jim Wormold, a vacuum cleaner distributor in Havana, is recruited into the British Secret Intelligence Service. He goes along with this because he needs money to keep his extravagant and motherless young daughter in a luxury he can ill afford.

After coming on board, Wormold shows a remarkable capacity for 'discovering' fresh agents in the field. In fact they are no more than figments of his imagination. He gets very creative: the more agents, the more money. To pull off his deceit, Wormold invents incidents and conscientiously reports them to London. The senior officers in London are genuinely pleased with the drawings he sends them of a new weapon, unaware that the sketches are only greatly enlarged versions of his vacuum cleaner design diagrams. They pore over their treasure:

'Fiendish, isn't it?' the Chief said. 'The ingenuity, the simplicity, the devilish imagination of the thing.' He removed his black monocle . . . 'See this one here six times the height of a man . . . what does this remind you of?'

Hawthorne said unhappily, 'A two-way nozzle.'

'What's a two-way nozzle?'

'You sometimes find them with a vacuum cleaner.'

'Vacuum cleaner again. Hawthorne, I believe we may be on to something so big that the H-bomb will become a conventional weapon . . .'

'What have you in mind, sir?'

'I'm no scientist,' the Chief said, 'but look at this great tank. It must stand nearly as high as the forest-trees. A huge gaping mouth at the top, and this pipe-line – the man's only indicated it. For all we know, it may extend for miles – from the mountain to the sea perhaps. You know the Russians are said to be working on some idea – something to do with the power of the sun, sea-evaporation. I don't know what it's all about, but I do know this thing is Big. Tell our man we must have photographs.'[1]

It is almost unbelievable that high-ranking officers in British Intelligence wouldn't spot the deception, or at least suspect that Wormold is taking them in, since the drawings do look like a vacuum cleaner, and after all, he is a vacuum cleaner distributor. Of course it is understood that Greene is satirising the intelligence world he'd entered during the Second World War, when no doubt he met up with some oddballs, and some dullards too. On the whole, British Intelligence justifiably had an almost unimpeachable reputation. But the lighter parts of the novel are simply good fun, poked at the expense of MI6. (The intelligence community in Britain was not amused.)

But where did he get such an idea?

Greene's man in Havana, Wormold, was inspired by two wartime agents: Paul Fidrmuc, code name 'Ostro', and Juan Pujol García, code name 'Garbo'. The humour of Greene's fictional Wormold ('old worm') is his own.

Fidrmuc, a young Czech businessman, looked like a blond German and in fact, in 1940, became a German citizen, worked for the Abwehr (German Military Intelligence) in Denmark and Rome, and then settled in Portugal. His reports to the Abwehr originated in Lisbon. British intelligence officers knew of him, Lisbon being a fruitful ground for spies: although officially neutral, the government of Portugal allowed the Allies to establish naval and air bases. For that reason alone the city was thick with German agents.

The SIS regularly intercepted and decrypted secret Abwehr reports. Even before Greene became an agent in March 1943, the Radio Security Service (RSS) had obtained thirty-seven Ostro reports emanating from a wide scatter of countries – Egypt, South Africa, India, the United States – supposedly from agents communicating in secret writing. British Intelligence were convinced that the reports dealing with Britain were fraudulent, though well-written, carefully structured and giving the impression that they were from various agents in the field. The Abwehr believed that Ostro had four or five agents in England and regarded him as one of their best sources. British Intelligence considered discrediting Ostro on several occasions, though such an action would have been difficult since he had such a high reputation (though based on an illusion) in the Abwehr. And all the time Fidrmuc was studying

English press reports, cooking up information, and 'managing' his completely phoney agents, Ostro was making a complete fool of his German employer.

Greene's second model, Garbo, was a brilliant amateur called García, also living in Lisbon. In 1942, Bletchley code-breakers realised that the Abwehr Enigma traffic between Madrid and Berlin contained reports presumably from a German agent in the United Kingdom – reports too ludicrous to be true – about drunken orgies in Liverpool, and Glasgow dock-workers prepared to tell any story for a litre of wine. The British were right to believe that the agent was not even living in England. García, a twenty-nine-year-old Spaniard of good family, was deeply devoted to the cause of British victory when he approached the Abwehr in Lisbon. He was recruited and given supplies of secret ink and questionnaires and an accommodation address in Madrid. In his room in Lisbon, he operated with a map, a *Blue Guide* to the United Kingdom, a Portuguese study of the British fleet and an Anglo-French vocabulary of military terms.

When the SIS arranged for Garbo to travel to the United Kingdom, he told the Abwehr that he was visiting London on behalf of Spanish security services. Once there, he continued his reports, and his imaginary sub-agents grew to almost thirty. Garbo, as did his fictional successor Wormold, asked for payment for his 'men'.

Greene determined he would draw on the exploits of Fidrmuc (Ostro) and García (Garbo), and their phantom assistants. We see the character Wormold selecting his own so-called assistants in the same way. But there was a radical difference. The odd bunch of agents 'recruited' in England by García were nonexistent – he invented the garrulous officer in the Royal Air Force working as an official at the Ministry of Information; the Venezuelan businessman in Glasgow; the communist Greek sailor operating in Scotland; the Gibraltarian waiter working in an army canteen; the Anglophobe sergeant in the US Army; and the Welsh nationalist in Swansea. Greene's agent takes a different tack.

To lend credibility to his confections, Wormold uses the names of real people with real jobs in Havana who have no idea that their identities have been handed on to British Intelligence as their sympathisers. These included Raul the pilot, too partial to alcohol, a dancer called Teresa, and other names gleaned from a country club membership list which included such men as Engineer Cifuentes and Professor Luis Sanchez. None could know that their lives are at risk. The situation is ripe for humour – Greene returned in the case of this novel to the term 'an entertainment'. But the plot soon begins to run into tragedy.

★

Let us drop into the story at the point when Wormold and his secretary, Beatrice, who has come out from headquarters, go for a walk after dinner. Wormold, anxious to get out of the spy business, weaves a story in which Raul fails, and dies in the attempt. But Raul is a real person, a real pilot. Beatrice is not yet fully aware of, but is vaguely suspicious about, what her boss is up to. At first she thinks that Wormold is worried about Raul, assigned to take aerial photographs of the made-up machines. According to the mythical 'agent Cifuentes' these weapons are being transported from army headquarters at Bayamo to the edge of the forest, where the terrain turns so rugged that mules must then take over.

Wormold reports to London in the style of an adventure story, creating the action as it comes into his mind. Since the equipment doesn't exist, it can't be photographed for London. The pilot must fail in his mission to get pictures, and Wormold decides on a crash. The way in which he concocts Raul's pretended demise is no doubt very like the way Greene worked on a plot line. Greene has never been funnier, but later the story becomes disturbing, as fact follows fiction.

In a few pages of the novel, we come to *know* Havana – the beauty of the women, the nightclubs, the wild weather streaming in from the Atlantic – our increasing knowledge running in tandem with the increasing danger being unearthed. Wormold's mental quickness is such that he can conjure up characters like a magician pulling a rabbit out of a hat – as could Greene. In this way, Wormold is closer to Greene than any other created character in the author's repertoire. Wormold cooks up *his* imaginary agents, as does the novelist.

Here, we are coming close to the creative mind in operation. This is what a great writer does – he tries to make his fictional characters live and breathe. The various possible permutations fashioned by Wormold, alias Greene, include Raul's being foiled, or perhaps he disappears into Captain Segura's tortuous clutches:

Wormold [mulling it over in his mind, with Beatrice in a restaurant] would warn London that he was going off the air in case Raul was forced to talk. The radio-set would be dismantled and hidden after the last message had been sent . . . Or perhaps Raul would take off in safety and they would never know what exactly happened to him over the Oriente mountains. Only one thing in the story was certain: he would not arrive in Jamaica and there would be no photographs.
    'What are you thinking?' Beatrice [asked] . . .
    'I was thinking of Raul . . .'

'Anxious?'
'Of course I'm anxious.'

Wormold is working out his story for the SIS in London, and he speaks aloud to Beatrice.

'If Raul had taken off at midnight, he would refuel just before dawn in Santiago, where the ground-staff were friendly, everyone in the Oriente province being rebels at heart. Then when it was just light enough for photography and too early for the patrol planes to be up, he would begin his reconnaissance over the mountains and the forest.'
'He hasn't been drinking?'
'He promised me he wouldn't. One can't tell.'

Both Beatrice and Wormold speak almost simultaneously of 'Poor Raul'. They leave the restaurant heading down the Avenida de Maceo. We are watching as Greene watches, seeing what he sees, knowing that it will lead up to creating a successful fictive scene: 'The rollers came in from the Atlantic and smashed over the sea-wall. The spray drove across the road . . . and beat like rain under the pock-marked pillars.' (We cannot doubt that Greene is describing his own physical experiences.) Wormold feels himself to be 'part of the slow erosion of Havana'. He tells Beatrice, 'One of those lights up there may be him. How solitary he must feel.' She replies, 'You talk like a novelist.' The conversation shifts and then returns:

'He should be over Matanzas by now. Unless he's been delayed.'
'Have you sent him that way?'
'Oh, of course he decides his own route.'
'And his own end?'
Something in her voice – a kind of enmity – startled him again. Was it possible she had begun to suspect him already?

She wants more details:

His lips were dry with salt and apprehension. It seemed to him that she must have guessed everything. Would she report him to Hawthorne? . . . 'What are you hinting at?'
'You mean there isn't to be a crash at the airport – or on the way?'
'How do you expect me to know?'
'You've been behaving all the evening as if you did. You haven't

spoken about him as though he were a living man. You've been writing his elegy like a bad novelist preparing an effect.'

She asks Wormold to promise her that nothing has been fixed. He doesn't answer because it is absurd. The answer comes in the form of Dr Hasselbacher, coming down the pavement, head bent, nervous and disturbed. He invites them to his home. A call comes; someone has died and he is even more upset. They talk. Hasselbacher disappears out of the room.

> 'There has been an accident,' Dr Hasselbacher said. 'Just an accident . . . A car has crashed on the road near the airport. A young man . . . He was too fond of the glass.'
> Beatrice said, 'Was his name by any chance Raul?'
> 'Yes,' Dr Hasselbacher said. 'That was his name.'[2]

Reality chasing the tail of fantasy.

★

Greene went to Havana to write his novel and later the film script. MI6 knew about his visits. He also met with a representative of the Foreign Office prior to departure. He would report on what he observed, attitudes of mind: he would criticise the British government in the press; would rightly vilify the corrupt Batista government; he would praise, and overpraise, Castro's government; he would criticise American government policy, as it often seemed he did, but, even so, *he would report to his one-time employers* – MI6!

One imagines that MI6 might be angry that a colleague was ridiculing them. I believe that was part of Greene's grand plan. It must have been suggested, perhaps in casual conversation, that if he made fun of British Intelligence, Cuba wouldn't take it, or him, seriously. If Greene were ever questioned by Castro, his novel would stand to minimise anything he might have told MI6. Those who thought the spying was significant would see that the lightness of the dialogue, along with the sheer fatuity of the head office in London, made it frivolous. As a camouflage, it would have its uses.

★

Greene left for New York early in October 1958, staying at the Algonquin. By the time he reached his hotel, he was exhausted, more tired than he'd ever felt after a trip. He shared a benzedrine with a fellow passenger to get him through dinner with Carol Reed and a Columbia Pictures executive, and a deal was struck over the film *Our Man in Havana*.

In a letter dated 2 October 1958 Laurence Pollinger, Greene's London literary agent, told A. S. Frere that the 'purchase price is the sterling equivalent of $100,000'. Frere responded jubilantly four days later, saying he saw no reason why the contract should not be prepared covering purchase.

★

Greene arrived in Havana with Carol Reed to start arrangements for filming exactly one week after *Our Man in Havana* appeared in the British bookshops on 6 October 1958. Dictator Batista was still hanging on by a shoestring, but America had withdrawn military aid and he wisely fled the country on 1 January 1959. This left Castro and his not much more than a guerrilla band to confront the world, marching toward revolution with a certain joyous ruthlessness. In those days, only his closest henchmen knew that he was a communist.

Soon after Batista escaped to New York, Greene embarrassed British foreign secretary Selwyn Lloyd in two letters to *The Times* (3 and 6 January 1959). Lloyd had stressed in Parliament that when the British agreed to export arms to Cuba, they had done so believing there was no evidence of a civil war. Greene, on the other hand, asserted that 'the province of Oriente was already dominated by Dr Castro and a military reign of terror [the Batista regime] . . . existed in Santiago':

> Any visitor to Cuba could have given Her Majesty's Government more information about conditions in the island than was apparently supplied by our official representatives: the mutilations and torture practised by leading police officers . . . the killing of hostages.[3]

This was disconcerting news, and after it broke, a biting article appeared in the *Spectator* on 16 January 1959 deriding Selwyn Lloyd, alluding to Greene's fictional hero, Wormold. It suggested that Greene's picture of inefficient, lazily inadequate intelligence, at least from that corner of the world, was not far from the truth.

On 7 January 1959, the magazine *Time and Tide* said that 'Mr Graham Greene's letter to *The Times* on Cuba has certainly fluttered the dovecotes', and added: 'It is really rather perturbing if an itinerant novelist can bring back better information on a country than Her Majesty's Ministers can obtain from Her Majesty's accredited representatives.' The *Manchester Guardian* also weighed in: 'It cannot be that our representatives abroad meet too few people; the trouble is that they meet the wrong ones. They would often do better to meet none at all, but to sit at home reading the newspapers.'[4] *Time and Tide* continued: 'Recent events in Cuba will have stirred yet again in many a British breast the unworthy suspicion that the amiable and well-bred gentlemen of the Foreign Office are in fact – amiable and well-bred gentlemen.'[5]

★

Greene made six visits to Cuba between 1957 and 1966, meeting several heroes of the revolution. He admitted he felt very close to the 'Fidelistas', especially during their early struggles:

> Santiago, the second city of the island . . . was now the military headquarters in the operations against Fidel Castro, who made periodic sorties from the mountains with his handful of men. It was the beginning of the heroic period . . . An unofficial curfew began at nine p.m., dangerous to ignore, there were arbitrary arrests, and often when day broke a man's body would be found hanging from a lamp post. That was a lucky victim. One building had an unsavoury reputation because of the screams which could be heard in the street outside, and after Santiago had fallen to Fidel a cache of mutilated bodies was found in the country.

Santiago could be reached only by air. In 1957 Greene was at a party in Havana late the night before he left. His Cuban friends were middle-class supporters of Castro. One, a young woman,

> had been arrested by Batista's notorious police chief, Captain Ventura, and beaten. Another girl claimed that she was a courier for Fidel. She was going [to Santiago] by the same plane as myself and she asked me to take in my suitcase a lot of sweaters and heavy socks badly needed by the men in the mountains. In Santiago the heat was tropical. There was a customs' examination at the airport, and it was easier for a foreigner to explain away the winter clothes. She was anxious for me to meet Fidel's representatives in Santiago – the genuine ones, she said, for the place was full of Batista's spies, especially the hotel where I would be staying.[6]

Years later, in an interview with the writer Marie-Françoise Allain, Greene returned to his experience helping the Fidelistas, taking them a 'large suitcase full of winter clothes'.[7] The danger was immense. Batista, in spite of large forces at his command, could not put down the young guerrilla Castro. And the Oriente Province, almost to a man, was on the side of Castro.

Santiago, Cuba's second city, located at the foot of the Sierra Maestra, was Batista's headquarters. Here, as Greene explained, everyone had to

137

go through customs as if coming from another country. He took the suitcase through, and after a comedy of errors, arrived at the secret meeting place, a house owned by a wealthy bourgeois family. Inside were the courier from Havana, her mother, a priest and a young man who was having his hair dyed:

> The young man was a lawyer called Armando Hart who later became Minister of Education in Castro's Government and then the second secretary of the Communist Party in Cuba. A few days before, he had made his escape from the law courts in Havana, he was being taken under military escort to trial.
>
> There was a long line of the accused – a soldier at each end. Hart knew the exact point beside the lavatory where the corridor turned and where momentarily he would be out of sight of the soldier in front and the soldier behind. He slipped into the lavatory and out of the window; his friends were waiting in the street outside.[8]

Greene speaks of the wife of Armando Hart, Haydée Santamaria, who left her hideout with Castro in the Sierra Maestra to be with her recently escaped husband. They had to move from hiding place to hiding place, for Hart was the most hunted man in Cuba at that time. Greene describes her as a heroine, known to all Latin America. She was a young woman, but haggard, as if she'd been 'battered into fanaticism by events outside her control. Before she married Hart she had been affianced to another young Fidelista. He was captured after the unsuccessful attack on the Moncada barracks in Santiago in 1953 and she was taken to the prison to be shown his blinded and castrated corpse.'[9]

Greene described this slightly differently to me at the Ritz Hotel on 28 June 1979, and also in the same year to Marie-Françoise Allain, giving more graphic details of Boris Luis Santa Coloma's torture and murder after he'd been found to be involved in the attack on the barracks at Moncada. 'Batista's police had dragged Haydée to the prison to show her his mutilated body with its eyes torn out.'[10] But the situation was worse than Greene allows, for in his version he contracts two torture episodes into one.

Haydée and attorney Melba Hernandez were involved in the raid. Haydée was with her brother Abel Santamaria, Castro's second in command, whose job it was to seize the hospital, and take it over during the attack on the barracks. The two women, in civilian clothes, were to act as nurses should any guerrilla be wounded.

The assault was only a partial success and Castro gave the order to retreat, which Abel, at the hospital, did not hear. The first he knew of it was seeing Batista's soldiers in the street below. The rebels realised they were encircled. One of their group was able to escape by simply walking out of the hospital and leaving his rifle at the door. Abel Santamaria decided to keep firing, to give the main group led by Castro cover to escape, until he ran out of ammunition. But he was very keen that Haydée and her friend Melba should make their escape. They did not leave. They instead went into the maternity ward to pretend to be nurses. Abel and other rebels were put into beds (Abel being taken to the ophthalmology ward with a bandage over one eye) to convince the arriving soldiers that they were patients.

By a devastating coincidence, a press chief of Batista's was also in the hospital. He told the authorities that a wanted rebel was in a hospital bed and two rebel women were hiding. Sometimes destiny appears to be in unspeakable collusion with the powers of darkness.

According to author Tad Szulc, 'Melba and Haydée saw Abel being yanked out of bed and beaten with rifle butts; his face was a bloody mass.'[11] Later, Haydée was forced to describe in court what happened to her brother Abel and her fiancé, captured in the attack on the barracks. The court found that thirty-three cadavers had 'smashed skulls and other signs of violent death by beatings or point-blank gunshots'. Szulc then recalls what happened:

> Astoundingly, it was Prosecutor Mendieta Hechavarria who through persistent questioning of Haydée Santamaria brought out . . . what the army had done to her fiancé, Boris Luis Santa Coloma, and her brother Abel before killing them. Haydée testified that . . . a guard approached, saying that Boris was in the next room and 'to tell me that they had extirpated his testicles' to make him talk. Jesús Montané [very much in the forefront of the attack on the barracks] had testified earlier that an army officer had approached him in the Moncada detention area, holding in his blood-covered glove a rotting ball of flesh, and said, 'You see this? If you don't talk, I'll do the same thing to you I did to Boris. I will castrate you.' . . . About her brother, Haydée said, 'They gouged out one of his eyes.' An army witness . . . added that Abel's eyes had been removed with a bayonet.[12]

The price Haydée Santamaria paid was great. Long years after, she committed suicide. Who is to say it was not a result of being forced to witness the vile and ignominious debasement of human flesh committed against her loved ones?

★

With *Our Man in Havana*, Greene made fun of his old employers, which must have made them laugh in Moscow. But as always with Greene we must look for untold layers of meaning. Was Greene sending up a kite to both Russia and the newly communist Cuba that if it came right down to it, he would speak out to the world on their behalf, even at the expense of his own country? He keeps on stressing in a variety of ways, and even more forcefully in his 1969 Hamburg lecture, as we'll see later, on 'The Virtue of Disloyalty', a parallel statement made long ago by novelist E. M. Forster: 'If I had to choose between my country and betraying my friend, I hope I should have the guts to betray my country.' But Greene is sending smoke signals that he is anti-American, a suitable man for Kim Philby to contact in the West with the notion of Philby's becoming a triple agent.

Remember, after Philby defected to the Soviet Union in 1963, Philby, when asked what he would like if he had a magic wand, replied: 'Graham Greene on the other side of the table, and a bottle of wine between us.'

13

Some Fidelistas, a Film
and a Firing Squad

A mighty, unifying thunderstorm,
marking the springtime of mankind.
— NIKITA KHRUSHCHEV

IN March 1959, Greene and Carol Reed went back to Havana to film. The omens were good, and we've seen their superb cast: Noël Coward as itinerant secret service man Hawthorne, Alec Guinness as Wormold, and Greene's friend Ralph Richardson as the chief of the secret service, 'C' himself. His performance, like Coward's, was immaculate. Here were three distinguished British actors, all eventually knighted, and to top it off, Sir Carol Reed directing. Columbia Pictures were concerned that there were no Americans, so the fine comedian Ernie Kovacs (then with a beard) took the part of Captain Segura, the head of the Secret Police.

By this time, the Fidelistas had inherited Cuba. They took offence at many aspects of the film, not least because it seemed to them that the beard as described in the character sketch in the script made Captain Segura (based on the notoriously cruel Captain Ventura) physically look like a young, revolutionary Fidelista. Beards were, in a sense, part of the required dress of these fighting men, whose tradition paralleled the Sikh vow never to cut their facial hair and always to be ready for war. Kovacs was ordered to shave. This was only one of the many changes the new communist regime dictated.

This novice government caused Carol Reed problems, sometimes absurd, but nevertheless impossible to ignore. According to B. J. Bedard in *Film Literature Quarterly*, 'Thirty-nine changes were required in the script, and a censor was assigned to the location shooting . . . The puritanism of the new government made it difficult to fully recreate the bawdiness of such Havana establishments as the Shanghai theatre (long known for its nude shows). The garish Tropicana was available for Milly's [Wormold's spoilt daughter] birthday as the casinos had not all been closed.'[1]

In the old days, according to Greene, for $1.25 'one could see a nude cabaret of extreme obscenity with the bluest of blue films in the intervals' at the Shanghai.[2] It was also there that 'Superman' appeared in a nightly live performance with a mulatto girl. Robert Emmett Ginna wrote an article recalling the event of filming there:

> Sir Carol found some of his most vexatious work in the Shanghai Theatre. During the Batista reign . . . [t]here was no more naked chorus in the world. In Graham Greene's novel and script, laid in the Batista period, the Shanghai is brought in when Wormold picks the name Teresa off its billboard to send back to London as one of the subagents he has hired. After Beatrice [his secretary] appears on the scene and they discover that real spies are operating against them, she dragoons Wormold into going to the Shanghai to warn Teresa. An uproarious scene follows, when they meet the stripper whom Wormold has pretended to hire for his fake spy ring.

Under Castro, the club had cleaned up its act and most of the old dancers were in jail. Sir Carol rounded up those he could, but they had to perform partially dressed. They were a 'beat up vision to behold'. A government censor was overseeing things and would jump up, ordering the girls' panties pulled higher – but how could they portray a bawdy show without showing anything?

> Sir Carol had the answer. He would stand up among the undulating damsels with the camera beside him pointing at the audience. He would throw some intimate apparel out toward the grateful spectators so that the camera would catch them grabbing for the items . . . The audience threw them back so the action could be repeated. This brought the censor up, howling that the show looked truly immoral. He stopped the filming. He demanded that the whole day's negative be turned over to him. Sir Carol, with thousands of dollars invested in it, held firm. Hours dragged by until Sir Carol signed some deposition concerning what he would or wouldn't do with the shot.[3]

Ironically, in Cuba, Greene the sometime spy was himself spied upon. In 1986 Professor Francis Nevins interviewed retired CIA covert action specialist David Atlee Phillips for the magazine *Espionage*. Phillips mentioned watching Greene while Greene was in Cuba working on *Our Man in Havana*. He gave Professor Nevins a fascinating morsel, which Nevins passed on to me:

I was stationed in Havana at the time, in deep cover, so I kind of wandered around, finding out what was going on. These were the days right after Castro had taken over. Graham Greene went to Havana to watch the making of the movie, which starred Alec Guinness. And at one point Greene said to the director: 'All right, we should change this line and have him say the following:' And Alec Guinness said 'Fine.' But then a *commandante*, a man with a star on his shoulder, a military censor, walked up and said: 'No, you can't change that line.'

I'll never forget the look on Graham Greene's face when he realised for the first time that there might be some flaws in the new Cuban society. And so they went ahead and cut it out, but I'm sure that later, when the film was pieced together, they put it back in. But I'll never forget the look on Greene's face when his work was suddenly subject to censorship.[4]

British newspapers published a succession of Greene's letters about Cuba. The following is typical:

One reads with distress of the bombing by Batista's forces of the beautiful seventeenth-century town of Trinidad – with more distress because the planes and the rockets used were very likely British, planes supplied because the Foreign Office acknowledge that they were unaware that there was such a thing as a civil war in Cuba.[5]

To some in the Foreign Office, Greene must have been an irritating mosquito, and no doubt they wanted to swat him. On 19 October 1959, Greene again wrote to *The Times*, on this occasion comparing the treatment the British government gave to the previous dictator Batista with its refusal to help Castro:

There will surely be little visible justice if the British Government refuses the replacement of jet fighters to Castro in time of peace (even though an uneasy peace) when it supplied jet fighters to Batista in the middle of a civil war.

Surely your Washington Correspondent's suggestion that Castro might employ his jet fighters against Miami, that is to say, the United States, shows a certain sense of unreality.[6]

Greene could not have written at a more inopportune time, since it did not take long for Castro to take over American property. But Greene saw no danger in providing Castro with jet fighters. Within fourteen months, America would break off diplomatic relations with Cuba.

*

After the book and film, Greene made his fifth visit to Cuba in 1963 at the request of Donald McLachlan, editor of the *Sunday Telegraph*, who had written to Greene in December the previous year to suggest that

> It is now possible to get into Cuba without a special visa and I am writing to ask if it would interest you to go there on our behalf? Obviously the sooner you could go the better, but the important thing from our point of view is that *you* should go . . . You told me once that a really different assignment wd. interest you.[7]

The political reasons for going were obvious. The new government of Castro had followed the pattern of the Soviet bloc, initiating political purges, suppressing opposition, and expropriating US and other foreign holdings, banks and industrial concerns. Suddenly, America had a communist country on its doorstep. A trade embargo was followed by the Bay of Pigs invasion of 17 April 1961, when a CIA-trained force, composed of mainly white professional Cubans, fell quickly. It was a pitiful humiliation for the newly elected President Kennedy. At this point, the Soviet Union increased support for the little island, and in the summer of 1962 Nikita Khrushchev, premier and first secretary of the Communist Party of the USSR, began secretly installing ballistic missiles. On 15 October 1962, US reconnaissance planes revealed the construction in Cuba of launching sites.

This was at once publicly denounced by Kennedy, who ordered an immediate naval blockade and promised that if a missile were launched from Cuba, America would retaliate at once with a full-scale missile attack against the Soviet Union. Khrushchev suggested to Kennedy that the United States should in return remove its own missiles from Turkey. Kennedy gave his word, contingent upon persuading NATO to agree, and promised not to invade Cuba. On 24 October, Russian ships carrying missiles turned back, and by the 28th, Khrushchev agreed to withdraw and dismantle the sites.

Because of fear of a holocaust on both sides, Khrushchev broadcast a hurried message of Soviet agreement by public radio, perhaps preventing universal death in two vast countries and several small ones. The confrontation ended as quickly as it began, but Castro was bitter that Khrushchev had left him to discover the Soviets' plan by means of the airwaves.

In light of such danger and trouble, the editor of the *Sunday Telegraph* wanted Greene to sniff around. He couldn't have picked a better man, for Greene was welcomed in Havana as a supporter of Castro, who rarely missed a chance to attack American foreign policy. It was unusual that the *Sunday Telegraph*, a conservative newspaper, should approach Greene, a near socialist, but given his fame, his access to the press, and his friendship with the Fidelistas, the editor must have felt it was worth the risk that Greene might be seen as partisan.

Greene's meeting with Donald McLachlan as late as March 1963 suggests that the *Sunday Telegraph* was willing to wait any length of time to haul Greene aboard. In response to McLachlan's December letter, Greene had written: 'You certainly put the most luscious temptation in my way. I've so far evaded prison and it would be interesting to see the inside of a Cuban one!'[8] He wanted to accept the invitation, but he had reservations: 'Really I would be keen to accept your assignment [but] I don't wish to leave Europe except during the months of July and August.'

By the time Greene *was* ready to go to Cuba, political interest was greatly diminished. But he was to be allowed a free hand, and the editor conjectured: 'The situation may be much more interesting there in July and August than now. May I suggest that we ask you definitely to go to Cuba at a date of your choosing in July . . . and do Haiti* as well if Cuba is in any way disappointing?'[9]

*

Getting into Cuba for Greene was easy – he had an open invitation from the government. They could hardly object to his travelling all over the island, and he knew where to go. The disadvantages were that he'd 'be shown a great deal of dull things such as collective farms and new schools'.[10]

Greene arrived without difficulty during the first week of August 1963. In his diary: 'Noticeably more news in [Havana] papers than usual – especially . . . Latin America. Nearly 40 cabarets [closed down].' He then refers to '7,000 small farmers in for a convention',[11] which translates into his *Sunday Telegraph* article as, 'When you drive out to the Country Club you pass the homes of the millionaires. Washing hangs from the balconies; the garage doors are open and classes of peasants sit before blackboards. (Seventy thousand are being educated in Havana.)'[12] Further diary notes: 'Aug 7 Plans postponed till midday

---

* Greene did 'do Haiti' on the same trip, and saw first-hand that ravaged country under the evil Dr Duvalier. If Greene had not made his third visit to Haiti he could not have given birth to one of his greatest political novels, *The Comedians*.

tomorrow . . . Dutch ambassador (self-invited) to lunch at Floridita. Fallen completely for Fidel & speaks of him (without truth I am sure) like a lover.'[13]

In the commissioned article he does not mention the ambassador:

In the Floridita, which was one of the great restaurants of the world, daiquiris may give out any day for lack of limes. I notice in my diary of 1957 that on 11 November I had for lunch there crayfish *au gratin* containing white truffles, asparagus and small peas. Now in 1963 I had some bean soup, tinned langouste and rice, one bottle of beer (served only with meals and never more than one), coffee – this meal cost me $6.80.[14]

But Greene felt some passion for Castro himself. He elaborates in his diary:

The huge crowd that gathered before the monument to Marti* to hear Castro's three-hour speech on 26 July was not the regimented or hypnotized crowd that used to greet Hitler.[15]

Greene calls it a cheerful Bank Holiday crowd that had come to take part in an amusing show. 'There were interludes of song, interludes of comedy, interludes of farce – a young man in front of me went down on all fours to make pig-noises when the [Bay of Pigs] invasion was referred to.'[16]

After Castro's speech, Greene noted in his diary: 'One has the sense of a people who are taken into the confidence of this government directly – perhaps only a small people (Cuba has 6,000,000) can accomplish this intimacy. It grows with the universal Fidel who may turn up anywhere at any moment to talk to students or a diplomatic cocktail party. Government of the western democratic kind is far more remote.'[17]

This is enlarged in his article:

There is a touch of ancient Athens about Havana today; the Republic is small enough for the people to meet in the *agora*. Castro walks unexpectedly into the hotels and starts a discussion; he stops at the café where foreign students are gathered and is interrogated on Khrushchev's view of art. 'Khrushchev is not a man of extremes. He is critical of everything, but I have never heard him criticize himself.' Lorry-loads of small farmers come up from the country to lodge in the great hotels and discuss the

* Jose Marti (1853–95) was the leader of the movement to liberate Cuba from Spain.

new agricultural policy. They meet Castro – he is more accessible than . . . [prime minister] Macmillan.[18]

★

There is one incident which Greene never spoke publicly about, though he intimated to me that he was aware of it. When he visited Havana in 1959, writer Kenneth Tynan was also in town. Tynan and Greene knew each other; both frequented the Floridita, and each would have heard the other was in town.

In that month, Kenneth Tynan, George Plimpton and Tennessee Williams were in the Floridita. The story is beautifully told by Plimpton in his book *Shadow Box*. Captain Marks, an American soldier of fortune, arrived and joined their circle in the Floridita. He revealed that he'd fought with Castro in the mountains, which was applauded, but then went on to say that his job now was at Morro castle, and that he was in charge of the execution squads:

> He was being kept very busy, especially in the evenings, and sometimes his squads didn't [finish] until one or two in the morning. We all stared at him. In fact, Captain Marks went on, that very evening there was going to be quite a lot of activity over in the fortress and he'd be just delighted if we would consider joining him [for] 'the festivities'. He made the invitation as easily as he might have offered a round of cocktails at his home. He counted us: 'Let's see . . . five of you . . . quite easy . . . we'll drive over by car . . . tight squeeze . . . I'll pick you up at eight . . .'
>
> At this point there was a sudden eruption from Tynan. He had been sitting, rocking back and forth, in his chair; he came out of it almost as if propelled . . .
>
> At first, I don't think Captain Marks was aware that these curious honked explosions of indignation from this gaunt arm-flapping man in a seersucker suit were directed at him, but then Tynan got his voice under control, and Captain Marks could see his opened eyes now, pale and furious, staring at him, and the words became discernible – shouts that it was sickening to stay in the same room with such a frightful specimen as an executioner of men ('l-l-l-loathsome!'), and as for the invitation, yes, he was going to turn up all right, but in order to throw himself in front of the guns of the firing squad! He was going to stop the 'festivities' – the word sprayed from him in rage – and with this he pulled his wife up out of her chair, and . . . he rushed for the exit.[19]

147

Plimpton, though troubled, planned to watch the execution of a young German mercenary, but first visited Ernest Hemingway, then residing in Cuba, telling him how Tynan, steaming with rage, had stunned Marks. Hemingway, Plimpton recalls, felt 'it had been a mistake to ask Tynan' to an execution 'since his emotional make-up . . . just was not suited to accept such things', that he would 'give the revolution a bad name'. However, he encouraged Plimpton to go.

But the execution was called off. Plimpton never knew for certain, but he always hoped that Ken Tynan's intervention saved the day:

> I like to think . . . that the officials had got wind of his outraged reaction to Captain Marks in the Floridita . . . that he was going to throw himself in front of the guns. No, it was best to let things cool down; to let this weird fanatic clear off the island. At least they would not have to worry that just as everything was going along smoothly, the blindfolds nicely in place, not too tight, just right, Tynan's roar of rage would peal out of the darkness ('St-st-stop this in-in-infamous be-be-behavior!'), and he would flap out at them across the courtyard, puffs of dirt issuing from his footfalls as he came at them like a berserk crane.[20]

So one man was saved – for a night perhaps.

★

Castro's battle-cry was noble-sounding at first:'Our only secret weapon is the human leg.' Yet once Batista had been driven out, Fidel Castro found himself suddenly in the high seat of power. He's on record as saying, 'I am determined to show no mercy.'

But the people did not know this. They awaited Castro's arrival in Havana, and gave the strapping six-footer, supposed destroyer of a corrupt government, an unprecedented welcome. Women wept (as did men), kneeling in prayer in the streets, as Castro, the victorious rebel, rode by, his beard flowing. What a victory for this destined liberator. Yet very soon, it would be revealed that there was a quality in him – an ability to create in people purgatorial fires, and just as quickly dampen them down. But in the early days of the success, it was a time for retaliation: we move from reform and democratic hopes to rage (easily kindled) and then to inevitable carnage.

The enemy, dictator Batista, had fled. It was time for Castro to kill Batista's supporters, those known to be, those thought to be, those who *might* be. The fever of vengeance was upon the people: they gathered in the great trial arena, the ring lit by floodlights, one man standing on the centre stage – every man his enemy. It was like a Roman spectacle renewed. But this Bastista man, Jesús Sosa Blanca, was no gladiator, his hands were manacled, he stood gaunt. He is allowed to speak amid jeers: 'I fought the rebels, because they were my enemies. There are deaths in war. You get killed or you kill,' he exclaimed, 'but by God, I'm no murderer.'[21]

One man, joking, put a noose around his own neck to mimic his enemy's impending death, the noose calling forth much laughter. The enemy, Sosa Blanca, is quickly sentenced to death by the tribunal, to the satisfaction and roar of the crowd: this is building a new country on a heap of corpses. The victims were now the victors. The black pot of Batista had suddenly become the black kettle of Castro.

Verdicts were quickly reached and sentences just as quickly carried out by Fidel's brother Raul, head of the exterminating gang – young, confident, monstrous, in control. Raul's firing squad worked in relays, hour after hour. Raul is reported as saying, 'There's always a priest on hand to hear the last confession.' He carried out a great bloodletting at Santiago's firing range. A trench 40 feet long, 10 feet wide and 10 feet deep was gouged out of the earth. A priest led two prisoners to the edge of the trench and then stepped quickly back. A firing squad fired and the two bodies fell. Two more stepped forward, and then two more and two more and two more, the mass grave quickly filling.

And Graham Greene, staunch admirer of Fidel Castro, never seemed to see that it was time to change views. And his famous statement, 'I am for the victim and victims change', should have determined this change. Would that he had acted like his friend Kenneth Tynan! Why could he not see that Raul's activities were reminiscent of the SS, rounding up Jews, taking them out of their villages, having them dig their own graves, and then standing them up so that once shot, they fell into the ditch. It saves time, don't you see?

Raul could have easily worked effectively for Commandant Hoess, killing millions of Jewish children at Auschwitz. And why not? Raul was surely a lineal descendant of the sabre-toothed tiger.

PART 7

Entering Father Damien Country

14

Another Escape Route

For my part, I travel not to go anywhere, but to go.
— ROBERT LOUIS STEVENSON

O N 15 September 1958, three weeks before the publication of *Our Man in Havana*, Graham Greene wrote to a friend in Belgium about a trip to Africa:

Dear Hansi, I wonder if you can help me. I want for the purposes of a book to spend some weeks in a hospital of the Schweitzer kind in West Africa or Central Africa (because already I have a certain knowledge of the background), but run by a religious Order. I have found a leper hospital in Bamaco, but this is the Sahara which I don't know and it is run by nuns and I wouldn't feel at ease with them! It occurred to me that there might be some place in the Belgian Congo. If you could help me I would be very grateful.[1]

'Hansi' was Baroness Lambert. Greene had chosen the right person to assist him.

Before his search for material had effectively begun, Greene already had a shrewd notion of what he wanted – a leper hospital 'run by a religious Order', in which priests predominated. Even while writing *Our Man in Havana*, he was thinking ahead to his next novel, in order to combat the awful void which arose when one project was over, another not started, with his terrible brooding of empty days.

Baroness Lambert wrote at once to the leprologist Dr Michel Lechat, already famous at thirty-one, who had worked under Francis Hemerijckx (Belgium's Dr Schweitzer), and was at the time director of the Leprosy Centre at Yonda, near Coquilhatville (now Mbandaka) in the Congo's Equator Province. Serendipitously, seven years earlier

Greene had dined at the home of Baroness Lambert when Dr Lechat was a fellow guest. It was natural for her to approach the young doctor.

★

In 1890, on that great Congo river, Joseph Conrad had captained the steamship *Roi des Belges*. He passed Iyonda (Yonda) and afterwards returned from Stanleyville (now Kisangani; Conrad's 'inner station') with the ailing head of station, one Klein, whom Conrad in *Heart of Darkness* called Mr Kurtz. (It was Klein, dying on board ship, who spoke the immortal phrase: 'The horror. The horror', and a servant who pronounced the fatal words: 'Mistah Kurtz – he dead.'*

As a young writer, Greene had worried about being influenced by Conrad's work. Coming to what he felt would be his last novel, it was perhaps his conscious intention to try his hand at setting a novel in Conrad territory. He had lived long enough with his own style and thoughts to confront the darkness in his own soul, just as Conrad had. But Conrad's characters are not so much reflections of his private self as they are depictions of decent men brought under the corrupting influence of the lawless Congo, revealing their hidden nature. The ivory hunters, planters, seamen, all are tested in Conrad.

For Greene, the precise observer of others, his Congo story is strangely different from his other novels. *A Burnt-Out Case* is an introspective study in crisis, written out of compulsion, thinking of what he'd become – and being sickened because of the sense he had of a deep desolate moment of failure. To the extent that Greene shared the skin of his scapegoat hero, Querry, in *A Burnt-Out Case*, he scrutinised his own spiritual barrenness. It is Greene's view of his own abyss which he gives over to Querry, who, pushed to the extreme, comes un-expectedly to death.

Greene is confronting an aspect of himself he did not like: the eating away of his own being as a result of long years of attempting 'that hard and selfish thing' – the curious disease well known to artists: self-expression, manifested in the inability to compose, paint, write, when the imagination is empty – something dead in the heart, though the body continues. This is Greene with his clock stopped, just on the brink of breakdown, a burn-out.

Though most of his leading characters are offshoots of Greene, no character is released and separate – they are chained to him.

★

* Though Conrad has his Kurtz buried in a muddy hole, Klein was buried downstream from Yonda in a Baptist cemetery at Chumbiri.

Baroness Lambert might well have been a bit afraid of Greene – not his fame, but his reputed willingness to twist the lion's tail. She, along with political authorities and governments, knew that Greene enjoyed fishing in troubled waters. *The Quiet American* had established Greene's proclivity for being perceived as anti-American. After his visit to Sierra Leone, he had poked fun at British colonists in *Journey Without Maps*. In *Our Man in Havana* he went after British Intelligence. He was no respecter of countries or leaders (political or religious). Not even the Pope was safe from a tongue-lashing. The Belgian colonial authorities, intimately aware of the dangers brewing in the Belgian Congo, might well have been disturbed, and would want to know what Greene was up to.

The Baroness asked Lechat to question Greene regarding his proposed length of stay in the Congo, and the precise dispensary and hospital he had in mind. Lechat was cautioned: 'He is very agreeable', but 'very problematic'.[2] She also wrote: 'It might be fun to have Graham Greene write a novel with the Congo as background.'[3] There was a suggestion in Lambert's letter that Greene should be introduced to ambassadors, governors and other high officials during his visit, not an agenda that would have enchanted Greene.

Lechat responded quickly about his hospital and other leprosariums in the Congo with scholarly detail. Describing the event thirty-two years later, he remembered a Sunday afternoon spent preparing a large chart describing two dozen places throughout Africa which in his opinion were 'better suited than Yonda to accommodate him and the gestation of a potential novel. I was not eager to shelter such a visitor in Yonda.'[4]

Writing in his native French, with characteristic directness, Lechat pointed out that there were two distinct groups: lepers, and those who nursed them. He himself was interested in the former, but he knew it was the latter who held Greene's attention. He added: 'But they are very different, and their attitudes are sometimes incompatible. I remember an American leprosarium, founded by Sisters who were buying leper slaves in order to marry them off and make them plant cocoa trees; and now [a century later], a Holy Sister declared to me: "Doctor, it is horrible. I don't have any more lepers. They have all left. They are all getting better."'[5]

Lechat's map ranged widely, mentioning various facilities: Ndan in Cameroon, Mikomeseng in Spanish Guinea, Ossiomo in Nigeria, Tshumbe Ste Marie in the Belgian Congo. He went on to describe three leprosaria in his area, founded in 1945 by Monseigneur van Goethem. In passing, Lechat mentioned Conrad's famous story, and this must have attracted Greene, for on his way to Yonda he carried his own copy of *Heart of Darkness*, which he hadn't read for thirty years. Lechat wrote that Yonda was located in a real 'Heart of Darkness' setting and belonged to the Missionaries of the Sacred Heart.

Yonda; 1,015 sick; three Fathers in management of the leprosarium, plus the Father Superior of the Mission; plus eight Sisters. Yonda has a unique characteristic, a leper ward that isn't an annex of a mission, but constitutes the whole mission. Situated on the banks of the river Congo, it extends down three kilometres of avenues into the marshy forest; 15 kilometres from Coquilhatville, (chief town of the province, 1,000 Europeans) . . . A government doctor [Lechat himself] lent to the Missions by its demand has lived in Yonda for six years. The leprosarium especially takes in complicated cases (ocular leprosy, etc.), and the maimed (340 sick with mutilations of the hands and feet). There is a well developed social activity: apprenticeship for crafts, carpentry, masonry, mechanics, clockmaking, reading classes for adults, schools for leprous children. The whole leprosarium of 165 houses was built by the leprous ones, paid the same wages as healthy workers. The medical facilities are not complete; the hospital research centre is under construction; pretensions of doing scientific research.[6] [Perhaps Lechat's little joke, for he was serious indeed about research.]

Lechat speaks of the Yonda hospital as a model leprosarium which had adopted modern methods to fight the disease. He says nothing of his own efforts in bringing this about, but is full of praise for the nuns and priests: 'Their spirit is extraordinary, made up of intelligence, devotion, humour and dynamism.'[7] He also reveals something of the standards which presumably he himself had instituted, indicating that because of extremely modest resources and extremely restricted personnel, the leprosarium sacrificed personal efficiencies: 'preferring to build houses suitable to patients rather than a church; to build a kitchen rather than to plot gardens'.[8] But to show the missionaries' fair-mindedness, Lechat points to the small Protestant church in the leprosarium.

Finally, Lechat describes Imbonga, on the River Momboyo, 'three days by boat from Coquilhatville (one boat per month), located in a barely penetrated region among the Pygmies, a leprosarium without medical [services] attached to a Mission'. Another was 'Wafanya, upstream on the same river, some 30 kilometres from an administrative post (staffed by ten Europeans); six days by boat from Coquilhatville. Hospital served by a Government doctor lent to the missions; a leprosarium attached with a nursery for children brought into the world by the lepers; served by ten missionaries.'[9]

Greene made up his mind swiftly. Lechat had written on 3 October 1958, and his letter must have gone by diplomatic pouch, for Greene replied four days later thanking Lechat for his extraordinary kindness and information. It was all he needed. 'In principle [I would like] to come out and stay at Yonda for some weeks towards the end of January . . . Then if I had not got all that I required at Yonda I might be able to visit one of the other stations by the Mission boat.'[10]

★

As usual, Greene was working without a break. But he was also considering what he needed to do prior to coming out to the lepers, and how long he'd stay. 'My problem is when? I am just starting a film script [*Our Man in Havana*] and I don't expect to finish it until early in the New Year. I gather that the time I proposed – the end of January – is about the worst period possible because of the rains. On the other hand I would like to see something of "the worst period".' He wanted to come at the end of the rains and stay a bit in the dry weather – in all for about six weeks. 'Would such a long period be asking too much of your hospitality and the hospitality of the other Missions?'[11]

Greene confessed some nervousness, 'as disease is always a little upsetting to me perhaps because I have been too lucky in my own health until now'. He mentions a Japanese test to see if one was prone to leprosy, and he felt the airline would let him know what inoculations were necessary, but asked about 'mosquito boots', and 'tablets . . . against malaria'.

Greene addressed the question he felt must be exercising the minds of the authorities, assuring them that the leper mission was to be purely background for an intended novel, and 'I have no intention, I promise you, of producing a *roman à clef*. Indeed the reason why I want to visit all three missions if that be possible is to produce some kind of composite picture which will not be a portrait of any one of them.' And then a surprise: 'Nor am I looking for any dramatic material. The more normal and routine-like that I can make the background the more effective it would be for my purpose.'

★

With the film script of *Our Man in Havana* and his play *The Complaisant Lover* completed, Greene's remaining difficulty, apart from 'a little ulcer trouble',[12] was rehearsals. He wrote to Lechat on 15 December: 'It also depends on when the rehearsals of a new play [John Gielgud's production] are likely to begin.'[13]

Greene also addressed Dr Lechat's fear that Greene would 'not have the same comfort' at his disposal, 'or the charm, of Avenue Marnix', the home of the Lamberts. 'There would be difficulties concerning water, showers etc., the installations being rudimentary.'[14] Greene dismissed his concerns: 'Please don't worry at all about my comfort. I can assure you that after three months, years ago in Liberia, and fifteen months during a war in Sierra Leone and nearly a year in all acting as a correspondent in Indo-China, I don't expect, while gathering material, to live in grand hotels!' Greene's fear of being a nuisance to Lechat and his wife Edith (herself a distinguished artist) made him add: 'and I will certainly be troubled if you take any special measures for my comfort. I want to see things as they are.'[15]

Again Greene came back to his novel, reiterating that he knew what he was looking for (and we now know to some degree the surprising intellectual concept from which this story begins), though in admitting it, he tried to put his future hosts' fears to rest regarding the subject of the novel – a theological and psychological argument which he does not go into 'for fear of destroying this still nebulous idea [that] should take place against a background of an African hospital settlement. If I can visit other stations besides Yonda there will be no danger of my composite picture being attributed to any one station.'[16] He ended his letter by promising he'd be on the Lechats' doorstep by February.

His forthcoming Congo journey had been made known to his friend Edith Sitwell, who, on 15 November 1958, a month after the publication of *Our Man in Havana*, wrote to Greene: 'What a perfect book it is! I don't know when I have laughed so much.' And about his trip: 'Osbert and I are horrified to hear of your proposed sojourn among the lepers. But we feel you ought to have a little preliminary experience, think of us as *moral* lepers, and come here on your way.'[17]

★

But much as Greene intended to go to the leper colony, his paramount interest was still Catherine Walston: he wanted to see her, to love her, and would hold off the day until he'd read her letters and replied to her. On 3 January 1959, three weeks before he left for the Congo, he wrote: 'If a holiday were possible before, I'd postpone the lepers.'[18] Catherine was again unable to meet him.

As we've seen in Volume Two, in 1950 Greene had desperately wanted to marry Catherine, and forced the issue. The result was that the gentle but scandal-shy Harry Walston had laid down the law: Greene could continue seeing Catherine, but away from Newton Hall. Such future meetings were mere crumbs to Greene. Unable to see her often, he began taking himself out of the country. He concentrated on being a natural nomad, spending six months in Vietnam; out of his journeying came *The Quiet American*, alongside *The Comedians*, which came from his experiences in Haiti, both illustrious political novels.

Nine years after Greene made his play for Catherine's hand, life at Newton Hall was becoming troublesome. Harry Walston was once more trying to become a member of Parliament. He contested Huntingdonshire as a Liberal in 1945, 1951, 1955 and 1957, and as a Socialist in 1959. He was seen at that time as an anomaly, a socialist who was very rich. Under such circumstances, it was quite impossible for Catherine to leave her husband for a holiday with Greene. Yet Harry Walston surely was generosity itself to Greene. A card from Harry 'which turned up too late',[19] forwarded to Greene from Paris to Havana, asks Greene to join the Walstons at Newton Hall after Christmas.

The novelist found the erratic relationship with his greatest love difficult to stomach. It seemed to get worse each year. Greene had persevered so long, but Catherine was impossible to capture. And he wanted so much more (as true lovers do): her lips to touch his mouth, his skin. He kept trying to persuade her to see him, or to make iron-clad promises to see him, but little could be definite in Catherine's life. They had arranged to see each other in Paris when he returned from the Congo in March, but it was now only 3 January and his leper trip didn't begin until February. Greene kept on trying to persuade Catherine even as he was planning his Congo visit. On 3 January, he wrote saying that Brazil would be too much, and offered to come willingly to the West Indies if she wanted. By 14 January, Catherine had denied him a meeting. Graham anticipated such and had 'already provisionally booked [for] the Belgian Congo'.[20]

In this dry period, Greene did not know what to do. The Anita Björk affair had ended in December 1958; the Catherine situation turned difficult. He was back to the directionless searching which was becoming routine. Feeling fundamentally unattached to Catherine left him psychologically out of gear. His only remedy was work, yet this consistent labourer felt blocked. When he was unable to love, he often found himself unable to write – hence his desire to escape to the Congo.

Greene was seeking escape in every direction; his manic busyness and socialising reflect his fear of facing his moods alone. He feared finishing the film script of *Our Man in Havana* because 'there's nothing to do but brood'.[21] At the same time, he was trying to write *The Complaisant Lover* and work out the date he should leave for the Congo, admitting to Michael Meyer: 'I have to fit in leper colonies in the Belgian Congo before rehearsals.'[22] Working on the play, writing a film script and a new novel, along with travelling to do research, kept his schedule tight, but once he was finished with these projects, and had no serious lover, despair set in. He assisted John Gielgud in casting *The Complaisant Lover*, grappling with fears of suspected cancer and preparing for the Congo: 'Now I'm off for a yellow fever injection.'[23] He must have sometimes felt he was hanging on to sanity by a thread.

★

Writing from Paris to Catherine about *The Complaisant Lover* on 14 January, Greene tells her, 'Scofield is going to be in it as well as Richardson, Gielgud directing, rehearsals in April.'[24] Not a word about these being the leading actors of his generation. Greene's trip to the Congo had to be gingerly wedged into his schedule.

For want of a true love, his life became a series of short dances with one girl after another, sometimes blatant, sometimes less so. 'Gillian's [Mrs John Sutro] no real trouble – nothing is a trouble which isn't mutual.'[25] Earlier he had spoken of her making a play for him: 'On New Year's day I took John & Gillian to the opening night of a new strip tease club . . . Gillian has started pressing again.'[26]

He goes on: 'I feel very far from you in this tired state – it's odd having no one to talk to – Anita & you so far away.' But then he speaks of other women, and truly one begins to think that not only was Harry Walston generous and gentle, but Catherine too, as he confesses he took his 'Hong Kong girl to *Expresso Bongo* last night – memories of the first night [with Catherine]. We drank till 2 & then there was such a thick fog that I had to bribe a taxi for £2 to take us as far as Eaton Place.'[27]

On his way back from Paris he travelled with Rex Harrison and Kay Kendall and wrote: 'Liked him but not her.'[28] Greene nevertheless invited them both to his daughter Lucy's twenty-sixth birthday party. He says: '*Express* journalists tried in vain to gatecrash.'[29]

Admitting that 'the Belgian Congo will be a good escape', he appeals to Catherine in the hope that after he returns 'we can find each other again'.[30]

The social whirl did not stop. He speaks of a 'trying dinner' with Ann Fleming (Ian's wife) and the Huxleys: 'Julian an *absolute* bore & very inimical to me.'[31] 'Today lunch with Moura [Budberg] & then a cocktail party & movie with Lucy. Tomorrow we lunch with Margaret & Jack [Huntington] . . . Thursday dreary Ronald Matthews.'[32] (Matthews, a journalist, loomed large in *A Burnt-Out Case*.)

Greene ends his letter to Catherine with a reference to writing to the '*Spectator, New Statesman* & Lit. Supp.'[33] This letter stirred up his old argument with John Gordon. Almost three years after Greene and Gordon had tilted over *Lolita*, and just as he was leaving for the Congo, Greene sent a request to the press, as if undertaking to write an unauthorised biography, '*The Private Life of John Gordon*, and I should be grateful to any of your readers for any unpublished letters or anecdotes that they can supply. Any letters will be carefully copied and returned.'[34]

Gordon was overjoyed with Greene's letter and saw a way of turning the tables on him. He replied urgently and publicly, saying he was thrilled that Greene would be his Boswell: 'To have the promise of immortality from a writer of such distinction is the most wonderful thing that has happened to me in all my humdrum life. Of course, I realise that such a task involving so much research can be tedious and burdensome. Would it be immodest of me to offer Mr Graham Greene my help?'[35] But Greene had the last laugh, his reply coming from the leper colony, explaining he couldn't accept the invitation. He extended his own invitation for dinner and a chat upon his return, but got in a jab: 'I doubt whether Mr Gordon can himself provide the best material on his life.'[36] John Gordon should have known to beware of the dog's tooth, the bull's horns, the stallion's hoof, and Graham Greene's smile.

*

Greene's restlessness ever seeking an outlet, he couldn't resist writing a poem on the extraordinary wedding of a famous member of Parliament, a popular socialist and well-known homosexual who decided to marry. Here are two stanzas of the poem, 'Ode on the Wedding of Thomas Driberg Esq. MP':

> Friends of yours and friends of mine,
> Friends who toe the party line,
> Labour friends who're gratified
> At being allowed to kiss the bride,
> Artistic friends, a few of whom
> Are rather keen to kiss the groom,
> Friends from Oxford, friends from pubs,
> And even friends from Wormwood Scrubs,
>
> Friends we always thought were dead,
> Friends we know are off their head,
> Girl-friends, boy-friends, friends ambiguous,
> Coloured friends from the Antiguas,
> Friends ordained and friends unfrocked,
> Friends who leave us slightly shocked;
> All determined not to miss
> So rare a spectacle as this!

The imp in Greene keeps itching to make mischief. There were in him at least five different personalities crammed into one tight skin. One was lawless, another had a godless impatience with life (often wanting it over), a third could not suffer bores. A fourth we see here in the high-flighted exuberance of his ode to Driberg and his letter to the press about undertaking Gordon's biography. The fifth was the no longer manic but profoundly depressed soul, full of that terrible sense of hopelessness of which the character Querry in *A Burnt-Out Case* is an expression. But where was his centre? Only Catherine was allowed to know something of his troubled nature. Greene kept his dark side dark, all the while looking for a hole (some dangerous, displaced and disturbing port of evil – Haiti for example) to hide in quietly, but ready to confront and subtly disturb, even control and ultimately to put to an end a further black spot of specific evil.

★

The leper colony Greene was to visit at Yonda was absolutely not an evil place. It was under the auspices of Christian ministers, in this case the Missionaries of the Sacred Heart. The priest most famous for ministering to lepers had done so on the Hawaiian island of Molokai, long a place of leper exile. Father Damien* died of leprosy in 1889, surrounded by those he'd cared for. Greene's interest in him – he had once considered writing Damien's life – was one reason for his wishing to visit a leper colony. In 1890, Robert Louis Stevenson had written a brilliant 'Open Letter' in support of Damien, who had been criticised as a 'coarse, dirty man, headstrong and bigoted'; his detractors asserted that since he was 'not a pure man in his relations with women . . . the leprosy of which he died should be attributed to his vices and carelessness'.[37]

Perhaps another reason Greene chose a leper colony as backdrop for his novel was that he felt ostracised by the woman he loved. The image of the leper, the ultimate outsider, was employed by Greene; he used it to describe Pyle in *The Quiet American*: 'Innocence', says Fowler, 'is like a dumb leper who has lost his bell.'[38]

Greene's link to his character Querry, the bored loveless voluptuary, emotionally spent, his religious faith dead within him, also drew him to Africa. Greene went to the leper colony perhaps with Querry in mind, but with the conclusion of the novel not yet resolved. Though personally depressed, he went to Yonda with hope: hope is a haven to a spiritual leper, suffering from the rotting of the soul as a leper suffers from the rotting of the body.

* Religious name of Belgian priest Joseph de Veuster (1840–89).

★

Although he converted to Catholicism in 1926, Greene did not begin to feel real faith until he returned from Mexico in January 1938. But two decades later, at the end of January 1959, he was a different man. He journeyed to the Congo because he knew he responded to what he called the primitive manifestations of the Catholic faith. He was tracking alongside the spiritually dead Querry in order to rediscover his own faith; to see the full tragedy of leprosy in the thousand patients in Yonda; to imagine what it must have been like for Father Damien, who among the terribly sick stood in the shoes of God; to see if he could look at living leprosy straight on.

How would Greene cope with such harrowing material: the abominable malformations, body parts missing, the sickness in the air? Would he see what Damien saw: a young woman of twenty whose right side was a swarm of worms, thousands of them, like Kafka's worms: 'as thick and long as my little finger, themselves rose-red and blood-spotted as well . . . wriggling from their fastness in the interior of the wound towards the light, with small white heads and many little legs'?[39] Would Greene find in Yonda a buttress for a flagging belief in his adopted faith?

15

In Search of a Character

The mercy of darkness was falling at last
over the ugly and the deformed.
                    — GRAHAM GREENE

GREENE, en route to the Congo, spent a night at the Palace Hotel
in Brussels before leaving by plane on 31 January 1959. He heard
rumours that in order to visit one of the outlying leper stations he
might have to go by water: 'About six days by canoe & I feel nervous!'
– and added to Catherine – 'However I'm in for it now, to go now
was the only way to have work to take away when we are together.'[1]
Catherine was pivotal to his travel and work plans. Later on, without
her, his work changed.

Greene begins his Congo journal on the plane with the seeds of
his novel: 'All I know about the story I am planning is that a man
"turns up", and for that reason alone I find myself on a plane between
Brussels and Leopoldville. The search for the character cannot end
there – X must have known Leopoldville, come that way, but the place
where he emerges into my consciousness is a leper station.'[2]

Once he's on the track of another novel, Greene feels depression
lifting: 'The business is all finished. Now I'm doing something again
I feel better.' And he ends the letter telling Catherine she's 'the only
real complete companion I've ever known & I long for you as much
as ten years ago'.[3]

Greene spent his first day in the Congo under the ugly outline of
Leopoldville's skyscrapers prior to going to Coquilhatville and the leper
colony. At the airport he noticed again the 'smell of Africa' which he'd
first encountered at Dakar in 1934. Later he was to recognise it at an
airfield at Casablanca, then again on the road beyond Nairobi. In 1942,
landing in Sierra Leone's capital, the great city of Freetown, he described
the scenery, the bay crowded with shipping, the strange bubble-like
mountains, the absurd Anglican cathedral built of laterite bricks – but

it was the smell he wanted to understand: 'is it the starved greenery and the red soil, the bougainvillaea, the smoke from the huts in Kru town, or the fires in the bush clearing the ground for planting?'[4] Arriving at Leopoldville airport, again he muses on what makes up that aroma – 'Heat? Soil? Vegetation? The smell of the African skin?'[5]

★

No sooner had Greene arrived at Leopoldville than the press surrounded him in relays. There had been riots for the previous two weeks and it was thought that Greene was up to his old trick of arriving at another of the world's hot spots before trouble escalated. Nothing could persuade them that his journey had not been occasioned by the unrest. The streets were patrolled by tanks, lorries and black troops walking single file, reminding Greene of the Indo-China war.

The next day, he left for Coquilhatville and then for the leper station at Yonda, fifteen kilometres further on. In Coquilhatville he discovered that the political unrest was serious. Many colonists were afraid. He heard of a man continually ringing up the Sûreté at night to say there were Congolese outside his house who were going to murder him and his wife. 'A lot of people at Coq now are sleeping with guns beside them – the chief danger is an incident provoked from fear.'[6] As it turned out, the colonists' fears were justified, for the Belgian army was losing its grip and within eighteen months the Congo would be fully independent – more 'red-haired devils' chased home.

Greene was met at the airport and taken to Yonda by Dr Lechat. They liked each other at once. Greene knew something of Lechat's nature from the detailed information he'd given about the leper stations, and he recognised his dedication (Lechat was the only doctor looking after 1,000 lepers). Lechat had turned his hospital into a highly organised garden-city, running down to the River Congo – and all done in the terrible heat of a place just a few miles distant from the Equator. He was a doctor who was sensitive, but without sentimentality, tough, quick, efficient, not deferring to the famous – quietly aware of his own worth.

★

Greene arrived exhausted. He'd met too many strangers, and in the blazing heat of the afternoon the Bishop insisted on giving him whisky neat. That night he watched the little groups of lepers round fires outside their simple homes in the hospital precincts. He felt the oppressive stickiness of Africa, a place where the evening air is at times so humid that it breaks upon the skin 'like a single spot of rain'.[7]

His first letter to Catherine begins: 'Here I am', and immediately tells her that Yonda, the largest and the best-run leprosarium, is 'quite a pretty garden village of 2,000 people except that everyone . . . the boy who serves the dishes & washes the laundry – is a leper' but these are non-contagious cases. 'There is still no way of saving the fingers or toes – but the disease can be stopped at the knuckles.' And Catherine had a surprise waiting for him: 'I was so glad as soon as I arrived to get your telegram.' First impressions: 'I've got to stick these next weeks, but it won't be easy.'[8]

Greene's room was bare, with nowhere to hang clothes, and in the communal shower were five large cockroaches. Typical citizens of Greeneland. He 'felt defenceless in this vast space which held only a washstand with a jug, basin and glass, a chair, a narrow bed under a mosquito-net, and a bottle of boiled water on the floor'.[9] He did not know he was the leper station's first visitor, the first human inhabitant of this bare room. The Father Superior followed him into the room and 'looked in the jug to see whether it was full. "You will find the water very brown," he said, "but it is quite clean." He lifted the lid of a soap-dish to assure himself that the soap had not been forgotten.'[10]

Greene's leper world, in contrast to restless Coquilhatville, was peaceful. At first he was prostrated by the terrible heat, the daily act of writing almost impossible in the deep torpor of that land. He kept blotting-paper under his wrists to absorb perspiration just so that he could make entries in his journal. The slightest movement sent sweat stinging into his eyes. After dark, the mosquitoes were hungry; the whining sound (from the horny membranes), their piercing sucking mouths feeding on human blood.

In his first letter a cry of anguish: 'Why do I have to write about places like this?'[11] But on the second day, everything changed. He was 'woken in the dark to the sound of prayer and responses in the little chapel next door, then slept again till seven. Bright sunlight and the air still fresh. No cockroaches in the shower.'[12] In *A Burnt-Out Case*, though, far from treating this experience as joyful, Greene entered immediately into the mind of Querry, which was a version of his own:

> The first morning when he was woken at six by the sound of prayers from the chapel next door, he felt the panic of complete abandonment. He lay on his back listening to the pious chant, and if there had been some magic power in his signet ring, he would have twisted it and asked whatever djinn answered him to be trans-ferred again to that place which for want of a better name he called his home. But magic, if such a thing existed at all, was more likely to lie in the rhythmical and incomprehensible chant next door.[13]

★

At Yonda, Greene saw the lepers, the countless cases of mutilation, but also, under such circumstances, the great good humour of the residents: 'The laughter of the African: where in Europe does one hear so much laughter as among these leper workers?' The reverse was also true: 'the deep sense of despair one feels in them when they are sick or in pain'.[14]

On the first day he heard a story of an 'old Greek shopkeeper who saw his clerk in bed with his Congolese wife. He said nothing but went and spent his savings on an old car – so old that it would only start when pushed.' No one understood why he wanted it. He said he wanted to drive a car just once before he died, so they all got behind and shoved until the engine spurted and started. He went down to his square in 'Coq' and 'hooted his horn to some of his clerks. He couldn't stop his car because then it would never have started again. He called to his clerk to wait for him, made the circuit of the square, twisted the wheel and drove over the clerk into his doorway', crushing his legs and pelvis. 'The old man left the car where it was and waited for the police. It was the first case of the new young commissioner. "What have you done?" he said. "It is not a case of what I have done, but of what I am going to do" . . . and shot himself through the head.'[15]

Characters seemed to just come to Greene. On the first day a leper boy with the extraordinary name Deo Gratias ('Thanks be to God') walked past his room: 'As I shave a worker goes by in sandals cut to fit feet without toes . . . The toeless man puts down his feet as though he were thumping the ground to level it with iron rods.'[16] The boy became Greene's assistant at the leper colony and (though Gratias never knew it) a memorable figure in *A Burnt-Out Case*.

Greene absorbed the nature of the Yonda leprosarium. He watched the fathers; and worried about the priestly chorus; they were right for Europe, but not for the missions. He added sadly that he had 'never yet found in a missionary priest either the naïvety which I want for certain of them, nor the harshness towards human failing, nor the inquisitiveness'. They were too busy to worry about motives: 'they are concerned with cement, education, electrical plant – not motives. How can I get rid of this falsity?'[17]

He watched Dr Lechat and made a note in his journal:

Scene in the dispensary yesterday when there was too much noise of children crying and the doctor called to his assistant who commanded, 'Put the children to the breasts', a command, he says, you hear frequently at Mass . . . silence suddenly reigned.[18]

Greene transferred this to *A Burnt-Out Case*: 'A baby began to cry and immediately like dogs all the babies around the dispensary started to howl together. "Henri," Doctor Colin called; his young African dispenser rapped out a phrase in his native tongue – "Babies to the breast" and instantaneously peace returned.'[19]

For the novel's Dr Colin, in 'this continent of misery and heat'[20] the smell of Africa is the smell of leprosy: 'in all the years he had never become quite accustomed to the sweet gangrenous smell of certain leprous skins, and it had become to him the smell of Africa.'[21]

Wonderful cures, terrible sights, every leprosarium was home to the living, the dying, the dead. Greene stood at Dr Lechat's side at his dispensary and hospital, observing the tattoos on old women:

> . . . the withered breasts like a pair of small empty gloves: the man without fingers or toes nursing a small child: the man with elephantiasis, testicles the size of a football: the tubercular woman (it seems unfair that if one is a leper one should suffer from other diseases as well): the old man with the sweet face and a gentle courtesy who has retired into the mud hut behind his hut to die (high blood pressure) – legs like a child and the face of a saint: the woman without legs who has borne a child: the man who retired to die and was not discovered at the back of his house for days.[22]

The medical references and incidents in his novel come straight from his day-to-day experiences of the hospital, and sometimes Greene's notes in his 'Congo Journal' are put virtually unchanged into the novel:

> On the verandah the walking cases sat out of the sun . . . a man who, when he moved, had to support his huge swollen testicles with both hands . . . A man without fingers nursed a baby on his knee, and another man lay flat on the verandah with one breast long and drooping and teated like a woman's. There was little the doctor could do for any of these . . . Nor could he help those in the first ward who were dying of tuberculosis or the woman who dragged herself between the beds, her legs withered with polio. It had always seemed to the doctor unfair that leprosy did not preclude all other diseases (leprosy was enough for one human being to bear) . . . He passed on and Querry tagged at his heels, saying nothing.
>
> In the mud kitchen at the back of one of the lepers' houses an old man sat in the dark on an ancient deck-chair. He made an effort to rise when the doctor crossed the yard, but his legs wouldn't support him and he made a gesture of courteous apology. 'High blood pressure,' the doctor said softly. 'No hope. He has come to

his kitchen [a mud hut] to die.' His legs were as thin as a child's and he wore a clout like a baby's napkin round the waist for decency. Querry had seen where his clothes had been left neatly folded in the new brick cottage under the Pope's portrait. A holy medal lay in the hollow of his breast among the scarce grey hairs. He had a face of great kindness and dignity . . . the face of a saint.[23]

Lechat's excitement in looking at his Japanese atlas of leprosy is described in Greene's journal: 'the plates resemble the warm landscapes of Van Gogh';[24] and in *A Burnt-Out Case*: 'the thick bright colours and the swirling designs resembled the reproduction of a Van Gogh landscape.'[25] Dr Colin is full of hope, expecting some new medical apparatus from Europe:

With it I will be able to take the temperature of the skin simultaneously in twenty places. You can't detect it with your fingers, but this nodule here is warmer than the skin around it. I hope one day to be able to forestall a patch.[26]

Sometimes Greene runs together tales and superstitions from two different sources, for example, from the Bishop, that 'wonderfully handsome old man with an eighteenth-century manner – or perhaps the manner of an Edwardian boulevardier',[27] and from Dr Lechat. The Bishop reported that 'many were persuaded that with a certain powder they could destroy walls. They pushed the powder under their nails and then they had only to beat on a wall and it would fall.'[28] Two pages earlier in his journal, Greene wrote: 'A man whom L[echat] has cured wrote a letter to his sister still [under the doctor's care] urging the death of L. and boasting of what he had done in Leopoldville in the riots.'[29] In the novel it is slightly rearranged:

In Leopoldville six months before, when the first riots broke out, the attack had been directed at the new glass-and-steel hospital intended for African patients. The most monstrous rumours were easily planted and often believed. It was a land where Messiahs died in prison and rose again from the dead: where walls were said to fall at the touch of fingernails sanctified by a little holy dust. A man whom the doctor had cured of leprosy wrote him a threatening letter once a month; he really believed that he had been turned out of the leproserie, not because he was cured, but because the doctor had personal designs on the half acre of ground on which he used to grow bananas.[30]

Greene saw that sometimes the treatment was almost as bad as the disease. On 3 March he heard from Dr Lechat of a problem caused by the chemical DDS: 'it sometimes has the effect of making a patient temporarily mad'. Greene noted in his journal the case of a man who asked to have his hands bound because of his desire to attack people. '"I told him", the doctor said, "that at eight o'clock you will feel worse. At eleven o'clock worse, but a few more hours and you will feel as you do now, and after that less."'[31]

In the novel Greene deepens the story. An old man is troubled by the treatment, fearing he will attack his own child. Apart from the introduction of the child, the rest is an authentic case:

'Trouble again like the other night?' the doctor asked.

The man looked over the doctor's shoulder as if someone he feared were approaching and said, 'Yes.' His eyes were heavy and bloodshot; he pushed his shoulders forward on either side of his sunken chest as though they were the corners of a book he was trying to close.

'It will be over soon,' the doctor said. 'You must be patient.'

. . . 'I am afraid for my boy. He sleeps beside me.'

The DDS tablets were not a simple cure. Reactions from the drug were sometimes terrible. When it was only a question of pain in the nerves you could treat a patient with cortisone, but in a few cases a kind of madness came over the mind in the hours of darkness. The man said, 'I am afraid of killing my boy.'

The doctor said, 'This will pass. One more night, that's all. Remember you have just to hold on. Can you read the time?'

'Yes.'

'I will give you a clock that shines so that you can read it in the dark. The trouble will start at eight o'clock. At eleven o'clock you will feel worse. Don't struggle. If we tie your hands you will struggle. Just look at the clock. At one you will feel very bad, but then it will begin to pass. At three you will feel no worse than you do now, and after that less and less – the madness will go. Just look at the clock and remember what I say. Will you do that?'

'Yes.'

'Before dark I will bring you the clock.'

'My child . . .'

'Don't worry about your child. I will tell the sisters to look after him till the madness has gone. You must just watch the clock. As the hands move the madness will move too. And at five the clock will ring a bell. You can sleep then. Your madness will have gone. It won't come back.'[32]

Standing behind the fictional Dr Colin is the real Dr Lechat, still a legend among the lepers, his story still sung, the big fetishist* who took leprosy from their bodies.

*

Lechat made a penetrating point about Greene: he was antipodean to a journalist – the unpleasant type as symbolised in *A Burnt-Out Case* by Montagu Parkinson. 'Greene never looked at people as though they were cockroaches. Greene inspired great confidence; he was becoming part of the landscape of the leper colony, with his own routine, even though his routine was the walking down to the river Congo: "The great trees with roots . . . like the ribs of a half-built ship" is how Greene described them.'[33]

Dr Lechat remembers how Greene would go to

> an old tin barge . . . [which] enabled him to avoid the ants; and he sat there until the sun, soon after nine, became too high for comfort. Sometimes he read, sometimes he simply watched the steady khaki flow of the stream, which carried little islands of grass and water jacinth endlessly down at the pace of crawling taxis, out of the heart of Africa, towards the far-off sea.[34]

Though Greene blended in, he had the power of reading people accurately, and had great insight. Dr Lechat, a young man at the time of Greene's visit, is made older in the novel in the form of Dr Colin, his wife already dead. But in fact, Greene, who often had dinner with the Lechats, knew and liked the quiet, genteel, civilised Edith (it is impossible not to, they are a marvellous couple).

According to Lechat, Greene foresaw future success for the Father Superior. Greene observed: 'Red beard never ceases to smoke except at meals: he stands around, bicycles around, strolls around, a veritable overseer.'[35] But Lechat described the Father Superior as a quiet man: 'A most inconspicuous character, he is an innocent piece of the decor, who does not see the difference between a bidet and a foot-bath.' (This incident is carried over into the novel.) However, '[Greene] tunnels into what people could have been, and could become at different times, in different circumstances.'[36] The Father Superior in the novel is led

> to make *en passant* a number of incisive remarks – that nobody in Yonda would have expected from him. Yet, several years later,

* A 'fetishist' in this context is an object or person regarded with great reverence.

he actually became archbishop, revealing himself to be much closer to the assertive and robust character displayed in the novel than to the laconic priest he was during his years at the leprosarium when Greene met him.[37]

It is also the Father Superior who speaks in his sermon of the importance of Christianity. It is a scene of genuine authenticity and simplicity. The Father Superior is saying mass. Querry and Dr Colin sit on the steps of the hospital in the cool of the early morning as the lepers enter the church, which has open sides and a lattice of bricks to break the sun. The nuns are in the front row on chairs, and the lepers behind them on benches of stone, which is more easily disinfected than wood: 'Beyond the doctor on the top step sat the old man with elephantiasis, his scrotum supported on the step below.'[38]

Querry and the doctor talk in whispers as the Father Superior delivers his sermon in a mixture of French and Creole and a word or two of Mongo, the tongue of the river tribes:

And I tell you truth I was ashamed when this man he said to me, 'You Klistians are all big thieves – you steal this, you steal that, you steal all the time. Oh, I know you don't steal money . . . You see a man who lives with one wife and doesn't beat her and looks after her . . . and you say that's Klistian love . . . But you are a mighty big thief when you say that – for you steal this man's love and that man's mercy . . . Why not say when Henry Okapa got a new bicycle and someone came and tore his brake, 'There's Klistian envy'?

The priest gives local examples of how non-Christians often act in a more Christian way, and how Christians can be un-Christian to their fellow man:

'All right. You tell me I'm number one thief, but I say you make big mistake. Any man may defend himself before his judge. All of you in this church, you are my judges now, and this is my defence . . .

'You pray to Yezu,' the Superior was saying . . . 'But Yezu is not just a holy man. Yezu is God and Yezu made the world. When you make a song you are in the song, when you bake bread you are in the bread, when you make a baby you are in the baby, and because Yezu made you, he is in you. When you love it is Yezu who loves, when you are merciful it is Yezu who is merciful. But when you hate or envy it is not Yezu, for everything that Yezu made is good. Bad things are not there – they are nothing. Hate means no love. Envy means no justice. They are just empty spaces, where Yezu ought to be . . .

'Now I tell you that when a man loves, he must be Klistian. When a man is merciful he must be Klistian. In this village do you think you are the only Klistians – you who come to church? There is a doctor who lives near the well beyond Marie Akimbu's house and he prays to Nzambe and he makes bad medicine. He worships a false God, but once when a piccin was ill and his father and mother were in the hospital he took no money; he gave bad medicine but he took no money: he made a big God palaver with Nzambe for the piccin but took no money. I tell you then he was a Klistian, a better Klistian than the man who broke Henry Okapa's bicycle. He did not believe in Yezu, but he a Klistian. I am not a thief, who steal away his charity to give to Yezu. I give back to Yezu only what Yezu made. Yezu made love, he made mercy. Everybody in the world has something that Yezu made. Everybody in the world is that much a Klistian.'[39]

I wrote to Dr Lechat about this sermon, and he remembered it as

outstanding . . . just like being in Iyonda. It is quite possible that we occasionally were sitting on the steps of the hospital. However . . . the Father Superior would not have spoken in Creole (Creole does not exist in the Congo). All the sermons were in Mongo, the local language, that all the missionaries spoke perfectly well. Therefore, the content of the sermon is not coming from such an episode. I suspect it is coming from some conversations between G.G. and the fathers . . . (Possibly Father Henri. He was the one closest to G.G.)[40]

Lechat indicated that patterns in this sermon were characteristic of others he'd heard. Greene was influenced by Father Henri, who travelled with Greene on the boat to the other leprosariums. Greene said sadly of Henri: 'the exhausted priest, what a life it must be to take one's rest in a leper-colony.'[41]

*

Greene did have the kind of conversations with Lechat that appear in the first chapter of *A Burnt-Out Case*. Much of the information comes from Lechat. Greene has Dr Colin plumb for the serendipity of accident, telling the tale of the old Danish doctor who, excavating an ancient cemetery, found skeletons without finger-bones. It was an old leper cemetery of the fourteenth century, and by taking X-rays the doctor 'made discoveries in the bones, especially in the nasal area, which were quite unknown to any of us', says Dr Colin. This information is taken from Greene's 'Congo Journal'.

Then we have a terrifying account of what used to happen to leprologists: Dr Colin says:

> Now that we can cure leprosy, we shall have fewer of those vocations of doom, but they weren't uncommon once . . . There used to be a high suicide-rate among leprologists – I suppose they couldn't wait for that positive test they all expected some time. Bizarre suicides for a bizarre vocation. There was one man I knew quite well who injected himself with a dose of snake-venom, and another who poured petrol over his furniture and his clothes and set himself alight.[42]

This is taken from another entry in the 'Congo Journal':

> What Lechat told me our last evening [before Greene went off on the Bishop's ship to visit other missions] about suicide among leprologists – a common phenomenon. The doctor who soaked his house and himself in petrol and then set himself on fire. The doctor who injected himself with an enormous dose of snake venom.[43]

In a conversation between Querry and Dr Colin, Querry is beginning to think he finds the doctor's 'vocation a little easier to understand', but says the 'fathers believe they have Christian truth behind them, and it helps in a place like this'. He adds: 'You and I have no such truth. Is the Christian myth that you talked about enough for you?' Dr Colin replies, wanting to be 'on the side of change':

> If I had been born an amoeba who could think, I would have dreamed of the day of the primates. I would have wanted anything I did to contribute to that day. Evolution, as far as we can tell, has lodged itself finally in the brains of man. The ant, the fish, even the ape has gone as far as it can go, but in our brain evolution is moving – my God – at what a speed! I forget how many hundreds of millions of years passed between the dinosaurs and the primates, but in our own lifetime we have seen the change from diesel to jet, the splitting of the atom, the cure of leprosy.[44]

Dr Lechat recalls saying something of this nature to Greene, but Dr Colin's further comments are Greene's natural extension of Lechat's thoughts. Greene had to expand the conversation to provide Dr Colin with deeper insight because at this point in the novel Querry must begin to feel that rehabilitation is possible even for a heart like his own, as dried as brown and fallen leaves.

Querry asks Dr Colin: 'You can really comfort yourself with all that? . . . It sounds like the old song of progress.' Dr Colin continues his argument:

> The nineteenth century wasn't as far wrong as we like to believe. We have become cynical about progress because of the terrible things we have seen men do during the last forty years. All the same through trial and error the amoeba did become the ape. There were blind starts and wrong turnings even then, I suppose. Evolution today can produce Hitlers as well as St John of the Cross. I have a small hope, that's all, a very small hope, that someone they call Christ was the fertile element, looking for a crack in the wall to plant its seed. I think of Christ as an amoeba who took the right turning. I want to be on the side of the progress which survives. I'm no friend of pterodactyls.[45]

★

There was one more thing I wanted to know. Was the young Dr Lechat, like Dr Colin in the novel, an atheist? I asked whether he was (A) a Catholic, (B) a Catholic, yet troubled about his faith, or (C) a non-believer. Dr Lechat's reply reached me on 30 March 1998. I think he did not much like my asking. He first referred to Greene: 'Your (A) (B) (C) questions. I see your question. Graham by the way never raised this question . . . the closest we ever came to that kind of issue, only once, was in the case of going to Mass on Sunday, to Coquilhatville.'

> Going back to your question, I have much difficulty to grasp its meaning. I guess I am missing that part of the brain dealing with philosophical issues and metaphysical concerns. It was probably lost somewhere on the way from the amoeba to the ape. Perhaps, I was a pterodactyl – though I do not remember – Let us say, if that may comfort you, that I am at the same time A & B & C. As for me, I am entirely satisfied as I am, no questions asked.[46]

A caring doctor, but a practical and non-spiritual scientist as well. The perfect companion for Greene while he created the world of Querry.

16

Down Tributaries of the River Congo: Happy Priests and a Gloomy Wanderer

From a beautiful girl 'in green with a fish'
to the tsetse fly's 'nasty little jet-styled wings'
— GRAHAM GREENE

AFTER Greene had been at Yonda eight days, Lechat tried to arrange a visit down the Ruki and Momboyo rivers to the more out-of-the-way leprosariums settled deep in the jungle, the home of pygmies. Such a trip was fraught with uncertainty. Greene writes about going to 'Coq with L[echat]' to get a boat on a terribly hot afternoon, a sense of despair upon him:

> A funny little high-built boat badly needing paint like a minia-ture Mississippi paddle-steamer. Received by the retiring captain, a tall priest with gold-stopped teeth and a long straggling beard who gave us beer in the saloon with big windows above . . . the bridge. A cupboard with a painted panel of the nativity. There was a difficulty in sailing . . . [as] the boat had for long been in bad condition and now it was dangerous: a hole or a rotten plank . . . in the bottom . . . A visit to Otraco [cargo-boat service on the Congo and its tributaries] – all berths to Wafania full as far as Imbonga.[1]

The visit to Otraco proved unsatisfactory. Only the Monseigneur could give the word for the dilapidated boat to go, and he was indisposed with a broken hip. Greene and Lechat returned to the cathedral, and Greene approached the 'ambiguous Father André':

> Perhaps the boat could go next week – or next month. Apparently the captain, Father Pierre, is 'a captain who hates the sea'. On every trip (about four a year) something is wrong. Father A. agreed to speak to the Bishop. The answer: the boat is to be examined

by two employees of Otraco and if they say it is safe it will sail. Otherwise no. I distrust the whole affair. I don't believe in a favourable decision.[2]

Greene's intuition, sometimes remarkable, this time failed him: 'Just as I sat down to dinner L. came in to say he had had a telephone call: all was well. I go on board Wednesday evening.'[3] Then in his journal he wrote: 'Perhaps the novel should begin not at the leproserie but on the mission-boat.'[4] And so it does.

*

With his first night on board ship over (Thursday, 12 February), Greene was awakened at 5 a.m. by the boat leaving and, opening his window, he saw the lights of Coquilhatville. There was a loud vibration from the great paddle as they crept on, keeping close to the bank.

Fearing he might lose his diary during his travels, Greene sent Catherine a detailed account (omitting references in his 'Congo Journal' to his returning sexual desires). In a letter dated Sunday Feb 15, 8.00 a.m., entitled 'On the River Momboyo', he describes mass at 6 a.m. in the deck house, an altar on top of a cupboard with the nativity panel behind. He breakfasts and writes in his journal:

> The captain, Père Georges who looks more like an officer in the French Foreign Legion than a priest, tried to shoot [a crocodile] – his first instinct with any wild thing.
>
> You would love this boat, a tiny version unpainted & decrepit of a Mississippi paddle steamer – very pretty. Apart from the crew with some wives & sweethearts – one very attractive – there is nobody on board but Père Georges, the captain, myself & Père Henri, a convalescent taking the trip for a rest, tall, & cadaverous & a joker. I have taught them to play 421. I have the Bishop's cabin which is quite roomy with a nostalgic photo of a church covered in snow over the bed.[5]

You can see how closely the opening of the novel *A Burnt-Out Case* parallels the journal and his letter to Catherine:

> The cabin-passenger wrote in his diary a parody of Descartes: 'I feel discomfort, therefore I am alive,' then sat pen in hand with no more to record. The captain in a white soutane stood by the open windows of the saloon reading his breviary. There was not enough air to stir the fringes of his beard. The two of them had been alone together on the river for ten days . . .

177

except for the six members of the African crew and the dozen or so deck-passengers who changed, almost indistinguishably, at each village where they stopped. The boat, which was the property of the Bishop, resembled a small battered Mississippi paddle-steamer . . .

The passenger would be woken at four in the morning by the tinkling sound of the sanctus bell in the saloon, and presently from the window of the Bishop's cabin, which he shared with a crucifix, a chair, a table, a cupboard where cockroaches lurked, and one picture – the nostalgic photograph of some church in Europe covered in a soutane of heavy snow – he would see the congregation going home across the gang-plank.[6]

On page 61 of his journal we see Greene trying out the beginning of the novel. The final change is very small: 'The passenger wrote in his diary: "I am alive because I feel discomfort."'[7]

In his 'Congo Journal' Greene describes their arrival at Lombo Lombo, a small leprosarium within a mere clearing in the forest: 'All day as we walked around questions shouted as to who I might be. The father replied, a big fetishist.' Greene comments on the natives singing about the events of the day. A note in the 'Congo Journal' considers beginning the novel with such a song, which may have been about Greene, sung by the African bearers in the 1930s during his extraordinary trip through Liberia. 'Here is a man who is not a father nor a doctor. He comes from a long way away and he goes to blank. He drinks much and he smokes and he gives no man a cigarette.'[8] The 'big fetishist' here is the priest, but again the song may well describe Greene:

'They call me the great fetishist,' he added with a smile and nodded at the Holy Family and the pull-out altar over the cupboard . . .

'What do they sing about me?' . . .

'Shall I translate . . . ? It is not altogether complimentary.'

'Yes, if you please.'

'"Here is a white man who is neither a father nor a doctor. He has no beard. He comes from a long way away – we do not know from where – and he tells no one to what place he is going nor why. He is a rich man, for he drinks whisky every evening and he smokes all the time. Yet he offers no man a cigarette."'[9]

Noticing that the water looks like polished pewter, Greene records in his journal that 'Men standing in [canoes] have their legs extended by their shadows into the water, so that they have the appearance of wading. Has some rationalist suggested this as an explanation of Christ walking upon the water?'[10] In the novel, it is Querry's idea: 'Two men . . . had their legs extended by their shadows so that they appeared to be wading knee-deep . . . The passenger said, ". . . Doesn't that suggest to you an explanation of how Christ was thought to be walking on the water?"'[11]

On Greene's first day on the Bishop's boat, he noted how the captain closely resembled 'many young officers of the [French Foreign] Legion one has known in Indo-China',[12] and that quality is transferred to another priest in the novel: 'One father, with a trim pointed beard, dressed in an open khaki shirt, reminded the passenger of a young officer of the Foreign Legion he had once known in the East whose recklessness and ill-discipline had led to an heroic and wasteful death.'[13]

But many of Greene's thoughts are simply passed on to Querry, who in the life of the novel has reached the point of complete mental burn-out. Greene remarked in his journal on the childlike simplicity of the priests he met, recalling their juvenile excitement while playing cards. The boat approaches Bokuma:

> [After] Arrival. Dinner in the mission and afterwards the fathers played a card game, with three packs, which they called Matches. You could deal five – ten – fifteen – twenty cards, and the stakes were made with matches . . . A kind of euphoria among the fathers. Continual jokes and laughter . . . Does this continual badinage and college humour go on through all the years?[14]

Greene's creativity is germinating: 'Can I make a value out of this euphoria, the continual jests and laughter around the enigmatic and unresponsive figure of X?'[15] 'X' later became 'Querry'.*

In the novel, little is changed from his journal, though the language and some of his reactions are more forceful. This allows him to develop Querry in *A Burnt-Out Case*:

> the too easy laughter, the exaggerated excitement over some simple game of cards with matches for stakes had the innocence and immaturity of isolation – the innocence of explorers marooned on an ice-cap or of men imprisoned by a war which has long passed out of hearing . . .

---

* Could Greene have combined for Querry the two words 'query' – because he questioned God – and 'quarry' – since, as he confirmed to me in interview, he hoped God was hounding him?

Their laughter irritated him, like a noisy child . . . He was vexed by the pleasure which they took in small things – even in the bottle of whisky he had brought for them from the boat . . .

The laughter rose higher. The captain had been caught cheating, and now each priest in turn tried to outdo his neighbour by stealing matches, making surreptitious discards, calling the wrong suit – the game, like so many children's games, was about to reach an end in chaos, and would there be tears before bed? . . . The face of the new Pope, looking like an eccentric headmaster, stared at him from the wall . . . The passenger wondered when it was that he had first begun to detest laughter like a bad smell.[16]

A photograph taken of Greene when ashore is full of laughter – there is no evidence that Greene, like Querry, detested laughter 'like a bad smell' at this point in his life; that would come later when he finally got down to writing *A Burnt-Out Case* – his most difficult book ever, when the nature of a burnt-out Querry increasingly becomes the nature of Greene. In fact, we have an example on film of Greene entering in the fun, dancing when 'the tall cadaverous joker' Father Henri pulled him up from his seat. To screams of pleasure from Dr Lechat's children, Greene, gloomy no more, and Father Henri put on a performance.

*

Greene was greedy with material he gathered; he'd use anything and everything which might provide authenticity to the leper background. However, his own personal experience with the two young priests making fun of him found its way into neither the journal nor novel.

I found this out when Father Henri recalled to me that Greene 'used to look everywhere with asking eyes'. He recounted the journey downriver with his young friend, Father Georges, the master of the ship. They were both twenty-four years of age, and somewhat troubled by the dour (and famous) Mr Greene:

Imagine our company: a very serious man and two young fellows, close friends . . . One day, he expressed his astonishment when we had a whisky and soda at 12, just before the noon meal . . . He told us a well-educated man wouldn't have a whisky before 6:00 p.m. . . . we proved to him we had learned the lesson he gave us. Next day at 6:00 p.m., as usual, he lay in his deck chair in front of the room. In secret, I had put an alarm clock under his chair, pointed at six. At the moment it started to ring he rose up, frightened, but at the same time Georges and I entered from the two doors behind him, Georges holding a tray with a bottle of whisky and I had another with three glasses and we both sang 'Whisky Time'. Seeing our faces, he burst out laughing.[17]

When the boat arrived at Bokum, Greene was wakened by the sanctus bell and walked ashore with Father Pierre. People ran up to the priest and shook his hand, mystified that Greene didn't speak the Mongo language. Others knelt and crossed themselves. Greene was vigilant, alert, scrutinising.

Greene is unlike his hero in one important respect: Querry is impotent; he has totally lost interest in sex, chiefly because he doesn't see the purpose in it any more, no longer caught up in that sensual music, 'the worst boredom [having] settled in'. He'd come to realise he'd been given love, but never returned it. Conversely, Greene, after two weeks in the Congo, noted in his journal: 'A girl with beautiful heavy breasts made me aware of how sex was returning after satiety, slowed by the heat and the strangeness but returning. Another girl with nipples like billiard balls.'[18]

The same day, he watched a woman pounding a cotton sarong as the dress she was wearing caught between her buttocks, and noticed 'the lovely smile of black women and the flirtation of their eyes'.[19] The priests on board the *Theresita* were well aware of Greene's interest in these young black women. Father Henri recalled: 'When the boat stopped somewhere he was looking very interested all around to see as much as possible . . . several times, he was charmed by the beauty of the young girls who usually tested the attention of the white people on the boat.'[20]

By the afternoon, it was 'terribly hot', making siesta impossible. When the ship stopped at a village, Ikonga, to buy cooking pots, Greene noticed 'A lovely young woman in green with a fish'. So enamoured was he that he approached the captain, Father Georges, and asked whether he 'could buy her as a wife for the trip'.[21] He seems easily put off: Father Georges 'explained that it would be hardly worthwhile. Any child would belong to the mother and for the birth she would return to her family. If I still wanted her then, I would have to put down the marriage price all over again.'[22] This was one occasion when Greene gave up the chase rather easily – but it *was* 'terribly hot'.

Later, on the Momboyo river, he observed the grooming styles of the local women: 'There are elaborate crossroads of partings on the scalp, the hair is twisted in thin cords to form a kind of bird's cage. The big toes often made up.' Black women here attracted Greene: 'I can never get used to the beautiful even colour of the young African women – the most beautiful *backs* of any race.'[23]

A storm gathered; there was thunder, lightning and heavy rain. Just as they were prepared to leave Ikonga, the steam engine blew a joint and they were held up for the night. 'Father Henri walked into the village to tell the people there would be Mass in the morning.' Once the lamps were lit, 'old women came creeping in to confession'. The next day, the ship's siren 'blew at five to signal the first Mass', and before dawn Greene watched 'a lamp-lit procession' coming down from the village. There were two Masses while the river 'smoke[d] with mist near the bank'.[24] The men working in the engine room came to the first mass and went back to work. Afterwards they breakfasted on eggs, bacon and rabbit, skinned by the captain. By lunch they'd reached Ingende, where Greene noticed a sign: 'Zone of sleeping sickness', and then the almost comic: 'Be careful of the tsetse fly.'[25]

By 14 February, the Bishop's boat had reached Flandria. This was to be a crucial stop, providing a setting used by Greene with great effect. He could not have known upon arrival that touring a palm-oil factory would become important in his novel.

★

The manager was English, and Greene a happy visitor: 'Yesterday we looked in at Flandria where there's an Englishman (ex-Indian army) in charge of a [Uni] Lever palm estate. His little girl [was so] excited by an English voice [she] stood on her head & was sick. He looked awful but turned out nice & intelligent: his wife very pretty & intelligent too.'[26]

Greene told Catherine that on his way back he would spend the night at the palm-oil factory. He did, nine days later. 'Arrived at Flandria around nine and L. met the boat. After beer on board sat up till nearly midnight drinking whisky at his house in the sheer pleasure of talking English to two intelligent people again.'[27]

Greene had been taken round the estate: 'The mill – nothing wasted: all that is not crushed into oil is fuel for the furnaces: no other fuel required. A smell of stale margarine.'[28]*

In a footnote, Greene wrote: 'There was nothing in common between my intelligent and charming host and the unspeakable Rycker', but at Rycker's factory too 'through the net of the window there blew in the smell of stale margarine'.[29] At a later stage when writing *A Burnt-*

---

* In June 2001, I received a letter from 'L.' after tracking him down through Unilever – the owners of the factory. They thought he might be dead, but happily I found him through the registrar's office at Cheltenham College. His name was Chris Lipscomb, and he graciously answered my questions and sent pictures. It was his little girl that Greene referred to as standing on her head. In February 2003, I heard that Lipscomb had died.

Out Case (in Jamaica, Tahiti and Paris), Greene used the physically repugnant palm-oil factory as the perfect setting for the morally repugnant Rycker – a wonderfully developed character carved in nastiness, a religious grotesque who after six years at a seminary school rejoins the world, much to the world's disadvantage.

Who was Rycker and from whence did he come? Can we find a source in the people Greene met in the Congo? Perhaps he came from the dark side of Greene's mind, and in any case Greene categorically states that it would be a waste of time trying to identify characters formed from the flotsam of thirty years as a novelist. But later I hope to make a good stab at identifying the original, though the original was not in any way appalling. Greene knew him no better than he knew Don Pelito, the source for the Judas figure in *The Power and the Glory*.

★

Greene left Flandria and continued to Imbonga: 'The boat punctual at the rendezvous looked very beautiful coming round the bend of the river into the sunset-stained reach.'[30] At Imbonga was a more primitive leprosarium; to Catherine he wrote of going miles in the forest, where there was no doctor, just sisters – very austere. He was looking to spend two days there and then another three at Wafanya for the third leprosarium, and then home to Yonda. His letter to Catherine is disturbing:

> Last night I had one of my awful dreams about you: jealousy. You told me you had slept with Douglas Jay & three other men since leaving home, & what right had I to be jealous anyway? In revenge I started making love to someone – not a bit like the person she was supposed to be – in bed in front of you. Then you became angry & the third person was amused & malicious. In the end we almost had made it up, & you said something profound about real love being always on the border of domesticity.
> Dear, dear, dear.[31]

This dream was not forgotten. He used it later in *The Comedians*. And in the 'Congo Journal' Greene refers cryptically to this dream: 'A disturbed hot night in spite of the pill. Dreamt angrily of someone of whom I have never waking thought angrily.'[32]

They arrived at Imbonga after dark and went ashore to eat and rest, but Greene again slept badly. He met a different Father Henri, with 'untidy red hair and bloodshot eyes and little red beard', whom he also liked: 'Sitting drinking in the deck-house by lamplight one touched the right mood.'[33]

They spent two nights at Imbonga, and the first morning Greene walked ten miles through the jungle to meet two lepers whose terrible cases he described: an old man 'cheerily waving goodbye with hands and feet, but without finger or toes', and the other a woman owning half a hut and living in complete darkness. He saw her as she 'crawled into the half light like a dog out of a kennel – no fingers or toes or eyes of course, & she couldn't even raise her head'.[34]

Weary, Greene dreams again of Catherine: 'We should get to Wafanya tomorrow, stay a few days & then start back towards Paris & you.'[35]* Anticipating that she'll keep her promise to meet him in Paris, he is full of nostalgia, wanting to hurry: 'The current will be with us then & we'll move quicker':

How I hope you can meet me, darling. Do you remember that time after Malaya when we met in Paris & didn't even dress for 24 hours? Just got up & sat in the sitting room in our pyjamas. And the meeting in New York when you cried. And the meeting in London about 1 in the morning when I came from New York & found you sleeping on my sofa. I'm glad it's the same sofa that I've got now. Dear love, I'm just as excited now as then to see you again. Don't be shy![36]

On 19 February, the trigger-happy captain brought down a bird: 'Père Georges has just shot . . . a beautiful fishing eagle. He always shoots a sitting target, and never one on the wing. The bird was only wounded . . . An African swims ashore and finishes the bird off . . . with a log of wood.'[37] By the time they reached Lombo Lombo leprosarium, Greene was getting very tired indeed: 'Staying here for two days & then start back. I shall be glad. I'm tired of being wet & hot & itchy all the time. I long for a proper bath & my first dry Martini with you. Dear dear dear.' But as they set out, they 'hit a snag in the river, [and] damaged the steering'. Next came a storm, and by dark the next day, rudder straightened, there was much rejoicing and 'a great deal of singing' by the black crew.[38]

The heat was devastating, exhausting, yet it was wonderful when night fell and the defeating sun ceased beating down. The stars appeared 'one by one and the large vampire bats went creaking over the forest'.[39] Greene felt happy.

They headed back in bad weather to Yonda. They were now in sleeping sickness country and Greene was aware of 'a lot of tsetse flies' with their 'nasty little jet-styled wings'.[40] He had many bad nights, but

---

* Long before Paris he goes back to Dr Lechat's leprosarium.

woke in the middle of one night '& wrote down the last sentences of the new novel. ['The fools – the interfering fools.'] I wonder if I'll ever get that far. (I've abandoned four in my time.)'[41] It is not the last sentence, but such is his preoccupation with his novel, he even dreams his characters' dialogue!

As he nears the completion of his fifteen-page letter to Catherine, his uneasiness grows: 'Hope – and fear that something may be stopping you meeting me. I love you, dear dear dear.'[42]

He learns he can leave the ship at Flandria, and get a lift next day by car. He seals his long letter to Catherine and promises to write again. His last sentence as he arrives in Yonda is telling, and typical: 'I'm getting so tired of being "jolly" with acquaintances ... And I'm tired too of sweat & bites ...'[43] The threat of disease from insects, the heavy debilitating heat, and having to pretend to be happy – all colluded to make Graham miserable.

17

The Trouble with Being Querry

I was already beginning to live in the skin of Querry,
a man who had turned at bay.

— GRAHAM GREENE

WITH the journey downriver over, we can turn to two characters: Father Thomas and the infamous Rycker.

★

'Father, why are you so against M. Querry?' Father Thomas asks the
Superior in *A Burnt-Out Case*. At the Superior's demur, Thomas
continues: 'What other man in his position – he's world-famous, Father
. . . would bury himself here, helping with the hospital?' The Superior
answers that he doesn't look for motives. Thomas replies, referring to
Querry's extraordinarily good deed:

> 'Well, I do look for motives. I've been talking to Deo Gratias
> [Querry's servant]. I hope I would have done what [Querry]
> did, going out at night into the bush looking for a servant, but
> I doubt . . .'
> 'Are you afraid of the dark?'
> 'I'm not ashamed to say that I am.'
> 'Then it would have needed more courage in your case. I have
> still to find what does frighten M. Querry.'
> 'Well, isn't that heroic?'
> 'Oh no. I am disturbed by a man without fear as I would be
> by a man without a heart.'[1]

Father Thomas fears the dark, yet has an intense desire to unburden
himself to the stranger at Yonda. He stands staring through his wire-
mesh door at the ill-lighted avenue of the leproserie. Behind him on
the table is a candle, 'the flame pale below the bare electric globe. In

five minutes all the lights [will] go out.' This is the moment he fears, and his prayers 'to heal the darkness' are of no avail. Each night 'when the dynamos ceased working, it needed an act of faith to know that the forest had not come up to the threshold of the room. Sometimes it seemed that he could hear the leaves brushing on the mosquito wire. He looked at his watch – four minutes to go.'

He has 'an enormous longing to confide', but it is 'almost impossible to confide in men of his own Order . . . He couldn't say to the Superior: "Every night I pray that I won't be summoned to attend [a leper] dying in the hospital or in his kitchen, that I won't have to light the lamp of my bicycle and pedal through the dark."' A few weeks earlier an old man had died, 'but it was Father Joseph who went out to find the corpse' and who gave 'conditional absolution by the light of the bicycle lamp because there were no candles to be found'. '"I want to talk, I want to talk," Father Thomas cried silently to himself as all the lights went out and the beat of the dynamos stopped. Somebody came down the verandah in the dark; the steps passed the room of Father Paul and would have passed [Father Thomas's] if he had not called out.'[2]

It is Querry, and Father Thomas tries his best to hang on to him because he must confide in someone, and Querry is to be his confessor. Father Thomas attempts to unburden himself:

'Sometimes I think if I stay here I'll lose my faith altogether. Can you understand that?'

'Oh yes, I can understand that. But I think it's your confessor you should talk to, not me . . . What I would say to you wouldn't help you at all. You must believe that. I'm not a man of – faith.'

'You are a man of humility.'[3]

Querry's central trait is his honesty – as was Greene's. He tells the truth about himself. Querry is believed by the intelligent Dr Colin, but disbelieved by Rycker and Father Thomas, each of whom feels strongly that he alone knows the truth about Querry. In such a context, it is impossible for Querry to be believed.

★

Greene did not have a specific source for the doubting Father Thomas, other than the obvious. He is, in fact, re-enacting a series of shocking and psychologically disturbing incidents which occurred soon after the publication of *The Heart of the Matter* in 1948. Priests sought out this wayward, troubled, nervous but famous Catholic to help solve *their* spiritual problems. This he couldn't do. Ten years later, Greene recreated this dilemma, sorting out his own fears and insecurities through his novel. He was too honest to pretend that he had climbed the mountain of knowledge; he was no guru dispensing wisdom. Any attempts to venerate him were stonewalled:

'If you knew the extent of my pride . . .'

'Pride which builds churches and hospitals is not so bad a pride.'

'You mustn't use me to buttress your faith, Father. I'd be the weak spot. I don't want to say anything that could disturb you more – but I've nothing for you – nothing. I wouldn't even call myself a Catholic unless I were in the army or in a prison. I am a legal Catholic, that's all.'

'We both of us have our doubts . . . Perhaps I have more than you. They even come to me at the altar with the Host in my hands.'

'I've long ceased to have doubts. Father, if I must speak plainly, I don't believe at all. Not at all. I've worked it out of my system – like women. I've no desire to convert others to disbelief, or even to worry them. I want to keep my mouth shut . . .' [But Father Thomas won't let him.]

'Then why do I get more sense of faith from you than from anyone here?'4

In a letter to Max Reinhardt, Greene refers to this unsettling period, enclosing a novel, the author's name a pseudonym, sent to him. He recalled the 'rather odd Dominican friar, a homosexual and rather consciously tormented spirit. At a certain period of my life when I seemed to attract confession from priests he haunted me, and I don't want to get in touch with him again.'5

★

Spiritual problems among priests like Father Thomas are one thing. Spoilt priests like Rycker – spoilt in the sense of being a frustrated musician or a would-be actor, longing for what might have been in life, but is not – are another.

Querry meets Rycker in a crowded store in the provincial capital of Luc. As a favour to Dr Colin, Querry is there to see whether an important piece of medical apparatus has arrived. He finds the equipment, goes to the European store to buy *haricots verts* (green beans), and quietly waits to be served. It is there that he hears Rycker give the colonial cry of Africa – 'Boy! Some *haricots verts* for this master' – before turning to Querry and saying more intimately: 'You know you have to shout at them a little. They understand nothing else.'6

Rycker assures Querry that the roads will be impassable because of the heavy downpour, and suggests that he should spend the night at his home.

Then suddenly, right there in the middle of Africa, Rycker unexpectedly remarks: 'You are *the* Querry, aren't you?', with that stupid underlined definite article, which he always uses when speaking to, and of, Querry. Although Querry claims that Rycker has made a mistake, Rycker firmly denies this, stating he can show a photograph of him in one of the papers they are saving at his house 'in case they may prove useful':

> This one certainly has, hasn't it, because otherwise we would have thought you were only a relation of Querry's or that the name was pure coincidence, for who would expect to find *the* Querry holed up in a leproserie in the bush? . . . I've buried myself too.[7]

Rycker takes Querry with him, and we are back at the palm-oil factory as seen in the previous chapter, with the stale margarine odour and hot air:

> the reflection of a furnace billowed into the waning light . . . 'The place functions,' [Rycker] said as the car bumped among the boilers, '. . . in its ugly way. We waste nothing. When we finish with the nut there's nothing left. Nothing. We've crushed out the oil . . . as for the husk – into the furnace with it. We don't need any other fuel to keep the furnaces alive.'[8]

Querry treats Rycker with chilly detachment, revealing him as an egotist, pious yet repellent (and sometimes farcical). Rycker has the patter of religion from his novitiate days and a fiendish desire to spout the rules of religion, intensified by his failure to become a priest. It is still the life he would like to live, though he is conflicted by sexual passion for his young wife. Greene plays off this character against a young, innocent, but ultimately dangerous wife: a 'girl in blue jeans with a pretty unformed face came quickly round the corner in answer to [Rycker's] call. Querry was on the point of asking "Your daughter?" when Rycker forestalled him. "My wife."'

Querry judges Rycker's wife to be an inexperienced child, out of her depth in a colonial world: '"I am very glad to meet you," she said. "We will try to make you comfortable." Querry had the impression that she had learnt such occasional speeches by heart from her governess or from a book of etiquette. Now she had said her piece she disappeared as suddenly as she had come; perhaps the school-bell had rung for class.' This childishness is also characteristic of Helen Rolt in *The Heart of the Matter*, from whom, unquestionably, Rycker's wife is in part derived. They share a dangerous innocence. (Could this be why Greene was later attracted to his future French mistress, Yvonne Cloetta?)

Rycker treats his young wife as if she were a pet monkey: 'Marie is fixing the drinks. You can see I've trained her to know what a man needs.' Querry asks Rycker politely: 'Have you been married long?' and Rycker answers more fully than is necessary. He tells Querry they've been married two years and continues: 'I know you are thinking that she is very young for me' – and it is *his* personality being stressed, *his* needs. 'But I look ahead . . . I've still got twenty years of . . . active life ahead of me, and what would a woman of thirty be like in twenty years? A man keeps better in the tropics.'⁹

Rycker spent six unsuccessful years in a seminary. The damage has been done: his religious thoughts are calcified along certain fixed lines, hardened into dogma that allows him to view himself in glorious self-pity, a stilted form of self-love. In conversation, Querry continues his defensive stonewalling:

'Why are you here, Querry?'
'One must be somewhere.'
'. . . no one would expect to find you working in a leproserie.'
'I'm not working.'
'When I drove over some weeks ago, the fathers said that you were at the hospital.'
'I was watching the doctor work. I stand around, that's all. There's nothing I can do.'
'It seems a waste of talent.'
'I have no talent.'

Querry, like Greene, is watchful of Rycker's childlike wife:

'Do you care for salad?' Her fair hair was streaked and darkened with sweat and he saw her eyes widen with apprehension when a black-and-white moth, with a wing-spread of a bat, swooped across the table. 'You must make yourself at home here,' she said, her gaze following the moth as it settled like a piece of lichen on the wall. He wondered whether she had ever felt at home herself. She said, 'We don't have many visitors,' and he was reminded of a child forced to entertain a caller until her mother returns . . .
'Not a visitor like *the* Querry anyway,' Rycker interrupted her. It was as though he had turned off a knob on a radio-set which had been tuned in to a lesson in deportment after he had listened enough.¹⁰

When Querry asks her directly: 'Do you like the life here?' she can answer only: 'It's very interesting.' Querry notices her staring through the window at the boilers, standing like modern statues in the yard.

At this point Rycker tells his wife to 'fetch that photograph' to prove that their guest is *the* Querry. His young wife trails off and returns with an ancient copy of *Time*.

> Querry remembered the ten years younger face upon the cover (the issue had coincided with his first visit to New York). The artist, drawing from a photograph, had romanticized his features. It wasn't the face he saw when he shaved, but a kind of distant cousin. It reflected emotions, thoughts, hopes, profundities that he had certainly expressed to no reporter. The background of the portrait was a building of glass and steel which might have been taken for a concert-hall . . . if a great cross planted outside the door had not indicated it was a church.
>
> 'So you see,' Rycker said, 'we know all.'
>
> 'I don't remember that the article was very accurate.'[11]

Rycker asks why Querry has come to a leprosarium: 'I suppose the Government – or the Church – have commissioned you to do something out here?' Again Querry stresses that he's retired. The sparring continues: 'I thought a man of your kind never retired.' Querry replies: 'Oh, one comes to an end, just as soldiers do and bank managers.'

Rycker's wife leaves as soon as dinner is over, 'like a child after the dessert', and Rycker suggests that she has gone to write in her journal about the arrival of their distinguished guest. He admits that in the early days he would look at his wife's diary. 'I remember one entry: "Letter from mother. Poor Maxime has had five puppies." It was the day I was decorated by the Governor, but she forgot to put anything about the ceremony.' Querry gently supports her:

> 'It must be a lonely life at her age.'
>
> 'Oh, I don't know . . . To be quite frank, I think it's a good deal more lonely for me. She's hardly – you can see it for yourself – an intellectual companion.'

Rycker continues complaining, now about spiritual matters which the seminary laid in his mind in deep and fixed tracks. Rycker has to drive many days to the leprosarium, to find only unsatisfactory fathers

> 'more interested in electricity and building than in questions of faith. Ever since I heard you were here I've looked forward to a conversation with an intellectual Catholic.'
>
> 'I wouldn't call myself that.'

'In the long years I've been out here I've been thrown back
on my own thoughts . . . [And then Rycker reveals what he really
wants to talk about.] I've read a great deal on the subject of love.'
    'Love?'
    'The love of God. Agape not Eros.'

Very soon Rycker gets down to his own concerns, as if his sense
of self disappears unless he proves he has problems, while Querry
watches the 'thin figure in a gold-leafed dress move towards the river'.[12]

As the evening wears on Rycker begins to drink heavily. He returns
to his disappointment with the priests. 'At least you listen. The fathers
would already have started talking about the new well they propose
to dig. A well, Querry, a well against a human soul.' Again he complains
of his wife: 'She's ignorant of almost everything . . . she doesn't even
cross herself at meals when I say grace. Ignorance, you know, beyond
a certain point might even invalidate a marriage in canon law.'[13] Querry
reiterates his incompetence in discussing such matters. 'In the moments
of silence he can hear the river flooding down.'[14]

Rycker has tried to teach his young wife the importance of loving
God because if she loved God, 'she wouldn't want to offend Him,
would she? And that would be some security. I have tried to get her
to pray, but I don't think she knows any prayers except the *Pater Noster*
and the *Ave Maria*.' As they talk, she returns. They hear her whistling
for her dog, and Rycker responds: 'That damn puppy . . . She loves
her puppy more than she loves me – or God.'

'I'm not jealous. It's not a man I worry about. She hasn't enough
feeling for that. Sometimes she even refuses her duties.'
    'What duties?'
    'Her duties to me. Her married duties.'
    'I've never thought of those as duties.'
    'You know very well the Church does. No one has any right
to abstain except by mutual consent.'
    'I suppose there may be times when she doesn't want you.'
    'Then what am I supposed to do? Have I given up the priest-
hood for nothing at all?'
    'I wouldn't talk to her too much, if I were you, about loving
God,' Querry said with reluctance. 'She mightn't see a parallel
between that and your bed.'
    'There's a close parallel for a Catholic,' Rycker said rapidly.[15]

Querry brings the evening to an end by stressing he has to be up early
the next morning to get the next ferry. His last thoughts spell out

Rycker's nature. The night thick with frogs and Rycker's croaking phrases: 'grace: sacrament: duty: love, love, love'.[16]

★

Initially, Rycker is a strong supporter of Querry, holding the view (not apparent in the passage above) that Querry is given to self-sacrifice. This is because Querry entered the jungle to look for his missing servant Deo Gratias, finding him lying in a ditch, too heavy to move. When Querry tried to go to the fathers for help, Deo Gratias 'raised a stump and howled, and Querry realized that he was crippled with fear'.[17] He did not abandon him.

Staying the night beside the hapless servant gives Querry a great reputation, promulgated by Rycker, who suggests that Querry 'may well be the greatest thing to happen in Africa since Schweitzer' simply because he has sought and comforted a runaway leper. Rycker exaggerates the real story, claiming that Querry 'spent the whole night with him in the forest, arguing and praying, and he persuaded the man to return and complete his treatment. It rained in the night and the man was sick with fever, so he covered him with his body.'[18] Later Rycker will become Querry's enemy.

So where does Rycker come from? At least one aspect of his character comes from the 'odd Dominican friar' already mentioned. Although a tormented spirit Rycker, of course, is not a homosexual. Rather, he is the product of Greene's creative alchemy, a melding of encounters and experiences, a touch of this, a dash of that. When Rycker first meets Querry, he recognises him from a photograph in a ten-year-old copy of *Time*. Dr Lechat recalled to me a similar real-life episode:

> On a Sunday we drove to the interior to visit an old veterinarian, a former colonial official turned planter. A primitive house on a small peninsula on the edge of a lake, a charming wife, much younger than he, nice children . . . In the colonial environment, it was perfectly normal on a hot and empty Sunday to go 200 kilometres, say hello and stay for lunch.
>
> I introduced Mr Graham (I never used his full name). When she had brought a bottle of beer, the wife glanced at Greene, growing a little restless. She turned to me, then to Graham: 'But you are . . . are you not . . . ?' She signalled to the husband. 'You know, this is . . .' He could not care less, the old veterinarian. A kind person, very open, but more concerned with the growth of coffee-beans than with writers. He had probably never heard of Greene, *The Power and the Glory*, *Brighton Rock*, or any trifles of that sort.

Then he suddenly stared at Greene, as if in a fit, speechless. 'But you were once on the cover of *Paris-Match*, were you not?' One of the kids was dispatched into the bedroom to rummage among old issues of *Paris-Match*. (Our host had the complete collection of *Paris-Match* for the last 15 years. 'For the children, when they go to college.')

Actually Greene was never on the front cover of *Paris-Match*, but he had been on the cover of *Time*, and in describing a young Querry, Greene is describing himself – appropriate given the parallels between Querry and Greene.

Greene assures us that Rycker is not based upon anyone he met at the palm-oil factory, which is true, yet I suspect one source. On 3 February 1959, Greene writes in his 'Congo Journal' that a man came to see him 'at the end of my siesta . . . He had written a novel . . . and wanted advice about an agent. Is there any part of the world, in the most remote corner, where an author who is known will not encounter very soon one who wishes to be a writer?'[19] The following day, the aspiring author returned, and Greene tells us no more than that he is 'pursued' by the writer, 'who now tries to exercise a kind of spiritual blackmail'. In a footnote, Greene remarks that 'for years . . . I found myself hunted by people who wanted help with spiritual problems . . . Not a few of these were priests themselves. I can only attribute to the heat my irritation with this poor [man] and to the fact perhaps that I was already beginning to live in the skin of Querry, a man who had turned at bay.'[20]

Perhaps the writer's 'spiritual blackmail' was the seed for the novel's treatment of the theme, which in turn grew into Rycker. However, there is nothing in the published 'Congo Journal' that indicates what Greene means by 'spiritual problems'. In the proof copy of the 'Congo Journal', there's a letter from an aspiring writer which irritated Greene – a letter, I might add, which would not have bothered others, but rather would have elicited sympathy. But Greene's irritation might have contributed to his creating a Rycker.

Dear Mister Greene, I thank you for the addresses of literary agents you have given me.

I am sure the Fathers and Sisters and especially your work will take most of your time, but if you still have a few minutes to spare I would like to talk to you once more about religion. I have lost mine . . . and I don't see how I will ever be able to come back to it . . .

I wished I could be of any use to you . . . Could I show you around the . . . mission . . . ? Very sincerely yours (I am not a reporter . . .)[21]

Rycker, though he has a young wife, has no children. But both he and the letter writer have spiritual problems to lay on another's lap – and so has Father Thomas. Turning 'Rycker' into a palm-oil factory manager was a necessary disguise. Querry listening to Rycker is Greene listening, not to one sad letter, but to hundreds of letters from troubled souls yearning to be heard. Greene gave attention to many, but lending an ear to others did not necessarily reflect a natural sympathy for the speaker.

Another source, and perhaps the most fascinating, concerns the 'innocent', child-like young woman, and even Rycker himself. I believe they are based in part on Yvonne and Jacques Cloetta, whom Greene would soon meet. Yvonne was to finish up as Greene's longest-lasting lover, staying until Greene's death, her innocence all gone. We will learn more in Chapter 33.

He struggled with *A Burnt-Out Case* in the early years of his secret relationship with Yvonne, and with his limited knowledge of Jacques, Greene, feeling guilty from the beginning, was a bit relieved to learn of Jacques's nature. We know that Jacques sometimes said unpleasant things – who doesn't? – but my first impression of him comes from one of Greene's dreams. The forceful directness of a Rycker is reflected in the dream Greene had on 1 April 1967 in which Greene is put through an inquisition, though Jacques is more kindly. 'Are you a good neighbour?' Greene answers: '"A neighbour, yes, but not a good man." He began to talk of my books and said, "You must run out of friends on whom to base characters . . . I saw he suspected I had used Y[vonne] and perhaps himself."'[22]

*

Inevitably, people will look at a celebrity as a prize goose, a beauty, or a genius. Greene, though grim and gritty, was also nearly always good-mannered, gentle and shy. He disliked being noticed, and to be tracked down in the Belgian Congo was precisely what he did not want, and feared most when it happened. He hated uncalled-for (and in his mind, false) adulation.* Greene believed it imperative that a writer not stand out, and endeavoured all his writing life to blend in. He managed well at Yonda. Dr Lechat recalls:

---

* An acquaintance of mine encountered Greene in Piccadilly and asked for his autograph. (Greene's photograph had appeared in *Look* magazine on 6 September 1955 in a feature called 'MEN WHO FASCINATE WOMEN'.) Greene refused. By the end of the street, Greene had capitulated, but said, after he handed back the signed book: 'It won't do you any good', probably thinking he would try to sell it.

The fathers went their way . . . [and] I went my own way. At times, habits overlapped – for the meals, the pre-dinner rest on the verandah at the fathers' or an evening at my house with my wife and the children. Nobody asked questions, each of us being engaged in his own task. This, when one comes to think of it, is quite remarkable.

Everybody should have been on the defensive, being exposed to such a formidable observer, one who was perhaps even preparing a book (although he did not miss an opportunity to say that the novel was not going well and that the book would abort before even being started, which I am convinced was true at the time). Nobody cared. He was the opposite of a journalist, and he inspired great confidence.

This trust was not, of course, misplaced. The explanation for it, as far as I can judge, was his perfect integration in whatever routine there might be, or however unusual the situation (and perhaps preferably when the situation *was* unusual).[23]

Greene wanted to be the observer, not the observed. He needed to see individuals unencumbered by their expectations of him. He didn't want to be their priest, or their friend. He sought to have the masks off, to 'take upon's the mystery of things/As if we were God's spies'. And Greene, with a writer's precision and deftness, took upon himself (as great novelists do) the very mystery of things.

18

Parkinson's Dis-ease

My friend, that felt like a Judas kiss.
— NORMAN SHERRY

O DDLY enough, it was more tragedy that was needed in *A Burnt-Out Case*'s secret leper world where the character Querry had so unpredictably arrived. And tragedy came in the shape of a journalist. Sly chance brings him to the colony in the Congo.

Montagu Parkinson, a roving journalist constitutionally unable to tell the truth, is the worm in the bud. Sent by a British family newspaper to write about disturbances in a British territory, he arrives too late. He then hears there is trouble in the Congo, but is again too late – and next he hears rumours of the famous Querry. Wanting *something* for his newspaper, Parkinson arrives unheralded at the Yonda leprosarium.

Rycker's lies about Querry, collected and exaggerated by Parkinson, set off a succession of events that culminate in Querry's death. Parkinson, for the sake of copy, makes myths of people's lives, is pathologically a truth-bender, insisting that his articles should 'be remembered like history'.[1] He sends back tabloid stories in an attempt to create a legend – a legend of a saint born in modern times.

*

Were Greene's difficulties with living, breathing journalists so infuriating that he determined to make a caricature of one, with zero integrity and not even a nodding acquaintance with accuracy, as his *deus ex machina* figure?

Greene was characteristically dismayed to find journalists waiting for him when he first arrived in Leopoldville on 1 February 1959. They were ruthless in their pursuit.

After having lunch fourteen floors up in a miniature skyscraper, and afterwards napping 'naked in the Sabena rest-house', he was awakened almost at once. He put on a macintosh, and was confronted by a young woman with such a bad stammer that he was unable to learn what she wanted. No sooner had she left than the press arrived 'in relays'. As we have seen, riots two weeks earlier had been so destructive that nothing could persuade them of any other reason for Greene's arrival.[2] *The Times* report of the uprising in January 1959 is indeed grim (most of the information came from Brazzaville, in French Equatorial Africa), with the casualty list much higher than the Belgians admitted:

> The death roll is now put at 'approaching 200 including several Europeans' and the wounded at some 1,000. First pictures of the riots . . . show extreme violence on both sides. The first target of the African rioters was 100 cars parked outside the Leopoldville zoo. Then they attacked a street of Portuguese shops, looting and burning [other sources suggest 40 shops left burning]. One terror-stricken Portuguese shot his wife and daughter and then committed suicide.

Even in Douala the reporters were after him. One, who was also a priest, managed an interview (no doubt because he was a priest) and Greene told his friend Lechat:

> I . . . felt extremely annoyed because I am reported as saying that I preferred the little leproserie of Dibamba to those in the Belgian Congo – better built, industrialized and less human! I am quoted as saying that I would have liked to have passed a fortnight at Dibamba. Needless to say I said none of these things – in fact I was rather repelled by the atmosphere of Dibamba. The journalist in question was a Jesuit priest and a poet, so apparently even a priest becomes a liar when he takes to writing for the press.[3]

Did Greene decide that these swarming locusts had to be punished for pestering him? Could Parkinson be a manifestation of generalised anger (as is Father Thomas) who has no particular individual source?

★

Greene makes the character Montagu Parkinson physically large, a loathsome slug, grotesquely fat, sweating profusely – a 'tub of guts'. He arrives unexpectedly, with a slight fever, a touch of malaria. The open door of the ship's cabin reveals the 'naked body of a very fat man. His neck as he lay on his back was forced into three ridges like gutters and the sweat filled them and drained round the curve of his head on to the pillow.'[4] Six men are needed to lift him and he wants a photograph of himself as he is taken ashore: 'Get as much atmosphere in as you can – you know the kind of thing, black faces gathered round looking worried and sympathetic.'[5]

As a journalist, Parkinson is profoundly careless about his facts; he employs instead the graphic distortions he feels his readers want, fables passed off as truths. On his Remington typewriter, he mimics the style of Conrad's *Heart of Darkness*, evoking the memory of the great explorer Henry Morton Stanley: 'The eternal forest broods along the banks unchanged since Stanley.'[6] From his bed in the cabin Parkinson speaks of the 'white man's grave', to which Querry, ever unromantic, with cold rebuke and a dry dislike similar to Greene's, responds: 'Your geography's wrong. This is not West Africa.' Parkinson retorts: 'They won't know the bloody difference.' Informed by Querry that 'Stanley never came this way', Parkinson repeats: 'They won't know the bloody difference', and then remarks casually: 'Oh well, if I hadn't had this malaria, I daresay I'd have had to invent it. It gives the right touch.'[7]

On the typewriter, his story partly written, lie follows lie: Parkinson struck down by both tsetse flies and mosquitoes; Parkinson carried ashore unconscious; Parkinson waking to find himself a patient in a leper hospital 'Where once Stanley battled his way with Maxim guns'. When accused by Dr Colin of telling lies, he answers: 'It's more than the truth . . . It's a page of modern history. Do you really believe Caesar said "*Et tu, Brute*"? It's what he ought to have said and someone on the spot . . . spotted what was needed. The truth is always forgotten.'[8]

Querry recognises that Parkinson cannot be insulted or shamed: 'Virtue had died long ago within that mountain of flesh for lack of air. A priest might not be shocked by human failings, but he could be hurt or disappointed; Parkinson would welcome any kind of failing. Nothing would hurt Parkinson or disappoint him but the size of a cheque.'[9] Querry challenges Parkinson to write the truth, and goes on to reveal it in all its grotesque unpleasantness. Even Parkinson admits that Querry is 'a cold-blooded bastard'. But though Parkinson now knows the truth about Querry, he will not tell it. Truth doesn't sell newspapers. His story must be chivalric, romantic.

★

On publication of *A Burnt-Out Case*, the journalist Peter Forster of the *Daily Express* predicted 'a lot of guessing in Fleet Street about the model here'.[10] There was indeed a lot of guessing, for enmity thrived between Greene and certain *Express* journalists whom he thought of as operating like the gutter press. But Greene's model was never discovered. Who could he be?

Could it have been Greene's old sparring partner John Gordon?

Unlikely, for Gordon was honourable, and was never a roving foreign correspondent: he stuck to his editor's desk at the *Sunday Express*. Greene could rightly argue that the *Daily Express* and the *Sunday Express* wouldn't print anything remotely risqué. The story which Querry offered Parkinson was one of cruelty to women, and would never be published by that newspaper. Nothing suggests that Gordon shared any of Parkinson's physical attributes, or his disdain for facts.

So I widened the search and looked at Greene's friends, and one in particular: Ronald Matthews. Matthews had never visited a leper colony. He was, in his early days, a fine journalist, but as opportunities and finances receded he had to take any assignment for any sum, and he made the mistake of writing a book about Greene, the very title of which irritated its subject: *Mon Ami Graham Greene*.

Greene refused Matthews permission to publish in English, allowing only a French edition, which appeared in 1957. Why did he forbid his friend to publish his book in the language in which it was composed?[11] In a strictly legal sense, Greene could not forbid publication, but I suspect that his fame and future usefulness made Matthews afraid to cross swords with him. According to Matthews's son, Greene absolutely hated *Mon Ami Graham Greene*.

> Graham . . . made it a condition that it should not be published in English. My father thought the agreement was binding only during his (Ronald's) own lifetime so after [my father's] death, I wrote to Graham asking whether that was also his understanding . . . I got a two or three-line note back saying that yes, he did still very much object because it was such a bad book. Can't remember the adjective he used – appalling? horrible? – anyway he made it clear he didn't like it.[12]

Greene's close friend Michael Richey confirmed Greene's attitude: 'I can tell you why Graham would not consent to the Matthews book being published in English. It was, he thought, extremely badly written. He [Matthews], according to Graham, had simply no idea of how to write dialogue . . . Perhaps the French was better than the original in English, in other words the translator was a better writer than the author.' But Richey added: 'It's years since I looked at it but I don't remember anything strikingly bad about the dialogue or anything else.'[13] I ask again, why did Greene hate the book so?

The French edition gives some evidence. Keep in mind that Matthews was writing his book between pub crawls with Greene, and under such circumstances errors accumulate. Matthews employed soft words and flattery to wheedle information out of Greene. Sometimes he used strong direct accounts, even about Greene's other friends – for example Claud Cockburn, whom Greene knew at Berkhamsted and at Oxford, and whose friendship meant a lot. Matthews in his book quotes Greene as calling Cockburn a hypocrite – the occasion is not known.

No doubt Greene felt somewhat betrayed but preventing Matthews's book from being published, except in another country and in another language, and even after the author's death, seems overpunishment. One wonders why Matthews didn't revolt. Given Greene's increasing, and Matthews's decreasing, fame, it was like hitting a gnat with a hammer.

My understanding is that Greene felt Matthews extracted too much out of him too slyly, and that the text went beyond what Greene knew he had said. In my own experience, Greene rarely failed to recall his own words exactly. For example, I suspect that Greene never declared, as Matthews reports in *Mon Ami*, that 'If we never shared the frightful treasures that introspection had dredged up in us, it was maybe because we had both recognised, from one buttonhole to the other, the invisible badge of despair.'[14] This is not the way Greene ever spoke. A doctoral student, Elizabeth Christman, wrote to Greene on 14 March 1971: 'It puzzles me that this book seems never to have been published in English.' And she asks the fundamental question: 'Do you, perhaps, disapprove of Matthews's report of conversations with you?'[15] It is a good question, answered by Greene in a letter of 5 April 1971: 'the book [is] a very poor one and the dialogue quite unreal.'[16]

I'm inclined to think that Matthews was perhaps somewhat careless in reporting Greene's answers to his questions. But Matthews was at one time a good friend and Greene should have corrected his errors, as he had done for others.

Did Greene see Matthews (as Querry sees Parkinson) in Parkinson's mirror? Querry tells Parkinson; 'I can talk to a looking-glass . . . It returns such a straight image. If I talked to Father Thomas as I've talked to you, he'd twist my words.'[17] Querry understands that Parkinson knows the truth – yet the truth will not be published. Parkinson's lies transform Querry's character. After hearing Querry's unpalatable confessions, Parkinson is determined to so overpraise Querry that they'll raise a statue to him by the River Congo. A genuine intimacy develops between the two; each knowing he can speak straight to the other.

If Parkinson does reflect Matthews, there is venom in Greene's portrait out of proportion to whatever Matthews may have done. Matthews had been a fine foreign correspondent for the *Daily Herald* and later for the *News Chronicle*, always in the front line. In this capacity, he entered Ethiopia with the British troops escorting Haile Selassie back from the Sudan; he reported on the British relief of Habbaniya, Iraq, on the recapture of Baghdad, on Syria and Lebanon's liberation from Vichy France. He sent the first reports of the forthcoming abdication of the Shah of Iran (the father of the last Shah). Some ten years after the Second World War, he joined the BBC Arabic department and covered the battle for Bizerte in 1958 and the Algerian War in 1959. Matthews was a respected journalist. Despite this, he never seemed to have enough money. After leaving the BBC, he washed up on the shores of Tunisia, a freelance writer trying to make ends meet.

Perhaps in exchange for stifling the English publication of *Mon Ami Graham Greene*, Matthews tapped Greene for sums of money: it was Greene who paid the school and university fees of Ronald Matthews's son Christopher, first at Downside School and then at Lincoln College, Oxford. It was a seven-year covenant, fulfilled by Greene. When Christopher took a couple of years off between Downside and Oxford and funds ran out, Greene made an extra *ex gratia* payment to cover his last year at university. (This curious arrangement Greene used as a tax write-off.)

Greene could harbour a grudge, but he seemed civil about this particular act of benevolence most of the time. Yet a young child can recognise anger. Once when Christopher was lunching with his father and Greene, Greene presented what Christopher Matthews described as a 'benefactor-enslaved story':

> On one of my days out from prep school [Graham came up with] an idea for a book or a story. The gist of the thing was that character A performs an act of generosity towards character B. But then finds himself entrapped and enslaved by B's abhorrent gratitude. I had the uncomfortable feeling that I, a ten-year-old, was the person that had given Graham the idea for character B.[18]

If Christopher Matthews is right, Greene was being monumentally tactless. I believe Greene never intended to write such a story, but it was an upper-middle-class Englishman's way of letting off steam without directly complaining. Besides, Greene's real target was Ronald Matthews, not the boy. Matthews did not debate the matter (how could he, for it would have meant further embarrassment in front of his son), but he was nobody's fool. He must have caught Greene's less-than-subtle point (his son did, after all) that Matthews was enslaving Greene by his excessive gratitude. Matthews thought he had the measure of the man; he knew what Greene was saying, but he'd rather take the cheque *and* the insult.

Parkinson's comment to Querry that he, Parkinson, is 'beyond insult' could apply to Matthews. He relied on Greene and had to disregard all else to keep his head above water. But Greene fought his own injunction which appears in *The End of the Affair*: 'What a cruel thing it is to humiliate a father in the presence of his son.'[19]

Matthews's letters to Greene generally seek assistance, monetary or otherwise, and are usually laced with praise.

I promised to send a cheque to Downside . . . for Christopher's school fees for the coming year and the extras that are outstanding . . . I wonder whether 'Graham Greene Productions' can see me through with the 400 pounds they did last year, and whether we can work out a pretext for the payment? The only thing I can think of at the moment is a sale of my half-share in the film rights (and t.v. rights) of TO BEG I AM ASHAMED.[20]

This was a book by the prostitute Sheila Cousins (not her real name), ghosted by Matthews, which today can sell at a very high price because it is thought (wrongly) that Greene ghosted it.[21] 'I haven't yet had the time to see your accountant about possible expenses to set against your last year's payment for Christopher,' writes Matthews to Greene. He is proud of Christopher, seeking more than financial support for his boy: 'Once more, I hate worrying you about Christopher. I wish you could see him before he goes back on September 13. He is an extraordinarily attractive and intelligent kid, with the kind of unexpected wit that would appeal to you, and I think you might feel that your money hasn't been thrown away.'[22]

*

Matthews's life in Tunis was a 'terribly hand-to-mouth existence as a stringer'.[23] His only fitful means of employment was translation work, when he could get it. Greene, as a director of The Bodley Head, was in a position to help his friend. Matthews wrote: 'If The Bodley Head had not told my bank manager that [I was involved] in a serious work, I would not have got an overdraft and couldn't have taken my July trip to Algeria in order to bring my work up to date.'[24] Matthews was preparing a book for publication entitled *African Powder Keg*, 'an analysis of the young states of Africa'. He wrote to Greene expressing the hope that this book might 'get [him] a new start in life . . . What I should really like is a staff job as African correspondent for some serious paper for three or four years.'[25] But he didn't have four years, or three. He was dead of a stroke in two.

Something about Matthews ate away at Greene. Matthews was putting him in a position where he couldn't easily say no. Greene's response was not the proposed novel of 'abhorrent gratitude' that young

Christopher remembers, but rather the creation of Montagu Parkinson. Greene called him a 'tub of guts', a deliberate physical exaggeration to prevent his friend from being recognised. Did Matthews recognise Greene's unfair portrait in *A Burnt-Out Case*?

I suspect he did, but he neither confronted Greene, nor did he admit it. At the very least his son received an education thanks to Greene. That itself to Ronald Matthews would have been worth the pain of an unfriendly and perfidious fictional portrait. But one can't help thinking that if Greene had allowed Matthews to publish *Mon Ami Graham Greene* in England and America, he might not have had to approach Greene with his unjustified feelings of inferiority. For whatever reasons, I suspect that Matthews had more or less given up by the time he landed in Tunis, and considered himself a failure. And what father wouldn't go, cap in hand, to help his own son?

★

A year before Matthews's death, extracts of *Mon Ami Graham Greene* were published in the Algerian government party French-language newspaper *L'Action*. Unfortunately, 'when [Matthews] got today's *L'Action*',

> I saw that the captions on the two pictures had simply been mixed up . . . and that the quite appalling representation of me, apparently daring heaven to visit me with its thunders, had been captioned Graham Greene and that the not very flattering but still almost recognisable picture of you had been captioned Ronald Matthews. I offer you on Mejdoub's [the newspaper's editor] behalf the profoundest apologies, and I do hope you won't feel tempted to sue him for libel, because he's a very good friend of mine.[26]

★

It is apparent that Greene changed Matthews's nature when he dreamed up Parkinson – but only somewhat. Matthews tended to be sycophantic, and his book is basically hagiographical, which must be what troubled Greene also.

Parkinson is myth-making *par excellence*, and to much lesser degree, Matthews was myth-making in his book. Greene felt vehemently that in biography, truth alone should survive. He admonished me: 'Tell the truth. If it's for me, fine. If it's against me, fine. But the truth, Norman, else I'll haunt you.' I believed him.

★

Greene was back in Yonda from his visits to the outlying leperosariums by midday 26 February: 'It was nice to run at once into the Lechats and have lunch with them – like coming home.'[27] He found enormous piles of mail and newspapers, some from Catherine. On the back of an envelope he wrote like a jubilant boy: 'Just back & found wire & letters. Do hope my plane's on time! Hurray.'[28]

Greene stayed seven more days at Yonda, visited Coquilhatville twice, and was seen off by the Governor and his wife. (Greene records that the Governor's wife gave him 'lessons on how one should write a novel, showing her method of taking notes for her next work' all of which she'd had to publish at her own expense!)[29]

Greene's first stop was Leopoldville, where, reluctantly, he underwent interview twice. The 'Congo Journal' records: 'Usual trouble with a journalist. Made an appointment for tomorrow evening when I shall be gone.' But the next day, the wily journalist caught up with Greene: 'Forced to give the interview I thought I was going to dodge, and caught a boat at 9.30.'[30]

He was happy to leave for Brazzaville, 'a far prettier, more sympathetic place than Leo'.[31] Greene observed that 'Colonialism [is] in hurried and undignified retreat . . . But one had the feeling all the same of the worst whites mixing with the worst blacks.'[32]

At Douala en route to Paris and Catherine, Greene's old police friend from Indo-China, identified in the 'Congo Journal' as 'B', took him to an hotel. It was what he had been yearning for: 'A genuinely air-conditioned room with a lovely view of palms, forest and water.' In the evening, there were 'pretty, well-dressed women, with good make-up, dancing, gaiety, unknown in an English colony'. Greene ends the 'Congo Journal' with the following evocative scene:

With B. and another man to the Frégate – black prostitutes and a tiny dance floor. Young French sailors standing drinks and dancing with the prostitutes cheek by cheek. One girl of great beauty with sad and humane eyes.[33]

In the manuscript draft I found a small addition: 'I would like to have gone with her but for fear of infection.'[34]

PART 8

The New Master of Farce

19

Graham's Final Success
in the Theatre

If yet I have not all thy love,
Dear, I shall never have it all.
– JOHN DONNE

G REENE attempted to leave Douala early, wanting to travel before
12 March 1959, but there was nothing available. If all went well,
he anticipated getting into London by 8.30 a.m.: 'Maybe I'll be able
to meet your plane! I fly non-stop from Douala–Marseilles.' He was
mindful that he and Catherine were to be together for only three days
(the longest she could arrange to be away from her husband).

They did have their beautiful time together. Sadly, it was but hours,
and it was over. Greene's love life didn't seem good any more, but
because of his play *The Complaisant Lover*, already written and awaiting
rehearsals, his professional life did. The next surviving letter is dated
simply Thursday 6.10 p.m. (probably 23 April 1959). Greene wants to
go away on 18 June, right after rehearsals: 'Shall we spend 2 nights in
Rome? Shall we go to Venice? Let's make plans so that I can get tickets.
So long to be away with you & quiet.'[1]

He'd been back in England for a while from the leper colony. The
play had its premiere in Manchester in late May. Afterwards Greene
sent review cuttings to Catherine: 'I never expected', the *Manchester
Evening News* critic confessed, 'to hail Graham Greene as a writer of
bedroom farce, but there are lines and situations which have the audience rocking in its seats', and, 'There is a moment in the second act
when the husband covers his face and weeps. And all the time he is
sitting on a trick cushion which blares forth: "Auld Lang Syne." The
triumph – for author, actor, and Sir John Gielgud, who directs the play
– is that no one laughed. This was one of the great moments in the
theatre.'[2]

Greene was in the audience and reported that moment to Catherine:
'Breathless hush & not one laugh when Richardson sat on the musical

chair & wept.'[3] Sir Ralph Richardson played the dentist, a bore given to practical jokes and schoolboy puns, who discovers he's been cuckolded by an antiquarian bookseller played by Paul Scofield: 'Curtain calls and thunderous applause left playwright Graham Greene very happy,'[4] said the *Daily Mirror*. And the *Manchester Evening News* stressed that 'the audience liked this well-made play. They shouted for the author. But Mr Greene, watching from the stalls, refused a speech.'[5]

Greene may well have been happy, but he still had a cast-iron reserve that could be a put-off. On 11 June 1959, *The Complaisant Lover* had its second airing at the Royal Court Theatre in Liverpool. In his autobiography, *Not Prince Hamlet*, Michael Meyer recalls how Greene invited him to travel up to Liverpool for the first night, which was also Meyer's thirty-eighth birthday. Greene promised to bring a bottle of Cheval Blanc 1953, the same vintage mentioned in the play, to drink on the train with their lunch. At Euston station they saw Gielgud and the well-known impresario Binkie Beaumont, who was presenting the play. Greene quickly told Beaumont and Gielgud: 'I'm afraid we can't join you for lunch. It's Michael's birthday and I've promised him this wine and there isn't enough for four.'[6]

'*The Complaisant Lover* proved a triumph', but, Meyer tells us, 'none of us could have foreseen that it would be Graham's last success in the theatre.'[7]

★

There comes around this time another rare gap in the Catherine correspondence. Greene writes from Steiermark, Austria, on 5 August 1959, a postcard showing a lovely mountainous village. He starts off with a bit of a grumble: 'Here I am till Sunday. You might send a chap a line – not a word since we *didn't* have a drink in Rome airport.'[8]

The letters begin again on 12 August. The note is unexpected: 'What I think *you* don't understand is that I don't want sexual freedom any more than you want theological freedom. I have it & don't want it . . . What tempts one is a kind of marriage . . . my tie to you, I think, is too great for anything to work. So I too fall back on platonic friendships. They become so dull in time . . . G.' His postscript is more important:

One also wants to be of use to someone as I can't be to you – perhaps I was, if Buzzie [her brother David] is to be believed, the first Achill time. To someone else perhaps one could be a Thomas . . . or a Father Sullivan.

This is all muddled because it's 2 in the morning & I've been drinking with Ralph R[ichardson] & trying to make little alterations in the play, & New York has been on the phone about a new *Living Room*, & I want to have someone other than myself to look after – not with a cheque book or at the end of a phone.[9]

He continues the following morning (Wed. 8.30):

> Shall we soon make plans for Brazil or would you prefer a quiet bungalow at Ochorios [in north-east Jamaica on the Caribbean]? How one is tempted by familiarity, & yet I don't want you to see new things only with other people. Until Thursday. I'll ring you tomorrow.

His perpetual love call goes on. And note the important lines: 'To someone else perhaps one could be a Thomas . . . or a Father Sullivan.' These do not make sense yet, but they will.

His next letter (undated, the envelope stamped 17 August) is written on *Graham Greene Productions* notepaper with two directors listed: Graham Greene and Catherine Walston. Greene is in some fear about Catherine's health:

> I'm so worried about you. You have an enormous pride about not giving way, but sometimes one must give way to avoid a complete breakdown. I'm sure Harry, just as much as I, would put your health before household responsibilities. You can't go on too long – I don't see why you need to go on till the election. No one is indispensable – except emotionally, as you are to me, but *that* doesn't stand in the way of hospital.

But then the tone changes. My guess is that this shift occurs because Greene is by now becoming friendly with the Frenchwoman, Yvonne Cloetta. It is her home (and her husband's) he'll stay in while in Antibes, the town Greene would move to a few years later. He writes:

> I'm off to Paris on Wednesday, & Thursday to Nice. I *had* promised, but nothing except company. If you can be platonic, so can I . . . I shan't be away more than four or five days at the most.

And then a slap across the wrist: 'Don't worry, except that I know you won't.' His suggestion:

> This to me is a passing shadow. What I want to say to you is if your sort of life is making you ill, come away quietly with me for six months & see if that's a better one. I want to live with

you just as much as when I argued with you in the garden at Anacapri in – oh 1947 I think. You'd probably find life with me dull – but give it a trial. Even dullness could be a good thing for you.

Greene seems to be working up his emotions and he speaks about their 'marriage': 'I love you, just as I loved you at Mass in Tunbridge Wells.'[10]

★

On 11 September, Catherine seems about to cancel their holiday: 'I do hope your note doesn't mean that you are changing your mind about Jamaica. You do need a quiet holiday & this time there would be no Anitas or fictitious Americans in the background. Personally I long for it – I've never felt so tired. I hope Paris will have periods of peace, & the boat too.'[11]

Then: 'Surprised and disturbed by a letter suddenly from Anita – the first for a year.'[12] And then two days later, 22 September 1959, Greene sent a letter to Father Caraman: 'My mother died tonight. Could I ask you to say a few masses. I feel there are few people who need them less, but all the same . . .'[13] He also sent Catherine a telegram: 'MOTHER DIED TONIGHT GRATEFUL FOR MASSES LOVE GRAHAM'.[14] He was concerned that the telegram should not awaken her by arriving in the middle of the night – 'I told them not to send it till the morning' – and described how he'd heard about his mother's death: 'I came in at 10 last night, after a nice solitary dinner, & after M. Ionesco, & found my brother had tried to ring me. She had died quite peacefully without coming back to consciousness. Raymond agreed with me that it was absurd to cancel my passage' to New York on the French liner *Liberté*[15] – the vagabond Greene was sailing to New York to meet Irene Selznick, who wanted to produce *The Complaisant Lover* in the US.

It looks from this as if he did not see his mother just before her death, since she died on 22 September and was unconscious on the 11th, and to Catherine on that date he says: 'I'm officially going to Crowborough, but there's not much point as my mother is unconscious, so I'm hiding . . . at Stonor [Park] tonight, & then seeing Vivien on Saturday. Back Saturday night. I leave about 11 on Sunday & I wish you'd ring me for a goodbye.'

In *A Sort of Life* Greene writes of his mother: 'When she was in an untroubled coma before death and I was watching by her bed, her long white plantagenet face reminded me of a crusader on a tomb. It seemed the right peaceful end for the tall calm beautiful girl standing in a punt in a long skirt with a tiny belted waist and wearing a straw boater whom I had seen in the family album.'[16] Perhaps Greene borrowed this impression of her coma from a brother, as he might well not have seen her; Greene was at sea before she was buried.

★

On the *Liberté*, Greene immediately regrets travelling first class: 'I had forgotten the awful servility of room stewards! . . . No one who looks the least interesting, but I have a comfortable cabin, a table to myself. A corner deck chair!'[17] His concern over creature comforts suggests a man older than his fifty-four years. He indulged in gourmet delicacies, and he, the one-time elongated tadpole (once described by J. W. Lambert as a Greene 'from that rangy line of East Anglian brewers . . . very tall and elegant'[18]), is putting on weight.

On the third day, Greene gets restless. He asks for a table by himself, but finds he's 'up against another solitary to whom I have to talk – the daughter of Blériot, the early flyer. Sixty if a day, but oh so flirtatious.'[19]

On board Greene is unfriendly. Efforts normally made for passengers' enjoyment do not appeal. 'A terrible little cocktail party of the captain the second day, & who knows what threatens one tomorrow.'[20] And what, indeed, threatened? 'O God. O Montreal! Cocktails with the purser tonight, & I've only got out of the captain's table for Saturday by using the excuse of my mother's death.'[21]

A fleeting happiness arises only on receipt of a telegram from Catherine and her promise to go on a holiday with him to Jamaica, where he would begin writing *A Burnt-Out Case*. Already, his experiences in the leper colony are six months old. He sends Catherine a telegram by ship's radio: 'SO GLAD FOR TELEGRAM'.[22] He is ecstatic at the prospect of a long stretch of time without the world interfering, where he could write: 'Do make our return in December as late as you can. It would be wonderful to have anyway five weeks *in* our house.'[23] But the question of 'peace' comes up whenever he speaks of a holiday with Catherine now, which must have its own psychological significance: the change he is beginning to see in Catherine, and the change he needs: it is almost as if she were a mother, *his* mother, and that is what he wanted.* In *The Heart of the Matter*, Greene has Scobie (who is almost a clone of Greene himself) describe his own conception of peace: 'Once in sleep it had appeared to him as the

---

* In his early life, Greene did not in any real sense receive a mother's unconditional love – as we have seen in Greene's character Mrs Callifer in *The Potting Shed*. The important mother in Greene's life was his nanny, whom he describes in *A Sort of Life*, her head bent over his bath, her hair in a 'white bun of age'. It was Nanny who lavished on him a warm unquestioned love.

great glowing shoulder of the moon heaving across his window like an iceberg . . . Peace seemed to him the most beautiful word in the language.'[24]

He begins to think about books he'll take to Jamaica: 'I shall bring the first volume of the new life of Proust. Why don't you bring Evelyn [Waugh, *The Life of the Right Reverend Ronald Knox*]? O God now it's almost time to give Mme Blériot her aperitif!'[25]

Greene was to be met by car in New York and then, as he writes to Catherine: 'the rush will begin: she [Irene Selznick] & Binkie [Beaumont] & Monica [McCall, Greene's literary agent] & Mary [Pritchett] and the man who's doing *The Living Room* & old Otto Preminger, I hear, is on my tracks. No time anyway for adventures [one-night stands]!'[26] ('Old' Preminger was two years younger than Greene.)

Writing from the Algonquin, he tells Catherine that he is 'pursued by letters about my mother which I have to answer in longhand & spend 15 cents a time, when I'd rather be writing to those I love. How I wish people wouldn't. They don't seem to realise what a hard hearted Hanna one is when once the thing is over.'[27]

He writes another letter to Catherine on the same day, 30 September 1959. He is busy meeting people. 'Last night I had dinner at Mrs Selznick's with Peter Glenville [director of *The Living Room* and producer/director of *The Comedians*] . . . Saw Mary Pritchett also. Tomorrow back with the McCalls & a couple of matinees (with an eye to casting). Friday I'm promised drinks or supper with my dream girl, Lauren Bacall, & my ancient dream girl Claudette Colbert. Then I may have to go to Chicago to see Ralph Bellamy. What a life in this weather.'[28]

At the top of his next letter (3 October) he writes '55 yesterday! and no wiser', and describes Mrs Selznick's birthday buffet for him: 'a chocolate cake with candles, & Claudette Colbert (a darling), Lauren Bacall (a disappointment), Ingrid Bergman, Margaret Leighton & a strange ghost from the past, Janet Gaynor [then fifty-two, but retired from the screen since 1939]. Some party you'll admit. I liked Ingrid's husband who spoke very warmly of Anita as a "great" actress.'[29]

He continued to worry about Catherine's health, and believed she should have been in hospital: 'It's sad that you haven't kept to your resolution of going into hospital instead of electioneering. Think how much more you would have enjoyed Jamaica if your health had been cleared up first. All this . . . is not right for you in the state you are in & I can't think how Harry allows it.'[30] It was his greatest wish to be writing his next novel in Jamaica with Catherine. Months were going by and he *had* to get started. But now he was in New York to see if Irene Selznick could succeed (as she was determined to do) in placing *The Complaisant Lover* for a run on Broadway. Five days later, when he's been and seen and gone, hating New York's excessive heat, he again refers to writing and Jamaica and Catherine: 'Haven't done a stroke of work except the Waugh review. I need you for that.'[31]

He leaves New York's hot weather to arrive in Montreal at his daughter's, where there is a 'hail disaster': Greene speaks of how 'one went from the humid 80s . . . to a snowstorm & 20°'.[32] On 4 October, a Sunday, 'after mass in the hideous little new church' (is there any description more Greeneian than that?), his daughter drove him into the Rocky Mountains – 'lovely colours, snow, yellow leaves & dark green pines'.[33]

Greene enjoyed Montreal and was developing an affection for things French: 'I do begin to love this city. Wonderful hearing French all round, having French street signs, & European faces moving along the pavement . . . I can imagine living here – except in winter.'[34]

And wherever Greene goes he carries books. On 5 October 1959 he writes to Catherine: 'Reading the 2nd volume of Casanova which is great fun. Much better than the first. Also Josephus's Jewish Wars which I think may be interesting enough to keep for Jamaica.'[35]

'On the plane between Calgary and Toronto', Greene hears the result of the British election. The leader of the Labour party, Hugh Gaitskell, had conceded: 'I felt a little treacherous at celebrating with whisky from my flask, because I know how disappointing it will be for Harry. I only hope he hasn't slipped in because five years of impotent opposition would be awful & he could never resign a marginal seat.'[36] Harry Walston did not try again for Parliament. Two years later, in 1961, he was made a Life Peer.

During Greene's short visit to his daughter's ranch, he was entirely preoccupied with Jamaica: 'I'm so impatient to hear about Jamaica & longing to be there *working, sleeping, loving, drinking, swimming*.'[37] He ends his letter with thoughts of yet another production: 'The new play is moving in my mind & may be a serious competitor with the lepers. A sad comedy. Title: "Can We Borrow Your Husband?" Setting: Cap Ferrat.' Eight years later, the play was no longer a play, but a short story with the title slightly changed: 'May We Borrow Your Husband?' Perhaps Greene never got beyond the first draft, for certainly, as it stands now, it was never in any way a serious contender with *A Burnt-Out Case*, lacking intensity, cynical at a limited social level, inferior Somerset Maugham.

On 30 October, he writes to Catherine, 'with only one week to go before we can be alone, really alone' for one fortnight.[38]

*

The Complaisant Lover, presented at the Globe Theatre on 18 June 1959, was a runaway success in London, a triumph in the provinces. But when it was produced in the summer of 1960 in Sweden, the play (and the author) ran into trouble. In the last act, the husband goes out to the garage quite casually, and gradually it dawns on the wife and lover that the husband may have left them (having received a letter proving her adultery) in order to commit suicide.

The husband has indeed gone into the garage to gas himself, but switches off the engine thinking of the headlines, an act not suitable in a domestic comedy. Michael Meyer recalls the reaction to the play in Stockholm by friends of Anita Björk and her husband Stig Dagerman, who had killed himself in just that way. '[Several Swedish writers] suggested that Graham had drawn the parallel deliberately, to wound either Anita or Stig's memory or both. In Sweden there was a good deal of envy of Graham for his having been Anita's lover.'[39]

Greene was exceedingly disturbed and wrote asking Meyer to assure Anita that nothing could have been further from his mind. Indeed the scene, precisely because it is a comedy, is not portrayed in a way that could suggest that Greene had this secret manoeuvre in mind. Greene to Meyer makes an obvious but important tactical point: 'After all, garage deaths are very common and there was no other form of playing with suicide that the husband could do. Anybody can sit in a car and imagine such a thing but you can't put cyanide in your mouth or a revolver in your ear without becoming melodramatic.'[40]

Meyer argues that:

Unlikely as it must seem to anyone who does not know Stockholm and the petty jealousies that exist in literary circles there (Strindberg, who suffered much from it, called envy 'the Swedish vice'), it was rumoured, I think falsely, that this antagonism was partly responsible for Graham failing to receive the Nobel Prize.[41]

*

But now, months later, Greene had come to New York on board the *Liberté* to plan the production of *The Complaisant Lover* with Irene Selznick, who had loved the play when she saw it at Liverpool. In her autobiography, *A Private View*, Mrs Selznick expressed her admiration for two English writer friends, Enid Bagnold and Graham Greene: 'Enid was drenched in words, while Graham was born edited.'[42] Mrs Selznick was a determined woman, and as it turned out, she needed to be, to bring Greene's play to New York after Binkie Beaumont had offered it to her in the spring of 1959. It wasn't produced on the New York stage until 2 November 1961.

The problem was casting. Greene and Selznick wanted Ralph Richardson, who'd done so stunningly well in London in the part of dentist Victor Rhodes, because of his understanding of farce and of how to play a cuckolded husband in a comedy of sexual manners. But Richardson wouldn't repeat the role. Next, Alec Guinness refused it; the distinguished Frederic March did too. So did golden-voiced Robert Preston, and then Ralph Bellamy, an admirer of Greene. The wonderfully adroit Robert Morley turned it down as well.*

Just getting the play on the road was impossible. Irene Selznick wrote to Greene offering to withdraw, and months later Greene himself sent her a cable: 'LET'S GIVE UP. NO FUN IN RAGBAG'. He followed this with a kind letter: 'I sent you a cable of despair, but I really think we shouldn't bother but call it a day. I'd naturally pay back the advance . . . Let's wait for another play.'43 Mrs Selznick 're-doubled her efforts' and decided on the lead actor for this demanding part – for there were in this farce moments of intense seriousness which, if not played right, could bring the play to its knees: the character of Victor Rhodes had first to be a farcical and rejected figure, later a somewhat sad heroic figure.

★

The play appeared in two great cities: a smash hit in London, a near flop in New York. So what went wrong? Greene did his best. He came to New York and had himself interviewed at length to give his play a good start. This piece was well covered in the *New York Times* on Sunday 29 October 1961 with the heading 'Life and Love: Graham Greene Takes a Triangular View in "The Complaisant Lover"'. Greene said: 'I'd always wanted to do a play in which awful emotional situations and practical jokes were exploding all over the stage at the same time.' The article continued: 'What's more, he said he had a jolly good time doing this one – rattled it off in four months, as opposed to two years' labor on *The Living Room* and a year and a half on *The Potting Shed*.'44

Greene argued against those critics who were always 'dredging for messages'. He took pains to stress that he was basically an optimist. Deploying the phrase 'Greeneland', first coined by Arthur Calder Marshall in 1940 and ever after overused by critics, Greene did make an inspired attempt to persuade his audience of journalists that they

---

* Greene might well have objected because, as he said of Morley playing the part of Dreuther (the character based on Greene's friend Alexander Korda) in the film based on his novel *Loser Takes All*, 'Robert Morley plays only Robert Morley.'

had him all wrong and that, certainly in this play, his was an essentially comic point of view:

> Some critics . . . have this idea of Greeneland, as they call it, as a fictional universe in which all one's characters are either drunken priests or adulterous wives. They call me a pessimist, but I'm not. I have often tried . . . to show the mercy of God. You cannot show it by portraying only virtuous people; what good is mercy to the virtuous? It is in the drunken priests that you can see mercy working. And I call that optimism. But they call it Greeneland, as though it bore no relation to the real world. And yet, one is simply trying to describe the real world as accurately as one sees it.

He further distinguishes between writing for the theatre and writing novels, much preferring for the moment to write for theatre, where one can 'see' the readers. And writing a play is less tiring than doing a novel:

> One lives with his characters for less time. When I was young, writing a book wasn't so bad. I could do one in nine months. Now it takes two years, and at the end of it one is flattened out. With a play, I can write one and a half minutes of playing time a day, and sometimes, when it is going well, two and a half. And I can be finished while I still feel a fondness for my characters.

As to the advantages of novel writing:

> A book is a one-man show . . . When one is writing a play the director says, 'Just write it as you fancy, don't mind how many scenes or any of that business. We'll straighten it all out afterward.' And I don't like that. I like things tighter and neater than that. I don't want somebody else putting right what I've done wrong.

And the difficulty of play writing? 'The dialogue is much harder for me in a play – every line must do so much more work.' In the novel there is 'an embarrassment of riches'.[45]

The part of the cuckolded husband was finally taken by Sir Michael Redgrave, who had been knighted two years earlier. Redgrave had been deservedly successful in classical parts – Hamlet, Macbeth, *Uncle Vanya, Mourning Becomes Electra* – and he was outstanding in films, especially *The Browning Version*. His most intense film role was as a ventriloquist tormented by his dummy in *Dead of Night*.

But perhaps in this play too much was expected of him. Mrs Selznick was convinced that she made an error: 'Not that it was Michael's fault, but he simply was not a good, stout fellow who happened to be a dentist – not remotely.'[46]

All along Greene fretted over the play. Six months before rehearsals, they were still casting. Mrs Selznick was keen for him to stay in New York to help, but privately he wrote to Catherine: 'I don't really care all that much who plays what in NY so long as I don't have a bête noire like Googie Withers they tried to wish on me by cable.'[47] Yet it was Googie Withers who finally played the part of the wife with a lover on the side.

In New York during the latter part of April 1961, he was 'trying to fit everything & everybody in', having a 'tiring time with Mrs Selznick seeing bits of film for casting'.[48] In early October, the play's first night less than four weeks away, Greene was back in town, the first two days exhausting: 'Mrs Selznick met me & drove me to the country (a beautiful little house surrounded by its own wood with a little lake on which I rowed her about!), but she kept me talking till 11.30 (4.30 a.m. our time) & I've lost the habit of sleeping late. Next day Bennet Cerf's to lunch & we "worked" all the afternoon & I only got to the Algonquin at midnight.'[49] And he no sooner arrived at the hotel than his daughter rang up to wish him many happy returns. It was close to midnight on 2 October. He was fifty-seven years old. She also told him he was going to be a grandfather in April: 'Slept badly.'

So even on his birthday, he (and the company) 'worked'. 'Yesterday I went to the run-through – all the small parts good (Dutchman, small boy, girl), but the three principals haven't got it yet, & Redgrave miles from knowing his lines. What the hell! *Tant pis*! I had to talk to them afterwards which I hate – everyone very nervous, then a conference with Glen [Byam Shaw, the director] & I went to bed with sandwiches & milk . . . to be woken . . . from next door by music & arguments which went on till about 3!'[50]

★

Greene stayed for the last rehearsal but not for the first night, as with *The Potting Shed*. He was back home in England by 31 October, and the play's first night came on 1 November at the Ethel Barrymore Theatre. From London he flew to Antibes to stay at the Hôtel La Mer, and from there sent Catherine the first reviews. Howard Taubman's review in the *New York Times* was somewhat disdainful, speaking of it as 'shocking without raising its voice . . . witty without being over-whelming', and whilst granting that the scene in an Amsterdam hotel room was rousing fun, ended with the judgment that it was 'thoroughly thin stuff". He says the cast did a serviceable job: Redgrave 'bumbling and foolish and then weak and wise'; Withers 'handles her two men like a lady'; and Gene Wilder, the valet, 'richly diverting'. Nevertheless he dismissed the play in a paragraph: 'In the English way "The Complaisant Lover" talks about sex without heat and outrages morality with scarcely the tinkle of a teacup. Very English – and a bit tepid.'[51] To Catherine: '*The Times* strikes me as silly & off the mark, probably written by an impotent husband.'[52] But Walter Kerr's first-night report must have pleased: 'One must be deeply grateful to Graham Greene for having such a hopelessly unconventional mind . . . he is stating a brand new truth for the theater . . . that adultery is a great deal funnier if you will only take it seriously.'[53]

★

In 1976, when I became Greene's biographer, he told a story at dinner at his sister Elisabeth's home in Crowborough. I was the only member of the intimate group not family. We listened avidly. He recalled how he hadn't stayed for the play's first night, but during final rehearsal, he witnessed a bizarre situation: Michael Redgrave failed to show, unheard of for a leading man:

> Something must have happened to Michael. He didn't turn up and we were all very worried. Had he taken ill? Had he had a heart attack? We telephoned his room but didn't get an answer. We rushed over to his hotel and we were told he had not come out of his room or responded to telephone calls. We got the janitor to take us up to his room and open his locked door. We anticipated that Michael was ill, and thinking of how we'd have to telephone his wife and children in England *and* find a hurried replacement.
>
> We opened the door and there was Michael, in good health, but struggling with the fact that he was roped to his bed and unable to release himself.

And Graham ended his after-dinner story: 'He'd had an argument with his boyfriend [who had] left him tied up as his answer to their disagreement.'* A not so complaisant lover.

---

* A director friend of mine told me that the catchphrase in the industry at the time, in answer to requests for Redgrave to take a part, was 'He's all tied up.'

PART 9

Incessant Wanderer

20

Round the World
in Forty-Five Days

Man needs escape as he needs food and deep sleep.
— W.H. AUDEN

THE play over, Greene was still counting on Catherine and Jamaica, to work on *A Burnt-Out Case*. When it seemed Catherine didn't wish to go, he offered Tahiti as an alternative. Catherine was still reluctant, so he sought to go with Michael Meyer.

Once the trip had been decided, Greene began watching the newspapers to see what was happening in the South Seas. He discovered with growing pleasure the anarchic state of affairs that might be found in Papeete, the Tahitian capital: 'We won't get entirely away from politics in Papeete,' he wrote to Meyer, and enclosed a cutting about the Prime Minister of French Polynesia, 'sent to prison [for] planning to set the town of Papeete on fire last year'.[1]

Four days later, on 30 October 1959, Greene sent Meyer an itinerary, an exercise which always raised his spirits.

The better itinerary seems to be the one which leaves England by BOAC on December 20th, first stop Sydney December 22nd at 1045 going on to Nandi in the Fiji islands at 1600, arriving 2215. We spend a night at Nandi, go on to Suva spending 24 hours in Suva on December 23rd and arrive in Papeete at 1400 on Christmas Eve. We are first class in all these flights except the Nandi Suva one ... Do you think we should stop off for Christmas in Fiji and go on to Papeete afterwards or do the whole journey?

He is leaning towards Papeete because he feels that, 'even though we are probably stuck in a hotel for Christmas Day, Christmas with the French is one degree better than Christmas Day with the British'.[2]

Before Tahiti came off, Greene did finally persuade Catherine to come on a short holiday in Jamaica at Noël Coward's home. The love which had burnt for almost eleven years was only flickering now, and he begins a letter to Meyer with an intriguing first sentence: 'The Dutch widow sounds interesting. Do get an introduction from Collins & write ahead. She might meet us at the airport.'

And continuing his letter from Jamaica, Catherine beside him: 'In spite of the pleasant life here (& my 500 words a day) my mind strays an awful lot to Douala [Yvonne] – not to speak of Stockholm [Anita]. Perhaps the Dutch widow is the real solution!'[3] Then an afterthought written on the surviving envelope: 'Do you want to see a private show of *Our Man in H* on Dec. 17?'

Once back in London, their short holiday over, he writes offering her the world (quite literally): 'I so long for you & miss you. I know now there's no substitute, but I don't believe the *good* things have changed. We have only had a shy (but to me lovely) fortnight together – let's have a month before long. One slips so easily back . . . Dear Catherine, Come with me to Brazilia or Tahiti or Capri or anywhere. We are nearly together again – put out your hand.'[4]

It was now nine months since Greene had first met the young Yvonne Cloetta in Douala. She was married, like Catherine. One suspects at the very least he must have been closing in on her.* After his monumental mistake in telling Catherine about Anita, was this a wiser Greene?

*

Meyer and Greene at last arrive in Sydney, Australia, with five hours' freedom before flying out again. To Catherine: 'A curious charm & some lovely little coloured houses with wrought iron balconies & a nice restaurant of the Victorian kind & of course the [Sydney] Bridge.'[5]

The two travellers were genuine friends, but the tiny beginnings of irritation were stirring in Michael Meyer:

> We travelled first class; I think my ticket, right round the globe, cost around £650. Graham had apologized for not being able to leave earlier, saying in his defence: 'We don't need to waste time in Singapore and Bangkok and such places' – rather a blasé obser- vation, I thought, for I would have loved to revisit them in his company, and also to see a little of Australia, where I had never been. But no; we had to be in Tahiti by Christmas.[6]

---

* This letter is dated 16 November 1959. Has a love affair with Yvonne already begun, or is it simply a secret attachment in Greene's mind at this stage? It *had* begun.

Meyer did persuade Greene to take a taxi ride around Sydney, and to eat 'a fine lobster lunch' at the Rex Hotel.

They were then off to the Fiji islands, travelling on Qantas. Greene speaks of the airport at Djakarta, and of 'an awful Vera Barry type of woman on the plane who is giving us useful information about Fiji & cockteasing two quiet Americans'. He ends his short letter to Catherine with the phrase: 'I love you & miss you & wish you were here & not Michael – though we haven't quarrelled yet.'[7] An ominous note.

Greene and Meyer arrived in Fiji exhausted, only to find the agent had made no further reservations. (To add to Greene's chagrin, the lock of his brand-new suitcase was already falling off, and his gold chain, given him by Catherine, had broken.) They'd anticipated spending the night at Nandi and then flying on to Suva. It wasn't to be. So they decided to go by car: 'Drove 20 miles around midnight & found rooms here'[8] at Lautoka. Greene was 'too tired to go to midnight Mass in Suva. The streets were full of woolly pates wearing masks & tinsel in their hair & garlands – all perfectly friendly, although the English had barred the door of their club with a table. Then last night on the way to the airport we passed a succession of huge churches crammed for midnight Mass again, everybody, men & women, dressed in white. Returning at 5 a.m. one saw them still drifting home.'[9]

'I so loved our last days with all the films & our last night & our last drink in your flat. I wanted badly to cry. But though I miss you I no longer want you to be with me. You wouldn't like this.' It was, he added later, 'the dreariest Christmas Day I've ever had'.[10]

Greene (to Catherine) and Meyer (in his book *Not Prince Hamlet*) speak of crossing back and forth over the International Date Line. Michael Meyer takes up the comic story:

> To get to Tahiti from Fiji, we had to take a New Zealand Airways flying-boat to Samoa and spend a night there [where Robert Louis Stevenson ended his days].

This entailed crossing the International Date Line, hence going back one day. On Christmas Eve they left Fiji and crossed into 23 December, but then:

> The pilot learned that the sea was too rough for us to land at Satapuala, so we turned and, in due course, found ourselves back in Fiji for our second Christmas Eve. Next morning a huge chambermaid woke us with cries of 'Merry Christmas!' Off we went

again in the seaplane, entered our third Christmas Eve, and in due course landed successfully at Satapuala.[11]

Greene, the man who hated Christmas, was getting his fill. But he soon changed his mind and described to Catherine things she would have loved: 'Drinking planter's punches above coral islands of incredible beauty in a nice slow flying boat.'[12] Greene did a diagram of the deep blue, then the peacock blue as one approaches the island, then white surf and bright yellow sand and in the centre of the island imposing trees. They went by car to Suva, which Greene found stunning; the food cheap:

> There's a little railway at Lautoka for taking sugar cane – passengers twice a week free of charge . . . oranges 12 for a shilling; tomatoes four gallon tin for a shilling . . . pineapples may cost 2d . . . Little girls sell huge prawns beautifully wrapped in banana leaves for a shilling a parcel by the roadside. All around the island . . . is the white circle of foam on the coral reef, so that everywhere the sea is quiet . . . and warm.

Then he mentions the chambermaid 'with hairy legs – she giggled all the time & when I said the day was very warm she seized my shoulder & squeezed it'. He had a drink

> with the Dutch widow who owns a copra island & then with the speaker of the Senate who has a police guard. The chief pilot of the airline turned up wearing a big Mexican hat & a false beard – Alec Waugh had warned everyone of my approach.[13]

On Christmas Day, Greene is stuck in Apia, forced to endure another Christmas Day: 'We started from Suva on time, but turned back half way because of a tornado in Samoa.'[14]

Greene and Meyer stayed at Aggie Grey's – she was renowned as 'one of the great characters of the South Seas'. Greene described the guest house as 'a terrible place like something out of Simenon'.[15] Meyer reports there were 'no mosquito nets . . . We had a nasty dinner, and a bad night on the uncomfortable beds, devoured by mosquitoes.' They had been told by Aggie, a tall old lady whose commanding presence seemed in the manner of royalty, that though dinner was bad, lunch would be 'special'. Meyer is hilarious: 'In due course and with ceremony, the feast began. The starter was a tinned crab cocktail, tasting mainly of tin with an undertone of rust, swathed in an evil bottled mayonnaise. This was followed by an indeterminate, dark-fleshed and sinewy bird.' They both thought there would be nothing to drink. There was, and the bottle claimed to be Armagnac, but it was not the colour of Armagnac. 'Graham's expression as it was poured into his glass was something to behold. It tasted like syrup of figs, a laxative much prescribed in his and my childhood, when all medicines were nasty to discourage malingering. Then the pudding arrived. This was a sickly white, like spotted dick, undercooked and suety. Graham and I agreed that we could not remember a nastier meal, even at school or during the war (though New Zealand Airways must have surpassed themselves next day, for in a little paperback volume of Gauguin's paintings which he bought me as a New Year's gift, Graham wrote: ". . . in memory of a terrible Christmas at Aggie Grey's and a worse Christmas meal Samoa–Papeete").'[16]

★

Greene went to the home of his mother's cousin, Robert Louis Stevenson: 'Yesterday in pouring rain I visited Valima', which he tells Catherine was 'very beautiful & a famous waterfall'.[17] It was too muddy to reach Stevenson's grave on the hill. Meyer noticed that the house had a 'grate for the open fire which [Stevenson] needed even in that climate'.[18]

Greene returns to what he sees as an extraordinary fact: 'Michael & I have not yet quarrelled, but it will be a severe test if we don't get off at 2 a.m. tonight. Between 2 a.m. & 4.30 are the only possible hours because we have to reach an atoll in the Cook Islands by daylight . . . Wind, swell & visibility all have to be right. One feels one might be stuck in this dreary spot for days. Tahiti will have to be awfully good':

> This looks like the last chance to visit a reasonably unspoilt Tahiti. The flying boat will be discontinued next year as they are building an airstrip & thousands of tourists will pour in from San Francisco. Already business men from Los Angeles & Honolulu are planning big hotels. It's sad. If we like Tahiti it will be sadder still.

It is very odd, says Greene in his letter to Catherine, that

> I'll have had 366 days this year. Yesterday your time was 12 hours earlier than mine & today your time is 11 hours ahead. Very confusing.[19]

On 26 December they still hadn't reached Tahiti because of the weather, and they 'fell into a tourist trap of dancing girls in a chief's hut. A lot of whisky before lunch cheered me up, but I'm no longer awfully looking forward to Tahiti. I fear it may turn out to be little better.'[20]

They got to Tahiti through the skill of the pilot who 'decided to fill up the [flying] boat with "gas" & fly direct to Tahiti – 1500 miles. We started at 7 a.m. It was the last chance for days, as time & tide would be wrong now for a night take-off.' And though he's surely travel-weary, he doesn't fail to notice an alluring woman: 'Just in front of me in the plane is the villainous American who is building a big hotel with his charming little Tahitian wife with eyes rather larger than her bottom.'[21]

They arrived fifty hours late – that's how they celebrated a second Christmas Day.

*

On the last day of the year, Greene was much happier and his letter to Catherine is full of their love: 'Next year [the following day] we'll have been "together" from 1947–1960. Dear dear dear, what a long time since Achill & yet in some ways such a short time. Only I miss the red dressing gown.* One day you must get another.'[22] He was happy because he was writing hard, reporting 700 words by 8.25 a.m. for the second day in a row, and Michael not even up.

> There is a flamboyant tree in the garden & the shape of Moorea across the water, behind the house mountains & across the flat warm lagoon full of bright blue fish darting in & out among the coral, the surf along the reef. The only bad thing a large cat in the kitchen last night, & I have to keep up a continuous fight not to be caught up socially – I throw Michael to the wolves. I invented a touch of sun to escape a Rotary dinner & of course that was the high spot in the local paper & so the shopkeepers inquire after one's health.[23]

Greene and Meyer had found a bungalow ten miles out of Papeete – the one Marlon Brando occupied during the filming of *Mutiny on the Bounty*. Meyer remembered finding Greene up early, keeping to a strict routine of rising at 6.45 and, after breakfast, sitting in a window seat

---

* On Achill, Catherine wore a red dressing gown which, as Graham told Vivien, was the sexiest image of any woman he had ever seen. What other man would share this with his wife? Well, perhaps Hemingway who went one step further and fondled other women in front of at least two of his four wives; and Joseph Kennedy, who is said to have taken a famous mistress home for dinner with the family.

on the verandah, with large double sheets of lined foolscap. Sitting on the verandah it must have seemed as if they were a mile apart, it being 72 feet long with three different suites of furniture.

> He wrote in longhand with a fine pen in a very small, almost illegible script, for two hours each day; no more, no less. In those two hours he would write seven to nine hundred words, the equivalent of two to three printed pages . . . At 9 a.m. he would stop. This was when I got up, and as I walked along the verandah to the shower room he would look up and say, somewhat complacently I felt: 'Nine hundred words this morning,' or, even worse, 'Finished my work for the day' – a depressing remark with which to be greeted when I hadn't yet begun and the thermometer was climbing towards ninety.

Then Greene would read for the remainder of the morning – history or a novel, maybe a detective novel – while Meyer

> struggled at my end of the verandah trying to translate Strindberg's *The Ghost Sonata* (and, later, Ibsen's *The Wild Duck*), incongruous texts in the sweltering heat with the Pacific twenty feet away.[24]

Greene's method was to not go out, confining his activities to his book. But this time Catherine was not there to fend off others so that he could write. This he had to do for himself, as he comically tells Catherine:

> Now again I wish you were with me. I realise now – apart from making love & reading & bathing & going to movies – what a protection you are. Here I'm rapidly getting the reputation a) of being a homosexual b) impotent c) sick or d) a religious fanatic.
>
> Next door is a very useful woman – Tahitian metisse 30 years married to an American who talks like a travelogue on the screen. She bought all our basic foods, but alas while looking like a handsome aunt she considers herself highly desirable, kisses one on the cheeks at all times with tender squeezes & sympathetic glances & wants to go for a walk in the mountains. The Tahitian doctor though is nice, & so is [Bengt] Danielsson of the Kontiki [expedition] and his wife. But I want to work & bathe & read & nothing else.
>
> We have a good male cook (a cripple) & a harmless maid – who is obviously puzzled because we don't attempt to sleep with her.
>
> A hurricane has wrecked the New Hebrides & perhaps we shall get a flick of its tail – so far it's been uninterrupted sun.[25]

On the envelope he tells her that he and Michael are staying four kilometres from where Gauguin had his hut.

Into January, Greene begins to get bored and troubled. His 3 January letter is five pages long because the post from Tahiti is only once a week. His first point is that he'd have been very happy in Tahiti if only Catherine had been there too, that a man's company cannot keep boredom at bay – 'never never never have I been bored in your company, excited, interested, happy, unhappy, irritated, angry, lecherous, loving – never bored'.

★

Greene is thrilled at the amount he is writing. He usually averaged 500 words a day (and did no more when he began the novel during his short holiday with Catherine in Jamaica where he completed more than 30,000 words). He's now doing a tremendous amount: 'For better or worse I've already done 3,700 words in 5 days! . . . [and] 4,500 words in six days.'

> I can't believe it's only 2 weeks today that we left. I begin to have erotic dreams. Come back to me, Catherine. There's no opium yet to comfort me for not hearing your voice on the telephone, going to movies with you, sometimes going to bed. How sweet & lovely & exciting you were when you broke the sound barrier [by telephoning him] two weeks & two days ago.[26]

But the next day's letter sounds a danger note: 'Don't be surprised if you suddenly hear that I've given up & am on my way home via San Francisco. In that case I'll finish the book in Brighton or Paris.' And then: '5100 words done in a week, but it doesn't make one cheerful as in Jamaica – nobody in the bed beside me & no drinking companion (I wouldn't have come with M. if I'd known that). Worst of all no opium. How I wish it were Capri & you with me.'[27]

Then after making provisional arrangements to leave as early as 23 January (they had originally planned to stay until 21 February), and after speaking with all the love at his command, he returns to the question of Michael Meyer. 'I'm trying to drive Michael out a week ahead of me. Then I might, of course, change my mind & stay! I better not put in a letter the degree he irritates me – it will make it worse. They are not things, like my cousin's shorts, which one can speak aloud. He has absolutely no sense of modesty & will wander about stark naked looking like a fat white slug. Ugh!' But then Greene backs off and acknowledges: 'However in ten days I'll be free of him & able to contemplate his very real virtues.'[28]

And it is not only Meyer who niggles, as his next line astonishingly admits: 'Something – not M. – which irritates me too is the sexual pressure. Nobody seems to think one can live for a little while without a girl & everyone is anxious to find one a companion. It doesn't seem to occur to them that one may prefer to be alone if one can't be with the person one loves.'

This was on the debit side, but on the credit side was the fact that he'd written 6,400 words in eight days, thus averaging 800 words a day, remarkable for Greene. Again he is radiant with love, and recalls something of the beauty of their relationship and sexual play:

Sometimes we are shy of speaking except with our bodies & on paper – & our bodies not a little (it's part of the fun) & pretend that it's all lust & savagery & not tenderness & love. Dear dear Catherine, all my love always.

In his postscript he writes:

I miss being able to read the book aloud at intervals & I miss being able to grumble to you at the major snags. There's one ahead just now. I'm trying to creep around, & I tell myself that it's the last before the plain sailing starts, but I know it won't be. Friday (today's Wednesday) I shall have passed 40,000.

He can't believe he left London so recently, less than three weeks before: 'I suppose with you everything has gone at normal speed. I shall soon be a very old man at this rate.'[29]

He is happy again with Michael: 'Personal relations go a bit better. Work surges on. If I keep up the present rate, I'll have passed 50,000 before I leave. God knows what the book will look like – it's awfully loose.'[30]

His enjoyment was increasing because of the Danielssons, his wonderful neighbours. He liked them both, and we find him writing to them from England once he'd returned, with British understatement: 'I find I'm missing Tahiti quite a lot.' He can't believe he won't return. (He actually did with Catherine the following year.) He offered the Danielssons the use of his London flat, no small recompense for their many kindnesses: 'I do hope that I shall be in England when you turn up and please don't hesitate if I am not there to borrow the flat. I can't help feeling that you will be more comfortable here than in a hotel.'[31]

And we can see how the Danielssons took care of him: 'Yesterday Mrs Danielsson & a Tahitian dancer – the girl friend of a dentist (how dentists always come into one's life) – paddled me out to the reef – an extraordinary thing to walk on & there seemed no reason why the great waves always broke three yards away. Then we fished – or rather they fished.'[32]

He speaks of a naval commander who turned out to be quite fun, and was investigating the possibility of a poet's offspring: 'I've unearthed a son of Rupert Brooke – possibly – anyway several of his girl friends – a new page in English literary history.'[33] But it was the Danielssons who gave him a drinking nightlife:

> Friday the Danielssons are giving us a Swedish acquavit party – they are really *very* nice . . . I'm changing my mind a little about Tahiti. I'd love it with you. In this house & the Danielssons' [who] just stroll over for a drink. We'd hire a canoe & make trips to the reef & begin to fish.[34]

By his last letter from Tahiti (22 January 1960) Greene has finished 20,000 words in twenty-five days. Tomorrow he would be off, but by the end of the day he'd found some opium and Meyer speaks of it:

> On one of our last nights, we managed to find someone who could provide us with opium. He was a French doctor, small and wizened, looking remarkably like the Graham Sutherland portrait of Somerset Maugham . . . The doctor greeted us in a long flowered robe. Somewhat to my satisfaction, Graham drew either too slowly or too fast on his first pipe, so that it went out prematurely, while I managed mine in a single deep inhalation. '*Bien, monsieur, bien,*' said the doctor, '*vous avez la disposition*' . . . I remember nothing else of that evening, as is often the way with opium. It was the second and last time I smoked it, an agreeable experience which left no hangover, but one which I have never had any particular desire to repeat.[35]

Greene's account differs:

> Right at the end I dug up some opium. Once very secretive in a dirty little Chinese hovel, but last night a Frenchman brought up the [opium] & we had a party in comfort in my bedroom . . . After the first two pipes I got the real hang & smoked about ten or twelve – slight nausea this morning but a lovely night & Michael has stopped complaining of his ills.[36]

Greene also speaks of the white flower which 'everybody wears . . .

at dinner & even in a crowded hot bar there's no human body odour as a result. Some of the scent is still in the flower.'

So they are leaving, and they should, because the rainy season, expected for the last twenty-six days, has arrived: 'the last two days the surf sounds as loud as an aeroplane & leaps the height of a house on the reef & the lagoon is too disturbed & the current too strong to bathe.'[37]

And in this 22 January letter he ends: 'Dear Catherine, I so love & miss you. Nothing is quite good enough without you. Now I'll seal this up & go & start packing.' But he can't end his letter: 'All love always. I miss you so in my room with two double beds & no one but you will believe one has been a month in Tahiti without a girl or even the desire for one.'[38] His postscript: 'O dear, this book whether good or bad is going to get me into trouble with the Catholic press!'

★

Meyer and Greene spent six happy days in San Francisco. (Apart from San Antonio, Texas, which he'd visited in the late 1930s just prior to his famous trip to Mexico, and many years later, in the 1980s, Washington DC, San Francisco was the only town in America Greene said he liked.) Meyer recalled that Greene's friends took them regularly to different (and very expensive) restaurants, but they themselves were happy at a cheap self-service eating house in Union Square (where the food was tastier). When on their own they 'made a bee-line for Lefty O'Dool's'. Greene admits his pleasure – even if his maths is somewhat suspect:

> I love this place. Very nice people ... Until 4 this morning I was at a beatnik party where the beatnik poet who is half negro, half Jew & half Catholic & very very drunk paid me his highest compliment by saying that I was the only true beat in English literature! Did you know?[39]

★

Graham's daughter Lucy arrived in a two-ton Chevrolet truck to drive her father and Michael Meyer across the Sierra Nevada mountains, a prodigious run, stopping at Reno and then on to Salt Lake City, where Greene and Meyer happily parted company. Michael was to fly back to New York and on to England. Graham was to drive with Lucy to Calgary. They started on 3 February. He jokingly told Catherine he wished he could pick up a divorce at Reno on the way 'but it takes 30 days'.[40] (Given Greene's ardent love for Catherine, we sometimes forget that though he and Vivien were separated, they never divorced.)

At the end of the gruelling journey, Graham felt 'tired, irritable &

old', and wished he were back in Tahiti with the book. To Catherine he wrote:

> San Francisco was . . . amusing; then about 270 miles with M. in the front of the truck – speed sometimes down to 20 because of snow – to Reno. Then our luck turned. After doing 500 miles, lunch & two stops for coffee, in only 10½ hours the truck came to a full stop.[41]

And to Peter Smith:

> We had a fairly good trip back – a little tough the first day to Reno as conditions on the Donner Pass were not too good. We broke down after 500 miles in the great salt desert but with incredible luck the truck broke down within a hundred yards of a garage, the only one for fifty miles . . .[42]

After being towed to another garage where they had to abandon the truck, they went on, tired and frustrated, another forty miles, Greene clinging to the briefcase Catherine had given him and his '20,000 words like grim death', to 'a ghastly hotel full of conventions'.[43] Then the car they travelled in took off with Greene's overnight bag and his washing gear.

Lucy's truck was ultimately repaired and ready to go, and it turned out to be a fine day. Greene was more cheerful, and with reason – a postcard to Catherine reports that his expensive night in an hotel was covered by his win with the first quarter he put into a fruit machine. Two jackpots in succession! Beginner's luck. So, Michael went on his way, and Greene and Lucy arrived safely – and happily – at her Calgary ranch, the world trip over.

★

Thirty-five years later Greene and Meyer's relationship was proclaimed in Waterstone's Hampstead bookshop, in a gladiatorial debate between biographers Shelden and Sherry. (According to the manager the shop had to be hosed down afterwards.) Meyer was there when Shelden called Greene anti-Semitic. 'BALLS!' shouted Meyer from the floor. 'I was his friend for forty years. As a Jew, I know that if he'd been anti-Semitic, we wouldn't have been friends for forty minutes. Nor would we have gone round the world together.'

21

I Shall Arise and Go Now

What of soul was left, I wonder, when the kissing had to stop?
                                              – ROBERT BROWNING

B Y 13 February 1960, Greene had returned to the Algonquin in
New York. He saw his agent Monica McCall, along with Mary
Pritchett and Carmen Capalbo, and watched a tape of a televised
version of *The Power and the Glory*: 'not at all bad, [directed] by Capalbo'.*

He was back in London the next day, and got down to masses of
mail, telling Catherine Walston: 'I have just done my 22nd letter (more
to come) and had lunch with Max [Reinhardt] on Bodley Head business.'[1] And he found an account of himself in William Hickey's 27
January column in the *Daily Express*:

RIDDLE OF THE VANISHING MR GREENE

Saying little to his friends of his whereabouts, author Graham
Greene has faded somewhat mysteriously into the fastness of the
South Sea islands.

He was last heard of in Tahiti with his friend Mr Michael
Meyer – the translator of Ibsen and Strindberg – with whom he
travelled out.

But Mr Meyer is now on his way home. And of Mr Greene
there is no sign . . .

___

* Carmen Capalbo told me in April 2002 that the morning after the first showing, the TV
station's phones were jammed with complaints from Catholics angry that such an 'anti-
Catholic' play was broadcast. It was to be repeated for six more nights as part of 'The Play
of the Week'. They rushed Capalbo to the studio, where he taped an introduction explaining
that Greene was a 'world-famous Catholic author and that the novel from which the play
was taken was considered one of the greatest books on a Catholic subject. The introduction was played before the show each succeeding night, and this quelled the uproar.'

Is Mr Greene writing a new masterpiece while he roams the Pacific? I am told he is not. That he is intent merely on taking a holiday and seeing a new quarter of the world. But no doubt we shall see one day the influence of this trip.[2]

*

Greene found no rest in London. He began 'to yearn for the comparative peace of Tahiti. My dream of getting down to Brighton [to finish *A Burnt-Out Case*] before the end of this month is shattered. The night before last I had dinner with Donald Lancaster [of the SIS] . . . Last night a dinner at Frere's to Mary McCarthy – the K. Clarks,* Tony Powell & his wife . . . Tonight cocktails at the Russian Embassy with Surkov, Jeanne [Lady Camoys] to dinner. At the weekend John & Gillian [Sutro] . . . Monday Vivien! O God. O Montreal.'[3]

Greene's meeting with Lancaster probably meant a briefing prior to his short, curious visit to Moscow as a guest of British European Airways. Amidst all these machinations, his desire for Catherine is laced with guilt and genuine sadness. He was leaving for Moscow on 1 April 1960 to return on the 5th. He wanted to meet her in Paris to lie in bed 'for hours & hours, see nobody & get up only for dry Martinis. Ever since I heard about your illness† I've been . . . vexed at being far away from you.'[4] And he speaks of his short story, 'A Visit to Morin', which appeared in January 1957 in *London Magazine*: 'Yesterday I had lunch with Frere . . . they are making a nice little book of "Morin" for Christmas.' He was having it specially reprinted as a present to friends, almost four years after its original publication.

*

Greene needed a way to renew himself. The whirl continued. He spent a 'liquorous' weekend at the Stonors', and saw his wife. He went out with the Sutros and Vivien Leigh, but work was on his mind:

On Sunday I break away from the London tentacles for Brighton & work. (If I find Brighton unsatisfactory I might try France – not too far from Paris.) I want to finish the first draft before I go to Moscow.[5]

* Sir Kenneth Clark, art historian, was to achieve fame in 1969 with his television series *Civilisation*.
† Catherine would be hospitalised several times within the next year, her illness undisclosed. I suspect it was to 'dry out', but at this point Graham was unaware of her condition.

He is still trying to reel Catherine in, inviting her to Anacapri to his roof patio: 'Let's sit on the roof . . . drinking wine & making out a list [of 'Morin' recipients].'⁶ On each copy is the following notice:

A Visit to Morin
was first published in the *London Magazine*
250 copies only have been printed
and the type has been distributed.

On Catherine's, Greene wrote: 'because you know you are in my mind, this first copy of all. Graham October 14, 1960'.

*

After a long run, *The Complaisant Lover* came off the London stage on 8 June, chiefly because Ralph Richardson was scheduled to make a film. Another invitation to Catherine: 'If we are not in Anacapri would you come to the last night with me? It will be exactly a year – & no nerves!'⁷ By 29 February, Greene wrote from Brighton, and the first part of his sentence is immensely revealing as to how passionately he viewed his career as a novelist – a passion that caused him acute concern and then sudden pleasure: 'Last night I reread with awful fear what I'd written in Tahiti, & do you know I think it's quite good! What it will all add up to I don't know, of course, but I was encouraged & this morning did 600 – making 53,000.' Still busy, he goes out 'to a pub & then a film' (*The Wreck of the Mary Deare*). The next day he went to London for lunch with a 'Russian of the Trade Delegation after work and then I'm flying to Paris, but I'll be back home by Saturday at latest & settle down', and mentions having lunch with Jocelyn Rickards.*

In the same letter to Catherine, he refers to the London Library having a manuscript sale in aid of themselves at Christie's in May. Some of the donations: 'Eliot has copied out *The Waste Land*; Forster has given *A Passage to India*; Evelyn [Waugh] *Scott King's* [*Modern Europe*], & I've given *The Complaisant Lover* (I didn't want to give a novel).' But on 7 March, *A Burnt-Out Case* is worrying him again: 'I'm not so happy now about the book – working very hard revising &

---

* Greene would later play down his affair with Jocelyn a bit to me: 'I met her at a cocktail party . . . very sweet . . . [she] fought her way to the bar and got me a dry martini . . . So that was the beginning . . . We had an affair which lasted over a few weeks, you know. And we remained friends ever after.' It was a wonderfully exhilarating love affair, as the interview Jocelyn gave me proved, and she inscribed a book to me with the legend: 'Everything I've told you is true.' (I did not doubt it – things like, they had made love on a train, and he took her from behind when she was bending over to brush her teeth – mild stuff like that.)

the day after tomorrow I shall have to take up the writing again. It all seems to me very muddled. What a hideous labour a novel has become. I wonder if I can ever get through another. I think I'll try to write long short stories instead.'

Catherine must have told him she was horrified at his trip to Moscow. He asks: 'Didn't you get my letter from America? It's a free trip . . . as Lord Douglas's guest; we are going to the Bolshoi & the State Circus – I've seen neither.' The trip to Moscow was to be a bit of a boisterous frolic. In *The Times*, 2 April 1960, an advertisement:

Sir Patrick Reilly, the British Ambassador to Moscow, was piped aboard a Comet IV B air liner at London Airport last night. The jet was inaugurating the British European Airways twice-weekly Comet service to Moscow, which is expected to take three-and-a-half hours on the 1,600-mile flight. Among other passengers [were]: Lord Douglas of Kirtleside, the chairman of B.E.A., and Mr Graham Greene, the novelist. The pipers . . . were to fly in the Comet and . . . pipe the passengers off again in Moscow.

★

Greene's call of love goes on. Sometimes he must have sounded to her like a sick moose. He asks Catherine to come to the first night of the film *Our Man in Havana*, but she can't. Again he sees the same set of friends, to-ing and fro-ing, one night ending up at a striptease club in Paris. He'd escorted a group of Australian women to a show. Even this dashing around is lived in reference to Catherine: 'One pretty girl & one obscene girl, but not to be compared with the *Crazy Horse*. What a long time since we've been there. In April let's go to my little restaurant & the Ritz Grill . . . & Maxim's & the *Crazy Horse*.' But behind this mad dance of socialising was the novel, boring a hole in his back: 'Dear Catherine how you are missed & particularly now, struggling with the beastly book.'

He feels a desperate need to flee the treadmill, dissatisfied by a sense of limited achievement. The danger comes from his fear, as he works through the descriptions of Querry's nature, that *he is* Querry, a ventriloquist's doll brought alive, the doll taking over the master. Then we discover he has secretly provided himself a bolthole. He is fifty-five years old, anxious and distraught – then suddenly made happy – transformed to an earlier, happier self. He is as effervescent as a boy. Graham, delighted to hear from Catherine, invites her to Paris for a 'TOP SECRET' reason:

Before you turn this page you must promise to tell *no one* without consulting me first – not even Harry or Thomas. The secret is . . .

He draws a line at the bottom of the page and, as in a child's game, we are forced to turn over to find – *voilà!*: 'I have yesterday bought an apartment in Paris.'[8] He sketches the apartment. Costing no more than £4,500, in the Boulevard Malesherbes, it was ten minutes from his agent, and no distance from Maxim's.

*

Graham is finally wrapping his mind around the possibility that Catherine is pulling away. Still working in Brighton on 19 March, he writes a sad letter:

> I expect this is the last letter I shall write. What a long time it's been. Perhaps the longest ever including Indo-China. I haven't only missed you: I've felt an *absolute aridity* the last weeks with you away – nothing seems amusing or worthwhile without you, at worst, at the end of a telephone. Nothing – & nobody – makes up for that for more than a stray half hour.
>
> Do you realise that when I come back from Moscow it will be 13 years since Shelburne? . . .
>
> I hate the book. There are bits I like, but I've had hardly a moment of pleasure in working this time & the result is muddled & shapeless. However I've passed the 60,000 & perhaps I'll finish in a week. This time in Capri let me just read & sunbathe & make love – I've *had* work.[*]

He mentions he's been invited to Japan 'all free of charge & no lectures', and tells her Francis is in love and that he's suddenly grown up and become an easy companion; also, the Sutros came down to Brighton to see the film *Our Man in Havana*: 'It seemed much better (apart from the girl [Jo Morrow]) & there had been a valuable cut. It's a tremendous success.'

Greene offers another tiny persuader, informing Catherine that he is a patron of an English theatre in Florence: 'I'm promised the Grand Duke's box any time *we* want to go!' He hates the long separation: 'One gets crazy.' In his next letter, two days later, he's back in London suffering from a hangover ('my hard drinking friend Richey having caught up with me'). He visits the empty Albany room:

---

[*] Greene states in the same letter: 'Nobody could type from the MS so this time I have a new system. I read it out onto the belts & then Miss R[eid] types & I correct & revise that & then it goes to a professional & I revise that & in the end it finishes with the roneo – awful thought correcting that.' Here is a whole new system of working for Greene, born out of his desperation over *A Burnt-Out Case*.

The curtains are all down in K3 [Catherine's rooms – Greene's are in C6] & the rooms look empty & blank without you. How I miss you. How would I have got through these 12 long years without you? Do try & see me if you are on your own (breakfast at the airport?) on April 1 [Greene was leaving for Moscow at midnight that day], but if you can't, darling . . . book at the Ritz any days that suit you . . . Try to make it 3 nights – so much to do & talk about – if not 4 or 5! Do you remember how we always used to say 2 was more than twice one – & three seemed almost twice two.[9]

Greene perseveres:

In spite of hangover I did my work before coming up – 750. I've staggered now to 61,750. When I left Jamaica I was at 32,200! How long ago it seems. I have always said it would be 65,000 – so I'm not far off. But what a beastly book. I don't mind getting into trouble [with the Church] over a good one but this . . .

I love you more & more & want you more & more . . . Dear Catherine.[10]

One has to feel sorry for Greene, eternally lonely, protractedly working on an impossible novel. The following night (22 March) he doesn't get to bed until 1.45 a.m.: 'Work with dexedrine & hangover [a potentially lethal mixture].'[11] He is getting very close to the end.

And in spite of being only a week away from his visit to Moscow, his thoughts are on Catherine: 'Oh, how welcome you'll be. Do come to a movie with me on April 7. I'm counting the days now. I know that five minutes after our first drink together all the tiredness will go.'[12] On 23 March, a day after his hangover, Greene sends a telegram to Catherine in New York: 'FINISHED THANK GOD 325 WORDS SHORT ORIGINAL ESTIMATE'. Astoundingly close.*

The day before he leaves for Moscow, and without seeing her for breakfast (another hope gone), he writes: 'Tomorrow I shall hear you on the telephone & in a week [after Moscow] see you. You are so welcome, dear, dear, dear.'[13] That meeting was not to be. Greene was not in touch for twenty-one days (and then only by letter), well after

---

* *A Burnt-Out Case* runs about the same length as *The Man Within*. Graham once 'calculated 65,000 words but at the moment it seems to be 64,875'. Another writer might think that 125 words was not a shortfall, or that in the swirl of creative activity, it should not count so much.

his return from Moscow, but he left for Russia with the first quarter of *A Burnt-Out Case* revised.

*

Only days before he'd finished his most formidable and demanding novel, the first since 1947 done mostly without Catherine, just hours before he leaves for Russia, he found time to write to the *Spectator* criticising a well-known journalist. Greene is always champing at the bit:

> As I am about to leave tonight to visit for the fourth time the city so strangely described by Mr Bernard Levin I feel a great interest in his account. What has happened to all those coffee houses – or ice cream parlours – which I saw in Moscow on my last visit, for Mr Levin says there are none? What has happened to the attractive 'bar' with stand-up tables on one leg where one drank and ate so cheaply? (Mr Levin says there are no bars.) What has happened to all the friends of mine who have written to me for books and who have acknowledged their receipt? (Mr Levin says it is dangerous to receive books from the West) . . . How odd it is that when a journalist describes a city he makes it seem so different from the one others have encountered as ordinary travellers with no need to melodramatize their impressions. The Beaverbrook press . . . teaches its young apprentices, of whom Mr Levin is one, that a story must 'stand up'. Mr Levin's story certainly does – as monumentally as a Cos lettuce.[14]

By the time Greene arrived in Moscow, Levin's reply had appeared below Greene's letter:

> What has happened to the bars is that they have been closed in the anti-drunkenness drive. There is a tiny counter in one of the big stores at which it is possible to buy a glass of wine. Here, again, 'the attractive bar with stand-up tables . . . where one drank and ate so cheaply' is another example of distance lending enchantment to the view. There are no tables in it, only a kind of ledge, and no seats, and it isn't attractive, and it isn't cheap. There is also a coffee-house, but the only time I tried to get into it there was a queue so long that I gave up. Mr Greene must not pretend to be even more naive than he is; some people in the Soviet Union are allowed to receive books and letters from outside without anything unpleasant happening to them until the next twist in the line, when they are apt to be rounded up and shot. But outside

the ranks of this *elite* it is dangerous to correspond with the West even while the line stays still. As for Mr Greene's reference to my work for Lord Beaverbrook's papers, I would be grateful if he could park his somewhat over-obtrusive artistic virginity in his new-found Wardour Street [symbol for the film world] cloak-room for five minutes and give me some tips on how to keep the cash and let the discredit go.[15]

Greene, usually so quick to shoot back, did not return to the fray. Uncharacteristically, he left Levin completely alone. It wasn't out of kindness, or a change of heart. He saw little of Moscow, for almost upon arrival he became ill. He did attend a performance in Moscow, and was provided with a hilarious dossier of *The Quiet American*. In the dossier appeared a 'series of action-photos of the actors. The characters are cardboard cutouts, with fixed stereotyped expressions . . . Greene still laughs as he thumbs through the album.'[16] But he was not well. What started as a brutal cough and cold deteriorated rapidly into pneumonia so that he was returned to England on a stretcher.

Back home recovering, he chanced a joke with his friend Edith Sitwell: 'It must have been a conspiracy of those wicked Communists in Moscow who nearly succeeded in killing me with kindness. However, I hope to be out on Tuesday and off to Stonor to convalesce.'[17] From there, weak as water, he wrote a less chirpy note to Catherine: 'I got down here all right − not too tired, but it's an awfully long walk to the loo . . . too many people looked in too often & Sherman came in & started quarrelling with Jeanne after dinner (he was a bit tight & in that state he's a wearisome bore).'[18]

In his letter to Edith, he assures her he'd be off to Italy by 1 May. To Catherine he tells the truth: 'Today I feel much better. All the same I wouldn't promise anything about Florence . . . I'm all this time for staying quiet & convalescing. Tiresome family letters today. I feel like a moneybox which everyone shakes when they feel inclined.'[19] All during this time, Greene's life changed. The woman he loved was not around when his need was greatest. And a new factor entered the equation: from 7 June until 16 July, he writes Catherine only post-cards, pedestrian ones, from Antibes on the Côte d'Azur, close to where Yvonne Cloetta and her husband were living.

*

At last he owns a Paris flat and is *in situ*. On 8 June 1960, he writes a card to Catherine about his apartment: 'Reconstruction of the flat begins immediately. But how much one has to spend on small things. Be my first & last guest in September.' He ends another postcard: 'Feel very well & not coughing.'[20] And for the first time he mentions the restaurant, Chez Félix, in Antibes, which in later years was to become a ritual for lunch.

The first regular letter is dated 'Thursday'. He pooh-poohs the doctor's fears – that he had a possible cancer of the lungs: 'My cough has gone – with my hay fever – I've been working like stink (on this paper which is the right fetish size for film scripts as single lined foolscap for novels), & done more than ½ the first [film] version of *The Living Room* . . . & I've never felt better.' No word about Yvonne, but Greene describes his publisher's brood, the Freres, with whom he lunched:

> Lovely house & such a nice happy easy family – everybody liking everybody . . . Dear love, of course I'll always tell you what the doctors say. Last week I could believe it. This week I can't. All the tiredness gone. I'll ring you up when I get in on July 6 – dinner with Sutro & the producer of *England Made Me* that night. 7th I have to have lunch with Rubins, but can we have a Claridge's before Picasso [exhibition in London].[21]

Once his meetings are over, he hurries back to Antibes, and Catherine receives a chatty postcard about being 'at the old *Voile d'Or* & drinking with Ralph Richardson'. On the front of this card is the fishing port at Antibes, a shot of the stairs leading down to fishing smacks: 'This is the scene for "Can We Borrow Your Husband?" I'm back on Wed. afternoon & will ring you before dinner with Sutro. Very well & script will be finished tomorrow. So much love. G.'[22] And then the last phrase: 'Your poor legs!' More charity, less passion.

Was it really a new love at work here, or was this a different Greene after the terrors of finishing *A Burnt-Out Case* and his pneumonia? Now in a different country, a different atmosphere, has a sea change taken place? Has he become mature, or even openly cynical?

*

'May We Borrow Your Husband?' is a story told by an older man (Greene's age), a novelist (Greene's vocation), who is in Antibes (Greene's home to be) writing a *Life of Lord Rochester* (as did Greene),* and who, in the way of Somerset Maugham, writes short stories. He watches a honeymooning bride lose her husband for a night to a homosexual. The old writer tells the story of a young pretty wife, oblivious to what's going on, so early and so unexpectedly cuckolded.

* John Wilmot, Earl of Rochester (1647–80), courtier, poet and notorious debauchee.

This is one aspect of the new Greene, putting Catherine into the shadows, beginning to reach out for Yvonne Cloetta. Yvonne was not the source for the young girl in the story, but she did seem young and innocent to the fifty-six-year-old Greene. The nature of Graham's and Yvonne's early relationship is best explained by a passage from 'May We Borrow Your Husband?' The girl, speaking to the middle-aged writer, says she thinks she'd die if she lost her husband. The narrator says:

> If I had been twenty years older, perhaps, I could have explained that nothing is quite as bad as that, that at the end of what is called 'the sexual life' the only love which has lasted is the love that has accepted everything, every disappointment, every failure and every betrayal, which has accepted even the sad fact that in the end there is no desire so deep as the simple desire for companionship.[23]

There is an account in this passage that reflects Greene's original view of Yvonne: 'I must have been very much in love or I would have found her innocence almost unbearable.'[24]

But innocence has a shelf-life, and then it spoils.

The letters to Catherine go on, as does his feeling that he cannot continue working, that he must stop or drop, though there is no evidence of this in the story. Tiny images slip out onto the page: 'the two flickered their eyes at each other like lizards' tongues';[25] a handkerchief the young girl-honeymooner has soaked with tears the storyteller, picking it up from the ground, feels 'it was like holding a small drowned animal'.[26]

'May We Borrow Your Husband?' could have been a story of sorrow, and Greene could have written it with great power. But he refused to do it that way. He seemed altered, almost genetically. Without Catherine in his life, his work was moving from tragedy to irony, to comedy and farce, and though he sometimes comes close to tragedy, as in *The Complaisant Lover*, there is peripeteia – a sudden shift away from immediate disaster to a sophisticated ending. What a long way Greene has travelled from *Brighton Rock*, and *The Power and the Glory*, and *The Heart of the Matter*.

At this moment, he is out to do small things well, even brilliantly: short stories, short plays, film scripts. But he tells Catherine that even this seems much too much: 'I feel so tired with this bloody script that I could drop. Perhaps Lichtenstein* will help me to retire. Other people do – generals & bank managers.'†[27]

---

* Code for Thomas Roe, the con artist who claimed that he could free Greene from paying exorbitant amounts of tax, with disastrous results. This is addressed in Chapter 32.
† Here Greene is using a phrase (with little alteration) found in *A Burnt-Out Case* (Penguin, p. 38). Rycker says: 'I thought a man of your kind never retired,' and Querry replies: 'Oh, one comes to an end, just as soldiers do and bank managers.'

Greene raises *directly* to Catherine the very real problem of their failed meetings. He writes before going to Brazil, invited by an ambassador he'd met on the *Liberté*. Catherine is keeping him on short rations. 'Somehow the pattern now seems to be a rendezvous of a few hours in London & then . . . the evening doesn't take place after all.'[28]

By 16 July, Greene has had word from his Swedish publisher, Ragnar Svanstrom, and between them they decide that *A Burnt-Out Case* will be published first in Sweden. And though they are drifting apart, Catherine still colours every moment:

I got an enthusiastic cable from Ragnar about the book, but it's all rather dead-sea when things are drear with us. I wasn't a bit afraid of cancer of the lung, but I am afraid of losing you & going on living.

By the third week in July, they seem to be at loggerheads:

I tried to say goodbye to you – it seems strange going off without a line or a word, but a lot has seemed strange the last few weeks. I was told you were 'somewhere in Ireland', but no one knew where – it sounded like the north of Italy last year. Funny that for 13 years with me you always had to leave addresses behind. There doesn't seem any point writing to you again till I hear from you
   a) as posts are so bad from Brazil, and
   b) I don't know whether you want to hear from me.
   Well, goodbye. I hope you are well & happy, but *I wish you hadn't forgotten how to talk to me.*[29]

He leaves a loophole: 'If things are all right, you *might* telegraph to me.' Going to an hotel in Antibes is a giveaway as to his intentions, though he's keeping the affair with Yvonne private. Was he thinking, if I can't have Catherine, I can have the younger Yvonne? Catherine was busy with a wedding, but did send a telegram.

By 15 September he is in Paris, nesting like a newly married housewife: 'sheets, pillow cases, bath towels, face towels, breakfast cups, wine glasses, whisky glasses, brandy glasses, cocktail glasses, water jug . . . & a Cocktail shaker'.

Up to the end of the year, apart from a few dullish long letters, Catherine receives picture postcards with little on them, or very short letters. The lamp of love is going out, and it's about time. One last stab at a rendezvous with Catherine amid her obligations: 'Give me a ring & let's fix Paris before every day becomes a duty. A lot of next week's gone already. I begin to think work is preferable.'[30] But who could stand having every plan to meet betrayed? It must have seemed to him a devastating end. What on earth was Catherine up to?

By early in December, he is still settling in: the cupboard and red chairs are 'entrancing'. His heating isn't working, so he is in an overcoat and '*Perhaps* a plumber etc may come tomorrow ... I've bought gin, vermouth, whisky, brandy & vodka – which all look well on top of the cupboard.'[31] He wants Catherine to see it before she leaves on yet another trip. And then he wants to go out the next day to buy other items, mostly linked with having a good cellar: champagne, soda water, beer, ice trays and bucket. His son, Francis, is coming and then the books will go in. 'I went for dinner with Mauriac's memoirs (rather pompous) to quite a nice quiet restaurant three minutes away – old & middle-aged customers. Could become one's local.'

★

With the publication of *A Burnt-Out Case* in England within the month, Greene is flying to London and back, drinking heavily, socialising, and going to Brighton to work. Happy in his Paris flat, he felt more protectedly alone there than in Albany. He found even the coloured towels comforting, but doesn't seem to be looking forward to his first visitor, his son. Graham doesn't like company, even his own flesh and blood. He *still* writes to Catherine out of habit or need, or perhaps there is no one else worthy: 'I like the aloneness of it so much. I think I'll come for Christmas – if the heating is on.' Suddenly he realises it is: 'Thank God – I feel the hot water's on anyway! And your ash trays look *lovely!*'[32] And the ill-at-ease father reports about his son, aged twenty-four: 'I had to sit up till 2 a.m. for Francis. How I dislike children.'[33] Good grief.

22

Crossing the Shadow-Line

I'll never write another novel.
— GRAHAM GREENE

'I don't know whether *A Burnt-Out Case* is a cause or a symptom — of a kind of emptiness, when nothing much seems worth while. Except our love & affection for each other, & a few toys – of which this flat is one.'[1] This is what Greene wrote to Catherine, but the Paris flat was not enough of a barricade against the world. He still carried his troublesome nature with him, 'like a passport'. He couldn't have known that during this phase, upon returning to London, Brighton, Paris, or even Antibes (though less often there), he'd be skulking around in the shadows of his own mind, trying to find the source of Querry's sense of parched barrenness, that void, which affected Querry *and* Greene.

In *A Burnt-Out Case*, Greene shoots at a succession of targets – one being respectable men of the cloth, who he had unexpectedly discovered were often unsure of their own religious convictions. Greene first dealt with a priest's loss of faith in his play *The Potting Shed*, and then again in *A Burnt-Out Case*. That such people came to him in droves after the success of *The Heart of the Matter* devastated and shocked Greene. He speaks of it in *Ways of Escape*, having received many letters from strangers – mostly women and priests:

A young man wrote to me from West Berlin asking me to lead a crusade of young people into the Eastern Zone where we were to shed our blood for the Church . . . A young woman sent me a rather drunken letter of invitation from a Dutch fishing-boat enclosing a photograph, and another wrote from Switzerland suggesting I join her 'where the snow can be our coverlet'.

A woman living in New Jersey telephoned Greene in the early morning hours demanding help with her marriage difficulties. This last must have intrigued him, because he and Catherine went to visit her:

> The awful little New Jersey house with its too feminine furnishings and an insolent black maid still come vividly to mind. The mistress of the house lay in a drugged sleep at midday with the curtains closed and an eyeshade hiding the face and a pink silk nightdress on the body. Our visit was as useless as we had anticipated; only death could save her, and save her it did a year later in London with the help of drink and drugs, abandoned by all but one of the Jesuits she had befriended.[2]

Greene's coldness here sends shivers. Having recognised this, what follows is his attempt at an excuse: 'This account may seem cynical and unfeeling, but in the years between *The Heart of the Matter* and *The End of the Affair* I felt myself used and exhausted by the victims of religion.' Greene grants that a 'better man could have found a life's work on the margin of that cruel sea' but then adds: 'I had no apostolic mission, and the cries for spiritual assistance maddened me because of my impotence. What was the Church for . . . ? I was like a man without medical knowledge in a village struck with plague.'[3]

★

In *Ways of Escape* he comes back to priests.

> A French priest pursued me first with letters of a kind which should only have been addressed to his confessor, and then in person: he even popped up unannounced and inopportunely, one evening in a narrow lane of Anacapri, as I was catching the bus to Capri with my mistress, trailing . . . dust from his long black soutane. Other priests would spend hours in my only armchair, while they described their difficulties, their perplexities, their desperation . . . It was in those years . . . that Querry was born, and Father Thomas too. He had often sat in that chair of mine.[4]

It is Father Thomas who admits to Querry that he has serious religious doubts which 'come to me at the altar with the Host in my hands'.[5] Greene is looking on with ice-cold eyes.★ We see these eyes

---

★ Only once do I recall feeling the pale compelling hardness of his eyes, and that was over my describing his friend, the spy Kim Philby, thus: 'There is nothing wrong with Philby except that he is a traitor, probably England's greatest.'

in his short story 'A Visit to Morin', referred to earlier. Pierre Morin is a Catholic novelist, once well-known:

'. . . there were always too many priests,' he said, 'around me. The priests swarmed like flies. Near me and any woman I knew. First I was an exhibit for their faith. I was useful to them, a sign that even an intelligent man could believe. That was the period of the Dominicans, who liked the literary atmosphere and good wine. Then afterwards when the books stopped, and they smelt some-thing – gamey – in my religion, it was the turn of the Jesuits, who never despair of what they call a man's soul.'[6]

Another target of Greene's emerges in *A Burnt-Out Case*: journal-ists. In novel after novel, he shows his contempt for that vocation: the lesbian with 'coarse hair, red lips, masculine voice', Mabel Warren in *Stamboul Train*; and uncertain males like Minty (who keeps a spider trapped to death under a toothglass) in *England Made Me*; the bully Granger in *The Quiet American*, and of course, as we saw in an earlier chapter, Montagu Parkinson in *A Burnt-Out Case* – all offer a singular indictment.

And we see the beginnings of Parkinson in 'A Visit to Morin's Dunlop.* Having talked at length about both priests and himself as ones who have lost belief, Morin tells the interviewer: 'You don't understand a thing I have been saying to you. What a story you would make of this if you were a journalist and yet there wouldn't be a word of truth.'[7]

In *A Burnt-Out Case*, Querry gives Parkinson an unsavoury account of his own cynical sexual adventures and the suicide of Marie Morel, and dares Parkinson to print the truth in his family newspaper. Here then is the truth that cannot be told, having its beginning in the Morin story:

'They used to come here in their dozens to see me. I used to get letters saying how I had converted them by this book or that. Long after I ceased to believe myself I was a carrier of belief, like a man can be a carrier of disease without being sick. Women especially.' He added with disgust, 'I had only to sleep with a woman to make a convert.'[8]

---

* We are aware of another source for Parkinson, as seen in Chapter 18, 'Parkinson's Dis-ease'.

Morin is Greene. Querry is Greene.

The genesis of Querry must have occurred when Greene, thinking long into the night of the nature of his encounters with priests, journalists and women, made them more extreme to give Querry a 'sinister resonance'. He began by looking into his religious experiences, his own success with women, and the effect this had on specific priests who swarmed around him. 'A Visit to Morin' is Greene's preliminary excursion into the minds of the disturbed priests surrounding him. Building up Querry's nature, Greene used more substantial experiences of his own, resulting in a significant fictional character. Greene looked into his own heart to see the triangular lines connecting himself and Morin and Querry; some he enjoyed, some mortified him and made him feel he'd lost his moral moorings. Dunlop, the narrator of 'A Visit to Morin', recalls that reviewers

> accused [Morin] of Jansenism [as reviewers did Greene] – whatever that might be: others called him an Augustinian [as they did Greene] . . . orthodox critics seemed to scent heresy like a rat dead somewhere under the boards, at a spot they could not locate.[9]

Morin's speculation that if Dunlop were a journalist it would make a good story, except there 'wouldn't be a word of truth in it', is realised exactly in *A Burnt-Out Case*. Querry presents himself to Parkinson with his human scars made paramount, arising from his success: he disguises nothing and with commendable honesty (a quality Greene shared with many of his characters) asks that his dark side be revealed. Greene must have known how tantalisingly close he was to describing himself.

But Parkinson, because he is a careless journalist, gets the facts wrong: 'Papers like yours invariably make small mistakes. The woman's name was Marie and not Anne. She was twenty-five and not eighteen.'[10] Querry then explains why Marie committed suicide, for the oddest reason: to escape the man she loved. Querry explains his love-making, as part of the impetus for her act: 'It must be a terrible thing for a woman to make love nightly with an efficient instrument. I never failed her.' Querry divulges his tricks to keep her in love. Once he used tears;

> another time an overdose of Nembutal, but not, of course, a dangerous dose. Then I made love to a second woman to show her what she was going to miss if she left me.* I even persuaded

---

* Remember Greene's dream of making love with another woman in front of Catherine while sailing down the River Congo; here, a fictional 'reality'.

her that I couldn't do my work without her. I made her think I would leave the Church if I hadn't her support to my faith – she was a good Catholic, even in bed. In my heart of course I had left the Church years before, but she never realised that.[11]

Did Greene borrow from Querry, and lie to Catherine in the ways Querry lied to his mistress? Probably, for both Querry and Greene took an overdose of Nembutal. Querry is Greene taken to extremes. He offers Parkinson advice on how to win a married women and why they are a surer bet.

Fame is a potent aphrodisiac. Married women are the easiest, Parkinson. The young girl too often has her weather-eye open on security, but a married woman has already found it. The husband at the office, the children in the nursery, a condom in the bag. Say that she's been married at twenty, she's ready for a limited excursion before she's reached thirty. If her husband is young too, don't be afraid; she may have had enough of youth. With a man of my age and yours she needn't expect jealous scenes.

Querry argues that even the loveliest of women feels gratitude to an ageing man if she learns sexual pleasure again:

Ten years in the same bed withers the little bud, but now it blooms once more. Her husband notices the way she looks. Her children cease to be a burden. She takes an interest again in house-keeping as she used to in the old days. She confides a little in her intimate friends, because to be the mistress of a famous man increases her self-respect. The adventure is over. Romance has begun. [Greene probably has in mind Yvonne, who was not used to famous people, while Catherine was.]

We've seen Parkinson's admiring response to this tirade of sardonic sexual knowledge: 'What a cold-blooded bastard you are.'[12]

*

After Greene's writing success while travelling round the world with Michael Meyer came the period of completing *A Burnt-Out Case*, in London and Brighton, revisions in Paris and Antibes. But Greene was deeply troubled. He was forced by the nature of his hero, Querry, to look at his own life, and the act of doing so created profound mental disquiet. In letters to Catherine there is a paralysing depression, descending out of nowhere. He feels 'very low . . . dreading tomorrow's flight (prescience? One will soon know.)' Here's another classic – only from Greene could this come: 'I wish I didn't have a sense of despondency, doom & failure, but I suppose it's just Christmas.' And on reading the second volume of Cardinal Newman's life, Greene comments: 'Very good . . . but it started [a] melancholic spell in me which is in its third week!'*

★

The fable told by Querry to young Marie Rycker (surely her revealed character is based on Yvonne Cloetta) as she lies abed is an outpouring of Greene's private disturbances, an allegory of disenchantment with his own achievement. It is also a parallel study of the void in Querry. Greene's belief in God and his sense of losing God are in every line. Finally it recognises that, though Querry might be separated from God's presence, God might still exist. The story is about a boy who believes in the King (God). His parents (and the community) also believe in the King. Though living far away, the King watches everything.

> When a pig littered, the King knew of it, or when a moth died against a lamp . . . When a servant slept with another servant in a haystack the King punished them. You couldn't always see the punishment . . . Sometimes it was postponed until the end of life [here is Greene's genuine fear that his punishment was simply delayed], but that made no difference because the King was the King of the dead too and you couldn't tell what terrible things he might do to them in the grave.

In almost every incident you can substitute 'Greene' for 'he', and 'writer' for 'jeweller' – a parable of Greene's own life.

> The boy grew up . . . He became in time a famous jeweller, for one of the women whom he had satisfied gave him money for

---

* Melancholy into its third week, and the cause is nothing more than his reading Volume Two of Cardinal Newman's life? We must not forget that Graham was a manic depressive (now called bipolar disorder) and after his deep depressions down into a disabling night, surrounded by hopelessness, there often followed severe mood swings, almost to a manic peak. We have seen how Greene would plunge himself into socialising. At such times he would abuse alcohol and drugs, but then just as suddenly he would long for peace and order, and come to hate noise and company. He longed for the peace Catherine often gave him. One thinks of other writers who suffered from the same malady: Poe, Byron, Hemingway – all alcoholics, and suicidal when depressed – characteristics shared by Greene. Greene's cousin, Robert Louis Stevenson wrote the classic novel of such changes in psyche: *Dr Jekyll and Mr Hyde*.

his training, and he made many beautiful things in honour of his mistress and of course the King. Lots of rewards began to come his way. Money too . . . Everyone agreed that it all came from the King. He left his wife and his mistress, he left a lot of women, but he always had a great deal of fun with them first. They called it love and so did he, he broke all the rules he could think of, and he must surely have been punished for breaking them, but you couldn't see the punishment nor could he.

He grew richer and the jewellery was better. Women were kinder and he had undeniably a wonderful time – but he became profoundly bored. Is this not Greene's eternal cry? And no one ever told him no.

'Nobody ever made him suffer – it was always other people who suffered. Sometimes just for a change he would have welcomed . . . the pain of . . . punishment . . . the King must . . . have been inflicting on him. He could travel wherever he chose and after a while it seemed to him that he had gone much further than the hundred miles that separated him from the King [as a boy Querry had thought the King only a hundred miles away on a star], further than the furthest star, but wherever he went he always came to the same place where the same things happened: articles in the papers praised his jewellery [a metaphor for his novels], women cheated [yes] . . . and went to bed with him [yes], and servants of the King [priests] acclaimed him as a loyal and faithful subject.

'Because people could only see the reward, and the punishment was invisible, he got the reputation of being a very good man. Sometimes people were a little perplexed that such a good man should have enjoyed quite so many women – it was, on the surface anyway, disloyal to the King who had made quite other rules. But they learnt in time to explain it; they said he had a great capacity for love and love had always been regarded by them as the highest of virtues. Love indeed was the greatest reward even the King could give, all the greater because it was more invisible than such little material rewards as money and success and membership of the Academy. Even the man himself began to believe that he loved a great deal better than all the so-called good people who obviously could not be so good if you knew all (you had only to look at the punishments they received – poverty, children dying, losing both legs in a railway accident, and the like). It was quite a shock to him when he discovered one day that he didn't love at all [when his love for Catherine was diminishing and his different kind of love for Yvonne had yet to flourish] . . .

'His King existed objectively and there was no other King but his . . . His second [discovery] came much later when he realized that he was not born to be an artist at all: only a very clever jeweller [Greene's sense of his own limitations]. He made one jewel in the shape of an ostrich egg: it was all enamel and gold and when you opened it you found inside a little gold figure sitting at a table and a little gold-and-enamel egg on the table, and when you opened that there was a little figure sitting at a table and a little gold-and-enamel egg and when you opened that . . . I needn't go on. Everyone said he was a master technician [this is repeated in countless reviews of his novels] but he was highly praised too for the seriousness of his subject matter because on the top of each egg there was a gold cross set with chips of precious stones in honour of the King [Greene's 'Catholic' novels]. The trouble was he wore himself out with the ingenuity of his design, and suddenly when he was making the contents of the final egg with an optic glass . . .'

It was, he began to think, a sad story, so that it was hard to understand this sense of freedom and release, like that of a prisoner who at last 'comes clean', admitting everything to his inquisitor. Was this the reward perhaps which came sometimes to a writer? 'I have told all: you can hang me now . . .'

'Suddenly our hero realised how bored he was – he never wanted to turn his hand any more to mounting any jewel at all. He was finished with his profession . . . Nothing could ever be so ingenious as what he had done already, or more useless, and he could never hear any praise higher than what he had received . . .'

Querry in the novel and Greene in life have reached the same tragic burn-out:

. . . A long time ago he had got to the end of pleasure just as now he had got to the end of work, although it is true he went on practising pleasure as a retired dancer continues to rehearse daily at the bar, because he has spent all his mornings that way and it never occurs to him to stop. So our hero felt only relief: the bar had been broken, he wouldn't bother, he thought, to obtain another. Although, of course, after a month or two he did. However it was too late then – the morning habit had been broken and he never took it up again with quite the same zeal. [After *A Burnt-Out Case*, Greene thought he'd never write again with 'quite the same zeal, or indeed, write another novel'.] . . . It isn't easy leaving a profession . . . people talk a lot to you about duty. People came to him to demand eggs with crosses (it was his duty to the King and to the King's followers). ['Why don't you write more Catholic novels? It's your duty to God.']

The jeweller tries to discourage his public, to show them how his mind has changed; he cuts a few more stones as 'frivolously' as possible, creating exquisite little toads for women to wear in their navels, and for men – 'soft golden coats of mail, with one hollow stone like a knowing eye at the top, with which men might clothe their special parts':

> So our hero received yet more money and praise, but what vexed him most was that even these trifles were now regarded as seriously as his eggs and crosses had been. He was the King's jeweller and nothing could alter that. People declared that he was a moralist and that these were serious satires on the age . . . [When] his jewels ceased to be popular with people in general [it] only made him more popular with the connoisseurs who distrust popular success. They began to write books about his art; especially those who claimed to know and love the King wrote about him . . .
>
> What none of these people knew was that one day our hero had made a startling discovery – he no longer believed all those arguments historical, philosophical, logical, and etymological that he had worked out for the existence of the King. [Greene had lost his intellectual belief in God.] There was left only a memory of the King who had lived in his parents' heart and not in any particular place. Unfortunately his heart was not the same as the one his parents shared: it was calloused with pride and success, and it had learned to beat only with pride . . . when a jewel was completed or when a woman cried under him, '*donne, donne, donne*'* . . .
>
> You know . . . he had deceived himself, just as much as he had deceived the others. He had believed quite sincerely that when he loved his work he was loving the King and that when he made love to a woman he was at least imitating in a faulty way the King's love for his people. The King after all had so loved the world that he had sent a bull and a shower of gold and a son . . .
>
> But when he discovered there was no such King as the one he had believed in, he realized too that anything that he had ever

---

* 'Give it to me, give it to me, give it to me.'

done must have been done for love of himself. How could there be any point any longer in making jewels or making love for his own solitary pleasure? Perhaps he had reached the end of his sex and the end of his vocation before he made his discovery about the King or perhaps that discovery brought about the end of everything? I wouldn't know, but I'm told that there were moments when he wondered if his unbelief were not after all a final and conclusive proof of the King's existence [Greene's expression of doubt and the possibility of continued faith revealed by Querry]. This total vacancy might be his punishment for the rules he had wilfully broken. It was even possible that this was what people meant by pain.[13]

Greene was just a body walking around with no heart, no soul. 'Total vacancy' had arrived.

From 'A Visit to Morin' came the same cry, a precursor to the fable:

I can tell myself now that my lack of belief is a final proof that the Church is right and the faith is true. I had cut myself off for twenty years from grace and my belief withered as the priests said it would. I don't believe in God and His Son and His angels and His saints, but I know the reason why I don't believe and the reason is – the Church is true and what she taught me is true. For twenty years I have been without the sacraments and I can see the effect. The wafer must be more than wafer.[14]

*

How then must Catherine, whose faith was all-encompassing – she said she believed the 'whole bag of tricks' – have felt reading 'A Visit to Morin', received in October 1960, and then how must she have felt only months later (16 January 1961) on receiving the newly published *A Burnt-Out Case*, reading of Greene's rapidly disappearing belief in Christ? Greene always felt, however incongruously, that Catherine had made him a true Catholic.

And now, after thirteen years, Greene had become a lawless Catholic. He was an anomaly, a Catholic without God.

Few men fulfil themselves before death, but that wasn't Greene's problem. Rather, he no longer believed in what he was doing, no longer valued what he'd done. This reality, coupled with his alter ego, Querry, was overwhelming. *A Burnt-Out Case* is a bitter, gruelling exposition of Greene's feelings about himself at this particular point in time, and, when in depression, about his own sense of failure. Often Greene felt so low, he had to 'reach up to touch bottom'.

Greene is Querry, and thus reveals himself at moments of chasmic despair as one of the undead, sucked dry by his work. Querry says: 'I have no interest in anything any more, doctor. I don't want to sleep with a woman nor design a building.'[15] (Change 'design a building' to 'write a novel'.) Greene's vampiric vocation was slowly devouring him – tortuously slow like a boa eating a goat – and his adventures with women sucking dry his spiritual life. Greene's judgment of himself (it certainly is not my judgment of him) exists in one of Querry's reflections:

I'm no genius, Rycker. I am a man who had a certain talent, not a very great talent, and I have come to the end of it. There was nothing new I could do. I could only repeat myself. So I gave up.[16]

Few writers were more successful than Greene, yet his bleak spells of depression seemed bottomless. He suffered from this inner despair, suffered like Querry the terrible emptiness – the sense of a wasted life, a barrenness sometimes so profound it left him in deep agitation, his sense of absolute failure and his feeling he was a moral leper – and in *A Burnt-Out Case* he is unbuttoning thoughts about himself, kept mostly hidden but revealed here as limitless darkness.

The novel was the most difficult Greene had written: 'Never had a novel proved more recalcitrant or more depressing.'[17] He told journalist Marie-Françoise Allain that his 'bout of depression, my worst, I think, coincided with the gestation of *A Burnt-Out Case*. I can find reasons for this in my private life, but also in my two-year cohabitation with the deeply depressive Querry.'[18]

Yes, he could find reason for his condition in his private life: the way Catherine was rigorously avoiding him. What was so terrible was he had to write *A Burnt-Out Case* at a time when Catherine had deserted him. He had finished *A Burnt-Out Case not* before he'd slept with Yvonne, but before he'd fallen in love with Yvonne. Catherine's departure from him at this time induced him to move in the direction of Yvonne and to leave England. At that point Greene's love for Yvonne began to grow, ultimately luxuriantly.

Greene explains: 'The reader had only to endure the company of the burnt-out character . . . for a few hours' reading, but the author had to live with him and in him for eighteen months.'[19] I believe Greene had to live with Querry most of his life; the two rarely parted. Being Querry was Greene's wound, his unhealable sore until old age, when his heavy depressions lifted somewhat. And this disability is set against his enormous writing abilities.

One compensation for his difficulty was the insight it gave him into morbid psychology – his own. And in countless ways and countless times he softened the deep hurt of his depressions, allowing him to hit again and again his creative targets. But he suffered from his wounds, which made him attempt to draw his creative bow; and novels of his, born in sadness and despair, sometimes were flawless.

★

Greene admitted to me that he was not at peace with himself except for brief occasions, but spoke more vividly to Marie-Françoise Allain after she'd asked where he hid to find peace: 'I crouch in a corner like a sick dog. I don't want other people's sympathy. I go to the doctor, but I don't want any "ministering angels" around me.'[20]

But Catherine *was* a ministering angel. For thirteen years, she touched and temporarily healed the heart of Greene's fractured psyche. He knew he wanted her at his side at the sharp, painful end of creation. He longed for her (even as he was falling out of love) because of the peace she bestowed. Here he is writing to Catherine with *A Burnt-Out Case* already published two months earlier: 'I keep on meaning to start on some work, but for twelve years I've practically always started with you around – writing letters or reading theology or Erle Stanley [Gardner], and I've got to wait till you're around again.'[21]

Catherine could alight upon a troublesome passage like a bird; never fighting him, never adding weight, but simply guiding, genuinely wishing the writing genius in him satisfied. Alert, generous in spirit, kind, not given to outbreaks of temper or jealousy, she was (no matter how extraordinary in the first instance it might seem to say this) the mother of perpetual help. It was with *A Burnt-Out Case* he needed her most (witness his letters). But partly because of her own illnesses, spanning the two years from Greene's initial leper experience to the novel's publication, she was less able (and understandably less inclined) to see him.

★

A Burnt-Out Case appeared in the middle of January 1961. In a diary entry on the last day of 1960, a concerned Evelyn Waugh admits that the *Daily Mail* sent him an advance copy of the novel to review. 'I suppose they would have paid £100. I had to refuse':

There is nothing I could write about it without shame one way or the other. Coming so soon after his Christmas story ['A Visit to Morin'] it emphasises a theme which it would be affected not to regard as personal – the vexation of a Catholic artist exposed against his wishes to acclamations as a 'Catholic' artist who at the same time cuts himself off from divine grace by sexual sin . . . It is the first time Graham has come out as specifically faithless – pray God it is a mood, but it strikes deeper and colder.[22]

'A Visit to Morin' and *A Burnt-Out Case* will for some be evidence of a loss of belief on Greene's part. Greene's frequent companion, Father Leopoldo Durán made an understandable mistake: 'Something put it into Evelyn Waugh's head that the character of Querry in *A Burnt-Out Case* was actually a portrait of his dear friend Graham, the author of the book.'[23] Writing to his friend, the biographer Christopher Sykes, on 2 January 1961, Waugh reported that 'Grisjambon Vert [Waugh's private name for Greene – French for 'grey ham green'] has written a very sorrowful novel.'[24]

★

Let's play along with Greene's 'time-old gag' that a 'writer cannot be identified with his characters'. Why does Greene, in book after book, make it almost his trademark to deny that his characters are based on living people? He is particularly firm in his preface to *The Heart of the Matter*:

No character in this book is based on that of a living person . . . I want to make it absolutely clear that no inhabitant, past or present, of that particular colony appears in my book.

But why did he feel it necessary to deny that his fictional characters have living models? There was a very practical reason.

Greene's first visit to Sierra Leone and Liberia in 1935 resulted in his writing one of the best travel books of the century. However, his book *Journey Without Maps* (1936) had to be withdrawn by the publisher a year and a half later because of a libel case. At a party in Freetown, Sierra Leone, Greene described a lively drunken character whom he called (giving him a false name) Pa Oakley. However, there was an Oakley in the Sierra Leone Medical Service, and he sued. Damages had to be paid. The book remained out of print until after the Second World War when Greene became a publisher at Eyre & Spottiswoode. This was a profound shock for him, not least because he'd had an early novel, *Stamboul Train* (1932), pulled from the presses over a character which offended J. B. Priestley.* They had the same publisher, but Greene's

---

* The popular writer J. B. Priestley, leafing through a review copy before it was even in the bookshops, recognised a fictional character, Mr Savory, as an 'unsavoury' portrait of himself. See Volume One, p. 435.

reputation was then still a plant of tender growth, and Priestley could command Heinemann to act. The jolt of Priestley's holding up his book, and the fear of further libel cases, led Greene in future work to stress that his characters were fictional. But nothing comes of nothing. We should take Greene's denials with a grain of salt.

In *A Burnt-Out Case*, the disclaimer comes in his dedicatory letter to Michel Lechat: 'It would be a waste of time for anyone to try to identify Querry, the Ryckers, Parkinson, Father Thomas – they are formed from the flotsam of thirty years as a novelist.' Another disclaimer appears in the dedicatory letter to his publisher, A. S. Frere, on *The Comedians*, where Greene makes fun of certain kinds of readers: 'Many readers assume . . . that an "I" is always the author. So in my time I have been considered the murderer of a friend, the jealous lover of a civil servant's wife, and an obsessive player at roulette. I don't wish to add to my chameleon nature the characteristics belonging to the cuck-older of a South American diplomat, a possibly illegitimate birth and an education by the Jesuits.' He puts it like this: 'A physical trait taken here, a habit of speech, an anecdote – they are boiled up in the kitchen of the unconscious and emerge unrecognisable even to the cook in most cases.' Even to the cook? I doubt that. Greene's truth lies in his fiction.

The Swedish critic Olof Lagercrantz says bluntly of *A Burnt-Out Case*: 'Religious and irreligious readers of Graham Greene can now freely discuss whether in this book he definitely takes leave of his Catholic faith.'[25] But Greene never publicly asserted that he had lost his faith until very late in the day – you wouldn't expect this tight-lipped man to do so.

In his diary, Waugh describes Querry as 'a bored, loveless volup-tuary'.[26] And he puts forward the Catholic point of view, that not only are Greene's fictional characters guilty, but Greene himself is as well. Even when they were close, these two could not easily agree. Waugh had written quite beautifully about Greene's *The End of the Affair* in 1951 for the *Month*. Yet in a letter to Greene written on receipt of *The Lost Childhood* (1951), Waugh freely admitted he could 'never hope to [agree with Greene] . . . this side of death'.[27]

But a private letter to his Swedish publisher, Ragnar Svanstrom, has survived which puts Greene's position in gentle yet decided terms. Referring to the unfavourable review by Olof Lagercrantz in *Dagens Nyheter*, Greene writes: 'No one yet seems to suspect that this book may be a farewell to Catholicism – I thought the Swedes might have spotted that aspect though the farewell is a friendly one.'

About his moving away from his faith he wrote gently to Catherine

– he did not wish to hurt her – a month after the publication of *A Burnt-Out Case*:

> I'll probably never succeed in getting any further from the Church. It's like, when one was younger, taking a long walk in the country & at a certain tree or a certain gate or the top of one more hill one stopped & thought, 'Now I must start returning home.' One probably went on another mile to another hill or another tree, but all the same . . .[28]

★

Greene did wander slowly back towards Catholicism, but with hesitant steps. Doubt became an important term for him, employed many times from then on. One might say that faith cannot exist without first some doubt, but when Greene was asked where the then-current Pope had gone wrong, he answered: 'I don't think he doubts his own infallibility . . . I have always believed that doubt was a more important thing for human beings.'

Greene's unorthodoxy is puzzling, and there is no rarer bird than he, with his refusal to conform whilst remaining in the Catholic Church. Yet he endured as a leading Catholic, writing novels that raised pertinent questions, breaking rules which to a lesser man would have prevented him from being a Catholic. He makes an odd, archetypal fence-sitter. Greene has left himself a crevice of belief, a speck of religious hope. In the very middle of a consuming desert, dry of inspiration and stimulation, he yet wrote two moving, dramatic and ultimately revealing pieces, 'Morin' and *A Burnt-Out Case*. He's crossed the shadow-line, after casting a savage sceptical look at his own face looking back from the mirror, over to a consuming vacancy reflected there, in an exhaustion as heavy as the sea.

PART 10

Intimations of Mortality

23

Death Is a Mole

And death *SHALL* have dominion.
– PROPHECIES OF ALLADOR

GREENE began losing friends to that little rodent: first, in 1965, John Hayward died; then in 1966 Evelyn Waugh, who, along with Michael Richey (the navigator criss-crossing the Atlantic as if on a morning stroll) must be accounted Greene's best male friend – Waugh, like Greene a Catholic convert, a Catholic novelist, equal in fame, equal in intellect, unequal in nature and personality. And in November 1971, Greene's one-time mistress, Dorothy Glover, died.

Greene's friendship with the crippled John Hayward began with a letter Greene wrote from Chipping Campden on 12 October 1931 – when he'd left London to live more cheaply in the country. Greene had now a wife to support, but he was short of cash – his second and third novels, *The Name of Action* and *Rumour at Nightfall*, were prodigious failures. In a sense, it was fortunate that they were. It made him reconsider the implications of being influenced by Joseph Conrad, and also gave him the opportunity to work in a different medium.

Greene took up the notion of writing a biography of the infamous Earl of Rochester, known as one of the wildest of those debauchees who surrounded Charles II. Rochester was remarkable in many ways – a considerable satirist and great wit, as shown in his *Satyr Against Mankind* (1675), brilliant, polished, licentious; a real roaring boy – but when he became ill he was moved to repentance by Bishop Burnet's intervention and experienced a religious conversion. This was the man whom Greene chose to write about.

John Hayward, a year younger than Greene, was an established writer, and had already in 1926 brought out an edition of Rochester's works. It was inevitable that Greene would try to contact him as the Rochester expert. But after finishing his short life of Rochester, *Lord*

Rochester's Monkey, Greene saw his book rejected, and realised that at a crucial moment in his career he had wasted valuable time. Heinemann were afraid that the biography could be viewed as pornography. Greene was warned about the dangers when he met Hayward, then editorial director of the *Book Collector*. Hayward's advice was to bear in mind that if a charge of obscenity were brought against him, it might possibly be extended to include Hayward, whose text he'd used, and his publishers. Greene recalled

> being 'warned' that I would find [John's] physical appearance ugly – an extraordinary misapprehension. That powerful head ugly? that twist of the half paralysed arm, as the agile hand seized a cup or procured itself a cigarette? the wicked intelligence of the eyes? A cripple yes, but there are few men I can remember with greater vitality, and with a greater appreciation of physical love.[*1]

Hayward might have been unattractive in the conventional sense, but according to Greene 'no man in London in his day was a repository of more intimate confessions'. He liked Hayward's outspokenness and lack of reverence:

> I can see him clearly as I write, throwing back his head and drawing in a long loud breath (his equivalent for laughter), while his left arm waved, like the tentacle of an octopus, and captured his silver cigarette case, as I asked him a direct and indiscreet question about some writer whom he did not regard with unmixed friendship. A pause and out came the atrocious anecdote – amusing and enlightening.[2]

Greene never forgot a favour, and remembered that when he was poor as a church mouse, 'established nowhere at all', the already well-regarded Hayward 'received me generously, & gave his time to me without the slightest hint of patronage'.

We see how much Greene trusted and admired his friend, for it was to Hayward he turned when he finished *The Heart of the Matter*, allowing him to sit in judgment on that great novel. (Hayward was a

---

* Because Hayward was crippled by polio, his only sexual satisfaction was in the mind. Greene would send him 'dirty postcards' from all over. A typical card sent two years before Hayward's death: a shocked nurse and doctor are standing over an anaesthetised patient, the nurse with scissors in her hand: 'But Nurse,' says the doctor, 'I said remove his spectacles!'

distinguished critic.) Greene admitted to being 'nearly cheered because John likes the book very much – I'm just off to see him now'.[3]

On 30 September 1965, in a letter to Catherine, Greene wrote about Mrs Cordery, who had looked after him when he was in London. He realised only after she was gone 'what she did for me all these years. The wings of death are very much around. Then John [Hayward] – his death seems to have been really peaceful & in the nick of time – he had lost the use even of his hands.'[4] A last word on Hayward by Greene was to a friend: 'I've done my tribute [in the *Book Collector*] . . . He was a wonderful friend and a very courageous man.'[5]

★

Evelyn Waugh was a religious conservative, a political reactionary, a brilliant, hilarious writer, a master of corrosive irony (recall his characters: Mrs Melrose Ape, Lady Fanny Throbbing). Unlike Greene, he had no doubts about his faith, and remained a convinced Catholic. Greene was normally reserved, civilised and good-mannered (hiding his thoughts in his manner) – an iconoclast. Waugh could be a snob. They were a match for each other. After reading an advance copy of *A Burnt-Out Case*, Waugh wrote to Greene:

> I could write much of my admiration for your superb description of the leper-village and for the brilliance with which you handle the problems of dialogue in four languages. I particularly admired the sermon of the Father Superior. But I am not reviewing it.

Waugh then makes a personal apology without speaking of his fears that Greene is suffering from a renunciation of faith:

> I know . . . how mischievous it is to identify fictional characters with their authors, but, taken in conjunction with your Christmas story, this novel makes it plain that you are exasperated by the reputation which has come to you unsought of a 'Catholic' writer. I realise that I have some guilt in this matter. Twelve years ago I gave a number of lectures here and in America presumptuously seeking to interpret what I genuinely believed was an apostolic mission in danger of being neglected by people who were shocked by the sexuality of some of your themes. In fact in a small way I behaved like Rycker. I am deeply sorry for the annoyance I helped to cause & pray that it is only annoyance.

This was of course a very real concern for Waugh, but his last line expressed a hope that would be for him of paramount importance:

'that the desperate conclusions of Morin & Querry are purely fictional'.[6]
Greene's response was immediate:

> With a writer of your genius and insight I certainly would not
> attempt to hide behind the time-old gag that an author can never
> be identified with his characters. Of course in some of Querry's
> reactions there are reactions of mine, just as in some of Fowler's
> reactions in *The Quiet American* there are reactions of mine . . .
> a parallel must not be drawn all down the line and not neces-
> sarily to the conclusion of the line.

Greene then goes on to analyse what he thought he was doing in the
novel:

> I wanted to give expression to various states or moods of belief
> and unbelief. The doctor, whom I liked best as a realised char-
> acter, represents a settled and easy atheism; the Father Superior a
> settled and easy belief . . . Father Thomas an unsettled form of belief
> and Querry an unsettled form of disbelief. One could probably dig
> a little of the author also out of the doctor and Father Thomas.[7]

Waugh would have none of this and came quickly to the point:

> I was not so dotty as to take Rycker as a portrait of myself. I
> saw him as the caricature of a number of your admirers . . . who
> have tried to force on you a position which you found obnox-
> ious. You have given many broad hints which we refused to recog-
> nise. Now you have made a plain repudiation.

Waugh added his fateful judgment:

> I don't think you can blame people who read the book as a recan-
> tation of faith. To my mind the expression 'settled and easy atheism'
> is meaningless, for an atheist denies his whole purpose as a man –
> to love & serve God. Only in the most superficial way can athe-
> ists appear 'settled and easy'. Their waste land is much more foreign
> to me than [Waugh uses a phrase Greene had once coined about
> certain Catholic attitudes] 'the suburbia of *The Universe*'.[8]

Greene felt the correspondence (and the fracas) was getting out of
hand, so he sent Waugh a postcard of Brighton pier, toned down to
stop the conflict with humour:

My love to Milton, Burns, Shelley and warn them that Spender and Day-Lewis are on the way. I shall be grateful for all your coppers. A voice from the Rear and the Slaves.[9]*

Waugh responded as only he could: 'Mud in your mild and magnificent eye. Hoping for a glad and confident morning.'[10]

Waugh was renowned for being rude and sometimes pointlessly cruel, to both men and women. Peter Glenville, Greene's director of *The Living Room*, in an interview he gave me in New York in 1978, remembered the first night of the play:

Evelyn . . . had a few drinks and was looking bellicose, and I was having first-night nerves and . . . one or two drinks, and I suddenly thought 'This man is being intolerable' because instead of just sitting and minding his own business . . . he was, I thought, carrying on a bit, and I remember thinking 'I'm going to hit that man', and there were about twelve of us in this tiny room, and a friend of mine told me . . . he remembered me going up and staring at him till we were practically forehead to forehead, and he had these huge bulbous eyes that were staring at me with glaring hostility, and I equally him apparently, and then the bell for the curtain going up rang, and so we fled.[11]

Waugh was never insulting to Greene, but Greene witnessed one of his tantrums at a dinner given by Carol and Pempe Reed. Alexander Korda, whom Graham loved, was the victim. (Greene had numerous times criticised Korda's films, but Korda never took personal offence.) Catherine Walston was also a guest, when 'suddenly Evelyn leaned across the table and launched an attack on Korda of shocking intensity, killing all the conversation around'. In Greene's view it was crude and unprovoked. The next day, sharing a taxi, Greene questioned Waugh, seeking a reason for his actions. 'I demanded an explanation,' Greene states. 'What on earth induced you to behave like that?' Waugh answered: 'Korda had no business to bring his mistress to Carol and Pempe's house.' Greene responded: 'But I was there with my mistress.' Waugh's droll answer was: 'That's quite different. [Catherine]'s married.' Greene wondered: '[Is] fornication more serious than adultery?'[12]

But Greene knew him too as generous with words for those he loved. An ageing Waugh† described 1965 as a bad year for him in a

---

* Greene is borrowing from Browning's 'The Lost Leader'.
† As early as 23 December 1957, in a letter to Catherine Walston, Graham noted that Evelyn had 'taken to a large ear-trumpet'.

number of ways, including dentistry: 'I had a lot of teeth drawn and find that the false snappers ruin my appetite for solid food';[13] deaths of friends; the 'aggiornamento' (the Catholic Church's modernisation campaign). He could not know that he himself had only a few months to live. He did know that Greene was to leave England and live in France. To Ann Fleming the same month he speaks with his usual flippancy: 'Graham Greene has fled the country with the [Companion of Honour] and a work of communist propaganda.'[14] (Greene was on his way to Cuba to interview Fidel Castro.) By 28 February Waugh wrote to his close friend Nancy Mitford (who lived in France) to give her Greene's Paris address, adding, 'I cannot tell you if he is alone there. I suspect not. But he is more social than his books would give one to think.'[15]

He wrote to Lady Mosley at the end of March, little more than a week before he died, making fun of his friend (and Greene's) John Sutro, who'd 'had hallucinations of poverty and was cured by electric shock'. He also complained about the recent change of liturgy which deeply troubled Waugh's Catholic heart:

> Easter used to mean so much to me. Before Pope John and his Council – they destroyed the beauty of the liturgy. I have not yet soaked myself in petrol and gone up in flames, but I now cling to the Faith doggedly without joy. Churchgoing is a pure duty parade.[16]

He was a firm believer, and had absolute confidence in the divine guidance of individual lives: 'God wants a different thing from each of us, laborious or easy, conspicuous or quite private, but something which only we can do and for which we were created.'[17]

We see the same sentiment in his diary's last entry at Easter 1965:

> A year in which the process of transforming the liturgy has followed a planned course. Protests avail nothing . . . I don't think the main congregation cares a hoot. More than the aesthetic changes which rob the Church of poetry, mystery and dignity, there are suggested changes in Faith and morals which alarm me. A kind of anti-clericalism is abroad which seeks to reduce the priest's unique sacramental position. The Mass is written of as a 'social meal' in which the 'people of God' perform the consecration. Pray God I will never apostatise but I can only now go to church as an act of duty and obedience.

Sadly, he spoke the truth: 'I shall not live to see things righted.'[18]

Greene thought that the changed liturgy of the Catholic Church quite literally broke Waugh's heart. To Nancy Mitford Waugh wrote: 'The buggering up of the Church is a deep sorrow to me and to all I know. We write letters to the paper. A fat lot of good that does.'[19] On 9 March 1966 he admitted to Diana Mosley that the Vatican Council had 'knocked the guts' out of him, and that in the previous two years, he'd become 'very old . . . Not diseased but enfeebled. There is nowhere I want to go and nothing I want to do and I am conscious of being an utter bore.'[20]

A month before his death, he wrote to his daughter Margaret that the 'awful prospect is that I may have more than 20 years ahead . . . Don't let me in my dotage oppress you.'[21] His first biographer, Christopher Sykes, recalls the last time he met him in White's Club, when Waugh described his lamentable condition: 'My life is roughly speaking over. I sleep badly except occasionally in the morning. I get up late. I try to read my letters. I try to read the paper. I have some gin. I try to read the paper again. I have some more gin. I try to think about my autobiography. Then I have some more gin and it's lunch time. That's my life. It's ghastly.'[22] Father Martin D'Arcy tells of his end:

> On the eve of Easter, April 1966, a priest came to see him and his wife Laura at their home Combe Florey. Knowing of a wayside Catholic chapel nearby, where Mass could be said, they asked him to stop the night and celebrate Easter by saying Mass at this chapel. He agreed, and so on Easter morning all the family who were at home went to Mass and to Communion together. After returning home, Evelyn left the room and fell dead.

Waugh was fortunate that his gentle Jesuit friend Father Caraman came to the rescue. Having just come from Norway for a few days, Father Caraman had the advantage of not needing higher authority to say mass in Latin. Christopher Sykes spoke of Evelyn being 'in good spirits, happy because he was to hear Mass said according to the time-honoured ancient rite'.[23] Waugh's later biographer, Selina Hastings, writes of Waugh as being 'in high good humour'.

Afterwards, at home with friends, he wandered off before lunch. He didn't return. He was found dead in the downstairs lavatory. 'A nanny tried to give him the kiss of life' without success and 'Father Caraman administered Conditional Absolution, the Last Rites given on the supposition that life may not yet be extinct'.[24] To the extent that anyone's death can be pleasant, Waugh's was what he would have wished. His son Auberon accounted his father's end as merciful: 'To die on Easter Sunday, after communion, among friends, with no lingering deterioration of the faculties'[25] must be reckoned a merciful death.

Graham heard another story from Sykes. When approached by Martin Stannard, Greene told him what he'd heard – that Father Caraman tried to interest Sykes in an account of what really happened. Stannard relates 'that Waugh had drowned in the lavatory, that there was water in his lungs and that an autopsy was necessary'. Stannard continues: 'And, ultimately, there remains a mystery. Greene was certain of his story. Fr Caraman denies it absolutely.'[26]

To drown in a lavatory bowl is just too unlikely for words. By the time Stannard wrote this, Greene and Caraman were at loggerheads, so that Caraman tried to, as it were, sell the story or (less appallingly) simply tried to interest the biographer in the story. If Greene had it right, it surely boggles the mind.

Greene's and Waugh's politics were miles apart, and Waugh regarded Greene's Catholicism as heretical, yet they stayed good friends. Writing to Greene on his fiftieth birthday, Waugh speaks of this milestone as a 'grand climacteric which sets the course of the rest of one's life', adding that it has for him been a 'year of lost friends . . . Not by death but wear and tear. Our friendship started rather late. Pray God it lasts.'[27] Greene was aware of Waugh's 'fine qualities: physical courage, private generosity, loyalty to friends'.[28] And Graham makes an arresting final statement: 'When I come to die, I shall wish he were beside me, for he would give me no easy comfort.'[29]

★

On 30 November 1971 there appeared in the local newspaper in Crowborough, Sussex, an obituary reference, brief enough to escape notice: 'GLOVER – On 23rd November, Miss Dorothy Glover, of Alberta, West Beeches Road, Crowborough.' Dorothy had been Greene's wartime lover, once of tremendous importance to him.

While writing *Brighton Rock* in 1939 Greene wanted to get out of the country, and when family life closed in, he had an enormous inclination to flee. Six weeks after the birth of Francis, Greene wrote to his brother Hugh: 'The baby is crying & I have ten books accumulated for review & this damned thriller to write.'[30] Greene told me that he saw an advertisement for a studio in Mecklenburgh Square, near Gray's Inn Road. He went to inspect it, and found 'Dorothy living with her mother. It was just a work room . . . it wasn't a studio in the French sense with a bed . . . Simply a room to work in. That is how we met. And she reduced the price because she thought I looked rather poor and I was a poor struggling author.'[31] Greene, thinking war would come soon, evacuated his family to his mother's home in Crowborough. War was declared on 3 September 1939.

Greene recalls the first air-raid warning (a false alarm) in a letter to Vivien: 'a woman in an unhurried manner, passed down the street, watching the huge barrage balloons rising into the sky; noting the odd scene of pigeons making a mass dive for shelter and feeling that this was the end of civilisation.'[32] But Greene told Malcolm Muggeridge (and he told me) that he was writing in his rented work room when war was declared and he looked out of the window to see 'barrage balloons rising in the sky and a sort of exaltation seized him. Looking behind him, he saw Miss Glover looking out of the window too and there was the beginning of this rather weird affair.'[33]

In the same interview Muggeridge spoke about Dorothy as 'Old Glover who rather strangely enough was very intimate with [Greene] and whom he was extraordinarily good to'. Clearly Muggeridge found the whole affair odd because he felt that Dorothy had very little going for her. Again, we see his opinion of her: 'on the grounds of attractiveness, [she] was absolutely a non-starter . . . a very ordinary kind of person and not the sort . . . you'd think in worldly terms he'd be attracted to, and yet he was devoted to her.'[34] David Higham, in an interview with me, called her 'little Dorothy . . . a strange little person – very small . . . She was nice, she lived [with] a parrot somewhere down in Kent . . . she was always breaking her leg or her wrist or something. She was a little spunky, courageous thing. She was short and a bit stout – [though not] a fat girl. I could see no sexual attraction at all.'[35]

But Dorothy's qualities revealed themselves almost as soon as the German blitz descended, beginning on 7 September 1940.

On that satanic night, the German Luftwaffe sent 1,300 bombers escorted by 600 fighters into the skies above London. That first day they did terrible damage. Indeed it was 'one of the dark places of the earth'. A. P. Herbert recalled what happened along the Thames. At Limehouse corner he witnessed a 'stupendous spectacle. Half a mile or more of the Surrey shore was burning . . . fires swept in a high wall across the river.' Going through that wall of smoke 'was like a lake in Hell. Burning barges were drifting everywhere.'[36]* But

---

* It was as if the whole world was on fire. On the docks they were breathing the fiery smoke of cargoes – pepper, burning rubber, barrels of rum, drums of paint exploding together. Tuning in British radio, one heard the Irish traitor William Joyce, known as Lord Haw-Haw, broadcasting from Germany: 'Germany calling, Germany calling', with that arrogant snobbish voice, telling Londoners ominously: 'Jews today are shaking in their shoes, but tonight there will be no more Jews.' Some undoubtedly must have been killed in the East End, for we know that that night the Germans chalked up a kill of 430 civilians, seriously injured 1,600 and made thousands homeless.

Greene did not run away, as those who could afford to often did.

And in that madhouse Dorothy stayed, on fire-watching duty (an inadequate term for dangerous patrolling on roofs of buildings watching for enemy planes, for bombs and the inevitable fires). This was the setting for their love affair.

On 16 April 1941, life was a maelstrom and Greene kept an account of it in his mind. It was too mad, too dangerous, too deadly to be written down during the blitz. In a single evening 2,000 civilians died, 100,000 homes were destroyed, and central London experienced its worst raid.

That night, Greene and Dorothy were having a drink in the Horseshoe Inn (later the site of the battle between John Gordon, Greene and Randolph Churchill). Leaving the pub, they went to Frascati's and then to Victor's, hoping to have dinner before the raid got under way: both were closed. They ended up at Czardas, sitting apprehensively next to the plate-glass windows. An hour into the raid, bursting bombs in Piccadilly shook the restaurant in Dean Street, and they left, walking back to the home they shared in Gower Street. Dorothy, on fire-watching duty, went to her post on the roof of a garage. Before she and Greene reached it, they saw flares from enemy planes drifting down 'like great yellow peonies'.

The bookseller David Low recalled that when one of the biggest bombs fell and hit on the corner: 'I saw Graham and Dorothy walking up Bloomsbury Street. As a result of the bomb, there were papers flying everywhere. Graham and Dorothy were picking up the papers whatever they were and reading them to each other in the street and roaring with laughter.'[37] Sometimes laughter was the only relief.

Greene was very happy with Dorothy as a comrade-in-arms. Dorothy's spirit shone courageously, and Greene loved her for it. I remember interviewing Greene in Antibes and talking of Dorothy. He was adamant about her marvellously unfeminine bravery: 'From the first raid, she . . . showed absolutely no fear of any kind.'[38]

Greene felt deep remorse over Dorothy.* He suffered in the break-up. He even allowed her to humiliate him – always the most terrible thing in life for him to bear. There is no question that she could be something of a termagant. Once, when she thought Greene was going to visit Catherine, she prevented it by hiding his trousers. Like Helen in *The Heart of the Matter*, Dorothy called her lover out:

---

* Greene told me thirty-three years after the event, Dorothy dead ten years, about giving up his wife and Dorothy. His face absolutely wooden, an ingrained melancholy painfully apparent: 'I've betrayed very many people in my life.' He selected only one for special mention: 'I betrayed Dorothy. Particularly Dorothy.' Dorothy had no marriage, no children – her only companion her widowed mother. She tried to resign herself to her role in life. What was there left for him to feel but enormous pity?

'You are not protecting *me*. You are protecting your wife . . . That woman . . . You'd never leave her, would you?'

'We are married,' he said . . .

'You'll never marry me.'

'I can't. You know that.'

'It's a wonderful excuse being a Catholic,' she said. 'It doesn't stop you sleeping with me – it only stops you marrying me.'[39]

Greene felt he had to confront Dorothy which he was loath to do. He decided on a roundabout method, taking her first to Paris, then Brussels, and giving her a letter which explained why he'd be leaving their apartment at the top of the stairs in Gordon Square. I asked him why he did it this way. His answer: 'I was suffering from terrible moral cowardice over Dorothy and wanted to let her down easily.'*

Graham wrote to Catherine, she a calm watcher of his manoeuvrings over Vivien and Dorothy, that in Paris with Dorothy: 'as for love (in the f-sense) we are two corpses',[40] and told Vivien that he hoped to take a flat by himself in London, and that the present set-up in Gordon Square would be materially altered: '*though I am trying if it's humanly possible to save some relationship there*'.[41]

Suddenly he had a letter from Dorothy – ungrammatical, in places indecipherable, pungent, direct, and the only one we have from her, written on 14 April 1948:

I had lunch with Mr Mellar today. Heard little except the story of you & Walston for an hour & a half. Everyone from Douglas [Jerrold] to the packers [at Eyre & Spottiswoode] it seems know you are behaving like a fool over an American blond [*sic*] as you have made no attempt to disguise it from anyone, everyone you know in London is talking about it too! Charles supplies the directors with information (he is in great demand as he has become part of the set up & drinks with you all) & your secretary deals with the lower orders & so on. They also know that you are prepared to break up Oxford for this woman.[42]

That Dorothy was unaware Greene had already left his wife indicates his secretiveness. She reported that though others had guessed about the Walston affair as far back as April 1947, their suspicions weren't confirmed until the autumn (while Dorothy was away), when the affair grew more intense and Greene completely 'lost his head'.

* Remember Graham's term 'moral cowardice' applied to T. S. Eliot when he moved out on John Hayward. Perhaps they were both too sensitive.

Then Dorothy speaks of herself, spewing out her anger and insults: 'They are of course "very sorry for the other woman" who they regard as a kind of Graham Greene specimen – something to be kept in private & never seen or mentioned . . . Mrs Greene feels that you are going out of your mind as no man in his right senses would behave as you do over an American blond [*sic*] with a yearning for culture!'

She speaks of a holiday he'd promised, suggesting he should cancel it because 'it would be awful [to be] with one woman when all your thoughts are on another'. And she added a note showing that in spite of everything, she wished to keep a foot in the Greene door:

> If at any time you want to make a life we can share, or this thing with Walston breaks tell me, but any advance now I'm afraid must come from you.[43]

In Paris, he gave her the 'Dear Dorothy' letter. He wrote to Catherine: 'I gave her the letter 24 hours before we left Paris. Ghastly, scenes, but we went on.' Now that the letter was delivered, he tells Catherine that half of each day could be pleasant and the other half 'an awful hell of tears, pain, melancholy'.[44] Dorothy worked out a plan that she would continue sleeping at Gordon Square and he would sometimes sleep there but have also another flat where he could work. They travelled to Fez, reaching it on 11 May, and then to Casablanca at four in the morning, and to Rabat. To Catherine, his emotional barometer: 'Everything is quieter now, & last night we went & saw a couple of very bad naked dancers in a native brothel & smoked a pipe of hashish.' But the next day, Dorothy had sexual proof of his affair with Catherine right in front of her gimlet eyes: 'Today I put on my corduroys & she spotted the guilt marks right away – in five seconds. She said she'd already found them on my grey flannels. However no scene – yet.'[45]

By 16 May they were at Marrakesh: 'Yesterday we arrived here, hell opened again from 2 till 6 & I nearly got the plane back but the office was closed. There is no longer a chance, I think, of avoiding a complete split & this time has cleared my mind a lot about that & wiped out a good many memories.' He was quite frantic: 'No more lies or worries of that kind . . . it will be a good time beginning & I'll write my best book yet . . . All the deception is over for ever.'[46]

*

With the publication of *The Heart of the Matter*, Greene was suddenly the most famous and most pursued writer in England, but Dorothy was on his mind. Not because he was still in love with her, but because she loved him totally. A statement by him in a different context was surely written with Dorothy in mind: 'Against the beautiful and the clever and the successful, one can wage a pitiless war, but not against the unattractive.' Poor Dorothy. In her case, Greene felt her all-too-human need: 'any victim demands allegiance,' he wrote in *The Heart of the Matter*, 'especially the victim you have created.'[47]

By looking at the inscriptions in the books Greene gave to Dorothy, we see what was for him the most important period of his love. There are no surprises. In *The Lost Childhood* (1951), his book of essays, he writes: 'For Dorothy with love from Graham with many memories of the blitz'. And in *The Ministry of Fear*, his inscription to her refers to the war years so crucial to their love: 'For Dorothy this book which is particularly yours, with love from Graham'. Greene's play *The Living Room*, first published in 1953, shows he had had the germ of it in mind ten years earlier. The volume had a printed dedication 'To Catherine with love', but the handwritten inscription might suggest Dorothy had more right to the dedication: 'For Dorothy in memory of Westerham & the flying bombs when we first discussed it, with love from Graham'.

The Heart of the Matter speaks of the period of their greatest love: 'For you, with ten years *real* love, from me. June 1948. D.G. G.G.' He also gave her an understanding of what he thought of himself in leaving her. He sent *Nineteen Stories*, published by Heinemann in 1947, the year he fell in love with Catherine and set about removing himself from Dorothy, and penned: 'For Dorothy Glover with so much love over so many years, 1939–1947 from Graham Greene – the bastard'.

★

In November 1951, three years after his break with Dorothy, Greene heard unexpected news: she had decided to become a Catholic and was under instruction from Father Philip Caraman. From that moment Dorothy became a friend of Catherine's and visited her home at Newton Hall.

Greene continued to keep in touch with her. They wrote children's books together, though this was not known at first. *The Little Train* came out before Catherine met Greene, in June 1946. Nowhere on the book is there any reference to Graham Greene as the author. In the first edition, the legend reads 'Story and Pictures by Dorothy Craigie'. But the truth was revealed when Greene sent a copy of *The Little Train* to Catherine, recording the little book's history in his own hand:

The name of Dorothy Craigie *in the case of this book only* and one as yet unpublished called *The Little Fire Engine* – conceals two characters, the author, myself, & the artist, my very great friend

Dorothy Glover formerly a stage designer and now a successful writer of boy's books, *Ride (Voyage of the Lune)*. It was written mainly in a pub called the Chester Arms near Regent's Park on Sunday mornings at the fly-bomb period of the war.* (One remembers the Scotch terrier who used to panic at the inevitable siren). We made a small dummy out of a notebook, & I made wild pencil suggestions as to how the illustrations should go & of what they should consist, so the book was written and designed simultaneously. 1st edition, I think, 20,000, of which 12,000 were quickly sold.

The Little Fire Engine was published in 1950, *The Little Horse Bus* in 1952, *The Little Steamroller* in 1953, with its exciting subtitle: 'A Story of Adventure, Mystery and Detection'.

Through the good offices of Father Philip Caraman, Dorothy completed her conversion to Catholicism. Graham and Catherine went to Dorothy Glover's confirmation on 16 June 1953.

*

During 1957, Greene visited Dorothy in Crowborough. She clearly had deteriorated in the previous eight years – not least because she had become an alcoholic after her lost love:

> I looked in at Dorothy & was shocked & horrified . . . She had [gained] weight again, after two whiskys couldn't stand straight, wept about her loneliness & how awful her mother was (I can believe it) & regretted leaving Gordon Square. It was an awful atmosphere with the mother listening outside the door.
>
> I've asked Philip [Caraman] to take her out. One feels awful – I don't seem able to do anything but make people unhappy.[48]

Two weeks later Greene told Catherine that he'd had Dorothy for three days: 'Seemed much better and more cheerful.' Becoming a Catholic seemed to do her spirits good, and her visits to Newton Hall helped, too.

Dorothy was to bring out a final book with Greene, one which was long in the making, originally being a collaboration with Hugh Greene, who had taken to seeking out Victorian detective fiction. This collection, compiled over many years, helped to make the three of them

* A week after D-Day, on 13 June 1944, the first pilotless plane crossed the English coast and fell on London. As many as 20,000 houses a day were damaged, and casualties were severe – 10,000 during the first week's bombing.

bibliophiles of distinction. The final aptly named catalogue, *Victorian Detective Fiction*, is awe-inspiring and unique. Graham and Dorothy began this endeavour after the war when there were few competitors in the field. The edition was limited to 500, each signed by Graham and Dorothy Glover, thus bringing their printed signatures together, along with John Carter, the well-known bibliophile who contributed an introduction, as did Greene. They had searched together, and they searched everywhere, even finding Victorian detective fiction outside a second-hand furniture store, including – to quote Graham – 'a parody of Sherlock Holmes by a fairly well-known writer of the time, cost 1/6d'.[49] At last they were in the same book.

★

Greene left England and was residing in Antibes writing *The Honorary Consul* when he got the sad news from his secretary. On 25 November 1971, Miss Reid received a letter from Dr Michael Walters:

> Miss Dorothy Glover died on Tuesday 23rd November. Her mother asked me to write to you. She says that she thought she had posted the letters to you but the poor soul was very upset & vague and I would doubt that this had been done.
>
> She will, against her will, have to be moved to a safe house and the Welfare people have the matter in hand.

Mrs Glover was moved to Furze House, Flimwell, near Ticehurst. Miss Reid telephoned Greene in Antibes and he flew to England for the funeral. He invited Malcolm Muggeridge, who'd known Dorothy, but he was unable to attend. In a letter to Greene he recalled the early days during the Blitz at Dorothy's place, when Graham fried sausages. But at the funeral, Conrad's phrase haunted Greene: Mr Kurtz, experiencing the darkness of his soul, dies lamenting: 'The Horror. The Horror.'

Greene paraphrases: 'D's funeral . . . the horror.'[50]

PART II

Carving Two Failures

24

A Flop of Biblical Proportions

Enough is as good as a feast.
— JOHN HEYWOOD

IN late March 1978, Georgie Stonor wrote to Greene: 'Muggeridge reviewed you on TV Book programme [*The Human Factor*]. Howlingly patronising – did you watch? You are "out of date" re MI6 but [have] "not lost his touch with words."'[1]

Muggeridge's comment was typical, and Greene admitted that he 'didn't hear Malcolm on TV, but I gather he was his old jealous self'.[2] Greene once said to me: 'Muggeridge is a good friend, but he always carries a stiletto in his stocking.' Off and on throughout their friendship and professional lives, Muggeridge and Greene had their tiffs, but Muggeridge suggested to me there was no real enmity between them.

There are two skittish references to him in Greene's play *Carving a Statue*. The teenage son of a sculptor, long years without a mother, wants his father to marry again: 'Don't you think there's a chance, just a chance, you might come to marry again? Your heart's not broken, is it? It's not mother's fault she died the way she did. Mr Muggeridge has married again. For the third time.'[3]

The boy is simply trying to evoke his mother's memory. But the sculptor is a narcissist, his world peopled only with those who can be of use to him in his attempt to sculpt a huge image of God. His admiration for himself is appalling:

BOY: Did you suffer when mother died?
FATHER: It was a shocking inconvenience.

The father is superb at speaking at cross-purposes:

283

BOY: What's the act of darkness, father? [*He gets no answer.*] . . .
FATHER: [*Speaking of his unfinished statue, two mighty stone legs crowding the stage, the rest going on up to the flies some fifty feet high.*] The right eye's not quite as it should be yet . . .
BOY: I wish you had come to my school just once. I used to boast about you, but nobody believed me. I needed evidence.
FATHER: At least I've got real power into the feet. I've done that. And I've got a *bit* of wickedness into His right eye . . . The trouble is – He isn't only power. He isn't only wickedness . . . Did He love? Didn't He love? What's love? There's the tricky question.
BOY: We loved you, mother and me.
FATHER: I can't avoid the question like Michelangelo did. [*He indicates the Pietà.*] The Son's dead. It's easy to love the dead – they cause no trouble. But they say He loved the world. They say He even loved his Son. It was a queer way He showed it though.
BOY: Did I love mother, father?
FATHER: The feet are right. I defy anyone to question the feet.⁴

Talking this way can be humorous, even farcical, which was how Greene wanted it played.

FATHER: The knees are an awful problem. He never knelt. His son knelt, and His son's mother knelt, but it's never recorded that He ever knelt. What would He kneel to? . . . It's an interesting point of anatomy. A knee is made to bend. If the knee never bends what kind of a knee is it? How do you represent it?
BOY: Perhaps he didn't have any knees.

The one-sided discussion goes on. The sculptor needs his son to do odd tasks, but is otherwise totally uninterested in him, or in his dead wife, obsessed as he is with the nature of the Almighty:

FATHER: I only have to carve what shows. All the same how do you carve a contradiction? He has to be wicked and He has to be loving at the same time and He can't suffer or He wouldn't have sent His son down here to die. He wiped out the whole world except Noah without blinking one stony eyelid. The Egyptians were drowned in the Red Sea like so many Chinamen. Of course I can understand His attitude . . . I wouldn't . . . suffer if I broke Him up with a crowbar. I would be free of Him as He was free of His son. I suppose I'd feel a bit of waste . . . But I wouldn't go so far as to say [I] suffered.

BOY: Dr Parker said that mother suffered. I can remember listening outside the door and I heard Dr Parker say to the nurse 'She's gone. It's a good thing she's gone. She suffered terribly.' Where were you, father?

FATHER: Perhaps the knees are not required under the circumstances. Or I could put in embryo knees, like a child in the womb has embryo gills, because if all had gone well with the world, who knows? . . .

BOY: Is unhappiness the same thing as suffering? Or is suffering something worse? I cried. I didn't scream. Mother screamed . . .

FATHER: It's a terrible thing to have nobody anywhere who has any idea what I'm trying to do.[5]

Done right, the play should come off as farce, but there is one imponderable ignored. Greene had given himself the task of pitting the father's ambition against the pain of a young man's profound loss – the death of his mother. So Greene is trying to put in unison what can never be joined. How did Greene not know this?

The whole thing misfires because the father is so engrained in self-love. In the final act, the son summons his courage to ask the question raised in the first act: 'Where were you when mother died?' The answer comes after a long pause:

When your mother died I ran out of the room before the breathing stopped. I began to work. It was all I could do. I can't take life except at second hand, but I work. I work. In dryness I work. In despair I work. As long as I work I can hold the pain of the world away from me. That's the only subject I've got – my indifference and the world's pain.[6]

This enormous egotist could have been played as a foolish figure, which is what Greene wanted, but the audience at the Haymarket Theatre did not laugh.

★

The sculptor makes his son in effect an orphan even with his father standing beside him. In the first act, the son's interest is his mother;

his father's interest is how, having got a wicked glint in God's right eye (he'd used a photo of Landru, guillotined in 1922 for murdering ten women and a boy), he could put love into God's left eye: 'But what infernal chisel stroke do I use for love?'

The same cross-talk continues:

BOY: Did you love mother?
FATHER: Give me another sandwich.[7]

And then the father links himself to the great: 'Michelangelo, Rodin and me. Nobody can deny we try to do big things.'[8] At this point, the father goes out in search of a model – a person with a loving eye. He meets Dr Parker (who has a lascivious eye), but the area is alive with fathers of the kind the sculptor is seeking. 'You'd think I could get a good idea for Him and his left eye with all those fathers around.'[9] So there's his problem: having found the means of showing divine wrath in the right eye, the sculptor has now in the left eye to chisel divine clemency.

★

The second act starts with the boy's attempts at making love. Greene describes the First Girl as having her 'hair rumpled and wet after a bathe. She wears blue jeans and a shirt . . . [and] has picked up many Americanisms from the movies. She has an air of toughness, but perhaps she is more vulnerable and inexperienced than she appears.' They have been drinking sherry.

She sees the statue and utters an oath: 'God Almighty, what's this?' and the boy answers (inevitably): 'God Almighty.'[10] The boy has a nice line of romantic talk; they smooch clumsily. He imagines for her that he is a sailor and she thinks of sailors: 'There hasn't been a ship in here for weeks, for months, it seems like years. I want to love the first man who comes ashore.'[11] Then she thinks of sleeping in a great golden bed with a net around, offering herself in a sleazy way. With the dream over, she wants to leave for another date. He tries to make her stay but fails; he pleads for her to come back, but there are no promises.

The father returns and the girl is immediately impressed. She twice whispers to the son: 'He's a big man', and speaks of 'carving a statue like that – he must need an awful lot of muscle'.[12] The girl seems to have forgotten the son. The father ignores her and asks his son to bring back a ladder. The boy leaves. The girl begins to speak to the father about the weight of the head which he is now moving up in the flies – 'Is it heavy?' – and mockingly the father answers: 'If I'd left it lying

1 Norman Sherry in Mexico, seeking the originals used in *The Power and the Glory*

2 Greene and his sister Elisabeth Dennys at Gemma's Restaurant, Capri

11 Jesús Sosa Blanco
unsuccessfully defended himself:
'By God, I'm no murderer!'

12 While filming *Our Man in Havana*:
sitting, (*left to right*) Alec Guinness,
Carol Reed, Maureen O'Hara,
Ernie Kovacs. Standing, (*left to right*)
Noël Coward and Greene

13 (*above*) Entrance to leper colony at Yonda, Congo

14 (*left*) Greene with Dr Michel Lechat

15 (*below*) Filariasis (elephantiasis) of the scrotum: 'It seems unfair, doesn't it, to suffer all that and leprosy too.' (Dr Colin in *A Burnt-Out Case*)

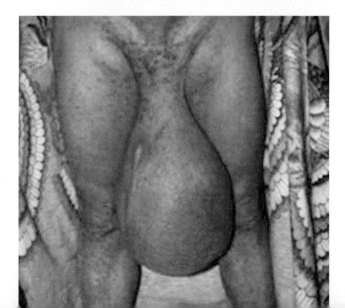

21 The bungalow Greene and
Michael Meyer shared in Tahiti

22 (*above left*) Michael Meyer and
Greene in Tahiti

23 (*above*) Evelyn Waugh with ear trumpet

24 (*left*) Sir Ralph Richardson

there much longer it would have sunk into the floor like a tombstone sinks in the grass.'[13]

Soon she is trying to excite: 'Your boy wanted to make love to me . . . He kissed me and touched me. Of course I was safe in jeans.' Again and again she returns to it, trying to intrigue the father while he talks in his usual way about his statue.

At last she has his attention:

FATHER: He's too young.
GIRL: He gave me a lot of drinks. He got me tipsy.
FATHER: You aren't tipsy. You want a man, that's all.[14]

The father begins to appraise her from every angle. She stands still and lets him. He makes up a naughty rhyme about his physician:

Botticelli
Showed the belly
And the little round tail
Through a muslin veil
But Dr Parker
Prefers 'em starker.[15]

FATHER: [*with a laugh*] You're no virgin.
GIRL: I am – sort of. Cross my heart.
FATHER: You mean you need to have the job finished?[16]

The girl speaks of his son's love for her: 'swoony. Like your boy said about "I love you for ever". It's silly, isn't it. But it's nice all the same.'

FATHER: You want me to show you something?
GIRL: What?
FATHER: Don't complain if it scares you.
GIRL: Something you've carved?
FATHER: Something my father carved for me . . . He carved in
         human flesh . . . Come over here and I'll show you. [*He
         moves towards the tool-shed.*]
GIRL: . . . What's in there?
FATHER: It's where I keep my tools.[17]

The father goes off with the girl following him nervously.

Back on stage comes the son, slowly pushing the heavy ladder. He assumes the girl has gone, but he's happy with the beginnings of a love adventure. He becomes, for the first time, rhapsodic with hope. He speaks to himself: 'If there are enough prayers some will be answered. It's the law of averages.' From the tool-shed the girl comes back onto the stage looking 'bemused and tousled. She is without her blue jeans. Her shirt comes down to her knees. She walks by the boy, paying him no attention at all.'

GIRL: Where's my jeans? [*The Father comes for a moment to the door of the tool-shed and tosses the jeans to her without speaking.*]

The girl asks for the bathroom; the father replies. The father goes back into the shed. The girl goes out, trailing the jeans after her.

For the first time, the boy criticises his father: 'You think you are strong, don't you. "My, he's a big man." You needn't feel so proud. She's only a little tart. I saw through her all the time.' The boy collapses in tears with his face pressed against the statue. The father enters dressed for sculpting. He is completely oblivious to his son's pain.

FATHER: Here. Help me with this ladder. I'm ready for a bit of work now.
BOY: Put up your own bloody ladder.
FATHER: I've got an idea about his left eye. What are you waiting for? I want to get the ladder up quick. I'm going to start right away. I'm in the mood. You wouldn't understand what it feels like when an idea strikes you. I feel giddy with it. It's like vertigo . . . It's like God Almighty on the first day. When He divided the light from the dark. You can't rest till you've made the first start, and anything may follow after that . . . I've been knocking my head against a brick wall over that left eye. But now I know. I don't have to worry about love. God doesn't love. He communicates, that's all. He's an artist. He doesn't love.
BOY: Did He hate his son?
FATHER: He didn't love or hate him. He used him as a subject. That's what the Son was for.[18]

The curtain falls on the second act.

*

This heinous father is not the end of difficulty for the son. The final act furnishes the son with another horror to sup on.

The play has a paucity of characters; the last act brings in two new ones. A month has passed; the son has found someone he really loves. The third act begins with his reading to his future wife the marriage regulations: 'The marriage must be solemnized between the hours of 8 a.m. and 6 p.m. with open doors in the presence of a Superintendent Registrar.' He is sitting beside the girl, reading out loud. 'The parties must make the following declaration. I do solemnly declare . . .'[19] and the silent girl is following the text with her eyes. One is aware that they are very close and in love.

The boy leaves, late for a job interview. Enter the lascivious Dr Parker, bringing in some welcome humour – at least at first. He sits down to take his own blood pressure and keeps up a rapid-fire conversation with himself, concerning the joy of not having to employ a bedside manner:

> A doctor may be clever, charming, assiduous, he may be loved by his patients, but he belongs to a world of fantasy. After telling a lot of frightened patients a lot of reassuring stories I find it hard to believe in my own reality. I tell little jokes – what is the difference between an elephant and a flea? – as I feel the cruel tumour under my fingers.[20]

And having patted the statue of God Almighty, he draws parallels between himself and the Lord, as the boy's father does throughout the play:

> My friend, I become like you, a block of stone, indifferent to human suffering. The thought of you soothes the dying. Just so they wait for my footsteps. Like you I offer false comfort. What other use have you? Can you tell the difference between an elephant and a flea?[21]

As he is talking to himself and then to God, the son's fiancée appears. The doctor speaks, saying his name, asking hers. She makes no reply. He admits to his harmless habit of talking to himself. Still no response from the girl.

> PARKER: You're rather a silent child, though a very charming one
> . . . Are you deaf? [*No reply.*] Are you dumb? [*The father enters.*]
> FATHER: She's deaf *and* dumb.[22]

The father tells Dr Parker that his son found her after she became lost on the Underground. Parker watches the girl, uttering words like 'poor child'. Clearly fascinated, he crooks his finger, and she approaches.

He puts his hand on her shoulder and turns her around, examining her figure with an experienced eye':

> A little Botticelli. I can see her rising from the sea in something silky and diaphanous, through which the pearly skin gleams like an oyster-shell. And what a gift of silence.[23]

We discover next that Dr Parker has the means of communicating with the girl using sign language. His fascination grows, and the whole time he is speaking to the father he has his eye on the girl. Soon after, the men argue and a disgruntled Parker shouts at the father: 'What makes you such a selfish old bastard? I've known you for twenty years and you've never faced pain yet.'[24]

The girl wanders out. She looks back and the doctor speaks to her in sign language. She smiles, and for the first time gestures with her hands before she goes. The father asks what he is saying to her and Parker replies: 'That she puts a flame in my old body.'[25] The doctor follows the girl. The father disappears up the ladder to work on his statue. The son returns.

He has much to tell his father: he is going away, he's found a job at Bentley's garage, been given a room above it, and eight pounds a week, and the central fact that he's getting married and he wants his father's permission. The boy and the deaf-mute are genuinely in love.

In the middle of their talk, as usual at cross-purposes, 'from somewhere outside comes the high squeal of brakes, a confusion of cries'. The boy pooh-poohs its significance: 'Only an accident in Elm Park Road. It's always happening. I'm going away, father.'[26]

While conversing with his father, the son keeps asking where his girl is, and the father, not thinking much about it, says she and Dr Parker were talking together in deaf and dumb language, which worries the boy. He talks more about his new job, of how his future wife is to help Bentley's wife in the house, and how he'll arrange for old Mrs Harris to attend his father.

Suddenly Dr Parker returns, crying: 'It was nobody's fault. Nobody's. The driver had no chance. She ran out into the street as if she were blind.' There is confusion, the boy asking the doctor where his girl is and Parker, as if mentally confused, saying: 'Oh yes, your girl. I forgot. She was your girl. We laid her on the bed in the spare room.' The boy goes past and Parker tries to stop him: 'There's nothing you can do.' Parker begins to explain to the father: 'She didn't suffer. If I'd known she was going to tear out of the door like that, I'd have stopped her, but she didn't say a word.'

FATHER: She was dumb.
PARKER: Yes, I'd forgotten that. The policeman saw it happen. He
knows it was no one's fault but hers. The driver put on
his brake. He sounded his horn.
FATHER: She was deaf. Why did she run out?

He replies: 'How would I know?' But his guilt is evident:

FATHER: What's that in your hand?[27]

Parker looks at his hand as though he doesn't know what it contains.
It is the girl's white panties. (On certain nights, a critic reported, her
panties were frilly lavender ones.) And Parker shrugs off the guilt: 'I
was only having a game. I meant no harm.' When the father says she
was a virgin, Parker can only add: 'How could I know that? I was
being kind to her.'[28] This sybarite has only one interest: copulation.

★

In this appalling play, the guilt lies with older men, men in responsible positions who play dirty little games that claim lives, or who, like
the father, are indifferent to sons in pain. So in this 'farce' we witness
two tragedies, the second more terrible than the first. The boy carries
the dead girl in his arms, and cries out to his father for help. The father
retreats to his tool-shed:

BOY: Father! She's dead. Come out of there and speak to me,
         father. I'm alone. I need you. Help me. I'm your son.

The boy, faced with his overwhelming loss, threatens to hang himself:

BOY: You are a father, aren't you? Indifference in the right eye
         and a bit of tenderness in the left. But you could never
         get round to finishing the left eye, could you?
FATHER: Why are you blaming me? I did nothing.
BOY: Nothing for me and nothing for mother. You know all
         about indifference, don't you, and nothing about love.[29]

And a message that seems at last personal and central to the father's
nature: 'There wasn't time for two lives with all I had to finish.'[30]

★

The play is neither fish, flesh nor fowl. It reached the London stage
after a try-out in Brighton, on 17 September 1964. Derek Patmore, in

an unpublished piece, recalls being with Greene at the Theatre Royal, Brighton, for the premiere, admitting: 'It is probably the most difficult of his plays but it has a number of profound moments. But watching it with him at Brighton, I could sense that he wasn't happy about it. During the interval, he turned to me and said, "The last act is all wrong. I must alter it before London."' And Patmore told Greene something Greene was well aware of: 'With the theatre you are at the mercy of so many elements: your producer & the actors & actresses. When you write a book it is exactly as you wanted it.'[31] This weighed on Greene, as is clear in a dream he had on 18 July 1965:

I have to direct a film for the first time in my life; I have no script . . . & I have done no homework – I have thought out no camera angles, cuts etc. Ralph Richardson is to star in it, & someone warns me that he intends to get me sacked humiliatingly on the first day. It is R. who introduces me to the *équipe*, about twenty men sitting at long tables having refreshments. I make the mistake of apologising for my inexperience & they shout back their mocking agreement. If only, I think, I can get through the first day's shooting, I'll be able to study the play at night. A remark of Ralph's gives me a clue. I say, 'I want to begin with an exterior shot of your monocle lying on the doorstep. We hear you cursing from a window above – whatever curses you are in the habit of using.' But after that promising beginning we begin to quarrel. He talks of appealing to his agent. I say, 'Are you threatening me?' 'Yes.' I say I shall appeal to no one, but I'll cut his face open with a riding whip.[32]

Carving a Statue was Graham's greatest flop. He was hopeful that with another triumph similar to the enormous success of *The Complaisant Lover*, he could give up writing novels, which since *A Burnt-Out Case* he'd found so desperately difficult. He was feeling that at sixty, youth had disappeared, and he was suffering the effects of his idiosyncratic darting round the world. He longed for another victory on the stage, fearing that his creative batteries would never recharge enough to write a lengthy story.

But he'd written an impossible play, a strange hybrid: his words were plainer than he'd ever written, monosyllabic, with hardly a rhetorical note. Given no more than simple speech, the actors had to contend with the set and the enormous size of the statue. It towered over all, monstrous and gelded (for it had no genitals), or as the *Daily Mail* put it, 'huge feet, massive legs, the hips, the agonised stone chest, the statue without gender'.[33] Numerous reviewers remarked on it.

John Holmstrom described how the statue's 'vast feet, legs and sexless crotch bestride the Haymarket stage like a cosmic reproach cast in coagulated boulders'.[34] In the *Lady*, J. C. Trewin admitted that 'I daresay I shall go on thinking of Desmond Heeley's extraordinary set, the legs and thighs of an immense statue that fills the stage, its head out of sight . . . We remember the decor . . . more than the play itself.'[35]

The mammoth statue dominated and overpowered, and the Brobdingnagian setting allowed the actors little space to act, to confront, to convince. The rejection of Greene's play by reviewers was almost universal, and *Punch* punched his lights out:

> Possibly the worst play by a reputable dramatist that I have ever seen. I can't think why H. M. Tennent and Donald Albery wanted to put it on, why Sir Ralph Richardson and Roland Culver were prepared to appear in it, why Peter Wood wanted to direct it or why Mr Greene ever let it loose outside his study.

Having trashed it, the unnamed reviewer goes on to bury it:

> The story is banal, the development inept, the characterisation is perfunctory and the observations about God (the play is about God) are more excruciatingly naïve than I would have thought possible this side of the Arian heresy.[36]*

The tirade did not stop: 'Greene's failure . . . lies in lack of material and lack of passion . . . Short as it is (under two hours playing time) *Carving a Statue* is nevertheless shamefully padded – with weak jokes, aphorisms, gratuitous comic turns and romantic fantasies . . . Practically nothing happens, and when it does, proves to be a jaw-cracking melodramatic cliché.'[37] Malcolm Rutherford in the *Spectator* seemed to enjoy dismissing Greene:

> Now it is perfectly possible that a play like this could have been written without the statue ever being shown. But imagine *Carving a Statue* without the figure there and there is absolutely nothing, neither dialogue, nor plot nor characterisation. It would be as reasonable to ask people to pay just to sit and look at the statue as for what is shamefully passed off as a play.[38]

Molly Hobman stressed that she 'left heavy with a boredom I had never expected this author to induce', and she added a final insult: 'The book

---

* As a priest, Arius (*c.* 318) taught that God created before all things a Son who was the first creature, but who was not equal to God. He taught that Jesus Christ was a supernatural creature, not quite human and not quite divine.

of Job, as enacted by an American group in a London church the same night, must have been less lugubrious than this portentous play.' In *Theatre World* the reviewer added: 'We are not sure if we are asked to ponder on God-forsaken Man or Man-forsaken God, or why sex should play such an important part in the author's current effort to unravel the mystery of God the Father and God the Son.'[39] A list of reviewers reviling Greene's play deserves entry in the *Guinness Book of Records*.

*

It is surprising that Greene could have written such a half-baked play, with such shallow characters. Here the consummate creator of the tightly-made plot tries unsuccessfully to fit obvious religious symbols into the story. If we were watching a Samuel Beckett play, we would expect a certain awkwardness, the partially unfinished, confused sentence – but Greene had given us three successful plays: *The Living Room, The Potting Shed* and *The Complaisant Lover. Carving a Statue* is not Greeneland: it is Beckett country, and the woodrot shows.

In this play, Greene's own character is nowhere to be seen. Yet unless Greene's own powerful personal interests are engaged, his work never comes alive. Displayed here is Greene's interest in parables, in the nature of the Godhead, and the rather obvious nature to boot, but its descent into cliché plunges us smack-dab into the realm of dullness.

*

Derek Patmore sheds light on the heroic side of Greene's nature when on the receiving end of critical blows to the head. He didn't think Greene was set back by the critics' reaction. He felt that Greene's strength lay in an 'almost Olympian detachment. Unlike so many authors he seems little worried by criticism, and just goes on writing the books & plays which he wants to write.' On this occasion however, Greene – for once and at last – had been chosen as a sacrificial victim of the press. He'd received such a battering – he, who'd been their darling these long years – it would have been inhuman not to be disturbed. Typically, he did not show his private feelings to Derek Patmore, though Patmore supported Greene:

> The theatre is different. Sir Ralph Richardson, who played the leading part, obviously had his own ideas of how to play the sculptor but these did not always correspond with those of the author, Graham Greene. This noble play did not succeed for Richardson, good actor as he is, could not project the agony and doubt of the creative artist which formed the whole basis of the play.[40]

Yet there *are* noble lines in the play, and looking at the collected reviews, there is some support for Patmore's stance. B. A. Young, reviewing for the *Financial Times*, praises the director, then faults the leading man: 'Ralph Richardson as the father seems to have given up completely and trudges through his lines as if he were reading them for the first time. When an actor of this distinction is defeated, one can hardly expect a sixteen-year-old to do much better.'[41] *The Times* did not agree:

> Hardly until the third act does [Richardson] address anyone directly, descending from the statue in goggles and covered in stone dust, he speaks and moves with unapproachable detachment, the eyes alternately glittering in the light of his private obsession and glazing over whenever any other topic intrudes. It is a performance that combines mystery and animal magnetism.[42]

And Milton Shulman of the *Evening Standard* saw Richardson as the 'booming, virile, eccentric, somewhat mad presence [the play] needs'.[43] One reviewer wrote that Richardson had the power of 'putting anguished flesh on the barest bones'; a second, that 'Richardson as the meretricious sculptor has nothing but the void of his own egotism to act against, but he acts as usual with commanding presence and authority.'[44]

*

Yet Greene blamed Richardson for the fiasco. In *Ways of Escape* (1980) he speaks of how 'The first act is, almost completely, farce . . . Alas! The principal actor saw the play quite differently from me. He believed he was playing Ibsen.'[45] In his 1979 interview with Marie-Françoise Allain, he speaks of having a weakness for *Carving a Statue* ('which was mauled by the press'). Greene gives examples of the power an actor has to make or break a play: 'It's this very metamorphosis that fascinates me: an actor, without changing a word, can ruin a play or bring it to life.'[46]

It was Greene's view that irreconcilable antagonisms develop in the theatre, never to be rescinded, not least because once a play has failed on a massive scale, news of it is blown by the four winds to every theatrical corner of the globe.

Richardson's biographer, Garry O'Connor, claimed there was a difference in interpretation: 'While Richardson tried, to no avail, to make him human, Greene, it appeared, wanted Richardson to "send him up".'[47] J. W. Lambert indicates the differences of approach: 'Richardson made him a Michelangelo; Greene made him a great ass.'[48]

When I interviewed Richardson, he did not mention their falling out, but gave me a copy of a fan letter Greene had sent to him on 26 June 1964, at a time when he had just finished writing *Carving a Statue*:

Dear Ralph,

I have just been to see the film of 'Long Day's Journey' & I must write to you before the emotion is eaten away by newspapers, telephone calls, drinks with friends. You are magnificent, it is magnificent, & so are the others. It's wonderful to see you surrounded by fine performers – & what a 'take' that was of you which lasted in closing for four minutes.

The piddling little journalists – who call themselves film critics – will say that this is a photographed play & not a film. If it were that, who cares? It's good enough to feel that your performance – & the others – in a great play can be seen by our grandchildren.

But of course what they say is nonsense. This is a great *film*. The stage couldn't have held you in close-up for four minutes – you would have been at the mercy of any one of the others making an inadvertent false movement which would have taken our eyes away. And in the theatre our eyes are inclined to wander from a kind of cheap curiosity – how are the others managing to deal with this silence? For me this film is the play more than any stage can present it – except on that one miraculous evening when all goes well.

I write you this a little drunk by the play & your performance in it. I've attended the miraculous evening – this was history.

Yours with affection,

Graham.[49]

★

Greene had also praised Richardson's performance in *The Complaisant Lover*. 'For Ralph with gratitude and affection from Graham (18.6.59).'

But the dispute over *Carving a Statue* was more than a gentlemanly falling out. Michael Meyer, who knew of the letter that followed the one full of praise from Greene, pronounced it fiercely deracinatory – a letter written to incite distress. Richardson pasted the letter into a book of Henry Moore's sculptures which he kept in his bathroom.[50] This mysterious letter Mrs Richardson would not allow me to see, but I saw Greene's first draft, which must have been close to what was sent, dated 4 October 1964. Greene begins in the manner of a schoolteacher chastising an unruly pupil; though speaking from the deepest anguish, paranoia comes bobbing to the surface:

Dear Ralph,

I consider that I have been very patient with you, but my patience is exhausted. I have only had one previous experience in the theatre comparable to the first night at Brighton, but that 'knight' at the theatre had at least the excuse of drink.

It seems to me that you have been sacrificing the whole cast to building up – with the minimum of work – your own idea of your own image. I have done my best to build you an image, and I see no reason to doubt that mine is the more valid one. I am a writer – you seem to fancy yourself as a writer, but I am afraid I have as little faith in your writing as in your ability to judge a play as a whole. You are apparently incapable of understanding even your own part.

I hear that after our common decision to freeze the play on Friday night – you have begun again – as you so lamentably did then – to play at the end of the first act lines not in my script, thus killing the Boy's curtain.

You'd think Greene was out to poke a stick into a rattlesnake's nest:

I attribute this to stupidity and not to jealousy.

If you do not act the play I have written, I shall see that this letter is distributed as widely as possible to the Press.

In France there is a law which protects the 'author's rights'. I would welcome libel action which might prove to be the beginning of such a law in England.

And the final insult, the rapier piercing the body:

The vanity of an ageing 'star'* is far more damaging to the theatre than any censorship exercised by the Lord Chamberlain.[51]

Responding to a letter I wrote asking his judgment of Graham Greene, Richardson replied:

Graham is a giant, I am a mouse, what can I say to you about him from my mouse's point of view. 'Very little', must be my reply.

Well you have asked me and

'Richardson refuses'

---

* Greene was two years younger than Richardson.

This is one peep that you can see from my mouse hole

I am alive but I am
by no means biting
Why would I bite
Graham has fed me
so well.

I have found this out
    in several friendships
        you strike the flint[52]

And there it ends.

After the foul reviews, Greene wrote to Michael Meyer on 18 September 1964, two weeks prior to Greene's letter to Richardson:

> One day I will account to you the extraordinary story of the rehearsals. Alas most of the fire was expended there and not in the performance! However I hope you'll look in at the play. It's not really quite as dull as the critics make out.[53]

On 12 November 1998 Meyer sent me his opinion of that night at the Haymarket Theatre thirty-four years earlier:

> I thought *Carving a Statue* a really awful play, and I am surprised that Graham could ever have thought otherwise, being the self-critical chap he always was. I don't think Ralph's casting made a bit of difference, except perhaps in the sense that any actor who has lost confidence in the part . . . tends to fall back on a particular mannerism; with some actors they shout, Ralph simply became extra eccentric, and you can imagine what that was like. I don't know what Graham meant by saying that Ralph thought he was playing Ibsen. Binkie Beaumont . . . should never have put it on, except that *The Complaisant Lover* had been such a success and *The Living Room* before it, both rightly so. My memory of the audience reaction is of an embarrassed silence, no doubt with some laughter at places where laughs were intended. When at the final curtain call it descended for the third time to tepid applause, I was amazed to see Ralph's feet jump and disappear. When I asked him why he said he was holding on to the curtain to make sure it didn't go up a fourth time.[54]

When *Carving a Statue* was published on 11 November 1964, Greene wrote a piece entitled 'Epitaph for a Play', and one paragraph helps us to understand his growing sadness and anger:

> Never before have I known a play like this one so tormenting to write or so fatiguing in production. I am glad to see the end of it, and to that extent I am grateful to the reviewers who may have a little accelerated the end.[55]

★

We can repeat some of the final lines of the play, where the sculptor makes his fundamental (and sad) comment about himself and the world:

> I work. I work. In dryness I work. In despair I work. As long as I work I can hold the pain of the world away from me.[56]

Graham Greene worked this way too, often in dryness and despair, but he never tried to keep the world's pain at arm's length. He embraced it.

We are dealing with the imperfect artist – the dedicated artist – whose passion for his subject makes him an unloving father. This is the age-old cry of the artist who must work at his creation, but who knows he is neglecting his family – who are his creation, too – in order to work. At the time of writing *Carving a Statue*, Greene suspected that his talent was running out, the same affliction we see in Querry in *A Burnt-Out Case*.

★

On 28 November 1964, Evelyn Waugh wrote movingly to Greene: 'You are a most loyal friend & I am deeply touched by your sending me your play . . . You told me that you were suffering annoyances during the production & I read in the papers of its premature removal . . . I am sure it is much better than the critics said & that it will have a successful revival. I know that you know that you will always be welcome here if ever it suits your purposes. I will not press invitations further.'[57] In the end, you just couldn't see the play for the statue, and it was a case of a father, a son, and a holy horror.

★

Even Greene's avid admirer, the distinguished poet Edith Sitwell was just a little mysterious about his troubled play.[58] Ill at seventy-seven, she wrote to him deftly, with great diplomacy, praising his gift of flowers, if not the play:

299

My dear Graham,

I am so grateful to you for sending me that strange, noble work *Carving a Statue*; I am very proud to have it from you and thank you also, again and again, for your share in the lovely lilies sent me by you, Jeanne and Sherman [Lady and Lord Camoys].

I should have written immediately, but have been in really agonising pain from a 'bug' caught in that infernal hospital in which I was incarcerated with pneumonia. I ought, of course, to be very grateful to them for not blinding me, which they do in some hospitals now (there is a great scandal going on in the medical profession about this).

Jeanne says you are in torture with sciatica. It is *hell* – as I know, having been the sciatica Queen while in Hollywood, the only thing which keeps the pain [away] is aspirin. (I used to have 8 aspirin tablets in 24 hours.) That and Bengee's Balsam, not rubbed but spread on.

Here comes one of the cats who has just had an accident, poor boy. He is guiding my pen.

Much admiration, love, and so *many* thanks from

Edith.[59]

Eight days later Edith Sitwell was dead. Her brother Osbert wrote to Greene:

My dear Graham,

Edith thought so much of you. I feel her loss intolerably. Before she died I was just going to write to you to thank you for writing the play which I enjoyed quite as much as the first one [*The Living Room*]. The boy is a character. But so is the father and the girl, as for that I can't think how it got bad notices, excepting that the press is so idiotic.[60]

The play might have failed, but his friends never did.

25

More Naked Than the Law Allows

Prouder than rustling in unpaid-for silk.
— SHAKESPEARE

IN October 2000, a recently discovered three-act play by Graham
Greene with the odd title of A *House of Reputation* was given its
world premiere in a special performance at Berkhamsted. The play was
set in a brothel. At one point, Greene denied he'd ever written it (a
Clintonic evasion, for I have all three acts, loaned to me by Greene's
friend, the multifaceted Bryan Forbes, actor, screenwriter, director,
biographer, novelist).* It is remarkable – even astonishing, Forbes thought
– to find a work by Greene not yet staged in a London theatre, the
more so because the play is quintessential Greene: curious, witty, fascinating and reflecting his view of brothels (at least the type represented
here) as being both unique and necessary. One might think that such
a place deserves to exist, but surely, in life, could not.

What accounts for Greene's disowning his play? Carmen Capalbo
told me that in the negotiations over *The Potting Shed* in 1956, he and
Stanley Chase wrote first refusal rights of Greene's next play into the
contract. Capalbo thinks Greene completed A *House of Reputation* by
the autumn of 1957, the success of *The Potting Shed* (1957) still fresh.
Reluctantly, Chase and Capalbo turned it down, thinking it wasn't viable:

---

* That Greene had written this play was known to very few. Part of A *House of Reputation*
(the first act and scene one of the second) is to be found in the Harry Ransom Research
Center in Austin, Texas. They at first were not aware that it was in their possession.
Originally, Greene wanted its existence hushed up. His letter in the magazine the *Stage*
(5 June 1958) states: 'Sir, There is no truth whatever in the statement appearing in your
columns that Messrs Capalbo and Chase have concluded arrangements to present a play
of mine "A House of Reputation" on Broadway next autumn. Not only have no arrangements been concluded, but no play has been written and I am not planning to write any
play with this title. I have no plans whatever for a play in the foreseeable future.'

301

You have to have two sets of eyes – the artistic one, the quality of the play as you see it, the other set . . . whether *this* play would attract enough finance . . . Such was the success of *The Potting Shed*, I had great hopes for Greene's next play . . . had my tongue hanging out . . . But . . . I felt it wouldn't work . . . it broke my heart to reject [it because of] my admiration for him . . . So my speculation about Greene's letter to the English magazine the *Stage* is that he wrote . . . after we had turned down his play. There was, I remember, some notice of it in the *New York Times*. Someone [must] have noticed the short note in [the] newspaper and Greene, hurt and upset, which he genuinely was, [denied] the play's existence.[1]

One reason the play was not acceptable in the somewhat repressed 1950s must be that Greene tried to turn a house of ill repute into something respectable. It was doomed to fail.

In the singular world of corruption, here is an orderly household where extremes of sexual and sadistic behaviour are not allowed and where the madam treats her 'girls' as daughters. One could ask, is this a fairy tale, a fable, a morality play – or all three? There is something about this madam, with her high standards of behaviour, that is incongruous. For one thing, gloom, guilt and shame are not to be part of her house. Her young prostitutes (apart from their nightly work) behave like schoolgirls. She is a well-preserved sixty-year-old, wearing an old-fashioned

evening dress like a uniform and her white hair is a little too good to be true. She has a kindly determined face and a manner accustomed to authority. She might well be the headmistress of a fashionable school.*

She shows a strong contempt for one of her clients, Dr Candolo, a dentist. (Greene's dentists usually fare badly.) 'The street door is pushed further open and a man enters the passage with a furtive air. His coat collar is turned up, his hat pulled down . . . The maid looks after him [as he disappears up the stairs] and spits on the floor, and takes up her rosary again.' Why is the dentist so disliked?

The response in the play is both realistic and allegorical. Dr Candolo comes down the stairs an hour later as secretively as he went up. Confronted by the madam and told he must pay 350 instead of the

*As this play was never produced or published, Greene never finalised it – the two scripts I have differ slightly.

usual 300, he at first refuses, but is told he won't be allowed to come back if he doesn't pay.

CANDOLO: Will you please explain? I'm an old customer . . .
MADAM: Yes. You've been getting on my nerves for a very long time . . . Every week you creep into this place as though you were ashamed. Nobody must know who you are. Nobody must see you. Why?
Pause
CANDOLO: (*in a low voice*) Because I *am* ashamed.
MADAM: Why?
CANDOLO: I'm ashamed to pay money to a woman like this . . .
MADAM: Other men do it.
CANDOLO: Perhaps from drink. I do not drink, Madam.
MADAM: Or loneliness.
CANDOLO: I have a young and beautiful wife, Madam. What am I then?
MADAM: A hypocrite.
CANDOLO: Oh no, Madam. You'll find your hypocrites among your noisy, cheery customers. Follow *them* home and see them creep empty into their beds . . .
MADAM: And you?
CANDOLO: I *have* enjoyed myself, but I'm ashamed of the enjoyment. It's not what a man was made for, Madam. Sometimes in the spring I take a holiday . . . under the trees, I seem to see the world God made. But men like me made this.
MADAM: And women like me? I suppose you believe I'm wicked to run such a house, and my girls are wicked to give pleasure . . .
CANDOLO: I accuse only myself, Madam.
MADAM: Is this the wisdom you learn from looking into people's mouths?
CANDOLO: Perhaps it is. One scrapes and drills and repairs . . . I peer into the crannies for decay — it's not a pretty job. And I can't make love prettily, Madam. So — I am ashamed.
MADAM: Do you know what would happen to these girls if I didn't keep them here? . . . Do you know what life at the corner of the National Square is like? I stood there once . . . I listened to you and you must listen to me. My beat was fifty yards. . . When a man spoke to me, he spoke to me out of the corner of

303

his mouth. Coat collar turned up like yours. Hat pulled down. Then he would dodge round a dark corner and wait for me to make his bargain. 150? Too much. 100? Will you do this and that? Ashamed to be seen with me, and we carried the shame with us in our cab, and up the stairs to my room . . . He undressed with shame. He hardly looked at me for shame – and I can tell you I was worth a glance in those days. More often than not he was impotent from shame. That is why I won't have shame brought into this house, to make my girls unhappy. The men who come here are not ashamed . . . A man can go home if he wants to: He needn't buy. But if he chooses to go upstairs he feels no shame, and the girl feels no shame. I won't have you bringing your shame here to infect them. This is their home.

CANDOLO: There can be shame in a home. There is in mine.

MADAM: Keep it there and don't bring it to mine.

CANDOLO: Here are your 350.

MADAM: You can keep them. Don't come back. (*Candolo turns and goes out into the passage. Madam, after a pause, follows him.*) Dr Candolo. (*He turns back.*) I'm sorry, Dr Candolo. But last time you were here you left a girl crying.

CANDOLO: I have never mistreated anyone.

MADAM: Not in the Jeronimo Street way. But I had to spend an hour persuading her that she wasn't dirty or wicked.

CANDOLO: I understand. I'll try to stay away.

MADAM: With a pretty wife it should be easy. Is she cold?

CANDOLO: Oh no. (*He gives a despairing gesture.*) It is only this terrible curiosity?* (*Dr Candolo leaves. He tips the girl . . . Madam watches him.*)

MADAM: (*to the maid*) Next time don't let him in.

*

One prostitute, Marta, comes in late because she has been to her mother's funeral. She doesn't look like a prostitute. She has never

* This is the cause of many of Greene's ventures into the seedy sectors of the world – his 'terrible curiosity'.

known romantic love and doesn't wish to. She has a hatred for her own body.

Two young men enter; one is thoroughly drunk, the other thoroughly sober. At first the madam tries to put them out, but then learns that the sober young man, twenty and sexually inexperienced, is the only son of the Minister of the Interior, and in such a country he has tremendous power. So the drunk is allowed to be drunk and to stay, and as his companion takes a woman upstairs, the sober young man stays below, looking with contempt upon the scene:

MADAM: Do you know what shocks you?
YOUNG MAN: Doing this. For money. Without love.
MADAM: That's like a lot of marriages, surely. Oh no, what
              shocks you is there's nothing shocking. Except
              your drunken friend. You thought you'd find vice.
              But there isn't any vice here . . . Only be a little
              human. After all it's a human activity.
YOUNG MAN: We share it with the animals.
MADAM: Do we? When animals have brothels, I'll believe
              they have souls.

Marta then comes on the scene and is told that the young man is waiting for his drunken friend and that this is his first visit. Marta persuades the young man to come upstairs lest his boastful drunken friend laugh at him. 'Don't look scared. We'll just sit and talk until your friend is through.' They go into the bedroom above the salon. The young man sits down in the middle of the sofa, leaving his jacket on. Marta casually slips her dress over her head and flings it across the bed. She takes a chair, as the young man has left her no room on the sofa, pulling her feet up under her. She tells him to take off his jacket, and gradually he begins to open up: 'Perhaps for the first time in his life he feels able to talk with the intimacy of being unknown, to an unknown.' He speaks of another kind of imprisonment, living with his parents, surrounded by reporters watching his house all day, cameramen following his mother when shopping, father never leaving without travelling in a bullet-proof car. The boy is scared to read the papers, a speech by his father, speeches about youth when he's never been young. The young girl tries to get his name. He is afraid to give it:

YOUNG MAN: Do I have to tell you?
MARTA: Your first name, idiot. It doesn't have to be your
              own. You can invent one. It's convenient to

remember you by, that's all. If you like I'll christen you myself.

Marta gets up and comes to the sofa. She stands in front of him and wets her finger in her mouth. 'I'll call you Martin. This is holy oil.' (She makes a cross on his forehead with her finger.) The young man tries to find out Marta's real name: 'I want to call you by a name the others don't use.' But she won't tell him: 'You're talking like a lover. You mustn't do that here.' 'Why?' asks Martin, and she answers: 'You are a customer. That's why.'

MARTIN: Your customers don't stand about and talk, do they? We are only talking. I haven't really bought you.
MARTA: (*smiling and trying to keep him light*) Oh, you bought me all right. You just left me behind on the counter, that's all.
MARTIN: Kiss me.
MARTA: That's never part of the sale. You know, for hygienic reasons.
MARTIN: I'm sorry. I didn't realise.

The two young people talk – the sober young man is curious about her life. Marta, partly skirting the questions, remains pragmatic:

MARTIN: Can I see you tomorrow?
MARTA: We open at six and close at two – if we can.
MARTIN: If I brought enough money with me, could we be together all the time?
MARTA: Eight hours is a long time to spend in a room like this.
MARTIN: Couldn't we go out?
MARTA: That's not allowed.
MARTIN: So you are a prisoner?
MARTA: Of course I'm not a prisoner. Madam looks after us, that's all. What do you think would happen if men were allowed to take us out? You'd have to look for us in a trunk at the Central Station or at low tide on the beach.
MARTIN: Do you never go out?
MARTA: I go to the post office and sometimes I go to the big store in the National Square. Today I went three miles on a trolley bus. And I spoke to the priest at the cemetery. I paid for two carriages and twenty

people walked behind the hearse. It was a real
funeral. There was even somebody crying. The priest
blessed me.

And then the conversation turns:

MARTIN: What happens to people here – in the end I mean?
MARTA: It's like any house anywhere. Some die. Some go
away. Last year somebody married. A farmer.

Marta asks Martin to put on his jacket. She's tired and wants to sleep.
And suddenly, perhaps in order to get rid of Martin, she holds him by
the lapel and gives him a quick kiss on the cheek:

MARTA: Perhaps I hope for somebody young and good
looking like you who will be very rich, who will
buy me an apartment, a motor car and a Pomeranian
dog.
MARTIN: I have a little, but I'm not rich yet.
MARTA: That's lucky for you. Because when he'd given me
all that, I'd say to this rich man, 'Thank you very
much, I hope I've given satisfaction, would you mind
going now because I've asked my lover to stay here
with me?' And my lover would be poor like you.
MARTIN: Young and good looking?
MARTA: Perhaps he would be ugly and old, but I would
make the bed with the best silk sheets all the same.
MARTIN: Why ugly and old?

And Marta answers the naïve young man with homely wisdom:

That's the way it is, isn't it. Love and kindness don't follow the
rules. They strike suddenly – anywhere.

Young Martin begins to feel jealous, and says he'll come the next day
at six. Marta responds: 'I'm not a restaurant table you can reserve in
advance.' But Cupid has let go the arrow: 'You said it strikes suddenly
anywhere', he says, and kisses her clumsily. Ah, but Marta has not been
struck; therein lies the danger.

★

In the second act Marta's nature is revealed. When the madam questions her about why she came to her house, Marta answers in rhetoric

pointed and raw. She is out to lay bare her paranoia – her form of self-loathing:

MARTA: Because I hate all this fuss people make about love. I hate sunsets and tenderness and moonlight. I hate the way they wrap up this thing between the legs. Let them all have it. I'd like to lie down before men as I would before a charge of cavalry. I want to have no features left. Something men have ridden over and gone on.

MADAM: What a strange girl you are. Aren't you happy here?

MARTA: Of course I'm happy. I'm the one who's really made for a brothel, Madam. I want to stab my body with men. But then this fool came. He touches me with fear as though I were something of value he might break. He talks nonsense to me. My child, my sister, he called me. What am I to do?

When the madam asks if she is in love with the young man, her response is uncompromising, reaching its apogee in self-hate:

I'm not in love. I'll never be that. You have to love yourself, don't you, before you love anyone else. You've got to have something to give you don't hate. My mother only taught me how to hate. She hated me, she hated the man she couldn't remember whom she got me with, she hated the surgeon who refused to wash me out. Madam, I'm a bit of refuse they didn't clear away. I want to be of use, and here you have a use for refuse.

★

In act two there is a song Greene composed, an account of poverty and the disaster of birth. The gramophone plays the first verse of the blues:

> I was born in a dive in Jeronimo Street.
> Between one striptease act and another.
> The men in the bar heard a baby bleat.
> And before they could turn
>   There was me with my mother.
> More naked
>   than the law
>   allows.

Halfway through this act we hear the second and third verses:

> I was laid by my first in Jeronimo Street
> Within one sleazy joint or another.
> The men in the bar heard a virgin bleat
> And before they could turn
> > There was me with the other
> More naked
> > than the law
> > > allows.

> They fished me out for good near Jeronimo Street
> Beneath one bridge or the other.
> The men in the bar heard patrol cars bleat,
> And who bothered to turn?
> > It was only another
> More naked
> > than the law
> > > allows.

This is Marta's birth and perhaps her death, though the play does not end with her demise. Instead the obsessed young man feels he can win her (he has already offered marriage and been refused) by persuading his rigid father to close the brothel. The prospects for the other girls do not matter.

Thus the House of Reputation is closed down, the furniture taken away, leaving the much cruder brothel in Jeronimo Street, with its violent reputation, alone thriving. The experiment in creating a noble house ends in failure.

Gradually, Marta realises that it's her young man who has brought an end to the only true home she's ever had. Her future (unless she chooses him) is as a prostitute on the street in the National Square. The greatest possible damage has been done from his need to possess her:

MARTA: How did you persuade your father to ruin us?
MARTIN: Not ruin *you*. I tricked him. I told him that I meant to come here every night to see you. I couldn't live without you. He thought he was getting rid of you by closing this place, and he's given you freedom instead.
MARTA: Freedom from what?
MARTIN: Your life here.
MARTA: And freedom for what?

MARTIN: Freedom to live with me. You can leave here
         tonight. I have our flat ready . . . I'm ready to take
         you away. Yes, and marry you . . .

MARTA: You are a sentimental ignorant fool who has ruined
         five girls by sending them to that dive in Jeronimo
         Street – and Madam who protected them. Where is
         she? If she's dead you killed her. Now clear out of
         here & hang yourself if you have any sense of justice.

MARTIN: You are only saying this because of the shock, Marta.
         I'm not giving you up. I love you.

MARTA: Love? Do you know what you mean by love? I
         know what I mean by hate and I hate you . . . Your
         love is just a wish to possess – and I hate you for it.
         You are one of dozens of fools who think they've
         possessed me, but I tell you not one of them ever
         has. I'm not possessable.

If Marta comes close to loving anyone, it is an old man with very little
money who waits the night out. It is Madam's gift to let him have
the girl of his choice for half price. He offers Marta an envelope
containing the half-price fee:

No, keep it. Tonight we are free. Free. No money. No duty.
Tomorrow I won't be here.

The dance is over, Marta's destiny is in the streets.

★

Where did Greene get this strange notion of an ideal dwelling of prostitution? In a few chapters, I'll try to reveal its origin.

PART 12

Voodoo Doc's Republic of Fear

26

Prelude in Blood

All the physicians and authors in the world could not give a clear account of his madness.

— CERVANTES

JOHN F. Kennedy was shot and killed in Dallas, Texas, in the eleventh month of 1963 – a date remembered by the whole civilised world. But early in 1964, a special emissary of President François Duvalier arrived at Kennedy's Arlington Cemetery tomb on a primitive and profane mission. His errand?

> to secure a bit of earth from each corner of the grave, a withered flower, and, in a bottle . . . a breath of grave-site air . . . by means of the ingredients obtained, Duvalier hoped to 'capture' the soul of Kennedy, render it subject to his will, and thus control future American policies toward Haiti.[1]

Dr François Duvalier believed he'd been instrumental in the death of Kennedy through the arts and spells of voodoo.

★

François Duvalier was outstanding in Haiti's farrago of tyrants. In all, twenty-nine heads of state were assassinated or overthrown. He stayed in power by means of arbitrary arrests, persecutions, summary executions. He was a dictator without pity who thought himself divine. Darkness fell on the island from 1957 to 1971, starting with Duvalier's election and ending only with his death. Total night was forced upon the Haitian people. Over Port-au-Prince flew a flag proclaiming, 'I AM THE STATE. I AM THE STATE.' Greene describes the scene in *The Comedians*, as his hero Mr Brown returns to Port-au-Prince:

In the public park the musical fountain stood black, waterless, unplaying. Electric globes winked out the nocturnal message, '*Je suis le drapeau Haitien, Uni et Indivisible.** *François Duvalier.*'[2]

Duvalier came from a dirt-poor family. His father was a primary school teacher; his mother was described by Diederich and Burt as a 'barefoot bakery employee'.[†] He was very much aware of his dark skin colour, and felt that the light-skinned mulatto elite, the upper class of Haiti, never let him forget it. But he seemed determined to elevate himself by the most effective of weapons: fear, torture, death. He also took unto himself the Creole adage: 'Every man betrays his neighbour',[3] and he saw to it that he betrayed every man. Politically, he gradually began to reveal himself chiefly as a hater of mulattos.

Duvalier in those early days, according to Diederich and Burt, rarely spoke unless spoken to, and his silence gave him an advantage among other politicians: he was an unknown quantity. He attracted enough attention to be appointed in the Fignolé government in 1948 as Under-Minister of Labour and then as Minister of Public Health. He aroused little enmity because he made a negligible impression. His mild manner turned wrath aside.

On 26 May 1957, Daniel Fignolé was made provisional president. He didn't last long. General Kébreau, a secret friend of Duvalier, allowed Fignolé nineteen days of high office, and then, according to Heinl and Heinl, 'marched upstairs in the Palais, slammed open the door of the council chamber, silenced the cabinet with a look, and marched off with the president before he could utter a word'.[4] Kébreau had Fignolé sign a letter of resignation and arranged for him to be sent out of the country. Fignolé's cabinet and many of his followers were imprisoned. The army took charge and Kébreau promised to restore order, conduct elections, and have a legitimate president emerge.

A rumour went round that Fignolé had been secretly executed. To a man, his supporters rose, attacking Fort Dimanche, a prison on the edge of Port-au-Prince. The military responded with machine-guns. Behind light tanks they moved into the lower city, shooting to kill the

---

* 'I am the flag of Haiti, united and indivisible'.
† Bernard Diederich and Al Burt's book *Papa Doc: The Truth About Haiti Today*, and its later edition, *Papa Doc: Haiti and its Dictator*, tell the story, often first hand, of the hell hole that was Haiti. In a country where the universities and libraries are not respected and preserved, there are few archives fit for research. This work, along with *Written in Blood*, by the late husband-and-wife team of Robert and Nancy Heinl and excellently updated by their son Michael, are the two definitive, diverse sources. Neither book, when once read, can be easily forgotten, and I urge all who wish for greater knowledge to read both.

stone-throwing, torch-bearing mob, with battles into the morning. 'The army gained the upper hand, trucks began picking up littered corpses, and the *pompiers* [fire brigade], after wetting down fire-desolated areas, hosed away whatever blood and guts the dogs left.'[5]

With Fignolé gone, the spread of propaganda began, implying that Duvalier had American support. More and more, Duvalier began to show not only his power but an enormous hidden vanity, released in a speech:

> They dare to keep Duvalier, most popular of the Candidates, in outer darkness . . . *They have gone mad*. Masses of . . . [the] middle classes of Port-au-Prince, intellectuals, Masters of thought and art, professors, teachers, students: they have decided to ignore you. *They have gone mad* . . . The mad coalition has decided that you and I have nothing to say.

He ended: 'They would decide without us. *They have gone mad*.'[6] With the army controlling the polling booths, the impossible happened: a few hundred inhabitants of La Gonave delivered 18,000 votes, and La Tortue's 900 registered voters delivered 7,500 ballots. Duvalier won the day.

★

The Haitians' fear of Duvalier sprang from the pits of their stomachs. People thought he was the earthly representative of Baron Samedi, who was death itself, the most powerful, most dreaded of the gods in the voodoo pantheon.

At his 1957 inauguration, Duvalier uttered one of his numerous lies: 'My Government will guarantee the exercise of liberty to all Haitians and will always give them the necessary protection in that exercise for their wellbeing.'[7] In his first press conference he identified the country and its people entirely in relationship to himself: 'I have no enemies except the enemies of the Nation.'[8] Before the month was out, a general strike was called by one of the failed presidential candidates, Louis Déjoie, but Duvalier was ready for it. Robert Heinl, then head of the US Marine mission in Haiti, describes how 'muscular *noirs* with dark eyeglasses and pistol bulges under their jackets persuaded shopkeepers to stay open'. Déjoie went underground.

Soon Duvalier was attacking on other fronts. A hundred political prisoners were taken to Fort Dimanche. Wiser and luckier souls were beginning to slip into foreign embassies to gain political asylum (a practice dramatised in *The Comedians*).* Duvalier next targeted the

---

* Duvalier's tentacles were far-reaching. If he wanted to destroy an enemy, his henchmen could find themselves on their way to New York and further still. Once Greene's novel was published, he was himself afraid that Duvalier would send killers after him.

independent press. Printing plants were bombed; kidnapping and terrorism were his tools. A well-known editor, Yvonne Hakim-Rimpel, was beaten and raped.[9]

General Kébreau, who had been instrumental in Duvalier's coming to power, realised that he would soon be picked up himself, so, also being a friend of Dominican president Trujillo, he slipped into the Dominican embassy. This was a good move, for Trujillo was an important ally of Duvalier. Duvalier did not go after Kébreau.

In December 1998 I interviewed for the third time Aubelin Jolicoeur, long known as the goodwill ambassador for Haiti.* Jolicoeur knew both Duvalier and Kébreau well. He explained that Kébreau had made him his press secretary.

*

Duvalier intended to marginalise the Haitian army. He began making his palace courtyard a base for arms, weapons and even tanks. He started building an army of thugs, the Tontons Macoute,† made up of bovine peasants. Duvalier's distrust of the regular army was intensified by a minor but remarkable invasion (which was almost successful) made up of five American mercenaries and three (one-time) Haitian officers: a curious band. Three of the mercenaries were ex-deputy sheriffs, one from Miami, Florida.‡ They set off for Hàiti in a fifty-five foot Key West fishing boat, the *Molly C*. The three ex-Haitian officers secured the mercenaries at $2,000 each, and expected to be supported by air, with a Second World War plane carrying 150 men, weapons and ammunition.

In the beginning, this miniature invasion was successful. The first piece of bad luck came from a peasant – the very kind of man the heroes were trying to assist, who noticed them and reported their arrival. A three-man patrol came quickly to reconnoitre, and were just

---

* Greene changed Jolicoeur's name to Petit Pierre in the novel, but hardly changed his personality. Petit Pierre is the journalist who meets Brown in Port-au-Prince, just as Jolicoeur had met Greene at the airport on his three visits to Haiti, facilitating easy passage through customs – no small service.

† 'Tonton Macoute' is Creole for 'Uncle Grab Bag' (a legendary bogeyman who stuffed little children into a sack). This band of thugs was founded by one-time schoolteacher and Duvalier aide, Clément Barbot. There were 5,000 Tontons Macoute on the great bogeyman's payroll, which was funded by money from America earmarked for the army or the needy.

‡ This manoeuvre, it was rumoured, was financed by the previous president, Magloire (1950–7), earlier unceremoniously expelled. Seemingly, Magloire's friends were now invading Haiti. (Surely such a small band could not have hoped to pull off a *coup d'état*.) There is little doubt that if the return of Magloire had been effected, Haiti would never have had to endure those years of torture, greed, mayhem and massacre.

as quickly dispatched, though not without consequence: Arthur Payne, a handsome thirty-four-year-old mercenary, was shot in the thigh. Their jeep broke down on the way to the capital and they had to hire a *tap tap* (a light truck turned into a passenger bus). But their bad luck with the jeep was fortuitous, since no one could have imagined an invasion composed of only eight men in a pitiful little *tap tap*.

Upon reaching Port-au-Prince, one of them drove straight for the Dessalines barracks, just behind the palace, shouted to the sentry that he had some white prisoners, the mercenaries' pale faces proof of the cry. The gates were opened. Once inside, they drove immediately to headquarters, ran up the steps and promptly shot the duty officer, roused the sleeping soldiers and locked them in their squad rooms.

The invaders expected to find plenty of weapons in the barracks, but Duvalier had been stockpiling them in the basement of his palace. The men should have rushed the palace, but instead they telephoned, and as the president packed a bag full of money in case he had to escape to the Colombian embassy with his family, he had time to raise the alarm and attack what they thought were hundreds of invaders inside the barracks.

Then events started to turn when one of the expatriates sent a soldier to get cigarettes. It got out that they were only eight men. The counter-attack began. The mob, led by a helmeted Duvalier, looking every inch a soldier going into combat, fired rifles as they approached the barracks. It was soon over. Morgue photographs show the bodies of the courageous eight riddled with bullets. Heinl and Heinl give an account of the end. Payne was 'pummeled to death' and

> Walker, the *Molly C*'s skipper, had his legs broken and his genitals pounded into blood-soaked hamburger. Riquet Perpignand, wounded, escaped from the *casernes* [barracks] but was run down by a mob, which found him hiding in a chicken coop. Kersten, one of the mercenaries, was also caught outside. The two [were] stabbed, shot, kicked, gouged, trampled, twisted, all but dismembered, their bodies were dragged naked through the streets, tugged into the palace, shown in triumph to the president, and then hauled about under the blazing sun until police gathered up the carrion and dumped it at the morgue.[10]

★

On 24 May 1959, but for the intervention of Duvalier's close friend Clément Barbot, there would have been tremendous rejoicing in Haiti. On that day, Duvalier suffered a heart attack, which was misdiagnosed as a diabetic reaction. His physician administered insulin, leaving the president comatose for nine hours. Seeing that Duvalier was not responding, Barbot sought another doctor who recognised the mistake. 'Barbot rushed out in the middle of the night, broke into the first pharmacy he reached, and brought back glucose',[11] and Duvalier began to mend.

During the president's convalescence, Barbot ran the country. He was the only one Duvalier trusted, though not for long. Barbot did an excellent job, and gossip had it that he would hold on to power. He still saw Duvalier as a friend, so he relinquished authority early in July. He lived to regret it.

*

By regulation, Duvalier's term of office was to end on 15 May 1963 (the year of Greene's visit), but on 6 April 1961, foreseeing the danger to his position, he dissolved one of the two legislative assemblies. He then arranged for fifty-eight 'freely' elected new members. For this he introduced simple ballot forms with DR FRANÇOIS DUVALIER in large letters at the top, and in small print, the name of the candidate, personally chosen by Duvalier. They alone were available for election. A Sunday was designated election day, and all civil servants were called out to vote. People were told to vote twice, sometimes three times for luck, on separate forms. Peasants were brought in to the voting booths, and foreigners were 'advised' to vote – the 'election' a foregone conclusion.

Afterwards, Duvalier played up to the crowd, offering his gratitude and, in his softest tones of pretended humility, expressing how thankful he was that they'd been inspired by God. They discovered that while he still had two further years as president, they had unanimously elected Duvalier for a fresh term of six years.

*

On inauguration day 1961, the excommunicated Papa Doc (excommunicated for persecuting the French archbishop, looting his home, and attacking various priests and lay people) was still determined to receive religious honours. He called for a *Te Deum* to be sung in the cathedral to celebrate his victory. The Papal Nuncio was coerced to attend, faced with a promise by Duvalier that he would close down all Catholic schools in Haiti if he refused the invitation.

The president, dressed in tails and top hat (regulation Baron Samedi garb) and an array of medals, gave a speech in French which was translated into tortured, uneducated English. It had the usual excessive references to himself:

United in thought with Me, you have realized, My brother Haitians, the urgency, the necessity of having a Chief chosen by the people, a Chief in whom the majority of the nation, in spite of the quarrels of parties and factions, can recognize the Manager of its essential interests and the dependable Trustee of its destinies . . . The people, the army, and you, have chose Me . . . I am facing history; I am facing the nation with a proud head, with a serene soul, a clear conscience and a firm cause . . . My brother Haitians! With Me You must procreate, give birth to the new Haiti, and make her live all the great dreams of which she has for too long been frustrated.

In 'Nightmare Republic', an article for the *Sunday Telegraph*, Greene gave a vivid account:

In the cathedral . . . when the excommunicated President puts in his one appearance at Mass, the Tontons arrive armed with sub-machine-guns and search, even behind the altar. Then they take up their position in the cathedral with their guns covering the diplomatic corps, while in the choir rifles dominate the congregation.

Greene defined the Duvalier regime:

There have been many reigns of terror in the course of history. Sometimes they have been prompted by a warped idealism like Robespierre's, sometimes they have been directed fanatically against a class or a race and supported by some twisted philosophy; surely never has terror had so bare and ignoble an object as here – the protection of a few tough men's pockets, the pockets of Gracia Jacques, Colonel Athi, Colonel Desiré, the leaders of the Tontons Macoute, of the police and of the Presidential guard – and in the centre of the ring, of course, in his black evening suit, his heavy glasses, his halting walk and halting speech, the cruel and absurd Doctor.[12]

★

The horrors worsened.

Blood splatters on the floors and walls of the Tontons Macoute's interrogation rooms were camouflaged by rusty brown paint. In an antechamber stood a 'coffin-shaped Iron Maiden, its interior spiked with stiletto blades'. Upon watching the young Eric Brièrre tortured to death in 1961, a former police chief, though hardened by witnessing much killing in those precincts, vomited, sickened by the barbarism.

In Fort Dimanche, survivors of flaying had their raw flesh rubbed with citrus juice and red pepper. The infractions that brought on these atrocities were often minor. For example, students, some still teenagers, scrawled on walls in Port-au-Prince a mild obscenity about Duvalier: '*Caca Doc*' ('Doc Shit'). Duvalier had the students, their relatives and some university professors arrested, beaten and tortured. Several were interrogated and then *executed*.

Charles Turnier, a black soldier of distinction, was involved with a few senior officers in a plot against Duvalier. There was a leak. Most of the officers were able to slip into the Brazilian embassy with their families. Turnier did not try to escape. He was picked up, beaten all night, and next morning an officer shot him through the head to end his agony. The Haitian command was determined to, as their saying goes, 'make his feet leave the earth', but even when Charles Turnier was dead, they weren't finished. His body was allowed to rot in the open, 'to decompose into a heap of offal in the hot sun'.[13]

Dead bodies were not the only thing Duvalier let rot in the sun. Haiti needed charity. Catholic and Protestant organisations along with the Church World Services had sent food for the poor, which Duvalier ordered kept in port. Tons of perishables were left to spoil in Port-au-Prince. Such inhumanities were going on before Greene's arrival in August 1963, and continued after he left. Town and countryside were starving. To Robert Heinl, a Haitian friend once said bitterly: 'Duvalier has performed an economic miracle. He has taught us to live without money and eat without food.'[14] The character Dr Magiot uses this phrase in *The Comedians*.

★

Back during General Magloire's presidency in the 1950s, Clément Barbot had gone underground with Duvalier. Later, when Duvalier became president, Barbot became his personal secretary and confidant. After nearly dying on 25 May 1959, Duvalier was healthy enough by 2 July to put down a minor revolt of his nominal supporters. If senior supporters did this, Duvalier would often move them to another country, making them ambassadors, far away from Haiti. Barbot was a different case. He had done too well in looking after the affairs of the country while Duvalier was ill. But Duvalier did not move swiftly against his pet. He waited until July 1960. Barbot's many allies in the Tontons Macoute caused Duvalier to fear that his friend might one day overthrow him, so he plotted Barbot's downfall.

On the night of 14 July 1960, after leaving the French embassy, Barbot and his wife were met at home by the presidential guard. Barbot's wife was placed under house arrest; he was put into a small cell in Fort Dimanche. After a year, Duvalier relented (rare for Papa Doc) and released him.* Then house arrest was enforced for his whole family. First, they lived quietly at home, but soon Barbot went underground with his brother, and others. To a few friends Barbot let it be known that he'd left for one purpose: 'To *remove* President Duvalier'.[15]

Nearly two weeks after Charles Turnier had been tortured, shot and left to decompose at the Methodist Bird College (just blocks from the palace), Duvalier's children arrived at school in the palace limousine. A car came alongside; shots were fired. Two Tontons Macoute guards and the driver were dead. The children ran into school unharmed. Barbot had not intended to harm the children – just to abduct them. The war between Barbot and Duvalier had begun.

Duvalier went into a rage. Barricades were thrown up around the palace, and 5,000 Tontons Macoute exercised the role of police. Duvalier was operating in the dark. He did not know who the culprit was, aware only that the gunman must have been an excellent shot.

In his ignorance Duvalier decided it must be the well-known marksman, Lieutenant Benoît. He must be guilty. Benoît had recently fallen under Duvalier's fierce glare and had wisely taken himself, alas, without his family, into the Dominican embassy. The president sent Major Franck Romain, a pitiless killer (on whom Greene's character, the infamous Captain Concasseur in *The Comedians*, is based) with a swarm of Tontons Macoute to search, Duvalier-style, Benoît's home.† In Greene's powerful article for the *Sunday Telegraph*, 'Nightmare Republic', appearing within a month of his 1963 visit to Haiti, he elaborated on the 'blackened ruins' of Benoît's house:

> Benoît, one of Haiti's prize marksmen, was suspected . . . in the attempted kidnapping of the President's children earlier in the year. He took refuge in [the Dominican] Embassy and his house was set ablaze with petrol by the Tontons Macoute, who machine-gunned the flames. Mme Benoît escaped, but no one knows whether her child is alive, nor how many servants were shot or burnt to death.[16]

*

On 30 April, the council of the Organization of American States (OAS) sent an investigating team of ambassadors from Chile, El Salvador,

---

* When Barbot got out of prison, he discovered that his wife and child had not been allowed to consult a physician when his son suffered a mental collapse.
† In *The Comedians* Greene describes Brown and Martha passing 'the blackened beams of [Benoît's] house that the Tonton had destroyed'.

Ecuador, Colombia and Bolivia. On their arrival, Duvalier had peasants in great numbers brought into the Place de l'Indépendance: Heinl tells us that there was an 'enormous sea of faces before the palace'.[17] When Duvalier spoke that day in front of thousands, his face showed no emotion, but his voice was fierce, every word spoken filling the vast square in front of the white magnificence of his palace. As if he had supernatural authority, he threw down this challenge:

> Bullets and machine guns capable of daunting Duvalier do not exist. They cannot touch me . . . I take no orders or dictates from anyone, no matter where they come from. No foreigner shall tell me what to do.

Then the incredible: 'I am even now an immaterial being.'[18] The crowd roared; the sacred drums beat.

In the spring of 1963, a few months before Greene's arrival, the body of a Captain Yvan D. Laraque, killed during a rearguard fight at Préville against Duvalier, was flown to the capital. 'There, on public view, facing the Grande Rue exit from the airport, the swollen, flyblown corpse, flung over a wooden chair, clad only in jockey shorts, was left to rot in public view.'[19] This was a favourite way to frighten the populace.

Duvalier demanded that the body be exhibited for three days to the morbidly fascinated passers-by, squawking like crows sighting a corpse, relentlessly gazing at the dead man, sun burning the watchers' crowns, eyes wide. Laraque alone ignored the sun and the crowd. He sat in the chair which had been stolen from his home. Opposite, a large sign proclaimed:

WELCOME TO HAITI.

27

Killing Is My Pleasure

The bullet that is to kill me has not been cast.
— NAPOLEON

As soon as Brown, a leading character in *The Comedians*, arrives in Haiti, he first meets his girlfriend, Martha, an ambassador's wife, and then leaves for the Trianon, the hotel he owns, which, because of Duvalier, is almost empty of tourists. Something horrible has occurred in the hotel swimming pool: the Secretary of Social Welfare has committed suicide. Philipot, who feared for his life after criticising Duvalier, has literally been scared to death. (Others had been executed for less.) Brown fears that if he reports the suicide, he will be suspected of being in a plot against Duvalier, so he and the unforgettable Dr Magiot move the body in the dead of night to find a place far enough away that Brown cannot be held account-able. The body is ultimately found.

During the funeral procession, Philipot's wife and child are stopped at a military barrier while riding in the hearse. The undertakers, driver and companion wish to return to town. Madame Philipot exclaims: 'They murdered him, and now they will not even allow him to be buried in our own plot.' In her company are Brown and two Americans, the Smiths, naïve, heroic and fascinating.

Mr Smith, once a presidential candidate (on the vegetarian ticket!), and his wife are passionate supporters of blacks in America. They cannot believe a black regime could be crooked. Mr Smith and Brown go to Madame Philipot's rescue. Mr Smith asks what is happening, and in his idealism, asserts that there must be some mistake. Madame Philipot responds, 'I told that *salaud* [bastard] to drive on through the barrier. Let them shoot. Let them kill his wife and child.'[1] They get through one barrier but are not allowed through the next, nor are they allowed to return to town. They are told they

323

cannot proceed without permission of the Secretary of Social Welfare (the so-recently deceased, yet still present in body, Mr Philipot):

> We all with one accord looked at the handsome coffin with its gleaming brass handles.
>
> '*There* is the Secretary for Social Welfare,' [Brown] said . . .
>
> 'But that's absurd,' Mrs Smith interrupted me. 'Does the coffin have to wait here till some fool mistake has been cleared up?'
>
> [Brown as narrator]: 'I'm beginning to fear it was no mistake.'
>
> 'What else could it be?'
>
> 'Revenge. They failed to catch him alive.' [Brown] said to Madame Philipot, 'They will arrive soon. That's certain. Better go to the hotel with the child.'[2]

They argue. Mrs Smith won't leave Mr Smith, so the undertakers take the child to the hotel for ice cream. They wait. They stare through the glass wall of the hearse at the coffin. A dog whines in the distance:

> Far away, in the land where the barking dog belonged, a car was taking the first gradients of the long hill. 'They're coming,' I said. Madame Philipot leant her forehead against the glass of the hearse and the car climbed slowly up towards us.
>
> 'I wish you'd go in [to the hotel],' I said to her. 'It would be better for all of us if we all went in.'
>
> 'I don't understand,' Mr Smith said. He . . . gripped his wife's wrist.
>
> The car had halted at the barrier down the road – we could hear the engine running; then it came slowly on in bottom gear, and now it was in view, a big Cadillac dating from the days of American aid for the poor of Haiti. It drew alongside us and four men got out. They wore soft hats and very dark sunglasses; they carried guns on their hips, but only one of them bothered to draw, and he didn't draw his gun against us. He went to the side of the hearse and began to smash the glass with it, methodically. Madame Philipot didn't move or speak, and there was nothing I could do. One cannot argue with four guns. We were witnesses, but there was no court which would ever hear our testimony. The glass side of the hearse was smashed now, but the leader continued to chip the jagged edges . . . There was no hurry and he didn't want anyone to scratch his hands.

Mrs Smith darts out and grabs the Tonton Macoute's shoulder. He turns and pushes his gloved hand into her face, sending her reeling backwards into the bushes:

> I had to put my arms round Mr Smith and hold him.
> 'They can't do that to my wife,' he shouted over my shoulder.
> 'Oh yes, they can.'
> 'Let me go,' he shouted, struggling to be free. I've never seen a man so suddenly transformed. 'Swine,' he yelled. It was the worst expression he could find, but the Tonton Macoute spoke no English. Mr Smith . . . nearly got free from me. He was a strong old man.
> 'It won't do any good to anyone if you get shot,' I said.

Mrs Smith sits down, bewildered. They lift the casket out and carry it to the car, wedging it into the boot, but it doesn't fit, so they tie it down.

> There was no need to hurry; they were secure; they were the law. Madame Philipot with a humility which shamed us – but there was no choice between humility and violence and only Mrs Smith had essayed violence – went over to the Cadillac and pleaded with them to take her too . . . [but] in a dictatorship one owns nothing, not even a dead husband. They slammed the door in her face and drove up the road, the coffin poking out of the boot, like a box of fruit on the way to market.[3]

Later, in the hotel, Madame Philipot comments: 'One day someone will find a silver bullet', and Brown speaks to his barman, badly crippled by the Tontons Macoute, about the affair:

> 'The people they very frightened,' Joseph said, 'when they know. They frightened the President take their bodies too when they die.'
> 'Why care? There's nothing left as it is but skin and bone, and why would the President need dead bodies anyway?'
> 'The people very ignorant,' Joseph said. 'They think the President keep Doctor Philipot in the cellar in the palace and make him work all night. The President is big Voodoo man.'
> 'Baron Samedi?'
> 'Ignorant people say yes.'
> 'So nobody will attack him at night with all the zombies there to protect him? They are better than guards, better than the Tontons Macoute.'

'Tontons Macoute zombies too. So ignorant people say.'

'But what do you believe, Joseph?'

'I be ignorant man, sir,' Joseph said.[4]

Was this Greene's fertile imagination weaving a tapestry of inhumanity and degradation? No. It was based on the painful and real experiences of Clément Jumelle, the Finance Minister under President Magloire which we go back to now.

*

The next in line to be despatched by Duvalier (because he'd been a presidential candidate and might later be a danger) was Clément Jumelle and not only he, but his family also. When Duvalier decided to charge him with the bombings in Port-au-Prince, Jumelle's two brothers, Ducasse and Charles, had to go on the run. They were tracked down. Both were innocent; both were shot in their bed. The Tontons Macoute dragged the dead brothers out, pressed pistols in their hands and had photographs taken. (During the time of President Magloire, when Duvalier himself had to go underground, Ducasse fed and protected him. His reward: a bullet in the head.)

On 6 April 1959, Clément Jumelle sought refuge, escaping into the Cuban embassy. The Cuban ambassador saw in his enclosure two persons dressed as peasants, one lying on the ground. It was Jumelle and his wife. He was suffering horribly with severe uraemic poisoning. A doctor was brought in specially from Cuba, without avail. Jumelle died five days later.*

And now the bizarre comedy began from which Greene drew his inspiration. The next day a hearse carried Jumelle on his way to the Church of the Sacred Heart. Hundreds of sympathisers followed. At Rond Point a police car, siren wailing, stopped in front of the hearse. They knocked down wreaths and mourners, leaving bloodied heads behind. Then, covering the crowd with sub-machine guns, they snatched the coffin from its bier, heaved it into the back of a truck and sped north to St Marc and a cemetery there. A priest tried to bless the Catholic Jumelle's interment, but the burial proceeded 'with Voodoo rites in a shallow grave'.[5] Gossip spread that the body had been taken back to the palace on orders from Duvalier 'so that Jumelle's heart could be removed to make a potent *ouanga*'[6] – a voodoo spell. Duvalier was making Haiti a tomb.

---

* As a perverted follow-up, the owner of the house where the Jumelle brothers were hiding, Jean-Jacques Monfiston, was tortured to death in Fort Dimanche and his family killed.

*

In 1961, Duvalier, seeming to address the needs of the poor, launched a programme called *Mouvement de Rénovation Nationale* (MRN), to build a new town named Duvalierville.

With this façade in place, Duvalier and his gang found new ways to extort money from the general populace and the business community, soliciting monthly contributions of $5,000. Duvalier had a licence to steal. It was still a year before Greene was to visit Haiti, and all the while, matters were deteriorating. The myth of Duvalierville was sent out:

> Everybody will come with what he has, one cent or one dollar, everything he has, to improve the general economy.
>
> Duvalierville is a pilot project to test our possibilities. It will be completed in six months. This is where the Haitian peasant is making more effort by himself than anywhere else. This is a voluntary effort . . . They know the government has no economy. This is not part of the Haitian budget. This is the people giving because of their great feeling for their President . . .[7]

Greene visited the miserable mess in 1963.* He brings Duvalierville into *The Comedians* to show the ways corrupt ministers hawk shamelessly for handouts. Greene's American character Mr Smith is told by the minister that there were once 'several hundred on this very spot. Living in miserable mud huts. We had to clear the ground. It was quite a major operation.' Mr Smith asks if the peasants once living there will be coming back. The minister answers that they're planning for a 'better class' of people and speaks grandly of how they are going to house five thousand. But now only one person is to be seen: 'a negro with white hair [sitting] on a hard chair under a sign that showed him to be a justice of the peace'.

Another Haitian, this time a beggar, seesaws around the corner of a great cockpit towards them. What follows cuts through the minister's pretence of helping the poor. Mr Smith is searching diligently for a site suitable for his project – a vegetarian centre. The minister implies that he and his friends expect kickbacks.

The beggar, while the minister is trying to grease his own palms, moves awkwardly towards them. He has very long arms, no legs, and makes his way nearer almost imperceptibly 'like a rocking horse' until he sees the

---

* In December 1998, I found Duvalierville no better. It was all rack and ruin, its buildings broken down, rubble and refuse everywhere, the glory that never was.

driver with the gun and dark glasses. He starts up a 'crooning murmur' and pulls out from his ragged shirt a carved statue which he presents to them. Brown remarks that they already have their beggars, prompting the minister to state that he's no beggar, but an artist. The minister has his driver go over and take the statuette, 'indistinguishable from dozens in the Syrian stores that waited for gullible tourists who never came'. Smith wants to give something to the cripple, but the minister refuses this and speaks airily of later providing a proper art centre at Duvalierville for artists to live and relax, whilst 'the beggar rock[s] to and fro, making sounds of melancholy and desperation'. Brown thinks he must have no roof to his mouth since no words are distinguishable.

Suddenly Mr Smith breaks away from the minister, runs back to the cripple and pulls out a bunch of dollar bills; the beggar looks at him with 'incredulity and fear'. Mr Smith makes it back to the minister and the car and says with a satisfied smile: 'He's made a sale all right.' The cripple then makes a furious effort to return to the pit. 'Perhaps,' thinks Mr Brown, 'he had a hole there in which he could hide the money.' But it is not to be. When they have taken their places in the car to return, Brown takes a last look:

> The justice of the peace was running fast on long loping legs across the cement playground, and the cripple was rocking back with desperation towards the cockpit; he reminded me of a sand-crab scuttling to its hole. He had only another twenty yards to go, but he hadn't a chance.[8]

*

Three months before Greene's arrival in Port-au-Prince, the personal battle between Clément Barbot and Duvalier was raging. Duvalier had huge advantages over his newly metamorphosed former friend. Hatred was on both sides. Barbot, the former killer for Duvalier, was now in the role of David against a not-so-giant Goliath who was fearsome (if only from the safety of his palace – torture chambers at the ready). Was this more a war between a scorpion and a tarantula?

Barbot's first aim was to ensure the safety of his wife and children. They were refused asylum by four embassies before the Argentine embassy (halfway up the mountain of Pétionville) allowed the three daughters and one sick son refuge. Once he'd found asylum for them, Barbot was ready to try the impossible, hunting down his target while the Tontons Macoute everywhere sought him and his men, with orders to kill on sight.

First, Barbot had leaflets dropped on Port-au-Prince threatening a revolt by 15 May, warning residents to leave the city because of an impending (as Barbot put it) 'dry-cleaning operation'. Everyone – the Tontons Macoute, the presidential guard, and the civilian militia estimated at 10,000 – turned nervous, gun-shy and trigger-happy. At the palace, a sergeant shot and killed two motorists who failed to heed his command to stop. There was fear of reprisals in the town. Wholesale arrests were made. Barbot began in earnest to harass the Tontons Macoute and attack Duvalier's militiamen. There were reports that Barbot and his small group of men killed forty-five militiamen.

There was about Barbot the stuff of which legends are made. Diederich and Burt pass on a strange account of voodoo warfare. Storming a stronghold in which Barbot was thought to be holed up, the Tontons Macoute riddled the building with bullets until it seemed nothing could possibly have survived. But the doors opened and one creature still living, a black dog, ran out and promptly disappeared. The voodoo-blinded locals felt that Barbot must have had the power to turn himself into a dog. Duvalier must have believed it too, because he gave orders that all black dogs be shot on sight.

Having lost his stash of weapons when his hideout was discovered, Barbot found another source. Major Jean Tassy, his successor as head goon of the Tontons Macoute, thinking Barbot would visit his wife and children in the embassy, scoured the town. But like the elusive Scarlet Pimpernel, Barbot was neither here nor there. Tassy surrounded the area, while Barbot, with his brother fighting at his side, successfully raided Fort Dimanche miles away, escaping with a cache of weapons.

Barbot somehow arranged for a letter to be placed on Duvalier's desk. Haiti's telephone service was (and is) dismal, so surely only Barbot (now with a price of $10,000 on his head) could have reached Duvalier by phone, warning that his coffee was poisoned, promising to kill him. Duvalier's response was eerie: 'Clément, you will bring me your head.'9

★

On 19 May 1963, an American reporter risked his life by contacting Barbot at a canefield sanctuary. For two hours, Jeremiah O'Leary (who printed his account in the *Washington Star* of 22 May 1963) listened to Barbot talk about his struggle with the madman. Barbot told O'Leary that Duvalier demanded the Tontons Macoute kill 300 persons every year, guilty or not, to cause, one supposes, a predominant sense of terror among the populace. Barbot also asserted that Duvalier had more than a million and a half dollars in a Swiss bank. This seems a modest amount for someone thieving from his people on a vast scale, and also surely stealing from the US. The Tontons Macoute could be paid only by Duvalier because he siphoned off the money – it was a case of vanishing dollars – $8,500,000 in American aid. During Duvalier's period of office, at least 77 million dollars were given. Yet Haitians remained hungry, the poorest people in the Caribbean.*

During O'Leary's interview, the daredevil Barbot had his photograph taken at a time when the Tontons Macoute were seeking him everywhere. An unsigned account of another meeting with Barbot appeared in the *New York Times* on 23 May 1963:

> The door opened and a slight man in underwear held out his hand. 'I am Barbot,' he said.
>
> He was Clément Barbot, the most hunted man in Haiti . . .
>
> Asked whether he had enough men and weapons, Mr Barbot replied with a confident, softly spoken, 'Oh yes' . . .
>
> Expressing confidence that the army and many others would side with him, he said: 'I have many friends who say they are with Duvalier now, but inside they are with Barbot.'[10]

Barbot became a legend. Sources in the palace reported secretly that Barbot was frightening the president himself. One diplomat described how it was for the ordinary citizen:

> The people are petrified. Nobody sees anybody and nobody talks to anybody. After the 8 o'clock curfew they sit in their houses, each family alone, and wonder what the shots down the street are about.[11]

Richard Eder, writing a special for the *New York Times*, admitted that

> it is not unusual in this country for important figures to take on an aura of something approaching witchcraft in the eyes of ordinary people . . . In this atmosphere the enmity between Mr Barbot and the President has developed the quality of a combat between two magical forces.[12]

---

* When first elected, Duvalier announced that he would take a cut in salary; in fact, it is reported that he received an estimated $3 million of annually in secret funds from government monopolies in tobacco, soap and other articles. In his article on the 'Nightmare Republic', Greene gives his projection of Duvalier's wealth: 'All trade which does not offer a rake-off is at a standstill. A whole nation can die of starvation so long as the Doctor's non-fiscal account is safe. The public revenue of Haiti in a reasonable year should be around $28 million, but the non-fiscal account which is paid into the President's pocket amounts to between $8 million and $12 million.'

Given his bloody background, many hoped that Barbot would put an end to Duvalier's regime, and then himself be put aside.

But Barbot and his followers were betrayed by a peasant. On 14 July 1963, led by 'Fat Gracia', the presidential guard ringed the area where the rebels were hiding out. Barbot and some followers managed to escape into a sugarcane field, but the Tontons Macoute set fire to it, forcing Barbot, his brother and others to break cover. They were 'shot . . . like rabbits' as Diederich and Burt describe it.

Many could not believe that Barbot was dead. His wife and children in the Argentine embassy refused to accept it. In the town many superstitious Haitians were sure Barbot lived on, and as *Time* described it: 'black dogs on the street draw fearful sidelong glances'.[13] But pictures of the dead Barbot, the bullet hole through the heart clearly visible, left no doubt. These pictures were displayed everywhere in Port-au-Prince. Like all other corpses on show, Barbot's must have bloated up, flies laying eggs in the corrupting flesh, maggots crawling in and out of the bullet holes.*

★

Greene remarked, while writing of Papa Doc, that 'Heroes are produced by tyranny.'[14] Looking at the heroes Haiti produced, one sees honourable young men, without exception idealists and courageous, enormously keen to bring down Duvalier, but disorganised. Hector Riobé was one of these. He revolted because of what happened to his father, a sugar-cane planter.

We've seen that after the attempt to abduct Duvalier's children, the Tontons Macoute began picking up any other possible suspects. Two seized Riobé's father as he drove home. His car was confiscated and he himself disappeared. They then took everything the family owned, claiming it was to ensure the elder Riobé's safety. It was all a lie. The Tontons Macoute had murdered Hector's father before they had reached the jail. Young Riobé went underground and, two months later, into action.

By the time Greene arrived in Haiti, Riobé's heroics were over, but it is clear that Greene picked up his story – it was less than three weeks old. Greene records it in his diary soon after his arrival:

20 August 1963: Absurdity of rumours. S[eitz, owner of Oloffson's] says that 3 out of the 4 Kenscoff fighters were captured after the attack on the police station.

---

* When I was in Haiti thirty-five years later in December 1998, a Haitian businessman told me: '[Duvalier] just got rid of bad grass.' Another mulatto businessman had no doubt as to the evil one's nature: 'Duvalier was the prince of fucking darkness.'

> They had gone to K[enscoff mountain] to 'make' a bomb – cautiously they had made a flame thrower. One man hurt in the night & killed 100! Govt. figures 23. Other stories 18.[15]

It was a home-made armoured car, and a home-made flame-thrower. Their fight was extraordinary but they'd run out of luck. 'Just after dusk', the day Barbot was killed, 'their vehicle overheated in front of the barracks.'[16] The soldiers at the barracks offered to help, thinking the rebels were militiamen. The young men declined, but when one of the soldiers looked into the back of the truck and noticed the flame-thrower, someone panicked. The group had no option but to blaze away at the barracks, leave the car, and take to the mountains ahead on foot. Diederich states that the post was captured and the ensuing alarm brought the Tontons Macoute. The boys retreated 'to a cave previously stocked with food, water, and ammunition.'[17] They fought for three days, killing over a hundred of Duvalier's army. Finally, Duvalier sent Hector Riobé's mother 'riding a donkey bareback, up to the cave's mouth to plead with her son to surrender'. He refused. He shot himself with his last round: 'The boy, the last survivor in the cave, had given Duvalier his answer.'[18]

*

More valiant young men were to die.

Jeune Haiti ('Young Haiti'), a group of thirteen mulatto men from good families, landed on 5 August 1964 at the extreme south of the island, disciplined and well trained, surely the type needed by any civilised country. Their initial notion was to take the town of Jérémie, but they couldn't get close. As they retreated into the mountains, they had at least ten serious engagements, including the disabling of a plane which was strafing them. Ultimately, to a man, *Jeune Haiti* died, their small force gradually eroded. They made their last stand in battle on 26 October 1964.

In the aftermath, Duvalier ordered the relatives of the invaders to be killed – fathers, mothers, daughters, sons. His method was to hand the mulatto families to the black irregular troops. The Heinls say 'whole families were slaughtered':

> [the] Villedrouins, Drouins, Guilbauds, Laforests, Sansaricqs . . . The Drouin and Sansaricq families were stripped naked and herded through the town to execution . . . When in tears tiny Stephane Sansaricq asked to 'faire pipi' [relieve herself] amid the slaughter of her family, ['Sonny'] Borges said he would wipe her eyes and did so – with a hot end of a lighted cigarette. Then he slashed her to death with a dagger.[19]

The Sansaricq family were killed in the belief that their son was a member of *Jeune Haiti*. He was not.

According to Diederich and Burt, women and children were shot first 'to enrage the male members of the family, thus giving the Tontons Macoute a little extra sport'. 'Children were hacked to death in their mothers' arms.' The family of the leader of *Jeune Haiti*, the Villedrouins, were killed first: 'The Tontons Macoute went after the two children, Lisa, eighteen, and Frantz, sixteen, and their mother. They died singing a church hymn.'[20]

On 28 October 1964 there were only three left of the original thirteen – Villedrouin, Roland Rigaud and Reginal Jourdan (who was related to Hector Riobé). Out of ammunition, they threw whatever they could at the militia – even rocks. They died. Their heads were chopped off and taken to Duvalier, and were photographed, appearing on the front page of *Le Matin*.*

★

In 1967, some three years before the devil carried away his soul, Duvalier found that his own Tontons Macoute were falling out with each other. He chose sides and dealt with it, slaking his thirst for vengeance.

On 15 April of that year, at the time Duvalier was celebrating his tenth anniversary as president, as well as his sixtieth birthday, two bombs went off near the palace, killing four people. Duvalier suspected his son-in-law, Max Dominique. There was known friction between Duvalier's two sons-in-law. Duvalier's wife supported Max Dominique, and Duvalier supported Luc Albert Foucard. Dominique's notion was to bring his brother-in-law into disrepute out of jealousy over Foucard's recent elevation to Minister of Tourism, but his plan backfired.

First, Duvalier demoted some of his most trusted presidential guard officers and sent them to remote areas. A few weeks later he brought them back, and according to Diederich and Burt they were happy to have returned. But that didn't last long, because they were taken to Fort Dimanche. Among those suspected by Duvalier was Sonny Borges, murderer of Stephane Sansaricq.

---

* Diederich and Burt recount Duvalier's speaking to the heads of his enemies, communicating, it was said, with their departed spirits. A year before *Jeune Haiti*'s downfall (a month after Greene had left Port-au-Prince) another young man, Captain Blücher Philogènes, fought with General Cantave, who'd also invaded Haiti. Duvalier demanded that Philogènes' head be chopped off, packed in a bucket of ice and flown to the palace. According to Robert and Nancy Heinl (p. 638), Duvalier 'interrogated the spirit of Philogènes and conversed at length with the head'. From a different source: wearing only his top hat, he talked to Philogènes from the bath, no doubt reminding him what happened when you opposed the great Duvalier.

Close to midnight on 8 June 1967, the chief of the army staff, General Comfort, and eighteen others were awakened. There were nineteen senior officers, including Duvalier's 6′ 7″ tall son-in-law, Colonel Dominique. They were summoned to the palace and, as was Duvalier's wont, were kept waiting two hours. He then appeared surrounded by machine gun-sporting Tontons Macoute. Duvalier ordered the rounded-up officers to follow him and they were escorted to Fort Dimanche. There were no explanations.

They were taken to the rifle range. Imagine their terror in seeing exactly nineteen other senior militiamen, Tontons Macoute and presidential guards, friends of theirs, each tied to a stake. The new arrivals were each issued a rifle with one round in the breech and told to face a brother officer tied to a stake. Their relief must have been palpable – it wasn't their turn – yet. Duvalier, as master of ceremonies, gave the command in a high nasal voice like the spirits of the dead. The nineteen died at the hands of their friends, who'd been forced to be the firing squad. Sonny Borges, the child killer who put a cigarette out in little Stephane's eyes, was also shot that night. We will not mourn.

Papa Doc was as bereft of human decency as Emily Brontë's Heathcliff, who set a trap over a lapwing's nest so that the mother bird could not feed her young: 'We saw its nest in the winter, full of little skeletons.' What bastards fill the world.

★

Duvalier allowed his son-in-law Colonel Dominique to become Haiti's ambassador to Spain, but he always felt he'd been cheated out of a body. At the airport, as the plane took off for Spain with Dominique and Duvalier's daughter, Duvalier had Dominique's chauffeur and bodyguard shot. Everyone connected with Colonel Dominique was sent out of this world hard.

Duvalier, after Hitler, after Stalin, has disfigured our notion of dictatorship still further. George Orwell comes to mind: 'a boot stamping on a human face forever'.

PART 13

Coming Up Close
to Creativity

28

Two Shades of Greene

Me and my shadow, strolling down the avenue . . .
— song by BILLY ROSE

AFTER discovering a rabid killer-president in Haiti, Greene was temporarily cured of his internal torment; his fears became external. Dr Duvalier was a perfect opponent. Focusing on this death-dealer's regime allowed Greene to escape from himself: to become preoccupied with planning his novel, craving a victory, both moral and creative.

Greene (on his third visit) heard stories of the young opponents of Dr Duvalier fighting in the hills, sometimes on the outskirts of the country, in the fields and the harsh mountains of Haiti, always obscenely outnumbered by the forces of evil. He came to know some of those who had survived and crossed the Massacre river to safety in the Dominican Republic. He recalled the death of two young heroes:

I made a trip in 1964 . . . along the Dominican-Haitian border. It was in San Domingo that I met one of the group leaders, Fred Baptiste, who became a friend of mine; so did his brother Raynald (who played the part of a Tonton Macoute in the film version of *The Comedians*). The Dominican government had allowed them to set up their headquarters in an old lunatic asylum, just as in the novel. Later, Fred Baptiste and his brother returned to Haiti to fight. They were captured and died in prison.[*1]

* In 1971, at the International Journalists meeting in London, in a Q&A session Greene spoke out. Asked if he'd go back to Haiti now that Papa Doc was dead, he quickly answered that he would be only too glad to return to Haiti and take note of every change for the better but on one condition — 'that my friends Fred and Raynald Baptiste met me at the airport. I'd learnt that Fred had gone mad in prison, and that his brother's condition was grave. And I thought: if they go ahead and kill them now because of my declaration, at least they'll be free of their sufferings.' (Marie-Françoise Allain, *The Other Man: Conversations with Graham Greene*, pp. 79–80.)

These romantic young men knew little of guerrilla warfare. Greene, aware of the odds against them and wanting to fight on their side, found he was able to put depression aside and enter the fray, and was no longer weighed down (as he had been) by the 'grace of misery'.

But Greene's greatest battles had been waged in childhood, so the youthful yet derisively small band of Haitian heroes fighting in the mountains above the capital against immensely superior forces profoundly touched him. Heroism, idealism, courage and self-sacrifice came alive. 'In childhood,' Greene wrote, 'we live under the brightness of immortality – heaven is as near and actual as the seaside. Behind the complicated details of the world stand the simplicities: God is good . . . there is such a thing as truth, and justice is as measured and fault-less as a clock.'[2]

Greene aligned himself with the young men struggling for a cause. 'I began with the intention of expressing a point of view and in order to fight – to fight the horror of Papa Doc's dictatorship.'[3]

In *The Comedians*, the individual consciences of his created characters – the witty liar Jones (ultimately a hero), the narrator Mr Brown (his illicit love affair paralleling Greene's own) and the Smiths (at last, sympathetic Americans in a Greene novel) – have powerful feelings to contend with. Brilliant plotting makes this novel a major achievement, but it is not melodrama, and there is much in Duvalier's world that would have made it easy to descend into melodrama.

Greene, however angry, wrote his novels coolly. He did not explore in detail the human disasters of the Duvalier regime. That was not his way. He knew that unless he was going to write a tome as extensive as *War and Peace*, the terrible listing of crimes would not work. Yet these horrors are in the background, and one hears as much and as freshly as strangers, arriving in that swarming nest of human vipers, would hear.

Greene takes us into the minds of characters such as Brown's mother and her black lover; the brilliant Dr Magiot; the evil Concasseur; the visitors to the island: the Smiths, Jones, and Brown (while he lives in Port-au-Prince, it seems as though, like Greene himself, he would always be a visitor in any society). Because they are visitors, as they learn of this world bit by bit, we do as well, piecing together information about the nature and impact of Duvalier upon these characters, as Duvalier's Haiti takes root in their minds. Greene suggests that the difficulty in such a novel is making one's way 'through the thick jungle of savagery, incompetence, greed and superstition'.[4]

Greene's novel captures the sense of brooding terror in Port-au-Prince, reflected in these strangers' reactions. The Smiths come to feel that nothing can be done in Haiti (after going there with such chivalric hopes of doing good for blacks), bringing us closer to their despair. They are out of their depth in the face of Satan's apprentice.

In the end, what is remarkable is Greene's fine-tuning. What he did in *The Quiet American* he does again in *The Comedians*. The two detailed historical studies of Heinl and Heinl, and Diederich and Burt vividly chronicle facts and list atrocities of Duvalier's reign, but until these facts become unified and woven into the fabric of life (as only a novel can do), we cannot be too deeply moved. It is like the tragic events recorded on the television news; they exist of course, but somehow do not go deep into our psyche, though the overall historical knowledge of the work of the Heinls *does* touch our hearts – and that also applies to the work of Diederich and Burt. With Greene's Haiti, we know its taste, its sights, the sounds of traffic: we sense the smell of fear, know its terrible autocracy, for we've seen it within a living community, portrayed in the novel with unerring accuracy.

Greene's Haiti comes alive as soon as Brown arrives at his hotel, as we've seen in the episode about Philipot, a powerful minister psychologically pushed to the edge. That he had irritated, simply irritated, President Duvalier drove Philipot in terror to kill himself. Everyday life in Haiti goes on amidst political madness: 'Poor Haiti itself and the character of Doctor Duvalier's rule are not invented,' said Greene in his dedicatory letter to A. S. Frere, 'the latter not even blackened for dramatic effect. Impossible to deepen that night.'[5] The book offers thrilling evidence of what a canny fighter Greene was, writing tight, writing light, and often with austere lyrical strength.

★

Greene visited Haiti twice before Duvalier took power. His initial notion was to use it as a backdrop for an 'entertainment', which he abandoned as being too light-hearted. His first visit was in 1954, during the time of Paul Magloire, a popular head of state who helped bring tourists to Haiti. Aubelin Jolicoeur recalled meeting Greene in Port-au-Prince:

> Peter Brook [the theatrical director] was here and Greene came to meet Brook. He was waiting for him but he was all by himself. I remember I went to El Rancho, a very handsome place, fantastic. There was a war-torn bar and when I arrived I saw two young couples in bermuda shorts and one shouted: 'Over here, Jolicoeur. I want you to meet the great author of *The Power and the Glory*', and to tell you the truth I did not know what *The Power and the Glory* was. Graham Greene was very humble and he left his seat at the bar where he was all by himself and came over to me. He

shakes hands with me and we talk. The young couple were working with Mr Brook on *The House of Flowers*. Yes, we used to go out together gathering information about brothels. *The House of Flowers* [a musical] is about brothels.[6]

Jolicoeur was universally known in the capital as 'Mr Haiti'. It was he who arranged for Greene to go to his first voodoo ceremony and to the brothel where he met the madam who so impressed him (the source for Mère Catherine in *The Comedians*), Georgette John-Charles.

Greene returned to Haiti on 28 June 1956. This trip was simply to find a setting for an 'entertainment'. He stayed at the Oloffson Hotel, which was swiftly becoming a popular place for the rich and famous. Sir John Gielgud would stay there, and had an ornamental suite named after him.*

The Oloffson, used by Greene in *The Comedians*, was a huge mahogany house, festooned with spires, cupolas and towers on the hundred-sided roof with every filigree, scroll, and magnificent fretwork, amid palatial gardens of coconut palms, casuarinas and other tropical foliage. On this trip, Greene brought along Catherine Walston. Roger Coster, then the owner of the hotel,† recalled Greene's visits:

> Mr Greene came here with Peter Brook . . . I remember Graham Greene as a vague person. He was tall, very gentle with an ironical smile, but with watery eyes which covered quite a lot of mysterious little twists of malice . . . Malice in a certain way, because I felt that with his watery eyes . . . he was grabbing the mood and the atmosphere of the people at the same time.

Coster described Greene's eyes as a

> window through which you cannot see too much. On his next visit in 1956, Graham Greene came with a very beautiful lady – he was always with beautiful ladies, English ladies – a very grand salon lady, very hospitable, greyish hair, probably a very great beauty ten years ago, but still very striking . . . statuesque . . . It was just before the beginning of the political troubles in Haiti.[7]

---

* In December 1998 I stayed in the John Gielgud suite at the Oloffson. It had seen better days. I was chased out of the room by a swarm of bees who were determined to take over my bathroom.

† Coster, born in Paris, was a photographer who'd come to Haiti to make money, and he bought Oloffson's. He says, in his French accent: 'To be a photographer, one must be completely nuts. But to be a hotelkeeper is the epitome of insanity.'

At the same time, Greene was writing to a Dr Lherisson (one source for the philosophical and wise Dr Magiot in the novel):

If there is any chance of being . . . at a voodoo ceremony . . . I would very much like the opportunity. I saw one . . . with Mr and Mrs Brook two years ago but Mrs Walston has not been present at one. [Notice, Greene does not pass her off as his wife or girlfriend, but refers to her as a married woman.]

Coster's report of a watchful Greene is spot on: 'Graham Greene walking along the street, not making any fuss (always slightly aloof and a little bit reserved) but *absorbing plenty*.'

★

An interview with Greene conducted in Port-au-Prince on 16 August 1963 by a local journalist appeared in the *New York Times* on the 18th, three days after his arrival on his third visit to Haiti. The article began with three headings: 'GRAHAM GREENE, IN HAITI, TALKS OF DOUBLE TROUBLE'; 'Author Finds His Name Used by Indiscreet Adventurer'; and 'Other Man's Activities Lean to Theft and Gun-Running':

Graham Greene writes about men pursued by divine love. But he himself is pursued by an adventurous, rather indiscreet man by the name of Graham Greene.

The British novelist arrived in Haiti the other day. He is thinking about writing another entertainment . . .

If the entertainment is written, it will begin with a hotel proprietor returning from abroad and finding his hotel has only two guests. Mr Greene is staying at the Hotel Oloffson, which has only three guests. Because of the uncertain political situation, Haitian hotels are almost deserted.

Shadowy Encounters: Mr Greene sat on the verandah of the Oloffson, a turreted gingerbread structure that looks as though the jungle were about to repossess it. The author, who has extraordinarily light blue eyes and a ruddy seamed face, sipped a Scotch and discussed his shadowy encounters with the other Graham Greene.[8]

Greene seems the essence of relaxation, but we know from his terse diary entries that he was sometimes afraid. Issa el Saieh, a Syrian who worked on occasion for Al Seitz, a later owner of the Oloffson, remembered Greene: how he gave him a big crucifix – huge – at least three feet tall and easily two feet across – to be laid on his pillow nightly.

Greene's comic tale to the local journalist concerns an impostor, a man masquerading as Graham Greene in different parts of the world. It would have been quite possible for someone to double as Graham Greene and not be caught, because while Greene liked publicity (it improved book sales) he did not like celebrity. Every time a book was published his picture surmounted the review, but his face and physique were not well known. For a man who had been famous ever since his first novel, *The Man Within*, in 1929, Greene was timid. He never wished to be a household face and this made it eerily possible for a crook to masquerade as Greene in faraway places. The false Graham Greene used his name and fame to impress women, and engage in small-scale swindling.

The first hint of trouble came when the editor of a French magazine asked the real Graham Greene to write an article, saying in passing that they'd met at the Cannes Film Festival. Greene had never been to the festival. Sometime later another French editor of a film magazine apologised for a member of his staff who had tried to blackmail Greene. It was the first time Greene had heard of it. After Greene returned from Vietnam (where he was collecting material for *The Quiet American*), the phone rang in his Paris hotel room. 'This is Valerie,' said a woman's voice, asking why he had changed his mind about staying at the Hotel George V and inviting him to dinner. He had never met anyone with that name. He arranged to meet her for a drink. Sending an intermediary, Greene sat at the far end of the bar. She didn't recognise him. Clearly *her* Graham Greene looked different. His friend told him that Valerie was an American who'd met Graham Greene in Arabia.

The next headlines about the spurious Graham Greene were that he had got himself jailed in Assam, charged with selling guns to the Nagas and then with harassing the Indian authorities. Greene II (as we'll call him) had the chutzpah to send a telegram to the *Picture Post* stating that he, 'Graham Greene', had lost his baggage and passport, was in trouble with the Indian police, and needed them to send £100 forthwith. The editor wisely sent someone to Greene's Albany chambers to enquire if Greene was in town, but the porter there said Greene had not been seen for several days, so the *Picture Post* telegraphed the money to India, no doubt expecting a good story in return. Headlines in the Indian press announced the following: 'Graham Greene Convicted. Sentenced to Two Years'. The real Greene even had a copy of a long letter that the bogus Greene had written to the *Picture Post*, making no attempt to imitate his namesake's style. Greene kept a growing file on Greene II and had hoped some day to meet him. He never did.

With his tremendous capacity for looking perfectly innocent, in this case we see Greene using the amusing and apolitical tale of his double to indicate to the authorities in Haiti that he was not in Port-au-Prince to gather damning political material for a serious and devastating novel. He kept silent about the tribulations in Haiti. Not until he'd written his *Sunday Telegraph* account would his hatred of the Duvalier dictatorship become known. By referring to his novel vaguely as 'an entertainment about a hotelier with three tourists', Greene misdirected Duvalier's Tontons Macoute. His story of the doppelgänger Graham Greene II no doubt warded off further attention.

The Haitian journalist ended his interview with a description of the *real* Graham Greene:

> Mr Greene is a quiet-mannered, innocent-looking man to whom things have been happening for at least 40 of his 59 years from Vietnam to Africa to Cuba.

In *Our Man in Havana* one sentence states a firm belief of Graham's philosophy: 'There was always another side to a joke, the side of the victim.'[9] Greene *was* an innocent-looking man, but that's where his innocence ended. He was secretly seeking information about Duvalier's victims: a great work was beginning in his mind, quietly, inextricably taking root.

29

To Haiti by Sea

Sometimes your hero ends up bleating like a billy goat.
— LUCINDA CUMMINGS

GREENE could have opened *The Comedians* conventionally, with Brown, the hotelier, travelling to Haiti by plane. Instead the pace is leisurely. The four central characters arrive by ship. Michael Heinl told me in a letter of 28 November 2001 that during the early fifties, some tourists did go to Port-au-Prince by two aged ships of the Panama line, the *Ancon* and the *Cristobal*. However, I've found no evidence that Greene himself travelled to Haiti by sea.

Before the first page of *The Comedians* has ended, we are in the Atlantic aboard the *Medea*, bound for Port-au-Prince. The journey from New York by sea is a wonderful prelude, moving calmly towards the dangerous world ahead.

The advantage of beginning this way is that it allows Greene to develop his main characters: Brown, the hotel owner returning from New York; the Smiths, friendly and honest Americans on their first visit; and Major Jones (his title suspect), a quack, a con man. The opening strikes the proper note of discord, revealing Brown's sardonic nature and introducing Major Jones as one who plays the part of a hero with a valiant wartime past, but who is actually a liar, a mountebank, a cheapskate — and yet . . .

*

What does Greene know of travelling by sea? His knowledge derives from experiences during the Second World War, over twenty years before. Unlike the journey from New York to Port-au-Prince, that trip of three weeks from the port of Liverpool to the port of Freetown in December 1941–January 1942 was extraordinarily dangerous.

When Greene made that journey, Hitler's U-boats were sending

344

huge tonnages of British ships to the bottom of the sea, attacking not only at periscope depth by day, but on the surface by night, making use of their greater speed, hunting in wolf packs.

On the cargo vessel to Freetown there were twelve passengers. On the *Medea* there are seven, but there are parallels between the real and the fictional. Early on in *The Comedians*, Brown goes to the purser's cabin before dinner only to find:

He was blowing up a French letter till it was the size of a policeman's truncheon. He tied the end up with ribbon and removed it from his mouth. His desk was littered with great swollen phalluses . . .

'Tomorrow is the ship's concert,' he explained to me, 'and we have no balloons. It was Mr Jones's idea that we should use these.'

A party is being thrown to celebrate the cargo ship's approach to Port-au-Prince. The captain and the chief engineer honour the guests with their presence: 'one at the head of the table and one at the foot, they sat with equality under dubious balloons'. There is an extra course to commemorate their last night at sea, and, with the exception of the Smiths, the passengers drink champagne. The captain speaks:

'I understand', the captain said gloomily, 'that after dinner there is to be an entertainment.'

'We're only a small company,' the purser said, 'but Major Jones and I felt that something must be done on our last night together. There is the kitchen-orchestra . . . and Mr Baxter is going to give us something very special . . . I have asked Mr Fernandez to help us in his own way, and he has gladly consented . . . We shall end by singing Auld Lang Syne for the sake of our Anglo-Saxon passengers.'

And the kitchen musicians are a diverting embellishment. Is it just from Greene's imagination?

The purser said gaily, 'Chins up,' and began to beat his hands softly on his plump knees as the orchestra entered, led by the cook, a cadaverous young man, with cheeks flushed by the heat of stoves, wearing his chef's hat. His companions carried pots, pans, knives, spoons: a mincer was there to add a grinding note, and the chef held a toasting-fork as a baton.[1]

No, this strange orchestra made up of pots and pans originates in Greene's sea journey to Freetown in 1941. Greene's diary entry on his arrival is terse: 'The cook arranged a musical farewell as I got on the launch: the gong, tinpans, etc.' In his *Collected Essays* Greene adds: 'A kitchen orchestra of forks and frying-pans played me off the . . . ship into a motor launch where my temporary host . . . awaited me.'[2]

But just as on the fictional *Medea*, there was also a party on the ship bound for Freetown:

> As Christmas approached, there were more parties . . . [Greene] went down to the steward's to help with Christmas decorations . . . 'French letters blown up the size of balloons and hung over the captain's chair . . . The cracked second steward . . . the recitation in a tin helmet'.[3]

The poem recitation on the Elder Dempster cargo ship was about the Merchant Service, and 'recited for no apparent reason in a steel helmet'.[4] In *The Comedians*, the same situation exists but the poem is about the Blitz in London, and in the novel it is the fictional Mr Baxter, a pharmaceutical traveller, who does the recitation. He enters, as did the steward on the Elder Dempster ship, wearing a steel helmet and with a whistle clenched between his teeth, and after blowing it to demand silence, he makes an announcement: 'A Dramatic Monologue entitled "The Warden's Patrol" composed by Post Warden X'.

We discover that Mr Baxter was Warden X, and on the *Medea* he often feels the need to speak of the bombing: 'He had been, he said, a warden in civil defence and he had an urge to recount the usual bomb-stories, as obsessive and boring as other men's dreams . . . the chemist went on and on about the bombing of a Jewish girls' hostel in Store Street. ("We were so busy that night no one noticed it had gone.")'[5] Greene himself was involved in the raid that Warden X speaks of, and his own description of that terrible night is one of the most gripping to come out of the Blitz.[6] But Greene could not here exceed his character's abilities.

*

Now we can address the genesis of Greene's design for an ideal house of ill repute. The answer lies in his visits to Haiti, out of which comes the allegory in his play, *A House of Reputation*. He also puts an extraordinary brothel into *The Comedians*, a more realistic example of such a place, but the madam has characteristics which parallel the madam in his play. The brothel is seen as a private oasis of sanity in a desert of insanity.

In *The Comedians*, Brown is returning to Haiti from New York after trying to sell his hotel. Papa Doc has brought tourism to a halt. No hotel, not even Brown's once successful Trianon, can survive. He goes to the usual meeting place that he and his mistress use, the statue of Columbus, as we have seen before. (This landmark is gone for ever now, having been knocked down and tossed into the sea.) Unexpectedly, Martha is there. Soon after, Brown is invited to the embassy, little wishing to go:

> I would have much preferred to know nothing of Martha's normal surroundings . . . Now I knew exactly where she went when her car left the Columbus statue. I knew the hall which she passed through with the chained book where visitors wrote their names, the drawing-room that she entered next with the deep chairs and sofas and the glitter of chandeliers and the big photograph of General so-and-so, their relatively benevolent president.

Brown sees Martha's husband as a lonely man: 'What did he do when there was no official party and his wife was out meeting me?'[7]

When Brown arrives, Martha takes him upstairs to see her son, Angel, who has mumps. Brown suddenly desires her in one of the empty ambassadorial rooms – her husband is engaged in a discussion downstairs – but the attempt comes to nothing. Stung by failure, he leaves and drives along the edge of the sea, the road pitted with holes, in the direction of a brothel, Mère Catherine's – the 'long long day was not yet over':

> Midnight was an hour or an age away . . . On my right hand were a line of wooden huts in little fenced saucers of earth where a few palm trees grew and slithers of water gleamed between, like scrap-iron on a dump. An occasional candle burned . . . Sometimes there were furtive sounds of music. An old man danced in the middle of the road – I had to brake my car to a standstill. He came and giggled at me through the glass – at least one man in Port-au-Prince that night who was not afraid.[8]

It is two years since Brown visited Mère Catherine's, 'but tonight I needed her services. My impotence lay in my body like a curse which it needed a witch to raise.'

He reaches a roadblock and is allowed to pass. A great placard announces '"The USA-Haitian Joint Five-Year Plan. Great Southern Highway", but the Americans had left and nothing remained . . . but the notice-board, over the stagnant pools, the channels in the road, the rocks and the carcass of a dredger' in the mud.

Brown arrives at Mère Catherine's compound to discover it is almost empty. The stalls, the 'quarters for love', are dark, but a light is burning in the main building. Brown walks towards it, hating every step. He stumbles against a jeep – this rare vehicle surely belongs to some of Duvalier's private police. 'If the Tontons Macoute were making a night of it with Mère Catherine's girls, there would be no room for outside custom.'

Believing it too dangerous, Brown is yet 'obstinate in my self-hatred'. He goes on and the madam, hearing him stumbling in the dark, meets him on the threshold, holding an oil lamp. Immediately we are back in *A House of Reputation*, the principled and kindly madam concerned with her 'protégées':

> She had the face of a kind nanny in a film of the deep south, and a tiny delicate body which must once have been beautiful. Her face didn't belie her nature, for she was the kindest woman I knew in Port-au-Prince. She pretended that her girls came from good families, that she was only helping them to earn a little pin-money, and you could almost believe her, for she had taught them perfect manners in public. Till they reached the stalls her customers too had to behave with decorum, and to watch the couples dance you would almost have believed it to be an end-of-term celebration at a convent-school.[9]

And she protects them:

> Three years before I had seen her go in to rescue a girl from some brutality . . . I heard a scream from . . . the stable, but before I could decide what to do Mère Catherine had taken a hatchet from the kitchen and sailed out like the little *Revenge* prepared to take on a fleet. Her opponent was armed with a knife, he was twice her size, and he was drunk . . . He turned and fled at her approach, and later when I left, I saw her . . . with the girl upon her knees, crooning to her as though she were a child, in a *patois* which I couldn't understand, and the girl slept against the little bony shoulder.[10]

As Brown enters, the madam warns that the Tontons Macoute are there and that the girl Brown likes is busy. (He discovers later that she is with Jones, who Concasseur, the leading Tonton Macoute, thinks is important to his president.) As Brown puts it, not having visited for two years, his one-time choice would now be eighteen: 'I hadn't expected to find her, and yet I was disappointed. In age one prefers old friends, even in a *bordel*.'

Brown decides to have a drink. The place has cleared out – it is unhealthy to be where there are Tontons Macoute. There is rum, but no Coke, now that American aid is over. He asks for rum and soda. Mère Catherine disappears into the bar; she still has a few bottles of Seven-Up.

> At the door of the *salle* a Tonton Macoute was asleep on a chair; his sun-glasses had fallen in his lap and he looked quite harmless. The flies of his grey flannel trousers gaped from a lost button. Inside there was complete silence. Through the open door I saw a group of four girls dressed in white muslin with balloon-skirts. They were sucking orangeade through straws, not speaking. One of them took her empty glass and moved away, walking beautifully, the muslin swaying, like a little bronze by Degas.[11]

Sitting at a table by the wall is the fiercely arrogant Captain Concasseur. Since Brown's return from New York, he has already seen Concasseur twice – in a police station, where there were snapshots on the wall of a 'dead rebel', and later, when Concasseur smashed the windows of a hearse. One disturbing quality of Concasseur's is the way he stares. Brown bows to him and goes towards another table. He is frightened but he holds his own despite his fear:

> The officer said, 'I seem to see you everywhere.'
>   'I try to be inconspicuous.'
>   'What do you want here tonight?'
>   'A rum and Seven-Up.'
>   He said to Mère Catherine, who was bringing in my drink upon a tray, 'You said you had no Seven-Up left.' I noticed that there was an empty soda-water bottle on the tray beside my glass. The Tonton Macoute took my drink and tasted it. 'Seven-Up it is. You can bring this man a rum and soda. We need all the Seven-Up you have left for my friend when he returns.'
>   'It's so dark in the bar. The bottles must have got mixed.'
>   'You must learn to distinguish between your important customers, and . . . the less important. You can sit down,' he said to me.
>   I turned away.
>   'You can sit down here. Sit down.'
>   I obeyed.[12]

The conversation goes on; all the time, Concasseur stares blankly through Brown 'with his black opaque lenses'. Mère Catherine returns with his rum and soda, while Concasseur sips from Brown's original glass: 'Mère Catherine brought me in my drink. I tasted it. The rum was still mixed with Seven-Up. She was a brave woman.'

Concasseur tells Brown that his white colour reminds him of 'turd' (perhaps a transposition of a coarse insult once hurled at Concasseur), and then demands that the girls dance: They 'dance together in a graceful slow old-fashioned style. Their balloon-skirts swung like silver censers and showed their slender legs the colour of young deer; they smiled gently at each other and held one another a little apart. They were beautiful and undifferentiated like birds of the same plumage. It was almost impossible to believe they were for sale.'

> Concasseur saw where I was looking; he missed nothing through those black glasses. He said, 'I will treat you to a woman. That small girl there, with a flower in her hair, Louise. She doesn't look at us. She is shy because she thinks I might be jealous. Jealous of a *putain* [whore]! What absurdity! She will serve you very well if I give her the word.'
>
> 'I don't want a woman.' I could see through his apparent generosity. One flings a *putain* to a white man as one flings a bone to a dog.
>
> 'Then why are you here?'
>
> He had the right to ask . . . I could only say, 'I've changed my mind,' as I watched the girls revolve, worthy of a better setting than the wooden shed, the rum-bar and the old advertisements for Coca-Cola.[13]

A superior brothel in the evil world of Haiti.

★

On 31 May 1978, visiting Haiti, I interviewed Roger Coster. Greene in *The Comedians* described the scene I later viewed: 'We entered the steep drive lined with palm trees and bougainvillaea . . . The architecture of the hotel was neither classical in the eighteenth-century manner nor luxurious in the twentieth-century fashion. With its towers and balconies and wooden fretwork decorations it had the air at night of a Charles Addams house in . . . [the *New Yorker*] . . . But in the sunlight, or when the lights went on among the palms, it seemed fragile and period and pretty and absurd, an illustration from a book of fairy-tales.'[14] In *The Comedians*, Brown has a possessive love for his 'fairy-tale' hotel, the Trianon, as had Coster for the Oloffson, even after he'd sold it, something the character Brown had been trying to do.

Coster recalled in interview seeing the film of *The Comedians* in

Paris with his wife, after a rough time in Haiti. He remembered: 'Suddenly we saw the Oloffson, my hotel was all the mood, and it was absolutely magnificent.' It was Coster who took Greene to the local brothel, Georgette's, on which Mère Catherine's is based. In the same interview he reflected:

> Sex has never been like in America which before you give your-self away you need to have life insurance . . . Here it is like eating a mango. But . . . Georgette [would take] from a certain class, not . . . poor . . . not very rich, some young chicken who is quite agreeable, and teach them the trade.[15]

He recalled how once the actor Maurice Evans, a homosexual, went with him to Georgette's:

> [She] opened the door [wearing] a peignoir . . . two enormous bosoms sticking out, and I said to her, 'Georgette, I want to present Mr Maurice Evans, he . . . is looking for a young man.' She said, 'A young man, let me think.' She . . . was a completely under-standing woman. She would take her girls to Cuba, Puerto Rico to learn about life, not only on a pleasure trip, but on knowing the world's business.[16]

Also staying at Oloffson's during Greene's third visit were an American couple, the husband a skilled artist whom I interviewed in New York, 23 March 1981, when he was a young ninety years of age.* Harry Gottlieb recalled how he and his wife were in Georgette's one night with Graham, when all the girls who were not working watched him sketch. 'They had lovely young voices, and seemed very pure, very simple, very clean. My wife and I have always loved coloured people.'

Greene, in his introduction to *The Comedians* in the Collected Edition, is more evocative:

> There were three guests in the Oloffson hotel (I call it the Trianon in the novel) beside myself – the Italian manager of the casino and an old American artist and his wife . . . One night the three of us braved the dark to visit the brothel I have described . . . as Mère Catherine's. There were no customers except a couple of

---

* During my first visit to Port-au-Prince, like Greene, I stayed at the Oloffson. Checking the register for August 1963, I found an American artist and his wife. The only other name was the casino manager. With their address in hand, I looked them up and interviewed the artist almost twenty years after their stay at the Oloffson. His wife had just died.

Tontons Macoute. 'Mr Smith' began to draw the girls who had been dancing together decorously . . . they gathered round his chair like excited schoolchildren, while the Tontons glared through their dark glasses at this strange spectacle of a fearless happiness and an innocence they couldn't understand.

Given the nature of this brothel in Haiti, Greene's decision to make it a refuge was superb, the only place apart from foreign embassies that might be a haven for the displaced and pursued. Unquestionably, for all his adult life Greene had a passion for brothels, but especially this one. This is the source for Greene's *House of Reputation*. Gottlieb continued:

> One day, in Oloffson's, Graham Greene says: 'I want to visit a house of prostitution' . . . My wife went along too . . . There was nothing that went on that anyone would be ashamed of . . . we came into this charming little place with tables – people were sitting around and soft music playing. Young women, very nice, dressed in summer clothes . . . they'd . . . go off in the rear [to] their little cottages . . . [there] they had their romance . . . I remember I did a drawing of a young lady at the next table and when I finished I gave it to her. She was entranced. She apologised and left her young man and [left] the drawing in the safety of her little cottage . . . it was so absolutely harmless, the brothel . . . so tame. In no sense could you figure out just by being there for the first time what it was . . . it was a charming little café and bar.

Greene hired a car to take the three of them from Oloffson's to the brothel. On the way back, he said softly: '"In a certain sense I'm sorry that we took your wife because there was a young woman that I would have liked to have made contact with." And he didn't because we were along and he thought it would be discourteous.'

Even in a brothel, Greene remained an English gentleman.

★

Here we see the origins of the delightful Americans, fighters for the civil rights of blacks in their country. They enter the desperate island of Haiti, but find the political nature of that country quite beyond their understanding.

Greene didn't find it difficult to take up the nature of the Gottliebs and transfer it to the Smiths. On meeting the artist and his wife, he recognised the genuine love they bore each other; this he carried over into the novel. He knew why they were in Haiti, but writing seven-teen years later in *Ways of Escape* he tells only the minimum, describing the Gottliebs as 'a gentle couple whom I cannot deny bore some resemblance to Mr and Mrs Smith of the novel'.[17] The differences are telling. The Smiths have a strange vegetarian philosophy and, because of this, are figures of fun. In real life, the Gottliebs kept to a kosher diet, and were there to teach Haitian artists silk screening, so that poverty-stricken local painters could earn a better living by selling reproductions in the States.

Greene tells us, as Gottlieb told me, that they had been promised the necessary material for teaching the local people by the Haitian Consul-General in New York, but after weeks of waiting, nothing arrived. The Gottliebs had no personal axe to grind and wanted only to do charitable deeds. They consulted various officials but none would assist. If the Gottliebs had offered a kickback, they would have had assistance, but that was intolerable to them. They could not have come to Haiti at a worse time.

In *The Comedians*, Greene's Smiths are naïve; their diet composed of products like 'Nuttoline' and 'Slippery Elm Food'. As for drinks, it's Barmene with hot water or Yeastrel, or Vecon, and at the party on board ship a typical line is 'Mrs Smith . . . gave [herself] a second helping of Nuttoline.' To some extent they are caricatures; he with his 'large innocent hairy ears . . . one lock of white hair standing up like a television aerial in the wind', she with her willingness to stand up on all occasions for her husband, and for anyone who is being victimised. Mr Smith ran on the vegetarian ticket the year President Truman was elected. Smith got only 10,000 votes, but that was a victory of a sort, in a battle they knew they couldn't win.

The American couple's most wonderful quality in fiction and in life was indestructible integrity. What makes the Smiths absurd is not their adamant but naïve belief in the innate goodness of all blacks. No, it is their firm notion that acidity in one's diet makes for violence that would disappear if all humans gave up eating meat and refused alcohol. His motto: World discord ended by universal vegetarianism! There is a contrast between the Smiths' very real integrity and their failure to believe in the possibility that a black government could be corrupt. This was also true of the Gottliebs. However, the Smiths gradually made the necessary step to realising that, as we've seen, in Haiti, evil flourished.

They are told of the attempt to kidnap the president's children, and of Duvalier's Tontons Macoute surrounding the falsely accused Benoît's house, setting the house on fire and machine-gunning anyone escaping. Sardonically Brown adds: 'They allowed the fire-brigade to keep the flames from spreading, and now you see the gap in the street like a drawn tooth.' Mr Smith gives his answer for the black race: 'Hitler did worse, didn't he? And he was a white man. You can't blame it on their colour.' And Brown answers: 'I don't. The victim was coloured too.'[18]

★

Brown goes to a voodoo ceremony, after which his barman, Joseph, disappears. Brown waits up for him – Joseph is, after all, the only worker left in the hotel – but finally falls asleep at four o'clock. He is awakened at six by the Tontons Macoute.

Brown is confronted by the appalling Concasseur, while his men search the kitchen and the servants' quarters. There is a 'banging of cupboards and doors and the screech of smashed glass'. Brown asks Concasseur, who lies 'on a wicker *chaise longue* with the gun in his lap' pointing at Brown, what he wants. There is no answer. He tries again: 'We have no refugees here. Your men are making enough noise to wake the dead.' With 'reasonable pride' (for tourists were no longer coming to Haiti), Brown adds that he has guests. Mr Smith is something of a celebrity because the authorities think he might have influence in America which could be used against them.

Gradually the sky reddens over Concasseur's shoulder, the palm trees turn black and distinct. Concasseur begins to question Brown, about 'Colonel' Jones (Brown notices that Jones has been promoted) and about Joseph, suggesting that both Brown and Joseph had had a rendezvous with the rebels. It turns out that '[at] four o'clock that morning a police station was attacked', with one policeman killed. (This is the real attack dealt with earlier, when young Hector Riobé attempted to avenge his father's death. Greene transfers this incident to the servant Joseph and to young Philipot, who is out to avenge his father's suicide.) Told of the attack on the police station, Brown now knows why the Tontons Macoute have called on him.

Concasseur's men return from smashing up the kitchen, and Brown finds himself surrounded by the Tontons Macoute, their dark glasses on even in the murky dawn. Concasseur makes a sign and one of them hits Brown in the mouth; Concasseur tells Brown that his body will be shown to the British Chargé d'Affaires. Brown feels his nerve going, and we have a beautiful Greene aphorism: 'Courage even in the brave sleeps before breakfast.' Concasseur signals again and Brown is kicked. As he is falling, another pulls the chair from under him and he falls close to Concasseur's feet. The Tontons Macoute close around him on the floor as he tries to stand up. He is afraid:

If only I could have seen one pair of eyes and the expression . . .
I was daunted by the anonymity. Captain Concasseur said, 'You
. . . have pissed in your *pantalons*.' I realised that what he said was
true. I could feel the wet and the warmth. I was dripping humiliatingly on the boards. He had got what he wanted, and I would
have done better to have stayed on the floor at his feet.

'Hit him again,' Captain Concasseur told the man.

'*Dégoûtant*,' a voice said, '*tout à fait dégoûtant*.'*

Mrs Smith appears at the end of the verandah, quite terrible to
behold. She recognises Concasseur and calls him a woman-striker.
Incredibly she is able to force him to give up his gun. She asks for his
warrant. Then, in her atrocious French, she says: 'You have searched.
You have not found. You can go.'[19] Concasseur knows now that she
is the wife of a one-time US presidential candidate, enough to frighten
the bully in him.† Soon after, the Smiths decide to leave Haiti, seeing
no hope of establishing, nor indeed wishing to establish, a vegetarian
centre in such a country.

★

Martha, Brown's lover, begins to visit him regularly at his hotel when
only the Smiths are staying there. The lovers are sweet together. Brown
has never been more at peace:

Somewhere from far away in the town came the sound of shots.
'Somebody's being killed,' I said.

'Haven't you heard?' she asked.

Two more shots came.

'I mean about the executions?'

'No. Petit Pierre hasn't been up for days. Joseph has disappeared. I'm cut off from news.'

'As a reprisal for the attack on the police station, they've taken
two men from the prison to shoot them in the cemetery.'

'In the dark?'

'It's more impressive. They've rigged up arc-lights with a television camera. All the schoolchildren have to attend. Orders from
Papa Doc.'

---

* 'Disgusting, completely disgusting.'
† This event happened in real life, too, not to Greene but to Issa el Saieh. Greene knew
him well. El Saieh was picked up by the Tontons Macoute at the Oloffson hotel and
imprisoned briefly in Fort Dimanche. But el Saieh had no wife of a presidential contender
to come to his aid.

Later, as Martha leaves, they pass the open door of the John Barrymore suite: 'Mr Smith sat with his hat in his hands, and she had laid her hand on the back of his neck. After all, they were lovers too.' Mrs Smith calls to Brown as he comes back up the stairs after Martha has left. Brown expects that, like the old inhabitants of Salem, he will be denounced for adultery. Instead she tells him that they have given up their hopes:

'We go home tomorrow,' she said. 'Mr Smith despairs.'
'Of a vegetarian centre?'
'Of everything here.'
He looked up and there were tears in the old pale eyes. What an absurd fancy it had been for him to pose as a politician. He said, 'You heard the shots?'
'Yes.'
'We passed the children on the way from school.' He said, 'I had never conceived . . . when we were freedom-riders, Mrs Smith and I . . .'
'One can't condemn a colour, dear,' she said.
'I know. I know.'
'What happened with the Minister?'
'The meeting was a short one. He wanted to attend the ceremony.'
'Ceremony?'
'At the cemetery.'

The minister knew they were leaving and tried to bribe Smith with a share of his ill-gotten gains, as noted in a brief diary entry written two days after Greene's arrival in Port-au-Prince. Greene weaves the diary passage into the novel with Mr Smith explaining why he is leaving:

The Minister had been thinking . . . and had come to the conclusion that I was not after all a sucker. The alternative was that I was as crooked as himself. I had come here to get money, not to spend it, so he showed me a method . . . The Government would guarantee wages. We would hire the labour at a much lower wage, and at the end of a month the labourers would be dismissed. Then we'd keep the project idle for two months and afterwards engage a fresh lot of workers. Of course the guaranteed wages during the idle months would go into our own pockets . . . He was very proud of the scheme.[20]

★

Hope gone, the Smiths head for home. No good can be done amidst the nightmare. But what could one expect from a head of state who, according to Diederich, 'studied goat's entrails for guidance'.[21]

Of the real young men belonging to *Jeune Haiti* who had fought so hard, one, Marcell Numa, was a black Haitian. The rest were sons of the elite mulatto groups in Jérémie. These young men, only thirteen in number, left wives in America, saying they were going off for the weekend. They never came back. The tiny group fought hard, but no peasants came to their aid. After eighty-three days they had their last engagement and died. Their heads were chopped off, and photographed for local newspapers.

Two who had already fallen into Duvalier's hands, Numa and Louis Drouin, were taken to Fort Dimanche and tortured, and the next day, on the morning of 12 November 1964, they were driven to the cemetery. It was 7 a.m., so while it might have been dark initially, the sun must have come up quickly, the palm trees becoming outlined, red light over their shoulders. As Greene described it in *The Comedians*, they had 'rigged up arc-lights with a television camera'. And yes, all schoolchildren had to attend on 'orders from Papa Doc'. They were taken by bus to the cemetery, and peasants from outlying parts were brought in by trucks, to stare at the men, one black and tall (Numa), twenty years old, one mulatto and short (Drouin), twenty-eight years. Both were pinioned to pine posts sharp and dark, silhouetted by the rising sun. The two faced cameras, radio equipment recording every sound. Their graves already dug, the young men refused a priest's assistance in their last moments and, it is said, 'hurled insults' at Duvalier.

Diederich quotes from a leaflet handed out to the thousands watching the 'ceremony' in the cemetery:

Dr François Duvalier will fulfill his sacrosanct mission. He has crushed and will always crush the attempts of the antipatriots. Think well, renegades. You will not enjoy the gold with which they filled your pockets . . . Thus will perish the antipatriots . . . No force will stop the invincible march of the Duvalierist revolution . . . The Duvalier revolution will triumph. It will trample the bodies of traitors and renegades and those who sell out.[22]

Le Matin reported the huge crowd involved in 'mutual patriotic exaltation'. According to *Time* (27 November 1964) the government-controlled paper spoke of 'three volleys of Springfields, and submachine guns, and three *coups de grâce*'. Three finishing shots indeed, and then the great crowds, according to *Time*, 'marched to the National Palace', where Duvalier, acceding to its 'solicitations', appeared on the balcony 'to smile and wave'.[23] This exhibition of killers and victims was shown on local television for at least a week, impressing upon terrified Haitians how thousands of Tontons Macoute could put an end to thirteen young men.

★

In *The Comedians*, Brown takes the Smiths to the airport. Before they fly home, they make a last attempt to salve the poverty in Haiti, at least momentarily:

> Mr Smith asked me to stop the car in the centre of the square, and I thought he intended to take a photograph. Instead he got out, carrying his wife's handbag, and the beggars approached from all directions – there was a low babble of half-articulated phrases, and I saw a policeman run down the steps of the Post Office. Mr Smith . . . began to scatter . . . *gourdes* and dollars indiscriminately. 'For God's sake,' I said. One or two of the beggars gave high unnerving screams: I saw Hamit standing amazed at the door of his shop.

The police begin to close in, as

> Men with two legs kicked down men with one, men with two arms grasped those who were armless by their torsos and threw them to the ground.[24]

A new Darwinism: survival of the evillest.

30

The Real Mr Jones

Words at great moments of history are deeds.
— CLEMENT ATTLEE

THE other traveller on board ship to Haiti is Jones, the easy liar and phoney soldier, wanted by police in several countries. Brown first comes across him as Jones tries to bribe the bedroom steward into letting him swap cabins with Brown:

> He stood in [my] doorway . . . suitcase in one hand and two five-dollar bills in the other. He was saying, 'He hasn't been down yet. He won't make a fuss. He's not that kind of chap . . .' He spoke as if he knew me.

Jones, 'with the little black moustache and the dark Pekinese eyes',[1] is an admitted 'comedian' in the French sense of the word, meaning someone who plays a role in life. Greene felt we often play parts in life, as actors on the stage, but for him there was also a special aspect to the nature of a comedian. They are those 'who do not die', says Brown. Given the plot, it has to be said that while Jones is for most of the novel a 'comedian', he abandons this role and becomes willing to make the supreme sacrifice. Jones finds a role that his callow boasting suggests he had sought all his life.

It is only when his death is imminent that Jones confesses to Brown: his past as he has told it, the guerrilla activity, the heroics in Burma during the war, were all a sham. He discards his mask as a 'comedian' when he begins to realise his life is over.

★

After the Smiths leave Haiti, Brown calls on Jones and finds him full of bonhomie. Jones tries to tie Brown into his shady deal. He wants

Brown to take the reins when he's out of town. But it's a stand-off: Jones will not give details unless Brown promises to come in with him; in turn, Brown refuses to come into Jones's business unless he knows what Jones is up to. Jones refuses to tell Brown what is at stake, though he promises a fortune should Brown change his mind.

Jones speaks of the skirmish at Cap Haïtien, criticising the sloppy way the police station was attacked: the home-made armoured car with its home-made flame-thrower stalling, forcing the rebels to make their inadequate attack. Jones's assertion here makes sound military sense:

> Give me fifty Haitians with a month's training and Papa Doc would be on a plane to Kingston. I wasn't in Burma for nothing. I've thought a lot about it . . . Those raids near Cap Haïtien were a folly the way they were done. I know exactly where I'd put in my feint and where I'd strike.[2]

★

Aubelin Jolicoeur told me that Greene's title *The Comedians* came from him, but I'm dubious. During my third interview with him in Haiti, after Greene's death, he said he described his own people to Greene: 'These Haitians are comedians, they love stories, they love telling the great novelist stories.' No doubt there must have been rich talk. And Greene described his experience in his *Sunday Telegraph* article, 'Nightmare Republic':

> You reach your hotel, symbolically enough, in darkness . . . In the hotel you may find yourself the only guest (the tourists fled last spring and never returned). There were three others in my hotel . . .
>
> While you wait for the lights to go on, you sit around oil-lamps exchanging rumours – the rebels are only twenty-four hours from Port-au-Prince, one optimist declares; the army has suffered a hundred casualties (it is always a hundred when an optimist speaks); a military plane has been shot down . . . On the way to the hotel one night when I was stopped at a road-block, the man who searched me for arms, patting the hips, the thighs, laying a hand under the testicles, asked my companion in Creole, 'Is there any news?'
>
> But there is no such thing as news any more . . . The President's daughter is said to be on a hunger-strike to induce her father to leave; the President's wife has abandoned him and is in America . . . The Spanish Ambassador came home . . . to find a black dog in the Embassy, but none of his staff would touch it because it might house the spirit of Clément Barbot, the President's deadly

enemy, shot down a few weeks back . . . by the Tontons Macoute
. . . The Ambassador (the story grows and grows) had to put the
dog in his car himself and drive it away. He tried to turn it out
in the great square by the Presidential Palace, but it refused to
move – the dog was too close to Dr Duvalier. Only when he
reached the cathedral did he consent to budge, trotting off into
the dark to seek another sanctuary. Of course there was no truth
in the story, but it seemed probable enough in this city without
news and, between certain hours, without light.[3]

★

Brown leaves Jones and his dry martinis. A few days later, at his hotel,
Brown has an unpleasant dream in which someone calls sharply behind
him. He awakes and recognises the voice is coming from the verandah
below his bedroom, sounding faint through the 'holy mutter of the rain'.
It is Jones, but a different Jones, drenched, face smeared with dirt.

There is a vague reference to what Jones was attempting in Florida
– to make important contacts. Now all seems to have ended for Jones
and his particular swindle, as he stands inside the hotel, wet, smelling
of gin, breathing heavily, frightened, on the run from the government
he meant to cheat. He follows Brown 'like a dog, leaving wet patches
in his wake' as Brown pulls on his trousers:

'You are telling me . . . I was to be the fall guy?'
   'No, no, old man, you exaggerate . . . I'd have tipped you off
in time for you to get into the British Embassy. If it was ever
necessary. But it wouldn't have been. The investigator would have
cabled OK and taken his cut, and you would have joined us
afterwards.'
   'How big a cut had you planned for *him*? . . .'
   'I'd allowed for all that. What I offered you, old man, was net
not gross. All yours.'
   'If I survived.'
   'One always survives, old man.' As he dried, his confidence
returned. 'I've had my setbacks before. I was just as near the *grand
coup* – and the end – in Stanleyville.'
   'If your plan had anything to do with arms,' I said, 'you've
made a bad mistake. They've been stung before . . .'
   'How do you mean, stung?'
   'There was a man here last year who arranged half a million
dollars' worth of arms for them, fully paid up in Miami. But the
American authorities were tipped off, the arms were seized. The
dollars, of course, stayed in the agent's pocket. Nobody knew how

many real arms there had ever been. They wouldn't be taken for the same ride twice. You should have done more homework before you came here.'[4]

Does Brown know Jones is heading in a dangerous direction with his stupid boasting? Jones had worked as a non-combatant during the war, yet feels the need to speak of how he would deal with Papa Doc and the Tontons Macoute, always as if he were a specialist in guerrilla warfare.

Brown, in trying to save Jones from Duvalier's retribution, takes him to his mistress's home at the embassy. What Brown does not anticipate is that Jones (who he rightly suspects is a liar on a massive scale) will prove so entertaining to Brown's mistress: so he returns to persuade Jones, the boaster, to boast, and thus trap him into leaving. Brown entices Jones to become a leader of the raw young fighters struggling against Duvalier's powerful forces.

Brown comes to the embassy with the news that Hamit, the prominent Syrian shopkeeper, has disappeared:

'What can I do?' Pineda [Martha's husband] said. 'The Secretary of the Interior will accept two of my cigars and [say] Hamit is a citizen of Haiti.'

'Give me my old company back,' Jones said, 'and I'd go through the police station like a dose of salts till I found him.'

I couldn't have asked for a quicker or better response: [Dr] Magiot had said, 'You can trap a man who boasts.' When Jones spoke he looked at Martha . . . I could imagine all those domestic evenings when he had amused them with his stories of Burma.

'There are a lot of police,' I said.

'If I had fifty of my own men I could take over the country . . . I was proud enough of some of my own tricks.' . . .

'What a tragedy it is you are shut up here . . . There are men in the mountains now who only need to learn. Of course they've got Philipot.' . . .

'Philipot,' he exclaimed, 'he hasn't a clue, old man. Do you know he came to see me? He wanted my help in training . . . He offered . . .' . . .

'It's a great pity you didn't go with Philipot,' I said.

'A pity for both of us old man. Of course, I'm not running him down. Philipot's got courage. But I could have turned him . . . into a first-rate commando. That attack on the police station – it was amateurish . . .'

'If another opportunity arose . . .' No inexperienced mouse

could have moved more recklessly towards the smell of cheese. 'Oh, I'd go like a shot now,' he said.

I said, 'If I could arrange for your escape . . . to join Philipot . . .'

He hardly hesitated at all, for Martha's eyes were on him. 'Just show me the way, old man,' he said. 'Just show me the way.'

As he leaves the embassy, Brown hears Jones making some obvious joke, 'for he was unaware then that the trap had really closed – which set Martha laughing, and I comforted myself that the days of laughter were numbered'. He tells Jones he'll have to be ready at a moment's notice and Jones responds: 'I travel light, old man.'

Brown immediately revisits Dr Magiot, the communist who is organising the trip, since all (except Brown) think Jones is a first-class commando and mercenary. He finds Magiot in the dark, the lights having failed again. Brown is triumphant: 'I've hooked him. Nothing could have been easier.'[5] The journey to Aux Cayes is planned to coincide with severe expected storms, in the hope that the many road-blocks will not be manned during pouring rain.

Jones is not in a position to back down. All we know is that he is pleased at the chance to live up to the boasts with which he has saddled himself for much of his life, when throughout his career he has been but a small-time crook, card-sharp and 'spiv', and as sad as a clown living on dreams.

★

Jones confesses that he did not have the money or contacts to buy guns for Papa Doc: 'My scheme was not exactly that. In fact there were no arms at all. I don't look like a man with that much capital, do I?'[6]

Prospecting for the source of this story of an attempted sting on Papa Doc unearths a small nugget that Greene uses in the psychology of composition. We have heard that Hamit has disappeared. While Hamit is well known in the European community of Haiti, he is otherwise a typical Syrian shopkeeper and, as we discover, just another Duvalier victim. According to Petit Pierre, Hamit has disappeared (picked up secretly by the Tontons Macoute) because 'he has too many foreign friends'.[7] Soon afterwards his body is found in an open sewer on the edge of Port-au-Prince.*

---

* The source for the character Hamit is the handsome Issa el Saieh, who was also a secret partner with Al Seitz, owner of the Oloffson, still very much a successful businessman, now in his eighties, whom I met for the third time in December 1998. He remembered Greene with clarity.

Brown's story of phoney arms dealers taking in Duvalier is based on the true story of a deal gone bad, when Duvalier was taken to the cleaners for a quarter of a million dollars. The weapons were seen and seemingly bought for Duvalier, to make up for the arms that used to come by way of American marines. Duvalier went to a private dealer, an American from North Carolina called Etheridge, and two others, an Arab-Jew called Bustani, and a member of a well-known Haitian family, Carlo Mevs. Duvalier gave Etheridge $250,000 to buy arms. Etheridge and his two assistants disappeared to Miami with their loot. They bought $10,000 worth of weapons in Miami, had them loaded onto a plane, and promptly called the CIA and the FBI revealing that guns were being shipped to President Duvalier. Of course the shipment was seized.

There had to be a fall guy, and Issa el Saieh was chosen. The three sent Duvalier a telegram saying they were truly sorry but the guns had been seized, adding that it was the man who ran the Oloffson who had tipped off the Americans. The Haitian authorities, operating in their characteristic way, tried to have a bully pick a fight with Issa. Though he refused to fight, they put him into the dreaded Fort Dimanche. The penalty for suspected betrayal usually was death.

Greene spoke daily with el Saieh during his nine days in Port-au-Prince in the cruel year of 1963, and after he heard the story of el Saieh's arrest Greene felt sure that his friend would soon be executed. The Syrian was released, having been jailed for only a month. Powerful friends of the regime spoke up for him. Issa could not be released instantly, lest Duvalier be seen as a weakling. But perhaps because the real culprits had all escaped and no money came to el Saieh, his captors came to accept that he was not guilty.

*

As Greene was leaving for the Dominican Republic, he felt a letter pressed into his hand. On the plane he discovered the letter was addressed to a former presidential candidate (this must have been Louis Déjoie) then in exile in Santo Domingo. Greene passed it on when he arrived, but he was afraid until his plane was in the air.

The day Greene left the island described by Dr Magiot as 'an evil slum floating a few miles from Florida',[8] his third visit over, with fear in his heart (he never visited Haiti again), another stranger arrived in Port-au-Prince. The *New York Times* recorded that he was Colonel Hubert Julian, called the Black Eagle, 'one of the world's best known arms dealers':

His clients were Central American rebels who wanted to over-throw their governments and Central American governments that did not want to be overthrown . . .

His arrival here Saturday coincided with reports that the Haitian Government was making a desperate effort to buy weapons. These reports have centered on a trip to Europe made two months ago by a Government official's wife, who was said to have taken with her a sum estimated variously at $500,000 and $3,000,000.[9]

The journalist believed that Julian was in Port-au-Prince to sell arms. Julian strenuously denied it, but he protested too much: he was there for just that purpose. Here, then, is one source of the fictional character Jones.

Julian initially came into prominence when he showed up in Katanga, in the Congo. In Greene's original entertainment dealing with Haiti (not finished and not published), his lead character had fought in Katanga and came to Haiti to sell arms. How serendipitous that must have seemed. So the plot to con Duvalier out of money for arms is derived in part from Colonel Julian, who arrived in Port-au-Prince as Greene left.

There is a sense in the interview that Julian is a bit of a fraud. It comes through easily enough: he is conceited, gregarious and enjoys making fun of the poor local Haitian journalist – clearly a man who likes to hear his own voice:

'Did you come here to sell arms, Colonel?'
'I won't answer that question. Listen, I used to be a licensed dealer in arms, but since Katanga I'm not any more. I wouldn't do anything contrary to the wishes of anybody. I'm too old [the photo taken at the time shows a man of youthful middle age] and too rich to start any foolishness.'
'How much money do you have?'
'In round figures: zero zero zero zero.'

After further foot shuffling, the journalist comes back to his question:

'Did you come here to sell arms?'
'Are you trying to insult me? I have no arms to sell and nobody has asked me for any. I don't know anybody here. Anyway, where in the hell are they going to get money to buy arms? If they asked me to sell them arms, I would laugh at them.'[10]

It is difficult to believe that even a cocky Colonel Julian would laugh at a country run by a self-exalted killer, or as Shakespeare put it, 'behold a great image of authority: a dog's obeyed in office'.

Greene would have read of Julian's visit in the *New York Times*. The idea of Jones seeking to be an arms dealer without money would have sparked his creativity. As always he was alert for any morsel of information he could use creatively. Greene would rummage through the news, seeking material he felt he could use, and finally work out the direction his story should take. The story he heard of Issa el Saieh's set-up and imprisonment, and of the arms dealer Etheridge from North Carolina, must have contributed to Major Jones's plot, too. However, there is a more significant, and curious, source for Jones which determined his nature.

★

We know from Greene's interview when he arrived in Haiti in August 1963 that he was reflecting upon the double who used his name, got himself jailed in India, and conned bail money out of *Picture Post*. The *nature* of Graham Greene II clearly fascinated Greene, for here was a petty cheat, yet a man of daring, and it seems always in the good graces of ladies he met. Because of Greene II, the character of Jones came (almost) ready made.

Greene was thinking hard about his fake namesake, and knowing what he knew, or was coming to know, about the conditions in Haiti, he began to recognise that Graham Greene II could easily become part of his plot. He must have been thinking of people who would find their way to Haiti, big-time and small-time crooks. Wouldn't the man who was wandering around the world using his identity fit perfectly into the squalid world of Port-au-Prince?

He would make his character Jones a friend of the Smiths. In the novel they immediately take to Jones. Everyone seems to take to him, especially women, just as they did to Greene II. Jones will befriend Brown, because Brown is a variant of Greene. So Greene pits Brown's shrewdness – with himself as Brown – against Jones's crooked naïvety. Of course Brown is less than Greene, lacking Greene's brilliance and understanding, but nevertheless, he is a partial portrait of Greene. The whole scheme of his plot and the characters must have begun to churn just this way in his mind.

And the Smiths/Gottliebs? The artist Gottlieb and his wife came into Greene's mental periscope because they were in Haiti, staying at the same hotel as he, during the moment he was deeply into the nature of his characters, all residing in the torture chamber called Haiti. Greene never wasted material. When I interviewed Gottlieb, he had no idea that he and his wife had been made part of a novel, though after reading *The Comedians* at my suggestion, he immediately recognised their portraits. I have said it before: Greene's truth is in his fiction. He might have written only two hours a day, which so galled Michael Meyer in Tahiti, but his eyes were on duty at all times. Greene worked every shift of the clock: he never took a break: as long as he was awake and watching, he was on the prowl. What we are seeing up close is his method of work, following the mysterious paths of his mind. We are, in an eerie way, God's spies.

Greene never tracked down Greene II, though he did offer to interview him for *Picture Post* when he was jailed in India. Alas, Greene II broke bail, and *Picture Post* feared there might be repercussions, including Greene's probable arrest, if he arrived in Assam. However, if Greene had been able to observe Greene II closely, it might well have hampered his imagination.

Greene did hear of a number of women who'd met Greene II, and from them learned that he was an intriguing, civilised man with stories of adventures which only the real Greene knew to be fraudulent. 'The Other certainly seemed to leave strong impressions behind, particularly on women.'[11] A letter from a lady in Bournemouth came to the real Graham Greene, but she also knew and believed in Greene II, and reflected upon his gifts:

> Mr Graham Greene is a man of courage and is not indifferent to principles, and although he may have been in a forbidden place, due to his roving adventurous spirit, I do feel sure that the charge against him is without much foundation.[12]

He seemed especially good company. In *The Comedians* Greene makes good use of the story-telling talent seen in Greene II by transferring that talent to Jones – Jones telling his stories, and women liking him.

*

When Jones comes back to the table at Mére Catherine's, where Brown has been waiting with Concasseur, Brown finds that Jones is the 'someone important' who has been with Tintin, Brown's special girl at the brothel. Later Brown gets a chance to ask her if Jones had been kind to her. She replies that she liked Jones a lot.

> 'What did you like so much?'
> 'He made me laugh,' she said. It was a sentence which was to be repeated to me disquietingly in other circumstances. I had learnt in a disorganized life many tricks, but not the trick of laughter.[13]

Brown's generous action (in taking Jones to Ambassador Pineda's embassy) later troubles him, as we've seen. The affair he has with Martha Pineda seems to be fading. They fight, and Brown becomes jealous over Martha's growing interest in Jones (or what he thinks is her growing interest), ensconced as Jones is in her home. Brown's jealousy grows. He says to Martha:

'We spend half our time now talking about that damned crook.'
'You brought the damned crook to our house.'
'I didn't know he was going to become such a friend of the family.'
'Darling, he makes us laugh, that's all.' She couldn't have chosen an explanation which worried me more.

And then there are all the old stories Jones told on the ship: his time in Burma battling the Japs, his guerrilla fighting, the platoon he'd lost, his having a nose for seeking out water in the jungle, his prize cocktail-case. (This was actually a favourite possession of Greene's which he lent – as it were – to Jones; Greene admired it immensely.) Finally Brown learns that Jones has asked one of the servants to take this special symbol of good luck to Hamit's shop to be inscribed. 'So there it is,' says Martha to Brown, 'we can't give it back. Such a quaint inscription. "To Luis and Martha from their grateful guest, Jones."'[14]

Brown agrees to take Jones up country – and Martha asks why. The danger if they are caught is immense. He tells her: 'I don't like Concasseur and his Tontons Macoute. I don't like Papa Doc. I don't like them feeling my balls in the street to see if I have a gun.'[15] But mostly he is doing it to clear the decks for himself. He wants Martha's love to continue. Success lies in taking Jones from the embassy to join the rebels.

★

Brown thinks that Martha has slept with Jones. Early on a wildly stormy morning, the two men leave the embassy. They are aware of the real possibility that Jones will die should he succeed in joining the rebels. Brown notices that Martha has been crying and that there is a trace of lipstick on Jones, and, Brown, desiring to hurt her says: 'You seem upset at losing Jones?'

'Yes, I've been happy having Jones here – hearing people laugh at his bad jokes, playing gin-rummy with him. Yes, I'll miss him till it hurts. How I'll miss him.'

As they leave, Jones goes out first and Brown returns for a moment to say goodbye. She kisses him indifferently because she doesn't like his motive for taking Jones up into the mountains to the young rebels:

'Have you slept with Jones?' I regretted the question even before the last word was said. If the heavy peal of thunder which followed had drowned it I would have been content, I would never have repeated it. She stood flat against the door as though she were facing a firing squad . . .

'You've been asking me that for weeks,' she said, 'every time I've seen you. All right then. The answer's yes, yes. That's what you want me to say, isn't it? Yes, I've slept with Jones.' The worst thing was I only half believed her.[16]

★

In their car to the rendezvous with the rebels, Brown questions Jones:

'I got the impression she was fond of you.' . . .
  'We got on like a house on fire.'
  'I sometimes envied you, but perhaps she's not your type.' It was like stripping a bandage from a wound: the more slowly I pulled the longer the pain would last, but I lacked the courage to rip the bandage right away . . .
  'Old man,' Jones said, 'every girl's my type, but she was something special.' . . .
  'As [special] as Tintin?' I tried to ask in a casual clinical way.
  'Tintin was not in the same class, old man.'

They are both drinking whisky to keep their courage up:

'How did you get on with the husband?' I asked him cautiously.
  'Fine. I wasn't stealing any greens of his.'
  'Weren't you?'
  'She doesn't sleep with him any more.'
  'How do you know?'
  'I have my reasons,' he said.

They are practically down to walking pace; Brown has to watch the road, threading his way between rocks, the track becoming plain laterite – only mud to clog the passage. It is close to one in the morning and they've been travelling for three hours. The time has come for Brown to 'push the question home':

'Was she a good lay?'
  'Re-markable,' Jones said, and I clung to the wheel to keep my hands off him.[17]

369

But later he finds he can't sustain his anger.

The journey to the cemetery where Jones is to meet the rebels is difficult. The axle of Brown's car breaks and they have to walk three kilometres in the dark over rock and low wet scrub. Brown's flashlight picks up the cemetery. (A Haitian cemetery looks like a 'city built by dwarfs, street after street of tiny houses'.*) They lie there waiting for the small group of rebels or whoever is going to pick up Jones.

Now that his car has broken down, Brown himself has an almost impossible problem to overcome: how to get back to Port-au-Prince. Sitting there in the dark, a flashlight between them, it comes upon Jones that the game has turned serious – this playing at soldiers could lead at last to blood.

Jones has a desire to confess, and suddenly admits to Brown he's a liar: he's no leader; he knows nothing about being a guerrilla. It turns out he is half-Indian, his father a tea planter and he a bastard. He has a final confession:

> 'Martha filled the shaker for me,' he said. 'I've never known a girl so thoughtful.'
> 'Or such a good lay?' I asked.

After an obstinate silence and an expression of his desire to be truthful, Jones says:

> 'I'm an awful liar, old man.'
> 'I've always assumed that,' I said.
> 'What I said about Martha – there wasn't a word of truth in it. She's only one of fifty women I haven't had the courage to touch.'

And so the confession goes on: 'Old Man, I've never been in a jungle in my life – unless you count the Calcutta Zoo'; he has never been in the army (rejected because of flat feet); never used a Bren gun. Among the Haitian tombs, Jones pleads with Brown:

> I flashed my torch around the acre of grey tombs. I said, 'Why the hell are we here then?'
> 'I boasted a bit too much, didn't I?'
> 'You've let yourself into a nasty situation. Aren't you frightened?'
> 'I'm like a fireman at his first fire,' he said.

---

* Just such a 'tiny house' is now Duvalier's final home.

370

'Your flat feet won't enjoy these mountain tracks.'

'I can manage with supports,' Jones said. 'You won't tell them, old man? It was a confession.'

'They'll soon find out without my telling them . . . You've spoken too late. I can't smuggle you back.'

'I don't want to go back.'

And so it continues. Seeing parallels between Jones's life and his own, Brown observes (pointing to Jones's origin – Greene's fake twin): 'Jones and Brown, the names were almost interchangeable.' Greene spoke of what he called 'the Other': 'I like you, Jones.'[18] But there can be fraud in fame.

★

Unable to return to Port-au-Prince, Brown waits at the border crossing into the Dominican Republic and sees what's left of the small Philipot group, a mere tail, limp with fatigue, wearing the expressions of children who have broken something of value.

Later, Philipot is able to talk to Brown about Jones:

'Our weapons were so old, so out of date. I had to teach him. He was not a good shot, he went through Burma with a walking stick, he told me, but he knew how to lead.'

'On his flat feet. How did the end come?'

'We came up to the border to find the others, and we were ambushed. It was not his fault. Two men were killed. Joseph was badly hurt. There was nothing to do but escape. We could not go fast because of Joseph. He died coming down the last ravine.'

'And Jones?'

'He could hardly move because of his feet. He found what he called a good place. He said he'd keep the soldiers off till we had time to reach the road – not one of them was anxious to risk himself very close. He said he would follow slowly, but I knew he would never come.'

'Why?'

'He told me once that there was no room for him outside of Haiti.'

'I wonder what he meant.'

'He meant his heart was there.' . . .

Philipot said, 'I had grown to love him. I would like to write about him to the Queen of England . . .'

They hold a mass for the dead in Santo Domingo and the priest, no older than Philipot, preaches a short sermon on words by St Thomas the Apostle:

'Let us go up to Jerusalem and die with him.' He said, 'The Church is in the world, it is part of the suffering in the world, and though Christ condemned the disciple who struck off the ear of the high priest's servant, our hearts go out in sympathy to all who are moved to violence by the suffering of others. The Church condemns violence, but it condemns indifference more harshly. Violence can be the expression of love, indifference never. One is an imperfection of charity, the other the perfection of egoism. In the days of fear, doubt and confusion, the simplicity and loyalty of one apostle advocated a political solution. He was wrong, but I would rather be wrong with St Thomas than right with the cold and the craven. Let us go up to Jerusalem and die with him.'[19]

Brown becomes one of the cold and the craven.

★

Greene, by basing Jones primarily on Greene II, allows 'the Other' to be counted a hero, no longer cold and craven. But the false Greene maintained his cheeky charade even after the real Greene's death. The following letter from Patrick Marnham, then living in Paris, appeared in *The Times* in 1994:

Earlier this week a skilled and dependable removals man noticed that I possess books by Graham Greene. He noticed these books because, as he assured me, earlier this year he personally had helped Graham Greene to move house.

I thought that your readers would like to know that, even after the master's death, the Other remains active.[20]

★

After the publication of *The Comedians*, Greene felt threatened. He knew that Duvalier had a long arm and never forgot an enemy abroad. Those who offended him might have escaped from Haiti, be living in different parts of the world, yet Duvalier's goons would go far to kill them. Greene admitted to me that 'Fear penetrated deep into my unconscious.'[21]

Papa Doc did not, as far as we know, hire a hit man to attack Greene. Instead, he produced a glossy pamphlet of fascinating lies accusing

Greene of racism. *Graham Greene Démasqué: Finally Exposed* was written by Lucien Montas, then Head of Cultural Affairs in Duvalier's government, and included other signatories, among them the Haitian Minister of Information and the Foreign Minister.

> With *The Comedians* he achieves a double coup; he assuages his sadistic instincts, gives himself leisure to exercise his negrophobia and at the same time rounds out his bank account by serving . . . those who would denigrate the world's First Black Republic . . . especially under the leadership of Dr François Duvalier who means to inspire the Haitian people with pride about his origins and who pursues, with success and determination, the battle for the economic and cultural independence of the Haitian nation.

There follows Greene's seemingly deliberate attempt to bring down the black man:

> A proud, a dignified black man has to be humbled at all costs and, if possible, eliminated. Called in to meet this challenge, Graham Greene finds the game all too easy, for the task is admirably suited to his innate tendencies.

It seems that Greene had a 'thoroughly perverted and unbalanced ego', and was moreover 'a drug addict, a spy of an unnamed imperialist power', 'a liar, a *cretin*, a stool-pigeon . . . unbalanced, sadistic, perverted . . . a perfect ignoramus . . . lying to his heart's content . . . the shame of proud and noble England . . . a torturer'.[22] (This last puzzled Greene, eliciting in my company that funny grin of his.)

British television traveller Alan Whicker visited Haiti on 17 June 1968 and was allowed an interview with Papa Doc in his black Mercedes – perhaps Duvalier intended to counter the adverse publicity that the novel and the film of *The Comedians* (released late in 1967) were spreading. Whicker wrote:

> It seemed unreal to be riding around with one of the world's most feared men, broaching subjects which no Haitian would dare *think* . . . I wondered how he felt about Graham Greene . . . 'He is a poor man, mentally, because he did not say the truth about Haiti.'[23]

When the film appeared on American television, the Haitian embassy in Washington echoed Duvalier's views:

The author claims the plot of the story is based in Haiti. Such is not the case. Haiti is a land of smiling, singing, dancing, happy people with a joy of living. It is not a country of crime, of witchcraft or of diabolic excesses of any kind . . . the Haitian Government is convinced that this television programme is propaganda intended to adversely affect tourism and its efforts to improve its economy and the lives of its people . . . it is an affront to the dignity of the Haitian people, to all black communities and to all the Third World.

Duvalier was enraged. Most assuredly in his mind he must have had the culprits, Greene and film director Peter Glenville, killed many times.

It did not work out well for the 'Renovator of the Nation' (one of Duvalier's admiring descriptions of himself). Impotent, he sought revenge another way. He sued the film company and Greene in the French courts for ten million francs. He won – sort of . . . and was awarded *one* franc.

★

Long ill with diabetes and heart disease, Duvalier died at the age of sixty-four on 21 April 1971, thus ending fourteen years of dictatorship, his tenure one long atrocity. He was buried with full honours. People wailed and screamed, 'Papa is dead! Papa is dead!' Women tried to throw themselves on to the glass cover of the coffin. Others writhed on the floor in paroxysms of grief. In the coffin with the body was a crucifix and a copy of his book, *Memoirs of a Leader*. The funeral was comparatively mild, with the usual pomp and circumstance. The *New York Times* records that sudden panic gripped the mourners during the funeral march:

> It began inexplicably . . . one mile from the palace . . . No one . . . could explain how it started.
>
> But suddenly the street was churning in a wild melee of Haitians who ran madly about in search of escape. They were slammed against the metal shutters of closed stores. Two men fell out of sight down a sewer manhole.[24]

An absurd conclusion, especially with these words sung by a popular Haitian tenor to the chorale movement of Beethoven's Ninth: 'We thank thee François Duvalier for having given so much to us. You are great and beautiful and just. Up there in the skies you will watch over our Fatherland.'

374

Duvalier's reign was one man's long night of cruelty. His memorial is a ruthless autocracy: torture and execution both as the daily instrument of power whenever the fancy took him.

Soaking up everything, Greene richly revealed the specific and general nature of this madman, with the blood of his own people upon him. His friend Conor Cruise O'Brien wrote that Greene was 'looking for Hell all his life and . . . found it at last in Haiti'. Duvalier, as observed by Diederich and Burt, was, in our time, the first 'black Caligula'.

PART 14

The 'Priest Thing'

31

He's Over the Wall

What is this mania for sleeping each night, in a different bed?
— PETRARCH

'My darling, be careful. Don't you understand? To you nothing
exists except in your own thoughts. Not me, not Jones . . . You've
turned poor Jones into a seducer and me into a wanton mistress
. . . My dear, try to believe we exist when you aren't there . . .
None of us is like you fancy we are. Perhaps it wouldn't matter
much if your thoughts were not so dark, always so dark.'

I tried to kiss her mood away, but she turned quickly and
standing at the door said to the empty passage, 'It's a dark Brown
world you live in. I'm sorry for you.'[1]

And it was a dark Greene world Greene lived in. Catherine knew this
only too well, and one wonders if, during an argument with Graham,
she might have spoken in this way. We'll discover more of her world
in this chapter, from an eyewitness who saw much of what was going
on during a few summers in Catherine's realm, and more than could
be revealed to the naked eye. And the eyewitness? Who better to show
such a slice of Catherine's home life than her sister, Bonte? Moreover,
once we know what Bonte has to say, we can work back to the novels
mentioned, to discover complications that prove how cleverly and
deliberately Greene used such incidents to comment on Catherine,
often as a release from the pain she'd caused him.

The interplay in *The Comedians* between Brown and Martha, her
husband and Major Jones is part of that concealed history, an underground narrative reflecting the secret concerns of Greene's life, not
Brown's; Catherine's distresses, not Martha's; Lord Walston's vexations,
not Ambassador Pineda's, and to introduce a new name, Thomas, not
Jones. Let's follow the trail, a thin red thread leading back from fictive
descriptions to the real world and the people in it.

379

★

In *The Comedians*, we know that Brown imagines he is being cuck-olded by his friend Jones: it is sufficient that he himself has made a cuckold out of Martha's husband. His jealousy has been increasing. He can't leave Martha alone over Jones: 'We'll have peace together when he's gone. You won't be torn in two between us then.'² Earlier Brown has remarked that Jones sees her all day long.

'Not in your way.'
'Oh, Jones has to have his periodic woman – I know that. I've seen him in action. And as for me I can only see you for dinner, or cocktail parties of the second order.'
'You're not at dinner now.'
'He's climbed the wall. He's in the garden itself.'³

At the beginning of the novel Brown returns to Haiti because he misses Martha. Earlier, in New York he had found a call girl on East 56th Street, just as Greene had done, on that same street. Brown writes to Martha grudgingly, suspiciously, jealous because he feels that Martha will not have waited for him, as he has not waited. She writes back 'with tenderness, without rancour'. This passage, applied in the novel to Martha, gives a remarkably close description of Catherine Walston. Martha is a better person than Brown, chiefly because she does not suffer from jealousy, and she is rigorously honest. We see this at the embassy party:

I took her wrist and drew her down the corridor. 'Who sleeps in this room?'
'No one.'
I opened the door and pulled her in. Martha said, 'No. Can't you see it's impossible?'
'I've been away three months and we've made love only once since then.'
'I didn't make you go away to New York. Can't you feel I'm not in the mood, not tonight?'
'You asked me to come tonight.'
'I wanted to see you. That's all. Not to make love.'
'You don't love me, do you?'
'You shouldn't ask questions like that.'
'Why?'
'Because I might ask the same.'
I recognized the justness of her retort and it angered me, and the anger drove away the desire.

'How many "adventures" have you had in your life?'

'Four,' she said with no hesitation at all.

'And I'm the fourth?'

'Yes. If you want to call yourself an adventure.'

Many months later when the affair was over, I realized and appreciated her directness. She played no part. She answered exactly what I asked. She never claimed to like a thing that she disliked or to love something to which she was indifferent. If I had failed to understand her, it was because I failed to ask her the right questions, that was all. It was true that she was no comedian.[4]

When Greene asked Catherine Walston about her other lovers, she would tell him the truth. But it is also a fact that such truthfulness profoundly attracted Greene. His latest *amoureuse*, Yvonne Cloetta (whose love for Greene lasted thirty-two years until his death, and continued a decade longer until her own death), had this quality too. Perhaps because she is by nature almost strident in her expressions of her beliefs and attitude towards her lover, we will see Martha as a creation from Greene's knowledge of both these ladies, Catherine and Yvonne. We know that Yvonne, in reading the novel, identified herself with Martha.[5]

Martha doesn't like to pretend. She is not a dissembler like Jones and Brown.* In a letter to Brown in New York, she writes with great understanding and compassion of her fourth betrayal of her husband:

Perhaps the sexual life is the great test. If we can survive it with charity to those we love and with affection to those we have betrayed, we needn't worry so much about the good and the bad in us. But jealousy, distrust, cruelty, revenge, recrimination . . . then we fail. The wrong is in that failure even if we are the victims and not the executioners. Virtue is no excuse.[6]

A profound thought from Greene's pen – one that might be either from Catherine to Greene, or it might come from notes for a novel she was writing in the form of a diary.

*

If we go back to Greene's novel *The End of the Affair*, published fifteen years earlier, and Bendrix's great love, Sarah, we see that Brown suffers from afflictions parallel to Bendrix's: both are jealousy personified. There is a strong feeling that Brown is Bendrix's twin, and Martha is Sarah's.

---

* *The Dissemblers* was an early title given by Greene to *The Comedians*.

Bendrix is a writer, and the hotelier Brown is, according to Martha, like a novelist who uses real people as characters.* Martha's cool, organised mind is also reflected in Sarah's calmness in *The End of the Affair*. Pressed by her lover Bendrix to meet, Sarah explains at a moment's notice how she will arrange it. He says she thought

> carefully . . . collectedly, quickly, so that she could give me straightaway the correct answer. 'I'm giving Henry a tray in bed at one. We could have sandwiches ourselves in the living-room. I'll tell him you want to talk over the film – or that story of yours,' and immediately she rang off the sense of trust was disconnected and I thought, how many times before has she planned in just this way?

Sarah and Bendrix make love at her house, her husband on the floor above:

> and in the room below, on the hard-wood floor, with a single cushion for support and the door ajar, we made love. When the moment came, I had to put my hand gently over her mouth to deaden that strange sad angry cry of abandonment, for fear Henry should hear it overhead.[7]

Similarly, as we've seen in *The Comedians*, Martha and Brown try to make love in the house as her husband is climbing the stairs. And Martha – like Sarah, like Catherine – never suffers guilt while cheating.

This is the Unholy Triad: Brown and Bendrix and Greene (along with Ambassador Pineda, Miles and Harry) on the male side, with Martha, Sarah and Catherine the distaff. *The End of the Affair*, despite its fictional cover, was a precise and intense account of the love life of Catherine Walston and Graham Greene, with Henry as Harry Walston.

> I think I had an idea that the sight of Henry might have roused remorse, but she had a wonderful way of eliminating remorse. Unlike the rest of us she was unhaunted by guilt. In her view when a thing was done, it was done: remorse died with the act.[8]

Brown's jealousy of Jones, once Jones climbed the wall into the garden, is constant. Brown saw Martha only at parties, or at his hotel in his bed, but Jones lived in her house. Both Brown and Bendrix measure love by jealousy.

---

* We also saw Greene do this with Wormold in *Our Man in Havana*.

Martha deals with the crux of the problem, putting her finger on Brown's secret thoughts. They are discussing Jones's charisma, and the fact that her husband, having taken him in as a refugee, is probably becoming *persona non grata* to the Duvalier regime – and may have to leave the country.* The one advantage, Brown thinks, is that Jones will be left behind. Martha jokes:

> 'Who knows? Perhaps we could smuggle him out in the diplomatic bag. Luis likes him better than he does you . . .'
> 'It's strange to me,' I said, 'how easily he makes friends. Luis and you. Even Mr Smith was fond of him. Perhaps the crooked appeals to the straight or the guilty to the innocent, like blonde appeals to black.'

Neither can leave the subject of Jones. Brown plies Martha with questions, even about her husband: 'How often does he make love to you?' She answers: 'You think me insatiable, don't you? I need you and Luis and Jones.'9

In *The End of the Affair*, the cuckolded husband is a senior civil servant; in the Haiti novel, an ambassador. What would have led Greene to turn Lord Walston from a civil servant in one novel, into an ambassador in *The Comedians*?

★

If it's true that the affair in *The Comedians* between Brown and Martha, and the affair in *The End of the Affair* between Bendrix and Sarah, share similarities, then they share similar origins as well. The portly Ambassador Pineda is different in character from the civil servant, Henry Miles – one quintessentially South American, the other quintessentially English. But their situations replicate each other.

When Brown arrives at the embassy soon after returning from New York, he finds Pineda alone. 'He seemed tired and out of spirits. He carried his weight of flesh slowly, like a heavy load, between the drink-table and the sofa.'10 Conversely, Henry Miles is British, upright and moral – the perfect civil servant. Both husbands love their adulterous wives: Bendrix remarks that Henry has his 'blinkers firmly tied', and Brown hated Pineda's blinkers even when he had benefited from them, knowing that others could benefit too.

Later, Brown, calling on Martha one night, confronts the ambassador who has returned unexpectedly from abroad. Pineda answers the

---

* Duvalier often sent ambassadors packing. Even American ambassadors were booted out, in spite of providing Duvalier with millions of dollars over the years.

door to an unsuspecting Brown and tells his befuddled visitor: "'I came in on tonight's plane." He put his hand to where his tie should have been. "There's a lot of work waiting for me to do. Papers to be read . . . you know how it is." It was as though he were apologizing to me and proffering humbly his passport – Nationality: human being. Special peculiarities: cuckold.'[11]

This surely is Greene looking at his own character in 1951 during his early years with Catherine Walston, and reflected in *The End of the Affair*, and Greene looking again at his own character in 1966 while writing *The Comedians*. Time has taken its toll, the relationship between married woman and 'bachelor' man now in tatters. But Greene is Bendrix; Greene is Brown, older, colder and irritated now that his love for Catherine is disappearing. In all three, jealousy rules mind and action.

★

Greene's private history, when decoded, is most often found in his novels, because personal memoirs would have revealed too much, too directly, of this shy man who remained shy until the end of his days. His memoirs, *A Sort of Life* and *Ways of Escape*, do not illuminate the inner man.

But biography is characterised by revelation, as it must be. In Greene's case, given his profound reticence in his memoirs, he is open only in his novels, because novels are fictions after all, and the truth, he must have felt, would not be unearthed. The style of his memoirs is straight-forward and limited. You can sniff around for years and not decipher the first clue. But the tense, nervous, fidgety man needed to unburden himself somehow. Disguise was well-deep in Greene, and the clues lie silently, awaiting discovery, however strongly he desired them to remain hidden. I sometimes believe that his novels and their veiled disclosures are the only kind of revelation he could give.

Let us tap into part of Greene's secret history, and the clandestine crises in his life shadowed forth in fiction, at least a cunning form of it, as engrained as etched glass – an imitation of truth.

★

No novel can be believable if the novelist does not tap into the truth of his own experiences, even when disturbing. Greene needed to deal with his past: and we, in turn, need to excavate his private history. Greene's style often mimics clinical detachment, but the serious novelist can never ignore personal passions, and sometimes in Greene's case personal furies. The intimate side breaks through the defences of even the most seemingly detached of writers, revealing an author who could offer himself as sacrificial victim, as Greene does in his last master-piece, *The Honorary Consul.*

Catherine Walston was Greene's fixed star for more than a dozen years. She was a deep-rooted need. He needed a woman sitting beside him, not to obstruct, but as a line of defence. Catherine was calm, temperate, not given to the depressions that Greene's flesh was heir to. I sincerely believe that she saved his life. Without her, in the 1950s, he would have committed suicide. To Bonte, Catherine made a wise and gentle point: 'Graham's misery is as real as an illness', and suggested it was because he had 'no family, no friends whom he has any respon-sibility for, he has nothing to plan for or no one to consider'.[12] He could be thoughtful and sympathetic, but the twists and turns of manic depression were part of his genetic lineage, a birthmark that stayed with him, not diminishing until late in life.

Again we turn to Greene's focus on Lord Walston, fictionalising him first as a leading civil servant (and in some senses, Harry really was) in *The End of the Affair,* and now in *The Comedians* making him an ambassador. Why the promotion? Perhaps it was to confront and diminish the personal pain and suffering which the failure of true love brings. Greene's misery had to be shed. Let us be a witness to that torment.

*

Graham Greene wrote two anguished letters to Catherine Walston, on 25 and 26 April 1950: in the first he refers to Catherine's affair with the American General Lowell Weicker during the war, before she'd even met Greene. Catherine, while visiting her mother in New York in 1950, has met Weicker again. Greene writes to her from England:

> Now that you know that this L. affair isn't dead – would you *try* not to have times alone with him? – or have you found that after all he's very important, more than we are? . . . If we crash there's only tarting & self-disgust & three women a week.[13]

In the previous day's letter, Greene has discovered that she is having an 'adventure' with a 'Swiss friend':

> I can't keep my imagination quiet yet. It's morbid & I hate it . . . There's so much to understand too: that story of *not* meeting your Swiss friend . . . Please *make* me understand. I feel hopeless. Suppose [Harry Walston] had become Ambassador, this would have happened all the time. Please try to make me see what

happened, how. Would you have ever told me yourself? I'm lost.
I don't know what to believe any more. Please pray for me as
you've never done before.[14]

There was worse to come. We've seen Greene's own affair from late
1955 to mid-1958 with the Swedish actress Anita Björk, which so
uncharacteristically disturbed Catherine. However, there was a second
love affair in Catherine's life which took place before Greene met
Anita Björk, and well before Yvonne Cloetta, his last love. Like Jones,
this man was popular (and more intelligent than Jones), and often spent
time in the middle of the Walston family circle. You could most
certainly echo Brown's reference to Jones: 'He's climbed the wall. He's
in the garden itself.'

★

Letters survive written by Catherine's sister, Bonte Durán, a year older
than Catherine, and married to the famous Spanish Republican General
Gustavo Durán.* She and her three young daughters spent the summer
holidays of 1952 and 1953 at Catherine's home. These vacations were
taken without the General, chiefly because Senator McCarthy did not
look kindly upon Durán, thinking him a communist. Thus, Durán felt
it unwise to accompany Bonte in case he was not allowed to re-enter
the United States. Bonte dearly loved her husband, and, ever watchful,
wrote daily to him in New Hampshire. Her letters paint a remarkable
picture of the Walston household, and of the times Greene visited as
a welcomed guest.

Bonte recalls arriving at Newton Hall (probably in 1952):

> Finally we arrived & Bobs [Catherine's family nickname] &
> Harry . . . drove us to Newton & were very loving & cordial.
> Newton is really lovely & charmingly furnished & my only
> regret is that you aren't here to see it for it really is just your
> cup of tea. It is all done in yellow & white with wall to wall
> carpets, beautiful hangings, lovely *objets d'art*, lovely & varied
> pictures.
>
> We had a delicious supper & the table was rather like
> Shakespeare's 'burnished throne' set with fantastic silver with two
> men to wait on table, turkey, & meringue with strawberry ice
> cream. Buzzy [her brother David's nickname] was fairly cordial
> which as I expected him to call me an old bitch or something
> like that was an unexpected joy. You know, I like Father Caraman.

* Ernest Hemingway admired Durán, and mentions him in *For Whom the Bell Tolls*.

He is very civilized & amusing & not in the least sinister, as I had been led to expect.

Bonte describes Harry Walston as she knew him in 1952–3 – and Walston's character did not change. She mentions Graham and someone called 'Thomas' as being close to her sister. Thomas was enlarged upon during our interview:

Harry was in no way disagreeable to anyone. He certainly didn't show to Graham or to Thomas any kind of dislike. In fact he had such a bland character that I never was anything but surprised when later on in his life he turned a little horrid to me. But he really was always very kind and thoughtful with my sister. I think he really loved her, but he wasn't strong enough to show her directions. Yes.

Later on, she spoke of Catherine's marriage to Walston:

I only knew Harry one weekend. We went on a skiing weekend . . . to our house in New Hampshire – and Bobs had hurt her ankle. Harry stayed back with her, and the rest of us went skiing. And then Bobs and I were both at Barnard College in New York, and we came back at the end of the weekend, and on Monday morning Harry Walston telephoned and proposed to Bobs over the phone. So it just took him three days, and Bobs said yes right over the phone . . .
So then my sister was married in New Hampshire, and the day that she was going to get married, she went for a walk with me and said: 'I am not in love with Harry.' And I said, 'But Bobs, you cannot marry a man that you're not in love with.' She said, 'I like Harry, he's very nice, and I can't stand life here.'
They married in Wilton, New Hampshire, and then sailed to England.[15]

In 1969, in a letter to her younger sister Belinda, Catherine spoke of life with Harry:

I'm pretty sure that [my marriage] with Harry was NEVER a marriage. At the time I married him I decided that I would give it a try, and if I found anyone I liked better, I would leave Harry and marry X. Our sex life broke down before it hardly got started. We have never decided whose fault it was, and of course, it doesn't matter. However, in our 33–34 years of marriage,

we have become very loving friends, almost like twins – brother
& sister.[16]

In Catholic terms Catherine was Greene's goddaughter and he her
godfather – that's how they came together. We saw in Volume Two
how Greene met Catherine, and the moment he fell in love – 'In a
plane your hair was blown'[17] – thereafter to be in love as he had never
been before, and never – in spite of his final companion, Yvonne
Cloetta (I might be wrong) – would be again:

I can't get you out of my heart. You've splintered inside it and
surgeons are useless. They say one day I may die of the splinter,
but it cannot be removed.[18]

Catherine was *special*.

★

Catherine's elder sister tried to give me some notion of her mystery.
'It was hard to analyse what it was about my sister that was deep and
moving and generous and imaginative, and at the same time very difficult to understand how it was that orthodox religion – which I don't
understand at all – had such a grip on her.'
    Bonte was an atheist, and genuinely surprised by Catherine's passion
for Catholicism. Moreover, she discovered that men whose calling was
religious were all too human:

Having a Catholic household was not just having a household of
Catholics, but a household [of] bigots. And that is the thing that
made me dislike a great many of the priests that I met at her
house. And I think that the priests, who . . . in my unimaginative way I think should be sort of sublime beings, were in fact
very impressed with the amount of money, the number of servants,
the beautiful objects, the freedom that everybody had – on the
whole – to say what they felt, but on the whole they all felt the
same or had the same orthodox views as the next person.

This was, for Bonte, a revelation: 'I found myself absolutely outside of
this as though it [was] some play that I was watching and I couldn't
understand how anyone took seriously such [religious] matters.' And
she found the priests' attitude towards her beautiful sister stranger still:
'clergy [who] stayed a long time in the house would gradually all turn
out to have the same rather craven dogmatic attitude to my sister'.
    Bonte was an excellent observer, if a less careful guide. I asked her

if she felt that Catherine's house was in a sense being taken over by the priests:

> I think that they wanted, for some reason, to possess her. I don't think physically possess, but one after another, even gentle Father Booth, who nobody thought was going to react this way . . . as the other priests said at night, 'I'll see you upstairs later, Catherine' . . . that meant that there would be some final conversation upstairs which had to do with − I don't know what . . . in her study . . . it would be the sort of last admonition of the day or it would be some discussion . . . Father Booth was probably . . . a gentle and rather plebeian man . . . I think that he had not the sophistication of somebody like Father D'Arcy* and Father Caraman and the other various Fathers, he was just trying very hard to be the same. And when he said, 'I'll see you later upstairs, Catherine,' my sister looked at me and she winked. And I know that she knew that this was something that had taken probably all his courage to say.[19]

Two years after this interview, Bonte added something else. She was sometimes critical of her sister, but knew she possessed a mysterious personality:

> BD: Catherine was unlike anyone I've ever known.
> NS: Because of her generosity?
> BD: No. Because of everything . . . she was always a mystery . . . I never knew whether she was really happy, or whether she was covering up agony.

★

Life at Newton Hall seems idyllic: 'Darling. We all leave in a few minutes on our giant boat expedition − four cars from here, & 40 people altogether, including cook − up the river to Ely by boat & back, everyone going.' But amid the bliss, the letter mentions a little contretemps, not explained because Bonte did not understand the problem. She then describes famous guests, and a party:

> I forgot to tell you about the weekend guests . . . George Brown, a Labour MP & former Minister of Works [a flamboyant, controversial figure] & Cecil King [owner of the *Daily Mirror* and the

* Prominent and fashionable Jesuit of his day − handsome, attractive, friend of wealthy Catholics.

Sunday Graphic], a great hulk of a man with a blotched face & a watchful manner. George Brown was very quick & witty, & so we all became equally so, & I ended the weekend by giving a lecture on sex-life in the high plateaus of Tibet in the native costume (with among other things a wicker flowerpot on my head) which was if I say so quite a success. I forgot to tell you that the week before in the Stokes ballroom,* I did a dance of ancient India as understood by a lady traveller from Kansas City, complete with a sari & flute. You will have to take my word for it when I tell you that Harry, Bobs, the Stokes & John Hayward were crying with laughter, & I was forced to give many encores. I have to boast now & then! But you are very forgiving, so you won't mind. I love you. Bonte.[20]

Bonte gives a description of Catherine's study, from where she often wrote to her beloved: 'What a beautiful, silent sunny day. I am in Bobs' study. The only sound is the buzzing of a solitary fly. The parrot gazes at me silently without moving. The clock ticks.'

She has met Evelyn Waugh, and is hostile to him, perhaps reciprocating Waugh's proverbial hostility to others.

Did I tell you Evelyn Waugh came to lunch a few days ago? He possesses no charms that one could say are spiritual at least on the surface (resembling more King Farouk than Erasmus). He is fat with beady eyes surrounded by pouches & a red face & a small rose bud mouth.

And she reports shopping for art by calling on Henry Moore, and spending the evening with him. She bought a painting for £27 and a drawing for £12. She then adds:

We sat and drank & chatted until midnight. He is a cheerful, unpretentious, lovable man, a man one liked & trusted immediately, warm & humane & serious & gay, unworldly in appearance, quick in wit & intelligence, and in fact all one hoped that such a man would be. His wife is very pleasant, easy & straightforward, and friendly. It was really one of the nicest evenings of the summer.[21]

That night David Crompton, Bonte and Catherine's brother, invited Bonte and Father Booth – the first priest he'd ever asked – into his home. It was a delightful evening, talking, laughing and playing cards.

* Named for Walston's friend Richard Stokes, who superfluously willed money to Catherine.

Bonte describes Booth: 'He is small & round faced with spectacles & a habit of closing his eyes when he says something earnest. He has been here two weeks & I have the greatest liking for him.' They returned to Newton Hall at eleven thirty and found 'Bobs & Harry & a couple called Zaberman, & an amazing priest called Thomas, whose conversation so electrified me, who was so totally unorthodox that he left even me behind him quite out of breath. We talked until two o'clock in the morning. I wish you could have heard him.'[22]

★

Bonte's letters are out of order, undated and often unsigned, sometimes separated from the envelope, but I suspect that the following letter was written a year later, in 1953. In August of that year, Greene visited Kenya to write on the Mau Mau. His first letter to Catherine from Kenya is dated 24 August 1953. Bonte must have written just before that trip to Africa, when Greene visited Newton Hall.

The first morsel of information Bonte sends to her husband is about a visit to Stratford-upon-Avon, getting home late. Greene also visits Stratford, with Catherine and their old friend Dottoressa Moor from Capri, a doctor. Bonte notes:

> We set off Tuesday after lunch, Graham, Bobs, Dr Moore [*sic*] & I, getting to the *Welcome Hotel* in Stratford by six. The country-side was gentle & pleasing, but not breathless in any way. Graham was in a good mood, considering that the night before the sounds of his irate quarrelling that came from Bobs' study made me feel sure that he was about to commit murder.
>
> I had gotten in rather late from Buzzy's and I shivered in bed a long time, as doors banged & there were shouts & tears. Next morning, however, it was exactly as tho nothing at all had happened and perhaps these storms are the normal part of their odd relationship.[23]

And then Bonte adds in the next sentence, perhaps ominously: 'Thomas was away for two days.'

The letter starts out. 'After walking home I bathed both children in the huge bath tub . . . even if you lie down full length you don't reach the end.' Then:

> Bobs had her troubles yesterday; the arrival of a very *distraught*, hysterical woman from America who had attempted to beard Graham in his den without an appointment, whom he had repulsed & left in tears. She had then gone to Father D'Arcy . . . [who]

391

was foolish enough to refer her to Bobs. Her purpose to write a book on Graham but she came to England without having made any contacts beforehand . . . he just wouldn't see her.

Catherine was not in, so Bonte gave the woman tea, but noticed her eyeing the liquor, and so offered a drink. She

> seemed to feel better after she had had a few swallows. She was one of these pathetic ones, [a] sensitive, rather 'precious' woman who looked to me as she might believe in 'spirits' & indulge in séances. Thomas thought it dreadful of Father D'Arcy to involve Bobs and in fact the evening before ripped Father D'Arcy limb from limb, saying he was a snob & many other things.[24]

On another occasion Bonte describes a visit from Dorothy Glover: 'Harry is away. Bobs has a writer of children's books here, an old flame of Graham's, and [Dottoressa Moor]. The old doctor is a sweet & real person, very fat with protruding teeth & china blue eyes, all wrinkles & wisdom.'[25] They all went to see Shakespeare's *Antony and Cleopatra*. Bonte stresses: 'Graham was in the best of humours.'

She then tells her husband of a funny poem she'd written about Thomas which she read at the table the previous weekend, and also the verses for the Thriplow Ballet: 'Bobs got me to read both of these to Graham who thought they were very funny & asked me if I would collaborate with him in writing a musical comedy. He was really serious & [wanted] to begin right away. He is going to Kenya in a few days to have a glimpse of the joys of the Mau Mau.'

And then, as if by arrangement, the following:

> We dropped at 12 Dr Moore [sic] & Graham at the station & they went on to London, & we picked up Thomas at the same station and rode on home, getting there at about five.[26]

Has Catherine three lovers – her husband, Greene and the verbally exhilarating Thomas?

*

Most of the long-ago days of that summer on the surface seemed paradisal. Conversation was rich: 'Last night . . . an extremely intelligent Jesuit, Bobs and I sat talking until one on the nature of God, what sin is & what forgiveness is, and many other things.'[27] She continued: 'In the evening Graham arrived.' His presence didn't stop Catherine from spending the evening with Ernesto (brother of Bonte's husband) as well as Gigi and Buzz. Bonte, not surprisingly, found herself with a gaggle of priests: 'Fathers Booth, Caraman & Wills are all here in the room with me which is somewhat confusing.'[28]

Gradually, over many letters, we begin to realise who Thomas really is. On 1 July 1953 the Walston children have returned from boarding school and Bonte comments to her husband:

> For two days I've scarcely seen my own for they are out in the fields & meadows, sailing their boats on the stream, and running & talking and laughing together. Last evening before supper they all got into the impressive boat built by Father Gilby and it was the most charming sight as they rowed about. The company last night consisted in Father Caraman, Father Gilby, Bobs, Harry & Dr Straus [Greene's physician]. Food was excellent. Sweetbreads & partridges and fresh fruit. Conversation was light & personal.[29]

The Walstons were clearly given to entertaining. Bonte writes of a huge event, the company suggesting that Harry was having important members of the Labour Party to Newton Hall. It was clearly to be a grand weekend. The guest list: Hugh Gaitskell – former Chancellor of the Exchequer and future Labour Party leader – Lord and Lady Wimbourne, the Yugoslav ambassador, and Graham Greene.

Everyone had things to attend to in preparation. Bonte collected flowers; Harry 'planned excellent meals for the weekend, a thing he enjoys very much doing'; Thomas was busy on the boat. The sharp mind of Bonte was disposed (for the moment) to like him:

> Harry was out last night & Bobs & Thomas & I had a long talk in her sitting room on various aspects of the Faith, which was interesting. I have fortunately lost my extreme distaste for Thomas and I see him now as any other weak spirit, self-absorbed and unfulfilled.[30]

It is at the Gaitskell party that, for the first time, Thomas shows his true colours. Bonte, in a letter dated 22 July 1953, tells us: 'People were still up so I joined them in the living room where Father Thomas, dressed for the first time since I have known him in his white Dominican habit, was holding forth on whether perfection was possible, and whether or not there was such a thing as a perfect Catholic, etc. Graham was arguing against him rather mildly, & Cecil King was needling him with an ironic expression on his face.'[31] A few days earlier, on 9 July 1953, Bonte noted: 'Bobs seems more relaxed in these last days & Thomas less aggressive.'[32]

But whether Thomas was truly liked by Bonte or not, Catherine was certainly enamoured. Moreover, Harry Walston liked him enough to take him to Paris along with Catherine!

Bonte silently observes, silently records.

I learned last night from Buzz who said that Bobs had told him that Father Philip Caraman had so resented his 'place' having been taken by Thomas that he had spread the most terrible stories about Thomas's life & person, as well as Thomas's relation to Bobs, & that was the reason that Father Booth came down for a few days, to talk it all over with Thomas, Bobs & Harry. That accounts therefore for some of the extreme tension of Bobs & Thomas when I arrived & her continued preoccupation. She has seen that even priests are vulnerable . . . with the weaknesses of human beings. With Thomas (who by the way is a non-mass priest, whatever that means, I don't dare ask) our talk is more varied than with Philip & Bobs has lost her intense interest in the ritual of the church.

It is Buzzy's theory that the church will become less & less important to Bobs, but I myself don't think so.

You know how grateful I am to Bobs for her generosity & kindness to us. My weaknesses are not her weaknesses & my temptations are not hers. I would have liked to give her pleasure & enjoyment in companionship this summer, but she is really wholly absorbed in Thomas & what is left over is for Harry. A little example of this is that she, Thomas & Elizabeth Gilby go this weekend to Paris & she didn't ask me.[33]

For a time, the scandal of Bobs and Thomas is dropped. Fathers Booth and Gilby still show up in her letters, and everything seems homely and harmonious: 'Bobs has gone out for the evening to visit Henry Moore with Thomas Gilby & Ernie O'Malley, Harry & Father Booth are bridge playing with Buzz & Gigi.'[34]

By now, Bonte thought Greene tolerable, Thomas unendurable. A letter from Catherine to Bonte shows some of Bonte's kindness to Greene. Acknowledging Bonte's invitation to Greene to her home in America, Catherine states: 'That's particularly nice of you as I know you don't awfully like him and I gather he is frightfully tired and knows very few people in the USA.'[35]

Another night, Bonte was staying at a friend's house and was not due back at Newton Hall, but she returned unexpectedly:

When we got back Bobs was in the living room, with Max Hapsburg, the little Prince of Florence, a tubby plebeian boy exceedingly dull, & Thomas. She hadn't expected me until the next day, so she & Thomas had made plans to go out to a pub for supper. Max & I had supper with the children. There is no doubt, & let me say no more on this subject & *let* it go no further than you, that *poor Bobsee is entirely absorbed in Thomas to the exclusion of everything & everyone else. It seems to be mutual.* Philip Caraman comes here very seldom (at present he is still in the hospital) but their entire morning is spent reading & writing together, & their entire afternoon is spent gardening or doing the boat & then according to who is here the evening is spent with everyone else, or not. She is very kind, both to me & to the children, but just not intensely interested.[36]

The same month Harry and Catherine left for the Riviera for three days, where they were to be joined by Thomas Gilby on a yacht belonging to his friends.

Bonte reports the arrival of the intelligent and sensitive Father Booth, on a mission:

He was very shy . . . but warmed up and by supper time, he was quite at home. He came for a special reason, to give advice to Father Gilby & I think in some rather grave matter. What the matter is I don't know, but Harry hinted that there were certain members of the Catholic clergy and even conventional Catholics who wouldn't stay in the house with Father Gilby, & certainly his behavior is odd to say the least . . . Father Booth has a nice sense of humor in spite of his earnestness, and we continued to talk upstairs in Bobs's living room . . . such subjects as 'How can God who is Perfect understand imperfection in man?' 'Are saints freaks?' 'Does Christianity despise the life of the senses more, or less than other religions?' . . . At eleven, Bobs suggested that we go to bed . . . she told me that Father Booth had a special purpose for having come & had to have a talk with her & with Father Gilby, so I retired to my room. I think they must have talked until very late.[37]

*

In the light of Bonte's letters, our picture of Catherine is close-up. Yet judgment is never simple. There are always shades of difference, the sunny side merging with the shadow-line. In my interview with Bonte, we discussed Harry Walston's attitude towards the two contenders for Catherine's love: Graham and Thomas. Surely the trouble must lie in part with Catherine's relationship with Harry. (We remember Catherine was not in love with Harry sexually.) In my interview with the Walstons' friend Lady Melchett, she spoke of Harry Walston's attitude and nature:

> One never saw them intimate . . . They sat next to each other and that was the only sort of outward sign that there was a deep bond between them. Certainly Harry must have felt that he did have this beautiful jewel of a wife. There was a sort of mystery about their relationship. I couldn't think . . . why this great beauty . . . could have married him. I mean, Harry was very nice, but he was a man's man.[38]

*

Catherine did not develop what her sister saw as an attachment to the clergy until three years after Graham had fallen in love with her. The first priest visitor to Newton Hall was Father Tell. Bonte met Tell in Vienna and thought him a lonely man who'd never seen the outside of a monastery. In his whole life, he'd never been out to lunch. From boyhood he'd been cooped up. When he visited Newton Hall he was unhappy, and this was, according to Bonte, the beginning of 'the priest thing'. But the relationship between Graham, Father Gilby and the whole group was a mystery to Bonte:

> I don't know how many years Graham's relationship with my sister lasted. In my letters there are times when Graham [and] Father Gilby [are] there . . . a whole lot of priests . . . all these people together, and the centre was my sister. She was extremely beautiful until her health broke down.

About Thomas Gilby and her sister, Bonte recalled with precision:

> Feelings were something that she didn't talk about, and in that way, somebody could make her feel like hell. My dislike of Father Gilby was about his brutality, and also his sense of power. He had a terrific sense of power.
>
> When Lucy was three years old and she was afraid of water, Bobs said it was Father Thomas who would show her how to get used to the water, so the bathtub was filled and Lucy was put into it and Father Thomas put his head into the water and came up and said everything was fine. He just held his breath and he more or less pushed Lucy's head down and she, of course, opened her mouth to yell and all the water came in and up her nose and so she was terrified.

But my sister was so hypnotised by this man, and he also, and the other priests that came, were fascinated by my sister ... And Father Thomas would stay up a long time ... after everybody had gone to bed talking and then he'd ... say: 'Catherine, I'll see you in your room upstairs afterwards.'

Was that a call to prayer or to sex? The whole business about the nest of priests troubled Bonte:

[The priests were] very possessive of her, even about small things, possessive even with a desire to be the one that rides in the jeep with her, or the priest who was to take her to the pub ... I couldn't understand it except I thought it demeaning to my sister. I never got into a discussion with her about religion because where that's concerned I am ... blind ... I couldn't understand ... mumbo-jumbo dogmatism, the feeling that the people who worked in the house ... who took care of the children ... all were genuflecting and doing [things] I'm sure mystic gods would not appreciate.

If it had been just my sister that had had these feelings I would have felt that that's her ... insight and I don't have that ... But when I saw everybody kowtowing to this, including my little girl of three and my other girl of six and [how] they thought it was really marvellous that one should become a Catholic ... should cross ourselves and do all the things that seemed to me so impossibly dogmatic.

Near the end of the interview, Bonte stressed how she felt about her sister, elucidating the relationship Catherine had with Father Gilby. We can set it against Gilby's powerful and commanding personality. Surely he was wrong-headed, wrong-principled, to take extreme advantage of a devout believer:

I feel that my sister was a very deep, very compassionate person *who put no value on herself*. She married Harry to change her life, because her mother didn't understand her, was less sophisticated. She didn't understand [Catherine's] agony ... [Catherine] thought that she would somehow change her life if she got away. And I suppose she did change her life.[39]

*

The bitterness of losing a lover is the sub-plot of *The Comedians*. What was Greene up to? Even before Brown suspects Jones of having an affair, he is jealous over Martha. When Brown, upon his return from New York, goes to the Columbus statue, their meeting place, he approaches, and sees her waiting, yet he doesn't rush forward as a true lover would. Instead, he spies on her. No other man comes, and they make love:

> I was half-happy, half-miserable . . . Even while I made love to her I tested her. Surely she wouldn't have the nerve to take me if she were expecting another man . . . [but] it wasn't a fair test – she had nerve for anything. It was no lack of nerve that tied her to her husband.[40]

Greene is jealous, and not least because he doesn't live with Catherine at Newton Hall – the wondrous place so often filled with an abundance of food and fun, with saintly priests (and some not so saintly) and socialist politicians alongside writers, talkers – some incessant such as Gilby – in the vast country house. All seemed like cormorants voraciously devouring Catherine.

And Greene on his visits saw it all, and objected in public (we have seen him arguing with Gilby) – but mildly, because that was his way. He could be wallflower-shy at dinner parties, but in the secrecy of Catherine's room, or in her bed, he would let his temper fly, in anguish and horror at what was going on. Gilby, just like Jones, had climbed the wall and come through the door, but Gilby was bolder; he went through the garden and up the fine stairs to the bedroom. But Graham didn't want to shake the Catholic tree, so he based Jones on Graham Greene II and on Father Gilby in only a vague way, and made Jones a bit of a cad, because he couldn't use Gilby as a pure source for his fiction. Priestly scandals, while flagrant today, were rare back then, and even though Graham hated Gilby and his access to Catherine, he didn't hate his Church, and he did not wish to harm it with bad publicity, even disguised in a novel.

Greene always suspected Catherine, but he now knew the truth, the truth spilled out originally by Father Caraman, and it stayed with him. Less than two years before his death, Greene wrote to George Russo, a former priest living in Australia, about Caraman, whom he once thought of as a friend:

> I am afraid that Father Caraman is a Jesuit whom I dislike very much. He was a man who tried to intervene in my private life and he knows nothing of my conception of the priesthood except that his own priesthood has been to me very suspect.[41]

So now we know the source of Greene's dislike for Father Caraman. We know that Caraman let the cat out of the bag to the Catholic authorities – hence the arrival of Father Booth, who had the task of Church inquisitor. Greene would protect Catherine to the end, but he knew that the Gilby cat was playing the sex game with her. He felt the need to seek relief by revealing his knowledge in a disguised form in this distinguished novel. Still, while Greene is limiting Caraman's interference (by implication) to Catherine and himself, Booth was obligated to send to the church authorities a direct account of Catherine and Gilby, and I'm sure about Greene, too – and the story of the whole grim and shabby secret affair must to this day be lying in some Catholic file to be kept secret to the end of time. Father Gilby was a priestly libertine and debauchee.

Greene was hurt by Thomas Gilby, and at the time he was writing *The Comedians*, the sting was still in his blood. But Greene made Jones's danger as a Lothario nil. Jones hasn't that kind of courage. He is a gentle fraud, and I think Greene is probably not far away from guessing what the masquerading Graham Greene II was really like. Greene must have thought that Greene II's frauds were like Jones's, using fame to flirt with ladies, but visiting a brothel to satisfy his needs, for fear of rejection in a real relationship. We see the prodigal bitterness that finds its way into the portrait of Martha unexpectedly ordered, as it were, to disappear at the end of the novel, as Brown's love for her has vanished, just as Greene's sexual love (a more complicated story) for Catherine finally did too.

★

After the mass in honour of the fallen young guerrillas and Jones late in *The Comedians*, Brown finds himself standing beside Martha and her child Angel. She takes Brown by the arm and leads him into a side chapel and tells him that her husband has been transferred to Lima. She also tells him she never slept with Jones. Here Brown confides to the reader, not to Martha: 'the fact that after all she had been faithful to me was ironic, but it seemed singularly unimportant now. I almost wished that Jones had had his "fun".'[42] This is a further expression of Greene's sardonic coldness, but it's also a pointer to his bitterness at the time of writing this book.

Martha then tells Brown of Dr Magiot's death, killed by the Tontons Macoute, and also, in a short piece of dialogue, we are witness to the death of love:

'Where are you staying?'
I told her the name of the small hotel in the city. 'Shall I come to see you?' she asked. 'I can this afternoon. Angel has friends.'

'If you really want to.'

'I leave for Lima tomorrow.'

'If I were you,' I told her, 'I know that I wouldn't come.'[43]

How woefully Graham's love for Catherine had deteriorated.

Flashes of salvation continued to be glimpsed when they saw each other well into the late fifties and early sixties, but we begin to see that for Greene it has become a time for strained and bitter laughter, a domestic comedy of a woman who wants to eat her cake and have it too: keep her husband and, as in Greene's play *The Complaisant Lover*, allow for the survival of double relationships, the classic triangle enduring, not through secrecy, but because all the parties concerned are in full knowledge. This, of course, is the arrangement Lord Walston allowed. But in his case, there came to be two lovers servicing his wife.

Catherine and Graham continued writing letters to each other. Graham's letters to Catherine still carry love as their message, but this decreases substantially in 1966 when he leaves England to settle in France to be with Yvonne. A clue lies in the death of Brown's love for Martha: 'If I were you . . . I know that I wouldn't come.' Thus the end of Greene's greatest love? It would seem so. Greene is moving on, committing the same sin with a different married woman. This sin with Yvonne was of the same degree as that with Catherine – achieving the same level of separation from God. But in spite of that, Greene needed something stable in life around which his adventurings could revolve. Yvonne was that fixed centre for the rest of his life.

His turmoils did not end until his death, nor did he stop his cease-less rushing around the world, 'never', as Vivien Greene said to me, 'staying in the same place for more than weeks together'.[44] But he wanted to be able to return to a settled home, not a circus. The world was his circus, and his apartment in Antibes, the town where Yvonne lived, his base. Greene and Yvonne did not live in the same house – not until he was dying. Yvonne told me in my last interview with her that she loved Graham, and when her husband objected, her answer to him was not delicate but direct. If Jacques loved her still (and he did), it must have caused him acute personal pain: 'If you make me choose between you and Graham, it will be Graham.'[45]

PART 15

Farewell and a Kiss

32

Bonjour la France

('Twas a Bad Year for Pigs)

One for you, nineteen for me.
— GEORGE HARRISON, 'TAX MAN'

O N 1 January 1966, 'Henry Graham Greene' was made a Companion
of Honour. Such awards were a dicey thing for Greene. Ten years
earlier, he'd turned down a knighthood. This was revealed by Claire
Tomalin, who, before she was herself well known, worked as a secre-
tary/editorial assistant at Heinemann. One of her tasks was to forward
mail to authors.

Claire records that one day Greene received 'an elaborately formal
letter' in care of the publisher. Miss Tomalin's boss, Roland Gant (who
had been in intelligence during the war), steamed it open. Inside was
the offer of a knighthood.[1] Greene never spoke about his refusal publicly,
but there is a reference to it in a letter to Catherine Walston: 'Did you
see the New Year Honours? I wonder whether it was [L. P.] Hartley,
Osbert Sitwell — or *Agatha Christie* who took my place! I'm surprised
at Osbert accepting.'[2]

In those days it was more or less a convention among writers that
knighthoods (which Joseph Conrad also refused) were not to be
accepted. I raised the matter with Greene, asking if his correspondence
would reveal anything. He answered: 'The private secretary of the
Prime Minister writes saying would it be acceptable. I simply wrote
back and said "no".'[3]

But the award of a Companionship of Honour *was* accepted. This
acceptance coincided with the publication of *The Comedians*, Greene's
twenty-seventh book and his first novel in five years. This was a canny
move since it resulted in maximum publicity. Evelyn Waugh wrote
about both achievements:

I was on the point of writing to congratulate you on *The Comedians*, and to thank you for your loyal friendship in sending me a copy, when I opened the newspaper to see the exhilarating news of your having been made a Companion of Honour. Am I not right in thinking that one of your characters remarks that it is the only public recognition worth having?[4]

Waugh told Graham cordially: 'What staying power you have. It might have been written 30 years ago and could be by no one but you.' But he couldn't help aiming a squib at Greene in a letter to Ian Fleming's wife Anne: 'Graham Greene has fled the country with the CH and a work [*The Comedians*] of communist propaganda.'[5]

And fleeing he was, for France. On 7 November 1965, as his exit date approached, Greene wrote to Yvonne Cloetta, his lover now for almost seven years, showing a sympathetic heart:

This afternoon I am happy because of you, but a little sad too. So many letters have shown me how good & sweet & patient people have been to me. If only I'd been as good to other people.

But in thinking of his departure: 'Life became better yesterday when you telephoned.' He tells her he has been 'cleaning drawers, destroying letters, preparing for the new life'.

He speaks to Yvonne almost as if she were a child: 'So many arrangements to make so that I leave England "for ever" before Christmas. My darling . . . I love you & want to look after you & make you feel rested & happy & hopeful.'[6] And something of this shows in the beautiful nickname he gave her, which appears often in letters to friends: 'HHK sends a loving embrace to both of you [Pat and Alexander Frere] and so do I.'[7] Only a few people would know then that the initials stood for 'Healthy Happy Kitten'.

Even when corresponding with Yvonne, he continued to write to the ailing Catherine. He was deeply troubled. From Antibes on 'Sunday' he writes: 'Do send me a line of when I may see you – out of hospital & in hospital & then I hope out of hospital for good & all – or at any rate for 20 years.'[8] By 8 November, Catherine's operation was over and Greene speaks of the last time they'd met before he leaves for France: 'I loved our evening together. Let me come down to Newton [Hall] when you come back home, & we'll make plans for meeting out of Albany.'[9]

He receives a 'sweet letter' from Catherine (undated, but probably the last day of November) and replies, explaining that he has to leave England. On 5 December he gives Catherine his movements: 'I now plan my UDI* for January 1.' On the penultimate day of December, he finds time to give her details: 'The day after tomorrow I leave by Golden Arrow & there is so much packing & cleaning to be done that I don't feel the real *angoisse* – I expect that will come later.' He ends: 'I love you, dear Catherine, forever.'[10]

On 17 December 1965, prior to the book's publication, Greene writes to Yvonne referring to the film script of *The Comedians* and to his first meeting with director Peter Glenville on 2 January. In the same letter, a half playful and half plaintive Greene asks Yvonne 'You'll go on loving me if I become rich won't you?'[11] What vast amounts of energy Greene expended (writing for the film so quickly on the heels of the book) in order to climb his endless Everests, yet often now exhaustion pursued him. He tells Catherine: 'January 5 I go to Antibes & then the hated job of film scripting.'[12] It wasn't greed driving him, but it *was* money. He stressed: 'My purpose is to make all the money I can during 15 months – & then perhaps I can return to Albany.' He was desperately short of funds. He goes on: 'Everybody – even Francis – seems sad at my leaving, & I long to say, "It's sad for you, but it's sadder for me."'[13] Here, the good manners of Greene: he longs to let people know how personally hard it is for him, but he doesn't.

Having sent Yvonne an early copy of *The Comedians*, he writes: 'Dearest Love, I think your book is on the way with a discreet *dédicace*,'[14] – discreet because it was going to her home and her husband Jacques might see it. But then he adds that the novel is 'too long to read in English', which I take to mean that at this point Yvonne's English was not much better than the average Englishman's French. He ends a 23 December letter to Yvonne: 'Dorothy [Glover] came for the night, spluttering & coughing all over the flat, & Miss R[eid] goes round with the face of a corpse . . . I long to be away.'[15] Greene's world was changing.

*

As his leaving loomed, Greene needed to say his goodbyes. He spent Christmas with the Stonors† and Archbishop David Mathew. Greene told Catherine he'd enjoyed himself, 'but I ate & drank too much & put on 5 lbs!'[16] Yet he remained the curious observer, standing watch

---

* Rhodesia had recently (11 November 1965) announced its 'Unilateral Declaration of Independence' without international recognition; Greene expresses his departure in the same terms.

† One of England's oldest Catholic families, who offered asylum in subterranean rooms of their great house during Queen Elizabeth 1's persecution. Edmund Campion, the great Jesuit missionary, was also hidden by the Stonors. He was caught, condemned, suffered the rack, his limbs pulled out and his body hung, drawn and quartered.

in life, scouting for material. According to Jeanne Stonor's daughter Julia, Greene was transfixed by their home's history and theatricality, and its ghosts, known to frequent the huge library. Julia remembered him emerging very red-eyed from sitting up all night awaiting spirits in the freezing room.

A. S. Frere, whom I interviewed in Barbados, knew Greene well and, referring to Greene's incessant desire to travel the world, he maintained it was not restlessness that drove Greene, but 'divine curiosity. He's madly curious about everything. He does not have a possessive instinct; he has never had a possessive instinct and the lack of that has made him [and did make him], a strange child, a strange adult.' Greene was always seeking out the sorrow and anguish of the human soul: searching, questioning, prying into this, probing into that, thoroughly and unabashedly nosy, but gently and silently.

Before his exit, Greene was unable to return to Stonor Park to see his friend Archbishop David Mathew, who had become resident priest to the Stonors upon his retirement. Coming up to his last days of living in London, having to give up his Albany chambers, with all the bother of trying to complete everything by the end of the month, Greene abandoned the notion of a final visit. He had time only to see *Thunderball*, the latest James Bond film, but sadly, this time without Catherine. She was simply not up to it. They'd had a tradition to keep up with Her Majesty's Secret Agent 007.

On his last official night in town, Greene dined with the Sutros, Max and Joan Reinhardt and his secretary, Miss Reid, who had arranged a farewell dinner that John and Gillian Sutro recalled to me, in Monte Carlo on the night of 10 May 1977, our interview running on into the early hours of the 11th. According to Gillian:

> Greene had treated her with great generosity. She was troubled by his departure to France. She saw him every day he was in town and now he was leaving permanently . . . On that last night . . . we were at the Connaught and we sat and sat and sat, and drank and drank and drank, and all of a sudden, she got up – Graham had gone off to telephone or something – he disappeared for a minute and Josephine Reid got up and said, 'I'm leaving. Tell Graham I'm leaving.' And she disappeared into the night.

He had written to Yvonne that his last days were to be 'terribly crowded with small things [such as] complicated emigration forms. I shall give a sigh of relief when I get on the train.'[17] He lists his agenda after he has left the country of his birth and arrived in Paris:

Gare du Nord Jan 1 [1966]
Jan 2 Peter Glenville.
Jan 3 The Prefecture.
Jan 4 Barclays Bank
Jan 5 You.
Jan 8 (I hope & pray) the Colombe d'Or [an hotel where they
       made secret love]

He arrived at the Gare du Nord at 6.15 p.m., as he puts it 'a free man'. Gillian Sutro told me that

> on his first day in Paris . . . he was surrounded by reporters. He was very nervous – nervy. He went to his flat [which] was next door to a police station. It had got into the papers that Graham Greene had . . . chosen France to live in, so the reporters were after him. And one was outside his flat, in Boulevard Malesherbes. Greene had gone in to change, and when he came out, the reporter took a flash of him. Graham was furious and pushed him into the police station and had the whole thing stopped because in France, it's against the law to interfere with another's privacy.

In any case, Greene couldn't stand the invasion, hated the interruption of his interior thoughts. Throughout his life, he closed a lot of doors on a lot of people – especially the press. In a private note to Catherine:

> An unknown journalist rang me up on the phone wanting a photograph. I refused & he was persistent & impertinent & I put the receiver down. Apparently he had . . . taken the names off the concierge's list & began to try them all on the phone until he got me under Verdant. When we went out into the street there was a flash of light & there he was with his camera. I turned my back & a flash from another direction. Luckily the police station was next door. He was hauled in & interrogated & his film destroyed. But it left a nasty taste – I don't like having the police on my side.[18]

He was usually more receptive to French journalists. They were aware (and delighted) that Greene had chosen to live there, at a time he was being designated in the Queen's New Year's Honours List. He adopted the French, and they adopted him. On 1 January 1967 he was appointed Chevalier of the Legion of Honour, proof that for the

French, he was *their man*. In March 1967, his collection of short stories came out with its head story 'May We Borrow Your Husband?' and Greene, in interview with V. S. Naipaul, mentioned that sales had reached 25,000 soon after publication. French critics surely went just a bit over the top: 'Each story [a] masterpiece' is how the weekly *L'Express* described them, though they were right to recognise the beginnings of an amused tolerance towards human sexual behaviour in his latest work. French passion for Greene had begun much earlier with *Brighton Rock*. This pre-war novel did not appear in France until 1947, and then was heralded by *Le Monde* as 'the most important foreign novel to reach us since the Liberation'.

*

On 8 February 1967, a year and a month after Greene had urgently left his own country, there appeared in *The Times* an account of a trial. The place was Switzerland, the case criminally intriguing, but not, one would imagine, even marginally touching Greene's life:

> Thomas Roe, a director of the former Cadco pig project, which collapsed in November 1964 . . . is on trial in the Lausanne district court, charged with abuse of confidence, fraud, and passing coun-terfeit dollar notes.

Thomas Roe was Greene's accountant, who Greene hoped would provide a tax haven in Switzerland to save him from having to pay exorbitant taxes to the British government. The last court charge refers to the circumstances of Roe's arrest on 28 July 1965, when he was stopped on the Geneva–Lausanne motorway. It is alleged that he had earlier in the day exchanged fifty-nine counterfeit $100 bills at five Geneva banks, part of a consignment of such notes, their face value totalling $375,000 (about £134,000), which had been sent to him from the United States by Denis Loraine, another former Cadco director.

Upon hearing the sorry tale, about a week after Roe's arrest, Greene was profoundly disturbed. On 24 November 1964, in a postscript to his son Francis: 'I'm going through a period of some anxiety in case most of my savings have gone down the drain, but I shall know better in a week or two's time.'

Roe, a man with a brilliant mind and excellent military record, provided a shelter in Switzerland for Greene and others – in Greene's case, to protect money earned from books published abroad. In August 1965, Greene wrote to Catherine:

My man in Lausanne has been arrested for having in his possession 400,000 forged American dollars! If he's guilty, what else is
he guilty of? I'm flying to Geneva on the 10th to see Charlie
Chaplin's banker & take his advice over Verdant. You can imagine
what an anxious time this is so forgive a very short letter. So
much love, darling. G.[19]

Eighteen days later Greene wrote to Catherine: 'My peaceful August
has been ruined by Roe (not only my August!). I've been to Lausanne
. . . & have now got a very nice Swiss lawyer working for me.' Jean-
Félix Paschoud was a fine lawyer and a good man. Greene had chosen
well. Sadly he admitted to Catherine: 'We've locked the stable door
even though the horses have got out.'[20] Back in Antibes on 30 September
1965, he seems resigned: 'My Swiss lawyer comes over for two days
on the 10th for conference with me & my English lawyer, & in the
meanwhile my French lawyer . . . I'm tired & fed up with all this, but
it's my own fault.'

According to *The Times* Roe admitted in the Swiss court to accepting
a proposal by the one-time managing director of Cadco, Denis Loraine,
that Loraine would send Roe 'a supply of counterfeit dollars with the
object of Roe using these to meet the most pressing of his commitments'. The trial did not resume until 2 November 1967, when the
court was told that Roe had run up debts totalling £480,000 in five
years.

Roe had been a director of the failed Cadco piggery project at
Glenrothes, Fife, in Scotland, and was charged not only with possession of the counterfeit dollars, but also with fraud, and misappropria-
tion of £183,000 in funds belonging to people who had entrusted
him with the management of their investment:

> The prosecutor alleged that Roe had unwisely risked other people's
> money even before going into Cadco. He said that in 1960 Roe
> had availed himself temporarily of more than 27,000 pounds
> belonging to clients, among them Mr Graham Greene, the author,
> to cover some of the expenditure on a 130,000 pound villa which
> he had built in a Lausanne suburb.[21]

The prosecutor told the court that 'Roe had an outstanding war record,
had married a wealthy woman, the former wife of Lord Inchcape, had
set up companies in Liechtenstein and other "paradises of tax evasion"
. . . [The prosecutor] said that by 1965 Roe was using falsified stocks,
emanating from financial gangsters, a group controlled by the chief of
the Mafia.'[22]

The court's verdict was announced on 24 February 1968. Roe was sentenced to six years' imprisonment. The sentence was not as severe as it seemed, since he had already been awaiting trial for nineteen months; with good-conduct remission of one-third, he could be released by the summer of 1969.

More punishing to Roe was that he was stripped of his CBE. On 9 August 1967 an announcement in *The Times* stated: 'The Queen has directed that the appointment of Mr Thomas Chambers Windsor Roe to be a Commander of the Civil Division of the Most Excellent Order of the British Empire dated 1st January 1953 shall be cancelled and annulled, and his name erased from the Register.'

★

Roe had enjoyed good standing in Lausanne, and was admired by film stars, writers and great comics, many of whom trusted him with their investments. In *The Noël Coward Diaries* there is an entry for Sunday, 11 August 1963: 'My investments, looked after by Tom Roe in Switzerland, are doing fine.'[23] And on 5 November in the same year, Coward writes: 'A satisfactory "summit" conference about finance. I am now definitely to be a Swiss resident and Tom Roe is working to get a satisfactory tax arrangement with the Swiss government. If he succeeds it will mean that my financial life will be far less complicated.'[24] Coward's biographer, Cole Lesley, reveals:

> before Tom was sent to prison (he has been out for some years now, as cheerful and Micawberish as ever) he performed more than a few good services for Noël, for which we have to thank him to this day. Tom it was who fell back in astonishment when we told him that Noël's royalties were still not flowing directly to him, and who flew immediately to London and goosed everybody concerned.[25]

Then it was that Coward began to get his own cheques. But Roe did Coward another favour:

> Tom then saw the authorities, and Noël's Swiss income-tax was fixed at just over seven per cent; a reasonable figure to pay . . . and certainly an improvement on the fifty he had been paying in England. Need I say that like everything else the figure increased before very long but remained, and remains, reasonable.[26]

Roe operated a tax-avoidance scheme for his clients, some of whom were in danger of prosecution. Coward was not imperilled, since he had received special dispensation in the form of 7 per cent Swiss tax, after he'd sought residency in Switzerland. Another Roe client, Charlie Chaplin, was already resident there. But Greene resided in England and was in danger. Noël Coward and Charlie Chaplin, as tax exiles, were not.

★

Why was the keenly intelligent and astute Graham Greene taken in by Roe? According to his close friend Peter Glenville, Greene was very sharp where business was concerned. Glenville recalled to me a time when he'd half-boasted to Greene about a minor triumph in the stock market. Greene told him he was actually wrong about the whole thing: 'And suddenly he came out with the most astonishing knowledge of Wall Street and the inner workings of corporations which absolutely amazed me. I thought him a dreamer who wouldn't know about these things.'[27] But Greene was indeed snookered by the creative Roe.

Brian Aherne, biographer of the film star George Sanders, in his 1979 life, *A Dreadful Man*, reveals the astonishing set-up that Sanders, Denis Loraine and Thomas Roe were involved in. Its purpose seemed to be the spending of other people's money. The holding company, Cadco, derived its name from Sanders's autobiography *The Memoirs of a Professional Cad* (1960) and was to be an investment for Roturman, S.A., another dubious holding company, of which Aherne writes:

> Exciting plans were made for this company, including investment in Swiss real estate, the purchase and storage of Scotch whisky in bulk, Canadian oil wells and other projects about which, it seemed to me, they knew nothing. [Roe] began to invest money that had been entrusted to him by clients in various parts of the world, while George [Sanders] bought a new Rolls-Royce and once more talked of abandoning the profession in which he was so phenomenally successful in order to become a business tycoon.[28]

The money for Sanders's Rolls-Royce came from Greene and others. Roe was extremely clever, smooth and sympathetic even when on trial. His defending attorney spoke the truth: 'Maître Lob also emphasized that the persons who had lost money bore Roe no ill will; they had earlier done very well out of their investments placed through him.'[29] He certainly succeeded in persuading Greene that the failure of the Royal Victoria Sausage Company, an endeavour close to Greene's heart, or at least his gullet, was not Roe's fault.

Greene loved English sausages, and missed them terribly when he left the country. French sausages were just not the same.* So it was right up his alley to put money – something like £100,000 – into a meat company, especially one making sausages which supposedly had pleased King Edward VII.

According to the report issued in the UK by the Board of Trade, Roe's friend, Denis Loraine (real name Denis Edwards), acquired a small butcher's shop just outside Greene's favourite city, the seaside resort of Brighton, in Victoria Terrace, Hove. This was the beginning of the Great Sausage Scandal. The wife of Denis Loraine had run up a bill at the butcher's of £180, which was 'discharged in a somewhat unusual manner: her husband entering into a partnership with the butcher . . . and eventually taking over the business'.

Loraine expanded the company rapidly; chiefly by making it known that he had found a letter from King Edward VII praising the sausages. Within a few days of the company's incorporation, he managed to get misleading advertisements inserted in newspapers about the Prince of Wales taking pride in their sausages.† Edwards/Loraine changed the shop's name to the Royal Victoria Sausage Company and, with the royal crest appearing on his fleet of vans, he was away and riding high. But it was all a lie, as the Board of Trade document reported: 'Loraine registered it as the Royal Victoria Sausages Ltd. on the strength of a "wholly untrue" story that King Edward VII, when Prince of Wales, had enjoyed the sausages so much that he had had regular supplies sent to him.'

Loraine, then living in Hollywood, established the Glenrothes piggery firm in league with the actor George Sanders.‡ Sanders was made a director, and 'encouraged Loraine in his excesses'. Sanders was materially

---

* When he'd return to England, Greene would see his sister Elisabeth Dennys. Often I would join them at her home in Crowborough, Sussex, and we'd go to a pub for this delight. Gillian Sutro described him perfectly: 'Cold sausage and a glass of beer. That's happiness for Graham.'

† Another version of the story appears in Brian Aherne's life of George Sanders. In this version, 'a local butcher . . . found the recipe in a pile of old papers' in the basement of his shop, with a 'letter from Queen Victoria's secretary saying on a visit to Brighton, Her Majesty had enjoyed these remarkable sausages very much and wished to order more'. Harris, a cipher for Loraine, 'put a copy of Queen Victoria's letter in the window'. It went on from there: 'A factory was leased in Sussex, machinery and workers installed, and contracts were in process of negotiation with railways, schools, institutions and restaurants over the southern counties for the supply of Royal Victoria Sausages.' (*A Dreadful Man*, Simon & Schuster, 1979, p. 97.)

‡ Sanders, whose roles capitalised on his English voice, did a roaring trade: 'On screen George has seldom stopped sneering [and had] an elegant assumption of superiority over the other cast members. He made an extraordinarily successful career out of it.' (David Shipman, *The Great Movie Stars*, Crown Publishers, 1970, p. 484.)

responsible for the venture launched at Glenrothes, a project that served as a device to recoup substantial losses of the Royal Victoria Sausage company (mostly through reckless spending by Loraine, Sanders and Roe). The government report stated that if it hadn't been for the 'world-famous figure' of George Sanders supporting the endeavour it would never have got under way.*

Glenrothes was a new town and councillors anticipated that once the piggery was established it would employ some 2,000 people. Loraine, Sanders and Roe, as Cadco, approached the Scottish Development Corporation and persuaded it to shell out, £763,911. Additionally, Cadco obtained from the Royal Bank of Scotland an overdraft sum rising to £460,000.† The money was lent on specific terms, terms that were immediately abused on 'a vast scale'. The firm submitted 'fraudulent documents . . . including accounts which had been materially altered! The Royal Bank of Scotland admitted, following the collapse of the Cadco piggeries, that it was not always possible to protect itself against false statements. The cost to the Glenrothes corporation of the Cadco buildings was a sweet £1,100,000, including £626,000 spent on standard factory and office accommodation.'[30]

As the authorities studied the books, they discovered that monies raised for the project had been swiftly transferred to other associated companies outside Glenrothes and overseas. Enormous sums left the country in the form of traveller's cheques and business allowances.

The Cadco Development Company requested that its subsidiary, the Cadco Building Company, should build the piggeries and factories for this project. But the new company had no financial status whatsoever. Its entire paid-up capital was £2! On the part of government officials, it was a case of poor judgment, negligence, incompetence and gullibility. It didn't take a crackerjack market prognosticator to pronounce it a bad year for pigs.

*

* The original press handout listed other famous names – Robert Mitchum, William Holden, Charlie Chaplin, Graham Greene – connected with Cadco. This, generally speaking, was not true. At the last moment it was dropped because Roe, a shrewd operator, thought it was too blatant and therefore too dangerous.
† Why were such large sums offered? How could the authorities have been so careless? One reason was that the Scottish authorities, especially the Secretary of State, saw the piggery as a glittering example of how to attract industry to their country. Officials (certainly not themselves corrupt) *wanted* to be convinced, so investigation was minimal. There was a social need – it was a distressed mining area – to bring employment to Glenrothes. Collieries were closing, leading to widespread unemployment. This factory, if successful, would diminish unemployment, providing facilities for handling some 20,000 pigs.

Greene was invited by the Board of Trade to appear before them on 15 April 1965. He had been taken in by Roe, persuaded by his glib self-serving talk. So much so that he had reported to Catherine in a letter written probably in December 1964: 'I had a long reassuring letter from Roe waiting for me' when he arrived in Antibes. 'I don't think I'll have lost more than my few shares in Royal Victoria.' But George Sanders's wife, Benita, much closer to the events that were coming apart, described Roe as 'a terrible disease in our lives'. It was only when Roe was charged in Switzerland that doubts arose in Greene's mind, by which time the damage was done.

The extent of Greene's holdings entrusted to Roe is alluded to in a letter to his son Francis, sent to the National Provincial Bank, headed in Greene's own hand, 'To be opened only in event of Mr H.G. Greene's death'. In it, Greene explains the division of property between Francis and Lucy Caroline and states that all American and foreign translation rights and the Paris flat are included, and, remarkably, admits that Roe was going to set things up in order to 'avoid the death duty. Verdant SA have always retained a proportion of the monies coming in from these rights and passed the rest on to a Trust called Pasture in Liechtenstein which is run by the same man Roe. Pasture holds certain investments as well as cash.' Greene made suggestions as to the liquidation of certain properties, and recommended a visit to Mr Roe 'when the time comes'.[31]

So Greene must have known that he'd lost his investment, and would, in a sense, have to start again. Interviewed in New York, Peter Glenville was categorical:'I would be extremely surprised to find Greene a rich man. Graham, through Roe, lost *all*, repeat lost *all*.* The Swiss venture just about finished him.' And was it so terrible to want to avoid paying huge sums to the Inland Revenue on books *published abroad*? At least *fifty per cent*? It must have been heart-breaking. Thus, Roe was punishment enough for Greene. He survived financially, but he'd sustained a severe haemorrhage. In the *Times Literary Supplement* of 21 May 1982, Malcolm Muggeridge is quoted describing Roe as a 'shark [whose] real specialty was floating phantom companies . . . and passing forged dollar bills'. He continues: 'When Roe began to steal his authors' money, [Robert] Graves lost 65,000 Swiss francs' and he names Greene among 'shrewder' men who suffered as well.

*The *Toronto Star* of Sunday, 1 December 1991, indicated that when the contents of Graham's will were disclosed, his mistress received nothing, and Vivien, his '86-year-old widow', shared the estate with her two children. The article debunked the notion that Greene was worth 10 million pounds, stating that 'the personal estate of the man . . . is about 200,000 pounds'. I doubt that this is the whole story, but I know he gave away vast sums to friends and family through his corporation Verdant.

★

Greene's literary agent, Laurence Pollinger, believed in Roe too, and thought the only villain in the Great Sausage Scandal was Denis Loraine/Edwards. In a letter from Pollinger to Roe addressed 'Dear Tom', of 23 December 1964, he empathises with Roe, and puts the blame on Loraine. He expresses profound sympathy in having such a partner, though it is expressed carefully so that no one is accused publicly: 'I do hope for your sake the situation will rapidly clear itself. What a frightful worrying and anxious time it has been for you.' He then thanks Roe for his personal willingness to cover the loss of £10,000 of Greene's money, again spoken of with some delicacy:

> I saw Graham late yesterday afternoon and took the liberty of letting him read your letter to me of 17 December from which we note you accept the responsibility to reimburse International Authors [Pollinger's name for those authors earning royalties from publications abroad – in this case the responsibility to reimburse Greene] the sum of 10,000 pounds provided this is not repaid by Royal Victoria Sausage, Ltd.

That looks like the offer of a true gentleman. It was never honoured. Roe wrote to Greene in December 1964, reassuring him, when the truth was that he was appropriating enormous sums from Verdant SA, the Swiss company that he set up for Greene. The smaller organisation, Graham Greene Productions, with Catherine and Greene as co-directors, continued in business in England.

There are other references to Roe in Greene's correspondence with Yvonne at the time of the 1965 crisis, when Roe was picked up by the Swiss police. Greene knew something of Roe's tussle with the police, because a day before Roe was charged, 3 August 1965, Greene wrote to Pollinger from his flat in Paris mentioning the scandal Roe had brought down on himself, 'and therefore to a degree on us too'. The next week he tells Yvonne over the phone: 'I'm afraid I was at rather a low point.' He had heard about Roe and the counterfeit money by way of his French lawyer, Paschoud. 'He telephoned me from Lausanne . . . (I wonder whether Jacques [Cloetta, who was Swiss] knows Paschoud.)'

★

It might have been only a matter of paying back taxes for a number of years, but there was always the real possibility of the matter snow-balling into a devastating scandal, not so much because of the tax angle, but because Roe had involved himself in greater crimes, and British newspapers would have played up the story of a rich and famous writer cheating the tax authorities. This would have been maximised by the strange case of Roe as the conduit for forged banknotes, a messenger boy for the Mafia on a large scale. These facts, strictly speaking, were not relevant to Greene's case, but if it had made the papers, such was the Catholic magic of Greene's name that the whole matter would have been sensationalised. There was a chance that the British authorities, if Greene had not become domiciled in another country and had he not been willing to pay back what he owed, might have attempted to secure his arrest. But there were, I suspect, good reasons why the authorities were disinclined to take action against Greene. It was in part because he was immensely famous, and also perhaps because he was to be made a Companion of Honour, a considerable distinction.

During this stressful time, Lord Snowdon, then married to Princess Margaret, took a series of profoundly impressive photographs of Greene, almost grinding a new lens for a close-up, revelatory of Greene's character. The sixty-one-year-old face in Snowdon's photograph reveals a well-dressed exile, bold, yet as fearful as if he were a fugitive. Greene seems to be surveying evil's wide-ranging territory. His blue eyes bulge and dare, ready to hold terror at bay – as if he were the last man alive. Could it be that we see fear of possible scandal in his face?

Greene recalled to Catherine that he'd had a 'terribly busy week – & wasn't at all in the mood for Snowdon on Thursday morning. But I found him quite sympathetic – naïve, I'd say & lonely, & at 11 in the morning he drank my awful vodka with red pepper.'[32] Indeed, Lord Snowdon's portrait is exemplary photographic biography. The paramount quality of innocence once so evident in Greene had left his face by the time of his troubles with Roe. (Although it should be remembered that as early as 1929, Douglas Jay, meeting Greene in the offices of *The Times*, one young sub-editor to another, recalled that his main memory of Greene was his 'worried look, and I used to glance at him particularly in the Tube and think, "Is that just the cast of feature or is he really worrying terribly about something?"'[33])

*

Two and a half months before he left his native shores, Greene wrote to Catherine on 14 October 1965: '(strictly between you & me) I shall have to be domiciled in France . . . all very complicated & I long to talk to you about it.' The postscript illustrates how important Catherine still was: 'I see from my dream diary index that I have dreamed of you 22 times this year!'

Very soon, his letters to Catherine take on a gentleness. She is in hospital with a broken hip, and from the time of this incident onward, she is to be constantly in hospital. For the next six years we are going to see the heroic side of Catherine. On 20 May of that year, Greene writes to Yvonne:

Poor Catherine is in hospital again & comes back to England [from Dublin where she was first hospitalised] on Sunday. This time inflammation of the pancreas. There seems to be no end to it.

In an undated letter he writes: 'Dearest dear Catherine. I was horrified to hear that you were back in hospital in Dublin. You seem to be given no rest at all – you really are doomed to be a saint. But I would rather you were happy & well than a saint.'[34] He had planned to take her to their special place, Capri, but now they both knew that they might not be able to make another trip together: 'My darling, don't worry & let's leave the tickets booked for July 6 for the time being. Cancelling at the last moment is easier than booking . . . You don't have to make up your mind till July . . . My darling I think of you so much & pray for you to the best of my ability. You are very brave & patient. This bad time must come to an end like winter.'[35] In November he writes: 'I keep on thinking about you – it's 10.30 & the operation must be going on. I do pray so hard that this is really the end of your troubles. I had lunch with Jeanne [Stonor] yesterday – she says that you have to be prepared for some sickness & weakness for a few months afterwards & then it's like a renewal of life.'

Obviously, their carefree travelling days were over. 'St Lucia wouldn't be very wise, would it? I can't very well suggest though that Laos or Liberia would be better. Spanish Cove? I wish I was rich enough to suggest it for both of us, but I don't see the *Sunday Times* paying.'[36]

Catherine must have known he would have to give up his Albany apartment to prove to the tax authorities he had no legal British residence. Sick herself, she yet offered to help:

Dear Catherine, your letter was very sweet & dear I won't hesitate to ask your help if necessary in storing things. I can't let you & Harry be involved in taking over C6. After all he's a minister of the Crown. Speaking now *very* confidentially, Frere has offered to take on the remainder of the lease & notionally – but with real money – buy the furniture. This would give a breathing space until June '67 & anything might happen before then.[37]

Five years after Greene had privately (at the time of the publication of *A Burnt-Out Case*) turned away from the Church, he was back astride a Catholic horse and ready for whatever might happen between the stirrup and the ground. He speaks of Sherman Stonor (Baron Camoys), his close friend, who had been very sick, but had suddenly improved. Greene writes with a certain amusement about the strongly Catholic Sherman, who feared somewhat for his immortal soul:

> Sherman is better, but [Archbishop] David [Mathew] took the chance of anointing him & then suggested the sacraments which he hadn't had for years. David told him 'you don't have to make a confession – just an act of contrition, that's all.' Immense relief on all sides & he began to take the sacrament every day. David told Jeanne it was a real God-sent opportunity because if Sherman had been less bad, he couldn't have dispensed with the confession & then Sherman would have been scared off.

Greene turns serious, and we see a foreshadowing of his destined future need of a Father Leopoldo Durán:

> If I'm ever delirious in Paris you & Jeanne will have to send David over by plane. J. says he has been simply wonderful & an enormous help.[38]

*

Into his penultimate month of residence in England, Greene was still hopeful that his enforced stay out of his own country would not last long. Catherine had asked about the blue bed – their lovers' bed – in C6 Albany. She was loath to see it disappear:

> Of course, there's no question of *really* selling the bed. Officially, Frere will buy everything, but I shall be able to buy them back just as they are, if, as I hope, I will be able to return after 18 months or so of exile, with everything straightened up. If that day doesn't arrive, you shall have the bed & the chairs.

He ends his letter to Catherine: 'Look after yourself really carefully, dearest Catherine.' And he lets her know he wants to see her still:

> I go to Paris with Y. on Wednesday now & return on the 22nd or 23rd [November]. The 25th I have to attend the St Catherine's Day (!) dinner at Balliol as a Fellow! Is there any chance of coming to Newton [Hall] the week-end of the 27th 28th?[39]

Greene apologises to Catherine in a letter probably written on the last day of November 1965: 'I love you & that's a permanent thing which can't change now. I feel very much this going away, but it simply has to be.' He then speaks without explaining even to Catherine what this apprehension is, though presumably he is worrying he might, while in England, be arrested over his tax problems: 'Until I'm safely abroad I shall have the nagging anxiety which has [been] going on now for more than a year. I still hope that it will be temporary & the time will pass quickly.' However he offers Yvonne another opposite possibility: 'So many arrangements to make so that I leave England "forever".'[40]

★

According to his diary, Greene was received by the Queen on 11 March 1966. He was invested with his honour for the whole body of his work, a distinguished award, in terms curiously worded: 'for conspicuous service of national importance'.★ To Catherine, Greene complained that he was ill at ease, saying it was entirely his fault, and no doubt in part due to his situation – on the one hand nearly ostracised, on the other receiving a great honour – but nonetheless he was required to return to France urgently the following day. The extended group photograph of those receiving honours shows the Queen in the centre of the group, Greene appearing to be at his most gloomy. *The Times* of 12 March 1966 reported the occasion in the Court Circular:

> Mr Graham Greene had the honour of being received by Her Majesty when The Queen invested him with the Insignia of a Member of the Order of the Companions of Honour.

Upon leaving Buckingham Palace, with journalists and photographers hounding him, he hid his face behind a newspaper. He hated celebrity. In a letter to Catherine from Antibes the escapee told her: 'I come to London with permission [from the British tax authorities] on March 10 because I have to go and see the Queen on March 11 at 12.40 – it seems an odd time – to get my decoration. So apparently I shall be all alone and not in a crowd. I shall have to spend the night at an hotel on March 10 and fly back to France on the evening of March 11. If you are better do come and have dinner and do a movie with me on March 10.'[41] Nine days later, he writes again: 'You poor darling – let's go to Stone's & I'll drink beer & you'll drink nothing.'

★

★ Could this refer to his service in MI6?

Seventeen months earlier Greene had a dream of the Queen. Part of it appears in the undated extracts posthumously published in *A World of My Own: A Dream Diary*. Here is the printed version:

> quite by chance, I found myself sitting beside the Queen during a service in Windsor Chapel. The officiating clergyman preached an absurd sermon and I found myself in danger of laughing. So, I could see, was the Queen, and she held the Order of Service in front of my mouth to hide my smile. Then Prince Philip entered. I was not surprised at all that he was wearing a scout-master's uniform, but I resented having to surrender my chair to him. As I moved away the Queen confided to me, 'I can't bear the way he smiles.'[42]

The dream is basically as Greene wrote it. However the last sentence misses out a phrase (which is emphasised below), and two gorgeous final sentences are omitted altogether:

> The Queen confided to me, *like a promise of favours to come*, 'I can't bear the way he smiles.' What happened later I can hardly describe, for a man is not bound to give evidence against himself, & the crime was high treason. No crime could ever have given greater satisfaction to the criminal.

Would Her Majesty have laughed at this 'thought crime'? Or, like her great-great-grandmother, uttered the immortal: 'We are not amused'?

33

Le Petit Chat

O lovely Pussy! O Pussy, my love,
What a beautiful Pussy you are,
You are, You are!
What a beautiful Pussy you are!
       — EDWARD LEAR

T HE filming of *The Comedians* took place before the novel was published, reversing the usual order of events. The film's producer/director, Peter Glenville, employed a first-rate cast. Richard Burton, according to Quentin Falk, received $750,000 for his part in the film; his wife, Elizabeth Taylor, half a million; Alec Guinness surely another half a million, and a goodly sum went to the brilliant Peter Ustinov. Add to these Lillian Gish (heroine of silent films) and Paul Ford of the *Bilko* television series — MGM seemed to have no financial limits. Greene described how it went: 'Liz was hell',[1] he wrote in a letter to Michael Meyer, but he was impressed by all the other stars. They were shooting parts of the movie in Dahomey (Benin) — not far from where he'd met Yvonne, his final mistress, for the first time. To film in Haiti once the novel broke would have been madness.

In a long letter to Yvonne, he speaks of the death by drowning of a carpenter on the film crew, and how Glenville and his friend Bill look like 'skeletons':

> The day after one of the *equipe* was drowned, both of them only just escaped after half an hour's struggle, although they had been careful not to go in below their waist. Alec [Guinness] who was on the shore tried to get help & went to an old black mammy who only shook with laughter![2]

That night, Greene, in the company of Peter Glenville and Peter Ustinov, saw '50 minutes of rushes without sound — very impressive & encouraging'.

Old Lillian Gish & Paul Ford superb. Richard Burton perfect –
there were no rushes of Liz. I like them both – in the afternoon
she sat in the hot sun for *camaraderie* although she had no work
to do, but when they are both off they knock it down in their
little trailer – he beer & she *pastis*. How they can in this heat
[which is saying something for Greene, the prodigious drinker].[3]

Greene speaks of an 'incident' involving the famous pair, who forgot
a dinner party for 200 given by the Minister of Information. They
were contrite, and another dinner was put on, this time supposedly for
just eight. There were 150. A huge fuss was made including a German
TV crew filming the event. It was midnight, and still no dinner. 'Burton
after four hours of beer blew his top, told the minister he was a bloody
bore. All the same they are a cozy pair.'[4]

Greene was impressed with the couple at first, but later thought that
for his purposes Miss Taylor, at least in this kind of film, could not, or
didn't care to, act well. Quentin Falk thought the acting 'uniformly
good' with Burton's 'world-weariness and cynicism', and Guinness was
'just right'. The others:

Ustinov is unusually low-key as the cuckolded ambassador.* Lillian
Gish and Paul Ford as the rapidly disillusioned Smiths descend
with dignity. The main black actors – James Earl Jones as Magiot,
Raymond St Jacques as Concasseur and, particularly, Roscoe Lee
Browne as the impish Petit Pierre – are excellent.[5]

The exception, Falk believed, was Elizabeth Taylor:

Taylor's ineptness as the German Martha almost tends to devalue
the other performances. . . . Greene agrees that Taylor was a
mistake. 'She had, though, just made *Who's Afraid of Virginia Woolf?*
and certainly when I saw her in that I thought to myself, "My
God, she *can* act." Anyhow it was a disaster having her in *The
Comedians*, and she was also a very difficult person too.'

When I interviewed Glenville in New York on 15 December 1978,
I asked about Taylor. He thought Graham was right:

I thought she was quite wrong, not that she's not talented, but
she wanted to play the part, and she wanted to be with Burton

---

* Alec Guinness thought Ustinov's performance was 'frightfully underrated and . . . one
of the most distinguished pieces of work he's done'.

in Africa, so she did it for half her normal salary, which at the time MGM thought was the great coup of all time. Greene found her the exact opposite of what he sexually had imagined.

Taylor had a clause in her contract letting her keep any jewellery worn in her films, and she asked Glenville if she could go to Bulgaria to purchase some. Glenville told her she was playing an ambassador's wife from a poor country, in a poor country, and that no jewellery would be appropriate, maybe just '"little coral beads is about as far as you can go". But the lack of comprehension there . . . And . . . that big love scene on the bed, Graham had come to watch that being filmed, he was absolutely turned off . . . In the end it was cut from the movie, and Graham was right.'

In a letter to Catherine Walston, 6 April 1967, Greene sums up: 'Liz Taylor – beautiful head, bad body, slightly vulgar voice, "a good sort" & kind!'

*

It wasn't by chance that the movie was to be made before the book came out. That was the original idea, to shoot it quickly in Haiti, all the while watching for the book's appearance. Once published, with its contempt for the Duvalier regime revealed, they knew Duvalier could come after them.

Yet Glenville felt he could never do the film without seeing the terrain. So, he went to Haiti himself, taking along a photographer, the film's art director, François de Lamothe. When Glenville made it known to Greene that he wanted to visit Haiti, Greene thought there'd be no danger until the book's appearance.

Glenville arrived in Port-au-Prince in December 1965 and wasted no time arranging to see President Duvalier. The fact that he was a film director interested Duvalier. Here might be a method of manipulating the media in his favour. Glenville sparked his interest, prompting Duvalier to ask him to write a book on Haiti. Glenville pleaded the need to study Haiti further, knowing he could do his research before Graham's book hit the shelves and Papa Doc took his revenge. Glenville had gone to the police station near the palace to get permission to travel north, something which earlier had been refused to Greene. Greene advised Glenville to drop by the police station to photograph the gruesome posters he'd seen on the wall showing dead bodies of Duvalier's enemies, especially the famous Barbot brothers, with captions implying that such a fate awaited all the president's enemies (which he did – see the specific photos).

★

One day in January 1966, when many of the photographs of the Oloffson Hotel for the early action shots had already been taken, and Glenville was hard at work, he was confronted by the owner, Al Seitz, who was holding a copy of Greene's newly-published novel. Said Seitz: 'This has been sent to me from the Embassy and I hear that it's all about this hotel. It's going to cause a lot of trouble here.' Glenville told me: 'my blood ran cold. I rushed off to the travel agent and got to the airport. Jolicoeur, then head press man, told me he'd looked at the book, and exuberantly expressed, "I am the character Petit Pierre in the novel."'

Next, according to Glenville, a 'great big military boss' said to him: 'You must read this' and handed him a copy of the *New York Times*, showing 'the whole front page, the book, and a picture of Graham in the middle'.

Since Glenville had bought the rights, he was afraid there'd be a reference to him as director of the film and they'd know why he'd been snooping around. The military boss began to read passages from the review to Glenville: 'I haven't had many occasions to fear in my life, but I had a nasty wave of cold fear through me then.' The boss suddenly said as he was reading: 'You must excuse me, I have to go to the Palace.' Glenville didn't ask anyone to excuse him but raced to the airport. He recalled: 'Through the loudspeaker came this voice saying that the plane had been delayed for three hours.' He knew he could be in real danger, since his ambassador had told him that if he was put into prison, 'Nobody can do any good. No one can help.'[6] Once his plane took off, the terror which had almost overcome him was replaced by relief and pleasure. He drank, forcing himself to sip slowly.

★

Since they couldn't use Haiti as their film location, various sites in Africa were considered, but it occurred to Glenville that Dahomey had a similar background of slavery, and was still under the influence of the French (just like Haiti before the Haitians successfully revolted). In both cases, French was the official tongue. In his letter to Yvonne (written from Dahomey during filming), Greene concludes:

The Haitian Ambassador left a few days ago, recalled by his government. François de Lamothe left also some days ago in a sick state believing that he was going to die & that there was a voodoo spell on him.[7]

Poor de Lamothe feared – as did all Haitians – the powers of Papa Doc. His people still thought he haunted the graveyards as Baron Samedi.

In letters Graham wrote to Yvonne during the filming in Dahomey – where her husband spent three quarters of every year as a prominent French consular official – Greene keeps insisting upon his attachment to Jacques: 'I haven't yet seen Jacques but he comes to dinner tonight . . . and tomorrow we have dinner with him.'[8] Greene was close to Jacques, and Jacques was still unaware that Greene was sleeping with his wife.

So the movie is being made in Jacques's vicinity, but Yvonne is living in the Cloetta house near Antibes with her two children. Two months earlier, Greene had asked her to meet him in Nice 'two weeks from the day after tomorrow. Then quick to the Colombe d'Or.' He ends with: 'I love you always for always . . . *Tout à toi* [wholly yours].'[9]

When I met Yvonne, she was no longer young. But what was she like in 1966? A good description of her came during my interview with Peter Glenville. Glenville first spoke of Catherine Walston, whom he described as having a 'stately . . . beauty'. Glenville had never talked to Catherine, but had to grant that she 'was a splendid-looking girl, big and tall – but not Graham's usual thing perhaps'. He spoke similarly of Elizabeth Taylor: 'She didn't fit the kind of woman Greene was attracted to. He . . . liked [ladies who] were always a little bit deprived, or vulnerable or sad and not too fleshy.' Glenville recalled an incident when they saw someone who seemed Greene's perfect type:

> I remember we went into a chemist's shop and there was a sad little girl with sort of wispish hair and a very white skin and very large beautiful eyes, looking like some orphan from *Oliver Twist*.

Perhaps close to the type of child in Charlie Chaplin's 1931 *City Lights*? But it was another movie star who came to the mind of the director:

> Yvonne is a little waify, rather boyish. I don't mean masculine, but [he liked] boyish-looking women. Graham hated the masculine type of woman, but sort of elfin. If Graham had lived in another world, he might have fallen for Audrey Hepburn.[10]

Gillian Sutro described Yvonne, knowing her well:

> She's minute . . . She's got a little Pekinese face. Rather a funny little face. She obviously was very pretty once, because she has

a daughter who is exactly like her. She is very pretty – Martine – she does TV and radio. Yvonne is very chic – very well-dressed, but she's tiny. It's extraordinary – she makes every other woman appear a clodhopper. I've never seen anyone so tiny in my life.

And John Sutro added:

He likes bottoms I think. She's the most minute woman I've ever seen. She wears very high heels. A very animated face . . . She's good for him because she's a gay character.[11]

According to Shirley Hazzard's memoir on Greene: 'No pretty woman was ever more suited than Yvonne to the adjective *petite*. Heart-shaped smiling face, short shock of strong white hair; slight, perfectly proportioned compact body dressed in trousers and a pastel shirt, with a shawl at evening. Good English, spoken with a charming accent . . . A use of Italian enabled her to act . . . as intermediary during their Capri visits.'[12] Hazzard also tells of the strength of Yvonne's love for Greene: 'Yvonne loved – one might say, idolised – Graham.'[13]

For thirty years, until Graham's death, their love continued. My experience: I remember standing in front of them in Antibes, they deliberately kissed for me to witness and photograph. He was always thoughtful and good-mannered towards her. He seemed to treat her (at least in public) as if she were a child and he the grown-up. That's how it was, but I suspect that Yvonne was not a youngster in character, simply she took such a part (as I suppose an actress does) because Greene wished it. After his death, I recall she seemed much tougher, I felt she was out to prove to herself (and the world) that Graham Greene loved her, Yvonne, better than any other previous lover. As the book proceeds, we'll be in a better position to judge whether Yvonne's view was justified. Love she felt for Greene. Absolutely. Was she taking herself in? I suspect to a degree this was so. Lying to one's self is not entirely unknown to humans.

★

From 1959 Greene was indulging his proclivity for adultery. I remember asking A. S. Frere during an interview in Barbados in 1981 why Greene went after married women. His answer was male-oriented and a bit self-serving:

SHERRY: Why do you think he needs to have affairs with married women?

FRERE: For a very simple reason. Any man in his right senses doesn't get entangled with an unmarried woman!

I interviewed Lady Read (Herbert Read's wife), at Old Byland Hall in 1977.

SHERRY: How does he remain on such good terms with husbands? Why don't they take a shotgun to him?

LADY READ: Quite a lot of men are quite content that somebody should take their wives off their hands because women are left with seething energy long after men are, and men want to get on with their own lives. And to have a wife who is longing for sex – I think [husbands] are grateful to someone who comes along and takes them off [their hands].

Her novelist son, Piers Paul Read, suggested:

READ: Greene's not an obviously competitive man. I mean I don't think any man would feel humiliated and he wouldn't be a particularly humiliating person, would he – I mean for a writer and a family man?

SHERRY: You mean he would be shy and wouldn't make a fuss about it, and so it would be as if it hadn't taken place?

READ: That and the fact that we mustn't underestimate the gullibility of husbands. I mean, you know, a writer might seem to them like a priest – might think, 'Oh they are just good friends.'

Frere mentioned that Greene had many affairs which were 'short, sharp and pretty tempestuous while they lasted'. He added: 'I think his sexual appetites are voracious, frightening.' Again I quote David Higham in an interview in his London house in late 1978, making the same point: 'Without any question, he is a highly sexed man.' Peter Glenville added: 'His sexual stamina anyway has always astonished me, because it is endless.' Then I moved on to the husband issue – 'but it's amazing to me that he keeps so well in with husbands. Husbands don't turn against him.' I asked the same of the Sutros. Said Gillian:

GILLIAN: Because he is well-known.

JOHN: I think to a great degree that is the reason.

GILLIAN: They turn a blind eye . . . It's much easier for the husband to keep up the pretence game because they've got to keep up their side, you see. If husbands dropped the mask then this makes it much easier for everyone, doesn't it?

And then John Sutro told me more about the case of Jacques Cloetta:

JOHN: For the first dozen years, until he retired, [he] was for eight to nine months always away in Dahomey doing Consular work . . . Yvonne's husband you see was always in Africa.

GILLIAN: He obviously knows now, that's the trouble. [My interview was in 1977, some eighteen years after the Cloettas' first meeting with Greene in Dahomey.]

JOHN: And during the few months when Jacques came back from Africa, Graham went away to Paris, so for some years that is what happened.

GILLIAN: But if Yvonne goes off with Graham, she'll always say she is going off with a girlfriend. This is always the excuse.

I think this must be so. The Sutros were very close to Greene, both were his confidants. For fourteen years Jacques just did not know. And in an interview in a Fifth Avenue suite in New York, Otto Preminger told me:

When I was with Greene in his apartment in Antibes I told him that I'd be coming back . . . in June, July and August and he answered that he wouldn't be in Antibes during those months. And I said 'Why? I thought you lived there.' He said: 'Well, during these months my girlfriend's husband is coming home and I don't want to be in the way.'[14]

I remember Gillian Sutro's 1977 comment: 'Jacques obviously knows now.' Can we pinpoint when Jacques discovered the affair? I'd guess some time in 1973.

★

A letter of 9 October 1972 to Michael Meyer advises that Greene would love to see him on the Côte. Greene hoped Meyer and Yvonne could meet, but there was a problem: 'Yvonne's husband is now in retirement which is awkward but I hope we can arrange a meeting with the four of us.'

Yvonne had years of becoming more important in Greene's life, which dovetailed with Catherine's waning importance. Greene's love for Catherine Walston was, as we've seen, of an entirely different kidney from what he felt for Yvonne. For Catherine, Graham felt an urgent sexual attraction from the very beginning. Even after they parted, as her son Oliver personally confirmed to me, she was the same 'bewitching, exciting, unpredictable, shocking and sexy woman she had always been . . . still able to turn every male head when she walked into a crowded room'.[15]

David Higham, Greene's one-time agent, confirms this judgment. Higham met Catherine late in her life, then badly crippled with only two years to live.

I only saw Lady Walston once – she was a smashing blonde [actually light auburn], that one. Very tall Viking girl with a fine figure. I saw her at a party and I don't remember even talking to her, but I do remember being distinctly impressed.[16]

Oliver Walston describes his mother: 'energy, excitement, generosity and unpredictability' but not a traditional mother. 'She liked her children in short sharp bursts between the exciting episodes in her life . . . My mother would appear, preceded by a bow wave of Guerlain's Mitsouko perfume, and enthral us with an account of where she had been or was about to go.'[17] Oliver says that though he was only eighteen, in looking back on that period 'it is plain that my mother's long and painful decline started at almost exactly the time that she and Greene parted in 1959'.

I have heard from a different source that Greene taught her to drink – as if anyone could 'teach' that, but drink is what finally helped bring this beautiful woman down. And certainly, well past 1959, Greene tried to carry on with Catherine.

We have seen how difficult it was for Greene and Catherine to get together even before she broke her hip. Once that happened, it was almost impossible. I do not know how many operations she underwent, but in a letter written on 6 September 1969 to her younger sister, Belinda Straight, the total up to that date is shocking:

Dearest Binny, I suddenly heard the telephone ringing & I woke from a deep sleep to hear your voice . . . As I never keep a record of letters that I write . . . I can't remember telling you that I was to have operation No. 13 in October. I certainly didn't MEAN to tell you. It has completely stunned me. At first I wouldn't accept it.

She tells her sister she's too 'old and weak to face' the surgery, and even daily activities tire her. After bathing she has to lie down for ten minutes – all a 'bore' and an inconvenience. She asks no pity, wants no 'hand-holding':

> One is either OK and under drugs or pretty miserable without them. It's not like it was in Athens: what a good visit that was. I shall always be grateful to you for having come at that time . . . I had forgotten that in Athens the Dr thought it was an attack of DTs but finally diagnosed it as 'nutritional deficiency named Pellagra'.*

Catherine was out of the love stakes.

I asked Belinda why people, men and women (but mostly men) were so struck by her sister. In restaurants, people would notice her. Even as a teenager she carried herself well:

> She held her head high. She was dark, sort of auburn-coloured hair and wonderful eyes and short hair . . . fine cheekbones, rather widely spaced eyes, dark eyebrows. Her charisma was enormous. Also she wore her clothes with great flair. She was extremely modest physically. She didn't wear clothes that were daring.

She had her own style, consisting of 'raw silk, Thai silk, pyjama suits or cotton suits which she wore for twenty to thirty years in wonderful colours'. And she would go barefoot: 'She might wear a mink coat, some old blue jeans and bare feet.' Her sister did not think anything frightened Catherine. She was later worried over her health, but that was natural. She was afraid, though, of

> what would happen to her and Graham. As lovers they both knew as Catholics that they couldn't take communion, so certainly she was frightened and Graham was frightened too.

SHERRY: What drew your sister to Greene? Because he was good-lookingish? Because he was well known?

DR STRAIGHT: I am sure his writing was important to her, his dedication to that. His conversation to her . . . I mean I thought his face was sometimes quite tender and soft, often lively. But it was a face that haunted one and at times looked quite impenetrable.

---

* Her sister Belinda told me that the physician there, who was the King's doctor, was lying – it *was* delirium tremens – he was just covering up.

Not only was it a face that haunted, but also, in his depressions, he himself looked haunted, so sad and so pained.

*

While Catherine declined, Greene too began to grow old before his time. In June 1954, aged fifty, he wrote to Ragnar Svanstrom, who had himself just turned fifty, admitting that at their age 'one seems to have the same desires as at 20 and the same fears'. Greene tied these same desires *and* fears to Ragnar: 'Are you not still delighted when the stranger catches your eye at a crowded party, and are you not still daunted on arrival at the same party, voices echoing hollowly back, like they did in the school baths when we were 14?'

Into his sixties and seventies, he went through some illnesses: severe pneumonia had left him with a weak chest, and there was thought to be trouble with his liver. He was having tests constantly. Greene lived life hard. Only later, during his years with Yvonne, did he drink less. In these more reckless years, he moved around the world as much as ever, and needed to, for (as John Sutro said) 'if he had stopped travelling he would suddenly have become an old man'. John went with Graham to Amsterdam and Berlin:

> In Berlin we crossed over the border into East Berlin. Into the communist side to look at it and then walked back, and there was a sense of adventure. You have that feeling when you are with him. You never know what's going to happen. In Amsterdam, that was more normal Greene. We went to the streets where there were prostitutes but the women were ugly and so that was that and we went back to the hotel.

And Gillian added: 'He has a definite quirk for brothels. He likes them.'*

From a conversation with the Sutros and his other great friend A. S. Frere, we see his absolute need to move about. John Sutro answered one of my questions thus:

---

* He sought information about brothels. They fascinated Greene. Another friend I visited in South America tried to remember the kind of questions he asked. He recalled Greene asking about 'different prices according to what you wanted. The normal would cost about a dollar, something like a thousand pesos . . . there were several other ways, the price increased accordingly. Well you understand what the normal is. Then there [was] half-French, [with] a little bit of mouth work, if you see what I mean. Then the whole French was the mouth and normal. And then there is [the] complete or "the works" and that was the French and the rear approach – the whole thing. I can't [remember] the prices . . . but I just went and had a chat with one of the girls and she told me.'

Why all of his foreign journeys? The . . . curious thing about him . . . is the deep boredom because his work is finished rapidly and – then what does he do in the meantime? . . . He does so many words a day and then he stops. He kills time after that. There is a *time void* because he does his work with such swiftness.

In 1977, less than a year before Catherine died, Gillian Sutro echoed her husband's words regarding Yvonne:

They go off to Paris – they went to Greece just recently together. They go to Capri, they go to London. It works. I think if he didn't keep moving round the world he would become an old man. He needs it. He must do it. He doesn't smoke . . . He drinks much less. It is his hobby moving about like that.

In the summertime, he doesn't like it in Antibes, and he 'hops it':

Off he goes . . . [and] comes back in September. He leaves [at] the point when it is not nice. But he is here because of Yvonne. She's in her husband's home and he's in his apartment, which is almost side by side. He has chosen to live here because of her . . . He is very fond of her.

But was it love?

Well, something clearly approaching it. Frere, speaking as one who deeply admired Greene (Greene tried to help him at Heinemann's), referred to Greene's long years with Yvonne. He said others

were just short affairs. The present one has lasted so long and it is a great tribute to Yvonne, who has made a great deal of differ-ence to him . . . understood him and made him comfortable . . . She makes no intellectual demands on him.

SHERRY: But that's an incredible suggestion. A man of intense and superior intellect yet wants no intellectual demands made on him?
FRERE: I think other women did and it probably irked him a great deal. But this one, no.
SHERRY: That's a question I never asked. I assumed a great creative imagination, also something of a dialectician – masterly in argument – such natural quickness of perception, of penetration, wouldn't he desire a female with parallel sharpness of intellect? Without that,

Greene would feel he had been buried alive. I can't imagine Greene being attracted to a pretty girl who was a bimbo.

FRERE: It isn't quite like that. I think he found Yvonne restful. She was very nice and he was *very, very* fond of her.

SHERRY: Fondness, even great fondness, is not love.

FRERE: It works for him, and he can keep up the pretence of it being an affair still. There's a husband in the background after all. There's always trouble if a man gets involved with an unmarried woman. He liked having mistresses. I don't think he would think of it positively, but he had a Vietnamese mistress.

One's sexual life slows down a bit, surely, and so you haven't got the same urges . . . Yvonne's such a darling – so good for him . . . makes absolutely no demands on him at all. Insofar as he's happy being comfortable – she makes him comfortable. There were some considerable periods in Graham's life when he was only *happy* when he was being *unhappy*.

Here is a last word from Frere:

> One reason he can work in Antibes is that Yvonne doesn't bother him. He's always alone when he wants to be. She only comes when he wants her. That's why he likes it there.

*

If Greene is only 'very, very fond' of Yvonne, he's careful never to say anything that suggests comparison to previous lovers, Anita Björk or Catherine Walston. Greene continues to write to Catherine at the time he is also writing to Yvonne. Ultimately, Catherine becomes too sick to see Greene, and the correspondence tapers off.

Writing to Yvonne from his favourite New York hotel, the Algonquin, on 30 December 1964, Greene breaks into sometimes sexual French phrases in the middle of letters written chiefly in English:

> I'm completely quiet – not even erotic dreams. I'm only excited by you now & have only curiosity about you & only want to think of your body – the *petit chat, tes seins, tes fesses*.[*]

---

[*]'Little pussy, your breasts, your bottom'.

We notice even in the middle of 1964, five years on in their love affair, how Greene takes great care not to press Yvonne:

> Unless you tell me No, I shall be at Nice the 11th & 12th [August 1964]. Darling heart, think carefully about that & whether it will make things for you better or worse. I return to London to drown myself in [*Carving a Statue*] . . . Send me word if you can to Anacapri & where I'm to go. I asked Mimi to try to get me a room at the Royal or the Hotel de la Mer, but then I realised that you would have no car. Perhaps the Grand Hotel Juana would be better so that you could just walk over . . . I long for news of you. All my love forever, *comme* Everest – *avec la neige*, & a kiss [which I presume, loosely translated, to mean 'as Everest always has snow, my love is forever'].[18]

In 1964, his love for Yvonne is still tentative. He is older, but not yet the 'Old Fox'. He is in fact uncertain:

> Darling, I'm a little anxious because there's no word from Mimi about an hotel. Will you . . . tell me whether you still want me to come . . . The rehearsals start today & I *must* be back on the 13th. Perhaps it will be too difficult . . . to see each other for a few hours & then be off again. I shan't think you don't love me if you say no! . . . I have no problem like you & I'll come happily if you telegraph me the name of the hotel . . . My darling in my case I love you & only love you & desire no one but you. It's still easy to be *sage* [well-behaved]![19]

Greene then mentions how he arrived at six at Anacapri and took Dottoressa Moor to Capri for a drink, looking at all 'the pretties – but there were no *fesses* to compare with *les plus belles du monde* [the most beautiful in the world'.*

The affair seemed to be escalating towards commitment. Is Greene being cagey? In 1949 he'd used every verbal weapon at his disposal to persuade Catherine to leave Harry. The contrast in his communication with Yvonne is startling, but without making the comparison with his previous love, what Greene writes seems fair, honest, and the expression of a man in love. To Yvonne:

---

* Greene continues: 'We had dinner at Gemma's who was very sweet & welcoming (I am her favourite!) but her husband is going off his head & 3 days ago attacked the waiters & tried to strangle them in the middle of dinner, but last night he was here & [fine] – the waiters & no one would have known. That's very Capri.'

My darling, I wish I could help you more & be near you. I want you to live with me — but I want you to live with me without regrets. If we could stand the present situation for one year more — or two at most — the time would have arrived when it would probably be *better* for the children to be *en pension* [boarding school]. But if the break comes earlier I'll do all I can to make you happy.[20]

Greene is trying his level best to prove his love, if not now at least *in a year or two*. It looks as if Yvonne wishes, as early as 1964, long before Jacques took retirement, for Greene to acquaint him with the fact that a love affair is going on. Four days after his 20 August 1964 letter, Greene composes a letter to Jacques which he describes to Yvonne:

It's 10 o'clock in the evening. I've eaten a small trout & drank a glass of Guinness . . . & I've thought a great deal! As a result I've written — but not sent! — the draft of a letter to Jacques, explaining things & proposing things, in a reasonable & friendly way. The letter seems to me to make sense for all of us. I'll show it to you when we meet & see what you think. It might be a good thing to send it — say a month or two before he returns again, so that he could think about it & perhaps meet me & talk about it when he comes back.

I feel so sure, my darling, that we can live together without hurting the children.[21]

The letter was not sent then, and never was.

A surprising trait in Greene's letters to Yvonne, as opposed to those to Catherine, is his tendency to fill them with details of meals and drink. Is this because he has little to say, or feels the need to add on to the short letters in a language not her own, or because, as an older man, he's less concerned with 'adventures' and more with food? Perhaps he's weary and finds that small-talk takes less out of him. We can't know, but life does not become less interesting because he is in France, on the Côte. Soon he will be travelling extensively into South America, Nicaragua, Panama, and becoming involved in mini-wars. Undoubtedly much of his energy is taken by his journeys, and only a minuscule amount is needed for writing love letters to Yvonne.

Yvonne was a lively person. Her smile is what I remember — that, and a certain sense of self-satisfaction. I suspect that the matter of her leaving Jacques was allowed simply to percolate down into nothing.

She returned to her husband after Graham died, never having really left Jacques completely. After her mother's death on 3 November 2001, Martine said in interview with a journalist in the *Sunday Mail*, 17 March 2002, that the affair between her mother and the writer distressed her father 'greatly'. But Shirley Hazzard indicates that Martine was not the least bit disturbed by their relationship. Greene treated her as a daughter.

I've said (because others have said it to me) that she was thirty when she met Graham. I have now heard that she was eighty when she died and must have been therefore thirty-eight when she met Graham. Also Yvonne put it about that she did not sleep with Graham immediately but another source suggests it happened on their first meeting.

★

Greene expected rehearsals of *Carving a Statue* to be over by 5 September 1964. He is fed up with life, with his play (as we've seen), and even his family. Yvonne seems the only hope:

> My darling, darling, darling, I can't believe that in two weeks I'll be free from this bloody play – all the bickerings & intrigues that go with it, & we'll be together. I have never in England had such an awful time with a play. Ralph [Richardson] is *impossible*. Last night I lost my temper completely with him at 2 in the morning. I go to bed too late, I work like a slave, I drink too much in order to keep going. There has been no fun whatever in this production. If I could get out of going to the first night I would. I hate the whole affair & am determined never to do a play again. All other annoyances come too – my son telephones – he still hasn't got a job, & I said I was too busy to see him. Then today a cable from my American agent saying my wife wants 500 dollars . . . I say yes, but I'd paid her passage first class and given her 700 dollars for expenses and a few weeks ago she had more than £3000 from the MS sale. I long to break away completely . . . I long to say you can't have any more because I have another family to look after [he has in mind Yvonne's two daughters]. My darling, this is rather a hysterical letter, but I feel lonely without you & I'm tired, tired, tired.

On 19 September 1964 he is to meet Yvonne: 'Oh how good it will be that everything, including the play, is over & you beside me with peace & excitement at the Colombe d'Or. I long for it.' Later Greene asked Miss Reid to book from Paris 'for October 2 & 3 & touch wood. Two dry Martinis for my birthday and a long siesta', and adds: 'oh, what joy it will be when *le petit cheval* [the little horse] takes me up the road to St Paul'.[22]

There are still letters to Catherine during the rest of that year. Two weeks later, right after his sixtieth birthday, he writes from Antibes 'My dearest Catherine':

> Your letter made me miss you a great deal. Those years – even with their melancholies & anxieties – were the best of my life. I will never love ever again as I loved you. What I experience now is a kind of second-best, a sweet second-best but second-best all the same. I feel very much my age, I no longer get a great deal of pleasure out of the sexual life & could easily if I were alone give it up. But without intending to I've altered Yvonne's life a great deal & I have a responsibility & she is very attached to me & keeps solitude at bay. [Had Yvonne any more significant a role than this?] You will always be the most important to me of all.
>
> I'm so sorry things are so slow & still so painful. Let's think of Capri in terms of next year & plan well ahead – what about Easter there? and why not, in November or December or January go back to Vienna & see the Dottoressa working on her autobiography with her 'ghost' – I have arranged it all.[23]

But if he stayed true to Yvonne in real life in Antibes (or at least until he had travelled out of the country), before the end of the year, on the night of 20 December 1964, he was not so faithful in his dreams:

> An erotic entanglement of which it's difficult to disentangle the details. I was to go to Hong Kong with Y. to work, when a friend of mine . . . told me that Madame X, an attractive woman of about 40 with short curly black hair, asked me directly if my friend had spoken to me [the sexual meaning here is apparent]. I said yes, but there were difficulties on this occasion. I would ring her up from London if she would give me her telephone & arrange a special trip. (I was unable to say No directly to a woman.) The party broke up & a woman took me on one side to give me Mme X's telephone number. She said she was sorry to do it; she hated the idea of my betraying Y. I explained to her the situation & that I had no intention of betraying Y, but a little later – I think in a carriage – I found myself pressed against Mme X who touched my 'cig' which was in erection through my grey

flannel trousers. Y. was in the carriage just opposite to us & I tried to detach myself. 'If I can't do it to you, you can do it to me,' Mme X said & began to engage Y. in conversation while I put a hand below her & felt for her under her olive corduroy skirt. Strange to say that with my fingers only I could tell that she wore a black slip & black culottes [knickers].[24]

Just a dream, but what a dream . . .

★

Greene was, during the autumn and winter of 1964, feeling strange. In the letter written to Catherine five days after his birthday, he describes a puzzling physical episode while eating an egg and tea when he got a 'pins & needles' sensation in his fingers, 'which turned white & I thought I was going to faint & lay down & then I really thought I was in for a stroke'.

After the gruelling experience putting together *Carving a Statue*, his trouble with Ralph Richardson, the long hours in rewriting, late rehearsals sometimes past four in the morning, and his feeling that a stroke was imminent, he presses on and seems much better. 'Yesterday & today I'm much better. I work hard – I've done more than 7,000 on the novel [*The Comedians*] since I came away – apart from an opening page of a book called *The Last Decade* to be published post-humously, & *The Night Life of a Sexagenarian* which is a dream diary.' If Greene had overseen the publication of the selection of dreams, I suspect it would have had the more sexually provocative title above, rather than the tame one eventually chosen. He began his first dream diary on 6 October 1964, and worked unceasingly on it for twenty-six years, training himself to wake up and record his dreams. Sadly, the present published version is heavily abridged, and has the tedious title of *A World of My Own*. The soul of it has been diluted by heavy cutting, the genius of Greene taken away.

★

The news from Newton Hall is that Harry Walston was joining the Foreign Office as a junior minister. Greene admits to Catherine: 'The Foreign Office, I can't help feeling, is more amusing than agriculture, & a sprinkling of lemon is badly required by that dull fish, [Patrick] Gordon Walker.'* And he ends his letter of 21 October by inviting

---

* At that time Foreign Secretary, and father-in-law of Graham Carleton Greene, Hugh's son.

Catherine to see the latest James Bond movie, *Goldfinger*. He has set himself a quota of writing 6,000 words a month, but adds he's 'not very happy about *The Comedians* & it becomes more Communist day by day – which won't help it with the critics'.[25] It was almost as if the novel were writing itself, at least determining the direction it should take, and there's real truth in this thought so far as Greene is concerned. He liked his subconscious to influence his material.

He's heard from his secretary that Catherine is up and about, and admits that, 'in the end', he went to see *Goldfinger* without her, which he didn't enjoy, 'perhaps because you weren't there'. He tells her he's not feeling well, 'the buto-solydin I've been taking for sciatica, perhaps just age. Anyway nothing really to complain about to you, my poor darling.'[26]

In an undated letter Greene reveals his hopes that Catherine might recover: 'I was so relieved when I rang up Harry early on Friday that the examination had been satisfactory. Lots of people have been praying for you. Now for the hip to mend properly. Perhaps the worst is over?' It was not.

He tells her he'll 'be coming back (before the dreary visit to Canada) not later than December 18. I do hope the operation will be over & you well enough to be seen.'[27] Catherine underwent surgery in early December, and Greene wrote to her after learning of her ordeal from his French literary agent: 'My poor darling thank God that's over & perhaps the healing will really begin now with proper speed.'[28]

*

Back on 4 December 1964, writing *The Comedians* in Antibes, we see Greene's lonely life, but it is a self-imposed loneliness. In writing, especially with *The Comedians*, he was striving to get figs from thistles; and in light of the failure of *Carving a Statue*, he was under the strongest pressure:

Last night, walking down the ramparts all alone to my dinner at Félix [his favourite restaurant], I saw the most extraordinary falling star, if it was a star. It fell like lightning behind the mountains, but of enormous size & brilliance, the size of a child's balloon. I wonder whether it was a satellite coming to an end.
. . . after that I'll read the papers, & then . . . [finish the day] at Félix with an escalope & a half bottle of Pouilly.

Greene seems to be writing to Catherine every two days. She had written to him and their letters crossed: 'Thank goodness that awful operation's over' and 'of course I'll see you before Canada. I'll be back on Thursday, the 17th. If you feel up to it, can I come & see you during the weekend. I'd leave my Christmas present.' But we learn she's not at home: 'If you want to give me a nice Christmas present give me a tie & socks to go with it, though, poor darling, I don't see how you can really choose them in the London Clinic.'[29]

★

With Greene, what he sees is what he speaks – his pale magnetic eyes never missing a trick. Here's a letter to Yvonne from the Taj Mahal Hotel, Bombay, on Christmas Eve, 1963:

> It was a long long journey here I hardly slept at all. I was met by an Indian Professor & two girls who had stayed up from 4.30 am . . . my friend arrived last evening & I had an orgy – for Bombay in my room – with my bottle of whisky. The two girls . . . an Indian priest, my friend and I and the professor (he was the only one who didn't drink). We were breaking the law, of course, but it didn't matter as all the hotel servants are Catholics! I had tea with the Cardinal, a magnificent creature, taller than me, with his dark face & scarlet cap. Very easy & very intelligent & very virile. He walked back with me down the street, lepers sitting with begging bowls outside his house.

This Cardinal is a main source of *The Comedians*' wonderful Dr Magiot, a 'tall elderly Negro with a Roman face blackened by the soot of cities and with hair dusted with stone', who is most upright, who gives 'the kind of bow with which a Roman emperor might have brought an audience to an end' – Greene's impressive Cardinal in Bombay.

★

Into 1965, before the end of January, and still *The Comedians* goes on. Greene tells Catherine he has reached 67,000 words, then:

> I think I shall stay here [Antibes] till about Feb 16 . . . With any luck I shall have reached 75,000 by then & be really on the last lap. After my dry Martini in the evening at Félix's, I keep on writing different last pages! I & the old patronne are great buddies now, as I am generally the only person there [it's winter and no tourists are about] & her son is away in Cannes playing bridge in one of the hotels.
>
> Do send me a line how you are, darling, & when you expect to be up.[30]

Now, even so close to finishing his novel, he feels duty bound to visit Dottoressa in Vienna. 'I must keep my promise to her if only for a few days.'[31] He stops working for a while. (Also he has to find time to write an article on the recently deceased Pope John XXIII for the *Sunday Times*.) The next communication is a postcard from Vienna: 'Here we are, eating, drinking hard (the Dottoressa has drunk half a glass of beer) & missing you. The book [her memoirs] takes great strides except today when the two publishers & the ghost have hangovers.'[32] Though Greene could not know it then, he would himself have to complete her book:

> Today I lunched with the publisher & the ghost: they are absolutely delighted − only two more weeks of typing needed, & they'll publish in the autumn of next year. There are stories which even you & I have never heard! . . . I really feel I've created a scandalous best seller.[33]

Returning to Antibes, he had difficulty getting back to his novel. For one thing he'd been under the weather and had cancelled a date with Ronald Matthews and French writer René de Berval. When he did see Matthews for a drink, Greene learnt that his friend had undergone prostate surgery:

> My generation seems to have entered a decade of operations, breakdowns, deaths. Harold [Acton], John Sutro, Ronald [Matthews] − and there are rumours that Evelyn is ill. [Waugh had a year to live.] And I talk of flus & colds when poor you . . .[34]

In early March Greene visited Catherine in the clinic, but by 16 March he is deeply troubled by her condition, and by her determination to travel, presumably with her husband:

> My poor darling, I'm so sorry about the pain. You seemed so much better when I saw you in hospital & I hoped the worst was over. What do the surgeons say? I'm rather terrified of your Far East trip. When would you leave? Do do be prudent. Pain in Tokyo may not be worse than pain in Newton [Hall], but you'll be tempted all the time to do too much.[35]

★

He is now back at work on *The Comedians*, having finished 79,000 words. But it is still not finished. He complains of fever and of having to take antibiotics, and he yearns for an old remedy − hot whisky and aspirins! Even illness is something to be angry over: 'I'm maddened because I'd planned to reach 85,000 this March & finish the book in April. Now it looks like dragging into May.'³⁶ But, like the 'little railway engine that could', he keeps on keeping on. He writes again to Catherine on 25 March, quite open about his mistress, the references casual:

> I'm going to Paris with Yvonne on the 30th & she will stay till the 6th . . . I'll come back to London on April 7 or 8. Will you be out of the London Clinic by then? Can I make you a visit? Perhaps a mid-week is better than a week-end to avoid politicians* . . . I don't suppose I'll stay in London more than ten days because I'd determined to get the draft of this devilish book off my shoulders by the end of April – the flu has put me behind schedule. I'll work on it alone in Paris.

In England his brother puts him back on antibiotics, and Greene decides to go back to his friends the Stonors 'to continue a regime of mornings & afternoons in bed. Then if all is well, I'll go to Paris (alone) [he has now twice stressed he will be alone in his flat in Paris] to continue work on Wednesday after Easter.'³⁷ But he can work mornings only, because of visitors, including Réné de Berval and Peter Glenville, 'absolutely unchanged after 15 years with the same Bill Smith'.³⁸

So he's off to Antibes to finish *The Comedians*, but on the back of the envelope is a message: 'You see I arranged another revelation in Santo Domingo, but it's come too soon & is interfering with the last chapter of the novel', indicating he gave Catherine the manuscript to read, trusting her literary savvy. 'I saw Harry's *bon mot* about sailing ships – you obviously don't vet his speeches as you used to do his writing.'³⁹ And in a letter written the same day from Antibes: 'The donkey smells the carrot. I've reached 90,000 today – longer than any book I've ever written & there should be another 8,000 to come.' He adds: 'I feel it's as long as *War & Peace*.'

By 10 May, he was able to pronounce that 'the book is rushing to an end – I've passed 95,000 & tomorrow start the last chapter in Santo Domingo. It will reach 100,000 which is enormous for me – almost a quarter as long again as *The Heart of the Matter*.' He hoped to return to London on Sunday, 16 May, with the book finished. His American agent was coming through that week to pick it up.

---

* As we've seen in Bonte Durán's letters, leading Labour politicians congregated at Newton Hall at weekends.

Catherine went back into hospital. She thought the plans for Capri should be cancelled, but Greene decides to hold on to the tickets until the last moment. Also, he suggests that Catherine's personal attendant come along: 'Would it be easier for you to take Miss Bitoff, for helping dress etc. She could live in the big house & we need never see her for meals!' And: 'Shall we go direct to Naples? Can you fit into a helicopter? . . . But perhaps it would be less tiring to go straight to Capri.'[40]

And the book, on 13 May, is still not finished: 'Reached 98,000 today. About 3,000 more to go.' That is the end of Greene's comments, only 3,000 to go. But he does not stop. A postcard dated well into June – the 28th – from Antibes tells the latest score: 'Got up at 6 a.m. on Saturday & finished revision of first typescript. Now for second in Capri. Terribly hot.'

Catherine actually *did* make it to Anacapri, after being in a Dublin hospital in May with inflammation of the pancreas. On 11 July, Greene writes to Yvonne about Catherine: 'The days in Anacapri have passed very peaceably & well with no strain. I think C. already looks much better for the holiday. She sleeps a lot & reads.' What follows may be minimised for Yvonne's sake: 'I'm really glad that I've done this for her.' And, lying in bed, Catherine, the most generous of women, would have worked on Greene's second revisions of his manuscript of *The Comedians*. It was published at last in January 1966, in the United Kingdom and America.

*

On 5 July 1965, aboard a plane to Antibes, 'for more than half an hour we were tossed about the sky like a ball – I said many Hail Marys! It must have been the edge of the awful typhoon which hit North Italy yesterday morning.' Could this be fear of death? But there are numerous examples of his desiring life to end:

> I'm not working well & I don't like my life, but I've made it, & it's not the fault of anyone but myself. Thank God, ⁶⁄₇ths of it is over. The thought of another sixty years would be intolerable, but the years 1948–58 remain the best of all & make up for all the rest.[41]

So his love for Catherine endures: to her alone the title of 'his best years' belongs. His fondness for Yvonne is strong, despite his deliberate playing down of the sexual side of his life in his letter to Catherine, and the idea of not being able to see Yvonne when he wants her physically, because of her husband's schedule, deeply troubles him.

There is a diary entry on 16 February where Graham notes: 'Woke up finding myself in a state of erection and putting my hand down found I was enclosed in Y's *petit chat*. She said, "You've kept it there a long time."'[42]

34

Warming Up to the Cold Scots

'A Serbonian bog of politics'
— PROFESSOR BLACK

IN another month, near the end of August 1965, Greene has a letter from Catherine, who is flying back to England to go into hospital. He writes to Yvonne: 'Gall bladder again, & a fourth major operation in two years. All this & the Roe business will make a summer to remember. My God.'[1] By November, Catherine has had yet more surgery. During this time Greene visits his childhood home, Berkhamsted, which makes him very unhappy.

To Catherine from Paris he writes of planning a trip to the capital of Georgia, on 17 January 1966: a journey he did not make. In the same month he read a good book on Paraguay – 'which I've always wanted to visit' – *The People and the River* by Gordon Meyer. It was Paraguay (and the adjoining Argentina as well as Chile, Panama and Nicaragua) that he later did visit, and there he found his destined creativity.

By 3 April, Greene hears from his French literary agent that Catherine has been in the London Clinic again, and this time (one suspects) she's to be 'dried out'. He writes to Catherine, genuinely distressed. His feelings for Yvonne are a few rungs lower on the ladder of love:

I feel so out of touch. If only you could realise how much you are loved – not only by me. There has never been anyone in my life whom I have loved as I love you – & I hate not knowing when things are bad for you. (OK, We are not lovers now in the technical sense – but like it or not I'm your lover as long as I'm alive & I want to know about you & share bad things with you.)

He then gives her his phone number in Paris. He comments that

Catherine writes only when she has good news (and that is rare) and tells her: 'You are the bravest woman I've ever known . . . but thank God you can be cured at the end of all this appalling pain, disappointment . . . For God's sake I don't want you only cheerful.' Then he refers to the mysterious marriage: 'For better for worse applied at Tunbridge Wells & applies now.'[2]

By April, Greene was working hard on the film script for *The Comedians*. To Catherine: 'I get up each day at 7 & begin work before 8. I've done about 60 pages now (out of 180) of the first rough draft. Every three days or so I go over to Cap Ferrat & spend a night to go over the stuff with [Peter Glenville].' Dinner with the Freres was so 'delectable' that it put him out of action for twenty-four hours with a 'crise de foie'.[3]

★

Sometimes we get the impression that Greene would not have married again even if he had divorced Vivien. He didn't seem to have the temperament. In his sixty-second year, he is easily irritated and grouchy when his personal space is encroached upon. In his Antibes apartment he hosts his son, now in his thirtieth year, and a friend – a girl:

> (pretty, intelligent, Catholic – but I have no conviction that they do anything) to this Antibes flat. How I hated the squalor of other people's things everywhere, & the young are wildly egotistical – they would only have semi-cleaned up the kitchen etc. if I hadn't insisted. And I'm cross-eyed with work. Easter no Easter for me . . .
>
> Now I'm going to have a sleep before getting back on to script & then walking to Félix for dinner & dry Martini. Thank God, the young people have gone with their toothbrushes & their hair lacquer & I've washed the artificial eyelashes down the wash basin.

As we saw in the last chapter, he is happy about the film script of *The Comedians*:

> More cheerfully Peter & I suddenly hit on an idea for an end which will cut off an hour playing time & at least ten days work. Burton has written me a very nice enthusiastic letter accepting the part of Brown. Alec Guinness is keen to play Jones, & Vanessa Redgrave who has just made a huge sexy success in America with a film called *Morgan* wants to play Martha. Nothing settled. All between me & you & the London Clinic bedpost.[4]

He labours hard. Here is a day in the life of Graham Greene:

> Miss Reid is back in London for two days fetching clothes as Peter G. (or rather MGM are paying for her to stay on till the end of June) – it makes all the difference having her. My routine now is to get up at 7 & begin work at 7.30. By the time Miss R looks in at 10 I've done about 8 m.s. pages – she brings it in typed at lunch time & takes letters. Then back at 5 for more work.

It was the same on Saturday and Sunday:

> but [she] has a lot of spare time all the same. Usually P. has me fetched Tuesday morning & I stay till Wednesday after lunch going through things. Tuesday Alec Guinnes & his wife are staying . . .

He hated the work, but hoped for a rough version by the end of May, and then felt it would come easier:

> P[eter] is much better to work with than Carol – more imaginative & more grasp of character. Bill Smith, of course, is there, & P. has mellowed a great deal – perhaps because of riches. He owns his own apartment building in New York!

We have diaries proving the obvious – Graham's love of books – but now he has no time for reading 'except at dinner & in bed, so I've only finished one book about the retreat from Kabul which I found fascinating & horrifying – *Signal Catastrophe* by Macrory'.[5]

He hears of an additional saga of Catherine's illnesses, which seem to go on and on. Greene's frustration is in his reply to her on 16 May 1966: 'Again! Why do those bloody doctors allow you out too soon? My darling, I'm so sorry. Let this be the last time & come & rest up a little in Capri in August.'

He is to leave in two days, 'to entertain a dozen Haitian exiles in the Paris apartment'. And all the time he is trying to get ahead with the film script. His habit had always been to get up at 7 a.m. to begin work at 7.30. Now he's up before 7 in order to begin by 7, and he's hoping to have the 'real script finished by the end of June'. And while we know that the film was finally shot in Dahomey, at this point they didn't know if it was to be 'Brazil, Martinique, or even Madagascar'.

It is Catherine he first tells that he's putting an initial payment on 'a really beautiful little flat, brand new, all windows, even the kitchen, facing the sea . . . looking out over the port [of Antibes], the fort,

Nice & the mountains . . . I expect to be installed by the autumn. This will be the present the film makes me.'[6] He also tells one of his closest friends, Michael Meyer, in an undated letter that out of 'detestable film work on *The Comedians*, I have bought a flat in Antibes the brand new looking out over the guaranteed old, the Port, Vauban's Fort, Nice & the Alps & now having installed the necessary sticks I return to Paris'.[7]

Greene is happy. He is working well, tells Catherine he's written in longhand more than 250 pages, and promises that she can read the script as soon as it's finished and properly typed – for her judgment still mattered to him. Also (referring to the great Harry Ransom library at the University of Texas in Austin), he wonders 'what Texas will pay for all the drafts. I've unloaded *The Comedians* on [them] & a lot of bits & pieces for 15,000 dollars.' This money will not be going to a Tom Roe trickster; that sort of loss cannot be sustained again. 'Furthermore, I'm taking the money myself this time & not giving it to the family.'

We get a good account of his day: 'I'm reading practically nothing as I work all the morning, sleep in the afternoon & work again after dinner.' In a postscript he mentions that his friend Archbishop David Mathew is 'ill with jaundice & [David's brother] Gervase as usual being a nuisance'.[8]

The next letter to Catherine is undated, but was probably written in June:

> Soon I'll have been nearly six months out of England. I haven't had the time to miss roast beef or beer, only people – & of people you are the only serious 'miss'.[9]

Working flat-out now, he is up by 6.45 a.m., takes a dexedrine and works all day, takes a sleeping pill at night. 'I do this for two days & then for one day I drop the dexedrine. Anything to finish the script.' He is pushing hard. To Catherine he writes:

> Capri, darling . . . I pray to finish the script on June 30. I've postponed the usual 10 day spring holiday with Y until July 2. If all goes well I could meet you in Paris or Rome say July 15 . . . Or I'd meet you & the boat wherever you arrive – Venice? – at the end of August & we'd have a fortnight of September.

His enduring love for Catherine is intensified because of her physical decline – he wants to look after her, and again presses her:

This after-work, after-dinner letter is muddled. I'd love for us to have a holiday — whichever suits you best — either between July 15 & Aug 5 — I'd deliver you to the boat — or between your return at the end of August & Sep 15 — I'd fetch you from the boat. Dear love, love.

On 10 June he tells Catherine that he hasn't yet received payment for his novel: 'I live on a shoestring & a Swiss overdraft', and that he's 'never in my life felt so tired. 4 days on dexedrine. The last night up till 2 & every day giving myself breakfast between 6.30 & 7. Today a load has dropped off one's shoulders. In actual handwriting I must have written the length of a novel in 3–4 months.'

*

But Greene did not take Catherine to Capri. Instead he went to Cuba, invited by the *Sunday Telegraph* to assess Castro's first seven years in power. Clearly Greene's fancy was tickled: 'The *Telegraph* want me to go back to Cuba — but it depends a) on Peter [Glenville] b) on Castro's attitude & c) on my laziness. I would have to fly from Prague or Madrid . . . the weather would be terribly hot & it's the hurricane season.'[10]

By 16 August, he's going to Havana by way of Madrid, with limited expectations: 'I expect to . . . wander around much more, but I think it will be a sadder Cuba than even three years ago . . . I hope we've got a nice ambassador in Havana.'[11] Instead he 'came back loaded with presents', including 'a crocodile brief case from the woman [the heroine Haydée Santamaria] I met in hiding in 1957, who is now in charge of Latin American relations'.

Greene recounts meeting Castro, on his last night in Havana. The British ambassador had put on a private dinner for Greene, but before it had truly begun, Greene was fetched away by a messenger — and that was the end of his dinner with the ambassador. Greene had a three-hour conversation with the dictator, and the ambassador 'was quite jealous as he hasn't spoken more than two words to Castro . . . Altogether it was quite a show — I wish I didn't have to write about it.'[12]

Greene liked Castro enormously, but his attitude towards the dictator would vacillate when he was discouraged by what Castro was doing. To Catherine, referring to her husband, who by this time had met Castro and praised him, Greene stressed his delight that Harry liked Castro: 'He's the only Great Man I've ever met whom I thoroughly liked & admired.'[13]

A postcard to Catherine gives some notion of how well he was being treated:

Got back yesterday, after 3 weeks averaging 4 hrs sleep a night – wonderful time. Fidel gave me a lovely flower painting by this man Portocarrero whom I like . . . Had a car at my disposal, & a . . . military plane! Saw all my old friends including my taxi driver of 1958 and 1959.* I'll write properly when I get rested & to Antibes (tomorrow) . . . No socialist realism in Cuba! Lots of love.[14]

Greene wrote Catherine a long letter on 28 November. He was upset by the way his correspondence sometimes failed to reach her. So he tells the story again – an enlargement of what appeared on the post-card:

I had a wildly energetic and fatiguing time there. Real red carpet treatment. A cadillac car with a French-speaking chauffeur, my friend Pablo as companion, and I went from one end of the island to the other. Raul Castro gave me a military plane to take me to the Isle of Pines and Fidel (whom I liked enormously, I spent three hours of my last night with him) gave me a lovely flower painting by Portocarrero which he inscribed on the back.

His willing hosts wanted to put him up in style, but instead he went to an hotel:

My articles (not very good) are coming out in the *Weekend Telegraph* on December 2 and 9. I've written to Harry [Walston, now a Foreign Affairs minister] asking him to give some messages for me there. Portocarrero gave me a very nice drawing and Milian [an important painter] whom he lives with and I like generally better (though the flower painting is brilliant) gave me a painting and another one of his was given me by Franqui, one of Fidel's henchmen . . . All are hanging now in Antibes, quite a Cuban gallery.[15]

So Greene was given VIP treatment, indeed almost like a head of state. Many left-wing leaders and left-wing dictators in South America found it politically prudent to treat the famous Greene well. He was a useful and worthy friend. How could this brilliant mind be so easily taken in?

* A man who gave Greene and Catherine a harmless powder which they thought was cocaine. A year later Greene met him again and he apologised and ran them all over the island for free.

★

Writing while Catherine is abroad, he asks her to telephone after her trip to Italy and Greece. He expects to be in Paris until the end of October and lets her know that Yvonne will be with him for a week. Greene's determination to inform her when he's with Yvonne must have exhausted Catherine, but this man leaves nothing out of his letters,[16] including, lately, boring things like the fact that he's going off lunch because food never seems to agree with him: 'hope it's not an ulcer – probably effect of too much rum.'[17] He also mentions that he gave an impromptu broadcast in French to Haiti from Havana. It would be the strongest stuff he could muster against the hated Duvalier regime. Papa Doc, still in power, had more than four years to live.

Six days after his return to Paris from Havana, Greene went on to Capri for a short holiday and then back to Paris to meet Glenville to talk about the film. He tells Yvonne they'd gone to 'an awful rich socialite dinner' with various guests including 'an absurd Marquis de Something who was once married to Gloria Swanson & even sent me [when Greene was a film reviewer] anonymously (I think he had forgotten) an envelope full of shit because I had made fun of his terrible film'. He did not go to bed until 2 a.m. He tells her he feels the film is 'about 20 pages too long but no one can see where to cut it & everyone is enthusiastic. Alec [Guinness] has written that it's the best script he's ever read!' Graham mentions his fear that Jacques Cloetta 'might be invalided back to France'.[18]

Back on the island of Capri he writes to Yvonne:

Such a drama when I got here yesterday at 7.30 by the Aliscafo boat because they told me at the airport there was too much wind for the helicopter. No one to meet me at the port – I was glad, but my taximan told me a long story in Italian about the Dottoressa & Aniello which I couldn't understand. Near the house, I came on the Dottoressa in tears. She said, 'But you are dead!' Apparently, she and Aniello had met every boat until they thought the last one had arrived, & then they learnt that a helicopter had fallen into the sea between Ischia & Capri coming from Naples & the two passengers had been drowned & they had decided it was me! *Quelle drame!*[19]

He is seeing only the Dottoressa, and he's working:

I lead a very quiet routine here. Carmelina, Aniello's wife [both Aniello and his wife looked after Greene's house and attended to him], comes & gives me breakfast at 8, then I work on a *nouvelle*, then I find an excuse to walk up to the village, Carmelina gives me lunch at 12 – one dish, then I work again, have a siesta, perhaps go for a walk with the Dottoressa, & then down to Capri with her, a drink in the piazza, dinner at Gemma's, bus home to bed. I shall have had enough of the poor old thing by the 9th [August].[20]

★

Suddenly in an undated letter to Catherine, probably around July 1966, we come across the story which the Sutros mentioned in interview with me describing Greene's nerves. They told me how the relentless drilling in the street one night pushed him to take an electric bulb out of its socket and throw it down at the workmen. Greene tells only part of the story here: 'For 11 hours an electric drill has been going on outside the window, but I escape to Paris tomorrow.'[21]

He gives Catherine his new address: 'Résidence des Fleurs, Avenue Pasteur, 06 Antibes with a few sticks of furniture only to have the road drill start up'. He's very happy with his new apartment – not a good omen for any possible return to England when and if his tax problems are resolved.

★

On 26 October 1966, Greene sends another telegram to Catherine, this time to Athens, for she is ailing again. Just the now familiar: 'SO SORRY TO HEAR YOUR ILLNESS GET WELL QUICK LOVE GRAHAM'. He probably was not told what was now her major problem: alcohol.

Catherine had suffered much pain over the original hip break when she slipped on some steps at the airport, followed by a first operation, botched at an Irish hospital. Never to be well again, often confined to bed, either preparing for another operation or recovering from one, she began to drink more and more. Her husband tried to stop her. The tale I heard was that a favoured servant kept smuggling in whisky, which no doubt Catherine asked for – this led to at least the one attack of delirium tremens mentioned earlier, and I suspect her many visits to the London Clinic were for periodic dry-outs. Both Catherine's sisters, the eldest (Bonte Durán) and youngest (Belinda Straight), spoke to me about this terrible decline. Catherine, the most beautiful of women, was becoming haggard – her beauty daily consumed, though Greene, the loving gentleman, never spoke of it.

About the time of Catherine's illness in Greece, Greene's letters become less considerate, for a time. He seems preoccupied with his new apartment in Antibes; a child with a new toy. Answering Catherine's desire to visit his other apartment in Paris (which she originally helped him furnish) he pulls no punches: 'I'd *love* to see you, but I'd almost rather it was Antibes where you could see . . . all the pictures from Cuba.'

He offers good reasons why it shouldn't be Paris: because he's going to be there on business only, seeing film tests, finishing off the film script, preparing to go to Dahomey for the exteriors to be shot there. And then further excuses: 'Think carefully whether Paris is a good idea for *you* – I believe Antibes would be better. Here I think it would be a mistake to sleep in the flat – the concierge is so accustomed now to Y. coming.' (How could we believe that Graham Greene would be worried about a concierge?!) He asks: 'Would one be happy & at ease with you in a hotel & me sleeping here?'[22]

One would have thought the solution obvious: take Catherine to a hotel. (He'd tried to get her to do that often enough – he'd been sleeping with her for almost twenty years.) Clearly he doesn't want her with him in Paris. Surely Catherine would be able to see through his final sentence: 'Capri is so much easier because *it belongs only to us.*'

If Greene's letters to Catherine lost some tenderness, they remained interesting nevertheless. But his letters to Yvonne, as we've seen, are sometimes dull, reflecting the tired love of an older man, listing what was on his mid-day plate: 'I gave myself a great treat today – lunch at Fouquet's with my papers. Your phantom is always there – but *there* it's a happy phantom. I nearly took the haddock, but I had a *gigot* instead.'[23]

★

Old as Greene is getting (he's sixty-two), he can come up trumps in a crisis. In the 10 November letter to Catherine he added a shocking postscript. His friend Yves Allain, whom he knew in French Intelligence during the Second World War, had been murdered. In a postscript to Catherine:

A great friend of mine & Y's has been murdered in mysterious circumstances in Morocco & I've had to fight for the widow & children with the authorities here – who would like it to have been suicide. What with all that & general tiredness have done no work at all – except film.

He returns to the subject in his next Catherine letter, all worked up:

We [Yvonne and Greene] have to go to Paris on Thursday for the funeral of poor murdered Yves. The papers now say he was tortured before death, but his department, Radio-Television, are

behaving abominably to his wife. I feel like copying Zola* &
writing another 'J'Accuse'.[24]

Greene tried to publish an account of his friend's death, but the
French newspapers showed little interest, so he wrote his account in
a letter to *The Times*. That paper also refused it, on the spurious grounds
that, according to their correspondent, there was no official trace in
Paris of Yves Allain's assassination. Greene retorted that their correspondent hadn't taken the trouble to read *Le Figaro* or *Le Monde* of 8
and 9 November 1966. They published his letter belatedly on 24
November 1966 – but they *did* publish it and Greene was a cannon
who knew exactly how to blast an unknown enemy.

The brutal murder of Yves Allain in Morocco less than two weeks
after his arrival to take up the position of Chief of Post for the
ORTF Rabat will come as a shock to his many English friends.
He was a man of great courage, loyalty and integrity, how much
courage was shown very early, when he was hardly out of college,
as one of the '*grands résistants*' [member of the resistance movement
during the German Second World War occupation] in Brittany. He
directed the famous Bourgogne escape network to which some
250 Allied airmen owed their freedom, and he personally accompanied to the Spanish border many men who spoke not a word
of French. He received as his British award a modest MBE like so
many heroes and heroines of the Resistance; his French decorations included the Croix de Guerre with palm, the Medal of the
Resistance and the Legion of Honour and his American Medal of
Freedom.

In the 13/14 November 1966 edition of *Le Monde*, an account of
Allain's death appeared, quoting the Moroccan evening paper *Al Nassa*.
Apparently 'a foreign ship' with several businessmen on board had
arrived in Kenitra around the same time. 'While the ship was in the
wharf in Kenitra, Mr Allain's assassins committed their crime.' *Le Monde*
stated that the victim was killed by 'a blow delivered to the left side
of the head, his face burned, and he was most likely tortured with
electricity', and added that his body was found 'aboard a passenger
liner *Monique–Shiaffino* in Casablanca and [was now] destined for Rouen,
where [it] will be sent to the Allain family home in Vannes'.

* Thus Greene's thoughts about the Zola title were in his mind in 1966, long before his
battle with the French Mafia (le Milieu) in 1982, when he actually did use it.

Graham told Yves Allain's daughter that when he attended the 'strange funeral' of her father, he 'realised that there were, in and around the church, as many undercover men, *barbouzes*, as mourners'. And Greene tells us that 'The Elysée had apparently issued instructions to the press that no further allusion was to be made to the circumstances of his death, which had already been kept hidden, even from his family, for the last seven days and more.'

Greene, thinking he might one day write about Yves Allain's end, 'made notes of the lies which were told me and of the moral blackmail exerted' upon the Allain family 'by French Radio-Television, who were his official employers; but the circumstances of his death have remained deeply buried, in Morocco as in France'.[25] Nothing could be more mysterious than this, and Greene tells us that if he'd been younger he would have sought out the necessary secrets in Morocco.

Yet there was another secret. Some weeks prior to Yves's assassination, on 14 October 1966, Greene dreamed of it. In his dreams he had been 'very preoccupied for two weeks' with his friend's death – all the way back to the beginning of the month of October, *before* Yves's disappearance.

*

And then there was news from the University of Edinburgh. Greene tells Catherine he's been offered a DLitt and will 'receive the degree in July if the tax people allow me!'[26] By 20 May 1967, permission comes through: 'in July to England & Scotland . . . I want to take two nights in London *before* Scotland . . . & about 5 nights after.' But the authorities refused to allow him this:

> Snags have arisen over my visit. The accountants want me to go straight back to France after the degree . . . Would it be possible for you to have dinner with me on July 3? . . . Or dinner on July 6 (perhaps at the airport) on my way home? I can't stay longer. If it's impossible I'll try to slip over quietly in the autumn.[27]

You can never tell with these letters, sometimes from week to week, whether he's going off Catherine. Here's a backhanded compliment: 'I always think how nice your father must have been because your mother could never have produced you.'[28]

*

Greene was soon off to Dahomey for the 'exteriors to be shot', but going to such a place, which paralleled Haiti in character, brought back his genuine fears of Duvalier. 'Hope Duvalier has not arranged an assassination in Cotonou [capital of Dahomey]!'²⁹

His dreams anticipated such trouble, no doubt because, as we have seen, Peter Glenville, in visiting Haiti, had already got the fright of his life. Glenville's departure from Haiti was in January 1966. Greene's dream took place on the night of 16 November 1965, before Glenville had even arrived in Haiti. We have in Greene's dream Glenville, his friend Bill Smith, and Greene, in Port-au-Prince. Greene encounters Al Seitz, but 'while greeting Peter and Bill, he turned his back on me: "If you knew the trouble I had with the [authorities] because of you."' Glenville in 1966 was able to escape, but in the dream escape is impossible. Greene records: 'Upstairs I encountered two other people I knew – one a doctor – they were astonished to see me and more and more I wanted to get quickly away.' Graham looks out into the yard, where there are a number of cars. An old lady stands by one of them. He recognises her as Madame Duvalier, and then the President arrives and they ride away. Greene tries to hide his face behind his hands, and in this dream, is 'very much afraid'. When they started off, the way was blocked by a wooden gate. Bill got out to open it but 'opposite at the entrance of a yard stood an armed sentry who said the barrier could not be raised without the President's orders. We were trapped.'

*

Because of festivals at Cannes and a hydrographical congress in Monte Carlo, many people were descending on Greene, good friends like Michael Richey, but also others, an admiral, his French agent Marie Biche, a Cuban and a priest:

> always Haitian revolutionaries seeking money. I had one fun evening at Peter Glenville's with the Rainiers. I thought Grace Kelly very beautiful & very 'square', but I liked him immensely, kind, simple, gentle & amusing & intelligent as well.³⁰

Next he was off to Edinburgh, to receive his honorary doctorate, but he could see Catherine for only one night and a morning after. They went to a show over which Greene lost his patience, but Catherine calmed him down. In spite of his saying they were no longer lovers physically, perhaps they connected that night.

In the letter the following day from his flat in Paris, he writes full of joy that 'everything went well in Edinburgh'.³¹ Before going, he'd written to his old friend Michael Meyer: 'I wish you'd come to Edinburgh and support me.'³² But Michael was unable to drop tools and go. On 14 September 1967 he admits to Meyer that he 'enjoyed

Edinburgh in spite of my horror at having to make a Toast'. And, Greene wrote: 'I told Angus McIntosh [friend of Meyer], whom I liked, that one day we'd come back together and really do the town.' He'd overcome his lifelong shyness for a short time, anyway. (His sense of sadness that he couldn't return easily to England without permission is evident: 'I'd love to . . . once the authorities have reached agreement with me over taxes.')

To Catherine he speaks first of another Companion of Honour being there: 'Dover Wilson, the Shakespearian – a sweet old man who knew my uncle & aunts at Harston.' And with her, he felt he could boast a little: 'I spoke without looking at my notes & was a "smash hit" as the previous speeches had been serious & dull.'[33] A smash hit indeed:

As a writer of stories which are not devoid of sex, crime and violence, indeed an Edinburgh bookseller has refused to stock my last book,* I am particularly happy to be here tonight so close to Kirk O'Fields [residence where the husband of Mary, Queen of Scots, was murdered].

I wonder whether those who live in Edinburgh realise the romantic picture we have of it in the south. As a boy I loved what Professor Black of St Andrews has called your 'Serbonian bog of politics'.† That James the Sixth founded this university in the quarter where his father had been murdered removes any hint of dullness or pedagogy; you are truly here in the centre of the bog. The bog of politics, and what better situation is there for a university? The great universities have never in their finest days been ivory towers.

At my college, Balliol, we had a close attachment to the Scottish universities. The dour men who came south as undergraduates puffing out a cloud of John Cotton and knowledgeable about whisky had more glamour than any old Etonian. These were men bred in the Serbonian bog when we were boys aping men.

I had a friend, Claud Cockburn, now a distinguished contributor to *Private Eye*, who confirmed the sense of romance. He was a southerner, but in the long vac he would voyage north by boat – no tedious tourist flights of BEA in those days – and come back whispering of wonderful encounters with kind blackhaired girls in

---

* I assume this must have been his then-recent short story collection with the provocative title *May We Borrow Your Husband?* published in March 1967.
† A lake in ancient Egypt, which, dried out, is now a bog. In it whole armies were said to have sunk.

lands and *wynds*. I knew about these from Robert Louis Stevenson.

My first visit to Edinburgh was no disappointment. I came on tour with my first play [*The Living Room*]. At 2 a.m. on the first night I found myself struggling on the floor of the Caledonian Hotel with a heavy stranger who proved to be a breeder of prize bulls. He had resented my claret coloured tie and biography of Tchehov under my arm. The Serbonian bog of politics. The next morning I was accosted in the bar by a middle aged man who confided to me that he had escaped from a lunatic asylum. Our conversation was interrupted by two polite strangers who led him away. That night returning from the theatre I found the Caledonian Hotel full of men in kilts fighting each other on the stairs. I walked crabwise up to the first floor keeping close to the wall. A brawny body hurtled by me. What will happen, I wonder, on this trip?

Well, whatever else, the great honour of a doctorate at Edinburgh University. In other days I would have been slaughtered by the *Edinburgh Review*. For those of us who live in Europe a doctorate is not only a great honour, it is very useful too. I have a friend who even obtained a telephone from the French Post Office by means of his title. By the time they realised he was a doctor of law it was too late.

To say that a doctorate for a European is useful is an understatement. It is essential.

Perhaps you remember the Italian film producer. He went to a bank in Milan to borrow a billion lira for a film – the kind of tidy sum a bank prefers. They gave him a long document with 26 conditions for the loan. 'I cannot read,' he said. They read the document aloud to him and he agreed to the conditions. Then they asked him to sign. 'I cannot write,' he said. They asked him to make a cross. He did so. 'Please,' he said, 'will you write Dottore beside it.'

Like the Italian producer I lack learning. I cannot praise Edinburgh University as she should be praised. You founded the first Chair of English Literature in the world thirteen years before you were discovered by Dr Johnson, and is there another university in the world which has a section for what must be a terrifying Frankenstein study, Machine Intelligence?

As you can imagine most of what I know comes from the pages of my illustrious cousin (forgive the boast) Robert Louis Stevenson.

When I look at you I see the awe-inspiring figures of the Speculative Society: Scott, Brougham, Jeffrey, and I can hear

Professor Fleeming Jenkin rebuking my flippant cousin: 'We are not here to be happy but to be good.'

All the same Stevenson *was* happy and he was not good. You remember the passage where he compares the free life of Edinburgh University with the cloistered discipline of the south.

> The frost tingles in our blood, no proctor lies in wait to intercept us; till the bell sounds again, we are the masters of the world; and some portion of our lives is always Saturday.

Tonight and tomorrow we can share your Saturday and forget the long Sundays that go on and on.[34]

Greene, in some ways the gloomiest of novelists, had already begun his comic novel *Travels with My Aunt*, and his autobiography, *A Sort of Life*, as well. In Scotland, his humour blossomed.

35

Confessions Near
an Egyptian Shore

Nay but you, who do not love her,
Is she not pure gold, my mistress?
– ROBERT BROWNING

O N 4 September 1967, Greene wrote a letter to *The Times* – another
stunner, for on this occasion he takes a different tack. Not another
broadside against America: this time it was a shot across the bows of
the Soviet Union. He felt he was in trouble again, this time against
the opposite political side, a 'Serbonian bog of politics' to be sure. To
Yvonne: 'You will see from the enclosed that I get into a fight when
you aren't there!'[1]

Sir – This letter should more properly be addressed to *Pravda* and
Izvestia, but their failure to publish protests by Soviet citizens at
the time of the Daniel–Sinyavsky trial* makes it doubtful that
mine would ever appear.
  Like many other English writers I have royalties awaiting me
in the Soviet Union, where most of my books have been published.
I have written to the Secretary of the Union of Writers in
Moscow that all sums due to me on these books should be paid
over to Mrs Sinyavsky and Mrs Daniel to help in a small way
their support during the imprisonment of their husbands. I can
only hope that attention will be paid to my request as this might
encourage other writers with blocked royalties to follow suit. I
have no desire to make use myself of my royalties by revisiting
the Soviet Union so long as these authors remain in prison,
however happy my memory of past visits.

* See Chapter 51, 'A Kinder, Gentler Moscow'.

One can see that he's not just sounding anti-American – he is anti-anyone, any time, any way, any how, wherever he feels that justice is not being served. Greene is a thorn in the flesh of any establishment, and often more, a spike poking the nerve of the insensitive. (Though indeed, Greene himself could be on occasion monumentally insensitive.) He is the odd man out, a filibusterer who will engage in unauthorised warfare against one-time enemy or one-time friend, the highest (or the lowest) in the land if, in his view, his sense of repugnance risen, the attack is deserved.

But then, as if in the middle of transports of anger he has second thoughts, he suddenly damns his own case:

> There are many agencies, such as Radio Free Europe, which specialize in propaganda against the Soviet Union. I would say to these agencies that this letter must in no way be regarded as an attack upon the Union.

That is a distinction worth making, but what follows is an obvious absurdity, bringing him into disrepute, opening him up to the charge of being politically immature, unripe, callow, jejune – all of the above:

> If I had to choose between life in the Soviet Union and life in the United States of America, I would certainly choose the Soviet Union, just as I would choose life in Cuba to life in those southern American republics, like Bolivia, dominated by their northern neighbour, or life in North Vietnam to life in South Vietnam. But the greater the affection one feels for any country the more one is driven to protest against any failure of justice there.

But Greene knew that the genuine life of the people, during his journeys to both North and South Vietnam, was always richer in character, more attractive in the south. The people of North Vietnam he found (as I did too when following Greene's footsteps) a gloomier, more sour-eyed, unfriendly people. Of course Greene is trying to stay in with Soviet officials so that they might treat him as a friend, and perhaps act on his suggestion, perhaps even look closer at the case of Daniel and Sinyavsky. These words of Greene are indeed a sop to Cerberus, a bribe.

Still, Greene's remark about the choices he'd make – living in the Soviet Union rather than America, Cuba rather than Bolivia, North Vietnam rather than South Vietnam – is just poking his snout into a hornets' nest – but then he often did. Many intelligent people tried

461

to sting him, as he himself did to too many people over many years. When Greene writes a letter to the press, it's a lightning rod for shoals of letters to be poured out in answer, swords drawn.

A Mr Roger Pool responded by suggesting that Greene belonged to a certain type of westerner:

> Here we have writers who openly deny any sympathy for the West while reserving the right to speak freely and the right to protection which the outspoken individual enjoys in the West. Thus their beliefs are in open conflict with their life. . . . [They are] longing for an order under which they could not live, and then rejecting it in a kind of disillusioned self-righteousness, as Mr Greene does in his last line, for 'any failure of justice there' reflecting that they are out of touch.[2]

Mr Richard Harman remarks:'it is difficult to understand Mr Graham Greene's reasoning. He makes a dramatic protest against the imprisonment of Daniel and Sinyavsky by offering his blocked royalties for the alleviation of their sufferings and then goes on to say if he had to choose between life in the Soviet Union and life in the United States of America he would choose the Soviet Union.' And Harman catches Greene nicely on the hip:

> Would Mr Greene tell us, in the event of his going to live in the Soviet Union and if through his writings he, too, received a savage sentence of imprisonment, would he still prefer life in communist Russia?[3]

On 9 September in *The Times* Greene made fair answer to the swarm of criticism:*

> How very odd! I thought that my letter was about the unjust imprisonment of Mr Sinyavsky and Mr Daniel. All your correspondents seem to have forgotten these two men. I advise them to read *On Trial*, in which they will see how the process has been condemned by such devoted Communists as Monsieur Aragon and Mr John Gollan. This is not a simple matter of being Communist or anti-Communist.

★

* For other letters to the press: *Graham Greene: Yours, etc.: Letters to the Press*, selected and introduced by Christopher Hawtree (Reinhardt Books, 1989). This is an excellent selection of letters to the press spanning most of Greene's writing life.

Greene writes to Michael Meyer concerning rumours of Meyer's baby: 'Will he be called Henrik [after Ibsen, subject of Meyer's brilliant biography]?'* Then Greene adds: 'I have to go to London for two nights on March 28 for a PEN protest about Daniel and Sinyavsky.'[4] Parts of Greene's speech recovered from the *PEN Newsletter* of summer 1968 appear in the endnotes to this chapter.[5] Excerpts show his affection: 'I am an admirer of the Soviet Union, and an admirer of the Communist system. But in any government there grows up a hideous Establishment of stupid men. I have slight hopes because I notice that a distinguished officer of the KGB . . . criticised the Daniel–Sinyavsky trial . . .'

All such missives proved that disagreement, argument, mattered to Greene, who wrote letters on principle – he was for the underdog, the hunted, the persecuted (sometimes the case was personal – he writes on a personal level when irate, angry, disturbed). He could not help but make enemies, for he had a flair for seeking trouble.

In some of the letters, his contempt for the perpetrator of evil is almost palpable. He was often acutely aware of another's pain, the mix-ups natural to human life, the lies, the unnerving incompetencies, the foul-ups. His letters to the press are his battles on the front line, and the assault escalated into an onslaught beginning 21 February 1947 and ending 21 December 1989 when he commented to a journalist: 'The United States has no business interfering in Panama . . . I hope General Noriega will harass the invaders from bases in the mountains.' Not a last letter but close to one. This is decidedly a political comment, but in later chapters we'll see that Greene began his numerous visits to Panama from 1974 on, exhibiting a powerful sympathy for that country. Irritated, contemptuous, or simply bloody-minded, whichever side he is playing on, the body of his letters is to be viewed as a fire-wall against injustice, the voice of conscience that every generation hopes to find but rarely does. He has no personal axe to grind (at least until he becomes overwrought over Panama, and later Nicaragua). Thus, even when he is most political he often rises above the political swamp.

In another letter quoted in the endnotes of this chapter,[6] Greene deals with a horror brought to our attention in the *Daily Telegraph* of 6 November 1964: he cites the pictures in the newspapers depicting torture inflicted on Vietcong prisoners by the Vietnam army. He recognises torture as a tool of war, but adds:

The strange new feature about the photographs of torture now appearing in the British and American Press is that they have

---

* The child was a girl, named Nora after the heroine in Ibsen's *A Doll's House*.

been taken with the approval of the torturers and are published over captions that contain no hint of condemnation. They might have come out of a book on insect life: 'The white ant takes certain measures against the red ant after a successful foray.' But these, after all, are not ants but men. The long, slow slide into barbarism of the western world seems to have quickened . . .

Injustice, yes. I suspect part of Greene's uniqueness comes from the fact that in the large body of his letters to the press he is taking a shot at solving problems bigger than life, trying to cast beyond the moon.

★

At long last, he took Yvonne to Capri. Catherine's last haven was taken from her. He had been loath to do it, but I suppose by now he was beginning to realise that Catherine would never recover. They could not go back to the paradisal days and nights in Villa Rosaio. Here is the reference which must have told her all she needed to know:

Y. did a lot of gardening. I found it too hot for work – & we found a nice new restaurant . . . Bathed three times only. And finally returned by hovercraft![7]

It is at this point, his work on his autobiography and new novel (*Travels with My Aunt*), still going at a snail's pace, that he tells Catherine he's thinking of heading off to Israel.

There is never just one reason why Greene suddenly shifts into top gear. After his experience in Capri with Yvonne, she went home to France and he spent two months on his own. He tells Catherine that he's 'rather bored'. Max Reinhardt is coming to see him, but this is not enough to uplift him, and he writes: 'I've half made up my mind to go to Israel. I'll return to Antibes the last week of October.'[8] And to Michael Meyer on 14 September 1967 (only three months after the Six Day War of 5–11 June 1967), he writes that he is leaving for Israel at the end of the week, with the *Weekend Telegraph* paying his expenses, though 'I don't know what kind of articles I'll find there if any. However if my reputation is to remain intact the situation should hot up during my visit or immediately after.' But there were other reasons; I suspect there was more afoot than we know – perhaps some nego- tiations between Greene and the Israelis.

I'm sure Israel would have scouts looking for someone, not a Jew, perhaps a well-known writer, who would not be opposed to them. And here was a fighter who, if he could be persuaded to view their conflict with the Arabs sympathetically (especially after the Six Day War), might help Israel in her battle of words with the Arab world. They'd know that Greene could capture the ears of the press, and if he came out on their side it might well be a political plus. Fidel Castro recognised this, and, I suspect, so did General Moshe Dayan, the famous Israeli leader, then Minister of Defence, whose reputation had been increased by his success in the Six Day War. I found the following telegram deep in Greene's files:

WELCOME TO ISRAEL STOP RESERVATION IN DAN HOTEL TEL AVIV FOR TWO DAYS A WEEK IN KING DAVID HOTEL IN JERUSALEM STOP LATER ON ACCORDING TO YOUR WISH LOOKING FORWARD TO MEET YOU [9]

And it worked out for the Israelis since on Graham's return the diary in *The Times* (25 October 1967) provided a well-placed headline: 'Graham Greene's Views on Israel', and the following paragraph:

Graham Greene, back in his Paris flat after a four-week visit to Israel, tells me his stay there has confirmed him in his view that it is unreasonable to expect the Israelis to withdraw to their old frontiers: 'I was impressed mainly by the necessity of certain changes in the frontiers, especially having visited the Syrian Hills, where the Syrian lines were so near the kibbutz. I don't really see how you can turn back the clock, and it's fantastic to expect the Israelis to do so.'

Later, in the same column Greene adds: 'I was pro-Israel long before the Six-Day War and I am more so now.'

When Greene arrived in Israel, the *Guardian* newspaper reported his arrival in Jerusalem and his simple statement (a line for a reporter): 'I'm here because everyone has to see Israel once in his lifetime.'[10] In his diary he records a meeting with the Dayan family:

Dinner with Yael Dayan, her husband, General Dayan [her father] & his wife in the small courtyard of an Arab restaurant in Jaffa. D[ayan] a rather withdrawn man with a smile that doesn't move much & his wife voluble & full of good words for the Arabs. Yael pretty (prettier than her photos), dynamic, ready to quarrel even with her father. Her husband a charming young officer. The General all the time having to shake hands with strangers, most of them American, but after autographs – the half-indignant astonishment of those who act as if it were they who come

honouring him. I said, 'Sometimes you must want to do something unpopular.'[11]

His diary at this time consisted of notes written into a notebook
without a desk, little incidents run together in time. Gaps are due to
indecipherability:

> Sept 20
>
> Summoned from my lavatory seat by a madman. Misunder-
> standing on telephone. Tirade against atomic reactors of madman
> in Prague. To Jerusalem. The unmoved cars of the War of
> Independence with their wrecks. The flat plain before the police
> station at [unreadable] where the journalist had been sent up
> to fight straight from his boat at Jaffa not knowing how to use
> a rifle.
>
> The Wall of the Temple on the Jordan side excavated deeper
> by [King] Hussein, more impressive than the Wailing Wall – less
> impressive now. The little streets have been cleared, railings to
> separate men & women . . . Piety swamping faith . . .
>
> Awful dinner in the grill of King David. Food [compared] with
> the holiness of the place. A tourist can hardly complain after a
> visit to Calvary & then the King David bad mixed grill.[12]

In a letter written the same day, he tells Yvonne he feels a little lost
– 'too many famous things to see & nothing to write about'.[13] Here
is the very first scribble in his diary three days earlier:

> Sep 17 1967
>
> Arrived at Tel Aviv airport 5.15. Met by Moshe Pridan (dark,
> hawk-like Czech origin) – was a boy in Auschwitz & Abraham
> Shaler (Teutonic in appearance but a Sabra*) both producers . . .
> making a film of Six Day War. Prejudice against the orientals . . .
> A certain resentment against Yael Dayan for writing in English.

He is in the King David Hotel, Jerusalem: 'a huge railway station of
a "hotel" & I have a huge suite twice as big as our little home in
Antibes'.

Then Greene returns in his letter to his affair with Yvonne and the
difficulty of handling it with her husband around: 'I've booked a return
flight on October 8 – October 7 in the Dan Hotel. When you know
J's movements write or telegraph to me here & I'll try & keep in

---

* An Israeli-born Jew.

touch with the hotel when I leave.' We have to remember that in his 20 September letter he's only about two and a half days into his scheduled programme: 'Mrs Dayan is taking me to the Gaza strip, I think, & Tuesday the young husband is going to try to take me to the Suez Canal. Another colonel is taking me round occupied Syria. A lovely view from my window.'

He sends Yvonne a postcard from the Wailing Wall on 22 September: 'I am wailing for you cherie. Last days have been walking around by myself for three or four hours a day. Tomorrow I go to Jericho & Bethlehem & then up to Galilee . . . All my love & want.'[14] And the card is sent to his own address, Résidence des Fleurs, Avenue Pasteur, to be collected by Yvonne privately. He sends another postcard (written the same day) to the Cloetta home: 'Madame Jacques Cloetta, Le Villa Ty Nevez, Chemin de Cantogril, 06 Juan Les Pins.' It is, under the circumstances, a more modest postcard, mentioning the unexpected beauty of Bethlehem and saying that he anticipates Mrs Dayan taking him to the Gaza Strip and on to Suez, then north to Galilee. He ends the innocuous card with a word of love, carefully made out to the couple: 'Love to you & Jacques.' Their adultery, after eight years, was still hidden.

On 26 September he is with the military officer Major Shimon Levinson:

The debris of battle before El Arish. Tracks like abandoned snake skins. Tanks still upright but most of the trucks on their sides or upside down. Food tins, jerry cans, shell cases. A tourist bus arrives at Arish. Quiet women in funny hats & elderly globe trotters with American accents.

Greene, the eavesdropping novelist, keeps his ear cocked:

'The Hilton Hotel.' Dominating, Teutonic – born in Austria. 'I would never let a daughter of mine marry a gentile.' 'Why have they come? There's nothing to see. The war cemetery.' 'He got better.' Young economists all with English for their liaisons with the U.N. Strong point in the house. Shared a room with Shimon in side of [?]. Col. Ben. Don't go into the road outside. If there's firing, it's certain death. Make fear travel outside your room. Horrible dinner cooked by one of the officers. Cola drink with pizza . . . and cold welsh rarebit. Only soft drinks. Egypt only 1000 yards away. 4 casualties a few weeks before. At night cats kept on getting through little doors in mosquito wire. Little sleep.

But Greene found a story for his article the next day. Here are his diary notes:

Sep 27.
With Shimon meeting U.N. officers. The length of the canal to Port Tewfik. First stop the bridge where we left the col., the Australian commander. The sandbags at a useless height. 'Everything peaceful.' To Ismailia with Burmese officer. The U.N. building [indecipherable] the way. Not allowed to talk to his B[urmese] colleague though all his pay is there. The two Swedes who laughed. All peaceful but a crowd of cheerful soldiers arrived with cameras. Next point – no post. A pontoon bridge. ¼ hr wait. 'All peaceful.'

Meeting with Swedish colonel. Skinny. Was military, very formal. Decorative uniform badges. Followed him down to Tewfik.

. . . Thirteen stranded ships. Suez like a rubbish dump at the canal edge. Hideous white amateur statue looking at the desert with the moving inscription in Hebrew: 'I looked death in the face & death lowered his eyes.' To be remembered after. Another awful lunch . . . 'All peaceful.' Chair of observation: Kantara – Jerusalem – Ismailia. 45 minutes to complete cease fire arrangements. Has U.N here any point? 'Yes because there's no communication between the combatants.' But nor is there on the Jordan border. Started back. Stopped by soldiers near artillery post & held. We were not to go on because of shooting in the road. Stood for 20 minutes undecided listening to distant bimbooms. Sounds on the horizon. Suddenly the whistle & a mortar shell exploded half a kilometre beyond us. Rush to sand dune. Two truck drivers, soldier, our driver, Shimon & I. About 2.30. For some reason changed our dune twice & then mortar shells began coming over rapidly all beyond us, overshooting. [Not in diary but in his article: A red-headed sentry – Greene envied him his steel helmet – the only professional soldier, advised them to move to different dune, and then another; they never knew why.] Afraid they were bracketing & we were protected only from the canal side. The truck driver [in the article it mentions two truck drivers making their escape] decided to try & get away. We hesitated too long & the shelling increased.

In his article he tells how the truck drivers after about an hour 'abruptly took off, running doubled up the 50 yards to their truck exposed to the Egyptian shore, which was less than half a mile away. I watched them with selfish apprehension (sooner or later I might have to take

the same track), but they made it successfully; one started the engine
and they disappeared from sight in the direction in which most of the
shells were falling.'[15]

> Anti-tank guns – flutter flutter flutter . . . like a secretive bird
> seeking a mate. Bothered with flies. Shimon's face cut & flies
> setting there (they were horse flies like cats round a saucer of
> milk).

Lying there, Greene begins to analyse the emotional stages of a man
under fire:

> Moods, fear, resignation [from the article: 'Well, if this is the end,
> it's the end. At least I shan't die of cancer or be humiliated by
> senility], then irritation & at the end fear again of dying just
> before the ceasefire.

Greene admits he was encouraged to see the fear in the eyes of the
others lying with him. The diary entry carried over unchanged into the
article: 'It would have been lonely to share the sand dunes with heroes.'
    There was a final fear that once the Israelis responded to the Egyptian
firing the Egyptians would have a better judgment of where to shoot,
but they continued to overshoot. At five o'clock firing was much less,
though machine-guns continued. They decided to make a dash for it.

> Made it fast. Fear of a different death. [In the article Greene writes
> 'it would be an absurd chance to be killed by the last mortar
> shell . . . so we made a run for the jeep and took the next five
> exposed kilometres at a speed which would have been reckless
> if it had not been prudent'.]

He describes his experience first to Yvonne:

> This time yesterday afternoon, I thought all was over. I had gone
> down to the canal for two days to see what the situation was &
> I didn't take *Ted** with me. So I got involved in the . . . worst

---

* A baby teddy bear, a mascot from his dear friend Alexander Frere. Frere almost drowned
once and he rescued his mascot – a teddy bear. Frere gave Greene a bear for the same
purpose, to carry as he moved around the world, touching, it would seem, every pillar
and post. It was for Greene (as it was for his publisher Frere) a good luck talisman. When
he travelled to Goa in December 1963 he spent the first night in Bombay, and coming
through customs the officials looked at him in an odd way as he carried the teddy bear
in plain sight. He did not explain.

incident in two months at the worst place. From 2.30 till 5.15 in the afternoon, poor Graham lay flat against a sand dune, sudden artillery, mortar & machine gun fire. My companion got a chip out of his cheek, but I've only got sunburn & a sore elbow! I'll tell you all about it when I see you. I've finished with war! The odd thing is that I worried most about your being upset – in between Hail Marys & trying to appear blithe & quite accustomed to this sort of thing. In a way, it was worse than the blitz because for two days I'd drunk nothing stronger than lemonade! How I longed for whisky when at last we got away – but no, lemonade was all. All the same it's given me a good article. I go to Jerusalem tomorrow . . . Perhaps there'll be a letter waiting for me at the King David. *You were so much in my thoughts yesterday* . . . I love you and long for you.[16]

Three days later he writes joyfully because he did get a letter. He first tells Yvonne about his movements: 'Tomorrow I go with an officer along the Syrian hills, then a night in Haifa, back to Jerusalem, October 7 Tel Aviv & a week today back to France.' And what is driving him (and why should it not – it drives most men) is his desire to be with Yvonne: for sex:

My darling, now anyway we can say 'Next month the Colombe d'Or, *toutes nos petites habitudes*'* . . . Send a line to Paris if there is Jacques news – I'll fly down if he goes off . . . In December when the film [*The Comedians*] opens we'll come to Paris together & have a very private party of two.[17]

While in Israel, he attached to a letter of 1 October 1967 (one day before his sixty-third birthday) what seems a simple poem. It could indicate the beginnings of senile dotage (this I can't believe, since when I met him nine years later he still had *all* his marbles – so many that I thought he had his and somebody else's too). More likely is that poetry in English was not Yvonne's forte and thus, he was trying to cater to a limited sensibility. Perhaps. Here is the somewhat schoolboyish poem:

> Just push the gate & we'll be there!
> The loo's out of order, but what do we care?
> The garden's a mess, there are rats on the roof
> But in the big bed I can give you the proof

---

* 'All our little ways'.

That the HHK
Is by far away
Loveliest & best and *la plus belle derrière*.

The poem is strangely juvenile, ending on a sexual note. And in the case of Yvonne he saw her as being very young – not because she was, but because she *looked* young. On 6 December 1964, he'd had a dream: 'Came into the room & found Yvonne taking a bath in a metal tub. She was standing up & from behind her body looked like that of a 13 year old girl.' And with this sense of her seeming so young goes the inclination for fatherly protection.

A final dream on 16 April 1965, set during an air raid: he's seen the flash and heard the planes. Fearing for her life he takes her in his arms on the bed, 'partly to reassure her, partly to be able to cover her body. I picked up my keys also, thinking "if I'm killed she will hear them fall on the floor & be able to find them".'

*

The same day Greene wrote to Yvonne about the Sinai, he wrote a detailed letter to Catherine Walston, detailing an incident in the Suez canal while visiting the Israeli military:

> Dearest Catherine,
>   . . . For 2¾ hours two of us & a driver were lying flat in a sand dune under artillery mortar & gun fire . . . I said 'Hail Marys' & thought a lot! My companion got a chip out of his cheek. I only got a sore from leaning on my elbow & a hell of a sunburn . . . As you can imagine one thought a lot about one's life between flattening for an explosion.

Here he tells the utter truth:

> And you are so much of my life. My darling, I know how unjust I've been, & I don't suppose you'll believe me when I say that you are the greatest love I can ever have – & it continues. It was a tormented love – love which made one more happy & sometimes more miserable than I'll ever be again. I have a real quiet love for Y 'peaceful as old age'. I don't want to do any more harm. I'm afraid now of our love – so often nothing & nobody could stand against it. But it stays there – Tunbridge Wells is in my heart also. Only at 63 I haven't courage or strength – except for artillery bombardments. But you are part of my life & always will be. I was scared of [taking Yvonne to] Capri, but it was all right only because

471

it was very different. I never try to reproduce our life. That belonged
to you & me. I go back to Paris . . . & to Antibes at the end of the
month.

Always with the deepest love, my darling.

G

And the follow-up:

Sept 27

I re-read my letter this morning & there's nothing I want to
[take] out only to add a little explanation. My darling with you I
found a strange, beautiful . . . world like Cousteau's and nothing can
ever make me forget it. Now I live by a clear stream, no secrets,
nothing inexplicable. I am sometimes bored as I never have been
with you (but that is my nature). I receive great tenderness, kindness and there's intelligence and taste and charity comparable to
yours.

But here's the rub:

You would often present one with broken appointments, secrets –
and when you wouldn't tell me with whom you were going to
North Italy, your innocent movements I often learnt only by asking
Mrs Young [Greene's & Catherine's secretary] – and I stopped doing
that because it seemed like spying. I wasn't spying, I just wanted
to share your life. It was pure accident the time I was unwell &
looked out of my window and saw you kissing Skunkburgh.* I was
less angry with the jealousy than because you didn't tell me. Jealousy
was created not by anything unfaithful in you but keeping secrets
(wholly unimportant secrets which are a protection [for] you. This
[is] tolerable as man and wife, but dangerous when that can't be. I
loved and admired the dark waters and the coloured fish and I'll
never forget that world, but I wanted to [open the area] and
couldn't; it was a contradiction and then I began to have secrets,
too, but I could never keep them for very long. You wanted the
clear water as much as I did, but you didn't realise I wanted it too.
Now I'm too old for diving. I don't love the other stream more
than your ambiguity and when I'm bored (that side of my melancholy which still remains) I always remember that never for a
moment have I ever been bored by you – enraptured, excited,

---

* This is a made-up name for secrecy's sake. It refers to Father O'Sullivan, an absolute
snake, hated by Harry Walston as well as Graham.

nervous, angry, tormented, but never bored, because I lost myself in searching for you.

Now he is pedalling furiously:

Darling, now this seems a carping letter . . . but it isn't. It's an attempt to explain, not to justify. That Paris business does not come from my side or even from Y's — she always knew when we went to Capri, but she has a temperament which makes concierges, butchers, bakers fond of her and possessive. They romanticise her as a sweet wife, she couldn't care less (as a Catholic) whether we are officially married or not; like you once in Italy she finds herself unwittingly accepted in a false role, and suddenly she doesn't want to disappoint and worry the simples.

In Italy (for her) there wasn't any problem because nobody could force a false role on her. Everybody knew that I loved you and I made it plain that we still love each other and see each other. She was taken probably for [an] adventure but that she didn't mind. But the concierge pours out all her troubles . . . and the fatal moments have passed when she should have interrupted and said, 'But I'm not married to Mr Greene.' It's the years of lying now (without meaning to) that makes it all difficult.

My dear darling Catherine, you'll never get through all this letter — or even be able to read it because my fountain pen has been stolen, but somehow the day before yesterday when I was sure that I was going to die, made me want to explain everything.

And this is what we must remember:

My love for you wiped out all small loves — they couldn't grow — Vivien, Dorothy, Anita — all that is left is affection, but Y cannot wipe out my love of you (nor would she want to*) nor can you wipe out my love of Y (& wouldn't want to either). You never wanted to with the others — it just happened.
Dear dear dear for always
Graham[18]

Greene's love for Catherine was at times intensely noble; as he wrote above, 'so often nothing and nobody could stand against it'. She *was* the love of his life, and for many years he was 'wildly, crazily,

* I strongly suspect that Yvonne would have wished to wipe out Graham's love for Catherine. Yvonne would not wish to go on record about such a matter but she *was* jealous of his previous loves.

hopelessly' in her sway. Shakespeare's description of the power of love applies to Graham: 'A lover's eyes will gaze an eagle blind.' This is a love that needs to be known, to be celebrated. Catherine was the sun of his life in the beginning, and later the winter of his despair.

PART 16

A Weird Speech and a Zany Aunt

36

The Virtue of Disloyalty

I fawned and smiled to plunder and betray
– JAMES BEATTIE

GREENE'S letters written from the Dan Hotel, Tel Aviv, to both women in his life, reveal his sea-deep, richly coloured, subtle yet complex love for Catherine. But inexorably, given her health, such love could not continue. In a dream Greene had on 29 April 1967 we see how touched he was by Catherine, suspecting there would be no recovery for her battered body, thinking she might remain fearfully crippled. He realised, too, that she was well on her way to becoming an alcoholic; he even had a premonition as early as 1957 (7 May) in a strange dream about finding her in an awful boarding house: 'very ill in your bones'. His powerful intuition was at work again. The dream preceded by seven years the medical event which ultimately destroyed the woman he loved.

> C. said a very sweet thing to me which brought tears to my eyes: 'After making love with you once I don't want to make love again with anyone.'[1]

Catherine, loved by her children, loved deeply by her husband, never seemed susceptible to guilt. Lord Walston, the best of husbands, did not enforce fidelity. Harry was the least possessive of men, and if he had his share of male pride, he was not touched by that stark jealousy which wanders wild around the world.

Greene himself had this possessive quality – many of us do, we the jealous ones, nursing resentment, envious of another's success, especially in love. But Graham Greene's problem was a very different one. He felt the full weight of guilt, but persisted in sinning. In one dream, recorded on 3 October 1966, a bull with a human voice turns to him, saying: 'You are like me. You are marked superficially with sin.'

Greene believed this. But in the depths of his subconscious, his changing nature is also reflected. In a dream on 29 July 1965, he envisions Yvonne as quite young, as we've seen before, looking in one dream during their first years together as no more than a schoolgirl; in another, his description is close to a real photograph, 'Yvonne looking very lovely in skin-tight honey-gold pants & a little tight jacket'.[2] He was fifty-five, she was in her mid-thirties when they met, small-boned with a tiny frame. On 25 June 1965, we see how anxiety about his age creeps remorselessly upon him in his sleep. He sees himself as an old man, writing in his diary, 'Sad discussion with Y. I say that at my age we can count the yearly spring holidays left to us on my fingers. I ask whether she would really still like to live with me.'

Greene is part of all the five great loves he knew. Some of his dreams inevitably are about Catherine. He is seeing less of her. He is not seeing Yvonne regularly at this time, and his letters reveal that they have to meet in secret, and not too often, since Jacques, her husband, knows nothing of their affair. He does dream of his separated wife, but the dreams of Vivien are rooted mostly in his sense of guilt.

One month after the *petit chat* episode which appears in Chapter 33, on 9 March 1965, he dreams his wife has told him she is dying of cancer: 'She looked young and beautiful & I was horrified at how I had treated her. I took her in my arms & tried to convey to her that in spite of everything she had been my only love.'*

Still more moving were dreams about Anita Björk: one took place on the night of 13 October 1964. In it, he is 'cruising at night off some point of Arabia':

In the interior not far away was the ruined castle of Orbutum. There were stories that somewhere along this coast were the lost mines of Solomon. Mysterious lights in the sky, & there was a legend that if you named someone you had loved a light would fall & indicate where the treasure lay. I whispered the name 'Anita' but nothing happened – perhaps I had not loved enough.

Three years later (though dates don't matter in the slumber world, time and space shuttling back and forth), in June 1967, Greene was again having dreams of Anita. The first and last:

---

* Vivien Greene died at the age of ninety-nine in August 2003.

25 Husband and wife artists
Harry Gottlieb and Eugenie Gershoy

26 Sketch showing the variety of
Aubelin Jolicoeur's personality

27 Françoise 'Papa Doc' Duvalier
with Tonton Macoute bodyguard

28 The Barbot brothers, Clément and Harry

29 'Famed novelist, Graham Greene' at the Galleon Club, Jamaica

30 A dapper Jolicoeur ('Petit Pierre') on the steps of the Oloffson Hotel (*The Comedians'* Trianon)

31 Father Thomas Gilby

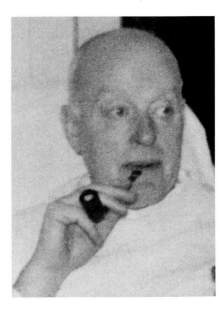

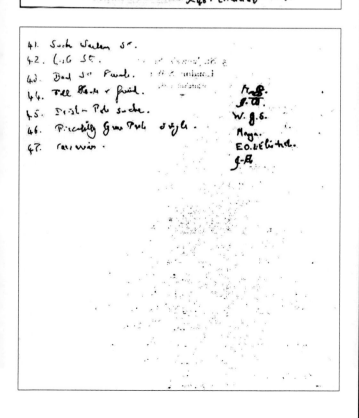

5 St. James's Street
London S.W.1
Whitehall 9680

32 'A list of prostitutes Graham Greene had as a young man' (see Appendix 2)

33 Greene on his way to recieve an honorary doctorate at Cambridge University, 1962

37 (*above*) Greene
returns to the City
Hotel in Freetown,
Sierra Leone

38 (*right*) Greene
with Mario Soldati
in Freetown

39 Poster of Jesus with a rifle slung over his shoulder, distributed in Argentina and other South American nations by Cuban government information service (Malcolm W. Browne/*New York Times*)

40 (*right*) General Omar Torrijos

41 (*below*) Greene with Daniel Ortega

42 An older Catherine Walston

43 Postcard of church at Thriplow which Greene bought
and marked with an X the spot where Catherine is buried

St. GEORGE'S CHURCH,
THRIPLOW

June 23

Met Anita quite unchanged by the years and we kissed tenderly, but I was aware that my body still loved her.

June 30

Met Anita at a dinner party. We kissed tenderly.

The middle one was more moving:

June 27

I had heard Anita was in town and suddenly at the entrance of a shop I saw a woman with a child and believed it was her — the child, I thought, was the right age, the colour of the woman's hair was different, but that signified nothing. We came face to face and it was Anita and she fainted. I leant over her and kissed her face and encouraged her back to consciousness.

A year earlier, he'd dreamt that Anita resembled Yvonne, raising the question: 'Was Anita the only one I really loved?' But now it is Catherine who is losing out, and this becomes apparent as early as 1964:

Sad scene with C. in a crowded bar where I was ordering drinks . . . Suddenly C. began weeping for the end of our relationship. I longed to comfort her & to tell her that I loved her still more than Y., but my loyalty to Y. stopped me.

This dream might seem to go against his Tel Aviv love letters, but note that it is his loyalty to Yvonne that stopped him, not his love. The Israel letters were written with his life on the line, under duress, and Catherine was paramount. Yet it is undeniable that Greene carried within him all the loves of his heart.

★

Greene's friend Michael Meyer stressed Greene's fascination with things sexual:

I always thought that Graham had a rather schoolboy attitude towards sex — never for a moment gay, but fascinated by mild divergences from the norm. Not a sadist or a masochist certainly. But I remember the night we went to the Crazy Horse . . . at the interval he suggested that we find a brothel where two women could put on a lesbian exhibition, which I found deeply uninventive and boring – it was so obviously faked . . . The Crazy Horse was so popular simply because it was by far the best of its kind, with stunning girls and imaginative presentation.

We know Greene was drawn to prostitutes. Meyer continued:

Doesn't he write somewhere something to the effect of: 'If a man has a tart he can leave a banknote on the mantelpiece and go out', meaning sex without responsibility or the need to linger afterwards? I could never understand the attraction of having a prostitute, which seems to me like paying someone to let you beat them at tennis.

I asked if Greene was in any way a deviant:

I don't think he was unusually deviant . . . I often heard him say of a woman, 'Nice little bottom she has,' which never interested me. He was a very sexy man . . . He told me once how Catherine and he had had it off together in the back of a car while Harry was driving (manually I imagine). That pleased him. I also remember once driving him from Stockholm airport to Anita's house . . . and how visibly excited he became as we approached the house, and how they could scarcely wait for me to leave so that they could start, she as much as he.[3]

I also asked him to compare Greene's loves:

Catherine, Anita and Yvonne. You ask, 'Whom did Graham truly love?', and I think the answer is all three in different ways. Catherine I met only once and disliked, but I can see how men could fall for her. She was handsome, intelligent and I imagine witty, but hard as nails. Yvonne I met twice . . . and liked greatly – attractive, calm and caring. Anita of course I have known for over forty years, and you know her. She has just about everything – [she's] beautiful, talented, highly intelligent, a linguist and very sweet-natured – and very sexy . . . I am sure [she and Graham] would have settled down permanently but for Anita's unwillingness to continue her career abroad, despite her being fluent in both French and English, and her wish to bring up her children in Sweden . . . Graham was still very much in love with her when we went to Tahiti.[4]

In Meyer's inscribed copy of *The Lost Childhood*, Greene had written privately for his friend: 'The lost Berkhamsted – the lost Stockholm – the lost Tahiti.' And sadly, the lost Michael Meyer.*

*

Countess Cerio – from a leading family on Capri - sent me an account of her good friend Greene on the island. I had interviewed her years earlier and we'd become friends. I was not to meet her again for twelve years – at Graham's funeral in Switzerland. Laetitia Cerio was not able to speak much of Catherine. They'd met only once, after Catherine's health had dwindled:

> I was living in New York during Graham's first years on Capri . . . The Dottoressa told me that we were to meet on the piazza. When I approached the Caffe Vuotto she was sitting there with Catherine. Graham had gone on an errand. I hesitated, but the Dottoressa waved at me enthusiastically: 'He is coming! He is coming!' Soon after Graham joined us. Catherine rose saying that it was time for them to be on their way to dinner at Gemma's. She was on crutches then. It must have been after the end of the affair. I felt that one was made to feel as if one had intruded.

But in the early sixties, Dottoressa Elisabeth Moor had news for Laetitia:

> The Dottoressa hinted at a mysterious new mistress (Graham seemed to enjoy using the very word when speaking of Yvonne) – very attractive – the Dottoressa said with a mischievous wink – and FRENCH. I spotted them at once as they were emerging out of the Funicolare from the Grande Marina. She was a striking looking person, a miniature woman of perfect proportions on high thin heels. Large blue eyes and a broad smile irradiated a warmth from under a head of thick white hair. She walked confidently beside him as if under the protecting wing of her great man.

Laetitia recalled a journey on a hot August day and how she watched Yvonne and Graham together. On the way back she remarked to

---

* I reached this point in the book just after noon on 4 August 2000, when I telephoned Michael Meyer in London, myself in Texas, to speak of Graham. His daughter took the phone with the news that her father had died the previous day. He was both brilliant and good, as man and biographer.

Graham that for her the summer heat sometimes made one 'feel voluptuous'. Graham chuckled and said: 'I didn't feel a bit voluptuous.' But
Laetitia observed: 'I noticed an appetite in his eyes that moonlit night.
At my urging, we all jumped into the pool with a minimum of
clothing. I watched him push Yvonne shimmering into the water.

Laetitia's view of Greene and Yvonne Cloetta:

> I was allowed to share Graham and Yvonne's devotion to one
> another which made their friendship valuable to me. It was the
> kind of love which impressed me as being supreme because of
> the many difficulties they had to surmount in order to have any
> time together. One sensed a profound mutual respect as they
> listened to one another. There was such dignity in Graham's cour-
> teous ways, a fulfilment in the interests they shared, a spice of
> humour throughout.

But, she added, 'the affair was still then secret'.

In the swing of debate about the women Greene loved, Catherine
Walston has not always fared well, depending on who was making the
argument. I'll end this discussion with a comparison by someone who
knew and admired Greene over a long period of time – Gemma, the
restaurant owner. She loved to have him in her café:

> Mr Greene could have the most beautiful women in the world
> but look who he chose? . . . Yvonne Cloetta is minuscule, a little
> thing, but Signorina Catrina, now *there's* a LADY.

*

The French took tremendous delight in Greene's leaving England to
take up residence in France. That was one up the nose for the Brits.
Increasingly, France came to see Greene as one of their own. They felt
he had the kind of tolerance for 'affairs of the heart' more characteristic of the French than the British. Greene's first collection of short
stories after his exile seemed, for the staid English gentleman, somewhat
light-hearted, without spiritual drama, but rather with a kind of amused
laughter at the sexual scene, especially with the title story, 'May We
Borrow Your Husband?' Here Greene shows a sad understanding of
human folly, as two predatory homosexuals 'steal' the husband of a
honeymooning couple. One French review had a nice twist, reversing
the English: 'Would You Lend Me Your Wife?' What could be more
French, or rather what could be more like what the English would
expect the French to be? France enjoyed the sense of having appro-
priated one of Britain's greatest writers, whom they thought of as a

grand personality, and who was, as Robert Frost said in a different context, 'occupying the land with character'. Greene was a new Frenchman.*

In that same year, Greene travelled to Paraguay for the *Sunday Telegraph* and to Argentina. The visit to Paraguay helped greatly with his new and unexpected novel, *Travels with My Aunt*, which appeared on the bookstalls in November 1969.

★

Earlier in 1969, Greene had been awarded the Shakespeare Prize at Hamburg University. On that occasion, he spoke to established authority *against* authority.

When Greene was an immature twenty-two-year-old, already down from Oxford but still seemingly strait-laced, he wrote to Vivien, perhaps trying to impress her, acting out the part of one naturally of the bourgeoisie, middle class to the core, dominated by a desire for conventional respectability. He thought she would be troubled by his sometimes outrageous beliefs, and tended to be careful, for he wished to marry her, and did so within a few months. Yet what he wrote to Vivien, given his true nature, takes some stomaching:

> This evening I happened to be reading that nasty fellow Shakespeare's sonnets. At least two thirds of them are clearly addressed to a young man. Why, in about 30 sonnets he either calls his love 'he' or 'dear boy' or something! How pastors & masters do shut their eyes to the regrettable propensities of the national poet.[5]

This is a letter from a young man (younger than his age). But as we've seen, he was to grow to be world-famous, world-wise, worldly, and ultimately, world-weary. Sometimes in later years, he was sulphuric, sophisticated, yet curiously, still shy. At Hamburg on 6 June 1969, four decades after his letter to Vivien, he was on entirely different ground, for entirely different reasons, using brilliant arguments opposing Shakespeare, the older Greene at his best – four months away from his sixty-fifth birthday.

Greene was no conformer, he was more of a maverick, a loner, a provocateur, a rebel (and this aspect grows as he ages), an anarchist (for he had no genuine political agenda except in the fundamental sense that he was almost always against the government). It is as if Greene had from childhood hated the authority of adults. There is more than a trace of that resentment in his early life and first stories, and as a young man he bore a certain contempt for the authority of

---

* In Singapore, I was hunted down by a French consul who, knowing I was Greene's biographer, wanted to shake the hand that shook the hand of the great one.

headmasters (somewhat odd, since his father was one). He chafed less under the authority of mothers, though in at least two works he shows a secret anger there, too.

There is nothing of the insurrectionist in Greene. However, he *was* against authority, and the greater the authority, the stronger his desire to make such his whipping boy. He often has in mind the most powerful country in the world – for him that usually meant the United States of America.

Also, Greene felt the Pope had too much assurance, too little doubt, and lumped this head of the Church together with US President Ronald Reagan, both becoming for him figures of opposition, ready-made ninepins in Greene's bowling alley. They are in heady company. Greene's attack on Shakespeare is subtle, not so much an attack on his body of work (though that takes place in his textual quotations) but against the man.

He was not alone in his time in attacking Shakespeare. George Bernard Shaw had a go at him in his short play *Shak versus Shav*, suggesting, none too seriously, that he was greater than Shakespeare. Not so Greene – his method is more in the manner of Ford Madox Ford in his *March of Literature*, each a polemicist in different ways.

Greene gave his speech standing at a lectern, in pinstripes, looking uncharacteristically like a well-dressed businessman. The title of Greene's address, 'The Virtue of Disloyalty', sums up his creed, and is deliberately provocative. He is testing, or we might think so, one of our strongest needs – the need for loyalty: loyalty to family, friends, school, to country, to a religious faith.

Surely we know instinctively what we need to be loyal to; most of us carry out periodic examinations of what we believe in – our own secret notions of ourselves – and what we don't any longer. Rebecca West considered that Graham Greene and Evelyn Waugh 'would not sympathise with treachery . . . But they have created an intellectual climate in which there is a crackbrained confusion between the moral and the aesthetic . . . people who practise the virtues are judged as if they had struck the sort of false attitude . . . while the people who practise the vices are regarded as if they had shown a subtle rightness of gesture . . . the sign of the born artist.'[6] West is dealing with the Nuremberg Trials.

★

Greene was happy and wrote to Catherine:

This time I finished the beastly novel, a load off my mind, and did my speech for Hamburg on the virtue of disloyalty. Tomorrow

I go to Paris and Miss Reid comes over to fetch the typescript [*Travels with My Aunt*], on the 5th to Hamburg . . . I feel so much better now the book's finished.[7]

Don't you feel that at times, writing a novel was for him a disease, and when it was completed finally – the disease and the pain disappeared for a while?

On 12 June 1969 he tells her of his trip to Germany:

I had an awful time in Hamburg getting the Shakespeare prize – I really earned the 25,000 Deutschmarks & the 90 gramme gold medal. Only Germans could be so pompous. The ceremony started at 10.30 in a huge university hall with an orchestra & choir playing & singing Purcell. Then a professor made a long speech. Then the Rector who wore a gold chain & looked like a life-guard read a citation. Then I made a speech attacking Shakespeare. Then a Professor Pascal, a nice old man, my fellow prize-winner made another speech. Then the choir sang a rollicking sailors song, all female voices. Then there was a gathering at the Atlantic hotel with bad sherry. Then an interminable lunch (with very good Moselle) & another speech from an old grain merchant who supplies the loot. What made it worse was that I had a severe acute attack of piles!

Despite his physical discomfort, Greene performed brilliantly, though many listeners must have been unwilling to accept his premise, convincing as it was:

Surely if there is one supreme poet of conservatism, of what we now call the Establishment, it is Shakespeare.

In none of his plays, Greene's argument runs, did Shakespeare get close to his own troubled time, 'receding from the dangerous present, the England of plots and persecutions [especially of Catholics], into the safer past'. He chastises Shakespeare for mocking 'poor Jack Cade* and his peasant rebels'.

Greene suggests we should 'revolt against this bourgeois poet on his way to the house at Stratford and his coat of arms', that, moreover, 'we sometimes tire even of the great tragedies, where the marvellous

---

* Cade led an insurrection in 1450 against Henry VI, marching to London. After a promise of a pardon he and most of his followers dispersed, but Cade was killed attempting to reach the coast.

beauty of the verse takes away the sting and the last lines heal all, with right supremacy re-established by Fortinbras, Malcolm and Octavius Caesar'. And Greene suggests somewhat indirectly, though he puts it gently enough, 'that we are inclined to use against [Shakespeare] the accusation flung at Antonio in *The Merchant of Venice.* "You have too much respect upon the world/They lose it that do buy it with such care."' Greene never showed 'respect upon the world', and he didn't lose it either!

Greene carefully takes us towards Shakespeare's superb rhetoric about England, lines from the third act of *Richard II*: 'This happy breed of men, this little world' then misses four lines and goes on: 'This blessed plot, this earth, this realm, this England'. Having played this up for all it was worth, Greene reveals that these 'complacent lines' were published in 1597. Two years before,* Shakespeare's brilliant fellow poet Southwell had died on the scaffold after three years of torture. 'Southwell disembowelled for so-called treason . . . If only Shakespeare had shared his disloyalty, we could have loved him better as a man.' Greene suggests that Shakespeare (whose father was Catholic) thought it wise to be politically careful — and careful he was.

Greene then speaks of honours, the honours that Shakespeare sought, and dares also, in front of his special audience, to speak even of the prize he is receiving in Hamburg: 'Honours, even this prize-giving, State patronage, success, the praise of their fellows all tend to sap their disloyalty. The house at Stratford must not be endangered.' From then on Greene begins to look at the nature of the true writer, not a Shakespeare with his notions of loyalty, but what a sympathetic writer must be and do, and where his 'disloyalty' must lie. Greene speaks with the same fervour about the need for *dis*loyalty as most people speak of the need for loyalty.

In stressing the need for individuality in a true writer, Greene thinks of himself as the freest of men, refusing to be linked with parties or governments. It is difficult from this moment on not to warm to what Greene sees as a necessary form of rebellion; this subtle man has caught us out and drawn us into his type of disloyalty:

> It has always been in the interests of the State to poison the psycho-logical wells, to encourage cat-calls, to restrict human sympathy . . . Isn't it the story-teller's task to act as the devil's advocate, to elicit sympathy and a measure of understanding for those who lie outside the boundaries of State approval? The writer is driven by

---

* The play was actually produced in the same year as Southwell's terrible punishment and death. Southwell was a poet indeed, but also a Jesuit priest who led a saintly but short life.

his own vocation to be a Protestant in a Catholic society, a Catholic in a Protestant one, to see the virtues of the Capitalist in a Communist society, of the Communist in a Capitalist state.

And he 'should always be ready to change sides at the drop of a hat'. Greene follows this with a phrase deserving to be savoured in full:

> He stands for the victims, and the victims change. Loyalty confines you to accepted opinions: loyalty forbids you to comprehend sympathetically your dissident fellows; but disloyalty encourages you to roam through any human mind: it gives the novelist an extra dimension of understanding.

He makes a further assertion about propaganda, perhaps unexpected in one who in the past had sided with the Soviet Union against the United States:

> I am not advocating propaganda. Propaganda is only concerned to elicit sympathy for one side, what the propagandist regards as the good side: *he too poisons the wells* [emphasis added]. But the novelist's task is to draw his own likeness to any human being, to the guilty as much as to the innocent – there, and may God forgive me, goes myself.

He uses another image when speaking about *duty* (in most people's language such a term inevitably linked with loyalty rather than disloyalty):

> If we enlarge the bounds of sympathy in our readers we succeed in making the work of the State a degree more difficult. That is a genuine duty we owe society, to be a piece of grit in the State machinery.

He wound down by quoting the moral decision of Dietrich Bonhoeffer, the German Lutheran pastor and opponent of Nazism:

> A great German theologian confronted, in the worst days of our lifetime, this issue of loyalty and disloyalty: 'Christians in Germany,' he wrote, 'will face the terrible alternative of either willing the defeat of their nation in order that Christian civilisation may survive, or willing the victory of their nation and thereby destroying our civilisation. I know which of those alternatives I must choose.'
> Dietrich Bonhoeffer chose to be hanged like our English poet Southwell. He is a greater hero for the writer than Shakespeare.

Perhaps the deepest tragedy Shakespeare lived was his own: the blind eye exchanged for the coat of arms, the prudent tongue for the friendships at Court and the great house at Stratford.[8]

Here ended Greene's lecture. I use the word 'lecture' because that's what it was – and certainly he did flutter the dovecotes. He told me his attack on Shakespeare, after whom his prize was named, 'disquieted the professors but pleased the students'. Greene also said that when he was offered the Shakespeare prize, 'for no reason that I could rationally understand', he thought the question of loyalty and disloyalty was a suitable subject for a German audience.

Though the students would not have experienced the horror of Hitler in any personal way (the Nazis had long since disappeared) the academic elders present surely would have. It was probably a distinctly painful experience for some. His last remarks about Bonhoeffer are like waiting at the pass to cut down the enemy. How could that respected and respectable audience of scholars and academics have felt (they had, after all, let the rascal in among them) other than that they were under attack – blindsided, not with a blunderbuss, but a moral rapier, handled by a master, knowing where and when in this discourse to strike, light lines of blood marking the body at points of his own choosing.

Did Greene think Shakespeare was the greatest of writers? He did. But Greene was interested in introducing to this particular audience (tongue slightly in cheek) a new moral imperative – disloyalty.

37

A Strange Dottoressa

. . . the startlingly blue eyes, the tough electric hair as alive as a bundle of fighting snakes.

— GRAHAM GREENE

GREENE wrote his lecture on 'The Virtue of Disloyalty' at the time he was close to completing *Travels with My Aunt*. In the novel the prim and prissy Henry Pulling, Aunt Augusta's nephew, is a dull dog until she gets her hands on him and shows him how to do his own thinking. He, who seemed early in the novel to be the last of the pipsqueaks, bland as pablum on milk toast, begins to have thoughts verging on the unconventional well into the story. He reconsiders his aunt's nature and takes the first steps to stop being a dullard – this the retired bank manager, precisely correct in all business matters, as only bank managers can be, with only one passion: tending his dahlias. Growing out of his tedious provincial life, he begins gradually to think like a stalwart from the Greene camp.

The early Henry Pulling is a sort of amalgam of the decent men Greene knew at *The Times*, when working as a sub-editor in 1926. What Greene feared most in those days was that he wouldn't escape to a more exhilarating future. In a letter to Vivien he speaks of his older colleagues:

How is it that all these sub-editors between 40 and 50 years old . . . seem perfectly happy – attending to their small garden at Streatham in their spare time . . . &, I am quite certain, feeling no acute disappointment with things.[1]

Greene felt even then the fear he'd carry throughout life, that he would be a slave to an occupation, with love alone (for Vivien at this early stage) keeping him sane: 'Without you life seems to be made up of an endless sub-editing till death.' Is Greene wondering how he can escape from this form of slavery? He did soon escape from sub-editing, yet he started on an unending track of seeking new (and unexplored) avenues throughout the world, looking for material for novels, and after that, endless writing in many fields, and yes, it was 'till death'. Is life simply different forms of slavery?

In the novel, the police are interested in Aunt Augusta's present lover, Wordsworth, a giant black man from Sierra Leone, and at the same time they are investigating a past lover of hers, a Mr Visconti, a one-time war criminal, thought to be dead, or well into his eighties if alive. Interpol and the British police are called upon to catch this brilliant crook.

Gradually Henry Pulling casts off the carapace formed over a lifetime in the provinces, and is finally rescued by his aunt (she is seventy-five), who refuses to settle down and continues her sexual life apace. She, under all circumstances, celebrates LIFE. Indeed, thinking about Pulling, you might call this novel *The Education of an Innocent Abroad* – a relevant description if a dull title (but then some would say so is *Travels with My Aunt*). Henry's enlightenment continues by train, plane and sea, specifically journeys to Paris, to Istanbul by way of the famous Orient Express, and a disturbing visit to his father's grave. Pulling is taken to Brighton, important to Greene throughout his childhood as well as in later years, and finally to Argentina and Paraguay. Throughout most of the trip, as his aunt regales him with stories, he sheds layer after layer of his past. Pulling angers her when he proves to be a prude and we find ourselves in two worlds: the past, as purveyed through the aunt; and the present, when Pulling's eyes are gradually opened. She is out to break any rule, but never considers herself unethical. By her nephew's original standards (and by most standards), she most certainly *is*, but at the end of the novel, Greene educates us out of our prejudices.

Just prior to Pulling's departure for Paraguay, when he's separated from his aunt but thinking about her, it seems that he has lived his life quite rigidly.

> I wondered whether she had ever forged a cheque or robbed a bank, and I smiled at the thought with a tenderness I might have shown in the past to a small eccentricity.[2]

★

Travels with My Aunt received some rave reviews, but mostly sympathising with Greene's escape from Greeneland. If it is a gem, it is a flawed gem.

Greene told Marie-Françoise Allain that when he started the novel he didn't expect to finish it. Moreover, he tells us he wrote for his own amusement, 'with no notion of what might happen [in the story] the next day'.³ He saw it as a series of short stories, and that must account for its slight sense of plot, akin to scraps stitched together, a quilt of picaresque adventures. Greene continued: 'A number of ideas I expected to use in short stories became recollections of old Augusta. I was surprised that they all cohered into a logical sequence, and that the novel became a finished product.'⁴ But they really didn't.

They remain a series of short stories, or stories only loosely connected. Greene told me that he usually had the title before he began a novel, and then worked at the beginning and the end, seeking to join them. This was not the case with *Travels with My Aunt*. Large portions of the first part come off as desultory, and we wait a long time for the brilliant short second section.

It *is* picaresque, and that form allows for a story to be miscellaneous. But it lacks pace, and even though we continue reading (as consistent admirers of Greene's) we are not compelled by the nature of the story to read on. I want to say Aunt Augusta is not wickedly interesting, but merely a naughty old lady. This is reminiscent of the style of *Moll Flanders*. Greene gives a sexual autobiography of Augusta, as Defoe does of Moll. In both cases, the incidents are sometimes funny, sometimes tedious.

In the case of *Travels with My Aunt*, the story is made more commonplace because of Henry Pulling. Of course Henry is drawn this way in order to make the aunt seem extraordinary. It is a literary device and the stitching frays at the seams. For example Augusta tells the story of an affair she had in her middle years with a Monsieur Dambreuse, married with six children, whom she loved greatly. They would spend time together, and then he would leave. She thought he went home to the country. But Dambreuse didn't travel on weekends. He never left Paris and was in fact a Parisian. He had four children, not six, and his wife lived only a ten-minute walk from the hotel he stayed in with Henry's aunt. More daring still, he had another mistress installed in a suite in the adjoining hotel. While the aunt thought her lover was at work, he was really with the other mistress, Louise. Dambreuse thought of Augusta as his 'lady of the night' and his other woman as his 'lady of the afternoon'. Dambreuse damned himself:

It was a weekend and he had led his wife and two younger children to the Louvre to look at the Poussins. Afterwards his family wanted tea and his wife suggested the Ritz. 'It's too noisy,' he said . . . 'Now I know a quiet little garden where nobody ever comes . . .' The trouble that afternoon was that both of us came – I and Louise.

They didn't know each other, but because there was no one else there, and perhaps because they had spent six months in a hotel room with one man, they were soon talking together and discovered that their 'husbands' worked at the same metallurgical firm,

> when into the garden walked Monsieur Dambreuse followed by his rather stout wife and two over-grown children . . . Louise cried, 'Achille,' and when I think of his expression as he turned and saw the two of us sitting at tea together, I cannot help smiling even today.

He introduced his wife to the two girls as wives of two fellow directors of the metallurgical firm. But it was over.

Of course the stuffy nephew can't understand his aunt, who in his mind had been treated most scurvily: '"But surely, Aunt Augusta," I exclaimed, "you couldn't bear the man after you discovered how he had deceived you all those months?"' This makes Aunt Augusta angry, and striding up to him (he's fifty years old, remember) she says: 'You young fool . . . Monsieur Dambreuse was a *man*, and I only wish you had been given a chance of growing up like him.' It was the 'end of an idyll' she told her nephew.[5]

★

But the most interesting villain, whom Aunt Augusta loves beyond all others, is Mr Visconti, known as 'The Viper'. She calls him a twister. He is a confidence trickster, an embezzler, a forger. Henry offers his moral view, which she strenuously rejects. She tells how Visconti came back and walked in on her while she was working part-time as a prostitute:

> . . . how happy we were . . . Just to see each other again . . . It was one o'clock in the morning. We didn't go upstairs. We went straight out into the lane outside. There was a drinking fountain . . . and he splashed my face with water before he kissed me.

The goof of a nephew doesn't guess his aunt's occupation:

> But surely you must have despised the man after all he had done to you?' . . .
>
> She turned on me with real fury . . . 'I despise no one,' she said, 'no one. Regret your own actions, if you like that kind of wallowing in self-pity, but never, never despise. Never presume

yours is a better morality. What do you *suppose* I was doing in the house behind the *Messaggero*? I was cheating, wasn't I? So why shouldn't Mr Visconti cheat me? . . . [And his Aunt adds] Your poor father didn't have a chance. He was a cheat too, and I only wish you were. Then perhaps we'd have something in common.'[6]

Having a passion to tell all she can, Augusta says: 'Visconti was a quite impossible man . . . but I loved him and what he did with my money was the least of his faults.'[7]

★

In section two of *Travels with My Aunt*, the past meets up with the present. Here Greene returns to being a novelist of merit: it's almost as if in the first 180 or so pages he has been meandering casually through the story, though of course there are flash points when his skill is apparent.

There are a number of 'characters' in the sense that Aunt Augusta is a 'character', and the young American girl, Tooley, is one. On her way to Istanbul, Henry meets her on the train. She is worried that she's pregnant. She is bright, lovely, immature at eighteen years old – and she smokes pot constantly. Her boyfriend Julian wanted her to go with him to Vienna and then to Istanbul. He made a demand:

> 'He was angry because I forgot the pill. He wanted to hitch-hike to Istanbul . . . He gave me an ultimatum. "We've got to leave now or never," and I said, "No", and he said, "Find your own fucking way then."'

Young Miss Tooley, who is also worried, but not too much, about losing her boyfriend, takes another cigarette, longing to abort the baby she thinks she might be carrying. She drinks brandy and ginger ale because at school they said that did the trick, meaning it could cause a miscarriage. Then she tries something else: 'I slept with a boy in Paris when Julian walked out because I thought, well, it might stir things up a bit. I mean the curse comes that way sometimes right on top of the orgasm, but I didn't get any orgasm. I guess I was worrying about Julian because I don't often have difficulty that way.'[8]

From young Tooley, we move to Wordsworth, the lover of old Aunt Augusta. His broken English is beautiful with love for her. Henry sees him when he suddenly shows up to meet the Orient Express. Wordsworth tells Henry: 'I wan my bebi gel.' Henry remarks:

Such an expression used in connection with Aunt Augusta offended me and I turned away . . . 'You jig-jig with my bebi gel,' he accused me.

'You're preposterous, Wordsworth. She is my aunt. My mother's sister.'

'No humbug?'

'No humbug,' I said, though I hated the expression. 'Even if she were not my aunt, can't you understand that she is a very old lady?'

'No one too old for jig-jig,' Wordsworth said. 'You tell her she come back here to Paris. Wordsworth wait long long time for her. You speak her sweet. You tell her she still my bebi gel. Wordsworth no slip good when she gone.'

. . . I stood on the top of the steps as the train began to move out . . . and Wordsworth followed it down the platform, wading through the steam . . . Suddenly, staring at a window beyond me, he began to sing:

'Slip gud-o, bebi gel:

An luk me wan minit

Befo yu slip.'

The train gathered momentum and with a final jerk and strain it had left him behind.

I squeezed down the corridor to my aunt's couchette . . . my aunt leant out of the window waving and blowing kisses . . .

[She] pulled in her head; her face was smeared with smuts and tears. 'Dear man,' she said. 'I had to take a last look. At my age one never knows.'

I said with disapproval, 'I thought that chapter was closed.'[9]

★

For a year Aunt Augusta disappears and Pulling thinks she may have died. Two British detectives come seeking information about Visconti, 'The Viper'. This novel is a real crossword puzzle, clues up, down, diagonal. Where did it spring from?

It was born of Marjorie Bowen's *Viper of Milan*, a children's historical novel set in sixteenth-century Italy greatly loved by Greene in his youth. In Bowen's book, her character della Scala turned to dishonesty and died a failure, failing even at treachery. Not so Visconti. Greene's viper can sit and joke 'in the wine light'. In this odd book (for Greene), *Travels with My Aunt*, he describes Visconti: 'his patience and his genius for evil'.[10]

Greene's detective is called Sergeant Sparrow, not based on but nevertheless named after that generous Oxford scholar and poet, John

Sparrow. As for Augusta's black lover, Wordsworth, he was based on the brother of the district commissioner in Liberia, whom Greene met in 1935 while walking through the jungles. This man seemed drawn to Greene. In one of their last conversations, he told the young Greene that the Buzie people had a wonderful cure for venereal disease – 'You tie a rope round your waist' – adding: 'I guess you white people aren't troubled with it [venereal disease].'[11] The Wordsworth we meet in *Travels with My Aunt* is less naïve and lives in London and Paris.

As the detectives search his aunt's home above the Crown and Anchor, Henry watches their moves. They have suggested that she might be in danger from her unfortunate associations, 'Particularly from that viper Visconti'. As the chapter ends, Pulling is resigned that 'my aunt might be dead and the most interesting part of my life might be over. I had waited a long while for it to arrive, and it had not lasted very long'.[12]

★

In Part Two, Henry Pulling is no longer prim and prissy. He has matured under Aunt Augusta's tutelage. After a year with no news of his aunt he receives a letter from her, now far away, in Buenos Aires. She encloses a cheque so that he can buy a first-class ticket, tells him she will not be returning to Europe, and asks him to dispose of all her furniture, but to keep one photograph of Freetown harbour: 'a memento of dear Wordsworth . . . Preserve it in its frame which has great sentimental value because it was given me by Mr V.' She wants Henry by her side as 'a member of my family whom I can trust in this rather bizarre country'.[13]

When Henry arrives in Buenos Aires, he finds a room reserved for him and a letter from his aunt apologising for not being able to greet him. It also advises that she had to leave for Paraguay, 'where an old friend of mine is in some distress'. She has left a ticket for the river boat. The boat will be met. On board, he has his hand read and meets a CIA man called O'Toole, who turns out to be the free-spirited young girl, Tooley's, father.

O'Toole himself pretends to be investigating the cost of living, malnutrition and illiteracy in the area. After having lunch together, they later stand side by side in silence in a urinal. Afterwards, Henry watches as O'Toole takes out a book and makes notes. They seem to be figures. When he's finished, he says: 'Excuse me. It's a record I keep.'[14] Henry sees him the next morning and again he takes out his notebook, writing down 'mysterious columns of numerals'. Henry asks if he is conducting research. O'Toole says: 'Oh, this is not official.' Henry thinks he's making a bet on the ship's run:

'No, no. I'm not a betting man.' He gave me one of his habitual looks of melancholy and anxiety. 'I've never told anyone about this, Henry,' he said. 'It would seem kind of funny to most people, I guess. The fact is I count while I'm pissing and then I write down how long I've taken and what time it is. Do you realise we spend more than one whole day a year pissing?'

'Good heavens,' I said.

'I can prove it, Henry. Look here.' He opened his notebook and showed me a page. His writing went something like this:

July 28

7.15	0.17
10.45	0.37
12.30	0.50
13.15	0.32
13.40	0.50
14.05	0.20
15.45	0.37
18.40	0.28
10.30	? Forgot to time

4 m. 31 sec

He said, 'You've only got to multiply by seven. That makes half an hour a week. Twenty-six hours a year. Of course ship-board life isn't quite average. There's more drinking between meals. And beer keeps on repeating. Look at this time here – 1 m. 55 sec. That's more than the average, but then I've noted down two gins. There's a lot of variations too I haven't accounted for, and from now on I'm going to make a note of the temperature too. Here's July 25 – 6 m. 9 sec.'

Why would such a mundane endeavour occur to any man? O'Toole the CIA agent sees a possible use:

'Are you drawing any conclusions?' I asked.

'That's not my job,' he said. 'I'm no expert. I just report the facts and any data – like the gins and the weather – that seem to have a bearing. It's for others to draw the conclusions.'

'Who are the others?'

'Well, I thought when I had completed six months' research I'd get in touch with a urinary specialist. You don't know what he mightn't be able to read into these figures. Those guys deal all the time with the sick. It's important to them to know what happens in the case of an average fellow.'

'And are you the average fellow?'

'Yes. I'm [a] hundred per cent healthy, Henry. I have to be in my job. They give me the works every so often.'

'The CIA!' I asked.

'You're kidding, Henry. You can't believe that crazy girl.'[15]

Of course he *is* CIA. And the fact that he takes care to note how long it takes him on every occasion he passes urine is indicative of his quirkiness. But where did this spring from? Well, Greene did his own research, as evidenced in columns of numbers written in his diary in his own hand. So the peeing incident is based on Greene's own calculations. But where did O'Toole come from? O'Toole is based on Professor Trevor Williams. Greene met him at the point when he was stuck: 'He needed a CIA agent,' Williams wrote to me on 28 September 1993, 'for his plot. I was American [and] a Professor of Statistics, so he made O'Toole an amateur statistician. I was also having trouble with one of my children. I . . . displayed those signs of anxiety he so tellingly noted.'

★

Arriving in Paraguay, Henry is met by Wordsworth, sent by his aunt. Their unexpected meeting gladdens both:

'Hi, man . . . You in number one hurry' . . . [he] advanced towards me with both hands out and his face slashed open with the wide wound of his grin. 'Man, you not forget old Wordsworth?' he asked, wringing both my hands, and laughing so loudly and deeply that he sprayed my face with his happiness.

Henry wonders what he's doing there:

'My lil bebi gel,' he said, 'she tell me go off Formosa and wait for Mr Pullen come.' . . .

'How is my aunt, Wordsworth?'

'She pretty OK,' he said, but there was a look of distress in his eyes and he added, 'She dance one hell too much. Ar tell her she no bebi gel no more. Ef she no go stop . . . Man, she got me real worried.'

'Are you coming on the boat with me?'

'Ar sure am, Mr Pullen. You lef everything to old Wordsworth. Ar know the customs fellows in Asunción. Some good guys. Some bad like hell. You lef me talk. We don wan no humbug.'

Henry protests he's not smuggling anything. Wordsworth doesn't hear, and answers: 'Man, you lef everything to old Wordsworth. Ar just gone tak a look at that boat and ar see a real bad guy there. We gotta be careful.'

He suddenly takes Henry's fingers:

'You got that picture, Mr Pullen?'
  'You mean of Freetown harbour? Yes, I've got that.'
  He gave a sigh of satisfaction. 'Ar lak you, Mr Pullen. You allays straight with old Wordsworth. Now you go for boat.'

And Pulling admits: 'Whatever trouble [Wordsworth] might have caused me in that dead old world of mine, I was overjoyed to see him now.'[16]

★

Who is the source for Aunt Augusta? Greene told me that it was his friend, Dottoressa Moor. Moor, who lived for many years as the medical doctor in Capri, would attend the poor on the island and take whatever they could provide in payment, which was sometimes vegetables and fruit. Perhaps because she was so accustomed to being paid on the barter system, she once agreed to sexual payment for appliance repair. Greene remembered in a letter to Yvonne Cloetta, 4 August 1966: 'Horrifying thought (remember she [the Dottoressa] is very fat & 82): Boris, Gracie Fields' husband & her last lover, came to fix her radio & insisted she make love with him in return. "I was quick," she said, "but oh, he went on too long." As she began at 16 it seems a long long sexual life [66 years] . . . Mind you, Boris was 63 years old. Does a 63-year-old feel young when he sleeps with an 82-year-old woman? Good question.' A tremendous character, greatly loved, she was older than Greene, but immensely attracted to him. Greene would go to endless trouble to please her.

The Dottoressa liked men – all kinds. She had a black lover on Capri, but his name was not Wordsworth. Neither Augusta nor the Dottoressa was good-looking, but they *were* remarkable. Here is how Greene describes Augusta, and it fits the Dottoressa exactly:

I was surprised by her brilliant red hair, monumentally piled, and her two big front teeth which gave her a vital Neanderthal air . . . 'You must be Henry,' Aunt Augusta said, gazing reflectively at me with her sea-deep blue eyes.[17]

The Dottoressa loved sex and took it wherever it was offered, as does Aunt Augusta, but the way Augusta speaks is very different from the

Dottoressa. She had an odd way of speaking, almost as unique as Wordsworth's in the novel:

'Darling Dottoressa, you are hopeless.'
'Please?'
'Hopeless. Crazy.'
'Crazy, yes, you tell me a truth. But this with me is no new affair. What I must do I must do. You are right, I am a wild one. So I am, so let me be.'[18]

Greene helped immensely in writing her memoirs, *An Impossible Woman*, keeping up the pretence that he was simply the editor, and in the epilogue, he writes: 'She had possessed even in her seventies a quality of passionate living which I have known in no other woman.' He adds: 'I tried to give it another form and habitation in Aunt Augusta in *Travels with My Aunt*.'[19]

★

Greene had a favourite memory of the Dottoressa. She'd come to visit Catherine Walston at Newton Hall. While she was in London, Greene played for Moor on his gramophone Kurt Weill's setting of Brecht's song 'Wie Man Sich Bettet' ('As You Make Your Bed'): 'She listened with her thick legs apart like a Henry Moore figure . . . Three times I had to play the record, while she listened with her blue eyes alight and her great teeth bared.'[20] In the epilogue of *An Impossible Woman*, Greene describes her: 'the startlingly blue eyes, the tough electric hair as alive as a bundle of fighting snakes'.

Shirley Hazzard, in her memoir, describes the Dottoressa not too differently: 'A squat, categorical figure, formless in winter bundling . . . [a] russet complexion . . . prominent paleolithic teeth, and memorably pale blue eyes.'[21]

The Dottoressa had strong views on her own gender:

Women are lying things. One has to drag them by the hair, as I did with my only girlfriend . . . Frieda. I was never sorry for her for a single moment. I would like to live in a state of men only. Women should be eradicated.[22]

Greene further adds that the Dottoressa 'in her moments of bawdry . . . resembled the Wife of Bath, and when she was happy and rambling over her sexual memories I was often reminded of Mrs Bloom's mono-logue, "and yes I said yes I will Yes".'[23] The rambling sexual memories in *Travels with My Aunt* are different from those in the Dottoressa's memoirs and Greene, in writing what amounts to successive memories spread out over Part One of *Travels with My Aunt*, inevitably produces an impression of not having control of his plot, a phenomenon almost unknown in this novelist. Part Two is a much more powerful performance because it is so well-structured, and because it is based on Greene's recent experiences travelling in Argentina, especially Corrientes, and in Paraguay, where he was seeking fresh information for a new and perhaps final masterpiece. Greene's customary alertness to character is missing from his descriptions of Henry because Henry is not a specific person Greene knew in life – he's initially a bore who is to be transformed.

★

Henry Pulling's meetings with Wordsworth are dotted about the novel: in the streets of London, on meeting the Orient Express and now, on the ship to Paraguay. But they meet once more, late in the novel, when Wordsworth knows he's lost out. Aunt Augusta has dropped him for an older man – a nastier one too, the shrewd, cunning, ruthless Visconti. Wordsworth tells Pulling on board that his 'bebi gel' has left him for Visconti, and that he is too old for her. Henry says:

> 'You aren't exactly young yourself, Wordsworth.'
> 'Ar no got ma big feet in no tomb, Mr Pullen, lak that one. Ar no trust that fellah. When we come here he plenty sick. He say, "Please Wordsworth, please Wordsworth," and he mak all the sugar in the world melt in his mouth. He live in low-class hotel, but he aint got no money. They go to turn him out an, man, he were plenty scared to go. When your auntie came he cry like a lil bebi. He no man . . . but he plenty plenty mean. He says sweet thing alright alright, but he allays act mean. What wan she leave Wordsworth for a mean man like him? Tell me that . . .' He let his great bulk down on my bed and he began to weep . . .
> 'Wordsworth,' I said, 'are you jealous of Aunt Augusta?'
> 'Man,' he said, 'she war my bebi gel. Now she gon bust ma heart in bits.'

And we know Augusta and we know that her passion for the evil one is, sadly, true, yet Wordsworth's love is real:

> 'I love your auntie. I wan for to stay with her like the song say: "Abide with me; fast falls the eventide: the darkness deepens: oh with me abide . . . Tears have not bitterness," but man, these tears are bitter, tha's for sure.'[24]

Wordsworth's departure is wrenching, and we have here something of the toughness of Augusta paralleling the old Dottoressa: Wordsworth is soon dismissed:

'I am not your bebi gel, Wordsworth, any more. Understand that. I have kept enough money for you to return to Europe . . .'

'Ar no wan yo money,' Wordsworth's voice replied.

'You've taken plenty of my money in the past . . .'

'Ar tak you money them times because you lov me, you slip with me, you lak jig-jig with Wordsworth. Now you no slip with me, you no lov me, I no wan your damn money. You give it *him*. He tak everytin you got. When you got noting at all, you come to Wordsworth, and ar work for you and ar slip with you an you lov me and you lak jig-jig all same last time.' . . .

'Don't you understand, Wordsworth, all that's finished now I have Mr Visconti back. Mr Visconti wants you to go, and I want what he wants.'

Henry Pulling witnesses this and tries to shake Wordsworth's hand to palm off a fifty-dollar bill, but Wordsworth deliberately presses the money-less hand: 'Goodbye, Mr Pullen. Man, darkness deepens, sure thing, sure thing, she no abide with me.'

Augusta comes down the steps, and shows that cruel dismissal that sometimes it seems only women without a sense of guilt can accomplish:

'Oh, I'm sorry for poor Wordsworth,' she added, 'but he was only a stop-gap. Everything has been a stop-gap since Mr Visconti and I were separated.'

Henry asks if he's worth it:

'To me he is. I like men who are untouchable. I've never wanted a man who needed me, Henry.'[25]

★

Greene is doing all sorts of things in this novel. He told me that it was chiefly about old age and death. But there is only one death. It takes place the night of a great party, still going on at four in the morning:

As I entered the little hollow I trod on something hard. I stooped down and picked the object up. It was Wordsworth's knife. The tool for taking stones out of horses' hoofs was open – perhaps he meant to open the blade and in his hurry had made an error. I

struck a match and before the flame went out I saw the body
on the ground and the black face starred with white orange petals,
which had been blown from the trees in the small breeze of early
morning.

Henry bends to feel his pulse but there is no life in the body and his
hand is wet from the wound:

Poor Wordsworth . . . I thought how his bizarre love for an old
woman had taken him from the doors of the Grenada cinema,
where he used to stand so proudly in his uniform, to die on the
wet grass near the Paraguay river, but I knew that if this was the
price he had to pay, he would have paid it gladly. He was a
romantic . . . he would have found the right words to express his
love and his death. I could imagine him at the last, refusing to
admit that she had dismissed him forever, reciting a hymn to keep
his courage up as he walked towards the house through the hollow
in the little wood:

> 'If I ask Her to receive me,
> Will she say me nay?
> Not till earth and not till heav'n
> Pass away.'[26]

*

The novel reveals many connections with Greene's own life. But it
also indicates something of Greene's philosophy – an urgency seated
in a refusal to settle down, and his constant uprooting of himself.

Greene as a teenager, through reading Marjorie Bowen's novel, discovered as he termed it 'human nature is not black and white but black
and grey'[27]. Well, must we throw the saints away as never existing? If
this is so, then the world is a tragedy striking us all. And sometimes
darkness creeps into our minds, as soundless as a feather falling. The
Viper in contrast, acted with cunning and not too secretly, the young
and old Greene seems on occasions to admire the diabolical hero, overcoming good as symbolised by the simple creature Wordsworth.

*

Greene had a philosophy of life which he put into the mouth of Aunt
Augusta, reported by Pulling. To her, everything is possible – hasn't she
had many 'careers': a prostitute, a tax evader, a smuggler, a lady willing
to break laws because she 'never read any laws'? When Henry suggests
he might finally marry a gentle lady, Augusta argues against it:

Do you know what you'll think about when you can't sleep in your double bed? . . . You will think how every day you are getting a little closer to death. It will stand there as close as the bedroom wall. And you'll become more and more afraid of the wall because nothing can prevent you coming nearer and nearer to it every night while you try to sleep.

Henry answers: 'Isn't it the same everywhere at our age?' Greene replies through Augusta:

Not here it isn't. [Henry has just arrived in Paraguay.] Tomorrow you may be shot in the street by a policeman because you haven't understood Guarani, or a man may knife you in a *cantina* because you can't speak Spanish and he thinks you are acting in a superior way . . . My dear Henry, if you live with us, you won't be edging day by day across to any last wall. The wall will find you of its own accord without your help, and every day you live will seem to you a kind of victory. 'I was too sharp for it that time,' you will say, when night comes, and afterwards you'll sleep well.[28]

And Greene continued to cross the line, break taboos, ignoring at times propriety. An example? His list of forty-seven prostitutes with pet names like 'Russian boots' and 'Irish-Pole sucker' – those girls he sought out in London streets two years after marriage, and even before, as his first novel, *The Man Within*, reveals.

That is the way Greene lived, seeking the perilous, and this he continued until finally doing battle with death. He would write like a lifer sentenced to hard labour, breaking rocks in the hot sun, with no hope for parole. Yet, however much he wished to go out of the world in an heroic battle of his own choosing, it didn't happen. The wall didn't find him; he slowly found the wall.

PART 17

A Masterpiece from the Old Fox

38

How *Not* to Snatch a Diplomat

'That one always wanted to exceed the normal limits by which men usually live: that was what he was seeking.'
— CORRIENTES AIRPORT DIRECTOR VERMUDEZ

I N late 1967, Greene went off with his old friend Mario Soldati to Sierra Leone and wrote for the *Observer* an article with a compelling title, 'The Soupsweet Land', about coming back to the place where he'd worked for MI6 during the war. He was returning for a happy visit, though his enjoyment is not evident in the photograph taken there, showing a tall, slightly forbidding Greene, and Soldati, confident and at ease in West Africa.

Mario Soldati was immensely fit and energetic, two years younger than Graham, a lover of good food and red wine. Greene called him 'that nice but hysterical Italian film director' and used him in a minor role in *Travels with My Aunt*, but he was much more than that – a novelist in his own right, and a character of characters.

On this, Greene's third journey to West Africa, he and Soldati visited the University in Sierra Leone.* We see Greene in photographs standing among students and the Vice-Chancellor, Davidson Nichol – to whom Greene had been kind when that young man was at Cambridge. But there is another photo which shows Greene, and especially Soldati, walking through groups of black students with undeniable pleasure and assurance. I met Soldati near Milan, at his home in Tallaro on the Bay of Lerici – where Percy Bysshe Shelley drowned. He lived in D. H. Lawrence Street, and though he must have been expecting me, he opened the front door and stared. I introduced myself. He did not offer his hand, nor did he welcome me. He had his left arm in a sling, and his first words were: 'What do you think of a wife who shoots

---

* I never thought that years later I would teach there so that I could follow in Greene's tracks through Sierra Leone and into Liberia.

you in the arm just because you've had an affair with the servant?' My immediate thought (which I didn't utter) was that she'd aimed too high. When our interview was over, after I'd reached my hotel in Milan, Soldati telephoned to tell me one more item. He had considered keeping it secret, but then thought it would do no harm to let it out of the bag, since he was sure that Greene and he would be dead before I completed the biography. (He was right.)

In his comic, outrageous way, Mario spoke graphically of his last conversation with Graham, crude, but too funny to censor: 'We were having dinner and we talked about everything under the sun, but we finished our conversation talking about the women we had loved and ended the night in laughter, confessing the varieties of oral sex we'd performed – each story diverse, and each story had to be about "strange pussy".'[*]

In Sierra Leone, Greene and Soldati visited brothels together and smoked opium. Greene enjoyed Soldati's company, though he was never entirely happy travelling with men (as we saw with Michael Meyer). In writing to Catherine on 18 January 1968, he said he hoped she'd see Mario upon his return, and recalled one night in Freetown's old City Hotel (a source for Greene's early novel *The Heart of the Matter*) when they were

> unable to buy a single drink for ourselves, and then moved for comfort to a brand new characterless [hotel]. We found my old house and several old beachcombers. We had two days at the diamond mines in great luxury and went up to Makene to see the old Italian bishop there (I don't know why I say old – he's younger than me). Mario was a good companion but a bit tiring. Too much making love in public to attract attention, dramas over health, clothes, woolen underpants, but I'd have been bored without him.

In 'The Soupsweet Land'[1] article Greene returns again to the wonderful City Hotel: 'It was a home from home for men who had not encountered success at any turn of the long road and who no longer expected it.' Greene was much touched by these men, and they had not forgotten him. He felt like 'a ghost – a *revenant*' – his memories unaltered. Indeed

---

[*] Many years later, Greene had died and Michael Shelden published his life of Greene in which he accused Greene of being a homosexual. I telephoned Soldati, then aged eighty-seven, and one of his sons told me he was in his sick bed. I explained the outlandish charge, and heard Soldati shout through the phone: 'You tell Mr Shelden that I'll come over to England and knock the lies out of his mouth.' That was Soldati.

he wished to be invisible, and was therefore shocked that he was fresh in their recollections: 'Coming back to Freetown and Sierra Leone last Christmas, I thought I belonged to a bizarre past which no one else shared. It was a shock to be addressed by my first name on my first night, to feel a hand squeeze my arm, and a voice say, . . . "Don't you remember we met in Pujehun? . . . Let's have a drink at the City."'

Greene recalled vividly the experiences he'd put into *The Heart of the Matter* when he saw that physically the City Hotel had not changed a bit. The 'kindly sad Swiss landlord was still the same; he hadn't left Freetown in more than thirty years . . . his shabby bar the "home from home"'.* Everyone welcomed Greene, and he was warmly treated by men who, these many years later, were still doing the same job, though 'the turbaned Sikh was absent who used to tell fortunes – in the communal douche for the sake of privacy'. And Greene goes quickly back to how it was at the old City Hotel, which he'd made famous with his hero Scobie, the police commissioner. The real commissioner on whom Scobie was based went out of his mind under the pressure of overwork; the strain of controlling corrupt officers, the badgering of MI5 bureaucrats from home. The holidays loomed: 'A Sierra Leonian played sad Christmas calypsos in the corner of the balcony and a tart in a scarlet dress danced to attract attention (tarts were not allowed).'

Little was forgotten of that hotel – steps leading up to the balcony where he sat long before, formulating Scobie, his hero to be. He put the following words into the mouth of his character Wilson, just recently out from England, but they apply to Greene, and helped make him the writer he was. Watching a figure in the street below,

> he couldn't tell that this was one of those occasions a man never forgets: a small cicatrice had been made on the memory, a wound that would ache whenever certain things combined – the taste of gin at mid-day, the smell of flowers under a balcony, the clang of corrugated iron, an ugly bird flopping from perch to perch.[2]

Greene and Soldati went to midnight mass, and he recalled the priest he knew during the war, Father Mackie (who used to preach in Creole) . . . And Greene, always observant, noticed:

> the girl in front of me wore one of the surrealist Manchester

* As I write these lines in December 2000, I have learned that the hotel has been stricken by fire and sadly, the Swiss landlord gone to his grave.

cotton dresses which are rarely seen . . . The word 'soupsweet' was printed over her shoulder, but I had to wait until she stood up before I could confirm another phrase: 'Fenella lak good poke.' Father Mackie would have been amused, I thought, and what better description could there be of this poor lazy lovely coloured country than 'soupsweet'?[3]

*

'Tomorrow I'm off,' Greene writes to Yvonne on 15 July 1968, and his leaden melancholia is suddenly lifted: 'I feel more cheerful now it's too late to change my mind.' This sixty-four-year-old man gained release by surrendering to the guileless boy still within him – 'the missed heartbeat, the appalled glee', venturing towards the edge, and perhaps over it.

Greene went to Paraguay by way of Buenos Aires and Corrientes. Just prior to that visit, he let Yvonne in on his excitement, the secret conflicts, even political skullduggery in Paraguay, speaking of plans, plots, rebellion – how such matters exhilarated him always:

A Paraguayan musician-refugee is coming to see me with letters to other exiles in Buenos Ayres, so the old political pattern of the trip is forming again. A few days ago *The Times* reported a plot against the President, & three colonels arrested – so I seem to have picked right again.[4]

He arrived first at Villa Victoria, Mar del Plata, one of the homes of his friend Victoria Ocampo.*

She was unconventional for the times, and later, as a publisher, she attracted to her magazine Albert Camus, André Gide, Aldous Huxley, William Faulkner – and Graham Greene. She kept away from politics, though at one time she was jailed by Perón for making anti-government speeches. She expressed her philosophy precisely: 'I do not ask an author about his political convictions. I ask him only to produce good literature.'

Greene's fame was reaching stratospheric proportions, and having arrived in Argentina, he expresses his annoyance in letters to Catherine about the 'film-star welcome':

Everything from little girls asking autographs at the agricultural

---

* An article in the 24 March 1961 *Time* tells how during the Depression in 1931, Ocampo founded a new literary magazine, *Sur* [*South*], and though it contained Picasso drawings, Argentina thought it just another 'butterfly magazine that would die by the summer's end'. The butterfly had grown into an eagle, reaching thirty years of age!

510

show to lunch with the Foreign Secretary. I've felt like Elizabeth Taylor, but she enjoys it.[5]

and to Yvonne:

I'm staying, very comfortably, with Victoria Ocampo – but oh the film star welcome in Buenos Ayres, the cameras, the 'royal' visits. I go to bed . . . exhausted.[6]

Greene had an urge to reverse the natural order, to grow younger. Most of us as we age turn from socialism to conservatism, from revolution (often enough found only in a teenager) to a desire to keep the status quo. Age often moves us in the direction of safety, but not Greene. Certainly not.

★

Greene meant to stay at Victoria Ocampo's home for a few days and then journey by boat to Corrientes. He had not yet started writing *The Honorary Consul*, but had made strides with *Travels with My Aunt*. Indeed, one reason he was going to Paraguay was because he'd thought of a better ending for *Travels with My Aunt*.

Earlier in 1968 he had met in his old haunt of Anacapri a friend, Alberto Cavalcanti, the Brazilian film producer: 'He told me that I would like Paraguay which was a very mysterious country – the only South American country where the Indians had retained their pride & language & music.'[7] And no doubt Cavalcanti had whispered stories to Greene about riches made by smuggling – stories, perhaps, of the special relationships established between smugglers, police and customs. It was this aspect which Greene saw as a possible denouement for his story. Greene tells Yvonne that 'when I woke up I suddenly saw a different rather happy ending to *Travels with My Aunt* & I felt encouraged.'[8] He travelled up the Paraná river, meeting with the odd passengers, and this did the trick for the unfinished novel.

He had trouble getting from Buenos Aires to Corrientes, the northern town next door to Asunción, Paraguay. From San Isidro, where Ocampo had her home, he tells Yvonne: 'I'm a bit stuck because all the boats to Asunción are full & I can't get away till August 2 – arriving August 6 . . . Dear love, this may be the last letter I'll post because communications from Paraguay are very bad.'[9]

Greene arrived at the Grand Hotel de Paraguay, Asunción, on 5 August 1968 and he tells Yvonne of the characters he'd met on the boat, some of whom he transferred almost without change into *Travels with My Aunt*:

Four nights & days on the boat with eccentric characters . . . the 83 year old fortune teller, the alcoholic woman of 60 who tried to rape me, the Hungarian plastics manufacturer with two million plastic straws which no one will buy.

Greene speaks of the jacaranda in flower, of the two colours on the same tree, the orange blossom everywhere, 'a decayed enchanting place'. But again, his fame is such that he cannot escape people, cannot watch, cannot observe:

At the little port of Corrientes, the Press came on board at 11 at night, & here they were again when we tied up, plus the Argentine Minister & his wife & an attaché, plus two people from the British Embassy.[10]

To be a celebrity is to see nothing, and Greene's frustration is plain: 'One can't dig around at all in this atmosphere of diplomats, journalists, photographers & endless' book signing. His modus operandi (which had always worked for him) of privately searching for material was being threatened by his fame. But he watched anyway, he saw what he could. He wouldn't have been Greene if he didn't. He had a ready smile and high, gentle English voice which helped disguise his spying-out the land. Listening to his new friends in Corrientes and Asunción he was impeccably polite. When seeking material, Greene spoke softly, seeming only to scratch the surface of life, the imprint on the clay delicately left behind.

In *The Honorary Consul*, the friends of Dr Plarr, the protagonist in the capital city of Argentina, are astonished when they learn that he's going to practise medicine in the northern port of Corrientes, only a bit more than a stone's throw away from Paraguay's capital, Asunción. 'He would find a hot humid unhealthy climate in the north, they all assured him of that, and a town where nothing ever happened.'[11]

This reflects comments made to Greene during his visit to Victoria Ocampo's lovely colonial home at Mar del Plata, but to Catherine, he gently rebuts their judgment:

We walked the beach and went to the movies every night and it was rather cold. Then I went up to Corrientes near the Paraguay border which I'd seen from the river boat on my way to Asunción two years ago. Nobody could understand why I was going there. It's very hot and humid, they said (and that was true) and nothing ever happens there.

His celebrity did, however, have its advantages:

> I flew up in the same plane as the governor who passed a decree making me a guest of the province so I paid for nothing . . . hotel, drinks all free. In 8 days there was an archbishop under arrest, a priest was excommunicated (I liked him), a murdered man in a field (I photographed the body), a bomb in a church, a consul kidnapped, four churches closed by the archbishop, and a man who committed suicide with his whole family by driving his car into the . . . river just opposite my hotel. So I still seem to bring trouble . . .[12]

Greene did see the corpse of the murdered man, guarded by two policemen:

> A piece of brown paper had been spread over the body: only the feet protruded at one end. I wanted to photograph the strange package, but a policeman with too friendly zeal took off the brown paper and left only an uninteresting corpse. We took a small path down through the trees to the waterside: a trickle of blood had not yet been dried by the sun.[13]

★

I visited Corrientes and Asunción, Paraguay's capital city, in July 1978 and interviewed the director of the airport who'd shown Greene the dead body. When I asked him to show me the place where the murdered man had been, Director Vermudez told me that he hadn't meant for Greene to see such a sight. 'The airport was then under construction. I had promised Greene I'd take him out to see the work . . . It was impossible to hide him because he was lying there in the middle of the whole thing. He was dead and ants had already begun to eat his body. The man had been killed about dawn and we arrived about 4 hours later.'

The man had been murdered in a fight during a pay-off between contrabandists, not by the police. The airport was not near the city of Corrientes but very close to the Paraguayan border, and Greene was pleased to be so close to this kind of action. The director continued: 'A man pays for what he does. It was truly a struggle between men – someone lost and someone won and it didn't involve any appeal to the authority, to the police or anything else.' And then Vermudez had a surprising insight when speaking to me about Greene: 'That one always wanted to exceed the normal limits by which men usually live: that was what he was seeking.'

In his diary, Greene makes a reference to Vermudez's kindness and courage, evident when he took Greene out to observe things as they were, and went ahead of him (in case of snakes) to a small, open hut:

> a disused wooden jetty & the huge rafts of logs which come two thousand miles down the river, for shipping out. Families build shelters & live on the rafts for two to six months. We passed the dead body of a man murdered last night. The police had covered the body with a sheet of paper, the toes sticking out. There'd been a fight & all the way down the path to the river were patches of blood. I wanted to photograph it but I hadn't expected the police to raise the cover. A man of about forty, thin, lying on his back with patches of blood on his chest – peaceful. V. had seen his killer. 'Why did you do it? He was your friend.' 'He would have killed me, but I am alive.' 'What will you do?' 'I will have to send for the police.'[14]

Greene asked the director if he'd been afraid, and he'd answered: 'Not really. These people are my friends,' which Greene then used in *The Honorary Consul*, applying the phrase to the cunning chief of police, Colonel Perez.

The director told Greene what he told me more indirectly: 'An affair of smuggling. Paraguay's just over the way. Perhaps a dispute over 3 pesos!' And Greene added the following note in his diary: 'Deaths like this not taken very seriously. No death sentence. If he can argue passion – which includes excitement as well as sex – a matter of a year or two in prison.'

★

Greene made a second material-seeking visit two years later to Corrientes and Asunción in March 1970. He is as ever aware of his limitations – since he doesn't have an intimate knowledge of the local people or the Guarani Indians, their presence is kept to a minimum in the novel, but he knows very soon what he wants to know.

On his return to Corrientes, he gobbles up the scenery of the port, used first in *Travels with My Aunt*, and soon after its publication, he starts seeking characters for *The Honorary Consul*. What he saw in Corrientes in northern Argentina made him realise there was much more to mine in Asunción. Greene probably recognised that he might have an opportunity to write a more serious – even a superlative, novel from all he was taking in.

★

A single line in his diary, his tiny handwriting ever more minute as he ages, now more or less a constellation of dots: 'The seventy-year-old teacher of English . . . at the residencia hotel'.[15] Nothing more is said about him in the diary. In the novel, he is called Dr Humphries, an English school teacher, who lives in a dilapidated hotel, typical of Greeneian seediness − and Greene needed seediness.* Humphries' life is carefully drawn, a nearly exact reflection of where and how the model lived.

The character through whose eyes most of the story is seen is Dr Eduardo Plarr. Early in the first chapter of *The Honorary Consul*, Plarr sits reading a novel by a friend, Dr Saavedra, entitled *The Taciturn Heart*. As he reads, Plarr feels 'a sudden desire for company which [is] not Spanish', but there are only two Englishmen other than himself (and Plarr is British only on his father's side), 'an old English teacher who had adopted the title of doctor without ever having seen the inside of a university, and Charley Fortnum, the Honorary Consul'. However, 'since the morning months ago when he had begun sleeping with Charley Fortnum's wife, Dr Plarr found he was ill at ease in the Consul's company; perhaps he was plagued by primitive sensations of guilt; perhaps he was irritated by the complacency of Charley Fortnum who appeared so modestly confident of his wife's fidelity.'[16] (Was Graham ever plagued by a sense of guilt while in the presence of a confident Jacques Cloetta, Yvonne's husband? I believe so, and as we shall see later, my interview with Count Creixwell in Spain confirms it.)

On this night, Plarr doesn't go back to his own rooms, anticipating that Clara Fortnum may telephone and request his company because her husband is dining with the governor, acting as an interpreter to the new American ambassador. But Plarr knows something else − something 'he had no right to know in advance' − namely that Charley is likely to return unexpectedly early because the dinner is sure to be cancelled. An attempt will be made to kidnap the ambassador.

So Plarr, not wishing to be caught *in flagrante* by the return of the Honorary Consul, avoids his telephone, and instead calls on Humphries at the Bolivar Hotel, to discover he has gone to the Italian Club. Plarr describes Humphries' room:

> There was hardly space for a bed, a dressing-table, two chairs, a basin and the douche . . . Doctor Humphries had pasted a new picture on the wall, from the Spanish edition of *Life*, showing the Queen perched on a horse at Trooping the Colour. The choice

---

* The journalist Colm Brogan recorded how on one occasion, he was sitting between Evelyn Waugh and Graham Greene when Waugh suggested to Greene he should write a novel about Brogan. And Greene replied: 'Brogan's no good to me. He'll never end in seedy decay.'

was not necessarily a mark of patriotism or nostalgia: patches of damp were continually appearing on the plaster of the room and Doctor Humphries covered them with the nearest picture which came to hand.[17]

When I visited Corrientes, some eight years after Greene, I met the same old Englishman Greene had met, and visited his single room. He sat on his bed marking school papers, the walls indeed streaming with water from a leak in his roof. A fine old gentleman, he was lonely, and conscientious to a fault. He did not speak of England because he could not afford to return home. His voice, refined, bespoke a good public school, even if (as Greene suggests in his novel) he had no justified right to the academic title of Doctor of Letters. 'Yes,' he told me, he'd 'met Greene once. We shook hands. That's all.' 'Humphries' could not know that he had achieved, on the basis of a simple handshake, the distinction of a place in literature.

Plarr remembers the first time he met Charley Fortnum and Humphries, just a few weeks after he arrived in Corrientes. As he was passing the Italian Club, 'an elderly gentleman leant from the window . . . and called to him for help', because his friend was exceedingly drunk and '"the bloody waiter's gone home," he explained, speaking in English'.

Plarr asks Humphries who the drunk is. It's Fortnum:

'The gentleman you see sitting here on the floor and refusing to get up is Mr Charles Fortnum, our Honorary Consul . . . I'm Doctor Humphries. Doctor of Letters, not medicine. We three, you may say, are the pillars of the English colony, but one pillar has fallen.' . . .

'Is he celebrating something?' Doctor Plarr asked.

'His new Cadillac arrived safely last week, and today he's found a purchaser.'

The good consul, in his drunkenness, wants to go to a brothel, Señora Sanchez's:

'A friend of his?'

'Of half the men in this town. She runs the only good brothel here . . .'

'Surely they are illegal,' said Doctor Plarr.

'Not in this city. We are a military headquarters – don't forget that. The military don't allow anyone in [Buenos Aires] to dictate to them here.'

'Why not let him go?'

'You can see why – he can't stand up.'

'Surely the point of a brothel is that one can lie down?'

'Something has to stand up,' Doctor Humphries said with unexpected coarseness.[18]

Humphries and Plarr lug Fortnum across the road to Humphries' little room.

*

The brothel in Corrientes is important in this novel, because there the Honorary Consul is to meet his young wife. Plarr goes to it. Only Humphries is not a regular. Greene himself visited Corrientes' only brothel; he called there within forty-eight hours of arriving in the town on 25 March 1970, his diary entries kept to the minimum:

> Home after 4.30. Walk to the port taking photos . . . afterwards to see best local brothel. 1000 pesos a girl, divided 50/50 by madam, a fat lady in spectacles reclining with a friend in deck chairs outside. Open patio surrounded by very clean little rooms.

This is how Madame Sanchez's brothel, based on a real brothel called *El Tiburón*, is described in the novel.*

Peter Keene, an Englishman working for the Ford Motor Company, took Greene to *El Tiburón*. Greene put him into his novel in a minor way. He describes him without giving his name in *Ways of Escape*:

> There was a certain character – a friend of a friend – who would certainly know if any such brothel existed anywhere, and from his appearance I felt certain of his authority on sexual matters. I borrowed his features for one of my minor characters, Gustavo Escobar: 'his face, brick-red as laterite, resembled a clearing which had been hacked out of the bush and his nose reared like the horse of a conquistador'.[19]†

In the novel, Don Escobar is married to a society woman (whom Dr Plarr has also slept with, but then Plarr is not averse to sleeping with his patients.

---

* This translates as 'The Shark'; other possible translations are Pike, Wolf, Raider, and one last which seems appropriate, *Don Juan*.

† When I met Keene I did not note such a red face, or that his nose reared so dramatically.

We can tie Greene's description of the brothel in his diary more closely to his description in the novel: Greene has Dr Plarr make his visit with his friend, the Spanish novelist Saavedra:

> Señora Sanchez sat in a deck-chair outside her house knitting. She was a very stout lady with a dimpled face and a welcoming smile from which kindliness was oddly lacking . . .
>
> They passed through the narrow lighted doorway. Except for Señora Sanchez in her deck-chair there were no exterior signs to differentiate her establishment from the other houses in the respectable street . . .
>
> It was a house very different in character from the clandestine brothels he had occasionally visited in the capital where small rooms were darkened by closed shutters and crammed with bourgeois furniture. There was a pleasant country air about this house. An airy patio about the size of a tennis court was surrounded by small cells.

Teresa, one of the girls, joins Saavedra and finally goes with him. Plarr sees another whom he is attracted to:

> A cell door opened and a man came out. He lit a cigarette, went to a table and drank from an unfinished glass. In the glow of light . . . Doctor Plarr could see a thin girl who was straightening the bed. She arranged the coverlet with care before she came out and joined her companions at their communal table.

Later Plarr notices on her forehead 'a little below the hairline, a small grey birth-mark, in the spot where a Hindu girl wears the scarlet sign of her caste'. Saavedra talks on, but while Plarr answers he has in mind the thin girl with her small flaw: '[He] thought how agreeable it would be to take the girl to her room. He had not slept with a woman for more than a month, and how easily sexual attention can be caught by something superficial, like a birth-mark in an unusual position.' As Saavedra goes off with Teresa, he asks his friend Plarr:

> 'Isn't there a girl here who pleases you?'
> 'Yes, there is one, but she has found another customer.'
> The girl with the birth-mark had joined the solitary drinker and they were proceeding together to her cell. She passed her former companion without a glance and he hadn't enough curiosity to look at his successor. There was something clinical in a brothel which appealed to Doctor Plarr [and I suspect to Greene too].[20]

As both Plarr and Saavedra leave, the madam is joined by a friend and they both sit knitting.

In the novel Plarr does not go back to the local brothel for a year: 'He looked in vain then for the girl with the birth-mark on her forehead.' And as cold a fish and unemotional as he is, Greene writes: 'He was neither surprised nor disappointed.'[21] The girl with the distinctive mark is Clara, and she is no longer a prostitute because she's accepted an offer of marriage from Charley Fortnum, the bumbling, outspoken (yet in his way clever) drunk, our Honorary Consul.

★

There are four major characters in the novel: Humphries, the schoolteacher; Dr Eduardo Plarr, a medical doctor; the Honorary Consul, Charley Fortnum, and Rivas. To 'Father' León Rivas, Plarr says: 'Charley Fortnum's veins run with alcohol, not blood';[22] in some sense alcohol is his God, and before his marriage, his only need. His friend Humphries describes him harshly: 'His father was a notorious drunkard and so is Charley Fortnum.'[23] Granted, he is a flop as an Honorary Consul, and Fortnum knows it.

Father León Rivas, a one-time priest, now a guerrilla leader and kidnapper, hopes that by kidnapping the new American ambassador he'll be able to persuade the Paraguayan leader General Stroessner* to release twenty prisoners (later reduced to ten); he is soon aware of their error in kidnapping the Honorary Consul. Maybe the plan would have worked if they'd bagged the right man, but what inefficiency in picking up Charley instead, the monumental drunk. These terrorists are amateurs.

Because the Honorary Consul is only honorary, he can have no political influence whatsoever in persuading the dictator General Stroessner to release the prisoners languishing in his jails. To Father Rivas, Plarr says:

'Charley Fortnum's no good to you as a hostage.'

'He is a member of the diplomatic corps,' Aquino [Rivas's helpmate] said.

'No, he isn't. An Honorary Consul is not a proper Consul.'

'The British Ambassador would have to intervene.'

'Of course. He would report the affair home. Just as he would for anyone British. If you kidnapped me or old Humphries it would be much the same.'

'The British will ask the Americans to bring pressure on the General in Asunción.'

---

* General Alfredo Stroessner, a Nazi sympathiser, took over as president of Paraguay in a *coup d'état* in 1954 and ruled until he was overthrown in 1989.

'You can be sure the Americans will do nothing of the kind. Why should they? They don't want to anger their friend the General for the sake of Charley Fortnum.'

'But he is a British *Consul.*'

Doctor Plarr began to despair of ever convincing them of how unimportant Charley Fortnum was.[24]

It is initially beyond the understanding of the revolutionaries that Her Majesty's government would have no interest in seeking concessions from the General's government, thus saving them from having to kill poor Charley.

*

While a prisoner in the squalid hut in the barrio, Fortnum tells Father Rivas (who catches him crying): 'I'm not a brave man.' He is afraid of dying, and he has every expectation that his kidnappers will shoot him. As Honorary Consul he is the weakest reed in the diplomatic corps; he knows he has no pull and the prisoners will not be released – the kidnappers will have to prove their machismo and shoot him. He denies he's crying out of self-pity; he says he just doesn't want his wife to be alone when she dies.

'Father Rivas made a gesture – it might have been an attempt to sketch a blessing in the air which he had forgotten how to give: "God will be there," he said without conviction.' But Fortnum's answer is firm: 'Oh, you can have your God. Sorry, Father, but I don't see any sign of him around, do you?'[25] The old boozer is no believer.

*

Nowhere in Greene's diary, nor in his notes for writing this novel, is there any indication of the origin of Charley Fortnum. Might we then believe that Fortnum was pure invention?

Greene was aware that the Tupamaros, Uruguayan urban guerrillas dedicated in the 1960s to making a revolution in that country, were unquestionably professionals. They, if Greene had used them to do the kidnapping, would have made no errors. How inefficient are Greene's fictional urban guerrillas.*

---

* Kidnapping was in the air in the 1960s and 70s. The most famous case took place in America when the heiress Patricia Hearst was kidnapped on 5 February 1974 by the Symbionese Liberation Army. The SLA persuaded the Hearst family to distribute $2 million in free food to poor areas. Patricia Hearst took a lover and chose – or was compelled – (for a time) to fight alongside her kidnappers.

I checked with a number of people during my stay in Corrientes. I was less willing to ask questions in Asunción, still under strongman General Stroessner, about any Honorary Consuls or consuls who'd been kidnapped or who would have held a position that revolutionaries might think useful for barter. Usually it had to be at least an ambassador, certainly not an Honorary Consul. Having failed to find anyone remotely paralleling Charley Fortnum (his name Greene took from the famous London shop Fortnum and Mason, and Charley's nickname is in fact Mason), I examined Greene's diaries, and the many letters in my possession. As I was doing this, it became clear that I had earlier discovered the origin of Charley Fortnum without realising it. There was a man Greene knew, a Consul-General whom he met twenty years earlier, and in a different part of the world.

★

It was back in 1949, soon after the film of *The Third Man* was released. Greene was busy trying his hand at dramatising *The Heart of the Matter* in collaboration with Basil Dean (who had been head of ENSA troop entertainments during the Second World War). They worked hard on the script and, as he often did when overworked, Greene returned to taking benzedrine 'to try to get the bloody thing finished this week', but felt he was 'trying to flog a dead horse into life'.[26] Completing the play on his forty-fifth birthday, he and Dean decided to travel to Sierra Leone, the setting for *The Heart of the Matter*, in December.

In Paris Greene had trouble getting a yellow fever certificate from the French officials, and feared he'd have to return to England to get it. After a heavy day with French authorities, he was finally allowed to travel without the certificate.

Two days later, Greene was stuck at Dakar in Senegal, and again officials were unhappy about his lack of a yellow fever certificate, Dakar having a disturbing record of the disease. Greene had been warned in Paris by Air France that if there was a problem with the lack of a certificate in Dakar it would be useless to try to solve it. Greene and Basil Dean finally tracked down the British Consul-General for assistance, but were warned that that wouldn't work either, as he was always drunk by 8.00 a.m.! Greene and Dean had no alternative:

> We called at 4 & after ringing twice, the door opened, not by a servant but by a white man, who swayed slightly. 'Is the Consul-General in?' I said. 'It's him in person,' he said. We stayed about half an hour, unable to get any sense out of him, & he developed a strong dislike of Basil & an embarrassing liking for me – perhaps

he scented someone who liked a drink too. He insisted on Basil photographing him and me & a black servant . . . on the steps under the Royal Arms & urged me to come and stay with him: 'Got two beautiful women to dinner tonight. Your friend – don't know his name – nor yours – looks short tempered. You stay with me any time. Always have a room for you . . .' Another of his *bons mots* was after an embarrassing silence (he had been too drunk to get his telephone to work) he spread his arms wide and with a twinkle at me, 'Tell me the latest story from London.'[27]

It was through this Consul-General that they were able to leave Dakar, obtaining a bogus medical certificate to say that he and Dean were unfit to be inoculated, which allowed Air France to put them on the plane. That Consul-General must have lain fallow in Greene's mind waiting to be reborn.

Perhaps more so than even in his earlier masterpieces, *Brighton Rock, The Heart of the Matter* and *The End of the Affair*, Greene has in *The Honorary Consul* got under the skin of his characters and their experiences, and none more so than Charley Fortnum. A guzzling drunk, often humorous, underneath Fortnum is sometimes pathetic, yet chivalrous, and, unexpectedly, genuinely in love with Clara, his young wife, the one-time prostitute. He is open and direct, as was the Consul-General in Dakar. And like Greene's original source, his behaviour and speech are unpredictable. Poor Charley, captured by bungling revolutionaries, confined in a bleak hut on a dirt floor, his bed a coffin as a reminder that after four days (the time limit the guerrillas set) he will be shot.

At this stage, Charley doesn't know that his friend Dr Plarr has slept with his wife. Such are the dangers of a complacent husband. The child in Clara's belly is not his, it is Plarr's. And Plarr, brilliant, but, to use a description from Conrad's *Heart of Darkness*, 'hollow at the core', laconic in speech (but not in thought), kind to the poor in the barrio, is yet another of Greene's burnt-out cases. His declaration is real and for him, fearful: 'Caring is the only dangerous thing.'[28] In Plarr's case, with his character gradually changing (handled so well by Greene), caring is most assuredly dangerous.

★

Searching for material in Corrientes and Paraguay, Greene came across a case that clearly disconcerted him. Here is the worried diary entry, 26 March 1970: 'Overtaken by events. Kidnapping of a Paraguay consul in a town in Corrientes.' This was a curious case which appeared in *El Litoral*. But eighty hours after the Paraguayan consul had been kidnapped, surprisingly, he was released and the stir subsided.

Why would the urban guerrillas go to the trouble of kidnapping a consul and then release him without achieving their goal? Here's part of the newspaper account translated from Spanish. First the headline: '*Tras 80 horas de Cautiverio Liberan al Consul*' – 'After eighty hours of captivity the Paraguayan Consul is freed'.

The case then: a Paraguayan consul, Waldemar Sanchez, was kidnapped by members of the Argentine Liberation Front – and then set free. Just as in Greene's fictional account, the consul was bait to compel General Stroessner to release the prisoners Carlos Domingo Della Nave and Alejandro Rodolfo Baldu. The government refused a trade, adding that the first had no wish to leave Paraguay, and the second was presumed dead, and if alive was a fugitive.

How did the kidnappers make contact with the consul? The method was odd and Greene took notice. It seems that three young men showed an interest in the purchase of a car which Consul Sanchez had brought to Buenos Aires.

The consul was saved, released about four blocks from Florida Station. When he got rid of the blindfold, he found his way to the León Hotel where he was staying. Inevitably journalists congregated and began asking questions, but not before his ambassador (and the police) were at his side. It seemed an exercise in futility. Taken from the transcript are a number of questions and answers:

Q. Have you any idea of the place where they were holding you?

A. (Looking at the ambassador) I don't know, because they took me there blindfolded.

Q. What was the place like where they locked you up?

A. It was a room which had been wallpapered.

Q. Did they treat you well?

A. Yes, in fact they did treat me well, very well . . .

Q. Were you afraid to die?

A. (Looking at his wife) They had threatened to kill me . . . I don't know if it was fear but I felt bad.

Q. What else was there in the room?

A. . . . I think that the room was dynamited.

Q. Did they tell you that?

A. I found out about it when they were talking to each other saying they were putting explosives in.

Sanchez was asked if he could recognise his kidnappers: 'They always were wearing masks.' The investigating journalists asked the right questions:

Q. Did they wear any uniform apart from the hoods?
A. No, they were always in shirtsleeves.
Q. Did they carry arms?
A. Yes, of all kinds. They had sub-machine guns, pistols, all kinds . . . an arsenal.
Q. Could you explain more fully the reasons why they set you free?
A. Well, they said that they were behaving like gentlemen towards the country.

Greene's detailed knowledge of this event influenced him in a number of curious ways. Knowing the consul was allowed to bring a car into the country every two years – this was his perk – Greene has Charley Fortnum make such an arrangement. Car imports were restricted and a handsome profit could have been made by Sanchez. The young revolutionaries knew that their feigned interest in the car would bring the consul into their orbit, that he would trip unsuspectingly into their trap. Thus the kidnapping was a cakewalk.

39

'As Mystery-Laden as Life Itself'*

The novel, properly handled can reveal the most secret places of life.

— D.H. LAWRENCE

I N 1963, *Newsweek* magazine reported Cardinal Richard Cushing of Boston as saying, some five years before Greene's first visit to Argentina and Paraguay: 'I feel like starting a revolution myself.' And the reason? 'In many areas, Catholics have been heard to say, "I have never seen my pastor; I don't know what parish I'm in."' He felt this complaint was justified.

The problem was twofold: the shortage of priests, and widespread poverty and illiteracy: 'You can't teach religion,' the Cardinal said, 'when the stomachs of little children are blown up four times normal size.'[1] Archbishop Hélder Camâra argued that the biggest problem in Brazil was poverty, 'which is the ideal garden for Communism to grow in'.

The archbishop took Pope Paul to visit the poor. Then there were the Fathers Houtart and Pin, who suggested three alternatives in Latin America: 'prolonged anarchy, violent Communist upheaval, or peaceful and ordered revolution'. They noted that 'the sign of the Church of Christ [will be] visible to the world [through] her social concern and social action'. This was the only way the Catholic Church in Latin America would survive.

The social upheaval really began much earlier than Greene's initial visits. He was late in seeking material for *The Honorary Consul*, and in studying Third World Liberation Theology.

In the 1970s, the rubric of Liberation Theology emphasised that the God of the Bible blesses the poor. Liberation Theology demanded a 'preferential option for the poor', arguing that the Catholic Church

* Machado d'Assis.

must necessarily be involved in the struggle for economic and political justice, especially in the Third World. When Pope John XXIII convened the Second Vatican Council in 1962, he said he fondly hoped it would help make the Catholic Church once again 'the church of the poor'. The Church modestly accepted 'pilgrim' status alongside the rest of mankind and began to see human progress as evidence of God's working in human history. For Catholics, the decrees of the Second Vatican Council offered an open-ended charter for the Church to tackle hunger, illiteracy, social injustice.

At the Second Latin American Bishops Conference, in Medellín, Colombia, in 1968 (the year of Greene's first visit to Buenos Aires, Corrientes and Asunción), there was a movement to persuade the Church to be a prophetic voice, and even to accept violence after the failure of peaceful means. Moreover, the declaration was that the region's church should not ally itself with the powerful and the privileged. One priest, Father Gustavo Gutiérrez, argued in his book *The Theology of Liberation* that 'theology is the second act: the first act is commitment to the poor'.*

The direction, now away from the privileged, led hundreds of nuns and priests at schools and hospitals in wealthy areas to move, *en bloc*, into the slums and shanty towns. Living among the poor, they read the Gospels with new eyes: the poor were to be liberated, for had not God once liberated the Israelites from Egypt?

*

The shock waves that had spread throughout Latin America following Castro's Cuban revolution of January 1959 had begun to shake the Catholic Church itself. Some priests even became terrorists, certainly liberationists (to coin a phrase). Camilo Torres, a handsome priest from a well-to-do Colombian family, scandalised the Church more than any other when he tried (unsuccessfully) to create a revolutionary mass movement to seize power, if necessary by means of violence, for the poor to build socialism. Torres believed (later in 1986, in a speech in

---

* And on 13 July 1969 the *New York Times* recorded a strange and growing phenomenon: 'The Roman Catholic Church, traditionally a pillar of Argentine conservatism, has suddenly become a major problem for the Government. The Catholic Primate, Antonio Cardinal Caggiano, has remained at the president's side at all public functions, but at least 400 priests have been in open rebellion, partly against the church hierarchy but mostly against the military Government and its policies. Some of these priests have provided moral support for students and workers, and some [priests] have gone even further – they have led protest marches, set up strike funds and taught the techniques of labour organizing . . . The new interior minister General Francisco Imaz pointedly warned these priests in a recent speech that the Government expected nothing less than the total backing of the church, [but] the priests remained adamant and their followers grow.'[2]

Moscow during the Gorbachev era, Greene made similar suggestions) that one could be a Christian *and* a revolutionary, that Marxists and Christians could unite. A 'painting depicting Jesus with a rifle slung over his shoulder, . . . distributed in Argentina and other nations' and reproduced in the *New York Times* (12 August 1970) reveals the astonishing change that was taking place among Catholic priests. Torres found no incompatibility.

Pope Paul VI asked the faithful poor not to put their trust in any form of revolution. He was, as many leading ecclesiastics were, worried that the Church would be perceived as an instrument of 'ideological domination'. But fifty priests in Colombia challenged the Church hierarchy, declaring that they were willing to commit themselves to 'different forms of revolutionary action against imperialism and neo-colonial bourgeoisie'. Called the Golconda Group, they fused one famous statement by Camilo Torres – 'the duty of every Catholic is to be a revolutionary' – with Castro's almost parallel assertion that 'the duty of every revolutionary is to make the revolution'. Early on Fidel *had* felt there was a need, at least in Latin America, to forge a 'strategic alliance between revolutionary Marxists and revolutionary Christians'.*

Torres had a remarkable, if short, life. Soon after his death in February 1966, he was hailed as a martyr. He was born (and lived) in Colombia. Without his lead I suspect it would have been less likely that Greene would have turned his fictional priest Rivas into an urban guerrilla.

We might ask, where did Greene find his revolutionaries? We've seen where the drunken consul Charley Fortnum comes from, but what of Father Rivas, the guerrilla leader who had been a priest, who still had the mannerisms and character of a priest? What of his activities as a kidnapper, and why did Rivas create for himself another situation with the Church by marrying Marta (a favoured female name Greene used at this time), herself part of the revolutionary group involved in the kidnapping? Were these creations based on a dream, as Greene himself claimed? He says:

> The origin of my next novel, *The Honorary Consul* . . . lies in the cave of the unconscious. I had a dream about an American ambassador – a favourite of women and a good tennis player whom I encountered in a bar – but in my dream there was no kidnapping, no guerrillas, no mistaken identity, nothing to identify it with *The Honorary Consul* except the fact that the dream lodged

---

* It wasn't until the 1980s (led by Pope John Paul II) that there were substantial criticisms of the new theology and those supporting it. The accusation was obvious: that they were wrongly supporting violent revolution and the Marxist class struggle.

inexplicably in my head for months and during those months the figures of Charlie [*sic*] Fortnum and Dr Plarr stole up around the unimportant ambassador of my dream and quietly liquidated him.[3]

★

I have three of the six volumes of Greene's dream diaries, but found no reference to this particular plot. I suspect that in this particular case the source was his travels in Argentina. The reference to his dream was, I think, an attempt to disguise the story's origins. In *Ways of Escape* Greene helps us, though somewhat indirectly: his 'fictional' guerrillas certainly did not come from the well-known terrorist group in Uruguay:

> It remained for me to discover the scene of the action. Of Uruguay I knew nothing and the Tupamaros were far too efficient an organization to make the mistake of kidnapping an unimportant English honorary consul in place of an American ambassador. Paraguay was quite another matter. Under the heavy rule of Stroessner no guerrilla organization had been able to grow, and it seemed plausible that a small inexperienced group working across the border into Argentina might make the blunder which I needed for my story.[4]

For many years, it's true, the Tupamaros were a highly organised urban guerrilla force, also known as the National Liberation Army. By the late 1960s the Tupamaros were involved in urban terrorism, kidnapping and murder. Greene writes in *Ways of Escape*: 'I was certainly right about the Tupamaros who almost at the same time as I was finishing my novel succeeded most efficiently in kidnapping the British Ambassador in Montevideo. His story when he came to write it contained some interesting parallels to my own. There was even, he believed, a priest among his kidnappers.'[5]

This smacks a little of Greene's using the original idea of the seizing of a British ambassador and simply transferring it to an unknown group of amateurs for his particular purpose. Indeed, Greene had to defend himself when Sir Geoffrey Jackson's *People's Prison* was published a few months before *The Honorary Consul*. On 9 October 1973, Greene wrote to the *Daily Telegraph* about David Holloway's review of *People's Prison*: 'I was very interested in the parallels Mr David Holloway found (4 October) between my novel *The Honorary Consul* and Sir Geoffrey Jackson's *People's Prison*, which I look forward to reading. Just for the sake of the record – my novel was more than three years in writing and I began it some fifteen months before Sir Geoffrey was kidnapped.'

528

In Greene's correspondence, we see he was in the throes of thinking of this story as early as 1968. And Greene needed time to ensure the quality of his novel – he revised it seven times.

★

There were at least two well-known guerrillas who had been priests, and in their own remarkable way extraordinarily sincere priests, wishing to serve Christ and their flocks. In July 1968, Greene, staying at the Grand Hotel in Asunción, writes to Yvonne about such characters whom he met and later developed in *The Honorary Consul*:

> So far the only really interesting contact . . . is with a group of violent young revolutionary Catholics plus students, married priests plus their wives. The movement is named after a priest who was killed with the guerrillas in Colombia.[6]

You can sense his excitement. You almost feel he's already found his subject – revolutionary married priests and their wives. Have we found a source for his ex-Catholic priest, the beautifully developed Rivas? It is Rivas who is tormented by the nature of God (as Rivas sees God). Here is a priest who has broken his vows, yet he is the most poignant figure created by Greene since the whisky priest in *The Power and the Glory*. We sense Greene 'knows' what is going on in Liberation Theology. He is fast gathering his material to deal with Third World revolutionaries within the Catholic Church.

We have the references above to 'revolutionary Catholics' and 'married priests plus their wives' (notice the plural). We know that his fictional hero, Father Rivas, is married to Marta, though she continues to call him Father – using such a title is where her pleasure lies – and the movement 'is named after a priest who was killed with the guerrillas in Colombia'.

Let's look at the life of that priest, Camilo Torres. This priest-leader knew what he was doing and where he was going:

> I took off my cassock to be more truly a priest

> The duty of every Catholic is to be a revolutionary
> The duty of every revolutionary is to make the revolution

> The Catholic who is not a revolutionary is living in mortal sin[7]

But Camilo Torres was not the only revolutionary priest. There were some 300 priests who felt the same. Revolt was in the air and in the blood of the young Catholics of Latin America in the late 1960s and 70s. Police reports of conditions in the capital city of Colombia estimated that there were 10,000 abandoned children wandering the streets and more than 40,000 prostitutes.[8] Many accounts of police brutality exposed practices such as hanging prisoners by the hands, and electric shocks to the breasts of women and genitals of men.

★

Was there another source for Greene's Father Rivas, in the role of leader of the guerrillas, as the story moves into a hut in the barrio? I suspect so, and it involves another excommunicant.

By 1970, Greene was beginning to write this novel. *The Times* of 6 April 1970 reports his attraction to revolutionaries of all breeds:

> *Buenos Aires, 5 April*: Mr Graham Greene . . . on a visit to Argentina has praised the 'third world' movement of young Roman Catholic priests in Argentina, saying they are doing 'great work'.
>
> Mr Greene, who left Buenos Aires yesterday, returned from Corrientes province where a dramatic confrontation between a priest of the movement and the archbishop of the diocese is taking place.
>
> Four churches in the diocese were closed today after police intervention and a clash last week involving Father Oscar Marturet who has been excommunicated by Msgr Francisco Vicentin.

Could Marturet also have contributed to our priest-cum-revolutionary? This question is not easily answered. Greene's brief entries in his diary reveal a strong interest in Father Marturet. Moreover, while he was in Corrientes, Greene picked up information about him as well as his archbishop, and later sought Marturet out:

> *March 24* [1970]: Earlier – the affair of the arrested archbishop & the rebellious priest. The armed police outside the church door.
>
> *March 26*: Story of the archbishop, more & more confused.
>
> *March 27*: After siesta photographic walk. Many of the walls *Viva Marturet* Marturet Cure de Pueblo. A confused story I must get right.

He must get it right indeed, for here is the second source, and it is happening in Corrientes, where he is seeking material. Next day Greene is flown to the governor's house.

March 28: Tea at Patricia's. A lot of books to sign. The enormous, & agreeable, difference between this rich family which works the land & the dried-up conservative rich Englishmen of Cap d'Antibes. They helped the guerrillas against Stroessner with food. 'Perhaps we did wrong. All the young men were killed.' Men of the centres not unduly critical of Father Marturet . . . The Paraguayan Consul has been released. More & more like my own story. They even think they kidnapped the wrong man. What was a Consul doing at a small town in Corrientes & how was it he had a Mercedes Benz? Smuggling?

Stroessner, of course, cared nothing about [the Consul's] life. No one was abused [by the young guerrillas] & the kidnappers took pity on their victim.

March 29: Went back after lunch with the Bittlestons . . . to Marturet's church. Now practically no one around . . . Father M[arturet] was asleep upstairs. Finally he came down – a good head, lay clothes, a quite possible leader. A lot of telephoning. An interpreter would be found – eventually she came . . . I said, looking round, 'You seem to have the support of the middle-class?' The son answered, 'It is true. The third world priests were as yet supported mainly by students. The working class still regards their employers as patrons. They had to be taught to be rebellious.' I remembered the excellent cottages of the governor's employees. Which paternalism is the better.

The photo on the wall of the young student killed by the police. There were always martyrs created by coincidence. He wasn't more dead than the peasant in the field.

M's troubles had begun in 1964 when he had taken the part of the peasants who had been turned off their land & their houses bulldozed on Christmas night because they were squatters on land intended for French immigrants. Today M had a meeting – very fraternal – with the archbishop but totally without result. He now had to work out his appeal to the Nuncio. Then a court of 3 bishops in Argentina would probably be appointed to judge his case. But he had little confidence in the result. The small bomb in the Church of the Cross probably planted by the right wing Catholic organisation . . . 'I've seen their names on the wall – in an attempt to inculpate [Marturet]'.[9]

Greene made friends with Michael Bittleston, an Englishman married to an Argentinian. He took Greene around to show him as much of Corrientes as could be studied in the time Greene had available:

Michael had described the real danger of the police – illiterate peasants who had never been taught to use their rifles. If they want to defend or attack they had only the one weapon which they had never learned to use. They would fire at random – they wouldn't know how to fire at the legs or over the head. [This Greene uses in the novel as the illiterate Guarani Indian who plays with his machine-gun all day, like a child with a toy gun.][10]

*

Greene's article 'The Worm Inside the Lotus Blossom'* is an account of Paraguay's General Stroessner, whose dictatorship lasted thirty-five years.

There were ugly stories of his early days [when Greene visited Paraguay Stroessner was in his third term of office] of opponents thrown from aeroplanes into the forest, and bodies washed up with bound hands on the Argentine bank of the Paraná – the dead are always lucky. Perhaps 150 political prisoners have been lying in the cells of police stations up and down the country for ten years or more, forgotten by all but their families and an occasional priest.[11]

The key figure in Greene's novel is Rivas, the priest, excommunicated and married, leader of the revolutionary kidnappers and yet, in his manner, very much a priest. Greene's ritual drunk, Charley Fortnum, notices that quality of priesthood about him. We see through Greene's eyes as he fits together this subtle novel, modifying material picked up on his travels.

We've reached the point in the novel where the Honorary Consul, no longer drunk, is aware that he is a prisoner and that he is likely to be shot. Eduardo Plarr is at home with his mistress Clara, Charley's wife. Suddenly there is an announcement on the radio:

The authorities, so the speaker said, believed the kidnappers were Paraguayan. It was thought that the Consul might have been taken across the river and the kidnappers were making their demands through the Argentine government in order to confuse the trail. Apparently they had demanded the release of ten political prisoners who were held in Paraguay . . .

The kidnappers had chosen their time with some skill, for General Stroessner at the moment was on an unofficial holiday in the south of Argentina. He had been informed of the kidnapping and he was reported to have said, 'That is no concern of

* *Daily Telegraph Magazine*, 3 January 1969.

mine. I am here for the fishing.' The kidnappers had given the Paraguayan government until Sunday midnight to agree to their terms by an announcement on the radio. When that time expired they would be forced to execute their prisoner.[12]

Plarr thinks of approaching 'Father' Rivas (whom he had known as a schoolboy) to release Fortnum 'in the name of our old friendship' – but no doubt also because he is sleeping with Fortnum's wife:

> But León [Rivas] was a man under orders [from the terrorist leader] and in any case Doctor Plarr had no clear idea of where to find him. In the *barrio* of the poor all the marshy tracks resembled one another, there were the same avocado trees everywhere, the same huts of mud or tin, and the same pot-bellied children carrying petrol tins of water. They would look at him with their blank eyes which were already infected by trachoma and reply nothing to any question. It might take him hours, even days, to find the hut where Charley Fortnum was hidden.[13]

We are first introduced to Rivas and his assistant Aquino when they visit Plarr's surgery some time before their guerrilla activity. Plarr immediately becomes aware of Rivas's singular physical characteristics: his protruding ears. Greene describes his 'bat-ears and the attentive eyes of a good servant'.[14] And: 'He made the gesture of putting his hands against the protruding ears. They flattened and sprang back.'[15] Greene has already met this aspect of Rivas. In his diary, he speaks of another priest 'with his bat ears, his little body – atoning for his ugliness, poor devil'.[16] But, I repeat, it is not this priest whom Greene primarily uses. Father Rivas's internal nature is taken from Father Marturet, who was in the process of being excommunicated at the time of Greene's visit.

★

Eight years after Greene's visit, I travelled to Corrientes and met 'Father' Marturet. He was working as a journalist. Although he was still excommunicated, I could recognise his priestlike ways: he was part-martyr, part-saint. But he did not feel himself to be a priest: 'Many people still call me Father and I don't correct them. I don't feel myself to be a priest of the Church now.' The breach occurred long before he was actually excommunicated. 'When there was a change of archbishop I tried to open a dialogue with the new archbishop. There were four or five other priests involved as well – Fathers Pascal, Tiscornia, Babín and Niellas. The last one went back to the Church and was reincorporated into it. He had to accept all the conditions imposed by the Archbishop of Corrientes, to renounce all his earlier activities.'[17] Marturet said

> The third world movement developed about 1966 in Argentina . . . [emphasising] human needs . . . All Latin America was living in a situation of a large and exploited population . . . the [problems of the] great majority of the people . . . could not be solved by small charities, donating a blanket or giving them a little bit of milk . . . really profound changes in the social, economic structure of the country were necessary.[18]

I asked him when he was excommunicated and why. He said it was during Holy Week right before he'd met Greene, who'd also asked him why this had happened. At first Marturet evaded the question, emphasising instead his interest in social change. He didn't mention his sermon on 'Father' Camilo Torres, but I heard from Greene that Marturet had spoken of him and Greene had transferred this into his novel as the words of Father Rivas, referring to Father Torres who was 'shot with the guerrillas in Colombia'.

Greene's account in *The Honorary Consul* fits in with what Father Marturet told me:

> The police reported me to the Archbishop and the Archbishop forbade me to preach any more. Oh well, poor man, he was very old and the General [Stroessner] liked him, and he thought he was doing right, rendering to Caesar . . .
>
> It is not the same Archbishop now. He was a fine priest, an excellent old man, but very conservative, and very closed. He worked very hard. A very meritorious man.[19]

Marturet's honesty is passed on to Rivas. Marturet told me he enjoyed his work as a journalist: 'I interview, I report, editorialise and also do what they call "cook". I "cook" the news, that is I take things that come in and put it into journalese – newspaper language.' When I asked if he still felt himself to be a priest, he said that he no longer did: 'I continue to question many of the things the Church does. I maintain my faith in Christ.'

M: People who knew me as a priest still continue to come and consult me over problems that I used to treat as a priest. I try to treat the problems religiously. They are medical problems often. I counsel them to go and see their priest first but if

they insist then I counsel them. My answers are always framed
within the reference to the Church, as if I were a priest.

NS: Do you still pray?

M: I still pray but in a different way. I don't use the ritualised
prayers, the rosary and so forth any more, and I don't go to
mass. Given the norms of the Church and my excommunica-
tion this is one of the *benefits* of the Church that are closed to
me now.

NS: And the sacraments?

M: For me the real presence of Christ is not in the bread and the
wine. I look more to the commandment that Christ gave in
the first communion, that is to share with all. I see more the
symbolic sense of the priest acting as Christ and the sharing
with those who are in the presence, and I don't need the real
presence of Christ in the bread itself. What I think more
important is to fulfil Christ's commandment of sharing.[20]

Unquestionably, as a result of the Third World Movement (Liberation
Theology), many priests were forced out, and Marturet was one. But
he was never quite able to hide the fact that he had been a priest, and
he stood for that movement's aspiration to be the voice of the oppressed.

And Greene makes it plain in the novel that Rivas's spirit, that
internal sweet shadow of priesthood, cannot be shed, whatever he says
for God or against God. In spite of the ex-priest's disturbing, even
outrageously irreligious, comments, it is as though God, even if seen
as an enemy, cannot be eluded. God is the hound of heaven pursuing
a wayward human soul, and Rivas the chivalric knight daring the outer
darkness. Rivas is a profoundly sensitive man, as is Marturet, but he is
also, like so many others in the canon of Greene's work, a failure.
Certainly Rivas fails as a kidnapper.

★

As the clock ticks, decisions have to be made before the amateur guerrillas are discovered by the police. They have to escape – already they
hear a helicopter over the *barrio* and feel (rightly) they are being surrounded.
But Rivas does not focus (as a true man of action would) on how to
escape. He hides his head, ostrich-like, in a dialogue of religious conflict
and a determination to dispute the nature of God. The minutes go by
as Rivas feels compelled to provide us with a God who partakes of some
of the characteristics of Satan; it is implied that there is no Satan, there
is only a God who is like the best of us and the worst of us – a reminder
almost of the sculptor in *Carving a Statue*, seeking to provide us first
with the supposed evil eye of God but then seeking to sculpt the

good eye. These are breathless moments in the novel, as we sense the police closing in on the hut, while Rivas holds forth on his heretical views.

Reviewers of the day criticised this religious interpolation on the singular nature of God, which was nothing to do with the working out of the plot, except as it might have led to the killing of the Honorary Consul and the escape of the kidnappers.

But this is the heart of the book. Greene, through Rivas, says something so terrible and so disturbing: that all but the most assured might have to wait until death to discover whether our trust is justified. His arguments almost paralyse by their unexpectedness, as if a new theology were being revealed in the statements of 'Father' Rivas and the counter-charges of Dr Plarr.

This book came late in Greene's life. Greene cannot leave religion, belief, faith, doubt alone; we find it in all his serious novels, always different aspects, growing slowly first one way then another, looking at his religious world, changing, moving, though no faster than a finger-nail grows.

Are Rivas's views about God Greene's own views? Does Greene feel at this stage and age that Catholic fundamental beliefs are wrong? It is the subject of all Greene's serious novels – and this *is* a very serious novel, 'as mystery-laden as life itself'.

40

The Ultimate Story

'I always thought there was some code of honour for doctors, Plarr, but of course that's an English notion, and you are only half English . . . What a swine you are, Plarr.'

— CHARLEY FORTNUM

THE first discussion of Liberation Theology in *The Honorary Consul* is a conversation between Charley Fortnum and León Rivas, with Rivas trying to explain the Third World Movement's viewpoint. Charley listens, feigning sympathy because his life depends upon the leader of the kidnappers. He asks why Rivas, a one-time priest, has broken faith by marrying, and then fears he may have touched a nerve:

He came and crouched down on the floor beside the coffin [in which Charley has to sleep nightly]. He said in a low voice (he might have been kneeling in the confessional box himself), 'I think it was anger and loneliness, Señor Fortnum. I never meant any harm to her, poor woman.'

'I can understand loneliness,' Charley Fortnum said, 'I've suffered from that too. But why the anger? Who are you angry with?'

'The Church,' the man said and added with irony, 'my Mother the Church.'

Charley responds by recalling the anger he sometimes had towards his father, but he can't relate to anger towards an institution, the Mother Church:

'She is a sort of person too,' the man said, 'they claim she is Christ on earth — I still half believe it even now . . . how ashamed I felt of the things they made me read to people. I was a priest in the poor part of Asunción near the river . . . On Sunday I had to read them . . . the Gospels.'

'What's wrong with the Gospels, Father?'

'They make no sense,' the ex-priest said, 'anyway not in Paraguay. "Sell all and give to the poor" – I had to read that out to them while the old Archbishop we had in those days was eating a fine fish from Iguazú and drinking a French wine with the General. Of course the people were not actually starving – you can keep them from starving on mandioca, and malnutrition is much safer for the rich than starvation. Starvation makes a man desperate. Malnutrition makes him too tired to raise a fist . . . Our people do not starve – they wilt. The words used to stick on my lips – "Suffer the little children", and there the children sat in the front rows with their pot bellies and their navels sticking out like door knobs. "It were better that a millstone were hung around his neck." "He who gives to one of the least of these." Gives what? gives mandioca? and then I distributed the Host – it's not so nourishing as a good *chipá* – and then I drank the wine. Wine! Which of these poor souls had ever tasted wine? Why could we not use water in the sacrament? He used it at Cana. Wasn't there a beaker of water at the Last Supper He could have used instead?' To Charley Fortnum's astonishment the dog-like eyes were swollen with unshed tears.

The man said, 'Oh, you must not think we are all of us bad Christians as I am.'[1] [An expression first applied by Greene to the whisky priest in *The Power and the Glory*.]

It becomes more difficult to converse as the police are surrounding them with blaring loudspeakers heard by the whole *barrio popular*. Their discovery comes immediately after Rivas's long account of the nature of God and Christ. Plarr is an atheist, but a kind and generous doctor to the poor. Partly through boredom, he begins the discussion with his one-time schoolboy friend Father Rivas. Rivas is speaking of his own father: 'He was a good *abogado*, but he never worked for a poor client. He served the rich faithfully until he died.' Plarr begins the argument after Rivas's personal account:

'And God the Father, León? He doesn't seem to provide much. I asked last night if you still believed in him. To me he has always seemed a bit of a swine . . .'
'The trouble is . . . we have Jehovah in our blood. We can't help it. After all these centuries Jehovah lives in our darkness like a worm in the intestines.'[2]

The conversation leads to Plarr's assertion (not within Fortnum's hearing, he thinks) that he'll finally leave Charley's wife whether

Fortnum is shot as a prisoner or not. Then he asks Rivas if he'd known in his heart that he'd leave the Church. Rivas answers that he'd never thought that for one moment. In fact he'd been happy at seminary — he called it his 'honeymoon' phase. But something rang off-key with one old professor in a moral theology class:

'I've never known a man so . . . sure of the truth . . . Oh well, I used to think, a little difference of opinion, what does it matter? In the end a man and wife grow together. The Church will grow nearer to me as I grow nearer to her.'

'But when you left the Church you began to hate it, didn't you.' . . .

'I have never left the Church. Mine is only a separation . . . not a divorce. I shall never belong wholly to anyone else. Not even to Marta.'

'Even a separation brings hate often enough . . .'

'It will never happen in my case. Even if I cannot love, I see no reason to hate . . . I think she could have used me easily for a good purpose if she had understood a little better. I mean about the world as it is.'

And Rivas's first astonishing declaration is in answer to Plarr's challenge, 'I thought you thought that the Church was infallible like Christ':

'Christ was a man,' Father Rivas said, 'even if some of us believe that he was God as well. It was not the God the Romans killed, but a man. A carpenter from Nazareth. Some of the rules He laid down were only the rules of a good man. A man who lived in his own province, in his own particular day. He had no idea of the kind of world we would be living in now. Render unto Caesar, but when *our* Caesar uses napalm and fragmentation bombs . . . The Church lives in time too. Only sometimes, for a short while, for some people . . . I think sometimes the memory of that man, that carpenter, can lift a few people out of the temporary Church of these terrible years, when the Archbishop sits down to dinner with the General, into the great Church beyond our time and place, and then . . . those lucky ones . . . they have no words to describe the beauty of that Church.'

This statement is beyond Plarr's understanding. But Plarr now tries to charge his old friend with extreme villainy:

All the same, when you shoot Fortnum in the back of the head, are you sure you won't have a moment's fear of old Jehovah and his anger? 'Thou shalt not commit murder.'

Answer (another disturber of our mental peace):

'If I kill him it will be God's fault as much as mine.'
'God's fault?'
'He made me what I am now. He will have loaded the gun and steadied my hand.'
'I thought the Church teaches that he's love?'
'Was it love which sent six million Jews to the gas ovens? You are a doctor, you must often have seen intolerable pain – a child dying of meningitis. Is that love? It was not love which cut off Aquino's fingers. The police stations where such things happen . . . He created them.'
'I have never heard a priest blame God for things like that before.'
'I don't blame Him. I pity Him,' Father Rivas said . . .
'Pity God?'

'Let this comedy end in comedy. None of us are suited to tragedy,'[3] says Dr Plarr, as disaster is almost upon them. But Father Rivas hasn't finished his discourse, though it's Plarr who continues the colloquy: he'd been speaking about one particular atrocity he'd faced:

I have seen a child born without hands and feet. I would have killed it if I had been left alone with it, but the parents watched me too closely – they wanted to keep that bloody broken torso alive. The Jesuits used to tell us it was our duty to love God. A duty to love a God who produces that abortion? It's like the duty of a German to love Hitler. Isn't it better not to believe in that horror up there sitting in the clouds of heaven than pretend to love him?

Father Rivas's answer is long and powerful, and what he experiences in this strange, sacred drama is aberrant – a raging in the dark. And Greene, through Rivas, expounds upon the disorder in the world in which some have found a certain fascination:

I have always wanted to understand what you call the horror and why I cannot stop loving it. Just like the parents who loved that poor bloody torso . . . In my first prison – I mean in the seminary – there were lots of books in which I could read all about the love of God, but they were of no help to me. Not one of the Fathers was of any use to me.

Rivas thinks they 'never touched on the horror' but were comfortable with it:

> ... and they talked about man's responsibility and Free Will. Free Will was the excuse for everything. It was God's alibi. They had never read Freud. Evil was made by man or Satan. It was simple that way. But I could never believe in Satan. It was much easier to believe that God was evil.

Rivas believes in the evil of God, but in the goodness too:

> 'He made us in His image – and so our evil is His evil too. How could I love God if He were not like me? Divided like me. Tempted like me . . .'
>
> 'I find my disbelief a lot easier to understand than your kind of belief. If your God is evil . . .'
>
> 'I can see no other way to believe in God. The God I believe in must be responsible for all the evil as well as for all the saints. He has to be a God made in our image with a night-side as well as a day-side. When you speak of the horror, Eduardo, you are speaking to the night-side of God. I believe the time will come when the night-side will wither away, like your communist state, Aquino, and we shall see only the simple daylight of the good God. You believe in evolution, Eduardo, even though sometimes whole generations of men slip backwards to the beasts. It is a long struggle and a long suffering, evolution, and I believe God is suffering the same evolution that we are, but perhaps with more pain.'

But Plarr isn't sure about evolution,

> not since we managed to produce Hitler and Stalin in one generation. Suppose the night-side of God swallows up the day-side altogether? Suppose it is the good side which withers away? If I believe what you believe, I would sometimes think that had happened already.

Yet Rivas says he believes in Christ, the cross and redemption and in the redemption of God as well as Man. He thinks:

that the day-side of God, in one moment of happy creation, produces perfect goodness, as a man might paint one perfect picture. God's good intention for once was completely fulfilled so that the night-side can never win more than a little victory here and there. With our help. Because the evolution of God depends on our evolution. Every evil act of ours strengthens His night-side, and every good one helps his day-side. We belong to Him and He belongs to us. But now at least we can be sure where evolution will end one day – it will end in a goodness like Christ's. It is a terrible process all the same and the God I believe in suffers as we suffer while He struggles against Himself – against His evil side.

Plarr, you'd think, puts an effective spoke in the wheel of Rivas's argument, but Rivas has his own answer:

'Is killing Charley Fortnum going to help his evolution?'
   'No. I pray all the time I shall not have to kill him.'
   'And yet you will kill him if they don't give in?'
   'Yes. Just as you lie with another man's wife. There are ten men dying slowly in prison, and I tell myself I am fighting for them and that I love them. But my sort of love I know is a poor excuse. A saint would only have to pray, but I have to carry a revolver. I slow evolution down.'
   'Then why . . . ?'
   'Saint Paul answered that question, "What I do is not that which I wish to do, but something which I hate." He knew all about the night-side of God. He had been one of those who stoned Stephen.'
   'Do you still call yourself a Catholic, believing all that.'
   'Yes. I call myself a Catholic whatever the bishops may say. Or the Pope.'

Marta, Rivas's wife, expresses fear at the things her husband is saying, but he continues, speaking to Plarr, saying God demands evil things, even to the point of creating 'monsters like Hitler'. Rivas says that one day, God, with our help, 'will be able to tear His evil mask off forever. How often saints have worn an evil mask for a time, even Paul. God is joined to us in a sort of blood transfusion. His good blood is in our veins, and our tainted blood runs through His.'[4]
Soon the radio announces that the kidnappers and the kidnapped are surrounded. So how does Plarr die, and how does his schoolboy friend Father Rivas die?

★

As events leading to their martyrdom begin to unfold, Aquino questions Plarr as to why he should not open the doors to enemy police. Aquino sees no sense in what Plarr intends to do, he'll try to save all of them, but especially Charley Fortnum.

> 'I'm jealous because he loves her. That stupid banal word love. It's never meant anything to me. Like the word God. I know how to fuck – I don't know how to love. Poor drunken Charley Fortnum wins the game.'
>
> 'One doesn't surrender a mistress so easily,' Aquino said. 'They cost a lot of trouble to win.'
>
> 'Clara? . . . I paid her with a pair of sun-glasses . . . There was something she asked me before I left home . . . I didn't bother to listen.'
>
> 'Stay here, Eduardo. You cannot trust Perez.'

Plarr opened the door to bright sunlight, and the world was again in focus. Mud stretched out before him with no sign of life.

> The police had probably cleared the people from the neighbouring huts . . . Doctor Plarr walked slowly and hesitatingly on. No one moved, no one spoke, not a shot was fired. He raised his hands a short distance above his waist . . . He called, 'Perez! Colonel Perez!' He felt absurd. After all there was no danger. They had exaggerated the whole situation . . .
>
> He didn't hear the shot which struck him . . . in the back of the right leg. He fell forward full length, as though he had been tackled in a rugby game . . . unaware of any pain. He for a time lost consciousness, but it was peaceful and when he opened his eyes, he felt sleepy.
>
> He wanted to crawl on into the shade and sleep again. The morning sun here was too violent. He was vaguely aware that there was something he had to discuss with someone . . . Thank God, he thought, I am alone . . .
>
> He heard the sound of breathing; it came from behind him, and he didn't understand how that could be. A voice whispered, 'Eduardo.' He did not at first recognize it, but when he heard his name repeated, he exclaimed, 'León?' He couldn't understand what León could be doing there. He tried to turn round, but a stiffness in his leg prevented him.
>
> The voice said, 'I think they have shot me in the stomach.'
>
> Doctor Plarr woke sharply up.

He was not safe and needed to reach the cover of the trees:

> The voice which he now knew must be León's said, 'I heard the shot. I had to come . . . Are you badly hurt?'
> 'I don't think so. What about you?'
> 'Oh, I am safe now,' the voice said.
> 'Safe?'
> 'Quite safe. I could not kill a mouse.'
> Doctor Plarr said, 'We must get you to hospital.'
> 'You were right, Eduardo,' the voice said. 'I was never made to be a killer.' . . .
> 'I have to talk to Perez . . . You have no business to be here, León. You should have waited with the others.'
> 'I thought you might need me.'
> 'Why? What for?'
> There was a long silence until Doctor Plarr asked rather absurdly, 'Are you still there?'
> A whisper came from behind him.
> Doctor Plarr said, 'I can't hear you.'
> The voice said a word which sounded like 'Father'. Nothing in their situation seemed to make any sense whatever.
> 'Lie still,' Doctor Plarr said. 'If they see either of us move they may shoot again. Don't even speak.'
> 'I'm sorry . . . I beg pardon . . .'
> '*Ego te absolvo*,' Doctor Plarr whispered in a flash of memory. He intended to laugh, to show León he was only joking . . . but he was too tired and the laugh shrivelled in his throat.
> Three paras came out of the shade . . . [carrying] their automatic rifles at the ready. Two of them moved towards the hut. The third approached Doctor Plarr, who lay doggo, holding what little breath he had.[5]

★

The Honorary Consul was published with great success in England and in the United States in September 1973. Greene used a new American publisher. He had fallen out with Viking, primarily because, as we saw, Viking had dared to suggest that *Travels with My Aunt* should have a different title. Another of their famous writers, John Steinbeck, had used a similar title:* But Greene was shocked, and sent a cable to the

---

* Steinbeck had been dead two years by the time *Travels with My Aunt* was published, but in 1962 he had published *Travels with Charley*, an account of his trip across the US, in the company of his pet – two elderly creatures on a trek: one man, one dog.

head of Viking, saying that he'd rather change his publisher than change the title of his book. Greene then approached the vice-president and chief editor of Simon & Schuster, Michael Korda,* who was delighted to take Greene off Viking's hands.

He tells Catherine that Simon & Schuster will pay $150,000 advance on the new novel and $30,000 for his autobiography, and that '*The Honorary Consul* will probably be my last book.' Greene ends this letter, dated 30 July 1970, almost as if he had neatly parcelled away their love (and therefore Catherine too) as past history, 'I long to see you & think of you so much. I had the happiest days of my life with you – & the most anguished. I expect the two go together.'[6]

So Simon & Schuster brought out *The Honorary Consul*. There could have been no better beginning to their relationship, for this story is vintage Greene, but until he had it in his hands, Michael Korda could not have known that. However, the mighty reputation of Graham Greene by this time would have ensured acceptance, sight unseen. *The Honorary Consul* became a Book of the Month choice, as had *The Heart of the Matter* (1948), *A Burnt-Out Case* (1961) and *Travels with My Aunt* (1970). But none received such a salvo of praise as this one, enough to make a saint blush.

*

The critic Reynolds Price's front page piece for the *New York Times Book Review* voiced his unmingled praise: 'He has found at last the ultimate story for which his work has been a search.' The chorus rose: 'It is a rare achievement for a writer of fiction to impart such conviction to his characters that their independent existence can't be doubted';[7] 'Matches the most memorable effects in *The Power and the Glory, The End of the Affair* and *The Comedians*. What higher recommendation need a book carry?';[8] 'Literally stunning, a major book';[9] 'A masterfully crafted story';[10] 'Beautifully told'.[11]

In England Greene's new novel was made the Whitefriar's Book of the Month in September. Its review is signed by 'Whitefriar', who ends it: '*The Honorary Consul* isn't far away from being a masterpiece.' In the *Illustrated London News*, Victoria Brittain compares Greene with a galaxy of other modern novelists: '*The Honorary Consul* is a memorable novel, a reminder of a standard most modern fashionable novelists no longer even try for' (December 1973). The *Chicago Tribune Book World* strikes a similar note: 'A major novel. It proves anew (as if further proof were really needed) that the novel as written by almost everyone else is in a truly sad state of decline.' David Holloway, literary editor of the *Daily*

---

* Nephew of Greene's friend Alexander Korda.

Telegraph, began his review: 'The scene is unmistakable from the first sentence: this is Graham Greene land although this time it is called Argentina', and after praise throughout, he ends with: 'the story has been perfectly constructed – never can a flashback have been more effortlessly slipped in – and the writing is calmly exact.' I quote one passage for the sheer pleasure of it:

> No dogs barked. The birds ceased to sing, and when rain began to fall it was in heavy spaced drops, as infrequent as their words – the silence seemed all the deeper between the drops. Somewhere far off there was a storm, but the storm was happening across the river in another country.
>
> ('Simple, but quite perfect.')

I will end the great torrent of praise with the words of Auberon Waugh, who shows his genuine admiration for his father's great friend:

> Graham Greene is an enormous, brooding presence over the English novel. Week after week, we reviewers lavish the most extravagant praise on anything which shows a pale shadow of his narrative skill, his extraordinary, forgiving intelligence or his quirkish black humour. He taught us not only a way to look at the novel, but a way to look at our fellow human beings. Now, approaching his 70th year, he gives us a new novel, which is as enjoyable as anything he has yet written: where the hopeless outrage of a 30 year old idealist is wedded to the cynical, faultless precision of an old master. One can only gasp and cross oneself and vow never to compare another novelist to him again.[12]

And a final American reviewer, Timothy Foote, in *Time*:

> What an indulgence for the reader. Temporarily, at least, everybody can sidestep this fall's avalanche of novels – many of them apparently the work of rude boys rubbing sticks together to make fire – and enjoy a Promethean storyteller at work . . .
>
> 'How blessed are they who know their need of God.' In a secular century, no writer has dramatized that message so variously or so powerfully as Greene.

★

But surely someone, somewhere, attacked Greene? There was one – a friend of sorts. On 20 September 1973, Anthony Burgess, who was in competition with Greene, spoke on BBC Radio Four in the series

Kaleidoscope. The presenter was Paul Vaughan, with Burgess speaking from Rome. A few years later much fur would fly between Burgess and Greene. Here Vaughan details the nature and conditions of Greeneland, a recognisable Greene cocktail:

> We're very firmly back in standard Graham Greene country; a forlorn landscape with many familiar features that appear almost like stage props. The seedy exiled Englishman, a tormented priest struggling to free himself of his faith and a foxy Police Chief who likes avocado mashed in whisky. Well today I've been talking about *The Honorary Consul* with the novelist Anthony Burgess, who . . . had mixed feelings.

We can understand Burgess's reaction, a genius in his own right, yet ultimately less successful than Greene. Might Burgess be irritated because he knew he could never be like Greene? Burgess did not reach the heights of Greene's standing, and he resented it. When Burgess was still an unseasoned novelist (he was thirteen years younger than Greene), I believe he expected in due course to rival this giant.

Burgess starts out praising Greene, but then quickly suggests that Greene has produced a caricature of his own work:

> I read the book with great pleasure, and indeed I would say, it's been to me the most pleasurable fictional experience of the year, because it's by Graham Greene, whom I love as a man and a writer this [side of] idolatry, but I do feel it comes very very close to self-parody. I'm wondering if Greene wasn't perhaps deliberately saying goodbye to the novel, especially to the kind of novel for which he is best known.

Burgess could not have known; yet he did guess correctly: Greene never wrote a greater or a more typical novel than *The Honorary Consul*. He was ageing, and troubled also by a conviction that a novel as great as this would in future be beyond his powers. Burgess knew that instinctively. He argues that Greene and Greeneland would have to come to an end, ultimately

> indeed, saying goodbye to the whole territory of Greeneland because there doesn't seem to be anywhere else for him to visit. He's been everywhere now. He's been in my own territory of Malaya and in the East Indies generally. He's been in Mexico, he's been in Africa, been in Cuba, everywhere and now all we have left is this corner of the Third World and I don't see what

else he can do. I'd be delighted if he'd give us another comedy like *Travels with My Aunt*.

Vaughan then asked Burgess, 'Did you find that there was any diminution for you in his descriptive powers?' Burgess replied, 'I felt there was. I felt that some of the images were very very false.' He then takes the first paragraph in Greene's novel, which has often been praised:

> This Anglo-Argentinean, or Anglo-Paraguayan, character, the Doctor, in exile from Buenos Aires, standing looking at the river, the Paraná. We have a typical dream image: 'Doctor Eduardo Plarr stood in the small port on the Paraná, among the rails and yellow cranes, watching where a horizontal pool of smoke stretched over the Chago. It lay between the red bars of sunset like a strip on a national flag.'

It does not seem a typical dream image to me. I visited Corrientes and saw the same sight. The passage is painted exactly. It is what Greene saw; comparing the view with the national flag is, in context, germane. And now Burgess attacks more directly:

> I think there is a diminution in imagery, . . . in the capacity to create new characters and every single character I would say is out of stock. It's out of Greeneian stock, admittedly, but here we have you know, the failed abroad, the man from a spurious public school, the man who cannot love, the man who wants to love, etc, etc, and so it goes on, in a beautifully planned, a beautifully plotted novel but I would say no more than an entertainment . . . It is just something we're glad to read because Greene has written it but from the angle of the novel as a serious art form, this is nothing; this is nothing new.

Vaughan asks how Burgess would place Greene as an influence on other writers.

> It's very hard to say, I myself am a novelist and naturally am open to the influence of writers temperamentally similar to myself; well, I say that Greene is temperamentally similar to myself in that he is a Catholic. I am a cradle Catholic whereas he of course is a convert. I recognise his influence in my own work but I think it's a dangerous influence because it normally takes the form of a particular kind of property. To use your admirable

abbreviation again, because it does suggest staginess, he is a great influence so far as props are concerned, but I've not been able to learn anything from him in the wider field [here comes another devastating blow] and I don't think many other authors have in the sense of you know dealing with the soul, the problems of compassion, the problems of love, because Greene is not really interested in those. He pretends to be. What he really is interested in is the set of anomalies or paradoxes that can be contrived out of Catholic doctrine and the actual circumstances of men's lives and of course this he did best of all in *The Heart of the Matter*, where he produced a marvellous paradox, a marvellous anomaly, which turned a man who commits suicide, an obvious sinner, into a saint.

And when a reference was made to Burgess's *A Clockwork Orange* (which novel Burgess denied liking), he got one more dig in: 'I think possibly Kubrick made a better job of that one book of mine than any of Greene's directors have made of any of his books.' What a cad Burgess could be.

★

Greene was working on *The Honorary Consul* on 22 October 1970, in Anacapri. He sees his old friend the Dottoressa there: 'I found her unchanged except too blind to read. She had made the journey on her own from Zurich' . . . He then tells Catherine he's asked his secretary, Josephine Reid, to 'find out about the talking books – tape recorded – because that's what she needs most. I was alone and it was a bit exhausting as I had to give her dinner every night at Gemma's . . . and also she came up nearly every day . . . and had lunch too with me.' But Greene is jubilant, his one powerful thought: 'I was able to work on my novel [*The Honorary Consul*]. 27,000 words done, but Lord knows if it will ever be finished.'

In his next letter on 28 November, Catherine is in hospital again – she tells him it's only for a check-up. Travelling incessantly, he wants to see her:

I return to London tomorrow. Then off book-hunting with Hugh. Then a couple of nights at Berkhamsted, & then at the Ritz Dec. 4 & 5. Dec. 6–10 in Switzerland for Lucy's divorce, & I'm thinking of being in England again between the 13th & 20th. I'll gladly come down & see you in hospital (or would you hate that? Do tell me).[13]

Greene enjoys his brother's company:

> Hugh & I did Cheltenham, Bristol & Bath ... the Royal Crescent
> seems to me more beautiful than anything in Europe − more
> beautiful than the Piazza in Venice or the Place Vendôme − & in
> the whole of Bath hardly an ugly building to be seen.

He makes another suggestion: 'Let's go to the Sherlock Holmes film
... & then have dinner ... Of course you shall see the corrected
proofs [*A Sort of Life*, published in September 1971] − early in the
year.'[14]

★

An Impossible Woman, reportedly an edited life of the Dottoressa, appeared
in 1975, two years after *The Honorary Consul*. I believe that most of
the book we now have is the work of Greene. His friend (and the
Dottoressa's too) Kenneth Macpherson, who originally was helping to
edit the memoir, died, and Greene felt he had to take over the task,
despite having to finish his own novels. The Dottoressa could be enormously trying. To Catherine he wrote:

> For once life in Anacapri was a bit of hell due to the demands
> of the Dottoressa. I managed to work, but with great difficulty.
> Misery, complaints, accusations against Giulietta [the Dottoressa's
> daughter, kindness itself to her mother] all the time. Finally I
> really broke out and said, 'You have two people seeing you every
> day, doing all they can for you, looking after your affairs, and you
> do nothing but sit there saying how unhappy you are. If I had a
> month of you I would be underground.'

In spite of his outburst, we can see how far Greene would go for a
friend:

> At last I got everything planned. She agreed to sell her house
> (if she died now Lodovico's children who have behaved abom-
> inably to her would claim a half share with G[iulietta] and there
> would be an 80% tax). I put it all into the hands of Guido
> Adinolfi, the lawyer who once wanted to marry Giulietta, I got
> Polak [Hans Polak, Greene's Austrian publisher] to find a comfort-
> able retreat in Vienna (she hates Switzerland), and Boris is willing
> to buy. The trouble is she must have foreign currency and he
> has only lire, but I've found a man in Rome who will buy dollars
> and transfer them for a modest premium and I hope all will be

well. But what with D., the heat and trying to work it was not a fun holiday.[15]

★

So many matters had Greene allowed to get in the way of completing *The Honorary Consul*. We learn that his politics had interfered – he went off (at the instigation of the *Observer*) to Chile, where President Salvador Allende was trying to build a socialist society within the framework of a parliamentary democracy. Allende met with widespread opposition from business interests *inside* the country, and the CIA *outside* the country, and was overthrown in September 1973 by a military junta led by General Augusto Pinochet. He was too good, too open, too compassionate to succeed in politics. To Catherine, Greene describes Allende:

> I liked him, though he's a very different type to Fidel. He gave me a car and a woman to take me south – we drove 1600 kilometres and then flew back . . . I loved the desert – most beautiful colours, all the shades of yellow and green which looks like vegetation till you come close.

Back in London, trying to catch up

> and clear the desk for my yearly visit to the Freres in Barbados in January. I've done a rather dull article on Chile for the *Observer* colour magazine and they are using some of my photos. Now I'm revising four books of short stories . . . and I have to write two introductions (much more difficult for short stories than for a novel). Then . . . an intro to a collection of my old film criticisms . . . Not till all this is done can I get back to my novel which is already too long. I feel a bit frustrated because I've done nothing on it for more than two months.[16]

★

At last Greene completed *The Honorary Consul*, or almost . . . To Yvonne he wrote: 'The book goes limpingly – I shan't reach 80,000 I'm afraid. If I crash in a plane do remember to make two things clear – to would-be biographers that I was never Jeanne's boy-friend★ & to Max

---

★ When we travelled together to Berkhamsted School to see the famous green baize door, the border between his father's home (which he loved) and the school (which at times he disliked heartily), I remember him stressing that 'whatever Lady Camoys tells you [I was to interview Jeanne Stonor later that week] don't believe her story of a love affair. It never took place.' Liking Jeanne Stonor, Greene yet had a hatred of lies.

[Reinhardt] a note in the unfinished book that the Honorary Consul was to survive & Dr Plarr & the priest were to be killed!'[17]

This was not how Greene had originally wanted it to end. A number of pages surviving in Greene's hand contain short pieces which are like sketches of the characters, their speech. We can watch their development. Close to the end of these notes is one marked simply 'Sep' – I suspect it is a note made soon after his letter to Yvonne dated 30 August 1971: 'A completely different ending – it is Plarr who dies', then, 'from self-disgust'. This last is crossed out, and instead Plarr 'saves the HC as a substitute for his father'. And a short note in October: 'Plarr is the character who grows & changes. His sacrifice coincides with his discovery of a kind of love.' And on the following page: 'It's EP who dies & the HC names his child after him.'

Initially, Greene intended that the Honorary Consul would die, and that Plarr would be with Clara, but clearly not for ever, not even for long. This enormous change occurred I think because while Greene was writing the book, Jacques Cloetta finally discovered that his friend Graham Greene was having an affair with his wife, and that made Greene feel an absolute rake, and it changed his character's fate.

Plarr, like so many of Greene's heroes (seldom too far removed from the character of their creator), thinks little of himself, knows he's led a life of cheating sex. But characters in his works such as Jones in *The Comedians*, and Dr Plarr here, suddenly commit acts of goodness, and Greene felt the need to commit a similar redemptive act fictionally. Though he did not do it in real life, there are aspects of a letter dealing with Jacques that suggest he would like to do something heroic and therefore break with his misdeeds in a permanent way. He couldn't give up Yvonne, though he was willing to accept a sort of capitulation for his adulterous behaviour where women and husbands were concerned: his hero should be punished by death. This may seem small punishment, but to the extent that Plarr is based on his creator, it is a serious decision – a kind of acting out a suicide.

*

Greene left London on 10 September 1971 for Buenos Aires. But first he went to Paris: 'This will enable me to get more of my book on the dictaphone in case I run into trouble! And I shall be able to speak to you [Yvonne] on the telephone.'[18] On 9 September, the day before he left for Argentina, he wrote to Yvonne: 'All my love darling. Oh, & I've reached my target for all but the last part of the novel. I thought of it as 80,000 words & it's turned out to be 80,040! Only the last 7,000 (?) to do when I come home. I love you, so much.'

Writing on 24 October 1972, Greene tells Catherine that he'll 'be in

London around the end of November for [an] unpleasant operation on my bottom – 8 days in hospital & then two weeks more to heal. Nothing malignant, but I'm feeling a bit drained. The novel, thank God, is finished.' On 1 November he writes further that he'll send her a copy before Christmas. 'People seem to like it, but it's been an awful chore.'

The novel finished, Greene wants out of Europe: 'For the first time in 3 years this summer I didn't go to South America, but in January I hope to be off on my New Year trip to the Freres in Barbados.'[19] He tells Catherine more of his up-coming operation: 'My operation is painful & ignoble. I have a large internal pile to which a polyp is attached & Sir Edward Muir insists on removing them.'[20] On 3 January 1973, he reports correcting proofs of *The Honorary Consul* in hospital.

When he recovered, he began revising his life of Lord Rochester, which had not been accepted for publication at the time it was written forty years before, when Rochester's poems were thought to be pornographic. *The Honorary Consul* took him three years, and 'unless necessity drives it seems too late to begin a new novel'. He called it a 'change of métier like my brief appearance in Truffaut's *Day for Night*!'*[21] He tells Catherine that the Dottoressa's memoirs ('a bit written by myself') are coming out in the autumn, and that he visited her in Switzerland: 'She is now very very old and not a bit easier. Giulietta must have an awful time, but I calculate she won't make less than about £5000 with the memoirs.'

He fears that writing another 'serious' novel might well be beyond him, and we see him looking out for something less demanding:

I have taken to the theatre again and done a comedy about Raffles, the gentleman burglar, which the Royal Shakespeare propose to put on in London in the autumn.

He is 'tiring for the big performance'. He feels too old: 'Plays are so much easier to write than novels – it took me 5 weeks while *The Honorary Consul* took 3 years.'[22]

★

* In October 1972, François Truffaut, the famous film director, was in Nice shooting a scene which required an English insurance agent. Michael Meyer, in Nice at the time, tried to get the part. They turned him down because he was wearing a beard. Michael mentioned to Greene what had happened, and the upshot was that at a party put on by Truffaut, Greene was 'discovered' as the perfect type to represent an English insurance agent. When it was revealed that 'Henry Graham' (Greene's two Christian names) was really *the* Graham Greene, Truffaut's staff were afraid he'd be angry. Instead he thought it a terrific wheeze.

However close to completion he thought he was before returning to Argentina, it would take a lot more time to do the revisions on *The Honorary Consul*. By the middle of the next year he writes to Yvonne, whom he addresses as 'My dear dearest love for ever & a day'. Working in Paris on the revisions, he's alone and feels 'a lack of you'. By the third day:

> I feel so bored & lonely. Even Fouquet's was closed. I had lunch at the Swedish restaurant – it was very good & one day we must go together, but then the weight of a long day without you came over me. I went to a movie – an early Leone, it wasn't bad – at the same cinema where I took you & Martine to *Once Upon a Time in the West*, & then I've walked back & seen two dogs like Sandy with sad eyes, & I want so much to be with you both.

He was going to get a snack and start back on the book:

> How I wish you were here – then we'd sit down at gin rummy & have our whisky & the depression would lift.
> I love you so much . . . You are so missed – work has no interest when there's no hope of you interrupting it.[23]

A week later he is in London at the Ritz, Piccadilly, each minute jam-packed:

Sunday.	August 6. Lunch at Stonor [Park].
Monday.	Lunch with an editor. Dinner with Raymond.
Tuesday.	Fitting at Toutz. Lunch with my agent. Dinner with Sutros.
Wed.	Lunch with [Joseph] Losey [American film director].
Thurs.	Lunch with Max [Reinhardt].
Friday.	?
Saturday.	To Zurich.
Monday	14th (probably back to London, but I might come via Paris. If I do I'll send a telegram to the apartment)

> I have to be back in London for a lunch on the 17th & then on the 18th I go to Bepton with Max & try to work. There's a lot to do, but I don't feel much interest in anything when you are not around to talk to. Time goes very slowly. It's our worst separation because one doesn't know when & how it will end. I miss you so much, my darling. You keep me alive.[24]

At long last it looks as if Jacques had made his discovery: indeed this was their 'worst separation' because the secret love was no longer secret.

Back in Latin America, in Chile and again meeting Allende, Greene received a 'royal reception at the airport . . . Three Chileans & two people from the British Embassy. A huge suite at this hotel (as a guest).'[25] He becomes friendly with President Allende, who 'promises [we'll meet] by ourselves, except for an interpreter . . . I get pretty tired, like yesterday when I had a meeting with about 30 priests! . . . I can have a siesta (full of thoughts of you) before cocktails with the British Ambassador.'[26]

But something else is going on while he is revising. I think one of the changes he made was the introduction of Charley Fortnum's hearing his friend Eduardo Plarr admitting to Father Rivas that he's having an affair with Fortnum's wife. Charley really loves her:

'Speak lower,' Father Rivas said, 'even if you are jealous of the poor man.'

'Jealous of Charley Fortnum? Why should I be jealous? . . . Jealous because of the child? – but the child's mine. Jealous because of his wife? She's mine as well. For as long as I want her.'

'Jealous because he loves her.'[27]

Later Fortnum confronts Dr Plarr. Fortnum accidentally knocks down his whisky bottle (what is left of it). Plarr brings him a light and Fortnum answers: 'Oh no, you won't. I don't want to see your fucking face ever again, Plarr.'

On 27 September 1972, Greene writes to Yvonne from his apartment in Paris. Here it is clear that after thirteen years, Jacques has found out that his wife has had a long sexual engagement with Graham Greene, the friend, Jacques thought, of both of them. What a mess. You can see something of what Jacques knows:

My poor darling . . . I hate your anxieties about the future without me there to talk to. I agree with Eliane about J[acques] & I think I would go even further. I think he's probably ready to accept that we remain lovers – intermittently. He will take trips & expect us to be together, but that's not the same as being together nearly every day. My own feeling is that he'll begin to realise that it doesn't work & that an amicable separation will be possible [it never came about until Greene's final illness, when Graham went to Switzerland and Yvonne followed and stayed until Greene's death] – maybe for a while we'd have to keep on the Antibes flat so that he wouldn't lose touch . . . I suspect for a while he'd even accept the comedy of Capri with Emmy – but I'm sure all that would be temporary. I'd be happy to remain 'a friend of the family' – but not by losing you. Anyway I do strongly feel that if we are not too selfish at the beginning, things will work out & we shall be together. The difficulty of arranging things in a gentle & friendly way would arise if he wanted to go & live in Switzerland. [Jacques is Swiss.] Then a decision would be forced on you. My darling, we shall soon be together (less than a month now) & we can talk about things together.

But the fact is that Greene, as the fictional Plarr, has himself shot, and for the same reason: Plarr goes out from the hut into the barrio towards the police to save Fortnum because he cheated on him. So, is this payback time for Graham's sin?

There are minor characters: Clara, as we've seen, the ex-prostitute, now wife of the Honorary Consul; and Colonel Perez, the shrewd chief of police, who finally forgoes the truth so it won't interfere with his promotion. At the end of the novel the Argentinian novelist Dr Saavedra speaks about Plarr, addressing his coffin:

'You were a friend of each of your patients – even to the poorest among them. All of us know how unsparingly you worked in the *barrio* of the poor without recompense ... What a tragic fate then it was that you, who had toiled so hard for the destitute, died at the hands of their so-called defenders.'

Good God, Charley Fortnum thought, can that be the story Colonel Perez is putting out?

'... not seeking whether [the] cause were good or ill ... you walked out to your death from the hut, where these false champions of the poor were gathered, in a last attempt to save their lives as well as your friend's. You were shot down without mercy by a fanatic priest, but you won the day – your friend survived.'[28]

Charley and Clara return home. He knows that

there had been no ceremony at [Father Rivas's] funeral. He had been shovelled quickly away in unconsecrated ground, and Charley Fortnum resented that. If he had known about it in time he would have stood by the grave and said a few words like Doctor Saavedra ... He would have told them all, 'The Father was a good man. I know he didn't kill Plarr.' ... He thought: at least I'll find out where they stowed him and I'll lay a few flowers there. Then he fell into a deep sleep of exhaustion.[29]

★

The last few years of writing *The Honorary Consul* had been a nightmare. And we can tell how Greene felt it almost impossible to write a great novel. But, I believe, along with the critics, that he did.

After the publication of *The Honorary Consul*, forty-three years after the publication of his first novel *The Man Within*, Greene spoke of how he was finding writing increasingly difficult. He considered this last novel probably his best, but said:

> It certainly gave me the most trouble. There were moments when I realised perfectly why Hemingway shot himself one day.

PART 18

Torrijos and Buying Bullets

41

My Pal the General

Dictators ride to and fro upon tigers which they dare not dismount.
And the tigers are getting hungry.

— WINSTON CHURCHILL

O N 27 May 1970, *The Times* reported that Graham Greene had
'resigned from the American Academy of Arts and Letters in
protest against American involvement in Vietnam'.[1] Greene sent his
letter of resignation to the Academy from his Paris apartment on 19
May. To attack such a prestigious organisation was a real thumb in the
eye. 'The Academy has failed to take any position at all in relation to
the undeclared war in Vietnam.' This might have been a justified point
of view, but Greene, hardly the honourable schoolboy, seemed determined to bring this august institution down:

I have been in contact with all your foreign members in the
hope of organising a mass resignation. A few have given me
immediate support; two supported American action in Vietnam;
a number considered that the war was not an affair with which
a cultural body need concern itself; some were prepared to
resign if a majority of honorary members were of the same
opinion.

He expresses 'small respect for those who wished to protect themselves
by a majority opinion', and stresses: 'I disagree profoundly with the
idea that the Academy is not concerned.' However, his final point,
whippet-smart, is disturbing:

I have tried to put myself in the position of a foreign honorary
member of a German Academy of Arts and Letters at the time
when Hitler was democratically elected Chancellor. Could I have

561

continued to consider as an honour a membership conferred in happier days?*

Greene received a thoughtful and eloquent reply from George Kennan, president of the Academy. A distinguished author in his own right, who had served as US ambassador in Moscow in the 1950s and finally as Professor of History at the Institute for Advanced Study in Princeton, Kennan holds his own against this wily literary maverick.

He first admits that he has no choice but to accept Greene's resignation, and then responds to the accusations:

> The chartered commitment of these organizations is to the further-ance of the arts and letters, and it is to this purpose that their efforts, as organizations, have been directed. Many, including myself, have voiced opinions on political subjects outside this organiza-tional framework; but it has not been our judgment that the arts and letters would be furthered, or that our effectiveness as an entity devoted to their furtherance would be enhanced, by attempts on our part to take positions as an organization on questions outside our chartered field of interest. It would be very unfair to our members – and particularly, I may say, in the present instance – to interpret this forbearance as the evidence of support for any particular governmental policy and to hold them, by implication, responsible for that policy.

Greene's attempts to bring about mass defection were unsuccessful. His only supporters were Herbert Read and Bertrand Russell, and both soon died. Thus, his personal rebellion failed – it was on to the next conflict.

*

Two years earlier, a man who was to become a great friend of Greene's did succeed in *his* rebellion, the man whom Greene called in a letter to Catherine Walston, 'my pal General Torrijos'.[2] Omar Torrijos came to power for a brief period as military dictator of Panama shortly after the 1968 election. President Arnulfo Arias (who had held significant high position already in 1940 and 1948) was President on this last occa-sion for only eleven days before Torrijos and Boris Martínez ousted him in a military coup.[3] We shall see more of this later.

---

* One wants to ask, are the situations comparable? A Nazi dictatorship set against a demo-cratic country – a living bonfire of diverse opinions, with their own powerful disdain for the way the Vietnam war was being waged. Why blow up the house of Arts and Letters?

Greene never wrote about Panama in a novel in those early days, though *The Last Word and Other Stories*, which appeared in 1990, contained a fragment of a novel he had titled *On the Way Back*, a story about Torrijos and Jose Martínez.* It never materialised beyond a short story, called (as if it were a chapter heading) 'An Appointment with the General'. But Greene did write about the Canal Zone in his 1984 account of Torrijos, *Getting to Know the General*, and in his final novel, *The Captain and the Enemy* (1988).

In the latter, young Victor Baxter meets the Captain on the first page, when Victor (later called plain 'Jim' by the Captain) is enrolled in a private school (reminiscent of Greene's own school at Berkhamsted) when the Captain takes him away from his real father:

> there in the middle of the quad stood our formidable headmaster talking to a tall man in a bowler hat, a rare sight . . . he looked a little like an actor in costume – an impression not so far wrong, for I never saw him in a bowler hat again. He carried a walking-stick over his shoulder . . . like a soldier with a rifle. I had no idea who he might be, nor, of course, did I know how he had won me the previous night . . . in a backgammon game with my father.[4]

Eventually, Victor/Jim leaves Liza, his putative mother, only to return as she is dying. They hear from the Captain, a good-hearted and like-able crook who's been away from them both for many years, that at last he's in the chips. He sends £1,500 and advises the ailing Liza to pack her bags and fly to Panama City. This is how Victor (without revealing that the beloved Liza is dead) turns up in Panama again to meet the Captain. While Victor/Jim is waiting for the Captain, the bodyguard Pablo, provided by Colonel Martínez (a name borrowed from the unique Chuchu), shows him around the city. In his description, Greene compares it to the Canal Zone, which after many years still belonged by sovereign right to America. It is a city of steep hills and rainstorms, which

> lasted for less than a quarter of an hour and yet made miniature Niagaras down the streets, leaving cars stranded. It was also a city of slums . . . In the quarter which was called ironically Hollywood it was a shocking contrast to see the tumbledown shacks on which the vultures lodged and in which whole families were crowded together in the intimacy of complete poverty only a few hundred

---

* Martínez, known as Chuchu, was General Torrijos's friend, and Greene's too.

yards from the banks . . . it was even more of a shock to gaze into the American Zone across the mere width of a street, and see the well-kept lawns and the expensive villas on which no vulture ever cared to settle.

Jim 'wondered what had induced the Captain to settle in this city', and on a drive with Pablo over the Canal Zone, he felt the juxtaposition:

I forget what words I used to express my amazement, but I remember Pablo's reply. 'This is not only Panama. This is Central America. Perhaps one day . . .' He patted the holster at his side. 'One needs better weapons than a revolver, you understand, to change things.'[5]

★

The power of America in the Canal Zone was total, and to many, justified. This is the viewpoint that was later championed by Ronald Reagan in his criticism of leading members of his own Republican party in the post-Nixon Gerald Ford administration for their 'mouse-like silence' in the face of 'blackmail from a Panama dictator'.

But let's go back to how the 1964 riots began, back to the Avenue of Martyrs. In their useful book, *Panama*, Weeks and Gunson's descriptions parallel Greene's own to a degree:

In this tropical enclave, with its neatly mowed lawns, swimming pools and white picket fences, native Panamanians were tolerated rather than welcomed. US citizens earned three or four times as much as Panamanians doing the same jobs.[6]

And Greene, in his intimate portrayal of General Torrijos, *Getting to Know the General*, provides a similar view:

Panama is not the Canal, and the Zone was a whole world away from Panama. You could tell the difference the moment you entered the Zone from the neat . . . houses and the trim lawns. There seemed to be innumerable golf courses and you felt the jungle had been thrown back by a battalion of lawn mowers.[7]

★

President John F. Kennedy had decreed that the Panamanian flag, up to that time not allowed to fly inside the Canal Zone, could now be raised* – an issue fraught with emotion. After Kennedy had introduced the notion that both the Stars and Stripes and the Panamanian flag could fly together over the Canal Zone,

> the Zonians, effectively settlers born and brought up in the canal strip, were in no hurry to put the new rule into practice. Many of them were rabidly anti-Panamanian, and on 9 January 1964 the simmering resentment of Panamanians at their second-class status in a part of their own country boiled over.[8]

Settlers living in the Zone began dismantling flagpoles and placing round-the-clock guards on some flags.

Panamanian students attempted in turn to raise their own flag at Balboa High School, where it was promptly pulled down, followed by American students raising their flag on the Canal Zone campus. Massive rioting by the Panamanians resulted: it was met by a force of United States soldiers. The government of Panama broke off diplomatic relations with America. The riots continued for three days, leaving twenty Panamanians (most from the 'Hollywood' district) and four American marines dead.

In *Getting to Know the General*, Greene doesn't mention the marines killed and lists the Panamanians dead as eighteen. He elaborates on what transpired after the American students raised their Union flag. 'Two hundred Panamanians marched into the Zone to hoist their own flag beside it according to the agreement. In the mêlée that followed the Panamanian flag was torn in pieces' and the response grew fierce. The dividing fence went down, the railway station in the Zone was attacked, 'shops were looted, and the riots spread all the way across the country to the Atlantic at Colón'.[9]

Omar Torrijos asked: 'What people can bear the humiliation of seeing a foreign flag planted in the very heart of its nation?'[10]

At the end of 1964 President Johnson announced negotiations for a new treaty. The new talks were slow off the mark; still, three sets of new treaties were drafted. But Johnson didn't seek another term, so, in the end, nothing was ratified.

*

Then, in 1968, a new element came into historic play. It looked as if Arias was very much in line to possibly achieve greatness for

---

* Greene tells us in *Getting to Know the General* (Pocket Books, 1984, p. 17) that it was President Eisenhower who 'agreed that the Panamanian flag might be flown alongside the American at one spot where the Zone and free Panama touched'. President Kennedy expanded the areas where the Panamanian flag could be shown.

Panama – he'd become the president-elect. He'd been at the 'centre of a rich and disturbed career for four decades . . . [He] has been shot, jailed, deposed, exiled and stripped of his citizenship yet he has always bounced back to face another storm.' He was said to have 'an almost magical hold over ordinary people [who carry] his picture in their pockets, proudly confide that they saw him or shook his hand, drop what they are doing to run for a glimpse of him'. It looked as if here was an old but well-tried, well-liked hero ready to take charge.

The *New York Times* in its profile on Arias remarked that 'at the age of 67 he is once again ready to assume the presidency, barring some unforeseen incident'.[11] The 'unforeseen incident', as we've seen, came in the form of two leaders of the National Guard – Boris Martínez and Omar Torrijos – who took power with almost no opposition eleven days after Arias's inauguration. As early as 21 May 1968, five months before the coup, the *New York Times* said in a prescient editorial: 'The National Guard, with a strongly anti-Arias commander, will be tempted to stage a military coup if Dr Arias is declared the winner. With its American advisers, equipment and training, the Guard is regarded as an American instrument by many Panamanians.'[12] Well, the National Guard may have been trained by America, but it certainly was not in America's pocket.

At first there was much talk about democracy stemming from the new leaders, but basic constitutional freedoms were suspended: there was little freedom of expression, and none in the press, radio or television. There were also firm guidelines which smacked of censorship: there could be no articles which were counter-revolutionary, no news of acts of terrorism, no statements by political exiles or others who opposed the military dictatorship. One newspaper, *El Mundo*, was allowed to be squeaky clean, but that had been the *only* newspaper opposing Arias.

Panamanians were asked for their ideas of how to clean up politics. The National Guard made promises to fight corruption in government, especially nepotism, but the National Guard had not, according to prevalent and justified gossip in the streets, freed itself from such favouritism. As for cleaning up corruption, David Wilson of the Boston *Globe* told a never-to-be forgotten story. In the city of Panama he observed a member of the National Guard in an off-limits bordello. The trooper, 'his brass ablaze, his boots gleaming, his truncheon dangling from his belt, knife-edge creases in his khaki shirt and trousers, stood at rigid attention while one of the girls performed an intimate service on her knees. Laundry is a costly matter for the military in the tropics, and this particular hero did not wish unnecessarily to rumple his uniform by taking it off. In return for the service, the trooper placed the house under his protection.'

Both Torrijos and Arias tried to pin the communist label on each other. Perhaps Torrijos had a point, since American newspapers reported that those who'd been rounded up and jailed by the National Guard were primarily communists. If Torrijos was a communist, that message didn't get through to the American government, since it did in fact recognise the coup and the junta of two who carried it out.

At the time of the coup, Torrijos, aged thirty-nine, the son of two schoolteachers, had been a National Guard officer since 1952, and was known for his toughness. His affable and gracious sidekick, Boris Martínez – not to be confused with Jose Martínez, his friend Chuchu – in character was more like a real dictator – rigidly moralistic – and had been a militant anti-communist since his schooldays; Greene called him a 'rightist' but one suspects that Greene was learning towards Torrijos, with whom he was becoming increasingly friendly.

At first, Torrijos and Martínez shared equal power. Then Torrijos offered Martínez a less important post in Washington with the American Defense Board, which he refused. At the beginning of March 1969, much to his chagrin, Martínez found himself suddenly banished to the 'Valley of the Fallen', otherwise known as Miami, where he and Torrijos had earlier sent Arias.

Henry Giniger reports in the *New York Times* of 4 May 1969 that no one quarrelled with Torrijos's aims – how could anyone argue against strengthening the economy, better education, stepping up investments in banking, tourism, agriculture and mining, and the elimination of corruption? 'Questions were being asked . . . about the future: General Torrijos having turned on Colonel Martínez . . . might not others [now] turn on General Torrijos?'[13]

Not long after Martínez was pushed out by Torrijos, Torrijos was himself tossed aside. On 16 December 1969 newspapers reported: 'Chief of Panama's Junta Ousted by Aides While out of Country'; 'General Torrijos Ousted in Bloodless Coup'.

Again two officers led the coup: Ramiro Silvera had been trained by Americans in guerrilla warfare at the Jungle Operations Training Centre in the Canal Zone; and Amado Sanjur, who had built a broad base of support in the ranks.

In considering the second overthrow, it was pointed out that Torrijos (after booting out Martínez) gave himself the title of 'maximum leader of the revolution'. The new leaders commented that 'a cult of personality had no place in a revolutionary regime and that too much power had been concentrated in the hands of one person'.[14]

There was no high drama. Silvera simply gathered eighty officers of the National Guard in their turreted headquarters to say that he was taking over and that General Torrijos was out.

Did they expect Torrijos also to retire to the Valley of the Fallen? He did not.

He and a small group of friends chartered a light aeroplane from Mexico, where Torrijos had been attending a horse race, to Panama's north-western Chiriquí province, and landed at night, aided by a loyal garrison who lit the runway with torches. It was easy going from there. The news of Torrijos's return led to a revolt at headquarters, and pro-Torrijos officers raised the garrison. Early on Tuesday two captains carrying sub-machine guns arrested Silvera and Sanjur and others, ending an ill-prepared rebellion.

Torrijos's reinstallation as Maximum Leader inspired a celebration. He and his men rode a motorcade east from Chiriquí, Torrijos in green fatigues and an Australian bush hat, to public acclaim. There was wild rejoicing. The country knew they didn't want Silvera, talentless and unpopular, and the failed coup placed Torrijos in a position almost above challenge.

★

Though Greene became a friend of Torrijos, two articles he wrote about Panama, as well as *Getting to Know the General*, reveal that his attachment in no way hindered his hatred of other dictators in Central and South America. Appearing in January 1984, *Getting to Know the General* is a curious work, dealing with his own experience of an unusual character – Torrijos, the man, politician, friend, leader, dictator. It was not intended to be the history of a troubled country; rather it was about Torrijos's struggle with America, and about Greene's friendship with a head of state. It takes us behind the scenes, where matters of government are on a personal level, and where there is no separation between the public and the private world. Because of their friendship, Greene was intimately concerned with the battle for the return of the Panama Canal and the American Canal Zone to Panama. Greene gave advice and help along the way.

The Greene/Torrijos saga began mysteriously. In the winter of 1976 Graham received 'a telegram in Antibes from Panama signed by a certain Señor V – a name strange to me – telling me that I had been invited by General Omar Torrijos Herrera to visit Panama as his guest and that a ticket would be sent to me at the flight bureau of my choice'.[15]

Given Greene's suspicious nature, he must have been able to work out a number of possible scenarios to account for his unexpected summons. It wasn't because Torrijos was a fan. Torrijos hadn't read his novels: Torrijos was strictly anti-intellectual.*

Greene learned that Torrijos was a friend of Fidel Castro's; indeed Castro advised Torrijos to be prudent in redrafting the Panama Canal treaties – something Torrijos found difficult. Castro probably told Torrijos of Greene's help with his own struggle with Batista. Castro, a very shrewd man, knew that at crucial and early moments of his battle with his own predecessor, Greene had been useful. Then again, a good friend to both Castro and Torrijos was Gabriel García Márquez, author of *One Hundred Years of Solitude*, and it is possible that he advised Torrijos to invite Greene. In later years, Greene thought Fidel might have suggested his name because he had contacts with the world press. So Greene's famous pen would make a mighty weapon. Given Greene's increasingly critical view of American foreign policy, Panama might win a doughty fighter to its side.

Torrijos and his military friends, especially Chuchu, who *had* read Greene's work, knew of his powerful letters to the press, and world-wide reputation. Indeed Chuchu (on the one occasion I saw Torrijos for a minute or two, I chose the wrong time to visit – President Carter had arrived) told me what an exceptional thing it was to have a renowned writer as a friend. 'He could speak up about our little country everywhere in the world.'

Greene knew what he was up to. He enjoyed laying into Uncle Sam, tossing barbs around, because he saw certain American leaders as bullies. His urge again and again was to be David against Goliath, shooting many different stones from his sling. Shirley Hazzard, in *Greene on Capri*, quotes Seneca about Hannibal: 'to side with any king at war with Rome'[16] – this was Greene. He would know before he'd even arrived that the invitation came in the hope that he could drum up support for Torrijos's battle for the Canal Zone's return.

★

* At the beginning of their meeting, Greene did his best to deny that he was an intellectual – an impossible task, you'd think: 'With a sidelong look at me [Torrijos] attacked intellectuals. "Intellectuals," he remarked, "are like fine glass, crystal glass, which can be cracked by a sound. Panama is made of rock and earth."' Greene's response was that Torrijos 'had probably only saved himself from being an intellectual by running away from school in time'. And he told the story of his grandfather and great-uncle, of how at fifteen his grandfather joined his brother in the management of the family sugar plantation in St Kitts; and that his great-uncle died of yellow fever a few months afterwards. Then came the kicker which fascinated the highly-sexed Torrijos: Greene told him that though his grand-uncle was only nineteen at the time of his death, he left behind thirteen children: 'It was as though I had opened a door to the General's confidence. His whole manner eased. No one with a great-uncle like that could possibly be an intellectual.'

Greene made his first trip directly to Panama from Amsterdam, a flight of over fifteen hours. Though he'd reached a station in life where he was 'oversaturated by air travel' to Africa, Malaya, Cuba, Haiti and Vietnam, he felt again a sense of adventure. In Amsterdam, the ageing Greene took to describing meals and drink with the same insight as he describes character, plot and scenery. Travelling first class (thanks to General Torrijos), at Schiphol Airport he had use of the famous Van Gogh lounge, 'with its deep armchairs and heavily laden buffet', and there was his favourite gin – Bols.[17]

Is this increasing sensuous preoccupation with comfort, food and drink, a characteristic of old age, or simply of Greene's old age? I remember his friend Frere telling me that the lack of good conditions never troubled Greene – unlike most of us, he didn't seek comfort: a simple uncomfortable life appealed. This was once true, but it's not found in *Getting to Know the General*. The creature comforts of the man, once bound to adventure and danger and sex, were beginning to turn towards lush and expensive food.

*

To better navigate Panama, Greene consulted Bernard Diederich, whom he'd known in Haiti and the Dominican Republic, who was in 1976 the *Time* correspondent for Central America. He was just the man.

Torrijos was a friend of the Sandinistas waging battle against the pitiless Somoza regime in Nicaragua. As a young lieutenant, Torrijos had fought against Somoza, and in due course it would be Torrijos who would introduce Greene to leaders of the Sandinistas – another liberation movement that would seek (and receive) his support. The long arm of Greene's journalism, the letters to the press he wrote on the Sandinistas' behalf, came about through Torrijos, his new compadre.

*

Greene did not meet Torrijos on the day of his arrival, and Diederich was a bit late, but the evening picked up as soon as the two friends were drinking together. They gossiped over whisky, and spoke about a subject that was to become central to Greene: 'the negotiations for the return of the Canal Zone'. Diederich told Greene the talks were dragging, as usual, that General Torrijos was getting impatient and that the Americans in the Canal Zone were also increasingly impatient. The leading American agitator in the Zone, a policeman named Drummond, was claiming that his car had been blown up by a bomb, and was scheduled to lead a demonstration against any negotiation in three nights' time.

The next day Greene, with Diederich in tow (for Greene asked if his friend could come along), met the General. Greene and Diederich went to a modest house belonging to the dictator's friend, Rory Gonzalez, then in charge of the important newly federalised copper mine. It was all very casual:

Two men presently joined us. They wore dressing gowns and underpants, one had bare feet and one was in bedroom slippers, and I was doubtful which to address as General. They were both men in their forties, but one [had] a youthful and untroubled face . . . the other was lean and good-looking with a forelock of hair which fell over his forehead and giveaway eyes (he was the one with bare feet). At this encounter what the eyes gave away was a sense of caution, even of suspicion, as though he felt that he might be encountering a new species in the human race. I decided correctly that this was the General.

Through the next four years I got to know those eyes well; they came to express sometimes an almost manic humour, an affection, an inscrutable inward thought, and more than all other moods, a sense of doom, so that when the news of his death in a crashed plane came to me in France, with my bags packed for yet another flight to Panama − accident? bomb? − it was not so much a shock that I felt as a long-expected sadness for what had seemed to me over the years an inevitable end. I remember how I had once asked him what was his most recurring dream and without hesitation he had answered, '*La muerte*.'[18]

*

Greene returned to Antibes after his first visit to Panama, his relationship with Torrijos now a genuine friendship. A letter to Diederich tells of the joy of his visit, which ended in December 1976:

I am writing after my return from one of the most charming countries I have visited! I was very grateful for your support those first days and as you can imagine we had a running struggle with Mr Verlarde.*

In the course of his visit, Greene had been chaperoned by Chuchu. His admiration for his companion knew no bounds, perhaps because

---

* Verlarde was a supporter of Arias, kept on by Torrijos. He was charged with watching over Greene and Chuchu: 'In any case the General on, I think, our second meeting had told us to do the opposite of anything Mr Verlarde required.' No wonder Chuchu and Greene got along; two boys bucking the headmaster.

he found him to be his twin in many ways – in his refusal to obey
rules, his sense of adventure, and in his left-wing politics.

> [Verlarde] told Chuchu to report at every Guardia Nacional on
> the routes we took so that he could know where I was, but
> Chuchu completely disobeyed instructions . . . Chuchu was a
> tower of strength though, unlike what you thought, he always
> carried a revolver in his pocket! In fact his car had been blown
> up by a bomb a little before my arrival and so we travelled always
> in one of the General's cars.

We can watch from the vantage point of Greene's letter to Diederich
his growing attachment to both men:

> I saw a great deal of the General and liked him more all the time.
> He soon came to realise that I was not an intellectual! I got
> involved even in his private life as well as Chuchu's. Altogether
> it was a complete holiday and, apart from Mr Verlarde and the
> fat translator [two people Diederich had advised him to be cautious
> of], I liked everybody. My only dislikes seemed to have been
> shared with the General.[19]

Diederich, a wise and sensitive journalist, kept in close contact with
the two unusual men: 'a Central-American strongman and an Oxford-
educated Briton [who] sat beneath a coconut tree on a tropical beach
philosophizing'.[20] This is a justified journalistic ploy: every reporter,
like every police detective, needs to keep an ear to the ground for
information.

Greene was compelled to report his evidence, no matter who was
guilty – friend or foe, President or Pope, and he was no respecter of
persons or positions. If attacked first, he responded with the sting of
an adder. But in this particular case, he is abandoning his Hamburg
principles: 'I am not advocating propaganda in any cause. Propaganda
is only concerned to elicit sympathy for one side, what the propa-
gandist regards as the good side: *he too poisons the wells* [emphasis added].'

Was Greene on his way to becoming a dictator's right hand, as
Chuchu (justified in his case) was Torrijos's left – a dictator's propa-
gandist? Greene was seeking powerful friends. He was not seeking a
promised land. He was not a Marxist. Later in his life, in 1986, he felt
tremendous admiration for Secretary Gorbachev, as many did, but
somehow it seems a weakness in Greene the fighter, Greene the rebel,
Greene the anarchist – and even, as he put it incongrously and later
in life, Greene the Catholic agnostic. And sometimes I wonder, if the

First and Second World Wars had not put paid to the British empire (on which once 'the sun never set'), would Greene have acted in defiance of his own country's power? His heroes never changed – David, not Goliath; Robin Hood, not the Sheriff of Nottingham.

★

In conversation with Greene, I found he rarely deviated from the truth; but what was his truth? Having dealt with the divided mind his whole life long – wanting at school to be on the side of the boys, but being troubled that his gentle father, governed as headmaster by the rules of a school, had a justified point of view, too. He was pulled apart by both sides. He tried to belong to both. This often gives the impression of being uncommitted to either, like Fowler in *The Quiet American*. Graham abhorred the name 'journalist', wanted to be called a 'reporter', reporting accurately, scrupulously, exactly as humanly possible – but not without bias where Torrijos was concerned.

For most of his life, Greene was a defender of free, critical thought. And it wasn't exclusively against the Devil that he'd set his jaw – for him, disagreement was a rule of life, almost an orientation. He was a strange compelling figure who became tougher as he grew older.

But Greene was never gullible. He had a strong attachment to Torrijos, yet he would never have been in his pocket. Graham must have seen through him at times. He thought Torrijos was heroic, that he was compelled to carry on: *la lucha sigue*: 'The fight continues' – that is, until death intervened in Torrijos's case.

42

That Old Goat and the
Dictator in a Hammock

I don't want to enter history. I want to enter the Canal Zone.
        — GENERAL OMAR TORRIJOS HERRERA

I T was with characteristic self-deprecation that Greene opened a
clever piece in the *New York Review of Books* of 17 February 1977.
Entitled 'The Country with Five Frontiers' some portions of it are
repeated in *Getting to Know the General*, that work which appeared in
Greene's eightieth year, dealing with Greene's experiences in Panama
during his first guest holiday:

> The American worked in the Canal Zone, but he lived in Panama,
> so he was generally regarded as an agent of the CIA, but nobody
> now seems much afraid of the CIA. When he heard that I was
> moving around, he asked my friend Chuchu, 'What's the old goat*
> doing here?'

*

Three draft treaties were negotiated by United States and Panamanian
teams between 1964 (soon after the riots there) and 1967. By September
1969, Torrijos was making serious efforts to talk about a new treaty.
In 1969, Richard Nixon, thirty-seventh President of the United States,
showed little interest in the strong hints by Torrijos that he'd like the
long-stalled talks to resume. The argument used by Nixon was shrewd:
the United States government could not engage in long-term commitments on militarily and politically sensitive issues with the 'military-
type provisional' government then ruling Panama.

We can understand his reluctance. Military dictatorships in Central

---

* This is reminiscent of what the flamboyant mayor of Nice, Jacques Médecin, called
Greene: 'un vieux gâteux' – 'an old dotard'.

and South America were not noted for honesty, stability or longevity. But the real factor must have been that Nixon didn't want America to lose either the Canal or the Canal Zone, sovereign property that provided an obvious and powerful political influence in Central America. The US had in the Zone an army of 10,000 troops, as well as 40,000 Americans well paid for the work they did. A wise Nixon knew what he was saying when he declared, in the year of the riots in Panama, that Washington should negotiate with Panama on the little things, but not on essentials.

When President Jimmy Carter came to power, one felt that here was a politician not in the usual mould (and neither was Torrijos). Carter was a seemingly God-fearing Southern gentleman, though, regrettably, those traits do not necessarily make for a strong chief executive in times of conflict. Nevertheless, Torrijos was fortunate to have such an honest politician in power. President Carter went to enormous trouble to bring about a solution. He knew he couldn't follow the road Nixon had started down. For Carter, there were two facts that had to be faced: 'We would have to begin immediately [which so many of his predecessors had not done]; and the eventual agreement would have to include a phasing out of our absolute control of the Canal, as well as the acknowledgment of Panamanian sovereignty.'[1]

*

In 'The Country with Five Frontiers', Greene gives an excellent example of why it was necessary to return Panama to the Panamanians (which he also used in *The Captain and the Enemy*). After speaking of the original inequitable 1904 treaty, signed on behalf of Panama by a French engineer, which cut the country in two and left the Canal Zone as sovereign American property 'to the entire exclusion of the exercise by the Republic of Panama of any such sovereign rights, power or authority', Greene asks the reader to 'Imagine yourself a Panamanian suspected of a crime in the Zone; you can under the law of the United States be hauled off for trial in New Orleans even though your home is on the other side of the street in which you were arrested, beyond a boundary line less visible than a traffic line.'[2]

I believe that Greene's article had an ulterior motive. It was a form of propaganda directed at particular political individuals in the hope that they would begin to think carefully about Panama. The first cheeky reference to the newspaper man-cum-CIA agent was a tactic to hook their attention.* And what would the CIA look at carefully? What

---

* Here is the source of Quigley, the journalist/CIA man in Greene's *The Captain and the Enemy*.

would President Carter and his chief negotiator Ellsworth Bunker, and indeed all who were going to be involved in the forthcoming negotiations (in particular Sol Linowitz whom Carter specially chose), be searching out?

For fourteen years, according to President Carter, the two countries hadn't been able to come to an agreement, but in December 1976 the Linowitz Commission had called the dispute with Panama 'the most urgent issue to be faced in the hemisphere'. In appointing Ambassador Linowitz as a special representative, Carter chose someone who believed as he himself believed. It was necessary to have the assistance of a man like Linowitz, for there were powerful senators and congressmen who were known to be vociferously opposed to any new treaty. Perhaps because Greene had once used the name 'the refrigerator' in reference to Bunker in his work with Linowitz, Bunker became much gentler; his fierceness and stubbornness, the coldness seen in Vietnam, gone.

Greene provides an angry litany of the American arguments for the numerous delays in returning the Canal and the Canal Zone to the Panamanians, and slips deliberate warnings innocuously into the article, material which came from private conversations with Torrijos. Greene's admiration for Torrijos shines through as he asks how much longer they will go on – 1965 to 1977 is a long time:

> General Torrijos said to me: 'The year 1977 will exhaust our patience and their excuses.' After the mild student riots last October he announced, 'If the students break into the [American] Zone again, I have only the alternative of crushing them or leading them. I will not crush them.' He has also said, 'I don't want to enter history. I want to enter the Canal Zone.'

Chuchu burst out, saying he wanted a confrontation, not a treaty, and shot a nervous glance over to Torrijos, who 'lay resting in his hammock. The General said, "I am of your opinion."'[3]

And all the time, Greene is revealing Torrijos's true nature. There is an advantage to American officials reading this article: they would learn Torrijos's character, and understand that he was not to be trifled with. He was not a politician by nature, but a soldier. He speaks of providing grass-roots democracy – yet he is a dictator!

This was not your typical Latin American strongman. Torrijos took Greene to visit a farming village where the community was worried about the low price of the yucca they grew. The villagers gathered round and Torrijos spoke as a father to them, and finally, though not without haggling, increased the price in the farmers' favour. Greene observed that this form of democracy was 'closer to the Agora [public square for meetings in ancient Greece] than the democracy of the House of Commons'.

Perhaps. It looks more like the sort of system that used to operate in the English countryside – the local squire able to put up or pull down the price of his workmen and labourers, all living in his houses on his land – more paternalistic than democratic, sometimes successful on a small scale in the hands of a good man.

Still, Torrijos's nature fascinates, and one does believe he'd rather have a simple confrontation in spite of the terrible loss of life it would mean among his own people. 'Death . . . lies very close to him . . . He said he had premonitions of death, violent death.' Torrijos dreamed rarely, but when he did, Greene said, it was 'always bad'.

'I see my father across the street. There is a lot of traffic . . . I am afraid he will try to join me. I call out to him: "What is death like?" but I never hear his answer. I wake up' . . . On one occasion he said to me, 'Like you I am self-destructive.'

And Greene describes the 'charisma of rhetoric':

Castro and Churchill are obvious examples. Torrijos is totally unaware of his different charisma – the charisma of desperation.

To be only forty-eight and yet to feel time running out – not in action but in prudence: to be establishing a new system of government, edging slowly toward socialism, which requires of him almost infinite patience (and yet on his travels he hasn't the patience to take a canoe or wait for a bridge over a river – he swims across) to live day by day with the Canal problem, dreaming, as a soldier, of the simple confrontation of violence and yet acting all the same with the damnable long-drawn out prudence Fidel advised.

At a meeting with Torrijos among the people, Greene was impressed by a black speaker who 'talked with great dignity and confidence and fire. "We have the moral authority of those who work for low wages." Again and again the Zone cropped up in his speech – "We are waiting to go in, we are with you, you only have to give the order," and all the drums rolled.' Did this tiny country – the mouse that roared – really believe it could take on the colossus of the world? Indeed it did.

Greene's article expresses a general view held by Panamanians, which was also Torrijos's considered view, of what would happen if it came to war, a realistic estimate:

They believe they could hold the city of Panama for two or three days and temporarily close both ends of the Canal. After that it would be guerrilla war for which Panama is peculiarly suited: the Central Cordilleras rise to 3,000 metres and extend to the Costa Rican frontier on one side of the Zone and the dense Darien jungle, almost as unknown as in the days of Balboa, crossed only by smugglers' paths, stretches on the other side of the Colombian border. Here they believe they can hold out for two years – long enough to rouse the conscience of the world and American public opinion. For the first time since the Civil War American civilians will be in the firing line – there are 40,000 of them in the [Canal] Zone.

The Panamanian special brigade, the *Machos de Monte*, believe themselves to be second to none and the General goes out on training patrols himself twice a month and reports high morale. He hears a song sung by the recruits:

No one wrote the song; it is improvised a little by every squad to go with the beat of the feet. The theme is this:
I remember that January 9 when they massacred my people, students armed only with stones and sticks, but I am a man now and I carry a gun. Give the order, my general, and we will go into the Zone, we will push them into the water, where the sharks can eat *mucho Yanqui, mucho Yanqui*.[4]

There was also information which Greene knew but did not use, because it was decided it should be leaked, as it were, to the journalist who was a CIA agent. This was probably the most potent secret information of all. After telling Greene they could hold Panama City for forty-eight hours, Torrijos added how easy it would be to sabotage the Canal by blowing a hole in the Gatun Dam, allowing the water to drain out into the Atlantic. 'It would take only a few days to mend the dam, but it would take three years of rain to fill the Canal.'[5]

*

Greene, by the end of his article, had written a superb piece of propaganda which may well have played its part in affecting the negotiators. In a letter dated 13 April 1977, Bernard Diederich said he'd received a copy of the 'Five Frontiers' article in the *Telegraph Magazine* and heard that it also appeared in the *Chicago Daily News*. Greene had been working very hard in Antibes on *The Human Factor*, and so delayed replying to Diederich for a month: 'I've finished my novel which I don't like but which has met with approval of others who are perhaps better judges.* Now I am free to contemplate the Panama book [*On the Way Back*, never completed].' Greene remarks on who accepted his piece on Panama. 'The French refused to publish my article although it's been published twice in America, in England, in Sweden, in Brazil, and in Spain and I think Holland. The French attitude is a bit strange.'[6]

Chuchu wrote to Greene, delighted with the article. Diederich records the satisfaction in Torrijos circles: 'I don't know what Chuchu wrote you about your piece, but . . . I watched him read it with sheer joy. The General's reaction was probably the same.'[7] (And sheer propaganda pleasure it must have caused in the hearts of Greene's Panamanian friends.)

Chuchu translated the article for a Panamanian newspaper, including a passage where Greene revealed what Torrijos had privately told him – that some senior officers in the National Guard had special privileges in the way of housing, because, as the General said, 'If I don't pay them, the CIA will.' Chuchu asked Torrijos whether he should leave out Greene's reference to the National Guard officers. The General advised Chuchu not to touch a word of Greene's, and that included Greene's adverse comment about Torrijos's Chief of Staff: 'I hoped that there would be no *coup d'état* while I was in Panama.' Torrijos told Greene: 'You describe me as a real person and not a computer.'[8]

★

The second article Greene wrote about Panama was entitled 'The Great Spectacular'. This piece elucidates what the 'old goat' was doing in Panama. He was being used, and wished to be used, by his new friends. After all, he was slapping America's rump.

'The Great Spectacular' was published on 26 January 1978, in the *New York Review of Books*. Greene was trying, as he told Marie-Françoise Allain, to upset the US: 'I would go to almost any length to put my feeble twig in the spokes of American foreign policy. I admit this may appear simplistic, but that's how it is.'[9] And Greene was to have a ringside seat in Washington for the official reception and the signing of the Canal Treaty which Torrijos brought about.

★

* In a letter to Catherine Walston, he reports on *The Human Factor*. 'I was very uneasy about [the book] and would have liked to put it into a drawer for publication after my death, but, Frere proved unexpectedly and irrationally enthusiastic.' The book was published in March 1978, the year of Catherine's death.

In July 1978 I was in New York interviewing Otto Preminger when suddenly Preminger said: 'Let's phone Graham in Antibes.' Greene had only recently returned from Washington, where he'd travelled as part of Torrijos's entourage. The conversation started with Preminger: 'I have your biographer in my office. I'm telling him about how . . . we one day ran into each other in a Parisian brothel.' I could hear Graham's nervousness, that troubled little giggle of his: 'Oh yes. I can't be all that sexual else I wouldn't have had time to write twenty-nine novels.' Quickly Greene changed the subject to his trip to Washington. He was proud of the venture and had travelled on a Panamanian passport. I remember the glee in his voice, like that of a child who gets his way. But in his memoir on Torrijos, Greene seems a reluctant recruit:

> In the evening Chuchu came to see me. He told me that Omar wanted me to go with the Panamanian delegation to Washington . . . for the signing of the Canal Treaty, the terms of which had at last after all these years been agreed.

There would be an immediate transfer of fifty times more territory to Panama than under the old agreement. American military bases would exist until the year 2000, at which time the Canal would become the property of Panama. Except for the bases, from now on the Zone would no longer exist. But, Greene said, 'I felt unwilling to go to Washington. I had booked my return flight, and it was time I returned to France and to my proper work. I told Chuchu that I had no visa for the States, a white lie for it was no longer true.' Chuchu replied:

> 'That doesn't matter,' he said, 'you will have a diplomatic passport, a Panamanian one.'
> 'I don't want to come back all the way here to catch my plane to Amsterdam.'
> 'You won't have to. The General will book you on the Concorde direct from Washington to Paris.' He said the General was already being attacked because the Treaty was not as good as people had hoped. He had made a speech to the students, saying, 'I am making what progress I can, but if I don't have the support of the progressives, what can I do more?'
> I gave in. 'If the General really wants me to go,' I said.
> 'He really wants it.'[10]

This seems to indicate that the General was increasingly relying on Greene. Or perhaps Torrijos hoped for another brilliant article. Greene didn't fail his friend. In 'The Great Spectacular' Greene treats the signing of the Panama treaty as a night at the Oscars, laden with suspense over who wins the statue from the Academy.

> Kissinger, before the delegates had settled in their seats, could be seen button-holing his way around the hall of the Organisation of American States with his world-wide grin: five rows in front of me I could see Nelson Rockefeller being strenuously amiable to Lady Bird, as though [they] were sitting out a dance together, ex-President Ford more blond than I had imagined . . . or had he been to the barber?

He listed the Mondales, Mrs Carter and Andy Young.

> All of them looked strikingly unimportant, like the stars in *Around the World*. They were not there to act, only to be noticed, party-goers having a night out together, pleased to feel at home with friendly faces – 'What, *you* here?'

But it was not a Hollywood ending. Greene felt the real characters were on the platform – an unpleasant sight but more impressive than the stars below:

> General Stroessner of Paraguay, whom I had last seen in uniform one National Day in Asunción saluting the cripples of the Bolivian war as they wheeled by and the colonels stood stiffly upright in their cars like ninepins in a bowling alley (he had reminded me then of some flushed owner of a German *Bierstube*, and in civilian clothes he looked more than ever the part): General Videla of Argentine with a face squashed so flat there was hardly room for his two foxy eyes.

Then he describes General Banzer of Bolivia, 'a little frightened man with a small agitated mustache' who would have looked 'more like a dictator if he had worn a uniform', feeling he'd been 'miscast and misdressed'. And then, the 'greatest character actor of them all – General Pinochet himself, the man you love to hate'. Greene compared him to Boris Karloff, and acknowledged he'd 'attained the status of instant recognition, he was one who could look down with amused contempt at the highly paid frivolous Hollywood types below him'. Pinochet (who brought about the death of Greene's friend Allende, and was responsible for more than 2,000 political assassinations) had clever, humorous, falsely good-fellow eyes which seemed to tell us all not to take too seriously all those stories of murder and torture. (A week before I had listened in Panama to an Argentine refugee. She broke down as she described how a bayonet had been thrust into her vagina.)

And it is time to bring on the two heroes:

> We all stood for the national anthems as Carter and General Torrijos* entered to sign the treaty, a bit shop soiled since it had been fingered and corrected for thirteen years, ever since negotiations began after the riots of 1964, when Torrijos was an unknown young officer in the Guardia Nacional and Lyndon Johnson was alive and nobody dreamt of Nixon, Ford, or Carter.[†]

President Carter spoke first, then General Torrijos.

> Carter looked miserably unhappy. He made a banal little speech and was almost inaudible from five rows back in spite of all the microphones.
> It was a different kettle of fish when Torrijos took the stand.[11]

While I don't see in the photos an unhappy President Carter, the part about the speeches has some truth, for Carter, an intelligent man, was not a dramatic public speaker. Torrijos was as handsome as a film star, and certainly as charismatic. But Greene saw Torrijos while he was writing his speech, and knew he was very troubled about it. Greene admits helping with 'a sentence' – I suspect perhaps with much more than a sentence, though maybe not, since Torrijos had only to deliver a four-minute talk after each leader had signed the treaty. But certainly Torrijos wanted Greene's judgment before they left for Washington:

> I felt proud . . . as a temporary Panamanian, of General Torrijos who spoke in a voice with a cutting edge very unlike Carter's.

---

* Notice that Greene gives Torrijos his title but not Carter.
† There are two illustrations of Carter and Torrijos on stage, Carter looking happy, and Torrijos in a white suit, right arm gaily raised at the signing ceremony on 16 June 1978, in Carter's autobiography, *Keeping Faith*, p. 179. There are pictures of Greene towering over President Carter – Greene standing with the Panamanian delegation. The actual signing of the new canal treaty by President Carter and General Torrijos had taken place 16 September 1977 – a ceremony Greene witnessed. William J. Jorden's *Panama Odyssey* (University of Texas Press, 1984) shows a photo of Carter and Torrijos standing happily together.

It began abruptly (no conventional 'Mr President, your excellencies', etc.) so that even the stars began to listen – it sounded for a moment like he were attacking the very treaty he was about to sign: 'The treaty is very satisfactory, vastly advantageous to the United States, and we must confess not so advantageous to Panama.' A pause and Torrijos added 'Secretary of State Hay, 1903.'[12]

Greene reminds us that Torrijos signed the new treaty with reluctance; he had said himself it was only 'to save the lives of 40,000 young Panamanians'. Two clauses stuck in his gullet: 'the delay till the year 2000 for Panamanian control of the Canal and the clause which would allow the United States to intervene even after that date if the Canal's neutrality is endangered'. Greene adds that Torrijos wouldn't have signed it if he had not liked President Carter.

Greene clearly enjoyed the affair and felt he had indeed put his 'twig into the spokes' of American policy. In 'The Great Spectacular', he speaks of the mixed bag of members of the Panamanian delegation which included a student leader, and the mother of a student killed by American troops in the riot of '64, as well as novelist Gabriel García Márquez, and then adds: 'Remembering how once I was deported from Puerto Rico I savoured a gentle revenge when I arrived in Washington with a Panamanian passport.' Of course, Greene was happy, too, to find someone to befriend and to be used by. There is little doubt that without these journeys and the ensuing activity, he would have aged more rapidly. Panama and Nicaragua gave him a chance to escape the writer's solitude that he needed but which fuelled his isolation. He was exhilarated by being able to play games of state with Torrijos.

Torrijos was a fine man, not only in Greene's view, but also according to President Carter, who exposed the sentimental side of Torrijos, not at all what one might expect of a Central American dictator. President Carter and the General received eighteen heads of state from throughout the hemisphere (mostly the dictators of whom Greene wrote so unpleasantly). But for Mr Carter, 'the most impressive aspect of the evening was the deep emotion with which General Omar Torrijos approached the ceremony'. They were waiting in a small office before entering the assembly hall, and the General tried to thank President Carter for 'ending generations of frustrations and despair'. As Carter described it:

But before he could finish his statement, he broke down and sobbed as his wife held him. During the months ahead, the more my colleagues and I learned about this man, the greater the respect and affection we had for him. I was certainly convinced that night that we were doing the right thing, and that all our efforts were indeed worthwhile.[13]

★

The General's life was short: fifty-two years. Greene, in the foreword to his memoir *Getting to Know the General*, wrote:

In August 1981 my bag was packed for my fifth visit to Panama when the news came to me over the telephone of the death of General Omar Torrijos Herrera, my friend and host. The small plane in which he was flying to a house which he owned at Coclesito in the mountains of Panama had crashed, and there were no survivors.

The news flashed around the world that Torrijos had died in an airplane crash in western Panama on 31 July 1981. One obituary said that his death created a power vacuum in Panama and that his reign brought to an end (to use the phrase coined by Torrijos) 'a dictatorship with a heart'.

★

The National Guard trusted Torrijos. They did not trust each other. Colonel Florencio Aguilar, a Torrijos loyalist, succeeded the dead dictator, but he did not last long. By March 1982, having completed twenty-six years of military service, he was forced to retire, and was replaced by General Rubén Darío Paredes. Paredes considered himself Torrijos's rightful successor and became President. (Many suspected that Paredes had struck a deal with Colonel Manuel Noriega, who had been assistant chief of staff for intelligence since 1970.) Noriega assumed command of the National Guard in December 1982, Paredes the Presidency in 1984.

Torrijos's influence did not end with his death. Military and civilian leaders sought to wrap themselves in his mantle. Everyone of importance seemed to be claiming to be his true heir . . . not least Noriega. Torrijos had been greatly loved. Even President Reagan, who once described him as a 'tin-horn dictator', changed his mind, and upon learning of his death, praised him as 'one of the outstanding figures in Panama's history'.

Torrijos's funeral was held on 4 August 1981; the *New York Times* headline of 5 August reported: 'Thousands Mourn Torrijos at Funeral in Panama'. His funeral was a gathering of opposing clans who once would not have thought it possible to sit together under 'the white,

584

vaulted arches' in the Metropolitan Cathedral: the American Chairman of the Joint Chiefs of Staff sat next to military officers from China, Barbara Bush (her husband was then vice-president) in the nave with the vice-president of Cuba's Council of State and the Nicaraguan delegation.

Typical banners, quoting phrases from Torrijos, faced the cathedral: 'Oligarchy doesn't have a nationality'; 'Colonialism is the jail of the free man'. And at least 10,000 Panamanians carried the red, white and blue Panamanian flag.

At the funeral mass, Archbishop Marcos McGrath of Panama described the death of General Torrijos as putting them in a 'point of suspension, for the social and political history of our fatherland, and in some degree, for Central America and the third world'.

The coffin rested on an orange fire truck, and the procession on the final journey to the Amador cemetery was led by Torrijos's riderless horse, black riding boots placed backwards in the stirrups, his Australian bush hat atop.

Because Torrijos was not an ideologue, he could not be pigeonholed under any particular political classification. He acted not as a politician, but as a human being, responding to aspects of his nature which were rare – he was tender, he was kind, he saved many people from the violence of war in Nicaragua, in San Salvador, Paraguay, Argentina, and Panama.

★

Greene returned to Panama after Torrijos's death, in 1983. On his arrival at the new Omar Torrijos International Airport, he said, 'I was more sad than happy to see him commemorated in the great dead letters.'[14] Greene had been provided by Colonel Diaz, head of security and cousin of Torrijos, with a security guard on round-the-clock duty to look after him. Greene had a mission.

Greene spent the first evening, of course, with Chuchu, for they were great friends – more than ever now that Torrijos was gone – and with Colonel Diaz. That night they talked until midnight: 'Diaz was finding his own position difficult. With the signing of the Canal Treaty and the death of Omar the heroic days seemed over for little Panama; there was no one now who could talk like an equal with the world leaders as Omar had talked to Tito, Fidel Castro, Carter, the Pope, and all the heads of state on his tour of Western Europe in 1977 after the signing of the Canal Treaty.' (Greene tells us of a slight deception reflecting Torrijos's character: when he saw the Pope, the General introduced Chuchu as his Minister of Defence.)[15]

Before Greene went off on his mission to Nicaragua, he had to go to the Presidencia, where the new president, Ricardo de la Espriella, presented him with the Grand Cross of the Order of Vasco Núñez de Balboa. Greene admits that in his view he had done nothing to justify such a decoration except to have been a friend of Torrijos, but he thought there might have been a tactical reason behind the ceremony – a signal to the Sandinista leaders that 'they could trust me as the messenger'. And then Greene adds: 'In the end I had a certain sense of happiness because the kindly gift made one feel a little closer to the country which had produced Omar Torrijos.'[16]

★

Two years earlier, when Chuchu had telephoned Greene to tell him of the death of Omar Torrijos, he described where the plane went down, and added the shocking news: 'There was a bomb in the plane. I *know* there was a bomb in the plane, but I can't tell you why over the phone.'

Greene didn't hear anything further about a suspected assassination of Torrijos until he came on his mission to Panama in 1983. But what he heard from Chuchu, 'who was convinced that Omar had been murdered' and who knew of 'mysterious events' which had preceded the crash, did not persuade him: '[Chuchu] gave as an example two articles which had been published containing attacks on Omar by President Reagan, and it seemed flimsy evidence. I was not convinced. Omar . . . had been on good terms with Carter, [and] was a very useful intermediary for the Americans in spite of his social democracy – surely the only people who might have desired his death were the military in El Salvador and perhaps some conservatives at home.'

> But there was certainly one mystery, which I learned later from his friend Rory González (who told me also that he disbelieved in the bomb): the last four nights before Omar was killed he had spent with his wife. It was as though he had felt some sort of premonition of his end and wanted to show his kindness and his consistent loyalty to the past, which went so much deeper than his infidelities.[17]

But Greene's view ought to have been influenced by a little-noticed reference in the *New York Times* on 3 August 1981, a very short paragraph with a small headline: 'Torrijos's Body Flown To Panama's Capital', and then: 'General Torrijos . . . was killed Friday when his light air force plane crashed into the side of a mountain in western Panama . . . Killed with him were a pilot, co-pilot, mechanic, two bodyguards and a dentist.'* There followed the news that the General's body was carried away separately and that three Panamanian Air Force helicopters flew out the other bodies. But then appeared an unexpected reference: In Moscow, the Soviet radio alleged that General Torrijos might have been assassinated by the United States Central Intelligence Agency: 'The CIA has been behind several attempts on the life of the Panamanian leader,' it said.

Why didn't Greene pick up on that? Perhaps because the CIA's reputation throughout the world is such that it is often chosen as the fall guy. We have to look at the source: this could have been a chance for Moscow to stir the pot.

*

On 8 June 1987, six years after the death of Torrijos, information from Reuters came to light. Colonel Roberto Diaz Herrera, leading officer of the Panamanian Defence Force and Omar Torrijos's cousin, blew the gaff. Keep in mind that Diaz had been head of intelligence and following that, chief of the general staff, and was the chief aide to the then leader of the country, General Noriega – nicknamed 'Pineapple' by Panamanians because of his scarred and pitted brown face.

Among many serious criticisms, Roberto Diaz admitted that he himself was involved in electoral fraud (which kept an earlier winner of the presidency out of office), and accused Noriega of killing a widely respected critic, the opposition leader Hugh Spadafora.† But what shocked Panamanians more was that according to Torrijos's own cousin, their beloved Omar had been murdered: Diaz claimed that a top aide of General Noriega's was involved in the death, that the July 1981 plane crash had been planned.

This was the beginning of a succession of reports in most of the leading papers and magazines. It stirred tremendous protests and riots in Panama; the next day the *New York Times* spoke of clashes between protesting students and police. The reason for the clashes? 'Panamanian strongman was accused . . . of being involved in the death of the country's former leader, Brig Gen Omar Torrijos Herrera.'

Diaz's accusation was direct enough, and extraordinary. He claimed that Noriega as armed forces chief conspired with Lieutenant-General Wallace Nutting, commander of the United States Army Southern

---

* A dentist? How very Greeneian!
† In September 1985, in a grotesque assassination, Spadafora was followed, killed, decapitated and his head dumped over the border into Costa Rica. Spadafora had charged Noriega with being a drug smuggler – which he was, and on a huge scale. Spadafora paid the penalty for his honesty.

Command, and the CIA 'to plant a bomb aboard the aircraft in which General Torrijos was killed when it crashed in the mountains'. 'Hundreds of university and high school students, demanding that the Government investigate the charges, hurled rocks and sticks at policemen . . . Police responded with tear gas and water cannon.'[18] In Washington, a CIA spokeswoman denied that the agency had been involved, and President Reagan's administrative officials said they 'support[ed] the efforts of Panamanians to get all the facts out in the manner that is fair to all'.

Diaz had broken rank. Two days later, on 12 June 1987, the *New York Times* released fascinating information: 'Colonel Diaz said a bomb disguised as a radio transmitter was placed aboard the plane on orders of General Noriega, who was then the country's second-ranking military officer.'[19]

This was corroborated by a report in the *New York Times* on 2 August 1987, reiterating Diaz's charge that the bomb was placed on the plane 'on orders from General Noriega, who was at the time chief of military intelligence'. Diaz added that 'rivalry and bitterness between [Torrijos and Noriega] had become intense'.

But why had Diaz taken so long to reveal the story? Diaz explained on Sunday, 14 June: he was a 'self-described sinner' and said that 'he had the fear that God would punish him if he remained silent'.

A previously unknown letter of 6 February 1990 leaves us with strong suspicions of Noriega's part in the affair, and perhaps the CIA's. Greene, two months before he died, wrote to Diaz:

> You rightly draw attention to the doubts surrounding the 'accident' in which Omar Torrijos, a man I knew well and loved, lost his life. One fact is not generally known. According to custom the Canadian builders of his plane sent their insurance company down to Panama to investigate. What was very unusual, the inspectors returned without visiting the scene of the 'accident' as they were assured by certain high officers of the National Guard, who included Noriega, then connected with the CIA, that the destruction of the plane had been so complete that there was nothing useful to be seen there.

And so it seems that the insurance inspectors, who seemed either scared, naïve or lazy, accepted as proof the word of 'certain high officers' including Noriega, the unsolicited opinion that the destruction of the plane was so complete that there was 'nothing useful' to see, and so, they would not be going to the site of the crash. Noriega languishes in a Florida prison, not for murder but for drug-running. Poetic injustice.

43

Dashing Around
Central America . . .

... they castrated him, gouged out his eyes, pulled out his fingernails, cut the flesh from his legs, broke every bone in his body,
and shot him.

— GRAHAM GREENE

For Greene, Torrijos's spirit did not die in the explosion on the plane.
His influence never left — it was a wind that swirled around Greene
when he travelled to Panama, and especially so when he visited Nicaragua.

At this time, British and American newspapers were full of the civil
war in Nicaragua between the dictator Anastasio Somoza Debayle and
the Sandinista resistance. Somoza's was an inherited dynasty. His father
had deposed Juan Bautista Sacasa in 1937 and did what dictators do:
exiled his political opponents. (Omar Torrijos did the same, to a lesser
degree.) Somoza Snr amassed a huge personal fortune, retaining power
until he was assassinated in 1956. His sons followed in his footsteps.
Anastasio, his last son, who took over in 1967, was cruel beyond the
usual measure for dictators and, like his father, amassed a vast fortune.
Greene was drawn, not surprisingly, into this ferment as if duty bound.
Greene's habit was to ride up to the sounds of war.

In 1978, during the conflict, a young mathematician and activist,
Rogelio, arrived in Antibes and called on Greene. At this time, Somoza's
air power had the upper hand, and for lack of anti-aircraft guns the
Sandinista guerrillas were often badly mauled. Rogelio's mission was
to raise money for arms. Greene 'could only send off a small check of
my own to Panama in the hope that it would buy a few bullets, one
of which might put paid to Somoza'.[1] He was out for blood.

We don't know how small 'small' was in Greene's case — perhaps he
was being modest — but his fierce antipathy towards Somoza is clear.
It is certain that he later split the Spanish royalties for *Monsignor Quixote*
between the Sandinistas and the monks at Osera monastery. In a later
letter to his Swiss attorney Jean-Félix Paschoud about the unexpectedly large sum of money Greene received from royalties:

The Latin-American and Spanish advances have now been paid and I have to fulfil my promise to the Monastery and to my mystery friend in Panama.* The advance on the Spanish rights is much heavier than I expected and so ... I suggest that you divide that into two halves, one to Panama and one to the Spanish Monastery and I think they will be very happy at the result.[2]

*

Back during his second visit to Panama in 1978, Greene had been scheduled to meet Sandinista prisoners released by Edén Pastora, a one-time conservative who with astonishing daring strode into Somoza's palace and captured it. Greene described the events rather flatly:

There had been an outbreak in Managua, the capital, and the National Palace had been seized by a small group of a dozen Sandinistas, who were holding a thousand deputies and officials hostage and demanding the release of their comrades in prison.[3]

Richard West, in *Hurricane in Nicaragua*, describes the situation:

Edén Pastora led a band of men that stormed the National Palace, taking the deputies hostage, and using them to release from prison fifty Sandinistas, including [Tomás] Borge.[4]

It was a stunt worthy of legendary heroes, achieved by a mere dozen men. Because of this incident, Omar Torrijos decided to go to the Sandinista commandos, and asked Greene and Chuchu to be at the airport very early. (Chuchu indulged in too much merriment the night before and ran late so they didn't go.) Torrijos wanted to pick up the commandos and the released prisoners, and even some of their hostages (who in this sortie had changed sides), and take them to Panama to celebrate. For Greene, 'Life had become interesting again.'[5]

Here lies the root of the friendship between author and dictator – at heart, they were both adventurers. But there was a further reason. As Greene got older he seemed to take more risks, made up his mind in favour of those leading dangerous lives. It was for Greene a bulwark against ageing and boredom. The battle begins a little late for some of us, but Greene's adventures started long before the Second World War. He continued collecting new and dangerous experiences until he died.

Through Torrijos, Greene made two further influential political friends. Tomás Borge was a leading Sandinista who would advance

* One of the tasks of Greene's 'mystery friend' was to buy weapons with the money Greene sent him in order to assist in bringing down Samoza.

from guerrilla to an immensely powerful position as minister of the interior, a semi-Marxist and semi-Catholic. Strange bedfellows rubbed shoulders in Central America. In contrast, Greene's other new friend was the unassuming prime minister of Belize, George Price.

Greene first met Tomás Borge when Torrijos brought to Panama those whom Pastora had rescued from Somoza's terrible jail. Borge had been captured by National Guardsmen in February 1976, 'hooded, manacled and tortured for nine months . . . tried by a military tribunal, sentenced to 180 years in prison [a somewhat immoderate term unless you are Methuselah], and kept in solitary confinement until his dramatic release'.[6]

It is difficult to know what to make of Borge, who became a close friend of Greene's after the Somoza dynasty was overthrown on 19 July 1979, and especially after the death of Omar Torrijos in 1981. Here is a story which, if authentic, is very moving – although there are elements of propaganda in it, Marxist as well as religious, which invite suspicion. In his introduction to *Christianity and Revolution*, an anthology principally dealing with Tomás Borge, Andrew Reding tells of the horror suffered by Borge's wife just months before the demise of the Somoza dynasty: 'Yelba had been seized by the dreaded *Guardia Nacional* . . . She had been savagely raped, tortured, and killed.' A defeat of Somoza a few months earlier might have saved her. Reding tells us that within days of Somoza's overthrow Borge was able to confront his wife's murderer 'as Nicaragua's new Minister of the Interior'. 'My revenge', Borge told the prisoner, 'will be to pardon you.' Would even a saint have done this?

Certainly, Greene thought highly of Borge. Critical of other journalists' condemnation of the Sandinistas, and also in those days critical of both the Pope and President Reagan, Greene tells a simple touching story, addressing it to the *Tablet*. Greene was then eighty-one years old.

The Pope when he speaks of religious persecution in Nicaragua seems to be lamentably ill-informed. I have just returned from that country, and I can only speak of what I saw – big placards displayed on the roads marked 'Revolution Yes, But Christian', the open churches and the traditional celebrations on the eve of the feast of the Immaculate Conception held in the cities and villages. I walked between six and eight in the evening along the streets of Leon in the barrios of the poor. Every little house stood open to the crowds and displayed altars decked with flowers and the image of the Virgin. The crowd would shout 'Who has brought you happiness?' and the answering cry was 'Mary the Immaculate' while the host of each house distributed sweets, if he could afford or find them, or cheap jewellery or in one case small home-made brooms. This may be described as Mariolatry but hardly religious persecution, nor were the celebrations a protest against the government. My company that night in the streets of Leon was my friend Tomás Borge, the Minister of the Interior, whom no security guard could possibly have protected in those crowds.[7]

On 14 June 1986, Greene was interviewed by John Mortimer. Echoing a phrase of the 1950s, Greene described himself as 'An Angry Old Man'. Greene could not leave the subject of Nicaragua alone, and Mortimer, a shrewd interviewer, inevitably asked Greene if he'd been to Nicaragua lately. Greene's answer:

> Three times in the last few years. You know, it's really not communist. The President's [Daniel Ortega] a doubtful Marxist and the ministers of foreign affairs and education are both priests [Father Miguel D'Escoto and Father Ernesto Cardenal]. Can you imagine communists leaving education in the hands of a Jesuit priest?

And then Greene trotted out the story of strolling in a neighbourhood, told it a bit differently, and this time he directly denies that Borge had guards with him. All the information I've been able to gather suggests that this, if true, was a rarity.

> I went down to Leon, the second city, with the Minister of the Interior who is a Marxist but an agreeable friend, and we walked through the crowds at the Feast of the Immaculate Conception. The minister had no guards and all the houses were lit with statues of the Virgin and people were calling out: 'To whom do we owe our happiness? Maria Immaculata!' The conservative and liberal posters were all still up on the walls. Do you know that 75 per cent of the people voted in the Nicaraguan election? That's 25 per cent more than vote for an American President. Well if that's communism all I can say is that communism is improving enormously and we all ought to encourage the improvement.

Mortimer then turned to Contra[*] terrorism in Nicaragua, and Greene described one terrible incident he'd heard, too terrible, it seems, to be a lie:

> I heard from an American Sister, a Californian, and she described

---

[*] The Contras (or *Contrarevolucionarios*) opposed the Marxist Sandinistas who came to power in Nicaragua after the overthrow of Anastasio Somoza.

the body of a young Nicaraguan churchman murdered by the Contras. His eyes had been gouged out and the skin taken off his legs and he'd been castrated.

Greene sent the story in a letter to *The Times*. They found it both interesting and distressing, but said they couldn't print it. Greene sent it next to the *Daily Telegraph*. They also turned it down, so he sent it to America's *Time* magazine. They published it. Greene was angry that neither leading British newspaper had, as he said, the courage to do so. It was stronger and more detailed stuff: 'One of our Catholic cate-chists, Donato Mendoza . . . they castrated him, gouged out his eyes, pulled out his fingernails, cut the flesh from his legs, broke every bone in his body, and shot him.'[8] The article appeared on 21 May 1986. The Contras had originally assembled in the summer of 1981, some 8,000 of them, and soon began systematic attacks across Nicaragua's border.

★

Writer Richard West recalls a visit he made to the Intercontinental Hotel in Managua, where he met Borge *and* Greene:

> At the door of the bar, a Nicaraguan grabbed my arm, 'You don't want to go in there. It's full of gunmen. They're Tomás Borge's bodyguard.' Like most of the Commandantes and even quite lowly army officers, Borge, the Minister of the Interior, goes around with a bevy of strong-arm men, like a gangster boss from old . . . Chicago. I went to the bar and bought a drink then, turning round, saw Borge with Graham Greene.
> The next evening, Borge and his bodyguard had gone but Greene was there with a young woman interpreter and a bearded, goat-like man who proved to be Chu-Chu, the Panamanian Marxist mathematician and army sergeant . . . Greene was reluc-tant to talk about Nicaragua.

But then West, who'd had a lifelong admiration for Greene, was trou-bled to see that Graham was in such company:

> consorting with men like Borge, whom I regard as a terrorist . . . Why does he now support the Popular Church, defying the Pope? His friend Tomás Borge, when asked to define the Christian element in Communism, answered that 'State coercion is love'.[9]

This smacks of Orwellian doublethink, the gobbledegook of Tomás Borge.

★

Torrijos sent Greene on a mission in 1978 with Chuchu to meet the prime minister of Belize, George Price. Price and Torrijos were bosom friends, and indeed all three became mates. Torrijos assessed Price and Greene correctly when he told Greene: 'You'll like Price. He's a man after your own heart. He wanted to be a priest, not a prime minister.'

There seemed no reason to send Greene, except that Torrijos had promised to be Greene's tutor in the affairs of Central America. Greene and Torrijos discovered they could be on naturally easy terms with each other. Just how easy is revealed in Greene's interview with Martin Amis for the *Observer*'s commemoration of Greene's eightieth birthday (8 October 1984), when Amis asked Greene how he felt when a friend died: 'Does it leave the life that remains feeling thinner?' Greene said: 'One is shocked when a bit of one's life disappears. I felt that with Omar Torrijos . . . a whole segment of my life had been cut out.'[10]

★

Greene did like Price enormously: 'He still lives as a priest might live, celibate [for which Greene admired him] . . . [He] goes to bed around nine at latest, for he rises early at 5.30 in the morning for Mass and his daily Communion, and at 8.30 he is back at his desk in the new capital.'[11] But the local opposition newspaper in Belize, *Democracy*, had this to say: 'a so-called writer called Green[e]' had been 'sent by the Communist Torrijos to see his fellow Communist Price for reasons which were unknown and certainly sinister'.[12] Price remained popular and, off and on, remained prime minister until 1993.

Chuchu in the meantime was meeting one of his 'dubious contacts', and the next day moved to San José, capital of Costa Rica. Like the Captain in Greene's last novel, *The Captain and the Enemy* (1988), who carries arms into Nicaragua for the Sandinistas, in his small plane Chuchu took the same dangerous journey. Greene describes the manoeuvrings. Costa Rica 'was very conveniently situated for his clandestine activities, and he had several times delivered arms to the Sandinistas on its border with Nicaragua with the help of his second-hand plane'.[13] It is just such a plane the Captain uses, and here is fiction copying fact, for it is the story of Chuchu's gun-running. Greene felt he could not finally write a novel about Chuchu and Torrijos, and he tried hard, because they were like statues and would not be changed. But he did use Chuchu's activities for inspiration.

★

Once Somoza was thrown out, the Contras emerged with the aim of bringing down the new government of the Sandinistas. Fuelled by the cruelty of the Contras, Greene's arguments against America grew. He argued against the brightest and best: Jeane Kirkpatrick, noted for her anti-communist stance, then the USA's Permanent Representative to the United Nations under President Ronald Reagan. She and Greene crossed swords in the press. In *The Times* of 15 October 1983, he challenged her evidence which showed that

'The Sandinista regime is subjecting many thousands of Misquito Indians to the most brutal maltreatment' ('Spectrum' October 12). Will she publish her documentary evidence?

When I was in Nicaragua last January I interviewed an American sister of the Roman Catholic Maryknoll Order who had been living in Nicaragua for ten years. She had visited the camps outside the war zone to which these Indians had been transferred and she stated to me categorically that they were 'well housed, well fed, and well cared for'.[14]

Six months later, Greene argued the subject again, this time with a Dr Norman, who'd spoken of the removal of the Misquito Indians in Nicaragua from the Atlantic war zone as an outrage. Clearly Greene had not put a stop to criticism in spite of his public letter to Kirkpatrick. He again quotes the sister of the Maryknoll Order, and, on the warpath, contends that Dr Norman is using his words carelessly:

I cannot accept his remarkable understatement of the issues in Central America. 'Many of the existing governments subject to subversion are not themselves very creditable.' The death squads in El Salvador and the murder of Archbishop Romero – are they in his eyes 'not very creditable'? Yet he regards the removal of the Misquito Indians in Nicaragua from the Atlantic war zone, penetrated by the Contras of Somoza's National Guard and Pastora's *Arde*, where noncombatants are a serious encumbrance, as an 'outrage'. Tomás Borge . . . has frankly admitted that the removal was clumsily done without proper explanation, but I have talked to an American nun . . . [etc.][15]

Greene's willingness to accept Borge's remarks may just be because they are the remarks of a friend. In any case, what does it mean to say 'Tomás Borge frankly admitted that the removal [of thousands of Misquito Indians] was clumsily done without proper explanation'? Could this be semantic trickery? Is the phrase 'clumsily done' in Borge's mind parallel to Kirkpatrick's stern judgment of 'subjecting many thousands of Misquito Indians to the most brutal maltreatment'?

Greene himself should have made enquiries, but one has the strongest feeling that he was so determined to support his new friends that he was willing to accept everything they said, without his characteristic cynicism. In this context, he has lost his acidic eye. He is too tired to find out the truth. What has happened to the man who so brilliantly enunciated the principle for writers of truth above all? Clearly when the Sandinistas were in power, theirs was the accepted opinion. What happened to the Virtue of Disloyalty, his belief that 'it has always been in the interests of the State to poison the psychological wells'? Wasn't Borge, now in charge, doing just that? Was old age clouding Greene's once sharply sceptical mind?

Greene had a further desire to bicker with Dr Norman, who wrote that in Nicaragua, 'a unitary Marxist state' was 'in the course of construction'. Greene's blood was up: '"Unitary"? With the Foreign Minister a Catholic priest, the Minister of Culture a Catholic priest, and a Jesuit priest in charge of education and health?'[16]

Greene was always ready to fight for the Sandinistas. When the *Spectator* stated on 15 August 1987 that education in Nicaragua 'was indistinguishable from indoctrination', Greene offered a series of searching questions, thinking to catch out the *Spectator*:

> You write that 'education is now indistinguishable from indoctrination'. Can you give us details with what the schools are now indoctrinated? What books are the children reading? What subjects are they taught?
>
> You might indeed have reason to fear that under a minister of education who is a Jesuit priest the 'indoctrination' may be too Catholic though that seems hardly necessary in a country quite as Catholic as Poland.[17]

Had the *Spectator* even tried to get hold of school textbooks? Greene finally seemed to have scored.

But a Charles Morley replied that he had 'seen a first-grade reader published under the imprint of the Ministry of Education, Managua, Nicaragua'. He provided many examples of indoctrination (too many, alas), not subtle, which in a first-grade reader would do the job effectively. Here are a few:

> On page 48 it says '¡Viva el FSLN! [Frente Sandinista de Liberación Nacional]' . . .
> On page 59 the text reads 'DEFENCE – The valiant militia march

in the square. They hold their rifles in their hands. The militia are of the people. The people are ready for defence. The militia defends peace. Long live the militia . . .'

On page 100, illustrating the two letters 'gu' (used frequently in Spanish hence translated here as one letter), is the single word 'guerrilleros'.

On page 73 . . . Sandinista children use neckerchief. They take part in the tasks of the Revolution and are very studious.

On page 127 the text reads 'The children of the Revolution – We children are the fledglings of the Revolution. We study to prepare ourselves and be useful to our country and our people. We children help in the defence of the Fatherland . . . We are the fledglings, the Revolution concerns itself with giving us education, health and recreation. And above all it guarantees us peace.'[18]

Of course, Greene couldn't refrain from answering:

I remember as a boy of 11 being indoctrinated by posters of Lord Kitchener pointing his finger at me from the hoardings and apparently saying, 'England has need of you.'[19]

Morley came back with references to Sandinista terrorism – 'well-documented instances of . . . attempted genocide, arbitrary arrests followed by torture, assassination of political opponents'.[20]

Greene had the last shot, saying that the 'Contras . . . have been condemned for many atrocities by Amnesty, while the few atrocities on the Sandinista side have been condemned and punished by their own leaders'.[21] The punishment of their own men one assumes must have come from known leaders, especially Borge, as an aggressive minister of the interior.

In spite of his belief in the 'Virtue of Disloyalty', Greene wasn't thinking straight here, and this deficiency had sprung up from a fierce loyalty. It was his habit to stir the waters, he was ready to set a whirlpool in motion for someone whom he called 'friend'. In any case, Greene was at home in the eye of the storm.

PART 19

The Girl with the Coral Harp Bracelet

44

His True Love Dies

Sweetest love, I do not go, for weariness of thee . . .

— JOHN DONNE

GREENE finished *The Human Factor* on 13 April 1977. It was published simultaneously by The Bodley Head in London and Simon & Schuster in New York, in March 1978. However, as with *The Tenth Man*, some parts of the novel were written long before publication. 'I began *The Human Factor* more than ten years before it was published and abandoned it in despair after two or three years' work.'[1] In a letter to Catherine Walston on 23 December 1975 he says that after *The Return of A. J. Raffles* he felt flat and wanted to get back to 'the novel I abandoned six to eight years ago'.[2] He'd written 20,000 words of it, but had to give it up. He recalled when *The Human Factor*, then without a title, 'hung like a dead albatross around my neck', and his 'imagination seemed as dead as the bird'.[3]

Another reason for the dry spell was the sensation made by his one-time MI6 boss Kim Philby when it was discovered that he was a traitor (not the term Greene would use to describe his friend): Greene abandoned the work 'because of the Philby affair'.[4] Philby absconded to Moscow in 1963, as does the main character in *The Human Factor*, Maurice Castle, both for the same reason, and though Greene's fictional character is vastly different from Philby he realised that readers would think it was derived from that source. He put the book aside. When it did eventually come out, Philby criticised the novel, but in Kim Philby fashion. Greene had sent a copy to Moscow addressed 'to my friend Kim', and Philby's reply began with the phrase 'My dear Graham'. The letter is dated 25 April 1978 and speaks of how warming it was 'to see the familiar handwriting so well preserved':

I won't follow the reviewers in writing of 'the maestro's touch'
. . . the book gave me much amusement, wry and otherwise. Was
[Doctor] Percival an import from CIA? It seemed so at times
[since he was a doctor who killed one of his own colleagues] yet
poor Lankester also must have caused havoc among officers and
secretaries by eccentric diagnosis and prescription.

With his usual care, in his letter Greene calls Dr Lankester, who had
attended to intelligence officers, simply 'L'. He admits that Philby was
right, Lankester's diagnoses were eccentric, and while he wouldn't have
poisoned a man, he was notoriously inaccurate – he misdiagnosed
Greene with diabetes. Philby's letter continued:

Castle's treatment [once he landed in Moscow] was shabby and
most un-Russian, however marginal his importance may have
been. I got the lot, down to a shoehorn, an article I had never
before possessed.

Greene reminds us in *Ways of Escape*: 'It was true [Philby] . . . was a
more important agent than Castle.'*
   The Human Factor is brilliant in parts. Perhaps because Greene is
ageing, he longs to go back to childhood. His hero, Maurice Castle
(the same first name as the hero in *The End of the Affair*), and Sarah,
his black wife (called after the heroine in the same novel), are living
in Berkhamsted, Greene's boyhood home. Here, Castle takes Sarah's
son for a walk over the grounds that he'd known as a schoolboy. His
solitary troubles are revealed to the boy in Castle's child-like fantasy:

He took Sam by the hand and introduced him to the forgotten
hiding-places and the multiple dangers of the Common. How
many guerrilla campaigns he had fought there as a child against
overwhelming odds. Well, the days of the guerrilla had returned,
daydreams had become realities. Living thus with the long familiar
he felt the security that an old lag feels when he goes back to
the prison he knows.[5]

Castle tells the boy about his old haunts, about his unhappiness at
school, and about his pet dragon, all fodder from Greene's childhood.

---

* Irrelevant to *The Human Factor* but reflective of Philby's regret: 'mankind moving so
slowly, and so often backward. But then old age creeps up slowly too!' And: 'I was recently
approached by Professor Sherry, with a request for reminiscences about you. To my chagrin,
I found that I could remember very few facts about those unreal days.'

When he was a child he 'thought there was a dragon living in the old dug-out'.

'Did you ever see a dragon?'

'Once I saw smoke coming out of a trench and I thought it was the dragon.'

'Were you afraid?'

'No, I was afraid of quite different things in those days. I hated my school, and I had few friends.'

'Why did you hate school? Will I hate school? . . .'

'We don't all have the same enemies. Perhaps you won't need a dragon to help you, but I did.'

Everybody wanted to kill his dragon, but he fed it and kept it alive:

'But did that *really* happen?'

'No, of course not, but it almost seems now as though it had. Once I lay in bed in the dormitory crying under the sheet because it was the first week of term and there were twelve endless weeks before the holidays, and I was afraid of – everything around. It was winter, and suddenly I saw the window of my cubicle was misted over with heat. I wiped away the steam with my fingers and looked down. The dragon was there, lying flat in the wet black street, he looked like a crocodile in a stream. He had never left the Common before because every man's hand was against him – just as I thought they were all against me . . . You see he had heard that school had started again and he knew I was unhappy and alone . . .'

'You are pulling my leg,' Sam said.

'No, I'm just remembering.'

'What happened then?'

'I made a secret signal to him. It meant "Danger. Go away," because I wasn't sure that he knew about the police with their rifles.'

'Did he go?'

'Yes. Very slowly. Looking back over his tail as though he didn't want to leave me. But I never felt afraid or lonely again. At least not often. I knew I had only to give a signal and he would leave his dug-out on the Common and come down and help me.'[6]

But we remember that Graham did cry under the sheets when he was a boarder at school. Lurking in so many crevices in his novels are pages and pages of his secret history. This was his life at Berkhamsted.

★

The fictional guerrilla fights he had in his dreams as a boy ultimately came to pass in his grown-up battles on behalf of Panama and Nicaragua, and earlier in Haiti and Vietnam.

V. S. Pritchett, in *The Times* of 18 March 1978, two years after Torrijos's telegram inviting Greene to Panama, asks rhetorically: 'Where is Graham Greene now and what is he up to? The most accomplished of English novelists has been making only fitful visits to London in the past ten years and, anyway, in the manner of the old Jacobite spies, he is a man of disappearance in mysterious company.' He answers his own question: 'The last I had heard of him was that he had turned up with Brigadier-General Omar Torrijos at the recent Panamanian Conference in Washington – strange for one who has never been a conference man.'

Pritchett speaks quickly of the places Greene visited. Reporters routinely travel, but novelists less so. But he tells us that Greene was invited to return to Europe by Concorde. And Pritchett knew also of his visit to Northern Ireland:

[He] skipped off to Belfast . . . for a cold whiff of fear – but he might as well have been in Asunción drinking with his Honorary Consul, or in Cuba, Haiti, Hawaii, Saigon, the Congo, his house in Anacapri, or with the Third Man in Vienna or on the Lawless Roads of Mexico at the time of the persecution of the Church.

The brilliant Pritchett, a long-time friend, telephoned Antibes to arrange an interview, enjoying Greene's 'flat, conspiratorial, laughing voice which, of itself, makes him the best company I've known in the past 40 years'.

Pritchett found him gleeful, but notice the subtlety of his description:

[He] welcomed me as usual with a quotation. He'd just found the right words in Conrad for his state of mind. He had done no work for weeks – he was waiting for his new novel, *The Human Factor*, to appear – and 'felt the leaden weight of an ir-remediable idleness'. Writers love words: the word 'irremediable' spoken with his curious near-French 'r' and its overtones of glee in being beyond hope, was Greene in vintage condition.

★

I have no doubt that Greene had in mind the treasonable activity of Philby when creating Maurice Castle in *The Human Factor*. And after all, Greene and Philby often worked closely, if not in the same office, then in the same building and on the same floor, both as spies, though Philby was a double agent, working for his own country and his country's enemies. We know, too, in certain essentials, that Greene drew on Philby's reception in Moscow when he finally defected in 1963. He used descriptions of the Moscow flat from Philby's third wife, Eleanor (*Kim Philby: The Spy I Loved*, 1968).

Would Greene have come to write *The Human Factor* if he hadn't worked with Philby in Ryder Street, and been directly under his command during their wartime service in MI6? I doubt it. He wouldn't have had the urge: he wouldn't have had sufficient knowledge, the exactitude he demanded of himself when writing, that urgent claim to do the job unerringly.

If Philby had not defected after being revealed as a betrayer of his own country, I'm sure that Greene would not have been inspired to write the book. But the book is *not* substantially about Philby or Philby's character, and as we saw previously, Greene abandoned it precisely because he didn't want it to be thought of that way: it is much more about Greene, about hidden deposits in his *own* character, while seeming to mine fictional depths. Simple aspects of Greene show up in the first paragraph:

> Castle, ever since he had joined the firm as a young recruit more than thirty years ago, had taken his lunch in a public house behind St James's Street, not far from the office. If he had been asked why he lunched there, he would have referred to the excellent quality of the sausages; he might have preferred a different bitter from Watney's, but the quality of the sausages outweighed that. He was always prepared to account for his actions, even the most innocent, and he was always strictly on time.[7]

Greene is describing two aspects of himself: his ability to account for his actions and his regulated life. He *was* always on time. He did visit a public house behind St James's Street (where he used to drink with Philby), just a short walk from his flat.

Greene also used his surroundings in creating Colonel Daintry. Daintry is the new broom, in charge of security. Greene fits him firmly in his one-time home: 'Colonel Daintry had a two-roomed flat in St James's Street.'[8] And what Daintry does in looking after himself, and what he sees both inside and outside the flat, is what Greene saw and experienced. Greene describes well-known people living in other flats; the names alone are changed: there was a famous general living above him — a household name during the war.

When Daintry meets his daughter, Greene has his own daughter in mind, and his own wife, whom he'd once loved (a fact he now found hard to understand). Daintry asks after her mother

> as if they were speaking of an acquaintance whom he hardly knew – it was odd to think there had ever been a time when he and his wife were close enough to share a sexual spasm which had produced the beautiful girl who sat so elegantly opposite him drinking her Tio Pepe.[9]

What Greene could see from his flat at 5 St James's Street is what he gives to Daintry. He showed it to me once from the outside and took me round to the back, so that I'd know the tiny court area of one portion of *The Human Factor*:

> Daintry was no cook and he usually economized for one meal by buying cold chipolatas at Fortnum's. He had never liked clubs; if he felt hungry . . . there was Overton's just below. His bedroom and his bathroom looked out on a tiny ancient court containing a sundial and a silversmith. Few people who walked down St James's Street knew of the court's existence. It was a very discreet flat and not unsuitable for a lonely man.[10]

Greene had made simple meals for himself, and sometimes, like Daintry, his lunch didn't last beyond four minutes. Not divorced, Greene had companions, yet he was a lonely man, always a lonely man.

★

Daintry is troubled by the death of the young Davis, who he thinks has been deliberately and undetectably killed by their MI6 doctor. Daintry first thinks of 'Dr Percival' and 'C', Sir John Hargreaves, going 'down the street in front of him when [Davis's funeral] service was over, their heads bent like conspirators'.[11]

How was it done? Here is Greene, writing nine years earlier, on 15 May 1967, to ask his brother, Dr Raymond Greene, how his character could be killed off without it being suspected or even known:

> Could you help me with a suggestion? . . . I am writing of a man in the Secret Service who is suspected of being a double agent [who] has to be made to die apparently naturally from some disease or other. The bacteriological War Establishment is at the disposal of the Secret Service. Is there some bug that they could use with the help of those experts? . . . The death has to appear

a natural one to escape an awkward inquest and questions in Parliament about security.[12]

Raymond's response has disappeared, but we see through Greene's reply that he made fruitful suggestions:

Many thanks for your long and useful letter. The impression I get is that the Aphlatoxin* is what I want. The man concerned is a rather heavy drinker and as long as he is put out of action for a while and dies at leisure that is all that is required.

Greene repeats why he must have the double agent put to death without involving any suspicion of this:

An officer of the Secret Service in London is suspected of a leak. It is not an important leak, but obviously a deliberate one. The chief feels that to put the man on trial will do far more damage than his leak in destroying confidence especially with the Americans. He wants to have the leak definitely traced to the man and then for the man to die a more or less seeming natural death which won't require an inquest. A false suicide would result in an inquest where he would be described as belonging to a department of the Foreign Office which would arouse the attention of papers and of members of Parliament. Publicity is the last thing desired. A man is put in charge of the case who is the liaison officer with the Porton Bacteriological Warfare outfit and is also a doctor . . . Could the liver damage be hurried up?[13]

Greene is still corresponding with his elder brother about the matter in October 1972, five years later! Here is Raymond's reply:

Yes a good knock on the head plus morphia would work. Adult lethal dose of morphine is 300 mg.
    To give an intravenous drug needs practice. I know hippies do it but they must make a lot of shots before they get the knack. Also the 'victim' would have to be dead still or the vein would be missed. The best immediate drug would be pentothal. It works in 5–10 seconds. 'Instructions' from a doctor would be useless.

---

* A toxin made by a bacteria-like organism found in some moulds that contaminate grains and nuts. It is a powerful immunosuppressant and carcinogen, especially in the liver. More commonly 'aflatoxin'.

Only practice under his supervision would work and the 'victim' must be acquiescent or unconscious.[14]

Greene takes care painting his Greeneland scenery.

★

Daintry's father and mother fit Greene's father and mother to a tee, except of course that the fictional parents lived in an obscure rectory in Suffolk with its vast basement kitchen, which was based on the headmaster's house at Berkhamsted School. And the way the mother dealt with her husband is the way Graham's mother, Marion, dealt with her husband Charles:

> Confessions came to him [Daintry as a security officer and Greene as a young man still at school], if they came at all, second-hand, for people did confess sometimes to his mother, who was much loved in the village, and he had heard her filter these confessions to his father, with any grossness, malice or cruelty removed. 'I think you ought to know what Mrs Baines* told me yesterday.'[15]

Here is evidence that Mrs Greene would tamper with confessions she heard. We remember that she would read aloud to her husband and cut out suspect phrases in their own son's book. She had another part to play in the novel as Maurice Castle's mother. And some of the feelings Vivien expressed during the war when she and her children were evacuated to Crowborough (where Greene's mother and father retired to) are repeated here. Having changed them from Daintry's folks to Castle's, Greene gives another description fitting Marion Greene:

> Mrs Castle was invariably standing there on the porch waiting for them, a tall straight figure in an out-dated skirt which showed to advantage her fine ankles, wearing a high collar like Queen Alexandra's which disguised the wrinkles of old age. To hide his despondency Castle . . . greeted his mother with an exaggerated hug which she barely returned. She believed that any emotions openly expressed must be false emotions. She had deserved to marry an ambassador or a colonial governor rather than a country doctor.[16]

---

* Mrs Baines is also the name Greene gave to the married woman who is killed by her husband in his famous short story, 'The Basement Room', made later into the moving film *The Fallen Idol*.

Replace 'country doctor' with 'headmaster' and we have a portrait exactly true to his mother and father.

Greene's sister, Elisabeth Dennys, told me that her mother kept a tight hold on her emotions. Writing to her daughter about the death of her father, she ended with her full signature, 'Marion R. Greene'. Elisabeth recalled that Marion would never throw her arms round one of her children or kiss one: 'I remember when I went abroad on special duty during the war, she didn't make any fuss.'[17]

Vivien Greene complained similarly that Graham, during the war, 'wrote seldom' from Sierra Leone, but added fairly: 'some [letters] may have been torpedoed, etc. [His] father's death: Nothing: Marion nothing that I can remember . . . I shouldn't think so. She was very "inhibited about emotions".'[18] And Graham's cousin Barbara Greene (the Countess Strachwitz), writing to me on 15 May 1977, referred to her mother's view of Marion that 'she was a most formidable and cold woman'.

★

Catherine Walston, at the time of the publication of *The Human Factor* in 1978, had six months to live. Greene gave her a walk-on part in the novel as the wife of Sir John Hargreaves, he who conspired with Dr Percival (using Raymond Greene's expert medical knowledge) to find a way to secretly murder the young agent Davis, whom they mistakenly think is responsible for leaks of vital information to the enemy Russia. (The betrayer is really our hero, Maurice Castle.) Davis appears to have died from natural causes, so that at autopsy, it seems a normal death. They commit the rash act, and later discover that they have put to death the wrong person.

The Hargreaves's home life is derived from the weekend parties that Catherine and Harry Walston organised. Greene is inspired for fictional purposes by typical conversations in the Walston household:

> 'Drinks are waiting,' Lady Hargreaves said. 'Help yourselves. Lunch in ten minutes.' . . .
>
> 'And your famous steak-and-kidney pudding?' Daintry asked. 'I've heard so much about it.'
>
> 'My pie, you mean. Did you really have a good morning, Colonel?' Her voice had a faint American accent – the more agreeable for being faint, like the tang of an expensive perfume.

The evening wanes:

> 'John,' Lady Hargeaves called down the table, 'wake up.' He opened blue serene unshockable eyes and said, 'A cat-nap.'

'Serene unshockable eyes' were characteristic of Lord Walston.

Hargreaves has been made head of intelligence, 'C' himself. Walston was a peer in the House of Lords. Greene has some envy for Harry, as does Daintry for Hargreaves. Can you imagine this internal rumination (the differences necessary for the story's sake)?

> He envied him in the first place for his position. He was one of the very few men outside the services ever to have been appointed C. No one in the firm knew why he had been chosen – all kinds of recondite influences had been surmised, for his only experience of intelligence had been gained in Africa during the war. Daintry also envied him his wife; she was so rich, so decorative, so impeccably American. An American marriage, it seemed, could not be classified as a foreign marriage: to marry a foreigner special permission had to be obtained and it was often refused, but to marry an American was perhaps to confirm the special relationship . . .
>
> Sir John Hargreaves limped round, handing out cigars, pouring out whiskies, poking the fire.[19]

Harry Walston did limp sometimes. He did hand out cigars, usually Cuban, and poured whiskies for his guests. Catherine's voice had a faint American accent, but she was not known for her cooking. Graham had now stopped using Catherine for important characters in his books – she is peripheral here.

Yet it is impossible to read the two letters Greene wrote to Catherine and Yvonne in his dangerous desert foray in Israel* without noticing that he never stopped loving Catherine. And if his love for Catherine was fading to not much more than caricature, this is evidence that even the greatest love dies from separation. Love is never stationary, it is in flux, as the movement of the tides.

★

Catherine was fighting two crises: Greene's receding affection, and a series of illnesses from which she was never to recover. I remember calling on her in July 1977, the interview arranged by Greene. I had seen some photographs of the stunningly handsome Catherine. She hadn't lost her exciting character, but she had lost her beauty. She was an ailing old woman, and had a need for whisky – initially to alleviate pain. And Greene, I suspect, was in part guilty, though not deliberately, and her family blamed him for this. In order to deal with his depressions, Graham for many years drank too much, and his compan-

---

* See Chapter 35 'Confessions Near an Egyptian Shore'.

ions – Dorothy Glover, as well as Catherine – followed his habit. But unlike the weaker gender (physically, at least) Greene had a great advantage: he was a man, and a big one. And he could stop drinking when working, such was his dedication to his craft. He was not like so many writers who destroy themselves while suffering from the loneliness of long active writing years. Writing was, is, a hazardous occupation.*

★

Few letters of Catherine's survive, though those that have, written late in her life, are revealing. First we notice that in spite of her dreadful condition, she never complained. In fact, she was in the habit of praising Greene. She did so when I interviewed her, and some of her comments were almost a replica of those she wrote to Greene, at a time when it must have been apparent to her that she had lost forever her great and famous lover. She was herself in part to blame through never wanting to see him, and by not marrying him when he was so desperate for her to do so. In the end, I rather fancy, he knew that being married again wouldn't work for someone whose whole life was primarily given over to writing. His books came first, absolutely, not the comradeship of men, not even, in the last resort, the love of women. In spite of his modesty, he wanted to be a giant in the field of literature. He wanted to belong to the first rank. He rarely believed he did. But did ever anyone in the long history of literature work harder?

Greene was never without his work. He refused to retire. Death alone retired him. And just look at his output: unending correspondence (sometimes he had fifty letters a day to write before he could begin working); his many diaries; his six volumes of dream books; thousands of love letters. Tally the novels, the plays, his collected essays, his travel books, his two biographies, his letters to editors of *The Times*, the *Daily Telegraph*, the *Tablet*, his screenplays – an exhausting output, prodigious energy.

★

Back when Catherine was healthy but unavailable most of the time, Greene became attached to Yvonne, and by the mid-1960s, when he left England for France, Catherine had little chance. It was inevitable they'd see less of each other, even if she hadn't become terribly crippled. His physical love for Catherine gradually dwindled and finally choked on itself. We see it happening in the way he writes about Mrs

* Didn't Hemingway commit suicide because he came to feel he'd destroyed his enormous talent by drinking, which led to ill health on a massive scale? One day he got hold of his best double-barrelled shotgun, put two canisters in and blew away his entire cranial vault.

Hargreaves. Near the end of June 1971, we see that he doesn't even want to refer to their being lovers, but you'd expect that: she's sick, he's in a different country, and he's extremely close to Yvonne.

More and more, Graham felt part of the Cloetta family. He'd grown close to Martine, Yvonne's eldest daughter, as if she were his own child, aged six when he first met her, now, at eighteen, a woman. Greene had never been close to his own children when they were young and he had his career to make. Here, at the age of sixty-six, he was more comfortable playing the role of father, even if a surrogate one.

★

Catherine would know what Graham was saying on that crucial day, 25 June 1971, that this was the final brush-off:

> You must by this time know I love you dearly – I would have had to live out of England in any circumstances because of losing all that money to Roe – so I wish we could write to each other as special friends . . . We've both got things to reproach ourselves with, so can't we leave all that out.[20]

He then tells her she'll be getting a copy of his autobiography, *A Sort of Life*, when it appears in September. This letter sounds a personal cry about the difficulty he is having in writing *The Honorary Consul*: 'The novel goes very slowly & with difficulty. About 60,000 done out of, I suspect, 85,000.'[21] In a later letter (after eight months' further work) he writes: 'the novel – all has been rewritten about five times, except the last chapter & I don't want to begin that before the rest is tolerable . . . I doubt if it will be ready before the summer (publication perhaps in 73 [it appeared in September 1973] – old age – 67 now – write slowly.)'[22] So the letters are sparse, no love left, even between the lines.

When she asks a favour he turns her down bluntly, at least for a man usually so sensitive. She could not help but know now that it was all over. The fat lady had sung:

> Dear Catherine,
>
>   I would love you to go to Anacapri any time, but I don't think it would be a good thing to go together. For myself I know it would be horribly depressing under the changed circumstances – one could go anywhere new together in this new relationship of special & loving friends, but then everything would seem unnatural & artificial – not going to bed together at the end of the day.[23]

Greene adds, slightly coolly: 'But I'd like you to see the place & tell me what you think of the changes.'

On 2 August 1974 he expresses his sadness that Catherine is back in hospital: 'I do hope this the last time.' He speaks of his own health problems that year: 'A rather dreary one for me – six months of dentistry (21 teeth capped & five out) . . . A lot of anxiety too about Y's daughter Martine, who was operated on for a cancer spot on the leg at the end of 1972 and had a baby last February.' Catherine could no longer expect anything more than friendship. In the same letter he is clearly disappointed with his writing and the tedium of life. He could not know that in two years' time his adventures in Panama and later in Nicaragua would suddenly enliven his world.

So he writes to Catherine less often now, only out of concern when she's sick. She was soon severely disabled. In a letter of 20 November 1975, he offers a possible solution: 'I'm terribly sorry to hear how badly crippled you are – I had no idea of it. The last time I saw you you seemed better.' He writes about a Capri friend, Laetitia Cerio whom Catherine knew well and her 'miraculous cures', and suggested she see the same physician. Catherine's reply has survived:

> Thanks for suggesting the Swiss Clinic. I don't think I could face it. I've seen all the best Doctors and surgeons in London and Cambridge and have been having acupuncture but with no success. I am just going to have to learn to live with it.[24]

Catherine began this note of 13 December 1975 by thanking Graham for his 'most welcome letter' and mentioned that she had heard from his former agent Mary Pritchett, who was visiting London. Mary told her that Greene was in town for rehearsals. This was the play with plenty of sexual deviance, *The Return of A. J. Raffles*: 'I had a letter from Bobbie Speaight the other day and he said "Graham's play is gloriously funny. I haven't laughed so much in the theatre for years."' Suddenly her letter turns serious:

> We are all getting older, alas, and now to-day, after Thomas's death and funeral, I see that David Mathew has died. Poor Gervase.*

---

* Gervase was Archbishop Mathew's younger brother, also a priest, to whom Greene had dedicated *The Power and the Glory*. In a copy given to his wife, in March 1940, beneath the simple printed dedication 'For Gervase', he had written, in his minute hand, 'but far more for you, dear love'.

'Thomas' is Father Thomas Gilby, Greene's rival in love.

> Thomas was largely living here and going back to Cambridge
> occasionally but I'm so glad that he died in his own house with
> the Fathers and Brothers around him, dressed in his habit and
> white socks, so one of the lay Brothers told me. I think he had
> been preparing for death for the last six months so what could
> have been better than to die instantly between the soup and the
> main course.
>   And she adds simply: 'He will be a great loss to me.'

She has accepted that she is a past love of Greene's; it's all over.
Speaking of the fact that he's much 'in the press these days', she
expresses her hope that he is not depressed. Catherine was witness
to some of Greene's desperate depressions, and ends her letter: 'I think
of you so often and with such pleasure. What a vast amount you gave
me.'[25] These last two sentences were repeated by her to me in
interview.

Greene replied in ten days' time (a quick response at this stage, the
embers all but ashes). Speaking of *The Return of A. J. Raffles*, he had
to admit that 'the theatre reviewers certainly don't like me . . . [They]
will have successfully prevented a commercial management taking on
the play. However this time I thoroughly enjoyed the rehearsals.' Thus
Greene had 'two failures in a row & the cast & I got on very well.
The theatre is like roulette – the croupier has won. This odd thing is
that the reviewers all seemed a bit shocked – I thought nothing shocked
anyone nowadays.' In his heart he felt poor, alone, naked, unsuccessful,
and exposed to a public that no longer liked his plays.

It was then that Greene commented on the death of Father Gilby:
'I was sorry to see about Thomas's death – sorry for you & his other
friends.' He then adds what the young would find passing strange:
'Death as one gets old [Greene was then seventy-one] seems more &
more a friend.' And again he mentions the death of Archbishop Mathew:
'I wrote a piece about David to *The Times*, but they neither acknowledged it nor published it.'

But illness was also upon his brother Raymond, and Greene was
very anxious:

> Poor Raymond has been having an awful time with cancer of
> the throat. He diagnosed it himself very early & they said the
> cancer was cured, but he suffered terribly afterwards & went back
> for a few days to hospital last week & says he's 'better,' – but I
> don't know.

One would have thought his worry over Raymond suggests that death is no friend, yet he ends his letter to Catherine mentioning his 'fear of surviving too long'.[26]

★

In the winter of 1976, Greene received his first invitation from General Torrijos, but before that, whilst still struggling with *The Human Factor*, he was seeking to enter the belly of yet another beast, or where the beast in 1976 still raged: Belfast. His visit to Ireland was short. He was testing the water to see if it intrigued or distracted him. Thus V. S. Pritchett was right to remark that Greene had 'skipped off to Belfast for a cold whiff of fear'. Whatever his purpose, he thought four days would prove something. What it proved was that he 'hated' his time in Belfast. There are no descriptions of the scene, just of meetings with political people in the news, and two famous writers in Dublin:

> Belfast – more frightening than the blitz, but I liked Merlyn Rees a lot. I just went over to have a look & then went on to lovely peaceful (by contrast) Dublin & had dinner with Sean O'Faolain who seemed . . . old [O'Faolain was then seventy-six but he lived ninety-one years], & with Conor Cruise O'Brien whom I liked very much. I forgot to say I had one wild pub crawl north of Belfast with Gerry Fitt in his bullet-proof car & his armed detective.[27]

Greene had been asked if he'd like to visit Northern Ireland. In reply to the invitation by the Northern Ireland government, Greene specifically laid down that he'd go only if he met Gerry (now Lord) Fitt.

★

Gerry Fitt's background was tough. He was a merchant seaman from 1941 to 1953, serving in wartime Artic convoys to the USSR, and then entered local politics, representing the Dock Division of Belfast as a Republican Labour MP. In 1970 he co-founded the Social Democratic and Labour Party (SDLP) which he led for nine years. Fitt only resigned in 1979, and so was still SDLP leader at the time of Greene's visit. Fitt was an opponent of violence and had to endure the animosity of Republican and Loyalist extremists. It must have been his daring and obvious courage that attracted Greene.

No doubt, when together, they talked politics, but the story I heard from Mary Kenny, a friend of Fitt's, was that it was something prodigious in the way of a pub-crawl up the Antrim coast. They went on

615

and on and on, drinking whiskey, and kept going well into the next morning, finishing up with an early breakfast of bacon and eggs. Greene received his first defeat at the hands of the Irish. He reached his limit at 4 a.m., leaving Fitt a note saying that it had been a wonderful evening, but he couldn't stand any more and had flaked out.

In 1979, Greene, in his interview with Marie-Françoise Allain in Antibes, had revealed an unexpected attitude towards the provisional IRA, which he described as terrorising the Catholics in Northern Ireland. Ms Allain objected to his alluding to the IRA in unflattering terms: 'In view of your habitual partialities, and bearing in mind the fact that you are a Catholic, should you not be on their side, on the side of the underdog?'

And Greene really let go, criticising the Provos:* '[They] are not the underdog. They are the executioners . . . [they] have turned into out-and-out gangsters, devoid of ideals. One might as well be in Chicago. They bully little shopkeepers who, unless they give way, are punished by knee-capping. They terrorize the Catholics. They own the taxis. They own the big self-service stores. They win fortunes thanks to terrorism . . . In fact it's no longer a question of "Protestants" versus "Catholics" but of two terrorist gangs.'[28] I suspect that during his drinking session with the splendid Fitt, Greene was made knowledgeable, in the long evening and dawn to follow, of the two sides. As always, Greene was a sponge. In my travels with him, I was acutely aware of how he soaked up information at the speed of sound.

*

On 1 September 1976, Greene spoke to Catherine of his first trip with Leopoldo Durán:

> Then off to Spain travelling 3,500 kms in a tiny Renault 5 with a Father Durán who has written a book on my theology!
> We stayed in monasteries, a pious home, a hostel, an occasional hotel, & had as driver an ex-student & as companion two cases of Galician wine which we drank as aperitifs along the road.

But then it's back to the grindstone: 'Now I have to get back to work on reviewing Evelyn's *Diaries* & picking up a novel [*The Human Factor*] that won't go right.'

---

* In 1970, guerrilla activity was renewed by the IRA, which had split into two groups: the Officials, concerned with political action, and the Provisionals (Provos), dedicated to the reunification of Ireland at any cost. Terrorism was intensified, resulting in many deaths and the assassination of a Stormont senator.

Just before Christmas, Catherine mentions that she's been without pain for four days ('which is very encouraging') and relief allows her to think of Graham. The letter is dated 14 December 1976: 'I thought you had a play ready . . . I wish you would let me see it and I [hope] the novel is going better than when you last wrote.' Then with genuine concern and love she writes: 'I hope you are well, dearest Graham. I think about you, worry about you, and love you very much.'[29] She wrote this with not much more than a year to live.

By 6 April 1977, Catherine was very sick, or so I infer from Greene's response to information which came from Marie Biche, Greene's French agent and special friend of the Walstons:

I was very anxious about you after what Marie had told me of your experiences in Italy. You do seem to be going through an appalling purgatory.

I don't know the full story, but Catherine had gone to Italy with Father Donal O'Sullivan (probably the man called 'Skunkburgh' by Greene). They were both alcoholics. When Catherine took ill in an hotel in Venice, Father O'Sullivan acted out the part of her husband. Catherine worsened, and O'Sullivan, caught out, had to send a telegram to Lord Walston, who travelled to her and brought her home.

Lord Walston had a profound dislike for O'Sullivan, though he'd had feelings of fellowship for Gilby, an engaging figure who was no drunk, a fine scholar, and did not rashly spend the Walstons' money. He was altogether a verbally outrageous and ever engaging Irishman. The one letter of O'Sullivan's I have read struck me as sharp, cunning, a betrayer of God.

It was at this time, on 6 April 1977, that Greene approached Catherine about my visiting her. His next letter, dated 19 May 1977, might have put the fear of God into her about his biographer, for he spoke of an interview I'd had with John and Gillian Sutro in Monte Carlo: 'I hear that Sherry kept the Sutros up till half-past five in the morning the other day. You mustn't let him do the same to you if you see him.' When I did visit her in the summer of that year, Greene wrote anxiously: 'I wonder if you saw Norman Sherry & if you like him?'[30]

I did see her. I went to her upstairs study and did not recognise her. There was nothing left of the beauty that had been so admired. Only her eyes had retained a glint of her great powers of attraction. (Mrs Woodrup, who knew both Greene and the Walstons, told a friend of mine that she was with an acquaintance who suddenly nodded towards a certain lady and said: 'That's Catherine Walston over there!' Mrs Woodrup could not believe it. It couldn't be, such an old lady, when Catherine had been so beautiful. It could not be; but it was.)

*

Catherine's decline was irreversible. When she visited her elder sister in Athens, Bonte 'was horrified at what had happened to her beauty'. While there, she had a terrible pain and Bonte's husband, General Durán, got a doctor to give her an injection. The doctor was just washing his hands when they all heard a terrible cry. 'Apparently she had bitten her tongue and the blood was all over the wall. She was unconscious and we got her to hospital.' When they arrived, there were no beds and 'poor Bobs was put on the floor along with a crowd of accident cases'.

Bonte tried unsuccessfully all night to contact Harry Walston, in Mexico on a mission, or Catherine's son Oliver. The next day they were able to get her a suite in the Liavangalismos hospital.

*

Greene would still periodically see Catherine, usually at her home. He had to be in London to meet the Foreign Press Corps: 'I've done this several times before and it is always quite amusing as one has Russian, German, American, Swedish correspondents etc. etc.' He was also to be 'a judge on an Irish Book Prize* given by Mrs Ewart-Biggs in memory of her murdered Ambassador husband', killed by the Provos in July 1976. When it was over, he wanted to visit Catherine at her Cambridge home, 'but would it be all right for you or have you got a lot of people?'[31] (It's almost as if Greene didn't realise that her party days were over.) Catherine offered to 'send a car to Royston or Audley End (Liverpool Street) at any time that you arrive. I might even be brave and come myself although I can't drive a car yet.'[32] Sadly, she never would again.

Greene's next letter to Catherine comes seven months later, on 12 May 1978, when he writes about the enormous publicity surrounding *The Human Factor*. He is disgusted with himself. Odd that he is still full of his own problems, his own sicknesses, at a time when Catherine is near death. He seems selfish, and it seems that such phrases as 'How are you?' would be especially painful. He chats on: 'It all came of my giving my niece Louise [Dennys] permission to do an interview for a Canadian paper & the *Sunday Telegraph*, so I couldn't refuse *The Times*, the *Sunday Times*, the *Observer* & so on & so on. Never again will I

---

* Not to be confused with the Guinness Peat Award (see Chapter 53).

let myself in for this.' He tells Catherine he's coming over to England after his 1978 tour with Father Durán, 'whom [my friend] Maria Newall calls my "pocket saint",' but not before he's gone to Anacapri for three weeks. He admits it's been 'an awfully long time since I've heard of you. How are you? And how is the treatment going?' His last letter wasn't even in his own hand, but dictated to his sister Elisabeth: 'I am off for my usual visit to Panama and my pal General Torrijos,' he writes on 10 July 1978, 'In between Spain and Panama I hope to be in England for some days and I'll see if I can come down to see you.' (He did not.) He concludes his short note: 'That poor Norman Sherry who has been trying to follow in my footsteps in Mexico, Haiti, and Paraguay has returned to England very unwell. I do hope I'm not going to be the death of him.'[33] He was worried about himself, and me; but he should have been downright alarmed about Catherine, but then he hadn't near the end kept in close touch and did not know how near she was to death.

Catherine replied happily, delighted he'd written because she had not heard from him since his visit the November before:

> And now today, or maybe a week today that you go to Capri. What happy times I had there with you and won't ever forget them from the day we walked through the gate for the first time . . .
>
> I am just out of a stint in hospital so I am not yet back at my typewriter. But my treatment goes excellently: all is well.

She had but months to live.

She is surprised he goes to Spain and Portugal every year with a priest: 'Have you a real priest chum in Paris or Antibes? I hope you do: they are fun and I miss no longer having one.' I'm assuming that Father O'Sullivan is out of the picture, perhaps advised by Harry Walston never to darken their door again.

Catherine talks cheerfully about what she's reading: Tolstoy's letters. Then she comments on the last novel she would receive from Greene, expressing the view that *The Human Factor* might have been the most difficult he had ever written; she then refers to his *Collected Essays*: 'of course I read them all . . . some eighty essays altogether, such brilliant essays they are.'

Even in dire sickness Catherine reminisces, uncomplaining, asking very little of her old lover, her life now lived alone in her bedroom:

> A few more letters and the odd telephone call when you are in London would be a pleasure. But can I complain? What a vast

amount of pleasure you have given me playing Scrabble on the roof at the Rosaio and the 7/30 Bus to Gemma's and teaching me [to] swim underwater at Ian Fleming's house; smoking opium and Angkor etc.

She refers to Greene's long-time friend John Sutro: 'I didn't know he was so ill.' But she is in much worse condition. 'I hope Lucy and the children are well and happy also, but most especially *you*.' Finally, seeming to sense that this might be her last communication with him, she writes: 'There has never been anyone in my life like you . . . Love Catherine.'[34]

★

Catherine Walston died on 2 September 1978 in Addenbrooke's Hospital in Cambridge. Only Harry and son Oliver were present at her death. Some sixteen years later, Oliver consented to be interviewed about his mother's death and spoke of his father's attachment to her: 'I sat with my father and he was still utterly devoted to this woman.'[35] Twenty days later he wrote beautifully about his mother (and father) in the *Spectator*:

> The strange thing is that even in her final days, when my mother's mind wandered and her body could scarcely move, the men in her life remained constant and devoted. Chief among these was . . . my father. They had been married 42 years earlier and – in spite of the sort of pressures which would have smashed most marriages – they shared a family, a home and a bedroom . . .
>
> During her last night I sat in the hospital room while my father stroked her hand and talked quietly about the old days. With tubes sticking through her papery grey skin, she drifted in and out of consciousness. From time to time she would open her eyes, smile an exhausted smile, and close them again. Towards dawn she died and my father sat silent. Only then was their marriage finally over.[36]

The service prior to interment took place at St George's Church, Thriplow, on the 7th. Her once beautiful face and body had inched with painful slowness towards death. Greene should have pressed to see Catherine, but she didn't want him to see her in that condition. She was suffering from leukaemia, the disease which would bring Greene himself to his end.

Following her death, Harry Walston wrote to Greene, showing a desire to be proper, yet also cool. The letter should be read carefully.

Greene's letter to Lord Walston about his wife's death has not survived. This reply is all we have. Walston's letter is dated 18 September, sixteen days after Catherine's death.

Dear Graham,

I've left your letter to the last to answer because it's the most difficult. I've thought a lot but still don't know what to say.

You should not have remorse. Of course you caused pain. But who can honestly say that he has gone through life without causing pain? And you gave joy too. One cannot draw up a balance sheet of pluses & minuses. But you gave Catherine something (I don't know what) that no one else had given her. It would not be unjust to say it changed her life: but it developed her into a far more deeply feeling human being than before; & gave her a love of reading that had begun already, but matured because of you. What she read had a profound effect upon her.

One knew that death would come sooner rather than later: but, altho' during those last months pain became more frequent & she grew weaker, her mind became brighter & her interest in people & things returned. So my innate optimism remained. The end came from haemorrhage caused by the persistent ulcer. An operation was out of the question. By the evening I had no more hope, & she died next morning. She had no pain – tho' discomfort: the priests came. Marie will tell you of the funeral – if you wish to hear . . .

Yours

Harry.

I find I've omitted the ostensible purpose of this letter – to thank you for writing. I do.

How very gentlemanly. But it's hard not to notice little flashes of anger. Walston was a good man, and Oliver Walston describes his father well: 'He never got angry, or sad, or cried, or shouted.'

When Greene returned from seeing General Torrijos he was unaware that Catherine was dying, and there were no obituaries I've been able to uncover. The death was reported to him a day after her burial on 7 September, by Marie Biche, who had just returned from Thriplow and the funeral. Thinking that Greene was away, she called at his Paris apartment because she'd left something there. Marie disturbed him asleep in bed, and it was in his bed that he received her news. She told him then what she knew about the end, and later sent him a letter:

I hated having to be the one to break the news of Catherine's death to you. What is somewhat consoling is that everyone here says she was in exceptionally fine form mentally for the last few weeks; that after having been very frightened of death since leukaemia was discovered she spoke of it in a far more peaceful frame of mind as something to come in the non[e too] distant future (tho' by no means the immediate one) talked to the ones & the others of what she thought they should do – regarding themselves – when she would be gone. *Porter*, the ex-chauffeur you must remember, told me that when he drove her to the hair-dresser (in Harston, I believe) on the day before she went (again) into hospital she was particularly lively & cheerful.

Dying on the 2nd, Catherine was not buried until the 7th and must have lain in the hospital morgue for days. Services took place on the day before burial, but the oddity of Marie's English makes certain things a little doubtful:

(That was on the Wedn). In hospital Thursd p.m. and Friday a.m. all the 'entourage' had particularly good chats with her – then the [ulcer haemorrhage] (can't spell that in English) set in. In view of her general condition the Doctors/Surgeons would not attempt (I say, thank God) – another operation. She was put under strong drugs, for the first time, I believe. The sort she'd theoretically wanted but had not needed, such as (did I understand right) heroin.

   Harry and Oliver spent the night by her. On Sat a.m. the Drs attempted another X-ray – when she passed out (as I understand) unconsciously at about 10 a.m.

(From this, it looks as if she died mid-morning, but Oliver suggests it took place at dawn.)

At long, so long, last out of pain. The amount of physical pain she had to endure over those innumerable years since she broke her hip-bone in that Dublin airport is beyond record – and inhuman.

   I only know victims of multiple sclerosis (that of recent expe-rience) to have had to face the like. And those have the advantage (?) that Drs . . . know the different stages & types of crippling pain they are subject to, whereas with Catherine it has been so many, if not every, time(s) that it was a different one with a cause to be discovered & only then could [she] be treated or palliated, and, in between, all too easily attributed to psychosomatic causes ('Tu parles', as we say!).

Friday, the 7th, a *suitably* cool, grey, drizzly morning (that's my opinion, unshared by some of the younger generation!) the service was short but good and the 'atmosphere' was particularly 'chaude et veulerie' [warm and listless], as tho' the church was [chock] full, it was only with people who really cared (place, date and time had only been made known to such). All the 'children' – but does the word apply when the youngest is verging on 30? – Binny [Belinda Straight], Bonte, Buzzy [Catherine's brother David] & Gigi [David's wife] (all of those on affectionate speaking terms at last thanks to Catherine's enduring efforts!). Several of the grandchildren – of those she was closer to, were all there.

Father Gilby is given an honourable mention:

The one person that was deeply missed by all was dear Fr Thomas Gilby. (I know he wasn't a favourite of yours but he was a 'universal' favourite of all who were close to C over the past dozen or so years). He really should have survived an extra 18 or whatever the number of months is, to help her thru' the particularly hard ones those months were, and to officiate on Friday.

Extraordinarily, the clergy were not allowed a voice:

As always, there was a comical (& to most [a] mysterious) feature. No 'words' – if that's the term – said by any of the clergy: the local Catholic priest & 2 or 3 from Blackfriars. That['s] because the one who should have had 'the honour', the senior chap from Blackfriars is an excruciating bore who had made the service for Fr Thomas past the unbearable for C and all present. So Harry had had to say 'No, thank you' when he'd offered to make a speech – and therefore 'no words by anyone'. Actually, any such would have been superfluous as every person present was so aware of the indelible mark C had left on him or her through being given her love, affection, friendship or concern.[37]

The prayer was Psalm 23: 'The Lord is my Shepherd, I'll not want'; the lessons II Corinthians, chapter 4, v. 16, and chapter 5, v. 10. And then the final prayer.

★

Marie Biche's letter is confusing as to dates, but I suspect that Greene visited Catherine's grave within days of her burial. After buying a post-card of St George's Church, where the last ceremony took place and where her grave lies, he marked the spot with a cross in black ink and wrote beside it the date of her burial. Standing in front of Catherine's grave, he must have regretted that he had not returned sooner from Panama, and feeling her absence, must have said his final goodbye, perhaps whispering a tender word, or even a line similar to Thomas Hardy's, 'Woman much missed'. Catherine's son, William Walston, felt that even if the family had invited Graham 'he would not have attended out of consideration for my father. He would have known that his presence would have been unwelcome, and I think he was too much of a gentleman to have ever contemplated such an intrusion.'

On the gravestone, the Walston family's friend (and Greene's too) Henry Moore later completed a bronze relief of a woman and child.

*

Years before, at the height of their love, Greene had given Catherine a special pair of charms which she attached to her Cartier wristwatch. One was a gold and coral musical harp, the other a tiny gold book with individual pages. Catherine wore them from the moment she received them, and never took them off. According to William Walston, she wore them even during her final illness. The rest of the family knew of it, of course, and William, in his recent letter to me, felt that the charms were 'romantic in the extreme'. They were removed only after her death.

*

On 22 September 1979, when the first year of mourning was over, Lord Walston married Elizabeth Scott, formerly the wife of Nicholas Scott, MP.

When I visited her in Bath on 1 June 1992 Elizabeth's first comment about her late husband was that 'he was a most uncommon man'. And she added that he had allowed the affair between Greene and his wife as a result of his belief that everyone was an individual in his own right, and thus Catherine had every right to do what she wished.

Throughout her married life with Harry Walston, Elizabeth Walston was aware (I do not mean *made* deliberately aware), according to William Walston, her stepson and good friend, that 'she was secondary in her husband's thoughts and feelings':

Despite everything, Catherine remained the love of my father's life and Elizabeth was realistic and honest about this. It was her decision to reunite my father with my mother, by pouring his ashes* over her grave (I was the only person present with her at

* Lord Walston was to die just weeks after Greene, on 29 May 1991.

the time). Although I think she knew it was what he would have wished, it was still an act of courage and generosity on her part . . . No ashes of my father were kept. All the ashes were scattered on my mother's grave by Elizabeth. Ashes scattered on grass are unlikely to blow away, more likely they would have been absorbed into the ground with the first rain.[38]

PART 20

Going Out with a Bang

45

Angry Old Man

Truth is on the march; nothing can stop it now.
— EMILE ZOLA

I N the waning months of 1980, when writing letters to the press
urging the government to end corruption in Nice, Greene began
to receive death threats. He never needed to stand on a soapbox in
Hyde Park to get attention.

Greene had received the appointment of the Chevalier of the Legion
of Honour early in 1969. He'd decided to approach the French government with an offer of resignation: 'It is with great regret that I am
returning to you my insignia as Chevalier of the Légion d'Honneur
granted me during the presidency of Monsieur Pompidou.' He stated
that he'd been an unhappy witness of the corruption of the police. In
the department of justice,

> Assaults on the person remain unpunished and indeed have not
> even been heard by the court. Plaints have been killed at birth
> because police officers and at least one official at the office of
> the Procureur of the Republic have been bribed with gifts from
> members of the criminal milieu of Nice (their identities are
> common knowledge).

He asked that his name be struck from the honours list: he would
then 'feel at full liberty to speak out on behalf of the victims'.[1] The
reply came swiftly from the Chancellor of the Legion of Honour,
Général Boissieu:

> I must inform you that I share your concern in seeing the victims
> of [the acts] assured of reparations and protection, to which they
> have a legitimate right. In light of your exposé, I can do nothing

but deeply and sincerely deplore the impunity in fact, from which it appears the perpetrators of the unlawful acts have benefited. As you know, it isn't quite within the purview of the Grand Chancellor of the Legion of Honour to remedy this regrettable situation.

He advised Greene to appeal to Monsieur le Garde des Sceaux (the Minister of Justice) and to the Minister of the Interior, the only men competent in the Chancellor's eyes to give good results.

You have, nevertheless, assumed the duty of returning your badge of Chevalier de la Légion d'Honneur in order to, as you have written, 'be completely free to speak in the highest regard in the name of the victims' in renouncing this distinction. I have the honour of informing you in this respect that, save for penalties of a disciplinary nature, whoever is decorated with the Legion of Honour carries it for life. Thus . . . I cannot accede to your request . . . I consider indeed that the high distinction that has been conferred on you because of your outstanding merits in no way whatsoever constitutes an obstacle to free and sincere expression of the feelings you have in this case. I estimate on the contrary that this French decoration carried by a universally renowned author such as yourself gives your statements a particular trustworthiness.[2]

On the same day Greene wrote to Boissieu, he also wrote to the Minister of Justice, Alain Peyrefitte, enclosing a copy of his resignation and reasons for submitting it. He tells the minister that the case to which he refers has been going on for two years, and involves violence against two young women and threats against small children. The perpetrator of these offences? Daniel Guy, son-in-law of Yvonne Cloetta, married to her daughter Martine. Greene speaks of Guy's stints in prison, four times in ten years, and of how 'with the help of gifts to certain police officers & to a member of the Procureur's office in Nice he has proved invulnerable to all *plaintes*. The man is unbalanced & I fear a tragic end to the affair. This is a call for help.'[3]

Peyrefitte replied quickly, admitting that he was 'stupefied'. During his tenure, he'd been aware of a few cases of 'magistrates' mental and sexual unbalance', but:

Never have I known any that had reference to a lack of integrity or an indelicacy. To me the French magistracy, and I say this very sincerely, appeared deeply honest and truly incorruptible. It is you who say that the importance that I would attach [to this affair] would quickly shed light on the matter to which I am deeply grateful that you have drawn my attention. I have charged the Inspector General of Judicial Services, M.RIBIÈRE, with immediately making an inspection so that we may understand it more clearly.

Then he states that M. Ribière will visit Greene to talk over matters he might not have been able to write about:

Since we met in Cracovie a quarter-century ago and you visited my home, you have known the loyal admiration that I have for your work. Your sense of precision and your taste for detail lead me to place greater weight on the testimony that you will want to give to M. RIBIÈRE.

This high magistrate would be ready to come to see you during the course of the day 10 January in Antibes, at whatever time is most convenient for you . . .

Thank you again for the help . . .

Loyally yours,

Alain Peyrefitte[4]

Greene records that the inspectors arrived on Saturday, 10 January; 'they are staying at least until Tuesday and they are doing a very good job . . . very pleasant people too. One is the Inspector General for *les affaires juridiques* and the other a young magistrate. Everything is being done in great secrecy and they will be reporting back to Peyrefitte in person.'[5]*

★

Nothing prevented Greene from publicising his coming pamphlet. He began by writing a letter to *The Times* on 25 January 1982, entitled

---

* Here is a private undated dictabelt note to Greene's sister Elisabeth Dennys recorded a year before the publication of *J'Accuse*: 'Things are moving. I have spoken to Peyrefitte on the telephone and he has sent down two Inspectors here who are doing a wonderful job I think and I think the net will close round Daniel. I can't remember if I sent you a photocopy of my letter to Peyrefitte, the Minister of Justice. If I haven't done so I will let you have a copy because all this will be material for Norman Sherry! I will also no longer be able to use the blackmail about the Légion d'Honneur because I have had a letter from Général de Boissieu, de Gaulle's son-in-law who is head of the Légion d'Honneur saying that only death or disciplinary action removes one but I am at complete liberty to talk. He even suggests what I had already done – to communicate with Peyrefitte – of which I will send you the original eventually. All this will make a little history for Norman Sherry at the end.'

'Corruption in Nice', starting his attack on Guy and others in the criminal world of Nice. He opens with a reference to a mysterious phone call, clearly a set-up, where he was asked if he would be ready to receive three members of the Red Brigades who'd murdered a general on the streets of Rome around Christmas 1980. They had someone wishing to meet Greene. They were seeking publicity: a reporter with an Italian magazine was under arrest for publishing an interview with the members of the Brigade.* Greene suggests that Nice was a likely Red Brigade hideout.

> The criminal milieu of Nice, a city noted for its corruption, has an Italian connexion which has led to the closing of the casinos . . . and the disappearance (and almost certainly the murder) of Mlle Roux, the owner of certain key shares in the Méditerranée [casino]. Whether the man who spoke to me on the telephone . . . was really a member of the Red Brigades, or whether he was a member of the milieu of Nice, one of those party members, who had been imprisoned in Italy for theft, I had to some extent exposed [Daniel Guy], I cannot be sure.
>
> The corruption of Nice by the criminal milieu, of police officers, certain magistrates and some avocats, is a subject which has been well described in a novel by Monsieur Max Gallo . . . If old age permits I hope to deal with it too in a non-fiction book based on personal experience. As for the title I shall have to borrow from Zola, *J'Accuse*.[6]

Articles sprouted up everywhere: Greene's reputation preceded and followed him. This must surely have alarmed the mafia. What creature had come to live in their midst, that the world's press followed him, and the local police paid attention to him? It just wasn't cricket.

But Greene had a powerful adversary in the mayor of Nice, Jacques Médecin, who had ties with the criminal underworld. Médecin owned the local newspaper and wrote in an editorial that the only real scandal was Greene's incredible impudence.

Guy fought back too. He let the cat out of the bag to the general public, assuring journalists that Martine's mother was Greene's mistress, a disclosure which placed the Cloetta family in a quandary. Greene

---

* The Red Brigades in Italy were ruthless left-wing urban guerrillas active between 1970 and 1988. Their most infamous act was the spectacular kidnapping in March 1978 of Aldo Moro, key leader during the sixties and seventies of the Christian Democrat party, and five times Prime Minister (1963–8 and 1974–6). The Red Brigade left five security guards dead on the streets of Rome, and Moro's bullet-riddled body was found fifty-five days later.

spoke of how they had met long ago, and of his current relationship with the family as being simply close friendship. What other response could he give?

★

In 1981, Greene received the Jerusalem Prize, but not before there was some adverse publicity about his allegations of corruption in Nice. Earlier the previous year, he was in Vienna to publicise the German translation of *Ways of Escape*. The French trouble followed him. His publisher told the audience that Greene was extremely shy (I concur) and that he didn't wish to give interviews or any after dinner speeches. Greene did offer to answer questions asked by his audience.* He said what he had to say like a reluctant witness. When the question of Greeneland was raised during the dinner, Greene denied its existence: 'Once one has seen a dead child in a ditch in Vietnam or Mexico in the time of religious purges or Haiti under Papa Doc or Cuba under Batista, one is not inventing fictions called *The Quiet American*, or *The Power and the Glory* or *The Comedians* or *Our Man in Havana*. This is not my land. It's the world as it is.'

Then came a somewhat devious question: 'With so many subjects for a writer to look into, why pick such a small and silly subject as the corruption of Nice?' Greene didn't take umbrage at the description of Nice's corruption as 'small and silly'. His answer was straightforward: 'It has affected my friends personally and even my own life.' Asked what precautions he took to protect his safety from the mafia, he answered, 'A tear-gas bomb.'

Bryan Forbes recalls the occasion when he learnt that Greene believed, truly believed, he would be attacked and very probably shot to death. Forbes was filming *Ménage à Trois* in France and met Graham for dinner. He described the evening in Antibes with a vulnerable Greene, he himself feeling none too safe:

> [Greene] turned up at Chez Félix, his usual watering hole in the old port of Antibes, carrying a plastic supermarket bag which he said contained a gun and a bottle of Mace . . .: 'If they do succeed in killing me,' Graham said, '. . . you'll be the only one to know who did it.' It was not a confidence I wished to harbour. Since we ate in the open, every time a black Citroen cruised by I

---

* That's what he did in Washington when he visited Georgetown library and in London when speaking about his films. It's what he did in my case when we met for interview. I had to offer the question and he would answer – precisely, scrupulously, dispassionately honest. But he never suggested further questions.

instinctively shifted my position. I thought, if they're out to kill him and their aim isn't too hot, I'm the one who'll get the bullet between the eyes. He elaborated on the drama while we had our meal, betraying no fear, merely stating the situation in a way that echoed the revolver in the corner cupboard of his childhood. Perhaps throughout his life he had always invited a violent death for himself . . . putting himself in the firing line.[7]

★

As the pamphlet neared publication, telegraphic headlines appeared from the Associated Press: 'WRITER FINISHED BOOK ON CORRUPTION.'

Once Greene mentioned in the newspapers that he was to publish *J'Accuse*, his correspondence from supporters increased ten-fold. James Baring, expressing sympathy, admitted that he knew 'from personal experience how difficult it is, as an Englishman, to criticise the country of one's voluntary adopted domicile', but he echoed Greene: 'However, the matters under discussion go beyond the barriers of race and geography and there is no way of living with them.'[8]

Soon Greene was inundated with letters from all over the world, admiring his stand and detailing appalling experiences they'd suffered from the police and the judiciary: 'You are my knight in shining armour,' wrote one lady who then went on to tell her story. She had been deeply scarred as a young girl, and when she saw him on television, she relived 'all the anguish which I suffered . . . at the hands of the French legal mafia'.

A divorcee wrote to Greene about France's most prominent lawyers, whom her family had hired to defend her in her split from her husband, George Ortiz-Patino: 'Such was the power of the Patinos and their immense wealth that not only were they all bought, but also the judge and even the Bolivian Consul disappeared with my passport leaving me unable to move anywhere out of my husband's grasp.' Another ends her letter on the note that it is 'an inspiration to see the depth of your humanity'.[9] And another, who'd had many personal tussles with the French mafia, closed her letter: 'with all my renewed respect for you as a writer and as a man of courage and a believer in justice'.[10]

By 1 February the political furore was easing, and *The Times* described the events as reported by Jonathan Fenby from Paris:

The 'Graham Greene Affair' developed into a political dispute in France today as opposing figures from the Riviera exchanged rhetorical punches over the British allegations of police-protected crime and corruption in Nice. M. Jacques Médecin, the Mayor of Nice, was first into the fray with an interview accusing Mr Greene of fouling the Riviera nest. He said the allegations, first made in a letter to *The Times* a week ago and enlarged upon in an interview with the *Sunday Times* published yesterday, were romanticized conclusions drawn from the unhappy experiences of one of Mr Greene's friends threatened by her criminal ex-husband.

'Once again, I note that a writer who likes the Côte d'Azur to the point of settling down to live here fouls the nest in order to gain a bit of publicity and promote a novel through scandal,' he added.

This was too much for M. Max Gallo, Socialist Deputy of Nice, a long-time political opponent of the right-wing mayor and author himself of a recent novel about crime and corruption of the area. 'To suggest that a writer of Mr Greene's standing needed publicity was grotesque, and only lent strength to the Greene thesis.'

Greene recalled to me in interview that sixteen years earlier, 'Funnily enough I called the Côte d'Azur the Côte d'Ordure ['Filth Coast'] when I first came to live here, and aroused the wrath of Monsieur Médecin.'[11]

★

On 9 May 1982 the first, slightly abridged, version of *J'Accuse* appeared in the *Sunday Times*. In article form it seems longer and strangely more powerful than the pamphlet. Near the end, Greene sharpens his attack: '*J'Accuse* – yes, I accuse – but it's not merely a petty criminal I am accusing, a man unbalanced, perhaps paranoiac, even pitiable.' Here Greene disparages the 'pitiable' Guy and makes the point that without the corrupt cooperation of officials, he would have been a crook of little moment, 'powerless without . . . the support [given] by certain police officers, magistrates and lawyers'. Greene said this gave Guy 'a good reason to believe he can obtain any impunity he may need. He feels fully justified in his corrupt view of the world.' Greene goes on to clarify:

No, it's not the man Guy I accuse. I accuse a lawyer of having helped to deliver a young woman and two children to an unbalanced criminal.

I accuse certain police officers in Nice of protecting criminals, of encouraging them in their crimes by guaranteeing them immunity whether for the sake of the information they provide or for money and favours.

I accuse certain magistrates of having deliberately shut their eyes to a problem concerning the emotional stability of two children . . . just as we have found everything blackened and blocked locally, we now discover the same obscure forces working away to prevent justice being done elsewhere.

Greene had contempt for Guy and enormous sympathy for Martine and her young children. She was attempting to deal with a crook who had power, despite his limited intellect, over certain segments of the police and judiciary.

★

Biographer Michael Shelden claims that in *J'Accuse* 'Greene turned a minor divorce question into a major international feud.'[12] The 'minor divorce question' was the dissolution of Yvonne's daughter's marriage, and Greene might well have been prejudiced in favour of his lover's child. The birth of *J'Accuse* lies here, in the feud that began as love but moved to hate during the six short years of the marriage of Martine Cloetta and Daniel Guy.

Greene was a formidable foe, but likewise Guy, with his intimate connections to the Nice mafia, would hardly be afraid of a 'mere writer'. With the mafia's influences, both known and covert, Guy had tremendous backing. He could frighten regular folks such as the Cloetta family, the lawless confronting the law-abiding.

It was most assuredly not an ordinary break-up of a marriage, not with Guy's willingness to use the Milieu's brutality. Nor could Greene, by writing a pamphlet no longer than twenty pages, excluding appendices, turn 'a minor divorce question into a major international feud', no matter how much weight he wielded. At the time Greene published *J'Accuse*, in May 1982, he could, and did, command the interest of the world's press. But to transform the split into an international matter? That Greene could not do, unless Shelden simply meant that for a few months the divorce was in the news, or that the relationships, usually under cover, between officials from the police all the way up to the mayor of Nice, were exposed. This Greene did, but at a high cost.

★

Greene had a genuine fondness for Martine, and according to Yvonne, Martine returned his affection all her life. During the nasty divorce proceedings, Greene would accompany Martine to court, and she'd emerge crying, 'saying that she hadn't been allowed to open her mouth, either herself or her lawyer, in front of a judge'. Greene was not permitted inside, but 'would wait outside, and he saw with his own eyes'[13] her distress.

636

Though Greene's life thus far can be characterised as having been a charmed existence – he must have carried an angel on his shoulder (though if true, Greene surely sometimes made her weep) – this mafia fight, this burden of battle and having to hunker down in the trenches for the duration (taking him into his eighties) aged him immensely. Photographs taken at the time reveal it.

Yvonne Cloetta describes Greene's close involvement in Martine's conflict having known her most of her life. That was the way he operated. He had to see things for himself.[14] Yvonne's influence, and her desperate need, swayed him profoundly. She must have talked to Greene about her daughter's marriage in 1973, and then grown more and more anguished as Guy's true nature was revealed. Martine's fear of the next thunderbolt must have been manifest, especially as the relationship was folding up.

One of Shelden's assertions in this regard is probably accurate. 'Realising that a mere personal problem would not attract substantial attention, Greene widened the dispute by claiming that corrupt officials in Nice were protecting Guy.'[15] But the claims were valid, so the plot thickened.

★

It is obvious that Greene interwove white lies with truth in his pamphlet, but only on a minor, personal level. It comes in the fifth paragraph of *J'Accuse*, and refers to his first meeting with the Cloettas in the Cameroons, and how, many years later, they met again in Antibes. A certain amount of prevarication was necessary here. He was dodging the strict truth. On the one hand he did not want to let Martine down, and on the other, he couldn't let Yvonne down. Greene's position was a delicate one. It was not the time to speak publicly of their affair, and it was never made public. Such information probably would have doomed the case from the beginning – never mind that Martine really was being terrorised. Greene is clever:

> Twenty-three years ago I met and made friends with Monsieur and Madame Jacques Cloetta at Douala in the Cameroons, and their daughter Martine, a child of seven. Monsieur Cloetta, a Swiss, worked for the United Africa Company . . . Later when I settled in Antibes they became my near neighbours, as they had a house in Juan-les-Pins, and my close friends.[16]

In the *Saturday Review* a few further nuggets are revealed which may well have come from Greene too: 'They renewed their friendship, the wife became Greene's secretary, and the daughter, Martine, a surrogate niece.'[17]

Shelden writes: 'The problem of corruption in Nice obscured the real question. Was Guy a crooked man who had mistreated his wife?' His question needs to be dealt with. My own reading of *J'Accuse* indicates that Greene proved just that.

From the look of the title, one would assume that Greene meant to launch a major attack on the criminal element in Nice, but the surprising thing is that he barely mentions the subject. Médecin's name comes into the work only a couple of times, and no specific evidence is presented to back up his claim of pervasive corruption.

Now Shelden pounces: 'The "J'Accuse" phrase is wildly inappropriate for a pamphlet which is mostly concerned with a blow-by-blow account of Martine's divorce and custody battles. It is absurd for Greene to suggest a comparison with Zola and the Dreyfus case.' For Shelden, this 'borders on the obscene, given his [Greene's] history of anti-Semitism'.[18] This last charge was and is totally unfounded, and has never been taken seriously. I suspect that Shelden might be following an early article, by Jonathan Raban (brilliant but wrong-headed) which appeared in the *New York Review of Books*. There, among other dismissive comments, Raban writes that *J'Accuse*'s 'invocation of Zola and the Dreyfus case is so ill-founded that it seems frivolous'.[19] People who had been victimised like Martine did not think so. One wrote: 'We are glad that, in the great tradition, you are calling your book *J'Accuse*.' From another supporter, the pamphlet earned bravos 'for exposing the rot behind the mimosa of our Côte d'Azur'.[20]

*

In an appendix to *J'Accuse*, Martine records some of the things that terrified her during her marriage. Daniel never stopped speaking of his exploits in the OAS,* of his sorties in the Aurès Mountains, his narrow escapes. 'There was nothing I did not know about his exploits in Algeria,' she said. In the spring of 1978, things were deteriorating between the couple. One evening they decided to go out to eat:

The atmosphere between us was heavy, painful. To try to break the ice I turned the conversation towards the OAS and Algeria, the period of his life about which he had always spoken to me

---

* Organisation de L'Armée Secrète, a secret army organisation, founded by dissident officers of the French regular army which waged a terror campaign in Algeria and France in 1961–2 in an effort to prevent Algerian independence.

with such passion and enthusiasm. He then gave me some appalling revelations, details of tortures he had inflicted on the 'fellaheen', how he had coolly slit their throats, especially at the beginning, 'to learn the ropes'.*

As he spoke, his face changed and his mouth found difficulty articulating. She goes on:

A sort of froth began to show at the corners [of his mouth]. He concluded the account of his exploits with a grin and I was looking at a monster in the flesh; I was seized with panic. That night I did not sleep. I listened to him breathing.[21]

Additional reasons for the break-up included Guy's jealousy of Martine's friendships, her closeness to her mother, and her interest in the arts, which he disdained. She quit her job twice to please him and, in the hopes of placating him, even got pregnant a second time. 'She put up with blows and violence for the sake of [their first daughter] Alexandra.' But, not surprisingly, things worsened and, after a terrifying scene where Martine thought he'd strangle her, 'she went away with her child. She was now four and a half months pregnant with her second daughter, Sandrine.'[22] Even after leaving him, Martine remained desperately afraid of Guy. He was cunning, maniacally jealous, and totally unforgiving. Once, he burst into her apartment and attacked her while she was sleeping.

*

A curious divorce was granted. Even the Minister of Justice thought it odd: Martine was forced to live within a radius of five hundred metres of her ex-husband's home, and she was forbidden to work after 8 p.m. This precluded her continuing her work in television. But even these concessions did not ensure her safety. Greene overheard a telephone conversation between the two of them: 'Up till now I've shot with blank ammunition, and I've had a lot of trouble stopping my friends in the *milieu* from intervening. But in despair you know I can't control myself, and then anything can happen. At the end of the day you will have to slug it out with them.'[23] As Greene wrote, 'It is one

---

* The *New York Times* of 31 December 2000 reported that General Aussaresses, formerly of the French security apparatus, had revealed in interview in *Le Monde* that in Algiers torture was routine and widely condoned, that 3,000 suspects had 'disappeared' and that he, General Aussaresses, now eighty-three, had personally executed twenty-four suspected guerrillas.

of the essential laws of the *milieu* to punish disobedience, and by leaving Guy she had been disobedient!'[24]

★

Greene's research for *J'Accuse* led him to inquire at Lyon, near Guy's birthplace. He discovered that Guy had been 'condemned to prison there three times between 1960 and 1970 for various offences: violence, fraud, theft, receipt of stolen goods, and a fourth time in Italy for theft. In fact, his sentences amounted to more than five years in that decade.'

Greene decided to confront Guy, and he kept a heavy statuette within reach in case he needed to protect himself when they met on 15 January 1980. In the face of Greene's proof, Guy admitted his jail sentences: 'He spoke of them in quite an offhand way, dismissing them as mere youthful peccadilloes. Nevertheless, he had taken care to make no mention of his past before his marriage.'

One of the reasons Martine received such a poor settlement out of the divorce was because of a phoney dossier about an alleged affair with a man named Marc. In their interview, Guy glibly admitted to Greene that the information about her infidelity was untrue: 'Of course I know it's a lie. This man Marc, I paid him for his testimony; then Bonito [another *milieu* friend of Guy's] and I went and beat him up', just to make certain of the result.

Greene's confrontation did not disturb Daniel Guy in the least, and 'the acts of violence and menaces increased'. On 1 April 1980, Guy telephoned Yvonne 'threatening to blow her brains out . . . and an hour later [attempted] to break into [Martine's] grandparents' home'. On 2 April, 'Guy assaulted Martine's father who had driven home with Martine and little Alexandra.' Martine had to resort to using a tear-gas bomb. A gardener heard their cries and came to their assistance, 'but Guy drove off, taking with him the child Alexandra'.[25] So though officially Martine had custody of her six-year-old daughter, the child was forced to live with her father, who had seized her without legal authority.

Someone had to speak the truth. That someone was Greene.

★

One can understand Martine's terror upon finding out that her own attorney was linked with Guy. Ostensibly working for her, he was 'in constant touch with Guy by telephone'.[26] The lawyer, looking very much like a pawn for Guy, tried to corrupt Martine herself. He asked her to come to his office to take stock of her situation, and then suggested they 'spend the evening in a Nice nightclub'. This was innocuous, but then they went to a 'cinema with two of his friends

640

the next night'. His efforts intensified, and inevitably Martine became afraid of her attorney. I quote Greene's words:

> After the film they dined in a Nice restaurant where they were joined by two girls of a certain class, who were deposited at the end of the evening at a night club, the Camargue. Maître T then pressed her to go with him next day to a '*partouze*' at a house in Cannes notorious for such parties, a proposal which she rejected. (A *partouze* is a private sex party at which people swap partners and copulate in public.)

Though Maître T tried to deny it, it was discovered later that he was 'addicted to such parties'.[27] An obvious view, and one that Greene espoused, was that if her attorney could have manoeuvred his client into attending the *partouze*, just as a bystander, Guy could have used it to obtain custody of the children on moral grounds.

Shelden's original question about Guy is unequivocally answered by Greene: 'Guy waged a ruthless undercover war against his ex-wife: constant surveillance, spying on her every moment from the apartment she had been forced to take five hundred metres from his own, endless telephone calls lasting hours at a time to her flat and to her parents, threats to take the baby.' And Martine, fearing revenge, put up with everything. She listened to him bragging on the phone for hours, boasting of his conquests: 'This summer I and my *copain* [chum] lived a mad life. We screwed forty girls in two months.'[28] And inexplicably, Daniel succeeded in taking custody of his child Alexandra. It did not seem to matter what he did: no judge, magistrate or policeman took any notice. Guy boasted of his power to handle police and the judiciary:

> 'We (the *milieu*) have our antennae in the police and it costs us a packet. Besides,' he added, 'I haven't yet even scratched the surface!'[29]

46

Toe to Toe with the French Mafia

What a fool a clever man can be.
— EMILE ZOLA

IN his novels Greene creates pathetic though sometimes courageous heroes, their moral character twisted by events, using his style of detachment, sometimes tapping into his own self-hatred. But *J'Accuse* and his numerous letters to the press came from a different place in his heart. They voiced Greene's direct, committed political, social, religious and personal fury, his novelist's detachment not to be seen, and his hunger to fight the victimisers of the world on behalf of the victims.

In many letters one sees his temper boil. Greene aimed to sting authorities wherever he felt they'd overstretched themselves, when they were subtly enjoying the inequities of power (in his mind a form of corruption). Writing helped to diffuse his anger, and remained a necessity up to his last years. It was his means of venting the angry man within, in order to repel his own melancholy, that ball and chain which held him in thrall for most of his life. Greene could be tart, acid, ironic and outrageous, his letters acerbic and confident, as if he knew he had an ace up his sleeve.

In *J'Accuse*, he was out to display a tale of villainy. As always, he felt it was his duty to reveal the knavery of men. Far more fervent and disturbed than any of his fictions, the pamphlet is like his letters to the press, intended to highlight true stories of injury to the weak. But *J'Accuse* could have been written whether or not Greene had been personally close to the Cloettas. His lifetime of battles against authority is recorded in his large body of letters to the press. He had been practising for this crusade much of his life. Taking a stand was necessary because Martine was patently not at fault, and her husband, a hoodlum and killer.

*

Michael Shelden writes of Greene losing the court cases Guy brought against him:

> The interesting thing is that Greene was completely defeated on the legal front. Guy won a decision in a Nice court to ban the book in France, and later in a Paris court, he won libel damages of 52,000 francs against Greene and his publishers. Thanks to large sales of *J'Accuse* in Britain and elsewhere, Greene was more than able to pay the damages from royalties.[1]

This was not, however, accurate. While there were modestly large sales in Britain and elsewhere, the royalties were not used to pay damages to the court. A letter Greene wrote to his Swiss attorney, Maître Jean-Félix Paschoud (his attorney during the Thomas Roe affair) proves again that Martine, the focus of Guy's hatred, was at the centre of Greene's fatherly love:*

> I gather from Max [Reinhardt] that he has sent you a cheque for royalties on *J'Accuse*. I don't want to make money out of this myself so would you of course following the usual method of withholding 25% for Verdant pass the money on to Martine.

Here is another indication Greene was not trying to fill his own pockets. In June 1982, he sold his working drafts and papers of *J'Accuse* at Sotheby's, where they were bought by a Californian dealer for $7,000. Greene sent the money to the Society of Authors to be used for authors less fortunate than himself.

*

There must have been times when Greene was utterly exhausted. Knowing the methods of the *milieu* he stood up to them, a writer pitted against gangsters, too old not to be sapped by the situation.

We can sense Graham's deep disquiet from Bryan Forbes, reporting an encounter which occurred before the dinner related in the previous chapter (while in the South of France directing *Ménage à Trois*):

---

*Vivien Greene was upset about Graham's parental concern for Yvonne's daughter. Graham arranged for Martine to work for his attorney, and he bought her a house right down the street from his own daughter, Lucy Caroline. Vivien thought it was 'not good taste to get his mistress and her daughter involved with the family'.

After the film had been shooting for a couple of weeks, I dropped a note into [Greene's] letterbox on my way to the location, telling him that I would be at the Hyatt, Nice, for the next three months and would love to take him to dinner.

Forbes returned later that night and found a message to ring Greene, which he did around 10 p.m. Greene answered, and

without further ado plunged into a bizarre and complicated account of what he was currently experiencing. He told me that he felt his life was in danger because of the stand he had taken about corruption on the Côte d' Azur. Much of what he related that night eventually appeared in his published pamphlet *J'Accuse* but at the time I was in ignorance of the background. He told me that a girl had disappeared and had probably been murdered. I listened and made sympathetic noises from time to time, and finally was able to break into his disturbing account.

'Look,' I said, 'you're obviously having a rough time, why don't we have dinner and talk about it? How is Friday for you?'

Friday was okay.

'Well, if I'm on location I'll call for you at seven-thirty and if I'm at the studio, we can make it eight-thirty.'

Graham said: 'Are you anything to do with the Bryan Forbes film?'

Not unnaturally this took me by surprise. 'Graham,' I said, 'This is me, this is Bryan you're talking to.'

There was a long pause, then he said: 'Oh God, what have I told you.'

'Nothing that I can't forget. I don't know the people concerned, so don't worry about it.'

To this day I have no real clue as to who he thought he was talking to. Perhaps I woke him out of a deep sleep or perhaps he was expecting somebody else to call at the time. Graham's life was never far from a mystery of one sort or another.[2]

Forbes also recorded on the following page a 'shocked cry' from Greene. He shows that Greene was under grave pressure. Remarkable, too, that this is revealed in a comic account, a sense of tragedy creeping in during Greene's pause in his conversation. Once more he is facing powerful adverse forces through the unexpected confluence of circumstances which led him yet again to protect others.

★

Greene kept sending his sister Elisabeth recorded material, a running account of developments, mostly dealing with Guy's mysterious riches made in a corrupt casino scheme. This was dictated 10 February 1982:

> The plot thickens here . . . a visit today from Madame Roux the mother of the girl who has disappeared completely [Greene was convinced, as were others, that the girl was murdered] and who was the owner of the Méditerranée Casino and she is giving me all the support she can. A formidable woman too and she knows the *milieu* very well. I returned from lunch and there was a man on the phone who won't give his name and I say I can't receive you unless you give me your name and he says Oh I am a detective privé so I said to him that I have no need of a detective privé as I have all the sources of information I required. But you can see that things are fairly hot here . . .
>
> It's all beginning to connect up and is very interesting if a bit tiring. Perhaps in the case of anything happening [i.e., if he gets killed by the *milieu*] you had better keep this dictabelt. At the week-end at the place where Madame Martine Escrivant works, the ex-mistress of Guy who has given information . . . when nobody was there the door was broken into and all the furniture broken up. This was after her photograph had appeared in some of the French press. Quite a business.

Also 'quite a business' is the further tale of Escrivant:

> This same month of December 1980, during an argument with his current mistress, Mademoiselle Escrivant, [Guy] smashed her nose. A doctor diagnosed the fracture, confirmed by an X-ray, and ordered her off work for a month. Mademoiselle Escrivant went to the police at Antibes and brought charges. Guy was advised of them an hour later and he telephoned her: 'Withdraw your charges or things are going to get rough.' The girl persisted. Two days later she too had to call the Antibes police: she had spotted Guy's Rolls outside her apartment block. Guy, cocksure as ever, defiantly announced, 'I don't give a damn. Your charges, like all the others, will get shoved away in a drawer . . .'
>
> On 22 June 1981, no doubt because Mademoiselle Escrivant had made some embarrassing disclosures about Guy's activities to the Ministry of Justice, a thug broke into the office where she was employed on a construction site; it was late afternoon, after the workers had all gone home. The thug, according to the report the girl made to the police, cut the telephone wire, threatened

her with his revolver and said, 'So busting your nose wasn't enough, eh? Now I've come to shoot you.'[3]

A lorry arriving on the site probably saved the girl's life. She was hit on the head with the butt of the revolver. That it was to be a killing we know, because Guy had driven up to her in his Rolls a few days earlier and told her she wouldn't live to see the end of the year. Mademoiselle Escrivant's complaints were examined on 6 December 1981 at Nice. Despite the evidence, the tribunal discharged Guy.

★

Things did not go well for Greene in France. Having appeared in May 1982, copies of *J'Accuse* were seized under French invasion of privacy laws. There were several libel actions against Greene by December 1982. On the 6th, writing to a Monsieur Sabov, he returns to the same matter:

> I think at the time you came to see me the pamphlet had already been seized after the appeal in Aix. There is an appeal now against the appeal. I don't know when it will come on, probably not until some time next year. In the meanwhile there are various writs for libel against me and a great many papers, both American, English and French and the cases are likely to come on in Paris (thank God!) in February. ['Thank God' because Paris avocats and magistrates were infinitely less corrupt than those in Nice.]

But forces were working against Greene. On 24 May 1983 a letter from Anthony Whitaker, the legal manager at *The Times*, informed Max Reinhardt that the Tribunal de Grande Instance had awarded Daniel Guy 'FF.52,500 against ourselves and Graham Greene on the basis of our Review Front piece on 9 May, 1982'.[4] They had a month to file notice of appeal. Whitaker was running for cover:

> In your letter of 25th June 1982, *you confirmed your agreement to indemnify us against the financial consequences of publication* [emphasis added] and for that reason we would obviously wish to consult closely with you before incurring the further expense any appeal would involve.
> On a first reading of the judgment, I am bound to say my immediate inclination is to leave the matter where it is. I say this for two reasons.
> First, because the award which is equivalent of about 5,000

pounds, is very modest indeed by English standards in view of the highly defamatory and damaging allegations of corruption the Court has decided were unproven. If the case had been heard by an English jury, I would have anticipated an award of at least 50,000 pounds.

Second, the Court appears to have held against us at least partly on the basis that the bulk of the documentary evidence on which we and Graham Greene relied to demonstrate Guy's perfidy appears (see the bottom of page 10 and the top of page 11 of the judgment) not to be admissible as valid proof once ten years have elapsed since the events in question.

Unless there is some very firm prospect of getting this ruling reversed on appeal, I would have thought it better not to throw good money after bad. The award seems to be partly based on the extent to which our piece amounted to an invasion of Guy's privacy, a tort unknown – as yet, at any rate – in English law.[5]

★

Mayor Médecin and the police circled their wagons to repel this impudent English enemy: 'Insisted former Police Superintendent François Guillon:"Major crime in Nice is practically nonexistent."' And wouldn't any loyal citizen react strongly to the provocative opening sentences of *J'Accuse*, describing their city?

> Let me issue a warning to anyone who is tempted to settle for a peaceful life on what is called the Côte d'Azur. Avoid the region of Nice which is the preserve of some of the most criminal organisations in the south of France: they deal in drugs; they have attempted with the connivance of high authorities to take over the casinos in the famous 'war' which left one victim, Agnes Le Roux, the daughter of the main owner of the Palais de la Méditerranée, 'missing believed murdered'; they are involved in the building industry which helps to launder their illicit gains; they have close connections with the Italian Mafia.[6]

Greene's powerful headlines, appearing in so many countries, were enough to dry up Nice's lucrative and booming tourist trade to a trickle for a while.

At the time of publication, the right-wing political authorities in Nice were already facing serious troubles. It was natural that Mayor Médecin would think *J'Accuse* was somehow engineered by the socialists, who certainly took advantage of its criticism of Nice – the weekly *Nouvel Hebdo de Nice* (*The New Week in Nice*) carried Greene's photograph on the cover. Jonathan Fenby, in his article entitled 'Dirty tricks, says le patron, and takes the Gloves Off', speaks of 'bitter political in-fighting, economic pressure, shutdown casinos, tension with the central government in Paris and, now, *l'affaire Graham Greene*'.[7]

The popular mayor might well have believed that Greene was in a conspiracy to bring him down. Médecin had been mayor for fifteen years, his father before him for thirty-seven years. As Fenby writes, though Médecin receives only small mention in *J'Accuse*, he nevertheless felt he had 'to climb into the ring to fight for the good name of his city'. He fought rough, as we see in the interview he gives to Fenby: 'Nice's current notoriety, M. Médecin told me, had a simple cause: "The left hates me because I am one of the most combative right-wing politicians in the country. They hate my guts and I hate their guts."' Fenby concluded: 'The carnival will go on, but Graham Greene's private war may play its little part in deciding whether it dances to the familiar Médecin tune or to a more left-wing air.'[8]

The city council decided it would sue Greene for defamation. The predominantly left-wing police union wanted to take legal action, too. The Médecin-owned local paper demanded that Greene 'provide immediate proof of his allegations of high-level corruption in Nice or make a public retraction'. Médecin knew what Greene thought of him. He had been a journalist himself. The mayor telephoned Greene, identifying himself only as a reporter, and 'made a recording of what was said. I can tell you, if you print what he said about me it will cost your newspaper a lot of money.' And the mayor knew how to get the city on his side: 'I'm not fighting for myself. I am fighting for the good name of my city. We spend more than ten million francs a year promoting tourism in Nice, beautifying the city ... and here is Mr Greene claiming we are corrupt and putting down the work of hundreds of dedicated people who love Nice and want to work for the good of it.'

And even Daniel Guy had his say: 'Greene is moved by a desire for vengeance; he is being pushed by my former mother-in-law.' And Guy put forward a ludicrous view of himself (given what Greene had quoted of their conversation, in which he admitted his crimes and boasted about them): 'I am an honest man. Everyone in Nice knows that. I have nothing to hide.' Guy acted out the part of a citizen falsely accused, declaring that he 'wanted this insidious campaign aiming to establish my participation in crooked deeds at the gambling table to stop'.[9]

Greene told me in interview that this self-proclaimed 'honest' man's vicious attacks on Martine and her father Jacques Cloetta, and the 'theft' of their child Alexandra, were methods of punishing Martine. Guy also threatened that if Greene carried on poking his nose into his affairs, he (Greene) would be involved in a sudden and tragic car accident, 'just like that . . .' and Greene flashed one hand in a slicing movement against the other, indicating the mafia's willingness to execute him.

On 23 March 1983, a civil court in Paris convicted Greene and three French publications of defamation. The court ordered Greene to be fined 30,000 francs, and levied fines of 10,000 francs each against the directors of a newspaper and two magazines, *Le Matin de Paris, Le Nouvel Observateur* and *VSD*. The court's ruling was that Mr Greene 'knew perfectly that his affirmations were susceptible of doing damage to the honour and esteem of the plaintiff'. Guy, it seemed, had won hands down.

No action was taken on Greene's investigation into corruption in Nice or on his charge that Guy was a racketeer protected by a corrupt police force. Greene had been told by the Minister of Justice that 'Nice has a wall. It consists of the *milieu* of dishonest police, dishonest judges; not all but some.' He had been assured that Guy's police officer friends were being watched, and that the corrupt officials 'formed a wall which was difficult to pierce, but one day they would find a breach'. As for Médecin, this colourful mayor who spoke perfect English (with an American accent) and was married to a much younger woman, heiress to the Max Factor empire, looked to all the world to be an exciting, glamorous figure. Still there was fear in the Médecin camp that Greene's fame and, as Médecin termed it, his sense of 'obsession with a minor personal matter' could bode further trouble.

★

By August, three months after *J'Accuse* was published both in English and French in the same document, the French version was banned. In a letter to *The Times* on 7 August 1982 Greene wrote bitterly:

> Sir, It is often dangerous to write the truth. I have already had one book of mine – *The Comedians* – seized and suppressed by Papa Doc in Haiti nearly 20 years ago. A second book of mine – a small pamphlet called *J'Accuse* – was condemned rather curiously in my absence, and in the absence of my lawyer, by a court in Nice and the condemnation has now been confirmed by the Court of Appeal in Aix.
>
> I admit I feel the condemnation in France rather more than the condemnation in Haiti for ever since the age of 19 I have considered France my second home. However, I hope this will not deter me from continuing to write for any cause the justice of which I believe in.[10]

The pamphlet was too hot to handle. Two publishers quickly dropped out: Norstedt, Greene's Swedish publisher, where his friend Ragnar Svanstrom was a director; and his American publisher, Simon & Schuster. Norstedt, via Svanstrom, basically declined on the grounds that *J'Accuse* was being serialised in the *Sunday Times*: 'And newspapers all over the place including Sweden will undoubtedly use the opportunity to quote extensively from it. Consequently a later serialisation in this country would be rather effectless.' Greene had made the suggestion that just as *J'Accuse* was published in English and French within the same booklet, in Sweden it should be published simultaneously in English and Swedish. Their answer was it would take too long: 'The spring and summer lists are already closed [a hoary old method of rejection] and the book trade would be unprepared to take care of it. It would, so Norstedt tells me, in fact be impossible to publish until early autumn. And that would be altogether too late.'

I am sure that Svanstrom, by using the phrase 'so Norstedt tells me', was signalling to Greene that he personally was against the rejection, as implied in his final remarks: '*J'Accuse* strikes me as a very brave, shocking and from a human point of view deeply moving piece in line with all you have fought for ever since you started writing.'[11] Greene's reply was abrupt: 'I quite understand Norstedt's decision.'[12]

The letter from Simon & Schuster (to Max Reinhardt) takes the same line, though they weren't quite sure what to say about *J'Accuse* other than that it was fascinating, and 'wonderful in its way':

> but essentially it's a pamphlet (on a subject that will seem at best remote to readers here, where we have plenty of similar cases). Also, if you're sending it out to *Time, Newsweek,* the *New York Times*, etc, we'd be scooped on this by the media.[13]

Their basic argument is that they were 'simply not equipped to sell a 30-page pamphlet, and it would get in the way of *Monsignor Quixote*, given the short attention span of bookstores and salesmen'. Fear of lawsuit has many eyes.

The *Evening Standard* of 23 June 1982 spoke of the seizure and banning of Greene's pamphlet: 'Graham Greene must relish the irony. After publication of his paperback, *J'Accuse*, the exposure of police corruption in Nice, the French Courts have banned it. They also ordered him to pay Daniel Guy, a local housing developer, whom Greene allegedly libelled, 100 francs (about £8) for every copy seized plus interest.' It went on: 'But all is not lost. People have only to nip along the Riviera coast to Monte Carlo, an enclave independent of France, to snap up a copy, and this they are doing by the thousand.'[14]

The novelist Stephen Vizinczey was outraged on Greene's behalf:

Ever since the 1930s it has been fashionable to argue that evil is too banal, too commonplace to pay serious attention to ... organised crime seems to be treated with the sort of disdain for moral considerations that was used to gloss over Hitler's actions before the war. Only quick averting of sophisticated eyes can explain what has happened to *J'Accuse*. It was banned in France without anybody protesting. In America, where Graham Greene's novels are best sellers and earn fortunes for their publishers, no one would publish it. There is always paper for thick novels glamourizing gangsters and crooks, but the printing of Greene's 69-page pamphlet against a particular injustice is beyond the spiritual/financial resources of American publishers.[15]

If Simon & Schuster reneged on their most celebrated author, Lester & Orpen Dennys of Canada did not; they had the courage of their convictions:

We have been informed that seizure of Graham Greene's *J'Accuse*, to be published in Canada in early August, has been ordered in France. The author and his British publisher The Bodley Head, are being sued for 'intrusion of privacy' (a suit, under French law, which can be brought even when it is acknowledged that libel is not in question). The book is now banned in France where it was released last month.[16]

Lester & Orpen Dennys took command, rushing it through the press, with copies 'to be shipped within the next few weeks'. They were wise in this approach, knowing that bringing out *J'Accuse* could start a battle. They, unlike other publishers, were not found wanting: 'We would like to take this opportunity to confirm that *J'Accuse* will be on sale in Canada.'

In reviewing *J'Accuse* in the *Sunday Telegraph*, Auberon Waugh, with sudden epiphanous insight, wrote: 'It just seems a pity that our senior and best writer – the only one with an international reputation – should be forced to spend his later years in an exhausting battle which others should be fighting for him.'

And Greene *could* have done with some help. He was losing friends fast, those detachable friends who crowd around until things get hot. Auberon Waugh admitted that the British settled on the Côte d'Azur were not 'pleased with the way he is stirring things up. Go native, they say, adjust.' And Waugh adds that Greene 'has been living in a state of siege for near three years. As he approaches his 78th birthday he finds he has taken on the legal and municipal establishments as well as the criminal fraternity of the Côte d'Azur more or less singlehanded.' Waugh describes Greene's unquestioned nature:'a brave, intelligent and a tenacious man'.[17]

★

But let us look at Jonathan Raban and his thoughts on Greene's pamphlet.What troubled Raban was Greene's seemingly sudden surprise at corruption and evil. Greene dealt with subjects such as 'martial warfare, bayonets and revolvers, the mechanics of espionage . . . staple ingredients of Greene's world in the past: why, then, is he so shocked by them now?' Raban quotes a passage where Greene details Martine's life after her divorce and the treatment she suffered during her marriage, how Guy boasted over sexual conquests, how he beat her and stole her child away, and how she discovered his extensive criminal record and corrupt business operations. He made this judgment:

> The story of Martine's unfortunate marriage is ordinarily foolish, ordinarily unhappy. The account that Greene gives of malice and brutality makes one squirm; but then so would most reports of most divorces in the newspapers if so well told . . . What does astonish is Greene's own astonishment. For fifty years his novels have been dealing coolly with terrorism, murder, and betrayal, and treating viciousness as one of the most instinctive of human motives. Yet faced with the plight of Martine, Greene goes into a peculiar state of literary shock.

Quoting a passage where Greene refers to the court's order that Martine live within a radius of five hundred metres of her brutal ex-husband and not work after 8 p.m., recalling how a member of the mafia group kept in a safe deposit three revolvers and a bayonet, Raban expostulates:

> Greene is the last writer one would have expected to break out in this rash of italics and exclamation points. They are the characteristic devices of someone who can't make language sufficiently emphatic to express his intensity of feeling. They are, predictably, the favourite grammatical crutches of the subliterate. They signal clumsily at the reader that words are failing the writer.[18]

In contrast, Stephen Vizinczey, whom one would not wish to have in the same trench if you were an enemy during a war, is scathing in attacking Raban's arguments:

A moving and shocking document, *J'Accuse* highlights one of the saddest truths about our age: it is possible to hurt people openly and *endlessly*, because hardly anybody cares, or cares very much . . . [Raban] thinks it is a sign of *old age* for Graham Greene to get wrought up at all. He speculates that Greene 'has softened in age and now finds intolerable things that a few years ago he could cast a cold and unwavering eye upon.' Or alternatively, 'the impression of unillusioned poise, so central to the working of Greene's novels, is really no more than a convenient piece of artifice, a front that quickly crumbles when it's tested in actual flesh and blood.' In other words, if Graham Greene had really been as worldly-wise as he pretends to be in his novels, he wouldn't have been so shocked by the agony of his old friends and wouldn't have made such an unseemly fuss.

. . . consider this richly vile sentence: 'The account that Greene gives of malice and brutality makes one squirm; but then so would most reports of most divorces in the newspapers if they were as well told.'

. . . It is simply not true that most divorces involve violent criminals who have the police and judiciary on their side. But even if it were true, it would make each instance more serious, more significant, not less so. To Raban both thugs and the people whose lives they ruin are just too numerous, too common to worry about. 'We all know men like Daniel Guy,' he asserts dismissively. In fact, most people don't; if Raban does, he should get in touch with the police. At all events, he is bored by *J'Accuse*, a plea for living victims in desperate trouble, because he knows it all; it covers 'well-trodden ground – corrupt officialdom, private dishonour, cruelty, violence . . . The story of Martine's unfortunate marriage is ordinarily foolish, ordinarily unhappy . . .' In short, there is nothing new about wickedness, so why make an issue of it?

What is perhaps even more nauseating is the sort of condescending admiration Mr Greene has been receiving for his pains . . . Raban, too, is guilty of this ultimate piece of impertinence. He writes: 'Greene has stirred up a lot of trouble for himself in Nice with the publication of the pamphlet, and one would be churlish not to admire his courage, even if the mission in which it's exercised seems quixotic.'

How odd it is for someone to try to protect the defenseless! How foolish, how absurd, how *quixotic* it is for a great writer with millions of readers behind him to think that he could prevail against a little crook! The Mafia looks after its own better than the literati.[19]

Greene's first letter to me about *J'Accuse* reflected a curious hope, and one, given his sometimes suicidal nature, not unexpected. He wrote that he might go out 'with a bang instead of a whimper'. He was thoroughly exhausted over the Martine affair, wrung out like a wet rag; it never seemed to end. He and the Cloettas lived in perpetual tension, the brunt borne by Greene because of his great fame – journalists never left him alone.

With this life-changing episode, Greene would never really be fit again. I knew him well by the time of *J'Accuse*, but I never heard even a twinge of hesitation in his voice when he spoke of the fight forced upon him. One concerned correspondent said Graham would go out for a walk with no police protection despite all the threats. Greene's philosophy was that he'd rather die with a bullet to his head than in a geriatric home.

Auberon Waugh reported on the hoped for future in the South of France: 'Sooner or later, someone in Paris is going to have to pick up the civil administration of the Côte d'Azur and shake it until all the fleas drop out.'[20] But it would take time, and could not come about until Mayor Médecin, the biggest flea of all, had his long career brought to an end.

Médecin was flamboyant and energetic – a live wire. Despite his flaws it was difficult not to like aspects of him. Even Greene at one point spoke up in his defence:

> I have a very low opinion of Médecin but he is not the worst part of the Nice atmosphere. The corruption I suppose has grown under his leadership as it grew for twenty-three years of centre-right government, but I don't think one can blame it all on the mayor. The magistrates, police and lawyers have all played their part. Nor do I think Nice typical of France. It's too close to the Italian frontier.[21]

Greene was praised by Médecin, who pretended that he could not understand why Greene was so critical of Nice: 'The man is a brilliant author, I love him – the Socialists have taken advantage of his advanced age, to mislead him. All Socialists hate me because, no matter what dreadful stories they tell about me and the rackets, I keep getting elected.'

However, a few months before Greene died, Jacques Médecin resigned unexpectedly, contending that the socialist government was hounding him with corruption charges:

His resignation, announced in a local newspaper when Mr Médecin was visiting Japan, aroused speculation that he might not return, out of fear of prosecution on charges of owing $3.1 million in taxes and illegal use of city money.[22]

Médecin did fly the coop but no matter what he did he still retained to an astonishing extent the love of the people of Nice. There is a famous photograph of the mayor, handsome with his pencil-thin moustache, his lovely wife holding on to one arm, and another gorgeous woman holding on to the other. The ladies are glamorous and one – not his wife – is wearing a dress which prominently and expertly displays her very obvious charms.

Médecin fled France in 1990 with the law closing in on him. He was faced with a claim for payment of 20 million francs in back taxes and criminal prosecution for misuse of 13 million francs of public funds. He attempted to settle in Uruguay, but the government there forcibly returned him to France.

Even then, when he was brought back to Nice, he was still popular. A typical headline from *The Times*, 'Skeletons rattle as Nice faces Médecin's return'; 'He is a gangster and a bandit but he was king of our castle and he was a great mayor.' At least one café patron was heard to say, 'He robbed us blind for years and he deserves everything he gets.'

*

And what was happening to the sadist Guy? Did the net, as Greene predicted to his sister, close round him? Not so. On 14 May 1985 Greene wrote to his friend Joseph Jeffs, librarian of Georgetown University Library in Washington: 'Our enemy in Nice is still alive & kicking. He tells his little girl of ten* (her mother now has guardianship) that when I'm gone – from old age – he'll have her grandmother Yvonne killed!'[†]

Eventually Greene felt the whole matter was over. In a letter written in late December 1986, he tells Max Reinhardt that he'd rather not have *J'Accuse* republished in Dutch: 'I feel it has served its purpose and we have won most of our case.'[23]

*

On 26 March 1986, Greene wrote to Elizabeth Brinck Moller, a teacher in a College of Education in Copenhagen. Her students were a group

---

* Although Martine now had custody of her daughter Alexandra, the girl spent school holidays with her father.
† He didn't. Yvonne died of natural causes on 3 November 2001.

of senior citizens studying English literature, including Greene's novels. Finally their teacher 'gave a talk on your booklet *J'Accuse*'. The class then wrote a letter together and signed their names:

> We admire your courage in exposing the *milieu* and hope that they won't be able to harm you. But as most of us are grand-mothers, we were much concerned about poor Alexandra's fate and are wondering what has happened to her. We understand that you have to be very discreet, that's why we won't ask any questions about Martine and the rest of her family, but we would be very grateful for a few lines telling us about what has happened to Alexandra.[24]

Greene replied:

> I was very touched by your signatories' interest in Alexandra's fate. We eventually won our actions in the Cour de Cassation and the Cour de Nîmes, her father refused to hand her back but we had her legally kidnapped* from her school and she is now very happy in Switzerland with her mother . . . The great thing is that she gets on very well with her younger sister and she is very content with life in Switzerland.[25]

His most wearisome battle was over, but he was left exhausted and thoroughly drained. He'd stood toe to toe with the *milieu* and placed his hand in the fire for Martine. Greene rang his friend Father Durán on the morning of 2 July, and shouted down the line: 'Leopoldo, we won.'[26]

*

The task of every biographer is to tell his story unfeigned, undistorted – and when necessary to stitch up a wounded reputation should it bleed beyond need. Greene was still *almost* fearless, but he did fear, and on some occasions he panicked – as shown by Bryan Forbes. All the same, for most of his life he had embraced the possibility that he would die before his time, preferably when his voice and strength and wealth were needed, where victims were being oppressed. Greene could have left France and the dangers there – he never considered himself an exile: 'I visit England half a dozen times a year.' He felt that one could never turn one's back on the enemy. To Father Durán, he admitted:

---

* On 7 June 1984, a legal officer and a policeman collected Alexandra from school to return her to her mother.

'If it would prevent those who I love from suffering so much . . . I would give [up] every one of the words that I have written. Without any doubt whatsoever.'[27]

PART 21

Windmills of Doubt

47

Sancho and the Saint

'Father, I feel as though we are saying goodbye for ever.'
He answers, 'No, no . . . for a Christian there's no such thing as
goodbye for ever.'

— GRAHAM GREENE, *Monsignor Quixote*

*M*ONSIGNOR *Quixote* is not simply a novel about a journey made
by two friendly antagonists – one a priest, an innocent, and the
other a communist ex-mayor. It is also a theological and political
pilgrimage, in a series of parables, light-hearted and sober, between
two putative friends, on a picaresque excursion. They are on the loose
in post-Franco Spain, determining by whim where they'll travel. They
are constantly chatting, the conversation rich in humour, dotted with
exchanges arising naturally between a Christian and a Marxist. The
conversations are illustrative narratives, mixed with gossip, sometimes
argumentative, but they never fall out.

Almost every other character exists to highlight the nature of these
two shadow-boxers. We meet the stiff, excessively correct Father Herrera
(who has taken over Father Quixote's parish), and their bishop. Both are
images of the small-minded in life, prissy, petulant, rule-bound creatures.
And the scenery of Spain, the flesh-pots and the sometimes extravagant
shrines and monasteries allow the short novel to centre itself. This is the
first novel in which Greene's purpose is running commentary. It breaks
new ground for him to make the plot nugatory.

*

Monsignor Quixote, with its short chapters, must have come as a godsend
for Greene at the time. He could not have handled more while locked
in conflict with the criminal underworld in Nice. That painful time
caused him great strain. (In 1984, 'When asked why his works were
getting shorter and shorter, [he] replied, "Because I get older and
older." '[1]) Cervantes' *Don Quixote* embraced the notion of resurrecting
chivalry, just as Greene was attempting to restore chivalry in Antibes.

And in creating Father Quixote, he was attacking his own windmills. For Don Quixote, the 'windmills' were giants: for Greene they were the mafia, and in particular Daniel Guy.

Monsignor Quixote is an allegory, reflecting the conflict between the pure of heart – the lovable Father Quixote, who has no weaknesses – and society's representatives, with their rules and rigidities, in politics, (the Guardia Civil) in religion (the bishop, a tyrant). Father Quixote's battles exhausted him just as Greene's did him.

The gentleness in *Monsignor Quixote* carries with it an element of dottiness that could in no way apply to Greene. Moreover, Father Quixote is totally innocent to the world's ways, unlike Greene. But there are parallels between the fictional character and his creator, especially in the concern they shared for others.

I remember Greene's smile as kind, with a natural (and genuine) modesty – rare in the truly famous. There was no elephantiasis of the ego in him. He had no sense of narcissism. He thought himself good at his trade, but he never allied himself with the greatest; he put himself down among the second class, not a Dostoevsky, not a Tolstoy. Yet, looking back over Greene's many literary achievements, surely he has a right to be wedged in there somewhere among the great.

Monsignor Quixote ultimately doubts his faith, and Greene's central theme in this book is the need to doubt. The priest's Sancho sees Marx as his spiritual leader, and tries to make nonsense of his friend's religion. Ultimately, as we discover what is to become of this man, we feel that, like his fictional ancestor, Monsignor Quixote's days are numbered. Greene, as he has in the past, brings this novel to a powerful and emotionally charged conclusion.

*

Where did this story come from? It is unlike any other Greene wrote, at variance with his other 'theological' classic novels, *Brighton Rock* (1938), *The Power and the Glory* (1940), *The Heart of the Matter* (1948), *The End of the Affair* (1951) and *The Honorary Consul* (1973). In each, apart from the last, there is no doubt where Greene stands. He is very much a Catholic novelist. In *Monsignor Quixote*, doubt becomes the central theme, as the pair motor about the countryside or sit under a tree enjoying wine (they bring cases and cases with them) and cheese (lots of that too).

Greene based his novel in large part on trips with Father Leopoldo Durán, his close comrade, going round Spain as Durán describes in his book, *Graham Greene: Friend and Brother*. Whilst the tone of the lengthy arguments in *Monsignor Quixote* does not run through Durán's book (and should not because Graham's novel is more fable than fiction, more fiction than *roman à clef*), the subtitle of Durán's book fits exactly the relationship between the Monsignor and the former Mayor: friend and brother.

As I read *Monsignor Quixote*, I had an urge to pronounce it slight, or something 'approaching a novel', but found its ending undeniably moving. Greene felt he could no longer take three gruelling years writing a major novel, as with *The Honorary Consul. Monsignor Quixote* was an easier birth.

★

Just how tired Greene was during this time is evident in the photographs taken by Father Durán at the time Greene was doing battle with the French-Mafia.* Durán, who was close to him, sets the span of Graham's suffering as running from 1979 to 1985. The experience made Greene age faster than he might have if he'd not been damaged by threats from Daniel Guy and his bone-wearying confrontation with the mafia. It was Greene alone who wrote constant letters, consulted lawyers, sought help from powerful men in the French government, stood up to the tough Mayor of Nice. It was an unutterable burden. He'd often taken risks in his life, but here was the stuff of paranoia: threats that he'd be run down by a truck, that at any moment he could be shot by his enemies. Durán puts it robustly:

> I knew two Grahams: one belonged to the period before 1979 and the battle with the mafia; the other, to the period afterwards. The struggle against the wretched mafia affected his nerves and his sleep more than ever . . . one had to bear in mind the colossal mental and psychological pressure on the man during those ghastly years. He was very tired and he would get upset much more easily.[2]

Given this observation, and his age (according to Durán's dates, Greene was over eighty when the conflict ended), the Cloetta family, surely aware of his nature, should have known he'd fight for them, but that at this stage in his life, the fight was too much. Yvonne, genuinely fearing for her daughter and granddaughters, turned to the one person

---

* Yet sometimes, when not disturbed and despairing, the glamour of a kind of youth crept back into his face. It returned when he made a visit to Georgetown University in Washington, DC (where his friend, the librarian Joseph Jeffs invited him for a visit) on 25 October 1985, twenty-three days into his eighty-first year. On this, his last trip to America, Greene spoke in the same hall where his friend Evelyn Waugh had spoken in 1949. Waugh's talk then was on 'Three Catholic Converts', of whom Greene was one.

she knew could not resist her request for help. Whatever the price. And the price was high. If Greene saw it, he felt it, and if he felt it, he had to correct it, come what may.

★

The plot: Father Quixote, through his kindness to a visiting bishop with car trouble, is made a Monsignor, the bishop telling him: 'I would like you to go forth like your ancestor Don Quixote on the high roads.' This angers his own local bishop who holds Quixote in contempt. Receiving an 'utterly incomprehensible' letter from Rome about Quixote's promotion, his bishop responds with 'cold rage', thinking at first it was 'a joke in the worst of taste',

> I have today received an abrupt letter confirming . . . that the Holy Father has seen fit — for what strange stirring of the Holy Spirit it is not for me to inquire — to promote you to the rank of Monsignor, apparently on the recommendation of a Bishop of Motopo, of whom I have never heard, without any reference to me, through whom such a recommendation should naturally have come — a most unlikely action on my part, I need hardly add.[3]

Father Quixote had no wish for promotion and doesn't want to leave his little parish of El Toboso.

His friend Sancho, having lost the re-election for Mayor, decides they should take a journey. The map they follow, made up by Greene and Durán to show the route of the trips that the two protagonists would take, was kept in Greene's archives at his sister Elisabeth's house.

The first part of the trip is quiet. Sancho is determined that the Father buy purple socks and purple bib, necessary equipment for a Monsignor. The priest is reluctant. (In the end they buy the items in Salamanca.) Their first stop in the priest's old car, a Seat which Quixote calls 'Rocinante' after his predecessor's horse, is a shady place by the road to eat cheese and drink wine. They settle under the ruined wall of an empty outhouse where 'Someone had painted a hammer and sickle crudely in red upon the crumbling stone.' Verbal play runs as a vein throughout:

> 'I would have preferred a cross,' Father Quixote said, 'to eat under.'
> 'What does it matter? The taste of cheese will not be affected by cross or hammer. Besides, is there much difference between the two? They are both protests against injustice.'
> 'But the results were a little different. One created tyranny, the other charity.'

'Tyranny? Charity? What about the Inquisition and our great patriot Torquemada?' . . .

'Torquemada at least thought he was leading his victims towards eternal happiness.'

'And Stalin too perhaps. It is best to leave motives alone, Father. Motives in men's minds are a mystery.'[4]

They argue without bitterness.

The central theme in *Monsignor Quixote* – this meditation on Faith and Doubt, one as necessary as the other – is religious and political doubt. Greene came to believe that to doubt is necessary for ultimate faith, and is more edifying than to simply believe:

'I hope – friend – that you sometimes doubt too. It's human to doubt.'

'I try not to doubt,' the Mayor said.

'Oh, so do I. So do I. In that we are certainly alike.' . . . It's odd . . . how sharing a sense of doubt can bring men together perhaps even more than sharing a faith. The believer will fight another believer over a shade of difference: the doubter fights only with himself.[5]

Soon afterwards the Father has a terrible dream:

that Christ had been saved from the Cross by the legion of angels to which on an earlier occasion the Devil had told Him that He could appeal. So there was no final agony, no heavy stone which had to be rolled away, no discovery of an empty tomb. Father Quixote stood there watching on Golgotha as Christ stepped down from the Cross triumphant and acclaimed. The Roman soldiers, even the Centurion, knelt in His honour, and the people of Jerusalem poured up the hill to worship Him. The disciples clustered happily around. His mother smiled through her tears of joy. There was no ambiguity, no room for doubt and no room for faith at all. The whole world knew with certainty that Christ was the Son of God.

Quixote experienced a profound despair upon waking of having taken up a useless profession, and that he

must continue to live in a kind of Saharan desert without doubt or faith, where everyone is certain that the same belief is true. He had found himself whispering, 'God save me from such a

belief.' Then he heard the Mayor turn restlessly on the bed beside
him, and he added without thought, 'Save him too from belief,'
and only then he fell asleep again.[6]

*

At last the travellers reach a place Greene came to love, Salamanca,
with its university and scholars, where once the question of doubt was
raised. We see the distinguished old city through the eyes of the two
characters, but it is also what Greene and Durán saw:

> They crossed the River Tormes into the grey old city of Salamanca
> in the early afternoon . . . This was the university city where he
> [Father Quixote] had as a boy dreamt of making his studies. Here
> he could visit the actual lecture room where the great St John
> of the Cross [greatly admired by Greene] attended the classes of
> the theologian Fray Luis de León . . . 'This is a holy city, Sancho.'[7]

Sancho, a communist, had had what he called a 'half-belief' as a student.
Recalling his days at Salamanca University, Greene's Sancho says:

> There was one professor with a half-belief and I listened to him
> for two years. Perhaps I would have lasted longer at Salamanca if
> he had stayed, but he went into exile – as he had already done
> years before. He wasn't a Communist, I doubt if he was a Socialist,
> but he couldn't swallow the Generalissimo [Franco].

Greene recalls his and Father Durán's experiences at Salamanca and
transfers some rich elements into his novel, for example his depiction
of the famous Spanish philosopher and writer whom he greatly
admired, Miguel de Unamuno.* Greene describes his statue in *Monsignor
Quixote:*

> In a very small square, above folds of rumpled green–black stone,
> an aggressive head with a pointed beard stared upwards at the
> shutters of a little house. 'That's where he died,' Sancho said, 'in
> a room up there sitting with a friend before a charcoal burner
> to keep him warm. His friend saw suddenly that one of his slip-
> pers was on fire and yet Unamuno had not stirred. You can still
> see the stigmata of the burnt shoe in the wooden floor.'

* Unamuno (1864–1936), a Professor of Greek and Rector at Salamanca, was author of
The Life of Don Quixote and Sancho (which Greene studied in preparation for writing
Monsignor Quixote), and the brilliant *The Tragic Sense of Life in Men and in Peoples.*

Father Quixote speaks of what he sees in the square:

> 'Unamuno.' Father Quixote repeated the name and looked up
> with respect at the face of stone, the hooded eyes expressing the
> fierceness and the arrogance of individual thought . . .
>   'Many priests gave a sigh of relief when they heard of his death.
> Perhaps even the Pope in Rome felt easier without him. And
> Franco too . . . In a sense [says Sancho] he was my enemy too
> for he kept me in the Church for several years with that half-
> belief of his which for a while I could share.'
>   'And now you have a complete belief, don't you? In the prophet
> Marx. You don't have to think for yourself any more . . . How
> happy you must be with your complete belief.'
>   'Have I complete belief?' Sancho asked. 'Sometimes I wonder.
> The ghost of my professor [Unamuno] haunts me. I dream I am
> sitting in his lecture room and he is reading to us from one of
> his own books. I hear him saying, "There is a muffled voice, a
> voice of uncertainty which whispers in the ears of the believer.
> Who knows? Without this uncertainty how could we live?"' [In
> an earlier draft, further words of Unamuno concluded the passage:
> 'Doubt and belief are two halves of the same hinge, neither is
> defined without the other.']
>   'He wrote that?'
>   'Yes.'[8]

They find he is in a spartan grave, numbered 340.

These events took place in reality on 19 July 1976. Father Durán
in his book *Graham Greene, Friend and Brother*, describes their experience thus:

> We set off early for Salamanca, passing by the [Valley of the
> Fallen] . . . or 'The Valley of the Dead' as [Graham] called it,
> and as a result he felt a complete antipathy for this entire memo-
> rial. He wrote a cruel paragraph about the basilica there . . .
> The grandiose setting and Graham Greene's taste for simplicity
> simply could not be reconciled. For Greene [it] resembled 'a
> huge Ancient Egyptian tomb in very bad taste'. As we have seen,
> Graham never understood Franco's political and spiritual
> ideology.
>   *19 July 1976.* We are in Salamanca . . . It is true to say that Salamanca
> cast a spell over Graham from the very first moment . . .
>   It was Unamuno's tomb that had brought us to Salamanca.
> Greene had a deep affection for this writer . . . Graham and

Unamuno had much in common: their rebellious natures, and their constant struggle with their beliefs.

The cemetery at Salamanca. At the entrance we ask for Unamuno's grave.

. . . 'Unamuno is number 340.'

Graham Greene had understood what was said. Nevertheless, he asked: 'What did that man say?'

'He says Unamuno is number 340.'

Graham did not expect a mausoleum to have been erected to Miguel de Unamuno – he would certainly have disliked that – but for Unamuno to be known by a number![9]

What Father Durán says is in its own right fascinating, for he was with Graham and witnessed the birth of the idea for this novel:

> *Monsignor Quixote* was born in the cemetery at Salamanca. Miguel de Unamuno's tomb would become almost a place of pilgrimage for us on our summer jaunts, but the attitude of the cemetery officials . . . on our first visit had appalled Graham . . . As he stood there in front of the numbered box – 'one cannot call it a tomb' – the idea for his novel entered his mind.

Greene said to Durán that the book would be 'based on material from our journeys'.[10]

*

It would be wrong to focus only on this serious note, for there is much fun in *Monsignor Quixote*. Greene told Durán he would base Father Quixote on him, but I doubt this was done. Father Durán is an amiable Spanish priest, but in his book on Greene, we are made aware that on matters of principle, he was not willing to allow Greene to win arguments easily. Sometimes Durán would, and rightly, take offence. (On one occasion, Greene, having had too much to drink, tried to haul down the Pope himself!) I met Father Durán on the steps of the Savile Club in London in 1974, where on the following day, Greene and I were introduced for the first time. Durán was warm, endearing – absolutely not simple, not a Father Quixote in any obvious sense.

*

There are two examples of Father Quixote's utter simplicity and almost powerful naïveté: a scene in a brothel and a visit to a pornographic movie. Of course, the humour depends upon our accepting Quixote as a total innocent – as in a fable. Here he is extolling the amenities in what he believes is a pleasant hotel in Salamanca:

'The *patrona* was truly welcoming,' Father Quixote said, 'unlike that poor old woman in Madrid, and what a large staff of charming young women for so small a hotel.'

'In a university city,' Sancho said, 'there are always a lot of customers.'

'And the establishment is so clean. Did you notice how outside every room on the way up to the third floor there was a pile of linen? They must change the linen every evening after the time of siesta. I liked to see too when we arrived the real family atmosphere – all the staff sitting down to an early supper with the *patrona* at the head of the table ladling out the soup. Really, she was just like a mother with her daughters.'

'She was very impressed at meeting a monsignor.'

'And did you notice how she quite forgot to give us a *ficha* to fill in? All she was concerned with was our comfort. I found it very moving.'

There was a knock on the door. A girl entered with a bottle of champagne in an ice-bucket. She gave Father Quixote a nervous smile and got out of the room again quickly.

'Did you order this, Sancho?'

'No, no. I don't care for champagne. But it's the custom of the house.'

'Perhaps we ought to drink a little just to show that we appreciate their kindness.'

'Oh, it will be included in the bill. So will their kindness be.'

'Don't be a cynic, Sancho. That was a very sweet smile the girl gave us. One can't pay for a smile like that.'

While Father Quixote wanders around the room, Sancho tries to open the champagne and the Father says: 'What a good idea. They provide a foot-bath.' (It is actually a bidet.*) Next, the Father, seeing a little square package, opens it. Sancho, finally getting the cork out of the champagne bottle, turns and finds the priest 'blowing up a sausage-shaped balloon' which explodes:

'Oh dear, I'm so sorry, Sancho, I didn't mean to break your balloon. Was it a gift for a child?'

---

* Greene first heard this error made when he was at the leper colony in Yonda; it was also a priest who made the same mistake there.

'No, Father, it was a gift for the girl who brought the champagne. Don't worry. I've got several more.' He added with a kind of anger, 'Have you never seen a contraceptive before? No, I suppose you haven't.'

'I don't understand. A contraceptive? But what can you do with a thing that size?'

'It wouldn't have been that size if you hadn't blown it up.'

He asks where Sancho has brought him, and finally the truth dawns:

'To a house that I knew as a student. It's wonderful how these places survive. They are far more stable than dictatorships and war doesn't touch them – even civil war.'

'You should never have brought me here. A priest.'

'Don't worry. You won't be bothered in any way. I've explained things to the lady of the house. She understands.'

'But why, Sancho, why?'

'I thought it was good thing to avoid a hotel *ficha* for at least tonight. Those civil guards . . .'

'So we are hiding in a brothel?'

'Yes. You could put it that way.'

The Father laughs on the bed:

Sancho said, 'I don't believe I've ever heard you laugh before, father. What's so funny?'

'I'm sorry. It's really very wrong of me to laugh. But I just thought: What would the bishop say if he knew? A monsignor in a brothel. Well, why not? Christ mixed with publicans and sinners. All the same, I think I had better go upstairs and lock my door.'[11]

In chapter nine, they go to a small cinema advertising a film called *A Maiden's Prayer*. Not even Sancho knows it's pornographic (though mild enough for our day). He simply foresees an evening of 'boredom and piety'. The answer to the maiden's prayer turns out to be a handsome lover:

The photography at that point became soft and confusing, and it was a little bit difficult to discern whose legs belonged to whom since the private parts, which distinguish a man from a woman, were skilfully avoided by the camera.

There is no dialogue, only grunts and squeals:

> To make things even more difficult the scenes had obviously been
> shot for a small screen (perhaps for a home movie) and the images
> became still more abstract when enlarged for a cinema. Even
> Sancho's enjoyment waned: he would have preferred more overt
> pornography.

The ending is a wedding, a kiss at the altar, with the Father still not
having a clue:

> a quick cut to a tangle of limbs in bed – it occurred to Sancho
> that for the sake of economy they had simply repeated one of
> the earlier scenes with the anonymous limbs . . . The lights went
> on and Father Quixote said, 'How very interesting, Sancho. So
> that's what they call a film.'
> 'It wasn't a very good example.'
> 'What a lot of exercise they were all taking. The actors must
> be quite exhausted.'
> 'They were only simulating, Father.'
> 'How do you mean, simulating? What were they pretending
> to do?'
> 'To make love, of course.'
> 'Oh, so that's how it's done. I always imagined it to be a great
> deal more simple and more enjoyable. They seemed to suffer such
> a lot. From the sounds they made.'[12]

That night in bed, the Father thinks about the scenes of love-making:
his response in the cinema had been to laugh, but there was such a
silence that he was afraid to embarrass others. In afterthought,

> He still found himself . . . worried by his failure to be moved by
> any emotion except amusement. He had always believed that
> human love was the same kind as the love of God, even though
> only the faintest and feeblest reflection of that love, but those
> exercises which had made him want to laugh aloud, those grunts
> and squeals . . . Am I, he wondered, incapable of feeling human
> love? For, if I am, then I must also be incapable of feeling love
> for God. He began to fear that his spirit might be stamped
> indelibly by that terrible question mark . . .
> The dreaded question mark was still stamped on his spirit when
> they set out next day.

The next day as they rest during their travels, Sancho becomes aware of the Father's unhappiness and asks what is wrong: 'Again today you are the Monsignor of the Sorrowful Countenance' (a description used by Cervantes about Don Quixote):

'I have sometimes thought, may God forgive me,' Father Quixote said, 'that I was specially favoured because I have never been troubled with sexual desires.'

'Not even in dreams?'

'No, not even in dreams.'

'You are a very lucky man.'

Am I? he questioned himself. Or am I the most unfortunate? He couldn't say to the friend who sat beside him what he was thinking – the question he was asking himself. How can I pray to resist evil when I am not even tempted? There is no virtue in such a prayer. He felt completely alone in his silence* . . . He prayed . . . O God, make me human, let me feel temptation. Save me from my indifference.

Sancho suggests: 'if you have taken a vow of silence go into a monastery. There are Carthusians at Burgos and Trappists at Osera. Take your choice, Monsignor, which way we go.'[13] He also proposes that they open a bottle of wine which has been cooling in the river, and the Father goes to get some cheese from his car.

The Father is gone a long time. When he finally returns, he is accompanied by one of the Guardia Civil. Throughout the ensuing questioning Father Quixote answers only in Latin, completely perplexing the policeman, who finally asks if the priest is a foreigner. The Guardia takes an interest in the Monsignor's old car, complaining that he'd left the key in the starter, and then asks if they've seen a man in a false moustache, with a bullet hole through his right trouser leg. Asked what the man has done, the officer tells the travellers that he 'robbed a bank at Benavente. Shot the cashier . . . it's not safe leaving your car unlocked like that with the key in the starter.' Quixote's response is again in Latin:

'*Laqueus contritus est . . . et nos liberati sumus.*'

---

* Greene in his numerous depressions 'felt completely alone in his silence', though these spells softened as he aged, partly because Yvonne did not give him any reason to be jealous. Catherine was different; his feeling that he'd lost her led him to agony. But he also made the choice to be alone. No professional writer can help but be alone – he must work in solitude. Such loneliness, as in a *Château d'If*, prompts a searching of the soul, and Greene was driven to do this his whole life.

'What's the monsignor saying?'

The Mayor said, 'I'm not a linguist myself.'

After advising the two comrades not to give a lift to any stranger, the Guardia salutes the Monsignor and leaves. Sancho then asks the Father why he's speaking in Latin. He replies that he wanted if possible to avoid a lie:

'What had you got to lie about?'

'I was confronted very suddenly with the possibility – you might say the temptation.'

And then Sancho asks him if he found any cheese:

'I found a quite substantial piece, but I gave it to him.'

. . . 'You mean you've *seen* the man?'

'Oh yes, that was why I was afraid of questions.'

'For God's sake, where is he now?'

'In the boot of the car.'

Sancho is worried. He is a communist in a state where (until General Franco's death) he is likely to be arrested on suspicion of holding opposition views. Fearing the Guardia, Sancho has had the plates changed in Valladolid: 'The garagist there is an old friend and a member of the Party.'

'Sancho, Sancho, how many years in prison have we earned?'

'Not half as many as you will get for hiding a fugitive from justice. Whatever induced you . . . ?'

'He asked me to help him. He said he was falsely accused and confused with another man.'

'With a revolver hole in his trousers? A bank robber?'

'Well, so was your leader, Stalin.'

And so they argue until Sancho realises that while they are talking, 'our wounded man is probably dying for lack of air'.[14] They rescue the bank robber, who turns out to be a miserable wretch who holds a gun on the men who tried to save him. The thief's shoes are rotten so he forces the priest to take off his, and to drive him to the cathedral at León. The crook's last words to the priest, when Father Quixote leaves the car to see if it is safe to escape: 'If you betray me I will shoot your friend.' And when the Father, looking around, tells him it is safe, the man repeats his warning: 'If you are lying . . . the first bullet's for you.'[15]

Before they leave León, the Father telephones his trusted housekeeper in El Toboso and learns that the bishop has heard of his activities: a Monsignor staying in a brothel for the night, going to a cinema to watch a pornographic movie, hiding a crook in his car. She asks where he is, and he tells her he's in León.[16]

It is clear that both the bishop and the new parish priest Herrera are determined to bring Quixote down. The two men decide not to return home but go instead to the Trappist monastery and 'the silence of Osera'.

They nap in the afternoon. When Sancho wakes up, he cannot find his friend. He discovers that someone has snatched him, but doesn't know who and is afraid it must be the Guardia Civil. Then he discovers that Quixote was taken off in a stretcher, kidnapped by Father Herrera; the Monsignor's doctor gave him an injection so that he wouldn't wake up until he'd been returned to El Toboso. There he is imprisoned, his trousers taken from him and locked away to prevent escape.[*]

The old Father comes to himself, only to discover what has happened and speaks to the priest who replaced him, and the doctor:

> 'You two have been guilty,' Father Quixote said, 'of a criminal action. Abduction, medical treatment without the patient's consent . . .'
>
> 'I had clear instructions from the bishop,' Father Herrera replied, 'to bring you home.'
>
> '*Que le den por el saco al obispo,*' Father Quixote said, and a deathly silence followed his words. Even Father Quixote was shocked at himself. Where on earth could he have learnt such a phrase, how was it that it came so quickly and unexpectedly to his tongue? From what remote memory? Then the silence was broken by a giggle. It was the first time Father Quixote had ever heard Teresa laugh.[17]

Translated, he'd said, 'Bugger the bishop.'

So the priest is a prisoner in his own home. But the faithful Sancho finds his way back to El Toboso and, with the help of Teresa, frees the Monsignor. They are ready to make a second journey, this time into Galicia.

*

Greene, speaking through his characters, returns to the nagging question of assurance and doubt:

---

[*] This is an old Dorothy Glover trick; she hid Greene's trousers in anger so he couldn't leave her apartment.

'Perhaps it's not belief that really matters . . . I tell myself that I must be wrong. My faith tells me I must be wrong – or is it only the faith of those better men?'

It is at this point, the story well advanced, that Sancho tells Father Quixote what attracted him to the priest: 'You drew me to you because I thought you were the opposite of myself.'

'A man gets tired of himself, of that face he sees every day when he shaves, and all my friends were in just the same mould as myself. I would go to Party meetings . . . and we called ourselves "comrade" . . . we knew each other as well as each one knew himself. We quoted Marx and Lenin to one another like passwords to prove we could be trusted, and we never spoke of the doubts which came to us on sleepless nights. I was drawn to you because I thought you were a man without doubts.'

'How wrong you were, Sancho. I am riddled by doubts. I am sure of nothing, not even of the existence of God, but doubt is not treachery as you Communists seem to think. Doubt is human.'

And the Father echoes Greene's own cry of despair, repeated many times in his later years:

'Oh, I want to believe that it is all true – and that want is the only certain thing I feel.'[18]

In saying a hurried goodbye to his loyal housekeeper, Quixote had heard her say, 'Father, I feel as though we are saying goodbye for ever.' He answers, 'No, no, Teresa, for a Christian there's no such thing as goodbye for ever.' Leaving, 'he raised his hand from habit to make the sign of the cross in blessing, but didn't complete it.'

I believe what I told her, he told himself as he went to find the Mayor, I believe it of course, but how is it that when I speak of belief, I become aware always of a shadow, the shadow of disbelief haunting my belief?[19]

These are the fictional protagonist's concerns. They are also Greene's own disturbing concerns.

★

The two heroes start in earnest their second great journey, which is to be Father Quixote's last. They reach and cross into Galicia, halting

at a village where the Mayor enquires about a vineyard. He is advised
not to go near a place called Learig for the Mexicans are everywhere:
'Stay away from the land of the Mexicans. Their priests spoil even the
wine.'[20]

They make good progress and find a Señor Diego, who sells wine
to the Mayor and the Father. They sit under a fig tree, the same one
that was the actual meeting place for Graham Greene, Father Durán,
and the owner of the vineyard.

Señor Diego learns where they are travelling:

'They are going to Osera to the Trappists.'
   'The Trappists are good men, but their wine, I believe, is less
good . . . You must take a case of wine for them, and for yourselves too, of course. I've never had a monsignor here under my
fig tree before.'[21]

And it is under this tree that Father Quixote hears of the hard-working
Mexicans who made themselves rich, and who have an urge to seek
an ultimate place in heaven. Señor Diego tells the story, which deeply
disturbs Father Quixote:

'They give money to the priests here and they think they are
giving to the Church. The priests have grown greedy for more
– they prey on the poor and they prey on the superstition of the
rich . . . Perhaps some of the Mexicans really believe they can
buy their way into Heaven. But whose fault is that? Their priests
know better and they sell Our Lady. You should see the feast they
are celebrating in a town near here today. The priest puts Our
Lady up to auction. The four Mexicans who pay the most will
carry her in the procession.'
   'But this is unbelievable,' Father Quixote exclaimed.
   'Go and see for yourself.'
   Father Quixote put down his bowl. He said, 'We must go,
Sancho.'[22]

And so they go. This is the beginning of the end for Father Quixote.
They reach the village and see the procession of Our Lady, the swaying
to and fro of a crowned head, and Father Quixote crosses himself in
union with those about him. He is offended by the crudity of cash
bills stuffed in and on the statue of the Virgin. Sancho tries to persuade
his friend to leave before there's a riot, but Quixote is determined to
act. He takes two steps forward and confronts the priest organising the
sinful (in Quixote's mind) procession:

'This is blasphemy.'

'Blasphemy? . . .'

'Yes. Blasphemy . . . Put down Our Lady. How dare you,' he told the priest, 'clothe her like that in money? It would be better to carry her through the streets naked.' . . .

'Go on with the procession,' the priest commanded.

'Over my dead body,' Father Quixote said.[23]

And on being asked who he is and what right he has to stop the procession, Quixote gives his name and declares as his authority the right of 'any Catholic to fight blasphemy'.

The priest tries to swing his censer between the statue and Father Quixote and it strikes Quixote on the side of his head: 'A trickle of blood curved round his right eye.' Quixote, with a mixture of dismay and fury, thrusts the priest aside, and starts pulling a hundred-dollar bill off the statue's robe, then a five-hundred-franc note. Several hundred-peseta notes he rolls into a ball and tosses into the crowd. Ultimately the whole statue comes crashing to the ground. The Mayor takes a hand, grasps Father Quixote's shoulder and pushes him out of the way, saying: 'You've done quite enough for today.'

Sancho gets him into the car and takes over the driving. The Monsignor touches his bloodstained head: 'Did somebody hit me?' Sancho the communist answers: 'You can't start a revolution without bloodshed.'

They speak little during the final leg of the journey to the Trappist monastery at Osera, tucked above the shoulder of Portugal. At last the tough Mayor and the tender priest will reach a place of safety. In the final chapter of *Monsignor Quixote*, Greene takes us inside the monastery. All is silent, except when monks speak to visitors and break 'the silent world of Osera'.[24]

★

Greene, who had an affinity for few places on earth, loved Osera. On his first visit with Father Durán in July 1976, they stayed just a few hours, but he was, as Durán tells us, 'enchanted by the stark simplicity of the magnificent Cistercian monastery'. In the visitors' book he wrote: 'Thank you very much for these moments of peace and silence. Please pray for me.'[25]

Greene and Durán visited Osera on every occasion they went to Spain. Only at Osera, among those silent priests, for short periods of time, did Greene find respite from his almost terminal extremes of restlessness. Even this special spot he used as a setting.

Inside the monastery, as described in the novel, a priest and a visitor, a professor, are speaking. They hear 'an explosion outside . . . followed seconds later by two more, and the sound of a crash'.[26] The professor suggests it's a tyre, but the priest is sure it was gunshots. They move swiftly outside to discover a small car – Father Quixote's 'Rocinante' – has smashed against the wall of the church, after being chased by the Guardia Civil, which has been despatched to arrest the priest and the Mayor because of the near-riot at the festival for Our Lady. The Guardia shot at the tyres inside the grounds of the monastery, causing the car to crash.

Two officers of the Guardia Civil leap out of their jeep and approach the car with caution, guns drawn. A man with blood on his face is trying to open the door. He angrily calls to the Guardia: 'Come and help, you assassins. We are not armed.' The priest asks Sancho if he's hurt. He answers that indeed he is, but he is concerned for his friend. The Guardia try to arrest them but Father Quixote is out cold. They finally succeed in removing him from the wrecked car, and he is laid on the ground.

When it is obvious that Quixote is injured, the Guardia offer to send for an ambulance, but their determination to arrest both 'culprits' is in no way diminished. The head of the monastery knows how to deal with such small fry:

> The surly Guardia said, 'We can see about the doctor . . .'
> 'Not in this condition. I forbid it . . . these two will stay here in the monastery until the doctor allows them to leave. I shall speak to the bishop . . . I am sure he will have something to say to your commanding officer. Now don't you dare to finger your gun at me.'[27]

They carry the old man into the church and up to the nave. He is muttering to himself what they think might be prayers. He faints in front of the altar. They take him to a guest room. Quixote wakes up, worried that a doctor has been called, and tells his small audience, if only he could say mass.

The Monsignor is in dire condition. He faints again – twice. But he has a powerful longing to say mass; he is told, 'Perhaps . . . tomorrow . . . when you are rested.' The doctor arrives, examines Father Quixote, and thinks he will be all right after a rest.[28] Of course at his age . . .

About three in the morning, Quixote wakes again and speaks to himself, either dreaming or in delirium. He rambles: 'Excellency, a lamb may be able to tame an elephant, but I would beg you to remember the goats in your prayers.' 'You have no right to burn my books,

Excellency.' There is 'a short period of silence, then, "A fart," Father Quixote said, "can be musical."'[29]

The Father falls asleep again and then suddenly speaks from his bed, strong and firm: 'I don't offer you a governorship, Sancho. I offer you a kingdom.' He then adds, 'Come with me, and you will find the kingdom.' Sancho, troubled by the condition of his friend, replies: 'I will never leave you, Father. We have been on the road together too long for that.' In answer, Quixote throws off his bedclothes and begins to get up. He speaks in a trance to his dream bishop, 'You condemn me, Excellency, not to say my Mass even in private. This is a shameful thing. For I am innocent. I repeat openly to you the words I used to Dr Galván – "Bugger the bishop."' Then he walks to the door, turns for a moment and looks through the three standing there 'as though they were made of glass'. They decide to follow him but not wake him since it might be dangerous – he is clearly walking in his sleep. They let him play out his dream.

The priest and the professor follow, and Father Quixote begins to speak the mass in Latin. They are afraid to distract him. Father Quixote proceeds to go through the mechanics of communion, giving it all by rote, in a trance. The professor thinks that when he finds nothing there, he will stop and wake up. Father Quixote remains silent, swaying a bit at the altar. The Mayor positions himself to catch him, but the Father speaks again:

'*Corpus Domini nostri*', and with no hesitation at all he took from the invisible paten the invisible Host and his fingers laid the nothing on his tongue. Then he raised the invisible chalice and seemed to drink from it. The Mayor could see the movement of his throat as he swallowed.

For the first time he appeared to become conscious that he was not alone . . . He looked around . . . Perhaps he was seeking the communicants. He remarked to the Mayor standing a few feet from him and took the non-existent Host between his fingers; he frowned as though something mystified him and then he smiled. '*Compañero*,' he said, 'you must kneel . . .' He came forward three steps with two fingers extended, and the Mayor knelt. Anything [to] give him peace, he thought, anything at all. The fingers came closer. The Mayor opened his mouth and felt the fingers, like a Host, on his tongue. 'By this hopping,' Father Quixote said, 'by this hopping,' and then his legs gave way. The Mayor had only just time to catch him and ease him to the ground. '*Compañero*,' the Mayor repeated the word in his turn, 'this is Sancho,' and he felt over and over again without success for the beat of Father Quixote's heart.[30]

The next day the Mayor comes to say goodbye. He's decided not to attend the funeral, and he answers a query: 'What one does with the body is not very important, is it?'

The monastery has been informed by the bishop that Quixote must not be allowed to say mass even in private. Leopoldo, named for Greene's friend Father Leopoldo Durán, explains the sad circumstances which make it quite certain that his order will be obeyed – in the future.

'Why did you say "in future"? What we listened to last night could hardly be described as a Mass,' the Professor said.

'Are you sure of that?' Father Leopoldo asked.

'Of course I am. There was no consecration.'

'I repeat – are you sure?'

'Of course I'm sure. There was no Host and no wine . . . You know as well as I do that there *was* no bread and no wine.'

'I know as well as you – or as little – yes, I agree to that. But Monsignor Quixote quite obviously believed in the presence of the bread and wine. Which of us was right?'

'We were.'

'Very difficult to prove that logically, professor. Very difficult indeed.'

'You mean,' the Mayor asked, 'that I may have received Communion?'

'You certainly did – in *his* mind.'

The argument goes on with the professor insisting there was no Host, but the priest's answer is powerful:

'Do you think it's more difficult to turn empty air into wine than wine into blood? Can our limited senses decide a thing like that? We are faced by an infinite mystery.'[31]

And the Mayor's last thoughts on the last page of *Monsignor Quixote:*

An idea quite strange to him had lodged in his brain. Why is it that the hate of man – even of a man like Franco – dies with his death, and yet love, the love which he had begun to feel for Father Quixote, seemed now to live and grow in spite of the final separation and the final silence – for how long, he wondered with a kind of fear, was it possible for that love of his to continue? And to what end?[32]

★

By no stretch of imagination could Greene be accounted a holy innocent like Father Quixote. (His friend Shirley Hazzard once called his
humour 'the snowball that conceals the stone'.[33]) His longing to believe,
and to eradicate doubt, was real; yet he did doubt and was deeply troubled by it, despite arguing strenuously on several occasions in favour
of doubt. In his Catholic novel period he had not agonised over a
desire to believe – back then, he simply believed. It is odd that before
he published *Monsignor Quixote*, Greene, when interviewed in America,
said he was probably no longer a Catholic – that he no longer believed
in Christ except as an historical person who was crucified, a common
end for criminals in Roman times – then out comes this extraordinary novel.

Greene, in his old age, is aching to have faith. God remained central
in his life. Greene carried within himself a constant debate about God,
about belief and doubt. There arises a disturbing question: is faith real
only after a struggle with doubt? Earlier in this chapter, we saw the
priest's vision of a crucified Christ, saved by angels, stepping down
from the cross. There would be no question if this had occurred: Christ
would have been proved to be the Son of God. (But it would all be
futile – He would not have died for our sins.) This prompts Father
Quixote to exclaim, 'It is an awful thing not to have doubts.' Doubt
drummed constantly in Greene's mind, and surely during those long
journeys with his friend Father Durán, his confessions going on deep
into the night were about faith and doubt and *his* faith and *his* doubt.

Greene was unpredictable, but I strongly suspect that the heart of
the matter for Greene was this intense yearning for God, and after
Monsignor Quixote, such yearnings raced through his mind constantly
like a 'blood-dimmed tide' thrashing about, thrusting forward into his
conscious mind, with untamed velocity.

Now central to Greene was his restlessness. A soul in torment. The
contradictions within Greene were myriad.

As Auberon Waugh, sounding much like his father, Evelyn, wrote
in his review of *Monsignor Quixote:* 'Graham Greene seems to become
more and more Catholic, although he denies this hotly.'[34] Greene, to
the end of his life, had a powerful desire to believe in the Living God
and His Sacrificed Son. Only Greene would put truth so resolutely in
the centre of a fable, and wrap doubt snugly around great faith. As a
fox to the furrier, that's how Greene approached the Catholic church.

48

The Lamb and the Lion:
What Did Greene Believe?

The trouble is, I don't believe my unbelief.
— GRAHAM GREENE

IT is difficult to know Greene's real feelings towards Catholicism. We know they were strong once, but by the time of Professor John Cornwell's interview for the *Tablet* (on 23 September 1989), Greene's faith seemed almost nil. Had he given up belief? Graham once told Vivien that if he indeed had a soul, it was a 'small, dirty beast'.[1] His journey to faith was up and down, back and forth, high road and low road throughout his long life.

There is a sense in which Greene seems to be a believer only when he has a fight on his hands – clarifying mind and spirit. Graham 'discovered early [that] when under the necessary element of danger, when fear arose in him [from] going into dangerous unmapped places . . . he could do incredible things'.[2] His journey to Mexico in 1938 was a faith-building trip, amidst the desecration and destruction of cathedrals, the hunting down of priests. God was denounced from the pulpit, people were forced to destroy altars, all religious ornaments were ruined, even torn from people's necks. Piles of religious statuary were burned in the square and local red guards sang atheist songs. Priests were shot to death.*

We know, too, that Greene originally became a Catholic because he wanted to marry Vivien. But his conversion didn't really 'take' until this visit to Mexico. What he experienced there led him to move easily

---

* In Volume One, between pages 714 and 715, is a photograph of a martyred priest, killed first by being shot, then hanged (his feet just off the ground), facing his church, though his dead face looks downward. A sheet of paper nailed just above his kneecap states his crime: being a priest. This was the systematic creation of a Godless country. This is what Graham the young Catholic witnessed.

682

and joyfully into the great camp of believers. In the dirt of Mexico, Greene became an ardent Catholic.

★

We know of one dilemma for Graham, namely that his Catholicism prevented him from acting on his recurring desire to commit suicide, since to do so would be a mortal sin. But he sought a legitimate way to kill himself by travelling towards peril. Possible annihilation was his fix.

Greene was a secretive man. In private moments, or on occasions with his friend, Father Durán, I'm sure he was genuinely religious. But his public comments often hid this aspect, and the twisting nature of his racing thoughts unmasked the agnostic in him.

Greene's faith was influenced by Archbishop David Mathew, particularly during the times Greene visited Stonor Park, where Mathew had partially retired, living with the Stonor family. Graham wrote to Catherine Walston on 5 November 1965: 'If I'm ever delirious in Paris you and Jeanne [Stonor] will have to send David by plane.' I'm sure that David Mathew helped keep Greene in the faith, and when David died, long before Graham did, there were only two others who kept his faith alive. Clearly one was Father Durán. The other was Padre Pio,* whom Greene visited with Catherine Walston. Greene has little to say about Padre Pio in *Ways of Escape*. But in speaking about his novel *The End of the Affair*, he tells us of the discovery that Sarah had been secretly baptised by her mother when a child, and that it was looked upon as introducing the notion of magic. Then he adds:

> But if we are to believe in some power infinitely above us in capacity and knowledge, magic does inevitably form part of our belief – or rather magic is the term we use for the mysterious and the inexplicable – like the stigmata of Padre Pio which I watched from a few feet away as he said Mass one early morning in his monastery in South Italy.[3]

Greene raised the subject with Malcolm Muggeridge. According to Muggeridge's diary entry on 19 January 1950, they'd dined together and talked about Padre Pio,

---

* Padre Pio (1887–1968), a Franciscan friar said to suffer the stigmata, was proclaimed a saint in 2002.

who, according to Graham, has stigmata. Greene described these in his usual lurid way. Said miracles were done constantly by him, and that, in his view, the heavenly and devilish forces in creation were now exceptionally active in preparation for busting up the universe by means of the hydrogen bomb.[4]

Greene, I suspect, was leading Muggeridge on.

Yet there is no doubt that Greene was profoundly moved by Padre Pio. He'd been told that Pio was a holy fraud, enough reason for Greene to seek him out in a Franciscan monastery as he said mass at 5 a.m. in a side chapel. When I interviewed Greene in his eightieth year, he still carried Padre Pio's picture in his wallet and spoke in awe, remembering the blood, how it would start up, dry, and then start up again, on his hands and feet: 'those hands looked terrible, sort of circular pieces of dried blood'.

Pio invited Greene to meet him privately, but he declined: 'I didn't want to change my life by meeting a saint. I felt that there was a good chance that he was one. He had great peace about him.' (The subtext here is that he was afraid of losing Catherine Walston.) Yet Padre Pio helped Greene believe.

A female friend recalled Greene speaking about the question of Jesus as the Son of God, and speaking too of Padre Pio. Here is the evidence of Greene's own eyes, *known* evidence, and therefore easy to believe, not the faith of those who believe without seeing. She went on:

> I remember his saying to me once (we were walking together through some woods near Berkhamsted – I can remember his voice and his look as he quoted the words, one of my few flashes of imaginative insight into Graham Greene), 'Unless I shall see in His hands the print of the nails, and put my finger into the print of the nails, and thrust my hand into His side, I will not believe.' It was from Graham also that I first heard of Padre Pio, who bore the stigmata. It is obvious that for one of the types of mankind, this proof by physical evidence is crucial; to me I must confess, it really had no importance whether the Incarnation had, as historical fact, taken place or not.

Once I asked Greene when I visited him in Antibes if he, like his atheist character Bendrix in *The End of the Affair*, was hounded by God. His answer reveals his genuine sense of belief, or genuine desire to believe (which of course is not the same thing). He answered me:

'I hope so. I hope God is still dogging my footsteps.' Because if so, I assumed, he felt there was still hope.

Greene then picked up a French edition of *The End of the Affair*, and translated it into English as he read the passage about Sarah, the heroine, and her totally unexpected change of character:

If even you – with your lusts and your adulteries and the timid lies you used to tell – can change like this, we could all be saints by leaping as you leapt, by shutting the eyes and leaping once and for all: if *you* are a saint, it's not so difficult to be a saint.[5]

His reading was filled with fervent emotion. I was deeply moved. It was, in all my interviews, the most disturbing. I felt that he believed God has a special commitment to each of us, yet he was in some perplexity as to his own mission.

*

By the time of John Cornwell's interview, it was difficult to believe Greene was a sure and certain Catholic. He states categorically that he is an agnostic. But he had published four great Catholic novels – *Brighton Rock* (1938), *The Power and the Glory* (1940), *The Heart of the Matter* (1948), *The End of the Affair* (1951) – which reveal his history, thirteen years of tremendous, reassuring belief: no matter the character of Greene's Catholic heroes, some (like Pinkie in *Brighton Rock*) are bad; others, like the whisky priest in *The Power and the Glory*, cannot control their desire for alcohol and sex; one commits the ultimate sin in the Catholic list of sins (Major Scobie's suicide in *The Heart of the Matter*). Bendrix, the atheist in *The End of the Affair*, who we can sense will convert in spite of a current hatred of God, prays: 'leave me alone for ever'[6] – no matter, there is yet an underlying assurance.

*

When the young Greene arrived at Oxford to read history, he was an atheist. Round about the age of thirteen (the time he was persecuted by the schoolboy Carter), he had attempted suicide more than once. But in early childhood days he *was* a believer, and an original one, and original is what he has been all his life.

This is from the prologue of *The Lawless Roads*, when he is 'across the border'. It is a Saturday night in Berkhamsted. During the week, as a boy, he goes to school simply by walking through a door down a hallway:

If you pushed open a green baize door in a passage by my father's study, you entered another passage deceptively similar, but none the less you were on alien ground. There would be a slight smell of iodine from the matron's room, of damp towels from the changing rooms, of ink everywhere. Shut the door behind you again, and the world smelt differently: books and fruit and eau-de-Cologne.[7]

The boy Greene was 'an inhabitant of both countries: on Saturday and Sunday afternoons on one side of the baize door, the rest of the week on the other'. And he tells us that life on the border is restless: 'You are pulled by different ties of hate and love.' The boy Greene describes his escape from school music classes to the other side of the border, in the garden of his parents' home, where 'lay the horror and the fascination'. He would run off for an hour at a time, sneaking by the 'frontier guards', and he stood on the 'wrong side of the border':

> looking back – I should have been listening to Mendelssohn, but instead I heard the rabbit restlessly cropping near the croquet hoops. It was an hour of release – and also an hour of prayer. One became aware of God with an intensity – time hung suspended – music lay on the air; anything might happen before it became necessary to join the crowd across the border. There was no inevitability anywhere . . . faith was almost great enough to move mountains . . . the great buildings rocked in the darkness.
>
> And so faith came to me – shapelessly, without dogma, a presence above a croquet lawn, something associated with violence, cruelty, evil across the way. I began to believe in heaven because I believed in hell, but for a long while it was only hell I could picture with a certain intimacy.[8]

It is Graham's early unhappiness at Berkhamsted which ultimately provides his source for a belief in hell: 'In the land . . . of stone stairs and cracked bells ringing early, one was aware of fear and hate, a kind of lawlessness, where appalling cruelties could be practised without a second thought; one met for the first time characters, adult and adolescent, who bore about them the genuine quality of evil.'[9] So as a youngster, he unquestionably believed in the existence of hell, even if it was a hell on earth. In later years one of the chief attractions of Catholicism would be the Church's belief in hell: 'It gives something hard, non-sentimental and exciting.'[10]

When Greene was an intelligence agent for the SIS, he became acutely aware of the separation of hell and heaven. He had his character Major Scobie, in *The Heart of the Matter*, describe life in the British colony of Sierra Leone during the war by asserting that 'there was always a blacker corruption elsewhere to be pointed at. The scandalmongers of the secretariat fulfilled a useful purpose – they kept alive the idea that no one was to be trusted.' Scobie felt even this was better than complacence. He swerved the car 'to avoid a dead pye-dog', and asked himself why he loved that place so:

> Is it because here human nature hasn't had time to disguise itself? Nobody here could ever talk about a heaven on earth. Heaven remained rigidly in its proper place on the other side of death, and on this side flourished the injustices, the cruelties, the meanness that elsewhere people so cleverly hushed up. Here you could love human beings nearly as God loved them, knowing the worst.[11]

Greene's was an orderly world, full of meannesses and cruelties, but heaven was 'rigidly in its proper place on the other side of death'.

In the 1930s, 40s and 50s Greene's belief in Catholicism is pure. But by the time of the interview for the *Tablet*, he is far away from the assurance of those early years. The furthest he takes us while still seemingly believing in God (and then he was fast approaching three score and ten) is his theory as seen in *The Honorary Consul* – Father Rivas's strange notion of God having a daytime and a nighttime face. Rivas seems still a priest, and like many of Greene's Catholic heroes, he has sinned most alarmingly. But he does protect the poor and innocent; that is what he is doing in a sense by becoming a guerrilla leader and capturing an ambassador. Rivas is willing to kill the insignificant Honorary Consul if the enemy fails to release those he believes are wrongly in jail. How many Catholic priests have committed or been willing to commit such a sin, the murder of an innocent?

Rivas is a priest in many ways – his voice, his manners, his gentleness. And, just as Jesus helped prepare and serve breakfast to the disciples as recorded in John 23: 9–14, Rivas, kneeling before a stove, breaking eggs, reminds the Honorary Consul of the 'moment at the altar when a priest breaks the Host over the chalice'.[12] There are also other parallels with Christ and the priest Rivas.

Greene's religious heroes are not primarily interested in their own souls: they are concerned with saving others. But the theory promulgated by Greene and passed on to his character the guerrilla priest is astonishing by any standards. To recap Rivas's beliefs: there is a good day side of God and an evil night side of God. (Greene is truly astonishing here.) But he goes on: whatever good is done by man brings about God's 'redemption'. The good done by men makes God better, and thus in evolution God could, with man's help, become entirely good: thus also the sum total evil of men we have seen in the previous century, men such as Hitler, Duvalier, Stalin (and later, bin Laden, Saddam Hussein), would have the opposite effect.

We saw early indications of the development of this theory in *A Burnt-Out Case* (1960) when Dr Colin considers Christ not the Son of the Creator but as an evolutionary figure, even an amoeba:

> We have become cynical about progress because of the terrible things we have seen men do during the last forty years. All the same through trial and error the amoeba did become the ape. There were blind starts and wrong turnings even then ... Evolution today can produce Hitlers as well as St John of the Cross. I have a small hope . . . that someone they call Christ was the fertile element, looking for a crack in the wall to plant its seed. I think of Christ as an amoeba who took the right turning. I want to be on the side of the progress which survives. I'm no friend of pterodactyls.[13]

And a dozen years later Greene in *The Honorary Consul* had Rivas admit:

> 'I believe in the evil of God,' Father Rivas said, 'but I believe in His goodness too. . . . I believe the time will come when the night-side will wither away, like your communist state . . . and we shall see only the simple daylight of the good God.'

Rivas envisions that sometimes whole generations of men slip backwards to the beasts. 'I believe God is suffering the same evolution that we are.' Rivas's final answer is that he believes in Christ, the cross and redemption:

> The Redemption of God as well as of Man. I believe that the day-side of God, in one moment of happy creation, produces perfect goodness . . . Because the evolution of God depends on our evolution . . . But now at least we can be sure where evolution will end one day – it will end in a goodness like Christ's.[14]

*

In Greene's short story, 'A Visit to Morin', the protagonist Morin has lost his belief. This story caused Evelyn Waugh a great deal of pain because he thought Greene, the leader of the Catholic pack of writers, had also lost his faith. Indeed, the Morin character fits Greene like a glove – he's lost his *belief* but not his *faith*, and Greene makes much of the difference. He defined 'belief' as arguments in favour of theological propositions, the point being that whilst you may not be convinced by theological propositions, you can still have faith, even when you aren't convinced any more by rational argument that God exists (as if such a thing could be 'proven' by rational argument). So what we have is rational *dis*belief, yet faith survives. The case, fictional though it may be, approximates to Greene's religious condition closely as he comes upon the end-game. (I don't feel Greene ever reached a point where he could abandon all belief – perhaps he believed he *could* believe, if he just held on.)

Dunlop, who in the story interviews Morin, notes that neither of them took communion. They have an argument and Dunlop says he knows why Morin didn't participate: because he's lost his faith. But Dunlop has it wrong; such would not keep even a priest from admitting he'd lost his faith in confession. Here is Morin's conclusive answer, that for twenty years he stayed away from confession because he had a mistress and did not want to pretend that he would leave her:

> 'You know the condition of absolution? A firm purpose of amendment. I had no such purpose. Five years ago my mistress died and my sex died with her.'
> 'Then why couldn't you go back?'
> 'I was afraid. I am still afraid.'
> 'Of what the priest would say?'
> 'What a strange idea you have of the Church. No, not of what the priest would say. He would say nothing. I daresay there is no greater gift you can give a priest in the confessional, Mr Dunlop, than to return to it after many years. He feels of use again.'

He feels his 'lack of belief is a final proof' that faith is real; after years away, his

> Belief withered as the priests said it would. I don't believe in God and His Son and His angels and His saints, but I know the reason why I don't believe and the reason is – the Church is true and what she taught me is true. For twenty years I have been without the sacraments* and I can see the effect. The wafer must be more than wafer.[15]

---

* Greene did refuse to go to communion, not for twenty, but for thirty years.

This collection of short stories was published in 1963, enough time to believe that there was still hope for Greene as an abiding Catholic.

*

Responding to the Cornwell interview, *The Times* published a detailed summary *on the very day* that the *Tablet* article appeared. *The Times* postulated that Greene might be 'repaying a long-term debt of gratitude for an ancient favour' by granting the *Tablet* 'intimate access to his own private life', and stated that 'like [that of] a character from one of his own stories, it is revealed as the familiar teasing mixture of mysteries and mistresses'.

Greene is described as a 'rather nice kind gentleman, very old and very modern, very graceful and scandalous, very problematical'. The piece goes on to describe the *Tablet*'s 'rare, extensive and personal interview with the greatest English novelist alive today' as a

> literary event of some considerable interest, a terrific scoop . . . Greene is a trustee of the Catholic magazine and this is not the first time he has let it use the connection. It is appropriate, for John Cornwell, the interviewer, speaks the Catholic shorthand needed to pry some of Graham Greene's sexier secrets from him. Some will even call it a confessional statement, though there is no plea for absolution at the end – by 85, it seems, the shame with the libido, has all burnt out.[16]

The interview in the *Tablet* begins with a truth he had not so easily expressed to other journalists. Greene, we know, was wary of journalists, but not so this one, perhaps because Cornwell, a Catholic, had been a distinguished journalist and was now a Cambridge scholar.

Arriving in Antibes, Cornwell immediately asked Greene: 'Why here?' nodding at the forest of masts in the harbour. Greene didn't beat about the bush. It wasn't solely for tax reasons as Cornwell suggested, though as we've seen in Chapter 32, tax played its part. The reason given is the pre-eminent one:

> I came to live here so as to be near to the woman I love. I have a girlfriend, a friendship of some 30 years. She lives close by. We see each other most days. She is married, to a Swiss husband; but he is . . . *complaisant.** All parties are in agreement. My friend and I usually have lunch together; spend the afternoon together.

---

* Not so, for Martine's comments about her father indicate that he was hurt by the affair.

Cornwell then moved in fast as a sharp-shooter. In almost a single sentence he asked all the leading questions and finally the big one:

> You are perhaps the most famous Catholic layman alive . . . but what sort of a Catholic *are* you? Do you go to church? Do you go to confession? Do you even *believe*?

Greene's answer is astounding for a believer, for surely the term he used means '*dis*belief': '"I call myself now a Catholic Agnostic," he snapped.' Cornwell shows no surprise. (But doesn't 'agnostic' mean 'one who believes we cannot know that God exists'? Such a person denies the possibility of ultimate knowledge. Is Greene's answer not the ultimate oxymoron?) Agnostic or not, Greene still wishes to participate in the sacraments and go to mass:

> usually on a Sunday . . . I've got a great friend, a priest from Spain, Fr Leopoldo Durán, who has permission from his bishop to say the Mass in Latin and say it anywhere, so if he comes here [his Antibes apartment] he says it at that table. And if I'm travelling with him, he'll say Mass in the hotel room . . . although only on a Sunday.

Next come further denials which are especially interesting, and perhaps to a degree, deliberately misleading: 'And to please Fr Durán I make a confession now.' Was it that Greene could not stand to be seen by the world as vulnerable? Unlike Morin, we find Graham confessing, but the proviso is: it's for the sake of his special priest friend. This sounds phoney. I've always considered Graham to be a perpetual kneeler, but also a perpetual protester. What good does confession do for the soul if it's not heartfelt? No one does that, not even Graham Greene, *just to please a priest*. (In any case, the priest would know at once if the confession were suspect, done just to flatter. Idle chatter for our consumption *and* confusion.) He carries on the pretence: minimising the sessions, which he said lasted two minutes, 'although I've nothing much to confess at the age of 85; and I take the host then, because that pleases him'. Well, poor Father Durán. This conscientious priest would not have been taken in! I just don't believe it. But then Graham makes matters worse:

> There's plenty in my past to confess, which would take a long time, but there's nothing in my present because of age. And lack of belief is not something to confess. One's sorry, but one wishes

one could believe. And I pray at night . . . that a miracle should be done and that I *should* believe.

Cornwell asks about earlier confessions, and Greene goes straight to one he had many years before with an inquisitive priest, asking about prior incidents which, because he'd already confessed three months earlier, needed no confessing. The priest kept on about the recent past. Not wishing to repeat himself, Greene leaves, saying: 'I *told* you – it's three months since my last confession. And I'm wasting *your* time, and I'm wasting *my* time, and goodbye, Father!'

I'd heard this before in interview with Greene, so I know I'm not the only interviewer he'd told this to, but Cornwell recognised a tone I did not. 'As he repeated the words with which he had quelled the priest, his voice was suddenly cold, withering.' Cornwell backtracks: 'You say you take the host to please Fr Durán. But do you *believe* in communion – the Real Presence in the Eucharist?' Greene answers: 'I believe in it as a commemoration of what I think happened at the Last Supper. A *commemoration*. Not necessarily to be taken literally.' Says Cornwell: 'Every word was precisely enunciated. He was looking at me defiantly', and Greene further confuses the issue, deliberately I feel, and continues, citing places in Africa where they didn't even have bread for communion, and no way to make it. So he asks: 'How can one be too literal, too dogmatic, about the way in which the Eucharist is understood?' Greene would have made an excellent attorney.

More sparring follows. Cornwell refers to Greene's having 'plenty to confess in your own past life' and then asks him: 'But did you actually *believe* in sin in a theological sense?' In answer, we see that Greene doesn't believe in sin either. That's convenient. He doesn't like the word 'sin' and explains that:

It's got a kind of professional, dogmatic ring about it. Crime, I don't mind the word crime, but the word sin has got a kind of priestly tone. I believe that one does something *wrong* . . . and it may be a little wrong and it may be a big wrong. I never liked that strict division of mortal sin and venial sin in the Catholic Church. And then again, it depends on the consequences; some apparent little wrongs can cause more pain than apparent big wrongs. It depends on the circumstances and human relations.

Cornwell slips in:

'Your characters are often trapped between their weaknesses and their consciences. Do you think that temptation, a sense of guilt, adds to the spice of life?'

'No. I'd rather be without it.'

'And what about Satan? Do you believe in the devil, or in demons?'

Greene smiled wanly. 'No. I don't think so.'

'Do you believe in angels?'

A chuckle. 'No, I don't really.'

'Do you believe in hell?'

'I don't believe in hell. I never *have* believed in hell [this is not true, as we've seen earlier]. I think it's contradictory. They say that God is *mercy* . . . so it's contradictory. I think there may be *nullity*, and for others something that is conscious. But I don't believe in hell and I feel that purgatory may happen in *this* life, not in a future life.'

'By nullity you mean annihilation?'

'Yes. Hell is suffering; but nullity is not suffering.'

'And who would deserve nullity?'

'People like Hitler . . . he would be wiped out.'

'And what about yourself? Are you optimistic about your own survival beyond death?'

Cornwell's questions are fast and sure.

'Well, I would love to believe in it. And there is a certain mystery somehow. And one would like to let it be more than this world.'

And the ultimate question:

'Do you fear death?'

'No, and especially now . . . I'd like it to come quickly. What I fear is lingering illness. I had cancer of the intestine ten years ago. I assumed that that would be that, so I wrote a number of letters and tried to arrange things in a nice way as far as I could without mentioning why. But I didn't feel any fear of death.'

We need to remember this when death is close to him.

'And what about heaven?'

'I couldn't conceive what heaven could be. If it exists it's an entity I can't visualise in any way. My idea of heaven would be that it would be something active, rather than happiness with people one had loved, a form of activity in which we could influence life on earth . . . perhaps one's prayers in that state could influence somebody on earth.'

Then:

'How do you think about God?'
He fell silent. For a moment his eyes looked strangely shifty, haunted.
'Do you contemplate God in a pure, disembodied way?' I asked.
'I'm afraid I don't,' he said flatly.
'You think of God as Christ?'
'Yes, more . . . yes, that's closer to it.'

So Greene doesn't like the word 'sin', doesn't believe in Satan, doesn't believe in hell, doesn't believe in heaven, doesn't believe in angels, and an omnipotent God is a mystery. 'Sin' is too priest-like in tone, purgatory is something found on earth. He doesn't believe there is a rational basis for a belief in God. You might conclude that he doesn't believe in anything, isn't a Catholic or, if he dabbles in Catholicism in a semiserious way, he also enjoys rising up in mutiny against his past Catholic beliefs. We see Greene's disenchantment. It looks as if Greene is no longer a Christian, and certainly not a Roman Catholic.

Cornwell says that it sounds to him as if Greene's belief is a struggle. Greene admits it is worse than that: his belief is not strong enough to be called *belief*. Then he tells a story from the gospel of John which helps to keep his *faith* alive. The passage Greene says is almost reportage, the kind that might have been written by a good journalist:

where the beloved disciple is running with Peter because they've heard that the rock has been rolled away from the tomb, and describing how John manages to beat Peter in the race . . . and it just seems to me to be first-hand reportage, and I can't help believing it . . . I know that St Mark is supposed to be the earliest gospel, but there's just the possibility of St John's gospel having been written by a very old man, who never calls himself by name, or says 'I', but does describe this . . . which strikes me as true.

This scripture, and the Padre Pio history, have allowed him to keep his faith, or, as Greene puts it, laughing gently in self-mockery: 'Well, at any rate, it introduced a *doubt* in my *disbelief*.'

Cornwell brings out an assenting admission: 'If you hadn't had your mysterious experience with Padre Pio you might possibly have lost your faith?' Then, a little later, Cornwell says: 'Your faith, then, is tenuous.' Greene assents: '"One is attracted to the Faith," he said with a wry smile. "Believing is the problem."'

On the basis of this interview (but only this interview) it would be possible to argue that Greene, with but a year and a half to live – cancer of the blood soon upon him – was not a believer. Either that, or he is talking out of both sides of his mouth in deliberate obfuscation. It seems he certainly didn't want anyone to think he was a believer.

There are many strange things in Greene, paradoxes and contradictions; clearly he could not be said to be a leader of the faithful. We see plainly enough what Greene is saying about himself. He is not easily a believer because that entails analysis, but faith demands unconditional acceptance, belief with one's eyes closed so to speak. I find this approach disingenuous for one gifted with a brilliant mind, whom even priests looked up to.

Greene was way behind by this stage. He attended mass regularly, but had not gone to regular confession for thirty years. If he went, he would have to make promises – did Father Durán keep finding excuses during every individual confession to excuse his friend for the blanket transgression of a sexual sin perpetually committed? We cannot find out. The profession doesn't allow for double agents: there are no Philbys among priests. But there's an extraordinary development.

It seems that for a long time, and at least once a year during his summer jaunts with Father Durán, Greene did make confessions. Not wishing to tell Professor Cornwell too much, he implies that these were very short sessions, and we won't hear more from his private priest. Father Durán is a first: Greene's very own travelling priest!

So Greene must have felt he'd been forgiven, if, as a very old man of eighty-five (his earlier suggestion is that he did not sleep with Yvonne at his great age), he was not now sinning (sorry, wrong word for Greene), since at this point, a pre-Viagra Greene wasn't physically able to commit the sexual deed as had been his wont. (As if this were the only sin needing confessing.) Yet everything I know about him tells me that he retained an interest in sex even during his last terrible illness. I came upon Greene's soulmate in St Augustine (though unlike Greene, St Augustine was able to grow up and move on), who spoke to God:

> But I, a most wretched youth, most wretched from the start of my youth, had even sought chastity from you, and had said, 'Give me chastity and continence, but not yet,' for I feared that you would hear me quickly.

Chastity and continence to Graham Greene? Unlikely. Greene loved five women, all in their different ways fascinating – certainly Vivien and Dorothy Glover were, unquestionably Catherine Walston, his greatest love, was; and if the Swedish actress Anita Björk had allowed their affair to go on, she could have competed with Catherine (and did for two years). Then there's Yvonne, and her long-standing love for Greene right up to death. There is no doubt that in his years in France, Yvonne had Greene's powerful love. However, Greene also had, for many years, one-night-stands with other women, mostly prostitutes.*

★

Greene's statements are damning enough but I talked to his friend of many years, the navigator Michael Richey, a scrupulously honest man. He wrote to me on 17 January 2000, almost nine years after the death of his friend. The first thing he mentioned was that 'the Catholic faith was inevitably an element in [their] friendship . . . if only in providing a common language about some things'. The second point he made was a comparison: Edith Sitwell became a Catholic late in life. She was described by the well-known Jesuit Father D'Arcy as being 'an eccentric Catholic, but then she was an eccentric woman'. The point Richey is making is that Greene, too, wasn't a typical Catholic, but that he *was* a Catholic.

> Although he would sometimes refer to himself as an agnostic – or even an atheist – Catholic (in the sense I suppose that his faith exceeded his somewhat pared down beliefs) I never got the impression that Graham was at all lukewarm about his religion; indeed the mere fact of his difficulties is a sign of how seriously he took it rather than how little he thought it all mattered.

Richey had been reading Bernard Wall's autobiography, *Headlong into Change*. When Wall had visited Salamanca he spoke to an Irish rector there who had known Unamuno, whom Greene admired enormously. It was Richey's conclusion that Unamuno's attitude to Catholicism was 'ambiguous' (as was Greene's), and also that he was a deeply religious man, 'yet didn't seem to believe in the creed'. Still Unamuno remained a strong Catholic.

Richey evidently believed that Greene was a man of piety, and also that the story of Morin is Greene's story. He knew that Cornwell's interview delved into Greene's attitude towards confession and communion. This was a 'delicate area', he admitted. Yet he felt the

---

* The best description of this aspect of Greene came to me from his nephew James Greene: he told me that when his friend, the writer Jon Halliday, was introduced to Graham at a reception, his response was that 'he was happy to have looked into the eyes that had seen the inside of a thousand brothels'.

need to tell me that over the years he had gone to mass with Graham all over the world: 'Always, like Pierre Morin . . . he would stop short of going to communion. This seemed to define his status within the faith, perhaps as he once put it, keeping one foot in the door.'

Richey felt that originally Greene was 'simply not prepared' in communion 'to make pledges ("a firm purpose of amendment" and all that) which he couldn't trust himself to keep'. We know this to be true over Catherine Walston, and habit alone would have made it impossible during the long years he was with Yvonne. Quite clearly this created a real difficulty: Greene could not go to communion and confess, for him it would be a waste of time. But then Richey makes the following point:

> I am sure it is necessary to see Graham's faith as living rather than dying; and in the story, you'll remember, the fact that Morin lost his belief rather than his faith became for him the final proof that the Church was right and the faith true.

And here is the origin of that story, reflected upon by Richey:

> Well, I don't know if these reflections lead anywhere but I remember Graham, many years before that story was written, wondering whether his somewhat irregular practice might of itself lead to a further lack of belief and so on ad infinitum.

Richey ended his letter by referring to Father Durán's book on Greene, and speaks of the importance of Durán for Greene, arguing that Durán's presence was the 'means of reconciling him to the practices of religion and, ludicrous though some passages may appear to be, Durán's book gives a revealing insight into Graham's instinctive piety'.

★

In this Richey is right that Greene did have an instinctive piety. He was, certainly in his four famous Catholic novels, well aware of the significance of being a priest with the Catholic power to forgive sins – this in the days when he had no personal objection to the term 'sin'. Moreover, at that time Greene had told Father Caraman that a priest's power was more important than anything else in the world. A description of this power appears in James Joyce's *A Portrait of the Artist as a Young Man* – Greene knew the passage and he quoted from the priest's terrifying description of hell in the prologue to his book, *The Lawless Roads*. But here is Joyce's priest on the significance of all priests,

697

speaking to Stephen Dedalus, trying to persuade him to become a priest:

> To receive that call, Stephen . . . is the greatest honour that the Almighty God can bestow upon a man. No king or emperor on this earth has the power of the priest of God. No angel or archangel in heaven, no saint, not even the Blessed Virgin herself has the power of a priest of God: the power of the keys, the power to bind and loose from sin, the power of exorcism, the power to cast out from the creatures of God the evil spirits that have power over them, the power, the authority, to make the great God of Heaven come down upon the altar and take the form of bread and wine. What an awful power, Stephen![17]

★

As a young priest, George Russo was enormously impressed by Greene's 1940 novel *The Power and the Glory*, he loved the whisky priest, in spite of 'his lapses into serious sin', for his courage and his faith. Russo was aware of Greene's own personal failings as well as those of his priest hero. About Greene's failings, Russo put it this way in a letter to me:

> I believe fully that, after his conversion, he kept faithful to this Faith all his life . . . I think Graham's interest in the Catholic Church grew beyond the parameters of certain dogmas and Roman decrees to a faith in Jesus' Gospel, given to the Catholic Church and passed down through history . . . I think his encounters with Catholicism through Vivien and later Fr Trollope,* (& Fr Caraman & those other priests he met over the world) gave him examples of holiness, heroism, and leadership that impressed him. These people introduced him to truths about Christ and other human beings like the saints and sinners he wrote about.

And it is obvious that *The Power and the Glory* was still with Russo, so that he could come to Greene's 'rescue', in spite of Greene's comments to John Cornwell:

> Remember the priest in *Power*, the horrific conditions he lived under, and yet continued his priestly duties; saw them as obligations, as Graham did in the Catholic practices he followed till the end. He got the grace of a priest to administer to him at the time of death; what he wanted; and what mattered. These are ways of

---

* The priest in Nottingham who first helped Greene to accept Catholicism.

Catholic faith that Graham had to the full. If he did not always live it (and I think he did by prayer & the Mass which he attended regularly), he certainly wanted a priest at his death bed. I've experienced plenty of this in my life as a priest. He is a bit like his own whisky priest; likes alcohol and women, yet in the end faces the firing squad for his Faith. Forget Cornwell! I don't think he understood Greene.

I agree with Russo, and particularly what he says about Greene's strong need to have a priest at his deathbed. I'd go so far as to say that Greene's friendship with Durán (and tremendous loyalty towards him) stemmed from his future *need* of Durán. Graham knew he could call on Durán as he was dying. But Greene faced no firing squad for his faith, unlike his whisky priest – he simply organised his relationship with Durán so that he had his own priest to officiate over his final departure. He needed this security blanket, because increasingly as Graham grew older he felt the proximity of punishment after death for his sexual transgressions. Perhaps he believed in sin after all. But he never gave up cuckolding Jacques Cloetta.

Russo makes an important last point:

> One cannot write stories like *The Power and the Glory*, or 'The Hint of an Explanation' without faith, and these are totally Catholic, as are *The Heart of the Matter, Monsignor Quixote* and *The End of the Affair*. Remember Scobie, 'Human beings couldn't be heroic all the time: those who surrendered everything – for God or love – must be always sometimes in thought to take back their surrender. So many have never committed the heroic act, however rashly. It was the act that counted.' Graham did many acts of charity and faith that the world knows nothing of, but I'm sure he did them because of his faith in, and love of, God.[18]

★

At the end of his second journey in Spain with Father Durán, Greene decided he would like to have a portable communion set. His sister Elisabeth found a beautiful one for their third trip. In a letter to her on 8 August 1977, Father Durán wrote how extremely pleased he was: 'In a very small pretty box there is everything necessary to say Mass and that saves a lot of inconveniences when one travels.' This is how Durán was able to give communion to his travelmate.

On their yearly trips to Spain up to the monastery at Osera, they would have mass and communion and Greene would make his confession. A constant topic for Greene with Durán was the question of faith. Durán speaks of his nervous disposition. We will find unique evidence of this in the interview I had with the aristocrat, Count Creixell, later in this chapter. We have seen that Greene was restless to the point that though he loved to visit Osera, two days were all he could take before he had to move on.

★

Greene, at times, and sometimes quite suddenly, could feel tremendous remorse over things in his past. Father Durán has revealed some of these to us. Once he was angry with his friend Durán and felt the next day 'enormous remorse'.[19] I am sure that few of us who knew Greene escaped a private whipping.* But Durán could handle his rapid changes of mood.†

When Greene started attacking the Pope in letters to the press, he had an argument with Father Durán over the ill treatment of priests who were members of the Nicaraguan government. Greene wrote in a letter to the *Tablet* of 25 August 1984 that the Pope had made a fool of those priests. But this public criticism was mild in contrast to his own feelings and the public admonishment of Father Cardenal. He was extremely angry about this. In a letter on 2 March 1985 in the *Tablet*, Graham quotes Erasmus with contempt: 'It is neither safe nor pious to harbour and spread suspicions of the public authority. It is better to endure tyranny, so long as it does not drive us to impiety, than sedulously to resist.' He suggests that the Pope is a disciple of Erasmus: 'Small comfort there for the victims of the death squads in El Salvador or the victims of the *Contras* recruited from Somoza's National Guard in Nicaragua, both supported by President Reagan'.‡

Concerning Pope John Paul II, Greene had several bones to pick. He felt that the Pope's meeting with Reagan on the eve of the 1984, American elections had been timed to influence Catholics to vote for Reagan. He was offended by the Pope's treatment of the priests who were members of the Nicaraguan government and appalled that the Pope had not publicly spoken out about the murder of an Archbishop.

---

* Elisabeth once told me: 'Graham got angry with you Norman and I had to save your bacon.' My bacon has been saved often by the kindness of such souls – my bacon, loin chops *and* rump roast.

† One wonders if Greene could have really lived with anyone for long – perhaps his mistress who dropped by daily, but then went home. Yvonne was docile when there, and otherwise absent. I sometimes wonder how much of her real nature was evident to Greene.

‡ But I do believe that had President Reagan been in office during the terrorist attacks on New York and Washington, DC, and the abortive plane crash in a field in Pennsylvania on September 11, 2001, Graham might well have switched gears smoothly. After all, his famous motto was 'I'm for the victim, and victims change.' Here thousands of innocent victims were annihilated.

The two friends, Durán and Greene, parted tight-lipped, but the next day Graham apologised.

★

It becomes increasingly difficult to deny that Greene is a believer. He certainly doesn't always act like a non-believer. On one occasion, Greene asked Durán quite out of the blue: 'Do you think I have true faith?'
Durán's answer:

> You know as well as I do that there is no effect without a cause. Reading your books, I notice that the name of God appears constantly. But that's not all. Your work hinges on the existence of that Being . . . I genuinely believe that your faith is greater than mine. I have no doubt about it.

Greene was so astonished that he could only reply:

> Thank you very much indeed. Your answer is very comforting.[20]

What an uncertain fellow he is that he needs the yearly companionship of a priest to assure himself that he has faith. His life seems to me at times to be an unnecessary struggle, but also a worthy one as if that is what he needed to do in order to remain a Catholic and a Christian. Yet a struggle it remained. Greene was ever in a confused state about the condition of his faith. Durán reports that he prayed every day and with 'great intensity', and that the constant purpose of his prayers was to ask God that he might 'truly believe', that his faith might be increased.

Father Durán remarks about the daily mass he performed for his audience of one: 'It is amazing how much faith Graham set on his friend's Mass.' He adds: 'I will say just this: during the last ten years of his life Graham received all the sacraments with normal frequency.'[21]

One night in France, Greene saw on television a film starring Trevor Howard called *Catholics*. The film deals with an abbot who loses his faith, and ends with him reciting the Lord's Prayer, knowing that he is living a charade. Greene was hugely impressed and wrote a most telling note to the actor to express how 'moved I was by your performance: there were tears in my eyes at the end & I had to take a pill to sleep'. He says it was some of the finest acting he's seen on screen or stage, and to assure Howard that he was honestly affected he adds: 'I write this with the cold wisdom of next morning, not in the flood of first enthusiasm.'

*

Information came to me when, through the British Council, I was invited in 1987 to give a lecture in northern Spain, at the Fundación Creixell. The day after the lecture, sitting outside not far away from Father Durán, who was uncharacteristically scowling, was Count Creixell. I got the feeling that perhaps Durán wished me not to speak to the Count.

That afternoon Durán made a generous offer, never repeated, though not for want of prompting. He asked me if I would like to travel over the same ground he and Greene had, finishing up at the Cistercian monastery at Osera. I did have a desire to see the place.

I thought the reason Father Durán was so helpful and generous with his time then was that he wanted to help the authorised biographer of his friend Graham Greene. He knew Greene wanted me to follow in his footsteps to wherever he'd set a novel. But I never made it to Osera. I couldn't get the Father to renew his offer. I still long to visit what Greene called 'the stark simplicity'²² of that monastery.

Back then, I thought there would be plenty of time to make such a trip and did not take the Father up on it. After all, I was then close to finishing my first volume of *The Life of Graham Greene*, which came out two years later and went only up to 1939. Greene didn't start travelling in Spain with Durán until the mid-1970s. There was a long stretch of time (and enormous efforts to be made) before I could possibly reach that decade. I didn't reach it until I'd completed altogether eighty-two more chapters. (I confess I had no idea the height of the mountain that Greene's life would force me to climb, or how long it would take me overall.)* But I suspect Father Durán might have fallen out with the Count.

Count Creixell wanted to speak to me about Graham. Indeed, he went searching for me. It was a curious interview.

*

First, he told me that Graham said I was the 'only man who wished to write a serious book' and added that Greene had said, 'The only person I trust is Norman Sherry.' I confess that I felt his remarks might be a sop to Cerberus. Then he recalled the occasion that Greene invited him and his wife to visit Antibes. Greene booked rooms for them but didn't pay. (I didn't think this onerous. When I visited Greene in Antibes, it was natural that I'd be in some reasonable hotel near his home which I paid for myself. Still, as we shall see, the Count had been remarkably generous when Greene had visited his mansion, the

---

* It cost me more than a quarter century of life in fact.

Fundación Creixell, so reciprocity was a natural thought.) Next, Greene took them to Chez Félix, his favourite place, but the Count thought it an inexpensive restaurant. Greene did assume on this outing that he himself would be paying for dinner and chose a not very good wine. Immediately, the Count let it be known that he would be footing the bill. Greene responded by changing to 'a better more expensive wine'. (That I could believe. He was canny with his money.)* There was a further reason why the Count felt that he and his wife might have been treated more kindly, and not only because Greene continued to stay at the Count's home when he travelled in Northern Spain:

COUNT: Your novels are very important in the world.
GREENE: Your wine is very important in the world.

But then the Count was not offering insignificant words of praise:

COUNT: I should like to create a foundation which would bear your name.
GREENE: I should be delighted if this would give Leopoldo Durán a pension when I die.

The Count agreed to support Leopoldo Durán for life. Later, the Count had another suggestion. Not only would the Foundation perpetuate Graham Greene's name and give Leopoldo Durán a salary, but the idea should be widened. Students should be brought in. But Durán was opposed to students. I assume he felt the need of a priestly sinecure. Perhaps Durán felt the Count was too friendly with Graham and that this was a danger to him personally – that the Count's friendship with Greene would threaten his own. We'll see that he need not have worried.

And then there was a matter of money. Durán offered to sell Graham Greene documents to the Count. Presumably, Durán was short of the ready. What priest isn't? They were offered at a heavy price. The Count told me: 'Durán was the owner of Graham Greene's conscience.' (The Count never used Durán's title, but always just 'Durán' or 'Leopoldo Durán'.) He went on with his proof.

The Count's first point was that Graham Greene was 'profoundly Roman Catholic, and his problem was Yvonne Cloetta, the married one'. (Note that I haven't attempted to modify or correct the Count's

---

* Once I borrowed five pounds for my longish journey back to Lancaster University from London. I'd spent all my money at my club, the Savile, on Graham. He loaned me five pounds as I was catching a train from Euston, and said: 'Don't forget to return it to my sister Elisabeth', which of course I did.

English, which was serviceable enough.) He spoke of Durán's hearing Graham's confessions about this matter 'constantly':

> Seven days in Graham Greene's company. Leopoldo Durán always here. The relationship was absolutely astonishing. Leopoldo Durán would be in his bedroom until he went to sleep – Graham Greene was often nervous about his conscience – he drank so much – when he was living in this house, his breakfast was a glass of vodka – very little to eat and this eating was so he could drink. At his bedside table – a bottle of vodka and a bottle of whisky. Astonishing. The more he drank, the clearer his mind became. The last time he was here, in January 1987 he drank about 6 bottles of Marques de Murrieta [which comes into *Monsignor Quixote*] at the last . . . little left in the bottle, 'Don't serve it. Let the gods enjoy it.'

As to Greene's nervousness, well, he himself admitted this. He was asked in interview: 'The predominant trait in your character?' Answer: 'Anxiety.' Another question: 'Your present state of mind?' Answer: 'Disturbed.' And as to Durán being in Greene's bedroom until Greene went to sleep, I don't doubt it.

Father Durán was probably hearing Greene's confessions, those that Greene repeatedly denied to journalists, or those he claimed elsewhere lasted only minutes! Father Durán couldn't speak openly about such matters, but an interesting account comes in his book: 'Our routine was to take a shower, followed by "whisky time", conversation over dinner and, quite often, a further chat in our bedrooms before going to sleep.'[23] Durán is very careful not to over-step the particular line he'd drawn in the sand for himself. And Count Creixell:

> Durán gave him the night to pacify him with his confessions – he was a private priest Durán, a kind of midwife. Now the odd thing was that Greene was a competitor. He was a winner. He wanted to win even after death. In Leopoldo Durán he had the way to win even over death. He was funny. He had the fear of a perpetual spy. The door would suddenly open and he would half rise. In his home in Antibes it would be the same. Was it out of fear? I saw him get rid of a journalist suddenly.

So, if the Count is right, Greene was a great competitor 'wanting to win even over death'. He had a mortal's craving for immortality, but who among us doesn't? We're flesh and bones. Flesh and bones die, but does the soul need to? Even though he flirted with death and contemplated suicide his whole life, he told the Sutros he didn't want to die in a plane crash – despite saying the very opposite to Catherine – because then he 'wouldn't receive absolution from a priest'.

Greene referred to the priest jokingly as 'My Father Durán'. But it rather looks as if, given the Count's details, Durán could just as easily (and perhaps with more truth) have said, 'My Graham Greene', and it *wouldn't* have been a joke, for Father Leopoldo Durán also needed Graham Greene – he was his claim to fame. At the same time Durán often seems to present himself as somewhat submissive, though this probably was no more than a natural humility when in Greene's company. Goodness knows there *are* many reasons to love Graham Greene: first and foremost, his masterpieces, by my reckoning eleven novels, creative and great works. But Greene didn't need (never did) the world to agree with him – and certainly not Father Durán. Greene could not abide sycophants. He would sometimes march with mad determination in the wrong direction, on the wrong road.

Old Graham Greene, unquestionably a Catholic, cannot live a pure Catholic life, and is deeply troubled. But he remains a Catholic, and though in his middle years (at the time of *A Burnt-Out Case*) he almost completely lost his sense of belief (and faith), with his spirits barometrically measured, swept up and down the scale: his vacillations must have terrified him. But by the time he came nearer to death he returned to his own personal sense of sin, especially of sexual sin. Greene continued to be a sexual raider, and for him, this powerfully fed his sense of innate sin. The only relief could come in the hope of divine mercy. Count Creixell told me that Graham pursued his pleasures secretly as a 'voluptuary would and thought that the freedom he'd given himself could and probably would lead to punishment everlasting. Secret remorse often overwhelmed him. Now that Archbishop Mathew was dead, Father Durán was an absolute necessity, his final hope that the good Father could prevent him from being condemned.'

I think Count Creixell's account of Greene is fascinating. We know that at the time in question, Greene, in old age, was suffering from intense grief. His many regrets had quickened, and his lifelong adultery frightened him. Love sustained him, but in his mind his sin stood tall. It is doubtful that he ever spoke to Yvonne, a Catholic despite her years with Greene, about his great fears. I suspect that in order to make comparisons between Greene and other unusual seekers in history, we would have to return to medieval ascetics, for this is what he wished to be (his very opposite). Still, with the help of Father Durán he prayed, he confessed, and he died with his priest at his side. He wanted to be saved; wanted his soul after death to be vouchsafed to heaven, as determined (though so different) as an anchorite withdrawing from the world for the purpose of salvation.

A non-Catholic might think that Greene, as he reached life's end, was putting himself into a straitjacket. This is, it seems true to say, a revelation of Graham's humanity – his personality. He put himself into a narrow mould because he wanted desperately to believe, in order to die in quiet contentment. He knew the sacredness of life; he anticipated death. Is death the appalling unrelieved subjugation of humankind, or is it a foretoken of the sacredness of future mercy? Assuredly, all useful certainty lives in a penumbra of doubt.

PART 22

Accolades and Black Eyes

49

Raise the Plague Flag!

Another man's soul is darkness.
— RUSSIAN PROVERB

A secret battle was waged each year in the Swedish Academy. It was sincere work, going on behind the scenes, to determine who was worthy of the Nobel Prize for Literature. The outside world often nipped at the committee's heels, not least because candidates such as Greene were always being praised (overpraised, certain members thought), and arguments dogged their trail. Indictment followed indictment in British and American newspapers. If the Swedish officials were sensitive, and many were, then the comments — which were often disparaging — from the international press must have turned their stomachs. Being upbraided by the world of letters was bound to rankle when they felt themselves to be powerful and impressive representatives of that world.

One barrage came from Jonathan Yardley, a distinguished literary critic who could put the enemy down when needed. It appeared in the *Washington Post* of 25 October 1982 under the title 'Prejudices':

For the past several years the month of October has produced, with monotonous regularity, an annual proclamation of bad tidings called the Nobel Prize for Literature.

This time there was 'good news along with the bad':

The good news is the selection of Gabriel García Márquez, the author of *One Hundred Years of Solitude* and *The Autumn of the Patriarch*, for the 1982 award.

Surely no one could be disappointed with the Committee's decision

709

on this occasion, yet criticism in Greene's favour is potently offered by Yardley:

> But before reflecting on the pleasures that choice affords, let us contemplate the astonishing fact that the members of the Swedish Academy, in their collective ignorance and bias, have once again refused to give the award to the writer who deserves it above all others now living, Graham Greene.
>
> Not since 1970, when the award was presented to Alexander Solzhenitsyn, has the Nobel for Literature gone to a writer whose stature rivals Greene's: not Neruda, not Böll, not – sorry about that – Singer or Bellow.

He goes further, stating that if Solzhenitsyn could be seen as being honoured more for his 'implacable moral presence' than for his writing, then the comparison must reach as far back as 1949 and William Faulkner, passing up

> Sartre and Pasternak and Camus and Hemingway and assorted other worthies – before we encounter a writer as deserving of the honor as Greene.
>
> ... from 1929, with the publication of *The Man Within*, through 1982 and the publication of *Monsignor Quixote*, Greene has produced a body of literature matched in this century perhaps only by Faulkner's. Like all other writers who genuinely deserve to be called 'great', he has found a large general readership as well as literary and scholarly ones; he speaks to the world, not to the academy.

Yardley then asks the inevitable question. If Greene is so great, why has he lost out so often? This is how he puts it, the sharp edge gleaming:

> Why he has been denied the award is a mystery, since the workings of that geriatric ward known as the Nobel selection committee are swaddled in secrecy.

Nevertheless, Yardley has kept his ear close to the whispering gallery, and provides the following reasons:

> The grounds for its opposition are variously reported . . . his perverse insistence on writing from time to time what he calls 'entertainments', his irreverent view of orthodox Catholicism, his

departure from England and the punitive taxes it imposes on successful writers, and his contempt generally for authority whether secular or ecclesiastical.

That is quite a ragbag selection of excuses, but Yardley asserts that Greene's politics and ambiguous attitude of mind operate against him:

There is no question that a central reason for Greene's rejection is that his politics do not coincide with those of the Swedish Academy, which waits for Lefty; Greene is too bleak, too aware of life's ambiguities and compromises, for the apple-cheeked, idealistic, naïve Swedes.

Yardley seems to have persuaded himself to be firm about it, and the situation as he perceives it is:

If these considerations figure in the determination of the Nobel for Literature − *and make no mistake about it, they most certainly do* [emphasis mine] − then the integrity of the award is compromised and trivialised; best think of it as the Nobel Prize for Ideological Rectitude with Literary Embellishments, and accord it the respect it thereby merits.

★

No one would argue that Greene did not want the Nobel Prize; he wanted it more and more, perhaps because it eluded him year after year after year.

In the appendix, I have placed a copy of the criticism upon which the committee's secret judgment was based, accompanied by an English translation. This indicates that although Greene might have expected to be considered for the Nobel Prize as early as his first great novel in 1938, *Brighton Rock*, or with his 1940 masterpiece, *The Power and the Glory*, he was not. The first time the Swedish Academy allowed Greene on their list of possibles was in 1950. The novel was *The Heart of the Matter*.

On a later occasion, Greene allowed *A Burnt-Out Case* (translated by Torsten Blomkvist) to appear first in Stockholm. This was asking for trouble. Apart from anything else, it meant that both British and American publishers had to wait until the book was translated into Swedish before releasing the original English version. The book appeared in Sweden in 1960; not in England and America until 1961.

Almost immediately the *Daily Mail* printed an article, appearing on 12 November 1960, suggesting a reason for the change about. As a

711

result, Greene probably was persuaded that it might seriously jeopardise his chances of winning the Nobel Prize that year. The headline alone, one suspects, may wilfully have damaged his chances: 'IS GRAHAM GREENE'S NEW BOOK AIMED AT THE NOBEL PRIZE?'

The writer began by asserting that publishers would go to any lengths to publicise a book, but then suggested that Greene's publisher must have a good reason for *not* publishing his latest in England. The *Daily Mail* phoned Greene's British publishers, Heinemann. They had no comment. In Norway and Sweden the newspapers implied that *A Burnt-Out Case* was very likely the best book ever written by Greene.

But the journalist, referring to the fact that local people were flattered and intrigued, added: 'They are guessing that with *A Burnt-Out Case* Greene is making a bid for the Nobel Prize for which his name has often been mentioned as a candidate.' This was most likely the journalist's own conclusion. It seemed to the reporter that there had to be a reason for publishing first in Sweden and that reason must be to ensure that *this time* Greene won. Certainly Frere was troubled after attacks on Greene in the press about the early Swedish appearance, trying to link it to the Nobel. But Frere knew that Greene's Swedish publisher had pushed hard for the publication there. Frere advised Greene against it, but he didn't think it mattered (which was somewhat naïve of Greene).

Greene wrote to Svanstrom on 22 November 1960, adding that he 'had a certain apprehension about your prior publication but it seemed to be too farfetched to mention'. Greene adds ironically that 'my fans have been sending me the enclosed cutting. I hope it will do no damage on your side.'

Svanstrom's answer was immediate, calling the *Daily Mail* article absurd and stating that it wouldn't have any effect in Sweden:

> Norstedts' prior publication is being appreciated here as a great literary event and the great privilege which it is. Nobody would dream of throwing suspicions as to the motives of your consent.

Svanstrom makes a special point:

> The prior publication has undoubtedly greatly intensified the interest of responsible people in your writing. My own feeling is that your position in Sweden is stronger than ever. Several leading members of the Swedish Academy have talked to me about your book, expressing their deep admiration. So the situation is most satisfactory: there cannot be any doubt that your name will be

very seriously discussed in connection with the Nobel prize for next year.

I am entirely happy. I do hope that you have no regrets.[1]

I suspect that Ragnar Svanstrom, no doubt because of his admiration for his leading author, was somewhat innocent, for surely the old men of the Swedish Academy would have their suspicions – especially any who already had a powerful dislike for Greene. But it should be remembered that the world premiere of Greene's first play, *The Living Room*, had taken place in Stockholm in 1952 so this was not the first occasion that Greene had a work of his published first in Sweden.

Greene's next novel, *The Comedians*, appeared in 1966 and Svanstrom was once more hopeful, but Greene's short note poured water on his expectations. Greene refers to the 1938 winner, whom Greene held in little regard: 'Many thanks for your letter. But you know I don't feel we should set our sights so high – to those heights crowned by Pearl Buck.'[2]

In 1978, twelve years after Greene's letter above, a spirited Texan and poet, Mary Connell, wrote to Greene. Connell had a direct, even outrageous style. Greene still had not been awarded the Nobel, and Connell went into battle. Greene must have felt her first rifle shot immediately:

> Pray address no further thought to the issue of the scoundrel in Stockholm. Wax figures are our specialty, and we attended your order with dispatch and cunning. Being among the more civilised practitioners of juju, we rarely work with pins, but have opened the gentleman's cranium and administered a brain transplant. Ideally, he will wake tomorrow newly graced with wisdom, taste, judgment, and a sense of historical proportion.

She plays upon the notion that 'Ours is an inexact science (more an art) and mistakes do occur' and suggests (of course humorously): 'If he dies of a brain hemorrhage, I shall feel rather clumsy.' But she returns to the Nobel:

> Obviously you will win the prize, and it was naïve of me not to realize it was imminent. I can think of a dozen writers who have written some one book as good as some one book of yours. But no living writer has written any five books as good as any five books of yours. I recently enjoyed reading *The Quiet American* again. I can't think who's ever written a superior book. God, it's so beautiful!

★

In a letter sent to Graham from the distinguished Society of Authors on 22 December 1981 by Derek Parker, we see that the Nobel Committee is working as usual in mysterious ways:

> Although I dare say it's extremely tactless, I cannot resist writing to pass on to you what I take to be a considerable compliment from your peers! For the first time, as far as I know, the committee administering the award of the Nobel Prize for Literature wrote to me as current chairman of this Society, to ask whether we would suggest the name of a British author to whom we felt the award might properly be made. Your name was the one which instantly occurred to me, but I restrained myself to the extent of asking the other members of the Committee of Management (seventeen of them) whether they would consider the matter and let me have any names within a week or so.
>
> You might be glad, or at least interested, to hear that every single one of them put your name forward, all but two of them as the one name which seemed to them proper. Three actually used the same phrase: 'It is disgraceful' that the award had not been made to you before. I don't know to what extent the award itself would mean anything to you, but the unanimous opinion of such a committee as ours (plus, I might say, that of our President) may, at all events I thought it worth mentioning. I would be glad, however, if you would regard this letter as confidential!
>
> With best wishes, and my personal thanks for your work.

But again, no Nobel.

Greene's friend Michael Meyer, who'd lived in Sweden for twenty years, wrote a brilliant article about the Nobel. He knew members of the Swedish Academy, and was wise about the nature of the leading writers and academics in that country, and how decisions were made. Meyer spoke Norwegian and Swedish fluently, so the Stockholm establishment was not foreign to him. His article appeared in the *Daily Telegraph* colour supplement, 5 December 1975.

Meyer started by referring to the 1975 winner, of whom I suspect, unless you are very knowledgeable about Italian poets, you might not have heard. Eugenio Montale was never a household name and at the time of receiving the Nobel award, he was seventy-nine. Meyer begins:

> Eugenio Montale . . . is a worthy recipient. His output has been small, but distinguished: and he had the courage and integrity to turn his back on Fascism and Communism, as they successively became the literary fashions in Italy.

But then Meyer adds: 'His selection may help to restore at least temporary respectability to this, the most valuable and prestigious literary prize in the world, increasing yearly . . . and tax-free.'

Meyer now makes the same point as Yardley, namely, that for seventy-four years since the Nobel had been inaugurated in 1901, 'the choices and omissions have become so frequently ludicrous that the winning of it has come to be regarded (apart, of course, from the money) as a doubtful honour'.

Meyer goes on to survey the list of winners:

If one looks back on the names of the winners since the prize was inaugurated in 1901, they make a far less impressive list than those of the rejected. Who today, even in their own countries, bothers about Sully Prudhomme, France [this was the first award winner], Paul Heyse, Germany [1910], Rudolf Eucken, Germany [1908], Verner von Heidenstam, Sweden [1916], Grazia Deledda, Italy [1927], Carl Spitteler, Switzerland [1920], Karl Gjellerup, Denmark [1917], Pearl Buck, USA [1938]?

Next Meyer lists the geniuses who, though eligible, were not chosen:

Tolstoy, Ibsen, Zola, Hardy, Strindberg, Freud, Gorki, Proust, Conrad, Henry James, Rilke, Joyce, Georg Brandes, Croce, Valéry, H.G. Wells, Stefan George, D. H. Lawrence and Virginia Woolf (not to mention those who only became internationally famous after their death, such as Chekhov and Kafka).

There are some monumental absentees. Meyer asks: 'Why is the choice so whimsical?' and his answer impresses.

Alfred Nobel left 96 per cent of his immense fortune to a fund, of which the interest would be divided annually into five prizes. Three would be given to the person or persons who had made the most important discoveries in physics, chemistry, and physiology or medicine. The fourth was for what is now called the Peace Prize, and the fifth would go 'to the person who shall have produced in the field of literature, the most outstanding work *of an ideal* (sic) tendency'. Here lies the problem: what did Nobel mean by the term 'ideal'?

The biggest headache as regards the literary prize was caused by the 'ideal'. The relevant sentence has usually been translated as 'the most outstanding work of an *idealistic* tendency', and indeed is so rendered in the official calendar of the Nobel Foundation.
But Nobel did not write 'idealistic', the Swedish for which is

idealistick. He wrote *idealisk,* which simply means 'ideal', as in 'an ideal husband'. Nor was it a slip of the pen, for a facsimile reproduction of the will shows that Nobel had originally planned to write some longer word such as *idealistisk* but altered it to *idealisk,* inking in the last three letters heavily over whatever he had written before. *Idealisk* in this context is bad Swedish; what on earth can be meant by 'work of an ideal tendency'? But it seems most unlikely that Nobel meant 'idealistic' as signifying 'hopeful' or 'non-pessimistic' in the sense in which it was taken by the Academy for nearly 50 years for, although he disliked Zola's novels, he seems greatly to have admired Ibsen, of whose plays he owned over ten copies ... He even possessed a good number of Strindberg's works. Did he perhaps mean 'works of ideas'? Or did he mean 'idealistic' in a bigger sense, which would embrace such writers as Ibsen and Tolstoy, both of whom could much more truthfully be described as idealists than some of the sloppy optimists who got the prize?

We shall never know. But for half a century, the Swedish Academy, whom Nobel chose to pick the winners, took it that 'pessimists' were ineligible, and we know that it was for this reason that Tolstoy, Ibsen, Zola and Hardy ... were rejected.

As Meyer tells it, he had it from a member of the Swedish Academy that Hardy was persistently nominated, but 'the conviction had long since taken firm root among the members of the Academy that Hardy's deep pessimism and inexorable fatalism were not to be reconciled with the spirit of the Nobel Prize. For nearly 50 years many of the greatest writers were passed over.'

Meyer also writes that after the Second World War, 'partly because some of the older and more bigoted members of the Academy had died, the old bogey of "idealism" had died with them'. But still Meyer felt the need to explain what he saw, as an Englishman, to be a characteristic of Swedish critics not shared by British and Americans which created an unbridgeable gulf between British and American taste on the one hand, and Swedish taste on the other. Chiefly the difference was that for a writer to achieve real distinction, he must be 'deep-minded' – in Swedish, *djupsinnig.* According to Meyer, Swedish critical opinion distrusted 'anything which might be described as "entertainment"'.

Over the 20 years and more that I have lived in Sweden, I have continually noted how Swedish critics, consciously or unconsciously, separate literature into two classes: 'good' literature, and 'entertainment' literature.

Clearly, if you wrote 'entertainment' literature, you could not be considered for the Nobel Prize. Ever. Here Meyer homes in on the case against Greene:

> This, I am convinced, is why Graham Greene has never been awarded the Nobel Prize, though he has been nominated year after year and would be overwhelmingly voted in Britain to be our leading serious novelist (an opinion that would surely be echoed in France, and I should have thought in most Western countries and by a high proportion of past winners).

Meyer expands:

> Greene, even at his most serious, is compulsively readable, and is accordingly regarded by the members of the Swedish Academy with grave suspicion; how can a writer whose novels can be finished in a couple of sittings be truly *djupsinnig*? If he were to write a heavy novel full of abstract platitudinising . . . something that, for whatever reason, was difficult to read and fully comprehend, I think the Academy would yield to this annual pressure from various countries and choose him; but as he is mercifully, never likely to write that kind of book, I have little doubt that he will join Tolstoy, Ibsen, Henry James and the rest of that far more distinguished company of the permanently rejected.[3]

★

Did the anti-Greene feelings in the Academy run deep? Was it a general view or was there one particular powerful enemy of Greene, as fan Mary Connell hinted at, that 'scoundrel'? If so, who was he?

We know he existed in Greene's mind, because in 1979 he gives answer to Connell:

> Last year not only my Swedish publishers but the press in general believed that the Nobel was coming to me, but I have a deadly enemy in the Academy who just managed to swing it to [Isaac Bashevis] Singer. Perhaps you ought to make a wax image of him, and stick in some pins. His name is Arthur Lundkvist. He is proudly known as the only autodidact on the Academy. He got a sort of Lenin Prize in Yugoslavia but he hasn't been to collect it they think because it might put him in bad with Russia. This is all scandal and probably untrue. All the same a waxen image wouldn't be a bad thing.[4]

Greene speaks truly, for in the previous year, *in the Swedish press*, there was a considerable outcry, indeed an eruption, in protest against Greene's having been passed over by the Academy judges. Any man might think that by 1979, after a lifetime of writing, Greene had written many superb novels. Keeping in mind that Swedish critics value 'deep-minded' stories, I list those I believe qualify: *Brighton Rock, The Power and the Glory, The Heart of the Matter, The End of the Affair, The Quiet American, Our Man in Havana, A Burnt-Out Case, The Comedians, The Honorary Consul, The Human Factor*: here's ten, any one of which legitimately could be considered for the Nobel Prize.

And the process went on the following year with the choice of Odysseus Elytis, a Greek whose poetry was not then translated into English, or any other language, again leaving Greene out in the cold. This time John Mortimer spoke out, expressing anger and sarcasm towards the Swedish Academy of Literature because of their choice. Was it, one wants to ask, a deliberate insult, perhaps saying: 'We don't like your work Graham Greene; we don't like your principles; we don't like you as a man, and will *not* on any account award *you* the Nobel Prize'?

Greene himself must have begun to feel hopeless, since after the last two (and apart from the unexpected *Monsignor Quixote* in 1982) he did not write another major novel. He was too old, too tired, and a great novel was now *almost* beyond him.

But then, on 1 September 1982, one month from his seventy-eighth birthday, he must have recovered some sense of hope, at least momentarily. He received out of the blue a letter from the Swedish Royal Society:

> As the Secretary-General of the Swedish Royal Society it is my honour to inform that you have been elected to Honorary Member of the Royal Society 1982.
>
> The Royal Society was founded 1901 by the Swedish King His Majesty Oskar II (1829–1907). Every year a committee of 12 persons elect very carefully 'a person of any category who during his or her lifetime, with his or her work, contributed in the development of humanity'. The committee consider that you fulfill the demands on account of the work you have done during your career as author.

Greene accepted the honour. Yet it made no difference. The next year, 1980, the Nobel went to the Polish poet Czesław Miłosz.

★

I tried to visit the Swedish 'scoundrel' in Stockholm in 1978. I wrote and made an appointment, but when I arrived at his home, a woman (I think his wife) told me, 'Dr Lundkvist is sick and cannot be interviewed', which, given the money I'd spent to make the journey from my home in England, made the day memorable to me.

Two others were more fortunate than I: Peter Lennon, who interviewed Lundkvist in 1980; and Miron Grindea in 1989. Peter Lennon's account of his interview appeared in *The Times* on 23 November 1980 and Miron Grindea's in a London-based literary magazine *Adam*, which he edited.

Lennon was a tough interviewer. At first he encouraged Lundkvist to talk about his background (about being originally very poor), and how he had educated himself. He learnt English the hard way, translating Virginia Woolf's *Orlando*. Lundkvist also told Lennon that he had travelled to Australia to meet Patrick White even before 'the Australians had heard of him'. Then quite suddenly Lennon changed tactics. From listening to Lundkvist's excited account of himself, he blurted out: 'Why didn't you give the prize to Graham Greene?' (This in the veiled underground world of the Nobel, where the process of decision-making was kept rigorously secret.)

Unexpectedly, and uncharacteristically for a discreet and leading member of the Swedish Academy, Dr Lundkvist immediately offered Lennon his reasons:

'Thirty years ago I was very impressed by him . . . I thought *The Power and the Glory* was a very good book. But I think his work has declined.'

'But Steinbeck (1962) got it 23 years after he wrote his last good book, *The Grapes of Wrath*, and Sholokhov (1965) wrote *And Quiet Flows the Don* nearly 40 years previously.'

'I know. But Greene is too popular,' he said sulkily. 'And anyway, he doesn't need the money.'

'That cannot be a condition,' I said. 'Most Nobel Prize winners are too well-known already and don't need the money.'

'Well, personally I will not vote for him,' Dr Lundkvist said exasperatedly.

The other powerful committee member was also the oldest – Dr Anders Osterling, aged ninety-six. He expressed his regrets about Greene:

'It is a pity England has been so neglected,' he said. 'I regret Graham Greene never got the prize. His name would have adorned our list very well.'

The youngest on the committee, Lars Forssel, aged fifty-two, echoed his senior: 'It was a great mistake that in the 50s they didn't give the Nobel Prize to Graham Greene.'

In his interview with Grindea, Lundkvist gave an entirely different reason. Lundkvist's attitude had not changed: it was still combative. When Grindea asked what had motivated his objection over the years, he received the extraordinary answer: 'Because he was Catholic.'

*

Well, they didn't give it to Greene in the 1950s in spite of three members of the judging committee suggesting that's when it should have been done. That was when Lundkvist claimed to have considered *The Power and the Glory* a 'very good book', though it could hardly have been seen as anything other than a work by a *Catholic* writer, and the damnable implication of what Lundkvist said to Grindea was that he didn't like Catholics. In any case, *The Power and the Glory* was published much earlier than the 1950s, in 1940 in fact, and we now know that the first novel of Greene's to be considered was *The Heart of the Matter*, published in 1948. There's something fishy here.

I do not think for a moment that Lundkvist ever intended to vote for Greene, or that Greene was, in his mind, even a possibility. Michael Meyer told me, and he told Greene, that Lundkvist was ever a determined enemy and had expressed himself most forcefully. 'Greene will never receive the Nobel Prize except over my dead body.' Well, Lundkvist won the battle royal. Greene died the spring before Lundkvist, who died in December.

Greene, I know, was bitter over Lundkvist's attitude, and he thought, as did Meyer, that an unspoken reason for the ostracism was Greene's affair with Anita Björk. There was a curious jealousy here. But I see this as just a further excuse, and it doesn't get to the source of Lundkvist's genuine hatred for Greene.

*

I suspect that Greene had forgotten an earlier event which I quoted in Volume Two, though I did not then tie it neatly to the Nobel debacle. I feel that Lundkvist couldn't help himself. The hatred for Greene was yawning deep, and stretched out for the duration of Lundkvist's life.

As early as October 1952 (perhaps around the date he said he was impressed by Greene's work), Lundkvist reviewed Greene's *The Living Room* when that play had its premiere in Stockholm. Lundkvist's dislike is palpable: it is prejudice run riot. As the review continues, his animosity is raging. If Greene had read the review, how could he have forgotten it?

Lundkvist admitted that there were times in the play when 'the theatre public were deeply moved', but stated that it troubled him when the audience 'tittered delightfully every time the priest on the stage spat out the word psychology or the name Freud'. This was contempt for a person Lundkvist admired. Further, he described the play as Catholic 'propaganda of the most vulgar type',

> to which is added artistic and intellectual cheating. The most dangerous and unpleasant thing about Greene's play is the way in which it attacks modern psychology. The means are clearly dishonourable – a number of foul blows below the belt.

Lundkvist felt that Greene disdained psychology. (He was mistaken of course.) More galling was that the theatre audience (*his* Swedish theatre audience!) shared what he saw as Greene's contempt for those who kept guard over their

> tangled complexes, dread elucidation and analysis . . . And yet it is psychology that we have to thank for the progress . . . made during the latter generations as regards candour, naturalness, inner freedom and increased consciousness.

Moreover the doctor in the play didn't command even the rudiments of general knowledge of psychology and clear reasoning which should counteract the priest's misleading mystifications. From that point on, his review becomes outraged, his fury welling up, and we recognise Lundkvist's hostility for both play and playwright. Not only is the play 'a monstrosity of anti-psychology', it is from start to finish 'sadistic in the name of human sympathy'. Sympathy becomes terrorism, it falsifies its claims 'so that only self-sacrifice is possible'. 'This Jesuistically exploited sympathy coerces, oppresses, lies and is used as rank blackmail. The result is the girl's suicide.'

> The one person in the company who is most able to cope with life [Rose] must be sacrificed in order that obsolete dogma and morbid hysteria shall triumph . . . What sort of victory has been won? Catholicism's claims to oppression have triumphed, the Church has been avenged against one who dared to escape her, reason and human feelings have been trampled underfoot. Mr Greene and his sympathizers should feel satisfied.

Lundkvist felt that there were few who refused to agree with 'this cynicism or perverse charlatanism'. Yet he believed that the play unmasked itself as 'a warning against Catholic distortion, its inhuman demand for sacrifice, its abuse of power behind its so-called solicitude for the soul'.

And Lundkvist's last blows?

Graham Greene's development (degeneration) has long been suspect. In this play he reveals himself as a morally dangerous writer in league with the darkest powers of present-day western reactionism.

When we recall the power Lundkvist wielded in the Swedish Academy, we cannot be surprised by his last sentence – his hatred is visceral: 'The plague flag should be raised over the Dramatic Theatre Studio.'[5]

50

Kudos in a Bundle

What a smack in the eye [the OM] is to those pedestrian Swedes.
— VICTOR, A FRIEND OF GRAHAM GREENE

A year after Catherine Walston's death in September 1978, Greene was made an honorary citizen of Anacapri. Greene behaved admirably that night of 18 October 1979: 'the ceremony – held, at Graham's request, at evening in the eighteenth-century church of San Michele . . . without press or publicity and in the presence of an invited audience – was simple, dignified, sincere. Graham . . . made his fine little speech and was glad.'[1] Promising he wouldn't keep his audience long, he came to the island, he said, just thirty years before,

> with no idea of staying more than a few days. Within hours I found the house *il Rosaio*, & since then I have lived part of every year there. More important I found at once two friends who made my life on the island a happy one – Gemma [owner of the restaurant] & Aniello Marinello [who looked after his property]. There is also friendship, affection, tenderness at first sight. Aniello opened the door of his home to me. I felt myself part of his family. Carmelina has been like a sister – I was going to say like a mother, but she is far too young for that.

He refers to Edwin Cerio's book on the magic of Capri:

> I know the magic of Mont Solaro. All my books for thirty years have felt the influence. Here in Anacapri, in 4 weeks I do the work of six months elsewhere. For me there is a quiet & happiness in Anacapri which I have found nowhere else in the world. I have been a restless traveller – in Africa, South America, the Far

East – I will always be restless, but Anacapri more than my native land is Home, & like a pigeon I always return.[2]

Mr Vacca, a Capri council member, when asked why Greene had written about so many places but never about Capri, replied: 'because only at Anacapri, he can contemplate a divine Nature without trying to discover the "infernal" aspects of most of a world which becomes more and more flat, more uniform, and where "all human illusions" become impossible'.

★

I'd promised Greene that wherever he had set a major novel, I would follow in his footsteps. This took me to Liberia, Sierra Leone, Thailand, North and South Vietnam, Hong Kong, Tokyo, Malaya, Kenya, Panama, Tabasco and Chiapas in Mexico, Barbados, Monte Carlo, Antibes, Switzerland, Argentina, Paraguay, Eire, Spain . . . In planning to make a trip to Africa on 23 February 1979, I telephoned Graham's sister Elisabeth in Crowborough, with news that I'd soon be off to Sierra Leone and Liberia (where Greene had been both before and during the Second World War). I was somewhat daunted by the upcoming journey, as I thought it would be a terrible one, especially the tremendous trek through Liberia.* I asked Elisabeth what would be the most opportune and authentic time to travel through Liberia, in reference to Graham's experiences. Her answer was distracted, that sharp mind of hers rattled. She told me that at 8 a.m. that morning Graham had undergone an operation lasting four hours. His physician, Lionel King-Lewis, had removed a malignant but localised tumour in his intestine. The cancer was caught early and had not spread. With relief in her voice, she added: 'Graham will recover.'

Graham had been conscious of a swelling only a week before his operation. A letter to me on 16 February 1979, must have been written immediately after it was discovered. In a letter to Yvonne, addressed 'Dearest love of my life' and dated 20 February, he speaks of the operation and, in case she is fearful, reassures her that it's 'nothing to worry about'. He describes the impending surgery: 'the polyp was very conveniently placed. A bit of intestine has to be cut & then the ends joined again. Four days of intravenous feeding & keeping very still to avoid pain as they have to cut through a muscle. Out of hospital in about 12 days. Operation is early

---

* Greene and his cousin Barbara undertook this dangerous trip in 1935, going to places where no white man had ever been seen before. (See *The Life of Graham Greene, Volume One*, and *Journey Without Maps*.) I travelled by jeep more than forty years later – a much easier mode. Graham and Barbara had walked through Liberia!

Friday morning . . .' And at the end of the letter, Catherine dead and gone: 'My darling, I love you so much & how good it will be to see you after this nasty spell. You have given me so much love & happiness over these 19 years which have been the best of my life.'

The operation took place at the King Edward VII Hospital for Officers. But Greene decided to return to a hospital in Paris. He had an ardent desire to move, which troubled his sister, though his arguments were sound: the National Union of Public Employees was on strike, and it would seriously affect hospitals, with no ambulances operating, no sheets cleaned, no food, no assistance for the doctors. He was not going to stay in a British hospital under these circumstances.

*

Greene's first offer of an award started an academic bell ringing that (almost) never seemed to stop. It came in 1962 from Cambridge University – a Doctorate of Letters (*honoris causa*). The public orator introduced Greene perspicaciously in Latin. Here are extracts from a translation by the classical scholar Professor Colin Wells. First, a reference to his entertainments that soothe and delight – 'mere enjoyment, pleasing indeed and welcome, but scarcely worthy of this academic solemnity':

> He displays the same force in his arguments, the same verisimilitude in his descriptions [as in his entertainments]; but now he sees deeply into the hearts of men, how they conduct themselves towards their own persons, towards their fellows, and finally towards God. He himself professes the Catholic teaching of the Church of Rome, but he is not a man who assigns the roles of the upright and of those who are good examples to others like himself, and of the depraved to those who disagree, but rather the other way round. Victims indeed we are, all living our lives under God, at the mercy of evil from forces both inside and outside ourselves; for us the Father himself willed that 'the way to worship should not be easy', and that only those who seek God, however feebly, have any hope of safety . . .
>
> Throughout the whole earth [he] seeks the material for his work and new themes for his novels. For whatever things everywhere touch mortal hearts, these he observes. For this he is read everywhere in the world, and being read, is praised.
>
> I present to you the illustrious author
> GRAHAM GREENE

After this, awards seemed to rain down upon him: the next from Balliol, in May 1963. Greene heard that a college meeting on 29 May

1963 passed a resolution: 'subject to your consent, you should be invited to accept an Honorary Fellowship of the College.'

But it wasn't until June 1979, some seventeen years after Cambridge's honour, that Oxford University offered an honorary Doctorate of Literature. Just as at Cambridge, Greene was introduced by a Latin citation hailing him as 'a most gifted novelist'. The long citation ends: 'I present to you Graham Greene, CH, a glorious pillar of the Republic of Letters, to be admitted to the degree of Doctor of Letters *honoris causa.*'

We have already seen his awards of an honorary Doctorate of Literature from the University of Edinburgh in 1967, and the Shakespeare Prize at Hamburg University in 6 June 1969. It would be tedious to list all the honours showered (or perhaps it might be said inflicted) upon him. Fearfully he once said to me: 'I want no more scalps', and he turned many down. Indeed, he stated: 'I want no more honours' a year prior to receiving the greatest honour that can come to an Englishman: the Order of Merit. He put it differently when Sir Brynmor Jones, Vice-Chancellor of the University of Hull, offered Greene the degree of Doctor of Letters in 1971. Greene refused on the grounds that he'd turned down Sussex University, and because he'd 'already received honorary degrees at Edinburgh and Cambridge, and to receive in absence would be like notching up marks on the handle of a revolver'.[3]

These gatherings never pleased Greene, but once he was roped in, he worked hard. He did accept the 1973 Thomas More Medal for *The Honorary Consul*.

Since this organisation is not well known in England, it was good that the popular Catholic magazine the *Tablet* explained to him that the Thomas More Bookshop, located in Chicago,

> is probably the best Catholic bookshop in the world . . . One of its major achievements is to have founded the Thomas More Medal annually awarded for an outstanding achievement in Catholic literature.

The editor of the magazine of the Thomas More Association was Joel Wells who was concerned whether Greene would accept it:

> I would be grateful if you could let me know . . . As I say, it requires absolutely no response on his part, but we mean it to honor him and not cause him displeasure.[4]

He added the names of some of the previous winners: 'Flannery O'Connor, Teilhard de Chardin, Daniel Berrigan, and Muriel Spark'.

Greene's answer was short but not without humour: 'I think the head-less corpse of Thomas More would turn in his grave, but naturally I would be only too glad to receive the medal and join the ranks of the previous winners.'

The citation which accompanied the medal begins by noting his forty-seventh book and his nineteenth novel:

> It is a story of a man's struggle with God – with a God whom he resists and even resents, but whom inevitably he cannot avoid because he resides within. No accolade or honour can possibly add to Mr Greene's stature as a writer . . .

Greene also received the Raymond Chandler medal, his acceptance written in his own hand, and recalling gladly that he had met Chandler once:

> I am much honoured by this medal, though I don't think I can compete with him as a mystery writer – perhaps our mysteries were different ones.
>
> I feel all the greater pleasure because this is an Italian prize & since 1949 I think all my books have been partly written in the tranquillity I have enjoyed in Italy.[5]

★

In 1964, Greene was approached about receiving the title of Companion of Literature. No writer can receive such an award (there are only ten Companions at a time) unless the Council of the Royal Society of Literature is satisfied that the recipient has achieved exceptional distinc-tion. In his invitation, the president of the society listed the current holders of the title as Edmund Blunden, Sir Winston Churchill, E. M. Forster, John Masefield, W. Somerset Maugham, Dame Edith Sitwell and Evelyn Waugh. At least four were friends of Greene's, Blunden, Maugham, Sitwell and Waugh, enough to warrant that he would, at least on this occasion, jump at the chance to join his friends. But Greene's answer nineteen days later was curt. He was honoured but stated, 'I hope you will forgive me if I decline the title.' And the last cut of all: 'I do not really feel at home in such ['such' is crossed out] a literary estab-lishment.' At the time, the president of the Society was Rab Butler, with whom he had sparred over the John Gordon Society,* which may have been the reason for his refusal. In 1984, Greene accepted. By then Butler was no longer in the picture having died two years earlier.

---

* See Chapter 5 'Is It Pornography?'.

In 1966, as we have seen, the Queen made Greene a Companion of Honour. The following year, by then living permanently in France, he was honoured by the French with the Chevalier of the Legion of Honour. Eighteen years later, his adopted country honoured him again by making him Commander of the Order of Arts and Letters – one of the highest awards for excellence in the arts. The award was presented by the French Minister of Culture who told him: 'We are touched, we are profoundly moved by the fact that you have chosen to live among us.'

*

In 1989, Graham was ill. He had a year and seven months to live.

The British Council produced an elaborate poster exhibition, mostly of Greene. They proposed 'to throw a small party on the 14th [of September], together with an associated book exhibition' which would accompany the posters to some of the countries that would be showing them. Harvey Wood, the director of the literature department, wrote delicately: 'I enclose a card and write to say how delighted we would be if by some miracle you could make it.'

But Greene couldn't come to the London exhibition because 'I shall be far away on September 14.' By that date, the chances are that he was already suffering from a blood disease. He was interested in the affair, of course, and asked if the British Council would simply send the posters to his sister's home in Crowborough: 'I will see them when I come over to visit her.'[6]

And not only did his own poster exhibition fail to lure him, dignitaries held no sway either. The famous came and went: Greene could not be moved. A letter he received from Seyid Muhammad on 26 February 1982 informed him that Indira Gandhi would be visiting the United Kingdom, and asked if he would like to come to Claridge's (hotel) on Wednesday, 24 March 1982 at 11.15 a.m., to have an informal coffee with the Indian Prime Minister. Written at the top of the letter in Elisabeth's hand the shortest ever R.S.V.P.: 'Rang & refused.'

*

When Greene was approaching his seventy-seventh birthday, the Oriental in Bangkok (the most famous hotel in the Far East) paid Greene homage by naming a suite after him. Two suites had already been named for authors: Joseph Conrad and Somerset Maugham.*

---

* Used by Joseph Conrad in those faraway days (it appears in his 1915 novel *Victory*), the Oriental was the base from which the foul Manager Schomberg operates. These days, it is a superlative hotel, which retains some of its more ancient rooms where Conrad stayed, and later Maugham in the 1920s. When I taught at the University of Malaya in Singapore in the 1970s it was still possible to hear stories of Maugham leaving a trail of unpaid bills.

On first being invited, he seemed willing to attend, though he mentions his age, possible date conflicts, and some doubts about his health. I think a primary reason for his hesitation was to entice the Oriental to invite Yvonne along:

> Would it be possible for you to extend your invitation to the companion who shares my life and who would be able to make the necessary funeral arrangements if I died in Bangkok! It would in any case be rather sad for me to occupy the Graham Greene suite alone.

By March the following year, however, he declines, saying that the 'slight warning note I sounded when I tentatively accepted your kind invitation is going to prevent me coming to Bangkok in October'. (He'd been advised after a medical check-up to call it off.) He suggests 'you would be better employed by a younger man! What about Paul Theroux?'[7] Failing that, Greene suggested his nephew, Graham Carleton Greene.

Theroux wrote to me on 9 November 2001 that he ultimately did go to the Oriental to act in Greene's stead but perhaps Graham felt he should have a family member there too. Graham Carleton Greene ultimately stood in for him. The Oriental asked Graham for two photographs of himself, and a short speech which Graham Carleton read on his uncle's behalf:

> I am highly honoured to have a Graham Greene suite in The Oriental of which I have very happy memories from nearly thirty years ago. Yes, very happy even though it was impossible to sit outside in the evening because of the mosquitos and a room with a bath meant a barrel on the balcony and a bucket to pour water over oneself into the barrel. This was all part of the atmosphere of The Oriental and I hope that its character has not changed with all the modern improvements and that it remains a hotel where almost anything may happen and one may meet almost anybody from a mere author to an international crook on his way elsewhere.

On 17 November 1981, nephew Graham reported to his uncle:

> Your speech was a big success and clearly thought to be extremely daring by the extremely respectable 70 or 80 guests. The point about international crooks at the Oriental went down very well.

Sadly, Graham's suite was in the new wing. It was accommodating, but offered little in the way of 'atmosphere':

Copies of your books are firmly under lock and key as I suppose businessmen, who would be the main users of the suite, are as likely to steal them as the occasional passing crook. I was shown the Somerset Maugham and Conrad Suites in the old wing which still does have some of the feel of the hotel you once knew and which was still recognisable on my last visit in the 60s and I would strongly recommend you to ask for one of them as your fee when you do eventually get to Bangkok. The hotel has been voted by American businessmen as the best in the world so they run to about 98% occupancy which I suspect means they will be fairly difficult about free stays.

★

From the Far East to the United States, Greene was being courted: Yale University wrote on 18 December 1986 to announce their wish to confer upon him the honorary degree of Doctor of Letters at the University's Commencement Exercises. The letter ended with their wishes 'to express to you how pleased we are to extend this invitation and how we hope that you will accept it'. But there was a way out for Greene, and he took it: the secretary referred to the Bylaws of the University requiring recipients of honorary degrees to receive them in person.

I am most honoured . . . [but] I very much regret that I am unable to accept as I would not be able to be sure of travelling to Yale to accept the degree in person.[8]

★

In his young days (in the 1940s), Greene received few awards. There was no tedium of prize after prize falling with a thump into his unwilling lap. An early example was the James Tait Black Memorial Book Prize, awarded every year by the Professor of English literature at Edinburgh University, to the author of the best novel 'or book of that nature published in the year': the year was 1948, the prize just £185, the book *The Heart of the Matter*, one of his most celebrated. The prize was well thought of, and the recipient could choose not to lecture which is what he did. In his reply Greene accepted the honour graciously: 'I, of course, accept the award with very great pleasure and with much appreciation of the honour paid to me.'[9]

Sometimes there seems little rhyme or reason for his acceptances or refusals.

★

In January 1980, Columbia University informed Greene that the Trustees invited him to receive the degree of Doctor of Humane Letters. He again declined: 'My health is at the moment rather uncertain, and I cannot undertake any long journeys.'

But at the same time he did accept a different, and perhaps to him more meaningful, award, from Longwood College, Farmville, Virginia. Refusing it at first (though proud to be nominated for the John Dos Passos Prize), he added: 'It is simply impossible for me to make the voyage as in my seventy-sixth year I have to live rather quietly.'[10] Longwood College did not give up easily. They replied, 'Wishing to make you welcome, I may have stressed too heavily . . . our hopes for your visit to the College . . . we understand fully the circumstances that prevent it, and wish to assure you that the award of the John Dos Passos Prize is in no way contingent upon it.' They ask to be allowed to consider him the winner and to send the prize and prize money directly to him. The letter ends: 'I join the Committee in their opinion that no living writer of English prose is more deserving of it.' They did ask him to write a short note to be read to the audience:

> When I was a young writer in the early thirties, John Dos Passos represented for me the contemporary American novel. I could 'take' his realism as I failed to 'take' the realism of Theodore Dreiser. His social commitment appealed to me all the more strongly because in England it was the period of the hunger marchers, and his experiments with form, for example, his use of newspaper cuttings, interested me as a novelist. Later after the war he became deservedly a European figure, admired, and a little imitated perhaps, by Sartre. I am very proud that you have chosen me as the first winner [over John Updike and Norman Mailer] of the Dos Passos Prize.

Other English universities, including Warwick, Lancaster and Liverpool, all sent invitations offering Honorary Doctorates of Letters: he refused most of them in the usual way, but in the case of Warwick, his reasons echo his refusal to Sussex University: 'Having received Honorary Degrees from Edinburgh and Cambridge and from my own University Oxford, I can't help feeling that to add to the number is a little like tuft-hunting.' The offers continued.

He turned down the distinguished Catholic Loyola University of Chicago in 1976 and the offer of an Honorary Doctorate from Loyola University, New Orleans, in 1978. In the latter case there was a twist. A seminar was also to be held on Greene by the Department of

Communications. This shocked Greene, their jargon appalled him: 'We propose an interdisciplinary seminar to study your complete signature. We believe your recent novel [*The Human Factor*] confirms that there is a coherent political and theological vision which transcends traditional morality and probes the mysteries of human motivation which link our private, interpersonal and social universes.'

> Loyola University wants to provide an American platform for your vision and hopes you could visit this quaint Latin city . . . to receive an Honorary Doctorate and attend the final sessions of the proposed seminar on Graham Greene: *The Politico-Moral Congruence of His Multi-Media Signature.*[11]

Greene refused the honour on the grounds that he had already refused one from their branch in Chicago and he didn't think he should discriminate. He was getting grouchy:

> I see that the Department of Communications is already confusing the ordinary person by its semantics. I have never seen signature used in the way you use it and I simply don't understand the title of your proposed seminar. Surely a Department of Communications should use the simplest and most precise language. Forgive this little criticism in return for your kindness.[12]

*

One of the most unexpected elections was an Honorary Membership, formerly held by 'the late G. K. Chesterton,' of the International Mark Twain Society. Greene's admiration for Chesterton prompted him to accept this particular tribute. At the time (15 March 1952), Harry S. Truman was the Honorary President and Winston Churchill the English representative.

Even the Athenaeum tried to grab him, obviously without checking their rosters, by first explaining that they sometimes selected 'a small number of persons of distinguished eminence in science, literature or the arts or for their public services . . . Would you please take this letter as an informal enquiry whether you would honour the Club by joining it by Special Election, which I need hardly say would give great pleasure to the General Committee and the Members of the Club?' Naturally 'a member so elected would not need to pay the Entrance Fee'.[13] Greene replied on 9 January 1979:

> I am highly honoured by your invitation, but I feel I must refuse it. I am a very unclubbable man and I am very seldom in England

and to tell you the truth I once resigned from the Athenaeum of which I was an ordinary member. However I do very much appreciate your invitation.[14][*]

★

In April 1981, Greene was visiting Jerusalem. It seems that he could never be offered an award without running into controversy.

The trouble started at the Jerusalem International Book Fair with the presentation of the Jerusalem Prize, offered every other year to the most distinguished of men and women, among them Bertrand Russell, Ignazio Silone, Jorge Luis Borges, Simone de Beauvoir, Octavio Paz, Isaiah Berlin – and Graham Greene. The award included a prize of $5,000.

At least two people criticised Greene's suitability. The first was Conor Cruise O'Brien, the Irish historian, editor-in-chief of the *Observer*, and mordant political columnist.[†] Speaking as a Catholic, O'Brien objected to Greene's early work on the special grounds that Greene did not seem to him to be the 'right kind' of Catholic. At the ceremony, O'Brien told a select audience of publishers and writers that Greene did not fit the prescription for the award, which was given on the grounds of dealing with 'the freedom of the individual'. O'Brien put his objections with subtle waywardness: 'I must confess that it would not have occurred to me unaided, that the freedom of the individual in society is what the writing of Graham Greene is all about. If he is expressing it, he is expressing it in a dark, complex, paradoxical way of his own.' This convert to Catholicism did not appeal to 'a born-and-baptised Catholic' like himself.

Harold Frisch, Professor of Literature, adds more weight to his criticism. He had looked at some of Greene's early work, *A Gun for Sale* (1936) and *Brighton Rock* (1938), and in the *Jerusalem Post* commented on the way Greene treated Jews in these novels:

There are few parallels in modern literature to the portraits of Sir Marcus, the Jew-devil, who, through murder and conspiracy, manipulates the fate of nations in *A Gun for Sale* or of Colleoni with his 'old semitic face' in *Brighton Rock* who 'owns the whole world – the cash registers, and the policemen and prostitutes' – to mention only two examples of the still-active power of the medieval archetypes in his writings.

[*] Hugh Greene was also invited to join by special election; he also refused.
[†] Greene and he met in Dublin 1976 – they talked and liked each other enormously.

The Mayor of Jerusalem, Teddy Kollek, who presented the prize, said: 'We knew beforehand that it would create an argument, but nothing that is worth doing doesn't create an argument.' Greene praised the givers of the prize:

> What strikes me more than anything about this honour is the generosity of spirit it shows in the judges. The tortuous history of English relations with Israel during the period of the mandate is not one of which an Englishman can be proud. Nor is the history of the Roman Catholic Church's relations with Jewry one of which a Roman Catholic can be proud.

He also criticised dogma, political and religious:

> The ideas of Marx wear out. Papal pronouncements are subtly modified. Even the international terrorist movement has its dissidents.

Greene praised the Mayor: 'Surely if anyone deserves this prize for the defence of the individual in society it is Teddy Kollek. He has defended the individual irrespective of race.'

But Greene had to answer Professor Frisch. Looking up the word in the Oxford English dictionary, Greene cited the definition of 'Semite' as a term that 'pertains to Arabs as well as Jews. What I find rather curious is that you are inclined too often to think that Semite means Jewish.' Greene is more successful in explaining the appalling character of Sir Marcus in *A Gun for Sale*: 'It was based on a real figure, a Russian Jew named Sir Basil, who was, in fact, a trader in arms . . . You can't be free entirely, as Jews, from undesirable characters, and Sir Basil was an undesirable character.'

To a minor degree *Brighton Rock* (1938) can also be considered anti-Semitic. Even as late as 1939, in *The Confidential Agent*, Greene describes Forbes/Furtstein with his 'raisin eyes', and 'domed Semitic forehead'. And Michael Shelden comments on *Brighton Rock*: 'The treatment of Colleoni and company is indeed a terrible strain on a great novel', and adds that 'the inescapable fact is that Greene's genius is marred by a wide streak of malice'.[15] Greene modestly and truthfully told Maria Couto in interview that some of his work could be perceived as being anti-Semitic:

> During those years we did not think in those terms, and I meant the term 'Jew' to be descriptive. When I reread it later because

44 Greene with Bryan Forbes in Antibes, 1981

45   Greene's last trip to
America, Georgetown
University, 7 October 1985

46   Greene with his
brother Hugh and sister
Elisabeth Dennys

47 'His Eminence,
Cardinal Greene',
from *Punch*

As They Might Have Been

IV GRAHAM GREENE

*THE crankiest Christian that ever was seen
Is surely His Eminence Cardinal Greene.
His creatures find s candal and degredation
The sole sure means to attain salvation.*

54 Finally at peace

the anti-Semitic idea was pointed out to me, I could see that it could be regarded as anti-Semitic.

Greene suggested the word 'tycoon' as a substitute, and added: 'It was not meant to be anti-Semitic.' But according to Shelden, 'The greatest absurdity is that someone needed to point out the problem to him.'[16]

But Greene's body of work throughout his life was enormous. Such an output should prove that he never had time to look over his shoulder at earlier books. Critics and students (and biographers) do that. Novelists move on and write fresh novels. Greene's generosity proves that he isn't anti-*anyone*. He is pro-victim. His secret benefactions, his willingness to fight for the underdog, had no limits.

Shirley Hazzard's graceful treatment of the subject of his anti-Semitism is gentle, wise:

> I don't believe that Graham was racist; nor, when we knew him, was he anti-Semitic . . . When – before its airing at his acceptance of the Jerusalem Prize in 1981 – the accusation of anti-Semitism in his early work was first publicly raised against Graham, he spoke to us of it, saying, as he had said previously, that he reread his past work with reluctance but had taken up the book most in question, *The Confidential Agent*, to see if the accusation held water. 'And yes, there is anti-Semitism in it. I don't believe I was anti-Semitic. I don't find it in myself, or in my past. But the thing was in the air, between the wars, an infection. Of course it would have been better not to fall for it at all. Many people didn't.'[17]

And Greene was reflecting his own times, his society. He was a novelist, and that is what novelists do. They walk in another's moccasins. They must allow their characters to have their own thoughts: how could a novelist speak with authority of a created character, his good, his evil, except by determining to take on board strange real selves? Great novelists are incessant creators in miniature; they hand out characters' motivations as God hands out noses: it's *subjective*. Shirley Hazzard again: 'To write fiction is to learn to inhabit other skins.' That should have been Greene's answer to critics. And, at the time of these early novels, anti-Semitism was rife throughout Europe, and to a lesser degree, in England. How could a great writer ignore what existed in society then? He created and used anti-Semitic figures because *they existed* in the world he was writing about. Distinctive novels must needs be inclusive. The powerful Jewish criminal, Sir Marcus, in *A Gun for Sale* existed in real life, and Greene, given the nature of *that* story, could not ignore him or change his origins – nor should he have.*

*

Early in January 1983, he was honoured with Panama's highest civilian decoration, the Grand Cross of the Order of Vasco Nuñez de Balboa. Named for the famous Spanish explorer who on one of his marauding expeditions climbed a peak and became the first European to look upon the Pacific Ocean (of which he promptly took possession for Spain), the device was bestowed at the National Palace.

It was next Nicaragua's turn, and Greene received his award from the hand of President Daniel Ortega in April 1987 (Greene in his eighty-third year). As in the case of Panama, Greene was offered the Sandinistas' highest award for literary achievement, the Ruben Dario Medal. According to the *San Antonio Express News*, 23 April 1987, Greene was inducted into the Order of Cultural Independence for his 'solidarity of the defense of the Nicaraguan national rights and his place in the fight against imperialist domination'. He received a standing ovation.

For an Englishman, there is perhaps no greater award than the Order of Merit. The *Guardian* of 11 February 1986 ran the headline: 'Graham Greene, by appointment'.

> Greene – viewed by almost everyone except the Nobel Prize judges as for over 40 years the world's greatest novelist – joins an order which has only 24 distinguished members eminent in the arts, sciences, politics or in human or intellectual achievement. They include his fellow artist, Sir Henry Moore, a member since 1966, Lord Olivier, who was appointed five years ago, Sir Isaiah Berlin, the Earl of Stockton [Sir Harold Macmillan] and Group Captain Leonard Cheshire, VC.

Two others were appointed: the inventor of the jet engine, Sir Frank Whittle, and Frederick Sanger, a double Nobel Prizewinner for chemistry for his discoveries about the structure of insulin, and for his work on nucleic acids.

In recalling that Moore had become a member of the order twenty

---

* There is another point, and Greene often made it, especially in *Ways of Escape*: 'It is a curious experience to read an account of one's own past written by – whom? Surely not by myself. The self of forty years ago is not the self of today . . . I read my own book, *The Lawless Roads*, as a stranger would.' (*Ways of Escape*, Lester & Orpen Dennys, 1980, p. 64.)

years before, and Olivier five, the journalist John Ezard asked the reason for tardiness in Greene's case, and offered the following:

> His long residence abroad. His frequent outbreaks of leftwing sympathy . . . his favorite causes over the years have ranged from Castro's revolution in Cuba to his recent defence of the Sandinista government in Nicaragua against US attempts to subvert it. He has also voiced sympathy for the master-spy Kim Philby's conflict of loyalties.

The OM was the personal gift of the Queen, entirely detached from political humbug. It was Britain's most exclusive club. He heard from his contemporaries. The honorary Secretary of the Eighteen Nineties Society, G. Krishnamurti, a friend of Sir John Betjeman,* wrote to tell Greene how pleased Betjeman would have been: 'I vividly recall his frustration, annoyance and even anger at quite a number of individuals and institutions for their indifference and timidity in some for failing to accord you proper public recognition.' And Krishnamurti expresses his admiration for Greene's achievement in beautiful rhetorical exaggeration: 'I personally feel that the Queen while honouring you has saved the nation from the greatest possible international ignominy.' Greene in responding admitted his pleasure and added (for Greene admired Betjeman): 'I think it completely wrong that your friend Betjeman did not get the same honour before he died.'[18]

Then came a voice from the past: Lord Walston wrote a short note, sad and wistful, offering 'Very many congratulations. I know you don't set much store by honours, but this one is really an honour. How glad Catherine would have been – tomorrow is her birthday.'[19]

And Lord Boothby (usually known as Bob Boothby), one of the greatest characters who ever graced the Houses of Parliament, wrote: 'At last our greatest living author has been given appropriate recognition. Warmest congratulations from one of his sincerest admirers.'[20] This was followed by a note from Alec Guinness addressed to 'My Dear Graham' 'Great rejoicing in this household, and indeed everywhere, over the OM. My congratulations. It should have happened half a lifetime ago. People still refer to *Mgr Quixote* with enthusiasm, which pleases me no end.'[21]

John Mortimer also sent congratulations, saying: 'I hope it was as much a pleasure to you as it was for your many admirers to hear about. Anyway, no honour could have been more entirely deserved.' But Mortimer had to come back to business:

---

* Betjeman listed himself in *Who's Who* as 'poet and hack' (and hater of bad architecture): 'Come friendly bombs, and fall on Slough. It isn't fit for humans now.'

I saw *Monsignor Quixote* and thought it beautifully directed and acted, a most moving piece. I do rank it very high among your works, and I was never disappointed. Alec was better than I've seen him for some time, and Leo superb I thought. He's coming back from Australia to do some more Rumpole this year, so we'll both have the benefit of him.

Much love from us both,
John*22

Michael Foot, one of those rare politicians, intelligent *and* honest, chimed in:

We can't let this moment pass without letting you know how over-joyed so many are by your OM. It is the best honour of all, & may be the only one you would accept. Anyhow, the decision has given widespread pleasure to those who know that never since *Brighton Rock* & even before – have you failed to stand against inhumanity in all its manifestations, against all powers & principalities.23

More telling, the comparison between the OM and the Nobel Prize by a friend. His name is given only as Victor:

What a smack in the eye the Award is to those pedestrian Swedes. And, by the way, how splendid that it coincided with the fall of Baby Doc! [Papa Doc's son] God has His Jokes!24

Michael Mewshaw sent felicitations, linking the OM with the fall of Duvalier. The happy coincidence was not lost on Greene I'm sure.25

And Greene's one-time lover Jocelyn Rickards, one of the most exciting women in London, wrote to express her pleasure:

I'm very glad about your OM, although it's taken such a long time coming that I rather think one should congratulate the Queen on catching up with her reading.

Now I'm going to concentrate on the Nobel prize, although if offered perhaps it would be more enjoyable to ram it back down their throats, although the money is always useful.26

---

* Guinness and Mortimer are referring to the TV film of *Monsignor Quixote* which was an exceptional success and basically, a two-man show – Alec Guinness as the Monsignor, and Leo McKern as the Communist Mayor. McKern acted brilliantly as Mortimer's Rumpole – almost to the point where he couldn't take any other part. But he did, and successfully, as Mayor Sancho, in *Monsignor Quixote*.

The Economist compared the relative significances of the OM and the Nobel:

> Men and women have to be very grand to get an OM. For those in the know it carries more kudos than a mere title – though 18 of the 24 living OMs have one of those too. Members of the Order can be anything so long as they excel at it. Music will do (Elgar, Vaughan-Williams), or science (Lister, Rutherford), or literature (T. S. Eliot, Hardy), or statesmanship (Churchill, Lloyd-George). Even odd foreigners qualify (Dwight Eisenhower, Mother Teresa) as honorary members . . . There has also been a shipful of admirals, the choreographer Sir Frederick Ashton, and Florence Nightingale.[27]

The Times, in its editorial about Greene, made the following unexpected comment:

> It is easy to believe that his work will be read a century hence, but will readers then accept Greeneland as reality? A strange world, my masters, they may say. In the real world due honour has been done to GRAHAM GREENE by his admission to the Order of Merit. Next the Nobel Prize? It is due.[28]

51

A Kinder, Gentler Moscow

... a nice smile, but he has iron teeth.
— ANDREI GROMYKO

GREENE travelled to Moscow once in 1986 and twice in 1987, after not having visited that city since 1961. It took a Gorbachev to bring him back. In interview I noted that Greene never prepared for my questions, because he had his life at his fingertips. After his 1986 trip to the Soviet Union, over the phone he talked to me, and the conversation was happy — *he* was happy — about his visit. However, he didn't answer my questions directly.

One of the latter visits to Moscow was not made to buttress Soviet society. Greene went to participate in a great peace jamboree, part of Gorbachev's radical attempt to make serious changes in a communist society.

Gorbachev was a man of immense will and skill. Mrs Thatcher said of him: 'I like Mr Gorbachev. We can do business together.' His friend Andrei Gromyko declared, when proposing him to the Supreme Soviet as party leader in 1985: 'This man, Comrades, has a nice smile, but he has iron teeth.' Gorbachev swiftly made his presence felt. Auberon Waugh pointed out what an incredible change it must have been for the ordinary Russian citizen to go 'from living a lie to being able to face the truth: from not daring to speak out ... to being able to discuss things openly'.

Greene was chosen to give a speech at the close of the Peace Conference held in Moscow in February 1987, with close to a thousand delegates. He delivered a sympathetic speech. Greene had become so popular in Moscow that he shared the podium with Mr Gorbachev. When they met, Gorbachev shook Greene's hands and said: 'I've known you for years.'

However Greene faced criticism by English journalists for going, and also for writing so supportively (and some might say flatteringly) in the introduction to Kim Philby's book *My Silent War*. Suddenly the militant in Greene was born again in Moscow, invoking a fiery rhetoric, very different from the cool language of his novels:

> Roman Catholics are fighting together with the Communists and working together. We are fighting together against the death squads in El Salvador. We are fighting together against the Contras in Nicaragua. We are fighting together against General Pinochet in Chile. There is no division in our thoughts between Roman Catholics and Communists.

This use of rhetorical parallelism is unlike anything I've read elsewhere in Greene. At our last meeting, he recalled to me how he had turned towards President Gorbachev and spoken seriously, almost as if they had been alone together, saying: 'I have a dream that, before I die, there will be an ambassador of the Soviet Union at the Vatican giving good advice.' And he added: 'There was Gorbachev, smiling at me like anything.' I smiled too in interview but did not comment, for I thought it pie in the sky, the illusory prospect of future benefits.[*]

Greene was fiercely criticised in a London newspaper for his passionate desire to praise all things Soviet. The *Sun* suggested that all his books, and Greene himself, should be dumped in Moscow.

★

The great Peace Conference inaugurated by Gorbachev was billed as 'The International Forum for a Nuclear-Free World for the Survival of Humanity'. A sceptical account appeared in *Time*, stressing the personalities there:

> Over there was Norman Mailer chatting with Yoko Ono. Through the lobby strode Gregory Peck wearing a name card. Gregory Peck with a name card? Claudia Cardinale was a stunning sight in a tailored black-and-white-striped suit. Peter Ustinov moved grandly about, with all the bearing and intonation of one of his best-known characters, Inspector Hercule Poirot. 'I can't believe it,' said an awed American tourist as she gawked around the lobby of the Kosmos Hotel. 'This could be Hollywood.'

---

[*] Greene's comments were given in the atmosphere of the peace conference, but even so, they must have seemed a poetic absurdity, as he seemed to be ignoring the bottomless suspicions that existed then between Catholics and Communists. Though his speech was warmly applauded by the Russian audience, it must have been received tepidly by everyone else, as open-minded as they all were.

Then came a quick reference to people known worldwide:

> Celebrity bashes are not the Kremlin's forte, but last week's coming-out party for Mikhail Gorbachev was worthy of Lifestyles of the Rich and Famous. The stars that shone at the glamorous gala ranged from literature (Graham Greene) through economics (John Kenneth Galbraith) to fashion (Pierre Cardin).

All these rich or famous (or both) 'were willing', says *Time*, 'to give a polite hearing to the Kremlin's pitch for peace'. And the list goes on, 'stargazing' at the 'cavernous marble lobby of the Kosmos Hotel where Soviet dissident Andrej Sakharov shuffled between round-table discussions'. Gorbachev, during one reception, 'shook hands with Yoko Ono'; 'Mailer quipped that he had "cemented a peace pact" over dinner with novelist Gore Vidal, with whom he has frequently feuded.'*[1] And Greene had a different view of the Kosmos Hotel – not luxurious (as reported by *Time*), but, as he told Kim and Rufina Philby, 'Terrible cockroaches scuttling in all directions and full of very dodgy characters.'[2]

Fay Weldon was there and wrote an account, drenched in irony:

> During the eighties I used to be a member of a team which went on 'cultural exchanges' to the Soviet Union at the behest of the Foreign Office: when relations were good we'd go over: when they froze we'd be withdrawn. When we got there we'd sit round making speeches with the Moscow Writers Guild.
>
> In the autumn of [1986] I got a telegram which I thought was some kind of *Readers Digest* exercise: offering a two-week holiday in Yalta. I binned it and a week later had a phone call from the MWG [Moscow Writers Guild]: the telegram had contained an invitation to a conference of intellectuals from Gorbachev – how to break the East-West arms deadlock – the two weeks in Yalta being the reward. I said okay to Moscow but not to Yalta . . .
>
> The Foreign Office tried to warn me off: 'It'll be all Mir, Mir, Mir (Peace, Peace, Peace, while preparing for war); Iris (Murdoch) isn't going, (not officially sanctioned, in other words) Graham Greene is – he runs a whisky factory these days, you know – (their way of saying he was an alcoholic, I assumed) – but I went all the same. Only two from Britain came – a communist journalist and me. Norman Mailer and Kris Kristofferson and various film stars from

---

* In a letter to me of 28 July 2001 Mailer wrote: 'The conference itself was big and full of liberal hope and relatively empty but for the real hope of all the Russians who were there – that was moving.'

the States were there as I remember. We were the writers: the scientists and journalists had their own sessions: we conferenced for two long days. (No such thing as a free lunch, the MWG told me when I got there: you have to get the chairman's attention and make a speech: it doesn't matter what about, you're our nomination, just so you're heard and noted. I managed.) Nobbled by the Free Speechers and the feminists before I left I was also delegated to a rights of man subcommittee where we (or rather it turned out me) had to re-write the world charter in three hours. I had an African chief on one side with fifty-three wives, which made the feminist approach complicated, and an Iranian on the other protesting about cannibalism on the battle front and I found myself solemnly recording 'the right not to be eaten after death'.

After two days of this sort of thing there was a plenary session in which the various congregations presented their conclusions. Graham Greene was our spokesman. He ignored our pieces of paper totally and instead made an impassioned plea for dialogue between the Kremlin and the Vatican, which was not something which had arisen in our discussions at all. And he had been drinking.

I don't think anyone minded much, not only because we hadn't been able to make any dent in the apparent impasse between East and West, and Greene's speech was as good as any other, if not better, because it became apparent in Gorbachev's speech that he was using the occasion to announce the end of the Cold War. The Communist Party, he told us, we 'world intellectuals', had come to the conclusion that war was not the continuation of revolution by other means: war had become too expensive. Russia could not afford it.

Mrs Thatcher went over the next year, Anglo-Soviet relations were restored, the Cold War came to an end, and the Foreign Office forgave me. In our discussions it hadn't occurred to us that the Soviet Union might just totally unilaterally back off.

★

I have to go back again to 4 September 1967, to when Greene (anarchist? socialist? near-communist?) suddenly bloomed as an anti-Soviet, in his letter to *The Times*:

This letter should more properly be addressed to *Pravda* and *Izvestia*, but their failure to publish protests by Soviet citizens at the time of the Daniel-Sinyavsky trial makes it doubtful that mine would ever appear.[3]

Greene was angry, as we've seen, over the internment of these two important writers because they had published their respective books in the West, when their books were not acceptable in their own country because of the legitimate criticisms they made. Greene had an original suggestion which must have made true-born Soviet communist officials profoundly angry. In any case, we know now that Greene, a writer once wholly admired by them, at this time was not to be spoken of because of his criticism of the Soviets in the West. Writes Greene:

> Like many other English writers I have royalties awaiting me in the Soviet Union, where most of my books have been published. I have written to the Secretary of the Union of Writers in Moscow that all sums due to me on these books should be paid over to Mrs Sinyavsky and Mrs Daniel to help in a small way their support during the imprisonment of their husbands.

The same letter went on: 'I have no desire to make use myself of my royalties by revisiting the Soviet Union so long as these authors remain in prison, however happy my memory of past visits.'

This letter brought a courageous reply from, of all people, Kim Philby. No one could understand Greene's ostracism better than he. The letter appeared with Moscow stamps on it, the first correspondence to Greene since Philby defected. He wrote his approval of Greene's decision and hoped conditions might change, 'not only because what you did is just and honourable, but because it might result for us in some unexpected gratification, some meal together, for instance, when we could talk like in old times'.

Greene kept his word about not returning to Moscow under adverse conditions for writers, and it was nineteen years later, in 1986, that he made his second visit. It's clear that he and Philby, in finally meeting, enjoyed each other's company. Rufina Philby, Kim's young Russian wife, recalls meeting Greene at their home, after Genrikh Borovik, a well-known Russian journalist and President of the Soviet Peace Committee, arranged for them to get together. (Incredibly Rufina had learned English by using *The Heart of the Matter* as her textbook.)

Soon after Rufina met Philby, they talked of Greene. Seeing a picture of Greene in 1970 in *The Times*, she pointed and said: 'He's a fantastic writer.' Kim replied quietly: 'He's a friend of mine.' Here, sixteen years later, she was to meet this famous man. She went downstairs to greet Greene 'in a state of anxious excitement'.

Each man, but especially Philby, held each other in high regard. It had been over thirty-five years since they'd seen one another, yet in a matter of minutes (after they'd, as Rufina puts it, 'hugged, clapping each other on the back in embarrassment and pleasure') they 'chatted like close friends', and within a short time they were 'remembering mutual acquaintances, laughing as they shared old memories'.

The Greene sitting opposite me was nothing like the Greene I had imagined. I was captivated straightaway. He was nice, delicate, soft-spoken, with the clear, naïve eyes of a child.

But the two were buddies there in Moscow. Rufina describes it: 'Twenty years later [Kim's] hopes were fulfilled, the two of them sitting around a table in a Moscow flat knocking back vodka, Greene's favourite drink.' Their talk turned spiritual. Philby was pleased that Greene was also burdened by religious doubts. Rufina takes a quotation from Greene's *Monsignor Quixote*, a phrase which deserves to be famous: 'Sharing a sense of doubt can bring men together perhaps even more than sharing a faith.'

Astonishing, almost as if the communist mayor was Philby (too late in the day doubting his communist faith) and Monsignor Quixote was Greene (late in his day, doubting his Catholic faith). Certainly Philby (Rufina tells us) 'rated *Monsignor Quixote* as one of Greene's best books'. At the end of that first night together, Philby walked Graham to his car. Upon returning, he said of Graham to his wife: 'He is burdened by doubt as well.' From having betrayed his own country, having worked might and main against England, Philby was having doubts, perhaps profound doubts. His last years must have been a kind of hell. Both men were ageing and Greene said to Philby: 'You and I are suffering from the same incurable disease – old age.'[4]

Philby needed Greene: he had no other friends from his past. His English friends had turned away. His special friend, Malcolm Muggeridge (as is evident in Gregory Wolfe's *Life of Muggeridge*) ripped strips off him as a traitorous dog: 'His treachery was abominable because it was directed against all the people he worked with for years. Philby was a cad's cad.'[5]

Rufina Philby saw Greene for the last time five months after her husband's death in 1988. Greene was marking his eighty-fifth birthday in Moscow. (He was actually coming up for his eighty-fourth. He explained: 'At my age a year ahead might be too late.') According to Rufina, the Institute of World Literature wanted to mark Greene's eighty-fifth birthday by a special ceremony, and Greene took it a bit early.

On this occasion, Greene brought Yvonne along. After the ceremony they took Rufina home, she still suffering terribly the loss of Kim. He had been an enemy to everyone in the Western world, and now he was gone; a victim of that star of death invisibly embroidered on all our foreheads at birth.

After Greene's . . . birthday celebrations, he, Yvonne and I had spent another evening together at the House of Writers . . . We said goodbye on that same stretch of pavement where we had first met. I remember, as though he had just spoken, Greene's last words to me: 'Talk to Kim before you go to sleep. You'll feel better. I don't know if there is anyone up there,' he said pointing to the sky, 'but if there is, he will hear you. And tell Kim I love him.'[6]

Rufina had a premonition that they had said their last goodbyes, as indeed they had. But, as old as Greene was, the ground had not yet begun to crumble beneath him.

★

In his letter of protest at the imprisonment of Daniel and Sinyavsky in 1967, Greene had ended with a somewhat ludicrous statement:

This letter must in no way be regarded as an attack upon the Union. If I had to choose between life in the Soviet Union and life in the United States of America, I would certainly choose the Soviet Union.

He came back to this statement many times, arguing that he was referring to the fact that in America, writers made money, but no one was interested in writers. In Russia there was a powerful interest in writing, to the point that you were very likely to suffer internment. Communist dictatorships took poets and novelists very seriously: of course, a closed society fears the outspokenness of writers. They are dangerous to the continued existence of that form of society. A writer might turn a country around and destroy the system, the dictatorship of the proletariat might suddenly find itself doomed by the proletariat.

★

In his excellent work *Nightingale Fever* (1981), Ronald Hingley deals with the poetry of four great Russians: Osip Mandelstam, Marina Tsvetayeva, Boris Pasternak and Anna Akhmatova, their lives and deaths. Hingley tells us the oldest story, the various ways each died.

Poetic genius Mandelstam was imprisoned by Stalin and disappeared forever. It had its beginning in the usual communist manner. The famous poet Marina Tsvetayeva 'vainly search[ed] for a hook from which to hang herself'.[7] On Sunday, 31 August 1941, she did so.

Fear and mutual suspicion were rampant in Russia then. What if Greene, given his urgent desire to unearth instances of injustice and living in Soviet Russia (as was his oft-stated wish), had discovered an injustice? If he had revealed it, would not a neighbour or an enemy quickly have reported him, especially in that hothouse of intrigue on which the Stalins of this world rely? He would have been found out. He would have been jailed.

As a youngster, Greene longed to die. Greene would never have needed to worry about reaching that end during Stalin's long reign. He might die at his own hand, as did Tsvetayeva, or broken down as in the case of Mandelstam, the Greene mind thrashing about with the conviction that every morsel of food was poisoned. He could be framed for treason, or his children incarcerated. Anna Akhmatova's son (not guilty of writing poetry, not guilty at all) was imprisoned and punished just because he was *her* son. She felt she had to take the course of personal humiliation, composing poetry praising Stalin in the vain hope her son would be released. She wrote these shocking and dishonest words: 'Where Stalin is, there too are Freedom/Peace, and Earth's Grandeur'. There was faint hope that Stalin might release her son from prison. He did not. The son was released after Stalin's death.

What would have been Greene's humiliation, if he were in her place, having to write such God-awful droppings? They could have deprived him of a needed ration card, or expelled him from the Moscow Writers Union, which would mean that whatever he wrote could not be published. Or perhaps, when he was writing in his own minute hand, the authorities could have sent the KGB to entertain themselves with an unfinished novel on his desk: they'd pick it up before his eyes, and shred it. Or Greene, like Pasternak, might have written a novel in secret, and then perhaps he might have been offered the Nobel Prize, and have had to refuse.

Or he might have been forced to find someone he could trust (that would have been difficult in Stalin's day) so he could dictate his 200–500 words a day to someone who would memorise the story, as did the cosmonaut who learnt *Our Man in Havana* by heart.* This is

---

* When Anne-Elisabeth Moutet interviewed Greene for the *Sunday Telegraph*, 10 May 1987, she noticed a tattered paperback copy of *Our Man in Havana*. When in Moscow, Greene had met a Russian cosmonaut. Greene was much touched that the cosmonaut had taken his novel *Our Man in Havana* into space. Cosmonauts were allowed to take only three books, and on that trek, he read Greene's novel three times. He handed it back to Greene with the following inscription: 'There are books which you forget as soon as you've read them, there are some which make you read a second and a third time; and as to this one, I've been reading it all my life, both on Earth and in Space. I've learnt it by heart; while in Havana, I specially visited all the places described here. This is the most valuable thing of mine, and I give [it] back to you in gratitude.'

what Akhmatova was forced to do, to whisper her lines to a trusted friend 'in fear [as Ronald Hingley tells us] of hidden microphones, and once memorised, the manuscript had to be burnt in a stove for the safety of the poetess and the memoriser'.

Could Greene's statement of choosing Russia over the United States have been thrown off without reflection, a thoughtless mouthing of words? I doubt it.

> I would certainly choose the Soviet Union, just as I would choose life in Cuba to life in those southern American republics, like Bolivia, dominated by their northern neighbour, or life in North Vietnam to life in South Vietnam.

Graham is knee-deep in deliberate political folly.

★

Greene was fiercely criticised for his passionate desire to praise all things Soviet. And his fraternising with an infamous British traitor – and in a sense a traitor to America too, since Philby distributed American as well as British secrets to the Soviets – did not go unnoticed in the British press. Perhaps the most extended attempt to deliver a knockout blow appeared on 5 September 1987 in the *Daily Mail* from A. N. Wilson, harshly ethical, but a rollicking account. It's vituperative if you don't take it too seriously, more terrifying if you do. Wilson is saying, in effect, a pox on both men.

The title of Wilson's article is telling: 'Graham Greene and a Companion of Dishonour'. One thing is certain – Wilson has no admiration at all for anything Greene has done in his life – certainly not his CH award, nor his novels – which Wilson in effect tells us are puerile in the eyes of 'those like myself who regard Greene as "the most grotesquely over-praised writer of the Twentieth Century"'.

Wilson speaks at length about the code of the public schools. And he explains to his *Daily Mail* readers (many, no doubt, working men) the code among the privileged classes, the old boy network. But the code is misapplied:

> By certain codes of conduct there could even be said to be something noble in Mr Greene's refusal to drop an old friend just because he happens to be a traitor who betrayed agents to their death . . . In the world of public school from which Mr Greene has never really escaped there is or used to be a code of heroic friendship. If you were friends with a chap you went on being friends even when all the other chaps said he was a rotter. Even

748

if he . . . was actually expelled from school for misconduct. This code to a large degree continues into grown-up life for a high proportion of middle-class Englishmen. A friend goes on being a friend however badly he has behaved.

And he goes on to describe Greene's position and class, and argues that the code is attractive but 'less attractive when you see it at work in terms of a privileged class looking after its own'. He uses as an example the British cryptologist Geoffrey Prime, who handed secrets to the Russians, less important than those Philby dealt with, now still in jail. 'He is not privileged with such marvellous friends . . . He was lower middle class.' But surely if Philby had not taken flight he also would have been imprisoned for many years, or even shot – his public school background would not have saved him.

Wilson himself had the most privileged education, going to Rugby, one of England's best-known public schools, founded in 1567. Greene went to a minor public school (but one founded in 1541), good in its way, having had excellent headmasters and staff over many years, not least Greene's own father. But no one would know the code better than Wilson.

Wilson plays with the idea of Greene in Moscow drinking pink gins (Greene only drank vodka) with Philby: 'it will all feel much as it did when they drank pink gins together in clubs and bars in the parish of St James SW1'. As we've seen, Wilson is spot-on as to where Greene and Philby drank in those days of the Second World War. But then Wilson stresses the enormous political difference:

> Moscow isn't the parish of St James. And Philby is not just a naughty boy who was thrown out of school for smoking behind the gym. He is a dangerous traitor.

Wilson goes on to excoriate Greene's behaviour:

> Having a holiday with Philby is morally on par with having a holiday with Dr Goebbels while this country was at war with Nazi Germany.[8]

Auberon Waugh answered this pronouncement with the following in the *Spectator*, on 12 September 1987:

> Fiddlesticks. The only 'secrets' involved are secrets about keeping secrets. Perhaps a few secrets-freaks murdered each other as a result of Philby's defection, but that is their nature. There is no

earthly reason why Graham Greene should not visit his old chum in Moscow, if that is what he wants.

It is here that Waugh expressed his fears that Greene might leave the country to finish his days in Moscow.

Greene might be goaded into one last, desperate practical joke. At eighty-two he has little to keep him in the West, beyond his books and his flat in Antibes . . . I see the temptation for him to do a Solzhenitsyn in reverse, fleeing Thatcher's oppression and [A. N. Wilson's] persecution to spend his last years – possibly only months – in Moscow.

And there might be a reason for this. The *Evening Standard* gives us one:

The novelist Graham Greene has just received a tribute from a fervent admirer: member of the Moscow branch of his fan club, Mikhail Gorbachev.

The 83-year-old writer travelled to Russia this week to collect an Honorary Doctorate from President Gorbachev's alma mater, the Moscow State University . . . It wasn't all their [the University authorities'] own idea, though; that honour, I hear, must go to Comrade Mikhail.

The veteran story teller and practised mischief maker visited the USSR three times last year and likes Gorbachev even more than he likes obscure left wing South American generals, which is saying something.

'I want to help you,' Greene declared when he first met the Russian leader. 'I want peace and freedom,' replied Gorby. It was love at first sight.

Greene came to the peace conference with a strong sense of its importance. Geoffrey Wheatcroft records in the *Daily Telegraph* (17 February 1987) that a journalist colleague suggested to Greene that the Forum 'was a publicity stunt of which ordinary Russians could not possibly get an honest account'. Wheatcroft tells us Greene 'was much miffed', for Greene believed in Mr Gorbachev, and the future proved Greene right.

*

I have a last word about Philby and Greene. Greene wrote the intro-duction to Philby's book *My Silent War*, published first in England. It didn't appear for many years in Russia, much to Philby's chagrin. Philby must have suffered years of agony and rage, for he had hoped to strengthen his position in the Soviet Union by its publication. But Philby had never received the trust he'd anticipated, or the importance he desperately wanted, even while he stayed true to his own country's enemies.

Greene, in all the time I knew him, never lost his temper at my hundreds of questions. Never, except once. It was on the occasion I mentioned Philby. I began by discussing again how his schoolboy friend (Wheeler, called Watson in his autobiography *A Sort of Life* (1971)) was his greatest betrayer.*

I got round to Philby surreptitiously: 'You remember Wheeler, how he betrayed and humiliated you to the extent that you couldn't forgive him.' Greene's blue eyes were all attention. His hatred for his betrayer was, I felt, still intense, and he wrote: 'I found the desire for revenge alive like a creature under a stone.'⁹ Yet Greene did not seek revenge. In fact he thought that if it hadn't been for Carter and Wheeler, he would never have become a writer, wouldn't have tried so hard.

I made a comparison between Wheeler and Philby, and told Graham that however painful it must have been for a sensitive boy of thirteen, still I wanted to quote to him a part of his introduction to Philby's book *My Silent War*: 'He betrayed his country – yes, perhaps he did, but who among us has not committed treason to something or someone more important than a country.' Graham got the drift of my thoughts. He didn't speak, just nodded. But I ignored the importance of country and turned to the importance of the agents Philby had trained.

Being Philby, he must have got to know the freshly employed agents well. They'd have become friends; only he knew they were to be sent off to Albania. He also knew that he had imparted the information to Moscow so when his agents arrived they'd be caught and shot.

I also added that, I assumed that over time, weren't there hundreds caught?

---

* What brought Greene to crisis was the theft of his diary which Wheeler stole from his locker or desk and passed on to his enemy Carter. To boys his age, it was almost a crime to read (and write) poetry, so when Carter read out loud passages from his private diary in class, he was devastated. There are too many references in his fiction and travel books not to know of these jibes: 'It played on my nerves . . . like being the one unpopular boy at school . . . "Oh, do just look at this," he crowed. ". . . I'll read you some. It's priceless. 'Beastly unhappy to-night. Everyone teasing as usual.' Diddums then."'

Don't you think this is not a betrayal of a country but the betrayal of friends, a betrayal that led to their deaths? He surely would have been much more worthy a candidate for revenge, perhaps like a creature under a stone you speak of, rather than Wheeler.

Greene was very angry. His fascination with betrayal in his novels did not reach the point of rejecting Philby. 'You'd think that despite the loyalties we bear to friends and lovers, there would come a time when the act committed is too great to be forgiven, or forgotten ...' I stopped there for his face was beet-red. He told me firmly that I didn't know Philby. That was strictly true, but he knew I'd corresponded with him.

His answer: 'Still YOU DON'T KNOW HIM. AND CANNOT JUDGE.'

Philby *did* have friends he'd worked with killed: he had blood on his hands. This last I did not repeat.

52

Boxing with Burgess

Them there are fightin' words.
– AMERICAN FRONTIERSMAN

I was astonished when I heard that Graham Greene and Anthony Burgess, once friends, were in the midst of a feud. I thought at first it was a publicity stunt – Graham was capable of playing such games.*
I rang Graham's sister for the real story: 'It's true.' she said. 'It's a real battle. Graham thinks it's . . . jealousy.'

Greene and Burgess, two brilliant novelists, at loggerheads? It seemed juvenile to carry on private battles in public; just fodder for gossip columnists.

It began with a telephone call to Greene from a stranger. Greene rang back and was told that Burgess had attacked him on the French television programme *Apostrophe*, and continued it in the magazine *Lire*. This stung Greene to the quick. He wrote Burgess a letter which only exacerbated the quarrel:

My dear Anthony Burgess,
    I hear you've been attacking me rather severely on . . . *Apostrophe* because of my great age and in . . . *Lire* because of my correspondence

---

* I remember once when I was at Graham's sister's house to interview him, Rodney Dennys, her husband, asked me a personal question. As soon as I'd answered, Greene followed up quickly with another, followed by another by Rodney. In no time at all I realised I was undergoing a tennis match back-and-forth form of third degree. They were trying to get a confession out of me. Of course this wasn't real – it didn't go on for more than a few minutes, and there was laughter at the end of it, with Greene saying: 'I think Norman's earned a scotch and soda.' I told them perhaps I'd bring a legal friend next time to try to 'shoot the two of you down'. More laughter. But the fact is that Greene hated being interviewed and was often gloomy before I arrived when he knew he had to go through the process of being questioned. He was giving me a taste of my own medicine.

with my friend Kim Philby. I know how difficult it is to avoid inaccuracies when one becomes involved in journalism but as you thought it relevant to attack me because of my age (I don't see the point) you should have checked the facts. I happen to be eighty-three not eighty-six. I trust you will safely reach that age too. [Burgess did not.]

In *Lire* you seem to have been quoted as writing that I had been in daily correspondence with Philby before he died. In fact I received ten letters from him in the course of twenty years. You must be very *naif* if you believe our letters were clandestine on either side. Were you misinformed or have you caught the common disease of journalists of dramatising at the cost of truth?

Never mind. I admired your three earliest novels and I remember with pleasure your essay on my work in your collection *Urgent Copy*, your article on me in May in the *Sunday Telegraph* and the novel (not one of your best) which you dedicated to me.[1]

This last aside must have stung.

I found the lively piece in the June 1988 edition of the magazine *Lire*, where Burgess was interviewed by Pierre Assouline. It is wonderful to watch his quick answers. His language seems to be in flight, but truth is often skewed, flung aside for the quick exciting retort about his friends, Kingsley Amis and Graham Greene, and even about Evelyn Waugh, whom he had not known but admired this side of heaven . . . yet at them all, he throws sharp stones, followed by a grenade or two:

ASSOULINE: Is jealousy a widespread sentiment among writers?

BURGESS: I readily believe that. But I'm not concerned, because I'm alone in this statement. When I'm in London, I hardly see Kingsley Amis, who is a friend and whom I admire. He is like me; he's a monster who drank too much and smoked too much. As for my neighbour on the Côte d'Azur, Graham Greene, who lives in Antibes, he has become very bizarre. He has no friends, he writes letters every day to Kim Philby, the British spy refuged in Moscow, and he spreads himself around in a funny manner on my account in the British newspapers. He pretends that I have attributed imaginary remarks to him by reporting one of our conversations in a book (which is false), that he had to look up my words in

a dictionary (which is also false), that I read a lot
but without discrimination . . . not very friendly, at
all.

ASSOULINE: Why is he like that?

BURGESS: He's a convert, whereas I am a Catholic from birth.
All of the difference lies there. In a recent novel
[*The Captain and the Enemy*], he pretends that only
Catholic converts understand the nature of religion
and that they are better theologians than others. He
doesn't realise that Catholicism isn't just religion
but a familial culture. What's more, I am half Irish.
My grandmother Mary-Ann Finnegan was totally
Irish, just as is my cousin George Dwyer, the arch-
bishop of Birmingham. In general, in England, the
faith is Irish. It's the Irish who've maintained it.
This situation displeases the grand writers like
Graham Greene and Evelyn Waugh, it forces them
to pray in the churches with Irish workers or
Italian boys. Not very aristocratic, all that – socially
unacceptable.[2]

Burgess was also offended by what he termed Greene's 'living arrangements'. Now it's true that Greene was having an affair with Yvonne
Cloetta, and had done so for what could be called a lifetime.* But he
wasn't actually *living* with her. She always went home at night. (When
Greene was in Antibes, most of the year but not in the summer, it was
Yvonne's habit to call most afternoons about two, leaving around five
or six at night.†)

Burgess didn't reply to Greene's letter, so he wrote a second time.

By 7 August 1988, Greene had sent a copy of his first letter to the
newspapers (the one I have a copy of is to the *Sunday Express*). The
fat was in the fire. The headline ran: 'Literary Giants in War of Words'.
The first paragraph:

---

* There is proof in Greene's dedication in his last novel *The Captain and the Enemy*,
published in 1988 (the year of Burgess's attack and Greene's replies): 'For Y with all the
memories we share of nearly thirty years.'
† I remember she cooked a nice supper for me the first night I visited. During my second
visit, they kissed in front of me. What stands out in my mind was Greene's remark: 'That,'
he said 'is a first. I've allowed no one to see us kissing.' Once, when she arrived at the
flat at her appointed time, Graham suggested gently that I should go, to continue our
interview later that evening so that they could be alone together. Bed before biography.

Graham Greene, our greatest living novelist, has plunged at 83 into a ferocious mud-slinging contest with the almost equally distinguished author Anthony Burgess, 71.

Burgess lives in Monaco just up the coast from Greene's South of France flat.

Greene has been deeply wounded by remarks Burgess has made about him on French TV and in the magazine *Lire* and especially resented Burgess's criticism of his friendship with the traitor Kim Philby. And Greene is appalled that Burgess, a fellow Catholic, has gone on to attack his private life.

He added: 'Burgess is just bad tempered and unpleasant.'

Greene first hit back by writing Burgess an ironic letter jeering at Burgess's writing, especially his newspaper articles.[3]

I remember Greene telling me that Burgess was 'either a liar or suffering from something wrong in his head. I hope it's the second. In which case he should see a doctor.' Greene echoed his sister's report: 'Some people think it's jealousy.'

*

Let us go back in time. These two had been friends for many years, by correspondence, but it was a friendship based on Greene as king and Burgess as a rather fearful courtier, a lower-level official. Burgess came close to being sycophantic, when really there was no need. After all, he was a critically acclaimed novelist himself, a distinguished verbal performer, the possessor of great linguistic energy, and an esteemed composer. And yet to Greene (and probably only to Greene) Burgess could at times be almost servile.

Greene was one of the greatest writers alive; Burgess, even in his early days, a writer of fine reputation. It was only very late in their friendship, as we'll see, that they locked horns.

An early contact was on 4 October 1958. Burgess, aged forty-one, was teaching in Borneo at Sultan Omar Ali Saiffudin College. Greene had just turned fifty-four.

A very brief note to a man undoubtedly busy. I remember with very great pleasure the lunch we had in London last year [1957]* and your graciousness in asking me to sign your copy of my poor novel *Time for a Tiger*. I have just completed my fourth novel

---

* Greene had asked Burgess to lunch because Burgess had brought him some of his favourite shirts from Malaya. Usually Trevor Wilson took on this errand, but this time Burgess offered.

about the East – *The Devil of a State* and I am wondering if you would be good enough to allow me to dedicate it to you. Nothing flowery, just 'To Graham Greene'.

Greene had been on Burgess's mind because he'd recently seen the film *The Quiet American*. He was living in the Far East, so books took a while to arrive: 'I fret because your new novel [*Our Man in Havana*, published 6 October 1958] won't reach me here for such a long time.'

If you're terribly busy, and don't mind about my dedicating my new book to you, please don't trouble to rush to your desk to answer. I shall be sending the novel off to Heinemann's in a week or so, and, if you're furious about my presumption, you can always intercept it there. But, believe me, it's meant as a real act of homage.

Greene was in Havana when Burgess's letter arrived asking about the dedication. He wrote back, 'delighted and complimented'. Burgess replied by describing some characteristics of Brunei, but really it was only to put in another word of praise, as if Greene would want it or believe it:

I feel that if you came here you could write something very pungent and significant about a quite incredible situation – it's just impossible to describe the peculiar odour of malevolence that breathes in from the river and the Malays' armpits, the weird immigration laws, the inefficiency, corruption . . .
    My own third novel about Malaya, in which I kill off my hero, is coming, they say, in January. With this fourth [the one dedicated to Greene] I shall stop writing about the East. I haven't exhausted it . . . but it's exhausted me. It needs a vision and a pen of your sharpness, not a minor comic talent like my own.[4]

At this time Burgess signed not just his given name but, John Burgess Wilson. Almost each letter has its freight of praise, as if Burgess feared Greene would stop writing back if he didn't lay it on thick. It's a wonder Greene allowed it to continue, for he detested anything that smacked of fawning. Here's another example:

It's late to add my own meed of congratulation and gratitude for *A Burnt-Out Case*. It was, as well as so much else, a heartening thing for an author to read. It made it seem worthwhile prac-tising the art if the art could achieve something like that.[5]

The next letter, written ten years later (1971), is in reply to Greene, who has written to him first: 'How delightful to hear from you again after all these years.' He remembers 'with unkillable lucidity meeting you in London in 1957 and bringing those shirts from KL. It doesn't seem long ago, and yet so much has happened. My first wife died in 1968 and I married an Italian girl and took her to Malta.'

Thirteen years after their first meeting we see how persistent Burgess's admiration is. He'd been asked by Michael Korda, chief editor and vice-president of Simon & Schuster, to report on Greene's *A Sort of Life* (1971). His answer:

Dear Michael Korda,
    I fully concur with you in finding the autobiography of Graham Greene remarkable, fascinating, sobering, heartening, inspiring, beautifully done, masterful, and I am most grateful to have been given an opportunity to read it before publication. Any author must find in it so much bitter and glorious truth that, over and above the gratitude he has long felt for the Greene novels, he must look for new modes of saying thank you to an author who has been a great inspiring pharos to writers, British and American alike, for so long. This is a new kind of Greene, and it is wonderful.[6]

In a letter to Greene in 1971, he praises *Travels with My Aunt* (though that had appeared in 1969), but not too obviously this time, sidestepping the novel by saying: 'I needn't bore you with more praise,' as he tries to persuade Greene to go to the Joyce festival. Greene replies that he never goes to festivals, though he hopes 'one day I shall see you in Antibes', but Burgess slips in a little tag of praise in his 18 May 1971 letter: 'As always, your most devoted admirer.'

So they were friends of a sort. But Burgess placed himself at a disadvantage; singing praises which Greene could not (and I suspect would not) reciprocate. Burgess later came to interview Greene for the *Observer* and found himself in an awkward position because of his early letters and their lap-dog quality. When Greene wrote to Burgess years later complaining about the attack on French television and in *Lire*, his short letter dripped with irony and scepticism. Burgess, I suspect, couldn't face replying in kind. He'd never done so. They were such different characters, such different writers.

★

Burgess wrote two autobiographies late in his life. Just before he and Greene fell out, he published in 1987 *Little Wilson and Big God*, followed in 1990 by *You've Had Your Time*. In his 1990 memoir, he tries to explain what went wrong between Greene and himself. Burgess describes his interview with Greene, how he had to travel from Monte Carlo for the *Observer* to Antibes. The trip was difficult for Burgess as he was having real problems walking:

I went to Antibes to interview Graham Greene for the *Observer*. I limped up the hill to Monte Carlo station, caught the stopping train [then Burgess lists nine stops]. Greene's apartment was only a hundred yards up the hill from Antibes station, but I had to take a taxi. Greene, in his middle seventies, living with a *chic* French *bourgeoise* whose leg was not broken, was fitter than I at sixty-three. We talked and I bought him lunch. He seemed pleased at what he termed my suffering venerability and, when I sent him the typescript of our colloquy, accepted that this was a true account. I did not, of course, use a tape recorder. Later he contributed to 'Sayings of the Week' in the *Observer* the following remark: 'Burgess put words in my mouth which I had to look up in the dictionary.' *This turned me against him.*

He had long, it seemed, had something against me: back in 1966 I wrote an article on him in which I suggested that he had been touched by the Jansenist heresy. In 1980 he had abandoned hell and sin and was on the way to dispensing with God, but the imputation of Jansenism still rankled. He was like a murderer annoyed at being called a shoplifter.

There was in him, I thought, a little of the smugness of the achieved writer, though, to give him his due, there was not more of it than when I had met him first in 1957. I do not think he liked my novels. I was pretty sure he would not care for *Earthly Powers*. I had elected the Joycean way in the sense of deliberate hard words (to check the easy passage of the reader, in the manner of potholes on a road) and occasional ambiguity, Greene had made the popular novel of adventure his model.

But I feel that the real barrier between us was that between the cradle Catholic and the convert. Greene has said that the cradle Catholics are weak on theology (does he include St Thomas Aquinas?) One who has become a Catholic by choice is bound to feel himself superior to one who, crying at the douche and then licking the salt is merely unwittingly baptised into it. Evelyn Waugh, despite the legend, had more charity. He was certainly the better Catholic.[7]

I think their difficulties began with the interview Burgess just mentioned for the *Observer*. He wrote to Greene on 16 January 1980, and his first sentence was an apology because he had neglected to offer

seasonal greetings. He then explains why he is more than a little inca-
pacitated: 'I've been struck down in my left leg by something vascular
and temporarily crippling.' Then comes the reason for the letter. 'I hear
from the *Observer* that your new novel comes out in March [probably
Doctor Fischer of Geneva or The Bomb Party].'

Burgess tells Graham the *Observer*'s features editor wants him

> to crawl over to you at your convenience and talk to you with
> a view to writing a 3,000 word article on the event [of the book's
> publication] and on you generally.

This looks like the first time Burgess has formally interviewed Greene,
yet off and on, they had corresponded since 1958, over twenty-two
years. And in that time, Burgess rose mightily in stature as novelist and
composer and was known the world over for *A Clockwork Orange*. But
notice how, in this later letter, Burgess turns shy:

> I don't know whether you'd want to do this or not. I'd love to
> come over and talk, but not necessarily with a view to writing
> it down. On the other hand, I suppose somebody has to write
> such an article and it might as well be by myself. No tape
> recorder,* not even a notebook.

If the interview was a 'go', Burgess wrote, 'being so agonised by the
novel I'm writing now, what I'd seriously like to discuss is the novelist's
agonies. And of course your new novel.' He was compelled to add his
tot of praise at the end of his letter: 'With my strongest as ever admiration and, always, affection.'

The interview went ahead, and a month later Burgess had the galleys
from the *Observer* and sent them to Greene, enclosing them 'with the
right trepidation'. He gave Greene a wide margin, asking him to 'amend
or erase what doesn't seem to be true'. Burgess tepidly challenges

---

* There *was* a time when Greene couldn't tolerate anyone using a tape recorder. I suspect
Burgess had heard this, but as a result of trouble Greene had with Penelope Gilliatt, who
interviewed him for the *New Yorker* and introduced into her article some howlers (stemming – it has been reported – from her being drunk during the interview), Greene became
extremely vigilant during interviews, and began criticising some of his personal friends
who interviewed him for what he saw as errors: friends such as Auberon Waugh, Michael
Mewshaw, Piers Paul Read and Michael Meyer. I knew he hated tape recorders – he'd
told me so after I brought along a tiny one bought in Tokyo on our first interview. I
pleaded a bad memory and used it anyway. Greene, finally disturbed by the many people
misquoting him, thanked me later for forcing his hand. But Burgess didn't know that
Greene had changed his mind.

Greene's criticisms: 'You told our consular friend [very likely the Honorary Consul of Nice, Ronnie Challoner] that I talked more than you did – this seems to be true, but it was you I talked about.' I think Burgess missed a chance to understand Greene's original half displeasure over the interview, during which Burgess did talk far too much – often without giving Greene a chance to reply. He would raise a question for Greene to answer, but then jump right in and provide a brilliant answer himself. He really was putting on a performance, almost as if he were the interviewee, not the interviewer.

★

Upon arriving at Greene's flat, Burgess immediately crossed over to Greene's library. He found what he was looking for. His first words: 'I see you have a volume of Borges here, the man who kindly calls himself the Argentine Burgess.' So there is Burgess, before the interview even begins, offering Greene his first boast. And then he sets out to prove his superior knowledge about the byways of literature, determined to show how very clever he could be, a bright-eyed sixth-former showing off his erudition, and at the same time seeking Greene's admiration for his inventive answers. Instead of doing a proper job of interviewing Greene, he offers instead a mixture of brag and bluster, a deliberate parade of information. There is little talk of the new novel (except obliquely), the purpose of the interview after all. Nor do we hear anything about the ordeals of novel writing which Burgess had said he wanted desperately to raise:

GREENE: You don't find Conan Doyle dealt with at length in the literary histories. Yet he was a great writer. He created several characters . . . [interruption]

BURGESS: T. S. Eliot admired him, but he didn't think him worthy of a critical essay – not like Wilkie Collins and yet Eliot lifted a whole chunk of the 'Musgrave Ritual'.*

GREENE: Where?

BURGESS: In *Murder in the Cathedral*. You remember – 'Whose was it?' – 'His who is gone.' – 'Who shall have it?' 'He who will come.' – 'What shall be the month?' And so on. In Sherlock Holmes' story we have 'Whose was it?' – 'He who has gone.' 'Who shall have it?' – 'He who will come.' – 'What was the month?' Almost identical.

---

* The passage does not appear in later versions of *Murder in the Cathedral*.

And then Greene praises Rider Haggard and H. G. Wells and mentions Bulwer Lytton: 'His *Pelham* deals with an illicit love in a thoroughly contemporary way.'

No answer to this, just an attempt to win the argument:

BURGESS: The bosun in *Nigger of the Narcissus* is reading *Pelham* when the story opens. Strange that that same bosun should have to sign his papers with a cross when the story ends. No matter. Why not write a book, or certainly an essay, on the literary snobbism which prefers symbols and ambiguities to the straight art of storytelling?

GREENE: [A palpable hit this time.] I leave that to you.

Burgess throws up questions like fists, which Greene answers, but only just. He starts telling Greene how Auden adored Lorenz Hart, 'but was responsible for the un-Hartian lines':

> *Is this a milieu where I must*
> How grahamgreeneish! how infra dig!
> *Snatch from the bottle in my bag*
> *An analeptic swig?*

Then Burgess brings up the question of how parochial the British novel is. Greene answers wisely that there was a time in the nineteenth century when it could be both parochial and universal. And so it goes, playing the 'not only as clever but cleverer than you' game. Ultimately tedious, it's a pleasure when Greene scores with a right answer. When Burgess refers to Bellow and White being awarded the Nobel, he gets caught off guard by his wily prey. He asks Greene bluntly: 'When are you going to get it?' Greene answers as if he had been waiting all the afternoon for this question, and stops his guest in his tracks.

GREENE: I look forward to getting a bigger prize than that.
BURGESS: Which one?
GREENE: Death. Let's go and eat lunch.

*

Basically, I think Greene found Burgess boorish.* The interview had been a good performance, but it wasn't the place for Burgess to do

---

* As late as 22 February 1989, Greene wrote to his friend, Bryan Forbes, referring to Burgess: 'He's a man I do not like and he does not like me.'

circus tricks. He was there to ask questions of Greene. Burgess wasn't
made to be a first-class interviewer; he was instead first-class material
to be interviewed. He wanted to leave his mark – that was his way. He
had an almost miraculous memory, and could outwit Greene in such
a setting, but Greene wasn't expecting a competition. I'm sure Greene
never had another interview like this, because it was only incidentally
an interview. Burgess never seemed to run out of quotes. He was happy
in this public duel. Greene was not.

After their argument, when Burgess first let forth his criticisms of
Greene on television and in the magazine, they never made up. Though
both were Catholics, Greene had 'developed', according to Burgess, 'a
highly idiosyncratic version of Catholicism, which could even accommodate a probable absence of the deity'. Burgess was also disturbed
about Greene's 'capacity to reconcile a spiritual system with a materi-
alistic one'.

But what did Graham think of Burgess? 'Clever? Yes, but in company
and in interview, he was an upstart, and really didn't know how to
behave socially.' As for Burgess's venerability – well, poor Burgess was
sick on the day of the interview. What a note to end on:

GREENE: We'd better leave. Can you walk as far as the station?
BURGESS: With the help of my stick.
GREENE: [mischievously] That stick makes you look venerable,
             Anthony. [With glee] Look at the respect you're
             getting from the patron.
BURGESS: [sourly, in pain] And you still have something of the
             look of a juvenile delinquent.

Look at Burgess's last words above – I've cleaned up what he actually said as suddenly, in great pain, his sentence was broken by an outcry
which his distress made irresistible: 'Jesus Christ, my leg's going into
spasm. God help me. Blast the bloody thing.'

In response to his mistake about Greene's age, Burgess rationalised:
'I over-estimated his age by a couple of years.' It was three – but
Burgess was naturally careless, and often answered extemporaneously.
I don't believe he meant to make a mistake, but mistakes of any order
were for Greene a red rag to a bull. Burgess wrote: 'This drove him
into a fury whose excess was not matched by the exquisite small handwriting in which it was couched.' And then he adds: 'I was indiscreet
to a reporter about the Greene *ménage*.' Yvonne Cloetta probably
reminded Burgess of his first wife, who quite thoroughly cuckolded
him for years, including with a Punjabi police corporal and Dylan
Thomas. His sympathies, understandably, would have been with Jacques.

763

But Burgess wasn't such an old fogey. His first wife, he tells us in his autobiography *Little Wilson and Big God* (1987), was something of a terror. Burgess reports: 'No husband likes to be told of his sexual short-comings. I was told too brutally and drunkenly.' He writes of how he consoled himself over the years with prostitutes and other women.*

And Graham, as we shall see, was not through fighting with the Irish.

---

* One was a Tamil of twelve, and quite coldly Burgess adds that he may have a 'brownish, thirty-year-old, bastard son'.

PART 23

Final Hurrahs

53

Greene's Last Stand

Dear Mr Greene:
Please do not throw this letter in the bin.
            – JOAN MCDONNELL

IT seemed at first an easy and happy match, in the sense that in 1989 the Guinness Peat Aviation company (GPA), headquartered in Shannon, was offering an enormous award, £50,000 Irish, for the best book (fiction and non-fiction) written in the previous three years by either a native Irishman or an established resident of Ireland. And the committee of judges could not have been bettered.

Hugh Kenner, who'd written so well about Joyce and Beckett. Fay Weldon, whom we have met in Moscow already.* The critic Philip French, who after having read 103 novels for the Booker Prize, turned to work on the GPA award. Finally there was Gerry Dukes, given the rank of Prize Coordinator. To this group was added Graham Greene, whose task was to be adjudicator, a sort of Inspector-General. His authority to make the final decision was immense. It was the GPA's ambition to make this Irish award famous, so they wanted someone of Greene's stature as overseer. It was a recipe for disaster.

*

The head of GPA, Tony Ryan, had made pots of money. He'd set up a company, bought planes to lease out and made not millions, but billions until, as Gerry Dukes put it (using an uncomfortable image for an aeroplane business), his firm 'took a nosedive' in 1992. But in 1989, before its downfall, Ryan spoke to Sean Donlon at the company, who had overall responsibility for the award. Donlon knew the Irish

---

* In 2001 I spoke to Fay, the lively and lovely novelist. I thought she was originally known for the slogan: 'Go to work on an egg.' Her husband said her first phrase was, 'Zip down a banana.'

Honorary Consul in Nice, Pierre Joannon, who was acquainted with Greene as a neighbour and friend. Joannon was able to persuade Greene to take on the task of Supreme Judge.*

Philip French, still work-lagged from reading so many books for the Booker Prize that year, now faced another vast stint: mostly novels, but non-fiction as well. French, Kenner, Weldon and Dukes were charged with looking at 185 books sent in from all over Ireland, to read and winnow so as to come up with (French tells us) thirty to forty books, all worthy candidates for the prize in the combined opinion of the four judges. Then they would sift and cull again until the list was brought down to five. The assignment was considerable.

What the judges were bound to leave to Greene was the reading of the five books on the short list, and then he was to choose the winner. No doubt the four judges felt that any writer on the short list would be a worthy winner. Each, no doubt, determined in their own mind whom they would choose. But the rules didn't allow that.

Gerry Dukes first called on Greene early in 1989 (as it turned out, he had to make three separate visits to Antibes) delivering the short-listed books right to Greene's door. They were Seamus Heaney's *The Haw Lantern*, Roy Foster's *Modern Ireland 1600–1972*, John Banville's novel *The Book of Evidence*; and two collections of short stories, Aidan Mathews' *Adventures in a Bathyscope* and Shane Connaughton's *A Border Station*.

Dukes travelled from Dublin to Antibes, made the short walk from the railway station to La Résidence des Fleurs with his heavy load, and took the lift to the fourth floor. Greene was waiting, standing tall at the door. Dukes faced his unblinking blue eyes.

Dukes had brought as a gift a fifty-year-old bottle of whiskey, from the GPA. Graham, not missing a beat, opened it for Dukes, but sat down to drink his own favourite, straight vodka. But they drank, and through the window, Dukes could see the myriad masts of the Antibes marina.

Greene pointed his finger at a book on his table entitled *The Broken Commandment* by Vincent McDonnell. Greene said: 'This is the book that's going to win the Guinness Peat Aviation award.' Dukes responded with the first thing that came to mind: 'I haven't got round to that yet.' Incredulous, Dukes asked himself: 'Why had I the job of carrying five books across the Atlantic ocean, and one was Roy Foster's *Modern Ireland: 1600–1972* – large, heavy, some 688 pages.'[1] From where he was standing, Gerry could see the back side of the McDonnell dust-jacket

---

* Rumour had it that the money that Greene would receive for his part was to be given to a writer in need.

revealing a powerfully favourable blurb from Greene: 'Sad, frightening, merciless – and unforgettable.'

Who was Vincent McDonnell?

★

Dukes told me in a transatlantic conversation that McDonnell's book had been turned down by more than half a dozen publishers, and in the end, McDonnell's wife (in some despair perhaps) sent the first chapter, out of the blue, to Greene in Antibes.

I finally tracked down McDonnell and his wife, Joan, who were willing to help me unravel the complications of the story. They are gentle Irish Catholics. Joan McDonnell didn't have the original of her letter to Greene, but thought she could recall it. This, a letter of fortune from a loving wife, dated 19 September 1986:

Dear Mr Greene,

Please do not throw this letter in the bin. Read it first then you can throw it in the bin but I hope you won't.

My husband Vincent is a writer, a great writer. All he has ever wanted to do is write. It is his life. I believe he is even better than James Joyce but no one knows because no one sees his work. And until he is published no one will. But it is almost impossible. Each time the book is sent off, it is rejected. But a number of publishers have thought it promising, one publisher wanted him to change certain things but he wouldn't. But from that I feel it must have something.

I know you are 82 but even at 82 you still have the power to do something if you want. I do not want praise. All I want is for you to take the five minutes it will take you to read the enclosed first chapter of his book, and give me your opinion so that I can continue sending it off to the publishers.

There is a saying that if we helped just one person going through life then our life has not been in vain. Will you help, Graham? I know it will probably take a miracle but I believe in miracles. Miracles just don't happen, all it takes is someone somewhere to care. Will you be that person, Graham? I hope you will.

If the news is bad I would appreciate it if you would not reply. So until I hear from you I'll say bye and God bless you for now.

Yours sincerely,

Joan McDonnell

Immediately Greene sent back a telegram: 'FIRST CHAPTER REMARK-ABLE PLEASE SEND THE REST. GRAHAM GREENE.' It was sent, and he had the book hardly any length of time before writing to Joan that he liked it and had sent it to his publisher recommending acceptance. One small matter was that he felt the title had 'rather a too biblical sound'.[2]

And, just to put further pressure on Max Reinhardt, Greene admitted to Joan: 'I have told Max if he doesn't take it to return it to me as I would like to try another publisher and that threat may do the trick!'[3] Then came a telegram from Greene: 'BOOK DEFINITELY ACCEPTED, HAVE PATIENCE'.

Greene had taken over. No doubt Max Reinhardt admired the book, but more than that, Max remembered Greene's genius as a critic and a bookman. So Reinhardt accepted McDonnell's book for publication early in 1988, and Greene wrote his enthusiastic puff, which Gerry Dukes could not avoid seeing on Greene's table, no doubt placed there deliberately. But did McDonnell deserve Greene's praise?

Read the first chapter and decide. I believe he did deserve the praise. Also, I think such praise was almost inevitable, for Vincent McDonnell was passionately fond of Greene's work. The novel seems close to Greene's earlier work, yet it is unquestionably McDonnell's own. It is also very much a Catholic novel. Greene's major work, almost all of it, is Catholic. In some ways the book owes something to *The End of the Affair*, for, in an even more fundamental way, it is The End of His Hero's Affair, even unto death. A literary sleuth might easily have thought it an unknown early Greene. Much of what McDonnell learnt came from reading Greene — he wrote as the young Greene had written.

★

Greene, now old, could not know that his journey to Dublin would be his last public outing. I suspect that McDonnell's novel was a renewal for Greene, his own methods and techniques reborn.

Moreover, Greene took to the McDonnells as if they were his children. In Vincent McDonnell, Greene found a surrogate son, one who'd followed in his footsteps. Just before publication, Greene offered a bit of fatherly advice: 'Don't expect it to be a best-seller — it is too good for that. I however expect good and encouraging reviews.'[4] The title by now was provided by Max Reinhardt (or as I suspect, it came from Greene, who did not want to take the credit). McDonnell's original, *The Fifth Commandment*, was wrong, though Greene treated it kindly.

I was talking about the title to Max Reinhardt . . . and he suggested what I think was a good title, *The Broken Commandment*, leaving it to people to think for themselves which Commandment was broken! I quite like too A FLAME FROM THE ASHES [I don't believe he really did] so I think it is for you and Max to decide between yourselves. I look forward to the publication of your book with great hopes.[5]

The fifth commandment is the rather uncontroversial 'Honour thy father and thy mother', and *Flame from the Ashes* couldn't set a box of matches alight. Clearly, the title change was imperative.

★

While all this was going on, Reinhardt's relationship with The Bodley Head, which Greene refers to in his letter to Joan McDonnell of 17 October 1987, was coming to an end. Greene's concerns about the McDonnells' anxiety are expressed gently, explaining the snags:

> His book has been delayed over here simply because of a take-over of The Bodley Head and its group, but [Vincent] will be with me published by Max Reinhardt who has resigned from The Bodley Head and joined the Penguin group. [Max] has told me that Penguin will publish Vincent's book after the hard cover edition. You may not have heard from him because he has been very busy and concerned with his battle of the books.

The *Guardian* was interested in McDonnell for an award. That one did not come about, but the newspaper thought enough of him to have him visit London. Greene writes to Joan late in July 1989, the year of the GPA award: 'I was delighted to hear he was runner-up for that prize and have every hope for the future.'

Along with missing out on the award from the *Guardian*, the award for fiction from the *Sunday Express* went to another as well, though Greene tried with might and main, even writing to his friend, the distinguished literary editor Graham Lord. On 20 August 1988, Graham writes to McDonnell: 'I saw Graham Lord, the Literary Editor of the *Sunday Express*, the other day and I spoke to him mainly about your book and I hope it had a good effect.' The *Sunday Express* Book of the Year award was worth £20,000. Greene asked that it be given to this comparatively unknown writer for *The Broken Commandment*. He seemed determined to procure an award for his protégé. The impression one got was that had he failed this couple, he'd have been as ashamed as a nudist caught with his clothes on.

★

The GPA judging committee had its favourites, five of them short-listed, but overall it was probably John Banville. He was already a distinguished novelist with a handful of successes including *Dr Copernicus* (1976), *Kepler* (1981) and *Mefisto* (1989), followed by *The Book of Evidence* (also published in 1989). Banville was certainly Philip French's choice: if the first prize *had* to be between the two novels, McDonnell's *The Broken Commandment* (which wasn't short-listed, a point brought up by many) and Banville's *The Book of Evidence*, there was no doubt Banville should be the winner, in the other judges' view.

Philip French published an article about the GPA award in the *Observer* of 19 November 1989 in which he declared that Banville's novel was similar to McDonnell's, 'but superior in every way (both are first person confessional narratives by condemned Catholic murderers), [and] it seemed inconceivable that [Greene] would prefer a book none of us felt worthy of being on the short list'. But he did. French mentions the rumours which had begun to circulate 'that Greene planned to bypass [the committee of judges] and choose McDonnell', and adds, 'for [Greene] to do this would have been like Michael Foot [a paragon of political virtue after all] getting up at the 1988 Booker dinner and announcing that he was ignoring the short list and giving the prize to his friend E.P. Thompson's *Sykaos Papers*'.

Was Greene providing his own short list of one, ignoring his colleagues' toil?

*

During this time, Greene seemed to have reached the limits of his energy and health, and was recognising that the time he had left on earth was dwindling. He cared passionately about justice and human dignity, and was ever a shield against victimisation. But in the GPA conflict, was Greene acting as a little dictator? Where was Greene's near-pathological receptivity to another's suffering?

*

The story I heard from Gerry Dukes starts with Greene in Antibes, asking, 'Do I have to read all these?' – the five short-listed books. (This struck Dukes as somewhat comic, since from May to September he himself had read 175 books.) Greene kept on returning to McDonnell's book. It was agreed between them that Dukes would return to Dublin and speak to the GPA to discuss Greene's strong desire to honour McDonnell. Indeed, Dukes told me that Greene more than once said: 'We must do something for Vincent McDonnell.' So Dukes did go back to Dublin on his appointed rounds.

A letter from Greene to GPA official Sean Donlon on 4 April 1989 enlightens:

I am very happy to agree to your proposals for the Irish prize. It is understood isn't it that Vincent McDonnell's novel is among the five from which I choose. Or at any rate it will be among the full list of books submitted?

Philip French, in his *Observer* article states:

The rumours persisted, and last week they reached the front pages of newspapers in Britain and Ireland; the view was expressed that Greene was treating his fellow judges with contempt and insulting the short-listed authors.

But well before the award ceremony, poor Gerry Dukes was meeting himself coming and going, back and forth from Dublin to Antibes. I asked why he thought Greene was so keen on McDonnell. Dukes attributed it to a rush of nostalgia: McDonnell's novel is like a Greene novel of the 1930s.

On Dukes's second visit to Antibes, Greene had a go at the short list. And Greene modified his position just a little, agreeing that, of the short-listed books, Banville's was the best, but adding, in Dukes's words: 'It would be a "gross injustice" not to give McDonnell the award.' It was clear that Greene had the right and the authority to ignore the short list if he wished.

On his next visit to Antibes, Dukes found Greene at Chez Félix. He reported to Greene, and later told me: 'I'd spoken to the GPA . . . they'd be willing to go to 60,000 and divide the pot . . . Graham seemed to agree to split it.' The GPA said nothing other than that they would underwrite it. 'I also learnt', said Dukes, 'that Greene had been in touch in recent times with McDonnell.' That's true, as we see from the letter written to Vincent McDonnell just fifteen days before the award was to be decided. Greene suggests they go along with the compromise: 'Unless this is satisfactorily arranged I shall simply refuse to turn up to the prize giving.'[6]

Returning home, Dukes had to contact both authors with the suggested 40/20 arrangement. Banville was outraged and outspoken: 'Fuck off if you're going to split the award. You can take a running jump at yourself. All or nothing.' And Dukes then went to meet McDonnell at Kong Castle. McDonnell didn't want the prize either, even though he was in great financial need. He was a kind-natured man and had genuine compassion for the other writer. He said that he didn't want the prize if it affected Banville adversely, nor did he want to be the cause of Banville's not taking it. McDonnell was a swan among barracudas.

Even the day before the award-giving ceremony in Dublin, speculation was going down to the wire. An article by James Dettmer spoke of how

> The literary worlds of London and Dublin were gripped by speculation after reports that a little-known Irish writer was on course to win, with his first novel, the most valuable literary prize in the British Isles. Mr Graham Greene ... is preparing to shock the literary world by selecting Mr Vincent McDonnell's *The Broken Commandment*. He is believed to have rejected a short list drawn up by a panel of judges that included John Banville's *The Book of Evidence* (a Booker Prize contender), and Seamus Heaney's *The Haw Lantern*.

With a switch of the pen, Dettmer added intrigue: 'The selection of Mr McDonnell's first novel would be a major upset.' And then: 'It is published by Mr Greene's own publisher, Mr Max Reinhardt. Mr Greene, aged 85, declined to comment last night.'

In his letter to McDonnell, already quoted, Greene spoke of wanting to give the first and only prize to McDonnell, but he'd been 'overwhelmed by arguments', and so he capitulated. What turned the tables? I believe it was an article in the *Irish Times* by journalist Eileen Battersby, in the form of an ultimatum. It had some effect on Greene. Let me add here that I know that Greene and French admired each other. Nevertheless, honourable French felt that he would need to complain if the short list were ignored:

> Mr McDonnell's novel had been submitted for the prize and read by the assessors; 'none of us though saw it as a book of any serious merit,' he said. Mr French also assured the *Sunday Tribune* that had Mr Greene chosen to ignore the five short-listed books when selecting the winner, 'I would not have stayed sitting. I would have protested and made my views clear.'

French and Greene remained friends. But the snowball was gathering speed.

★

What followed were frantic telephone calls from Dukes to Antibes. The GPA cobbled together two awards. The Best Book Award for Banville, with the whole of the offered sum, £50,000. Then, for McDonnell, a First Fiction Award of £20,000. The losers, the other four short-listed candidates, were each given £1,000. But, Dukes told me:

Greene did not give his confirmation about this. And I had the job of seeing about getting jacket bands for the books of Banville and McDonnell, the two winners, with special leather cases made, still not sure that Greene would go along with the double winners. Indeed the GPA bought up most of the stock of the Banville and McDonnell.

Greene made one last request – that his friend Lord Fitt should join him in Dublin. A plane was sent to Belfast for him. Graham and Yvonne flew from Antibes in Tony Ryan's private plane. 'They arrived on 28 November and the award ceremony took place in the old Bank of Ireland.'

But with Greene, it still seemed touch and go, nor was Dukes sure of his reactions: 'He was incommunicado. He didn't say whether he was happy or sad.' And then, a prescient statement: 'He didn't seem to be particularly well to me.'

★

French tells us that Greene made a graceful speech, and Dukes reveals that Greene was 'like a lamb'. None of the trouble Dukes feared occurred. French recalled Greene's speech: 'He spoke of his lifelong attachment to Joyce, Moore, Yeats and Synge and how he had visited Ireland in 1923 "because I wanted to see the country where these men were bred".' But French also (like a trained novelist) noticed more than his remarks:

He was by some way the tallest man in the room, a commanding presence. He stooped slightly, possibly because so many of the Irishmen around him were on the short side, and his gauntness made his eyes seem even more penetrating and protuberant. His voice, however, was firm, with that curiously metallic sound that gave the odd impression of English not being his first language. The speech – recalling his lifetime admiration for Irish literature and the impressive first visit he made to the country as a young man – was delivered fluently and without any notes. It went down extremely well, serving to mollify the people who had been affronted by the cavalier way in which he had been prepared to override the short-list drawn up for him and substitute his own candidate.

The photographs taken on the night of the award, 28 November 1989, seem to show real dislike in Banville's face. Keep in mind that Banville is being offered a prize, astonishing in its size (£50,000), but he keeps a stiff countenance. You'd almost think that Banville had lost! The famous and congenial Seamus Heaney is comfortable, and happy to be part of the event. The short-listed Aidan Mathews was on the platform and remarked that it was just a thrill to know that Greene had read his book.

McDonnell, a west country lad originally from Limerick, came along with his lovely wife Joan, a determined creature – as we've seen from her first letter to Greene. This is McDonnell's account of the evening:

> When we got to the venue, we were told to be there an hour or more before the official time – we were hidden away in a dark room – we were told the lights didn't work. So there we were huddled in the dark and to be honest, terrified. We were there for ages.* Then some people came for us . . . and we were taken out into bedlam. There seemed to be cameras and microphones everywhere. Journalists certainly speak fluent profanity . . .
>
> My first impression of Graham was of a very tall man (I'm only five feet so you can understand that) and I dare say it, a rather shy man. He had a very firm handshake and I think was just as much discomfited at being there as I was myself.

There was little chance for Joan and Vincent to talk with Greene at any length the night of the award. But the following day it was different:

> The next morning we met Graham, Yvonne, Sean Donlon . . . at their hotel. Here we met a much more relaxed Graham and for Joan and myself it was like meeting old friends. We were there for two hours or more and were joined by Trevor Danker [a freelance journalist] towards the end . . . I remember [Graham] asking Sean Donlon (in an aside) if he could use what had been said and Sean Donlon agreed that he could. I remember being taken aback when Graham said outright that he had wanted to give me the main prize and spoke so strongly of my book. It was as if he was confirming publicly that he was opposed to what had happened and this was his way of doing so . . .
>
> I remember that he was good company and liked his Guinness mixed with champagne, called Black Lady . . . My only regret is that the time was so short and that we were not to meet again. But I remember him with fondness and a great affection and whenever I'm down I pick up one of his books and the world isn't such a dark place any more.[7]

---

* We might ask why they didn't refuse to be put into a darkened room. I suspect they felt themselves somewhat lost in the capital city of Ireland. McDonnell struck me as an extremely honest man. He didn't embroider facts, so I feel it must be true.

Gerry Fitt was at the lunch, too, and they had a convivial meal. Gerry Dukes was also there and his story is different. 'Well at first there was idle chat' about the evening's festivities and the massive prizes given out by the Guinness Peat Aviation company, but then as they were leaving, Greene was stopped by a freelance journalist, Trevor Danker, who wrote for both the *Irish Times* and the *Irish Independent*. Dukes felt himself 'gob-smacked' and couldn't believe his ears. Greene was attacking his own side! The GPA, the judges, and Dukes's enormous effort in reading, lugging books, and looking after Greene – all this, and Greene was disowning the whole thing. All of the lunchtime guests were present at the time of his sudden outburst.

'Oh,' said Greene to Danker, 'the whole thing was a set-up and the prizes that were given shouldn't have been given. The person who really deserved the award was James Simmons for his book of poetry.'[8] This was a book that had never been short-listed (another one!), though it had been read and judged. Moreover, through all the wrangling, Greene had never mentioned Simmons.

If Greene did act as Gerry Dukes recalled, then it was an ambush, and as sneaky as a shark in shallow waters. But I believe that Gerry Dukes got it wrong. I found a copy of Danker's article, and what Greene was saying was that he thought Simmons's volume of poetry, which was not in the running, was better than Seamus Heaney's submitted poetry (again he is discounting the judges!) and should therefore at least have been on the short list. This changes the picture. If Greene had said, as Dukes remembered it, that 'the whole thing was a set-up' surely it would have been too juicy a disclosure not to appear in Danker's article.

I have no doubt that Greene admired McDonnell's *The Broken Commandment*. But Banville is a marvellously fluent and inventive writer and he deserved the prize. I do not want to take even a tincture of praise away from McDonnell's first novel, but crawl behind Greene's eyes a bit, and see what he saw in this young Irish writer.

Graham liked McDonnell's work. He liked McDonnell. I think his conduct may have had its deepest origin in his own constant failures, year after year, to win the Nobel Prize. Had Greene come to the conclusion that to win any prize was something of a lottery? Did he see it as a game of chance, a gamble? Greene's treatment at the hands of the Swedish Academy was never forgotten, and never forgiven (though in interview he gives the impression that he'd lost interest). Maybe he felt he had to prove that the best do not necessarily win. He was controller of the prize; the rules allowed this. Dare we say that Graham was trying on Lundkvist's robes? No. Such robes would never have fitted Greene. He, after all, did give way finally to Banville's superior performance: Lundkvist never did.

*

Sean Donlon telephoned me after I'd written this chapter, in answer to my letters. Here is his account given on 19 September 2001: it takes us back to the first approach to Greene:

> It was decided on a literary Irish award, offering 50,000 Irish pounds and it was natural to seek out the most famous and distinguished writer for that person. Thus we chose Graham Greene. I first visited Greene in Antibes. He was willing, but only under certain tight rules – he would not read more than six books chosen, and he would not accept any fee – but [and Vincent McDonnell's name came up almost at once] Greene wanted his fee (of £20,000) to be given to a deserving writer, one Vincent McDonnell – Greene had been very moved by McDonnell's wife's letters to him [proof of Greene's putting his money where his mouth is – a redeeming aspect of him]. Thus a fee of £20,000 would go directly to McDonnell. Also, I think he demanded that McDonnell, his book already published, *The Broken Commandment*, would also need to be read by the panel of distinguished judges.

Donlon added that he found Greene physically fading: this was the spring of 1989 (March or April).

Graham was flown to Dublin to stay at the Conrad Hotel. He got a shock when he arrived to discover that biographer Anthony Mockler had followed him to Dublin – he would come to feel Mockler was almost stalking him. Greene became quite emotional and disturbed. But he was strictly business on the night of the awards. Having read Banville's *The Book of Evidence*, Greene admitted that, in a straight competition with *The Broken Commandment*, Banville's was the better book. Yet he insisted on giving his judge's fee to McDonnell.

Whatever the reason for his pugilistic bent, there must have been within Greene, perhaps since birth, but certainly in his ageing years, a need to fight, and this anomaly grew like a tumour. I don't think it was only that he was a determined surrogate father,* longing as he neared death to have a surrogate son, who'd followed his career, read

---

* Michael Richey told me in a letter of 1 June 1998, that Anita Björk had wanted a child with Graham. When Michael remarked how unfair that would be, effectively making that child fatherless, Graham replied, astonishingly honestly: 'That's what happened in the case of my own children.'

his writing, admired him – Graham would have this son rewarded. He never tooted his own horn, but he would sound the trumpet for a young man like this. And in this case at least, his paternal instincts were correct: though McDonnell was nearly broken by his experience with the GPA award, he has matured into the writer Greene foresaw. In 2004, he won Ireland's Francis McManus award – with no help from Greene, unless it be of a kind unknown to the living.

★

Graham told me: 'Dublin killed me.' But if the life we lead leads to disease, then I'd say that from *J'Accuse* onwards, Greene was gradually being finished off, getting weaker as every month passed. And in the middle of the GPA award it was too much – he couldn't cope. I know it's not fair to blame his death on a single event, but Greene had had a bloody hard time of it in Dublin. This was the beginning of the end of his life. Illness was soon to be upon him. We learn from a letter to the McDonnells upon his return from Christmas in Switzerland that he'd been in and out of hospital. Graham Greene had leukaemia.

With the accumulating years Graham nurtured his secret self, the inward man changing. The burden of his existence grew, though he still devoted himself to the busy political world and to his desire to pull out of his mind the hidden masterpiece that might still be in him.

But the latter-day battles were damaging. It was his tragic flaw; he could never pass up a fight. The trouble in Nice, the Nobel committee's rebuffs, his presence in Panama, Nicaragua and Moscow, the feud with Burgess, and finally Dublin sent him down for the count. But long before, Graham had organised his complex world on wishing to win – he didn't mind the idea of 'dying with his boots on'.

54

Hugh and Elisabeth

And then there were none.
— NURSERY RHYME

Two months after the GPA award, on 9 February 1990, Greene wrote to Joan and Vincent McDonnell about how he enjoyed meeting them: 'It was a great pleasure having the good talk with you the day after all the horrors.' He'd delayed replying because: 'I went to Switzerland [to Lucy Caroline's home] for Christmas & the New Year & found myself twice in hospital.'

I think we can further gather from a letter to Anthony Mockler that Greene by now is physically failing: 'I'm afraid I am not in good form. I'm living between blood transfusions and injections at the moment in Switzerland so I have just received your letter.' He was still being pestered at this bleak time of his life. (He was to live seven more months.)

Graham objected strenuously to Mockler's seeking permission to write his life. Determined that Mockler should not receive help in his endeavour, Greene wrote forcefully to me: 'The man who threatens another biography has made an arrangement with an American publisher, but you may be sure that no one around me will give him any help at all.' And then a postscript informing me that:

Mockler is pursuing us even into Switzerland putting notes in my daughter's box. The mysterious thing is that he included among the notes a typewritten assignation for me to sign saying I would refuse him the right to use any quotations from my work. I signed this of course . . . Of course all my family have been warned to have nothing whatsoever to do with him.*

* Greene's last phrase fell on deaf ears. After his death two journalists were not prevented from writing biographies, one slight, the other malicious. (Father Durán described at the Berkhamsted Trust one biographer's work as 'the most mendacious and impudent book I have ever read', a powerful statement but 'mendacious' seems a little strong.)

★

Life began to go seriously wrong for Graham with the death of his younger brother, Sir Hugh Greene, soon after Graham returned from one of his trips to the USSR. Earlier he had gone to see Hugh in hospital, and had been appalled to find him seriously ill. Back from Moscow, he paid another visit and was shocked by his condition – cardiac trouble combined with prostate cancer. He had seemed to be improving, and had gone home, but pain forced him back into hospital. To see his younger brother's body broken was too much for Graham. He didn't stay long, but returned to the south of France. Hugh died shortly thereafter, on 19 February 1987.

Graham did not come back for his brother's funeral. Perhaps he should have, but he had his own reasons for not facing it. This was in part because as usual he had the tightest programme of duties all around the world, people to see. He detested being late and hated to make promises and not keep them, no matter what the circumstances – remember he had skipped his mother's funeral too. But below the surface, there was a deeper reason – the very idea of indulging his grief over the loss of Hugh disturbed him mightily.

To James Greene, Hugh's son from his first marriage to Helga Guinness, Graham wrote:

> I don't need to tell you how shattered I was by Hugh's death. I tried to return more quickly from Moscow, but there was no plane. It was terrible sitting beside him the day I returned, in a coma, and when you rang me up at Bentley's it was a sort of relief, knowing he wouldn't have to struggle any more with his breath.

Then the pith and poignancy:

> I'm sorry I couldn't come to the funeral, but Moscow and Hugh's death had knocked me out. I still find it difficult to do anything – the last sight of his face comes between the lines when I read.[1]

James, a translator of Mandelstam and a poet in his own right, wrote about his father in hospital. This watchful and sensitive son saw his father dying, and then saw him dead – all six feet six of him, a giant of a father:

> Later, a nurse – like an editor – presumes,
> To sponge his foreign body. One of us gawps
> At stalk and stump, their youthfulness and size

And ending:

> the naked man,
> Caught in the public glare of a son's eyes,
> About to be thrown into the waste-paper basket
> Like a discarded *Telegraph* . . .

In another letter, James wrote to his uncle (on 2 March 1987): 'Hugh looked still warm & un-corpsey when I had my last glimpse as two nurses washed him . . . I felt like one of Rembrandt's gazing medical students.'

*

Graham was beset by bad news, and was distraught when his sister (the youngest in the family) suddenly took ill. A letter to me of 5 March 1989 shows he is under strain:

> Dear Norman, Forgive a short note. Elisabeth has had a stroke [on 25 February] & is in hospital. No secretary. The Burgess/Greene storm has not blown over. He continues his lies in the last *Sunday Express*. I think he's mad with jealousy!

He felt hopeless without her and with reason. She was a perfect friend and adviser, and much went wrong after her illness. Her daughter filled in for her, but as competent as Amanda Saunders was, she could not easily replace Elisabeth. Graham told me that her absence caused him to consider committing suicide. Yet wasn't it moving when Amanda said to Greene: 'Uncle Graham, don't worry, I'll do my best. I'll take over and do the job while my mother is . . .'[2] leaving unspoken the hope that they all had for Elisabeth's recovery.

James Greene visited Elisabeth in hospital and wrote to Graham on 18 May 1989, saying she was 'able to *say* articulately how miserable it was not to be able to speak so as to be understood, so perhaps there's hope'.* She did not recover. Losing her was like drowning for Graham.

---

* I was close to Elisabeth Dennys and visited her in the Devonshire hospital just before I went home to Texas. From San Antonio, I wrote on 25 May 1989:

> I have good vibes about you. I believe you are going to recover – move a finger, then fingers, then your wrist, then arm – and you'll be away with it. Please, please don't lose belief in yourself. You are needed by your family – every single one of them. You are *universally* loved. Graham needs you and (forgive me for mentioning it) I need & love you. My heart went out to you when we met in hospital (almost before you made an effort to speak) and I embraced you. You are going to win this fight. I'm praying for you this night.

Nineteen eighty-nine was the year of troubles for Graham. The Dublin awards wrangle might not have been so difficult if Elisabeth had been at his side. He turned to no other. (His mistress was not well versed in English literature, but made great efforts to assist him in his professional life. Yvonne had perception and wit, was direct and outspoken, but perhaps had insufficient *nous*. This, Elisabeth had in abundance.) Yet Greene never gave up.*

★

In October 1990, Greene told Marie-Françoise Allain: 'If Yvonne didn't exist, I'd put a bullet through my head,'[3] for Yvonne surrounded him with love.

By February 1991, Graham was himself very sick. He sent me a letter from Switzerland, Résidence le Chien, Chemin du Chano 26, in Corseaux. He did not want me to visit because he was so ill. Later, he told me he'd regretted this decision, 'because tired as I am I think it is going to be more tiring answering your letter than meeting face to face'. He was sure his daughter would put me up for a couple of days, but 'unfortunately she is going to be away the whole of April'. Greene couldn't know that he would die early in April. He wanted us to meet again. We never did.

But as late as 11 March 1991, another letter expresses concern: 'Dear Norman, I regret more and more having put you off coming here.'

A further inkling of death in the offing comes in a painful letter of 20 March 1991, dictated to his secretary/niece, Amanda. It conveys a decision made two weeks before his own death, calmly, without anger or anguish, simply an unemotional statement of fact, ending sixty-six years as a writer. Greene, I believe, is returning to the nature I saw when I first met him in 1974: the high rhetoric gone. To Mrs Diana Shine of the Society of Authors, Amanda wrote:

Mr Greene is in such a bad state of health that he can no longer work and therefore no longer regards himself as an author. He is therefore resigning from the Society.

She responded in large print, using her other hand: 'With all my love Elisabeth'. Her husband Rodney wrote to me in his microscopic script: 'N. You are honoured as it's her first letter with her left hand. R.'

* I suspect he couldn't stand a vacuum. During our many interviews, we'd sometimes run through a hundred questions, and the evening would go something like this: he would sit very still, very quiet, as he waited for another question. Then, getting impatient: 'Norman, another question please.'

Greene's mother bore six children. Molly died of cancer on 18 July 1963, and Herbert, the eldest, died in 1968. Then there was a good space of life for Raymond, the Harley Street physician, he who climbed Everest in the 1930s wearing little more than a leather jacket, before mountain-climbing equipment ensured warmth and safety. He died on 6 December 1982. Hugh died on 19 February 1987. And Elisabeth, tall and beautiful, her intelligence sharp as a razor (though not wielded to attack), suffered a severe stroke at the wheel of her car on 25 February 1989 and was never to recover, though she outlived Graham by almost eight years, dying on 16 January 1999.

Consider this splendid generation of Greenes – Raymond (I thought him the best-looking old man in London); Hugh, the Director General of the BBC; Graham, without peer as a novelist; and Elisabeth, with such gentleness and understanding, who served her brother well. Death served her brother well. Death, and death alone, defeated one of the great families of the twentieth century.

PART 24

1991: Our Man Dead

55

Our Man Dead

One moment alive,
he strained to look
at death's lime-burnt face,
but death stared him down
      — NORMAN SHERRY

A T 5.30 in the morning of 3 April 1991 the phone rang in my home in San Antonio, Texas. It was the *Guardian* asking if I'd heard the news. Without waiting for an answer the caller told me that Graham Greene was dead. Would I, as his authorised biographer, give my reactions? I managed to put something together, but I couldn't at that moment express what I truly felt. The life of the man I'd been working on had ended; the man I had come to know through my research into his character, genius and history, I would see no more.

From then on my phone rang every three minutes, calls coming in from all over the globe. They went on all day without ceasing until three the next morning (the last one from New Zealand). Three hours' sleep and they began again.

It seemed to me that journalists the world over were seeking information about Greene, enjoining, in the words of the old music hall song, 'Shovel the dust on the old man's coffin and take up your pen and write.'* And the reporters instincts were sound, for though Greene had lived in France for many years, at the end, it was Britons on this day who chiefly felt such a powerful sense of loss.

Greene had been writing for seventy years, his first short story appearing in the *Star* in 1921, the work of a boy of sixteen. For millions round the world, there had never been a time when he'd not been

---

* Once in 1982, after I'd spent three days interviewing Graham at his sister's home, as we waited for a train to London, he said he'd heard (wrongly, it turned out) that his wife, from whom he was long separated, was going to write about their marriage together. He called on that old song quoted above – we were the only two in the early morning on the platform – and he sang with such melancholy that I was an entranced spectator of another's mortal sadness.

writing. In this simmering, volatile world, his continued existence made for security and permanence. With Greene's passing, a light in European literature had gone out and Death had sentenced a unique individual.

★

The creation of his characters (often deeply divided creatures) was an unequalled accomplishment. At his death, he'd left over sixty books, including twenty-eight novels, and eight plays. There were many movies based on his work. His books sold tens of millions of copies and were translated into dozens of languages.

As we've seen, by the time of Graham's twentieth birthday, he'd flirted with death by playing Russian roulette, and on the last try had spun the chamber a second time, resolving to commit himself to the 'end of the game'. His description of this is disturbing, but clearly a reflection of his character. 'The revolver would be whipped behind my back, the chamber twisted, the muzzle quickly and surreptitiously inserted in my ear . . . the trigger pulled.' The cool objectivity in describing so terrible an action against his own person is indicative of his style and a pointer to the strangeness of his character. His war against himself never truly ended, and only death could be the victor.

Meeting a friend at a bus stop in London, he described to her the heart-stopping experience of being on a plane when its engines ceased in flight, only to assure her: 'If the plane had gone down, I would have been happy to die, very happy to die.'

When Graham converted to Catholicism, he believed he could no longer attempt suicide in an overt way without committing a mortal sin. But he still invited suicide by proxy – in Malaya during the War of the Running Dogs, in Vietnam, Kenya during the Mau Mau insurrection, wherever there were clandestine wars (and not so clandestine dangers), in Papa Doc's Haiti, the Communist revolution in Prague, the leper colony in the Congo. He continued to shun the safe and the comfortable by getting involved with the dictator of Panama, General Torrijos; Tomás Borge of Nicaragua; Havana and Tahiti; the war between Israel and Egypt; the mafia in Nice. Towards the end of his life there were new venues: Moscow (and his new hero, Gorbachev); Dublin and the GPA award – trouble of a different kind.

But Greene was not perpetually unhappy, he could be exciting company, a wonderful conversationalist. A friend recalls seeing the unmistakable figure of Greene coming out of the Royal Albion Hotel, Brighton. He was with a companion and laughing, his face lit up with sheer *joie de vivre*. In old age, he was still the romantic (the boy in him thrived), but his rages were more frequent. His softness was softer, his rough edges more deadly, mixed with fret and fume.

★

I first met Graham in 1974 in his seventieth year, at my London club, the Savile. I had known him by reputation only – elusive, aloof and unpredictable. When he poked his head round the door of the morning room, I was struck by his truly mysterious face. The front view was strong and still, and for the first of countless times I noted that his sea blue eyes gave the impression of blindness. His smile seemed to go silently on beyond need, a smile strangely beatific. Full-face he was handsome, compelling, with a stern strength, even noble. Turn him sideways, and all had changed. His profile was like a brass shield, an upturned dinner plate, with an odd, even comic, blue-veined nose (the gift of drink?) stuck on its centre. His expression was difficult to judge. His hand shook mine, with only the bent forefinger belying a life of writing, his long elegant fingers otherwise firm and strong.

Whenever he had writer's block, he would go to his 'happy home' in Capri, high in the mountains. Greene's study was reached by a stairway (a leg-stretch in length), the door opening to a loft (incredibly small) with only a skylight. It contained a wooden trestle of rough unplaned wood and a rough wooden bed at right angles to it. Nothing else. The walls were whitewashed and without ornaments apart from a cross, not large, on one wall, his workplace a monastic cell.★

My last meeting with Greene was in Antibes, soon after he learnt he was suffering from leukaemia. I remember how slowly we walked down to the old town to Chez Félix. He ate very little, and that little only so that he could drink a martini. The interview was sad, for he was suffering also from amnesia, this man who had always had the

---

★ During the week I stayed at Rosaio in Anacapri, something strange occurred. One night, under a heavily moonlit cloudless sky, I fell asleep early. I was awakened at midnight by someone opening the guest bedroom door. I heard it close quietly. I got up, also quietly, and stuck my head into the passageway only to see the house's front door closing. It was too hot for pyjamas, and so, in my bare feet and bare everything else, I yielded to my curiosity, and pursued my interloper. I looked outside and spied a tall man stepping out into the road. The huge moon lit up everything like a torch except the solid moving figure. I went to the gate. The intruder was no longer in sight. The next morning, I called on Countess Cerio, whom I'd interviewed the day before. I told her a little about my strange and slightly fearful episode and I asked her if Graham was on the island. She said no and that she would know it if he were. The mystery stayed in my mind until it was solved at Graham's funeral. I talked to the Countess for the last time and she astounded me by saying: 'Norman, it *was* Graham who called on you at Rosaio – he told me he had to leave very quickly because you woke up with a start.' But why? She said: 'Graham felt if you had the right to be a detective following him – even into the brothels he'd visited, then he had the right to follow you.' He was, for a moment, my doppelganger instead of my being his.

most prodigious memory, able to put the young to shame. The end was approaching.

★

On his way to Switzerland he had a premonition that he might have a heart attack on the plane – it was 10 September 1990 – and he left a note for Yvonne:

> I feel nervous about this journey tomorrow so I'm slipping this cheque into my pocket. Be happy after the shock is over in the beautiful flat you made for me. I hope I shall be watching you! All my love, Graham.

In writing to the mayor of Antibes, explaining his move to Switzerland, he added: 'I am living between blood transfusions.' And it was at this time that his wife Vivien, learning he was desperately sick, offered to visit him:

> Really I want to be forgotten even by old friends to do perhaps half an hour's work a day . . . that act is a tiring one . . . I envisage being here . . . alone . . . It is pure coincidence that this flat is not far from Caroline [his daughter]. I nearly turned it down because I wanted to be alone, & not part of a family, to work on what is likely to be my last book. Really I cling to my semi-aloneness.

His last home, the final sanctuary, was in Switzerland, his anteroom to death. He shut the door on the world and would rarely see visitors. He didn't want to chance humiliation: 'They'll take advantage of my dying. They'll be looking at me to see a dying man.' Certainly he was looking at death and he spoke often of it, eyes huge, the skin drawn tightly over the bone.

I was to see him in December 1990, arranging to arrive soon after he'd had a transfusion so that his amnesia would be lessened. When I telephoned from the Savile Club in late November he persuaded me, as I've said, not to come: 'I'm too ill to see my own children: I'm very ill: I expect to die: I'm fighting to live but I don't expect to. I'm very tired after each blood transfusion and have to lie in bed all day. I'm very tired. If I gain more marrow, perhaps a miracle might come & I'll see you.' Greene, who drank life down 'like damnation', travelled at full tilt to every part of the globe, lived a passionate, strong life, was now, without fuss, with dignity, facing death. In a sense he had one relapse. That winter, Yvonne recalled, he broke down, a unique event. 'He was in hospital, and all of a sudden an expression came over his face . . . the expression of an upset child.' He seized Yvonne's hands and said:

'I love you; you know how much I love you.' And he burst into tears . . . It was the only time I saw him cry. He was really weeping. And shaking with emotion . . .

Finally Graham pulled himself together, questioning why he was crying and saying, 'I can't remember having cried since I was a child.'

He had four months to live, yet Yvonne realised (and she was 'in despair') that 'that was the day he said goodbye to me, the day I realised what was happening'.[1]

He knew this was his last battle, and knew he would lose. He was becoming frail – a life from bed to chair to bed – and had one fear: that his last work, based on his dream diaries, would be incomplete at his death.

But if he didn't feel he was a writer any longer, he did continue dictating letters into a dictaphone, his voice barely audible. He was exhausted, his body wasted, but his mind, after transfusions, was crystal clear, not a comma out of place.

In January 1991, I telephoned Graham in Switzerland with a special request. First I told him that I'd been rereading *The Heart of the Matter*. I thought I'd offer him (for the first time) my literary judgment – he didn't like praise. I'd never done it before and I thought I should, for he had very little time left. Sometimes he seemed in good spirits. I told him I felt in my rereading, that the first hundred pages of the Penguin edition were the best hundred pages I had read in my lifetime. I was not buttering him up. I said: 'I've never tried to praise your work to your face before, have I?' He laughed that little dry giggly laugh which broke off suddenly, and then, the Greene gargoyle of doubt whispering in his ear, he asked: 'What about the rest of it?'

But I needed a favour, and for a wonderful reason. I told him I was going to be a father. Graham said: 'Illegitimate I hope?' and laughed. I said: 'Legitimate it is.' Graham joked: 'I am disappointed with my biographer.' My wife, Carmen, and I had just learned through amniocentesis that we were expecting a boy. I told him: 'My mother had a son called John who lived only two weeks. My father was called Michael. I'd like to call my first-born John Michael, but I'd also like to add your name.' There was silence over the line. He said, showing that unique gentleness: 'Well Norman, there's an old Graham going out of the world. So it's a good thing a young Graham is coming in to take his place.' I think it was the last time we spoke to each other. He said to me once he did not want to live till ninety. He did not.

The day before he died, his niece, Amanda Saunders, walked into his room at the Providence hospital in Vevey. He was asleep and she did not disturb him. When he stirred, he had no thought of his own condition, but rather was concerned that she'd left her husband and daughter to visit. Dying, he remained an English gentleman, his gallantry still shining.* And on the penultimate day of his life, the last night on earth coming towards him, he looked out of the window to the great mountains, the far shore in the distance, with Yvonne holding his hand, until a light coma seemed to embrace him.

*

In Singapore, Somerset Maugham said: 'If you are small, and remain very still, death may quite likely overlook you.' I have heard that Beethoven shook a defiant fist at the storm. Henry James's last words were, well, quite Jamesian: 'So this has come at last, the distinguished thing.' Lytton Strachey's final contribution: 'If this is death, I don't think much of it.' Rabelais: 'I am greasing my boots for the last journey.' And Oscar Wilde could not leave without a quip, as he lay dying in a drab Parisian bedroom: 'Either that wallpaper goes, or I do.'

Greene's last words reflected his urgency and restlessness for adventure: 'Oh why does it take so long to come?' He looked forward to crossing the last frontier. Death, he believed, was the last state left to us that retains the bite of mystery, essential to man. He'd long before answered my question: 'How do you want to die?' He answered: 'Peacefully & quickly.'

His physician, Dr Morandi, recalled to me how 'As soon as I told Mr Greene that there was no hope, he faced it so easily and wanted to go at once.' Softly, Morandi added: 'He must have a deep faith.'

He was tranquil. Only once did serenity escape him: 'Look, I want to die. I don't want you to hold me back artificially,' he said. Incredibly, Greene spent his last days encouraging his doctor not to feel bad because he couldn't keep his patient alive. Graham might not have made it 'to heaven in a feather bed', but he was anxious to be on his way from his hospital bed.

The head nurse saw how Graham differed from other patients in his curiosity as to what would happen:

You could almost drown yourself in his eyes, so expressive. There were great things in those eyes and you could read from them

---

* On 2 April, he raised his pen for the last time. In the mid-1970s, Greene made me his authorised biographer on a handshake alone. In a nearly final worldly movement, he signed a document protecting me. See Appendix 2.

what he wanted you to know. He had his faculties right to the end. On the Tuesday morning he had difficulty in speaking and in the afternoon he didn't speak, but was very alert and understood everything.

Greene was deeply interested in the possibility of the afterlife. He once poked fun at his friend, the atheist philospher A. J. Ayer:

He always said that given just half an hour he would convince me that there was absolutely *nothing*. Professor Ayer began to hedge a little towards the end. He claimed to have died for four minutes in the Fulham Road hospital. I didn't find his near-death experience all that convincing.

But Greene's interest in near-death experiences was real. His daughter remembers that while Graham was in hospital he spoke about people who'd 'come back from the dead'. He mentioned one instance where there was a sense of a strong light coming towards one while travelling through a long tunnel. 'I wonder whether I'll see that very bright flash of light,' he asked of Yvonne, 'which all those who have been in a coma and came back to life talked about.'

Lucy Caroline was sure that her father was ready to start his journey towards that light: he was looking forward to getting on to the train. 'After all,' he said to Yvonne, 'it might be a very interesting experience. I will at last *know* what is behind the barrier.' All his life he wanted to cross the next frontier, and now that he'd reached his last frontier he had no fear. Dying, he faced death: 'Tell me where I'll be buried. I'd like it to be as close as possible to the flat [in Switzerland] – and you,' he said to Yvonne. Indeed, during his last weeks, and especially in the last days, he talked happily about himself in the past tense.

Greene expected even when very young to die early. His sister Elisabeth had a childhood autograph album, and on one page Graham wrote: 'Death being but a little while away'. He dated the entry 27 December 1924. He was twenty years of age.

★

Father Durán, on page 91 of *Graham Greene, Friend and Brother*, tells us – he puts it vaguely – that 'on an earlier occasion' Greene had said to him: 'Supposing I were seriously ill and in danger of dying, I would summon you to be with me at that time. I would try to make a good confession.' With only hours to live, Graham wanted his friend and priest to be with him: 'The end is coming and I am waiting for you.' Leopoldo tells it slightly differently in his account of the death: 'At last, on Easter Sunday, at 9.30 in the evening, the telephone rang. It was Yvonne: "Graham has reached the end. He wants you to come."' And most assuredly, Graham did want Durán to be there to perform the final rites when Graham was ready to cross to the silent shore.

Durán arrived at the Hôpital de la Providence at 11.45 on Tuesday, the day before Graham died. Graham was conscious, recognised his friend, but couldn't easily speak. Durán administered the sacraments, including the last rites, extreme unction and papal benediction, but not the Host because Greene was having difficulty swallowing and Durán feared he might choke. (This information differs slightly from Father Durán's account in his book, *Graham Greene: Friend and Brother*, but my account is based on notes I took direct from Durán at the Fundación Creixell.)

Greene had twenty hours left, but to his family he seemed far from death. He could not know that the countdown had begun. They suggested he stop using morphia so that he could speak with Father Durán and answer final questions I'd sent him, still lying on his table (I was told his three green Pentel pens lay to the right of my letters). Graham gave his agreement with a nod of the head and the sudden vivid brightness of those speculative eyes – perhaps he could just start to see that light, invisible to living eyes, but inviting dying eyes to walk into it. He was at peace, the 'peace that passes all understanding'. The next morning found him in a coma.

*

Looking at Homer's *Iliad*, one is aware that death was horrendous. For those without the Christian belief in an afterlife, there is no vision of hope. It is as vacant as the enemy dead, during wars, left on the battle-field for the crows, the dogs and wolves to make a bloody deed bloodier.

But after all, when we put our dead beneath the green grass, they inevitably comply with the wishes of the earth. Worms breed, and the handsome man with stunning blue eyes is host to a thousand sliding lascivious creatures, eating our flesh, turning us gradually into a sort of human jam. In the grave loud silence is his: he hears not the roots growing, nor the spread of flowers above the grave, while unseen, the underground activity nibbles slowly on, never gobbling up flesh with swift and hungry pleasure. Death's journey continues piecemeal, slow, turning dry bones to dust. All we know is that the dead are innocent of their loathsome disintegration.

Graham was in Room 11, on the first floor – on one wall a crucifix. He was in bright yellow pyjamas. He had one bare hour to live, and breathing was difficult, his mouth open. Father Durán felt his pulse, which seemed normal. After half an hour his breathing became shallower, his pulse slowed; life was dribbling out of him. Durán began speaking to Greene for the last time: 'I think this is the last moment, Graham. God is waiting for you. When you are with Him, *pray for us* and now I am going to give you the last absolution.' Greene's eyes did not open, but Durán had the strongest impression that he did not lose consciousness until the last second of his life. Father Durán described Greene's ending – he was alone with his hero. 'His breathing stopped as smooth as silk. There was no sound. I kissed his forehead and should have kissed his hand but I forgot.' So Graham never seemed to die of terrible old age, but faded away – beautiful to the beholder. He was on his way to the land of the dead: perhaps just a heartbeat away. Graham Greene's soul had departed, the Old Fox (his description) was gone; the call to the last hunt sounded. He *did* go 'gentle into that good night'. Death had lowered its eyes countless times before, but had looked away so that Greene could continue his pilgrimage. Now, death's gaze chose him, and his haunting in life was over: the circuit cut. Each of us has our own respective deaths, in sealed envelopes, the date, the time, hidden, not knowing our day of delivery. The mystery of death gently descended.

*

Is this what Graham Greene was aiming at by befriending Father Durán? Are we seeing Greene's concern for his own spiritual survival, a priest to ransack the scriptures for him, to prove the promises and gather them in to himself so that he could die at peace (as he most certainly did)? Is this what his death seemed like: a quiet slumber?

Greene was concerned about his promiscuity, wanted forgiveness to escape punishment in hell and be received in the arms of God. Father Durán was his knight, combating Greene's heavy sense of sinning with his mistress. This was the knot he hoped Durán could untie for him.

Caroline, his daughter; Amanda, his niece; and Yvonne, his companion, came in, followed by the nurse who closed Greene's eyes. Vivien arrived the day after his death.

In the mortuary, Greene's coffin was separated from the living by a sheet of glass. According to Father Durán, Greene was well dressed: 'a most beautiful white shirt and silk tie – silk shirt, cuffs, suit and tie dark blue, his head on a cushion'. Vivien felt he was hardly recognisable: 'his face so white, his high colour vanished'. 'But he looked so beautiful,' urged Countess Cerio. 'I felt it at once as soon as I entered the room. The lines had gone from his face . . . I missed seeing those blue eyes for the last time, and his incredibly long artistic fingers.' Many will miss those eyes. As the head nurse said, 'You could almost drown in them.' I see them so clearly, having that light fiery blue of a Siberian husky's – and that is why, however soft and friendly his English voice often was, his eyes could frighten.

★

In light of his passion to examine and record what other novelists had not often attempted, to live any other kind of life would have been impossible for Greene. These were some of my hidden thoughts. In Greene's last moments, Father Durán implored him 'to pray for us'. In this he was following Greene's own vision of heaven. Graham had written: 'Perhaps in Paradise we are given the power to help the living. Sometimes I pray not *for* dead friends, but *to* dead friends, asking for their help. I picture Paradise as a place of activity.'

There were no wild thrashings of Death; on this occasion, the Grim Reaper was not grim – Graham's was a good death. He seemed to relax into it, not to confront it. His niece thought he died with great dignity, seemed in fact to be in control of his death, 'as if he were monitoring it'. Now his work was over: no further daily miracles of speech and writing, those unexpected phrases whose light lingers like a firefly.

One thing he did not care about was his dead body. 'If I should die abroad,' he once wrote to his brother Raymond, 'I hope I shall be shovelled into the nearest convenient spot.' Well, he *was* 'shovelled', if you will, into a convenient spot in the village graveyard of Corseaux, the land sloping gently, beside grass and a hedge, in front of a pathway: in the distance the great lake and the undiminished beauty of the Alps. Graham Greene's mortal journey ending in plot number 528. There are no quotations, no verses, simply his name firmly carved.

It was, I thought, a windless calm that day, but my memory may be at fault, or perhaps there was a brief breeze, but then the breeze stopped. Masses of flowers lay on the coffin; to them I added a single red rose – not from me. I'd been asked by Anita Björk, who loved Greene once, and whom he loved, to place it there.

The newspapers of the day provided many photographs. His daughter, his wife Vivien and his mistress – each of them grieving, each one making efforts not to reveal in their faces the profound sadness that did not belong to the press and photographers around them.

★

Twenty years before he died, in 1971, Greene believed that he did not have long to wait for 'revelation or darkness'. Assuredly he has found one or the other, perhaps salvation 'between the stirrup and the ground'.

His daughter said: 'His spirit must now know what we don't know' – has it not been said that the dead know everything? The death of a great writer especially emphasises man's accidental and transitory presence on earth. Graham never felt a victim of death. To him it was not a shadow but a friend.

*

His funeral was on a Monday – he'd died on Wednesday. Durán recalls that 'three priests celebrated mass' and he gave a short homily:

> Dear Brethren and Friends,
>   Let us be reminded that Graham Greene is not dead . . . Greene was born to eternal life on April 3rd at 11.40 in the morning soon after I told him, 'My dear Graham, God is waiting for you just now. Pray for us, help us all, when you will be forever in God's presence . . . I give you the last absolution.'

Durán added his view:

> My faith tells me he is now with God or on the way to Him. Graham was administered all the sacraments including Extreme Unction and the Apostolic Benediction . . . I do beseech you to be convinced that Graham Greene was a real Catholic Believer.

What I recall of his day of burial is the church, the blaze of altar lights, the swell of the organ music and the sense that *Graham Greene was safe at last.* I remembered how, in his last years, he showed me a two-column list of friends recently deceased, and now he was counted among them. All motion and sound of him had ceased.

Father Durán offered up a prayer for Graham, now in his simplified essence. I stood in the crowd, as Greene lay in his coffin before our eyes, closed in and boarded down in the dark wood of the casket, and his aloneness struck me. He'd found his final destination, free from despair and doubt – he who had always seemed content without a home, now at home, in what Sir Walter Scott called 'that dark inn, the grave'.

*

At the memorial service held in Westminster Cathedral on 6 June 1991, a thousand people turned up, including representatives from the embassies of the world. The Requiem Mass, held in Latin, was impressive, with pomp and dignity for one of England's greatest sons, the music superb, especially the *Ave Verum* exquisitely sung and accompanied. Many were deeply moved. In the middle of the ceremony, an old female tramp came in (classic mackintosh, her worldly possessions in a plastic bag) and walked among the VIPs. Greene would have been delighted.

In Antibes, at Chez Félix at the time of the Requiem Mass, Monsieur Félix, his son and his cook raised glasses to their most famous and devoted customer, who had eaten with them for thirty years: 'That is what he would have wanted us to do,' said Félix.

★

A few years after his burial, I revisited Vevey and Graham's resting place to stand looking down, with the Swiss sky above me and the flawless lake and mountains nearby. I talked to him, though knowing that he must be by now moving into dust 'and under dust to lie'. He already was, and all of us must become, 'sans wine, sans song, sans singer, and sans end!' Listening to the whisper of leaves, I felt a sense of shadow behind, a flutter round the grave of the brave one. And he *was* brave. He stood tall to fight the persecutors, the inhumane, in all their manifestations – to represent them wherever and whenever he could, those who are the wretched of the earth. He was tricky like a fox, clever, his genius curious. In death, he did not need to walk in sorrow, though many of us did at the funeral. I recalled his saying to me: 'No lies please. Follow me to the end of my life.' He wanted the truth – about his life and his writing: grim and glorious, terse and condensed, vigorous and genuine. He was a prodigy, his courage proven, his international prestige deserved.

★

How did Yvonne come to terms with Graham's death, or her own a decade later? She spoke of it to Marie-Françoise Allain for their book of conversations, *In Search of a Beginning: My Life with Graham Greene*:

> 'For me . . . I harbour the hope of finding [Graham] again . . . It's the only thing that keeps me going . . . But if I didn't retain this hope of finding him again, I'd collapse into despair and I'd be devastated, because everything would go to pieces . . . I don't want to let myself go. It's a struggle against myself . . . When I get desperate I think of him and then I say to myself 'He wouldn't want that.'[2]

On the last page of the book, Yvonne relates how she became friendly with a Father Cuzon and she explains to him how she is missing Graham: 'You see, for me, it's the thought of never seeing him again, never hearing him again, never being able to touch him again,

798

that I find so unbearable.' And the priest answered in a way that was a tremendous help for Yvonne: 'You're a Catholic; you're not allowed to say that', and his final statement lifted her out of the shadows: 'Death is a beginning, not an end.'

She admitted it was the 'being able to say everything to him. That's what I miss so much. It's dreadful.' And 'choking a little, she murmured, "It's hard, you know . . ."'

Allain ends her work with a final account: 'Later on, the summer before she died . . . in the weakest of voices she sighed, "At least when I go, I'll go to meet him."'[3] Surely her love was rare, singular, and probably unparalleled.

*

We all carry within us the common enemy of man, a future death. We come like water, like wind we take our leave, and we see through a glass darkly. As his biographer, coming to the end of this work, I want to stress that I have tried to give an exact rendering of authentic memories, and to do so in a spirit of piety. 'A man's life of any worth,' wrote John Keats, 'is a continuous allegory and very few eyes can see the mystery.' There lies the hope – to be those eyes; to lift the stone and let in light.

Death looked on Graham Greene as it will look on each of us at our appointed moment; as Prince Hal said: 'We owe God a death'. But there is a wonderful return in this for a biographer. The child born this night – I completed the *Life of Graham Greene* on 8 October 2002 – wishing to know, perhaps with seventy or more winters on her head, what it was like during the life of Graham Greene (not far short of a century long) might explore Graham's (and our) world through the authorised volumes presented here. Just as we find the Victorian period rich in complexities and perhaps somewhat bizarre, she, looking at our generation as past history, might find us strange and intriguing and even (at least in Greene's case, his fame not diminished by death, standing in the shadow of immortality) extraordinary. And every reader will in a sense bring us, the long-forgotten men and women, momentarily back among the living. The rest is silence.

Leaving Greene

Leaving Greene

My great travail so gladly spent
Forget not yet.
— SIR THOMAS WYATT

To the memorialist biographer, what matters is that he alone loves, or he alone understands. To the biographer who specialises in scandal (and our age seems to have spawned many), his interest lies in bringing forth a new distorted birth. It is in such a book that Greene, the genuine if unorthodox Catholic, is found to be outrageously fraudulent; Greene, the winner of the Jerusalem Prize, is secretly anti-Semitic; Greene, the doughty fighter for the victims of this world, is interested only in self.

There are many ways in which falsification enters into biography and history, and one of ancient Rome's greatest historians, Tacitus, declares: 'The histories of Tiberius, Caligula, Claudius and Nero, while they were in power, were falsified through terror and after their death were written under a fresh hatred.' 'Fresh hatred' should be anathema in biography. Truth is paramount. You cannot cheat; you cannot lie; you must reflect the world as it is in the time of your subject, and Greene's time is our time.

The completion of *The Life of Graham Greene* came neither easily nor quickly, yet when I began it in October 1976, I felt that I'd soon bring it to heel. Upon reaching the end of the Greene biography on the early evening of Tuesday at 8.30 p.m., at my table in Bistro Vatel, 8 October 2002, in San Antonio, Texas, six days after what would have been Greene's ninety-eighth birthday, I had the quite inexplicable feeling that time had shortened and I'd spent very few years writing it. Reaching the end had often seemed beyond my strength and spirit. On very many nights I sensed cicatrices gathering on my mind, invisible scars dotting my thoughts and memories. So it was odd, and miraculous, when the day of completion arrived.

803

By following Greene's tracks, I hope I've succeeded in resurrecting the history not only of Greene, but of the many largely forgotten men and women along the way. With my final word on this *Life of Graham Greene*, the last page turned, I sit in the silence of night in calm thankfulness. I have out of fear left the last sentence incomplete. Why have I, as Schubert did his symphony, left this biography unfinished? It was Greene's belief that he would live to read the first volume of the biography – he did; that he would not live to read the second – he did not; and that, as he told Gavin Young in the Travellers' Club, Norman Sherry would not live to complete the third. My superstitious dread of Greene's powers of divination dictated this ending, which I type only now – not finished, to breathe fulfilment into Greene's prophecy. I haven't completed the work, so I still breathe.

. . . at the news of Graham Greene's death, the king of writers dead, the chair empty, many felt a deep sadness, and young men, thinking of the quiet spirit of the newly dead (who had published compulsively for almost seventy years), were, even in their youth, made aware of their own mortality. Look into the sky, Signore, his star is not yet out. Let peace . . .

APPENDIX I

Swedish Nobel Documents

*(translated by Susan Szmania of
the University of Texas at Austin)*

Comments by Mr Osterling
[Regarding the 1950 Nobel
Prize in Literature]

IN regard to the five proposals which, according to the committee's preliminary message, seem to be most important in this year's prize discussion, I have come to the decision that Bertrand Russell should be considered as a decisive priority both because of his superior intellectual knowledge and his extensive influence as a modern Enlightenment philosopher.

I am unfortunately unable to judge the factual aspects of Russell's authorship, such as his work concerning mathematical logic and his method of analysis. But, it is essential to me that his works have had a powerful influence on laymen, and he has shown the ability to keep the general philosophical interest alive. All of his achievements constitute an exceptionally stimulating justification for the sound reason of reality. With his free and reliable sense, his admirably clear style and his quick seriousness, he has developed the writing skills that can only be found in few people in our times. Thus such a work of his which came out a few years ago, *The History of the Western World**, as far as I can judge, has made him Nobel prize worthy; but in addition there has been a steady line of works that are just as meaningful that take up all of the problems that a modern community has to wrestle with.

Through his liberal humanism I believe that Russell represents the wishes and patterns of thought that led Alfred Nobel to establish his prize. I follow the last words of Professor Wedenberg's for my own formal report: To give the Nobel prize in literature to Bertrand Russell would be, according to my thoughts, a credit to common sense and to humanity's brightest speakers in our time.

Concerning William Faulkner I have entertained the thought in light of the deeply depressive themes that he often takes up. It is a given that *he seldom answers to the demand for a more positive outlook on*

* This should be Russell's *History of Western Philosophy*.

life. But his artistic integrity is so strong and distracting that one, in the end, does not hesitate to place that measure on his books. For my sake, I am ready to concur with other knowledgeable people's clearly well-judged estimation of his writing genius. Faulkner is a master of his trade, which is the morbid and lush environment of the southern states that he grew up in and that hold him spellbound. His influence on the world of literature is now so well-qualified that an honour to him undoubtedly would be welcomed with approval in America and Europe.

However, I find Hemingway's chances considerably weakened by his long-awaited new book *Across the River and Into the Trees*, which tells about an American officer's last days in Venice as an invalid and shows a debatable relaxation in the question of both technique and human-interest compared to his earlier works. The role that Hemingway has played as a stylist is remarkable and undeniable, but of everything there is to judge, there is his promise for the future, and a prize to him now would not fulfil any real purpose.

The nomination of Graham Greene, I believe, is a bit premature, even if, for example, a novel like *Heart of the Matter* seems to me to be a more remarkable achievement than this formal report can give credit. I find however, that I have no grounds to consider this candidate more closely this year.

As for the nomination of sharing the prize between the Greeks Angelos Sikelianos and Nikos Kazantzakis, I must admit I am a bit hesitant for I have not been able to convince myself that the latter, with all of his extensive and abundant talent, may be placed in the same category as his more exclusive poetic brothers.

Given all that has been said, let me suggest that Bertrand Russell receive this year's prize for literature.

Comments by Per Hallstrom
Graham Greene
1950

THIS English author was born in 1904, studied at Oxford and held Government posts, which took him abroad on long travels. Moreover, he spent considerable time, as is seen in the reference points in his writing, in vastly different environments such as Mexico and the USA. He has published a large amount of work, mostly novels. The literary critics in England revere him as an accomplished novelist, and a few even go so far as to place him in the range of the best of his generation.

He is obviously deep and filled with an intensely strong imagination concerning the ancient question of malicious human superiority in our world, in a large part during the time that he grew up and lived in [it]. He has a very sharp eye and clearly a predominant interest in more or less the hellishness that he has met in his changing life experiences, and his fantasy seems to be constantly trying to fill in the possible blanks with sharper atrocities and more glaring colours. All of this in order for the reader to understand these beginning stages as a fixed idea. But if he has a complement to this frightening tendency, it is that he converted to Catholicism and he believes in the Kingdom of Heaven as well as in the existence of Hell. This is just about how the author himself has explained his beliefs.

In Greene's novels, there appears to be no equilibrium between the two worlds; detest for Hell has, of course, been more richly depicted than hope for redemption. But, this hope shines through now and again, and in his best book *The Power and the Glory*, it blossoms, at the end, like a flower from damnation's trampled grounds. One naturally becomes surprised by this phenomenon because in the story's course of events, the hopefulness has been well concealed. The hero is also as unimpressive as could be imagined, and likewise, nothing that befalls him prevents him carrying out his martyrdom so that the reader cannot understand the possibility of his redemption. The novel takes place in a part of Mexico where everything that can be called religion is being eradicated. All the priests must flee and there are only two left. One has saved his own life and even has secured a pension while he has changed himself under duress and married. In this way, he is able to bear the ridicule of his religion. The book, however, centres on the other priest's narrow escape from death. He is, as mentioned, not a very impressive figure, he cannot overcome a deep-rooted spiritual longing and his morals are burdened by a child that he had with an Indian and is forced to leave to take care of itself. In countless depictions, the reader learns everything that he already knows about the priest through repetitions, and through it all, a persistent description of all the good and all the bad, in which the rural population lives. The little ordinary priest cannot give them more religious consolation than by saying masses for them and by allowing the sick and dying to confess their sins.

But in this way, he denies them their connection with the church and with that he feels he must fulfil their needs for redemption to some degree, even though the whole time he knows that he himself is forever a rejected soul. At the end, he meets his fate by knowingly giving up the possibility of freedom that the border might allow. He does this by refusing to turn off the road while on his way to give last rites to a dying murderer. He has done a powerfully heroic deed, but it cannot count as a merit. He is executed without knowing and without understanding that he is really a martyr. But as the shot is being fired in the town where the execution takes place, all the rational people there understand that a martyr's life has ended.

If the summary of the story that has been given seems a bit dry and colourless, then the same can be said of the story. It is only in the end that the story's meaning and main purpose come forth. What throws the reader off is that he or she does not feel any real emotion for the form of the book sooner in the story. The author is, if not afraid of making any bad moves in his work, very scared of allowing his own person to come through in his writing, and of writing words that would add consistency and clarity to the scenes. Perhaps, like so many other writers of his time, Greene is influenced by film. In this art form, there is no room for true storytelling; it is sufficient just to give scenes. In film, these scenes are held together by the composition, while in novels these scenes are picked up at random and surrounded by obscurity about where the scenes come from and where they are going. When it concerns the serious religious qualities that Greene has in mind, this formlessness is very disturbing. Only in one area, the depiction of the melancholy, humdrum scenes in the book, does the author allow his own voice to come through, and the author is able to satisfy his need to carefully describe every detail about the dead things and his belief in reality.

The book, however, ends poignantly even if the reader becomes somewhat tired of the winding path along the way.

In another of Greene's most well-known books *The Heart of the Matter*, the setting is a West African town. Here, we find a desert that is not as tragically brutal as the one in the book about Mexico, and the depictions are more varied but make too great a claim. The book's thesis is serious enough and deeply felt; it proclaims, much like Schopenhauer, compassion as the only way to achieve human kind's and life's inner meaning.

In another similarly admired book, *Brighton Rock*, his storytelling ability encounters some especially serious problems. It appears, if one questions the theme, that the book is a detective novel.

This form of lyricism has reached technical and stylistic perfection in today's England, most notably through the mathematical clarity that evolves from the overly realistic and sharp-sighted detective who figures out the murder. In *Brighton Rock*, the murderer is unnaturally equipped, while the role of the detective has fallen into rather weak hands. Likewise, the culprit's ruin is expected because of the persecution that forces him to make compromising moves.

Without a doubt, the innovation that Greene introduces to the genre is that he does not, for a moment, follow the requirement of clarity in style and story. To be on a hunt for a criminal without seeing right before your eyes, without knowing if a murder has occurred, is not a good thing. But even worse, is that the book's one real aspect, the murder, has a sculptural solidity but is made from material that is not quite real, so that the reader does not quite believe in him. He is seventeen years old but he has a perfectly finished character and a monumental ambition and the willpower to strive to be a powerful leader of criminals. He has no means to differentiate enemies or friends and has no other human weakness than perhaps a small penchant for listening to music. He becomes a construed character.

I have not read any of Greene's other novels mostly because I have not had the time, except for the premature and uninteresting book: *England Made Me*, which gave no promise for the future. It should be, in all probability, that the three books from his most fruitful time could give enough of a foundation on which to base an evaluation of his works. He is, without a doubt, a gifted author with a rich imagination and discovery and an unusual life experience. Moreover, he does not have any of the rambling qualities that so often determine how successful one might be at making books. Rather, he has serious and, in his own way, noteworthy ideas and his feelings are real, when one is able to track them in their short revelations. But, as an artist, he does not seem to me to have reached the height that should be considered worthy of a Nobel Prize.

Stockholm, the 31st of May, 1950
Per Hallstrom

APPENDIX 2

Document to Norman Sherry, signed by
Graham Greene on the day before he died, 2 April 1991

I, Graham Greene grant permission to Norman Sherry, my Authorised
Biographer, excluding any other, to quote from my copyright
material published or unpublished.

Executed on April 2nd 1991.

Signed

Witnessed:

Graham Greene's List of Favourite Prostitutes

Appendix. *diary notebook.*

5 St. James's Street
London S.W. 1
Whitehall 9680

X 1.   1st

2.   2nd

3.   ° Hotel in Lisle St.

4.   After appetite.

5.   Channel Island girl.

6.   while mackintosh.

7.   Dentist 1.

8.   flight 2 —

X 9.   dreadfully drunk. J

10.   second time.

11.   Sofa.

X 12.   will

X 13.   Curse.

X 14.   Blackmail. 10/-

15.   Newsagent —

16.   Dentist's assistant

17.   ° girl in Don Juan's. Brighton

18.   Ellisthian etc.

---

19.   ° Annette. —

20.   ° Molly. —

21.   ° Shaftesbury St. Oxford St. —

22.   the one who wouldn't.

23.   ° Corner in Jermyn St —

X 24.   Pat.

25.   Oxford Circus.

26.   ° Bishop Hooper X

27.   ° girl with studs & body.

28. } Sisters from country —
29. }

30.   shy but violent

31.   Russian boots. —

X 32.   Poor tough beggar.

X 33.   Flagellate.

34.   Black pants

X 35.   Seville.

36.   Paris.

37.   Drussilla.

X 38.   Regent St. Arbuckle Ave.

X 39.   Islington.

X 40.   Leicester Sq — Circus.

41.   Soho — Wardour St.

42.   Lisle St.

43.   Bond St. Purity.

44.   Tall blonde + friend.

45.   Prostitute — Pub suicide.

46.   Piccadilly. Green Park. style.

47.   rain, rain.

The following transcription is the result of the efforts of three different people attempting to read Greene's handwriting, but there is no guarantee of accuracy.

1.	1st	24.	Pot
2.	2nd	25.	Oxford Circus
3.	Habit in Lisle St	26.	Bishop Hooper
4.	After appendix	27.	Girl with stench & baby
5.	Channel Islands girl	28.	Sisters from country
6.	white macintosh	29.	＂　　＂　　＂
7.	Brothel 1	30.	Shepherds Market
8.	flagel. 2-	31.	Russian boots
9.	dress shop. mast. 3	32,	Real tough buggerer
10.	Second twin	33.	Flagellatee
11.	Safer	34.	Black pants
12.	Welsh	35.	Seville
13.	Curse	36.	Paris
14.	Blackmail 10/-	37.	Brussells
15.	Nurserymaid	38.	Regent St – Arbockle Av
16.	Dentist's assistant	39.	Islington
17.	Girl in Bon Marché – Brighton	40.	Leicester Sq – Circus
		41.	Sucker Wardour St
18.	Ellister & Cavell	42.	Lisle St
19.	Annette	43.	Bond St French
20.	Molly	44.	Tall blonde & friend
21.	Jermyn St – Oxford St	45.	Irish – Pole sucker
22.	The one who wouldn't	46.	Piccadilly Green Park single
23.	Course in journalism	47.	caesarian

On a separate sheet, Greene listed some of the same women, with slightly different descriptions; for example:

'Habit in Lisle St' is listed as 'Steady in Lisle St hotel'
'Russian boots' is further described as 'Girl with Russian boots – now in Oxford'
'Shepherds Market' is 'Girl with cross in Shepherds Market'
'Blackmail 10/-' may be 'Girl I quarrelled with over 10/-'

We also see some new names:

'Girl by mirror'
'Doctor's girl'
'Beautiful bottom in S. Kensington'
'Circus girl in Cranbourn St'
'Monique'

'Girl off Chester Place'
'Fish tea in Nottingham'
'Saville Row Group 6'
'Girl who went to Couts'
'Near B. B. C.'

and the poignant

'Absolute stray'
'Girl who tried to keep me'

Poem by Greene showing his method of revision

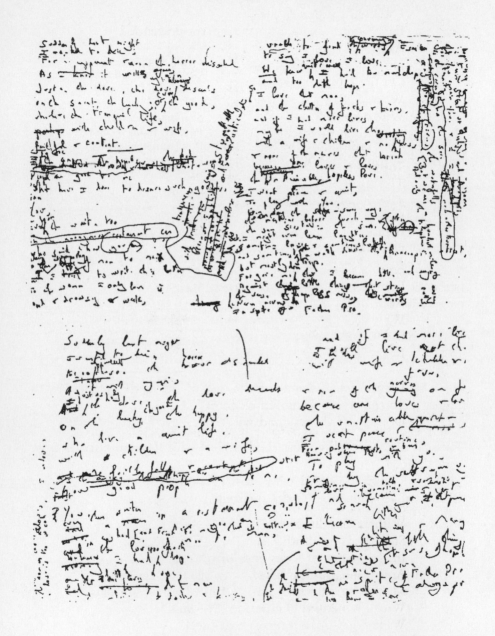

Suddenly last night
I wanted to die;
For no apparent reason the horror descended
As it will again,
Just as the dove, the dove always descends
On the saint, the good: even the lucky
Who live the tranquil aging life
With children and wife,
Faithful and content.

To me
The angry,
The hopeless, the bad
How strangely people are good to me,
Who have done nothing to merit such goodness,
From you,
From a priest at Padua,
From a stranger seen in the street,
Even from this waiter
Who said, "How are you?" with tenderness,
Seeing me stumble and inarticulate
In the anonymous restaurant car.

I try to write this letter
To the woman I only love,
Doped and drowsy and weak,
Unable to find the convincing words
To say, "I love. I love."
He knew too well I had too much dope
And too little hope.
So I love that man,
With his kindly breath
Staring at my death.
In the clatter of forks and knives.
And if I had more lives,
Maybe I would live thus,
With a wife and children and no fuss.
With none of the nerves that break
Because one loves and loves
The unattainable.

Letter from Greene to Dr Michel Lechat

La Résidence des Fleurs,

Avenue Pasteur,

O66OO Antibes

16th December 1984

Dear Michel,

A very belated thanks for your letter of November 29, but I have been moving around. Many thanks too for sending me the Chinese edition of A BURNT OUT CASE. Is this Taiwanese or from Pekin? They do seem to have begun to publish my books in Pekin. As a matter of fact I already had a copy but I didn't know what book it was!

I am afraid the cutting wont make me want to return to Pocos del Toro.

I am terrified of Norman Sherry going to the Congo. He caught the same dysentery as I did in Oaxaea, he had an operation on his intestines and I had an operation on my intestines, he nearly got involved in a revolution in Liberia, there were shots in the streets of Panama when he was there which in all my visits I have never heard and I fear he will catch leprosy if he goes to the Congo.

Much love from both of us

Acknowledgments

My sincere thanks go to Trinity University's Dr John Brazil, sensitive, meritorious, a most worthy President. Dr Michael Fischer, Vice-President of Academic Affairs and Dean of Faculty, overworked but never out of breath, a calmness pervades him. He was born honourable. Also Chuck White, Vice-President, another worthy, commendable and deserving: always busy yet always helpful, and always with a smile, sometimes leading to his infectious laughter. A number of distinguished scholars at Trinity read the manuscript, in particular Peter Balbert – for sixteen years a sterling Chairman of the English Department – a determined supporter of this biography, his judgments swift, sound, wittily expressed, always astute; and Dr Salomon, whose scholarship and character I've always greatly admired, when he gets up steam his judgment is scintillating. These, my colleagues and friends who worked through the final text. Thanks also to Richard West: so often I see him walking around the campus, earphones around his head. Listening to another recorded book? If he cannot read while walking, he can at least listen. I remember Professor William Samelson offering me strong encouragement, at moments when it seemed I'd never finish unravelling the complications of Greene's life.

The distinguished journalist John Maxim (of Mexico City). The brilliant novelist and winner of the 2003 National Book Award Shirley Hazzard, whose short study of Graham Greene – *Greene on Capri* – is superb. Stephen Vizinczey, Hungarian, author of (among many other novels) *In Praise of Older Women*, still after all these years a best seller in France. What else is Vizinczey? A genius. Bryan Forbes, a man lavish in talent who turned a film star as a youngster, later a film director, biographer and novelist – lavish indeed! For sheer beauty, coupled with intellect, his wife, actress and author Nanette Newman. When I visited their home she prepared three meals a day for four days. I witnessed that her cookbooks were inspired from real life. Carmen Capalbo, a superb director on the Broadway stage, producing Greene's *The Potting Shed*, read the final volume with the greatest care – a born editor he. The great leper specialist, Dr Michel Lechat and Father Hendrik Vanderslaghmolen, two men, both of whom earned my praise, thanks and admiration. And Robert Bolster – whose final comments on the manuscript offered sharp, penetrating, criticism (complete with swift unexpected flashes of humour), a strange watchfulness his, touching on the mystery of life.

My dear identical brother Alan Sherry (though he is half an hour older), went through the typescript, and his perceptive comments were well documented and well noted. 'Sir' Glenn Cummings and his gem, Ruby, always ready to look after a bachelor in need. Dr Bill Stone, distinguished biologist and good friend, living now in Spain and therefore much missed. Dr Joe Boyle, my dentist who rarely charges me – now there's a dentist to have, and the dazzling periodontist, the one and only Pam Berlanga. Eric Schaffer MD, who takes me – or I take him – for a monthly drink at our favourite bistro. (Most of us are dispensable, not he.) If I ever get lost on a desert island I hope I have the foresight to take Eric along. Michael Sarosdy MD, for his friendship and concern: the man to know when illness strikes. Bill Breit, Professor Emeritus, economist and novelist who excels in both fields. His subtle intellectual thrillers should not be forgotten. Before I forget, I'll tell you that Dr Breit has the wit of a reincarnated Oscar Wilde. Also Larry Hechler and Pat Ullman. My thanks to Irma Escalante, Senior Secretary in the English Department who is always professional, never flushed or flurried and above all friendly, and Suzanne Brown, with her smile and her attentive and warm manner.

Others I would call meritorious. Ralph Fiennes, a deservedly famous actor. Michael Holroyd, a rare bird surely one of England's finest biographers. Paul Theroux, admired as a writer by Greene, distinctly admired by Greene's biographer. Joan and Vincent McDonnell, Vincent proving Greene's judgment (see Chapter 53). Fay Weldon, a great novelist, a great character, she bubbles up, arch, impish and inspiring. Bruce Harkness and S. W. Reed, great friends to Conrad studies. Raymond Judd, University Chaplain, a truly good man and Christian.

These are special friends: Roger Watkins, David Pearce, Yan Christiansen from the Graham Greene Berkhamsted Birthplace Trust: all of whom I greatly admire. They also remind us of the love readers bear towards Greene and his novels. M. Fagin has a verbal dexterity that is unexpected, exhilarating, indeed, enough to keep the dying alive, unquestionably a friend to Greene's biographer. Edwin Thumbo, deservedly well known as a poet in the Far East, attached to Singapore University, where I received my first academic position. John Offord, a great friend and publisher. Jackie Loomis Quillen, who offers me free accommodation in this country's capital, she remains the kindest woman I know in Washington. Among the magnanimous in that city I include Rosemary and John Monagan, a beautiful purity is theirs. Kay Huey who directs her myriad kindnesses towards me.

And now I return to friends known by me at school and colleges in England. Ram Singh, confidant when I began my research of Greene in 1976 and still a true friend in 2004, twenty-eight years later. Dr Tony Bottomley, money sharp, his mind sharper, that slightly hoarse voice immediately recognisable. Cedric Watts, a scholar whose work borders on mine, a true friend whom I see rarely now, more's the sadness. Ian Carr, probably the best trumpeter of our time, playing his Yamaha custom trumpet, and Gerald Laing, much of his important work done in bronze (and brilliant sculptures they are) and myself, are old friends (and still today). I recall a photo taken in a saggy part of London where young ambitious men congregate – the photo vivid in my mind's eye – to see those three young graduates strolling, each one's secret ambition known to the other and believed by each. I wish we were neighbours in London now. A college friend, Dr Eddie Miller: when I knew him at college his passion was for music – he had a beautiful voice then – but he had to turn to the medical arts and practices in Saskatchewan, proving that to be a singer at University is an advantage to being a good doctor. What else? He was Chairman of 'SOC-SOC', and I can't remember now what SOC-SOC was! Dear, dear Mavis Leith, I knew her in childhood, then a bit of a tomboy willing to climb trees or ragged walls with the best of us. I loved her at five, I love her *still*. And Stanley Eveling, poet and playwright, a great creative force to many at university.

Dan Franklin, Publisher and Director of Jonathan Cape, who has now had the experience of having to deal with a biographer who tried to run, but I couldn't run fast enough! Kathryn Court, President and Publisher of Penguin, poised and highly intelligent, and the tremendously efficient Paul Slovak, Associate Publisher and Vice-President of Viking Books. Leigh Priest, the admirable indexer. Sue Bradbury, Editorial Director of The Folio Society – whenever I meet her in London, I always feel as if I'm royalty! So kind and warm and generous she is. Helpful Michael Korda of Simon and Schuster. Graham Carleton Greene, my literary agent, originally Managing Director of Jonathan Cape, my present publisher, whom I have been with since the first volume of the biography – I suppose we are both getting old together, skipping the same dance for twenty-seven years. Also James Greene, his brother, a poet of distinction and translator of Russian. Mrs Graham Greene (Vivien) who died at the age of ninety-nine years on 19 August 2003. She once told me in an interview that she was a supporter of the Protection of Tigers League and then went on to say that her husband, Graham, was the least domesticated and the wildest of creatures. I said to her that she must try to reach 100 years of age. She said 'I'll try Norman, but I'm very tired'. She had earthly rewards, but I am rooting for her eternal ones outdistancing them by far. Graham and Vivien's children, Francis and Lucy Caroline, and his niece Amanda Saunders, once met are not easily forgotten. Catherine Walston's family, both mother and father now dead: Bill Walston in Cambridge, very direct in speech, how wonderful to meet a man who tells no lies: Oliver, the eldest child, successful farmer, successful radio broadcaster and successful traveller.

Gracious thanks (though already mentioned in my text) to Bernard Diederich and Al Burt for their wonderful book *Papa Doc: The Truth about Haiti Today* (1969) and for a second long and inspiring work about Haiti, *Written in Blood: The Story of the Haitian People 1492-1971* (1978) by Robert and Nancy Heinl, now expanded to 1995 and updated by their wise and brilliant son, Michael. A new edition is expected in 2004. Aubelin Jolicoeur, rich in personality, living a dangerous life in Haiti. At eighty he still seems ageless. Márie Terèse Danielsson for help with material on Tahiti and Herbert Gold for assistance on Haiti. I must speak at once about George Russo who was originally a Catholic priest. He became attached to Greene's work by his brilliant description of the priest in *The Power and the Glory*. I need to state categorically that the remarks he made to me influenced the way in which I dealt with Greene in the chapter about his religion. Professor David Leon Higdon, author of the select bibliography that accompanies this volume, deservedly renowned for his accuracy and precision as a scholar.

I'd like to thank Tom Staley, Director of the Harry Ransom Humanities Research Center, interested in the *Life* and holder of one of the three great collections of original Greene material. If it is rivalled at all we need to go to two other centres of learning, Boston College and Georgetown University Library, both stockpiles of Greenery which no scholar can ignore. At Boston College, the collection was put together by Robert O'Neil, Director of the Burns Library (whom I call that grand acquisitor), and his special help-mate, John Atteberry, himself a successful bibliographer. At Georgetown University Library, Joseph E. Jeffs, whose friendship with Greene enormously benefited that library. In recent years, that indefatigable collector Nicholas Scheetz, a great librarian, a lover of books as his own personal library testifies, a scholar who is of swift mind, his lively tongue evidence of this. He is naturally good mannered and an honour to Georgetown University. He would run to the ends of the earth if it meant that his Greene collection could, even now, be further expanded. He is ever and ever a special friend. Also Scott Taylor, his excellent assistant. Ian Mayes, my newspaper stalwart at the *Guardian*. John Wilkins now retired from the *Tablet*, which journal he served most mightily as Editor. Laura Chandler, a wonderful opera buff. Randy Morris, a fellow Olmos Park traveller.

My one time students, author Dan Auiler and Sean Stratton, now successfully living and working in Hollywood. Leopoldo Durán – Greene's special priest and a special person. Pharmacists Israel Martinez, Bill Shuey and Stu Walker, also special in their field. Professor Francis Nevins long ago gave me information about Greene in Cuba, not forgotten and used in this final volume; and that neurosurgical genius, Dr Hilton.

My memories of friends during the writing of this final volume stretch wide and far. Neighbours in Lewes, England, good Samaritans they, Charles Revett and Bob Towner, a couple of 'backroom boys' I profoundly appreciate. Sister Thomas of St Mary's and her close associate Sister Camillus care for Sylvia Sherry with Catholic kindness, also the finance officer at St George's retreat, Pat Foster – always providing humour when we speak over the phone. Dr Siddiqui watches over Sylvia and I thank him for his gallant assistance.

For translations I have picked from the best; for German, Sarah Burke: for Latin, Dr Colin Wells, the Murchison Distinguished Professor of Classical Studies: for Spanish, Professor John Donahue, Professor of Sociology and Anthropology, all at Trinity. For Swedish, Susan Szmania, and for French, Christopher Kilmer, both from The University of Texas at Austin. Christopher even journeyed to Brussels to see and interview my friend, leprologist Dr Lechat, whose insights are spread over Chapters 15, 16 and 17.

Interested students who have helped with the volume (they kept me sane): Eric Faulk, Luke Petersen, Michael Slater, Shameela Keshavjee, Asif Rahman, Howard Wilen, Kira Kupfersberger, Wendy Montgomery, Elizabeth Walchuk, Ruth Anderson, Kathleen Fenske and Kristen Kylla. Austin's Sarah Mulvaney gave special attention to the Haiti chapters. Students of merit and maturity exist in Trinity University – here are five young reliables whom I suspect might well have dazzling futures if they refuse to lose their way, remember my words Bjorn Kruse, Kevin McConnell, Martin Lundeen, Lisa Sutherland and Michael Shay. Also Christopher Fisher, who developed a passion for the work of Greene, and took the pictures of his final resting place in Switzerland.

For Volume Three, I had two secretaries, Jonathan Plummer and Genie Beck. Genie proved skilled working the internet and her persistent endeavours are here acknowledged. Claire Smith came in at the end to ensure I broke the tape, her English good manners a comfort – her organisation a godsend.

Greene said to me on our first meeting that he 'didn't particularly care for academics, their life begins with the Adam's apple, goes upwards – never reaches the pants': the following absolutely do not fit Greene's exhilarating but somewhat twisted description. They are, without exception brilliant men. Professor John Carey a well known critic, so scholarly yet vivid, knowledgeable yet penetrating, an artful scholar in one of Oxford's oldest colleges. I must refer to Philip French who, during much of my working life, has published on many occasions material that I greatly admire. Also Alan Friedman, either Alan's following my career or I'm following his. His a genuine talent, ours a genuine friendship. But strange how he replaced me at Lancaster University for a year and I replaced him at the University of Texas in Austin. By such a move I was able to begin studying the original manuscripts of Greene, and among many other valuable items, a great assortment of letters to and from Greene.

Appreciation also to Christopher Matthews who gave information that allowed me to make an important literary detective scoop. A good friend, Dr David Kramer, who has successfully kept my blood pressure normal, an achievement in itself. Donna Madonna, a premier nurse, an angel on earth. Piers Paul Read, a friend to the second volume and a friend to this third. It is sad that we're out of touch so much. Max and Joan Reinhardt: Max's friendship valued to the very end. Michael Richey, a dear friend of Greene's, and mine too. Dear Julia Stoner (please forgive me if I leave out your many titles), a correspondent I have still to meet. Anita Björk, the famous Swedish actress, a beautiful lady who I found, on visiting Sweden, to be a darling. My love always to my elder brother Thomas Taylor Sherry and my dear sister Grace.

Special friends include Damien Vatel of Paris and Lille, he's *chef par excellence* in his own restaurant (the best in San Antonio). Well known in France and here in San Antonio for his prowess, he is by nature, uncannily, a philosopher. He let me be his mascot and gave me my own special room to work in while I ate, the third volume finally completed in Bistro Vatel at table number eight (let's not mention my manuscript catching fire on the candle – the remnants of that page now treasured and safely locked away for posterity). Sunny Tanner and Raymond Martinez, who work for Damien, are close friends. Patrick Kennedy Jnr (not Ted), attorney and entrepreneur; Paul Covey, financial wizard; Harold Wood, artist/wine connoisseur – often found among the scattered tables of the Bistro Vatel.

Not to forget that splendid fellow Bobby Cavender: a face unlined, unchanging, a mischievous look as he stares out from his office at Cavender Buick. He has kept me successfully on wheels for years now, and jokingly, promised to read this book, but only if it had lots of pictures! Rey Leal is hairdresser and photographer, excelling in both fields – also a trusted friend. Scott Cobb, a distinctive travel guru, but then Cobb is distinctive in many ways. Robert Callagy, renowned New

York attorney – he is a good friend: another friend, Robert Shivers, busy also as an attorney yet has a passionate interest in the byways and highways of literature. Ethan Casey, who calls me suddenly out of the blue (you never know where he'll be) approached me originally to be my biographer. Alas, I shied away – my secrets are my secrets!

Nellie the night janitoress, who nearly always caught me in the late hours working (while the rest of the world was at dinner). Tim McCollum, my postman – have you noticed how happy postmen are? Betty at the pharmacy who kept my coffee cup (and my life) full, and the smiling face of Gerald Wade and, almost finally, Herbert Rueppel – my favourite barman at Cappyccino's. Last in this line, Lloyd Brown.

Special friends in Texas also appear on the scene: Bernard Lifshutz, probably rich, I never asked, his friendship at the ready when I needed it. Dear Bill and dear Fay Sinkin, the earliest friends I had in coming to foreign parts – San Antonio! I love them both. Eleanor Kamataris, wise, totally trusted, and much missed. My friends, the Harrells, Robert and Lynne, of Horseshoe Bay, who have witnessed years of what they called Norman's single sadness, they responded with therapeutic invitations and wonderful interludes in their comfy home in the Texas Hill Country. Russ Newell, usually after the completion of a book Russ makes strenuous efforts to see that I go to his island at Ocacoke for a holiday, where I write poems, swig liquor and release myself from all tribulations, at least for a while. In his company it is impossible to do otherwise. And finally Lucinda Cummings, who came to me in the middle of the first volume, skipped the second, but rescued me at the airport in the midst of Chapter 3 of Vol Three. She kept my tea hot, my computer warm and my temper cool. A friend and editor, both of which I sorely needed, and need.

Auburon Waugh, the journalist terrier, who after reading four pages of an early chapter suddenly got up, knocked his coffee cup to the floor, and said: 'Surely you can't keep this standard up, can you?' After a pause, he said 'I'll review you, Norman. Absolutely I will.' He did not. A sudden heart attack prevented it. Michael Meyer also expressed a passionate longing to read and review the final volume – he read a portion of it regarding his trip around the world with Greene and he was just a little anxious as to what Greene might have said about him. I reassured him that there was nothing that would disturb him. He also did not review it, alas, death intruded again.

The old die, the young die, the gentle die, the brilliant die, even George Plimpton (of deserved recognition) is dead – but I thank him for his assistance. Always fertile in the ways of destruction, death continues merrily along, yet Jacques Barzan has escaped, now in his nineties and is cruising forward to one hundred years (in 2007), his mind alert and rich in knowledge. He is an inspiration to all writers including this biographer. H. R. Gaines (better known as ill-begotten), still in the north of England, still a recluse, still a fine English gentleman, whom Ian Carr introduced me to, now almost as old as the hills among which he lives. He and Jacques Barzan still stand proud – victors against nature's mutual enemy.

Finally Dulcie Sylvia Sherry and Carmen Flores Sherry: Sylvia a writer of adult and children's novels – her first book of fairy tales published when she was fourteen, Carmen an attorney and mother of and to my children: both kept me humble and gave of their great gifts. For my children John Michael Graham Sherry and Ileana Taylor Sherry, I feel intense love, in life and beyond.

Notes

1   1991: Our Man Dying

1. *A Burnt-Out Case*, Penguin edition, 1977, p. 46.
2. *The Heart of the Matter*, Penguin edition, 1982, p. 125.
3. *ibid.*
4. *The Power and the Glory*, Penguin edition, 1983, p. 125.
5. *ibid.*, p. 128.
6. *ibid.*, p. 130.
7. *ibid.*, p. 131.
8. *ibid.*, p. 128.
9. *ibid.*, p. 131.
10. Edward Sackville-West, *New Statesman and Nation*, 19 June 1948, p. 108.
11. Evelyn Waugh, *Tablet*, 5 June 1948.
12. Gilbert Burnet, describing how Lord Russell prepared to be executed.

2   His Noble Head of Hair

1. Letter to Ragnar Svanstrom, 26 February 1952.
2. Letter to Natasha Brook, 22 October 1954.
3. Letter from Natasha Brook, undated.
4. Letter from Peter Brook, undated.
5. Letter to Peter Brook, 7 January 1955.
6. Peter Brook, *Threads of Time*, Counterpoint, 1998, p. 29.
7. *ibid.*, p. 30.
8. *ibid.*, pp. 30–1.
9. Benedict Nightingale, 'And then he was heard no more', *The Times*, 9 December 1954.
10. T. C. Worsley, 'Producers at Play', *New Statesman and Nation*, 14 April 1956.
11. Gene D. Phillips, SJ, *Graham Greene: The Films of His Fiction*, Teachers College Press, 1974, p. 113.
12. Sir Laurence Olivier, quoted by Roger Lewis in *The Real Life of Laurence Olivier*, Applause, 1997, p. 84.

3   Greene on Broadway

1. Letter to Vivien Dayrell-Browning, c. 1925.
2. *Daily Express*, 17 April 1953.
3. *Brighton and Hove Herald*, 3 March 1953.
4. *ibid.*
5. *The Diaries of Evelyn Waugh*, ed. Michael Davie, Penguin, 1979, p. 721.
6. *ibid.*
7. *ibid.*, p. 747. Entry for 28 November 1955.
8. Letter from Evelyn Waugh, 5 December 1955, *The Letters of Evelyn Waugh*, ed. Mark Amory, Weidenfeld & Nicolson, 1980, p. 455.

9. Letter to Catherine Walston, 3 March 1955.
10. Letter to Michael Richey, March 1956.
11. 'London Diary', *New Statesman and Nation*, 22 November 1952.
12. *Ways of Escape*, Lester & Orpen Dennys, 1980, pp. 180–1.
13. *ibid.*, p. 181.
14. Letter from Jacques Barzun to author, 5 May 1984.
15. Telephone interview with Carmen Capalbo, 23 April 1996.
16. *ibid.*
17. Carmen Capalbo, 'Deal With Me As You Would Any Novice', *New York Times*, 14 April 1991.
18. Telephone interview with Carmen Capalbo, 23 April 1996.
19. Capalbo, 'Deal With Me As You Would Any Novice'.
20. Telephone interview with Carmen Capalbo, 23 April 1996.
21. *ibid.*
22. Letter to René Berval, 8 October 1956.
23. *New York Times*, 30 January 1957.
24. Telephone interview with Carmen Capalbo, 23 April 1996.
25. *ibid.*
26. *ibid.*
27. Telegram from Terence Rattigan, 29 January 1957.
28. Telephone interview with Carmen Capalbo, 23 April 1996.

4 Secrets of *The Potting Shed*

1. *The Potting Shed*, Viking, 1957, Act I, Sc. 1, pp. 29–30.
2. *ibid.*, Act II, Sc. 1, p. 61.
3. *ibid.*, Act I, Sc. 1, p. 18.
4. *ibid.*, Act II, Sc. 2, p. 90.
5. Introduction to *The Potting Shed*, Viking, 1957.
6. *England Made Me*, Penguin, 1973, p. 184.
7. Interview with Sir Cecil Parrot, 1977.
8. *England Made Me*, p. 9.
9. Letter to Vivien Dayrell-Browning, 24 February 1926.
10. *ibid.*, 10 March 1926.
11. Letter to Vivien Greene, 10 March 1957.
12. Interview with Felix Greene, 2 March 1977.
13. *The Potting Shed*, Act II, Sc. 1, p. 62.
14. *ibid.*, p. 59.
15. Interview with Zoë Richmond, 8 January 1985.
16. *The Potting Shed*, Act II, Sc. 1, p. 60.
17. *ibid.*, p. 61.
18. *ibid.*, Act I, Sc. 1, pp. 32–4.
19. *ibid.*, Act II, Sc. 2, p. 82.
20. *ibid.*, pp. 85–6.
21. *ibid.*, Act II, Sc. 1, pp. 78–9.
22. *The Potting Shed*, Penguin, 1971, Act II, Sc. 2, p. 72.
23. *The Potting Shed*, Viking, 1957, Act II, Sc. 2, p. 92.
24. *ibid.*
25. *ibid.*, p. 93.
26. *ibid.*, pp. 94–5.
27. *ibid.*, p. 90.
28. Edward Greene to Ben Greene, quoted in interview with Ben Greene.

29. Interview with Ben Greene.
30. *The Potting Shed*, Act I, Sc. 2, p. 42.
31. Letter to Francis Greene, 7 February 1958.
32. Henry Hewes, 'Resurrection Will Out', *Saturday Review*, 16 February 1957.
33. Letter from Evelyn Waugh, 10 January 1958, *The Letters of Evelyn Waugh*, ed. Mark Amory, Weidenfeld & Nicolson, 1980, p. 501.
34. *ibid.*, pp. 501–2. Letter from Evelyn Waugh, 6 February 1958.
35. *ibid.*, p. 502. Letter from Evelyn Waugh to Laura Waugh, 6 February 1958.
36. *ibid.*, p. 504. Letter from Evelyn Waugh to Ann Fleming, 10 March 1958.
37. Letter from Edith Sitwell, 14 April 1958.
38. *The Potting Shed*, Act II, Sc. 2, p. 94.
39. 'Mr Greene Promises No More Miracles', *Life*, 1 April 1957.
40. Richard Watts in *New York Post*, 10 February 1957.

5 Is It Pornography?

1. Letter to *The Times*, 5 June 1954.
2. Letter from Edmund Wilson to Jason Epstein, quoted by Brian Boyd in *Vladimir Nabokov: The American Years*, Princeton University Press, 1991, p. 264.
3. Boyd, *Vladimir Nabokov: The American Years*, p. 266.
4. Harvey Breit, 'In and Out of Books', *New York Times Book Review*, 26 February 1956.
5. John Gordon, *Sunday Express*, 29 January 1956.
6. Letter from Evelyn Waugh to Nancy Mitford, 11 January 1956, *The Letters of Evelyn Waugh*, ed. Mark Amory, Weidenfeld & Nicolson, 1980, p. 457.
7. Letter from Greene and John Sutro to *Spectator*, 10 February 1956.
8. Letter to *Spectator*, 2 March 1956.
9. Letter to Catherine Walston, 'Friday', 1956.
10. Letter from B. A. Young to *Spectator*, 2 March 1956.
11. John Sutro, 'Greene's Jests', *Spectator*, 29 September 1984.
12. Letter to John Gordon Society, March 1956.
13. Graham Greene, 'The John Gordon Society', *Spectator*, 9 March 1956.
14. Letter from John Gordon to John Gordon Society, 5 May 1956.
15. *ibid.*, 23 May 1956.
16. Sutro, 'Greene's Jests'.
17. Letter to Leonard Russell, 26 October 1959.
18. Greene review of *Wee Willie Winkie*, *Night and Day*, 28 October 1937, reprinted in the book *Night and Day*, ed. Christopher Hawtree, Chatto & Windus, 1985, p. 204.
19. William Barkeley, *Daily Express*, 26 July 1956.
20. *ibid.*
21. John Gordon, *Sunday Express*, 29 July 1956.
22. Letter from Vladimir Nabokov, 31 December 1956, *Vladimir Nabokov: Selected Letters, 1950–1977*, ed. Dmitri Nabokov and Matthew J. Bruccoli, Harcourt Brace Jovanovich, 1989, pp. 197–8.
23. Letter to *Spectator*, 1 March 1957.
24. *ibid.*
25. Orville Prescott, 'Books of the Times', *New York Times*, 18 August 1958.
26. Letter from Walter Minton to Vladimir Nabokov, quoted by Brian Boyd in *Vladimir Nabokov: The American Years*, p. 365.
27. Letter to Max Reinhardt, 3 September 1958.
28. Letter from Max Reinhardt, 3 November 1958.
29. Letter to Max Reinhardt, 5 November 1958.
30. *ibid.*

31. Letter from Max Reinhardt to Vladimir Nabokov, January 1959.
32. Letter from Max Reinhardt to author, 30 September 1998.
33. Robert Pitman, *Sunday Express*, 28 December 1958.
34. *ibid*.
35. Nigel Nicolson speech before Parliament, 29 March 1957.
36. *Sunday Express*, 28 December 1958.
37. *ibid*.

6 Love's Blind Dance

1. Letter to Catherine Walston, postmarked 24 January 1956.
2. *ibid*., 'Wednesday', 1956.
3. *ibid*.
4. *ibid*.
5. *ibid*., 'Thursday 4.30', 1956.
6. *ibid*.
7. *ibid*., postmarked 25 January 1956.
8. *ibid*., postmarked 26 January 1956.
9. *ibid*., 'Sunday 6 p.m.'
10. *ibid*., 17 January 1956.
11. *ibid*., 9 February 1956.
12. *ibid*., postmarked 6 February 1956.
13. *ibid*., postmarked 10 February 1956.
14. *ibid*.
15. *ibid*.
16. *ibid*.
17. *ibid*., undated, probably 14 February 1956.
18. *ibid*.
19. *ibid*., postmarked 7 March 1956.
20. *ibid*.
21. *ibid*.
22. *ibid*.
23. *ibid*., postmarked 16 March 1956.
24. A. J. Liebling, 'A Talkative Something-or-Other', *New Yorker*, 7 April 1956.
25. Letter to Catherine Walston, 7 April 1956.
26. *ibid*.
27. Postcard to Catherine Walston, 11 May 1956.
28. Letter to Catherine Walston, 19 June 1956.
29. Letter to Catherine Walston, 22 August 1956.
30. *ibid*.
31. Letter from Catherine Walston to Bonte Durán, 16 June 1950.
32. *ibid*., 13 March 1950.
33. Letter to Catherine Walston, 6 August 1949.
34. Interview with Graham Greene, 25 April 1981.
35. Letter to Catherine Walston, 5 August 1948.
36. *ibid*., undated, probably 31 August 1956.
37. *ibid*., 14 September 1956.

7 Actress in the Wings

1. Letter to Catherine Walston, early December 1956.
2. *ibid*., 9 February 1956.

3. Michael Meyer, *Not Prince Hamlet*, Secker & Warburg, 1989, p. 134.
4. Letter to Catherine Walston, 10 December 1956.
5. *ibid.*, 17 December 1956.
6. *ibid.*
7. *ibid.*, 23 December 1956.
8. *ibid.*, 25 December 1956.
9. *ibid.*, 27 December 1956.
10. *ibid.*, 30 December 1956.
11. *ibid.*, 9 January 1957.
12. *ibid.*
13. *ibid.*, 11 January 1957.
14. *ibid.*, 12 January 1957.
15. *ibid.*, 18 January 1957.
16. *ibid.*, 1 February 1957.
17. *ibid.*
18. *ibid.*
19. *ibid.*, 15 February 1957.
20. *New York Times*, 10 February 1957. Comments by Richard Watts Jr, *New York Post*; Brooks Atkinson, *New York Times*; Tom Donnelly, *Washington Times and Sun*; John McClain, *Journal-American*; and Robert Coleman, *New York Mirror*.
21. 'Greene With a Fine Edge', *Newsweek*, 11 February 1957.
22. Letter to Catherine Walston, 15 February 1957.
23. *ibid.*, 26 February 1957.
24. *ibid.*
25. *ibid.*
26. *ibid.*
27. *ibid.*, 28 March 1957.
28. Postcard to Catherine Walston, 30 March 1957.
29. Letter to Catherine Walston, 1 February 1957.

8 Cursing the Dragon

1. Letter to Catherine Walston, 15 February 1957.
2. Letter to Prince Chula, 26 March 1957.
3. 'A Weed Among the Flowers', *Reflections*, ed. Judith Adamson, Reinhardt edition, 1990, p. 308. Originally printed in *The Times*, 27 May 1985.
4. *ibid.*
5. Letter to Edmund Blunden, 16 May 1957.
6. Letter from Jack Dribbon, 26 March 1957.
7. *ibid.*
8. Letter from Father Connolly, 27 March 1957.
9. Letter to Father McGrath, 5 April 1957.
10. Letter to Catherine Walston, 27 March 1957.
11. 'Suggested intelligence information', Greene's notes, file entitled *Various Points*.
12. *The Lawless Roads*, Penguin edition, 1976, p. 19.
13. Greene's notes, *Various Points*.
14. Postcard to Catherine Walston, 9 April 1957.
15. *ibid.*, 14 April 1957.
16. Letter to Catherine Walston, 15 April 1957.
17. 'A Weed Among the Flowers', *Reflections*, ed. Judith Adamson, p. 309.
18. Letter to Catherine Walston, 15 April 1957.
19. *ibid.*, 16 April 1957.
20. *ibid.*, 'Holy Saturday' 1957 [20 April].

21. *ibid.*
22. 'A Weed Among the Flowers', *Reflections*, ed. Judith Adamson, p. 309.
23. *ibid.*, pp. 309–10.
24. *ibid.*, p. 310.
25. Interview with Felix Greene, 2 March 1977.
26. 'A Weed Among the Flowers', *Reflections*, ed. Judith Adamson, p. 310.
27. Letter to Catherine Walston, 'Holy Saturday' 1957.
28. *ibid.*, 28 April 1957.
29. Letter from Tu Nan, 27 June 1957.
30. Letter to Catherine Walston, 28 April 1957.
31. 'A Weed Among the Flowers', *Reflections*, ed. Judith Adamson, p. 312.
32. Letter to *Daily Telegraph*, 4 June 1957.
33. 'A Weed Among the Flowers', *Reflections*, ed. Judith Adamson, p. 312.
34. Letter from Lord Chorley, *Daily Telegraph*, 8 June 1957.
35. Letter to *Daily Telegraph*, 10 June 1957.
36. *ibid.*
37. Letter from Lord Chorley to *Daily Telegraph*, 20 June 1957.
38. Letter from present Lord Chorley to author, 27 September 1997.
39. 'A Weed Among the Flowers', *Reflections*, ed. Judith Adamson, p. 313.
40. Letter from Professor Lauwerys to *Daily Telegraph*, 24 June 1957.
41. 'A Weed Among the Flowers', *Reflections*, ed. Judith Adamson, pp. 313–14.

9 I Only Have Eyes For You . . . and You

1. Letter to Catherine Walston, 4 July 1957.
2. *ibid.*, 12 July 1957.
3. *ibid.*
4. *ibid.*, 18 July 1957.
5. *ibid.*, 27 July 1957.
6. *ibid.*, 17 August 1957.
7. Postcard to Catherine Walston, 23 August 1957.
8. *ibid.*, 26 August 1957.
9. Letter to Catherine Walston, 10 September 1957.
10. *ibid.*, 13 September 1957.
11. *ibid.*, 28 August 1957.
12. *ibid.*, 13 September 1957.
13. Postcard to Catherine Walston, 15 September 1957.
14. Letter to Catherine Walston, 13 September 1957.
15. *ibid.*, 24 September 1957.
16. *ibid.*, 6 October 1957.
17. *ibid.*
18. *ibid.*, 17 October 1957.
19. *ibid.*, 22 October 1957.
20. *ibid.*, 25 October 1957.
21. *ibid.*
22. *ibid.*, 8 November 1957.
23. *ibid.*
24. *ibid.*
25. *ibid.*, 23 December 1957.
26. Telegram to Catherine Walston, 26 December 1957.
27. Letter to Catherine Walston, 23 December 1957.
28. *ibid.*, 11 January 1958.
29. *ibid.*

30. *ibid.*, 8 January 1958.
31. *The End of the Affair*, Penguin, 1975, p. 55.
32. Letter to Catherine Walston, 8 January 1958.
33. Greene, quoted in a letter from Vivien Greene to Mr Bishchoff, 27 September 1948.
34. Letter to Catherine Walston, 8 January 1958.
35. *ibid.*, 4 February 1958.
36. *ibid.*
37. *ibid.*
38. *ibid.*
39. Telegram to Catherine Walston, 14 February 1958.
40. *ibid.*, 22 February 1958.
41. Letter to Catherine Walston, 25 February 1958.
42. *ibid.*
43. *ibid.*
44. *ibid.*
45. Letter to Catherine Walston, undated, probably 5 or 6 February 1958.
46. *ibid.*
47. Letter from Oliver Crosthwaite-Eyre, 4 March 1958.
48. Letter to Catherine Walston, 3 March 1958.
49. *ibid.*
50. *ibid.*
51. *ibid.*, 11 March 1958.
52. *ibid.*
53. *ibid.*
54. *ibid.*, 25 March 1958.

10 Lovers Come Tumbling Down

1. This is shown in a letter of 8 October 1956 to his friend René Berval, to whom he dedicated *The Quiet American*.
2. Letter to Ragnar Svanstrom, 22 April 1958.
3. Postcard to Catherine Walston, 4 June 1958.
4. Note to Catherine Walston, 20 June 1958.
5. *The Pleasure-Dome: Graham Greene: The Collected Film Criticism, 1935–40*, ed. John Russell Taylor, Oxford University Press, 1980, p. 75.
6. *Ways of Escape*, Lester & Orpen Dennys, 1980, pp. 206–7.
7. This is an estimated date since the letter simply shows 9.50 p.m.
8. Letter from Marie Biche to Catherine Walston, 24 May 1958.
9. Letter to Catherine Walston, 13 June 1958.
10. *ibid.*, undated, probably June 1958.
11. *ibid.*
12. *ibid.*
13. *ibid.*
14. *ibid.*, 4 July 1958.
15. *ibid.*, 9 July 1958.
16. *ibid.*, 14 July 1958.
17. *ibid.*
18. *ibid.*
19. *ibid.*, 8 August 1958.
20. *Our Man in Havana*, Penguin, 1962, introduction.
21. *Ways of Escape*, p. 191.
22. Interview with Malcolm Muggeridge, June 1977.
23. Letter to Catherine Walston, 'Monday', probably late August 1958.

24. Letter to Catherine Walston, 1958.
25. Greene's inscription of *The Potting Shed* to Michael Meyer, August 1958.
26. Letter to Catherine Walston, August 1958.
27. *ibid.*
28. *ibid.*, 5 September 1958.
29. *ibid.*
30. *ibid.*, 9 October 1958.
31. *ibid.*, 12 October 1958.
32. Postcard to Catherine Walston, 16 October 1958.
33. *Ways of Escape*, p. 215.
34. Telegram to Catherine Walston, 12 November 1958.
35. Letter to Michael Meyer, 24 October 1958.
36. *ibid.*, 15 November 1958.
37. Letter from Anita Björk to Michael Meyer, 16 March 1977.
38. Letter to Michael Meyer, 20 November 1958.
39. *ibid.*
40. Telegram to Catherine Walston, 19 December 1958.

11 Publishing Redux

1. Letter from Max Reinhardt to author, 30 September 1998.
2. Letter to Max Reinhardt, 18 June 1957.
3. Letter to Charlie Chaplin, late 1957.
4. Letter from Max Reinhardt, December 1957.
5. *ibid.*, March 1958.
6. Open letter to Charlie Chaplin, *New Statesman and Nation*, 27 September 1952.
7. *Sunday Times*, quoted by David Robinson in *Chaplin*, McGraw-Hill, 1985, p. 603.
8. Letter from Max Reinhardt, 18 December 1957.
9. *ibid.*, 3 March 1958.
10. Max Reinhardt interview with author, July 1978.
11. Letter to Francis Greene, 1958.
12. *Sunday Times*, quoted by Robinson in *Chaplin*, p. 603.
13. Introduction to *The Bodley Head Ford Madox Ford*, Vol. I, The Bodley Head, 1980.
14. Letter to Max Reinhardt, 16 January 1958.
15. 'The Lost Childhood', *The Lost Childhood and Other Essays*, Eyre & Spottiswoode, 1951, pp. 16–17.
16. Letter to Catherine Walston, 12 August 1959.
17. Letter to Max Reinhardt, 24 September 1959.
18. Letter to Max and Joan Reinhardt, September 1959.
19. Letter from Max Reinhardt, 13 October 1959.
20. Letter to Max Reinhardt, 14 October 1959.
21. Letter from Max Reinhardt, 6 November 1958.
22. Letter to Max Reinhardt, 15 December 1958.
23. *ibid.*, 3 April 1959.
24. Letter from Max Reinhardt, 3 April 1959.
25. Letter to Max Reinhardt, 6 April 1959.
26. Letter from Dr Hubert Eaton.
27. 'A Knife in the Jocular Vein', *Time*, 12 July 1948.
28. Letter to Leslie Nicholson, date unknown.
29. Letter from Max Reinhardt, 29 December 1960.
30. Letter to Max Reinhardt, 28 December 1960.
31. Letter from Max Reinhardt, January 1960.

12 Heroes and Heroines

1. *Our Man in Havana*, Penguin, 1971, p. 79.
2. *ibid.*, pp. 106–13.
3. Letter to *The Times*, 3 January 1959.
4. 'Our men in Havana', *Manchester Guardian*, 8 January 1959.
5. 'Graham Greene v. Selwyn Lloyd', *Time and Tide*, 7 January 1959.
6. *Ways of Escape*, Lester & Orpen Dennys, 1980, pp. 208–10.
7. Marie-Françoise Allain, *The Other Man: Conversations with Graham Greene*, trans. Guido Waldman, The Bodley Head, 1983, p. 60.
8. *Ways of Escape*, p. 212.
9. *ibid.*, p. 212–13.
10. Allain, *The Other Man*, pp. 60–1.
11. Tad Szulc, *Fidel: A Critical Portrait*, William Morrow & Co., 1986, p. 271.
12. *ibid.*, p. 289.

13 Some Fidelistas, a Film and a Firing Squad

1. B. J. Bedard, 'Reunion in Havana', *Film Literature Quarterly*, Vol. II, no. 4, Fall 1974, pp. 354–5.
2. *Ways of Escape*, Lester & Orpen Dennys, 1980, p. 206.
3. Robert Emmett Ginna, 'Our Man in Havana', *Horizon*, November 1959.
4. Francis Nevins interview with author.
5. Letter to *The Times*, 3 January 1959.
6. *ibid.*, 19 October 1959.
7. Letter from *Sunday Telegraph* editor Donald McLachlan, early December 1962.
8. Letter to Donald McLachlan, 4 January 1963.
9. Letter from Donald McLachlan, 5 January 1963.
10. Letter to Donald McLachlan, 10 May 1963.
11. Diary, August 1963.
12. 'Return to Cuba', *Reflections*, ed. Judith Adamson, The Bodley Head, 1990, pp. 216–17. Originally printed in *Sunday Telegraph*.
13. Diary, 7 August 1963.
14. 'Return to Cuba', *Reflections*, ed. Judith Adamson, p. 215.
15. *ibid.*, p. 217.
16. *ibid*.
17. Diary, August 1963.
18. 'Return to Cuba', *Reflections*, ed. Judith Adamson, pp. 217–18.
19. George Plimpton, *Shadow Box*, Lyons & Burford, 1977, p. 144.
20. *ibid.*, pp. 146–7.
21. See photo credit.

14 Another Escape Route

1. Letter to Baroness Lambert, 15 September 1958.
2. Letter from Baroness Lambert to Dr Michel Lechat, quoted in a letter from Lechat to author, 28 July 1998.
3. *ibid*.
4. *Bulletin*, 18 April 1991.
5. Letter from Dr Michel Lechat, 3 October 1958.
6. *ibid*.
7. *ibid*.

8. *ibid.*
9. *ibid.*
10. Letter to Dr Michel Lechat, 7 October 1958.
11. *ibid.*, 27 October 1958.
12. *ibid.*
13. *ibid.*, 15 December 1958.
14. Letter from Dr Michel Lechat, October 1958.
15. Letter to Dr Michel Lechat, 15 December 1958.
16. *ibid.*
17. Letter from Edith Sitwell, 15 November 1958.
18. Letter to Catherine Walston, 3 January 1959.
19. *ibid.*, 10 January 1959.
20. *ibid.*, 14 January 1959.
21. Letter to Michael Meyer, 20 November 1958.
22. *ibid.*
23. Letter to Catherine Walston, 19 January 1959.
24. *ibid.*, 14 January 1959.
25. *ibid.*
26. *ibid.*, 3 January 1959.
27. *ibid.*, 14 January 1959.
28. *ibid.*
29. *ibid.*
30. *ibid.*
31. *ibid.*, 20 January 1959.
32. *ibid.*
33. *ibid.*
34. Letter to *Spectator*, 23 January 1959.
35. Letter from John Gordon to *Spectator*, 30 January 1959.
36. Letter to *Spectator*, 20 February 1959.
37. Letter from Revd Dr C. M. Hyde to Revd H. B. Gage, 2 August 1889. Printed in the *Sydney* [Australia] *Presbyterian*, 26 October 1889.
38. *The Quiet American*, Penguin, 1977, p. 37.
39. Franz Kafka, 'A Country Doctor', *The Metamorphosis, The Penal Colony, and other Stories*, Schocken, 1975, p. 141.

15 In Search of a Character

1. Letter to Catherine Walston, 31 January 1959.
2. 'Congo Journal', *In Search of a Character: Two African Journals*, The Bodley Head, 1961, p. 13.
3. Letter to Catherine Walston, 31 January 1959.
4. 'Convoy to West Africa', *In Search of a Character*, p. 123.
5. 'Congo Journal', *In Search of a Character*, p. 14.
6. *ibid.*, p. 29.
7. *ibid.*, p. 25.
8. Letter to Catherine Walston, 2 February 1959.
9. *A Burnt-Out Case*, Penguin 1977, p. 16.
10. *ibid.*, p. 16.
11. Letter to Catherine Walston, 2 February 1959.
12. 'Congo Journal', *In Search of a Character*, p. 18.
13. *A Burnt-Out Case*, p. 25.
14. 'Congo Journal', *In Search of a Character*, p. 27.
15. *ibid.*, p. 17.

16. *ibid.*, p. 26.
17. *ibid.*, p. 39.
18. *ibid.*, pp. 27–8.
19. *A Burnt-Out Case*, pp. 18–19.
20. *ibid.*, p. 20.
21. *ibid.*, p. 18.
22. 'Congo Journal', *In Search of a Character*, p. 39.
23. *A Burnt-Out Case*, pp. 46–7.
24. 'Congo Journal', *In Search of a Character*, p. 21.
25. *A Burnt-Out Case*, p. 20.
26. *ibid.*, pp. 27–8.
27. 'Congo Journal', *In Search of a Character*, p. 29.
28. *ibid.*, pp. 33–4.
29. *ibid.*, p. 31.
30. *A Burnt-Out Case*, p. 43.
31. 'Congo Journal', *In Search of a Character*, p. 88.
32. *A Burnt-Out Case*, p. 104.
33. *ibid.* p. 26.
34. *ibid.* Dr Lechat felt this passage exactly described Greene's activities while at Yonda.
35. 'Congo Journal', *In Search of a Character*, p. 22.
36. Interview with Dr Michel Lechat, July 1999.
37. Dr Michel Lechat, *Bulletin*, 18 April 1991.
38. *A Burnt-Out Case*, p. 79.
39. *ibid.*, pp. 80–1.
40. Letter from Dr Michel Lechat to author, 29 March 1998.
41. 'Congo Journal', *In Search of a Character*, p. 18.
42. *A Burnt-Out Case*, pp. 121–2.
43. 'Congo Journal', *In Search of a Character*, pp. 59–60.
44. *A Burnt-Out Case*, pp. 123–4.
45. *ibid.*, p. 124.
46. Letter from Dr Michel Lechat to author, 30 March 1998.

16 Down Tributaries of the River Congo

1. 'Congo Journal', *In Search of a Character: Two African Journals*, The Bodley Head, 1961, pp. 40–1.
2. *ibid.*, p. 41.
3. *ibid.*
4. *ibid.*, p. 42.
5. Letter to Catherine Walston, 15 February 1959.
6. *A Burnt-Out Case*, Penguin, 1977, pp. 9–10.
7. 'Congo Journal', *In Search of a Character*, p. 71.
8. *ibid.*, p. 59.
9. *A Burnt-Out Case*, pp. 11–12.
10. 'Congo Journal', *In Search of a Character*, p. 49.
11. *A Burnt-Out Case*, p. 13.
12. 'Congo Journal', *In Search of a Character*, p. 51.
13. *A Burnt-Out Case*, p. 13.
14. 'Congo Journal', *In Search of a Character*, pp. 50–2.
15. *ibid.*, p. 52.
16. *A Burnt-Out Case*, pp. 14–15.
17. Letter from Father Henri Vanderslaghmolen to author, 26 April 1998.
18. 'Congo Journal', *In Search of a Character*, p. 52.

19. *ibid.*, p. 53.
20. Letter from Father Henri Vanderslaghmolen to author, 26 April 1998.
21. 'Congo Journal', *In Search of a Character*, p. 54.
22. *ibid.*
23. *ibid.*, p. 59.
24. *ibid.*, p. 54.
25. *ibid.*, p. 56.
26. Letter to Catherine Walston, 15 February 1959.
27. 'Congo Journal', *In Search of a Character*, p. 76.
28. *ibid.*, p. 58.
29. *ibid.*
30. *ibid.*
31. Letter to Catherine Walston, 15 February 1959.
32. 'Congo Journal', *In Search of a Character*, p. 51.
33. *ibid.*, p. 61.
34. Letter to Catherine Walston, 18 February 1959.
35. *ibid.*
36. *ibid.*
37. 'Congo Journal', *In Search of a Character*, p. 67.
38. Letter to Catherine Walston, 20 February 1959.
39. 'Congo Journal', *In Search of a Character*, p. 72.
40. *ibid.*, p. 67.
41. Letter to Catherine Walston, 23 February 1959.
42. *ibid.*
43. *ibid.*, 24 February 1959.

17 The Trouble with Being Querry

1. *A Burnt-Out Case*, Penguin, 1975, pp. 86–7.
2. *ibid.*, pp. 88–9.
3. *ibid.*, p. 91.
4. *ibid.*, pp. 91–2.
5. Letter to Max Reinhardt, 9 June 1959.
6. *A Burnt-Out Case*, p. 34.
7. *ibid.*
8. *ibid.*, p. 35.
9. *ibid.*, p. 36.
10. *ibid.*, pp. 37–8.
11. *ibid.*, p. 38.
12. *ibid.*, pp. 38–9.
13. *ibid.*
14. *ibid.*, p. 40.
15. *ibid.*, pp. 40–1.
16. *ibid.*, p. 42.
17. *ibid.*, p. 57.
18. *ibid.*, p. 63.
19. 'Congo Journal', *In Search of a Character: Two African Journals*, The Bodley Head, 1961, pp. 19–20.
20. *ibid.*, p. 26.
21. Letter from writer, proof copy, 'Congo Journal'.
22. Dream diary, 1 April 1967.
23. Dr Michel Lechat, *Bulletin*, 18 April 1991.

18 Parkinson's Dis-ease

1. *A Burnt-Out Case*, Penguin, 1977, p. 107.
2. 'Congo Journal', *In Search of a Character: Two African Journals*, The Bodley Head, 1961, p. 14.
3. Letter to Dr Michel Lechat, 2 April 1959.
4. *A Burnt-Out Case*, p. 97.
5. *ibid.*, p. 99.
6. *ibid.*, p. 97.
7. *ibid.*, pp. 98–9.
8. *ibid.*, p. 106.
9. *ibid.*, p. 109.
10. *Daily Express*, 17 November 1960.
11. One reason Greene stated for choosing me as his authorised biographer was my work on Joseph Conrad. Perhaps he deemed me acceptable because I was that curious hybrid: a scholar who travelled to the Far East and Africa, not as a tourist, but to ferret out information about my subject. Also, Greene did not want a Catholic biographer, and he did not want a friend. When I began my sleuthing in 1976, I knew as much about Greene as a blind man running for his life; that pleased him. I thought Greene's proscriptions stemmed from his hatred of the Evelyn Waugh biography written by Waugh's close friend, Christopher Sykes. Greene wanted no such performance. However, I now think that he might well have been afraid of a portrayal such as Ronald Matthews's.
12. Letter from Christopher Matthews to author, 2 February 1998.
13. Letter from Michael Richey to author, 21 March 1998.
14. Ronald Matthews, *Mon Ami Graham Greene*, Desclée de Brouwer, Paris, 1957.
15. Letter from Elizabeth Christman, 14 March 1971.
16. Letter to Elizabeth Christman, 5 April 1971.
17. *A Burnt-Out Case*, p. 116.
18. Letter from Christopher Matthews to author, 2 February 1998.
19. *The End of the Affair*, Penguin, 1975, p. 31.
20. Letter from Ronald Matthews to Greene, undated.
21. Greene, through Matthews, did know Cousins. Sometime in 1938 she solicited Matthews off Piccadilly, and he was struck (as was Greene) by her upper-crust accent. Her real name, which has remained unknown these many years, was Edith Margaret Emma Robinson.
22. Letter from Ronald Matthews, 6 August 1957.
23. *ibid.*
24. *ibid.*
25. *ibid.*
26. *ibid.*, 9 January 1966.
27. 'Congo Journal', *In Search of a Character*, p. 76.
28. Letter to Catherine Walston, 15–24 February 1959.
29. *ibid.*
30. 'Congo Journal', *In Search of a Character*, p. 90.
31. *ibid.*, p. 91.
32. *ibid.*, p. 93.
33. *ibid.*
34. Manuscript of 'Congo Journal'.

19 Graham's Final Success in the Theatre

1. Letter to Catherine Walston, 23 April 1959.
2. *Manchester Evening News*, 19 May 1959.

3. Letter to Catherine Walston, undated, probably 19 May 1959.
4. *Daily Mirror*, 19 May 1959.
5. *Manchester Evening News*, 19 May 1959.
6. Michael Meyer, *Not Prince Hamlet*, Secker & Warburg, 1989, p. 175.
7. *ibid.*, p. 177.
8. Postcard to Catherine Walston, 5 August 1959.
9. Letter to Catherine Walston, 12 August 1959.
10. *ibid.,* undated, postmarked 17 August 1959.
11. *ibid.*, 11 September 1959.
12. Postcard to Catherine Walston, 20 September 1959.
13. Letter to Father Philip Caraman, 22 September 1959.
14. Telegram to Catherine Walston, 22 September 1959.
15. Letter to Catherine Walston, 22 September 1959.
16. *A Sort of Life*, Penguin, 1984, p. 15.
17. Letter to Catherine Walston, 22 September 1959.
18. J. W. Lambert, *Listener*, 10 October 1979.
19. Letter to Catherine Walston, 25 September 1959.
20. *ibid.*
21. *ibid.*
22. Telegram to Catherine Walston, 24 September 1959.
23. Letter to Catherine Walston, 25 September 1959.
24. *The Heart of the Matter*, Penguin, 1971, p. 60.
25. Letter to Catherine Walston, 25 September 1959.
26. *ibid.*
27. *ibid.*, 30 September 1959.
28. *ibid.*
29. *ibid.*, 3 October 1959.
30. *ibid.*, 30 September.
31. *ibid.*, 5 October 1959.
32. *ibid.*, 10 October 1959.
33. *ibid.*, 5 October 1959.
34. *ibid.*, 10 October 1959.
35. *ibid.*, 5 October 1959.
36. *ibid.*
37. *ibid.*, 10 October 1959.
38. *ibid.*, 30 October 1959.
39. Meyer, *Not Prince Hamlet*, p. 188.
40. *ibid.*
41. *ibid.*
42. Irene Selznick, *A Private View*, Knopf, 1983, p. 354.
43. *ibid.*, p. 355.
44. *New York Times*, 29 October 1961.
45. *ibid.*
46 Selznick, *A Private View*, p. 355.
47. Letter to Catherine Walston, 27 April 1961.
48. *ibid.*
49. *ibid.*, 3 October 1961.
50. *ibid.*
51. *New York Times*, 2 November 1961.
52. Letter to Catherine Walston, 2 November 1961.
53. Walter Kerr, November 1961.

20 Round the World in Forty-Five Days

1. Letter to Michael Meyer, 26 October 1959.
2. *ibid.*, 30 October 1959.
3. *ibid.*, 16 November 1959.
4. Letter to Catherine Walston, 19 December 1959.
5. *ibid.*, 22 December 1959.
6. Michael Meyer, *Not Prince Hamlet*, Secker & Warburg, 1989, pp. 177–8.
7. Letter to Catherine Walston, 22 December 1959.
8. *ibid.*, 23 December 1959.
9. *ibid.*, 24 December 1959.
10. *ibid.*
11. Meyer, *Not Prince Hamlet*, pp. 178–9.
12. Postcard to Catherine Walston, 28 December 1959.
13. Letter to Catherine Walston, 24 December 1959.
14. *ibid.*, 25 December 1959.
15. *ibid.*
16. Meyer, *Not Prince Hamlet*, pp. 178–80.
17. Letter to Catherine Walston, 25 December 1959.
18. Meyer, *Not Prince Hamlet*, p. 180.
19. Letter to Catherine Walston, 25 December 1959.
20. *ibid.*, 26 December 1959.
21. *ibid.*
22. *ibid.*, 31 December 1959.
23. *ibid.*
24. Meyer, *Not Prince Hamlet*, pp. 181–2.
25. Letter to Catherine Walston, 31 December 1959.
26. *ibid.*, 3 January 1960.
27. *ibid.*, 4 January 1960.
28. *ibid.*, 6 January 1960.
29. *ibid.*
30. *ibid.*, 15 January 1960.
31. Letter to Bengt Danielsson, 15 February 1960.
32. Letter to Catherine Walston, 15 January 1960.
33. Postcard to Catherine Walston, 10 January 1960.
34. Letter to Catherine Walston, 15 January 1960.
35. Meyer, *Not Prince Hamlet*, p. 185.
36. Letter to Catherine Walston, 22 January 1960.
37. *ibid.*
38. *ibid.*, 22 January 1960.
39. *ibid.*, 31 January 1960.
40. *ibid.*
41. Letter to Catherine Walston, 5 February 1960.
42. Letter to Peter Smith, February 1960.
43. Letter to Catherine Walston, 5 February 1960.

21 I Shall Arise and Go Now

1. Letter to Catherine Walston, 15 February 1960.
2. William Hickey, 'Riddle of the Vanishing Mr Greene', *Daily Express*, 27 January 1960.
3. Letter to Catherine Walston, 18 February 1960.
4. *ibid.*
5. *ibid.*, 23 February 1960.

6. *ibid.*
7. *ibid.*
8. Letter to Catherine Walston, 13 March 1960.
9. *ibid.*, 21 March 1960.
10. *ibid.*
11. *ibid.*, 23 March 1960.
12. *ibid.*
13. Letter to Catherine Walston, 31 March 1960.
14. Letter to *Spectator*, 8 April 1960.
15. Letter from Bernard Levin to *Spectator*, 8 April 1960.
16. Marie-François Allain, *The Other Man: Conversations with Graham Greene*, trans. Guido Waldman, The Bodley Head, 1983, p. 178.
17. Letter to Edith Sitwell, Good Friday, 1960.
18. Letter to Catherine Walston, 20 April 1960.
19. *ibid.*
20. *ibid.*, 27 June 1960.
21. *ibid.*, 1 July 1960.
22. Postcard to Catherine Walston, 4 July 1960.
23. 'May We Borrow Your Husband?', *Collected Stories*, Viking, 1973, p. 28.
24. *ibid.*, p. 36.
25. *ibid.*, p. 16.
26. *ibid.*, p. 19.
27. Letter to Catherine Walston, 16 July 1960.
28. *ibid.*
29. *ibid.*, 21 July 1960.
30. *ibid.*, 7 October 1960.
31. *ibid.*, 7 December 1960.
32. *ibid.*
33. Postcard to Catherine Walston, 9 December 1960.

22 Crossing the Shadow-Line

1. Letter to Catherine Walston, 7 December 1960.
2. *Ways of Escape*, Lester & Orpen Dennys, 1980, pp. 216–17.
3. *ibid.*, pp. 217–18.
4. *ibid.*
5. *A Burnt-Out Case*, Bantam, 1961, p. 89.
6. 'A Visit to Morin', *Collected Stories*, Viking, 1973, pp. 251–2.
7. *ibid.*, p. 253.
8. *ibid.*, p. 251.
9. *ibid.*, p. 241.
10. *A Burnt-Out Case*, p. 108.
11. *ibid.*, p. 109.
12. *ibid.*, p. 111.
13. *ibid.*, pp. 150–6.
14. 'A Visit to Morin', *Collected Stories*, pp. 254–5.
15. *A Burnt-Out Case*, p. 41.
16. *ibid.*, p. 142.
17. *Ways of Escape*, p. 216.
18. Marie-Françoise Allain, *The Other Man: Conversations with Graham Greene*, trans. Guido Waldman, The Bodley Head, 1983, p. 142.
19. *Ways of Escape*, p. 216.
20. Allain, *The Other Man*, p. 144.

21. Letter to Catherine Walston, 1 March 1961.
22. *The Diaries of Evelyn Waugh*, ed. Michael Davie, Penguin, 1979, p. 779. Entry for 31 December 1960/1 January 1961.
23. Father Leopoldo Durán, *Graham Greene: Friend and Brother*, HarperCollins, 1994, p. 16.
24. Letter from Evelyn Waugh to Christopher Sykes, 2 January 1961, *The Letters of Evelyn Waugh*, ed. Mark Amory, Weidenfeld & Nicolson, 1980, p. 556.
25. Olof Lagercrantz review of *A Burnt-Out Case*.
26. *The Diaries of Evelyn Waugh*, ed. Michael Davie, p. 779. Entry for 31 December 1960/1 January 1961.
27. Letter from Evelyn Waugh, 17 March 1951, *The Letters of Evelyn Waugh*, ed. Mark Amory, p. 346.
28. Letter to Catherine Walston, 13 February 1961.

23 Death Is a Mole

1. Manuscript draft for 'John Hayward, 1904–1965: Some Memories', ed. John Carter, *Book Collector*, XIV (Winter) 1965, pp. 443–86.
2. *Lord Rochester's Monkey: Being the Life of John Wilmot, 2nd Earl of Rochester*, The Bodley Head, 1974, p. 9.
3. Letter to Catherine Walston, 21 August 1947.
4. *ibid.*, 30 September 1965.
5. Letter to Mademoiselle Mesnet, 1 November 1965.
6. Letter from Evelyn Waugh, 3 January 1961, *The Letters of Evelyn Waugh*, ed. Mark Amory, Weidenfeld & Nicolson, 1980, p. 557.
7. Letter to Evelyn Waugh, 4 January 1961, *Ways of Escape*, Lester & Orpen Dennys, 1980, p. 219.
8. Letter from Evelyn Waugh, 5 January 1961, *The Letters of Evelyn Waugh*, ed. Mark Amory, pp. 559–60.
9. Postcard to Evelyn Waugh, January 1961, *Ways of Escape*, p. 220.
10. Letter from Evelyn Waugh to Lady Diana Cooper, 21 January 1961, *The Letters of Evelyn Waugh*, ed. Mark Amory, p. 560.
11. Interview with Peter Glenville, 1978.
12. *Ways of Escape*, p. 226.
13. Letter from Evelyn Waugh to his brother Alec Waugh, 6 March 1966, *The Letters of Evelyn Waugh*, ed. Mark Amory, p. 637.
14. Letter from Evelyn Waugh to Ann Fleming, January 1966, *The Letters of Evelyn Waugh*, ed. Mark Amory, p. 636.
15. Letter from Evelyn Waugh to Nancy Mitford, 28 February 1966, *The Letters of Evelyn Waugh*, ed. Mark Amory, p. 636.
16. Letter from Evelyn Waugh to Lady Mosley, 30 March 1966, *The Letters of Evelyn Waugh*, ed. Mark Amory, p. 639.
17. Father Martin D'Arcy, SJ, 'The Religion of Evelyn Waugh', *Evelyn and his World*, ed. David Pryce-Jones, Little, Brown, 1973, pp. 78–9.
18. *The Diaries of Evelyn Waugh*, ed. Michael Davie, Penguin, 1976, p. 793. Entry for Easter 1965.
19. Letter from Evelyn Waugh to Nancy Mitford, 5 September 1965, *The Letters of Evelyn Waugh*, ed. Mark Amory, p. 633.
20. Letter from Evelyn Waugh to Lady Diana Mosley, 9 March 1966, *The Letters of Evelyn Waugh*, ed. Mark Amory, p. 638.
21. Letter from Evelyn Waugh to his daughter Margaret FitzHerbert, 6 December 1965, *The Letters of Evelyn Waugh*, ed. Mark Amory, p. 635.
22. Christopher Sykes, *Evelyn Waugh: A Biography*, Little, Brown, 1975, p. 445.
23. *ibid.*, p. 446.

24. Selina Hastings, *Evelyn Waugh: A Biography*, Houghton-Mifflin, 1994.
25. Auberon Waugh, *Will This Do?*, Carroll & Graf, 1991, p. 185.
26. Martin Stannard, quoted in Norman Sherry, *The Life of Graham Greene*, Vol. Two, Jonathan Cape, 1994, p. 491.
27. *Ways of Escape*, p. 226.
28. *ibid.*, p. 225.
29. *ibid.*, p. 226.
30. Letter to Hugh Greene, 31 October 1936.
31. Interview with Graham Greene, 25 April 1981.
32. Letter to Vivien Greene, undated, 1938.
33. Interview with Malcolm Muggeridge, June 1977.
34. *ibid.*
35. Interview with David Higham, 1 July 1977.
36. A. P. Herbert, *The Thames*, Weidenfeld & Nicolson, 1966, p. 165.
37. Interview with David Low, 24 August 1984.
38. Interview with Graham Greene, 14 December 1983.
39. *The Heart of the Matter*, Penguin, 1985, pp. 178–9.
40. Letter to Catherine Walston undated, 1948.
41. Letter to Vivien Greene, undated other than 1948.
42. Letter from Dorothy Glover, 14 April 1948.
43. *ibid.*
44. Letter to Catherine Walston, 11 May 1948.
45. *ibid.*, 12 May 1948.
46. *ibid.*, 16 May 1948.
47. *The Heart of the Matter*, p. 318.
48. Letter to Catherine Walston, 1 February 1957.
49. Graham Greene and Dorothy Glover, *Victorian Detective Fiction*, The Bodley Head, 1966, p. viii.
50. Diary, December 1971.

24 A Flop of Biblical Proportions

1. Letter from Georgie Stonor, late March 1978.
2. Letter to Georgie Stonor, April 1978.
3. *Carving a Statue,* Penguin, 1972, Act One, p. 18.
4. *ibid.*, Act One, pp. 20–1.
5. *ibid.*, Act One, pp. 22–3.
6. *ibid.*, Act Three, p. 79.
7. *ibid.*, Act One, p. 24.
8. *ibid.*, Act One, p. 27.
9. *ibid.*, Act One, p. 34.
10. *ibid.*, Act Two, p. 37.
11. *ibid.*, Act Two, p. 45.
12. *ibid.*, Act Two, p. 50.
13. *ibid.*, Act Two, p. 51.
14. *ibid.*, Act Two, pp. 52–3.
15. *ibid.*, Act Two, pp. 54–5.
16. *ibid.*, Act Two, p. 55.
17. *ibid.*
18. *ibid.*, Act Two, pp. 56–7.
19. *ibid.*, Act Three, p. 59.
20. *ibid.*, Act Three, p. 61.
21. *ibid.*, Act Three, pp. 61–2.

22. *ibid.*, Act Three, p. 62.
23. *ibid.*, Act Three, p. 63.
24. *ibid.*, Act Three, p. 66.
25. *ibid.*
26. *ibid.*, Act Three, p. 71.
27. *ibid.*, Act Three, pp. 75–6.
28. *ibid.*, Act Three, p. 76.
29. *ibid.*, Act Three, p. 77.
30. *ibid.*, Act Three, p. 78.
31. Derek Patmore, unpublished manuscript.
32. *Dream Book 2*, p. 31.
33. *Daily Mail*, 18 September 1964.
34. John Holmstrom, private diary, 1964.
35. J. C. Trewin, *Lady*, 8 October 1964.
36. *Punch*, 23 September 1964.
37. John Holmstrom, private diary, 1964.
38. Malcolm Rutherford, 'God Only Knows', *Spectator*, 25 September 1964.
39. *Theatre World*, October 1964.
40. Derek Patmore, unpublished manuscript.
41. B. A. Young, *Financial Times*, September 1964.
42. 'See-Saw of Pride and Contrition', *The Times*, 18 September 1964.
43. Milton Shulman, *Evening Standard*, 18 September 1964.
44. *Tablet*, 19 September 1964.
45. *Ways of Escape*, Lester & Orpen Dennys, 1980, p. 204.
46. Marie-Françoise Allain, *The Other Man: Conversations with Graham Greene*, trans. Guido Waldman, Bodley Head, 1983, pp. 145–6.
47. Garry O'Connor, *Ralph Richardson: An Actor's Life*, Applause, 1997, p. 205.
48. J. W. Lambert, quoted by Garry O'Connor in *Ralph Richardson: An Actor's Life*, p. 205.
49. Letter to Ralph Richardson, 26 June 1964.
50. Interview with Michael Meyer, June 1999.
51. Draft of letter to Ralph Richardson, 4 October 1964.
52. Letter from Ralph Richardson to author, 1981.
53. Letter to Michael Meyer, 18 September 1964.
54. Letter from Michael Meyer to author, 12 November 1998.
55. 'Epitaph for a Play', *Carving a Statue*, Introduction, p. 11.
56. *Carving a Statue*, Act Three, p. 79.
57. Letter from Evelyn Waugh, 28 November 1964.
58. While a student at Oxford, Greene had read Edith's book of poems, *Bucolic Comedies* (1923), and, as he wrote to his mother, was 'absolutely out middle stump'. Sitwell was attracted to Greene when he wrote an article about her, young as he was, for the *Weekly Westminster Gazette*; the *Gazette* turned it down but Edith Sitwell heard of it, and she and Greene became friends. Later, much later, especially after Edith became a convert to Catholicism, they met and corresponded.
59. Letter from Edith Sitwell, December 1964.
60. Letter from Osbert Sitwell, January 1965.

25 More Naked Than the Law Allows

1. Interview with Carmen Capalbo, 28 October 1998.

26 Prelude in Blood

1. Robert Heinl and Nancy Heinl, *Written in Blood: The Story of the Haitian People 1492–1971*, Houghton Mifflin, 1978, p. 621. This essay first appeared in *The Washington Post*, 5 July 1964.
2. *The Comedians*, Penguin, 1977, p. 47.
3. Heinl and Heinl, *Written in Blood*, p. 584.
4. *ibid.*, p. 581.
5. *ibid.*, p. 582.
6. *ibid.*, p. 583.
7. 'Duvalier Sworn as President of Haiti', *New York Times*, 23 October 1957.
8. Heinl and Heinl, *Written in Blood*, p. 589.
9. *ibid.*, p. 591.
10. *ibid.*, p. 595.
11. Bernard Diederich and Al Burt, *Papa Doc: The Truth About Haiti Today*, McGraw-Hill, 1969, p. 141.
12. 'Nightmare Republic', *Reflections*, ed. Judith Adamson, Reinhardt Books, 1990, p. 224. Originally appeared in *Sunday Telegraph*, 29 September 1963.
13. Heinl and Heinl, *Written in Blood*, p. 629.
14. *ibid.*, p. 627.
15. Richard Eder, 'Ex Aide Plotting Against Duvalier', *New York Times*, 21 October 1962.
16. 'Nightmare Republic', *Reflections*, p. 223.
17. Heinl and Heinl, *Written in Blood*, p. 632.
18. *ibid.*, pp. 632–3.
19. *ibid.*, p. 641.

27 Killing Is My Pleasure

1. *The Comedians*, Penguin, 1976, p. 121.
2. *ibid.*, pp. 121–2.
3. *ibid.*, pp. 123–5.
4. *ibid.*, p. 127.
5. Robert Heinl and Nancy Heinl, *Written in Blood*, Houghton Mifflin, 1978, p. 597.
6. Bernard Diederich and Al Burt, *Papa Doc: The Truth About Haiti Today*, McGraw-Hill, 1969, p. 139.
7. *ibid.*, p. 174.
8. *The Comedians*, pp. 164–7.
9. Bernard Diederich and Al Burt, *Papa Doc: Haiti and Its Dictator*, Waterfront Press, 1991, pp. 219-20.
10. 'Barbot, Major Foe of Duvalier, Predicts Victory Over Dictator', *New York Times*, 23 May 1963.
11. Richard Eder, 'Ex-Ally of Duvalier is Hunted in Haiti as Archfoe', *New York Times* 10 May 1963.
12. *ibid.*
13. 'The Living Dead', *Time*, 26 July 1963.
14. Graham Greene, introduction to Bernard Diederich and Al Burt, *Papa Doc: The Truth About Haiti Today*, p. x.
15. Diary, 20 August 1963.
16. Diederich and Burt, *Papa Doc: The Truth About Haiti Today*, p. 244.
17. *ibid.*, p. 245.
18. *ibid.*
19. Heinl and Heinl, *Written in Blood*, p. 641.
20. Diederich and Burt, *Papa Doc: The Truth About Haiti Today*, p. 305.

28 Two Shades of Greene

1. Marie-Françoise Allain, *The Other Man: Conversations with Graham Greene*, trans. Guido Waldman, Bodley Head, 1983, p. 79.
2. *The Ministry of Fear*, Penguin, 1968, p. 95.
3. Allain, *The Other Man*, p. 80.
4. *The Comedians*, Penguin, 1976, Foreword, p. viii.
5. *ibid.*, pp. 5–6.
6. Interview with Aubelin Jolicoeur, December 1998.
7. Interview with Robert Coster, 31 May 1978.
8. 'Graham Greene, in Haiti, Talks of Double Trouble', *New York Times*, 18 August 1963.
9. *Our Man in Havana*, Penguin, 1971, p. 72.

29 To Haiti by Sea

1. *The Comedians*, Penguin, 1966, pp. 30–5.
2. 'The Soupsweet Land', *Collected Essays*, Penguin, 1969, p. 339.
3. Norman Sherry, *The Life of Graham Greene*, Vol. Two, Jonathan Cape, 1994, pp. 96–7, incorporating journal entry for 7 March 1942.
4. 'Convoy to West Africa', *In Search of a Character: Two African Journals*, Penguin, 1971, p. 99.
5. *The Comedians*, p. 28.
6. Greene's warden's post was in Gower Street (mentioned in the poem) and he was on duty the terrible night that the Jewish Girls' Club took a direct hit, 16 April 1941, as his journal shows. That night 2,000 civilians died; 100,000 homes were destroyed. Before he got to his warden's post, he saw enemy planes dropping flares. He had hoped to leave at 2.30 a.m. but the flares continued coming down on Tottenham Court Road. A parachute bomb fell on the Victoria Club in Malet Street where 350 Canadian soldiers were sleeping. At the Royal Academy of Dramatic Art ('women wearing dressing-gowns and bleeding from cuts on the face'), someone was hurt on the top floor; two wardens, a policeman and Greene, ran up four flights to find the heavy girl bleeding on the floor. They got her down with great difficulty. Outside, the flames were everywhere. Another stick of three bombs whistled down and Greene lay on the pavement when a sailor fell on him. Greene had cut his hand from glass, bled a great deal, and had to go back to the post to have it dressed. Yet another three sticks of bombs came down. Again Greene dropped to the floor (this time of the post); the windows blew in.

   Greene began an Act of Contrition, no longer believing he would survive the night. Even the trees were wounded. Later in the morning they discovered that a high explosive bomb had hit the Jewish Girls' Club in Alfred Place. It was changed into a black hole, belching flames and choked with smashed brickwork interspersed with mutilated corpses. Rescuers took out bodies for a long time, and for days the sweet stench of fleshly corruption hung in the air.
7. *The Comedians*, pp. 128–9.
8. *ibid.*, p. 141.
9. *ibid.*, p. 142.
10. *ibid.*, pp. 142–3.
11. *ibid.*, p. 143.
12. *ibid.*, p. 144.
13. *ibid.*, p. 146.
14. *ibid.*, pp. 48–9.
15. Interview with Robert Coster, 31 May 1978.

16. Georgette, unlike the brothel-keeper described as almost a school mistress, thin and proper, was proper but had enormous breasts.
17. *Ways of Escape*, Lester & Orpen Dennys, 1980, p. 230.
18. *The Comedians*, p. 20.
19. ibid., p. 185.
20. ibid., pp. 190–91.
21. Bernard Diederich and Al Burt, *Papa Doc: The Truth About Haiti Today*, McGraw-Hill, 1969, p. 355.
22. ibid., p. 312.
23. 'A Warning to Renegades', *Time*, 27 November 1964.
24. *The Comedians*, p. 193.

30 The Real Mr Jones

1. *The Comedians*, Penguin, 1966, p. 11.
2. ibid., p. 196.
3. 'Nightmare Republic', *Sunday Telegraph*, 29 September 1963, reprinted in *Reflections*, ed. Judith Adamson, p. 223.
4. *The Comedians*, pp. 207–9.
5. ibid., pp. 240–2.
6. ibid., p. 209.
7. ibid., p. 240.
8. ibid., p. 232.
9. Richard Eder, 'Black Eagle Evades Questions on Arms for Haiti', *New York Times*, 27 August 1963.
10. ibid.
11. *Ways of Escape*, Lester & Orpen Dennys, 1980, p. 261.
12. ibid., p. 264.
13. *The Comedians*, p. 150.
14. ibid., pp. 227–8.
15. ibid., p. 245.
16. ibid., p. 256.
17. ibid., pp. 258–60.
18. ibid., pp. 263–6.
19. ibid., p. 283.
20. Letter from Patrick Marnham to *The Times*, 22 January 1994.
21. Interview with Graham Greene, 28 June 1979.
22. Greene read these passages to me in interview on 14 December 1983 from his original copy.
23. Alan Whicker, *Within Whicker's World*, Elm Books, 1982, p. 317.
24. 'Death and Funeral of President Duvalier', *New York Times*, 25 April 1971.

31 He's Over the Wall

1. *The Comedians*, Penguin, 1976, pp. 229–30.
2. ibid., p. 229.
3. ibid., p. 228.
4. ibid., p. 138.
5. Yvonne Cloetta and Marie Françoise Allain. *In Search of a Beginning: my life with Graham Greene*, trans. by Euan Cameron, Bloomsbury, 2004, p. 83.
6. *The Comedians*, p. 139.
7. *The End of the Affair*, Penguin, 1975, pp. 54–5.

8.   *ibid.*, p. 56.
9.   *The Comedians*, p. 244.
10. *ibid.*, p. 129.
11. *ibid.*, p. 220.
12. Interview with Bonte Durán, 25 May 1992.
13. Letter to Catherine Walston, 26 April 1950.
14. *ibid.*, 25 April 1950.
15. Interview with Bonte Durán, 25 May 1992.
16. Letter from Catherine Walston to her sister Belinda Straight, 31 January 1969.
17. Letter to Catherine Walston, undated.
18. *ibid.*
19. Interview with Bonte Durán, 25 May 1992.
20. Letter from Bonte Durán to her husband, August 1952.
21. Undated letter from Bonte Durán to her husband.
22. *ibid.*
23. *ibid.*
24. Letter from Bonte Durán to her husband, 1953.
25. *ibid.*, 'Thursday'.
26. *ibid.*
27. *ibid.*
28. *ibid.*
29. *ibid.*, 1 July 1953.
30. Undated letter from Bonte Durán to her husband, written in 1953.
31. Letter from Bonte Durán to her husband, 22 July 1953.
32. *ibid.*, 9 July 1953.
33. *ibid.*
34. *ibid.*, 'Tuesday'; stamp shows the 2 June 1953 coronation – it could be 22 June 1953.
35. Letter from Catherine Walston to her sister Bonte Durán, 7 March 1951.
36. Letter from Bonte Durán to her husband, 3 July 1953.
37. Undated letter from Bonte Durán to her husband, written in 1953.
38. Interview with Lady Melchett, 15 August 1991.
39. Interview with Bonte Durán, 25 May 1992.
40. *The Comedians*, p. 47.
41. Letter to George Russo, 27 July 1989.
42. *The Comedians*, p. 284.
43. *ibid.*, pp. 284–5.
44. Interview with Vivien Greene, August 1977.
45. Interview with Yvonne Cloetta, 1977.

32 *Bonjour la France* ('Twas a Bad Year for Pigs)

1.   Claire Tomalin, *Several Strangers*, Viking, 1999, p. 5.
2.   Letter to Catherine Walston, 4 January 1956.
3.   Interview with Graham Greene, 11 August 1977.
4.   Letter from Evelyn Waugh, Midwinter [January 1966], *The Letters of Evelyn Waugh*, ed. Mark Amory, Weidenfeld & Nicolson, 1980, p. 635.
5.   Letter from Evelyn Waugh to Ann Fleming, January 1966, *ibid.*, pp. 635–6.
6.   Letter to Yvonne Cloetta, 7 November 1965.
7.   Letter to Pat and Alexander Frere, date unknown.
8.   Letter to Catherine Walston, 17 or 24 October 1965.
9.   *ibid.*, 8 November 1965.
10. *ibid.*, 30 December 1965.
11. Letter to Yvonne Cloetta, 17 December 1965.

12. Letter to Catherine Walston, 30 December 1965.
13. *ibid.*, 5 December 1965.
14. Letter to Yvonne Cloetta, 17 December 1965.
15. *ibid.*, 23 December 1965.
16. Letter to Catherine Walston, 30 December 1965.
17. Letter to Yvonne Cloetta, 23 December 1965.
18. Letter to Catherine Walston, 27 January 1966.
19. *ibid.*, 5 August 1965.
20. *ibid.*, 23 August 1965.
21. *The Times*, 2 November 1967.
22. *ibid.*
23. *The Noël Coward Diaries*, ed. Graham Payn and Sheridan Morley, Weidenfeld & Nicolson, 1982, p. 541. Entry for 11 August 1963.
24. *ibid.*, p. 548. Entry for 5 November 1963.
25. Cole Lesley, *Remembered Laughter: The Life of Noël Coward*, Alfred A. Knopf, 1976, pp. 432–3.
26. *ibid.*, p. 483.
27. Interview with Peter Glenville, 15 December 1978.
28. Brian Aherne, *A Dreadful Man*, Simon & Schuster, 1979, p. 96.
29. 'Cadco director expresses his regret', *The Times*, 11 February 1967.
30. 'George Sanders named as one of trio in Cadco "disaster"', *The Times*, 1 December 1966.
31. Letter to Francis Greene, 1965.
32. Letter to Catherine Walston, 5 December 1965.
33. Interview with the Rt. Hon. Douglas Jay, 1977.
34. Letter to Catherine Walston, 21 May 1965.
35. *ibid.*, undated but written in 1965.
36. *ibid.*, 5 November 1965.
37. *ibid.*
38. *ibid.*
39. *ibid.*, 15 November 1965.
40. Letter to Yvonne Cloetta, 7 November 1965.
41. Letter to Catherine Walston, 13 February 1966.
42. *A World of My Own: A Dream Diary*, Reinhardt, 1992, p. 68.

33 *Le Petit Chat*

1. Letter to Michael Meyer, 5 March 1968.
2. Letter to Yvonne Cloetta, 11 February 1967.
3. *ibid.*
4. *ibid.*
5. Quentin Falk, *Travels in Greeneland*, Quartet Books, 1984, p. 161.
6. Interview with Peter Glenville, New York, 15 December 1978.
7. Letter to Yvonne Cloetta, 11 February 1967.
8. *ibid.*
9. *ibid.*, undated except for year 1966, but probably December.
10. Interview with Peter Glenville, 15 December 1978.
11. Interview with John and Gillian Sutro, 2 June 1977.
12. Shirley Hazzard, *Greene on Capri*, Farrar, Straus & Giroux, 2000, p. 33.
13. *ibid.*, p. 34.
14. Interview with Otto Preminger, 14 December 1978.
15. Oliver Walston, 'The End of the Affair', *Spectator*, 30 July 1994.
16. Interview with David Higham, 1 July 1977.

17. Oliver Walston, 'The End of the Affair', *Spectator*, 30 July 1994.
18. Letter to Yvonne Cloetta, 31 July 1964.
19. *ibid.*, 4 August 1964.
20. *ibid.*, 20 August 1964.
21. *ibid.*, 24 August 1964.
22. *ibid.*, 31 August 1964.
23. Letter to Catherine Walston, dated only 'Sunday '64' but written in August or September.
24. Dream diary, December 1964.
25. Letter to Catherine Walston, 21 October 1964.
26. *ibid.*, 12 November 1964.
27. *ibid.*, 30 November 1964.
28. *ibid.*, 4 December 1964.
29. *ibid.*, 6 December 1964.
30. *ibid.*, 29 January 1965.
31. *ibid.*, 6 February 1965.
32. Postcard to Catherine Walston, February 1965.
33. Letter to Catherine Walston, dated only 'Tuesday'.
34. *ibid.*, 11 March 1965.
35. *ibid.*, 16 March 1965.
36. *ibid.*, 19 March 1965.
37. *ibid.*, dated only 'Tuesday'.
38. *ibid.*, 3 May 1965.
39. *ibid.*
40. *ibid.*, 13 May 1965.
41. *ibid.*, 21 April 1964.
42. Diary, 16 February 1965.

34 Warming Up to the Cold Scots

1. Letter to Yvonne Cloetta, 27 August 1965.
2. Letter to Catherine Walston, 11 April 1966.
3. *ibid.*, 25 April 1966.
4. *ibid.*, 11 April 1966. Greene never forgave Carol Reed, who after all had produced for Greene two of the best films of the decade in the early 1940s (*The Fallen Idol* and *The Third Man*), for his sloppiness in taking on Jo Morrow, the disappointing young lady who played the part of Wormold's daughter in *Our Man in Havana*. Perhaps if Korda had still been alive, he could have won out. Certainly Reed had a friend in Countess Budberg: she was hell-bent in getting Reed the chance to produce and direct *The Comedians*, and Greene was just as determined that it should go to Peter Glenville. Moura Budberg wrote Greene five letters of pursuance. I quote one:

> Dearest Graham,
> I know I have been a nuisance – and I apologise. But when you said Carol could see the book in proof I didn't think there would be much difference if he saw it in manuscript – and not at all because of 20th Century Fox, but for my own egotistic peace of mind I wanted it to be quicker! You see, I do believe he *is* a good movie-maker and from what I heard about the book – it would be wonderful for him. And for the first time for many years, you didn't sound *reluctant* that a film should be made of it. However, naturally you must do as you think best, only could he see it in proof in September when Max says it will be ready?
> But you see, darling Graham, I'll be just as frank with you as you were with me and say that I wouldn't have dreamt to make all this fuss if I hadn't thought

that you & Carol were more friends than just a novelist and a movie-maker. For some reason, Carol certainly led me to think so. I took it for granted and was surprised to find obstacles. Of course I wouldn't tell him that he can see the novel 'like everybody else' – he would be too upset!

I didn't resent at all Miss Reid not giving me your address & telephone – I know she was acting on your instructions and rightly too, – I was just trying to 'break the barrier' in some way. You've won, my dear dear friend.

And please don't let all this interfere with what is for me a very valuable friendship. I promise I'll never do it again. Love Moura.

And Greene's answer, dated 6 August 1965:

My dear Moura,

You know that I love you very much, so you must forgive my telling you that you are being a bloody nuisance. Miss Reid is only obeying my instructions – and so is the Bureau Denyse Clariouin – in refusing my telephone number and address. I tried to indicate to you gently that my novel is not particularly suitable for Carol. In any case I see no reason at all why he should see it in advance of other companies. When it appears, if he wants, he can make an offer like anyone else – if I have need of money, I shall sell, and if I don't need money, I shall refuse *any* offer. No one has yet made a good movie out of any *novel* of mine, and it's a long time since I've liked any of Carol's films – including *Our Man in Havana*. My dearest Moura, you are much too precious a human person to be a scout for Carol. Let Carol do his own scouting, with someone he knows as well as he knows me, and get his own rebuffs. He can see the novel in due course like anyone else, and I couldn't care less about his situation with 20th Century Fox. Miss Reid quite properly told him the other day that I was not available – I was with you and Jeanne Stonor and I will not have my private life broken into by movie-makers. She told him when to ring back, but he didn't do so.

I would like you to understand that when Miss Reid refuses an address or a telephone number, *I* am refusing it. In my parents' day one was allowed to be 'not at home' even to good friends – they didn't go on ringing at the bell. I think you owe an apology to Miss Reid who has *always* let me know when you've telephoned me.

Dearest Moura, it's only because we are such good friends that I write to you so frankly – but Max Reinhardt, my American agent, and Laurence Pollinger have all had instructions from me that this book is not to be shown to any movie-makers at this moment. Love,

5. *ibid.*, 5 May 1966.
6. *ibid.*, 16 May 1966.
7. Undated letter to Michael Meyer.
8. Letter to Catherine Walston, 25 May 1966.
9. *ibid.*, dated only '9.50 pm Saturday' but probably early June 1966.
10. Letter to Yvonne Cloetta, 8 June 1966.
11. Letter to Catherine Walston, 16 August 1966.
12. *ibid.*, 3 October 1966.
13. *ibid.*, 24 January 1967.
14. Postcard to Catherine Walston, 20 July 1966.
15. Letter to Catherine Walston, 28 November 1966.
16. In the undated letter to Catherine quoted above, Greene enclosed a copy of a letter he'd sent to the *Spectator*, printed 13 May 1966. Greene recalls how, when having a meal at the Havana Tropicana music hall, Khrushchev's son-in-law came over and

'stole the most attractive member of our party for a dance, and as she two-stepped by I called out to him, How did you get on with Pope John? He made a long nose at me as he passed. Later with the Soviet Ambassador, he joined our table, and I repeated my question. This time he replied with great gravity, "the Pope told me we were following different paths to the same end".' This phrase is used by Dr Magiot in the letter he writes to Brown before being shot by the Tontons Macoute. A beautiful source for the basic idea in that letter, borrowed and used awesomely by Greene. I quote a little of it here, changed a bit in the context since it is an extract from Dr Magiot's letter: 'So take it as the last request of a dying man – if you have abandoned one faith, do not abandon all faith. There is always an alternative to the faith we lose. Or is it the same faith under another mask?' (*The Comedians*, Penguin, 1976, p. 286.)

17. Letter to Catherine Walston, 3 October 1966.
18. Letter to Yvonne Cloetta, 28 July 1966.
19. *ibid.*, 30 July 1966.
20. *ibid.*, 4 August 1966.
21. Letter to Catherine Walston, undated but probably late July 1966.
22. Letter to Catherine Walston, 10 November 1966.
23. Letter to Yvonne Cloetta, 22 December 1966.
24. Letter to Catherine Walston, 15 November 1966.
25. Marie-Françoise Allain, *The Other Man: Conversations with Graham Greene*, trans. Guido Waldman, The Bodley Head, 1983, pp. 9–10.
26. Letter to Catherine Walston, 13 December 1966.
27. *ibid.*, 17 June 1967.
28. *ibid.*, 1 February 1967.
29. *ibid.*
30. *ibid.*, 30 April 1967.
31. *ibid.*, 7 July 1967.
32. Letter to Michael Meyer, 23 May 1967.
33. Letter to Catherine Walston, 7 July 1967.
34. Copy of Greene's speech is in his biographer's possession.

35 Confessions Near an Egyptian Shore

1. Letter to Yvonne Cloetta, 5 September 1967.
2. Letter from Roger Pool to *The Times*, 8 September 1967.
3. Letter from Richard Harman to *The Times*, 6 September 1967.
4. Letter to Michael Meyer, March 1968.
5. From Greene's speech, reprinted in *PEN Newsletter*, Summer 1968:

   I don't appear here as an attacker. I am an admirer of the Soviet Union, and an admirer of the Communist system. But in any government there grows up a hideous Establishment of stupid men. I have slight hopes – because I notice that a distinguished officer of the KGB, in an interview with a Western journalist, criticised the Daniel-Sinyavsky trial. This is my old friend and colleague, Kim Philby.

   One of the traces left on the world by Christianity, I think, is a phrase like, 'There but for the grace of God go I', or in Donne's more literary fashion, 'For whom the bell tolls'. We can sympathise with a forger, or a blackmailer, or even that man, even that genocide, who drops the bombs on innocent peasants in Viet-Nam. What seems to me appallingly absent among these stupid men is a feeling of community. I wrote – if you'll forgive me being personal – I wrote to the Union of Writers in Moscow, asking them to hand over my royalties which are banked there to the wives of Sinyavsky and Daniel. After about three months I got a cold response that they could not hand over *my* money to anyone but myself. Legal enough, fair enough. But I knew the answer to that, and so I wrote to Mr Alexander Chakovsky, the editor of the *Literary Gazette*, who is also a member of the Supreme Soviet, and asked him if I took out a deed of attorney at the Russian Embassy in Paris and sent it to him, whether he would draw out my money and hand it to these ladies. I didn't expect a very good response, but I didn't expect really such a reply, smooth as ice. Can I read it to you?

> My dear,
> It goes without saying that I remember our encounters quite well, and those are very pleasant memories indeed. There's no need to tell you that I am prepared to comply with any of your requests if it is within my power to do so. I am extremely sorry that in this case I have to start with a refusal. The fact is that we do not see eye to eye with regard to the matter raised in your letter. My attitude towards this matter being what it is, I would not like to be involved in it or get in touch with persons who in one way or another are connected with it. This is the reason why I cannot comply with your request. Please accept my best wishes for the New Year.

One must say that no bell tolls in Mr Chakovsky's ears: no thought that when we defend others we are defending ourselves. Because, one day, God knows, we shall need to be defended.

6. *Daily Telegraph*, 6 November 1964:

> In the past few weeks photographs have appeared in the British Press showing the tortures inflicted on Vietcong prisoners by troops of the Vietnam army.
> In the long, frustrating war – now nearly twenty years old – in Indo-China there has, of course, always been a practice of torture – torture by Vietminh, torture by Vietnamese, torture by the French – but at least in the old days of the long, long war hypocrisy paid a tribute to virtue by hushing up the torture inflicted by its own soldiers and condemning the torture inflicted by the other side.
> The strange new feature about the photographs of torture now appearing in the British and American Press is that they have been taken with the approval of the torturers and are published over captions that contain no hint of condemnation. They might have come out of a book on insect life. 'The white ant takes certain measures against the red ant after a successful foray.'
> But these, after all, are not ants but men. The long, slow slide into barbarism of the western world seems to have quickened . . .

7. Letter to Catherine Walston, 29 August 1967.
8. *ibid.*
9. Telegram from September 1967.
10. *Guardian*, 19 September 1967.
11. Diary, 19 or 20? September 1967.
12. *ibid.*, 20 September 1967.
13. Letter to Yvonne Cloetta, 20 September 1967.
14. Postcard to Yvonne Cloetta, 22 September 1967.
15. 'Incident in Sinai', *Sunday Telegraph*, 29 October 1967.
16. Letter to Yvonne Cloetta, 28 September 1967.
17. *ibid.*, 1 October 1967.
18. Letter to Catherine Walston, 26 and 27 September 1967.

36 The Virtue of Disloyalty

1. Dream diary, 7 May 1957.
2. Dream diary, 29 July 1965.
3. Letter from Michael Meyer to author, 5 May 2000.
4. *ibid.*, 21 May 1998.
5. Letter to Vivien Dayrell-Browning [Greene], 1926 or 27.
6. *The Meaning of Treason*, Rebecca West, 1949, p. 313.
7. Letter to Catherine Walston, 30 May 1969.
8. 'The Virtue of Disloyalty', *Reflections*, ed. Judith Adamson, Reinhardt Books, 1990, pp. 266–70.

37 A Strange Dottoressa

1. Letter to Vivien Dayrell-Browning, 5 July 1926.
2. *Travels with My Aunt*, Penguin, 1971, p. 177.
3. Marie-Françoise Allain, *The Other Man: Conversations with Graham Greene*, trans. Guido Waldman, The Bodley Head, 1983, p. 126.
4. *ibid.*
5. *Travels with My Aunt*, pp. 83–6.
6. *ibid.*, pp. 110–11.
7. *ibid.*, p. 117.
8. *ibid.*, pp. 102–3.
9. *ibid.*, pp. 93–4.
10. *ibid.*, p. 16.
11. *Journey Without Maps*, Penguin, 1976, p. 211.
12. *Travels with My Aunt*, p. 182.
13. *ibid.*, pp. 186–7.
14. *ibid.*, p. 194.
15. *ibid.*, pp. 198–9.
16. *ibid.*, pp. 204–5.
17. *ibid.*, p. 10.
18. Dottoressa Elisabeth Moor in conversation with Kenneth Macpherson, Capri, 1951, quoted in *An Impossible Woman*, The Bodley Head, 1975, frontispiece.
19. *ibid.*, p. 119.
20. *ibid.*, p. 204.
21. Shirley Hazzard, *Greene on Capri*, Farrar, Straus & Giroux, 2000, p. 26.
22. *An Impossible Woman*, p. 204.
23. *ibid.*, p. 205.
24. *Travels with My Aunt*, pp. 210–11.
25. *ibid.*, pp. 221–2.
26. *ibid.*, pp. 262–3.
27. Interview with Graham Greene.
28. *Travels with My Aunt*, p. 225.

38. How *Not* to Snatch a Diplomat

1. 'The Soupsweet Land', *Collected Essays*, Viking, 1983, pp. 455–63.
2. *The Heart of the Matter*, Penguin, 1982, p. 13.
3. 'The Soupsweet Land', *Collected Essays*, p. 462.
4. Letter to Yvonne Cloetta, 15 July 1968.
5. Letter to Catherine Walston, 28 July 1968.
6. Letter to Yvonne Cloetta, 20 July 1968.

7. *ibid.*, July 1968.
8. *ibid.*
9. *ibid.*, 20 July 1968.
10. *ibid.*, 5 August 1968.
11. *The Honorary Consul*, Penguin, 1973, p. 11.
12. Letter to Catherine Walston, 9 May 1970.
13. *Ways of Escape*, Lester & Orpen Dennys, 1980, p. 253.
14. Diary, May 1970.
15. *ibid.*, p. 4.
16. *The Honorary Consul*, pp. 12–13.
17. *ibid.*, pp. 17–18.
18. *ibid.*, pp. 39–40.
19. *Ways of Escape*, pp. 251–2.
20. *The Honorary Consul*, pp. 55–9.
21. *ibid.*, p. 60.
22. *ibid.*, p. 32.
23. *ibid.*, p. 150.
24. *ibid.*, p. 35.
25. *ibid.*, p. 205.
26. Letter to Catherine Walston, 7 September 1949.
27. *ibid.*, 9 December 1949.
28. *The Honorary Consul*, p. 237.

39 'As Mystery-Laden as Life Itself'

1. Cardinal Richard Cushing, quoted in 'The Revolutionary Cardinal', *Newsweek*, 26 August 1963.
2. *New York Times*, 13 July 1969.
3. *Ways of Escape*, Lester & Orpen Dennys, 1980, p. 250.
4. *ibid.*, p. 251.
5. *ibid.*
6. Letter to Yvonne Cloetta, 20 July 1968.
7. Camilo Torres, *Revolutionary Priest: The Complete Writings and Messages of Camilo Torres*, ed. John Gerassi, Random House, 1971, frontispiece.
8. *Time*, 23 August 1968.
9. Diary, 24–27 March 1970.
10. *ibid.*, 28 March 1970.
11. *Reflections*, ed. Judith Adamson, Reinhardt, 1990, p. 261. Originally appeared in *Daily Telegraph* magazine, 3 January 1969.
12. *The Honorary Consul*, pp. 94–5.
13. *ibid.*, p. 99.
14. *ibid.*, p. 112.
15. *ibid.*, p. 115.
16. Diary, p. 8.
17. Interview with Oscar Marturet, 6 June 1978. My translator was Professor Richard Slatta.
18. *ibid.*, 7 June 1978.
19. *ibid.*
20. *ibid.*, 6 and 7 June 1978.

40 The Ultimate Story

1. *The Honorary Consul*, Penguin, 1974, pp. 115–16.
2. *ibid.*, pp. 215–16.
3. *ibid.*, pp. 217–19.
4. *ibid.*, pp. 224–7.
5. *ibid.*, pp. 249–51.
6. Letter to Catherine Walston, 30 July 1970.
7. *National Observer*, September 1973.
8. Peter Wolfe, *Detroit Sunday News*, September 1973.
9. *Buffalo News*, September 1973.
10. *Wall Street Journal*, September 1973.
11. *Denver Post*, September 1973.
12. *Evening Standard*, 18 September 1973.
13. Letter to Catherine Walston, 28 November 1970.
14. *ibid.*, 4 December 1970.
15. *ibid.*, 14 August 1971.
16. *ibid.*, 21 November 1971.
17. Letter to Yvonne Cloetta, 30 August 1971.
18. Letter to Yvonne Cloetta, 2 September 1971.
19. Letter to Catherine Walston, 1 November 1972.
20. *ibid.*, 14 November 1972.
21. *ibid.*, 12 January 1974.
22. *ibid.*, 23 January 1975.
23. Letter to Yvonne Cloetta, 29 July 1972.
24. *ibid.*, 6 August 1972.
25. *ibid.*, 19 September 1972.
26. *ibid.*, 23 September 1972.
27. *The Honorary Consul*, p. 228.
28. *ibid.*, p. 254.
29. *ibid.*, p. 258.

41 My Pal the General

1. *The Times*, 27 May 1970.
2. Letter to Catherine Walston, 10 July 1978.
3. Upon his arrival in power, Torrijos was determined to bring the Panama Canal under the jurisdiction of the Panamanians. A hard struggle achieved by a distinctive and friendly dictator was surely a rarity in itself, but especially one waged against the mighty influence of the United States, an influence that disturbed, almost to a man, the people of Panama.

   Panama revolted against Colombia on 3 November 1904, and an American warship prevented Colombia from rescuing its own territory. When formally recognised, the new republic signed an American contract on the same terms earlier offered to Colombia: a cash payment of $10,000,000 and an annuity of $250,000. Despite the then-large sums of money offered, America's demands were hard to swallow – no wonder Colombia baulked: exclusive control *in perpetuity* of a Canal Zone, as well as other sites thought by the United States to be necessary for defence of the Canal. (Not until 1921 did America pay out $25 million to persuade Colombia to recognise the independence of Panama.) The fallout literally split Panama in two.

   It was a sweet achievement for America – making her a colonial country, the vast Canal Zone, with 'all the rights, power and authority [which it] would possess and exercise as the sovereign of the territory' guaranteed. Moreover, the Republic of

Panama would not have its own 'sovereign rights, power or authority'. With the Canal and the Canal Zone now American, the Americans had the Panamanians remove their judges and abolished their army.

4. *The Captain and the Enemy*, Penguin, 1988, p. 9.
5. *ibid.*, pp. 116–17.
6. John Weeks and Phil Gunson, *Panama: Made in the USA*, Latin American Bureau, 1991, p. 34.
7. *Getting to Know the General*, Pocket Books, 1984, p. 42.
8. Weeks and Gunson, *Panama: Made in the USA*, p. 35.
9. *Getting to Know the General*, p. 17.
10. *Observer*, 8 October 1954.
11. *New York Times*, 1 June 1968.
12. *ibid.*, 21 May 1968.
13. Henry Giniger, *New York Times*, 4 May 1969.
14. *The Times*, 15 October 1983.
15. *Getting to Know the General*, p. 21.
16. Shirley Hazzard, *Greene on Capri*, Farrar, Straus & Giroux, 2000, p. 80.
17. *Getting to Know the General*, pp. 23–4.
18. *ibid.*, pp. 28–9.
19. Letter to Bernard Diederich, 30 December 1976.
20. *Time*, 20 December 1976.

42 That Old Goat and the Dictator in a Hammock

1. Jimmy Carter, *Keeping Faith: Memoirs of a President*, Bantam, 1982, p. 155.
2. 'The Country with Five Frontiers', *New York Review of Books*, 17 February, 1977.
3. *ibid.*
4. *ibid.*
5. *Getting to Know the General*, Pocket Books, 1984, p. 63.
6. Letter to Bernard Diederich, 17 May 1977.
7. Letter from Bernard Diederich, 13 April 1977.
8. *Getting to Know the General*, pp. 89–90.
9. Marie-Françoise Allain, *The Other Man: Conversations with Graham Greene*, trans. Guido Waldman, The Bodley Head, 1983, p. 93.
10. *Getting to Know the General*, pp. 105–6.
11. 'The Great Spectacular', *New York Review of Books*, 26 June 1978.
12. *ibid.*
13. Carter, *Keeping Faith*, p. 161.
14. *Getting to Know the General*, p. 186.
15. *ibid.*, p. 189.
16. *ibid.*, p. 194.
17. *ibid.*, pp. 187–8.
18. *New York Times*, 10 June 1987.
19. *ibid.*, 12 June 1987.

43 Dashing Around Central America . . .

1. *Getting to Know the General*, Pocket Books, 1984, pp. 127–8.
2. Letter to Jean-Félix Paschoud, date unknown.
3. *Getting to Know the General*, p. 136.
4. Richard West, *Hurricane in Nicaragua: A Journey in Search of Revolution*, Michael Joseph, 1989, p. 173.

5. *Getting to Know the General*, p. 137.
6. Russell Bartley, Kent Johnson, and Sylvia Yoneda, introduction to *Have you Seen a Red Curtain in My Weary Chamber? Poems, Stories and Essays by Tomás Borge Martínez*, Curbstone Press, 1989, p. 13.
7. *Tablet*, 4 January 1986.
8. *Time*, 21 May 1986.
9. West, *Hurricane in Nicaragua*, pp. 29–30.
10. *Observer*, 23 September 1984.
11. *Getting to Know the General*, p. 144.
12. *ibid.*, p. 146.
13. *ibid.*, p. 147.
14. Letter to *The Times*, 15 October 1983.
15. Letter to *Spectator*, 21 April 1984.
16. *ibid.*
17. *ibid.*, 29 August 1987.
18. Letter from Charles Morley to *Spectator*, 17 October 1987.
19. Letter to *Spectator*, 31 October, 1987.
20. Letter from Charles Morley to *Spectator*, 5 December 1987.
21. Letter to *Spectator*, 16 January 1988.

44 His True Love Dies

1. *Ways of Escape*, Lester & Orpen Dennys, 1980, p. 256.
2. Letter to Catherine Walston, 23 December 1975.
3. *Ways of Escape*, p. 257.
4. *ibid.*, p. 256.
5. *The Human Factor*, Penguin, 1980, p. 18.
6. *ibid.*, pp. 59–60.
7. *ibid.*, p. 9.
8. *ibid.*, p. 84.
9. *ibid.*, pp. 85–6.
10. *ibid.*, pp. 84–5.
11. *ibid.*, pp. 168–9.
12. Letter to Raymond Greene, 15 May 1967.
13. *ibid.*, 2 June 1967.
14. Letter from Raymond Greene, 15 October 1972.
15. *The Human Factor*, p. 169.
16. *ibid.*, p. 109.
17. Telephone conversation with Elisabeth Dennys, 6 July 1984.
18. Letter from Vivien Greene to author, 1 October 1984.
19. *The Human Factor*, pp. 26–30.
20. Letter to Catherine Walston, 25 June 1971.
21. *ibid.*
22. *ibid.*, undated.
23. *ibid.*, 6 February 1972.
24. Letter from Catherine Walston, 13 December 1975.
25. *ibid.*
26. Letter to Catherine Walston, 23 December 1975.
27. *ibid.*, 1 September 1976.
28. Marie-Françoise Allain, *The Other Man: Conversations with Graham Greene*, trans. Guido Waldman, The Bodley Head, 1983, pp. 114-115.
29. Letter from Catherine Walston, 14 December 1976.
30. Letter to Catherine Walston, 18 September 1977.

31. *ibid.*, 14 October 1977.
32. Letter from Catherine Walston, 18 October 1977.
33. Letter to Catherine Walston, 10 July 1978.
34. Letter from Catherine Walston, 18 May 1978.
35. Oliver Walston, *The Times*, 8 July 1994.
36. Oliver Walston, *Spectator*, 30 July 1994.
37. Letter from Marie Biche, 9 September 1978.
38. Letter from William Walston to author, 11 July 2001.

45 Angry Old Man

1. Letter to Général Alain de Boissieu, Chancelier de la Légion d'Honneur, 22 December 1980.
2. Letter from Général Boissieu, 6 January 1981.
3. Letter to French Minister of Justice Alain Peyrefitte, 22 December 1980.
4. Letter from Alain Peyrefitte, 6 January 1981.
5. Dictabelt, 15 January 1981.
6. Letter to *The Times*, 25 January 1982.
7. Byran Forbes, *A Divided Life: Memoirs*, Mandarin, 1993, pp. 126–7.
8. Letter from James Baring, 18 March 1982.
9. Letter from supporter, Holy Monday 1982.
10. Letter from sympathiser, 2 March 1982.
11. Interview with Graham Greene, 25 April 1981.
12. Michael Shelden, *Graham Greene: The Man Within*, Random House, 1995, p. 451.
13. *ibid.*, p. 452.
14. I cannot help but think that if Greene had lived at the time of Jesus and known of Christ's authority and crucifixion, if he were one of the disciples, no one would have run more frantically toward the open cave where the body of the Saviour once lay. This would have been the greatest opportunity in anyone's life – to witness the crucifixion and then the empty tomb, the great stone rolled away. Above all, he would have wanted to report that event with the same astonishing accuracy with which he'd related other events in his superb travel books, brilliant journalism, and unequalled fiction.
15. Shelden, *Graham Greene: The Man Within*, p. 452.
16. *J'Accuse: The Dark Side of Nice*, The Bodley Head, 1982, p. 8.
17. 'Intrigue on the French Riviera,' *Saturday Review*, May 1982.
18. Shelden, *Graham Greene: The Man Within*, p. 453.
19. Jonathan Raban, 'Innocents Abroad', *New York Review of Books*, 4 November 1982.
20. Letter from supporter, 7 February 1982.
21. *J'Accuse*, p. 34.
22. *ibid.*, p. 9.
23. *ibid.*, p. 12.
24. *ibid.*, p. 11.
25. *ibid.*, pp. 12–14.
26. *ibid.*, p. 16.
27. *ibid.*, pp. 15–16.
28. *ibid.*, pp. 21–2.
29. *ibid.*, p. 14.

46 Toe to Toe with the French Mafia

1. Michael Shelden, *Graham Greene: The Man Within*, Random House, 1995, p. 453.
2. Bryan Forbes, *A Divided Life: Memoirs*, Mandarin, 1993, p. 126.
3. *J'Accuse: The Dark Side of Nice*, The Bodley Head, 1982, pp. 22–3.
4. Letter from *Times* legal manager Anthony Whitaker, 24 May 1983.
5. *ibid.*
6. *J'Accuse*, p. 7.
7. Jonathan Fenby, 'Dirty tricks, says le patron, and takes the Gloves off, *The Times*, 10 February 1982.
8. *ibid.*
9. *L'ACTUALITE*, 6–7 February 1982.
10. Letter to *The Times*, 7 August 1982.
11. Letter from Ragnar Svanstrom, May 1982.
12. Letter to Ragnar Svanstrom, 13 May 1982.
13. Letter from Simon & Schuster to Max Reinhardt, 13 May 1982.
14. *Evening Standard*, 23 June 1982.
15. Stephen Vicinczey (from Greene's own files).
16. Lester & Orpen Dennys, May 1982.
17. Auberon Waugh, *Sunday Telegraph*, 18 July 1982.
18. Jonathan Raban, 'Innocents Abroad', *New York Review of Books*, November 1982.
19. Stephen Vizinczey (from Greene's own files).
20. Auberon Waugh, review of *J'Accuse*, *Sunday Telegraph*, 18 July 1982.
21. Letter to Madame Bertrand, 29 July 1982.
22. Susan Heller Andersen, 'Chronicle', *New York Times*, 18 September 1990.
23. Letter to Max Reinhardt, 22 December 1986.
24. Letter from Copenhagen literature class, March 1986.
25. Letter to Copenhagen literature class, 26 March 1986.
26. Leopoldo Durán, *Graham Greene: Friend and Brother*, HarperCollins, 1994, p. 251.
27. *ibid.*, p. 15.

47 Sancho and the Saint

1. 'Greene Criticizes Film Adaptations of His Books', *New York Times*, 6 September 1984.
2. Leopoldo Durán, *Graham Greene: Friend and Brother*, HarperCollins, 1994, pp. 83–4.
3. *Monsignor Quixote*, Penguin, 1985, pp. 27–8.
4. *ibid.*, pp. 46–7.
5. *ibid.*, pp. 58–9.
6. *ibid.*, pp. 76–7.
7. *ibid.*, pp. 109–10.
8. *ibid.*, pp. 110–12.
9. Durán, *Graham Greene: Friend and Brother*, pp. 126–7.
10. *ibid.*, pp. 212–13.
11. *Monsignor Quixote*, pp. 114–17.
12. *ibid.*, pp. 137–8.
13. *ibid.*, pp. 140–2.
14. *ibid.*, pp. 144–7.
15. *ibid.*, p. 150.
16. *ibid.*, p. 154.
17. *ibid.*, pp. 175–6.
18. *ibid.*, p. 205.
19. *ibid.*, p. 197.
20. *ibid.*, p. 214.

21. *ibid.*, p. 217.
22. *ibid.*, pp. 222–3.
23. *ibid.*, pp. 228–9.
24. *ibid.*, p. 236.
25. Durán, *Graham Greene: Friend and Brother*, p. 128.
26. *Monsignor Quixote*, p. 238.
27. *ibid.*, p. 241.
28. *ibid.*, p. 243.
29. *ibid.*, pp. 245–6.
30. *ibid.*, pp. 250–1.
31. *ibid.*, pp. 253–4.
32. *ibid.*, p. 256.
33. Shirley Hazzard, *Greene on Capri*, Farrar, Straus & Giroux, 2000, p. 89.
34. *Sunday Telegraph Magazine*, 12 September 1982.

48 The Lamb and the Lion: What Did Greene Believe?

1. Norman Sherry, *Life of Graham Greene*, Vol. One, Jonathan Cape, 1989, p. 255.
2. *ibid.*, p. 133.
3. *Ways of Escape*, Lester & Orpen Dennys, 1980, p. 116.
4. *Like It Was: The Diaries of Malcolm Muggeridge*, ed. John Bright-Holmes, William Morrow & Co., 1981, p. 374.
5. *The End of the Affair*, Penguin, 1975, p. 190.
6. *ibid.*, p. 190.
7. *The Lawless Roads*, Penguin, 1982, p. 13.
8. *ibid.*, p. 14.
9. *ibid.*
10. Sherry, *Life of Graham Greene*, Vol. One, p. 260.
11. *The Heart of the Matter*, Penguin, 1982, pp. 35–6.
12. *The Honorary Consul*, Penguin, 1974, p. 109.
13. *A Burnt-Out Case*, Penguin, 1977, p. 124.
14. *The Honorary Consul*, pp. 225–6.
15. 'A Visit to Morin', *Collected Stories*, Viking, 1973, pp. 254–5.
16. Clifford Longley, 'The Greene party: faithful to mysteries and mistresses', *The Times*, 23 September 1989.
17. James Joyce, *A Portrait of the Artist as a Young Man*, Penguin, 1983, pp. 157–8.
18. Letter from George Russo to author, 10 September 2001.
19. Leopoldo Durán, *Graham Greene: Friend and Brother*, HarperCollins, 1984, p. 81.
20. *ibid.*, pp. 94–5.
21. *ibid.*, p. 128.
22. *ibid.*, p. 121.

49 Raise the Plague Flag!

1. Letter from Ragnar Svanstrom, 30 November 1960.
2. Letter to Ragnar Svanstrom, 13 April 1966.
3. Michael Meyer, 'Head and Tails', *Daily Telegraph*, 5 December 1975.
4. Letter to Mary Connell, 3 April 1979.
5. Artur Lundkvist, *Morgon-Tidningen*, 4 November 1952.

50 Kudos in a Bundle

1. Shirley Hazzard, *Greene on Capri*, Farrar, Straus & Giroux, 2000, p. 61.
2. Speech accepting honorary citizenship of Capri, 18 October 1979.
3. Letter to Sir Brynmor Jones, 10 December 1971.
4. Letter from Joel Wells to Monica McCall, 6 September 1973.
5. Undated letter to Raymond Chandler Society.
6. Letter to British Council, 17 August 1989.
7. Letter to the Oriental Hotel, 23 March 1981.
8. Letter to Yale University, 10 January 1987.
9. Letter to James Tait Black prize committee, 13 January 1949.
10. Letter to Longwood College, 20 December 1979.
11. Letter from Loyola University, New Orleans, Louisiana, 25 April 1978.
12. Letter to Loyola University, New Orleans, Louisiana, 10 May 1978.
13. Letter from The Athenaeum, late 1978/early 1979.
14. Letter to The Athenaeum, 9 January 1979.
15. Michael Shelden, *Graham Greene: The Man Within*, Random House, 1995, p. 154.
16. *ibid.*, p. 152.
17. Hazzard, *Greene on Capri*, pp. 76–7.
18. Letter from Greene to G. Krishnamurti, 25 February 1986.
19. Letter from Harry Walston, 11 February 1986.
20. Letter from Lord Boothby, 11 February 1986.
21. Letter from Alec Guinness, 11 February 1986.
22. Letter from John Mortimer, 23 February 1986.
23. Letter from Michael Foot, 13 February 1986.
24. Letter from Victor (only name given) 14 February 1986.
25. Letter from Michael Mewshaw, 13 February 1986.
26. Letter from Jocelyn Rickards, 17 February 1986.
27. *The Economist*, 15 February 1986.
28. *The Times*, 11 Feb 1986.

51 A Kinder, Gentler Moscow

1. 'A Party to Remember', *Time*, 2 March 1987.
2. Rufina Philby, *The Private Life of Kim Philby*, Fromm International, 1999, p. 178.
3. Letter to *The Times*, 4 September 1967.
4. Philby, *The Private Life of Kim Philby*, pp. 173–7.
5. *The Times*, 12 May 1988.
6. Philby, *The Private Life of Kim Philby*, p. 180.
7. Ronald Hingley, *Nightingale Fever*, New York: Knopf, 1981, p. 232.
8. A. N. Wilson, 'Graham Greene and a Companion of Dishonour', *Daily Mail*, 5 September 1987.
9. *A Sort of Life*, Penguin, 1981, p. 60.

52 Boxing with Burgess

1. Letter to Anthony Burgess, 13 June 1988.
2. *Lire*, June 1988. Translated from the French by Christopher Kilmer.
3. 'Literary Giants in War of Words', *Sunday Express*, 7 August 1988.
4. Letter from Anthony Burgess, 2 November 1958.
5. *ibid.*, 19 June 1961.

6. Letter from Anthony Burgess to Michael Korda, 4 May 1971.
7. Anthony Burgess, *You've Had Your Time*, Weidenfeld & Nicolson, 1991, pp. 358–9.

53 Greene's Last Stand

1. Telephone interview with Gerry Dukes, 26 July 2001.
2. Letter to Joan McDonnell, 20 October 1986.
3. *ibid.*, 15 December 1986.
4. Letter to Vincent McDonnell, 31 March 1987.
5. *ibid.*, 15 January 1988.
6. *ibid.*, 13 November 1989.
7. Letter from Vincent McDonnell to author.
8. Telephone interview with Gerry Dukes, 26 July 2001.

54 Hugh and Elisabeth

1. Letter to James Greene, 26 February 1987.
2. Yvonne Cloetta and Marie-Françoise Allain, *In Search of a Beginning: My Life with Graham Greene*, trans. by Euan Cameron, Bloomsbury, 2004, p. 16.
3. *ibid.*

55 Our Man Dead

1. Yvonne Cloetta and Marie-Françoise Allain, *In Search of a Beginning: My Life with Graham Greene*, trans. by Euan Cameron, Bloomsbury, 2004, p. 190.
2. *ibid.*, pp. 202–3.
3. *ibid*, p. 205.

Bibliography to Volumes One, Two, Three

SECTION ONE: PRIMARY TEXTS

This section lists, in roughly chronological order corresponding to the organisation of the biography, works by Graham Greene consulted in the writing of this work. The place of publication is London, unless otherwise noted. The edition used, usually a Penguin, is also noted. For a fuller bibliography of writings by and about Greene, see R. A. Wobbe, *Graham Greene: A Bibliography and Guide to Research* (New York: Garland, 1979). Unpublished materials, by Greene and others, are listed in the second part of this section.

'The Poetry of Modern Life.' *The Berkhamstedian* 41 (March 1921).

'The Tyranny of Realism.' *The Berkhamstedian* 42 (March 1922): 2–3.

'The Trial of Pan.' *The Oxford Outlook.* 5 (February 1923): 47–50.

'John Drinkwater.' *The Oxford Outlook.* 6 (February 1924): 120–23.

'The Improbable Tale of the Archbishop of Canterbridge.' *The Cherwell* n.s. 12 (14 November 1924): 187, 189, 191.

'Poetry by Wireless.' *The Oxford Chronicle,* 30 January 1925, p. 15.

'Lord Love when will you . . .' *Weekly Westminster Gazette* 24 October 1925

Babbling April. Oxford: Blackwell, 1925.

'Sad Cure. The Life and Death of John Perry-Perkins.' *The Cherwell.* n.s. 16.5 (20 February 1926): 139–40.

'Unsigned article.' *The Times,* 27 December 1928.

The Man Within. Heinemann, 1929. (Penguin, 1977)

The Name of Action. Heinemann, 1930.

'Obermmergau.' *The Graphic.* 127 (17 May 1930): 345.

'Save Me Only from Dullness.' *Evening News,* 23 January 1930.

Rumour at Nightfall. Heinemann, 1931.

'Casanova and Others.' *The Spectator* 149 (9 July 1932): 54–55.

'Fiction.' *The Spectator* 150 (10 February 1933): 194, 196.

'Fiction.' *The Spectator* 150 (7 April 1933): 508.

'Fiction.' *The Spectator* 150 (21 April 1933): 579.

'Fiction.' *The Spectator* 150 (5 May 1933): 654.

'Fiction.' *The Spectator* 150 (19 May 1933): 728.

'Fiction.' *The Spectator* 151 (28 July 1933): 128.

'Fiction.' *The Spectator* 151 (22 September 1933): 380.

'Fiction.' *The Spectator* 151 (3 November 1933): 638.

'Fiction.' *The Spectator* 151 (15 December 1933): 910.

'Fiction.' *The Spectator* 151 (29 December 1933): 973.

'The Domestic Background.' *The Spectator*, 154 (26 July 1935): 164.

'The News in English.' *The Strand Magazine*, June 1940.

'The Sense of Apprehension.' *The Month*, n.s. 6 (July 1951): 49–51.

Stamboul Train. Heinemann, 1932. (Penguin, 1981)

'Fiction.' *The Spectator*, 150 (5 May 1933): 654.

'Gold Bricks.' *The Spectator*, 150 (3 March 1933): 308.

'Fiction.' *The Spectator*, 151 (31 June 1933): 956.

'Two Capitals.' *The Spectator*, 151 (20 October 1933): 520–21.

It's a Battlefield. Heinemann, 1934. (Penguin, 1981)

ed. *The Old School*. Jonathan Cape, 1934.

'Fiction.' *The Spectator* 152 (1 June 1934): 864.

'West Coast.' *The Spectator* 154 (12 April 1935): 620, 622.

'The Cinema.' *The Spectator* 155 (5 July 1935): 14.

'The Domestic Background.' *The Spectator* 155 (26 July 1935): 150.

'The Cinema.' *The Spectator* 155 (6 September 1935): 353.

'The Cinema.' The Spectator 155 (4 October 1935): 506.

'The Cinema.' *The Spectator* 155 (11 October 1935): 547.

England Made Me. Heinemann, 1935. (Penguin, 1980)

The Bear Fell Free. Grayson, 1935.

The Basement Room. Cresset Press, 1935.

Journey Without Maps. Heinemann, 1936. (Penguin, 1978)

'The Cinema.' *The Spectator* 155 (27 December 1935): 1068.

'Two Tall Travellers.' *The Spectator* 157 (11 September 1936).

A Gun For Sale. Heinemann, 1936. (Penguin, 1974)

'A Chance for Mr. Lever.' *Story* 8 (January 1936): 9–22.

'The Cinema.' *The Spectator* 156 (17 April 1936): 703.

'Short Stories.' *The Spectator* 157 (22 May 1936): 950.

'The Cinema.' *The Spectator* 157 (4 September 1936): 379.

'The Cinema.' *The Spectator* 157 (20 November 1936): 945.

'The Cinema.' *The Spectator* 157 (11 December 1936): 1037.

'The Cinema.' *The Spectator* 157 (18 December 1936): 1081.

'The Cinema.' *The Spectator* 155 (25 December 1936): 1122.

'The Cinema.' *The Spectator* 158 (5 March 1937): 403.

'The Cinema.' *The Spectator* 158 (2 April 1937): 619.

'A Typewriter in the Desert.' *London Mercury*. 25 (April 1937): 635.

'Subjects and Stories.' *Footnotes to the Film*. Ed. Charles Davy. Lovat Dickson, 57–70.

'The Cinema: Pawn's Move and Knight's Move.' *Night and Day* 1 (19 August 1937): 30.

'The Cinema: What's Left is Celluloid.' *Night and Day* 1 (26 August 1937): 30.

'The Week's Films.' *Night and Day* 1 (30 September 1937): 38–39.

'The Films.' *Night and Day* 1 (7 October 1937): 38.

'The Films.' *Night and Day* 1 (21 October 1937): 31.

'The Films.' *Night and Day* 1 (4 November 1937): 31.

'Cinema: The Great and the Humble.' *Night and Day* 1 (8 November 1937): 38.

'Ideas in the Cinema.' *The Spectator* 159 (19 November 1937): 894–95.

Brighton Rock. Heinemann, 1938. (Penguin, 1975)

'The Cinema.' *The Spectator* 161 (5 August 1938): 232.

'The Escapist.' *The Spectator* 162 (13 January 1939): 48–49.

'Bombing Raid.' *The Spectator* 163 (18 August 1939): 249.

'Fiction.' *The Spectator* 163 (22 September 1939): 296.

The Lawless Roads. Heinemann, 1939. (Heinemann Uniform, 1955)

The Confidential Agent. Heinemann, 1939. (Penguin, 1971, 1981)

'Fiction.' *The Spectator* 163 (10 November 1939): 662.

'The Cinema.' *The Spectator* 164 (12 January 1940): 44.

[as Henry Trench]. 'Finland.' *The Spectator* 164 (8 March 1940).

The Power and the Glory. Heinemann, 1940. (Heinemann, 1960; Penguin, 1977)

'Notes on the Way.' *Time and Tide* 21 (19 October 1940), pp. 1021–22.

[as Henry Trench]. 'The Strays.' *The Spectator* 165 (25 October 1940).

'The Theatre.' *The Spectator* 165 (1 November 1940): 440.

'Great Dog of Weimar.' *The Spectator* 165 (8 November 1940): 474.

'The Unknown War.' *The Spectator* 165 (6 December 1940): 578.

'A Lost Leader.' *The Spectator*. 165 (13 December 1940): 646.

'The Theatre.' *The Spectator* 166 (24 January 1941): 87.

'A Pride of Bombs.' *The Spectator* 166 (14 February 1941): 178.

'Domestic War.' *The Spectator* 166 (28 March 1941): 348, 350.

'The Theatre.' *The Spectator* 166 (11 April 1941): 395.

'The Last Buchan.' *The Spectator* 166 (18 April 1941): 430, 432.

'The Theatre.' *The Spectator* 166 (25 April 1941): 447.

'The Theatre.' *The Spectator* 166 (25 May 1941): 472.

'Bed-Exhausted.' *The Spectator* 166 (23 May 1941): 558.

'The Theatre.' *The Spectator* 166 (30 May 1941): 580.

'The Theatre.' *The Spectator* 166 (6 June 1941): 607.

'The Theatre.' *The Spectator* 166 (13 June 1941): 630.

'The Theatre.' *The Spectator* 166 (27 June 1941): 677.

'The Theatre.' *The Spectator* 167 (11 July 1941): 34.

'The Theatre.' *The Spectator* 167 (25 July 1941): 82.

'The Theatre.' *The Spectator* 167 (1 August 1941): 106.

British Dramatists. Collins, 1942.

'Men at Work.' *Penguin New Writing*. Penguin, 1942.

The Ministry of Fear. Heinemann, 1943. (Penguin, 1972, 1978)

'The Maritains.' *New Statesman and Nation* 28 (9 September 1944): 173.

'Graham Greene on Books.' *The Evening Standard*, 22 June 1945, p. 6.

'From Crafts to the Conveyor Belt.' *The Evening Standard*, 13 July 1945, p. 6.

'They Wanted to Use Another Name.' *The Evening Standard*, 10 August 1945, p. 6.

'That Gay Deceiver Dickens.' *The Evening Standard*, 31 August 1945, p. 6.

'It May Be Dangerous.' *The Evening Standard*, 17 August 1945, p. 6.

'Theatre.' *New Statesman and Nation* 34 (13 September 1947): 20.

'Books in General.' *New Statesman and Nation* 34 (22 October 1947): 292.

Nineteen Stories. Heinemann, 1947.

'Across the Border.' Penguin New Writing. Vol. 30. 1947.

The Heart of the Matter. Heinemann, 1948. (Penguin, 1983)

'Letter.' *News Chronicle*, 27 February 1948.

'Behind the Right Pupils.' *The Month*. 2 (July 1949): 7–8.

The Third Man and The Fallen Idol. Heinemann, 1950. (Penguin, 1971)

The Lost Childhood and Other Essays. Eyre and Spottiswoode, 1951.

The End of the Affair. Heinemann, 1951. (Penguin, 1975; Heinemann, 1976)

'Letter.' *The Times*, 21 June 1949.

'Letter.' *The Times*, 24 June 1949.

'Letter.' *Dieu Vivant*, 17 November 1950.

'Malaya, the Forgotten War.' *Life* 31 (30 July 1951): 51–54, 59–62, 65.

'Books in General.' *New Statesman and Nation* 43 (21 June 1952): 745.

'A Stranger in the Theatre.' *Picture Post* 59 (18 April 1953): 19–20.

'Indo-China: France's Crown of Thorns.' *Paris Match*, 12 July 1952.

'London Diary.' *New Statesman and*

Nation 44 (22 November 1951): 593.

The Living Room. Heinemann, 1953. (Penguin 1970)

'Kenya As I See It.' *Sunday Times* (27 September, 4 October 1953):

Twenty-One Stories. Heinemann, 1954. (Penguin, 1973)

'Letter.' *Le Figaro littéraire*, 7 August 1954, p. 1.

Loser Takes All. Heinemann, 1955. (Penguin, 1955)

'Last Cards in Indo-China.' *Sunday Times*, 28 March 1955.

'Last Act in Indo-China.' *New Republic* 132 (9 May 1955): 9–11.

The Quiet American. Heinemann, 1955. (Penguin, 1974, 1975, 1977)

'The Novelist and the Cinema – A Personal Experience.' *International Film Annual No. 2*. Ed. William Whitebait. Calder, 1958. 54–61.

The Potting Shed. Heinemann, 1958. (Penguin, 1971)

Our Man in Havana. Heinemann, 1958. (Penguin, 1962)

The Complaisant Lover. Heinemann, 1959.

A Burnt-Out Case. Heinemann, 1961. (Penguin, 1977)

In Search of a Character. Two African Journals. Bodley Head, 1961.

A Sense of Reality. Bodley Head, 1963.

'Security in Room 51.' *Sunday Times*, 14 July 1963.

'John Hayward, 1904–1965: Some Memories.' *Book Collector* 14 (Winter 1965): 443–86.

Carving a Statue. Bodley Head, 1964.

The Comedians. Bodley Head, 1966. (Penguin, 1981)

The Third Man [1949 film script]. Lorrimer, 1968.

'Introduction.' *My Silent War*, by Kim Philby. Panther Books, 1969.

Collected Essays. Bodley Head, 1969. (Penguin, 1970)

Travels with My Aunt. Bodley Head, 1969. (Penguin, 1972)

A Sort of Life. Bodley Head, 1971. (Penguin 1974)

'Letter.' *Daily Telegraph*, 15 November 1971.

The Pleasure Dome: The Collected Film Criticism 1935–1940. Ed. John Russell Taylor. Secker & Warburg, 1972.

Collected Stories. Bodley Head and Heinemann, 1972.

The Pleasure Dome: Collected Film Criticism, 1935–1940. Secker & Warburg, 1972.

'Letter.' *The Times*, 26 November 1971, p. 17.

The Honorary Consul. Bodley Head, 1973.

Lord Rochester's Monkey: Being the Life of John Wilmot, 2nd Earl of Rochester. Bodley Head, 1974.

'Letter.' *Daily Telegraph*, 22 November 1974.

'The Poet and the Gold.' *The Daily Telegraph Magazine*, 20 December 1974, pp. 25–26

An Impossible Woman: The Memories of Dottoressa Moor. Bodley Head, 1975. (Viking, 1976)

The Human Factor. Bodley Head, 1978. (Penguin, 1978)

'[Old Sayers].' *Irish Times*, 17 April 1978.

Ways of Escape. Bodley Head, 1980. (Penguin 1981).

Monsignor Quixote. Bodley Head, 1982.

J'Accuse: The Dark Side of Nice. London: Bodley Head, 1982.

Getting to Know the General. London: Bodley Head, 1984.

'I Do Not Believe.' *A Quick Look Behind*. Sylvester & Orphanos, 1983, p. 23.

'I'm not an angry old man, you see.' *The Spectator*, 14 June 1986, p. 9.

Reflections, ed. Judith Adamson. Reinhardt Books, 1991.

A World of My Own: A Dream Diary. Reinhardt Books, 1992.

UNPUBLISHED MATERIALS

Acheson, Dean. 'Undated note.' National Archives, Washington, D.C.

Blanche, Wendell. 'Secret report, dated 23 January 1951', in Indo-China: Internal Affairs: 1950–54. (see below)

———. 'Secret report, dated 31 March 1951', in Indo-China: Internal Affairs: 1950–54.

———. 'Secret report, dated 2 June 1951', in Indo-China: Internal Affairs: 1950–54.

———. 'Extract, 19 June 1951', in Indo-China: Internal Affairs: 1950–54.

———. 'Secret telegram, 22 June 1951', in Indo-China: Internal Affairs: 1950–54.

———. 'Secret telegram, 26 June 1951', in Indo-China: Internal Affairs: 1950–54.

———. 'Confidential Security Information', in Indo-China: Internal Affairs: 1950–54.

———. 'Report, 17 December 1951', in Indo-China: Internal Affairs: 1950–54.

———. 'Telegram, dated 19 December 1951', in Indo-China: Internal Affairs: 1950–54.

———. 'Secret memorandum, undated', in Indo-China: Internal Affairs: 1950–54.

———. 'Secret Telegram, dated 10 January 1952', in Indo-China: Internal Affairs: 1950–54.

———. 'Security report, 22 January 1952', in Indo-China: Internal Affairs: 1950–54.

Greene, Graham. 'After Two Years.' Unpublished [poem]

———. 'Anthony Sant.' Unpublished typescript. Humanities Research Center.

———. 'Diary.' Unpublished. Humanities Research Center, Austin, Texas.

———. 'Fanatic Arabia.' Humanities Research Center, Austin, Texas.

———. 'Journal.'

———. 'Notebook.'

———. '[nothing is more disquieting than the East. . . .].' Unpublished manuscript, dated 30 October (probably 1953).

———. 'Opium in Albany.' Unpublished manuscript.

———. 'Prologue to Pilgrimage.' Unpublished typescript.

———. 'A Sort of Life.' Unpublished typescript. University Library of Boston College.

———. 'University of Hamburg Address, 6 June 1969.' Unpublished typescript.

Greene, Raymond. 'Unpublished typescript.'

Greene, Vivien. 'Unpublished journal, various years.'

Heath, Donald. 'Secret Report to US Secretary of State, 14 June 1951', in Indo-China: Internal Affairs: 1950–54.

———. 'Secret memo, 4 February 1952', in Indo-China: Internal Affairs: 1950–54.

———. 'Secret memo, 14 February 1952', in Indo-China: Internal Affairs: 1950–54.

'Indo-China: Internal Affairs: 1950–54: Confidential US State Dept.' Central Files, National Archives, Washington DC.

McClintock, Robert. 'Letter to State Department, 31 October 1950.' National Archives, Washington DC.

OSS Files, National Archives, Washington, DC.

Pollinger, Laurence. 'In-house memo.' 25 September 1939.

Wall, Barbara. 'Unpublished diary.'

Will, Herbert L. 'Disseminate of Counter-espionage information to the X2 Branch, London.' X2 Headquarters, Ryder Street, undated.

SECTION TWO: REGISTER OF UNPUBLISHED LETTERS OF GRAHAM GREENE TO

Throughout his life, Greene wrote hundreds of letters. The following register lists, by recipient and by date, when possible, the numerous letters used. Often, no exact date can be established and a number of letters to Vivien Dayrell-Browning Greene and Catherine Walston are completely undated.

Anonymous supporter
    29 March 1982
Boissieu, General
    22 December 1980
Burgess, Anthony
    13 June 1988
Callendar, Louise
    11 October 1946
Cobb, Richard
Compton, Mackenzie, Mrs
    30 October 1941
Cooper, Diana
    26 June 1941
    22 October 1941
    23 October 1941
Copenhagan literature class
Crosthwaite-Eyre, Sir Oliver
    ? March 1958
Dayrell-Browning (Greene), Vivien
    14 November 1924
    6 March 1925
    14 April 1925
    ? May 1925
    18 May 1925
    19 May 1925
    21 May 1925
    6 June 1925
    8 June 1925
    25 June 1925
    26 June 1925
    29 June 1925
    13 July 1925
    17 July 1925
    22 July 1925
    24 July 1925
    26 July 1925
    27 July 1925
    30 July 1925
    6 August 1925

7 August 1925
9 August 1925
10 August 1925
11 August 1925
16 August 1925
17 August 1925
18 August 1925
20 August 1925
21 August 1925
25 August 1925
30 August 1925
31 August 1925
10 September 1925
11 September 1925
12 September 1925
24 September 1925
30 September 1925
7 October 1925
8 October 1925
10 October 1925
12 October 1925
15 October 1925
21 October 1925
22 October 1925
26 October 1925
28 October 1925
2 November 1925 (two letters)
3 November 1925
4 November 1925
5 November 1925
8 November 1925
10 November 1925
11 November 1925
13 November 1925
14 November 1925
16 November 1925
17 November 1925
18 November 1925
21 November 1925

23 November 1925
(? first week), December 1925
7 December 1925
9 December 1925
11 December 1925
13 December 1925
15 December 1925
16 December 1925
21 December 1925
24 December 1925
29 December 1925
1 January 1926
7 January 1926
9 January 1926
10 January 1926
13 January 1926
14 January 1926
15 January 1926
18 January 1926
20 January 1926
23 January 1926
24 January 1926
? January 1926
2 February 1926
9 February 1926
10 February 1926
11 February 1926
12 February 1926
13 February 1926
15 February 1926
22 February 1926
23 February 1926
24 February 1926
26 February 1926
27 February 1926
1 March 1926
2 March 1926
3 March 1926
8 March 1926
9 March 1926
10 March 1926
11 March 1926
15 March 1926
16 March 1926
18 March 1926
21 March 1926
22 March 1926
23 March 1926
29 March 1926
31 March 1926
1 April 1926
5 April 1926
6 April 1926

9 April 1926
10 April 1926
11 April 1926
12 April 1926
13 April 1926
14 April 1926
19 April 1926
20 April 1926
21 April 1926
22 April 1926
29 April 1926
4 May 1926
5 May 1926
6 May 1926
11 May 1926
12 May 1926
13 May 1926
17 May 1926
19 May 1926
22 May 1926
25 May 1926
27 May 1926
31 May 1926
? June 1926
2 June 1926
24 June 1926
28 June 1926
5 July 1926
7 July 1926
9 July 1926
10 July 1926
14 July 1926
15 July 1926
16 July 1926
26 July 1926
12 August 1926
21 August 1926
? September 1926
29 September 1926
? October 1926
2 October 1926
3 October 1926
4 October 1926
7 October 1926
8 October 1926
13 October 1926
15 October 1926
18 October 1926
6 November 1926
7 November 1926
8 November 1926
17 November 1926
18 November 1926

19 November 1926
24 November 1926
25 November 1926
26 November 1926
11 December 1926
15 December 1926
25 December 1926
5 January 1927
10 January 1927
18 January 1927
19 January 1927
24 January 1927
25 January 1927
31 January 1927
2 February 1927
8 February 1927
17 February 1927
21 February 1927
22 February 1927
1 March 1927
4 March 1927
13 March 1927
18 March 1927
19 March 1927
21 March 1927
30 March 1927
12 April 1927
22 April 1927
24 April 1927
26 April 1927
3 May 1927
4 May 1927
13 May 1927
28 May 1927
30 May 1927
1 June 1927
9 June 1927
10 June 1927
11 June 1927
14 June 1927
17 June 1927
18 June 1927
20 June 1927
23 June 1927
26 June 1927
30 August 1927
31 August 1927
1 September 1927
9 September 1927
11 September 1927
20 September 1927
25 September 1927
26 September 1927

27 September 1927
? April 1931
18 August 1932
27 February 1938
28 February 1938
? August 1939
30 August 1939
21 September 1939
14 October 1939
15 October 1939
26 October 1939
6 November 1939
23 November 1939
4 January 1940
24 November 1940
24 December 1942
9 April 1943
(?) 1945
(? Spring) 1945
24 April 1945
12 December 1947
3 June 1948
12 August 1948
(? Autumn) 1948
Dean, Basil
   27 July 1950
Greene, Charles
   28 February 1926
Greene, Elisabeth
   15 October 1941
   20 April 1942
   2 June 1942
Greene, Herbert
   17 December 1952
Greene, Hugh
   January 1925
   15 November 1930
   22 October 1932
   18 August 1934
   26 November 1934
   29 February 1936
   11 June 1936
   30 July 1936
   31 August 1936
   19 August 1937
   19 December 1937
   16 January 1938
   22 January 1938
   7 April 1939
   1 August 1942
   26 January 1951
Greene, Marion
   2 January 1905

(? Wednesday) 1921
24 October 1922
November 1922
24 January 1923
11 February 1923
3 May 1923
19 May 1923
9 June 1923
4 November 1923
? November 1923
24 February 1924
12 March 1924
17 April 1924
27 April 1924
13 June 1924
14 November 1924
22 November 1924
29 November 1924
? February 1925
16 February 1925
6 March 1925
14 April 1925
15 May 1925
18 May 1925
22 May 1925
25 May 1925
3 June 1925
19 July 1925
August 1925
6 November 1925
24 January 1926
26 January 1926
29 January 1926
30 March 1926
? March 1926
4 June 1926
30 September 1926
10 February 1927
21 April 1927
21 December 1927
February 1928
12 April 1928
9 May 1928
31 May 1928
23 July 1928
27 September 1928
November 1928
7 January 1929
14 January 1929
11 February 1929
9 March 1929
18 March 1929
29 March 1929

24 May 1929
5 June 1929
28 June 1929
13 August 1929
3 October 1929
21 October 1929
29 October 1929
2 February 1930
23 March 1930
5 August 1930
18 August 1930
2 October 1930
11 October 1930
20 October 1930
22 January 1931
March 1931
2 March 1931
28 April 1931
31 May 1931
2 June 1931
12 June 1931
11 September 1931
? Monday ? 1931
15 March 1932
22 August 1932
25 October 1932
30 November 1932
? 2 December 1932
3 March 1933
21 April 1933
August 1933
2 January 1934
18 April 1935
9 May 1935
3 November 1935
3 April 1936
29 August 1936
8 September 1936
7 February 1938
13 April 1938
23 September 1938
4 October 1938
26 December 1938
? August 1939
4 September 1939
? September 1939
? September 1939
? 1940
2 July 1940
? October 1940
7 April 1941
18 April 1941
20 April 1941

2 September 1941
3 September 1941 (to father also)
? October 1941
? 1942
5 February 1942
14 February 1942
2 April 1942
19 April 1942
'Good Friday', 1942
4 May 1942
11 June 1942
22 June 1942
22 July 1942
19 August 1942
19 January 1943
23 June 1944
20 October 1944
(late March?) 1945
? May 1945
21 June 1945
(? July) 1945
(? September) 1946
? March 1947
(early?) 1947
? June 1947
20 August 1947
1 November 1948
1 March 1949
24 October 1950
26 October 1950
31 October 1950
3 November 1950
13 November 1950
19 January 1951
12 February 1951
29 October 1951
31 October 1951
8 November ? 1951
Hayward, John
20 October 1950
Heinemann Publishers,
11 October 1946
10 March 1950
Higham, David
? 17 April 1931
8 December 1937
3 January 1938
? 8 January 1938
11 January 1938
16 January 1938
26 March 1949
Hodges, Cecil
12 June 1981

Hostovsky, Egon
11 January 1949
Hubsch, Ben
9 April 1938
25 April 1938
29 April 1938
31 May 1939
12 June 1939
13 July 1939
James Tait Black Prize Committee
13 January 1949
Jones, Sir Brynmor
10 December 1972
Macleod, Joseph
24 November 1980
Kirkpatrick, Mr
4 August 1944
Krishnamurti, G.
25 February 1986
Lasky, Victor
17 December 1952
Lord, Graham
27 July 1989
McDonnell, Vincent
20 October 1986
31 March 1987
15 January 1988
13 November 1989
Oriental Hotel
23 March 1981
Pearn, Nancy
20 October 1935
21 October 1935
11 November 1935
7 January 1936
11 January 1936
13 March 1936
7 March 1938
22 July 1940
24 July 1940
? October 1941
Peyrefitte, Alain
6 January 1981
Pollinger, Laurence
? September 1939
? March 1940
17 May 1940
8 October 1941
14 November 1941
9 March 1942
22 May 1942
19 June 1942
1 July 1942

17 July 1942
22 July 1942
4 August 1942
29 September 1942
4 November 1942
4 March 1943
13 March 1943
4 August 1943
1 July 1944
Powell, Anthony
  16 December 1940
  12 November 1948
  ? 1948
Pritchett, Mary
  25 February 1933
  ? March 1941
Reinhardt, Max
  22 December 1986
Smith, Lints
  October 1929
Spencer, Conway
  1925
Spring, Howard
  23 May 1940
Stine, Mrs
  21 April 1969
Strachwitz, Countess
  11 January 1975
Svanstrom, Ragnar
  13 April 1966
  13 May 1982
Trewin, J. C.
  18 September 1944
  9 February 1945
  12 July 1948
Vosper, Margery
  12 August 1942
Walston, Catherine
  26 December 1946
  6 May 1947
  16 May 1947
  17 May 1947
  18 May 1947
  (? May) 1947
  ? June 1947
  4 June 1947
  11 June 1947
  27 June 1947
  29 June 1947
  6 July 1947
  2 August 1947
  4 August 1947
  5? August 1947

18 August 1947
21 August 1947
22 August 1947
24 August 1947
25 August 1947
27 August 1947
2 September 1947
5 September 1947
12 September 1947
15 September 1947
28 September 1947
30 September 1947
18 October 1947
16 December 1947
12 February 1948
17 February 1948
18 February 1948
1 April 1948
29 April 1948
11 May 1948
19 May 1948
2 June 1948
7 June 1948
21 June 1948
26 June 1948
4 August 1948
? August 1948
(? August) 1948
5 August 1948
14 August 1948
22 August 1948
23 August 1948
19 January 1949
Undated 1949
11 April 1949
9 May 1949
21 May 1949
25 May 1949
8 July 1949
10 July 1949
19 July 1949
25 July 1949
(Probably July) 1949
? August 1949
6 August 1949
7 September 1949
11 September 1949
26 September 1949
2 October 1949
3 October 1949
7 October 1949
9 December 1949
9–12 December 1949

SECTION THREE: UNPUBLISHED LETTERS
TO GRAHAM GREENE

'Anonymous supporter'
  8 February 1982
  2 March 1982
  'Holy Monday' 1982
Baring, James
  18 March 1982
Boothby, Bobby
  11 February 1986
Burgess, Anthony
  2 November 1958
  19 June 1961
Calder-Marshall, Arthur
  8 October 1977
Crosthwaite-Eyre, Sir Oliver
  4 March 1958
Douglas, Norman
  ? November 1950
Dyer, A. O.
  23 August 1953
Fonteyn, Margot
  ? Sunday, undated, probably 1951
  15 April 1953
Ginn, Captain
  29 September 1952
Greene, Hugh
  28 June 1942
Greene, Vivien (Dayrell-Browning)
  7 December 1939
  5 January 1940
  24 January 1940
  February 1940
  28 November 1940
  ? 1941
  12 March 1941
  15 March 1941
  4 April 1941
  26 November 1941
  10 January 1942
  28 February 1942
  ? March 1942
  9 March 1942
  23 March 1942
  6 April 1942
  14 April 1942
  28 April 1942
  25 May 1942
  7 July 1942

  12 July 1942
  14 July 1942
  1 August 1942
  26 August 1942
  May 1945
  10 May 1945
  31 July 1948
Guiness, Alec
  11 February 1986
Guinzburg, Harold
  4 February 1952
  13 February 1952 (cable)
Foot, Michael
  13 February 1986
Franklin, Olga
  26 November 1980
Higham, David
  22 May 1939
Hodges, Cecil
  12 June 1981
Huebsch, Ben
  10 May 1939
Kee, Robert
  29 October 1946
Lasky, Victor
  11 December 1952
Lehmann, Rosamond
  The Spectator, 18 July 1941
Mewshaw, Michael
  13 February 1986
Mortimer, John
  23 February 1986
Newall, Maria
  23 January 1955
Parsons, Ian
  30 December 1976
Pearn, Nancy
  13 March 1936
  8 May 1936
  25 July 1936
Pearson, G. L.
  11 February 1977
Pollinger, Laurence
  April 1940
  15 June 1942
  25 September 1942 (cable)
  17 December 1942

OTHER LETTERS

To Mr Bischoff, 27 September 1948
To Francis Greene, 12 October 1970
Martindale, Rev. C. C.
  To Vivien Greene, undated, 1948
  To Vivien Greene, undated
Muggeridge, Malcolm
  To David Low, undated
Pollinger, Laurence
  To Vivien Greene, 21 December 1942
  To Vivien Greene, 29 January 1943
  To Vivien Greene, 24 February 1943
Young, Mrs

To A. S. Frere, 6 February 1952
Waugh, Evelyn
  To Catherine Walston, 25 August 1951
  To Nancy Mitford, ? September 1951
Walston, Catherine
  To Belinda Straight, 31 January 1969
  To Bonte Durán, undated, probably
    early 1950
  To Bonte Durán, 13 March 1950
  To Bonte Durán, 19 March 1950
  To Bonte Durán, 16 June 1950
  To Bonte Durán, 23 May 1953

SECTION FOUR: BOOKS AND ESSAYS

Allain, Marie-Françoise. *The Other Man: Conversations with Graham Greene.* Trans. Guido Waldman. The Bodley Head, 1983.

Allen, Walter. *As I Walked Down New Grub Street: Memories Of A Writing Life.* Chicago: University of Chicago, 1982.

Andrew, Christopher and Oleg Gordievsky. *KGB: The Inside Story.* New York: HarperCollins, 1990.

Anonymous. '[Comment on Demobilisation Conditions].' *Sunday Times*, September 1945.

———. 'Mrs Greene's House.' *Oxford Mail*, 28 April 1945.

———. 'Greene Comments on US Visit.' *New York Times*, 18 November 1947.

———. 'Mr Graham Greene and Miss Dayrell-Browning.' *Morning Post*, 17 October 1927.

———. 'An Interview with Graham Greene.' *Saturday Review of Literature*, 10 July 1948.

———. '[Announcement concerning dramatization of *The Heart of the Matter*].' *The Times*, 1 March 1950.

———. 'Obituary [of George Anderson].' *Times House Journal*, June 1951.

———. *Strike Nights in Printing House Square*. Privately printed, 1932.

———. 'The Basement Room.' *Times Literary Supplement*, 23 November 1935.

Atkins, John. *Graham Greene.* Calder & Boyars, 1969.

Balsdon, Dacre. *Oxford Now and Then.* Duckworth, 1970.

Barber, John. 'Review: *The Living Room.*' *Daily Express*, 17 April 1953.

Barber, Noel. *The War of the Running Dogs: The Malayan Emergency, 1948–1960.* Weybright & Talley, 1971.

Bates, H. E. *The Blossoming World.* Michael Joseph, 1971.

Baudelaire, Charles. *Intimate Journals.* Trans. Christopher Isherwood. San Francisco: City Lights Books, 1983.

Bennett, Arnold. *Journals, 1921–1926.* Cassell, 1933.

Beresford, J. D. W. *E. Ford: A Biography.* Doran, 1917.

Betts, P. Y. 'The Snob's Guide to Good Form.' 157 (24 May 1936).

'Big Air Battle Over London: 65 Raiders Shot Down.' *Observer*, 8 September 1940.

Blakelock, Denys. 'Heart of the Matter.' *Universe*, 16 July 1948.

Blunden, Edmund. *Undertones of War.* Cobden-Sanderson, 1928.

Bodard, Lucien. 'L'Appel aux Américans.' *L'Express*, 1967.

———. *The Quicksand War: Prelude to Vietnam.* Trans. Patrick O'Brien. Boston: Little, Brown, 1967.

Bolitho, Hector. *War in the Strand.* Eyre & Spottiswoode, 1942.

'A Bomb Makes a Shambles of a Sunny Saigon Square.' *Life*, 28 January 1952.

'British Novelist Graham (*The Third Man*) Greene.' *Time*, 13 September 1954.

Brown, Anthony Cave. *'C': The Secret Life of Sir Stewart Graham Menzies*. Macmillan, 1987.

Brown, Bishop. 'Heart of the Matter.' *Universe*, 3 September 1948.

Brownrigg, Ronald. 'Heart of the Matter.' *The Tablet* 191 (10 July 1948).

Burgess, Anthony, 'God and Literature and So Forth. . . .' *Observer*, 16 March 1980.

———. *You've Had Your Time*.

Burstall, Christopher. 'The Hunted Man.' BBC Omnibus programme, November 1968.

Calder, Angus. *The People's War: Britain 1939–45*. Panther, 1971.

Cavafy, Constantine. 'Come Back.' Trans. George Valassopoulis. *Oxford Outlook* 1925.

Cecil, Robert. 'Cambridge Comintern.' *The Missing Dimension*. Ed. Christopher Andrew and David N. Dilks. Macmillan, 1984.

Clurman, Robert. 'The Quiet Englishman: Greene's Answer to Critics of *The Quiet American*.' *New York Times Book Review*, 26 August 1956, p. 8.

Cole, G. D. H. and Raymond Postgate. *The Common People, 1746–1938*. Hutchinson, 1946.

Coward, Noël. *The Diaries*. Ed. Graham Payer and Sheridan Morley. Boston: Little, Brown, 1982.

Creel, George. 'Interview with Tomas Garrido.' *Collier's Weekly*, 23 February 1935.

Cripps, Sir Stafford. 'Letter.' *The Times*, 23 June 1949.

Cronin, Vincent. 'Review: *The Living Room*.' *Catholic World*, September 1953.

Currey, Cecil. *Edward Lansdale*. Boston: Houghton Mifflin, 1988.

Darroch, Sandra Jobson. *Ottoline*. Coward, McCann & Geoghegan, 1975.

Dean, Basil. *Mind's Eye*. Hutchinson, 1973.

Dos Passos, John. *Orient Express*. New York: Harper & Row, 1927.

Driberg, Tom. *Ruling Passions*. New York: Stein & Day, 1979.

Durán, Leopoldo. *Graham Greene: Friend & Brother*. New York: HarperCollins, 1994.

Durgin, Cyrus. 'British Novelist Graham Greene Turns Playwright and Likes It.' Boston *Daily Globe*, 24 February 1950.

'[Editorial].' *Daily Telegraph*, 12 May 1988.

———. *New York Times*, 6 February 1952.

———. *New York Times*, 11 October 1953.

———. *Daily Telegraph*, 23 May 1988.

Edwards, Anne. *Shirley Temple: American Princess*. New York: William Morrow & Co., 1988.

Eliot, T. S. *Selected Essays*. New York: Harcourt Brace, 1950.

Elliott, Nicholas. *Never Judge a Man by His Umbrella*. Michael Russell, 1991.

Equinn, E. *Dublin Quarterly* (1950).

Farnman, Christopher. *The General Strike, May 1926*. Hart-Davis, 1974.

Farr, M. M. 'Heart of the Matter.' *Universe*, 16 July 1948.

Fenby, Jonathan. 'Dirty tricks, says le patron, and takes the Gloves Off.' London *Times*, 10 February 1982.

Fisher, Geoffrey (Archbishop of Canterbury). 'Address.' 8 May 1945.

Forbes, Bryan. *A Divided Life: Memoirs*. London: Mandarin, 1993.

Fussell, Paul. *The Great War and Modern Memory*. Oxford: Oxford University, 1977.

———. *Wartime*. Oxford University Press, 1989.

Garvon, Jeremy. 'Dark Journey into Greeneland.' *Daily Telegraph*, 16 January 1988.

'General Jean de Lattre de Tassigny.' New York Times, 11 January 1951.

Gibbs, Sir Philip. *Philadelphia Evening Bulletin*, 5 May 1926.

Golding, Louis. *Magnolia Street*. Gollancz, 1932.

Goodger, William. 'Letter.' *New Statesman and Nation*, 26 June 1948, p. 297.

'Graham Greene Says US Lives in Red-

Obsessed "State of Fear".' *New York Herald Tribune*, 15 February 1952.

'[Greene] Wins Catholic Literary Award.' *New York Times*, 20 February 1952.

Greenlees, Ian. *Norman Douglas*. British Council, 1957.

Greene, Barbara. 'Interview.' *News Chronicle*, 4 January 1935.

———. *Land Benighted*. Geoffrey Bles, 1938.

———. 'Undated letter to her mother from Monrovia.'

Greene, Charles. *The Berkhamstedian*. Berkhamstead, 1913.

Greene, Dennis. 'Letter.' *Sunday Telegraph*, 30 September 1979.

Greene, Herbert. 'I Was a Secret Agent of Japan.' *Daily Worker*, 22 December 1937.

Greene, Raymond. 'Letter.' *The Berkhamstedian*. April 1919, December 1919.

Hart-Davis, Rupert. *Hugh Walpole: A Biography*. Macmillan, 1952.

Havic, Ivar. 'Review: *The Living Room.*' *Expressen*, 1 November 1952.

Hawtree, Christopher, ed. *Night and Day*. Pref. Graham Greene. Chatto & Windus, 1985.

Hazzard, Shirley. *Greene on Capri: A Memoir*. New York: Farrar, Straus, Giroux, 2000.

Herbert, A. P. *The Thames*. Weidenfeld & Nicolson, 1966.

Higdon, David Leon. 'A Textual History of Graham Greene's *The Power and the Glory.*' *Studies in Bibliography* 33 (1980): 249–56.

Higham, David. *Literary Gent*. Jonathan Cape, 1978.

Hilton, James. *Goodbye Mr Chips*. Macmillan, 1934.

Hingley, Ronald. *Nightingale Fever*. New York: Knopf, 1981.

Hinsley, F. H. and C. A. G. Sinkins. *British Intelligence in the Second World War*. Vol. 4. HMSO, 1990.

———, with E. E. Thomas, C. F. S. Ransom, and R. C. Knight. British Intelligence in the Second World War. Vol. 1. HMSO, 1979.

Holroyd, Michael. *Lytton Strachey*. New York: Holt, Rinehart & Winston, 1980.

Howard, Michael. *British Intelligence in the Second World War*. Vol. 5. HMSO, 1990.

Huxley, Aldous. *Letters*. Ed. Grover Smith. Chatto & Windus, 1969.

———. *Point Counter Point*. 1928. Penguin 1974.

'[Interview].' *Boston Daily Globe*, 24 February 1950.

Jenkins, Alan. *The Forties*. Heinemann, 1977.

———. *The Thirties*. Heinemann, 1976.

Jerrold, Douglas. 'Graham Greene, Pleasure-Hater.' *Harper's*, August 1952.

John, Otto. *Twice through the Lines*. Macmillan, 1972.

Joyce, James. *A Portrait of the Artist as a Young Man*. 1916. Penguin, 1965.

Knightley, Phillip. *The Master Spy: The Story of Kim Philby*. New York: Knopf, 1988.

Korda, Michael. *Charmed Lives*. New York: Avon, 1981.

Lancaster, Donald. 'The Emancipation of French Indo-China.' Oxford University Press, 1961.

Lane, Margaret. *Edgar Wallace: Biography of a Phenomenon*. Hamish Hamilton, 1964.

Laski, Marghanita. 'How Well Have They Worked? – Brighton Rock.' *The Times*, 17 February 1966, p. 15.

Leaming, Barbara. *Orson Wells, A Biography*. Penguin, 1986

Le Carré, John. 'Introduction.' Bruce Page, David Leitch, and Phillip Knightley. *The Philby Conspiracy*. New York: Doubleday, 1968.

Liebling, A. J. 'A Talkative Something-or-Other.' *New Yorker*, 7 April 1956, pp. 136, 138–42.

'Review: *The Living Room.*' *Brighton and Hove Herald*, 3 March 1953.

'Review: *The Living Room.*' *Svenska Dagbladet*, 1 November 1952.

Longmate, Norman. 'London's Burning.' *Daily Telegraph*, 18 June 1940.

Lundkvist, Artur. 'Review: *The Living Room.*' *Morgon-Tidningen*, 4 November 1952.

Macaulay, Rose. *Letters to a Friend 1950–52*. Ed. C. B. Smith. Collins, 1961.

McCullagh, Francis. *Red Mexico*. Louis Carrier & Co., 1928.

Maclaren-Ross, J. 'Excursion in Greeneland.' *Memories of the Forties.* Alan Ross, 1965.

Martindale, Rev. C. C. 'Heart of the Matter.' *Universe*, 25 June 1948.

Matthews, Ronald. *Mon Ami Graham Greene.* Paris: Desclée De Brouwer, 1957.

Matthews, W. R. *St Paul's Cathedral in Wartime.* Hutchinson, 1946.

'Mau Mau Massacre of Loyal Kikuyu 150 men, women and children dead.' *The Times*, 28 March 1953.

Meyer, Michael. *Not Prince Hamlet: Literary and Theatrical Memoirs.* Secker & Warburg, 1989.

Meyers, Jeffrey. *Katherine Mansfield.* New York: New Directions, 1980.

Meyers, Michael. 'Memories of George Orwell.' *The World of George Orwell.* Ed. Miriam Gross. Weidenfeld & Nicolson, 1971.

Muggeridge, Malcolm. *The Infernal Grove: Chronicles of Wasted Time.* Vol. 2. Fontana/Collins, 1975.

————. *Like it Was: A Selection from the Diaries.* Ed. John Bright-Holmes. Collins, 1981.

Murphy, John. 'Heart of the Matter.' *Universe*, 18 June 1948.

'My Characters Live Themselves: Greene's Words on the First Night [of *The Living Room*].' *Stockholms-Tidningen*, 1 November 1952.

Nichols, Beverley. *Twenty Five: Being a Young Man's Candid Recollections of his Elders and Betters.* Penguin, 1973.

Nixon, Barbara. *Raiders Overhead.* Lindsay Drummond, 1943.

Norfolk, Stanley. 'Heart of the Matter.' *Catholic Herald*, 6 August 1948.

O'Brien, T. H. *Civil Defence.* HMSO, 1955.

Orwell, George. 'The Sanctified Sinner.' *New Yorker*, 17 July 1948, pp. 66, 69–71.

Page, Bruce, David Leitch and Phillip Knightley. *The Philby Conspiracy.* Intro. John Le Carré. New York: Doubleday, 1968.

Papers Concerning Affairs in Liberia, December 1930–May 1934. HMSO, 1934.

Parsons, Father. *Mexican Martyrdom.* 1936.

Paton, John. *Left Turn.* Secker & Warburg, 1936.

The Pentagon Papers. Senator Gravel Edition. Vol. 1. Boston: Beacon Press, 1979.

Philby, Eleanor. *The Spy I Loved.* Pan, 1968.

Philby, Kim. *My Silent War.* Panther, 1973.

Philby, Rufina. *The Private Life of Kim Philby.*

The Portable Graham Greene. Ed. Philip Stratford. Penguin, 1984.

Powell, Anthony. *Faces in My Time: To Keep the Ball Rolling.* Vol. 3. Heinemann, 1980.

————. *Infants of the Spring.* Heinemann, 1976. (Penguin 1967).

Pritchett, V. S. 'The Human Factor in Graham Greene.' *The New York Times Magazine*, 26 February 1978, 33–36, 38, 40–42, 44, 46.

Preminger, Otto. *An Autobiography.* New York: Doubleday, 1977.

Quennell, Peter. 'A Kingdom of Cokayne.' *Evelyn Waugh and His World.* Ed. David Pryce Jones. Weidenfeld & Nicholson, 1973.

————. *The Marble Foot.* Collins, 1976.

'Red's Time-Bombs Rip Saigon Center.' *New York Times*, 10 January 1952.

'[Report on London Bombing].' *Picture Post*, 28 September 1940.

Roberts, Cecil. *The Bright Twenties.* Hodder & Stoughton, 1970.

Rowse, A. L. *A Cornishman at Oxford.* Jonathan Cape, 1965.

Sackville-West, Edward. 'The Electric Hare.' *The Month*, September 1951, p. 147.

————. 'The Problem of Despair.' *New Statesman and Nation*, 19 June 1948, p. 108.

'Saigon explosions linked to Caodaist terrorists.' *New York Times*, 25 January 1952.

Shelden, Michael. *Graham Greene: The Man Within.* London: Heinemann, 1994.

'Shocker.' *Time*, 29 October 1951.

Shuttleworth, Martin and Simon Raven. 'Graham Greene Interviewed.' *Graham Greene: A Collection of Critical Essays.* Ed. Samuel L. Hynes. New York:

Prentice-Hall, 1973. 24–41.

Simpson, Howard R. *Tiger in the Barbed Wire*. New York: Brassey, 1992.

Soldati, Mario. *Fuori*. Trans. Mario Curreli. Rome: Mondadori, 1968.

Speight, Robert. *Francois Mauriac: A Study of the Writer and the Man*. Chatto & Windus, 1976.

Sykes, Christopher. *Evelyn Waugh*. Boston: Little, Brown, 1975.

Thomas, Hugh. *Spanish Civil War*. Billing & Sons, 1961.

Tracey, Michael. *A Variety of Lives: A Biography of Sir Hugh Greene*. Bodley Head, 1983.

Trevor-Roper, Hugh. *The Philby Affair*. William Kimber, 1968.

'The Un-Midas Touch' [editorial]. *Life*, 4 July 1949, p.18.

'US Legation warns Americans that Vietminh plans demonstration.' *New York Times*, 21 February 1952.

Wapshot, Nicholas. *The Man Between*. Chatto & Windus, 1990.

Waugh, Evelyn. *Diaries*. Ed. Michael Davie. Penguin, 1976.

———. 'Felix Culpa? A Review of *The Heart of the Matter*, with Additional Commentary.' *Tablet*, 191 (5 June 1948): 352–54; also *Commonweal*, 16 July 1948.

———. *Letters*. Ed. Mark Amory. Weidenfeld & Nicolson, 1980.

———. *Unconditional Surrender*. Butler & Tanner, 1961.

'When Greene Is Red.' *Newsweek* 1 October 1956, pp. 94, 96.

Williams, B. N. Garnons. *History of Berkhamsted School – 1541–1971*. The School, 1980.

Wilson, A. N. 'Graham Greene and a Companion of Dishonour.' *Daily Mail*, 1987.

Winterbottom, Derek. *Doctor Fry, Berkhamsted*. Clanbury Cotterell Press, 1977.

Woodruff, Douglas. 'Times Remembered.' *The Times*, 2 May 1977.

SECTION FIVE: INTERVIEWS WITH AND LETTERS TO NORMAN SHERRY

Acton, Sir Harold
  11 May 1977
Allen, Walter
  August 1976
  1977
Baker, Charles and Nancy
  1 February 1994
Barzun, Jacques
  5 May 1984 (letter)
Cairncross, John
  14 May 1977
Cloetta, Yvonne
  23 May 1994
Cockburn, Charles
  18 June 1977
Cockburn, Claud
  Undated
'Colleague of Greene in Vietnam'
  7 July 1974
Cranston, Grace

  27 May 1982
Crompton, David
  26 May 1992
Dennys, Rodney
  22 January 1992
  23 January 1992
  Undated
Dennys, Elisabeth
  18 March 1983
  August 1983
  1983 (Letters)
  6 July 1984 (telephone conversation)
  21 October 1986
Durán, Bonte
  25 May 1992
'Former CIA Senior Officer'
  Undated
Frere, A. S.
  1976
Getz, John

22 December 1986
Richmond, Zoe
    January 1985
Smith, Leslie
    1977
Soldati, Mario
    18 May 1977
Springer, Paul
    28 December 1992 (letter)
Stanier, R. S.
    1976
    24 August 1977
Strachwitz, Countess
    1976
Straight, Belinda
    26 July 1992
Sutro, John and Gillian
    1976
    19 May 1977
Swinnerton, Frank
    2 January 1977
Topping, Seymour
    13 July 1992
Topping, Seymour and Audrey

13 July 1992
Turnbull, Peter
    30 October 1981 (letter)
Turner, Vincent (Rev.)
    July 1991
Tranmire, Lord
    April 1977
    2 June 1977
'Unattributable source.' (See 13n9, 15,
    1929, 30, 32, 36, 37, 38)
    13n9 – 17 June 1977
Walston, Lady Elizabeth
    1 June 1992
    13 June 1992
Walston, William
    14 June 1994 (telephone interview)
Wilson, B.
    January 1976
    1977
    7 June 1981
Wilson, Trevor
    1976
    11 March 1977

Index

The Life of Graham Greene, Volume I
1904–1939

"Rich with fascinating, dramatic detail . . . Greene's prodigious energies and inspirations are well matched by Norman Sherry's intelligence, sympathy, and powers of analysis." —Joyce Carol Oates

Graham Greene was one of the most guarded and complex literary figures of our time. In the first volume of Norman Sherry's celebrated biography, Greene's early life is explored through letters, diaries, and hundreds of interviews, including a breakdown in his early teens, his years at Oxford, and most particularly, his long and tortuous courtship with his future wife. Sherry uncovers the origins of Greene's literary preoccupations, as well as reasons for his conversion to Roman Catholicism. Greene's development as a novelist, from the early success of the *The Man Within* to his masterpiece, *The Power and the Glory,* is also explored in full, as Sherry literally follows Greene's footsteps to West Africa and Mexico, penetrating the strange and emotional territory that Greene made into his own.
ISBN 0-14-200420-0

The Life of Graham Greene, Volume II
1939–1955

"A riveting picture of a man profoundly at odds with his life . . . whose anxieties and obsessions came to reflect those of his violent century. . . . One of the finest literary biographies of a contemporary writer."
—*Publishers Weekly*

The years from 1939 to 1955 proved to be the most prolific of Graham Greene's life. In Volume II, Sherry continues his award-winning account, delving deeply and emerging with a portrait of the author at the height of both his espionage and literary careers. Greene produced some of his best novels during this time—*The Heart of the Matter, The End of the Affair, The Quiet American*—and saw the filming of *The Fallen Idol* and *The Third Man.* The same period encompasses his passionate affair with the beautiful American Catherine Walston, who was married to a British peer; the disintegration of his marriage and of his long relationship with Dorothy Glover; his activities as a secret agent; and his forays into the conflicts in Kenya, Malaya, and French Indo-China. Above all, Norman Sherry has succeeded in unlocking the mystery of Greene's character and the alchemic nature of his creative genius.
ISBN 0-14-200421-9

"Graham Greene was in a class by himself. . . . He will be read and remembered as the ultimate chronicler of twentieth-century man's consciousness and anxiety."
—William Golding

Brighton Rock
Introduction by J. M. Coetzee
Greene's chilling exposé of violence and gang warfare in the prewar British underworld features Pinkie, a protagonist who is the embodiment of evil.
ISBN 0-14-243797-2

The End of the Affair
Introduction by Michael Gorra
A love affair, abruptly and inexplicably broken off, prompts the grief-stricken novelist Maurice Bendrix to hire a private detective to discover the cause.
ISBN 0-14-243798-0

The Heart of the Matter
Introduction by James Wood
The terrifying depiction of a man's awe of the Church and Greene's ability to portray human motive and to convey such a depth of suffering make this one of his most enduring and tragic novels.
ISBN 0-14-243799-9

The Quiet American
Introduction by Robert Stone
While the French Army in Indo-China grapples with the Vietminh, a young and high-minded American based in Saigon begins to channel economic aid to a "Third Force"—leading him to blunder into a complex political and cultural world he seems not to understand fully, with disastrous and violent results.
ISBN 0-14-303902-4

Orient Express
Introduction by Christopher Hitchens
Set on the Orient Express, this suspense thriller involves the desperate affair between a pragmatic Jew and a naïve chorus girl entangled in lust, duplicity, and murder.
ISBN 0-14-243791-3

Travels with My Aunt
Introduction by Gloria Emerson
Henry Pulling's dull suburban life is interrupted when his septuagenarian Aunt Augusta persuades him to travel the world with her in her own inimitable style.
ISBN 0-14-303900-8

FOR THE BEST IN PAPERBACKS, LOOK FOR THE

In every corner of the world, on every subject under the sun, Penguin represents quality and variety—the very best in publishing today.

For complete information about books available from Penguin—including Penguin Classics, Penguin Compass, and Puffins—and how to order them, write to us at the appropriate address below. Please note that for copyright reasons the selection of books varies from country to country.

In the United States: Please write to *Penguin Group (USA), P.O. Box 12289 Dept. B, Newark, New Jersey 07101-5289* or call 1-800-788-6262.

In the United Kingdom: Please write to *Dept. EP, Penguin Books Ltd, Bath Road, Harmondsworth, West Drayton, Middlesex UB7 0DA.*

In Canada: Please write to *Penguin Books Canada Ltd, 90 Eglinton Avenue East, Suite 700, Toronto, Ontario M4P 2Y3.*

In Australia: Please write to *Penguin Books Australia Ltd, P.O. Box 257, Ringwood, Victoria 3134.*

In New Zealand: Please write to *Penguin Books (NZ) Ltd, Private Bag 102902, North Shore Mail Centre, Auckland 10.*

In India: Please write to *Penguin Books India Pvt Ltd, 11 Panchsheel Shopping Centre, Panchsheel Park, New Delhi 110 017.*

In the Netherlands: Please write to *Penguin Books Netherlands bv, Postbus 3507, NL-1001 AH Amsterdam.*

In Germany: Please write to *Penguin Books Deutschland GmbH, Metzlerstrasse 26, 60594 Frankfurt am Main.*

In Spain: Please write to *Penguin Books S. A., Bravo Murillo 19, 1° B, 28015 Madrid.*

In Italy: Please write to *Penguin Italia s.r.l., Via Benedetto Croce 2, 20094 Corsico, Milano.*

In France: Please write to *Penguin France, Le Carré Wilson, 62 rue Benjamin Baillaud, 31500 Toulouse.*

In Japan: Please write to *Penguin Books Japan Ltd, Kaneko Building, 2-3-25 Koraku, Bunkyo-Ku, Tokyo 112.*

In South Africa: Please write to *Penguin Books South Africa (Pty) Ltd, Private Bag X14, Parkview, 2122 Johannesburg.*